Happy Bir[illegible]

Ken 7/8/77

HOW NEW ENGLAND HAPPENED

HOW NEW ENGLAND HAPPENED

A Guide to New England Through Its History

by Christina Tree

Illustrations and maps by Richard Egland

Little, Brown and Company Boston - Toronto

First Edition

T 04/76

Library of Congress Cataloging in Publication Data

Tree, Christina.
How New England Happened.

Includes index.
1. New England—Description and travel—1951
—Guide-books. 2. New England—History. I. Title.
F2.3.T73 917.4'04'4 75-41700
ISBN 0-316-85260-0

Designed by Janis Capone

Published simultaneously in Canada by Little, Brown & Company (Canada) Limited

Printed in the United States of America

To my father

Contents

Introduction

How New England Happened tells the history of a region in terms of things you can see. It draws you at once through time and space, describing countless things to see and do in the six Northeastern states, as each illustrates a phase in one evolving story. Roughly half the places described are museums, buildings and sites commonly labeled "historic." The remainder are corners of New England worth explóring. There are also descriptions and listings of organizations which can aid in the attempt.

The book is an outgrowth of a half dozen years spent writing frequent New England travel features for the *Boston Globe*. Gradually it became a nagging obsession. In the absence of either a trustworthy regional guide or history, I was forced into scratch research, relying on local sources for historical background. There were so many seemingly simple questions which only experts could answer: Why did one town die at the moment its neighbor was born? Why is each of the six states so distinctive in its own right, and yet what is that intangible something which they all so visibly share?

Many books, experts, and thousands on thousands of miles later (some of the way with my long-suffering husband, most of it with my two-year-old and his port-a-crib), I knew the answers to a great many more questions than I had ever thought of asking. And something had happened to my eyes. Now, wherever I traveled within the region, the very landscape told me a story. I knew why buildings, from Bridgeport to Bangor, looked the way they did. I understood why wilderness perseveres where it does, what busy places New England's sleepiest islands and its least touristed back country once were, and what they offer today. I was finally, so to speak, a botanist in the same forest in which for so many years I had seen only "trees."

The mechanics of using the guide are unusual, but simple. Within the text each reference to a specific site is in italic and numbered in the margin. The numbers correspond to those in the section of "Details" at the end of each chapter, in which information necessary for a visit is supplied. Telephone numbers are provided wherever possible because New England sites are maintained by countless extremely independent groups; open hours change, constantly. Numbers also correspond to the maps which accompany each chapter. Historic inns are mentioned but no attempt has been made to be critical or comprehensive on this subject since a choice of inn guides exists.

Within the context of its story the guide to sites open to the public is thorough. This story begins with traces of "Vague Voyages" by the earliest explorers to New England and with the whereabouts of those descendants of "Indian Inhabitants" who welcomed the newcomers. It ends with "Victorian Vignettes," for by the turn of this century, most of those things which we think of as distinctively New England had already appeared.

In *How New England Happened* I have attempted to share a skill for reading the New England landscape, stamped uniquely as it is with 350 years' use. The story alone should please armchair travelers. But the object is to entice readers not only into but out of their cars. Yankees are famously half-hearted in the welcome they extend to "tourists." But adventurous travelers who appreciate the genuine wealth of this proud little land will ever find a warm reception.

HOW NEW ENGLAND HAPPENED

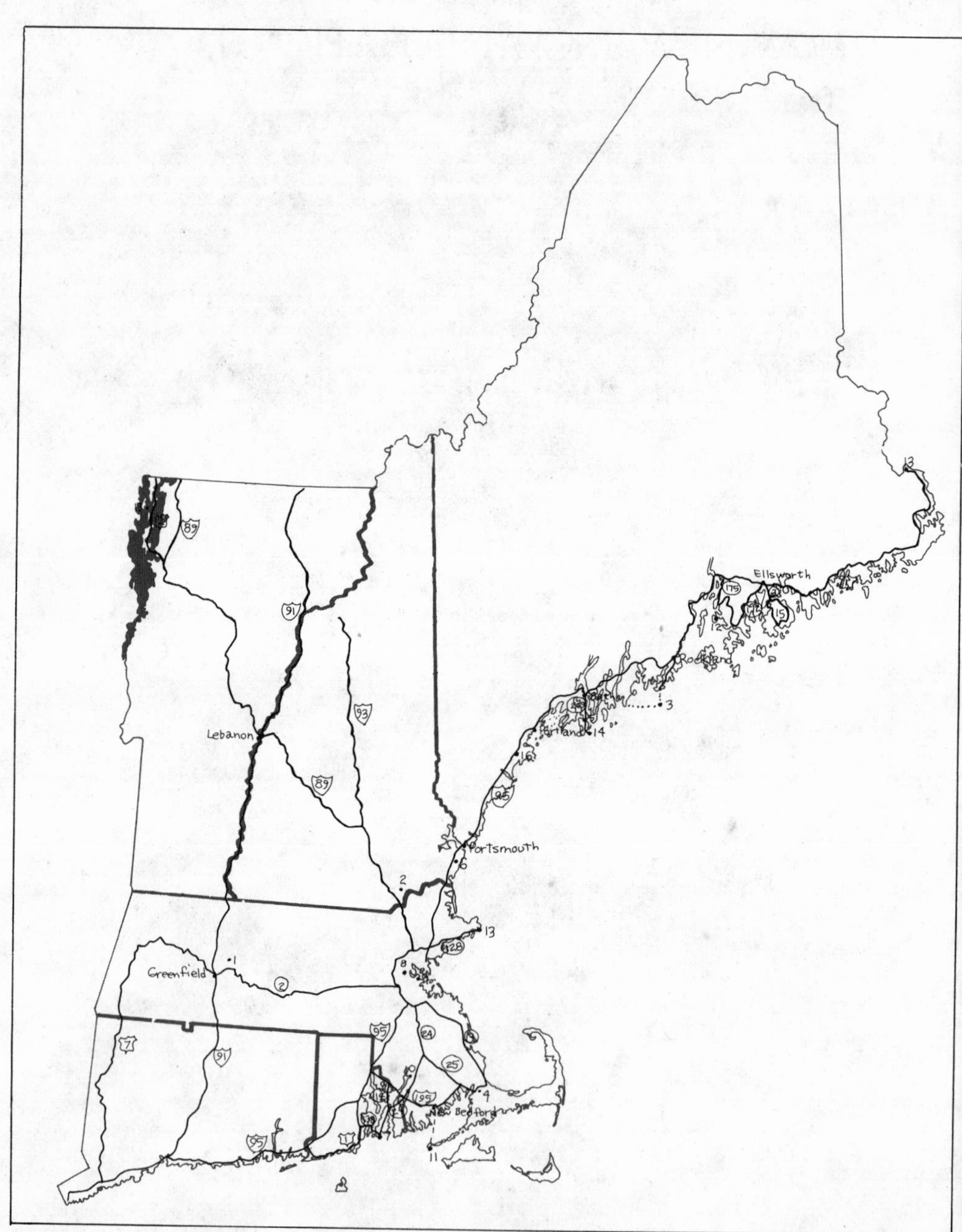
Ellsworth
Rockland
Portland
Portsmouth
Lebanon
Greenfield
Bedford

1

Vague Voyages and Short-Lived Settlements

We do not know who the first Europeans to discover New England were, when they did it, or why. The origins of the first explorers is a subject that sparks fierce debate, whether it is brought up in the halls of learned societies or the back rooms of ethnic bars. Irish monks and roving Vikings are the most popular candidates. But Portuguese mariners and off-course Phoenician merchants have their partisans too.

The Irish claim is based on the tales of a fifth-century sailor-monk, St. Brendan the Navigator. Brendan used his considerable nautical skills to seek out remote spots where he and his brother monks could practice their stark and celibate brand of Christianity, well away from female temptation.

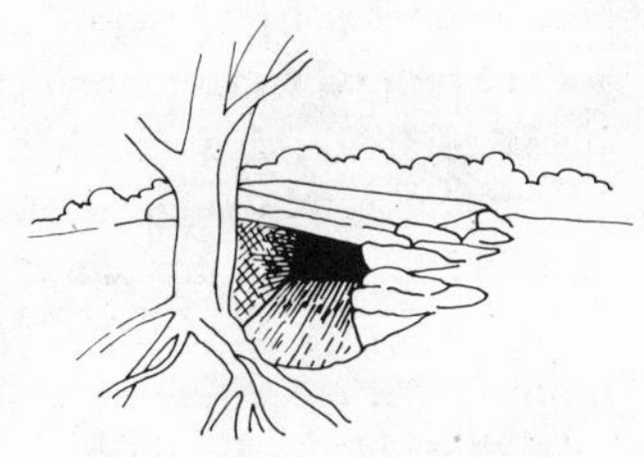

Beehive hut, Leverett, Mass.

Centuries of blarneying up Brendan's accounts of his voyages make it hard at first to take him seriously. His practice of picnicking on the back of a whale, for instance, seems a bit much – even for a saint. Many scholars believe, however, that he sailed to the Azores and to Iceland, where he established monastic communities. (One Icelandic loch still bears the unlikely Nordic name of Patrick's Fjord.) These Irish religious communities were swept away when a wave of Norse settlers broke over Iceland. Most of the monks probably went back to Ireland, but it is quite possible that some of them sailed off in search of "The Land of the Blessed" of Irish legend, which lay somewhere over the western horizon.

In New England, scores of stone structures resembling
the *Beehive Huts* favored by Irish anchorites have been 1
discovered. Some can be explained away as outdoor

ovens or root cellars, but there are many others for which no clear purpose is indicated. One theory is that these huts were links in a chain of monastic outposts, with the
head monastery at *Mystery Hill* in Salem, New Hampshire. 2
A twelve-acre complex of massive standing stones and eerie underground rooms and tunnels, Mystery Hill is New England's Stonehenge. Besides Irish monks, its construction has been attributed to the Phoenicians and to the same megalithic culture that built Stonehenge in England and Carnac in France. Skeptics say Mystery Hill was probably the work of an eccentric farmer who owned the property in the last century and the great grooved slab of rock known as "the sacrificial altar" was really a "lye stone," a common item in New England when lye was obtained by washing out wood ash. But visitors, helped out by Mystery Hill's guides – who suggest blood not lye ran along the grooves – usually have little trouble seeing some sort of pre-Columbian settlement in the tumbled stones.

We know the Vikings voyaged to North America, but it is still unclear where they landed – although Newfoundland is considered the likely site of the sagas' "Vineland the Good." Which by no means rules out the possibility of Viking voyages along the New England coast. In the nineteenth century, however, there was absolutely no doubt in Yankee minds: New England *was* Vineland.

By the middle of the last century, rune stones were turning up routinely in farmer fields all over New England. On closer inspection they usually turned out to be garden variety Yankee boulders, with perhaps a few more glacial scratches than usual.

Some of them, such as the stones found on the islet
of *Manana* off Monhegan Island, Maine; near the *Ap-* 3
tucxet Trading Post in Bourne, Massachusetts; on the 4
shore of *Spirit Pond*, Maine; and in *Hampton*, New 5, 6
Hampshire, have merited serious consideration by runic scholars. None, however, has been positively identified as Viking inscriptions.

The *Viking Tower* in Newport, Rhode Island, can at 7
least claim to be a literary monument even if it is not a Norse one. Now the centerpiece of a small city park, the tower is certainly old – but it is doubtful if it is the one thousand years old that some claim for it. Although they were an observant lot, the mariners who put into Newport's superb harbor in the early years of the seventeenth century seem not to have noticed it. Nowadays, it's gen-

erally believed that the tower was built around 1675 – by Benedict Arnold's grandfather – as a combination windmill and fortress, in case pirates or Indians attacked.

Back in 1830 – when the Viking mania was at its peak in New England – the legends about the tower, coupled with the discovery in Fall River, Massachusetts, of a skeleton bedecked with corroded metal plates, inspired Longfellow to write his narrative poem, *A Skeleton in Armor*, which fueled the Viking craze for decades. The skeleton turned out to be that of an Algonquin Indian wearing copper trade jewelry, but in the poet's romantic version he was a Norse warrior in the rusted remains of his armor, who had eloped with his true love to Newport where he built the tower "for my lady's bower."

One of the will-o'-the-wisps that obsessed New England's early explorers was the kingdom of "Norumbega," a fabulous place where the natives were extremely friendly – and lived in houses made of crystal and gold.

The name shows up on maps as early as 1529 and came to be used at one time for the whole region from the Bay of Fundy to the Hudson River. In the Algonquin Indian language, Norumbega means "a quiet place between the rapids" and is thought to have referred to a large Indian village in Maine. But, by the time yarn spinners like David Ingram got through with it, Norumbega was an American Shangri-La. Ingram was an English sailor who, after being marooned on the Gulf of Mexico in 1567, managed to talk and walk his way up to New Brunswick where he took ship for England – and lived off tall tales of his days among the Indians for the rest of his life.

At the height of the last century's Viking craze, an eccentric Harvard professor named Eben Horsford became convinced that Norumbega must have been an Indian mispronunciation of "Norwegian" and referred to Leif the Lucky's Vineland Colony. Horsford also decided that Leif's settlement was near Boston, in the Charles River Valley. The reason the Vikings would have selected this spot, according to Horsford, was the forest of great birch trees that flourished there in pre-Columbian times.

Because of their attractive spiral grain, the burl – or knob – of old birch trees was much prized by Norsemen, who used to hollow them out for beer jugs, among other things. This vision of a primitive beer mug factory operating in the environs of staid old Boston some six hundred years before the Pilgrims landed enchanted New Englanders. The name Norumbega was given to a now

defunct amusement park on the banks of the Charles River, outside Boston. A wealthy man, thanks to several
baking powder patents, Horsford built *a Norse style* 8
tower in this park to commemorate his version of how the Vikings came to Massachusetts.

Horsford was never taken too seriously, although "Norumbega" became a popular name for yachts and summer cottages, and Leif Ericson became a folk hero.
In the 1880s, a campy but imposing *statue of the lucky* 9
Viking was erected on Commonwealth Avenue in Boston's Back Bay, and Leif still stands – staring out on his vanished kingdom by the Charles.

In Berkeley, Massachusetts, near the tidal Taunton
River, there sits a large sandstone boulder called "*Dighton* 10
Rock" which has been puzzling people since its discovery in 1677. Now a state monument, the rock is covered with carvings and inscriptions of undoubted antiquity – but so overlaid with three centuries of graffiti that it is difficult to make much of them. Scholars seem to think that they are probably Algonquin Indian pictographs, but they have also been attributed to the Phoenicians, the Chinese, the Vikings, and even the Japanese! However, this part of Massachusetts has a large Portuguese population and the popular local candidate is the Portuguese explorer, Miguel Cortereal.

Miguel disappeared in 1502, while on a voyage to Newfoundland looking for his brother Gaspar – who had failed to return from a voyage of exploration to the same region the year before. The inscription on Dighton Rock, alleged to be Cortereal's, is dated 1511, putting him off course but still alive nine years after he left Portugal.

In the last decades of the fifteenth century, North America was being visited regularly by Europeans, particularly British and Portuguese fishermen who had discovered the great fishing grounds off Newfoundland and Labrador sometime around 1480. John Cabot sailed to Newfoundland and touched the mainland of North America in 1497 and again in 1498. It's quite possible that on one of the voyages he sailed as far south as Maine.

In 1524, Giovanni da Verrazano – an Italian sailing for France – went up the entire New England coast while looking for the fabled Northwest Passage to the Orient. He didn't find China, but discovered a large island which reminded him of Rhodes, thus giving our smallest state its name. He visited what is now Newport, noting that the harbor was so fine that "... any great Navy may ride safe without any fear of tempest or other danger." As he went up the coast, Verrazano noted thick forests "such as are wont to grow in cold countries" – probably a reference to the pines that still grow thick on the coast of Maine. He found that the Indians grew more hostile the farther North he got, suggesting that they had been in contact with the white man before!

The following year, a Portuguese mariner, Estevan Gomez, sailed to Newfoundland and then down the New England coast. Maps of the period suggest that he discovered the Penobscot River, Boston Bay, and Plymouth Harbor.

So, at the opening of the seventeenth century, Europe was well acquainted with the New England coast and the area was ripe for settlement.

In 1602, Bartholomew Gosnold set sail for North America from Falmouth, England, with two ships and a company of thirty-two men. After making a landfall near what is now York, Maine, Gosnold cruised down the coast – using Verrazano's account as a guide – naming Cape Cod and the Elizabeth Islands and discovering Martha's Vineyard. On one of the Elizabeths, *Cuttyhunk* 11
– off the southeast coast of Massachusetts – he landed on May 28 and attempted to plant a colony.

The settlers started well, planting a garden and building a stockade for defense, but the local Indians became increasingly menacing. By the middle of June, when a decision had to be made as to who would stay and who would sail back to England, everybody opted for the boat. The life of the Elizabeth Islands colony was twenty-two days.

The following year, two more ships, *Discoverer* and *Speedwell*, sailed from England under the command of Captain Martin Pring. This expedition touched land first in Maine, probably near the mouth of the Penobscot River, and then sailed down to what they called Mount Aldworth – believed to be near present-day Plymouth. Like the Gosnold party, Pring's men also threw up a stockade, but instead of planting a garden they began to harvest what they found waiting in the earth: sassafras. We don't use it much now, except to flavor some soft drinks, but in the seventeenth century, sassafras was used to treat "The French Pox" – venereal disease. Indians scared the Pring expedition away, too. Pring and company were particularly alarmed by bands of Indians setting fires in the woods around them. This may not have been a hostile act – just the ordinary Indian way of clearing underbrush. But the Pring expedition took no chances and headed home. There is no trace of Pring's aborted colony, but the voyage made a contribution to the nautical knowledge of Massachusetts Bay which the Pilgrims found useful seventeen years later. And the return of two boatloads of hitherto rare sassafras caused joy in some quarters, but sent the price plunging from twenty shillings to little more than three shillings a pound. The market was glutted.

By the early part of the seventeenth century, French fishermen – particularly the salty Bretons – had been fishing off Newfoundland and in the Gulf of St. Lawrence for more than fifty years. It was time for the French to have a try at colonizing North America.

In 1604, a colony was established on an island in the
St. Croix River on the present boundary between Canada 12
and the United States, and Samuel de Champlain explored
the Maine coast, discovering Mt. Desert and Isle au Haut
islands. Badly sited and built, the St. Croix Island colony
was moved to a new site on the Canadian side the following year, but Champlain continued his explorations.
During the next two years he explored the lake which
bears his name, and the Penobscot and as far as Bangor,
Maine, and the New England coast, noting and naming
the White Mountains and stopping by *Gloucester*, Boston, 13
and Plymouth (where he distributed rosaries). The French
probably would have settled in southern New England –
the harbors were good and the weather better than
Canada's – but the Indians were hostile and several of
Champlain's men were killed in disputes with the red
men. It was decided that Canada was colder – but safer.

In 1605, Captain George Weymouth arrived, sailing Nantucket Sound and the Maine coast. He sailed past Monhegan Island and traded successfully with the Indians on the mainland. Weymouth also discovered a great river, probably the Kennebec. He also kidnapped five Indians and brought them home as curiosities – and slaves.

Two years later, in 1607, a really serious attempt, partly
inspired by the tales Weymouth's Indians told, was made
to settle New England. Two ships carrying 120 colonists
arrived at the mouth of the Kennebec River and the
would-be settlers went ashore at *Sabino Head* in the 14
present town of Phippsburg. The expedition was financed

by Sir John Popham, the eighty-year-old chief justice of England, and led by his nephew, George Popham.

Things started off well for the Popham Colony. The Indians were friendly and the settlers began building cabins and even a pinnace, which they named *Virginia*, and were able to launch before winter.

This was the first boat built by Englishmen in what is now the United States and the beginning of the New England shipbuilding industry. Winter was particularly severe and the Popham Colony's luck ran out. In an effort to keep warm the colonists built such roaring fires that they set some buildings on fire, including their storehouse. Sickness broke out and George Popham, among others, died. Disheartened, the settlers left the following spring, some sailing south to the Jamestown Colony, others returning to England to tell tales of Maine winters they haven't lived down yet.

In 1613, the Jesuits established a mission on *Mount* 15
Desert Island, but were run off after a few months by the English, who considered it their territory. This was the first of a long and bloody series of clashes between the French and English to determine who would be master of this coast.

The English still dreamed of settling Maine. In 1616, Sir Fernando Gorges, a wealthy Englishman who had been a backer of the Popham Colony sent Captain Richard Vines and sixteen men to test the weather. Vines and his party
wintered over at *Biddeford Pool*, near the mouth of the 16
Saco River. The following spring, Vines returned home with a report that Maine winters were cold but bearable.

Two years earlier, Captain John Smith had sailed and mapped the New England Coast from Penobscot Bay to Cape Cod Bay. Smith made his first landfall at Monhegan Island, which by this time was being visited by as many as two hundred fishing vessels in a season. His book, *A Description of New England*, was just that, but also a shrewd bit of propagandizing for colonization, stressing the richness of the country, the availability of land, and the abundance of fish and furs. It was a best-seller and it gave this region its name.

So, when the Mayflower headed for the New World its passengers were not sailing into a void. They had read about the new land and seen maps of it and the ship's crew had picked up a lot of unwritten lore in fo'c'sles and waterfront taverns.

Although the Pilgrims had actually intended to settle

farther south on land for which they held a patent, when they did end up at Plymouth, they knew where they were: a promising place called New England.

DETAILS

1 *Beehive Huts.* Two of the easiest to locate and visit are in western Massachusetts, near the town of Leverett. From Amherst, follow Rte. 63 north, take the side road to North Leverett, continue through it to Locks Village and on by Lake Wyola (swimming and summer camping). Continue on through the crossroads just beyond the lake and take your first right. Park and follow the path, then the first side path on the left to the first hut. Return to your car and follow the road for a short distance, forking right on the dirt road marked Mineral Mountain; then left at the Temenos sign. The second hut is a couple of hundred yards in on the right, below a large tree. From the outside these structures look more like caves than beehives; the name derives from the intricate arched stonework within.

2 *Mystery Hill.* Southern New Hampshire, just north of the Massachusetts line. From I-93, exit 3 (Canobie Lake Junction), follow Rte. 111 east, 5 miles to North Salem. At the intersection just before Atkinson, take the Haverhill Road for a quarter mile. Mid-June–mid-Nov., daily; early April–mid-June, weekends: 9:30-dusk. Snack bar and gift shop. Admission charged. (603) 432-2530.

3 *Manana Islet.* Just off Monhegan Island, Maine, from which it is accessible by rowboat. Inquire at the Coast Guard Station. For more about Monhegan, see Chapter 3.

4 *Aptucxet Trading Post.* In Bourne, Massachusetts, on the south side of the Cape Cod Canal, just a few hundred yards west of the Bourne rotary. Follow signs from Bourne Village. April 1–Oct.: 1–5. Closed Monday, spring and fall. Admission charged. (617) 759-5171.

5 *Spirit Pond.* In Phippsburg, Maine. From Rte. 1 at Bath follow Rte. 209 south down the spine of the peninsula. The alleged rune stones found here are at the State Museum in Augusta, but archeological investigation at the site continues. Nearby summer resorts include Sebasco Lodge (207) 389-1161, and Rock Gardens Inn (207) 389-1339.

6 *Hampton, New Hampshire.* The rune stone is located in a wooded area off Rte. 1A in this old coastal town, near Great Boar's Head. It is a large boulder, alleged to be a memorial to Thorwald Ericson, Leif the Lucky's brother.

7 *Viking Tower.* In the heart of Newport, Rhode Island, off Bellevue Ave.

8 *Norse Tower*, Newton, Massachusetts. The tower stands in a small park offering picnic facilities and a path along the Charles River. From Rte. 128 exits 45 and 46 it is badly posted but very near (off South St.). For directions inquire at MDC police station just across the river from the Marriott Hotel; the hotel itself occupies much of the old Norumbega Park but a remnant of the park is adjacent to it, confusing since the tower itself is across the river.

9 *Leif Ericson Statue*, Boston. It stands in Commonwealth Avenue's green strip at Charlesgate East in Back Bay.

10 *Dighton Rock.* In Dighton Rock State Park on Assonet Neck in Berkeley, Massachusetts. From Boston, Rte. 24 south from Rte. 128, past Taunton to Rte. 79; follow the signs. Originally on the banks of the tidal Taunton River, the rock has been moved to high ground.

11 *Cuttyhunk Island, Massachusetts.* At the entrance to Buzzard's Bay, accessible from New Bedford. Now a summer colony with a year-round population of some forty people. Most transient visitors are sailors or fishermen. A pleasant walk from the town of Gosnold brings you to an

odd-looking stone tower, erected in 1902, which marks the site of the first stockade. There are two small inns, Bosworth House (617) 996-9295 and Allen House (617) 996-9292; meals must be reserved ahead. The Cuttyhunk Boat Line's M/V *Alert* carries passengers from New Bedford's Pier 3 daily in summer months, twice weekly the rest of the year. (617) 992-1432.

12 *St. Croix River.* The island is across from Red Beach, off Rte. 1, south of Calais. Dochet Island, where Champlain established his first colony – and where Christmas was first celebrated in the New World – is by mutual agreement a no-man's-land on the boundary between the U.S. and Canada. A marker commemorates this first settlement in the area.

13 *Gloucester, Massachusetts.* Terminus of Rte. 128 north from Boston, on Cape Ann. A marker on the road leading to scenic Rocky Neck, an artists' colony east of town, notes that Champlain landed in Sept. 1606, charting Gloucester harbor which he called "Beauport."

14 *Sabino Head.* In Phippsburg, Maine; from Rte. 1 at Bath, follow Rte. 209 south down the peninsula. A state historic marker has been placed on the Popham Colony site. It is near Popham Beach State Park, popular with swimmers and fishermen and Fort Popham, a massive granite bastion of the Civil War era.

15 *Mount Desert Island, Maine.* Rte. 3 off Rte. 1 at Ellsworth, Maine. Much of this extraordinarily scenic island is included in Acadia National Park. (See Chapter 10.)

16 *Biddeford Pool.* Part of the town of Biddeford, Maine, exit 5 off the Maine Turnpike (I-95). There is no trace of Vines' winter camp, but this is a picturesque little lobstering port.

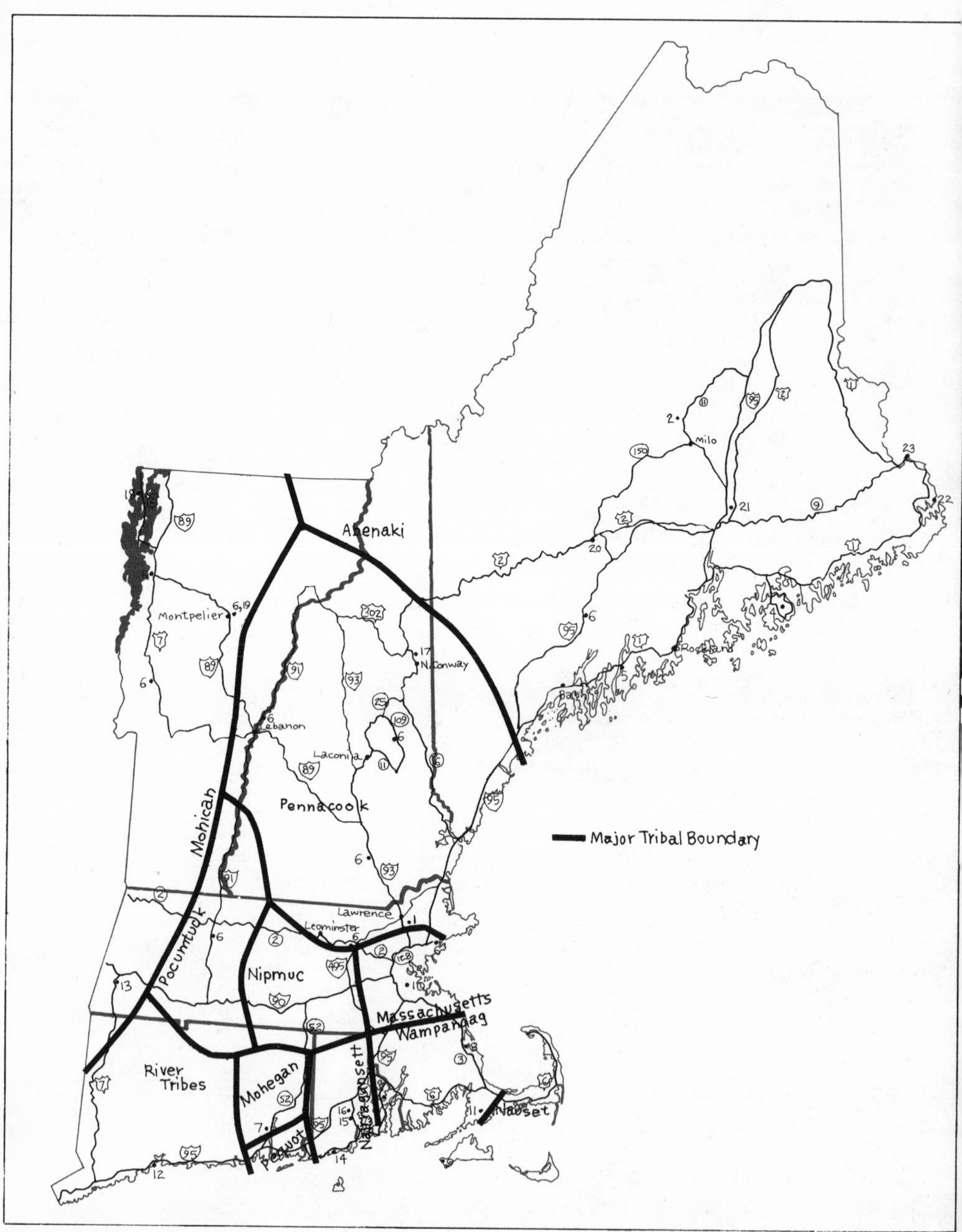

Abenaki
Mohican
Pennacook
Pocumtuck
Nipmuc
Massachusetts
Wampanoag
River Tribes
Mohegan
Pequot
Narragansett
Nauset
Major Tribal Boundary
Montpelier
Lebanon
Laconia
N. Conway
Lawrence
Leominster
Milo
Rockland

2

Indian Inhabitants

New England Indians showed the European newcomers how to survive in this land which they had inhabited for many thousands of years. They taught them how to plant corn, beans, tobacco and squash, to dig for shellfish and make snowshoes, sleighs, canoes and maple sugar. For this kindness and the loss of virtually all their land, they received trinkets, alcohol and the attentions of missionaries and the military.

Winnipesaukee, Penobscot, and Narragansett – not to mention Connecticut and Massachusetts – are among the many Indian names salting the New England map. But it usually comes as a surprise to learn that after more than three hundred years of "civilizing," some eleven thousand increasingly proud Indian descendants still live here.

18th-century iron weathervane

The three state reservations in Maine, the Narragansett communities in Rhode Island and remnants of "Praying Indian" communities in Massachusetts, preserve ancient traditions and serve as rallying points for tribesmen trying to rediscover their identity.

Estimates of the number of natives here when the first Europeans arrived vary between twenty-five thousand and three times that. No one bothered to count Indians into the United States census before 1890. We do know that there were ten major Algonquin tribes in New England, each divided into villages of roughly one hundred people, who migrated back and forth between their winter settlements in the interior and summer camps on the shore.

Collections of ancient Indian weapons and artifacts can

be found throughout the six states. In the *Peabody Foundation for Archaeology* in Andover, Massachusetts, nine-thousand-year-old stone implements unearthed at nearby Ipswich are displayed, along with the remains of a four-thousand-year-old fish weir (some sixty-five thousand wooden stakes, originally linked by woven grass nets) discovered when the country's first subway was being dug in Boston's Back Bay. Here you can also see artifacts from the graves of Maine's "Red Paint People," named for the red ocher found sprinkled in their burial sites, much of it now thought to come from the *Katahdin Iron Works*. And in the *Sidney L. Wright Museum of Indian Artifacts*, located in the Narragansett Bay town of Jamestown, Rhode Island, soapstone bowls and stone implements dating back thirty-four hundred years are displayed near the site at which they were found. 1 2 3

In the *Robert Abbe Museum*, Acadia National Park, a caseful of four-thousand-year-old implements found nearby includes an awl, pear-shaped net weights, a firestone made of iron pyrite and weights for hunting spears. Heavy woodworking tools indicate that the use of birchbark hadn't yet been discovered. 4

The birchbark canoe, carryalls and baskets, intricately decorated with porcupine quills, show what descendants of these people had learned to fashion by the early seventeenth century. There are also tightly woven brown ash and sweet grass baskets, bone needles and harpoons. Dioramas depict how Maine's first explorers found the Penobscots skillfully adjusting to the vagaries of local climate; camping at waterfalls in autumn to catch migrating salmon, moving farther inland to their permanent, birch-covered villages come winter, back down to sheltered coves in spring and to islands such as Mount Desert in summer.

Shell heaps dating back thousands of years are found along Maine's rivers and coast, marking these ancient spring and summer campsites. You can easily understand why they aren't better known when you see the most famous of these formations. It's on the *Damariscotta Estuary* and by now looks more like a shell beach than a "heap." 5

Uninspiring *collections* of ancient arrowheads, shards, wampum, bones, hammer-stones and flints are scattered in corners of hundreds of local museums around the region, with an occasional diorama of a mat wigwam or an early canoe. In Connecticut, once inhabited by sixteen 6

distinct tribes, a small museum, including a reconstructed stockade and longhouse, is maintained by Harold and
Gladys *Tantaquidgeon*, who claim descent from the 7
famed Mohegan Chief Uncas. At *Plimoth Plantation* a 8
carefully researched Algonquin Summer Camp of portable wigwams has been built. The Plantation's Indian staff demonstrates ancient crafts, weaving the grass baskets, for instance, which once served for cooking, toting water and storing beans, pumpkins and corn.

Captain John Smith, recounting his adventures along the New England coast in 1614, described the area around present-day Boston as "all along large corn fields, and great troops of well-proportioned people." Just one year later, however, intertribal warfare destroyed Indian villages throughout southern New England. In its wake came a plague, some bug brought by Smith's fellow fishermen-explorers. By 1617 one-third of the population between Rhode Island and central Maine had been wiped out.

The Puritans took this as a sign of God's favor to his elect. The Indians in turn regarded the new, imported disease as "white man's magic" and were sufficiently impressed by other signs of power displayed by these white men to consider adopting their ways, even their God. The Massachusetts Bay seal pictured an Indian pleading, "Come over and help us." By 1644 the Puritans were feeling secure enough to remember that their charter charged them to "Wynn and incite the Natives . . . [to] the only true God, and saviour of Mankind." Within a couple of years Congregational preacher Thomas Mayhew had converted fifteen hundred Indians on Martha's Vineyard where upwards of two hundred of their descendants live today. In the town of *Gay Head* they man a 9
crafts shop atop the famous cliffs.

In 1649 Roxbury minister John Eliot, who had already
begun preaching at *Pulpit Rock* to local tribes in their 10
own tongue, chartered a Society for the Propagation of the Gospell in New England, drumming up six thousand pounds per year from England to fund publication of a catechism, and later a Bible in Algonquin. Eliot's first and most important "Praying Indian Town" at present-day Natick has long since vanished, along with dozens of similar communities to be found in Massachusetts before 1674.

To the Puritan mind, "civilizing" and "converting" the Indians were two very distinct matters. "Praying Indian" was a title conferred on any native who dressed and wore his or her hair in English fashion, stuck to one spouse, lived in a wooden house, and refrained from drinking, "pow-wowing" and "howling." To become a communicant, however, required a genuine "conversion experience"; in 1670, for instance, there were fifty communicants at Natick out of 145 "Praying Indians."

The town of *Mashpee* represents, as it did in Eliot's 11
day, the Indian stronghold on Cape Cod. Outraged by the high-handed way in which colonists were taking over Indian lands at the time, the son of a wealthy merchant, Richard Bourne, persuaded Plymouth Colony to declare "Mashpee Plantation" Indian land in perpetuity. Bourne was subsequently ordained by Eliot as their minister and his church numbered five hundred members by 1674. Mashpee still has an Old Indian Mission Church and a little Indian Museum: a tidy saltbox, its parlor fitted out with lace curtains and furnished nineteenth-century Yankee style. The Mashpees stage a Pow Wow in July, more a homecoming event for their scattered tribesmen than a tourist attraction, but today "Indian descendants" constitute less than one quarter of the town's population.

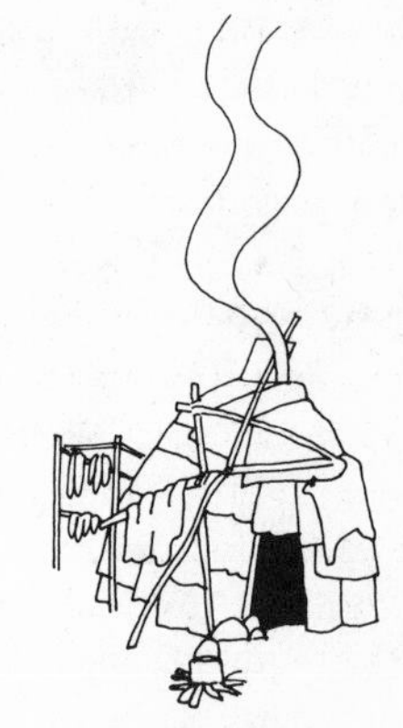

Early Dutch settlers in the Berkshires were content to trade and live with rather than civilize their Indian neighbors. But within a year after Massachusetts men moved into the present town of Sheffield, a young missionary
named John Sergeant was dispatched from *Yale College* 12
to propagate the Gospel at *Stockbridge* – a six-mile- 13
square township thoughtfully granted the local Housatonics (a sub-tribe of the Mohegans) who might wish to gather around him there. The town's unusually wide street dates from its early use as "the plain" on which these friendly Indians built their wigwams. Today only
Sergeant's *Mission House* survives, portraying how well a 13a
sophisticated white family could survive in these backwoods in the early eighteenth century, but little about the Indians. Despite their service to Washington during the Revolution (in gratitude for which the general presented them with a copy of the Declaration of Independence) the Stockbridge Indians were forced west by the end of the eighteenth century, carrying their heavy, leather-bound Bible with them. Today the Bible is back in the Mission House and other mementos of the tribe can be seen in the town's historical room, in the basement of its library.

In Rhode Island the Narragansetts continue to convene an August meeting which they claim to be America's

oldest annual event, held each year for more than three
centuries. It's staged on an *Old Indian Church* grounds at 14
Charlestown, near which a reconstructed Long House is
dedicated to teaching local Indian youth their traditional
crafts, songs, dance and language. The state is also home
of the annual *American Indian Federation Powwow* and 15
of *Dovercrest Trading Post*, a combination museum, shop 16
and restaurant which features ceremonial dances and Indian-style feasts.

In New Hampshire, Passaconaway, Chief of the Penacook Confederacy, received the first white settlers with kindness. His son, Wonalancet, had striven to keep peace with them throughout King Philip's War. After substantial provocation, his nephew Kancamagus attacked the town of Dover. That was it. By the end of the seventeenth century, the New Hampshire tribes had fled to join the St. Francis Indians in Canada.

In the village of *Intervale* there is an interesting memo- 17
rial to one Abenaki chief who returned to his ancestral home in the nineteenth century. Born on a Canadian reservation, Joseph Laurent began making summer visits to the Mount Washington Valley resort town in the 1880s, soon buying a few acres of land and building cabins in which a few of his tribesmen passed the tourist season, selling their wares at local hotels. Behind the little gift shop here, which his youngest son still runs, is a plaque dedicated to Laurent, a scholar who produced a lexicon and grammar on the Abenaki tongue. On the site of the annual summer encampment two birch wigwams, a drying rack, canoe and totem pole have been assembled. The 1970 census lists just 361 Indians in New Hampshire.

This same census counts 229 Indians in Vermont, the fewest in any state, but a big increase over 1960 when the count was 57. Few states, on the other hand, continue to yield such an assortment of ancient artifacts. The Abenakis, first to occupy this area, befriended Champlain in 1609, who in turn helped them defeat the Iroquois on
the lake which bears his name. On the Isle la Motte site
of *Fort St. Anne*, built by the French in 1666, a dusty 18
collection of stone artifacts, said to prove pre-Columbian settlement on the island, is displayed, in the corner of a snack bar. By the end of the eighteenth century Vermont's tribesmen had retreated over the Canadian border, but today practically every village historical society here has its display of arrowheads and pot shards. The best collection of these, garnered from throughout the state,

and dating from two thousand to two hundred years in
age, can be seen in the *Vermont Historical Society Mu-* 19
seum, Montpelier.

The ancestors of Maine's Abenakis are estimated to have once numbered as high as thirty-seven thousand. Today the tribes total fewer than three thousand. These Indians received a nasty impression of Englishmen from the start. In 1605 George Weymouth sailed up the Penobscot, kidnapping five natives at Port Clyde on his way home. These hostages so impressed Sir Fernando Gorges with their "great civility, far from the rudeness of our common people," that the English nobleman spent the rest of his life and fortune attempting to colonize Maine. The French, on the other hand, brought the Abenakis' handy and decorative items, showing no interest in acquiring their land, and the Jesuits worked tirelessly among them. It has been noted that the English colonists called the Indians "brothers" but treated them as wolves, while the French called them *loups* (wolves) but treated them as brothers.

Early French missions at Mt. Desert and Castine proved
to be battlegrounds between French and English: by the
end of the seventeenth century thousands of Abenakis
had retreated either to Canada or to the Penobscot community at Old Town and to the *Norridgewock* mission 20
on the Kennebec where Father Sebastian Rale insisted that the Indian lands "were given them of God, to them and their children forever, according to the Christian oracles." The site of this latter mission is now a pleasant riverside picnic area; there's a monument to Father Rale (who was killed by Massachusetts militiamen in 1724) and a version of the stockaded Indian village has been reconstructed across the road.

By 1760, when the French and Indian wars ended in Maine, only four tribes survived: of these the Micmacs and Malecites made the unlucky choice of siding with the Crown during the Revolution, after which they too fled to Canada. That left only the Penobscots and Passamaquoddies.

By 1786, the Penobscots deeded most of Maine to Massachusetts in exchange for the 140 small islands in the Penobscot River, and in 1818 Massachusetts agreed to pay them an assortment of trinkets for the land. When Maine became a state in 1820, a $37,400 trust fund was set up for the tribe, but it ended up in the state's general treasury. Today, the Maine Indians continue to sue to re-

cover that money (they estimate it's worth $150 million
today) and for back payments on the remainder of their
land, since leased to lumber companies. The Penobscots
now officially own forty-five hundred island acres in the
river which bears their name, but they live only on *Indian* 21
Island which is connected by a one-lane bridge with Old
Town. The 1970 census records 823 Penobscots, half of
whom live here.

Indian Island is believed to have been a campground for at least five thousand years, but present residents understandably refuse to excavate the old burial ground in which layer on layer of their ancestors are buried. They also discourage camera-toting tourists, although visitors are welcome to stroll around the little town which contains small Catholic and Baptist churches, the Indian Agent's office, a wooden school maintained by Catholic nuns, a general store, and a scattering of wooden homes, some with shops selling leather or beadwork and sweet grass baskets at prices well below what they fetch in coastal gift shops. Once a year, usually the third week in July, the tribe stages a two-day pageant that tells its story in song and dance.

The Passamaquoddies number thirteen hundred today
and occupy two reservations in Maine's northeast corner:
the hundred-acre *Pleasant Point* reserve which occupies 22
a bleak, windy point of land jutting into Passamaquoddy
Bay near Perry, and the eighteen-thousand-acre *Indian* 23
Township which begins near Princeton. While their land
reclamation cases continue to be argued, the Passamaquoddies have adopted "self-help" programs such as the logging operation at Indian Township and the crafts cooperative at Pleasant Point, which is also the site of an annual pageant, usually held the second weekend in August.

DETAILS

1 *Peabody Foundation for Archaeology, Andover, Massachusetts.* The first Andover exit off I-93, north from Boston; on Rte. 28, across from the Philips Andover Academy campus. Year round, Mon.-Sat.: 9-4; Sun.: 2-5. Closed national holidays. (617) 475-0248.

2 *Katahdin Iron Works, Brownsville Junction, Maine.* In the central region of the state, off Rte. 11, northeast of Dover-Foxcroft. A mid-nineteenth century blast furnace and charcoal kiln here have been restored by the state. The site was well known to early Indians.

3 *Sidney L. Wright Museum of Indian Artifacts, Jamestown, Rhode Island.* The town of Jamestown occupies an island in Narragansett Bay, linked to the mainland by the Newport Toll Bridge to the north and by the Jamestown Bridge to the south. The collection is housed in a wing of the Philmenian Library, North Road. Year round. Mon., Wed., Fri.: 1-5 and 7-9 P.M.; Tues., Thurs.: 7-9 P.M. (401) 423-0436.

4 *Robert Abbe Museum, Mount Desert Island, Maine.* Within Acadia National Park; Rte. 3 off Rte. 1 at Ellsworth, Maine. See Chapter 10.

5 *Damariscotta Shell Heaps, Damariscotta, Maine.* Rte. 1; ask at the town's chamber of commerce for directions to the site, which is accessible through private land.

6 *Scattered Indian artifacts collections worthy of note:*

Memorial Hall, Old Deerfield Village, Western, Massachusetts, off Rte. 5, south of Greenfield. The Pocumtuck Valley Memorial Association collection of local memorabilia includes a room full of Indian arrowheads, arranged in fanciful designs; also war clubs and Indian bones. April-Nov.; Mon.-Sat.: 9:30-5:00; Sun.: 1:30-5:00. Admission charged. For Old Deerfield Village, see Chapter 4.

Libby Museum, Wolfeboro, New Hampshire. Rte. 109 on Lake Winnipesaukee. A rare, authentic dugout canoe is displayed along with the usual artifacts. June-Labor Day: 10-5.

Haffenreffer Indian Museum, Bristol, Rhode Island, off Rte. 136. Displays of Indian artifacts from around the world, collected by a famous Rhode Island brewing family, currently maintained by Brown University. June-Sept., Tues.-Sat.: 1-4; Sept.-May, weekends: 1-4. Closed Feb. (401) 253-8388.

Fruitlands Museums, Harvard, Massachusetts. From Boston, Rte. 2 to Harvard exit, Rte. 120 one quarter mile south, right on Old Shirley Road, bear left when it forks on Prospect Hill Road. The American Indian Museum in this complex includes artifacts and dioramas of the Massachusetts tribe. May 30-Sept. 30, daily except Mon., unless a holiday: 1-5. (617) 456-3924.

Baker Library, Dartmouth College, Hanover, New Hampshire. Southwestern New Hampshire on Connecticut River, Rte. 10. The collection of Indian artifacts is outstanding.

Maine State Museum, Augusta, Maine. Opposite the Capitol Building. This new museum includes the usual artifacts. June-Sept.: Mon.-Sat.: 9-6; Sun.: 12-6. During the remainder of the year it closes at 4.

Manchester, New Hampshire. Southern, central New Hampshire, I-93. Both the Historic Association (corner of Pine & Amherst Sts.; Tues., Thurs., Sat.: 2-4) and the Institute of Arts and Sciences (corner of Pine & Concord Sts.; weekdays: 9-5, Mon.: 2-5) contain major exhibits from burial sites within the state.

Peabody Museum, Salem, Massachusetts. 161 Essex St. Extensive exhibits include an 18th century birchbark canoe from the area. Year round, weekdays: 9-5; Sun. & holidays: 1-5. Admission charged. (617) 745-1876.

Bronson Museum, Attleboro, Massachusetts. 8 North Main St. (Rte. 52), fifth floor. Artifacts dating from 9,000 years old to colonial times; diorama of a primitive Indian village. Maintained by the Massachusetts Archaeological Society. (617) 222-5470.

Sheldon Museum, Middlebury, Vermont, 1 Park St. A small but important display of locally found artifacts. June-Oct. 15, daily except Sun.: 10-5; rest of year, Tues., Thurs.: 1-5. Admission charged. (802) 388-2117.

7 *Tantaquidgeon Indian Museum, Uncasville, Connecticut.* Off I-95 at New London; follow Rte. 32. Besides a stockade and longhouse, the museum includes a mix of old artifacts, the dates of which have never been researched. There is also an early nineteenth-century Indian church here. The town itself represents the highest concentration of Indian descendants in the state. Heading north, follow directions to Fort Shantook State Park which includes a stockaded burial ground. Connecticut Indians are said to have numbered six thousand in the seventeenth century; today the count is two hundred with state reservations at Trumbull, North Stonington, Ledyard and Kent recording a total population of 21. May-Oct., Mon.-Sun., holidays, 10-6. Donation. (203) 848-9145.

8 *Plimoth Plantation, Plymouth, Massachusetts.* Rte. 3A, 1 mile south of Plymouth. The summer camp is part of the Plantation's Native Studies Program and represents the only New England-wide center for tribal study. See Chapter 3.

9 *Gay Head, Martha's Vineyard, Massachusetts.* Western tip of the island. The Aquinnah gift shop here is open seasonally. The Gay Head Baptist Church houses the congregation formed by Mayhew. For details contact Martha's Vineyard Chamber of Commerce, Box 853, Vineyard Haven, Massachusetts 02568. (617) 693-0085.

10 *Pulpit Rock, West Roxbury, Massachusetts.* Boston area, marked road from Veterans of Foreign Wars Highway.

11 *Mashpee, Massachusetts.* Cape Cod; from Rte. 6, exit 2, Rte. 130 to Fire Station, center of town, and ask directions to:

The Old Indian Church. Established 1637, moved to its present site 1717. Closed except for Sunday services, but the burial ground is interesting.

Mashpee Indian Museum. Displays of Wampanoag life; picnic tables out back. July 1-Sept. 10: 10-4; closed Sat. (617) 477-0494.

Mashpee-Wakeby Lake. Two large, connecting fresh water ponds with a sandy beach and picnic facilities in the Lowell Holly Reservation, maintained by Trustees of Reservations.

12 *Yale University, New Haven, Connecticut.* Founded in 1701 as the Collegiate School in Saybrook, it moved to New Haven in 1716 and changed its name to Yale College in honor of a benefactor. Free guided tours are offered during the academic term on weekends, departing from Phelps Gateway, College St. (west side of the Green). Details are available from the information office here. (203) 436-4771.

13 *Stockbridge, Massachusetts.* Western Massachusetts, follow Rte. 7 south from exit off Massachusetts Turnpike. A delightful Berkshire Hills town, best known today as home of artist Norman Rockwell and the Alice of restaurant fame.

13a *Mission House,* Stockbridge. Rte. 2 south from center of town. A beautifully restored and furnished eighteenth-century house, maintained by the Trustees of Reservations. May 28–Oct. 15; Mon.–Sat. 10–5:30; Sun. and holidays: 2–5:30. Admission charged. (413) 298–3383.

14 *Old Indian Church, Charlestown, Rhode Island.* Rte. 2/112; it can be approached either from the Hope Valley exit off I–95 or from Rte. 1. The church, built in 1859, replaces a 1750 mission; services are held here every Sunday, visitors welcome. The two-day powwow, usually held the second weekend in August, includes crafts sales, tribal dances and food. Sunday services, Palm Sunday–mid-Nov.: 11 A.M.

15 *American Indian Federation Powwow, Lafayette, Rhode Island.* Indian Hall on King St. (Rte. 873). First weekend in August. (401) 889–4826.

16 *Dovecrest Trading Post, Exeter, Rhode Island.* (Summit Rd., Acadia Village.) This complex includes the Tomaquag Indian Memorial Museum displaying general American Indian craftwork and a restaurant featuring periodic Indian festival meals. April 1–Thanksgiving, daily, from 11 A.M. weekdays, 11:30 weekends. (401) 539–7795.

17 *Intervale, New Hampshire.* Off Rte. 16, just north of North Conway. The Abenaki Indian Shop is opposite the old village railroad station. June 15–Oct. 15: 9:30–5:30. (603) 356–2417.

18 *Fort St. Anne; Isle la Motte, Vermont.* (On an island in Lake Champlain, accessible via Rte. 2 through Grand Isle from Burlington.) The site of the fort itself is outlined by a ring of cedar trees. This was the site of the first Catholic mass as well as the first settlement in the state, and is now owned by the Edmundite Fathers who maintain the adjacent shrine and cafeteria in which the artifacts are found. May 15–Oct. 15. (802) 928–8284.

19 *The Vermont Historical Society Museum, Montpelier, Vermont.* The museum occupies the ground floor of the Pavilion Building, next to the state capitol. Year round, weekdays: 9–5.

20 *Norridgewock, Maine.* Near Skowhegan; Rte. 201A, just south of Madison/Anson. Father Rale's grave is at the rear of the cemetery across from the new "Abenaki Village," a tourist come-on which includes a wax museum, a slide show and murals dramatizing the story of the mission and massacre. The actual Abenaki dictionary which Father Rale wrote during his thirty years in this community is now in Harvard University's Widener Library. The village is open April 19–Labor Day.

21 *Indian Island, Old Town, Maine.* Maine Turnpike to Orono, then north on Rte. 2. There are no tourist facilities on the island and photographs are discouraged.

22 *Pleasant Point, Maine.* Turn off Rte. 1 at Perry and follow Rte. 190.

23 *Indian Township, Maine.* Rte. 1 to Calais where information about the reservation can be obtained at the office of Legal Pine Tree Assistance.

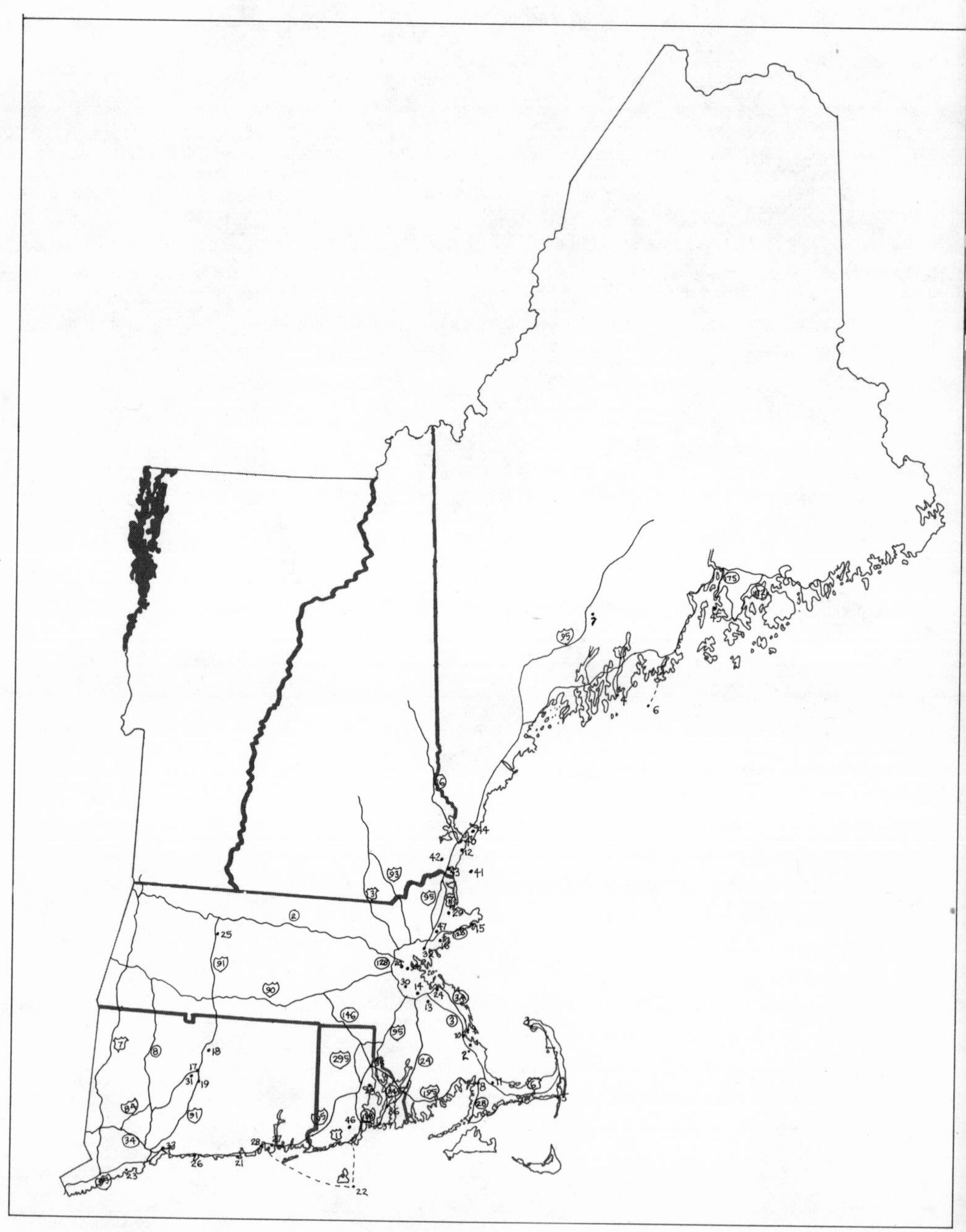

3

Colonial Crucible

PILGRIMS AND PURITANS

In *Plymouth* the very sight of *Mayflower II* 1, 1a
makes you wonder how 127 people could consider spending ten weeks on the autumn Atlantic in such a frail little rig.

Visit *Plimoth Plantation*, now re-created just south of 2
town, to learn the cause and upshot of this passage. You discover that some forty of the 102 passengers had already spent twelve years in Holland just for the privilege of practicing their "Separatist" beliefs, prohibited at the time in Anglican England. Still they felt as passionately about being English as they did about their religion. What they wanted was a place to put the two together and America looked like it. A profit-hungry London group agreed to finance the expedition on condition that all the land which they settled be shared and the money paid back within seven years. It also recruited a mix of farmers and tradesmen from the city to join the venture.

Mayflower, *Plymouth, Mass.*

These "Pilgrims" (the name by which all *Mayflower* passengers have since been known) wound up on Cape Cod's sandbars instead of in New York Harbor for which they were headed. Realizing that they were beyond reach of any law, the forty-one male passengers drew up an agreement to govern themselves according to what the majority decided was "most meet and convenient for the general good." The Mayflower Compact was a very new
idea at the time, as dramatic as the *Pilgrim Monument*, 3
that bizarre obelisk which now looms above the town of Provincetown, the spot near which the compact was signed.

The *Mayflower* sat in Provincetown Harbor for five
more weeks; by the time the pilgrims finally stepped off
onto *Plymouth Rock*, it was December 16, 1620, and they 1b
hustled to build temporary huts. Nearly half of them died
that first hard winter and were buried secretly on *Cole's* 1c
Hill. When the *Mayflower* set sail for England in March,
only the surviving crew went with her.

Plymouth itself had been the site of an Indian settlement, recently decimated by the plague. No wonder the
local Wampanoags took four months deciding how to react to the Pilgrims. Finally *Samoset*, a Pemaquid Indian 4
from Maine, strode in on a Plymouth Council meeting,
saluting it with his famous "Welcome." Soon *Squanto*, a 5
Wampanoag who had been kidnapped from Cape Cod a
few years previously and carried off to England (making
his way home via Maine where he had picked up Samoset)
introduced himself. Then Wampanoag Chief *Massasoit* 1d
appeared, declaring himself a subject to King James and
giving the white men all adjacent land. Throughout the
summer the Indians taught the Englishmen how to hunt,
fish and farm. By October there was plenty of excuse to
spend an entire week feasting and gaming in celebration
of the harvest with Massasoit and ninety of his braves.
This original *Thanksgiving* is celebrated over the Colum- 1e
bus Day weekend at the Plantation while the town of
Plymouth observes the date which the United States Government has since decreed.

A new ship arrived from England, bringing thirty more
settlers and a patent from the Council for New England
to all land in the vicinity, including Cape Cod. And the
London investors kept sending more settlers. Housing
and food became a problem. William Bradford, young
governor of the community, sent expeditions to beg food
from the fishing boats at *Monhegan*. The shallop which 6
they constructed for this purpose was also used in 1625
to sail up Maine's Kennebec River as far as present-day
Augusta, and here Edward Winslow of the colony bought
"seven hundred pounds of good beaver and some other
furs" from the Abenakis for "a shallop's load of corn."
The profits of the trade depended on maintaining a
monopoly, and in 1630 the Pilgrims procured a grant to
the Kennebec from Gardiner to a waterfall about half
way between Augusta and Waterville, and a strip of land
fifteen miles wide on each bank. At Cushnoc (*Augusta*) 7
itself they built a storehouse and by 1633 the proceeds
from beaver sales had taken care of the eighteen-hundred-

pound debt which the London merchants had agreed to in exchange for transfer of their interest to the colony.

In all the Pilgrims built a half dozen such trading posts. *Aptucxet*, founded in 1627 at Bourne, Massachusetts, 8
has since been reconstructed and contains samples of the "wampum" (white periwinkle and blue quahog shells) which Dutchmen taught them to use here in trading with the Indians for beaver pelts and otter skins. By 1627 the colony included fifty families, plus twenty-two goats, fifteen cattle and more than fifty pigs. This is the year in which you now walk into Plimoth Plantation, which looks much as a visitor of the day from New Amsterdam described it: "The houses are constructed of hewn planks, with gardens also enclosed behind and at the sides with hewn planks . . . surrounded with a stockade against sudden attack . . . upon the hill they have a large, square house, with a flat roof, upon the top of which they have six cannon . . . the lower part they use for a church."

Middle-17th-century meetinghouse

A dozen thatched houses have been recreated along the wide, unpaved street which slopes downhill from the "Fort-Meeting House." The Plantation's researchers admit that most of these are far too tidy, constructed as they were until recently with modern tools. Recent additions are visibly cruder, built by a dozen unskilled workers of daub (sand, mixed with grass and clay) and alder wattling. They are almost square with extremely small windows, covered with oiled paper.

The dimness of the interior would have been far more pleasing to its inhabitants than it is to us since fresh air was something they got plenty of from planting through harvesttime. And the wide chimneys let in too many cold blasts to satisfy the families huddled around their winter hearths. Most recreated homes within the Plantation are just one room with a loft above the "hall" which served as kitchen, living, dining and bedroom. Children, servants and boarders usually slept in the loft. Signs of wealth take the shape of what furnishings a family possesses: the iron utensils suspended from the "lug pole" above the hearth, the wooden, earthenware and pewter on the table, and the clothing encased in heavy chests. Not every house has a "bedstead"; "bed" at the time referred to what we call "bedding," usually stuffed with wool, rags and straw and laid out on the floor. Chairs were also garnishings, as was a planked floor.

Years ago Plimoth Plantation auctioned off its authentic eighteenth-century pieces or sent them to *Pilgrim Hall* 1f

Museum. The idea was to permit visitors to touch and move at will within the village, asking questions instead of listening to prepared spiels. Staff busy themselves with whatever their prototypes might have done: preparing what food their gardens, hunting or fishing might yield at a particular season, milking cows, drying fish, tending sheep. Late in the morning you can be sure to find stews bubbling in Dutch ovens on the various hearths.

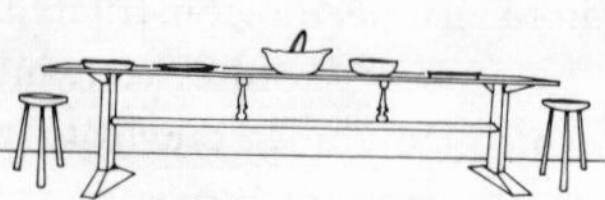

17th-century trestle table

The original Plantation was located on the site presently
occupied by Plymouth's two churches, a graveyard and a
post office on Leyden Street. Other sites in town, notably
the 1640 *Richard Sparrow House* and the *Harlow Old* 1g, 1h
Fort House, built in 1677 from the timbers of the original fort, trace life as it evolved here later in the century,
an era also depicted by the *John Alden* House in nearby 9
Duxbury, the *Major John Bradford* House in Kingston 10
and *Hoxie House* in Sandwich. 11

But it is the year depicted by the Plantation which best illustrates the Pilgrims' importance. By 1627 the community, just about to burst from its fortified cocoon, had demonstrated that a colony could be self-supporting in New England. It was about to be upstaged by a far larger group attempting that experiment.

A dozen other settlements had sprung up along the
New England coast by now, all basically fishing posts on
land granted from the Council for New England. In 1622
one immense grant, including all land between the Kennebec and Merrimac Rivers had been given two men – Sir
Fernando Gorges of Plymouth, England, and Captain
John Mason, a London merchant. These two speculators
sensibly divided it between them at the Piscataqua River,
much where the line between New Hampshire and Maine
now falls. An office clerk for the Council, David Thompson, also received a small patent to plant a settlement
within this domain which he did at *Odiorne Point*, now 12
in the town of Rye, New Hampshire.

Nearer the Pilgrims there was Wessagusset (now *Wey-* 13
mouth), from which an Anglican clergyman named
William Blackstone wandered off to build a farm on the
peninsula known then as "Shawmut," now Boston. At
Merrymount (*Quincy*) a group of Englishmen had set up 14
a Maypole and were so given to drinking and gaming with
the Indians that the Pilgrims managed to get their leader,
Thomas Morton, recalled to England. At *Gloucester* on 15
Cape Ann, yet another group, the Dorchester Company,
had set itself up.

It happened that most stockholders in this last company
were "Puritans," a sect as opposed to the Church of England as the Pilgrim separatists, but committed to "puri-
fying" it from within. A dozen of their leaders met at
Cambridge University in 1620 and agreed to come to
nearby *Salem* where Puritans led by John Endicott had 16
settled the previous year. This new group demanded the
right to govern the settlement, a point they won – along
with a royal charter for a "Company of Massachusetts
Bay in New England," the first to permit Americans to
govern themselves through a "great and general court"
held on their homeground.

More than four hundred of these Puritans led by their aristocratic Governor John Winthrop arrived in Salem that year, but didn't like it. They moved on down to Charlestown but found the water there briney and so scattered in various directions, settling Watertown, Lynn, Medford, Dorchester and Roxbury. One group accepted William Blackstone's invitation to join him on his peninsula.

Hundreds of these new arrivals died the following winter, but in 1630 more than a thousand more arrived. Persecution of the Puritans had increased back home in 1620: King Charles II had disbanded Parliament and begun ruling as a dictator, leaning heavily on his Anglican archbishop, chief enemy of the sect. By 1643 Massachusetts Bay numbered sixteen thousand residents – as many as the rest of British America (including Bermuda and the West Indies) combined. John Winthrop had become known as the "Moses of the Great Puritan Exodus."

His own regime was famously intolerant. Until 1634 a dozen "freemen," stockholders in the company, had made all the colony's decisions. Finally some minor officials demanded to see the original charter and found that law-making was up to the General Court. This they managed to expand to include representatives from each town. But every voter as well as officeholder still had to be a church member, a rule which hadn't applied in Plymouth.

Since most members of the Puritan exodus arrived in small groups, led by their home ministers – and since they had all taken the trouble to get this far in order to worship and live as they saw fit – it was a natural step to push out beyond the confines of Massachusetts Bay's rule. The first popular direction was Connecticut.

In 1633 the Dutch had established a "House of Good

Hope" trading post at present-day *Hartford* on the Con- 17
necticut River. The local Indians, looking for support
against their tribal enemies, invited both Pilgrims and
Puritans to settle along the river too. In a matter of
months a group of Pilgrims arrived at *Windsor*, just up- 18
river from Hartford, bringing with them a pre-fab house
which they quickly enclosed in a stockade, the "pala-
sidio." John Oldham, a Massachusetts Bay trader founded
Wethersfield, just south of Hartford, and a group from 19
Dorchester settled next to the Pilgrims at Windsor, eventually elbowing them out. Finally the man generally
dubbed "Father of Connecticut" arrived. This was Reverend Thomas Hooker, who had been serving as pastor
at New Towne (*Cambridge*), near Boston, until June of 20
1636, when he assembled one hundred of his followers
and 160 of the cattle, plus pigs and goats at Cambridge
Common and started off over Indian trails to Hartford.
This was the year in which England captured New Amsterdam, so the Dutch ceded them the spot. Connecticut
proved no refuge from the Winthrop family. In 1635
John Winthrop, Jr., had arrived in the Bay Colony with a
patent to land including all the present Nutmeg state.
But since he needed settlers as much as they needed his
patent, a bargain was struck, acknowledging Winthrop, Jr., governor of the three towns. He quickly founded a community of his own, building a fort at the
mouth of the Connecticut River in present-day *Old Say-* 21
brook.

Its first turned out to be this new colony's stormiest
year. In 1637 John Oldham was found murdered in his
boat off *Block Island*. Outraged Bay Staters sent ninety 22
soldiers off to pillage the island from which they moved
on to rampage the countryside around Saybrook. The
Pequots retaliated by roasting a local colonist alive. War
against the Pequots was declared that April. At the time
there were only three hundred settlers in Connecticut,
but the seven hundred Pequot warriors possessed just
sixteen guns and little powder. The settlers found backing
from the Narragansett and Mohegan Indians, and forces
from Massachusetts. It turned out to be less a war than a
massacre: a Pequot fort on the Mystic River was surrounded one dawn while its occupants slept off a night
of feasting. Within a half hour all but seven of the hundreds of men, women and children within were dead.
Massachusetts soldiers arrived in time to slaughter the last
fleeing members of the tribe near present *Fairfield*. Those 23

who did survive were sold as slaves to the colonists and friendly tribes or shipped off as such to the Caribbean.

Within a couple of decades more than eight thousand settlers were scattered through Connecticut, more than twenty-five thousand in Massachusetts Bay. But the Great Puritan Exodus was over. Civil War at home had pitched the King's Party against the Roundhead backers of both Puritans and Parliament. Many New World refugees returned to England to support their cause.

Still, new communities continued to "hive off" from the first New England towns: the colonies freely granted elbow space to the johnny-come-lately congregations which inevitably grew restless and land hungry as soon as they had found their land legs.

Typically these groups received six-mile-square townships which they turned into compact little communities, huddled around a "common" which in turn was surrounded by a stockade – a defense against both unfriendly animals and Indians. Beyond this place each settler cultivated his own fields, usually long strips of land which he had drawn by lot. Farther beyond lay fenced pasture, open to all, as were the reserves on which residents cut wood and quarried stone.

Such a layout required a high degree of cooperation, possible in part because these first "proprietors" had already weathered so many ups and downs together and in part because they believed strongly in that idea of self-rule which the Pilgrims first articulated. It had been quickly adopted by the Puritans at Salem and subsequently, decision-making by each congregation on secular as well as religious issues became the norm: instead of "Puritan" or "Separatist" churches became known as "Congregational."

Whitfield House, Guilford, Conn.

The term "church," however, they never applied to a building. Instead they built "meetinghouses," the center for all community life. Unfortunately, none of these has
survived, save that now known as the *Old Ship Church* in 24
Hingham, a late model (1681) and a unique one at that since its roof was built by ships' carpenters to resemble the inverted hull of a vessel. So fanciful were the early meetinghouses by comparison with their plain, box-
shaped successors, that the *couple which have been* 25
reconstructed would be difficult to believe if ample records didn't comfirm their shape, usually square with a steeply pitched roof raising almost to a central peak, capped by a belfry.

Occasionally the community's biggest home doubled for many years both as a garrison and meetinghouse. The
Henry Whitfield House in Guilford, Connecticut, built in 26
1639, includes an exceptionally long, wide "great hall" across the middle of which a wooden partition could be lowered to divide it when the town was not assembling. Built of stone and an extravagant five rooms with what must be the biggest of the region's big fireplaces, this building resembles those to be found in the north of England (home of Guilford's most influential founder), rather than anything else built here at the time.

Since wood is far more plentiful in new than in old England, it is a stroke of what the Puritans must have undoubtedly termed "Providence" that most of them hailed from the southeastern counties – one district in which quarrying stone is scarce and its residents accustomed to building in wood.

Whipple House, Ipswich, Mass., 1640

One thing no Englishman built at home was a log cabin. And they did not build them here. By the mid-1630s new arrivals could lodge in existing homes or even "burrow themselves in the earth for their first shelter under some hillside." They also threw up temporary "English wigwams" patterned on Indian models but with the addition of a wood or stone chimney. Samples can be seen at Salem's Pioneer Village.

Fairbanks House, Dedham, Mass., 1636

But carpenters and masons as well as brick and timber were plentiful and cheap. With a little help from your friends to help raise the wooden joints of a home – once the carpenter had numbered and laid them in place – you could have a sturdy if tiny house – a "hall" with bedroom above and chimney up one side – in no time flat. The most common model of its day, few examples of this "one room plan" house survive simply because a second set of rooms was soon added on to the other side of the chimney and soon after that a "lean-to" was tacked on behind, adding more cooking and bedroom
space, plus backing against north winds. The *Hempsted* 27
House in New London, the *Thomas Lee House* in East 28
Lyme, and the *Whipple House* in Ipswich all evolved this 29
way.

Many of the homes began as a four-room cluster around
the big chimney. Yorkshire wool dealer *Jonathan Fair-* 30
banks secured his "twelve acres more or less" in the brand new town of Dedham and here built such a dwelling (now America's oldest frame building) in 1636. His construction costs totaled a middle-class twenty pounds. Still

maintained by the Fairbanks family, this low-slung clapboard house with its picturesquely steep roof ranks among the best seventeenth-century homes extant. The sash windows along its southern face are later additions, but the essential look of the "parlor" with its formal Jacobean furnishings and the homier clutter in the keeping room are original. In the lean-to, you see Jonathan's toolbox and his oxen yoke along with many more wooden farm and kitchen tools. Walls are insulated with unburned brick, straw and dried grass, weatherproofed with carefully overlapping clapboards, now a deep brown. Since it was the custom for the oldest son to inherit the family property, another gambrel-roofed wing was added on for this lucky boy in 1648 – balanced by a similar west wing a half dozen years later. So it happened that by the time Jonathan died in 1668 his house, a medieval English cottage at its outset, had spread out unevenly along the land, adapting like the merchant-turned-farmer to the demands of a new land.

17th-century cottage, 1680

Fireplace

The picturesquely steep roof of the Fairbanks home, like many a contemporary, was pitched this way to permit water runoff from its thatch. Thatching was forbidden early in the 1630s by the Massachusetts General Court, but for decades after towns continued to set aside sections of marsh grass for the purpose. Over the years, however, split pine shingles proved a far more sensible defense against New England freeze and thaw.

The few homes (such as those of *Stanley Whitman* in 31
Farmington, *Buttolph Williams* in Wethersfield, and of 19a
the Iron Master at *Saugus*) which have been restored 32
complete with their casement windows, Elizabethan
overhangs and wooden "drops," show just how close to
medieval England these homes began. On the other hand,
you might easily take the *Cooper-Frost-Austin* home in 20a
Cambridge with its later sash casements and white paint
for a far newer model. Today only their unusually steep
roofs, outsized chimneys and occasionally the imbalanced
placement of their windows set many a modest seventeenth-century home apart from the typical New England
"saltboxes" of far later dates for which they served as
patterns. Less than half of the regions's 112 "first period"
homes have, in fact, been restored and opened to visitors.
For a listing, see the end of this chapter's details. A couple
of token houses in both *Guilford* and *Ipswich* are open 26a, 29a
to the public; dozens more dating from the seventeenth
century are private homes, a fact dramatized by an an-

nual July tour of old homes in the former and Old Ipswich Days, a week during which the latter town holds open house every August.

Be it said that none of these buildings now shelters anything like the number of people which they originally did, nor the variety of undertakings required merely to sustain life. The typical "hall" or "keeping room" was a clutter of fireplace gear, two spinning wheels (the big one for wool, little one for flax), its "settle" (that wonderfully high-backed, often curved bench set facing the fire), its cradle, high chair, plank table and chairs plus a bedstead and the cupboards required to hold a family's wooden "treen" ware, pewter, red pottery and horn cups, not to mention the wooden containers for water and grain, a butter churn and other wooden farm and implements too.

Fill this mentally with the typical family of six to eight during winter months: the women baking in the hearth's brick oven, minding the pot of beans, corn meal and stew, perhaps roasting eggs or potatoes in the ashes. This ash might also be made into soap or used to scour the plank floors.

Central though it was, the big old fireplace threw off nothing like central heating and frequently remained unlit in the "parlor" which, true to Puritan sense of decorum, contained the best high-backed chairs, maybe a round table and chests, and sat unused save for Sabbath and formal occasions – with the exception of that corner filled by the father and mother's bedstead, usually curtained both for privacy and warmth. Upstairs rooms were cold and sparsely furnished, aside from bedsteads and the chests which had brought the family bedding and clothes from England.

Iron kettles and pots were being produced as early as 1646 at "Hammersmith," an iron works set up by the
ubiquitous John Winthrop, Jr., in present-day *Saugus.* 32a
Advanced for its day, this operation included a "slitting mill" which produced durable "flats" which could be made into nails. Until the late eighteenth century, however, most iron hinges and nails continued to be imported from England.

It is interesting to note that Scots prisoners of war and a few Indians did the hot and dangerous work at Hammersmith. While 95% of the Puritans were small farmers or manual workmen, they had their pride. This fact is evidenced by their handsome doublets and full pants, the frocks which boasted lace to compensate for the forbidden jewelry. Crimson was the most popular color for stockings of the day.

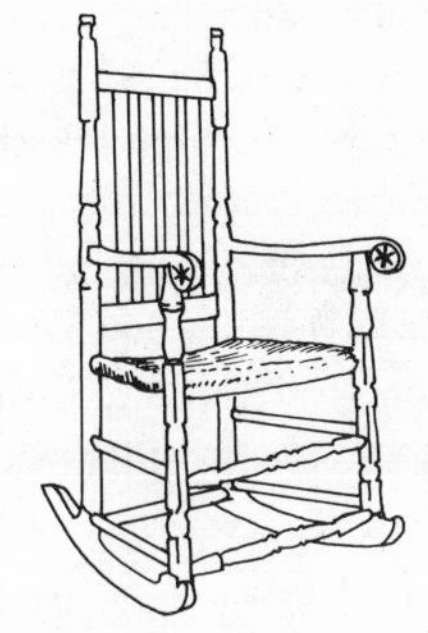

17th-century banister-back chair

If the family ate with wooden spoons and their hands (Governor Winthrop is reported to have possessed the only fork in the colony for many years and that he kept in a case), they also took care to conn the Bible, psalm book, New England primer or maybe an edifying poem like the "Day of Doom" after supper. If they ignored Christmas, they heartily celebrated Thanksgiving and the annual "training day" (on which men and boys mustered on the common and repaired to the adjacent tavern after).

The Congregational Church gave every man a say in religious affairs as the town meeting did in local government. Puritan doctrine taught each person to consider himself a significant, if sinful, unit. To be a church member, however, you had to be able to read the Bible, and to become a minister you had to have a university education – a problem before 1653 since English universities were closed to Puritans.

So in 1636, Massachusetts Bay granted four hundred pounds to open up a college in a small house on the Cambridge Cow Yard. It was named for *John Harvard*, who 20b
bequeathed it half his fortune and all his books. America's first printing press was installed here in 1639, scholarships were offered through contributions from all the colonies in the New England Confederation, and Harvard was soon famous enough to attract paying students from Bermuda, Virginia, and even England.

Harvard College, 1726. Cambridge, Mass.

A diorama of Cambridge in the 1670s in the University's Widener Library reveals the distinctive shape of early New England communities. Of course, no two towns were precisely alike, but the fact remains that grouping homes around a meetinghouse and a common remained a distinctively Puritan pattern until eighteenth
century towns began copying it a century later. *New* 33
Haven's core – a square divided into nine blocks with the central one forming the common, survives to this day. And the center of Windsor still retains the old "Palisado" name.

Boston, by far the region's biggest city, required no 34
manmade defense. It was a natural fort, connected only by narrow Boston Neck (now Washington Street) to the mainland. Given the fact that it has since entirely altered this shape, more than doubling its size, it is difficult to visualize what it looked like.

The Boston shoreline cut through the present *Common* 34a
and followed what is now Charles Street to the marshy
northern river bank, then back along a millpond (at the
outer rim of which North Station now stands) and back
around to Dock Square. The area was further divided by
three hills: Trimountain (itself composed of three peaks
which have since been filed down), Fort Hill (eventually
completely leveled to form the waterfront near South Station), and Copps Hill in the North End. *Three cemeteries*, 34b
the *Paul Revere House* and its oldest streets (which, con- 34c
trary to legend, were not designed by cows) are all that
survive of seventeenth-century Boston. Theoretically, the
streets radiated from the open-air market at Dock
Square. Here a big, gabled town house was built in 1657,
serving as the city's business center until 1711, when it
was replaced by the present *Old State House*. 34d

In 1663, English travel writer John Josselyn described Boston as "a metropolis, almost square" dominated by Trimountain and distinguished by "houses raised on sea banks and wharfed out with great industry and cost, many of them standing on piles." Josselyn noted that the streets were cobbled and lined with "many fair shops."

FRONTIER FRINGES

Rhode Island

Rhode Island's founder was a minister who objected to the tenets of the Puritan as well as the Anglican Church. He dared to say that church and state should be two distinct powers and that the king could not grant American land because it belonged to the Indians. For these views, Roger Williams was forced to flee Salem one bitter January night in 1636 after discovering that a ship was on its way there to deport him. Williams found refuge in Massasoit's camp that winter, and in the spring his family and a few friends joined him. Still they were within Plymouth Colony, which, although sympathetic because he had served as its minister, asked him to leave for fear of angering its powerful neighbor. So the group pushed on,
settling finally on a peninsula between two rivers; a site
which Williams named *Providence* having sense of "God's 35
merciful providence unto me." He dedicated it to complete freedom of conscience.

The new settlement grew quickly, expanding with new
refugees from Massachusetts Bay. *Anne Hutchinson*, the 34e

outspoken wife of a well-to-do Bostonian who had been
banished from Boston for daring to preach that salvation
lay in faith not works, arrived with followers enough to
found *Portsmouth* on the northern shore of that island 36
which the Indians called Aquidneck and the colonists
"Rhode Island." Soon thereafter a number of these, led
by William Coddington, withdrew to settle *Newport* at 37
the southern tip of that island. Samuel Gorton, still another dissenter from Plymouth, founded a community at
Warwick. Each of these four towns conducted its own 38
government in town meetings, and the informal arrangements soon proved inadequate against pressures from
the neighboring colonies. In 1643 the four towns sent
Williams to England to secure a charter, which he did –
writing his "Key into the Language of America" on ship
and paying for the voyage by establishing a post for trading with the Dutch at *Wickford* on his return. Again in 39
1633 he secured a second charter, New England's first to
guarantee full religious liberty (this served as Rhode Island's constitution until 1843). Williams also founded the
country's first *Baptist Church* at Providence but subse- 35a
quently turned his back on it. The *Friends Meeting House* 37a
and *Touro Synagogue* also bespeak his kindness to Quak- 37b
ers and to a distinguished group of Spanish and Portuguese Jews.

Rhode Island's climate is milder than the rest of New
England and its first permanent homes differed from
their Puritan neighbors. Many were "stone ender" story-
and-a-half, one- or two-room houses with stone chimneys
along one side, frequently built on one side of a large
room, the kitchen on a level below the entry, making it
cooler in summer. Many were also gambrel-roofed houses
such as the *Wanton-Lyman-Hazard House* in Newport. 37c
The town common was notably absent when these indi-
vidualists laid out their towns and frequently holdings
(termed "plantations") were larger than those to be found
in the Puritan colonies. The soil itself was enough to support a relatively large wealthy class who exported horses,
fish, beef, cheese, peas and flour to the West Indies. Newport, which soon became the colony's largest town, was
also an early shipbuilding center.

Unfortunately no records reveal what shelter the Reverend William Blackstone built for himself at "Study Hill" in Cumberland, northeastern corner of the state. This scholarly hermit, who had left his peninsula to Winthrop's intruding Puritans in 1634, is said to have visited Providence and Wickford occasionally, riding a tame white bull.

New Hampshire

Two London fishmongers had set up a fishing colony on the Piscataqua River for Captain John Mason, who supplied it with food, tools, cattle and even women. It prospered, especially after Mason died in 1635 and his widow left his employees to "shift for themselves," which they did by appropriating land, equipment and livestock. The first sawmill had been built in Dover, New Hampshire, in 1623.

In 1652 the Royal Navy began earmarking all white pine trees more than two feet wide for its own use as masts for its ships. This "mast trade," subsequently so resented by the colonists, initially meant booming business for New Hampshire. By 1665 this lower region of the Piscataqua boasted twenty sawmills and a dozen
shipyards. In *Portsmouth* sturdy homes like that which 40
Richard Jackson built overlooking his own shipyard, 40a
rivaled any dwelling to be found to the south. By 1671 the community was exporting shiploads of boards, staves, white pine masts, cod and beaver, and importing equal amounts of wine and brandy.

By the end of the century the settlement's first com-
pany "great house" disappeared, replaced by *Captain* 40b
Sherburne's modest two-room home of white pine, the first step in a subdivision which would form the town's
"Puddle Dock" area, now recreated as *Strawbery Banke*. 40c

Portsmouth was a frankly commercial-minded frontier
town. Just offshore were the *Isles of Shoals*, by 1670 41
home for five thousand fishermen, most of whom lived in sod and rock huts, surrounded by hundreds of wooden racks for drying fish. On "Smuttynose" there was a tavern, on "Star Island" a small stone fort, and on Hog Island a bowling alley and brewery. Even the mainland towns were far from being either political or religious
minded. The fact that *Exeter* and *Hampton* had been 42, 43
settled by Puritan dissenters from Massachusetts simply made the four towns less cohesive. In 1641 they accepted government by Massachusetts as a minor annoyance to be exchanged for protection. Shortly thereafter, a Puritan minister who is said to have berated his Portsmouth congregation, asking them why they had come to the New

World if not to be saved, received the famous reply, "Us'n came to fish 'n trade."

Maine

Scattered outposts along the coast above Portsmouth
had been peopled by fishermen from the rowdy seaports
of western England rather than by the sober Puritans
from southeastern counties. In 1635 Sir Fernando
Gorges had actually gotten himself declared "Lord Governor" of all New England, but the ship he was to sail
over on got wrecked in the launching. This Don Quixote
of Maine had to content himself with staying home and
drawing an elaborate government for "Gorgeana," which
was to be the capital of his feudal domain. In 1640 that
town boasted forty-three government officials – more
than half its male population. Through unlucky politicking Gorges wound up in prison, dying there in 1647.
His portion of Maine by then had shrunk to a small strip
between the Piscataqua and Kennebunk rivers, two other
companies claiming land between here and the Kennebec
– all of which was appropriated by the Massachusetts
General Court after 1652 (when it demoted Gorgeana
to a town named *York*). Districts west of the Kennebec 44
changed hands frequently during ensuing years – a fact
dramatized within the excellent little museum adjacent
to excavations at *Pemaquid*. The first stockaded fort 4a
planted by settlers from Bristol, England, here dates
from 1630 and word has it that pirate Dixie Bull made
off with a small fortune's worth of loot from this spot
two years later. In 1664 the Duke of York established a
trading post here – his attempt at controlling the surrounding area along with New York. *Castine* was settled 45
by the French who had built Fort Pentagoet there in
1611, and in 1676 the colorful Baron de Castine set
himself up as defender of France, the Indians and his
own trading interests; it worked for thirty years.

WAR AND WITCHCRAFT

King Philip's War

Having sketched the relatively bright side of the seventeenth-century life, we must admit to dark foils.

The first is remembered, when at all, as King Philip's War. By 1674 the Wampanoag Chief Massasoit had died and his oldest son had expired during a march which the settlers forced him to make to Plymouth. His second son, twenty-four-year-old Metacomet, whom the English named "Philip," now led the tribe and, according to tradition, was complaining: "But little remains of my ancestors' domain. I am resolved not to see the day when I have no country." Philip was more worried about his loss of power than land. A sachem could now be called to white man's court if suspected of brewing trouble and be punished if he did not mend his ways. Quietly Philip attempted to unite all tribes between the Hudson and Kennebec Rivers against the colonists who already outnumbered them.

In January 1675, an Indian preacher was found murdered in Middleboro Pond, having just informed the Plymouth Colony magistrates of what Philip was up to. Three Wampanoags were executed for the deed, after which some young braves killed nine Swanzey residents. Massachusetts Bay swiftly raised a small army to march on Philip's headquarters at Mount Hope, a high hummock on the eastern side of Narragansett Bay where Brown University's Haffenreffer Indian Museum now stands. They found it deserted. The tribe retreated to an eight-mile-long swamp at Tiverton, Rhode Island. Assuming that they had the Indians cornered, the colonists built a fort at the mouth of the swamp and sat down to wait until their prey starved. The Indians, however, built rafts, and fifteen hundred managed to float across an inlet one night, escaping to Nipmuc Country, the Connecticut Valley of Massachusetts. The chagrined soldiers rounded up the 160 men, women and children left behind and sold them into slavery.

During the fall and early winter Philip's warriors attacked one town after another in central and western Massachusetts. In December the colonists mustered more than one thousand men plus two hundred Mohegans, and surrounded the Narragansett winter camp, a palisaded fort within a swamp at South Kingston, Rhode Island. The six hundred wigwams within were fired. Of some five thousand Indians inside them, more than one thousand were slain and an unknown number taken prisoner. This "*Great Swamp* Fight" is the biggest battle fought in 46
New England, ever. It is commemorated each September by an Indian pilgrimage to the stone shaft which marks the grave of the Narragansett nation. (Great Swamp itself is a 2,600-acre wildlife reservation). Not far to the north

a second marker at *Smith's Castle in Wickford* stands 39a
above the common grave of forty colonists who died in the fray.

This battle marked the turning point in the war. Indians continued to burn towns and take captives and the colonists to take revenge wherever possible. But in May King Philip narrowly escaped an ambush while fishing at
Turner's Falls, and that August his son and wife were 47
captured and sold as slaves to Bermuda. Having retreated to his home ground, a swamp on Mount Hope Neck, he was slain one night, supposedly with a gun now in Pilgrim Hall. His head was carried to Plymouth and mounted on the stockade there where it stayed for twenty years, about the time it took New England to recoup from the war's damage. Of the ninety existing towns, fifty-two had been attacked, twelve destroyed entirely. Some six hundred colonists had been killed. Indian casualties are conservatively set at five thousand with an unrecorded number executed later or sold into slavery. And in its aftermath Indian raids continued on in Maine. In 1688 the Royal warship *Rose* razed the trading post at Fort Pentagoet and Baron de Castin's Abenaki friends retaliated by virtually destroying most western Maine settlements, including York.

Dominion of New England

The presence of the Royal warship *Rose* itself represents the second cloud which hovered over the colonists, this one originating in England.

Charles II, who had replaced Oliver Cromwell in 1658, chose to notice that New England had long been ignoring the Navigation Acts which bade her import only goods carried on English ships and coming either originally from or via England. The agent sent to investigate found ships flying a variety of European flags in Boston Harbor.

Massachusetts Bay first tried to placate the monarch with "ten barrels of cranberries, two hogsheads of special good samp and three thousand of cod fish." When that failed, she informed him that "the laws of England are bounded within the four seas and do not reach America. The subjects of his majesty here being not represented in parliament, so we have not looked on ourselves as impeded by them."

This declaration struck parliament as impudent. In 1684 it revoked Massachusetts Bay's charter and created the Dominion of New England. This included Plymouth

Colony, Rhode Island, Connecticut, New Hampshire, Maine and later New York and New Jersey, as well as Massachusetts Bay under one royal governor, Sir Edmund Andros.

Suddenly, after decades of virtual self-government, the colonists found themselves subject to laws, taxes and trade regulations which they had not made. Even funds for their schools were revoked.

Cape Codders, for instance, had been paying no land taxes; the towns received revenue from the oil they extracted from small whales washed up on shore. Now they were told that these were "Royal Fish," property of the crown. And all farmers were told that the lands they had cleared themselves were based on worthless Indian deeds, comparable to a "scratch with a bear paw," and now they must pay rent. Town meetings were forbidden, save once a year.

No colony accepted this new regime graciously. When Governor Andros arrived with sixty soldiers in Hartford to confiscate Connecticut's charter, he found the General Assembly gathered at the meetinghouse. The charter was laid out on the table and suddenly all the candles blew out. It was a gloomy October afternoon. By the time the room was relighted, the charter had vanished. The story goes that it was hidden in the hollow trunk of an old oak tree, part of which has since been carved into
a frame for the 1662 charter, still on display in the *Con-* 17a
necticut State Library, Hartford.

Luckily for New England, James II, the last of the Stuart kings, was replaced by William and Mary in January 1689. In April the news reached Boston that "all magistrates who had been turned out" should resume "their former employment." Andros was thrown in jail, and wine barrels were breached in the street; similar celebrations followed in Plymouth, Providence and Hartford.

All the colonies now hoped to get back their original charters and on to business as usual. But that is not exactly what happened.

In October 1689 a new French governor, Count Frontenac, arrived in Quebec and began dispatching Abenaki Indians led by Frenchmen to attack frontier settlements in Maine and New Hampshire.

Boston authorities reacted by sending seven hundred men to attack Port Royal in Nova Scotia. Their leader, Sir William Phips, had been born the twenty-sixth child of a gunsmith near present-day Bath in Maine, but had managed to get himself knighted for finding $2 million worth of sunken treasure in the Caribbean. He captured the fort, which theoretically meant that Nova Scotia and eastern Maine now belonged to Massachusetts. But then, with more than two thousand volunteers, mostly fishermen (including whaleboat fleets from Cape Cod), he tried to take Quebec and failed miserably. The French got Port Royal back.

England soon decided that Massachusetts could not handle her military problems and so created the royal province of Massachusetts Bay, which included Plymouth Colony and Maine. Sir William Phips became its first royal governor.

Witchcraft

It was a gloomy time for New England. The Quebec failure had both increased the Indian danger for frontier farmers and caused the colony to issue paper money, practically worthless. It was a good time for a witchcraft scare.

Everyone of that day believed that a person could bargain with and receive power from the devil. By 1692 there had already been forty-four cases of witchcraft and three hangings in Massachusetts Bay. Reverend Cotton Mather had written two books on the subject.

One of these books got into the hands of some girls in Salem who, as a prank, accused their half-Indian, half-black slave Tituba of being a witch. Flogged by her master, Tituba confessed to save her skin, and also indicted two respectable good wives in town. The girls persisted in their claims, and set off a chain reaction. Governor Phips appointed a special court to try witches, and its justices caught the frenzy.

Step into the "Sabbath Circle" in Salem's present
Witch Museum and watch the sorry tale unfold in thir- 16a
teen life-size scenes around you. Fourteen women and five men were hanged and one man pressed to death for refusing to concede that they were witches. At least four died in jail, and fifty-five others saved their skins by pleading guilty and accusing others.

Nearby in Danvers you can visit the early seventeenth-
century homestead of *Rebecca Nurse*, a large home for 48
its day and still set well off from its neighbors by the remnants of its three-hundred-acre estate. Rebecca had already raised eight children and was seventy-two years

old at the time she stoutly denied accusations that she was a witch. "Would you have me belie myself?" she replied, and so was hanged on Salem's Gallows Hill. That night her family, themselves risking death, stole her body and buried it in the grave near her homestead, now marked with a polished stone inscribed with the poem by Whittier: "O Christian Martyr/Who for Truth could die/When all about thee/Owned the hideous lie!"

The hysteria stopped short when people like Lady Phips herself began to be accused. The special court was disbanded in October 1692, and some 150 prisoners were released. In Salem actual records of the witchcraft hearings (some of which were held at *Witch House*) are exhib- 16b
ited both at the *Essex County Courthouse* and in the 16c
Essex Institute. This sorriest, most famous chapter in the 16d
town's history is dramatized as part of the "*Salem* 16e
Chronicles," sponsored by Historic Salem and presented from time to time each year.

Obviously life was bittersweet and varied widely in seventeenth-century New England. By the last decade of the century, however, one trait could be said to distinguish this region from other British colonies. It was a sense of belonging. People no longer talked of "going home" to Britain. The first person on record to use the word "American" for a colonist rather than an Indian was the Boston Puritan Cotton Mather. That was 1684.

DETAILS

1 *Plymouth, Massachusetts.* Rte. 3, south from Boston, just above Cape Cod. For tourist information write the Plymouth Chamber of Commerce, 65 Main St., Plymouth, Massachusetts 02360 (617) 746-3377 or Plymouth County Development Council, Box 1620, Pembroke, Massachusetts 02359 (617) 293-3551. During the mid-June to mid-September season, a money-saving combination ticket is available, good for nine major historic houses and museums in town, including Plimoth Plantation. Pilgrim-related sites to see in Plymouth which are not mentioned in the text include:

Jabez Howland House, 33 Sandwich St. The 1667 home of a pilgrim family, furnished to period. Late May-Oct. 15: 10-5. Admission charged. (617) 746-9590.

Burial Hill, head of Town Square. The site of the first fort, then a watchtower, this spot offers a fine view, old gravestones and a powder house. During August Pilgrims' Progress, a costumed reenactment of the procession to church by survivors of the first winter, begins 5 P.M. Fridays here.

Brewster Gardens, foot of Leyden St. The park includes the town brook and the spring which first induced the Pilgrims to settle here.

Edward Winslow House, 4 Winslow St. Built in 1754 by a great-grandson of the Pilgrim governor by that name; now national headquarters for the General Society of Mayflower Descendants, with twelve rooms furnished to depict life in the seventeenth and eighteenth centuries. May 27-Oct. 15.: 10-5. Admission charged. (617) 746-2590.

Jenney Grist Mill, Spring Lane. A reconstructed mill in which hand-dipped candles as well as meal ground on the spot are sold. May-Thanksgiving, daily: 9-6. Admission charged.

Pilgrim Monument and Park, Allerton St. An eighty-one-foot-high Victorian monument to the Pilgrims.

Plymouth National Wax Museum, 16 Carver St. Some 150 life-size wax figures depict the life of the Pilgrims in twenty-six scenes. July, Aug., daily: 9-9:30; March-June, Sept.-Nov.: 9-5. Admission charged. (617) 746-6468.

1a *Mayflower II,* State Pier. This full-scale replica of the original *Mayflower*, built in England in 1957, sailed across to Plymouth, taking fifty-three days, with a crew of thirty-three. Guides in period costume tell the story of its prototype's passage. July, Aug., daily: 9-5; April-June, Sept.-Oct.; Mon.-Fri.: 9-5:30; Sat., Sun.: 9-7; Oct. 15-Nov., daily: 9-5:30. Admission charged. (617) 746-1622.

1b *Plymouth Rock,* Water St., foot of North St. Two thirds of the rock is now below ground, all neatly fenced and weatherproofed beneath an elaborate stone canopy.

1c *Cole's Hill,* just opposite Plymouth Rock, above Water St. A sarcophagus contains bones of the early settlers.

1d *Massasoit.* A statue on Cole's Hill honors the sachem responsible for establishing peace with his tribe, permitting the Pilgrims to prosper.

1e *Thanksgiving in Plymouth.* Plimoth Plantation celebrates an annual Harvest Festival of "feasting, gaming, and exercising of arms" over the Columbus Day weekend. Unfortunately, state law prohibits visitors from actually feasting, but they can watch the preparation of the food and join in the period games during the most colorful weekend of the year at the Plantation. Town Festivities on Thanksgiving Day begin with a 10:00 A.M. service at the First Church in Town Square. A reasonably priced Public Dinner at Memorial Hall is served from 11:30 to 4 P.M. (no reservations). Afternoon events include a reenactment of the procession to church and a football game between the two local high schools with Miles Standish calling the plays. For details check with the Plymouth chamber of commerce.

1f *Pilgrim Hall Museum,* 75 Court St. This claims to be the country's oldest museum, dating from 1824. It includes an extensive research library and paintings, authentic Pilgrim furnishings and possessions. Year round, daily: 9-4:30. Admission charged. (617) 746-1620.

1g *Richard Sparrow House,* 42 Summer St. Built 1636-40, restored and occupied by Plymouth Pottery Guild. June-Oct. 15, Mon.-Sat.: 10-5. Admission charged.

1h *Harlow-Old Fort House,* 119 Sandwich St. Built in 1677 with timber taken from the original fort. Pilgrim crafts are demonstrated; crafts courses are offered during the summer season and Pilgrim Breakfasts are served periodically. June to mid-Oct., daily: 10-5. Admission charged. (617) 746-3017.

2 *Plimoth Plantation.* One mile south of Plymouth, Rte. 3A. The complex recreating seventeenth-century life occupies one hundred acres; its two dozen reconstructed and interpretive buildings include an orientation center and research library. July, August, daily: 9-6; Sept., Oct., June, daily: 9-5; April, May, Nov., daily: 10-4. Admission charged. (617) 746-1622.

3 *Pilgrim Monument,* Provincetown. Town Hill. This 252-foot-high tower sits atop a one-hundred-foot-high hill, making it the highest granite structure in the country. Adjacent museum. Year round, daily: 9-5; July 15-Sept. 15: 9-9. Admission charged. (617) 487-1310.

4 *Samoset Memorial, Pemaquid, Maine.* From Rte. 1 at Damariscotta, Rte. 130 south to the tip of the peninsula. A plaque set in stone commemorates the fact that this was Samoset's land which he sold to Englishman John Brown in 1625.

4a *Ancient Pemaquid Restoration, Maine.* This complex includes a restoration of Fort Henry, built in 1692 and the third in a series of four forts to occupy this site. Excavations adjacent to it have revealed a settlement dating from 1620, complete with seventeenth-century cobbled streets, a customs house, jail and homes. The story of this colony, established by a company from Bristol, England, is dramatized along with displays of artifacts found on the spot in an outstanding little museum. June 15 to Labor Day, daily, 10-6. Admission charged. (207) 677-2423. A seventeenth-century burial ground and twentieth-century lobster pound complete the scene.

5 *Squanto's Grave,* unmarked, one half mile south of Chatham Light.

6 *Monhegan Island, Maine.* Twenty miles off Boothbay Harbor, also accessible from Port Clyde and New Harbor, Maine. Monhegan Associates, a non-profit group of island homeowners, maintain walking paths which web the island; no private cars are permitted and there is no public electric lighting. The Island Inn and Monhegan House are the only two hotels with phones. For accommodations at the Trailing Yew or the Golden Gull phone Monhegan Store (207) 372-9600. For ferry service see Chapter 8.

7 *Fort Western, Augusta, Maine.* From downtown Augusta, cross Memorial Bridge and take Cony Street off the rotary; turn left on Bowman St. May 15-Labor Day, Mon.-Sat.: 10-5; Sun.: 1-5. Admission charged. (207) 622-1234.

8 *Aptucxet Trading Post, Bourne, Massachusetts.* Aptucxet Road on the Cape side of the Cape Cod Canal, a few hundred yards west of the Bourne Bridge rotary; also posted from the center of Bourne Village. The trading post has been reconstructed with bricks in its hearths from the original, and timbers from another seventeenth-century house; it now forms the center of a little complex which includes a Dutch windmill, a replica of a Cape Cod saltworks, an amateurishly reconstructed Indian encampment and a picnic area. April 1-Oct.: 10-5. Closed Mon., spring and fall. Admission charged.

9 *John Alden House, Duxbury, Massachusetts.* 105 Alden St.; north of Plymouth, off Rte. 3A.

John and Priscilla Alden lived here. Last Sat. in June–Labor Day: 10–5. Admission charged. (617) 934–2788.

10 *Major Bradford House, Kingston, Massachusetts.* Landing Road. Three miles northwest of Plymouth, Rte. 3A. Built in 1674 by a grandson of Governor Bradford, furnished to period; early crafts demonstrated. Late June–Labor Day, Mon.–Sat.: 10–5; Sun.: 1–5. Admission charged.

11 *Hoxie House, Sandwich, Massachusetts.* Rte. 6A, just beyond the Sagamore Bridge on Cape Cod; center of town, overlooking Shawme Lake. This is a classic saltbox, beautifully restored and furnished by the Boston Museum of Fine Arts. It's said to be the oldest house on Cape Cod. Mid-June to Mid-Oct., Mon.–Sat.: 10–5, Sun.: 1–5. Admission charged. (617) 888–1173.

12 *Odiorne Point, Rye, New Hampshire.* Off Rte. 1A, a state park which includes nature trails, the state's oldest cemetery, the site of its first grist mill, and Flake Hill where fish were dried.

13 *Weymouth, Massachusetts.* South of Boston, Rte. 3. A city which comprises a half dozen villages and many early homes. The Abigail Adams House, corner of Pearl and North streets, birthplace of the only American woman to be the wife of one president and mother of another, is restored to the mid-eighteenth century period. June–Sept., Tues.–Fri.: 1–4.

14 *Quincy, Massachusetts.* Rte. 3A, accessible from Boston via MBTA. Morton Avenue here commemorates the name of the merry leader of the settlement and a section of town is known as Wollaston for its co-founder. A portion of a cedar tree, said to have overlooked the famous maypole, is displayed in Adams Academy, new home of the Quincy Historical Society (8 Adams St., April 19–Sept. 30, Tues.–Sun.: 10–5. Small admission). For details about sites along the Quincy Historic Trail and a bus service offered to them during Bicentennial years, contact the city-wide information center, Quincy Heritage, located at the MBTA station: (617) 472–1776.

15 *Gloucester, Massachusetts.* Rte. 128, north of Boston. Today still primarily a fishing city. The site of the original settlement is preserved as Stage Fort Park. For details, contact the Gloucester Chamber of Commerce: (617) 283–1601.

16 *Salem, Massachusetts.* Rte. 1A north from Boston. Pioneer Village in the city's Forest River Park (off Clifton Ave., from the jct. of Rtes. 1A and 129) is a reconstruction of early Puritan dwellings which range from sod-roofed log dugouts and bark covered wigwams to the two-story Governor Fayre House. The Village is open April–Oct.: 10–dusk, admission charged. (617) 744–0180. For Salem details see Chapter 6.

16a *Salem Witch Museum.* 19½ Washington Sq. North, Salem, Massachusetts. A dramatic sound and light presentation of Salem's witch story. Summer months, daily: 10–7:30, spring and fall, daily: 10–5:30. Admission charged. (617) 744–5217.

16b *Witch House, Salem.* 310½ Essex St. One of the judges lived in this vintage 1642 restored house and held some of the actual hearings here. May–Labor Day, daily: 10–6; Labor Day–Nov., daily: 10–5. Admission charged.

16c *Essex County Courthouse.* Washington and Federal streets. This is a working courthouse which contains both documents and tools of torture used on the "witches." Open weekdays: 9–5.

16d *Essex Institute.* 132 Essex St. Year round, Tues.–Sat.: 9–4:30, Sun. & holidays: 2–5. Admission charged. See Chapter 8.

16e *Salem Chronicles.* Presented by Historic Salem, Inc., at regular intervals. For details, (617) 745–6299.

17 *Hartford, Connecticut.* On the Connecticut River, junction of Rtes. 44, 86 and I-91. Tourist information from Connecticut Development Commission, 210 Washington St. (203) 566–3336.

17a *Connecticut State Library.* Across from the State Capitol, Hartford. The impressive grand hall contains Indian material and early portraits as well as the famous constitution; a state museum of assorted memorabilia is attached. Year round, Mon.–Fri.: 8:30–5, Sat.: 9–1; closed holidays.

18 *Windsor, Connecticut.* Nine miles north, now virtually a suburb of Hartford. The town's history is told in the Fyler House and Museum (Rte. 159, 96 Palisado Ave.) which itself dates in part from the 1640s. April–Nov., Tues.–Sat.: 10–12, 1–4. (203) 688–3813.

19 *Wethersfield, Connecticut.* Off I-91, south of Hartford. This lovely community claims to be the "oldest permanent English settlement in Connecticut" and still boasts more than one hundred dwellings built prior to 1800. Besides the Buttolph Williams House (19a) the vintage 1692 Cove Warehouse and four colonial homes are open to the public. For details, (203) 529–0612.

19a *Buttolph Williams House, Wethersfield.* Broad St. An outstanding example of period architecture and furnishings which include a half-circle settle, trestle-foot tables, treen ware, a full array of fireplace gear, an early high chair and a hollowed-out log used for holding water. May 15–Oct. 15, daily: 1–5. (203) 529–0460.

20 *Cambridge, Massachusetts.* Just across the Charles River from Boston. The 1630 settlement here occupied a small area which now includes the Cambridge Common, Harvard University Yard,

Harvard Square and its nearby shopping streets. The Cambridge Bicentennial Office, Holyoke Center in Harvard Square, currently serves as the city's info source, supplying a leaflet, Cambridge Heritage Trail guide. (617) 354-5300.

20a *Cooper-Frost-Austin House,* 21 Linnaean St. This house marked the northern edge of Cambridge Common when it was built in 1690; today it sits a ten-minute walk up Massachusetts Ave. from the present Common. It's a charming little house, but you wonder how two families managed to survive here during the eighteenth century, with eight children on one side and seven on the other. June-Oct., Tues., Thurs., Sun.: 1-5. Admission charged. Maintained by SPNEA (617) 227-3956.

20b *Harvard University,* Harvard Square. The country's oldest university, now with an enrollment of more than fifteen thousand. None of its seventeenth-century buildings survived the Revolution, when troops were quartered in Harvard Yard (classes moved to Concord). Massachusetts Hall, oldest of the standing buildings, has been a dormitory since 1720. Other notable buildings include University Hall by Bulfinch, Sever Hall by Richardson, and Carpenter Center by Le Corbusier. The Fogg Museum, University Museum and Busch-Reisinger Museum all welcome visitors year round. During the academic year three daily tours leave from the Admissions Office; during the summer, twice daily from the information center (both departure points are in Holyoke Center, Harvard Square). (617) 495-1000.

21 *Old Saybrook, Connecticut.* A coastal resort town: I-95, exits 66-68. Handsome College Street is a reminder that Yale College was founded here as the Collegiate School in 1701 (it moved to New Haven in 1716). The community claims many early homes, all private save the Historical Society headquarters, Main St. (203) 388-2622.

22 *Block Island, Rhode Island.* Twelve miles off Point Judith, Rhode Island. For details about this resort and ferry service to it, see Chapter 10. The island's chamber of commerce phone is (401) 466-2436.

23 *Great Swamp Battle Site, Fairfield, Connecticut.* South from Fairfield on Rte. 1, across from Hull's Highway near Southport at Sasqua Swamp, a marker commemorates the destruction of the Pequot Nation on July 13, 1637.

24 *Old Ship Church, Hingham, Massachusetts.* South from Boston, Rte. 3A. Built in 1681, this is said to be the country's oldest church in continuous use. In 1930 it was restored to its original look with box-style pews and the old beamwork exposed. July and August, daily except Mondays: noon-5 and by appointment: (617) 749-1679.

25 *Reconstructed Seventeenth-Century Meetinghouses.* We are aware of only two. One serves as post office for Old Deerfield Village (see Chapter 4). The second is at Massacoh Plantation in Simsbury, Connecticut. Admission charged. (203) 658-2500.

26 *Whitfield House, Guilford, Connecticut.* Whitfield St., one-half mile south of exit 58, off I-95. This unusual home with its steeply pitched roof, small casement-style windows and big hall, is said to be the country's oldest stone house. Roughly one third of the building is original, furnished to period with exhibits of early crafts. Year round except Dec. 15-Jan. 15, Tues.-Sun.: 11-5. Admission charged. (203) 453-2457.

26a *Guilford, Connecticut.* Exits 57-59 off I-95. An unusually picturesque coastal town with a vast central green. In addition to the Whitfield house, the eighteenth-century Griswold and Hyland houses are open to the public; for details about the annual tour of old Guilford homes, contact the Guilford Keeping Society, 16 Fair St. (GL3-3514).

27 *Hempsted House, New London, Connecticut.* Corner of Hempsted St. and Rte. 1A (Jay St.). Only the western half of this wonderfully irregular, weathered clapboard home dates from 1640. The entryway and parlor are from 1678 and the rest from the early eighteenth century. Its unusually thick walls are insulated with brick and eelgrass. Built by a town founder, it was inhabited by his descendants until 1937 and is superbly furnished to period. May 15-Oct. 15, daily: 1-5. Admission charged. (203) 443-7949.

28 *Thomas Lee House, East Lyme, Connecticut.* Exit 72 off I-95. The oldest frame house in Connecticut (1660), it originally faced the opposite direction, the reason why its rare, original casement windowframe can be seen in what's now the attic. Its plaster is period oyster and clam shell and there are plenty of interesting details and furnishings. May 30-Oct. 12, daily except Tues.: 10-5. Admission charged. (203) 739-6070.

29 *Whipple House, Ipswich, Massachusetts.* 53 South Main St. The major part of this weathered clapboard home was built in 1640 by an affluent family, "clothiers of good estate." One of the country's first historic houses to be restored (1898), its furnishings include fine seventeenth-century chests, and its herb garden, sixty varieties of period medicinal plants. April 15-Nov. 1, Tues.-Sat.: 10-5. Admission charged. (617) 356-2811.

29a *Ipswich, Massachusetts.* Rte. 1A off Rte. 128, north of Boston. The original settlement clustered around South Village Green in front of the Whipple House, also along present-day East and High streets. More than forty of its houses built before 1725 are privately owned. A plaque at 33 High Street commemorates the home of seventeenth-century poet Anne Bradstreet with her famous lines: "I am obnoxious to each carping tongue/ who says my hand a needle better fits." A Historic Guidebook, also details about Old Ipswich Days, are available from the Ipswich Chamber of Commerce (617) 356-5525.

30 *Fairbanks House, Dedham, Massachusetts.* Corner of East and Eastern Ave. Apply at house next door. The rose-colored bricks in the hearths are said to have come as ballast from England. Various rooms depict various generations' life-styles. It's still owned by Fairbanks descendants, who hold an annual reunion here. May 1–Nov. 30, daily: 9:30–5. Admission charged. (617) 326-1170.

31 *Stanley Whitman House, Farmington, Connecticut.* Marked from Rte. 4, west of Hartford. Also known as the Farmington Museum, this classic seventeenth-century home (with a mid-eighteenth-century lean-to) is fully furnished. Later period farm implements and sleighs are displayed in its wagon shed, behind a herb garden. April 1–Nov. 30, closed Mondays, and 2–5, Sun., otherwise: 10–12 & 2–5. Dec. 1–March 31, Fri. & Sat.: 10–12 & 2–5. Admission charged. (203) 677–9222.

32 *Iron Master's House, Saugus, Massachusetts.* Rte. 1 north from Boston to Saugus exit, then Central St. until posted. Heavily reconstructed by Wallace Nutting in 1915, this was the 1640's family quarters of the manager of the Hammersmith community, also his office. Its hall includes a huge fireplace with hardware from the Iron Works. April through October, daily: 9–5. Admission charged. (617) 233–0050.

32a *Saugus Iron Works.* Rte. 1 north from Boston to Saugus exit; Main St. to Central St. and follow signs. The blast furnace, forge and slitting mill have been restored to their 1646 working order. The complex includes a museum depicting the history of iron-making and a working blacksmith. In 1650 only a dozen such mills existed in the world and this was the first in America. Maintained by the National Park Service. April 15–Oct., daily: 9–5. Admission charged. (617) 233–0050.

33 *New Haven Colony Historical Society,* 114 Whitney Ave., New Haven, Connecticut. The shape of the original settlement has been perpetuated in the grid system of blocks around the present common. A diorama of the way it looked in the seventeenth century can be seen in the Historical Society museum which also includes seventeenth-century local furnishings. Year round, Tues.–Fri.: 9–5, Sat., Sun.: 2–5. (203) 562–4183.

34 *Boston, Massachusetts.* What remains of the seventeenth-century city is best seen by following the Freedom Trail, a marked walking tour which begins at the chamber of commerce information booth, Tremont Street side of the Boston Common. A leaflet guide to sites along the way should be secured here and it's advisable to check by phone on the hours the sites are open. During 1976 phone (617) 338–1976. Otherwise, 536–4100.

34a *Boston Common.* Bounded by Park, Beacon, Tremont, Charles and Boylston streets. Purchased from William Blackstone with money raised from all Boston's first residents, this is now the country's oldest public park. The Puritans pastured their cows, held military musters and punished law-breakers at the ducking stool, whipping post, and stocks here; several "witches" were also hanged from its trees. Free speech is now a tradition on the Common, along with folk concerts and seasonal happenings. This is also the site of Boston's central MBTA stop, a playground and garage (underneath).

34b *Three Cemeteries.* The oldest of these is a small plot adjacent to King's Chapel (58 Tremont St.). The Old Granary Burial Ground down the street was laid out in 1660, named for the town granary which adjoined it. The plot now contains sixteen hundred graves, including those of Peter Faneuil, Benjamin Franklin's parents, Paul Revere, the Boston Massacre victims, Samuel Adams and Mother Goose. Copps Hill Burial Ground (Hull St.) was laid out in 1661 and here the British later planted their cannon for the attack on Bunker Hill, using the headstones for target practice.

34c *Paul Revere House,* 19 North Square. A wooden version of an English Tudor-style house, it was larger than most homes in the city when built in 1677. Paul Revere bought it in 1770, enlarging it to accommodate his sixteen children. It has been restored to its seventeenth-century shape and furnished by the Revere family, who still manage Revere Copper, founded by Paul's son. Year round, daily, 10–4. Admission charged. (617) 227–0972.

34d *Old State House,* 206 Washington St. Built in 1713, this handsome little building served the colonial and later the first state governors as an office. The Declaration of Independence was read from its balcony in 1776. Exhibits are a fascinating mix of relics from Boston history. Under restoration till summer, 1976. Then daily, 10–6. Small admission charged.

34e *Anne Hutchinson Statue.* In front of the "New State House," corner of Beacon and Park streets, overlooking Boston Common. Anne Hutchinson arrived in Boston in 1634 and soon began holding weekly meetings in her home (which stood on the site of the present Old Corner Bookstore). Since the point of these get-togethers was to criticize the weekly Sunday sermon, the city's divines soon began objecting to them. Ms. Hutchinson eventually settled on Long Island, where she was killed by Indians.

35 *Providence, Rhode Island.* Junction of I-95 and I-195, capital of "the State of Rhode Island and Providence Plantations." Sites commemorating the first settlement include Roger Williams Spring (North Main St.) across from which stood the state founder's first home, and Prospect Terrace (Congdon and Cushing streets) site of Roger Williams's burial place and monument, offering a fine view of the city. For a sense of the original lay of this land, before the "Cove" was filled in, see the painting of nineteenth-century Providence and other mementos from the city's history in the Rhode Island Historical Society Museum, John Brown House, corner of Benefit and Power Sts. "A Mile of History" leaflet guide to the oldest part of town can be secured from the Providence Preservation Society, 24 Main St. (401) 831-7440. See Chapter 6.

35a *First Baptist Church, Providence, Rhode Island.* 75 North Main Street at Waterman Street. The church was established 1638. The graceful 1775 building it now occupies was designed by Joseph Brown. April 1 to Nov. 30, Mon.-Fri.: 9-4, Sat.: 9-12. Otherwise by appointment, (401) 751-2266.

36 *Portsmouth, Rhode Island.* Route 138, north of Newport. Founder's Brook off Boyd's Lane marks the spot where the Boston settlers landed in 1638. The "Portsmouth Compact," said to be the first truly democratic form of government in the world, is inscribed on a marker here. The Portsmouth Historical Society (corner of East Main Rd. and Union St.) is a museum dedicated to telling the story of early Portsmouth. Memorial Day to Labor Day, Fri.-Sun.: 2-5, and by appointment. (401) 683-1195.

37 *Newport, Rhode Island.* Route 114 from north, Newport Toll Bridge from west. A city with a split personality: that of the old colonial harbor town and the Victorian era seaside resort. See Chapters 4 and 10. Chamber of Commerce, 93 Thames Street, (401) 847-1600.

37a *Friends Meeting House, Newport, Rhode Island.* Marlborough and Farewell streets. Enter from Broadway. Built 1699, recently restored. July, August, Tues.-Sat., 10-5, otherwise by appointment. Admission charged. (401) 846-3622.

37b *Touro Synagogue.* 72 Touro St., Newport. Built in 1763, oldest synagogue in America. The city's first Jewish families came here from Spain and Portugal in the late seventeenth century, and they were soon joined by a substantial number from the island of Curacao. Maintained by the National Park Service. June 24 to Labor Day, Mon.-Fri.: 10-6, Sun.: 10-6; rest of the year, Sun.: 2-4. (401) 847-4794.

37c *Wanton-Lyman-Hazard House.* 17 Broadway, Newport. The oldest house in Newport (1675), Jacobean style, the 1775 scene of Newport's stamp riots since it housed the local stamp master. Restored and maintained by Newport Preservation Society. July to Labor Day, daily 10-5. Admission charged. (401) 847-1000.

38 *Warwick, Rhode Island.* Off Rte. 1, west side of Narragansett Bay. The John Waterman House, Roger Williams Avenue, is a museum dedicated to the town's history. Year round, Sun.: 1-4, June to Oct., Sat.: 1-4. (401) 467-7647 (5-7).

39 *Wickford, Rhode Island.* In the town of North Kingston, off Rte. 1, south of Warwick. The site of Cocumscussoc, the trading post founded by Roger Williams, is now occupied by Smith's Castle, a 1678 home containing a chair said to have been used by the state's founder; otherwise delightfully furnished, eighteenth-century style. Mid-March to mid-December, weekdays except Thurs.: 10-5, Sun.: 2-5. Admission charged. (401) 294-3521.

39a *Smith's Castle.* See above detail. The burial site is marked by a plaque in the garden of this historic house.

40 *Portsmouth, New Hampshire.* Off I-95. A major settlement of one thousand people by 1700, it was stockaded and included two millponds; most homes were built fronting right on its streets. The Portsmouth Chamber of Commerce gives maps and guidance. (603) 436-1118. Also see Chapters 4 and 6.

40a *Richard Jackson House.* 76 Northwest St., Portsmouth. New Hampshire's oldest surviving building, constructed by a cooper-shipwright on Christian Shore, an early part of the city, but now off the tourist path. It is sheathed in weathered clapboard and retains its central chimney and extremely steeply pitched roof. Restored with its casement windows, furnished. June to Sept., Tues., Thurs., Sun.: 1-5. Admission charged. Maintained by SPNEA. (617) 227-3956.

40b *Captain John Sherburne House,* part of Strawbery Banke. Built in 1695 of white pine, it has a steeply pitched roof and casement windows. It has been restored, but left unfurnished to reveal its construction method.

40c *Strawbery Banke.* Hancock St., Portsmouth, New Hampshire. Puddle Dock had been filled in to form the city dump and the area was about to be razed by urban renewal when townspeople formed this non-profit corporation, buying the twenty-seven buildings around the site for $27,000. Lacking an endowment and major funding, Strawbery Banke must finance all restoration through its craft guild and admissions. The complex offers thirty-four exhibits to date. Late May through October, daily, 9:30–5:30. Admission charged. (603) 436-8010.

41 *Isles of Shoals, Maine and New Hampshire.* Ten miles off Portsmouth. Nine little windy outposts, first noted by Champlain in 1605, then carefully mapped by Capt. John Smith. An invisible line divides them equally between New Hampshire and Maine, and in 1652, when Massachusetts annexed Maine and began levying taxes there, the islands' fishing community took their household goods and paddled across from their first settlement on the Maine side to Star Island on the New Hampshire side. For details about Star Island, today the only one of these islands you can visit, see Chapter 10. Ferry *Viking Queen* tours the isles and drops passengers at Star daily during summer months. (603) 431-5500.

42 *Exeter, New Hampshire.* Southeastern coastal region, Rte. 111, off I-95. A proud, prosperous town settled in 1638 by John Wheelwright, brother-in-law of Anne Hutchinson and a dissenter from Boston's brand of Puritanism. It is best known today as home of Phillips Exeter Academy, founded in 1778, an outstanding prep school with a four-hundred-acre campus; its one hundred buildings include Gilman Garrison House, built c. 1650, 12 Water St., restored and open by appointment, through the Academy. (603) 772-4311.

43 *Hampton, New Hampshire.* Rte. 1, 10 miles inland. An early outpost of Massachusetts Bay Colony which erected a blockhouse here in 1635. Today famous as a summer resort which includes Hampton Beach State Park and a summer playhouse, housed in a two-hundred-year-old barn. Hampton Beach Chamber: (603) 926-8717.

44 *York, Maine.* Exit 1 off Maine Turnpike (I-95). The town of York today includes a half-dozen villages among which York Village is the oldest, including the Old Gaol which is said to be the country's oldest stone building (1653), now encased in a wooden warden's house. May 30 to September, Mon.–Sat.: 9:30–5, Sun.: 1:30–5. See Chapter 4.

45 *Castine, Maine.* From Rte. 1 at Bucksport, south on posted routes to tip of mini-peninsula. This gracious white wooden town marks the site of a long series of alternating French, English and Dutch trading posts. It was known as Pentagoet until Baron de Castine made it his headquarters. Its history is detailed on nearly one hundred signs, dotted around town. Local memorabilia is also contained in the Wilson Museum, Perkins St., open May 28 to Sept. 15, Tues.–Sun.: 2–5.

46 *Great Swamp, West Kingston, Rhode Island.* Off Rte. 2, an obelisk marks the location of the fight on December 19, 1675. For details about the annual pilgrimage contact the Rhode Island Development Council, Providence. (401) 277-2614.

47 *Turner's Falls, Massachusetts.* A plaque tells this story at the spot where Rte. 2 crosses the Connecticut River.

48 *Rebecca Nurse Homestead, Danvers, Massachusetts.* From exit 24 on Rte. 128, north on Endicott St., right on Sylvan St., left on Pine St. This fine old saltbox stands on a knoll overlooking its thirty acres, restored and furnished. The grave is a short walk out back. June to September, Tues., Thurs., Sun.: 1–5. Admission charged. Maintained by SPNEA, (617) 277-3956.

MORE SEVENTEENTH-CENTURY BUILDINGS OPEN TO THE PUBLIC

CONNECTICUT

Ansonia: David Humphreys House, 37 Elm St., Rte. 8 off I-95 at Bridgeport. The town's original parsonage (1695) with its seventeenth-century square hearth, otherwise restored to the eighteenth century. By appointment, (203) 888-2628.

Ansonia: Reverend Richard Mansfield House, 35 Sewett St. An unpainted saltbox restored to the days when Rev. Mansfield, who served as local rector for seventy-two years, lived here in the early eighteenth century. By appointment, (203) 888-2628 or 734-2300.

Cos Cob: Bush-Holley House, 39 Strickland Rd., one block south of Rte. 1. Jacobean fireplaces and a hidden stone staircase, otherwise eighteenth century with mementos from the leading early twentieth-century artists who lodged here when it was an inn. Admission charged. (203) 869-9849.

Essex: Lt. William Pratt House. Off Rte. 9 from I-95 at Saybrook. Pratt arrived in Connecticut with Rev. Thomas Hooker and later served as lieutenant in the Pequot War. It began as a one-room plan house, but its subsequent additions, including a gambrel roof, were early: fine structural detailing and locally made furnishings. June 1 to Oct. 31, Tues., Thurs., Sun.: 1-5. Admission charged. (203) 767-1003.

Greenwich: Putnam Cottage, 243 East Putnam Ave., off I-95. Built as a seventeenth-century home, but famous as a Revolutionary era tavern in which General Putnam was surprised by the approach of English troops. Year round, Mon., Thurs., Fri., Sat.: 10-5 by appointment. Admission charged. (203) 869-8034.

Guilford: Hyland House, 84 Boston St., off I-95. A 1660 saltbox with a later lean-to; completely furnished to period. June 25 to Sept. 9, daily except Monday: 10:30-4:30. Admission charged.

Milford: Eells-Stow House, 34 High St., off I-95. Basically seventeenth century and containing outstanding furnishings, including a portrait of the first owner and a period "turned" chair. Memorial Day to mid-Oct., Sun.: 2-5, holidays, 10-5. Other times by appointment, (203) 874-2664.

Stamford: Hoyt-Barnum Farmhouse, 713 Bedford St., off I-95. Town's oldest house, it retains three seventeenth-century hearths chinked with clay. As the Stamford Historical Museum, it also displays later local memorabilia. By appointment, (203) 323-1975.

Woodbury: Hurd House, Hollow Rd., Rte. 202, central-western Connecticut. A simple, basically one-room plan house under reconstruction at this writing. For details contact Old Woodbury Historical Society.

MASSACHUSETTS

Arlington: Jason Russell House, 7 Jason St., corner of Massachusetts Ave. Although built in 1680, this looks like a typical eighteenth-century home and it has been restored to dramatize the fact that its lame owner and a group of Minutemen were killed by the British Regulars here on April 19, 1775. April 1 to Nov. 1, 2-5. Donation. (617) 648-4300.

Beverly: John Balch House, 448 Cabot St., off Rte. 128. Construction of the 1636 original section is notable, seventeenth-century furnishings. June 15 to Sept. 15, Tues.-Sat.: 10-4 and by appointment, (617) 922-1186.

Beverly: John Hale House, 39 Hale St. The 1694 home of the town's first minister, furnished to reflect various periods. Tues.-Sat.: 1-4, and by appointment as above.

Chelmsford: Old Chelmsford Garrison House, Garrison Rd., off Rte. 110 at Westford town line (Garrison Rd.). This 1690 house and its later barn are both museums. June 15 to Oct. 15, Sunday afternoons, 2-5. (617) 692-6365.

Haverhill: John Ward House, 240 Water St. Extreme northeastern corner of state. Built in 1645, restored with seventeenth-century furnishings. Home of the Town Historical Society. June to mid-Sept., Tues.-Sat.: 1-5; Sept. to June, Tues., Thurs., Sat.: 2-5. Admission charged. (617) 374-4626.

Ipswich: Emerson-Howard House, 41 Turkey Shore Rd. (east end of Green St. bridge). Doubled in size since built in 1680, partially restored. Mid-June to Sept., Tues., Thurs., Sun., 1-5. SPNEA, (617) 227-3956.

Hingham: Old Ordinary, 21 Lincoln St. An authentically furnished 1780 house, later used as an inn and now home of the Hingham Historical Society; outstanding early furnishings and changing exhibits. Mid-June to Labor Day, Tues.-Sat.: 11-4, and by appointment, May and September. (617) 749-1028.

Quincy: John Adams and John Quincy Adams homesteads, 133 and 141 Franklin St. Both houses restored and furnished. Same hours, April 19 to Sept. 30, daily except Mon.: 10–5; Oct. to July, Tues. & Sun.: 10–5, and by appointment. Joint admission. Quincy Historical Society, (617) 773-1144.

Quincy: Dorothy Quincy House, 34 Butler Rd. A Georgian style house restored to the period when "Dorothy Q," wife of John Hancock, lived here, but retaining its seventeenth-century fireplace. Recently restored. April 19-Oct. 31, Tues.-Sun.: 10-5. Admission charged. (617) 472-5117.

Reading: Parker Tavern, 103 Washington St., near railroad station. A furnished seventeenth-century farmhouse built in 1694. May 1 to Nov. 1, Sun.: 2–5. Donation. (617) 944-5051.

Rockport: James Babson Museum, Beaver Dam. A 1658 cooperage, displaying early tools of the barrel-making trade. July–Aug., Tues.–Sun.: 2–5. (617) 596-2958.

Rockport: Old Castle, corner of Granite and Curtis streets in Pigeon Cove. This 1678 home retains its second-story overhang, restored and furnished. July 1 to Aug. 31, Sat. & Sun.: 2–5.

Marshfield: Winslow House, corner of Careswell and Webster streets. Built in 1699, but remodeled 1756; Daniel Webster's law office is on the grounds. July 1 to Labor Day, closed Tues.: 10–5. Admission charged.

Medford: Peter Tufts House, 350 Riverside Ave., near Spring St. Heavily restored and only partially open to visitors. Said to be the oldest brick house in New England. June to Oct., Tues., Thurs., Sun.: 2–5. Admission charged. SPNEA, (617) 227-3956.

Nantucket: Jethro Coffin House, Sunset Hill. This picturesquely weathered old place with a horseshoe set in the middle of its massive chimney, was built in 1686 by two founders of the island for their offspring as a wedding present, thus ending a feud. Beautifully restored and maintained by the Nantucket Historical Association. June 10 to Sept. 14, daily: 10–5. Admission charged.

Newbury: Tristram Coffin House, 16 High Rd., Rte. 1A. This classic began in 1654 as the one room which now serves as its ell. The home from which Nantucket's founding family set out. Partially restored and open. June to Sept., Tues., Thurs., Sun.: 1–5. Admission charged. SPNEA, (617) 277-3956.

Newbury: Swett-Isley House, 4–6 High Rd., Rte. 1A. Many later additions to its 1671 original building, but fine seventeenth-century furnishings. June to Sept., Tues., Thurs., Sun.: 1–5. Admission charged. SPNEA, (617) 227-3956.

Rowley: Platt-Bradstreet House, Main St., Rte. 1A. Built in the 1670s, now the town historical society museum; displays include an early shoe shop. June 27 to Sept. 5, Thurs.: 2–5. Admission charged. (617) 948-2488.

Salem: House of Seven Gables, Hardy and Turner streets, off Derby. Daily, year round, except Thanksgiving and Christmas, varying hours. Admission charged. (617) 744-0991.

Salem: Hathaway House (1682) and **Retire Becket House** (1655), on grounds of House of Seven Gables, but different months and hours, same phone. Admission charged.

Salem: Pickering Mansion, Broad St. The oldest house in town but delightfully face-lifted while retaining its old gables in the nineteenth century. Year round, closed Mon. Admission. Check hours, (617) 744-3390.

Watertown: Nathan Browne House, 562 Main St., on Rte. 20, west of center of town. Unpainted clapboard with casement windows; parlor painstakingly refurnished to 1698 period. June to Oct., Tues., Thurs., Sun.: 2–5. Admission charged. SPNEA, (617) 227-3956.

Chelsea: Governor Bellingham Cary House, 34 Parker St., near Cary Square. Said to be oldest house in Suffolk County, built 1659 by Governor Bellingham as a hunting lodge, period furnishings. Thurs.: 2–5 or by appointment. Donations. (617) 884-5386.

RHODE ISLAND

Newport: White Horse Tavern, Farewell and Marlborough streets, one block north of Washington Square. Heavily restored, but this claims to be the country's oldest operating tavern (built 1673). Open year round for lunch and dinner with traditional specialties like pork and apple pie and chicken in the pot. (401) 849-3600.

Pawtucket: Daggett House, Slater Park off Rte. 1A. Built in 1685, completely furnished but to later periods. Mid-June to mid-Sept., Sun.: 2–5, and by appointment, (401) 726-1532 or 761-8146.

NEW HAMPSHIRE

Dover: Woodman Institute, 182–192 Central Ave. (Rte. 16). Damm Garrison (1680–1712), a one-story log building; other exhibits from colonial era. Year round, daily except Mon.: 2–5. Free.

Exeter: Gilman Garrison House (1650), 12 Water St. By appointment only. Small charge.

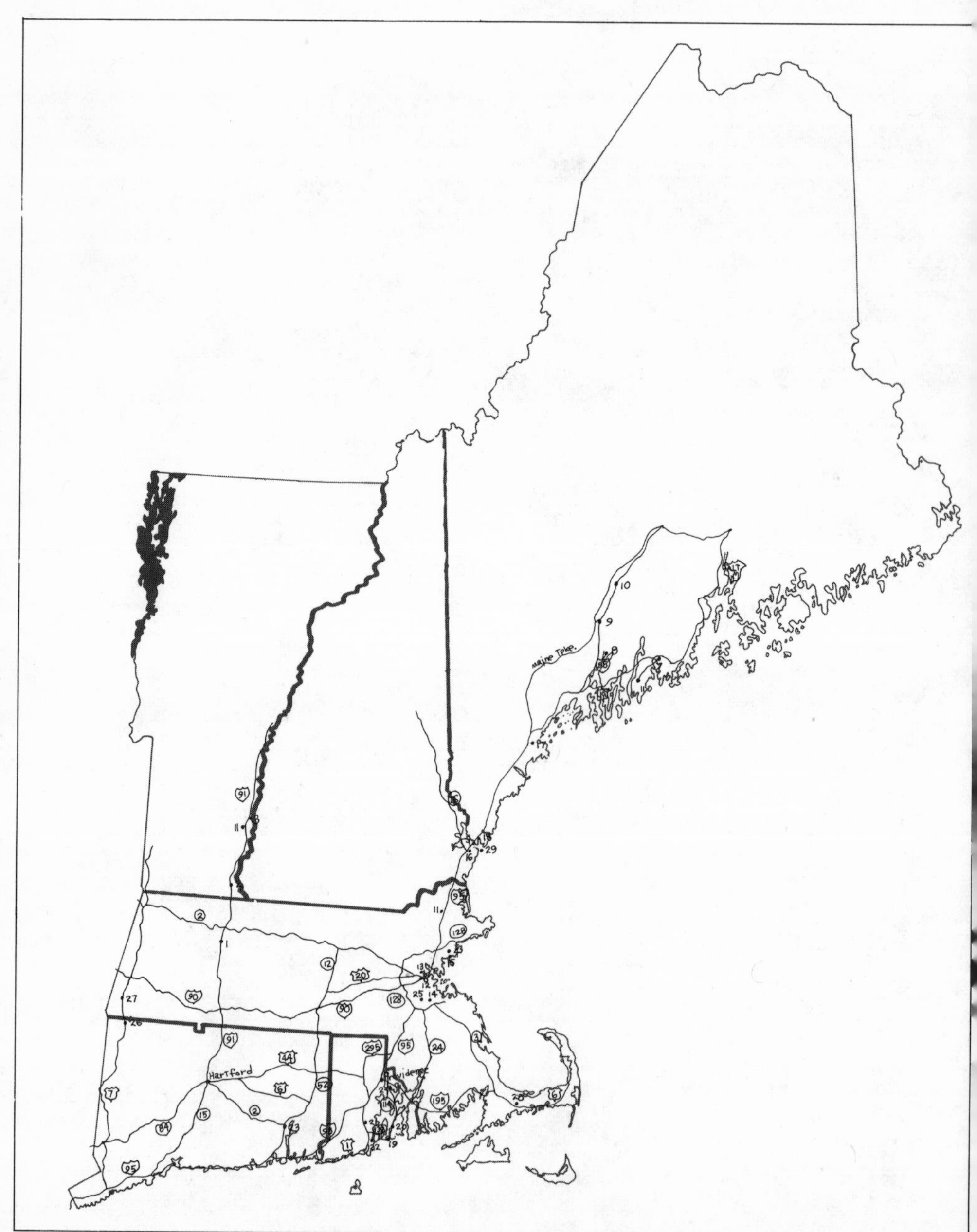

Maine Tpke.
Hartford

4

Growth and Grumbles

GROWTH

Despite the interminable series of wars, New England's population had been growing steadily. By the turn of the eighteenth century it had topped 130,000. Massachusetts with its Maine province counted 80,000 residents, far more than New York, New Jersey, Pennsylvania and Delaware combined. But understandably, not a single new town had been founded in New Hampshire or Maine since 1675.

No community illustrates the hazards for those who
dared to settle the frontier at this time better than *Deer-* 1
field, Massachusetts. Founded on a lush plain of the Connecticut River Valley in 1663 by twenty of Dedham's
more adventurous families, it had been left stark empty
for seven years following an attack at nearby Bloody
Brook during King Philip's War, which had felled most
of its young men.

By 1682 the Proprietors of Deerfield were back again, harvesting crops and listening to Sunday sermons in the square, tower-topped meetinghouse, now reconstructed on a smaller scale as a post office.

Then, one blustery February night in 1704, Frenchmen and Indians swarmed over Deerfield's stockade, carrying more than a hundred villagers off to Montreal. Even that tragedy didn't keep survivors from finding their way home again. By 1707 many of the same families were back. A few remain to this day. Ironically, having been erased twice, their efforts this time ended up being better preserved than those of any other eighteenth-century American community.

Georgian house, 1774

Old Deerfield Village's eighteenth- and early nineteenth-century houses add up to little more than fifty, fewer than a dozen New England towns can boast, but an impressive array, silhouetted starkly as they are against the flat openness of onion and tobacco fields. The fourteen buildings now restored for viewing provide a vivid sense of changing architectural and life styles of the period.

For a glimpse of the 1720s' western frontier days look into the central rooms of the Wells-Thorn House. Here you find rough weatherboard walls, a table off which the family ate from one trencher with horn spoons, and crude beds on which their few rugs were piled. But by the mid-century Ebenezer Wells had become a prosperous farmer, tavern keeper and merchant, enlarging his home to include an elegant carpeted and paneled parlor.

Chapin highboy, Ashley House, Deerfield, Mass.

The town no longer huddled around its common but dared to march out along its long, single street. And its clapboard homes, though still unpainted, now boasted sash windows, set with square panes of glass (still imported from England but, since it came in sheets as ballast, relatively cheap). These windows were now carefully arranged with a mind to symmetry: five across the second story and four flanking a wide, ornately framed door. Although they retain the old oblong shape, houses are a full two stories, front and back, many with gambrel roofs to permit comfortable living space on a third floor. The central chimney has been replaced by two smaller ones, set either behind or at the sides or back of the two front parlors, permitting a wide entry hall. A combination of the old seventeenth-century saltbox and styles now to be found in English architectural books, this building pattern is termed "Georgian" for the line of English kings who first appear in 1714.

Step through the wide "Connecticut Valley Doorway" of the Jonathan Ashley House, built by Deerfield's pastor for thirty-five pounds in 1733. Carved, built-in cupboards, filled with delicate china, flank the modern-sized hearth. Walls are handsomely paneled throughout and rooms are furnished with upholstered wing chairs, graceful, New England-crafted tables, desks and highboys.

The town's two taverns reveal the niceties which travelers had come to expect. Early in the century they would have had to settle for rum in the Hall Tavern's small taproom, and meals off the crude, long table in the family kitchen, served on wooden plates (tough luck if you hadn't brought along a knife and fork). After the mid-century they would have found individual tables set for them in the spacious taproom of the Frary House. Both buildings are long, double houses with separate entrances for family and guests, the likes of which can still be found serving both as inns and homes in many an upcountry town.

Deerfield's prosperity dates from the 1713 signing of
the Treaty of Utrecht, which formalized at least relative
peace, after forty years of continuous battling. But much
of its initial wealth came from supplying cattle to the
troops still fighting Frenchmen and Indians on the frontier which, by 1724, had moved up the Connecticut River
only as far as *Fort Dummer* (present Brattleboro, Ver- 2
mont).

It took another twenty years for a dozen families to advance this invisible line farther upriver, cleverly linking
their log homes into a fortified quadrangle, named *Fort* 3
Number Four in present-day Charlestown, New Hamp-
shire. No sooner had they finished than Indians began burning their crops and outlying buildings. Fifty colonial recruits arrived to help, but soon seven hundred Frenchmen and Indians surrounded the fort. The story of how this battle raged for three days during which the defendants never paused to sleep or eat, is dramatized in a film, now the first thing which visitors see on entering the reconstructed fort. It tells how the enemy finally retreated, starved and exhausted but taking a dozen captives.

Incredibly enough this incident is part of a war called
the "Austrian Succession" although locally labeled "King
George's War." It's best remembered for the 1744 capture
of Fort Louisburg, a $6 million (then) stronghold, the
chief French fort in America – by 3,000 recruits from
throughout New England. The colonists were led by a
Maine merchant named William Pepperell (later titled for
his feat) and it was a crazy attempt. But through a series
of flukes and pure brawn and guts (like lashing themselves to hundreds of sledges on which they hauled cannon through a swamp, under fire from the fort) they
won. More than a thousand died in the process. We have
both an exceptional *portrait* and a *mansion* to remember 4, 5
"Sir" William by, but nothing commemorates *Fort Louis-* 6a
burg itself, aside from the name of Boston's loveliest
residential square.

In the midst of all this military shuffle, city politicians and merchants continued to sell off large chunks of up-

country land. Bostonian Samuel Waldo, who had secured
a large coastal tract in Maine, settled it by importing forty
German families. Their yellow, wooden meetinghouse
still stands in *Waldoboro* and a marker in the cemetery 7
behind tells the story. "This town was settled in 1748 by
Germans who immigrated to this place with the promise
and expectation of finding a prosperous city, instead of
which they found nothing but wilderness."

In 1761 a group of German Lutherans were induced
to settle even more remote Dresden on the Kennebec
River (where *Pownalborough Courthouse* still stands). 8
This area had been bought from Pilgrim heirs by a group
of speculators who called themselves the Plymouth Company. They had built a *Fort Western* at Augusta and the 9
government had added *Fort Halifax* farther up the Ken- 10
nebec, both intended primarily to fill prospective settlers
with a sense of security.

In New Hampshire Governor Benning Wentworth was granting vast tracts left and right to friends, making it his practice in each case to reserve five hundred acres for himself, thus acquiring 100,000 acres plus fees for each of seventy-five townships chartered during his twenty-five-year term. His nephew, John Wentworth II, the colony's first Royal Governor, followed his example, albeit more conscientiously since he also built roads.

Settlers streamed into these new areas; property values in the older, southern New England towns were now high; all but the central common in most by now had been sold. And wilderness was still cheap, as low as thirty cents an acre. But there was a catch. The developers from whom individuals were now forced to buy were themselves required by law to make sure a minimal number of families were actually living on their land within a stated number of years. If they failed to induce enough takers, the land could be reclaimed by the colonial government and auctioned off. The settlers were never sure whether their fellow purchasers would show up to help them form a viable, defensible community; many did not. This fact is dramatized today by the roadside plaques throughout northern New England, informing you that a town was "founded" in the 1740s, "settled" in the decades after the Revolution.

The new towns in New Hampshire and present Vermont (then disputed territory between New York and New Hampshire) lacked a village common; instead they were strung out loosely along a river or the sides of a narrow valley and life was far more family- than village-

Rockingham, Vt., meetinghouse

centered. Still, townspeople gathered for Sabbath
services and town meetings in the *box-like meeting-* 11
houses of the day. They shared the community saw and
gristmill and gathered besides in the tavern or at house-
and barn-raisings. Neighboring farmers also frequently
banded together for the long winter trips to seacoast
ports where they exchanged game, produce, cheese, yarn
and homemade goods for imported and manufactured
staples and luxuries.

Faneuil Hall, Boston, Mass.

These expeditions must have been true adventures for the backwoods farmers. The contrast between New England's cities and these outposts, considerably less sophisticated than Deerfield, was much larger than it had been in the seventeenth century.

By 1722 *Boston* boasted forty wharves and more than 6
a dozen shipyards. By 1743, with 14,382 residents, it
was the largest community in British North America. Its
waterfront today is a sorry ghost of those years; in 1748,
for instance, 540 vessels cleared and 430 entered Boston
Harbor, not counting coastal fishing boats. It was also a
handsome city, distinguished by elegant brick public
buildings like the *Old State House*, *Old North Church*, the 6b, c
Old South Meeting House and *Faneuil Hall.* Judging 6d, e
from the few surviving commercial buildings like the
Old Corner Bookstore and the *Union Oyster House*, even 6f, g
these were graceful.

Unfortunately, most of its townhouses have vanished
since; the *Moses Pierce Hichborn House* is the only one 6h
you can visit. But a few mansions have survived nearby;
the *Craigie House* in Cambridge, *Usher Royall House* in 12, 13
Medford and the *Vassal-Adams Mansion* in Quincy give 14
us an idea of how stately these could be. Similar grand
homes along the shore to the north of Boston, notably
the *King Hooper* and *Jeremiah Lee* mansions in Marble- 15, 15a
head, itself sixth largest town in the colonies in 1765,
represent wealth accrued largely through selling dried
fish to the "slavers" which transported human cargoes
from Africa to the West Indies.

Portsmouth, New Hampshire, had also become a town 16
of considerable craftsmanship and pretension. By 1771
the city produced almost one-fifth of all ships built in

the colonies while maintaining its lead (although rivaled
now by *Falmouth, Maine*) in the lumber trade. Counting- 17
houses had sprouted around *Puddle Dock* where the 16a
Chase and *Clark Houses* now give us a glimpse of upper- 16b, c
and middle-class life. The splendid *Warner*, *Wentworth-* 16d, e
Gardiner, *Wentworth-Coolidge*, *Moffatt-Ladd* and *John* 16f, g, h
Paul Jones mansions are all truly grand.

York Village, Maine, not far north of Portsmouth, had 18
evolved into a cluster of graceful buildings – a jail, inn, school, church, burying ground and core of clapboard homes – which survive to this day, providing a rare glimpse of colonial coastal life in northern New England.

Newport, Rhode Island, was enjoying the very peak of 19
its sea-based glory. Some five dozen of its vessels were engaged in the Triangle Trade alone: transporting slaves from Africa to the West Indies where they were exchanged for sugar and molasses, which in turn was distilled into rum at home and shipped off to Africa to be sold for more slaves.

Newport's cultural tone had been set by Bishop
Berkeley, Dean of Derry, England. This worthy had 20
moved to nearby Middletown in 1729, bringing the English painter Smibert with him and suggesting the formation of the private *Redwood Library*. A building to house 19a
the collection of books was constructed by Peter Harrison, who also designed the handsome *Brick Market* and 19b
Touro Synagogue for the city. Harrison, who is remem- 19c
bered besides for his *King's Chapel* in Boston and *Christ* 6i, 12a
Church in Cambridge, is recognized as one of America's pioneer architects, along with Richard Munday who designed Newport's *Old Colony House* and *Trinity Church*. 19d, e
Ladies and gentlemen of Newport wore powdered wigs, high-heeled, gold-buckled shoes and rustling silks. They patronized a wide selection of shops and craftsmen and entertained Southern and Caribbean gentry who gathered here during summer months. Many of their houses have
been restored as private homes, and *Hunter House* pro- 19f
vides a glimpse of their gracious interiors. *Casey Farm* in 21
nearby North Kingston by contrast reveals the life-style
of Rhode Island's country gentry and the *Gilbert Stuart* 22
birthplace in neighboring Saunderstown that of a tradesman; the artist's father derived his income from the "genteel occupation" of grinding snuff.

Connecticut remained primarily agricultural, distinguished by handsome communities throughout. More than two dozen houses in the state now offer us views of the sophistication of this period and the *Leffingwell Inn* 23 in Norwich is, for our money, the best restored New England tavern of its day.

In all, the interiors of more than six dozen pre-Revolutionary, eighteenth-century homes can be visited and they are scattered throughout New England. For a detailed listing see the end of this chapter's details. Whether simple Cape Codders, rural homesteads or pretentious coastal mansions, they all support an impression of a distinctive and comfortable life to be enjoyed in this region at the close of its colonial day.

GRUMBLES

Boston as well as Newport and Marblehead had become heavily dependent on the "Triangle Trade" and early in the century England had begun objecting to this routine, especially to the Yankees' habit of trading with the French as opposed to the less prosperous English islands in the Caribbean. In 1715 she forbade trade with the French sugar islands and in 1733 promulgated the Molasses Act, permitting it but under a prohibitively high duty. The upshot was that New England's most prominent merchants became blatant smugglers. In 1761 Parliament, attempting to thwart them, declared a policy of searching and inspecting all colonial ships and homes, seizing what contraband she found.

Lean-to house, 1750

When you visit the Old Boston State House, picture James Otis, Jr., delivering his five-hour protest in its upstairs courtroom against these "Writs of Assistance," climaxing it with the words which were to become a slogan: "Taxation without representation is tyranny."

Next came the news that the Molasses Act, with lowered duty, was going to be strictly enforced with evaders tried in admiralty courts. Then in 1765 a Stamp Tax was levied on playing cards, newspapers, legal documents and liquor licenses. This was the first direct, internal tax ever imposed on the colonists. James Otis, Jr., proposed that a Stamp Act Congress, composed of delegates from all the colonies, be held in New York to form a protest to this act. Nine colonies accepted his invitation and the congress met for eighteen days, solving nothing, but demonstrating that the colonies could now form a united front against Britain.

The Stamp Act also sparked the formation of a secret society known as the Sons of Liberty, founded and headed by Samuel Adams, the son of a Boston deacon and prosperous brewer. While a boy, Adams had trailed his father around to Boston taverns, there discovering the existence of a little-recognized potential force in colonial politics.

At this time little more than one-fifth of New England residents could vote. Massachusetts and New Hampshire had remained royal colonies since 1691, but even Rhode Island and Connecticut which, regaining their original charters, had been acting virtually as small republics since the turn of the century, kept the vote limited to their landed aristocracy. In all four colonies, half of those who could vote filled the government offices. Naturally, the city working classes resented the high-handed way in which their interests were ignored, and they also resented the danger which they stood of being "impressed" (seized) as sailors in the notoriously harsh British Navy. For years they had been grumbling in the taverns. Now they were finding their voice through a new "Whig" party which also included businessmen, professionals, and merchants opposed to the Stamp Act. Basically this party advocated change in the status quo represented by the Tory party which supported Britain.

The Sons of Liberty was composed of the most left-wing, activist Whigs. It met chiefly in the upstairs room of a distillery at the corner of Boston's Essex and Washington Streets. Outside their window stood a big, old elm which they christened the *Liberty Tree.* 6j

On the morning of August 14, 1765, they hung a straw-stuffed effigy and a big boot with a devil peeping out of it from this tree. The boot represented the English Lord Bute, thought to be the author of the Stamp Act, and the effigy was of Andrew Oliver, distributor of the stamps for Massachusetts Bay. Come evening the symbols were paraded past the Old State House by a crowd who then set them afire and went on to fire the building which they believed would be used for distributing the stamps. Next they stormed Oliver's house. The frightened official appeared on his balcony and promised to resign his position. He formalized this promise the next morning under the Liberty Tree.

During the next few weeks the mob attacked a number of Tory homes, including Lieutenant Governor Thomas Hutchinson's mansion, now vanished. A few rioters were imprisoned but easily escaped. November 1, 1765, the day on which the Stamp Tax was to be imposed, came

and went without anyone daring to enforce it; the stamps remained stacked up in Castle William (today *Fort Inde-* 6k
pendence on Castle Island) and no business (for lack of legal papers) was transacted. On December 17 Oliver repeated his resignation at the Liberty Tree.

What impressed Parliament more than all this dramatized opposition was the success with which the colonists were also shunning British imports, causing a serious recession in English ports. Boston-born *Benjamin Franklin*, 6l
in England at the time, presented the colonists' case for repeal of the Stamp Act in the House of Commons, sensibly pointing out that, if enforced, it would consume all their scant reserve of cash within a year. George III finally repealed the act. When the news reached Boston in May, music filled the town, lanterns were hung from the Liberty Tree, and a wealthy young merchant named *John* 6m
Hancock held open house in his mansion overlooking the common and rolled huge barrels of his madeira wine out onto the Common for all to share.

The Stamp Act, however, turned out to be the first, not the last, of serious British attempts to meddle in colonial life. In 1767 Charles Townshend, Britain's Chancellor of the Exchequer, announced a new tax on paper, painters' lead, glass and tea. He also declared that revenues from the taxed items would go to pay the salaries of major colonial officials, thus freeing them from check by their legislatures. And he established an enlarged customs system with headquarters in Boston which gave the Writs of Assistance new teeth.

At a meeting in Faneuil Hall, Samuel Adams proposed that all British products be avoided again. He also wrote a letter to the other colonies, proposing that they send a joint petition to George III, requesting repeal of the Townshend Acts. (The Massachusetts legislature was subsequently ordered to disavow its support of this letter but refused, a victory which the Sons of Liberty celebrated, commissioning Paul Revere to make the big silver Liberty Bowl now displayed in the Boston Museum of Fine Arts.)

Early in 1768 the Sons of Liberty took to regularly parading past the Old State House and staging town meetings in Faneuil Hall and Old South Meeting House. On the anniversary of the repeal of the Stamp Act, they hung the new tax commissioners in effigy from the Liberty Tree. When *The Liberty*, a ship owned by John Hancock, was seized for contraband, they freed it and forced these same officials to take refuge on a British man-of-war in the harbor.

Two British regiments arrived in Boston, at first camping on the Common, in Faneuil Hall and the Old South Meeting House. But citizens protested so hotly at this use of their public property that the "lobster backs" were eventually quartered in warehouses and rented rooms.

On February 22, 1770, the Sons of Liberty mobbed the shop of a tea importer on Hanover Street in the North End. The shop owner responded by firing off a gun into the mob, mortally wounding a twelve-year-old boy. Samuel Adams arranged a huge funeral, beginning at the Liberty Tree and winding around town for this "little hero and first martyr to the noble cause."

On the chilly night of March 5 a soldier was standing in his sentry box outside the Customs House (just below the Old State House) when a captain passed by with a group of apprentice wigmakers on his heels, claiming that he had not paid his barber's bill. The sentry gave one of the apprentices a blow on his head, saying that the captain was a gentleman. Soon bells tolled and a crowd gathered. The apprentices continued to taunt the sentry and snowballs began to fly. A captain of the guard with six grenadiers arrived and one of these, after being struck to the ground, fired into the crowd. More firing, without orders from the soldiers' captain, and three colonists, including a black Bahamian named Crispus Attucks, were killed. Other colonists were felled by ricocheting bullets. Finally the captain managed to march his men away from the scene of what patriots
quickly dubbed the "*Boston Massacre*." (To the credit 6n
of the colonists, all of the soldiers involved later received a fair trial, six being acquitted and the other two getting off with branded thumbs.)

During the next few days a series of town meetings all demanded that the two regiments be withdrawn from the city. They were. And on April 24, news arrived that all the Townshend taxes, save that on tea, had been repealed.

Riot-weary Boston now remained calm for a while.
But in June of 1772, His Majesty's customs cutter *Gaspee* 24
was seized and burned by Rhode Island patriots (an act still proudly commemorated for an entire week every year). No one dared indict the prominent colonists behind this act.

That October Samuel Adams penned a proposal in the

Whig newspaper, the Boston *Gazette*: "Let every town assemble. Let associations and combinations everywhere set up to consult and recover our just rights."

In November Adams elaborated on this idea at a town meeting in Faneuil Hall, suggesting that twenty-one members of a Committee of Correspondence be named in Boston and that other towns throughout the colonies set up similar committees composed of local people which together would form a popular, new colonial government. (Now Adams was appealing to that large disenfranchised group in the backwoods and rural settlements as well as cities.) The response was enthusiastic.

A cause to rally this new force soon appeared. In March 1773 the East Indian Company, hovering on the verge of bankruptcy, asked Parliament for help and received it in the shape of a new "Tea Act." The tax on tea was retained but the price lowered to undercut that of Dutch tea being smuggled into the colonies at the time. And now it was to be exported directly to appointed "consignees" rather than to merchants.

On October 18 the Boston *Gazette* printed the names of Boston's consignees, comparing them to the hated stamp commissioners of 1765. Already four ships laden with tea, all owned by Massachusetts Bay merchants, had left London for Boston. Ships bearing similar cargo had also sailed for New York, Philadelphia and Charlestown, and in these other ports the consignees were bowing to public opinion and refusing to accept the shipments.

But in Boston the appointed distributors happened to include the sons of Thomas Hutchinson, now Royal Governor, and adamantly opposed to the local legislature which had petitioned for his recall. They refused to succumb to pressure from the Committee of Correspondence which now formed the *de facto* government of this city of 20,000 people.

On November 28, the *Dartmouth*, first of the tea ships, entered Boston Harbor; if duty on its cargo was not paid within twenty days, both the ship and its contents were liable to seizure by the crown. Public meetings, demanding that the tea be sent back, were now held daily and the consignees fled to Castle Island for protection. On December 2, the second tea ship, *Eleanor*, arrived, followed on the 7th by the *Beaver*. The fourth vessel, *William*, was totally wrecked on the 10th in a gale off Provincetown.

As December 16, the deadline for payment of the duty on the *Dartmouth*'s cargo neared, Governor Hutchinson ordered that no ship could leave Boston without a pass (thus cutting off the possibility of the tea ships quietly sailing off one night).

The artist John Singleton Copley, related to one of the consignees, attempted to intercede between the patriots and this group, making several roundtrips to Castle Island by rowboat, despite his horror of water. Still they refused to compromise, now claiming they were powerless to send the ships back without a pass.

The story of what happened December 16 is vividly
told through multimedia displays in the *Boston Tea Party* 60
Ship Museum adjacent to the reconstructed *Beaver*: thousands of Massachusetts Bay residents converged on the Old
South Meeting House. The *Dartmouth*'s owner appeared
and agreed to ride to "*Unkity*," Governor Hutchinson's 25
retreat in Milton, to request a pass for the final time.
When he returned with news that he had once more been
refused, Sam Adams turned to the throng and intoned
his famous signal: "This meeting can do nothing more to
save the country."

A band of patriots dressed as Indians responded with a war whoop and charged out of the building, thousands of spectators trailing behind. At Griffen's Wharf, where the three ships were docked, these "Mohawks" methodically unloaded 10,000 pounds of tea and dumped them in the harbor. It was all over by 9:00 P.M. The next morning citizens in small boats rowed out and beat down the tea crates which remained floating (a few of the historic tea leaves can be seen today at the Old State House, the Usher Royall House, and the Old South Meeting House).

Although this was the most famous, it was not the last Boston Tea Party. On March 6, 1774, the brig *Fortune* brought twenty-eight more chests to Boston, and again a band of "Indians" deftly disposed of them one night; this time at Hubbard's Wharf.

Governor Hutchinson made no immediate reprisal against Boston, having now resolved to resign. And the consignees spent an uncomfortable winter at Castle Island.

Then on Election Day, May 10, Boston learned that her harbor was to be closed within the month, until all the tea had been paid for. A set of "Regulation Acts" would also be enforced: all major officials would be appointed and town meetings would be forbidden without the governor's approval, save for one annual (now meaningless) election. That new governor was also to be commander-in-chief of His Majesty's troops in North America.

The governor was already a general, Thomas Gage by name, and he brought along four thousand soldiers, arriving within a few days. Even as he stepped onto Castle Island (it happened to be Friday, the 13th) Sam Adams was addressing a meeting in Faneuil Hall, denouncing the Port Bill. Throughout the year that followed, supplies were hauled overland from sympathizing farmers to the city. And although the new governor was formally welcomed with a grand banquet and salutes from all local militia, he soon found himself powerless. Jurors refused to serve in his court (which had been moved to Salem) and the officials he appointed were forced by popular pressure to resign.

Meanwhile, Committees of Correspondence in other cities were proposing a "Continental Congress," a meeting of delegates from all the colonies, deferentially leaving it to beleaguered Boston to pick the time and place. This Sam Adams did in the Council Chamber at Salem on June 17, 1774, announcing that it would be in Philadelphia on September 1.

Gage, understandably angered by this effrontery from his own assembly, dissolved it. In the ensuing months county conventions were held throughout the colony, reminding the king of rights he had previously granted and was now unquestionably denying.

Out in the Berkshires, *Sheffield* townspeople had drawn 26
up a set of fourteen such "Resolutions" the previous January. While acknowledging "Our Most gracious Sovereign," and "The Country on which we are and always hope to be dependent," they went on to observe that "Americans are entitled to all the liberties, privileges and immunities of natural born British subjects." The following August a Berkshire Congress dedicated to taking practical action in defense of such rights met at Stockbridge, and when the British ministerial judges attempted to convene at the courthouse in *Great Barrington*, they found 27
their way barred by fifteen hundred angry locals, supported by a few hundred farmers from Connecticut.

In September a similar group prevented the court from
meeting at *Barnstable*, shire town of Cape Cod. And on 28
September 9 the most famous of all the period's local protests was drawn up at the home of merchant Daniel
Vose in *Milton*. Again these "Suffolk Resolves" cheer- 25a
fully acknowledge "George the Third to be our rightful

sovereign," but declare the late "Acts of British Parliament are gross infractions of those Rights to which we are justly entitled by Laws and Nature, the British Constitution, and the Charter of the Province." Nineteen different reasons for disobeying these "Acts" follow.

Paul Revere galloped off to Philadelphia with a copy of the "Suffolk Resolves" which were in turn adopted by the Continental Congress on September 17, thus ending a struggle between radicals and conservatives within the Congress, in favor of the radicals. Now all the colonies were committed to suspending commerce with Britain, to raising troops and to paying taxes to a revolutionary organization.

Even before the committees to be chosen in "every county, city and town" could be picked, Massachusetts had held two provincial congresses, the first in Salem and the second in Cambridge. But the time for merely proclaiming fine sentiments soon proved past. On the afternoon of December 14, 1774, Paul Revere appeared in Portsmouth, New Hampshire, with news of an embargo on the export of arms and ammunition to the colonies, and of British intent to dismantle *Fort William* 29
and Mary here, as they had just dismantled the fort at Providence, Rhode Island.

The next day a couple hundred men and boys assembled in the falling snow, their number itself snowballing by the time they had reached the fort in nearby Newcastle. Since it was defended by only a token guard, they bloodlessly secured the one hundred barrels of gunpowder within and the next night sixteen cannon and military stores were also carted off and distributed along with the powder among New Hampshire towns.

General Gage next decided to seize the cannon and supplies stored in Salem. One Sunday morning in February, he dispatched a force of 250, hoping to make off with the loot while townspeople were in church. It didn't work. The Englishmen arrived at the *North Bridge* to 30
town, only to find it raised and a formation of Minutemen glaring at them from the Salem bank.

Luckily a local minister named Bernard, a loyalist but a sensible man, worked out a compromise, pointing out that even if these patriots were routed, the British would still have to march back to their hosts at Marblehead through a countryside now swarming with local militia. The colonel in command agreed to mind his manners if only the bridge would be lowered. It was and they did.

DETAILS

1 *Old Deerfield Village, Massachusetts.* Rte. 5, 3 miles south of Greenfield. The 14 buildings here now restored and open for viewing make a complex that differs essentially from New England's other outdoor museums. All but four were built here and most attempt to present only the life-styles which they sheltered. The point, underscored by the price and time required to see each house, is that you are expected to sample only a few in one visit. Each is a variation on the same theme. In 1962 Mr. and Mrs. Henry Flynt founded Historic Deerfield, Inc., which now maintains 11 houses plus the gracious Deerfield Inn, offering three daily meals and 20 delightful rooms (413) 773-3838. Its historic buildings are open mid-May to mid-Nov., daily, 9:30-12 and 1-4:30, Sun.: 1:30-4:30. Nov. to May 10-4 and Sun.: 1:30-4. Steep admissions charged but combination ticket available May-Sept. (413) 773-5401. Indian House Memorial is open summer months only, daily except Tues.: 9:30-12 and 1:30-5, Sun.: 1:30-5. Admission charged.

2 *Fort Dummer, Brattleboro, Vermont.* Southeastern Vermont off I-91; 1.4 mile south of town on Rte. 30. The fort itself was dismantled in 1763 and the site has since been covered by the Vernon Dam, but a plaque marks the approximate spot.

3 *Old Fort Number 4, Charlestown, New Hampshire.* On Rte. 11, one-half mile west of junction with Rte. 12. June 12 to Labor Day, daily: 11-5, Sat., Sun.: 11-5. May 30 to June 11 and Labor Day to Columbus Day, weekends: 11-5. Admission charged. (603) 826-9768 or 826-5516.

4 *Pepperell Portrait, Essex Institute, Salem, Massachusetts,* 132-134 Essex St. Year round Tues.-Sat.: 9-4:30, Sun.: 2-5. Closed holidays. Admission charged. (617) 774-3390.

5 *Lady Pepperell Mansion, Kittery, Maine.* Rte. 103, 4 miles east of Portsmouth, New Hampshire. Built by Sir William's widow, this splendid house with its Ionic pilasters and colonial revival porch is restored to period. Mid-June to mid-Sept., Tues., Thurs., Sun., SPNEA, (617) 227-3956.

6 *Boston.* During Bicentennial years a major exhibit depicting eighteenth-century Boston is housed in Quincy Market and details about all historic sites in the city are available from Boston 200, (617) 338-1976. Otherwise, to check the times at which Boston sites are open (since they are in flux at this writing) contact the Greater Boston Convention and Visitors Bureau. (617) 536-4100.

6a *Louisburg Square, Boston, Massachusetts.* Between Pinckney and Mt. Vernon streets. A must for every visitor to Boston, this private park contains the city's earliest outdoor statues and is ringed with some of the finest nineteenth-century townhouses on Beacon Hill. It's so exclusive that only residents and their guests are permitted to park here.

6b *Old State House, Market Square.* Built in 1713, the seat of colonial and early state government. Now a delightful mix of Boston memorabilia. For hours check Boston info sources. Admission charged except to Massachusetts schoolchildren.

6c *Old North Church.* 193 Salem St. Built as the New Meetinghouse in 1723, now Boston's oldest church. Most famous for its steeple in which that lantern was hung, starting Paul Revere on his famous ride to Lexington. Open: June–Sept., daily: 9–5; Oct.–May: 10:30–4; Services every Sun. (617) 523-6676.

6d *Old South Meeting House.* Corner of Washington and Milk streets. Built in 1729, saved from demolition in 1876 by the private, nonprofit group which still maintains it as a museum of Boston history. Year round, Mon.–Fri.: 9–5, Sat. and Sun.: 9–4. Admission charged. (617) 482-6439.

6e *Faneuil Hall.* Faneuil Hall Sq. at Merchants Row. Built in 1742 with a donation from Peter Faneuil, wealthiest merchant in town. It was designed by John Smibert and stood on the very edge of Town Cove. In 1805 Charles Bulfinch enlarged it substantially, adding a third story. Respecting Faneuil's wishes, its ground floor has always served as a market. The second story hall, still used for public meetings, was dubbed "The Cradle of Liberty" by James Otis, due to its frequent use for town meetings. (Year round, Mon.–Fri.: 9–5, Sat.: 9–12, Sun.: 1–5.) The third floor is headquarters for the Ancient and Honorable Artillery Company, the country's oldest military company, founded in 1637 (year round, Mon.–Fri.: 10–4).

6f *Old Corner Bookstore.* Corner of School and Washington streets. Built in 1712 on the site of Anne Hutchinson's house to serve as a combination home and apothecary shop. During the nineteenth century, as home of the publishing house Ticknor and Fields, it was frequented by the literary greats of the era. Restored by and used as an in-town office for the *Boston Globe*, with exhibits dedicated to the building's history. Year round, Mon.–Fri.: 10–6.

6g *Union Oyster House,* 41 Union St. Built in 1714 by Hopestill Capen, a sergeant in the Ancient and Honorable Artillery. Isaiah Thomas published his "Massachusetts Spy" here 1771–75, and in the early nineteenth century, exiled King Louis Philippe is said to have lived and given French lessons here for a couple of years before he returned home to become King of France. In 1826, the present restaurant opened. It serves lunch and dinner. (617) 227-2750.

6h *Moses Pierce Hichborn House,* 29 North Square. A three-story brick townhouse built in 1711. The original kitchen and staircase have been preserved and the entire house furnished to depict a middle-class home of the period. At this writing, its schedule is in flux. (617) 523-2338.

6i *King's Chapel.* Tremont and School streets. One of the few stone buildings in colonial Boston, built in 1749, with granite hauled from Quincy. Notice its gold-leafed Corinthian pillars, far more elaborate than any Puritan meetinghouse interiors. Year round, Mon.–Fri.: 10–4, Sat.: 12:45–4. Sun.: 10–11:45. (617) 523-1749.

6j *Liberty Tree.* Corner of Boylston and Tremont streets. A bas-relief marker on the third floor of a building, corner of Washington and Essex streets, marks the original site of this elm which was one in a row planted by the colonists in 1640. It was destroyed by the British. The new Liberty Tree, recently planted one half block away, is an oak.

6k *Castle Island,* connected to Day Boulevard, South Boston. In 1634 a mud-walled fort was built here, making it the oldest fortified site in Massachusetts. Castle William, built in 1701, was renamed Fort Independence in 1797. The present, five-bastion fort dates from 1867 and at this writing is in the process of restoration. The sixteen-acre park surrounding it includes a playground and picnic facilities. It's a favorite spot for watching passing ships.

6l *Benjamin Franklin Birthplace,* Milk St. The site is marked by a bust on the second floor of the narrow office building now occupying it.

6m *John Hancock Mansion Site.* Beacon St. The "new" Boston State House occupies what was once John Hancock's pasture. A plaque marks the site of his adjacent mansion which was demolished in 1863, despite the fact that Hancock's heirs offered to donate it to the state as a governor's mansion.

6n *Boston Massacre Site,* just below the Old State House, State Street, marked now by a circle of cobblestones.

6o *Boston Tea Party Ship Museum,* Congress St. Bridge, off Atlantic Ave. The replica ship was built in Denmark and sailed to Boston in time for the 1973 Bicentennial of the Tea Party. The adjacent museum contains graphics, a diorama, and slide-show dramatization of Boston in 1773 as well as events leading up to the historic event. Summer months: 9–sunset; otherwise: 9–6. Admission charged. (617) 338-1773.

7 *German Meeting House, Waldoboro, Maine.* Rte. 220, south of Rte. 1. Built in 1772, a mid-eighteenth-century style rectangular meetinghouse without a steeple. June to Oct., daily 9–5.

8 *Pownalborough Courthouse, Maine.* Rte. 128 between Brunswick and Augusta. A stockaded fort was built here in 1752, and in 1761, the present three-story house with its entire second floor occupied by the courtroom. It is now a museum dedicated to changing life and industries of the area. July, Aug., daily: 10–5. Admission charged.

9 *Fort Western, Augusta, Maine.* From downtown Augusta, across Memorial Bridge and around

the rotary to Cony St., left onto Bowman St. May 15–Labor Day, Mon.–Sat.: 10–5, Sun.: 1–5. Admission charged. (207) 622-1234.

10 *Fort Halifax, Winslow, Maine.* Rte. 120, one mile south of Winslow-Waterville Bridge. Look sharp, it's off to the river side of the road. Only one blockhouse for this complex of storehouses and palisade survives; it's said to be the oldest one in the country.

11 *Eighteenth-Century Meetinghouses*

West Parish Meeting House, Barnstable, Massachusetts. Rte. 149, off Rte. 6A. The country's oldest Congregational Church building, begun in 1717, substantially enlarged later in the century with a belfry added in 1852. It still retains the old side entrance and has been restored to its eighteenth-century internal look with the old box pews and exposed woodwork. Its weathervane was brought from England and its bell is by Paul Revere. Year round, daily: 8–5. Donation.

Rocky Hill Meeting House, Amesbury, Massachusetts. Elm St., just north of Rte. 495, apply at parsonage. Built in 1785 but retaining an earlier severe exterior and its original interior look, complete with box pews. June–Oct., Tues., Thurs., Sun.: 1–5. Admission charged. SPNEA (617) 227-3956.

Harrington Meeting House, Pemaquid, Maine. Rte. 32, south of Damariscotta. A rectangular 1775 building with a side entrance, restored as a museum of local history. July, Aug., Mon., Wed., Sat.: 2–5.

Rockingham Meeting House, Rockingham, Vermont. Rte. 103 from I-91. Built in 1787, a rectangular white clapboard building with its box pews and fine pulpit all restored and an old graveyard behind. June 26 to Sept. 1, daily: 10–4. For details about an annual "pilgrimage" here, contact Bellows Falls Chamber of Commerce, (802) 463-4280.

12 *Craigie-Longfellow House, Cambridge.* 105 Brattle St. An extraordinarily handsome home built in 1759 by Major John Vassall, a young Royalist who later fled to England. It is one of seven Cambridge mansions which form Tory Row. Presently maintained by the National Park Service as the Longfellow National Historic Site, restored to the period when the poet Longfellow lived here. Year round, daily: 9–4:30. (617) 876-4491.

12a *Christ Church,* Zero Garden St., facing the Cambridge Common. Built in 1761 for a Tory congregation. Simpler than King's Chapel, proof that Cambridge was Boston's country cousin: still more elaborate than Puritan meetinghouses of the day. Year round, daily: 7:30–6. (617) 876-0200.

13 *Usher Royall House, Medford, Massachusetts.* 15 George St. The shape of the original house here, built in 1637, can still be seen profiled in one brick wall of this imposing mansion which was built in 1732, patterned on a mansion in Antigua. Usher Royall himself came here from the West Indies and brought slaves with him. The salve quarters, the distinctive carving both on the mansion's interior and exterior, and its furnishings make this one of the most interesting eighteenth-century houses to be seen. May to Oct., Tues.–Sun.: 2–5. Admission charged. Advisable to check hours, (617) 396-9032.

14 *Vassal-Adams Mansion, Quincy.* 135 Adams St., corner of Newport Ave. Built by Major Leonard Vassal, a West Indies planter who paneled the study in Santo Domingo mahogany. Now the Adams National Historic Site, restored to the period when John Adams and John Quincy Adams lived here. Open April 19 to Nov. 10, daily: 9–5. Admission charged. (617) 773-1177.

15 *King Hooper Mansion, Marblehead.* 8 Hooper St. Built in 1728, it has been restored to period. Year round, daily except Mon.: 9–5. Admission charged. (617) 631-2608.

15a *Jeremiah Lee Mansion, Marblehead.* 161 Washington St. A three-story Georgian mansion built in 1768 for $50,000. Materials and furnishings to decorate its interior were brought from around the world on its owner's ships. May 15–Oct. 12, Mon.–Sat.: 9:30–4. Admission charged. (617) 631-1069.

16 *Portsmouth, New Hampshire.* Off I-95. For a map and guidance to touring the city, contact its chamber of commerce: (603) 436-1118.

16a *Puddle Dock, now Strawbery Banke.* Hancock St. This inlet was the city's commercial center during the eighteenth century; it was subsequently filled in and used as a city dump, rescued from urban renewal by townspeople who created the present museum village on the spot. Late May through Oct. 1 daily: 9:30–5:30. Admission charged. (603) 436-8010.

16b *Chase House, Strawbery Banke.* Built in 1762, gambrel-roofed with gables and corner quoins, restored and partially furnished.

16c *Clark House, Strawbery Banke.* A four-square house built in 1750 with interesting features like sliding pocket shutters.

16d *Warner House,* corner of Chapel and Daniels streets. The oldest brick house in Portsmouth (1718) and one of the most imposing for its day in all New England. Its three stories are capped with a cupola. Notable for its murals depicting Governor Phips. May 15–Oct. 15, Mon.–Sat.: 10–5, Sun.: 2–5. Admission charged.

16e *Wentworth-Gardner House,* 140 Mechanic St. A classic Georgian mansion with unusually long windows and facade detailing, built in 1760 on a terrace overlooking the harbor. It's restored and furnished. Early May–Oct., Tues.–Sun.: 1–5. Admission charged.

16f *Wentworth-Coolidge Mansion,* Little Harbor Rd. Off Sagamore Rd., a left just beyond South Cemetery. A rambling yellow mansion of forty-two rooms. May 25–June 22 and Sept. 2–Oct. 14, Wed.–Sun.: 10–5. June 22–Sept. 2, daily: 10–5. Admission charged.

16g *Moffatt-Ladd Mansion,* 159 Market St. A three-story mansion built in 1763 by a sea captain, later occupied by General William Whipple, a signer of the Declaration of Independence. Mon.–Fri.: 10–5. Admission charged.

16h *John Paul Jones House,* Middle and State streets. Built in 1758. The famous naval hero lived here during 1781–82 while supervising the construction of his ship *America.* May 15–Oct. 1, Mon.–Sat.: 10–5. Admission charged.

17 *"Falmouth" now Portland, Maine.* Off I-95. An important community by the midcentury as a shipment point for the white pine masts demanded by the British Navy. Coincidentally the city's outstanding museum house dating from this period is that of the mast agent George Tate. His gambrel-roofed home (1278 Westbrook St.) dates from 1755. Its long windows, illegally wide pine boards and eight fireplaces make it distinctive. July–mid-Sept., Tues.–Sat.: 1–5, Sun.: 1:30–5. (207) 774-9781.

18 *York, Maine.* Exit 1 off Maine Turnpike, Rte. 1A. Buildings open to the public here include: Jefferds Tavern, an eighteenth-century inn, restored as a museum; the Old Gaol Museum, a 1720 warden's home built around the seventeenth-century jail which now serves as a general historical museum for the town; the Emerson Wilcox House, 1740, restored to period; a mid-eighteenth-century schoolhouse; the eighteenth-century Elizabeth Perkins House, restored to its eighteenth-century interior look; and the John Hancock Warehouse, now exhibiting colonial era tools. All these sites are maintained by the Old York Historical and Improvement Society, open Memorial Day–Sept., Mon.–Sat.: 9:30–5, Sun.: 1:30–5. Admission charged.

19 *Newport, Rhode Island.* The colonial section of the city by 1761 included almost 900 dwellings plus half that many shops and warehouses. Its newspaper, the Newport *Mercury,* founded in 1758, continues to this day and its artillery company, the country's second oldest, maintains a museum at 23 Clark St. (June–Sept., Tues.–Sun.: 1–5; Oct.–May, Sat. and Sun.: 1–5.) Donation. The Newport Historical Society, 82 Touro St., contains exhibits related to the period. Newport Chamber of Commerce, 93 Thames St. (401) 847-1600. (Year round, Tues.–Fri.: 9:30–4:30, Sat.: 9:30–12.)

19a *Redwood Library,* 50 Bellevue Ave. Organized in 1730, this is said to be the country's oldest library in continuous use. Harrison's frame building resembles a Greek temple and houses an outstanding collection of period portraits; a delightful reading room was added in 1858. Year round, weekdays, except holidays: 10–6. In August: 10–5.

19b *Brick Market.* Corner of Thames St. and Long Wharf. Harrison designed the upper floor to be used as shops, the lower as a general market. In fact it served as a theater, then a town hall and is now home for Newport Crafts which makes and sells eighteenth-century-style Newport furnishings. Year round, Mon.–Sat.: 9–5. (401) 846-7243.

19c *Touro Synagogue,* 72 Touro St. Built in 1763, the oldest synagogue in America. Maintained by the National Park Service, June–Labor Day, Mon.–Fri.: 10–5; Sun.: 10–6; rest of the year, Sun.: 2–4. (401) 847-4794.

19d *Old Colony House,* Washington Square. The country's second oldest capitol building, colonial government's seat and, subsequently, meeting place for the state's General Assembly until 1900. The state's first Catholic Mass was celebrated here for French troops in 1780. A handsome brick building with a lantern cupola, today exhibiting local memorabilia and a full-length picture of George Washington by Gilbert Stuart. July–Labor Day, daily: 9:30–4; otherwise Mon.–Fri.: 9:30–12, 1–4; Sat.: 9:30–12.

19e *Trinity Church,* Church and Spring streets. A graceful white spire and airy interior reflect the influence of Christopher Wren. It retains its box pews, wineglass pulpit, 1702 bell and an organ, given by Bishop Berkeley, installed in 1733. Mid-June–mid-Sept., daily: 10–5. (401) 846-0660 or 846-0661.

19f *Hunter House,* 54 Washington St. Built in 1748, an elegant mansion with rich detailing and fine exhibits of locally crafted furnishings of the period. May 30–Sept. 1, daily: 10–5 or by appointment. Admission charged. (401) 847-1000 or 847-7516.

20 *Whitehall, Middleton, Rhode Island.* Three miles northeast of Newport, Berkeley Ave. Built in 1729, Bishop Berkeley's hip-roofed mansion is furnished to period. Noted for its eighteenth-century garden. July–Labor Day: 10–5. Admission charged. (401) 846-3116.

21 *Casey Farm,* North Kingston, Rhode Island. Rte. 1A below the Jamestown Bridge, just above Saunderstown. A four-square, hip-roofed house, still a working farm with horses, goats, hens and such, plus the menagerie of pets kept by the curators. This was a "gentleman's farm" and is furnished as such. June–Oct., Tues., Thurs., Sun.: 1–5. Admission charged. (401) 294-9182.

22 *Gilbert Stuart Birthplace, Saunderstown, Rhode Island.* Posted from Rte. 1-A, and Rte. 1. A gambrel-roofed house with its snuff mill in the kitchen, lower level. This is a snug home with corner fireplaces, period furnishings and paintings by Gilbert Stuart. In spring it's a spot to watch the spawning herring make their way via a fish ladder to the pond above the milldam. Year round. Daily except Fri.: 11–5. Admission charged. (401) 294-3001.

23 *Leffingwell Inn, Norwich, Connecticut.* Exit 81 off Rte. 52, 348 Washington St. The oldest section of this clapboard house dates from 1675. George Washington breakfasted here. The inn is furnished with elegantly, locally crafted desks, chairs, tables and clocks. Labor Day–Oct. 16 and May 16–31: Tues.–Sat.: 2–4: June 1–Labor Day: Tues.–Sat.: 10–12 and 2–4; Sun.: 2–4. Otherwise weekends: 2–4. Admission charged. (203) 889-9440.

24 *Gaspee Days, Pawtuxet, Rhode Island.* Alt. U.S. 1, south of Providence. An annual fair all the first week of June, climaxed by a parade, fireworks and pageant. For details contact the Rhode Island Development Council: (401) 277-2611.

25 *Governor Hutchinson's Field, Milton, Massachusetts.* Adjacent to 224 Adams St., Off Rte. 3, a ten-acre preserve; site of governor's country mansion "Unkity"; it is now owned by the Trustees of Reservations. Fine for a picnic, with a view of the Neponset Estuary below and Boston in the distance.

25a *Suffolk Resolves House, Milton, Massachusetts.* 1370 Canton Ave., off Rte. 3. South of Boston. This pleasant Georgian-style home was moved from the center of Milton Village and restored by the town's historical society. The story of the Resolves is told by a plaque on its facade. By appointment: (617) 333-0644.

26 *Colonel Ashley House, Ashley Falls, Massachusetts.* Well marked from Rte. 7 south of Sheffield. The oldest house in Berkshire County with splendid paneling throughout, beautifully restored and furnished. A copy of the "Resolves" is displayed. Late June through Labor Day, Wed.–Sat.: 1–5. Admission charged. (413) 229-8600.

27 *Courthouse, Great Barrington, Massachusetts.* Rte. 7. The present courthouse dates from the nineteenth century but a plaque tells the story of this confrontation.

28 *Courthouse, Barnstable, Massachusetts.* Rte. 6-A, Cape Cod. The present courthouse dates from the nineteenth century but just west of it, on the opposite side of the road, the Olde Colonial Courthouse has been preserved as a church. Inquire at new courthouse.

29 *Fort William and Mary (Fort Independence), New Castle, New Hampshire.* Rte. 18 east from Portsmouth. June 14–Sept. 1: weekdays: 10–6. May 24–June 13 and Sept.–Oct. 13: weekends: 10–6. Admission charged.

30 *North Bridge, Salem.* Rte. 114. The present bridge here divides the towns of Salem and Beverly. A plaque on the left just after crossing into Beverly tells the story.

MORE EIGHTEENTH-CENTURY BUILDINGS OPEN TO THE PUBLIC

CONNECTICUT

Danbury: David Taylor House, 43 Main St. Since this was the home of a Tory, it was spared when the British burned Danbury in 1777; its period rooms date from late eighteenth century to Victorian; the adjoining Dodd House contains the first hat shop in what has since been known as "hat city." The museum complex also includes a modern exhibit building and the 1780 homestead of composer Charles Ives plus a one-room schoolhouse. Year round, Wed.–Sun.: 2–5; closed holidays. (203) 743-5200.

Darien: Bates Scofield Homestead, 45 Old Kings Highway North. A 1736 saltbox with a later gambrel-roofed addition, furnished, mid- to late-eighteenth century. Year round, Wed., Thurs.: 2–4. (203) 655-9233.

Glastonbury South: Welles-Shipman-Ward House, 972 Main St. (Rte. 17). A fine example of mid-eighteenth-century Connecticut Valley architecture with rich detailing. June–Sept., Sun.: 2–4. Small admission charged.

Guilford: Thomas Griswold House, 171 Boston St. A saltbox with the grace of a mansion; furnished to period and also featuring displays of town artifacts. April–Nov., Wed.–Sun.: 11–5. Admission charged. (203) 453-3176.

Hamden: Jonathan Dickerman, "Old Red House," Mt. Carmel Ave. An unpretentious, story-and-a-half house, furnished to period. Mid-May–mid-Oct., weekends: 2–5. (203) 248-7064 or 248-0809.

Lebanon: Governor Jonathan Trumbull House, town green. Home of the only colonial governor to support the Revolution; handsomely furnished. May 1–Nov. 1, Tues.–Sat.: 1–5. Admission charged. (203) 642-7558.

Litchfield: Deacon Peter Buell House, Sawmill Rd. A 1734 saltbox, not only restored but lived in as it would have been in the eighteenth century. Visitors are permitted through "Heritance House" project, which conveys a genuine sense of period family life. By appointment only by writing Mr. Blaine A. Cota, Jr., Sawmill Road, Litchfield, Conn. 06759.

Tapping Reeve House, South St. The mansion and adjacent little law-school building are described in Chapter 7, "Details." May 15–Oct. 15, Tues. and Thurs.–Sun.: 11–12, 2–5. Admission charged. (203) 567-5862.

Manchester: Cheney Homestead, 106 Hartford Rd. Home of farmer, miller and early clockmaker Timothy Cheney; his son, who also raised nine children here, established a famous silk industry. Year round, Thurs., Sun.: 1–5. Admission charged. (203) 643-5588.

Meriden: Andrews Homestead, 424 West Main St. Built in 1760 with unusually fine paneling and detailing; now the town museum with collections of early chests, clocks and town products. Year round, Wed., Sun.: 2–5. Admission charged. (203) 237-5079.

Milford, Colonel Stephen Ford House, 142 West Main St. Built as a tavern and furnished early eighteenth-century style. Year round, Mon.–Sat.: 10–5. (203) 878-6669.

Mystic: Denison Homestead, Pequotsepos Ave. An exceptional early eighteenth-century home, well restored and furnished with family heirlooms. Exhibits include the builder's will, his bullet mold, and samples of his wife's needlework. The 125-acre preserve includes nature trails. May 15–Nov. 1, Tues.–Sun.: 1–5, winter by appointment. Admission charged. (203) 536-9248.

New Canaan: Historical Society House, 33 Oenoke Ridge. An eighteenth-century tavern, furnished as a period home. The grounds include studio of nineteenth-century sculptor John Rodgers, with displays of his work. Year round, Sun., Tues., Thurs., except holidays: 2–4:30. (203) 966-5598.

New Haven: Morris House, 325 Lighthouse Rd. (Townsend Ave. from exit 50 off I-95). Only the late seventeenth-century foundations and stone walls survived firing by British troops in 1779; it was promptly rebuilt and is now restored and furnished to period. May–Nov. 1, weekdays: 10–5, Sun.: 2–5. (203) 467-0764.

New London: Shaw Mansion, 11 Blinman St. A handsome stone mansion which served as Connecticut's naval office during the Revolution and is currently headquarters for the city's historical society. Altered in the nineteenth century, it is presently a mix of period rooms; the gazebo in its formal garden commands a fine view of New London. Year round, Tues.–Sat.: 1–4. Admission charged. (203) 443-1209.

Norwich: Nathaniel Backus House, 42 Rockwell St. A mansion in its own day; a museum with furnishings from various periods, including a table used by artist Jonathan Trumbell for mixing his paints. July, Aug., Wed.: 2–5 and by appointment: (203) 887-8737.

Ridgefield: Keeler Tavern, 132 Main St. Built as a private home and turned into a tavern in

1772, this served as patriot headquarters during the 1777 Battle of Ridgefield; a British cannonball is still lodged in one of its beams. It's well restored and furnished. Year round, Wed., Sat., Sun.: 2-5 and by appointment. Admission charged. (203) 438-5485.

Sharon: Gay-Hoyt House, Main St. A rare 1770s brick mansion, now the town historical society museum displaying costumes, weapons, furnishings, and tools. May-Nov., Tues., Sat.: 2-5.

Simsbury: Captain Elisha Phelps House, 800 Hopemeadow St. Built as a home in 1771, a tavern during the days of the New Haven and Northampton Canal. Gambrel roofed, with a massive central chimney and exceptional woodwork, it's now part of Massacoh Plantation, a complex of restored and recreated buildings maintained by Simsbury Historical Society. May-Oct., daily: 1-4. Admission charged. (203) 658-2500.

Stonington: Whitehall Mansion, Rte. 27. Notable for its unusually wide shingles, long windows and paneling. Handsomely furnished with late-eighteenth-century pieces. Year round, daily except Sats.: 2-4. Admission charged.

Stratford: Captain David Judson House, Stratford Academy Hill between Main and Elm streets. Notable for its ornate door frame, collection of tools, and a cellar originally used as slave quarters. April 1-Nov. 1 and by appointment. Admission charged. (203) 378-0630.

Suffield: Dr. Alexander King House, 234 Main St. Amply furnished with early chests, chairs and Bennington pottery; exhibits include a collection of wagons and sleighs, and a cigar shop which illustrates the history of cigar-making (the country's first cigar factory was established in town, in 1810). May-Nov., Wed.: 2-4. Admission charged.

Wallingford: Parsons House, 180 South Main St. A half dozen fireplaces, fine woodwork and collections of early pewter, silver, musical instruments, schoolbooks, Indian artifacts and old coins add up to an unusual museum house. June-Sept., Sun.: 2-5 and by appointment. (203) 269-6257.

Wethersfield: The Webb, Deane, Stevens Museum, owned and maintained by the National Society of Colonial Dames in the State of Connecticut, includes the three homes; all open mid-May to mid-Oct., Tues.-Sat.: 10-4; Sun.: 1-4. A combination ticket is available. (203) 529-0612.

Joseph Webb House, 211 Main St. Here in May, 1781, Washington spent five days planning with the Count de Rochambeau the campaign which resulted in the Battle of Yorktown. Unfortunately the murals by Wallace Nutting depicting that battle have been obscured to heighten the genuine look of the place, but still it's a gracious home furnished with fine local pieces, porcelains, silver and crewel work. Same hours as Wethersfield.

Silas Deane House, 203 Main St. Here Washington is said to have been apprised of plans to capture Fort Ticonderoga when he stopped by on his way to assume command of the Continental Army at Cambridge. Admission charged. Same hours as Wethersfield.

Isaac Stevens House, 215 Main St. A plain Jane by comparison with the other two houses, but a delightfully livable one, furnished with a stress on children's furniture, toys, books and clothes. Admission charged. Same hours as Wethersfield.

Wilton: Sloan-Raymond-Fitch House, 249 Danbury Rd. Built in 1757, now home for town collections of early furniture, clothing and such. Year round, Sat., Sun.: 2-5. Admission charged. (203) 762-7257.

Windsor: Oliver Ellsworth Homestead, 778 Palisado Ave. Ellsworth named this early central hall house "Elmwood" for the thirteen trees which he planted around it to commemorate the original states. It's said that when South Carolina seceded from the Union, the tree honoring it was struck by lightning. The interior is notable for its large parlor, French wallpaper, Chinese Chippendale furniture, silver, pewter, and china. May through Oct., Tues.-Sat.: 1-5. Donations. (203) 688-9444.

Woodbury: Glebe House, Hollow Rd. "Glebe" refers to farmland given a parish priest as part of his salary. The home was built in 1750 but its proudest day came in 1873 when the Episcopal bishop of Connecticut was elected here; he subsequently became the first bishop of that church with a see in the United States. Furnished late nineteenth-century style. Summer months: Sun., Tues.: 1–5; Wed.–Sat.: 11–5. Winter months: same days but closing at 4. Donations. (203) 263-3681.

MASSACHUSETTS

Braintree: General Sylvanus Thayer Birthplace, 786 Washington St., across from Town Hall. Headquarters for Braintree Historical Society with special collection relating to Thayer, War of 1812 hero. Year round, Tues. through Sat.: 1:30–4; open from 10:30 during summer months. Small admission charged.

Lexington: Buckman Tavern, Hancock-Clarke House and Munroe Tavern. All three buildings are open April 19–Oct. 31, daily: 10–5, Sun.: 1–5. Admission. A combination ticket is available from the Lexington Historical Society, Buckman Tavern. (617) 861-0928. See Chapter 5.

Melrose: Phineas Upham House, 255 Upham St. Notable for its massive fireplaces and oak beams. James Bailey Upham wrote "Pledge of Allegiance to the Flag." By appointment. (617) 665-3415.

Newbury: Short House, 39 High Rd. (Rte. 1A, opposite town common). Built in 1732, a brick-ended, wooden frame house with fine interior paneling and furnishings from the William and Mary period. June–Sept., Tues., Thurs., Sun.: 1–5. Admission charged. SPNEA: (617) 227-3956.

North Swansea: Martin House, Rte. 6. An early eighteenth-century farmhouse featuring period clocks, needlework, family portraits and pewter. May 1–Nov. 1, daily: 10–6. Admission charged. (617) 379-9616.

Norwell: Jacobs Farm, corner of Main St. and Jacobs Lane, Assinippi. Enhanced by its setting, open fields and numerous barns and outbuildings, a mid-eighteenth-century farmhouse illustrating farm life during its first and subsequent periods. June–Sept.: Tues., Thurs., Sun.: 2–5. Admission charged. SPNEA. (617) 227-3956.

Brookline: Edward Devotion House, 347 Harvard St., near Coolidge Corner. Built 1750, restored to period. Small admission charged. (617) 277-3663.

Chatham: Atwood House, Stage Harbor Rd. A gambrel-roofed cottage, considered a mansion in 1752 when it was built by a sea captain. Furnished to period and with new wings which house varied local historical collections. Late spring–early fall, Mon., Wed., Fri.: 2–5.

Charlestown: Warren Tavern, 2 Pleasant St. The sign on this working restaurant acclaims its building date as 1780. Named for Joseph Warren who died at Bunker Hill, it began as a tavern with a Masonic lodge upstairs, of which Paul Revere was warden. It has recently been restored to period after serving as a series of shops. Open from 11:30 for lunch, through the afternoon for sandwiches and 6–9 for dinner. It offers parking and traditional Yankee fare. (617) 241-8500.

Concord: Old Manse. For details see Chapter 9. April 19–May 31 and Oct. 15–Nov. 11, weekends and holidays: 10–4:30. June 1–Oct. 15, daily: 10–4:30. Admission charged. (617) 369-3909.

Gloucester: Sargent-Murray-Gilman House. See Chapter 8 for details. June–Oct. 15, Tues., Thurs., Sat.: 1–5. Admission charged. (617) 283-4505.

Hadley: Porter-Phelps-Huntington House, 130 River Drive. Junction Rtes. 47 and 9. Built in 1752, "Forty Acres" is furnished to period. May 15–Oct. 15, daily: 1–4:30. Small admission charged. (413) 584-4699.

Plymouth: Spooner House, 27 North St. A gracious mid-eighteenth-century home, furnished to depict changing life for the generations of one family which occupied it for two hundred years. May 25–mid-Sept., daily: 10–5. Admission charged. (617) 746-0012.

Provincetown: Seth Nickerson House, 72 Commercial St. Built by a ship's carpenter, most of its interior woodwork is said to be taken from ships wrecked off Cape Cod. Windowpanes are of Sandwich glass. Presently privately owned but shown during summer months. Daily: 10–5.

South Sudbury: Wayside Inn, Rte. 20. Built in 1702 and known as the Red Horse in the nineteenth century when Longfellow visited, setting his *Tales of a Wayside Inn* here. Restored in 1958 by the Henry Ford Foundation, it is a working inn offering Yankee fare and reasonably priced guest rooms. (617) 443-8846.

Weston: Smith Tavern, Boston Post Rd. (off Rte. 20, facing town common). A mid-eighteenth-century building which now serves as town offices and the site of community events; several rooms contain collections of the Weston Historical Society. Year round, Wed.: 2–4. Admission charged. (617) 899-4515.

Wollaston: Josiah Quincy House, 20 Muirhead St. (Turn off South Shore Boulevard at Bromfield St.). An impressive mansion built by the prominent Revolutionary-era merchant and patriot and partially restored, furnished in late eighteenth-century "high style." June–Sept., Tues., Thurs., Sun.: 1–5. Admission charged. SPNEA. (617) 227-3956.

Yarmouthport: Thacher House, Rte. 6A, across from town post office. Begun as a saltbox in 1690 but basically mid-eighteenth century, with a mix of period furnishings. June–Sept., daily: 11–4. Admission charged. SPNEA. (617) 227-3956.

MAINE

Camden: Old Conway House, Rte. 1 and Conway Rd. An eighteenth-century farmhouse restored and furnished. The complex includes a barn, blacksmith shop and museum of paintings, costumes and changing exhibits. July 1–Labor Day, Mon.–Fri.: 1–5. Admission charged.

Damariscotta: Chapman Hall House, Main St. opposite the town visitors' information center. Built in 1754 and restored to the period, complete with an herb garden. Mid-June–mid-Sept., daily except Mon.: 1–5.

Machias: Burnham Tavern. Main St., just off Rte. 1. For details see Chapter 5. Mid-June–Labor Day, Mon.–Fri.: 10–5; Sat.: 10–3 and rest of the year by appointment. Admission charged. (207) 255-4432.

South Berwick: Jewett Memorial, Rte. 236. (Center of town, next to the library.) An outstanding example of mid-Georgian architecture, also notable as home of the early twentieth-century author Sarah Orne Jewett, whose bedroom and study have been preserved as she arranged it. June–Sept., Wed.–Sun.: 1–5. Admission charged. SPNEA. (617) 227-3956.

South Berwick: Hamilton House, Vaughan's Lane. Splendid Georgian mansion overlooking the Quamphegan River. Setting for Sarah Orne Jewett's novel, *The Tory Lover*. June–Sept., Tues., Thurs., Sun.: 1–5. Admission charged. SPNEA (617) 227-3956.

NEW HAMPSHIRE

Exeter: Cincinnati Hall, Governor's Lane. A double house dating from 1721 which now serves as headquarters for the Society of Cincinnati. This elite group derives its name from the Roman senator who left his plow to fight for the empire. Membership is open only to those whose forefathers were officers (not just soldiers) in the Continental Army, and only the eldest son in each generation is eligible. An eighteenth-century occupant of the house helped draft the United States Constitution and his working draft is displayed, along with numerous Society possessions and portraits. May 1–Oct. 30, Tues., Thurs.: 2–4.

Keene: Wyman Tavern, 339 Main St. Built in 1762 by a veteran of the Indian wars who in

1775 led the town's twenty-nine minutemen from the front yard of his tavern off to Lexington. In 1770 it was also the site of the first meeting for Dartmouth College Trustees. Now restored, it serves as the museum for the county historical society. May 15-Oct. 15, Wed., Sat.: 2-4. Donations.

Manchester: General John Stark House, 2000 Elm St. An early eighteenth-century house which was the boyhood home of the hero of the Battle of Bennington and now serves as headquarters and museum for the Molly Stark Chapter of the D.A.R. May 15-Oct. 13, Wed., Sun.: 1:30-4:30. Admission charged.

Wolfeboro: Clark House, 5 Main St. (Rte. 28). Built in 1778 but an earlier design: six rooms around a central chimney, furnished and filled with local memorabilia. July 3-Sept. 5, Mon.-Sat.: 1:30-5:30 and by appointment. (603) 569-2324 or 569-2029.

RHODE ISLAND

Coventry: General Nathaniel Greene Homestead, Taft St., Anthony Village. Home of Washington's second-in-command, restored to reflect the 1770s. March-Nov.; Wed., Sat., Sun.: 2-5 and by appointment. Donation. (401) 821-8630.

Paine House, 1 Station St., Washington Village. Built around 1700 as an inn; now partially restored and furnished. May 1-Sept. 4, Tues.: 1-4; also Sun.: 1-5 during May. And by appointment. Donation. (401) 568-4047.

Cranston: Joy Homestead, Scituate Ave. A gambrel-roofed, ten-room farmhouse, now restored and furnished. For hours (not available at this writing) check with Rhode Island Development Council (401) 277-2611.

East Greenwich: General James Mitchell Varnum House, Pierce St. A gracious mansion noteworthy for its paneling and period garden. June 9-Sept. 8, Sun.: 1-5 and by appointment. Admission charged. (401) 884-4312 or 884-4622.

Newport: Bull-Mawdsley House, corner Spring and John streets. Built in the 1680s but enlarged with the help of English design books in the 1740s; its interior is furnished to depict later periods. June-Sept.; Tues., Thurs., Sun.: 1-5. Admission charged. SPNEA. (617) 227-3956.

Seventh Day Baptist Meetinghouse, attached to Newport Historical Society, 82 Touro St. Interesting in its design and for its early Clagget clock. The attached museum includes an extensive collection of eighteenth-century locally made furniture and other, varied Newport memorabilia. Year round, daily except Sat. afternoon, Sun.-Mon., 9:30-4:30.

Providence: Governor Stephen Hopkins House, Benefit and Hopkins streets. The early eighteenth-century home of Rhode Island's signer of the Declaration of Independence, later its governor. Restored. Year round, Wed., Sat.: 1-4 and by appointment. (401) 861-2935.

Admiral Esek Hopkins House, 97 Admiral St. Home of the first Commander-in-Chief of the Continental Navy. By appointment. (401) 751-4668.

First Baptist Church in America, 75 North Main St. The present graceful building dates from 1775; a must for every visitor to Providence. April 1-Nov. 30; Mon.-Fri.: 9-12, and by appointment. (401) 751-2266.

Old State House, North Main St. between North and South Court streets. "Rhode Island's Independence Hall," built in 1762 and site of the Rhode Island General Assembly meeting which established the "first free republic in the New World, May 4, 1776." Year round, Mon.-Sat.: 8:30-4:30.

Betsy Williams Cottage, near Elmwood Ave., entrance to Roger Williams Park. A small gambrel-roofed house owned by a descendant of Roger Williams and furnished with Colonial pieces. Year round; Mon., Tues., Fri., Sat.: 10-4; Sun.: 1-4.

Tiverton Four Corners: Chase Corey House, Main Rd. Built in 1739 and restored to serve as the local historical museum. May-Oct., Sun.: 2-4:30.

Soule-Seabury House. Built in 1760 as a home for a wealthy China Trade captain; a Georgian-style country home with many of its original furnishings. May through June, weekends: 11-5; July 1 through Sept., daily: 1-5. Admission charged. (401) 683-1270.

Warwick: John Waterman Arnold House, Roger Williams Ave. Notable for its beehive oven, paneling and nineteenth-century winding front stairway; now home of the local historical society. Year round, Sun.: 1-4; June-Oct., Sat.: 1-4. (401) 467-7647 (5-7 P.M.).

Westerly: Babcock-Smith House, 124 Granite St. Georgian-style home of the area's first physician and postmaster. July, Aug., Sat., Sun.: 1-4. Admission charged.

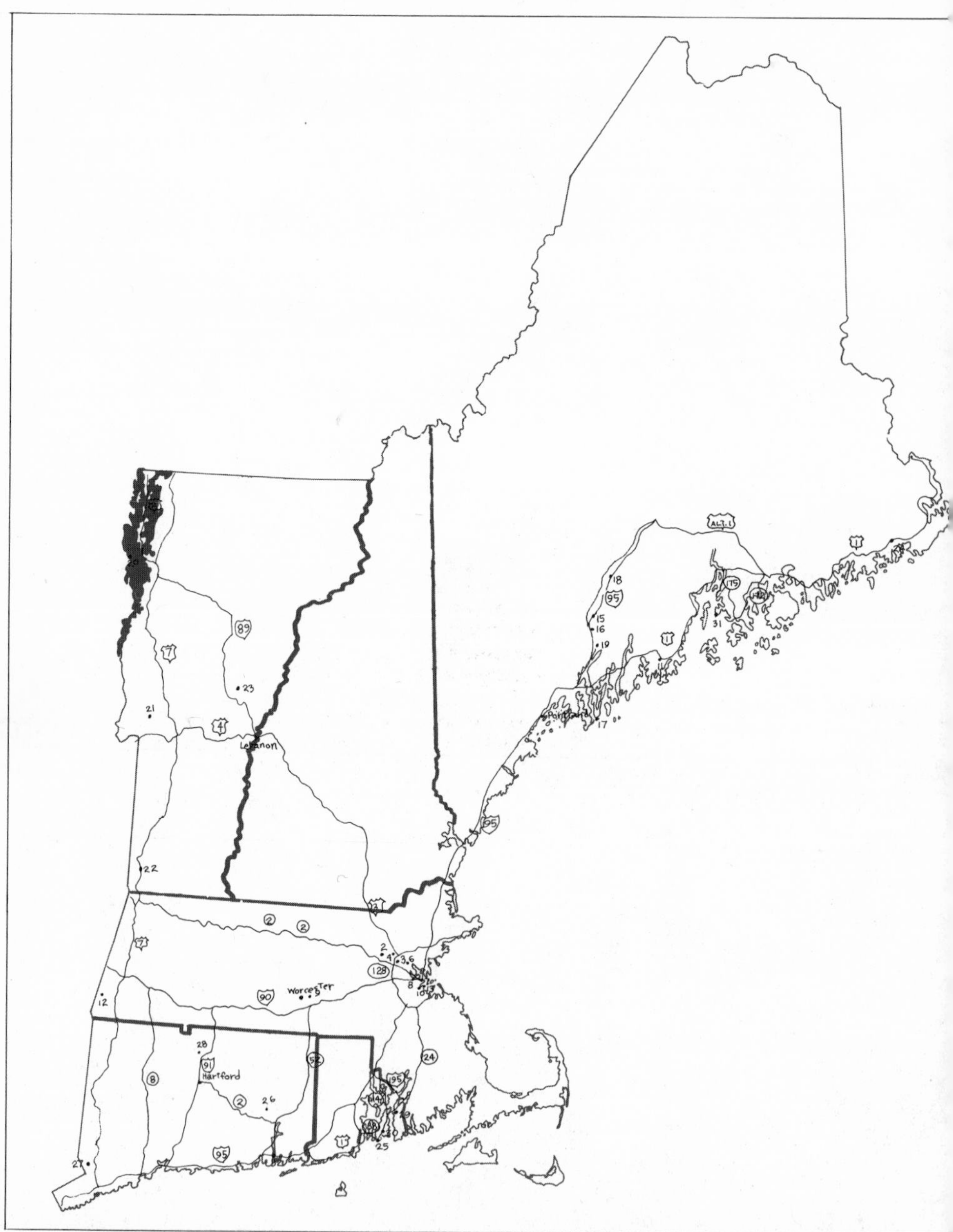

ALT. 1
1
18
95
175
15
16
19
31
Portland
17
89
7
23
21
4
Lebanon
95
22
2
2
2
4
3, 6
128
8
10
Worcester
90
12
7
28
91
Hartford
8
2
26
52
24
95
1
25
27

5

Redcoats and Rebels

Massachusetts was a bonfire waiting for a match
in the spring of 1775, as General Thomas Gage was well
aware. All through the winter, picked companies of militia called "*Minutemen*" – because they were pledged to 1
fight for provincial rights at a minute's notice – had been
drilling on New England greens, preparing for the clash
that seemed inevitable.

18th-century lantern

The Continental Congress voted authorization for an
army of 18,000 men, and then adjourned to drum up
support for the proposed force. Gage, who had only four
thousand men under his command, had been ordered by
London to move against the rebellious provincials while
they were still "a rude rabble" and not an army. Congress's adjournment created an opportunity Gage felt
compelled to seize.

The Congressional Committee of Public Safety had been
stockpiling guns and provisions at *Concord* – some of 2
these supplies stolen from Gage's own stores. The loss
of this stockpile would be a severe blow to the Continentals. But the provisionals expected some kind of
British foray and kept a close watch on all troop movements.

On Saturday, April 15, Gage tipped his hand by ordering the grenadiers and light infantry of his command
relieved from regular duties, supposedly to learn new
exercises. These were his elite troops, and some shrewd
Bostonians, among them Paul Revere, suspected something was up. Revere hurried out to *Lexington* where 3
John Hancock and Samuel Adams were lodging at *Jonas* 3a

Clarke's Parsonage, and warned them that the British were going to make a move.

After delivering his warning, Revere returned to Boston, arranging on the way back to signal a friend in Charlestown from the unusually tall steeple of Old North Church if the British marched out in force. This was the "one if by land, two if by sea" code immortalized in "The Midnight Ride of Paul Revere."

So, by the time more than seven hundred crack British troops assembled on Boston Common (then on water's edge) late on the night of April 18, steps had been taken to ensure that the expedition they were embarking on would fail.

Adams and Hancock still lingered in Lexington, but the precious arms and supplies were being loaded onto oxcarts and hauled away to new hiding places in the woods outside Concord and in the neighboring towns of Acton, Stow and Harvard.

About two hours before midnight, the troops boarded transports that took them across the Charles River. Barely were the first boats underway when two lanterns twinkled in the Old North steeple and Revere and fellow messenger William Dawes were off to spread the word. Revere reached Clarke's Parsonage around midnight, arousing the house with his cry that: "The Regulars are coming out!"

By 2 A.M. on April 19, some 130 Minutemen were assembled on Lexington's town common, now known as
"*Battle Green*." They were commanded by Captain John 3b
Parker, a forty-five-year-old French and Indian War veteran. They weren't looking for trouble, but the Minutemen weren't taking any nonsense either. Parker later said
the men decided "not to be discovered, nor meddle, nor
make with said regular troops, unless they should insult
or molest us."

The militiamen were uncertain what the British were
up to. All the scouts Parker sent out were picked up by
the British advance guard, as Revere had been. Just before daybreak, they began to disperse, some to their
homes, others to the taproom of the *Buckman Tavern* 3c
for a warming tot of rum. It was almost dawn when the
last scout Parker sent out – and the only one to avoid
British patrols – came back with the news that the troops,
several hours behind schedule, were now on the outskirts
of town.

The *Minuteman Drummer* sounded the alarm, and while Hancock and Adams beat a hasty retreat, seventy men – about half the adult male population of Lexington – lined up on the green. Parker deployed his unsoldierly-looking Minutemen in two ranks but ordered them to: "let the troops pass by, and don't molest them, without they begin first." A similar order, "on no account to fire," was issued by Major John Pitcairn as he entered Lexington with an advance guard of six companies of infantry. 3d

As the Regulars advanced onto the green – a splendid sight in their red and white uniforms – Pitcairn rode up to the Minutemen and ordered them to surrender their arms. Parker, an old soldier and concerned for the safety of his men, gave an order to disperse. Some Minutemen started to leave the green, while others – ignoring Parker's command – prepared to make a stand. No one, all eyewitnesses agree, dropped his musket.

What happened next is in dispute, and doubtless will remain so. Someone fired a shot and both sides immediately opened up on each other. The Americans, Parker among them, later insisted the British fired first – and "without provocation." Pitcairn, who died at the Battle of Bunker Hill a few months later, claimed the first shot came from behind a stone wall – from a rebel in other words.

Whoever fired first, the shot sent the British soldiers raging out of control, and the clash on Lexington Green was more of a military riot than a battle. Pitcairn finally restored order, as the main body of troops arrived, but eight Minutemen had been killed – most of them shot in the back.

The fight at Lexington looms large in history but in time took only a few minutes. Less than half an hour after they entered Lexington, the British marched out – rendering themselves the traditional victory salute before leaving. By 8 A.M., they were entering Concord Village where a force of 150 militiamen had assembled in front of the meetinghouse. The provincials marched out to meet the British, but when the regulars showed no sign of halting, they pulled back to high ground beyond town – many townsfolk fleeing with them.

Battle at North Bridge, Concord, Mass.

The Redcoats marched unopposed into the almost empty village and quickly consolidated their position by seizing the two bridges over the Sudbury River, South and *North Bridge*, and establishing a headquarters in 2a

Wright Tavern in the center of town. Most of the Con- 2b
tinental stores had been moved but the troops found
some supplies – including five hundred pounds of musket
balls and a quantity of flour. After knocking the wheels
off the jailhouse cannon, they made a bonfire out of
some barrels, which got out of control and spread to the
town house, as the town hall was then called.

The fire was extinguished before it did much damage,
but to the anxious Minutemen on the heights, the billowing smoke suggested that the British were burning
the town down. Reinforcements had been coming in
from towns like Acton and *Bedford* and the provincials 4
numbered around four hundred men. Word of the bloody
skirmish on Lexington Green hadn't reached them yet,
but the militiamen were still resolved to "March into
the middle of town and defend their homes or die in the
attempt."

With the Acton Company in front and fifers and drummers playing, the Minutemen marched in a double file toward North Bridge, defended by an infantry company – about one hundred men. The British fired on the attackers and they returned a volley of musketry that wounded nearly a dozen soldiers, three of them mortally. Unaccustomed to this kind of resistance, the soldiers panicked and beat a quick retreat back to town – abandoning their wounded.

The skirmish at North Bridge – "The Shot Heard Round the World" – lasted less than three minutes, yet was one of the most decisive battles in history, shaking empires and altering the course of history. No one knew that at the time, of course. The Minutemen were relieved to find that the British hadn't burned the town down after all, and marched back across the bridge, taking their dead and wounded to the John Buttrick House.

One of the last Minutemen to leave, a twenty-one-year-old Concord youth named Ammi White, stopped to examine a fallen British soldier when the man began to stir. This apparently frightened White, who finished him off with his hatchet. When a British force that had been searching for stores at an outlying farm returned to the village, they were startled to find the bodies of dead soldiers – one of them with his head hacked open – scattered around a battle-scarred North Bridge. Word of White's brutal act spread quickly through the British ranks, and with it a rumor that the Americans were scalping the dead, Indian style.

By noon, the badly shaken British were heading back
to Boston, some seventeen long miles away. The route
they marched along is still called "*Battle Road*," and 5
stretches of it have been restored as part of Minuteman
National Park. At *Meriam's Corner*, just outside Concord 5a
center, they got a taste of what lay ahead as local militiamen, concealed Indian fashion behind trees and stone
walls, fired volley after volley into the marching ranks.
About a mile beyond Meriam's Corner, where the road
took a sharp bend through heavy woods, the firing was
so intense – and accurate – that eight British soldiers
were killed and many others wounded, earning this
stretch the name "*Bloody Angle*." (Three Americans 5b
were also killed here.)

In Lexington, the dead had been hastily buried in a common grave and Captain Parker reformed his company and posted it on a hill just inside the town line where they could pepper the returning British as they passed. On Battle Green, scene of the "victory" earlier in the day, the battered British paused to rest – and contemplate the possibility that they might be wiped out.

Fortunately for them, reinforcements arrived; a thousand fresh troops with cannon, commanded by a British
earl, Lord Hugh Percy. While the troops rested and the
artillery kept the rebels at bay, the wounded were treated
in *Munroe Tavern*, where Percy made his headquarters. 3e
Shortly after 3 P.M., the British resumed their march
and the militiamen – now swarming over the countryside like a flock of angry bees – resumed their deadly
sniping. The enraged soldiers, who considered firing
from cover to be cowardly rather than sensible, began
breaking into houses suspected of sheltering snipers and
putting the inhabitants to death. Some of the bloodiest
such incidents occurred in a section of West Cambridge
called Menotomy, now the town of Arlington, one of the
worst at the *House of Jason Russell*, which fronted on 6
Battle Road. As the troops approached, Russell, an elderly man, built a crude barricade in front of his home
and prepared to defend his property. Seven Danvers
Minutemen, fleeing from the British flanking patrols –
sent out to flush snipers – rushed up and tried to take
shelter in Russell's home but the pursuing troops opened
fire and charged them with their bayonets, killing all
seven, and old Jason, too. Other militiamen were hiding
in the cellar of the Russell house but the first Redcoat to
try to enter was shot dead and the others retreated.

In the half-mile stretch of road around the Russell House, some twenty Americans and many more British soldiers died, making it the bloodiest single portion of the Battle Road. Among the dead were two noncombatant but luckless tipplers who were sitting over their ale in the Cooper Tavern when the British broke in and bayoneted them to death.

When the exhausted British stumbled into Cambridge, Percy decided on a change of route. Instead of continuing back through Cambridge to Boston, which would have meant crossing the Charles River under fire, the troops would detour across Charlestown Neck and bivouac under the protection of the guns of the warships in the harbor. (Tradition has it that if the British continued through Cambridge, they planned to burn the buildings of Harvard College. But, as all New Englanders know, God is a Harvard man.)

Minuteman statue, Lexington, Mass.

Percy's caution probably saved many lives, but even so, British casualties were heavy: 73 dead, 174 wounded, and 26 missing. About four thousand Americans played some part in the battle; 49 were killed, 41 wounded, and 5 were missing. The British commander found his enemy unconventional but disconcertingly competent: "Whoever looks upon them as an irregular mob, will find himself much mistaken; they have men amongst them who know very well what they are about . . . you may depend upon it, that as the rebels have now had time to prepare, they are determined to go through with it, nor will the insurrection here turn out so despicable as it is perhaps imagined at home."

The American Revolution had begun.

BUNKER HILL

By May of 1775, a force of some three thousand militiamen was camped around Boston and the British – who by now had a healthy respect for provincial military capabilities – were under siege.

A dashing militia captain and erstwhile druggist from Connecticut named Benedict Arnold had been given a colonel's commission by Massachusetts and dispatched to capture Fort Ticonderoga on Lake Champlain in upstate New York, joining forces with Ethan Allen of Vermont and his Green Mountain Boys, the Continentals. Led by Allen and his cousin, Seth Warner, they surprised the small garrison of the great fortress on May 10, capturing it, along with seventy-eight heavy guns and some mortars and howitzers.

The Continental Congress, meeting in Philadelphia, voted unanimously on June 15 to appoint a fellow delegate, George Washington of Virginia, as commander-in-chief of the Continental Army. Also, Congress agreed to send ten companies of Maryland, Pennsylvania and Virginia militia to join the predominantly New England force besieging Boston. But, before the new commander or his reinforcements could arrive, a major battle was fought in Boston.

Gage wanted to avoid a repetition of the Battle Road. But he realized that if the rebels mounted cannon on the heights in Charlestown Neck or on Dorchester Heights, his position in Boston would be untenable. He decided to occupy Dorchester Heights – now part of South Boston – but the Continental forces got word of the plan
and decided to forestall it by occupying *Bunker Hill* in 7
Charlestown first.

A force of about twelve hundred men, commanded by General Israel "Old Put" Putnam of the Connecticut Militia and Colonel William Prescott of Massachusetts, moved onto the Charlestown Peninsula on June 16, under cover of darkness. There had been a change of plan, however, and the men were ordered to occupy Breed's Hill rather than Bunker Hill, which gave its name to the battle anyway.

At dawn, the British spotted the hastily constructed redoubt and their warships fired on it, but with little effect. The Redcoats reacted quickly. General William Howe was sent out with a force of 2,400 men and orders to dislodge the entrenched Americans with a frontal attack, the kind of maneuver only disciplined regular troops could be expected to perform – or withstand.

It was June 17, a hot, muggy day, and the British went into battle wearing full packs. Twice they lumbered up the hill, closing ranks as a murderous fire decimated them. Twice, they were beaten back. For the third assault, Howe had his men take off their packs and ordered them to charge up hill as fast as possible, firing only when they reached the redoubt – and then to charge with their bayonets.

No reinforcements or supplies had reached the Continentals, their powder was getting low, and militiamen were not equipped with bayonets. Unable to meet a bayonet charge and without enough ammunition to hold the British off with gunfire, the Americans withdrew in the face of the third assault. It was a fighting retreat – not a rout – and the British paid dearly for the victory.

The Americans suffered about four hundred casualties, roughly a third of their force, but the British had more than eleven hundred killed and wounded – nearly half of all those engaged. "The success is too dearly bought," Howe admitted and never again during the war were British soldiers to go so arrogantly and confidently into battle.

SIEGE AND EVACUATION

On July 2, 1776, Washington arrived in *Cambridge* and 8
took official command of the Continental forces from
Artemas Ward. 9

The army he commanded had swelled to 14,000 men, but was a loosely organized and ill-disciplined armed mass rather than a real fighting force. As a Virginia aristocrat, Washington was put out – and put off – by the unkempt appearance and individualistic behavior of the New England volunteers. But he was also impressed by their accomplishments: "The deficiencies in their numbers, their discipline, and stores, can only lead to the conclusion that their spirit has exceeded their strength."

Washington commanded the army from Cambridge,
shifting his headquarters from *Harvard Yard* to the 8b
Craigie Mansion, now vacated by its Tory owner. His 8c
field headquarters was in an earthenwork redoubt, now
known as *Fort Washington*. The Continental forces were 8d
camped in a rough semicircle around Boston. Some of
the men were billeted in or around Harvard College –
which had shifted classes to Concord – using buildings
such as *Massachusetts Hall* and *Christ Church* as bar- 8e, f
racks. Others were in large fortified camps such as the
one in Roxbury on top of *Fort Hill.* 10

Washington was a hard taskmaster and soon had thousands of men digging trenches and throwing up earthenworks. Badly shaken by the losses they suffered storming the crude fortifications on Bunker Hill, the British looked at the formidable defenses surrounding them and abandoned all thought of attack. Which was just as well for Washington – and his army.

The Continentals kept such sloppy records that while Washington first thought he had sixteen tons of gunpowder, in fact there were only about ten thousand pounds – barely enough for nine cartridges per man. (A British soldier went into battle with enough powder and ball for sixty shots.) The situation was remedied, thanks to the resourcefulness of American smugglers, who bought powder in Bermuda and the Dutch West Indies and slipped large quantities of it through the British blockade. But for a while the Continental Army was very vulnerable.

British army recruit

By early September, Washington felt confident enough to propose an all-out assault on the British positions. His generals – reflecting Congressional opinion – opposed the attack on the grounds that peace might still be negotiated with George III and his ministers. So the Continental Army settled into its siege lines for another six months. The Continentals had the advantage over the British in what amounted to a waiting game.

Most of the men were near enough to home so friends and relatives could visit them, and there was entertainment to be found in the many taverns of Cambridge and neighboring towns. Food was plentiful enough and a soldier's ration often included a daily quart of beer.

Things were less comfortable for the British and their Loyalist allies. In October Gage sailed for England, relinquishing command to Howe, the unhappy victor of Bunker Hill. Howe's troops, paid threepence a day, compared to the six dollars a month a Continental soldier received, had to subsist on rations of rotten pork and wormy biscuit. Inefficiency and corruption in the army administration were partly responsible, but the flow of supplies was also frequently interrupted by daring American privateers – "George Washington's Navy."

During the siege the British revenged themselves on some Boston landmarks: Old South Meeting House was turned into a riding hall, King's Chapel became the officers' chapel for the garrison. Old West Church had its steeple knocked off to prevent patriot sympathizers from sending signals to the Continental lines, and the Liberty Tree was chopped down by the Tory mob.

The Americans realized that the only alternative to a bloody assault on the British positions was to bombard the city with heavy cannon – cannon they didn't have but were taking steps to obtain. In November 1775, Washington dispatched a fat young Boston bookseller
named *Henry Knox* to bring in the cannon captured at 11
Fort Ticonderoga the previous spring.

Dismantling these artillery pieces and lashing them to
forty-two ox-drawn sleighs, Knox and his men dragged
sixty tons of cannon and supplies more than three hundred miles through deep snow and thick forest, across
frozen rivers and over the steep Berkshire Hills. This
"Noble Train of Artillery" passed through thirty-four
towns in Massachusetts alone and each community turned
out to help haul, a fact which these towns remind us of
today through exhibits and events sponsored by the
Knox Trail Historical Society. The expedition was ex- 12
pected to be completed in two weeks. In fact it took
forty-seven days to reach Framingham, still twenty miles
from Boston. Knox rushed ahead with some of the lighter
pieces which he personally presented to Washington at a
spot now marked on the Cambridge Common.

Knox's cannon were slipped into the Continental line
– bales of hay were piled along the roadside so that the
British couldn't spot the bigger pieces. On March 4,
1776, Washington moved them onto *Dorchester Heights*, 13
a steep ridge commanding Boston Harbor.

The Americans had learned some lessons at Bunker Hill too. General John Thomas and his two thousand men were well supplied with powder, shot and prefabricated breastworks (mounted on 350 oxcarts). Under cover of darkness the Continentals rapidly constructed an almost impregnable redoubt. "The rebels have done more in one night than my men could do in months," General Howe is reported to have said when he saw the results.

Howe could either attack or evacuate the city, now
completely exposed to American cannon. Remembering
Bunker Hill, he chose the latter course and on March 17
the British garrison marched off *Castle Island* and onto 14
troop transports bound for Halifax, Nova Scotia. With
them went some one thousand Tories, some of Boston's
most prominent citizens among them.

The most enduring monument to the victory on Dorchester Heights – which raised American morale at a critical time – is a living one. Boston still celebrates Evacuation Day with a March 17 parade through South Boston, which passes in review by the victory monument.

March 17 is also St. Patrick's Day, a fact Washington noted by making the Continentals' password of the day "St. Patrick," to the delight of the many Irishmen in their ranks. By coincidence South Boston today is an Irish-American bastion: Evacuation Day *and* St. Patrick's Day are celebrated simultaneously and enthusiastically.

As the siege tightened around Boston, the Continental Congress received word that the British were planning to invade the northern colonies. There were fewer than one thousand regular soldiers in Canada, but the British were recruiting Indian allies whose raids could devastate scattered frontier settlements.

General Phillip Schuyler, assisted by General Richard Montgomery, was ordered to take a force of some eighteen hundred men and attack Canada by way of Lake George and Lake Champlain, using Fort Ticonderoga as a jumping-off point. Schuyler's objective was Montreal, but Washington proposed a second expedition to be commanded by Benedict Arnold, that would march on Quebec. Arnold was given a force of some one thousand picked volunteers and riflemen, including Daniel Morgan's famous Virginians. On paper, his route looked fairly easy: up the Kennebec and along the Dead River, across Lake Megantic and down the Chaudiere, which joins the St. Lawrence only four miles from Quebec.

Arnold expected that it would take about twenty days
to travel the 180 miles from *Fort Western* on the Kenne- 15
bec – now Augusta, the capital of Maine – to Quebec. But, because of the difficulty of the terrain and the faulty maps the expedition had been issued, the trip took forty-five days and the distance covered was three hundred fifty miles. Arnold's men had to drag their flat-bottomed "bateaux" over long portages. Later, when the boats – badly made of green wood – began to fall apart, they had to wade through swamps where they were nearly devoured by mosquitoes. About a third of the men turned back and only 675 exhausted, half-starved survivors reached the walls of Quebec. It is a tribute to Arnold's undoubted leadership powers that so many made it that far.

The other half of the expedition had reached and occupied Montreal. In the meantime, Montgomery, who assumed command when Schuyler became ill, took three hundred men and joined Arnold and his ragged men before Quebec. The survivors of the epic trek through Maine were in bad shape, their clothing "torn in pieces . . . hung in strips . . . few had any shoes but moccasins [*sic*] made of raw skins . . . many without hats, beards long and visages thin and meager."

On December 31, the combined force attacked the walled city in a blinding snowstorm. It was a disaster. Montgomery, one of the best young commanders in the American forces, was killed, and there were almost five hundred other casualties – compared to fewer than twenty for the British. Although wounded himself, Arnold stubbornly insisted on continuing the siege. His men survived the winter by plundering the countryside. This alienated the French-Canadians, who had no great love for the English, but grew to like the Americans even less.

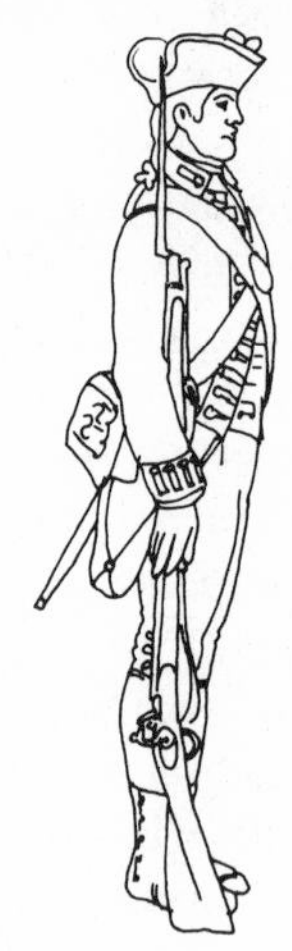

British officer

The besiegers got reinforcements in the spring, along with a new commander: General Thomas, the victor of Dorchester Heights. But British reinforcements had also arrived and the American army – now little more than a hungry mob – was in no state to continue a siege. Thomas ordered a retreat and by early July what was left of Arnold's force was safe inside Fort Ticonderoga – and Montreal and Quebec were safely British.

The Arnold Trail has been declared a National Historic 16
Place and thanks to the efforts of the Arnold Expedition Historical Society and other groups the American section, from *Fort Popham* at the mouth of the Kennebec 17
River to Coburn Gore on the Canadian border, is well marked, with some thirty-three interpretive panels at nine sites along the route.

Some of the buildings Arnold and his men visited on their march still stand, including Fort Western, *Fort* 18
Halifax in Winslow, and the *Old Pownalborough Court* 19
House in Dresden.

Arnold was a man of extraordinary energy, and despite the rigors of his wilderness march and the terrible winter in Quebec, he was back in battle again the following autumn. The British forces in Canada had grown to about thirteen thousand men, including Indian and German mercenaries. By September, their commander, General Carleton, was ready to march south.

The traditional invasion route, the one Schuyler had used in reverse, was over Lake Champlain. Arnold, who had some experience with ships during a stint as a West Indies trader, became a do-it-yourself admiral. Assembling a few captured lake boats and building others – some little more than glorified rafts – from standing timber, he put together a makeshift fleet of fifteen vessels manned by motley crews, most of them more accustomed to handling plows than hawsers. He had about seven hundred and fifty men, the British more than twice that number – along with a fleet of twenty fairly well-built vessels.

Arnold placed his little navy behind Valcour Island on the New York side of the lake, to surprise the British as they sailed by. It worked. On October 11, after spending the night in the lee of the Vermont Islands of North and South Hero, Carleton sailed south – bypassing Arnold. Spotting the Continental ships, he turned to do battle but had to sail into a wind blowing briskly from the north. This gave the out-gunned Americans a badly needed advantage, but they were still severely handicapped by a lack of skilled sailors.

One of the Continental vessels, *Royal Savage*, ran aground and was burned by a British landing party. Another small ship, *Philadelphia*, sank. Most of Arnold's guns were put out of action by British broadsides and only nightfall enabled the Continental fleet to escape. Carleton expected to finish off the Americans the following day, October 12, but under cover of fog, Arnold sailed his fleet in single file between the British and Valcour Island, escaping out into the open lake.

The British pursued, but both sides were hampered by lack of wind. On October 13 the wind picked up, and the British closed in, forcing one ship to surrender and another to run aground. Arnold avoided complete annihilation by rowing his flagship *Congress*, and what was left of his fleet, into *Buttonmould Bay* on the Vermont 20
side of the lake. The six ships – four of them flat-bottomed "gundalows" – were set afire, after Arnold nailed their flags to the mast so they would go down with colors flying. Arnold and the two hundred survivors of the battle marched to the fort at Crown Point, ten miles away. When the British approached, that fort was burned and the Continentals fell back on Fort Ticonderoga.

The Battle of Valcour Island was a sort of naval version of Bunker Hill. Both sides were brave, the British demonstrating discipline and professionalism, and the Americans, fighting spirit and ingenuity. Technically, the victory went to the British, who destroyed or captured eleven of the original fifteen American vessels, losing only three of their own. But the battle blunted what the British intended to be a sharp thrust and made General Carleton cautious in the face of an enemy that could fight so formidably with so little.

With winter approaching, and the Americans obviously far from vanquished, Carleton decided to postpone his invasion until spring – a decision that may have saved the American Revolution. Had he pushed on as far as Albany that autumn, American resistance might have collapsed entirely. Arnold's fierce holding action bought the cause of independence the thing it needed desperately – time.

Arnold was to distinguish himself in battle again, particularly at the decisive second battle of Saratoga, but his stubborn courage at Valcour Island may have been his greatest contribution to the cause he was ultimately to betray.

HUBBARDTON AND BENNINGTON

In the spring of 1777, the British finally launched their delayed offensive from Canada. The intent was to isolate New York and New England from the other colonies, setting them up for easy conquest. The plan was for General John "Gentleman Johnny" Burgoyne – who had assumed command of crown forces in Canada – to push down Lake Champlain and along the Hudson River to Albany, where they would join up with General Howe's forces, marching up from New York.

On June 17, Burgoyne and a force of nearly ten thousand men – a mixed bag of Canadians, American Loyalists, and German mercenaries – started south. On July 6, Burgoyne captured Fort Ticonderoga and a large quantity of American supplies. Retreating into Vermont, General Arthur St. Clair left behind a force commanded by Colonel Seth Warner of the Green Mountain Boys. Warner's orders were to collect the rearguard and any stragglers left behind when Fort "Ti" was evacuated, then join the main American army.

But, while St. Clair was retreating the British were pursuing. Warner and about 750 men were just having breakfast in their camp near Mount Zion, *Hubbardton, Ver-* 21
mont, when a British force commanded by General Simon Fraser suddenly attacked. The surprised Americans recovered quickly, and forming a semicircle on the hillside, they took cover and returned the British fire. They inflicted heavy losses and might have won the day if Fraser hadn't been reinforced by German troops –

singing loudly to the accompaniment of a brass band – commanded by Baron Friedrich Riedesel.

With half his command killed, wounded or captured, Warner ordered the remainder to retreat. The fight at Hubbardton lasted only forty-five minutes but was as bloody an engagement for its size as Waterloo. Warner has been criticized for getting involved in the battle at all, but there is no doubt that the stiff resistance of his men delayed the pursuit of St. Clair's army, which escaped to fight Burgoyne again. In Vermont, Warner – who fought
with distinction at the *Battle of Bennington* – is particu- 22
larly remembered for his stand at Hubbardton, and the state highway running from Manchester to Middlebury, passing near Hubbardton, is named for him.

After his victories at Ticonderoga and Hubbardton, things began to go wrong for Gentleman Johnny. The retreating Americans sniped at his marching columns and cut down trees in the path of his supply wagons, reducing progress to a crawl. A supporting force of Indians and Loyalists that was supposed to sweep through the Mohawk Valley retreated on learning that Benedict Arnold was advancing on them. And Burgoyne's provisions were running low.

He decided to detach 750 regular troops – half of them German – and some 300 Loyalists and Indians for a raid on Bennington, where there was reported to be a large store of militia supplies. On August 12, Colonel Friedrich Baum, a Hessian who spoke no English, started toward Bennington. Baum was unaware that a large militia force under Colonel John Stark was defending the Bennington stores. Stark decided to advance on his enemy and on October 14 marched an army of some 1,800 militiamen out of Bennington and into Baum's path. His force was made up mainly of men from the New Hampshire grants – which then included much of Vermont – but also volunteers from Massachusetts.

After two days of skirmishing, mostly in heavy rain, Stark attacked Baum's main position on a hillside three hundred feet above the Walloomsac River. Walloomsac Heights, where the "Battle of Bennington" was fought, is actually eight miles from Bennington and almost two miles inside the New York line.

The battle was fought on a steaming hot afternoon, and the shirt-sleeved militiamen – conscious that they were defending their own homes – swarmed up the heights and over the enemy positions. "We beat them today or Molly Stark's a widow," the dour, battle-wise Stark is supposed to have said before the attack.

Surrounded, and almost out of ammunition, Baum's dismounted dragoons – one of the things they hoped to find in Bennington was horses – tried to cut their way out with cavalry sabers. Baum was killed, and most of the Germans surrendered. An American victory appeared well-nigh certain and the militia were scattering to pursue the retreating enemy, when Lieutenant Colonel Von Breymann marched some six hundred Germans – late for the battle but lustily singing – onto the field. They should have participated in the earlier fighting but Breymann was a drillmaster in the Prussian tradition and insisted that his troops march with parade-ground precision – with the result that they only covered about half a mile an hour!

Stark's men turned Baum's captured cannon on Breymann's Hessians but were being forced back by the German regulars when Seth Warner's 350-men company from Manchester arrived to turn the tide. Stark took some six hundred prisoners and killed about two hundred of the enemy with only thirty Americans killed and forty wounded.

This victory by a hastily assembled force of backcountry farmers over regular soldiers commanded by professional officers had a tonic effect on American morale – which had been sagging. The dreaded Hessians, epitome of military professionalism, could be beaten. And, by backwoods squirrel hunters at that. For Burgoyne, the battle of Bennington was a total disaster. He lost time, some of his best troops, and failed to obtain the supplies he so desperately needed. Bennington paved the way for Saratoga where Burgoyne, abandoned by Howe whose army was engaged around Philadelphia, had to surrender his army to General Horatio Gates two months later.

Saratoga was the turning point, the victory that decided France to make an ally of the infant republic. Without that alliance, the decisive victory at Yorktown could never have happened. But without a victory at Bennington, there might not have been one at Saratoga.

There was no major fighting in Vermont for the rest of the war, but three years after the battle of Bennington,
the town of *Royalton* was burned by an Indian raiding 23
party led by a British officer. Few people were killed but

nearly thirty Vermonters were taken prisoner and brought to Canada. (Most were eventually ransomed.) The Royalton raid was a reminder to Vermont – at that time an independent republic – of how vulnerable a small country can be.

CONFLICT ON THE COAST

Britain's traditional dominance of the sea lanes gave her an obvious advantage in fighting the Revolutionary War. While Washington's troops were foot-slogging it up and down the thirteen colonies, British soldiers could move comfortably by ship and be quickly concentrated where they were needed. New England, with most of its population along the coast, was particularly vulnerable to British attack – and her superb harbors were coveted prizes of war.

Maine claims the honor of the first naval engagement – an American victory.

The British tender *Margaretta*, a small armed escort
vessel, was anchored in the little fishing port of *Machias* 24
on June 12, 1775 – just five days before the Battle of Bunker Hill – supervising the loading of a cargo of lumber for British Army barracks in besieged Boston. The townsfolk were reluctant to help the hated army of occupation and a force of militiamen led by Captain Jeremiah O'Brien – who took to rebellion against the crown with practiced Irish ease – attacked the tender, commandeering the sloop *Unity*; the militiamen, armed with muskets, swords, axes, and pitchforks, sailed alongside the tender and boarded her. After a sharp fight, in which the British captain was killed, the *Margaretta* capitulated.

By October of 1775, Bunker Hill had been fought, Washington was ringing Boston with entrenchments, and it was starting to look like a long war. On October 17, a British squadron bombarded and burned to the ground the town of Falmouth, Maine. No lives were lost but nearly a dozen vessels and several hundred buildings were destroyed. The town had to be rebuilt – in the process getting a new name: Portland (see Chapter 6).

The Falmouth raid wasn't in revenge for the attack on the *Margaretta*, but rather a reprisal for Falmouth's refusal to sell the Royal Navy ships' masts, at the time one of Maine's chief exports. The same month Falmouth was burned, the Rhode Island delegation to the Con-

tinental Congress – incensed because *Newport* was closed 25
to all American shipping by the British frigate *Rose* – 25a
introduced the bill creating the Continental Navy. Despite the existence of an American navy, on paper anyway, the British could sail pretty much where they pleased, and in December of 1776 a British force occupied Newport, remaining there for almost three years.

The British provided another example of what can be done with sea power. In April of 1777, two frigates put into Norwalk, Connecticut, and disembarked a force of some two thousand regulars who, virtually unmolested, marched thirty miles inland to Danbury. Connecticut
was known to the Continentals as "*The Provision State*" 26
because of its leading role in supplying the army, and the British burned a large supply depot and much of Danbury along with it. The Redcoats didn't have it completely their own way, however. On the return march from Danbury, Connecticut militia companies, led by the ubiquitous Benedict Arnold, harassed the British, inflicting close to two hundred casualties while suffering less than one hundred themselves. (Arnold had his horse shot out from underneath him and a grateful Congress voted to buy him another.)

The heaviest fighting took place in *Ridgefield*, where 27
the Americans built a barricade of farm carts across the
road and made a gallant but unsuccessful attempt to halt
the returning British. They did manage to take forty English prisoners early in the battle, who were sent to the
Continental Keep at *Newgate Copper Mine* in East 28
Granby.

The British raided the Connecticut coast again in July of 1779, plundering New Haven and Norwalk and meeting only slight resistance.

The British occupation of Newport, one of the finest natural harbors on the East Coast, naturally galled New Englanders and was an ever-present threat to their commerce. In the summer of 1773, emboldened by the new alliance with France, the Continental Army decided to drive the lobsterbacks out of Rhode Island.

In July, the French fleet took up stations off Newport, bottling up the British – but that was about as far as French-American cooperation went. The American General John Sullivan invaded Rhode Island in August, but the French failed to land troops to support him. And when a sudden storm scattered and damaged their fleet, they called off the blockade. Sullivan, with a Continental army of about ten thousand, laid siege to Newport for almost two weeks, abandoning the campaign and ordering a retreat late in August. The so-called Battle of Rhode Island was fought on August 29, during the retreat. This was little more than a large-scale skirmish with about thirty men killed on each side.

The Rhode Island campaign was notable for the participation of the Marquis de Lafayette, one of Sullivan's aides, and a Rhode Island militia company composed entirely of freed slaves.

The main American base for the Rhode Island campaign
was *Fort Barton* in Tiverton, Rhode Island. A well- 29
preserved earthenwork fortification built in 1777 to keep the British in check, the redoubt is named for Colonel William Barton, who was responsible for one of the daringest – and funniest – exploits of the war.

From spies behind the British lines, Barton learned that the British commander, General Richard Prescott, was spending much of his time outside Newport, at the country home of a Mr. Overton in what is now Middletown, Rhode Island. On the night of July 10, 1777, Barton and about forty men rowed across from Tiverton to
Portsmouth and marched on the *Prescott House*, as the 30
Overton Farm was to become known.

The general was surprised and captured in his nightgown. (Tradition has it he was in the company of a buxom lady at the time.) Prescott was later exchanged for a captured American general, Charles Lee, and returned to briefly command the Newport garrison – sticking to his townhouse this time.

The kind of non-cooperation between land and naval forces that doomed Sullivan's Rhode Island campaign blighted another Continental expedition the following year when an American – mainly Massachusetts – army tried to throw the British out of Maine, then a province of the Bay State. The British had established a naval base at Castine on Penobscot Bay, with an eye to making it the capital of a new Canadian province to be formed by detaching western Maine, which could serve as a refuge for Loyalists from the New England States.

Massachusetts assembled an army of two thousand men, both marines and militia, and a fleet of twenty-one transports and nineteen warships, including three ships of the Continental Navy. General Solomon Lovell commanded the army and Dudley Saltonstall commanded the fleet. This little navy was composed mainly of privateers whose captains and crews did not take kindly to discipline or nonprofit ventures. Lovell's army consisted of the scrapings of the Continental barrel – old men and young boys – all that was left after four years of war. The 1,200 militiamen had only five hundred muskets among them and the "artillery train" commanded by Colonel Paul Revere consisted of only three nine-pounders and four field pieces.

The British had their troubles too. They had only
about seven hundred and fifty men and two armed
sloops at Castine and work on *Fort George*, which was 31
to be its chief defense, had hardly begun. When the
American fleet sailed into the bay on July 25, 1779, its
ramparts were no higher than a man's chin and an immediate assault would probably have succeeded. But the
American command was confused and divided.

The generals wanted the fleet to support a land attack but the privateer captains refused to risk their valuable vessels. The American warships waited outside the harbor, refusing to do battle with the two British sloops – even though the odds were better than eight to one. This strategy succeeded in snatching defeat from the jaws of victory.

The British commander, General Francis McLean, was hopelessly outnumbered and knew it. When the Americans attacked he planned to put up some token resistance and then surrender. "I was in no situation to defend myself, I meant only to give them one or two guns, so as not to be called a coward, and then to have struck my colors . . ."

The expected American attack never came – but British reinforcements did. A squadron of seven men-o'-war sailed into the bay, capturing some of the American vessels and causing such panic aboard the rest that they were run aground and set afire. All forty ships were lost, making it one of the greatest naval disasters in American history. The survivors had to walk most of the way back to Boston and several of the footsore officers, including Revere, were court-martialed for their part in the debacle. (Revere was finally exonerated.)

Castine was the last British outpost on American territory to be relinquished, the garrison remaining until 1784, after the Treaty of Paris ending the war was signed.

In the fall of 1779, the British voluntarily abandoned Newport, permitting Continental forces to occupy it without firing a shot. The next summer a French fleet and an army of five thousand French soldiers arrived to a warm reception, remaining for a year before going on to play a part at Yorktown.

The war on the New England coast ended with a somber, savage incident: the British raid on New London, September 6, 1781. This was led by the hero of the Ridgefield fight, Benedict Arnold, who had turned traitor and was now a British instead of an American general. Using his intimate knowledge of his home state's defenses, Arnold caught the city by surprise, landing a force of 1,700 men and burning more than 140 buildings (his sister's among them).

While Arnold and some of the troops attacked Fort Trumbull, a detachment commanded by Lieutenant Colonel Eyre and Major Montgomery assaulted *Fort Griswold* 32
defended by some 160 men under Lieutenant Colonel Ledyard. After a short but furious fight in which Montgomery was killed, the fort's outnumbered garrison surrendered. Ledyard handed his sword to a British officer – apparently an American Tory – who ran him through with it! The British went on to finish off the survivors, killing eighty-five in all and wounding another sixty. This was the last Revolutionary War battle in the North; a bloody ending to a bitter conflict.

DETAILS

1 *Minutemen.* Many towns have reformed their Minutemen and Militia companies in recent years. During the summer, colonial style militia musters or "field days" are held on town greens and commons all over New England, featuring demonstrations of musketry and eighteenth-century military drill. Musters are also held daily in summer at North Bridge in Concord. For details of musters in Massachusetts and some parts of Connecticut, call the Council of Minutemen, Inc. (617) 485-8400.

2 *Concord.* Minuteman National Park incorporates most of the major sites connected with the events on Patriot's Day. A slide and sound program is presented every half hour at John Buttrick House, Ridge Rd., near North Bridge. Year round, daily: 8-5. (617) 369-6944. The Concord Antiquarian Society, Rte. 2A and Cambridge Turnpike, displays battle relics and period pieces. Mar.-Nov., daily: 10-4:30; Sun.: 2-4. Admission charged. The Concord Chamber of Commerce runs an information booth off Walden St. in Concord Center, May 30-Oct. 15, daily: 8:30-4:30, Sun.: 9-5.

2a *North Bridge.* Off Monument St., just to the north of Concord Center. The present bridge is a replica of the original. The famous Minuteman statue is on the opposite side of the bridge from the parking lot.

2b *Wright Tavern.* Corner of Main and Lexington streets in Concord Center. Built in 1747, now owned by First Parish Church, it houses a gift shop, an antique shop, and the town Chamber of Commerce, open year round, daily: 9:30-5:30.

3 *Lexington.* The Lexington Chamber of Commerce has a visitor's information one block east of Battle Green containing a diorama of the battle; April 19 – when townsfolk annually reenact the Patriots Day events – to Nov. 1, daily: 9-5. The National Park Service runs an information center at Fiske Hill on the Battle Road. Lexington Historical Society maintains Buckman and Munroe Taverns, also the Clarke Parsonage. (617) 861-0928.

3a *Jonas Clarke's Parsonage.* 35 Hancock St. Now also known as the Hancock-Clarke House, the old parsonage – built in 1698 – contains a valuable collection of early American antiques, open April 19-Oct. 31, daily: 10-5, Sun.: 1-5 P.M. Admission charged.

3b *Battle Green.* Intersection of Massachusetts Ave. and Hancock St. This triangular common is still Lexington's focal point. At the point of the triangle is a fountain topped by a heroic statue of a Minuteman. Under the ivy-covered Old Monument, seven of the eight patriots killed are buried. A boulder marks the Minutemen line.

3c *Buckman Tavern.* Hancock St., across from Battle Green, the town's oldest tavern (1690) was headquarters for the Minutemen who met in the taproom; April 18-Oct. 31, daily: 10-5, Sun.: 1-5. Admission charged.

3d *Minuteman Drummer.* The drum that called Parker's company onto the green is displayed in the Hancock-Clarke House. See Detail 3a.

3e *Munroe Tavern.* Massachusetts Ave., seven blocks south of Battle Green. Built in 1695 it houses an interesting collection of historical articles. Open Apr. 19-Oct. 31, daily: 10-5, Sun.: 1-5. Admission charged. Three blocks north of the tavern, at the intersection of Massachusetts

Ave. and Woburn St., a stone cannon marks the site of one of the fieldpieces that protected Lord Percy's headquarters.

4 *Bedford.* The flag of the Bedford Minutemen, displaying a mailed arm from heaven brandishing, is America's oldest flag. The original is in the town library of Bedford, five miles northeast of Concord Center. A replica is displayed at the North Bridge information center.

5 *Battle Road.* A four-mile corridor – parts of which include modern Rte. 2A – which has been restored and landscaped to look as it did in 1775. It's part of Minuteman National Park. Battle Road runs from Meriam's Corner, Concord, to Fiske Hill in Lexington. Its information centers are on Rte. 2A in Lincoln and on Fiske Hill near Rte. 128. Both are open 8 A.M. to sunset.

5a *Meriam's Corner.* At Rte. 2A and the intersection of Old Bedford Rd., east of Concord Center. The farmhouse for which the corner is named still stands but is not open to the public. Nearby is the Wayside, a unit of the National Park, in 1775 the home of Concord's militia muster master, and later of the Alcotts and Nathaniel Hawthorne; open April–May and Sept.–Oct.: Thurs.–Mon.: 10–5:30; June–Aug.: 10–5:30. Admission charged.

5b *Bloody Angle.* In Lincoln, just east of the Concord line, after crossing Tanner's Brook Bridge, Battle Road swerves north off Rte. 2A and onto Old Bedford Road, later swinging southeast and rejoining the Lexington Road. This is one of the few places on the Battle Road where the British were hit simultaneously on both flanks – with devastating results.

6 *Jason Russell House.* 7 Jason St. in Arlington, off Massachusetts Ave., open April 1–Nov. 1, weekdays: 2–5. Donation. (617) 648-4300.

7 *Bunker Hill.* Charlestown, Massachusetts. The 221-foot-high granite obelisk atop Bunker Hill (Monument Sq., Lexington and High streets) contains a spiral staircase to the top; the ground-level museum contains exhibits, including General Putnam's sword. (Year round, daily: 9–4; small admission (617) 242-9560.) Across the street the newly opened Charlestown Community Museum has more exhibits and a filmed reenactment of the battle. (Year round, daily; admission charged (617) 241-8220.) Also newly opened at Hoosac Pier, Water St., near the U.S.S. *Constitution*, the Bunker Hill Pavilion offers a multimedia rendition of the battle. Year round, daily: 10–8. Admission charged. (617) 241-7575.

8 *Cambridge, Massachusetts.* Just west of Boston, across the Charles River. A self-guiding Heritage Trail begins at Harvard Square where the leaflet guide is available, along with details about the diorama and multimedia exhibit depicting eighteenth-century Cambridge, from the Cambridge Bicentennial Office, Holyoke Center. Year round, daily: 9–5. (617) 354-5300. The City's Chamber of Commerce information booth in the square is also open summer months, daily: 9–5.

8a *Wadsworth House.* Massachusetts Ave. and Harvard Yard. Home of all Harvard presidents for a century, now the Harvard Alumni Assn. Office. For details about daily tours of Harvard University, phone (617) 495-1000.

8b *Craigie-Longfellow House.* 105 Brattle St., built by Tory John Vassall in the mid-eighteenth century. Washington's headquarters 1775–76, bought by Andrew Craigie after the Revolution, formerly home of Henry Wadsworth Longfellow, a national historic site open year round, daily: 9–4:45. Admission charged. (617) 876-4491.

8c *Fort Washington.* In the Cambridgeport section, opposite the intersection of Allston and Waverly Streets and adjacent to the St. Johnsbury Trucking Co. yard, well preserved, parklike remains of earthenwork redoubt.

8d *Massachusetts Hall.* On the west side of Harvard Yard, a three-story brick building just inside the gate, with a clock on the side facing Cambridge Common. Built in 1720, oldest college building in the United States. For details about daily tours of Harvard University, phone (617) 495-1000.

8e *Christ Church.* Zero Garden St., next to the Old Burial Ground and facing the south side of Cambridge Common; oldest church in Cambridge, designed by Peter Harrison, New England's first architect, still displaying a British bullet hole in the vestibule. Year round, daily: 7:30–6. (617) 876-0200.

9 *Artemas Ward Homestead.* 786 Main St., Shrewsbury; 40 miles west of Boston. Home of the militia general who commanded New England troops during the first weeks of the siege of Boston. May 15–Oct. 15; Mon.–Fri.: 10–12, 1–4. (617) 842-8900.

10 *Fort Hill.* At the top of Fort Ave., which runs off Centre St. in Roxbury, now a predominately black neighborhood, a small park with a memorial tower.

11 *Henry Knox.* Became a major general, Washington's chief of artillery and the first Secretary of War in his cabinet. His ebullient personality is reflected in the reconstruction of "Montpelier," his fine federal mansion on Rte. 1, Thomaston, Maine. May 30–Sept. 10, daily: 10–5. Admission charged. (207) 354-8062.

12 *Knox Trail Historical Society.* A nonprofit society which encourages research – and reenactments – of the artillery train trek from Alford in the Berkshires to Cambridge Common. There are historic markers in each of the thirty-four towns Knox passed through and there are long-range plans for a bike path along the trail. For information about Knox Trail events in bicentennial years, call the Massachusetts Bicentennial Commission hotline: (800) 242-0980.

13 *Dorchester Heights.* Actually in the South Boston rather than Dorchester section of the city. From the Southeast Expressway, take the Dorchester-South Boston exit and follow Day Boulevard along the shore; take the first left after Columbus Park. The site of the Continental redoubt is officially called Thomas Park and is marked by a steeple-like monument. Excellent view.

14 *Castle Island.* From Dorchester Heights, return to Day Boulevard and follow it all the way to the end. Present fort was built at the turn of the century on the site of earlier ones. There are plans to make it a military museum.

15 *Fort Western,* Augusta, Maine. Across Memorial Bridge from downtown Augusta; around the rotary to Cony St.; left onto Bowman St. The original barracks building, built in 1754, survives and was restored in 1919 by a descendant of the first commander. A blockhouse and stockade have been reconstructed. May 15–Labor Day, Mon.–Sat.: 10–5, Sun.: 1–5. Admission charged. (207) 622-1234.

16 *Arnold Trail.* Arnold's route of march through Maine, 194 miles from Fort Western at Augusta to Height of Land on the Canadian border near Coburn Gore, is a National Historic Place designated by markers and display panels. A schedule of reenactments and guided tours can be obtained from the Arnold Expedition Historical Society, P.O. Box 1775, Gardiner, Maine.

17 *Fort Popham.* At the end of Popham Point, Rte. 209 from Bath. A massive nineteenth-century stone fort, it stands on the site of the eighteenth-century wooden one. As an illustrated display panel at nearby Popham Beach explains, the Arnold Expedition picked up a Kennebec River pilot here.

18 *Fort Halifax.* On U.S. 201, a mile south of the Waterville-Winslow Bridge at junction of the Kennebec and Sebasticook Rivers. A blockhouse built in 1754, all that remains of a complex of buildings, is oldest in the United States.

19 *Old Pownalborough Courthouse.* Between Brunswick and Augusta on Rte. 128, built in 1761 within stockaded Fort Shirley and oldest courthouse building in Maine. July 19–Aug. 31, daily: 10–5, Sun.: 2–5. Admission charged.

20 *Buttonmould Bay.* The remains of the American fleet were beached and burned at Arnold's Cove on the eastern (Vermont) side of the southern part of Lake Champlain. Take Rte. 22A from Vergennes, Vermont, and follow signs for Button Bay State Park: campsites, picnic area, foot trails, swimming. (802) 475-2600.

21 *Hubbardton.* From Rutland, follow Rte. 4 west at Castleton, then north on Rte. 30. The battlefield, rimmed by the Green Mountains, is marked by a granite shaft. A small museum is open May 20–Oct. 20: 9–5. Admission charged.

22 *Bennington.* Although named for the Vermont town, the actual battlefield site is part of a New York State Park. From Bennington, Vermont, take 67A north and then go west on Rte. 67, following signs. The battle memorial, a 306-foot-high stone shaft, is in Old Bennington, Vermont, near the site of the supply depot the British wanted to capture. April 1–Nov. 1, daily: 9–6. Admission charge. The Bennington Museum, on West Main St. in Old Bennington, has a fine regional collection including battle relics. There are a number of paintings by Grandma Moses, including one of the Battle of Bennington – with troops fighting in front of the monument. Mar. 1–Dec. 1, daily: 9–6, summer; 9:30–4:30, winter. Admission charged.

23 *Royalton, Vermont.* Off Rte. 89, between Lebanon, New Hampshire, and Montpelier, Vermont. A granite monument beside Rte. 14 commemorates the Oct. 16, 1780 raid which helped convince Vermont that a state was safer than a small republic.

24 *Machias, Maine.* On Rte. 1 in northeastern Maine, some 35 miles south of Eastport. Burnham Tavern (Main St.) is now restored as a museum. (Mid June–Labor Day, Mon.–Fri.: 10–5; Sat.: 10–3; rest of year by appointment. (207) 255-4432. Admission charged.) Captain O'Brien's grave is in the O'Brien Cemetery on the west side of town. Fort O'Brien State Memorial, five miles east of town on Rte. 92 (commissioned by Washington in 1775) is open Memorial Day–Labor Day, daily: 9–sunset.

25 *Newport, Rhode Island.* Many buildings from the period survive, including: Colony House (1739), Touro Synagogue (1763), and White Horse Tavern (1673). Information and maps can be obtained at the Chamber of Commerce, 93 Thames Street (401) 847-1600.

25a *Rose.* Reconstructed in Nova Scotia in 1970, using material from the original ship, commissioned in 1756 and sunk off Savannah in 1779; tied up at the Newport Waterfront from April 1 through December. Open 10-sunset. Admission charged. (401) 846-1776.

26 *Provision State.* Lebanon, Connecticut, 11 miles outside Norwich on Rte. 87, was the home of Jonathan Trumbull, one of the few royal governors to back the cause of independence – and with money and supplies as well as words. His house, built in 1740, and the building he used as a "war office" are maintained by the Connecticut Daughters of the American Revolution. May-Nov. 1, Tues.-Sat.: 1-5. Admission charged. (203) 642-7558.

27 *Ridgefield, Connecticut.* About 10 miles south of Danbury on Rte. 35. A plaque on Main St. marks the spot where the militia built a barricade. Nearby is a Minuteman statue commemorating the town's defenders. The Keeler Tavern (132 Main St.), which served as headquarters for the patriots during the battle, is preserved as a museum (year round; Wed., Sat., Sun.: 2-5. (203) 438-5485.)

28 *Old New-Gate Prison and Copper Mine.* Posted from Rte. 20, East Granby, Connecticut. Established in 1707 as the Simsbury copper mine which yielded an extremely low value ore and ceased to operate in 1773. Thrifty Yankees turned it into a prison that very same year (its early inmates were required to mine copper) and during the Revolution it held a number of Tories as well as captured British soldiers; in 1776 it became the first state prison in the country and continued in use until 1827. Today it's a picturesque ruin, beautifully restored just enough to tell its story. Memorial Day through Oct.; Tues.-Sun.: 10-4:30. Admission charged. (203) 653-3563.

29 *Fort Barton, Rhode Island.* From Newport, take Rtes. 24 and 138 to Tiverton and follow signs to Fort Barton, on a bluff looking over the Sakonnet River. The earthenwork redoubt, General John Sullivan's headquarters during the Rhode Island campaign, has been restored to its original appearance.

30 *Prescott Farm.* 2009 West Main Rd., Middletown, Rhode Island, on Rte. 114. The house, built in 1730, is a private residence but a country store, nineteenth-century windmill, and museum in Prescott's old guardhouse are open June 1-Oct. 1, Tues.-Thurs. and Sat.-Sun.: 10-12, 2-4. Admission charged.

31 *Fort George.* Rtes. 175 and 166 from Rte. 1 to the tip of the Castine Peninsula. The fort, started in 1779, is in the center of town across from the Maritime Academy – which uses its parade ground as a drill field. Its present shape dates from the War of 1812 when the British reoccupied Castine. Illustrated panels inside the earthenwork walls explain the battle.

32 *Fort Griswold, Connecticut.* Groton exit off I-96. Head for the towering obelisk that marks Fort Griswold State Park. The earthen fort is roughly starshaped with a flagpole in the center. Memorial stones mark the spots where Major Montgomery and Colonel Ledyard died. A museum at the base of the obelisk is open May 30-Oct. 12, Tues.-Sat.: 1-3:45, Sun.: 1-4:45. Monument same dates: daily except Mon. and Thurs.: 8:30-11:30, 1-4:15, Sun.: 1-5. (203) 445-1729.

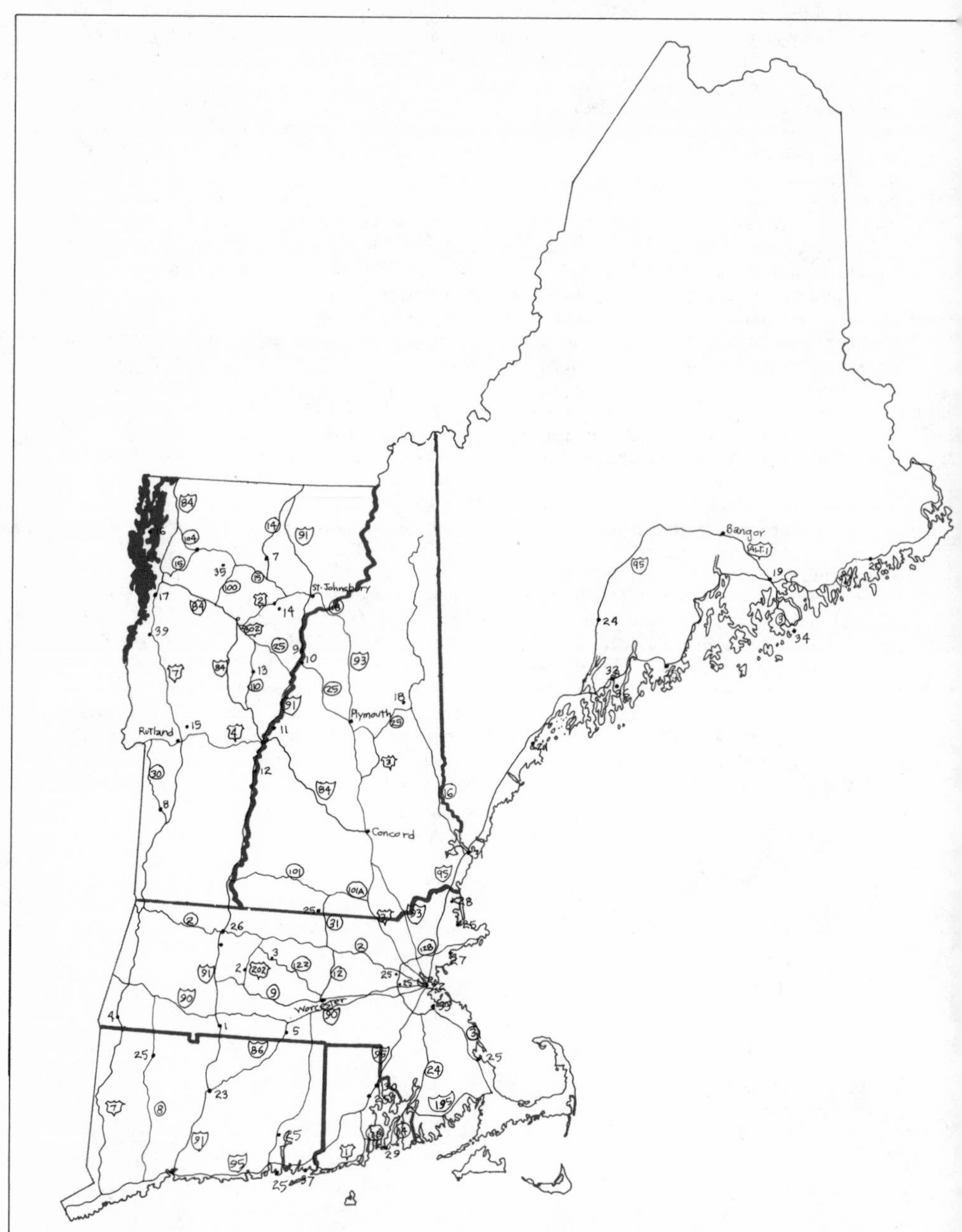

Bangor
ALT.1
St. Johnsbury
Plymouth
Concord
Rutland
Worcester

6

Rags to Riches

The next forty years, known as the Federal Period, revealed how drastically the Revolution altered the face and nature of New England. Many hundreds of families who constituted its pre-Revolutionary uppercrust had migrated to Canada, the Caribbean and England. And many hundreds of thousands of patriot families who now found themselves plagued with poverty and property qualifications which barred them from voting, sought escape from the older colonies by moving up north and out west. By 1790 New England represented barely more than a quarter of the new country, a downward trend which has continued to this day (when it accounts for less than 6%). On the other hand, this region acquired its full shape – both Vermont and Maine taking their places as states. Its unified if unpatriotic reaction to the War of 1812 proved it cohesive. It was America's first finished corner with a distinctive look and style all its own.

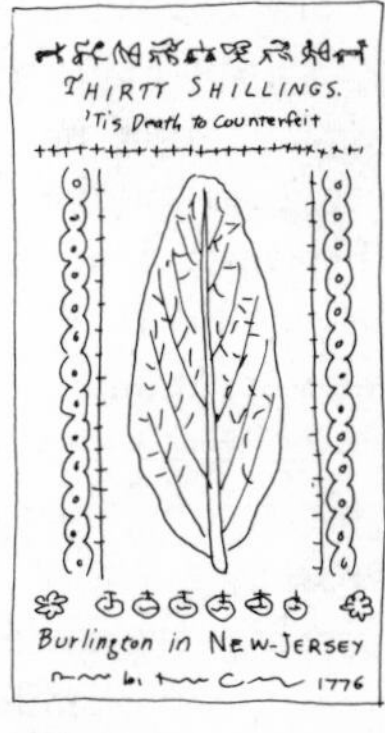

Colonial paper money

SHAYS'S REBELLION

During the long years of the Revolution, the most recently settled towns, those farthest from markets, found themselves hardest hit. City merchants had actually profited from filling war needs, and these men now took the places of the dislodged Tories, profiting too from the first revival of trade with Holland and Britain. Unsure of how to govern in the 1780s before the Federal Constitution was adopted, they imposed property qualifications for voting and attempted to halt inflation by substituting "specie" for the paper money which circulated during the war. Farmers frequently lacked this hard money, and their plight was increased by debts contracted when town merchants encouraged them to buy on credit the flood of imports which came with the end of war. A farmer who could not pay up could be stripped of his lands and thrown into prison. Sam Adams, now a member of the Massachusetts State Council, proposed hanging men who stormed local courthouses – the same methods he had encouraged a decade before.

At the height of this rural depression in 1786, farmers
held a three-day convention in Hatfield and decided to
attack the county courthouse in Northampton, Massachusetts. Their leader, Daniel Shays of Pelham, was a
debt-ridden war veteran who had been honored by
Lafayette at Saratoga. Next the rebels attacked the
arsenal at Springfield and failed miserably. A few for- 1
gotten plaques tell the remaining story. A marker beside the *Pelham* Town Hall commemorates the spot 2
where Shays, with half of his troops, camped from January 28 until February 3 in their stand "against unjust
laws." A marker in front of the *Petersham* Historical 3
Society gives another slant to the story – lauding General Benjamin Lincoln for the way he defeated these
same poor forces on February 4, refusing them amnesty.
Still another monument in a field near *Sheffield* records 4
the finale of the uprising: here one hundred rebels were
routed after they had plundered Stockbridge and Great
Barrington.

Shays himself escaped to Vermont and a recorded seven hundred families from western Massachusetts alone (there were more from Connecticut and the coast) followed him within six weeks.

Vermont at this time proved a refuge for many of
Shays's enemies as well as friends. Ebenezer Crafts, for
instance, a Harvard graduate and prosperous innkeeper
whose *Publick House* still serves the public in Sturbridge, 5
Massachusetts, had helped General Lincoln defeat the
farmers. But the war had left him as much in debt as
they. Casting about for a lawful way out of things, he remembered the Vermont property which he had bought
along with sixty other Stockbridge residents back in
1780. He set out with a few friends and reopened the
Bayley-Hazen Military Road from Cabot, Vermont. Af- 6
ter eighteen miles of this thankless work he reached his
claim and, clearing twelve acres, built a sawmill. In 1791

he led his family and one hundred fifty neighbors
to the hilltop outpost – soon known as *Craftsbury Com-* 7
mon, still one of Vermont's most beautiful communities,
steeped in a respect for education and culture which old
Ebenezer planted here.

VERMONT

How Vermont happened to be such a hospitable refuge at this point takes some explaining, especially since, before the Revolution, there was no Vermont at all.

The story begins with young Ira Allen who arrived in the area disputed by New York, New Hampshire, and Massachusetts in 1771, aged twenty. He was a surveyor and an operator. With his older brother, Ethan, he soon formed the Onion River Land Company, claiming a vast tract along Lake Champlain. When war broke, he suggested financing a local militia by confiscating Tory estates, a scheme which worked so well that the Green Mountain Boys were fielded within a week.

Constitution House, Winsor, Vt.

Having described the creditable mischief worked by this
group, we should point out that Ethan and Ira were busy
in the midst of it, mustering representatives from the
area's western towns at the *Dorset* Tavern to draw up 8
plans for a new state. A series of such meetings followed
– with control of the scheme teetering back and forth
between the "West Side" roughnecks (the Allens and
their friends on the western side of the Green Mountains)
and the more conservative "East Siders" from the older,
Connecticut River settlements like *Newbury*, *Haverhill* 9, 10
and *Hanover* (where *Dartmouth College* proposed itself 11
as cultural center of the new political unit), who favored
incorporating western New Hampshire into a state to be
named "New Connecticut." A compromise was finally
worked out and the "Free and Independent State of
Vermont" was proclaimed at a tavern ever since known
as *Old Constitution House* in Windsor, July 8, 1777. 12

But Vermont was in no hurry to get admitted to the Union when it saw other states being drained by the war debt. Calling itself a republic and fueling its own operations with money from the sale of land confiscated from the luckless "Yorkers" whom it ousted, it was willing to permit its case to rest while graciously welcoming the flood of refugees from the south. It inflicted no property qualifications to vote and besides accepted produce as legal tender. By 1791 when it was admitted as the first new state to the Union, it boasted 85,000 residents and enjoyed an 80% increase over this number in the next decade.

Jedediah Hyde log cabin, Grand Isle, Vt.

Its soil, enriched by centuries of rotting leaves, required no rotation at first, and yielded crops of corn and wheat plus kitchen garden staples the likes of which its new settlers had never enjoyed. Typically its new communities were perched on hilltops where growing seasons are longest. Many of these "hill towns," bypassed by
later "progress" – notably *Chelsea*, *Peacham*, and *Chit-* 13, 14, 15
tendon – retain their initial buildings and a charm which is rare even in Vermont today.

Travel anywhere in the Green Mountain State and you will find simple, deceptively small-looking clapboard homes patterned on those which were common in Massachusetts and Connecticut during the early eighteenth century. Their no-nonsense builders saw little reason to improve on what had already proven itself a sensible design. In the absence of water power for sawing clapboards in the northwestern Lake Champlain region, a few log
cabins were also built. One of these, the *Hyde Cabin* on 16
Grand Isle, has since been restored as America's oldest
log cabin. *Sawyer's Cabin*, another sample from Charlotte, 17
is now displayed at Shelburne Museum.

NEW HAMPSHIRE

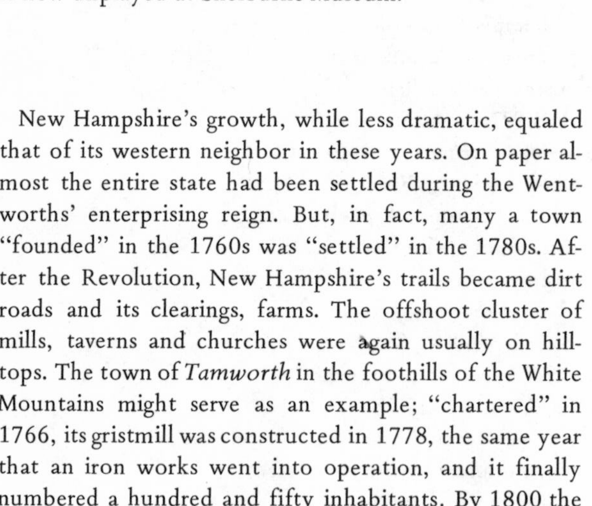

New Hampshire's growth, while less dramatic, equaled that of its western neighbor in these years. On paper almost the entire state had been settled during the Wentworths' enterprising reign. But, in fact, many a town "founded" in the 1760s was "settled" in the 1780s. After the Revolution, New Hampshire's trails became dirt roads and its clearings, farms. The offshoot cluster of mills, taverns and churches were again usually on hilltops. The town of *Tamworth* in the foothills of the White 18
Mountains might serve as an example; "chartered" in 1766, its gristmill was constructed in 1778, the same year that an iron works went into operation, and it finally numbered a hundred and fifty inhabitants. By 1800 the State counted 183,858 residents – most of them scattered on farms or working as lumbermen and fishermen – quite a contrast to 1741, when the Royal Province had included but 24,000 and these concentrated in the southeastern and coastal communities.

MAINE

At the close of the Revolution, the District of Maine
possessed a number of obvious advantages as a haven
over the more fertile but less known, less accessible and
certainly more Indian-dominated west. But Massachusetts' policy toward its vast adopted child discouraged
settlement. On one hand it favored speculators over
individual settlers by continuing to auction off vast
tracts at $2.75 per acre. On the other hand, by with-
holding clear title for many years and actually protecting the squatters who did come, it hobbled the big
investors. Still, a few of these left their mark, notably
a Philadelphia banker, William Bingham, who bought up
two million acres in 1791 but during an economic panic
the following year sold off half of this to Hope and
Company of London. This unlikely owner hired an unlikely representative, John Black, just eighteen at the
time. Black married the daughter of Bingham's own representative, who generously gave the couple three hundred acres in the present town of Ellsworth where they
built the sumptuous *Black House*, reportedly with bricks 19
brought by sea from Philadelphia and a gracious interior
which took workmen from Boston three years to complete.

Mansions are, in fact, the state's chief legacy from this
period. The elegant *Ruggles House*, forty-one miles far- 20
ther up the coast at Columbia Falls, was built by a lumber baron in 1818, and in *Portland*, the *McLellan-Sweat* 21, 21a
House, designed by Alexander Parris of Boston in 1800,
is easily one of New England's most beautiful Federal
homes. This in a town which had lost more than two
hundred and fifty buildings to the British in 1775, built
more than two hundred new ones in 1792, and incorporated itself with a new name (it had been Falmouth
until now) in 1796. If the Black Mansion represents
Maine's new wealth from land and the Ruggles Mansion
that from lumber (on the basis of which the towns of
Augusta and Bangor were also incorporated in the 1790s),
that of the McLellan-Sweat Mansion and the entire city
rests squarely on its ships. Climb the six steep stories of
Portland Observatory today (built 1807) and hear how 21b
local ship-owning families in the nineteenth century each
had a specially colored flag hung out from this post to
alert them when – literally – their ships came in. The
poet Longfellow, grandson of General Peleg Wadsworth

McLellan-Sweat House.

who had built the city's *first brick home* in 1785, de- 21c
scribed the Portland of this day:

I remember the black wharves and the ships
And the sea-tides tossing free
And the Spanish sailors with bearded lips
And the beauty and mystery of the ships
And the magic of the sea.

Longfellow himself never succumbed to the lure of the sea, but many of his less affluent contemporaries as those of his father's generation certainly did. Portland at the turn of the nineteenth century ranked second among New England ports. But Boston's tonnage surpassed that of its next three rivals combined.

BOSTON 22

Boston by 1794 boasted 18,000 people, 2,376 homes and eighty "quays" (wharves with brick warehouses atop them). The waterfront was, in fact, filled in to allow more streets full of warehouses. And rope-walks were thrown up on the marsh along the west side of the Common (now the Public Garden). Between four hundred and five hundred ships could be found on a given day around Boston Pier. The revival had been spurred by the appearance of an enterprising new class: former artisans, privateers and shipmasters who were not suffering from the new property taxes because they lacked property, nor from shipping losses incurred during the Revolution because at that point they had had no ships. These newcomers (with names like Cabot and Forbes, now Boston's old guard) soon dominated politics through their Federalist Party which represented immense profits for a few and opposed the reform-minded, typically poorer Republicans.

New England was unquestionably hurt by Britain's refusal to buy American-built ships, which were even barred from British West Indian ports. But the scene brightened after 1793 when war broke out once more between England and France and enterprising Yankees began helping France and her continental allies bring home produce from their West Indian possessions. These voyages, while yielding great profits, involved risking deadly scraps with British privateers; in Boston's Museum of Fine Arts today you can see a silver coffee urn shaped by Paul Revere, presented by a grateful shipowner to Captain Gamaliel Bradford for his "gallant defense, July 8, when attacked by four privateers off the Strait of Gilbraltar."

In 1784 Boston's Captain Samuel Shaw opened a new horizon for the region's seafarers when he accepted command of the New York ship *Empress of China*. Although the vessel (laden with ginseng, a herb which the Chinese believed revived male virility) reached China and returned with a cargo of tea, porcelain and silk, it was plain that America could not compete with Dutch and English expeditions to the Far East until it came up with something the Chinese wanted; our ginseng they frankly found inferior. A solution was foreshadowed when the *Columbia*, built on the North River in Scituate, set sail in 1787 and after rounding Cape Horn, traded its cargo of trinkets and hardware with the northern California Indians for furs, prized by the Chinese mandarins. It proceeded to Canton where it loaded up with tea, returning the autumn of 1790. The voyage was a financial flop but it paved the way for later, lucrative trade. It's worth noting besides as a link with Boston's most visible heritage of the era: a young architect named Charles Bulfinch was one of the *Columbia*'s six financial backers.

Bulfinch remains New England's single most famous architect, a status achieved not just through the buildings

he actually designed but those countless imitations which
soon added up to form the dominant look of New England's biggest city. His most celebrated work is the
"new" *Massachusetts State House*, erected on John 22a
Hancock's former cow pasture. It was completed when
he was just 32, after graduating from Harvard and collecting an impression of European styles from a two-year
visit. The July 4, 1795, cornerstone-laying of this building must have been a sight to see: seventy-three-year-old
Governor Sam Adams was on hand to watch the fifteen
white horses, representing the current fifteen states, haul
the stone into position. Paul Revere, who had fashioned
much of the building's metal work and the silverplate
inserted above the stone, also made a speech. (In 1802
Revere was to sheathe the entire wood dome in copper.)
Bulfinch had designed the graceful brick *statehouse in* 23
Hartford just a couple of years before, and he would furnish *Maine* with a granite *capitol* building at Augusta in 24
1826.

He also designed without charge Boston's first Catholic
church, which has since vanished, but a silver tray presented to him in gratitude by the "Catholics of Boston"
is displayed at Boston's Museum of Fine Arts. But his
St. Stephen's Church on Hanover Street in the North 22b
End, built for the "New North Religious Society," is
Catholic today. (Its massive classic facade distinguishes
it from later, slimmer steepled churches such as that on
the corner of *Park Street*, designed by British architect 22c
Peter Banner a few years later.) Bulfinch, it should be
remembered, was the first American architect to reject
the traditional boxlike meetinghouse with its side entrance and its tower, when it existed, simply tacked onto
one end. You enter St. Stephen's through the tower, flattened against the face of the building. The Palladian window above the entrance is another Bulfinch hallmark, as
is the cupola above.

The architect's other surviving public buildings are his
University Hall at Harvard University and the first building of *Massachusetts General Hospital*, granite, and 22d
capped by what later became known as the "Ether
Dome" when ether was administered in 1846 for the first
time during an operation in the room beneath it. Just up
Cambridge Street from the hospital stands one of Bulfinch's most influential buildings, the *Harrison Gray* 22e
Otis House, first of three mansions which he designed
for a Boston lawyer, politician and land speculator. Both

outside and in it epitomizes the "Federal Style": a self-consciously stark three-story brick facade with four windows, extraordinarily long on the first two floors, balancing in turn a handsome door with a glass fan and sidelights, a Palladian window on the second, with squat little windows flanking a "lunette" (semicircular) one on the third. The rooms within are high-ceilinged, exceptionally large and airy; dark paneling of the previous era is replaced by delicately carved classic motifs along the wainscoting, ceiling frieze and around the mantel. The mansion, now serving as headquarters for the Society for the Preservation of New England Antiquities (SPNEA), has been meticulously restored and furnished to period.

Harrison Gray Otis House, 1796

Another of the architect's unabashedly four-square mansions still stands at the corner of Beacon and Park Streets, across from the State House, all but unrecognizable with its street-level shops. The long row of colonnaded townhouses which once lined the Tremont Street side of the Common have completely vanished. But the second and third homes which he built for Harrison Gray Otis survive, intriguing variations on the first, as are
the *mansions* which echo their lines on *Beacon Hill* it- 25
self and *throughout New England.*

Asher Benjamin church, Windsor, Vt.

In fairness, Bulfinch cribbed many of his ideas from contemporary English architects, notably Robert Adam. Asher Benjamin, the second influential New England architect of the day, enthusiastically copied both Bulfinch and Adam's designs, producing his own versions. Benjamin grew up in Greenfield, Massachusetts, where he was apprenticed to a local carpenter and spent his first professional years designing *buildings* up and down the
Connecticut River Valley. Keenly aware of rural car- 26
penters' need for a "do-it-yourself" guide to the new architectural styles, he published *The Country Builder's Assistant* in 1796. In all he wrote seven books which went through forty-four editions and resulted in hundreds of handsome homes which continue to be mistaken for Bulfinch or Benjamin originals. In Boston itself he
designed a new facade and interior for the *Old West* 22f
Church and built the *Charles Street Meeting House* along 22g
with a number of distinctive Beacon Hill homes.

SALEM

In Boston the grace and scale of Federal design has
since been overpowered by high-rises. In *Salem*, however, 27

it still reigns supreme. This entire town, which ranked third after Boston and Portland in shipping tonnage at the time, still exudes an air of elegance.

The city's very seal is dedicated "to the farthest port
of the rich East" toward which its ships pioneered a new
route – around the Cape of Good Hope, tip of Africa.
Grand Turk, the first vessel to make an Orient round trip
this way, was built, along with the ship *Light Horse* (first
American vessel to visit Russia and the Baltic Sea), at
Derby Wharf, now a tidy park which abuts the city's 27a
handsome brick *Custom House* and the *Derby home* 27b, 27c
next door. Elias Hasket Derby was so enterprising that
he is generally credited with being America's first millionaire. A map on view in his mansion still impresses us with the world routes covered by his ships. In 1787, for instance, he made the Island of Mauritius, a refuge for French aristocrats after their own revolution, a base for trade with Java and Bombay.

Many a Salem ship did its owners proud. In 1799 the *Franklin* opened trade with Japan (closed until then to all but Dutch ships from Batavia); in 1801 the *Lydia* became the first American ship to trade with Guam; and the *Cadet* initiated a pepper trade with Sumatra which its sister ships so dominated in subsequent years that Sumatra and its neighbor islands became known as the "Salem East Indies."

In 1799 a group of the city's captains and "supercargoes" (passengers) formed the East Indian Marine Society to further their collection of "natural and artificial
curiosities" gathered from the four corners of the earth.
Anyone who visits the resulting *Peabody Museum* – 27d
oldest in continuous operation in the U.S. – cannot help
but be impressed by how far they got and what mementos they were able to come home with. In the imposing East Indian Hall, you enter one room through an archway made by two enormous elephant tusks to find a life-size scene depicting Salem Captain Benjamin Shreve buying textiles from a Calcutta merchant named Nasserwanjee. Look carefully and you discover that the cloths displayed were donated to the museum by Nasserwanjee himself in 1803, and the mannequins displaying them were carved by the city's own famous architect Samuel McIntyre. Scattered throughout the large (just expanded) museum are ship's models, reverse paintings on glass depicting the "hongs" – the warehouses which foreign traders set up in Hong Kong – and an endless wealth of

souvenirs, like a tooth extracted from Thankambau, "one of the greatest cannibal chiefs of Fiji," by a local sea captain, or a Marquesas chief's headdress and trumpet. The rooms dedicated to the "Ethnology of non-European peoples" are lined with cases full of extravagant relics from such places as Easter Island, Tahiti, the Gilbert and Caroline Islands, Tibet, Burma and Siam. Tucked away in a corner, a section dedicated to the Crowninshield merchant family reconstructs the stateroom cabin and saloon of their *Cleopatra's Barge*, America's first ocean-going yacht which attracted crowds everywhere on its maiden cruise through the Mediterranean in 1817. Later it was sold to Hawaii's King Kamehamaha. A picture of the family's own wharf by Georges Ropes, the deaf and dumb son of another of the city's wealthy families, vividly shows what the home base for these elaborate vessels looked like.

Elsewhere in town you can find intriguing booty from these expeditions: porcelain, inlaid ebony furnishings
and intricate toys. Both the *Crowninshield* and *Ropes* 27e, f
mansions contain outstanding examples.

To house their new-found treasures Salem families built
the lavish Federal mansions which line *Chestnut Street* 27g
and are sprinkled elsewhere around town. Many are architectural treasures in their own right, thanks to local architect Samuel McIntyre, who garnished the classic, square mansion of the period with intricate carvings, elegant interior arches and stairways. Frequently he also added his own furniture – a four-poster bed in the
Pierce-Nichols House, for instance, to complement the 27h
slim Sheraton and Hepplewhite chairs, sofas and tables.
His masterpiece is the brick *Pingree House* with its eleven- 27i
foot-high ceilings and intricate garlands, sheaves of wheat and fruit baskets festooning the woodwork.

Walk Salem's streets with a mind to what remains of these days of glory. Picture children buying their "Salem
Gibraltars" at "*America's oldest candy store*" and sailors 27j
shouldering each other in waterfront taverns. The waterfront itself, like that of Boston, receded at this time
from Front Street where the *Old Town Hall* stands, built 27k
like Faneuil Hall with the provision that it be used forever as a market. Here farmers from all over the North Shore brought their produce and traded with city merchants. The shipping elite themselves danced the sailor's hornpipe as well as quadrilles and occasionally dressed
in mandarin costumes for the balls at *Assembly House*. 27l

Later these dances were moved to *Hamilton Hall* where 27m
the pastor of the neighboring church who observed them is said to have muttered, "Back to back, breast to breast, they are dancing their souls down to hell."

NEWBURYPORT 28

A federal house, 1796

North of Salem the town of Newburyport at the mouth of the Merrimack River was also enjoying its peak day as a shipbuilding, fishing, rum-making and silvercrafting center. A substantial port before the Revolution, its population doubled between 1773 and 1803, and its tonnage now ranked fourth in New England. Along its two-mile High Street the newly wealthy built their square, tall mansions. The old elite had been replaced by the likes of Timothy Dexter, a former leather dresser who made a fortune selling bed pans to the West Indies (where they were used as dippers in the sugar mills). His home at 201 High Street still retains its cupola and rooftop minarets, but the statues he placed atop its forty columns, each honoring his favorite heroes and one depicting himself,
are gone. You can visit *Cushing House* at 98 High Street, 28a
home of the city's first mayor and subsequently both a minister to Spain and our first ambassador to China. On High Street there is also the courthouse designed by Bulfinch and the adjoining Bartlett Mall, a decorous park donated by a city merchant in 1800.

State Street runs downhill from High – past the *Li-* 28b
brary (a home where Washington slept), past the men's club (another former home where he once ate breakfast) and past the twin rows of brick *shops* (one of the 28c
first of the country's fireproof business blocks) to the vacant concrete triangle which was once busy Market Square. Along Water Street, also presently being restored, are the old two-story homes of artisans and tavern keepers who, from their first-floor shops, served the now-
vanished shipyards. The granite *Custom House* is due to 28d
reopen this year as a maritime museum dramatizing this era. It will also trace the history of the United States Coast Guard which the city claims to have launched along with the revenue cutter *Massachusetts* in 1791.

The very layout of "America's smallest city" reflects the political divisions of its heyday: Federalists lived along High Street; Republicans, nearer the water. Both parties supported their own fire companies, banks, insurance companies, Masonic lodges, and militia companies. When Republicans financed a turnpike to Boston, Federalists built a toll bridge at the northern (opposite) access to town!

RHODE ISLAND

While enjoyed by a relative few, the "Federalist"
wealth from maritime trade influenced every major
coastal New England city at this juncture, proving vi-
sually that this was a region of many small prosperous
seaports. Newport, so important before the Revolution,
had been drastically crippled by the English, who had
burned a large percentage of its wharves for firewood
during their unwelcome stay. One token *Federal mansion* 29
built on money from a local distillery, iron foundry and
machine shop rather than shipping has been restored
here. But it is plain to see that Rhode Island's commercial center shifted after the war to *Providence*, largely 30
because this happened to be the home of a family full
of sailors, adventurers and merchants named Brown.
Descended from the city's earliest settlers, it included
four brothers: Nicholas, Joseph, John and Moses. Although it was the son of Nicholas who gave his name to
the famous *university* and Joseph who designed some of 30a
the city's Federal period buildings, it was John who revived local commerce and spirits, in 1797 becoming the
first Rhode Islander to trade with the Orient and subsequently securing record profits from single voyages. His
ship *General Washington*, which cleared for Canton in
1787, returned two years later with a cargo of teas, silver, china, gloves, flannels, cottons and lacquered goods
which netted him $99,848. Another of his ships was the
first to fly the stars and stripes in Turkish waters. The
John Brown House, designed by Joseph and now head- 30b
quarters for the Rhode Island Historical Society, is filled
with exotic trophies as well as Newport-crafted furniture.
This was the first mansion to be built on "the hill" and
set a trend. Today it is surrounded by other Federal
homes and the length of *Benefit Street* on which it stands 30c
is lined with buildings representing the period's height of
fashion. The *Rhode Island School of Design Museum* 30d
contains a wealth of Providence relics from the era's
maritime trade.

NEW HAMPSHIRE

For *Portsmouth*, New Hampshire, this marked a final, 31
grand era of prosperity. The country's twelfth largest
town, it was still building ships and sending them to Europe and the West Indies. The *Governor John Langdon* 31a
House, built in 1784 by the patriot who had led the
charge on Fort William and Mary and subsequently became the first president of the United States Senate
(supervising George Washington's inauguration), is one
of the latest and finest of America's Georgian homes,
while the *Rundlet-May* and *Governor Goodwin mansions*, 31b, c
as well as many of the city's buildings now serving as
private homes, are Federal "high style." The Portsmouth
Public Library and *Portsmouth Athenaeum* as well as 31d
delightful Bow Street date from this period. Unfortunately a fire in 1813 destroyed the town's commercial
core and put a damper on the revival of shipping.

MORE MAINE

One small community is well worth mentioning here,
created as it was almost entirely on its shipbuilding and
sea trade at the turn of the century and little altered since.
Wiscasset, Maine, at the mouth of the Sheepscot River 32
was home port for thirty-five square-riggers; it was said a
man could walk across its harbor on the decks of vessels
lying at anchor. Wiscasset, like Portland, exported masts
and spars to Europe in exchange for salt, with which it
then dried its fish, which in turn went aboard West
Indiamen to the Caribbean along with more lumber,
there to be exchanged for molasses. There were also
local shipyards, and in 1806 a boy named James Feni-
more Cooper shipped aboard the *Stirling* here bound for
London and St. Petersburg, a voyage later described in
Cooper's *Tale of the Sea*. In 1811 a sturdy granite *jail* 32a
was built in town, a need created by the influx of seamen and woodsmen who congregated in this now sleepy
resort town. A fine *Academy* was also built and a *Cus-* 32b, c
tom House, both handsomely of brick. Its Federal
mansions still fascinate visitors, notably the *Nickels-* 32d
Sortwell House (five years in the building). One village
worthy even built himself a *copy of a Scottish castle* 32e
in 1807.

WAR OF 1812

While New England went about cornering three-quarters of this country's shipping, the country as a whole was turning its back to the sea. This division in land versus sea interests soon became obvious. In 1801 Boston Federalist *John Adams* was replaced by Virginia Republican 33
Thomas Jefferson in the White House. Jefferson reacted to the British interference with American merchantmen (climaxed by the British *Leopard*'s attack of the U.S.S. *Chesapeake* in 1807) by declaring an embargo against all foreign trade. On his own inauguration in 1809 James Madison went one step farther, declaring that British impressment of American seamen, its blockade of our coast, and prevention of neutral trade was cause for war. While the majority of New England senators voted against this war (ostensibly one defending their own interests), the country as a whole – a new generation feeling its oats – viewed such a war as a chance to conquer Canada and extend the western frontier. New England soon found itself not only financially ruined but alienated from the nation as a whole.

The lack of enthusiasm with which this region supported the War of 1812 is – from this distance in time at least – comic. The fisheries and coastal trade still lay open to our seamen and an amazing number of local sailors suddenly found themselves lost at sea. One captain from Maine's *Little Cranberry Island* finished haul- 34
ing for cod off the Newfoundland banks and discovered his vessel heading out of control for Portugal. Luckily he came safely to harbor at Oporto where he sold his cod at a handsome price and loaded up with enough salt to buy himself a new schooner on his return home. About this time a Bangor ship found itself in Antigua – en route from Newport to Castine. Boston clearance for Maine ports other than Portland increased ninefold between 1807 and 1808, while an unprecedented number of barrels of flour piled up in Eastport, Maine (a few miles away in Canada these fetched three times their price on the American side of the border).

Fort Edgecomb, Maine

The Vermont border proved itself just as full of loopholes. "Two-thirds of the army in Canada are at this moment eating beef provided by American contractors, drawn chiefly from the states of Vermont and New York," a military commander complained in 1814. Ver-

mont roads were filled with sleighs that winter carrying
produce to Canada. Cattle were hidden at "*Smuggler's* 35
Notch" before being herded across the border, and rafts routinely slipped across the Lake Champlain line between the countries at night (most famous of these was the *Black Snake*, reportedly a half-mile long and mounted with a bullet-proof top, powered by 500 armed crewmen).

The flip-side of this war was less comic. While the New England states refused to supply the nation with militia, they did provide the regular army with nineteen regiments and, in turn, found no national aid to their own
defense. A few forts, notably *Edgecomb* at Wiscasset 36
were financed locally, and the little town of *Stonington,* 37
Connecticut, repulsed a British landing fleet in August 1814 with its own militia and three cannons. Castine, however, fell to the British that year, the British going on to raid Bangor and take possession of the Maine coast from Castine east.

The region also attempted halfheartedly to do its part
by sea. In 1812, the U.S.S. *Constitution* had knocked 38
H.M.S. *Guerriere* helpless in an encounter, but after a run-in with H.M.S. *Java* was laid up for the remainder of the war at Boston. During the winter of 1814 Naval Commander Thomas McDonough managed to have seventeen vessels constructed at the town of *Vergennes*, seven 39
miles up Otter Creek from Lake Champlain. The following October this fleet actually defeated the British at the Battle of Plattsburgh. But in the balance this daring victory proved slight.

Unfortunately New England's own balance sheet was tipped toward discredit at the tail end of the conflict. In December of 1814 a convention of New England states met in the Old State House in Hartford to confer on mutual "public grievances and concerns." As it happened the moderate Federalists led by Harrison Gray Otis outvoted the extremists, who favored a separate peace between New England and Britain. Since the sessions were held secretly, the press of the day played them up as traitorous. The Peace of Ghent ending the war was actually signed Christmas Eve, 1814.

DETAILS

1 *Armory Museum, Springfield Arsenal, Springfield, Massachusetts,* Federal St. near State. Handsome brick complex occupying fifteen acres, all but the museum and commandant's house (under restoration) now form Springfield Technical Community College. The museum, begun as a research library in 1871, boasts "the world's largest collection of military small arms." Year round, Mon.–Sat.: 10–5. Admission charged. (413) 734-6477.

2 *Pelham, Massachusetts.* Rte. 202, just west of Quabbin Reservoir. Settled in 1730, noted for the beauty of its common and the town hall, oldest in the state (1743).

3 *Petersham, Massachusetts.* North from Pelham, Rte. 122. The plaque is at the town's historical society. June–Sept., Sun.: 2–4. (617) 924-3380.

4 *Sheffield, Massachusetts.* Rte. 7, southern Berkshires. The marker stands one and one-half miles from the town center on the South Egremont Road.

5 *Publick House, Sturbridge, Massachusetts.* Exit off the Massachusetts Turnpike onto Rte. 20. Landmark inn, featuring old-style food, lodging. (617) 347-3313.

6 *Bayley-Hazen Military Road, Vermont.* Northeast corner of the state. From the Connecticut River town of Wells River, unpaved to Ryegate Corner; from here, hard-topped to Peacham; a path from Erwell's Mills to West Danville, then a road past Joe's Pond through Cabot Plains to South Walden, unpaved from East Hardwick to Greensboro (by Caspian Lake) to East Craftsbury; hard-topped to Mill Village in Craftsbury, unpaved to Albany and Lowell. Well marked and known locally, this route links together some of Vermont's most beautiful villages, following ridges and hilltops.

7 *Craftsbury Common, Vermont.* Northwest of St. Johnsbury, from Rte. 15 at Hardwick take Rte. 14 north. So vast is the common itself that it dwarfs the surrounding old homes, academy and church. So high is it that the countryside around drops away on all sides. Few places convey such a supreme sense of tranquillity. In July this is the scene for an annual fiddlers' contest and in September of a smaller banjo blast. The village offers two lakes, tennis, canoeing and good cross-country skiing. The Inn on the Common is a tastefully converted nineteenth-century home. (802) 586-9619.

8 *Dorset, Vermont.* Southwestern Vermont, Rte. 30. The old tavern is gone, remembered with a plaque on the handsome town common. Today Dorset is a resort town with a summer playhouse and golf course. For lodging contact the Dorset Inn (in business since 1796): (802) 867-5500; also Barrows House, a converted nineteenth-century mansion: (802) 867-4455.

9 *Newbury, Vermont.* Rte. 5. This was the first settlement north of Fort Number 4. It remains an unusually handsome town. A monument in the center of its long common is dedicated to its founder, General Jacob Bayley; the Congregational Church dates from 1794 and the Ox-Bow Cemetery with its intriguing headstones, from 1761.

10 *Haverhill, New Hampshire.* Rte. 10 on the Connecticut River. Named for the Massachusetts town from which most of its first settlers came, this is an exceptionally handsome town, situated on a height above the river from which it commands a view of the valley and the Vermont hills beyond. The common is surrounded by Federal-era mansions, the brick buildings of Haverhill Academy (founded 1816) and mid-nineteenth-century public buildings. No traces

remain of its four early forts but the home of Captain John Hazen, co-founder of the Bayley-Hazen Road, still stands. In 1770 the town voted to give Reverend Eleazar Wheelock fifty acres of land if he would establish Dartmouth College here; it's never forgiven the college for declining the gift.

11 *Hanover, New Hampshire.* Rte. 10, Connecticut River. The town centered then, as it does today, around Dartmouth College. Guide service is available year round, departing during the academic year from the Admissions Office and during summer months from the town information booth on the common.

12 *Old Constitution House, Windsor, Vermont.* Rte. 5, on the Connecticut River, off I-91. This tavern was built in 1774, originally in the middle of town. It's since been moved a few miles north and partially restored: it serves as the town's historical museum. Late May-mid-Oct., daily except Mon.: 9:30-4:30. (802) 674-6628.

13 *Chelsea, Vermont.* Central Vermont, Rte. 110 from I-89. Settled in 1784, this is a delightful but untouristed town which clusters around its green, containing an unusual number of Federal-era houses, a handsome church, library and tiny business block.

14 *Peacham, Vermont.* Northeastern Vermont. South from Rte. 2, at Danville (just west of St. Johnsbury) or north from Rte. 302 at Groton. This elegant little town's 1763 land grant from George III can be seen in the town clerk's office. It boasts an early nineteenth-century academy and church and the town historical society, which is open in summer months and serves as the site for an autumn sugar-on-snow party. This is one of seven area towns which take turns during a week hosting visitors to church suppers, fairs and house tours. Usually held the last week in September, this Holiday in the Hills adds up to the most colorful foliage season event in all New England.

15 *Chittendon, Vermont.* Central-western Vermont; eight miles northeast of Rutland, marked from both Rtes. 7 and 4. Once known as "Flats City," this is now a ghost town and a resort offering swimming, golf and cross-country skiing. Lodging at the Mountain Top Inn: (802) 483-2311.

16 *Hyde Log Cabin, Grand Isle, Vermont.* Northwestern Vermont, Rte. 2 from Burlington. Crammed with local memorabilia. Memorial Day-mid-Oct., daily: 9-5. Admission charged.

17 *Sawyer's Cabin, Shelburne, Vermont.* On the grounds of Shelburne Museum, Rte. 7, south of Burlington. The museum is open May 15-Oct. 15, daily: 9-5. Stiff admission charged for its forty exhibit buildings. (802) 985-3344.

18 *Tamworth, New Hampshire.* Rte. 113 west from Rte. 16 at Chocorua. A delightful resort town with a famous old summer theater (the Barn Stormers), an old burial ground, meetinghouse and the nineteenth-century Tamworth Inn, year round. (603) 323-7721.

19 *Black House, Ellsworth, Maine.* Rte. 1. Said to be based on Asher Benjamin designs, its circular stairway is unusual for the day. Furnished to reflect the way it looked during the mid-nineteenth century. June 1-Oct. 15, weekdays: 10-5. (207) 667-8671.

20 *Ruggles House, Columbia Falls, Maine.* Rte. 1. A two-story mansion notable for its "flying staircase" and woodwork. Restored and furnished to period. June 1-Oct. 15, weekdays: 8:30-4:30, Sun.: 10-4.

21 *Portland, Maine.* Exits off I-95. Leaflet guides to Portland are available from the city's Chamber of Commerce, (207) 773-2811, from Portland Landmarks, (207) 774-5561, and from the Maine Publicity Bureau, (207) 773-7266.

21a *McLellan-Sweat House.* Corner of High and Spring streets. An airy mansion with a famous "flying staircase" and exquisite detailing: restored and beautifully furnished, attached to the Portland Museum of Art. Year round, Tues.-Sun.: 10-5, Sun.: 2-5. Admission charged. SPNEA, (617) 227-3956.

21b *Portland Observatory,* 138 Congress St. Built in 1807 this shingled lookout offers an easy climb to a fine view of the city. Memorial-Labor Day: 10-7. Small admission charged.

21c *Longfellow House,* 487 Congress St. This boyhood home of the poet was built in 1785; restored and furnished to period. June-Sept. weekdays: 9-4:40. (802) 773-3212.

22 *Boston.* During Bicentennial years a major exhibit depicting the city during the late eighteenth century is noteworthy here, both because it provides a sense of how drastically Boston was altered in these years which directly followed and because it is housed in the Quincy market building, a landmark in the classic revival style of the Federal period, built by architect Alexander Parris in 1824. It's advisable to check the times at which Boston sites are open, since they are in flux at this writing. For general Boston information phone: Greater Boston Convention and Visitors Bureau, (617) 536-4100, or during Bicentennial years, Boston 200: (617) 338-1976.

22a *"New" Massachusetts State House,* Beacon St., overlooking Boston Common. This handsome building cost state tax payers precisely $133,333.33 at the time. Its archives museum contains such treasures as the first Yankee musket to be fired at the Battle of Lexington, Bradford's *History of Plimouth Plantation* and the 1628 charter of Massachusetts Bay. The interior of this present seat of state government is well worth touring for the beauty of its working chambers. Year round, Mon.–Fri., except holidays: 9–5. Guided tours every half hour, 10–4; April–Oct. Weekend tours 10–3:30. (617) 727-2121.

22b *St. Stephen's Church,* Hanover St., opposite Old North Church. With minor alterations this is the way Bulfinch designed it.

22c *Park Street Church,* corner of Tremont and Park streets. Unusually graceful in design and possessing the highest steeple in Boston (originally higher but a gale caused its rebuilding). It is also known as Brimstone Corner due to the gunpowder stored here during the War of 1812. In 1831 "America" was sung here for the first time. The American Education Prison Reform, Mission and temperance societies all started here. Still a Congregational Church. Year round, May–Oct., daily 10–6. Winter months, Sun. 10–4. Sunday service: 10:30. (617) 523-3383.

22d *Massachusetts General Hospital,* Fruit St., off Cambridge St. Alexander Parris took over this job when Bulfinch moved to Washington to help design the national capitol. Greek revival style with mid-nineteenth-century wings. Tours offered: (617) 726-2206.

22e *Harrison Gray Otis House,* 141 Cambridge St., near Government Center. The restoration of the interior is precise – down to the paint, researched through chemical analysis. The museum house serves as headquarters for the Society for the Preservation of New England Antiquities (SPNEA) which maintains thirty-five properties open to the public throughout New England and offers a full program of lectures and events for its members. It pays anyone interested in visiting more than a few of its sites to become a member. Year round, Mon.–Fri.: 10–4. (617) 227-3956.

22f *Old West Church,* 131 Cambridge St. Designed in 1806, red brick with a distinctive projecting facade and unusual belfry, also a fine interior. Year round, Mon.–Fri.: 9–5. (617) 227-5088 or 227-8020.

22g *Charles Street Meeting House,* 70 Charles St. (Corner of Charles and Lower Mt. Vernon streets.) Benjamin's distinctive facade with arched doorways. Generally open. (617) 523-0368.

23 *Old State House, Hartford, Connecticut.* 800 Main St. The $52,480 to finance construction of this graceful brick capitol was raised through a lottery and private donations. It became city hall after state offices moved to the present nineteenth-century capitol and has since been restored as museum; it retains many original furnishings. Year round, Tues.–Sun., except major holidays: 12–4. Small admission charged. (203) 522-6766.

24 *Maine State Capitol, Augusta.* Exit 15 off Maine Turnpike. Follow signs. Granite and imposing both exterior and interior. Year round, weekdays: 9–5.

25 *Outstanding Federal mansions open to the public*

BEACON HILL

Women's City Club of Boston. 40 Beacon St. Said to be designed by Alexander Parris, in the office of Bulfinch. Year round, Wednesday tours: 10–4. Admission charged. (617) 227-3550.

Headquarters House, 55 Beacon St. Built in 1806 by Asher Benjamin: the home of famous nineteenth-century historian William Prescott. By appointment: (617) 742-3190.

African Meeting House, 8 Smith St. This is New England's oldest building specifically associated with black Americans. Said to be designed by Asher Benjamin, it was built by black craftsmen. Presently in the process of restoration. Inquire – Boston information sources.

Third Harrison Gray Otis Mansion, 54 Beacon St. Its striking exterior includes long second-story windows opening onto iron balconies. Weekdays, by appointment: (617) 227-2425.

Nichols House Museum, 55 Mount Vernon St. Built 1804, period townhouse. Year round, Wed. and Sat.: 1–5. Small admission. (617) 227-6993. For details about annual house tours of Beacon Hill contact the League of Women Voters of Boston. (617) 723-4583.

OTHER OUTSTANDING FEDERAL MANSIONS IN NEW ENGLAND

Gore Place, Waltham, Massachusetts. Rte. 20. Built in 1804 for Christopher Gore, who later became governor of the state, this is a long, low two-story brick mansion of twenty-two rooms with a distinctive bow-shaped front containing two oval rooms. April 15–Nov. 15, Tues.–Sat.: 10–5, Sun.: 2–5. Closed holidays. Admission charged.

"The Vale" or Lyman House, Waltham, Massachusetts. Lyman St., off Rte. 20 near the center of town. Designed by Samuel McIntyre in 1793, this grand wooden mansion includes an oval parlor, colonnaded ballroom and greenhouses built in 1800 and 1804 where pineapples, bananas and tropical flowers grew. July, Aug., hours in flux. Contact SPNEA, (617) 227-3956. Admission charged.

Codman House, Lincoln, Massachusetts. Codman Rd., off Lincoln Rd. just beyond the R.R. tracks. Built in the early eighteenth century with the third story and high Federal style look added in 1797 when merchant John Codman doubled its size, possibly with advice from Bulfinch. Just a fraction of the original surrounding estate remains (later surveyed by Thoreau) and its interior is restored to a later period. Admission charged. June–Oct., Tues.–Thurs., Sun.: 1–5. SPNEA, (617) 227-3956.

Barrett Mansion, New Ipswich, New Hampshire. Just above the Massachusetts line. Main St., off Rte. 124. A white wooden mansion with a third-story ballroom, superb eighteenth- and nineteenth-century furniture from Boston and Newport, also spinning and weaving implements, locally made highboys, tables and painted Hitchcock chairs. June–Oct., Tues., Thurs., Sun.: 11–5. Closed holidays. Admission charged. SPNEA, (617) 227-3956.

Antiquarian House, Plymouth, Massachusetts. 126 Water St. Built by a merchant and shipowner in 1809 and decorated to reveal changing styles from the Federal on through the nineteenth century. May 27–Oct. 15, daily: 10–5. Admission charged. (617) 746-9697.

Montpelier, Thomaston, Maine. Rte. 1. The original mansion, said to have been designed with the help of Bulfinch, was built for Major General Henry Knox in 1793. Rebuilt during this century's depression period, it contains many genuine Knox possessions, providing a vivid sense of its expansive builder and his equally fat but famously crotchety wife. Memorial Day–Sept. 10, daily: 10–5. Admission charged. (207) 354-8062.

Governor Sprague Mansion, Cranston, Rhode Island. 1353 Cranston St. A twenty-eight-room mansion built in 1790 for a politically and financially prominent Rhode Island family; altered substantially in 1864. Noteworthy for its display of Oriental art. July–Labor Day, Sun.–Tues.: 2–4. Admission charged.

Solomon Rockwell House, Winsted, Connecticut. 225 Prospect St. Known as "Solomon's Temple" for the many pillars in its classic revival facade, this is a grand and graceful mansion with rich detailing and fine furnishings. June 15–Sept. 15, daily except Sun., Wed.: 2–5. (203) 379-8433.

Deshon-Allyn House, New London, Connecticut. 613 Williams St. An elegant four-square mansion built in 1829 by a wealthy whaling captain, now furnished in late Federal style. Year round, Tues.–Fri.: 1–5 by request at the Lyman Allyn Museum. (203) 443-2545.

Rockwell House, Norwich, Connecticut. 42 Rockwell St. An imposing stone mansion built in 1818 containing an interesting mix of local memorabilia. July–Aug., Wed.: 2–5 and by appointment. (203) 887-8737.

Thomas Franklin Waters Memorial, Ipswich, Massachusetts. 40 South Main St. A Federal mansion built by a wealthy merchant in 1795; noteworthy for its graceful staircase, China trade furnishings, and the formal garden in its courtyard. April 1–Nov. 1, Tues.–Sat.: 10–5; Sun.: 1–5. Admission charged. (617) 356-2811.

26 *Asher Benjamin Buildings in the Connecticut River Valley*

Greenfield Public Library, Greenfield, Massachusetts. Off Rte. 2. The town was Benjamin's early home and this was one of his first works. (413) 772-6305.

Memorial Hall, Old Deerfield, Massachusetts. Rte. 5, three miles south of Greenfield. This was designed as the first building for Deerfield Academy, now a local museum maintained by the Pocumtuck Valley Memorial Association. April–Nov., Mon.–Sat.: 9:30–5, Sun.: 1:30–5. Admission charged.

Old South Church, Windsor, Vermont. Rte. 5, Main St. One of New England's most photographed white, steepled churches with Greek revival pillars. Open for Sunday services and special events.

27 *Salem, Massachusetts.* Rte. 1A north of Boston. The fame of this city as site of the seventeenth-century witch trials has long overshadowed that of its outstanding museums and nineteenth-century historic sites, but this is changing as more of the old port is restored each year. The chamber of commerce in the Hawthorne Hotel on Washington Square, (617) 744-0004, dispenses leaflet guides and rents a taped tour. During Bicentennial years visitor reception centers are set up in the city's churches (Salem Bicentennial information number: (617) 744-0798).

27a *Derby Wharf,* Derby St. Once the longest and busiest of forty-five wharves on Salem Harbor, an inlet of the Atlantic. Today this is a park: a replica of an original warehouse stands just west on Central Wharf.

27b *Salem Custom House,* Derby St. A handsome brick building but built in 1819 after the peak days of harbor traffic: several rooms have been restored, including that used by Nathaniel Hawthorne when he worked here. A Bonded Warehouse houses old charts, tea chests, rum barrels and other once-routine cargoes. This complex includes the Derby House and is maintained by the National Park Service as the Salem Maritime National Historic Site. Year round, daily except major holidays: 8:30–5. (617) 744-4323.

27c *Derby House,* Derby St. The oldest brick home in Salem, built in 1761. Notable for its slanting paneling indicating it was done by ships' carpenters; furnished with exotic imports. Same hours as Custom House. Admission charged.

27d *Peabody Museum,* 161 Essex St. Exhibits are divided into three categories: maritime history, natural history and ethnology. They include one of the world's largest collections of ship models. The building has been recently enlarged, permitting an extraordinary wealth of Far Eastern and South Pacific displays. The name of the museum was changed during the nineteenth century to honor its benefactor, George Peabody, a local boy who became a prominent London banker. A program of lectures and a fine research library on maritime history are also included. Year round, weekdays: 9–5, Sun. and holidays: 1–5. Admission charged. (617) 745-1876.

27e *Crowninshield Bentley House,* Corner Essex St. and Washington Square. Built in 1727 for the wealthy Crowninshield family: from 1791 to 1819 the Reverend William Bentley, chronicler of Salem's golden era, boarded here. Beautifully furnished. June–Oct. 15, Tues.–Sat.: 10–4, Sun.: 2–4:30. Admission charged. (617) 744-3390.

27f *Ropes Mansion,* 318 Essex St. Built in 1719, filled with exotica collected by the merchant family. May–Nov. 1, Mon.–Sat.: 10–4:30. Admission charged. (617) 744-0718.

27g *Chestnut Street.* This lineup of mansions is closed to visitors with the exception of occasional house tours. At this writing the Philips Home is expected to be open for viewing on a regular basis; check with the Chamber of Commerce.

27h *Pierce-Nichols House,* 80 Federal St. Samuel McIntyre was just twenty-four when he designed the delicately proportioned home; restored and beautifully furnished as the residence of the East India merchant, who commissioned it. Year round, Tues.–Sat.: 2–4:30. Admission charged. (617) 744-3390.

27i *Pingree House,* 128 Essex St. Built in 1804. Exquisitely furnished, fourteen rooms in all, with third-floor murals painted by an artist brought here from Naples to serve the merchant families. Year round, Tues.–Sat.: 10–4. Admission charged. (617) 744-3390.

27j *Ye Olde Pepper Companie,* 122 Derby St. Established in 1806 by an English lady whose family had lost all their possessions in a shipwreck en route to Salem. Sympathetic townspeople, hearing that she was a confectioner, donated the first barrel of sugar with which she made "Salem Gibraltars," a hard candy which is still produced in the present shop. Mon.–Sat.: 9–5, Sun.: 10–6.

27k *The Old Town Hall,* Derby Square, off Essex St. Built in 1816 in the Bulfinch tradition, it includes a handsome upstairs meeting hall in which a photo display of "Salem Streets and People, 1860-1930" forms a semi-permanent exhibit. Twenty-eight market stalls have been installed in the recently restored square here for the use of local farmers on Saturdays. For details about frequent special events held here, contact (617) 744-4580.

27l *Assembly House,* 132 Federal St. Built to house the assemblies, it was converted into a private home by Samuel McIntyre, who did it so cleverly that architects still puzzle over exactly where the original ballroom stood. It is furnished in late Chinese imports. Admission charged. (617) 744-3390. Year round, Tues.–Sat.: 2–4:30.

27m *Hamilton Hall,* 9 Chestnut St. The assemblies were moved here in 1805 and the building, also designed by McIntyre, is still used for lectures and functions. Year round, daily: 9–5.

28 *Newburyport, Massachusetts.* Rte. 1–A, northeast of Boston. During summer months a Chamber of Commerce information booth, Bartlett Mall, orients visitors; the chamber's year 'round offices are at 21 Pleasant St. (617) 462-6630. A walking tour guide is also available at the YMCA Civic Center and from the Newburyport Economic Development Commission, City Hall, (617) 465-0704. The city's Old Jail, built in 1834 with granite blocks hauled from Rockport (12 Auburn St.), is worth visiting (Mon.-Sat.: 9–5) as is the nearby Parker River Wildlife Refuge, a 4,650-acre nature preserve which includes Plum Island beach. Each August the city welcomes visitors with a weeklong series of festivities known as Yankee Homecoming.

28a *Cushing House,* 98 High St. The city's historical society museum displaying locally crafted silver and furnishings as well as standard memorabilia, May–Oct., Tues.-Sat.: 10–4, Sun.: 2–5. Admission charged. (617) 462-2681.

28b *Newburyport Library,* 94 State St. Notable for its maritime paintings.

28c *State Street Shops.* These shops have recently been restored, along with Inn St., a walking mall directly behind. They were built originally as one complete project after an 1811 fire wiped the area out, and represent an outstanding example of Federal-era commercial architecture.

28d *Custom House,* Water St. Not yet open at this writing. Check with Chamber of Commerce.

29 *Whitehorn, Newport, Rhode Island.* Corner of Thames and Denison streets. This is now one of eighty homes in town owned by Doris Duke's Portsmouth Preservation Society and is the only one open to the public. Lavishly restored with locally crafted furnishings and exotic imports. Summer months, Thurs.–Mon.: 10–12 and 2–4, otherwise by appointment. Steep admission charged. (401) 847-2448.

30 *Providence, Rhode Island.* Junctions I–95 and I–195. Many of the city's outstanding buildings date from this era. The Arcade (Westminster St.), built in 1827 and said to be the earliest shopping center in the country: its rose-colored glass roof shelters seventy-eight shops, half of them on a gallery level. The Round Top Church, Weybosset St., is one of the earliest Greek Revival buildings (1810) in the country. It's open Mon.–Fri.: 9–5, Sat. and Sun.: 9–1. The leaflet guide "A Mile of History" and visitors information is available from the Providence Preservation Society, 24 Meeting St., (401) 831-7440, and from the Providence Chamber of Commerce, 10 Dorrance St. (401) 521-5000.

30a *Brown University,* Prospect St. Chartered at Newport in 1764, the "college" was moved to Providence and named for its benefactor in 1804 (Nicholas was the class of 1786). University Hall (1770) served the patriots and French as a barracks and hospital during the Revolution. The John Carter Brown Library contains an outstanding collection of early Americana. Its current enrollment of men and women is almost six thousand. Guided tours leave from the Admissions Office, Prospect and Angell streets, year round except during exam periods, weekdays: 10, 11, 1, 3, 4; Sat.: 9, 10, 11. (401) 863-2378.

30b *John Brown House,* 52 Power St., corner of Benefit St. Built in 1786, this four-square brick mansion is outstanding, superbly furnished and containing a museum of city history and headquarters for the Rhode Island Historical Society. Year round, Tues.-Fri.: 11–4; Sat. and Sun.: 2–4. Admission charged. (401) 944-0750.

30c *Benefit Street.* Just above North and South Main streets follow signs for "Downtown Providence." Its name derives from the fact that between 1756 and 1758 the Town ordered the path here widened for "the common benefit." The Providence Athenaeum, 251 Benefit St., should not be missed; its architecture and portrait collection are outstanding and it was here that Edgar Allan Poe carried on his famous courtship. Year round, weekdays: 8:30–5:30. Closed Sats. mid-June–mid-Sept.

30d *Rhode Island School of Design Museum,* 224 Benefit St. One of the region's major art museums with an extensive display of local silver and cabinetwork. Year round, Tues.-Sat.: 11–5; Sun. and holidays: 2–5. Admission charged.

31 *Portsmouth, New Hampshire.* Off I–95. This was the country's twelfth largest city in 1800. For a leaflet map-guide and visitors information contact the city's chamber of commerce: (603) 436-1118.

31a *Governor John Langdon House,* 143 Pleasant St. John Langdon was the first to sign the Constitution and presided at Washington's inauguration. His mansion is a fine example of mid-Georgian design; the spacious interior is ornately carved and rooms are furnished in varying periods; the dining room in a later wing is said to have been designed by Stanford White. June–Sept., Tues.–Thurs.; Sun.: 1–5. Admission charged. SPNEA, (617) 227-3956.

31b *Rundlet-May House,* 364 Middle St. A four-square Federal mansion, restored and furnished with family heirlooms, many by Portsmouth's foremost cabinetmaker of the day, Langley Boardman. June–Sept., Tues., Thurs., Sun. Tours at 11, 1, 3, 4. Admission charged. SPNEA: (617) 227-3956.

31c *Governor Goodwin Mansion,* 30 Hancock St. Another four-square, three-story mansion, restored and furnished to reflect the late-nineteenth-century governor's residence; an intriguing contrast between the airiness of its Federal period design and heavy Victorian furnishings. Part of Strawbery Banke (See Chapter 3).

31d *Portsmouth Athenaeum,* Market Square. This narrow brick building was built as an insurance office immediately after an 1802 fire destroyed the city's commercial center. It's well worth a visit to see its elegant reading rooms. Year round, daily: 1–4.

32 *Wiscasset, Maine.* Rte. 1. A leaflet map and guide is available at shops and museums. General information is available from the Wiscasset newspaper, (207) 882-6210, and from a central information booth during summer months.

32a *Lincoln County Jail and Museum,* Rte. 218, posted from Rte. 1. Built with discouragingly thick granite walls, this three-story keep accommodated forty prisoners in twelve cells but frequently housed more, including debtors and the insane. It was used from 1837 to 1953. The first two floors now house exhibits and the jailer's house serves as a county historical museum. Mid-June–mid-Sept. weekdays: 10–5, Sun.: 12:30–5. Admission. (207) 882-7511.

32b *The Academy,* Warren St. This little brick building is now home for the Maine Art Gallery, which stages outstanding exhibits July–Labor Day and the rest of the year is open Sun. afternoons for lecture and discussion programs. July–Labor Day, weekdays: 10–5 and Sun.: 12–5. Admission charged.

32c *Custom House,* Water St. Handsomely restored to house a complex of gift shops.

32d *Nickels-Sortwell House,* corner of Main and Federal streets. An impressive early Federal mansion, built with its white clapboards flush to convey the illusion of stone; much of the facade with its ornate detailing is straight from Asher Benjamin's *American Builder's Companion.* Beautifully furnished to period. June–Sept., Tues.–Sun.: 11–5. Steep admission. Maintained by SPNEA: (617) 227-3956.

32e *Castle Tucker,* Lee St. at High St. Built in 1807, this unusual house is restored to its Victorian-era days. Summer months, daily: 2–5.

33 *Adams National Historic Site, Quincy, Massachusetts.* Corner of Adams St. and Newport Ave. This fine eighteenth-century mansion, built by a wealthy Tory, was purchased by the patriot who became our second president; it's restored to reflect the lives of John and Abigail and of their son John Quincy Adams, sixth president. April 19–Nov. 10, daily: 9–5. Admission charged. (617) 773-1177.

34 *Little Cranberry Island, Maine.* Two miles off Seal Harbor, Mt. Desert, accessible by ferry and excursion boats from Northeast and Southwest Harbors. The exceptional Iselford Historical Museum here contains exhibits depicting the history of the region. Guided tours by Park rangers during summer months. For details contact the Acadia National Park Visitors Center, (207) 244-3575, or the National Park Service Regional Headquarters: (617) 223-3793.

35 *Smuggler's Notch, Vermont.* Rte. 108, just north of the resort town of Stowe. An unusually scenic stretch of road, so high that it's frequently impassable in winter.

36 *Fort Edgecomb, Wiscasset, Maine.* Off Rte. 1, just north of the Sheepscot River from Wiscasset. An octagonal blockhouse which actually saw no naval activity, now restored by the state as a museum. A good picnic spot. Summer months, daylight hours. Small admission charged.

37 *Stonington, Connecticut.* Off I-95, just west of Rhode Island line: south of Rte. 1 on Rte. 1A. The two cannons are still displayed at Cannon Square. See Chapter 8.

38 *U.S.S. Constitution, Charlestown, Massachusetts.* Boston Naval Shipyard, posted from Mystic River Bridge. Known far and wide as "Old Ironsides" ever since her oak hull withstood shots from the British frigate *Guerriere*, this is the oldest commissioned ship in the United States Navy. Built in Boston in 1797, she has been lovingly restored and forms the centerpiece for the "historic park" which is presently taking shape on the yard's forty-three acres. Sites to see include the Constitution Museum, devoted to the ship's history, also the Rope Walk (in which all rope for the U.S. Navy was made until 1971), designed by Alexander Parris. Year round, daily: 9:30–4. (617) 242-3734.

39 *Vergennes, Vermont.* Rte. 7. One of the smallest and oldest cities in the country; a delightful, little-touristed community. The story of the war effort is told on a plaque in front of the library, which itself doubles as a local historical museum.

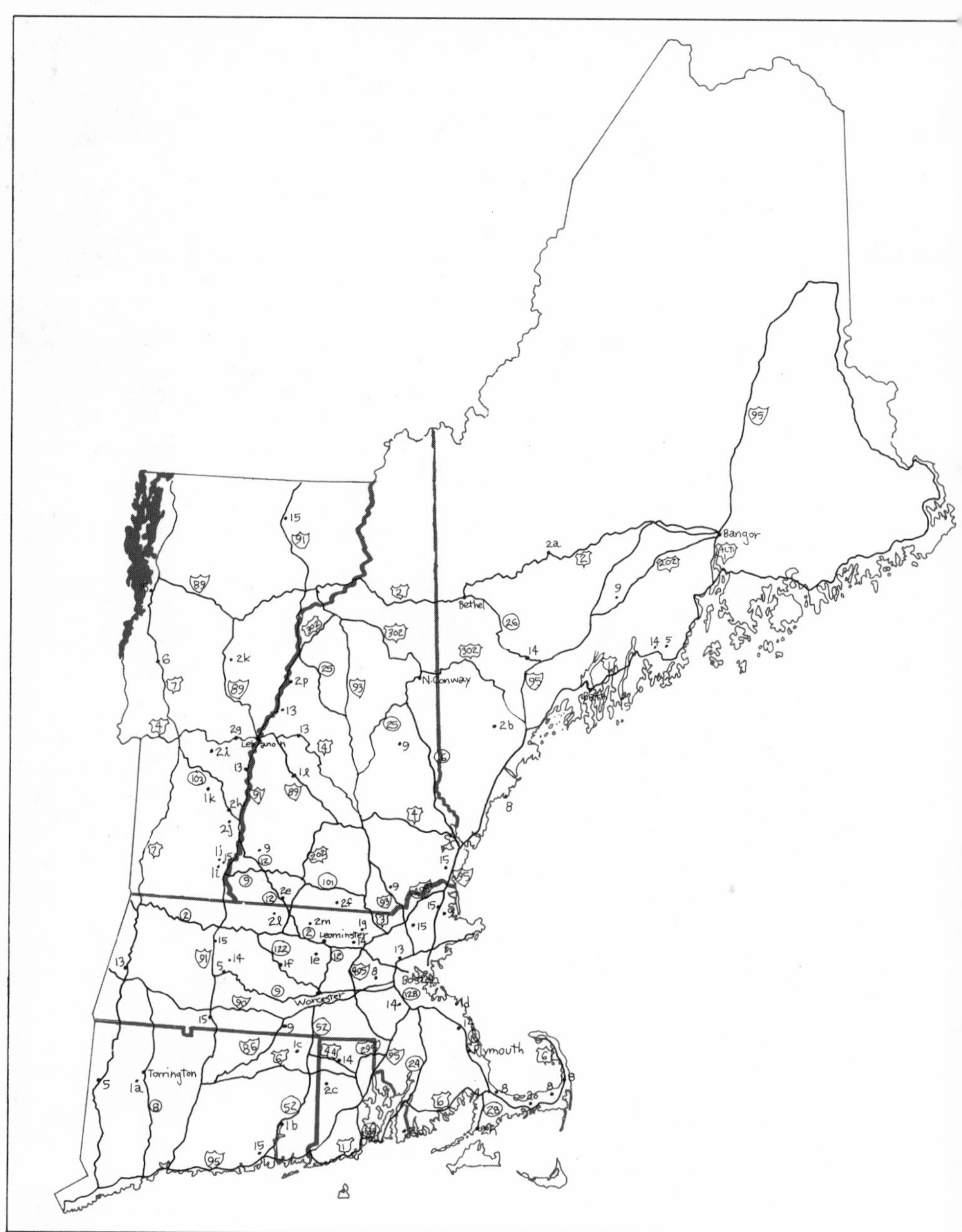
Bangor
Bethel
N. Conway
Lebanon
Leominster
Worcester
Boston
Plymouth
Torrington

7

Vintage Villages

To the entire world, a steepled church, set in its frame of white wooden homes around a manicured common, remains a scene which says "New England."

This familiar and frequent grouping is actually to the modern town what a formal head-and-shoulders portrait of some nineteenth-century forebear is to a family. The town's green, surrounded by its public buildings and handsomest homes, once formed the face of a community for which farms, shops, mills and an assortment of poorer dwellings formed the body. The green was a far busier, less tidy place than it is today, and the town as a whole was far more of a self-governing, self-sufficient unit than any now to be found in the United States.

The first decades of the nineteenth century marked the full growth of most rural, agricultural towns. While foreign trade spawned the elegant buildings and life-styles of coastal cities, with some spillover into the countryside, farming accounted for the livelihood earned by 90% of the population of the region. The Embargo extending from 1808 through the War of 1812 initially fostered those village industries already established, but its more dramatic effects – the advent of major industries – were just beginning to supply larger markets than household industry could serve and more inviting work opportunities for the rising generation than the family homestead could counter.

For the time being at least, the blacksmith, cooper, and village lawyer were still farmers as well. Daily rhythms continued to be set by those of the changing seasons, and tasks accomplished with the help of water-

wheel, oxen and long-familiar tools. Perhaps it is this lost human scale to things which enchants us about the era, tempting us to romanticize the life which we attach to
New England's handsomest town commons and those 1
picturesque *farming communities* which survive. We for- 2
get how drastically, if subtly, these places have altered with the intervening hundred and fifty years.

It is for this reason that we present outstanding, widely scattered vestiges of rural life at its peak under "Details" in this chapter. They are best understood when placed within the context of the one community, a nonprofit, outdoor museum, in which they have been assembled to form as complete a picture as we possess of village life in the years 1790 to 1840.

OLD STURBRIDGE VILLAGE 3

Most of the forty buildings at *Old Sturbridge Village* (OSV) are old, transported here from around New England and restored inside and out to look, sound and even smell as they did in the first fifty years of the Republic. The Village is peopled by day with "interpreters" in period dress who go about their seasonal tasks in this recreated setting in order to illustrate daily life and special events to visitors whose questions are welcome.

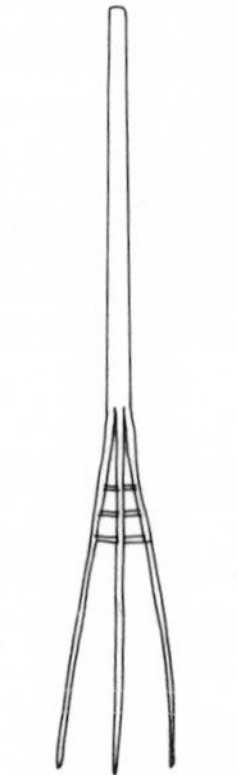

19th-century wooden hay fork

The real town of Sturbridge itself was laid out back in 1729 with land set aside for a meetinghouse and common. By 1820, it was home for some 1,500 people living on farms scattered twenty miles around. In contrast to the small, parklike common still to be seen in the heart of town, that at the center of the nearby two-hundred-acre recreated village is a long, open swath of scraggly
grass, kept in dubious trim by the town's *merino sheep*, 4
a breed eagerly adopted by the region's most progressive farmers at this time.

Morgan horse farm, University of Vermont

From this center, Old Sturbridge Village straggles along the Quinebaug River and out around a millpond. Perhaps the best place to begin exploring is the Pliny Freeman farm, representing as it does the dozens of farmlots, averaging one hundred acres more or less, on which the economy of this and every rural town was based. Fifteen acres here are planted in corn, pumpkins, rye, flax, oats, potatoes and hay, harvested and processed with the kind
of tools to be found in this region's *farm museums*. Near 5
the farmhouse stand the family provision plots: rows of

peas, asparagus, parsnips, onions, cabbage, squash, carrots, turnips and beans. An orchard supplies the staple cider and pie.

Beyond lie the woodlots, cleared in winter when it is
simplest both to get in and to haul logs out to lie sea-
soning a year in the farmhouse shed. Come March, the
maples are tapped for sugar. Progeny of that famous
steed *Justin Morgan* have not as yet appeared, so oxen are 6
here instead of horses, also a few shaggy-looking steers,
some milk cows and pigs. In autumn, you may find any
one of these animals dangling from the open barnway
while year round, dozens of "dung hill" fowl scratch in
the barnyard. Corn on the cob is left to dry during winter
months in the corn barn (elevated on stone stilts to insure
it against rodents and wolves), and hams are cured in the
smokehouse.

Farmer Pliny Freeman is lucky enough to have three sons among his seven children to help with the chores – at least until they drift away, one by one, to the west or local textile mills. Frequently, farmers still help each other to get in the harvest, but many also depend on hired hands. Somehow, everyone fits into the little gambrel-roofed farmhouse with its two rooms up and down, plus a homey kitchen and pantry.

West Dummerston bridge, Vermont

Stroll up along the millpond from the farmhouse – past
the tinsmith's, broom-maker's, and blacksmith's shops
and past the *carding*, *grist* and *sawmills*. With the excep- 7, 8, 9
tion of the carding mill (a harbinger of things to come),
all these buildings could have been found in town a century earlier. The *covered bridge* ahead could not have 10
been.

In those first decades after the Revolutionary War, as the country settled down to the job of knitting itself together with roads capable of conveying larger vehicles with heavier loads, it came smack up against rivers which were frequently wider and more flood-prone than any to be found in England. So inventors began producing longer and higher bridges, worrying about ways to protect their wooden joints against the rot which sets in through constant drenching and drying. Although a Philadelphia lawyer thought up the roof (actually a solution in use throughout Northern Europe for centuries), Yankees did develop the easy-to-assemble covered bridge such as this one from Dummerston, Vermont, a lattice truss model patented by Ithiel Town of Thompson, Connecticut, in 1829. This could be framed in any nearby open space, while stone abutments were taking shape in the river. On that day when the superstructure was hauled to the riverbank, the entire town turned out to watch it being "raised." Once in place, the contraption survived so well that almost two hundred covered bridges can be seen in New England today.

Beyond the bridge lies the foot of the common and two of its staples: the tavern (here a combination restaurant and museum) and the largest house in the village, this one, the home of Salem Towne. The mansion is a square Federal design with the predictable wide hallway and four spacious rooms to each of its two floors, a doorway and a fireplace copied from William Pain's pattern book. Its furnishings, many bought in Boston, include an English pianoforte, French wallpaper, a Simon Willard grandfather clock, fine china, silver and family portraits. The upstairs front rooms double as a long hall, the meeting place for a Masonic Lodge.

Salem Towne himself was the grandson of an Oxford minister and, having served in the Revolution (retiring as a brigadier general), he acquired money through marriage, lumbering interests in Maine and farming – in which he took an intellectual rather than a physical part. The orchard behind his home reveals his experiments with apple varieties of the time, for he was a member of the Massachusetts Society for Promoting Agriculture, one of a number of such organizations dedicated to improving the haphazard farming and breeding practices pursued up to this time (such groups also established many of the region's present *agricultural fairs*). 11

The few other homes around the common are simple farmhouses – a situation which will change as property values rise and local industrialists select this as the status place to build their homes. Meanwhile, the Fenno House, still unpainted, and built in 1704 in Canton, Massachusetts, is furnished with family possessions which have been passed down through the generations, simply because the family has never possessed wealth to replace them. Frequently it is filled with the smell of cooking food, drying herbs or the aroma of roasting coffee beans. The coffee, incidentally, might be sipped from blue Staffordshire cups, part of a teaset made in England, but celebrating the American victory at Saratoga. The British flooded our country stores with this cheaply priced china after the Revolution, frequently with eagles and similar themes to satisfy our newfound pride as a nation.

The gambrel-roofed Stephen Fitch House next door (built in 1735 in Windham, Connecticut) is noticeably more modern. It boasts a shallow reflector fireplace (designed to make the most of quickly vanishing woodlots). Its self-consciously formal parlor includes a wooden floor, painted in a diamond pattern, wallpaper and a stiff American Empire clawfooted sofa and *Hitchcock chairs.* 12
In its summer kitchen, the big loom and set of spinning wheels are perpetually in use, producing the still-essential "homespun." While working in the fields, the farmer wears a frock-like smock which falls to his knees over linen or cotton pantaloons. Come winter, he switches to store-bought corduroys and dons a heavy smock of homemade woolen cloth and, for dress occasions, a cloak. The women wear long frocks of homespun or purchased fabrics for home chores, also a small light "mob cap" or bonnet, both for modesty's and convenience's sake. Their Sabbath-day silk dresses with full sleeves are frequently passed from mother to daughter, restyled to satisfy changing fashions.

The Sabbath itself is still strictly observed but now in the churches of a number of denominations. Baptists, Methodists and Unitarians have in places reduced Congregationalists to a minority in town, and even Quakers are widely accepted. With the exception of the latter group (who, since they require no pulpit, still prefer the box-like meetinghouse of their forebears), each new denomination builds a church of its own, a steepled building to conform with the new notion of what *churches* should 13
look like. The village meetinghouse at the head of this village common is just such a Greek Revival model, built in Sturbridge for the Baptists in 1832. This was just one year before Massachusetts formally separated "church" from "state," the last of the New England states to do so. In many towns, you will find the "new" (1820s) church standing side-by-side with the town hall which, on close inspection, turns out to be the old meetinghouse.

Greek Revival church, 1832

Beside the church stands the burying ground, a grim reminder — as its counterparts are for anyone who takes the trouble to closely read gravestone inscriptions — of the life expectancy of these times: ten to fifteen years below the present. Due to the hazards and strains of childbirth, women died earlier than men, and it is said they attempted to time their deliveries for the spring months, giving their infants a full six months of life with which to face winter.

Just up the road stands the "*animal pound*," a high, 14
stone-walled holdover from the previous century. Animals caught straying are still herded into this little prison. Across the way is a shoemaker's shop; an indispensable craftsman to every town, he processes the hides which local farmers give him, fashioning them into heavy winter boots for the entire family.

But in summer, the children still come barefoot to school and the neighboring schoolhouse itself is a sorry revelation. Although Massachusetts and Connecticut both pride themselves on requiring schooling in towns of fifty or more families way back in the mid-1600s, the nature of this school varied drastically. During the Revolution, classes of any kind were suspended. Around the turn of the century, states divided their towns into "districts" in recognition of the fact that towns had long since straggled out over their entire six-mile-square spread, and offshoot villages had sprung up at crossroads and millsites, obviously more sensible school sites than the distant common (which might or might not at this time boast a schoolhouse). For decades now, children had, in fact, been attending "moving schools" – held for a few months at a time in local homes in which the local schoolmaster took up temporary residence.

The Village's *schoolhouse* is an unpainted, unclap- 15
boarded model, built in 1810 for "District 7" of Candia, New Hampshire, where it was in use until 1885. Its floors slope downward to the center of the room, putting every scholar within the schoolmaster's vision and within reach of his notorious rod. A small iron stove provides the only heat, and children whose parents neglected to stock their share of the woodpile found themselves in the room's coldest corners. Scholars were required to bring their own slates and slate pencils from home, as well as paper books (sewed at home from store-bought foolscap) in which they scratched with quill pens (in constant need of mending), using ink which had been boiled at home from powder, maple bark and coppers. In 1837, a survey of Connecticut schools reveals two globes, a few little-used blackboards and six school libraries in the entire state, information used to generate needed reforms in

this area. Vermont did not start providing texts until 1894. Attendance was rarely enforced.

Schoolmasters themselves needed no specific qualifications, and their $10 plus board monthly stipend ($4 for schoolmistresses) could hardly have attracted the town's brighter lights. Men taught the boys in winter months when they were freed from farm tasks, while in summer, women presided and girls attended. Rarely did a teacher stay at one school two years in succession and, since his charges varied in age from four to sixteen (frequently adding up to more than one hundred bodies to keep in tow), his familiarity with their varying needs and potentials is self-evident.

Since the level of this brand of public schooling rarely rose above the three Rs plus a heavy dose of Bible reading, the need for something more was filled by private academies, the first founded before the Revolution and hundreds (many of which still survive) appearing in upcountry towns at this time. As we shall see, many a "normal" school and university was also born at this juncture, but graduate schools were nonexistent – the would-be lawyer, for instance, typically apprenticed himself in a little free-standing wooden office such as the one here on the common. The Western World's sole law school was, in fact, currently in session in a similar little building at Litchfield, Connecticut.

The business block has not as yet found its way to the village, and each little enterprise (which includes, besides those we have mentioned, the cooper's, potter's and pewtersmith's shops) is housed in its own little building, somewhere in town.

Neither has Main Street yet replaced the common as the town's commercial as well as religious and social center. It is here you find both bank and general store. This village actually boasts two emporiums – one, the Grant store, features penny candy and like "oldie souvenirs" to be found in similar tourist traps around New England. The Asa Knight Store, in contrast, is a meticulously researched recreation of what this building stocked when it stood in the small southeastern Vermont town of Dummerston in the 1830s. A fraction of its 2000-odd item inventory was locally made (produce, cheese, boxes, butter tubs, milk pans, crockery, woven and knitted goods). The remainder includes city-made shoes, Italian silks, Indian dyed cottons, West Indian ginger, rum and

Country store

molasses, Shaker seed packets, threads, soaps, tooth powder, tobacco, patent medicines, English china, farm tools and countless other niceties which you might not expect to find.

How did it all get here? Twice a year, Asa Knight loaded a wagon or pung with the goods he had been accumulating in lieu of cash from local farmers – and headed for a coastal city. (As befited his status, he usually took the stage, hiring a farmer or teamster to drive in his load.) From the directory which Boston and other such cities published at this time, he knew which merchants could supply what goods. While some individual farmers still made the trip to market themselves, most by now were content to accept such a local representative as their middleman.

For our purposes, a tour of Old Sturbridge Village ends with the Thompson Bank, a mini- (one-room) Grecian temple the likes of which could now be seen in many busy rural villages. The first banks had appeared in big cities just after the Revolution, and their presence in these little communities is proof of how highly financial output of such places was already valued. Ironically, it also underscores the end of self-sufficiency (now that wealth is figured in hard currency instead of land and produce, other sources for accumulating it will quickly appear). This pretentious little building, in fact, augurs the end of the age of homespun.

DETAILS

1 *Town Commons.* If you are confused by the terms "green" and "common" remember that "common" was the land once shared by the town's first settlers. Today it may – or may not – be remembered in the shape of a mini-park, frequently known as "the green" on the site. Space permits only a token listing of towns with strikingly handsome commons; we have selected those which offer something besides for the visitor.

a. **Litchfield, Connecticut.** Junction Rtes. 118 and 63. western Connecticut. In addition to its long, broad green which sits some thousand feet high above the surrounding Litchfield Hills, this queenly dowager of a town boasts one of the most photographed churches in New England and more than one hundred late-eighteenth- and early nineteenth-century mansions, a sampling of which are open to the public annually on Open House Day, held early in June. It also includes a 4000-acre nature preserve and Bantam Lake, largest natural lake in the state. The Tapping Reeve Law School, 1784, South St., said to be the oldest formal law school in the English-speaking world, is a modest one-room clapboard affair, set in the garden of Judge Reeve's own Greek revival mansion. The distinguished lawyer's first pupil was his brother-in-law Aaron Burr; subsequent alumni include John Calhoun, Horace Mann, Samuel Morse and Noah Webster. Like the Litchfield Historical Museum (on the green) it's open May 15–Oct. 15, Tues.–Sat.: 11–5. Admission charged. (203) 567–5862.

b. **Norwichtown, Connecticut.** Exit 81 off Rte. 52. Norwich itself is the child of the later steamship and industrial era but the shape of the original settlement survives on and near *Norwichtown Green* just north. Buildings include a Congregational Church, two early taverns and schools and a plaque telling you that this is the place where "hides, merchandise, public business, military exercises, shows, sports, festivals and the general enterprise of the town found a center." It remains a frequent site for summer month festivals. The *Leffingwell Inn*, just south on Rte. 32, is a must for any visitors to the area (see Chapter 4).

c. **Woodstock, Connecticut.** Junction of Rtes. 169, 171, 197 and 198. Just five miles south on Rte. 169 from Sturbridge. Once part of Massachusetts, this town today lacks a commercial center, and the unusually expansive common is framed by handsome private homes, Woodstock Academy (opened in 1801 and now a public school) and *Roseland Cottage*, a Gothic revival style wooden mansion of a summer home complete with one of the earliest private bowling alleys in the country, formal gardens and ornate period furnishings. June–Oct., Tues., Thurs., Sun.: 1–5 Admission charged. Maintained by SPNEA: (617) 227–3956. Scattered around town you can find a number of antiques and crafts shops, notably *Woodstock Pottery*, still producing "redware" turned out here in the early nineteenth century. A leaflet guide to the community's Heritage Shops is available locally.

d. **Cohasset, Massachusetts.** Rte. 3A, south of Boston. Theoretically this town's history began when Capt. John Smith stopped by to look it over. Today it is primarily a bedroom town, one of Boston's loveliest, but in the early nineteenth century its wealth was based squarely on its own fishing, farming and shipbuilding. The common itself is broad and inviting; here the First Parish Meeting House dates back to 1745 and St. Stephen's Church exercises its 51-bell carillon daily. From the common walk to the *Independence Gown Museum* which displays nineteenth-century dress, to *Historic House*, built in 1810 and furnished accordingly, and to the *Maritime Museum*, all three at the junction of Elm and Main streets and maintained by the Cohasset Historical Society. Early June–Labor Day, Tues.–Sat.: 1:30–4:30. Admission charged. The Society also maintains Moore's Rocks Reservation, Jerusalem Road, overlooking the ocean.

e. **Princeton, Massachusetts.** Junction, Rtes. 31, 62 and 140. The town's old homes are strung out along ridge roads which meet at its long, sloping common which has a steepled church at its head and a genuine general store at its foot. Princeton is best known as home for *Mt. Wachusett State Reservation*, an isolated peak offering a grand view of the surrounding countryside, also hiking trails, picnic sites and a small ski area. The *Wachusett Meadows Wildlife Sanctuary* is crisscrossed with trails.

f. **Barre, Massachusetts.** Rtes. 32, 62 and 122. This central Massachusetts town is distinguished by its huge common, the site of band concerts and colonial musters from the county over. It's surrounded by shops, an 1880s hotel (Barre Guest House) and old homes, including one which serves as the local historical museum. (May–Oct., Sun.: 2–5. (617) 355-6614.) Cook's Canyon Wildlife Sanctuary, a thirty-five-acre preserve around a steep gorge, is off South St.

g. **Groton, Massachusetts.** Junction Rtes. 40, 119 and 11. The town's own impressive common, on which local Minutemen assembled April 19, 1775, is enhanced by the landscaped campus of Lawrence Academy. Prestigious Groton School, founded in 1884 by Reverend Endicott Peabody, is also in town (Farmer's Row). The First Parish Meeting House, dating from 1755 and remodeled with graceful columns and spire, boasts a Paul Revere bell. Governor Boutwell House, opposite Town Hall, is a mid-nineteenth-century mansion maintained by the town's historical society (May 30–Sept. 27; Sat.: 3–5). The *Groton Inn*, center of town, claims to be one of the country's oldest and features tavern style dining.

h. **Newfane, Vermont.** Rte. 30, north of Brattleboro. Bellows Falls and Brattleboro are the big towns in Windham County but Newfane, one dip in a twisty road, is shire seat. When court sessions began in 1787 the village was about the same size – twenty houses and two hotels. But it was in a different place: two miles up on Newfane Hill where a map of the first settlement still marks the site. Beams were unpegged and homes moved to the valley by ox-drawn sleighs in the winter of 1825. Still the *Newfane Inn*, (802) 365-4427, claims its birthdate as 1787 since its wooden bones once supported the hilltop Jones Vermont Coffee Pot. For over a century Newfane's inns have been well known. First it was because the whitewashed jail slept twenty-five paying guests, feeding them in the same room with the inmates. Both the Newfane Inn and the Four Columns behind it, (802) 365-7713, are now justly famed for their rooms and restaurants. This is also the boyhood home of Eugene Field of nursery rhyme fame ("Wynken, Blynken and Nod"). Gravestones in the fine old burying ground behind the railway station attest to the fact that Newfane reached its peak early in the nineteenth century. The town's most famous current resident is John Kenneth Galbraith.

i. **Townsend, Vermont.** A few miles north of Newfane, Rte. 30 dips sharply west along the rim of Townsend's vast common. The 1790 Congregational Church is flanked by white wooden, black-shuttered homes, by the stucco, columned town hall and the new buildings of Leland and Gray, the union school replacing a seminary founded 1834. There's a fountain and general store, too, also an adjacent state forest as well as outlet stores for the town's two industries: colonial-style furniture and stuffed toys.

j. **Weston, Vermont.** Rte. 100 in south central Vermont. The oval common was originally a shallow frog pond. Now it's truly the village center, flanked on one side by the *Farrar-Mansur House* which was opened as a tavern in 1797 and is now restored as a historical museum, complete with taproom. (July–Labor Day, daily: 1–5; weekends until mid-Oct.: 1–5. Admission charged.) It's owned, along with the reconstructed early gristmill (a crafts center) and the *Weston Playhouse*, by the nonprofit Weston Community Club. The *Weston Bowl Mill*, first opened in the 1890s, is still selling bowls. The *Vermont Country Store*, granddaddy of hundreds of similar emporiums featuring old style stock, is down the street and *Weston Priory*, a Benedictine monastery which welcomes visitors, is four miles north of the village, Rte. 100.

k. **New London, New Hampshire.** An exit off I-89, also via Rte. 11 from I-93. The expanse of town common is complemented by the grounds of the adjacent school, in this case Colby College, founded as New England Academy in 1836. The *New London Inn* is a rambling old stage-stop, obviously akin to the nineteenth-century houses which line Main St. Due to both the swimming and skiing available in Mt. Sunapee State Park it's open year round and outstanding (603) 526-2791.

2 *Farming Communities*

a. **Farmington, Maine.** Rte. 4 from Maine Turnpike exit at Auburn, most common route. The shire town of Franklin County, Farmington remains the bustling shopping center for farming towns scattered many miles around. The Franklin County Agricultural Society was incorporated in 1839 and still sponsors an annual September fair; the town also prides itself on the quality of its maple syrup. Its academy, founded in 1807, is now a branch of U. of M. In winter this is ski country (both Sugarloaf and Camelback are nearby). In summer there's theater and an art colony at nearby Skowhegan, and swimming in the area's numerous lakes.

b. **Standish, Maine.** Rte. 113 off Maine Turnpike from Portland exit, southeastern part of state. This is orchard country, settled in the mid-eighteenth century and still a handsome farming town. Its Unitarian Church (1806) has a square belfry and box pews. During the War of 1812 when it was feared that Portland would be invaded, coin from the city's banks was hauled here by oxen and stashed in the *Daniel Marrett House*, a Georgian-style home with Greek revival restyling which rambles out to its adjoining barn. Maintained by SPNEA, it's open June–Sept., Tues., Thurs., Sun.: 1–5. Admission charged. Nearby Sebago Lake is a summer resort area.

c. **Foster Center, Rhode Island.** Rte. 6 East from Providence, northeastern corner of state. Land here was purchased from the Narragansett Indians in 1662 and today is a pleasing cluster of eighteenth- and early nineteenth-century homes, a Town Meeting House (built 1796 for a second Baptist group in the community), deeded to the town in 1822, provided that it could still also be used for services. The Baptists eventually built themselves a second Greek revival church which also stands in the center, along with a nineteenth-century library (originally a one-room schoolhouse). Homes which have been built since the community's peak in 1820 blend in with the older buildings, giving a sense of the original hamlet, surrounded by its woods, hills and fields.

d. **Little Compton, Rhode Island.** Southwestern corner of the state, Rte. 77 south from Tiverton where it joins Rte. 24 to Fall River, Massachusetts. Permanent settlement began soon after King Philip's War and the land has remained unusually rich while the town's position (a peninsula between the Sakonnet River and the Atlantic) obviously lends itself to fishing. This is one Rhode Island township which does center around a common, due to the fact that it was founded as part of Plymouth Colony and remained within Massachusetts until 1746. Around this green are grouped several churches (all nineteenth century save the Catholic one), a nineteenth-century town hall and the school and library. A white marble statue here also commemorates the birth of the first white woman in New England, and in the graveyard New England's foremost seventeenth-century Indian fighter, Benjamin Church, is buried. The town also includes Sakonnet Point, a picturesque fishing village and summer resort. The Quaker Meeting House, West Main Road, dates from the early eighteenth century (open by appointment: (401) 635-4559). Wilbor House, West Main Road, serves as the town historical society, mid-June–mid-Sept.: Tues.–Sun.: 2–5 and by appointment: (401) 625-4559.

e. **Fitzwilliam, New Hampshire.** Rte. 119, southwest New Hampshire, Monadnock region. Today Fitzwilliam is known for its handsome inn but the town's first settler was so hard-put for shelter that his daughter had to be born under his ox-cart. The large, two-story frame Congregational Church, built in 1817, is distinguished by two pairs of slender Ionic pillars with an oval window in the pediment above and a four-story steeple rising in balustraded piers above it. The 1790s' *Fitzwilliam Inn*, (603) 585-9000, remains a favorite stopping place for travelers between southern Vermont and Boston, also a place to spend a quiet week year round. (It includes a swimming pool and in winter there's nearby downhill and cross-country skiing.) There's also a nineteenth-century town hall here at the neatly fenced common and three miles away is the Rhododendron Reservation, a mecca for flower lovers in late June.

f. **Mason, New Hampshire.** On Rte. 23 from Rte. 2A, just northwest of the Massachusetts town of Townsend. Just one house was painted and three rooms papered in this town when a boy named Sam Wilson moved here with his family. Sam was fourteen at the time, and later he made a reputation for himself in Troy, New York, where he supplied beef and pork to the army during the War of 1812, stamping his meats "U.S." It's said that passengers of Robert Fulton's river steamer one day questioned the meaning of the six-inch-high U.S. initials on barrels they saw piled on Troy pier and were told that those are "Uncle Sam's initials." The story grew. Meanwhile, with the help of a potato starch mill, some vineyards, and a quarry, Mason grew in size and dignity. Its houses were coated white, the lovely church, parsonage, meetinghouse and school were built, and the scene has changed little since. From shaded picnic benches on Knobby Hill you can see the cattle pound, built for $7 in 1771. There are also plenty of unpaved roads to hike, cellar holes to explore and a water-filled granite quarry to swim in.

g. **Woodstock, Vermont.** Rte. 4 from I-89, central eastern Vermont. Cradled between four valleys and in the crook of a swift river, Woodstock is a natural trading center and by the mid-nineteenth century was a "settled-down village of quiet and acquired beauty," already attracting admiring visitors from major eastern cities. It was the shire town of Windsor County when Vermont joined the union in 1791 and so attracted more than its share of lawyers, other professional men (a medical college thrived between 1830 and 1850), and merchants. It still boasts four Paul Revere bells in its churches (the oldest, on Elm St., dates from 1808) and two of its period inns survive, one as a museum house maintained by the Ottaquechee D.A.R. (22 The Green) and the second, the old White Cupboard Inn, as an office complex. The football-shaped green is surrounded by aristocratic early nineteenth-century homes in wood and brick, approached from one side by a brand new covered bridge. Around the corner, wedged between resort town specialty shops, the Dana House, a handsome white clapboard home with brick gables, houses an outstanding collection of period furnishings, costumes, toys and tools (open May 30–Oct. 30, maintained by the Woodstock Historical Society: (802) 457-1822). Some two dozen Federal-style mansions line adjacent streets, any one of which would qualify as the village aristocrat in a less splendiferous town. Biggest and most pretentious of all, the brick home built in 1805 and later Victorianized by railroad magnate Frederick Billings, is now a country home for Laurence Rockefeller, who married into the family. Rockefeller was also responsible for replacing the Victorian Woodstock Inn with a modern (colonial style) hostelry a few years ago: The *Woodstock Inn* (802) 457-1100.

h. **Chester, Vermont.** Junction Rtes. 103 and 11, eastern central Vermont. Chester is an unselfconsciously attractive town with three distinct centers to it. The proud Congregational Church with its three-tiered, cupola-topped steeple echoes Asher Benjamin's designs (built 1828), just up from the narrow strip of greenery which divides the Chester Inn (meals, lodging and swimming pool) from the brick academy building (now the historical museum) and large burying ground. Around a bend you come on Chester Depot, still terminus for an excursion railroad (see Chapter 10) and farther along is the "stone village," a stretch lined with more than two dozen buildings which are faced in "gneiss," a rough-hewn, gleaming mica schist quarried from nearby Flamstead Mountain (cool in the summer, warm in the winter and a rarity in New England). All are privately owned save the Universalist Church, a frequent site of church suppers and bazaars. Comparatively sleepy today, it's difficult to imagine Chester in its 1820s heyday when it boasted: four gristmills, nine sawmills, three fulling mills, an oil mill, one cotton and two woolen factories, three carding machines, five stores, taverns, one distillery, four tanneries, three lawyers, six doctors, the academy and two newspapers!

i. **Plymouth Notch, Vermont.** West of Woodstock on Rte. 4, then south on 100A. A typical Vermont "four corners" within a five-mile-square township which also included Plymouth Union, Plymouth Kingdom, Plymouth Five Corners, Tyson and Frog City – all of which once flourished, totalling 1,400 residents in the 1820s. Today three of these little centers survive, with a net population of 238. Undoubtedly Plymouth Notch would have disappeared long ago had not Calvin Coolidge happened to be born, to be sworn into office as president, and to die here. Today it has been restored and opened to visitors. The complex includes the Union Christian Church, its cemetery, a one-room schoolhouse, a cheese factory, farmer's museum, a little inn (formerly the Lakin Hotel, now a restaurant) and the Coolidge homestead itself. It's open daily, Memorial Day-mid-Oct.: 9–6. Admission charged. Lodgings are plentiful in the area and there's camping in nearby Coolidge State Park.

j. **Grafton, Vermont.** Junction Rtes. 35 and 121, southeastern Vermont. Like many a Vermont town, Grafton's population crested with that of its sheep (1,480 of the former, 10,000 of the latter). Local mills turned its wool into 75,000 yards of Grafton cloth annually, and soapstone from thirteen local quarries left town in the shape of sinks, stoves, inkwells, bullet molds, sashweights and foot-warmers. The boom tale is told in the town's little red historical society building. Vestiges of this past wealth can also be seen in the sumptuous, three-story Grafton Inn (which attracted literary and political greats of the nineteenth century and is once more a distinguished hostelry) and the row of Greek revival mansions along Main Street. The town reached its nadir in the 1940s, when its eighty-some houses were selling for $3000 with plenty of acreage. Then a New York financier (a descendant of the town's first pastor) who summered here restored the trompe l'oeil murals in the Congregational Church. His aunt, who frequently visited him here, left a fortune which was used to restore the Old Tavern and its three annexes, to build a new cheese factory, and in short turn the town into its current shape as a popular resort and retirement center for "out-of-staters."

k. **Brookfield, Vermont.** Exit I–89 at Randolf Center, then north on Rte. 12 to E. Brookfield. In 1830 people of this hilltop hamlet outnumbered those in Burlington. But the sole survivor of the thirteen mills which once lined its "brook" is a white frame house with a bell on top, now the Fork Shop restaurant. From its windows you look out on Sunset Lake, spanned by a floating bridge which was installed in 1812, buoyed up by 390 oak barrels (gradually these have been replaced by steel drums). The bridge leads to Allis State Park beyond. The Fork Shop itself is part of the surviving three corners, here completed by a general store, library (the state's oldest, established 1791), the site of an old wooden hotel, a post office and a series of white wooden homes, most of them part of a delightful resort named *Green Trails*, (802) 276–2012. The steepled church is down the road a piece and the historical society is housed in an early unpainted saltbox at another four corners within the town.

l. **Royalston, Massachusetts.** Rte. 68, north-central Massachusetts. An exceptionally handsome, sleepy hilltop hamlet with a green that's nearly a half-mile long, where even the general store has a fan-lighted doorway. The road runs through the middle of the common and leaves it in four directions. The town was named for Tory Isaac Royal of Medford (see Chapter 4) and contains an unusual number of mansions, most impressive of which is the square, hip-roofed Bullock House. Doane Falls Reservation here is a spectacular gorge crowned with pine and hemlock, through which the waters of Lawrence Brook plunge. The town hall and First Congregational Church complete the scene and the town has recently refurbished its historical museum (open by appointment). The Phineas S. Newton Library welcomes visitors daily.

m. **Ashburnham, Massachusetts.** Rtes. 12 and 101, north-central Massachusetts. The old Town Hall's museum features records from the town's part in the events of April, 1775; the town also maintains an Ashburnham Museum, built with material from the second meetinghouse (1791) which includes a nineteenth-century model schoolroom, bedchamber, parlor, and eighteenth-century kitchen. Atop Meeting House Hill (original center of the town) are the remains of an eighteenth-century animal pound and powderhouse.

n. **Falmouth, Massachusetts.** Cape Cod, Rte. 28. Bounded by Buzzards Bay to the east and Vineyard Sound to the west, this is a large township which includes Woods Hole (departure point for car ferries to Nantucket and Martha's Vineyard) and an exceptionally handsome center, clustered around its large green laid out in 1749. This triangular green at the west end of Main St. was the scene of a Revolutionary War encampment. The meetinghouse, built in 1796, has a Paul Revere bell; the fine elms around the green were planted in 1832. Impressive early homes include two maintained by the Falmouth Historical Society: the square *Wicks House* with its widow's walk, built by a sea captain in 1790, boasts eight fireplaces and town memorabilia; the 1770 half-cape *Conant House* is a less elegantly furnished museum. (Mid-June-mid-Sept.: 2–5, daily, nominal admission.) The town is the birthplace of Katherine Lee Bates, who wrote "America the Beautiful," and it's the summer scene of weekly summer band concerts, presented in a band shell at Marine Park (Scranton Ave.), Thursday evenings. Elsewhere in the town you can visit the *Saconesset Homestead* (a restored seventeenth-century Quaker homestead on Rte. 28A open late May–late Oct., daily: 10–6), and the Ashumet *Holly Reservation*, a forty-five-acre preserve maintained by the Massachusetts Audubon Society and offering a delightful year 'round show of blossoms set against the holly evergreens. During summer season the town is also known for its playhouse (July–Labor Day) and its warm-water beaches, among which Old Silver is the most famous.

o. **Yarmouth, Massachusetts.** Cape Cod, Rte. 6 (Nantucket Sound on south, Cape Cod Bay on north). Since this, along with just about every other town on Cape Cod, is now a popular retirement center, it's intriguing to know that one of Yarmouth's first settlers was seventy-five-year-old Rev. Stephen Bachiler of Lynn – who arrived in the winter of 1637 at the head of his congregation. Over the years this became a distinguished seafaring town, as its many fine homes attest. Oldest of these, the *Colonel John Thacher House* (basically 1680 but with major renovations and additions) reveals the lifestyles of generations of Thachers who inhabited it. Next door is the *Winslow Crocker House* (1780) with seven of its eleven rooms elegantly furnished. (Both houses are open June–Sept., Tues.–Sat.: 11–4. Admission charged.) Across the street, facing a tiny triangle of green, is the Greek revival *Capt. Bangs Hallet House* summer months (Mon.–Sat.: 2–4. Admission charged). Between these three homes and behind the village post office are the Botanic Trails of Yarmouth Port, 53 acres crisscrossed with walks which take you around Miller's Pond, one of the Cape's many "kettle holes" left by retreated glaciers. The town also includes a summer playhouse, eighteenth-century windmills, one on the end of Willow Street on the Bass River, South Yarmouth, and the second on the north side of Rte. 28 in West Yarmouth. And it offers beaches, a half dozen on its south and one on its north shore.

p. **Orford, New Hampshire.** Rte. 10 and connected by a bridge to Rte. 5 in Vermont. Orford is set high above the east bank of the Connecticut River and famed for its "Mansion Row": seven Federal-era square, hip-roofed homes in all, and so like those built by Bulfinch that they have been, until recently, attributed to him. This was one of the communities which pressed for incorporation of the state of "New Connecticut" instead of Vermont (see Chapter 6) and it remains one of the most fertile and handsome corners of New Hampshire. The mansions are complimented by a wide mall of elms below, and both a nineteenth-century church and academy. It's one of the local sites to see for visitors at the resorts located just across the river in Fairlee, Vermont.

3 *Old Sturbridge Village.* Massachusetts Turnpike to Rte. 20. The story of this prestigious outdoor museum dates back to a rainy weekend in 1926 when Albert Wells, a Southbridge optics manufacturer, went antiquing in Vermont. His enthusiasm was so fired by the old artifacts which he found that he began collecting them in quantities which soon outgrew his home. In 1935 his son suggested creating an early New England village in which to display them. The family bought a two-hundred-acre tract of meadow and wooded hills, watered by the Quinebaug River in Sturbridge. Gradually they moved a few early buildings here and reconstructed others in which to exhibit their collections of glassware, clocks, lighting devices and guns. These can still be seen, displayed much the way the first paying visitors saw them in 1946. But no longer is it possible to say that once you've seen OSV, you've seen it. The village changes constantly. From its inception it was dedicated to training apprentices in early crafts, and the potters, blacksmiths, coopers, tinsmiths, broommakers, millers and printers are constantly at work. More demonstrations, more buildings have been added year by year until there are now forty structures, "interpreted" by a part-time staff of two hundred. More subtle changes include refurbishings as historical research prove them necessary, new "old" plants and animals which are being backbred through "historical farming," and seasonal happenings: summertime musters, political debates and musical presentations, autumn butchering, wintertime special tours, and spring activities. Behind the scenes are a staff of historians, researchers, curators and archivists. The museum village also possesses an outstanding library of period diaries, town histories, atlases, cookbooks, sermons, agricultural journals, child-rearing manuals and such. Recently it has added both a new Museum Education Building and Visitors' Center. Lodgings are plentiful in the town just outside the village entrance. Admission charged. Year round except Christmas and New Year's. April–Oct., daily: 9:30–5:30; Nov.–March, daily: 9:30–4:30; Dec.–Feb., weekdays: 10–4, Sat. and Sun. until 4:30. (617) 347-3362.

4 *Merino Sheep.* The first Merino sheep are said to have entered the country as a present to a

Cambridge man who ate them. By 1802, however, their superior quality to that of local wool producers began to be appreciated, touted as it was by the new agricultural societies which were now attempting to improve the farmer's low yield. A former consul to Madrid brought a few hundred Merinos back with him, also a Spanish shepherd to drive them overland to his retirement farm in Wethersfield, Vermont. During the War of 1812 demand for home wool skyrocketed; so did the price of Merinos. Three sheep that sold for $300 in 1806 fetched $1,500 apiece a few years later. At the height of this craze in 1840 (now cited as the birth of the American wool industry) Vermont and New Hampshire together reported 2,250,000 Merinos. The boom ended abruptly with the opening of railroads to the West, luckily since farmers had been neglecting other aspects of agricultural improvement. In 1849 the sheep were sold cheap for hides and mutton. But many of the pillared, Greek revival mini-mansions still to be seen upcountry date from this never-equaled (before or after) source of rural, non-industrial wealth.

5 *Farm Museums:* Among the most notable are:

a. **Farm Museum, Hadley, Massachusetts.** Rtes. 9 and 47 between Northampton and Amherst. This trove of early wooden and iron tools is housed in a 1782 barn, moved here from a nearby estate and subsequently sheathed in clapboards. In all it's three floors full of carts, fences, churns, spinning wheels, cobblers' tools, pitchforks, plows, horse clippers, beehives, etc., etc. The early broom-making machines here deserve special attention since Hadley was once New England's foremost broom-corn center. This crop was first grown here for commercial purposes in 1798 and by 1855 the community was turning out 641,120 brooms, 3,500 switches a year in some forty small shops. The museum is set back behind a handsome nineteenth-century Congregational Church, in front of which is the long thin green with its adjacent pillared town hall, library and white clapboard homes. Open: May–Oct. 12, Tues.–Sat.: 10–4:30 and Sun.: 1:30–4:30. (413) 584-7122.

b. **Sloane-Stanley Museum at Kent Furnace.** Rte. 7 in Kent, Connecticut. (Rte. 7, far western central part of state.) This collection of primarily wooden tools is housed in a specially built barn on the site of the old Kent Furnace, which produced a high quality of pig iron for seventy years in the eighteenth century. Memorial Day–Oct., Wed.–Sat.: 10–4:30. For details contact Connecticut Historical Commission: (203) 236-5621.

c. **Union, Maine.** Rte. 17, near Rockland and Camden. The Edward Mathews Farm Museum, located on the Knox County Fair Grounds, houses "thousands of relics of early life in Maine." Best time to visit it is, of course, during the annual fair itself (held late August every year) but the town itself remains an essentially nineteenth-century farming center around its green, complete with bandstand and Civil War monument. Its industries are casket manufacturing, seasonal canning, and freezing.

6 **Justin Morgan:** Morgan Horse Farm, Middlebury, Vermont. A small, rough-coated colt left Springfield, Massachusetts, with his owner, schoolmaster Justin Morgan, late in 1789 to find greener pastures in Vermont. During his subsequent career he achieved fame under a number of owners, dragging heavy loads and outrunning other steeds. The Morgan horses descended from him are small (barely over 14 hands high) and weigh little over one thousand pounds, all muscle. Today they are found as showhorses and riding mounts throughout the world but their initial impact on New England was to furnish the ordinary farmer with a reasonably priced horse which he could use both for transport and farmwork. He was also a favorite for the long stage-lines of the nineteenth century. His memory is commemorated and thoroughbred descendants are both bred and trained at this delightful turn-of-the-century farm, maintained by the University of Vermont and open year round. May–Oct., daily: 8–5; Nov.–April, Mon.–Fri.: 8–5. Admission charged. (802) 388-2011.

7 *Carding Mill:* In 1794 plans for the first carding machines were brought to the United States by two brothers, John and Arthur Schofield, who set up a mill on which this one is patterned in Pittsfield, Massachusetts. The machinery is composed of different sized rollers, covered with leather and stuck full of fine wire teeth. The invention eliminated that time-consuming step between washing and spinning flax or wool which housewives had previously been compelled to do by hand at home. By the midcentury this machinery was incorporated into woolen factories. This water-powered mill comes from South Waterford, Maine, the lone survivor of thousands which once dotted the rural landscape.

8 *Grist Mills:* Grist mills were the earliest mills to be found in New England, a fact symbolized by

the Jenney *Grist Mill*, a recreation of that used by the Pilgrims, in the town of *Plymouth*. Its original was built by John Jenney in 1636 and the present model sells the corn which it grinds here by water power. Spring Lane, May–Thanksgiving, daily: 9–6, small admission.

On Cape Cod there are three early grist mills to be seen: At *Brewster* the *Stony Brook Mill* dates back to 1663 and was used until it burned down in 1871 (obviously the present one is a reconstruction). During summer months a miller is usually on hand to grind corn for visitors and there's a small museum on the second floor. The mill is backed up by a delightful millpond (a fine picnicking site) and Stony Brook, which spills on down past its wheel for a number of miles to the shore, is paralleled by a hiking path. Between mid-April and mid-May this is a famous site from which to watch the annual Alewife run, at which time the stream is sometimes choked with fish on their way up to the pond to spawn.

The Cape's best-known grist mill is one established in 1654 on the little pond which forms the centerpiece for the town of Sandwich, Shawme Lake. *Dexter Grist Mill* has been restored (its eighteenth-century and nineteenth-century alterations scaled off) to reveal how a water wheel, drive shaft and gears, all made of wood, actually worked. Corn meal ground here is on sale, along with free recipes (mid-June to mid-Sept., daily: 10–5, admission charged).

Eastham possesses one of the few working *windmills* which were once the norm on both the Cape and the islands. This mill was built where it stands, shipped up to Truro for a stint, moved back in 1793. The old wooden machinery, its massive octagonal shaft, peg wheel and gears are all original and with a good set of sails it works daily, early May to October. (On Route 6, Village Green, corner of Samoset Road.) Other windmills can be seen at *Heritage Plantation* in Sandwich and on *Nantucket* Island.

Near Boston a popular version of a working grist mill can be found producing flour and meal ground daily at the *Wayside Inn*, Rte. 20 in South Sudbury, April–Nov.: 9–6.

A later *Dexter Grist Mill* (1818) is open to the public in Dexter, Maine (now the Dexter Historical Society museum) but more intriguing is the Perkins Grist mill in *Kennebunkport*, Maine, one of the last survivors of an early tidewater mill. Built in 1749 and operated until 1939, its machinery was powered by tides rather than a stream. Most of that machinery survives and the building now houses a restaurant.

Connecticut grist mills can be found in Stonington (off Rte. 95, just up Rte. 216), in New London (under I-95 bridge), and Farmington (off Rte. 10 at firehouse on Mill Lane), Connecticut.

9 *Sawmills:* The Cheney up-and-down sawmill illustrates the way logs were turned into boards before the advent of the circular saw (in the 1840s). Like the grist mill, this was one of the first buildings to be put up in any new town – an essential to any permanent building. The mill itself is simply a long, wooden shed twice the length of the largest log to be sawed here, open on one side and unimpressive unless in operation, hatcheting the logs as they come one-by-one from the millpond and are dropped as lumber into the raceway. Among those which can be seen in action today are the *Taylor* sawmill in state-owned, 85-acre *Ballard State Forest, Derry, New Hampshire*. Here an eight-foot up-and-down saw, driven by a water wheel chops away on given weekends during July and August. Elsewhere in New Hampshire you can visit the *Chase* Mill in East Alstead, New Hampshire (off Rte. 123, near Bellows Falls, Vermont). Here its owner Herman Chase runs weekend shop classes for community children and welcomes visitors who call him in advance. The *Smith River* Company mill in Wolfeboro Falls, New Hampshire, just off Lake Winnipesaukee still produces excelsior (shredded wood for packing breakables) with waterpowered machinery installed in 1885; here a turbine has replaced the old water-wheel and it's a fascinating place to visit. Visitors are usually welcome but you might contact Charles Heard ahead: (603) 569-4228. In *East Vasselboro, Maine*, a water-driven turbine powers a circular saw. The red wooden mill was built in 1797 and is still used commercially, a site to see when the millpond is filled with logs. Check ahead before you come with Herman Masse or his son, Kenneth. (East Vasselboro is northeast of Augusta, next exit off I-95.) (207) 923-3461.

OTHER EARLY MILLS:

Three, not two mills, were built in almost every rural village from the seventeenth through nineteenth centuries. But fulling mills, last in this triad, have simply disappeared from the landscape. Fulling is that process which cleans, felts and shrinks the loose, dirty wool as it comes off the loom. First it was soaked in a vat of water with detergent (frequently animal urine), then pounded, wrung, turned and pounded. The first such mill was set up at Rowley, Massachusetts, in the mid-seventeenth century and by 1810, 1,682 such mills could be found in America. The water-powered Jewell Mill is open to visitors today in Rowley (on Rte. 1A) but is used to polish semi-precious gems sold within it.

10 *Covered Bridges:* An unchronicled number once dotted Vermont, nearly two hundred being destroyed in 1927 alone, but 112 surviving. The state publishes a mapped guide to these (write the Vermont Development Department, Montpelier, Vermont 15692), and protects them both with laws making it extremely difficult to remove one, and money for endangered members of the species. A brochure mapping and describing New Hampshire's 58 covered bridges is available from the New Hampshire Office of Vacation Travel, Concord, New Hampshire 03301. Maine publishes a leaflet guide to the nine remaining out of its nineteenth-century 120 total (write Maine Department of Commerce and Industry, Augusta, Maine 04330), and *Connecticut's Covered Bridges* (all five of them) is available from the Department of Transportation, 24 Wolcott Hill Road, P.O. Drawer A, Wethersfield, Connecticut 01609. In Massachusetts the number has dwindled from one hundred to ten, two of these at OSV and two in the town of Sheffield in the southern Berkshires. An excellent, amply illustrated overview of *Covered Bridges of the Northeast* by Sanders Allen is available from Stephen Greene Press, Brattleboro, Vermont, for $10.

11 *Agricultural Fairs:* As woodlands disappeared, streams dwindled, and soil began to give out, farmers began leaving New England in droves for the West, and agricultural organizations, first locally inspired and supported, later state-backed, attempted to counter this trend. The Massachusetts group ranks among the oldest of these groups, but the practical methods for stirring up local interest through fairs appears to have been pioneered by New York State, and it was a New Yorker who organized the region's first county fair and agricultural society in the Berkshires in 1811. The *Barrington Fair*, held early each September, at least claims to be New England's oldest. But so does the *Topsfield Fair*, which celebrates its 152nd season, the last week in September 1976. The *Eastern States Exposition*, staged mid-September in West Springfield, is the region's biggest and claims to be the only "regional" agricultural fair in the country. Among the most colorful autumn fairs (and no one dares to put a precise number on these annual occurrences in New England) are the *World's Fair* in the picturesque hilltown of *Tunbridge*, Vermont (mid-September), and that in *Bondville*, Vermont, usually the next week. Maine also boasts its World's Fair, held in North Waterford, late September, but the *Oxford County Fair* (early September, Norway) is usually ranked as most colorful. New Hampshire's *Rochester Fair* (mid-September) and Connecticut's *Danbury Fair* (mid-October) are justly famous and *Brooklyn, Connecticut*, is probably the state's oldest.

12 *Hitchcock Chairs:* See Chapter 8.

13 *Churches:* Any attempt to list New England's most beautiful churches is ridiculous. The nineteenth-century meetinghouse in *Bedford*, Massachusetts, possesses a striking facade, conveying the impression that it is four stories tall. The *Church on the Hill* in *Lenox* (1806) is frequently photographed, its handsome Asher Benjamin inspired facade enhanced by the height on which it stands (a nineteenth-century chronicler compares climbing this hill to "that of Zion" since it entails sweating in summer and slipping in winter). The *Old South Church* in *Windsor* was built by Asher Benjamin (not just copied from his *Country Builder's Assistant*) and its pillared entryway, and cupola top are exceptional.

The *Meetinghouse* (begun 1793) in *Canaan, New Hampshire*, represents a less pretentious style of the old rectangular meetinghouse with a narrow entryway tower (cupola on top of it) tacked onto the front. This building stands conveniently near Canaan Street Lake which is said to have served frequently for baptisms and the entire street on which it stands is little changed since its sixty buildings were built in the early nineteenth century. Another New Hampshire landmark is the Congregational Church at *Lyme* (1812) with a spire that's difficult to imagine improving on; it stands at the head of a long town green (the fine little Lyme Inn is just behind).

14 *Animal Pounds:* In the early eighteenth century courts were frequently clogged with suits between the owners and finders of stray animals. The subsequent creation of these chest-high stone corrals never quite solved the problem. Pity the poor poundkeeper (frequently an elected office) whose job it was to chase down any horse, goose or pig reported straying – and then collect the fine from its owner. Among those which survive intact to be seen are pounds in the towns of Leverett, Pembroke, Shirley Center and Westwood, Massachusetts; in Auburn, Gilmanton and Mason, New Hampshire; in Jefferson, Minot, Orrington, Porter, Sedgewick and Waldoboro, Maine; and in Chepachet and Little Compton, Rhode Island. All of these are open to the public; for directions, ask in towns.

15 *Schoolhouses and Academies: Brownington, Vermont* (Vermont's northeast kingdom, exit off I-91 at Orleans, west on 58 to unpaved, marked road, 3 miles). Built of local stone as a grammar school in 1823 when this was a half-shire town with Craftsbury (see Chapter 6) the building has been converted into an exceptional local museum of old implements, furniture, quilts and such. Open daily except Tuesday and Wednesday. It's composed of over thirty rooms, one for each town in Orleans County.

The region's famous academies which are still private prep schools include Deerfield Academy (Old Deerfield, Massachusetts), Governor Dummer at Byfield, Massachusetts, Phillips-Andover at Andover, Phillips-Exeter at Exeter. Others can be found through Maine and New Hampshire plus a few in Connecticut serving now as public schools.

ONE-ROOM SCHOOLHOUSES

The round schoolhouse in Brookline, Vermont (off Rte. 30 just above Newfane), was designed in 1821 by its first schoolmaster, Dr. John "Thunderbolt" Wilson who left town (and his wife) after he was discovered to be a former Scottish highwayman. Today it serves as the town library and meeting place for the local Ladies Benevolent Society (founded 1897) which supports its work by making fancy quilts sold annually at a bazaar and church supper (down the road at the Baptist Church) in July.

The oldest schoolhouse in Maine is an adventure to explore. Located at *Round Pond* within the town of Pemaquid, it's open to the public but at irregular hours. Ask around locally to find who is keeping the key (at present, it's the Yost Family, Valley View Farm) – and bring a flashlight. Built of stone with its benches ranged around the walls and doubling as desks like that in OSV, this is a prisonlike place indeed, one that's not easy to forget. The *Little Boston School* in East Lyme, Connecticut, is a far more cheerful place; it opened in 1734 and continued in use until 1933. This was in fact the first district school between Boston and New York and since local erudition was high it featured navigation, astronomy, Latin and Greek as well as the three R's (adjacent to the Thomas Lee House, see Chapter 3). In the town of Woodstock, not far south of Sturbridge, stands the *Quasset School*, in use from 1748 to 1943, built solidly of handmade bricks and seemingly well-equipped with double desks, book and slates, heated with a box stove. It's still used on various occasions by the adjacent, modern central elementary school and is open to visitors. Other exhibit schools can be found in the museum villages at South Sudbury and Storrowtown (West Springfield), Massachusetts, also at the Shelburne Museum in Vermont. One room, multigraded schools still function in the Vermont towns of Lyndon, East Haven, Kirby, Granby, Belvidere, Ira, Athens, Baltimore and Newark. They can also be found on Maine's offshore islands such as Cliff, Matinicus and Monhegan; also on the Massachusetts island of Cuttyhunk.

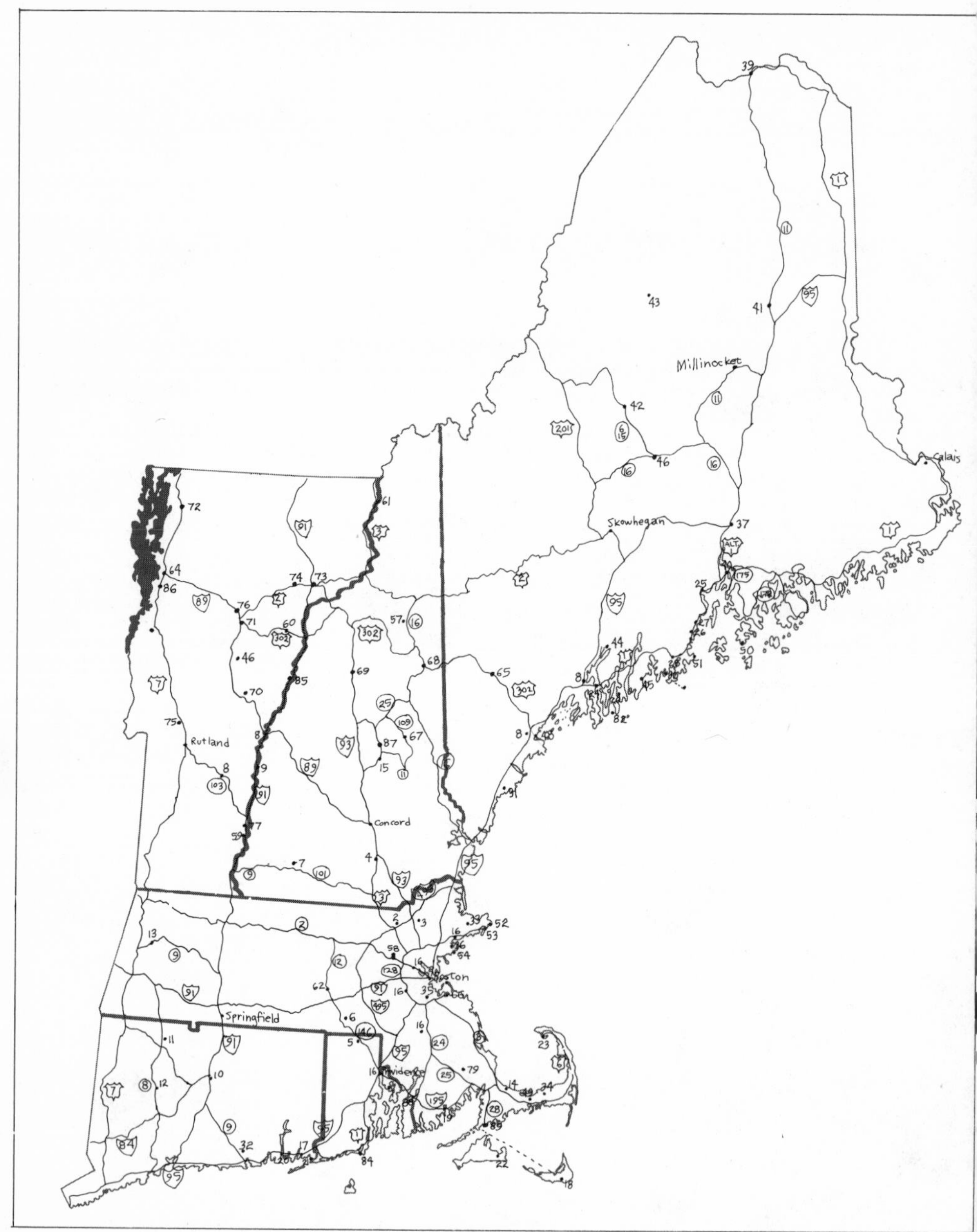

Millinocket
Calais
Skowhegan
Rutland
Concord
Boston
Springfield
Providence

8

Era of Enterprise

"It is an extraordinary era in which we live," Daniel Webster remarked in 1847. Webster was watching the first train roll into Lebanon, New Hampshire, the first rail link between the Connecticut River and the Atlantic. "It is altogether new," he continued. "The world has seen nothing like it before." And this was the feeling in New England throughout that "Anything's Possible" era ushered in by the Christmas Eve 1814 peace treaty which ended the War of 1812. It was a mood which characterized the entire remainder of the century. No longer awed by Europe, Americans eagerly tackled the challenge, first of self-sufficiency, then of world power. Their self-confidence and faith in "progress" knew no bounds.

During the war itself, profits accrued by privateering Yankee seamen were seeded into home industry, to the tune of $49 million. Stimulated by wartime demands, the usual foreign supply sources cut off, factories sprouted in every corner of the region. Fledgling enterprises were protected by postwar tariffs on imports and willingly backed by newly founded banks. Yankees soon became world famous for the new inventions with which they kept revolutionizing the world's traditional ways of getting things done.

New England's maritime interests – its shipbuilding, whaling, world and coastal trade, even its fisheries – revived quickly from the war which had seemingly clipped them in the bud. The region's golden age of sail was followed by a gilded era of steam.

At the dawn of this epoch New England was a patchwork of sleepy, rural communities – divided rather than connected by rutted dirt roads. At its close the region was knit more closely than it is today by a web of steel tracks over which inland products found their way to distant points, and residents of town and country alike journeyed on business and pleasure. While many young Yankees now filtered West, their places were taken by newcomers of widely varied stock. By the turn of the twentieth century New England had begun to assume much the look and atmosphere it bears today.

MILLS

Despite his legendary ingenuity, no Yankee could figure out a way to manufacture in quantity and cheaply that one product which all America needed most: clothing. In England the textile industry had been developed in the last decades of the eighteenth century. While flooding American country stores with the makings of Sabbath-day dress, it guarded the secrets of its factory system.

Slater Mill, Pawtucket, R.I.

Attempts at cotton spinning mills began appearing here in the 1780s, but bugs plagued every process tried. It was Moses Brown, Rhode Island's foremost shipping merchant (see Chapter 6), who arranged for recent English emigrant Samuel Slater to come take a look at his mill in Pawtucket in 1790.

Slater, who had just completed an apprenticeship in a leading British textile mill, rebuilt Brown's spinning and carding machines, then set about managing the mill, maintaining a continuous flow of materials at the pace which machines could process at full speed. Two years later the two-and-a-half-story clapboard building, now
the *Old Slater Mill Museum*, was built, and boys and girls, 1
aged seven to twelve, were operating its machinery; these young "operatives" were drawn from the foremost families in town.

Inside the Old Slater Mill antique machinery, much of it noisily demonstrated, dramatizes not only how the process worked but its relation to another innovation of the 1790s, this one by a Massachusetts-born inventor named Eli Whitney whose cotton gin unleashed a flood of cheap, raw cotton from the South. By 1810 the cotton mills they fed totaled eighty-seven, many of them – like the four-story Wilkinson Mill next door – far larger than the first successful model.

Still cotton thread isn't cotton cloth. Upstairs in the Slater Mill a display depicts the impact of power spinning on home manufacture: more than a decade passed before power looms were invented to meet the surplus of machine-spun threads and yarns. In the Sylvanus Brown house, home of one of Slater's employees, you see not only a loom but also flax and wool spinning wheels – testimony that most families could not even afford this early yarn and thread. Many of the new mills were in fact forced out of business under the deluge of cheap textiles brought with an end to the War of 1812. Over the next few years, however, a series of protective tariffs helped turn the tide.

Factory workers

A young Harvard graduate named Francis Cabot Lowell also helped. Having studied Robert Owen's model mill town in Scotland, Lowell returned home to Waltham, Massachusetts, where he installed a power loom developed by a local mechanic and set it to work as part of the world's first factory to manufacture raw cotton into finished cloth under one roof.

Today *Lowell* is best remembered through the town 2
which bears his name and which he conceived before his untimely death as a worker's utopia in which the company should provide fine but separate housing for its male and female employees, supply them with stores, education, entertainment and even burying lots. Overnight the brick town of Lowell (incorporated 1826) rose on the Merrimack River, attracting hundreds of farmer's daughters with relatively high wages. For a generation the Lowell factory girls, with their neat dresses, proud deportment and literary weekly, were one of the wonders of America – the first which Charles Dickens, arriving in New England, requested to see. This system's well-known excesses came later in the century with an enormous demand for cotton cloth, coupled with water power and available immigrant labor to produce it. The city itself is now attempting to recapture the beauty of its early period in an Urban Park, restoring its earliest working mills and its canals to use by barges and pleasure craft.
The Merrimack Valley Textile Museum in nearby North 3
Andover illustrates how this area's nineteenth-century woolen mills worked.

The "Northern New England Milltown" pattern spawned by Lowell was of course soon adopted by a number of instant cities. In 1793 Samuel Blodgett had begun building a canal around the "hideous waterfall"

in the Merrimack at the little town of Derryfield, New
Hampshire. He was in his eighties when he finished it,
prophesying, "Here at my canal will be a manufacturing
town that shall be the *Manchester* of America." The city 4
which fulfilled this boast began as a town designed entirely on paper, before a single lot was sold. Workers
entered the Amoskeag millyard, its centerpiece, by crossing over bridges and under archways; the yard itself contained its own noise, separated from boardinghouses and
shops by two canals which powered its machinery. One
after another, other large, water-powered mill cities
appeared overnight: Nashua, New Hampshire, Chicopee
and Lawrence, Massachusetts, Biddeford, Saco and
Lewiston, Maine, and Holyoke, Massachusetts.

Be it said that these centers initially drew young people who rarely stayed on. According to one chronicler of the period: "Young men and women who had spent their two or three years of probation . . . often returned to the old places, bought land, built their modest houses, and became new and prosperous heads of families. Some of the mill-girls helped maintain widowed mothers. . . . Many of them educated the younger children in the family and young men were sent to college with the money furnished by the untiring industry of their women relatives."

Southern New England factory villages at first adopted
a different, family-based pattern from those to the north.
Slatersville, Rhode Island, in which Samuel Slater himself 5
eventually located, grew up as a company town around a
green, but instead of boardinghouses, here, as in the nearby landscaped village around the old *Crown and Eagle* 6
Mills in *North Uxbridge*, Massachusetts, the housing is
for families, and company buildings include a school as
well as company store.

Harrisville, New Hampshire, is a delightful mix of both 7
patterns in which the human scale was never lost. This
little community of brick and granite, white-trimmed
buildings clusters around a millpond and along the steep
Goose Creek Ravine below. It includes a small, steepled
library, the church, post office and a mill-owner's mansion, all of brick. Behind are a string of neat wooden
workers' houses known as Peanut Row. Beside a small
bridge sits the old warehouse, now "Harrisville Designs"
and astride the falls is the brick, cupola'd Harris Mill
(1830); its former boiler house is a toy shop and the
granite "Cheshire Mill" (1846) now produces water

coolers and filters. There's also a woolen shop in the "Picking House," boutiques in the "Boarding House" and a pottery studio in the former school. What excites historians about this type of community is the uncanny way in which it echoes the shape of New England's earliest villages. But here life revolves around the mills instead of a meetinghouse, the mill-owner's mansion supplants the parsonage, and the mill and its waterway, the common.

Harrisville, Vt., General Store

Although *few early factory villages* survive in as com- 8
plete and pleasing shape as Harrisville, many early mill
buildings remain genuinely interesting places to visit.
Windsor, Vermont, for instance, calls itself "cradle of the
American tool industry" and the *American Precision* 9
Museum, housed in an 1846 brick, three-story mill building, tells a couple of interesting stories: how Asahel Hubbard perfected the rotary pump while serving as warden
at the state prison in town (still here and looking much
as it did when built in 1839) and used convict labor to
produce the pumps for his "National Hydraulic Company." Later Hubbard manufactured the Kendall Rifle,
a famous sporting gun of the day here at the mill, which
doubled as a machine shop and armory. Christian Sharp,
a mechanic in the firm, invented the breech-loading rifle
which bears his name, later produced in *Hartford* where 10
models are now exhibited.

Connecticut's own most-popular-to-visit mill occupies
the center of a four-corners full of homes, a church, a
general store and post office – all that's left of *Hitch-* 11
cocks-ville at Riverton. In 1818 when Lambert Hitchcock
chose this spot to begin mass-producing chairs, it was the
state's least peopled corner. Hitchcock had observed
how *Connecticut watch shops* turned out quantities of 12
wooden parts during the previous decade and thought
the time ripe for applying machinery to furniture-making. He began by producing just chair parts, carting them to Hartford from whence they were shipped south to be assembled for Philadelphia and Baltimore markets. This worked so well that in 1826 he built this three-story factory with a cupola and weathervane on top, employing over a hundred women, men and children to produce the finished chairs: men did the woodworking, children rubbed on a priming coat of red paint and women did the ornamentation, rubbing varicolored powders through stencils over the finished paint job. These hand-signed chairs are prized antiques today, but Hitchcock him-

self eventually ended up bankrupt, and the factory ended up producing rulers. Presently restored and enlarged, the old mill is now a showroom and outlet for Hitchcock reproductions and the Old Union Church down the street is open year round as a museum, displaying Hitchcock and other eighteenth- and nineteenth-century American furniture.

While textile mills dominated New England's early industrial scene, paper mills soon began coming in a close
second. Far from representative but also far more
interesting than the common species that evolved is the
handsome little stone building which serves *Crane and* 13
Company Paper as its museum in the northern Berkshires
town of Dalton. Founded by twenty-two-year-old Zenas
Crane in 1801, this company, still controlled by Zenas's
descendants, continues to make paper from rags (cotton
and linen fibers) and rags alone; since 1846 it has also
been the sole paper supplier for U.S. currency.

Perhaps the best remembered nineteenth-century Massachusetts factory is that of the Boston & Sandwich Glass
company. In 1825 the company was founded in Sandwich, not because of its sand (imported from the Berkshires of all places) but because local scrub forests
provided the fuel for its furnaces. Its most common product was pressed table glassware, the first which working
families could afford. It's best known for the blown glass
vases, the spiral-ribbed bottles and other ornate shapes in
kaleidoscopic colors which now fill a half dozen rooms
of the *Sandwich Glass Museum*. At its height in the 14
1850s–70s the factory employed more than five hundred
artisans, produced 100,000 pounds of glass per week.
Today the sole memorial to the huge brick plant itself is
a plaque on its site.

"Mill" and "mill town" are terms which still conjure
ugly memories for residents of many a New England city
where, later in the century, the size and demands of factories spawned makeshift, drab housing for employees
who worked long hours for low pay. In *Laconia, New* 15
Hampshire, the proposal to preserve the Buseil Company
Mill (1859) as a city hall was defeated for this reason.
Luckily the handsome building (predating the city's
dreary industrial period) was recycled as an office
building and the neighboring Belknap Sulloway Mill
(1823), acclaimed as the oldest brick textile mill in the
country, is under restoration as a combined museum, art

gallery and community center. The two mills are now set in park-like landscaping from which a walkway leads along the Winnipesaukee River.

Mill, Vermont

Long the ugly ducklings of the New England landscape, mill buildings have now begun to be recognized for their place in history and architecture, as typical of this region as steepled churches. Many an industrial city and village is now cited as the forerunner of the planned community. This new respect, coupled with rising construction costs, has turned many a nineteenth-century factory into 16
a new apartment complex, artists' workspace, and office complex. Smaller mills have been transformed into restaurants and community centers. Those major factories which have endured frequently include "factory stores," a phenomenon appreciated by thrifty Yankee families of the present era.

AGE OF SAIL

Mystic Seaport 17

Yards near the site of the present museum village began turning out small vessels in the seventeenth century and continued to produce sailing ships, including whalers and clippers, until the Civil War when it switched to manufacturing steamship machinery, finally specializing in small sailing yachts. The museum today is a vivid index to the entire range of New England's nineteenth-century sea ventures. On its forty acres stands a recreated shipbuilding village, complete with working boatyard, rope walk, chandlery, sail loft and one token tavern. Its sixty buildings include displays chronicling the story of whaling, the China, Atlantic and coastal trades, the local fisheries, and strides made during this period to make navigation a less chancy business. Its 170 ships and boats complete the picture.

Mystic Seaport, Mystic, Conn.

The *Charles W. Morgan*, last surviving wooden whaleship in the world, is the pride of Mystic Seaport. Built at New Bedford in 1841 and a veteran of thirty-seven voyages, the *Charles Morgan* netted more than $1 million for her owners before retirement in 1921. A full-rigged, bluff-bowed ship of 351 tons, she is open to visitors to poke around among her tools, tryworks and uninvitingly cramped and Spartan fo'c'sl. A short film shown daily on the premises depicts the ship's last voyage around Cape Horn. The museum also exhibits a fully rigged,

Double-topsail bark, the Charles W. Morgan

equipped, whaleboat, whale ship models, scrimshaw, harpoons, a bottle of whale oil, preserved whale lice and even a whale kidney stone.

New England Whaling

American whaling was almost exclusively a southeastern New England enterprise during its nineteenth-century heyday. Rarely in history has such a large, colorful fleet fanned out over so much of the world from home ports so close together.

Whaling is, in fact, both an ancient European and American Indian industry. Early seventeenth-century settlers on Cape Cod and Long Island towed in any whales found stranded in shallow water and removed their blubber on the beaches. Oil was extracted by cooking the blubber in large cast iron kettles called try pots. But within a very few decades this ready supply of convenient, liquid gold began disappearing.

Nantucket. The island of Nantucket, itself moored 18
like a mother ship thirty miles offshore, pioneered American whaling "on the deep." By the turn of the eighteenth century, its forty- to sixty-ton vessels were following migrating whales from the Guinea and Brazil coast in spring, as far north as Greenland come summer. The blubber they took was stored in casks and brought home to be "tried out." Nantucket whalers were also the first to specialize almost exclusively in capturing "sperm whales" valued for the spermaceti in its head which supplanted tallow in the making of candles, being far harder, yielding a stronger, less smoky light. In New England this valuable take was divided among ten manufacturers who set up a monopoly controlling its distribution.

In 1723 the first of Nantucket Town's five wharves had been built, a new focal point for the island, which frugally shifted its homes to the harborside. By 1730 the island was shipping oil directly to London, bypassing Boston middlemen. Nantucket ships were also gaining a reputation for being uncommonly well fitted and conscientiously manned. The vessels were, so to speak, caulked tightly by the island's predominant Quaker religion. Even those islanders not connected through marriage called and saw each other as "brothers" and "sisters." Each expedition was thus a communal venture: riggers, coopers, deck hands and captains all shared a pride in the voyage's success – and a piece of the proceeds.

A handsome brick building at the head of Straight

Wharf was built by Quaker merchant William Rotch as a countinghouse and warehouse in 1772. From here Rotch dispatched his ships *Dartmouth*, *Eleanor* and *Beaver* with oil bound for London and orders to bring back tea to Boston (where it formed the makings of that famous Tea Party). In 1783 the ship *Bedford* cleared from a customs house here (America's first), the first ship to flaunt America's colors on the Thames; London bought its oil.

During the Revolution this Quaker island remained neutral, a policy which destroyed 85 percent of its tonnage and caused one-third of its people to migrate. After a brief but spectacular comeback, the War of 1812 reduced its 116 vessels to 23. But again recovery was quick, followed by two decades during which Nantucket's whaling era reached its peak. The Pacific National Bank, still doing business at the head of Market Square, opened in 1818 and soon was one of five in business. Farther up Main Street, whaling merchant Joseph Starbuck built his three identical, tower-topped brick mansions, known locally as the "three bricks" (two of which are still owned by Starbuck descendants).

Both the island and whaling itself changed in these decades. Back in 1791 a Nantucket whaler had been the first to round Cape Horn, opening up the South Seas to the hunt. Whaling voyages averaged three years, and the ship became a factory alongside of which the leviathan, once caught, was reduced to the contents of barrels. The crew represented the range of specialties described in *Moby Dick* (set on a Nantucket boat in 1841). The island itself had become a boom town, its air filled with the scent of exotic spices and rich, malodorous whale oil. Nantucket's 9,700 residents (not counting the influx of seamen) were also a heady mix.

It is this era which Nantucket's Whaling Museum depicts. Upstairs in the grand hall of what was once an 1840s candle works, "nautical talks" describe how the whaling gear on hand was used. The exhibit whaleboat, a veteran of several voyages, was one of five attached to every mother ship. "Thar she blows" was the signal for lowering the boat with its crew of six who rowed furiously out after the prize, which measured twice the length of the boat itself.

The trick was to harpoon the leviathan, then keep a grip via a 1,300-foot rope while the whale sounded, diving deep – or plunged wildly off on its death run, an endurance contest between man and beast which became known the world over as a "Nantucket sleigh ride." Once exhausted, the whale permitted his killers to approach. They finished off the job by thrusting a lance into the prime artery just beneath his ear. Museum visitors are also told the intricacies of cutting up and boiling down that followed, using the tools and tryworks on display. The factory's original press reveals how the oil was eventually squeezed out, the residue molded into candles.

The museum is chock-a-block full of clues to life aboard such whaleships. Rows of dour-looking captains with names like Folger, Swain, Hussey and Coffin peer down from gilt frames. The effect is softened by baby clothes worn by the children born aboard and the souvenirs like sea fans, tapa cloth, war clubs, even a model of a New Zealand war canoe, picked up in the South Pacific.

It also includes one of the world's best collections of scrimshaw, an artform which Herman Melville defines as "the numerous little ingenious contrivances [seamen] elaborately carve out of the rough material [whale teeth or bone] in their hours of ocean leisure. Some of them have little boxes of dentistical-looking implements, specially intended for the skrimshandering business. But, in general, they toil with their jackknives alone." Although the display here includes dozens of ivory-headed canes, most scrimshaw is in the shape of sewing tools, pie crimpers and corset stays – obviously meant for wives or sweethearts, since they were never sold. From the constantly recurring female figures in the etchings (most of them taken from *Godey's Lady's Book*), it is easy to gauge sailors' thoughts during the idle sea hours they used to carve – and to visualize what happened when they put into friendly ports like Lahaina in the Hawaiian Islands after two years at sea. The results were a constant embarrassment to New England missionaries, the first boatload of whom arrived there in 1820.

The museum also displays a model of the "camels," floating drydocks employed from 1842 to 1859 when whaling vessels grew too large to cross the harbor's sandbar – a nuisance since the ships themselves had to be emptied beforehand. That sandbar by the 1840s had destroyed Nantucket's claim to lead the world as a whaling port.

Mansions like Hawden House continued to be built and when fire destroyed more than thirty-six buildings in Nantucket Town's core, the handsome store blocks now framing the square were built. Also white-columned public buildings like the Atheneum and Methodist Church. But within just a few years, islanders were flocking by the hundreds to California; one member of Nantucket's pioneer Macy family opened a store in New York on his gold rush proceeds. Oil, discovered in Titusville, Pennsylvania, in 1857 discouraged a comeback and the Civil War precluded it.

Luckily this fourteen-mile long, tipsy-shaped horseshoe of sand, moor and flowers was unsuited to any subsequent industry heavier than tourism. So it has survived – with more than six hundred homes still preserved, a shade tidier-looking and more self-conscious, but otherwise true in their appearance to the whaling era. As early as the 1870s these homes began taking in summer visitors. A three-story brick mansion built in 1830 by whaling merchant Jethro Coffin was converted into a hotel by the Nantucket Steamboat Company for its patrons (one of a half-dozen mansions to meet a similar fate but the only surviving example) and many a less elaborate dwelling, like the ropemaker's 1805 home which is now India House, do a whale of a tourist trade.

Pacific Club, Nantucket

A green fountain bubbles geraniums next to the old Rotch warehouse, known as the "Pacific Club" since the 1860s when veterans of the South Seas bought it as a clubhouse. Aptly it now also houses the island's chamber of commerce.

New Bedford. As early as 1820 New England's whal- 19
ing center had begun shifting from Nantucket to the Buzzards Bay port of New Bedford. While in 1846 some seven hundred whaling vessels sailed from two dozen southern New England ports, many of these retired the very next year. New Bedford's own fleet continued to grow, reaching its peak in 1857 with 329 whaleships; 95 more sailed from the nearby towns of Westport, Dartmouth, Fairhaven, Mattapoisett and Marion.

Unfortunately the New Bedford of whaling days has been all but erased – first by a heavy nineteenth-century load of cotton mills and most recently by urban renewal. Still the Whaling Museum stands across from the Seaman's Bethel on Johnny Cake Hill and the two together tell a vivid story.

The museum's centerpiece is an eighty-nine-foot replica of the square-rigged whaler *Lagoda*, but its real treasure is a set of huge canvases painted by seaman-artist Charles Raleigh during his 1870s "whaling cruise of the ship Niger." There is also an outstanding scrimshaw collection here which includes the log of the New Bedford ship *Timoleon*, carved on whalebone. (This voyage, you read, began Christmas Day 1831 and after rounding Cape Horn made its way up the coast of California and thence on to Japan, with two stops in the Sandwich Islands, returning July 3, 1835, with 1,589 barrels of sperm oil, netting $42,475.)

A display of paintings by artist William Bradford is by contrast devoted to Arctic whaling scenes. New Bedford's fleet managed to weather both the discovery of petroleum and the Civil War because it served a new fashion craze for tight-waisted dresses of the 1870s and 1880s. The whalebone known as "baleen" was used chiefly to make corset stays, was also turned into umbrella ribs, fishing rods, horse whips, carriage springs, women's hat frames, trunk frames and furniture stuffing. The best baleen (long, hornlike strips) grows in the mouths of bowhead whales, Arctic water creatures. With the completion of the transcontinental railroad in 1869, bone and oil could be shipped back to eastern markets overland and many a New Bedford whaleship shifted its homeport to San Francisco.

Scrimshaw on whale tooth

More Whaling Towns. Other whaling era collections can be found in the ports which ranked next after Nantucket and New Bedford in the 1840s. In New London,
the *Shaw Mansion* contains a small but fine collection of 20
harpoons, scrimshaw and flags of local whaling families,
and in *Stonington*, one in a row of whaling captain man- 21
sions houses like souvenirs. On *Martha's Vineyard* the 22
town of Edgartown grew, like Nantucket Town, around the needs of whalemen. Narrow side streets between North and South Water Streets formed a service center of chandlers, sail lofts, boardinghouses and boatbuilding shops which still survive. Townspeople proudly point out the home of Captain Valentine Pease under whom Melville shipped aboard the *Acushnet*, but claim he was more benign than Captain Ahab. The Dukes County Historical Society here also contains whaling memorabilia.
Provincetown is another resort town which once served 23
as a major whaling port in the era when seventy-five wharfs were built along Commercial Street. Rotting remnants of these can still be seen, along with whaling displays in the town's museum. And the "P-Town" fishing fleet is manned by descendants of Azorean and Cape Verdes whalemen, recruited aboard Provincetown ships.

Maine's active part in American whaling was small, but it was at Bath that most of the Arctic steam whalers were built. These vessels made whaling pay well after the turn of this century. But Arctic whaling was a chancy business. Arriving early in spring, whaleships made themselves fast to ice floes and drifted northward as the ice pack broke, ultimately rounding Point Barrow, Alaska, where they spent the summer in open channels. Their return trip was fraught with danger: in 1871, 32 ships were crushed by ice; the last steam whaler ended its days this way off Siberia in 1919.

SHIPBUILDING

Lumbermen's Museum, Patten, Me.

24

Whaling was but one among a variety of New England's nineteenth-century maritime enterprises – which created a corresponding demand for ships. Merchants requiring a sleek, specialized vessel – such as a packet ship to be used on the Atlantic run after the War of 1812 – could get it by paying the high price demanded by New York's East River yards. But a sturdy cargo carrier, such as those for the cotton trade, could be bought far more cheaply along Maine's Kennebec and middle coast.

Bath. The *Bath Marine Museum* chronicles Maine's shipbuilding decades superbly. The museum focuses on the decades beginning with 1862 when 80% of this country's full-rigged ships were built in Maine, almost half of those at the sixteen shipyards in Bath. The city's handsome granite and brick commercial buildings and its mansions along Washington Street all date from this era when "shipbuilding" and "Maine" were synonymous.

What is ironic is that by the mid-nineteenth century most shipbuilding timber had to be imported from Georgia and South Carolina since the "Pine State's" supply had about all been exported. Why the industry itself did not budge is explained through displays in the basement of a mid-nineteenth-century church, now the museum's "Winter Street Center."

These take you back to the seventeenth century when an England dependent on shipping for her world status decided that it was cheaper to export shipwrights to the colonies than to import the lumber and pay going wages in her own yards. The Long Reach of the Kennebec was a sensible place for these men to locate: the sloping banks are precisely the right gradient for laying keels, and the thirty-foot-deep channel offshore makes for safe and smooth launching, also access to the Atlantic, fifteen miles downriver.

Early attempts to take advantage of this seemingly ideal setup were snuffed out repeatedly by Indian raids through the eighteenth century. But by the time local lumber began to give out, this city-full of skilled craftsmen – who stubbornly refused to budge – had produced enough freighters, not to mention the glorious clipper ships of the 1840s, to command that the timber be brought to them.

A collection of models in the Winter Street Center depicts the array of vessles which followed: the downeasters (a compromise between the swift but small-capacity clipper ship and the old-style freighter) which plied the globe through the 1870s to 1890s, the big, multimasted schooners designed to ferry coal and local exports like ice, granite and lime for three decades thereafter. Here you also find relics of shipboard life during that entire era when whole families were as likely to be found in Shanghai, Hawaii or South America as at home on Washington Street.

Farther down the street the museum also maintains the Percy and Small Shipyard, the country's last in which large wooden sailing vessels were constructed. An 1840s Greek revival mansion built by the shipbuilding Sewall family serves as museum headquarters. The family firm built the bulk of the world's four-masted barks: steel-hulled but sail-powered vessels which ferried grain from California, Oregon and Washington to Europe during the late nineteenth century; these trampers also carried kerosine to China and iguano (seagull droppings) from Chile.

Searsport. Men of Searsport did not just build ships. 25
They built them to sail themselves. By 1845 the little town had constructed ninety-nine vessels, including a full-rigged clipper. In all, seventeen shipyards here produced two hundred sailing ships during the nineteenth century. Today its oakum shops, sail lofts and chandleries are all vanished, but an unusual *Penobscot Marine Museum* has appropriated the town's old center, a town hall, Congregational Church and the surrounding cluster of sea captain homes – all of which now house memorabilia from the farflung wanderings of Searsport's residents during this era.

Other Shipbuilding Towns and Sites. Searsport was

one of two dozen shipbuilding towns on Penobscot Bay
during the mid-nineteenth century (at which juncture
Bangor still reigned as queen of lumber ports). Most of
these are now small, private places today, but *Camden,* 26
perhaps the loveliest of all, extends an unusual invitation
to outsiders. Besides sharing its salty atmosphere through
numerous inns, it is home port for a fleet of eight wind-
jammers, most of them two-masted schooners which
offer week-long sails along the Maine coast in summer.
This is a fitting base for the country's largest group of
working schooners since Camden yards built their first
schooner in 1796 and later set a record by producing the
George W. Wells, first six-master in the world.

In Maine other former shipbuilding towns include *Bel-* 27
fast, *Thomaston*, *East Boothbay* (which remains a busy 28, 29
center for building small sailing craft) and *Friendship*, 30
famous for the sloops which have borne its name since
1753. Fine homes and public buildings in both *Kenne-* 31
bunk and *Kennebunkport* evidence a wealth to be had
from some of the state's earliest shipyards.

Like "the Kennebunks," *Essex, Connecticut*, is a town 32
which has sown its profits from shipbuilding back into
its handsome streets, insuring their appeal to visitors.
And like *Essex, Massachusetts,* it continues to service 33
tourists along with small craft. The latter town began
constructing vessels in the mid-seventeenth century and
it supplied Gloucester with its famous schooners in the
nineteenth century.

Clipper Ships. "Clipper Ship" is a much overworked term. Purists apply it to fewer than one hundred vessels that completed the New York to San Francisco run in 110 days or less (or got somewhere else with comparable speed) during the decade between the mid 1840s and 1850s. Topheavy with sail, which also consumed a third of their cargo space, these beautiful vessels began appearing when the opening of Chinese Treaty ports put a premium on the speed with which tea cargoes could be brought from Canton and Shanghai. Subsequently they helped the '49ers get around Cape Horn to San Francisco – a brand new city in which items fetched ten times their usual price. Although a few clippers paid for themselves within a few years, many were built too late to capture the profits of the pioneer models (some were saved by the Australia Gold Rush in 1851) and ended their days as hotels, beached at San Francisco, or in the unglamorous guano trade from Chile.

Boston and New York led the country in constructing
clippers; the rivalry was actually between Scotsman
Donald McKay (to whose memory a memorial stands at
Castle Island in South Boston) and William Webb of New
York. In the town of Dennis on Cape Cod, a plaque also
marks the spot of the once famous *Shiverick Shipyard* 34
where eight clippers in all were built.

China Trade

A very small group of New England aristocrats held sway over the most exotic of the period's shipping concerns, and the most vivid display of *China Trade* mementos is aptly housed in a mansion built on the proceeds by Robert Bennet Forbes, a scion of that famous Boston Brahmin clan.

As we have seen (Chapter 6), the China Trade had its
beginning in the 1790s, at which time one of Boston's
foremost merchants, Thomas H. Perkins, founded the
house of Perkins & Co. in China, the second largest foreign firm there until 1824 when it merged with Russel &
Co. and became number one. Perkins took his nephew
R. B. Forbes into the business, first sending him to sea
aged thirteen, subsequently making him captain of an
opium storeship at nineteen. Opium, picked up in Turkey, had by the 1830s solved the problem of what we
could exchange with the Chinese for their porcelain, silk
and tea. (Forbes and his colleagues rationalized its effects
away as less destructive than liquor.) The *Museum of the* 35
American China Trade (Milton, Massachusetts) exhibits
other trade items picked up en route: ginger, cinnamon,
camphor, and dried sea horses (an opium sample is simu-
lated). Fine brush paintings, the postcards of the day,
portray the "hongs," thirteen factories maintained by
the "fan-qui" (foreign devils) outside the walls of Canton. Presiding over a room full of Chinese imports from
the period is a portrait of Houqua, the wispy bearded
merchant through whom Forbes and most American
merchants dealt in Canton. (Houqua was said to be the
world's richest man; his fortune in 1830 was valued at
$26 million.)

While opium was technically outlawed during the Opium War (1839–44), the traffic continued surreptitiously. With the advent of peace, China's export tea center shifted from Canton to Koochow and Shanghai – ushering in still a greater era of trade for which the first clipper ships were built to take maximum advantage. Although the museum's displays chronicle this story only through clipper ship days, trade extended well into the twentieth century.

Salem

While *Salem* never recaptured its prewar glory (see 36
Chapter 6) its vessels still did a respectable amount of
prowling to the far corners of the globe during the revival that followed. The city seemed to specialize in
opening new markets – just as it had been the first in
the 1790s to pioneer a route to the Pacific around Cape
Horn, now it traded unbleached Massachusetts sheeting
(produced by its Naumkeag Steam Cotton Co.) with
Zanzibar and Guinea for gold dust, palm oil and peanuts:
between 1832 and 1864 more than five hundred vessels
from Africa cleared the city's customs house. In the *Essex* 36a
Institute, across the street from the Peabody Museum, display cases in the grand old balconied hall contain intriguing testimonies to this era. One, for instance, is devoted to Frederick Townsend Ward, born 1831 in Salem, who went to sea aged fifteen and after serving with the French army in the Crimean War, led a group of Western volunteers during the "Tai-Ping Rebellion" for which he was awarded the rank of General in the Mandarin Chinese Army. Ward married the daughter of a wealthy Chinese merchant, but was killed in battle, aged thirty. There is a picture here of the shrine which the Emperor ordered built for him, along with the actual bullet that killed him, his shoes and his hat.

Still, by 1845, when Nathaniel Hawthorne was appointed surveyor of Salem's port, he describes the once-bustling wharf as "burdened with decayed wooden warehouses" and the Custom House itself "cobwebbed, and dingy with old paint; its floor strewn with gray sand, in a fashion that has elsewhere fallen into long disuse."

Atlantic and Coastal Trade

New York now upstaged Boston as prime trading center for both the Atlantic packet and cotton trade. Boston attempted to compete, but Cape Cod kept getting in the way (the Cunard Line's inauguration of a Liverpool-Halifax-Boston route in 1840 was cause for city-wide celebration). Still, much of New York's foreign commerce was controlled by Yankee merchants, and ships continued to be manned by Yankee sailors. While New York accounted for 60% of the nation's imports in

1860, 46% of America's tonnage was "owned" (registered) in New England. New England's cotton now replaced cod as a trade staple with the Mediterranean; it was also the basis of exchange for hides and raw wool from South America. (Thus Lowell's textiles helped pay for the raw material for shoe factories in Lynn and Haverhill and the woolen mills in Lawrence.) The region's rum remained all-important in trade with the Caribbean (where Cuba and Puerto Rico had now replaced the French and British sugar islands as sugar and molasses sources). In 1860 alone this region distilled more than four million gallons, despite the current onset of the temperance movement.

Lumber

Cuba and the West Indies were also the prime customers for the billions of feet of lumber shipped from
the city of *Bangor*. Rum was consumed here by the 37
thousands of loggers who downed it by the dipperful (3 cents a dipper). Henry Thoreau described this unique port in 1846: "There stands the city of Bangor like a star on the edge of the night, still hewing at the forest of which it is built, already overflowing with the luxuries and refinements of Europe and sending its vessels to Spain, to England, and to the West Indies for its groceries – and yet only a few ax-men have gone up-river into the howling wilderness that feeds it."

Although Bangor had been chartered in 1791, its backyard sea of white pine aroused little interest at the time. But as lumber vanished from the coast, big city merchants began taking a look at the upper reaches of the Penobscot and Kennebec. It is no coincidence that 1820 – the year cited as dawn for New England's golden era of lumbering – also marks that in which the District of Maine became a state, planting its white pine in the center of its new official seal. Massachusetts, however, did not let go gracefully. With her coffers at their usual low, she stipulated that an even division of all previous undeeded wilderness be part of the agreement. The remaining woodlands were quickly sold off at a few cents per acre, bought by groups in order to cut losses from what were still deemed high-risk investments.

So the "Unorganized Townships" or "*Maine State* 38
Forest District" was born and persists to this day. A glance at the state's official highway maps reveals no public roads through the 6½ million acres bordered on

the north and west by Canada. In fact, this area is webbed with almost 5,000 miles of lumber roads. The green, mountain- and water-spotted carpet over most of Maine's interior is still privately owned – in small part by descendants of the original purchasers (one vast tract by descendants of Salem merchant David Pingree, who bought it in 1820).

By 1835, land brokers' offices shouldered the saloons and houses dedicated to taking in "gentlemen's washing" along Exchange Street in Bangor. Timberland that had gone for six to twelve cents an acre just a few years before now sold for the equivalent in dollars. That year a Baltimore paper reported that two paupers had escaped from Bangor's almshouse and by the time they were caught the next morning, had cleared $1,000 apiece by speculating in timberland (the land offices worked around the clock). Unfortunately most of old rip-roaring Bangor has since disappeared: what a 1911 fire did not get has been eaten by urban renewal. Only a few mansions built by lumber barons, a 31-foot high statue to Paul Bunyan, and a Penobscot Heritage Museum of Living History in city hall perpetuate the story of the days when a man could walk across the harbor via vessels, of the thousands of men who spent quickly here what they had earned, treading logs down the swollen northern rivers.

The speculation boom burst quickly but as loggers
kept hacking away to the north, the question of precisely where the new state ended and New Brunswick began became a hot question. The resulting hullabaloo in
the Maine legislature was heard in Washington, but to
little effect. In 1839 the state loaded brass cannon onto
oxcarts and scows and sent militia to man Forts *Kent* 39
and Fairfield up near the border. A treaty with Britain
was worked out (Daniel Webster representing Maine
lumbermen) in 1842 ending this "Aroostook War," but
the state remained uneasy, constructing formidable *Fort* 40
Knox near the mouth of the Penobscot a couple of years
later, just in case.

Lumbering continued to boom through another couple of decades, cresting in the 1850s, dying by 1880. In the process came new discoveries: the "peavy" invented by Stillwater blacksmith Joseph Peavy in 1858 turned the traditional heavy old pick used to untangle floating logs into a flexible light tool, and the intricacies of the river drive – from boom to beans – were worked out through practice. The entire story of early lumbering is told today

Sewall Mansion (Bath Marine Museum), Bath, Me.

in the *Lumberman's Museum*, way up in Patten, Maine. 41
While "lumbering" itself has long since been replaced by
the pulp and paper industry, towns like *Greenville* on 42
Moosehead Lake (which itself has made the shift) remain
intriguing woodsman's frontiers, while not far away sits
Chesuncook Village, still a wilderness outpost built by 43
and for loggers. Here a recently erected totem pole is dedicated to that breed – fashioned from old logging tools and pieces of Exchange Street taverns and brothels. It's capped with a beanpot.

Ice

New England's last major export of the period strikes us as unlikely today as it did Frederick Tudor's contemporaries. "The ice trade," this enterprising Bostonian later explained, "which I originated in 1805 by the shipment of a single cargo of 130 tons, in a brig belonging to myself, to the island of Martinique, excited the derision of the whole town as a mad project; but the ability of transporting it successfully had been fully calculated. The first cargo arrived in perfect condition."

Tudor had conceived the idea of sending ice south when he heard of a disastrous yellow fever epidemic in the West Indies the previous summer. Ice would have helped, he reasoned. That first boatload was hard to sell, but gradually the idea caught on, and after the War of 1812 Tudor secured a monopoly of the trade in Jamaica, from thence moving on to Cuba and South America. In 1833 he sent off 180 tons to Calcutta, two-thirds of it arriving unmelted and eagerly consumed by the British in residence. Trade with India had in fact all but died with the advent of American cotton; it was now revived, giving Boston the corner on gunny sack, indigo and linseed imports. The ice trade itself expanded to virtually every New England village with access to tidewater, prompting Thoreau, while watching the ice-harvest at Walden Pond, to observe that "the sweltering inhabitants of Charlestown and New Orleans, of Madras and Bombay and Calcutta, drink at my well." Later in the century the trade became dominated by large companies, with their own fleets of vessels and vast ice house complexes along
the Kennebec and Penobscot Rivers; a scale model of
one of these has been constructed at the *Pownalborough* 44
Courthouse, while a genuine survivor still stands in *Bris-* 45
tol, Maine, and a couple of towns stage annual *ice* 46
harvesting festivals.

Unfortunately Boston's own Atlantic Avenue and East
Boston wharves leave much to the imagination today,
but a film titled *Boston and the Sea*, shown at the city's 47
aquarium, reconstructs the story of this port in the century ending with the Civil War. In *Portland*, the Old Port 48
Exchange neighborhood offers a vivid idea of maritime
wealth accrued during the mid- to late-nineteenth century.

The protective law of 1817 (still in effect) barred foreign carriers from United States coastal traffic. Tonnage and traffic between Eastern ports exceeded that from all foreign enterprise combined. Besides carrying cargo, these vessels were also the most popular transportation of the day, preferable to the rutted overland routes.

On Cape Cod every village harbored two or three packet boats which competed in ferrying "mail and people"
between coastal towns and cities. The *Donald G. Trayser* 49
Memorial Museum, a brick customs house (one of thirty-
one in New England at the time) built in Barnstable Village, 1856, commemorates this business and its role as a
schooling ground for Cape captains who went on to skipper a lion's share of the nation's foreign-bound vessels.

"Downeasters" and multimasted schooners were the
workhorses of the coast, sturdy and inexpensive to operate. Their cargoes were far from glamorous. Thomaston, Maine, for instance exported lime, a tricky cargo
since if wetted it burst immediately into flames. Granite,
quarried at *Stonington* and *Vinalhaven*, Maine, also 50, 51
Rockport, Massachusetts, sailed forth in gigantic blocks, 52
the makings of bridges, breakwaters and the public buildings in the Greek revival vogue.

Fisheries

New England's oldest maritime activity also reached new heights during this era. Yankees netted 80% of the country's cod, herring and mackerel. Profits from this small-fry catch equaled those from whaling, and the dangers, though far less celebrated, were also equal.

In the first part of the century Cape Cod yielded its
old prominence in the field to the Maine coast, and *Glou-* 53
cester superseded *Marblehead* (which shifted to shoe- 54
making) as New England's first fishing port. It remains a
work-a-day fishing city with a fleet of more than 110
vessels, and the industry itself remains only slightly less
chancy than a century ago when Rudyard Kipling commemorated the hazards of the Georges Banks in *Captains*

Courageous. It's no wonder that Gloucester's Portuguese and Italian skippers are a religious lot. The Saint Peter's Day Fiesta, held the weekend closest to June 29 of each year, is a colorful four-day affair of dances, fireworks and band concerts, climaxed by a Pontifical Mass and blessing of the fleet. This fleet itself is composed of small vessels, more than one hundred of them under five tons, colorful modern replacements for the famous old "Gloucester Fishermen," the schooners of the previous century on which the city's fame was built. One surviving model, the schooner *Dunton*, can be seen at Mystic Village, where a Fisheries Exhibit also acquaints non-salts with the history and present importance of this industry to the region.

Navigational Aids

Plymouth Gurnet Light, Plymouth, Mass.

Efforts to mitigate the perils of New England's shoals and tricky harbor channels began in the eighteenth century with construction of a few lighthouses: rickety wooden affairs in which whale-oil lamps were kept burning through the night by men who frequently also worked as harbor masters or fishermen. North America's first lighthouse was built on Little Brewster Island in Boston Harbor in 1716, replaced by the present stone tower in 1784. Nantucket built its first, Brant Point light, in 1746. Both Gurnett light off Plymouth and New London light predate the Revolution; the present Portland light was completed in 1790. Of more than 150 manned *light-* 55
houses maintained by the U.S. Coast Guard today, 83 are in New England, a number of them easily accessible and open to visitors.

Eastern Point Light House, Gloucester, Mass.

In 1797 the federal government also undertook the establishment and maintenance of coastal buoys. Still vessels continued to pile up along this treacherous coast. The Humane Society of Massachusetts, founded in the eighteenth century, with the assistance of local private groups, constructed huts along the backside of Cape Cod and similar bleak coastal strips. In 1807 they built America's first lifeboat. Its offshoot U.S. Life-Saving Service was independent until merged in 1915 with the Revenue Cutter Service to form the present Coast Guard. It maintained a number of *life-saving stations*, examples of which 56
can still be seen on *Nantucket*, at Coast Guard Beach on Cape Cod and at Mystic Seaport.

As important as buoys and lights at the time was the publication of the *New American Practical Navigator* by

Nathaniel Bowditch of Salem. This became the Bible for negotiating these waters and has been cited as this country's first international best-seller. Aptly enough, both early life-saving gear and Bowditch memorabilia are preserved in the *Peabody Museum of Salem*, founded itself 36b
as one of the country's earliest "marine societies," which recommended sites for lighthouses and lobbied for legislation to protect maritime commerce.

TRANSPORTATION TRANSFORMATION

Water, be it ocean or river, formed the substance of New England's communications system through colonial times. Land routes had evolved haphazardly from Indian trails, widened where more frequently used by horsemen or ox-carts, obstacle courses for the first stages which began linking Boston with New York, Providence with Portsmouth, in the 1770s.

Josiah Quincy describes one week-long journey by stage from Boston to New York in 1773: "We reached our resting place for the night, if no accident occurred, at 10 o'clock, and after a frugal supper, went to bed with a notice we should be called at three, which generally proved to be two, and then, whether it snowed or rained, the traveler must rise and make ready . . . and proceed on his way over bad roads, sometimes getting out to help the coachman lift the coach out of a quagmire or rut."

Toll Roads

The Revolution ushered in an era of long-overdue road improvement. The war had necessitated movement of men and supplies over long distances, in the process widening the horizons of many a previously village-bound boy. The sorry state of roads had been due to their dependence on individual town funding, and now, since the states themselves were strapped with war debts, the financing for physically "securing a more perfect union" was sought from private individuals who were encouraged as a patriotic duty to form semi-public turnpike corporations ("turnpike" referred to the traditional English device used to stop travelers and elicit their tolls on English roads). Theoretically turnpike charters were to expire after the companies earned back their investment plus profits averaging 12% per year.

In 1800 two-thirds of the seventy-two toll roads in the

United States were in New England, twenty-three of these in Connecticut which, since it had no one center of wealth and commerce, threw up an array of links sponsored by competing townspeople. Elsewhere the turnpikes tended to radiate from centers like Boston or Providence, or to link the Connecticut River and Lake Champlain with the coast.

Soon it was possible to journey all the way from Boston to Burlington via turnpikes. Like the earlier roads these were usually ridge routes which offered the least resistance from swamps and rivers, frequently following the old Indian trails and spawning still more hilltowns along the way. We rarely stop to consider a road as part of the scenery it affords, but its age frequently determines that of the homes and walls which line it. The point is brought home by many a presently unpaved route, lined with handsome late eighteenth- and early nineteenth-century homes, proof of the long-lost importance of the "high" over the "low" road.

Ironically, the game of finding such roads today is labeled "shunpiking." Since travelers soon became adept at bypassing tollgates via frequent roundabouts – the true "shunpikes" of the era – financial backers rarely collected their promised due. Following a brief decline with the embargo and war years, another spurt of road-building and improvement, this time publicly financed, brought farming villages within the orbit of manufacturing towns. A few privately financed turnpikes continued to be constructed, notably the *Mount Washington* 57
Summit Road, begun in 1853, which remains a private toll road to this day.

Passenger transport, of course, improved dramatically with road conditions. Now every farm family possessed a four-wheeled wagon, and long-distance travelers could take advantage of the numerous stage lines. In 1826 the advent of the *Concord Coach*, with its nearly oval body 58
resting on an indestructible cushion of leather running strips, transformed punishing bumps from the road into a soothing rocking motion – a breakthrough soon appreciated from California to Africa. Still, the cost of freight transport was prohibitively high ($10 per ton in the twenties and thirties), and the advent of new industries in the interior of the region demanded new transport solutions.

Canals

Man-made waterways appeared to be the answer, and
an epidemic of canal fever swept the region.

At *Bellows Falls, Vermont*, a set of canal locks were 59
constructed in 1802 – thus lengthening the distance
which freight could travel down the Connecticut by 220
miles. Along the upper reaches of this river valley major
lumbering soon ensued, both on the *Vermont (Northeast* 60
Kingdom) side and in New Hampshire, where three adventurers carved out a vast wooded territory for themselves, its residents forming the *Indian Stream Republic* 61
in 1832 when state officials tried to bring them to toe.
The Connecticut remained a springtime river of wood
throughout the nineteenth century; rafts queued up at
Bellows Falls and their crews at the town saloons while
waiting their turns (the steamboats which eventually replaced barges proved too wide to fit in these early locks
and had to be transported by ox-carts around them).

Both the Middlesex Canal, opened in 1808 to service
Lowell, and Blodgett's Canal, which extended traffic as
far up the Merrimack as Manchester, were initial successes.
So was the Blackstone Canal, forging a link between
Providence and *Worcester*, which suddenly became an 62
important industrial city. But the *Farmington Canal*, 63
launched that same year by New Haven in the hopes of
finally upstaging Hartford once and for all as the state's
commercial center, was a disaster; leaks and dike failures
soon put it out of business.

Among surviving canals the most important remains at
Champlain. Initially it turned the direction of lake exports around completely. In 1810 alone (in defiance of
the embargo) *Burlington* had shipped $60,000 worth of 64
white pine across the border to Canada. For the next
half century, however, this, the world's third largest lum-
berport, found its market in New York and the West (via
the Erie Canal). Although Burlington's old waterfront
has all but disappeared, the Victorian mansions lining its
hillside streets attest that the palmy days lasted through
the 1870s. The Champlain canal itself continues as a link
to the Hudson.

The locks at Windsor Locks, Connecticut, still permit
small craft to ply the Connecticut between Hartford and
Springfield, and *Songo Lock*, constructed between 65
Maine's Long and Sebago Lakes in 1830, are still heavily
trafficked in summer, but New England's grandest canal

schemes – those linking Lake Champlain and Boston to the Connecticut River – never got beyond the drawing boards.

Railroads

The future of all canals was quickly decided by the appearance of railroads. *Quincy*, just south of Boston, 66
claims America's first commercial railroad on the strength of a horse-drawn contraption which hauled granite bound for the Bunker Hill monument. That was in 1825, the same year the world's first passenger train appeared in Britain.

But hampered by lack of state support, New England was actually a late starter in the steamtrain business. Its farmers saw nothing to be gained by watching western produce chug past their doors to coastal cities. Such was the opposition to extending the Providence and Worcester to Albany in the 1830s that owners of the company sent a letter to all churches in the state, asking that sermons be preached on the beneficial moral effects of railroads.

Soon, of course, the tide of public opinion shifted overboard in the opposite direction. Hundreds of old town centers turned to sleepy suburbs while new brick business blocks sprouted around the new depots. Major Vermont cities like St. Albans and St. Johnsbury date from this period, as do its quarrying centers of Proctor and Barre, and north New Hampshire's lumber towns and resorts.

Although passenger service within New England has since atrophied to a near nothing, its history can still be appreciated through passenger excursions, rail museums and the communities spawned by the golden era of railroading.

New Hampshire. The Granite State offers four rail excursions today, among them the most ambitious tourist gimmick of New England's railroad era.

"Might as well build a railway to the moon," skeptics scoffed when Sylvester Marsh secured charters from the state legislature to build railways to the top of Mount Washington in the late 1850s. But July 3, 1869, the world's first mountain-climbing cog railway engine pushed its inaugural load of passengers up to the summit of the region's highest mountain. Every bit of equipment, including the first locomotive, shipped in pieces from Boston, had been hauled over a rough road, twenty-five miles in from the nearest train, to the station at the western base of the mountain (now known as Marshfield). Logs for the three and one half miles of track and three miles of trestle were hand hewn along the way.

Today, passengers reach the *Mount Washington Cog Railway* via a high gear climb from Crawford Notch, and it's still through the woods. "Peppersass," the original engine on display, looks a shade different from the seven steam engines now used on the run, but not much. Interiors of the nineteenth-century cars conjure up visions of gentlemen in cravats, ladies in hobble skirts. The view offered by the ride is spectacular. The average grade of the climb is 25%, considerably sharper at Jacobs Ladder, which tips front seats in the coaches fourteen feet above the back. 57a

Railroad Station, Wolfeboro, N.H. Locomotive "Ossipee," Wolfeboro Railroad, Wolfeboro, N.H.

Like Mount Washington, Lake Winnipesaukee – seventy-two, island-studded square miles of it – was virtually wilderness until the mid-nineteenth century when railroads began importing summer visitors from the country over and exporting an amazing variety of "manufactures." Steam passenger service between Wolfeboro, northeastern corner of the lake, and the depot village of Sanborton, was offered first in 1872 and revived a little more than a century later. Aptly, since this never was just an excursion line, the *Wolfeboro Rail Road Co.* is a common carrier, 67 meaning that it must provide year-round regular service for residents along its twelve-mile run. It continues to haul freight and to connect daily in summer with the lake's excursion boat. The two-hour round trip takes you across lake and woods to the ghost depot which once served as northern division headquarters for the Boston and Maine.

The traditional route north from here would have been up through the White Mountains via the "Conways," recently connected once more by the *Conway Scenic Railroad.* 68 The eleven-mile, one-hour round trip between Conway and North Conway traverses the dramatic Saco River Valley. The onion-steepled North Conway depot (1874), brightly restored after ten demeaning years as a warehouse, is now a museum housing an extensive assortment of old ticket cases, daters, timetables, maps, brakemen's whistles and such.

Logging engines and track were once as plentiful around here as those used to haul passengers and through freight. A little woodburning locomotive which regularly hauls passengers around its two and one-half miles of track at *Clark's Trading Post* in Franconia Notch nicely com- 69

pletes northern New Hampshire's present rail excursion
picture.

Vermont. Three railroads through Vermont were chartered in 1835, but no rails were laid for another decade.
In 1848 the first train from White River Junction had
inched along only as far northwest as Bethel, spawning
the picturesque depot town of *South Royalton* in its 70
wake. The very next year the first locomotive chugged
into Burlington, but politics had dictated a devious path
for the line: both the state capital of Montpelier and the
quarrying center of *Barre* were bypassed in favor of the 71
governor's little hometown of Northfield, where he set
up Vermont Central offices and an unduly elaborate
station. As a result the Barre & Montpelier was founded;
this short line still hauls granite slabs from the quarries
to Montpelier. (A tourist train which carts summer visitors around the Barre Rock of Ages quarry is said to be
the steepest standard-grade railroad this side of the Rocky
Mountains.)

Up along the northern tier of the state the St. Johnsbury and Lake Champlain R.R. (for decades now better
known as the "St. Jesus and Long Coming") still serves
as lifeline for many a small town. Long ago it helped
turn the towns at its either end into major cities. At its
western terminus is *St. Albans*, once the largest rail depot 72
in New England.

The city's three-story brick station, still with many of
its matching sheds, hotel and surrounding commercial
buildings, survives. Although no longer home of some
other offshoot industries from the railroad (the world's
largest creamery and a big flypaper factory), it remains
one of the country's major maple sugar and sugar-making
machinery producers, scene of New England's most
colorful annual "sugaring" festival – and a delight for
those who enjoy late nineteenth century upcountry
work-a-day towns.

So is *St. Johnsbury*, at the eastern terminus of the line. 73
In "St. J." railroading coincided happily with home invention. In the 1830s Thaddeus Fairbanks, a direct
descendant of that Jonathan who built New England's
oldest surviving house, patented the world's first platform scale and built a factory here. Still, St. Johnsbury
must have looked like nowheresville to passengers aboard
the first train from Boston arriving in 1850. None of the
present commercial blocks along and behind Railroad St.
had yet been built, and nearby *Danville* (itself a delight- 74

fully sleepy town today) remained the shire seat of Caledonia County. But that very year St. Johnsbury House was built on "the plain" above, its 150 rooms lavishly appointed to attract "pleasure-seeking travelers to the white mountains." The town's population and importance skyrocketed in ensuing years; between 1842 and 1857 the scale business alone doubled every three years, and mansions in a variety of shapes appeared along with business blocks. Ultimately, the Fairbanks proved outstanding philanthropists, endowing the city with an academy, Atheneum and Museum of Natural Science.

Proctor's marble quarries also certainly profited from 75
convenient rail service at nearby Rutland. Although marble quarrying in the state (and North America for that matter) dates from 1785, in Dorset, Vermont, this tidy town of marble houses, marble public buildings, even marble sidewalks and great long marble mills, appeared almost overnight – along with the Vermont Marble Company – in the 1880s. Today Proctor is also site of the "world's largest marble exhibit."

Since Vermont is New England's sole entirely inland state it may have gained more than its neighbors from railroading; certainly it offers the lion's share of this region's tribute to that era. In Montpelier, in the Vermont
Historical Society's museum in the *Pavilion Building* 76
(itself an 1876 brick confection which might be described as "railroad rococo") you can see a slide show presentation of the state's railroading story, illustrated through
dozens of surviving stations. And "*Steamtown*" at River- 77
side, just above Bellows Falls, claims the largest and best collection in the world of steam locomotives, rolling stock and rail curios to go with it. An excursion train regularly steams away from the museum's depot, taking passengers on a 22.6-mile circuit through farmland and woods, across an assortment of spidery bridges, to Chester Depot and back. In addition it sponsors off-season specials to Rutland and back (one hundred miles round-trip).

At this writing Vermont's "*Historic 1876 Transporta-* 78
tion System," utilizing eighteen Steamtown cars and two engines on two 135-mile circuits of the state during the summer months of 1976, 1977, the bicentennial of Vermont's own birth, looks likely to come off. Vermonters are backing the project with the same enthusiasm with which they helped revive regular passenger service in 1972 (when they swung support in their favor over an alterna-

tive New York routing – by turning out with bands and placards at towns along the way to greet a trial run). All told thirteen different railroads still operate within Vermont, three of them run by the state itself.

Massachusetts. The Bay State offers but one token
excursion ride and that aboard a little narrow-gauge
work train which winds its way around a five-mile loop
through the cranberry bogs of South Carver. This is the
Edaville R.R., most popular both during the early Octo- 79
ber cranberry harvest season and at Christmas time when
the grounds are a blaze of lights. There is also a museum
here, housing locomotives and old rolling stock. The
Hoosac Tunnel, a 4.73-mile bore through Hoosac Mountain, which was the world's longest railroad tunnel when
it opened in 1873 – having cost 195 lives and $14 million
in the building – is also occasionally open to passenger
excursions sponsored by the *Mystic Valley Railway So-* 80
ciety, the region's most active railbuff group which currently offers a wide choice of passenger trips throughout
New England. *Railroad Enthusiasts*, the country's biggest
railbuff club and also based regionally in Massachusetts,
offers periodic upcountry runs.

Connecticut. Most large towns in this state were on
some rail route before the end of the century, a necessity
here since every major Nutmeg State community harbors
at least one factory. Several years ago the century-old
Connecticut Valley Railroad which once linked Old Saybrook and Hartford was revived – at least the nine miles
which lie between Essex and Chester – as the *Valley* 32a
Railroad. Excursionists board the nineteenth-century cars
for this run behind a steam locomotive at the Essex
depot, another mini-rail museum complete with pot-
bellied stove and a stationary dining car.

Maine. The Pine Tree State still enjoys extensive rail
freight service and one little-known passenger run aboard
the Canadian Pacific from the semi-wilderness outposts
of Jackman, Greenville and Brownsville to Montreal.
Maine's sole rail museum and short excursion run, the
Boothbay Central Railroad, gives visitors disappointingly 82
little for their money. One annual *autumn excursion* is 83
sponsored by Portland rail buffs to Island Pond, Vermont.

Rhode Island. A shore-side excursion run, 14 miles 84
round trip, is offered during summer months by the Narragansett Pier Railroad with the Peace Dale Depot as
departure point.

Steamboating

While people of the Connecticut River towns of Orford, New Hampshire, and Fairlee, Vermont, were all in church one Sunday morning of 1793, Samuel Morey gave his first little steam-powered paddlewheeler a successful test run. It chugged along at four miles per hour. For the next few years, Sam kept tinkering with the boat and improving it. In 1797 he built a new model at Bordentown, New Jersey, on the Delaware, but at this point Robert Fulton and Chancellor Robert Livingston, both of whom had encouraged him freely to discuss and demonstrate his invention with them, turned around and went into the steamboating business themselves, using a boat clearly patterned on Morey's. It's said that Morey, depressed by this betrayal, sank his boat in the little Vermont lake which now bears his name. 85

Fulton sent his paddlewheeler *Clermont* up the Hudson from New York to Albany in 1807, establishing a record for the journey: sixty-two hours round trip! The very next year America's second passenger-carrying steamboat, *Vermont*, entered service on Lake Champlain at Burlington. A plaque commemorating the spot gets unusually high readership today from would-be passengers queued up in their cars to board the present ferries operated by the *Lake Champlain Transportation Co.*, de- 64a
scendant of the line which, founded in 1828, claims to be "the oldest steamboat company on earth." This lake is said to be the world's first to enjoy regular steamboat service: north-south at first to link up with the Hudson River boats, carrying a sizable percentage of Vermonters on their first leg west and a steady stream of immigrants south from Canada to New England. Beginning in the '60s traffic shifted to its present east-west pattern, initially connecting the twin rail lines on either bank of the lake; the *Oakes Ames*, launched in 1868, even had railroad tracks across her lower deck, enabling a small train to make the connection via the boat's self-adjusting railroad bridge. The last of the lake's tall-funneled, wood-
fueled steamers can still be seen. The *Ticonderoga* (1906) 86
has come to rest a few miles inland and south of Burlington at Shelburne Museum, her lavishly paneled saloon with its gold stenciling on the ceilings, its eagle-topped mirror at the head of the grand stairway, the comfortable staterooms and even the barber shop and captain's dining table restored.

The *Ticonderoga*'s sister ship *Chateauguay* (1888) had

been turned into a clubhouse for the Burlington Yacht
Club by 1940 when the owner of the former *Mount
Washington* (which had burned at her dock the previous
December, after sixty years of service on Lake Winnipesaukee) found her and decided that here were the
makings of *Mount Washington II*. The *Chateauguay*'s hull 87
was carved into sandwiches of steel and shipped 150
miles overland to the lake which she still plies, known as
affectionately as her predecessor simply as "the Mount,"
a local landmark and delight to all.

Coastal service represented a greater challenge than inland runs, but since the profits were correspondingly
higher it didn't take the Fulton-Livingston Line long to
inaugurate a run from New York to New London (1816).
Connecticut objected to the monopoly which New York
had granted Fulton, so one company shifted to Providence where passengers connected with stages for
Boston. After the monopoly was broken in 1824, New
London, Norwich and Stonington all launched their own
highly competitive lines, but the real solution to easing
the New York City–Boston trip wasn't solved until 1847
when the Fall River Line Rail and Steamship Service
opened. It offered one and one-half hour by rail service
from Boston to Fall River. Here passengers could board
a sumptuous liner and enjoy fine food, music and staterooms during the overnight sailing to New York.

For ninety years "Fall River" was a byword for steamship elegance and safety, and although none of these
legendary boats has survived, their memory is commemorated through large-scale models, photos, menus
and furnishings in their hometown's *Marine Museum*. 88
Today's visitor finds it difficult to believe the extrava-
gance of these "floating palaces": the *Pilgrim* (1883–
1913), "largest steamboat in the world," demanded a
crew of two hundred to serve her one thousand passengers and boasted one thousand electric lights, ornate
chandeliers, rich carpeting, mirrors and potted palms, a
full band to drown the thunder of her twin paddlewheels
and a four-course dinner menu, including a steak or half a
lobster, priced at $1.50; a glass of wine was 15¢ extra. The
Pilgrim was also one of the first ships equipped with water-
tight bulkheads and a crew trained in lifesaving techniques. On the northbound route the passenger lists
regularly included magnates bound for Newport and
immigrants for whom the $1 steerage fare bought passage
to a new life. When the Fall River Line went out of

business in 1937 it had carried 19 million passengers and lost the life of just one passenger through a freak accident.

Long before its demise, the Fall River Line had become
a part of the New England Steamship Co., a subsidiary
of the New York, New Haven and Hartford R.R., in this
capacity managing all major steamboat services on Long
Island Sound. The present *Woods Hole, Martha's Vine-* 89
yard and Nantucket Steamship Authority is the sole surviving offshoot of this monopoly, servicing the islands of
Nantucket and Martha's Vineyard year round. The present *New England Steamboat, Inc.*, based in Haddam, 90
Connecticut, is no relation at all, an enterprising up-
start which offers river cruises and summer excursions to
Greenport, Long Island.

Ferry Sabino

Unfortunately no museum commemorates the colorful
story of those steamboats which once plied north from
Boston through the rough waters of the Gulf of Maine to
downeast cities and resorts. One venerable company does
still serve a tiny but heavy-weather swatch of this territory: the *Casco Bay Lines*, founded in 1845, claims the 48a
dubious title, "oldest firm of its kind in the nation."
Based in Portland's Custom House Wharf, itself a genuine
nineteenth-century holdover, the company's red, white
and orange boats make daily year-round runs to six of
the 138 Calendar Islands scattered offshore. Come summer a few of these milk runs are titled "excursions," and
there are some actual moonlight and narrated trips for
tourists besides.

New England's sole working steamboat today is a veteran of twenty years with Casco Bay Lines. The *Sabino* 17a
was launched from East Boothbay where she ended her
first life (and that of her engineer) in a freak sinking. At
present she carries excursionists upriver from Mystic Seaport.

"Steamboatin'" days may have vanished, but in their
wake a *flourishing flotilla of ferries* serves two dozen of 91
the 1,200 islands scattered between (in the words of the
U.S. Weather reporters) Eastport and Block Island. These
are all relatively small craft, most of them maintained by
small companies, and since it's relatively difficult to locate them we've only attempted to list the lot here under "details." We have also listed a sampling of excursion
sail boats which encourage you to forget that the age of
steam and its successors have ever happened at all.

DETAILS

1 *Old Slater Mill Museum, Pawtucket, Rhode Island.* From I-95, exit 29 south and 28 north, follow signs. Just as this was New England's first successful mill, it was the first to be salvaged and recycled; it was opened as a museum in 1955. Exhibits have been substantially expanded in recent years. Spring-fall; daily: 10-5; Sun.: 2-5. Winter weekends: 1-5. Admission charged. (401) 725-8638.

2 *Lowell, Massachusetts.* Rtes. 495 and 3, northwest of Boston near New Hampshire line. The Lowell Heritage Park is currently taking shape. A hiking-biking tour of the city has been prepared to help you explore the Locks and Canal system, nearly six miles of which crisscross the city. Sites to look for include Francis's Gate (built 1850 on the Pawtucket Canal) and the Boott Mill (1835) complex. The home of artist James Abbott McNeil Whistler is maintained by the Lowell Historical Society, 243 Worthen St. (summer months; Tues.-Fri.: 10-5; Sun.: 12-5). At the John F. Kennedy Civic Center secure maps, also details about the new museum which will chronicle the social history of Lowell.

3 *Merrimack Valley Textile Museum, North Andover, Massachusetts.* Exit off I-93, north from Boston. Machinery and prints trace the process of wool manufacturing both before and after the Industrial Revolution. Year round, daily: 9-5; weekends: 1-5. Admission charged Sun. only since demonstrations are held then. (617) 686-6191.

4 *Manchester, New Hampshire.* On I-93, less than one hour north of Boston. The original, continuous canyon of factory walls on both sides of the Amoskeag River has been broken by urban renewal and the canals have been filled in. Still the lineup of mills is memorable. More than forty manufacturing firms now occupy the area and the nearby rows of company homes still house workers. The centerpiece Pandora Tower has recently been restored; new pride in the city's industrial past is reflected in collections to be seen at the Currier Gallery of Art, 192 Orange St., year round; Tues.-Sat.: 10-4; Sun.: 1-5, (603) 669-6144, and at the Manchester Historical Association, 129 Amherst St., year round; Tues.-Fri.: 9-4; Sat.: 10-4.

5 *Slatersville, Rhode Island.* Rtes. 5 and 146, near Woonsocket and just below the Massachusetts line. Samuel Slater eventually became dissatisfied with his role in the Pawtucket mill and moved to this site where he set up shop in partnership with his brother John. The common which they laid out in the center of town is the only one to be found in the state (aside from those which were originally part of Massachusetts). Around it are ranged the church, school, John's mansion (now the Congregational Church parsonage) and tenements designed for mill workers' families. Both the 1804 wooden and the 1826 stone mills survive.

6 *Crown and Eagle Mills, North Uxbridge, Massachusetts.* Rte. 122, south from Massachusetts Turnpike exit 11. A stone village set in landscaped grounds around the handsome stone textile mill, obviously built, with little mind to expense, in the 1820s. At this writing the complex has just been gutted by fire.

7 *Harrisville, New Hampshire.* Monadnock region; from Rte. 101 at Dublin, north on unmarked road. Nonprofit "Historic Harrisville" now owns six buildings, five of them already restored, and controls the future of twenty more. The possibility of an inn or restaurant ever opening in town is unlikely but ample facilities are available in the area.

8 *Other Mill Villages.* Many an unrestored mill village can be seen in New England today, some sagging picturesquely, others still generating work for their locales.

PROCTORSVILLE, VERMONT

Rte. 131 between Ascutney and Ludlow. The handsome little mill, and the adjoining post office and company store, are still in use, but company housing surrounding them is sagging. For details, check with the Cavendish Historical Society, (802) 226-7396.

LUDLOW, VERMONT

Rtes. 131 and 100. The striking early mill here now produces General Electric small aircraft engine parts.

QUECHEE, VERMONT

Off I-89. The old mill is a summer playhouse and a developer has transformed the village into a resort community.

WESTBROOK, MAINE

Just west of Portland. An outstanding example of an early planned mill village with a dozen shingled workers' cottages, a mill agent's home, boardinghouse and mill-owner's mansion.

PEJEPSCOT PAPER COMPANY MILL, TOPSHAM, MAINE

The state's oldest wood pulp mill (1869) and one of the most picturesque mills in New England. It stands next to Brunswick Falls on the Androscoggin River, just off Rte. 1, north from Brunswick.

9 *American Precision Museum, Windsor, Vermont.* Off I-95, exit 8 to Rte. 5. A delightful hodgepodge of machinery, eighteenth to twentieth centuries. Ask here for directions to the early nineteenth-century dam, hidden off a side street up behind the millpond. May 31-Oct. 15, daily: 10-5.

10 *Connecticut State Library, Hartford, Connecticut.* Capital Ave. across from the state capitol building. The Sharp rifle is displayed as part of a major collection of locally made firearms which also includes early revolvers by Samuel Colt and muskets which Eli Whitney produced by the thousands for the United States government.

11 *Hitchcock Chair Factory, Riverton, Connecticut.* Rte. 20 from Rtes. 44 and 8, northeast from Winsted. Connecticut House. the factory outlet, is open year round, Wed.-Sat.: 9-5; and the museum, May through Nov.; Tues.-Sat.: 10-5, (203) 379-1003 or 379-8531. The Old Riverton Inn just across the river (1796) offers guest rooms as well as lunch and dinner (203) 379-8678.

12 *Connecticut Clocks.* In 1814 Eli Terry patented the shelf clock which made his fortune. When Joseph Ives of Bristol invented a cheap brass clock in 1832, his hometown became known for its kitchen clocks; the American Clock and Watch Museum (100 Maple St., April through Oct., Tues.-Sat.: 1-5, (203) 583-6070) tells the story. The most popular name in clocks by the mid-century was Seth Thomas, who established the handsome factory in the town now named for him (Thomaston, Rtes. 6 and 202) which is now a division of General Time Instruments.

13 *Crane & Company Paper Museum, Dalton, Massachusetts.* Rte. 9 near Pittsfield. Dalton itself is a handsome northern Berkshire town, obviously well endowed by its leading family. The museum stands beside the Housatonic River. Ask for directions to one of the best preserved large stone mills in the country, on East Housatonic St. and Hinsdale Rd., now a Crane Co. warehouse. The museum is open June 1-Oct. 1, weekdays: 2-5. (413) 684-260 ext. 202.

14 *Sandwich Glass Museum, Sandwich, Massachusetts.* Rte. 130 off 6A, just east of the Sagamore Bridge. Displays include cut glass, clear and colored, blown and pressed glass in literally thousands of shapes. May-Oct., daily: 10-5; July, Aug.: 9-6. (617) 888-0251. Admission charged. Visitors interested in watching glass blown should proceed to the small cement factory building of Pairpoint Glass Works (beneath Sagamore Bridge) where master glass blowers can be seen in action. Year round, Mon.-Fri.: 10-4:30. (617) 888-2344.

15 *Laconia, New Hampshire, Mills.* I-93, exit 20 to Rte. 11. The Belknap Mill's bell was cast by a Paul Revere apprentice with silver dollars donated by townspeople. Its power house remains intact and the gears, cogs and wheels are said to be the last of their kind in the country (before

the turn of the century this mechanism generated electricity for the entire city). At present only the building's exterior has been restored. Those interested in contributing to the project should write Save the Mills, Box 702, Laconia, New Hampshire 03246.

16 *More 19th Century Mills.* New uses for old mill buildings turn up daily.

BOSTON, MASSACHUSETTS

The former Chickering Piano Factory (791 Tremont St.), billed as the country's largest commercial building at its 1855 opening, is now home of the Piano Craft Guild, a combination loft and living space for artists, musicians and writers. The former Thomas E. Plant shoe factory (370 Centre St., Jamaica Plain), opened at the turn of the century, has also been converted into lofts.

PROVIDENCE, RHODE ISLAND

The Brown and Sharpe complex, Promenade St., now contains offices, including some branches of the state government.

NORTH EASTON, MASSACHUSETTS

An entire mill village designed by H. H. Richardson has been recycled as an industrial park.

AVON, CONNECTICUT

The town hall complex, 40 West Main St., now serves as town offices and a crafts center.

NEEDHAM, MASSACHUSETTS

The Mill Dam Restaurant occupies a period mill.

ARLINGTON, MASSACHUSETTS

The Old Schwamb Mill, Mill Lane (turn off Massachusetts Ave. at Lowell St.). The picture frames for which this little factory was long famous are still produced with nineteenth-century machinery, which is also used for classes in home carpentry. Crafts items produced by resident artists are sold, and evening classes are offered in a variety of crafts. (617) 643-0554.

PROJECTS STILL IN THE WORKS include the Bristol County Textile Museum, a memorial to the titanic stone textile mills, still to be seen in Fall River and New Bedford. (For details, write Bristol Textile Museum, 64 Durfee St., Fall River, Massachusetts.) In North Adams, Massachusetts, the nineteenth-century Windsor Print Mill is being converted into a performing arts and crafts center by the Hoosac Community Resources Corporation.

Factory Store Guide to All New England by Pequot Press lists and critiques 167 parent outlets plus plentiful branches of these discount shops. Bristol County also publishes its own free guide (available from Bristol County Development Council, 154 North Main St., Fall River, Massachusetts) and an Industrial Tours of Rhode Island booklet is available from the Rhode Island Development Council (see Helpful Hints).

17 *Mystic Seaport, Mystic, Connecticut.* I-95 exit onto Rte. 27. This extensive outdoor museum encompasses ships, artifacts and craftsmanship of nineteenth-century maritime America. Year round, daily. Winter months: 9–4; summer months: 9–5. Steep admission. (203) 536-2631.

17a *Steamboat Sabino, Mystic Seaport, Connecticut.* During summer months this craft, built in 1908, makes regular excursions up the Mystic River; to take the ride it is not necessary to pay admission. For details, contact the Seaport. (See detail 17.)

18 *Nantucket Island, Massachusetts.* Accessible by ferry from Woods Hole and from Hyannis (see listing at end of this chapter's details) and by air from Boston and Hyannis (Air New England: (617) 569-5510). Nantucket Chamber of Commerce is good for walk-in guidance, but the best source to contact before coming is the Nantucket Town Information Bureau, 23 Federal St., (617) 228-0925, which is adept at finding lodging in every price category and which dispenses the excellent Nantucket Historical Association leaflet guide to the island sites. A dozen of these are maintained by the Association, among them the Nantucket Whaling Museum, Hawden House, the Old Mill, Old Gaol, Jethro Coffin House and Peter Foulger Museum which depicts island life through three centuries with displays ranging from Indian

relics to portraits of whaling captains by Eastman Johnson. All are open, mid-June–mid-Oct., daily: 10–5. All charge admission but a combination ticket is available.

19 *New Bedford, Massachusetts.* Rte. 6 off I–95. A Moby Dick Trail, linking thirty local attractions, is outlined in a leaflet guide available at City Hall, (617) 999-2931, and at the information office in the historic waterfront district. New Bedford celebrates its salty past with Whaling City Days which include a parade, fish feast and a blessing of its commercial fishing fleet, usually the first week in July. Lesser known whaling era sites include the City's Free Public Library, built in 1865 as a combination drive-in market and town office building; also the early nineteenth-century Marine Bank Building, Mariners' Home, the Third District Courthouse, the Custom House and Mechanics Bank Building. The Seaman's Bethel remains an active church and its hours depend on those of the sexton who, incidentally, explains that the ship-shaped pulpit which Melville described here has been installed since the publication of *Moby Dick*. Across the street the Old Dartmouth Historical Society and Whaling Museum (18 Johnny Cake Hill) is open Feb.–Dec., Tues.–Sat.: 9–5 in summer months, and otherwise: 1–5. Admission charged. (617) 997–0046.

20 *Shaw Mansion, New London, Connecticut.* 11 Blinman St. A handsome home built in 1756 and the state's naval headquarters during the Revolution. The whaling display includes harpoons, scrimshaw and such. Year round, Tues.–Sat.: 1–4. Admission charged. (203) 443–1209.

21 *Whitehall Mansion, Stonington, Connecticut.* Rte. 27 off I–95. The 1775 mansion which serves as headquarters for the Stonington Historical Society, includes local memorabilia from whaling days. Year round; Sun.–Fri.: 2–4. Admission charged.

22 *Dukes County Historical Society, Edgartown, Martha's Vineyard, Massachusetts.* Corner of Cooke and School streets. The island's whaling story is told through a major display of memorabilia here in the vintage 1756 Thomas Cooke House. June through Sept., Tues.–Sat.: 10–4:30; rest of the year, Tues.–Sat.: 10–12 and 1–4:30. For details about the island, check with the Martha's Vineyard Chamber of Commerce, Vineyard Haven, Massachusetts. (617) 693–0085.

23 *Provincetown, Massachusetts.* Tip of Cape Cod, Rte. 6. Provincetown Museum (on Town Hill, adjacent to Pilgrim Monument) displays a full-scale replica of a whaling captain's quarters among many exhibits from the town's whaling days. Year round, daily: 9–5 and mid-June to mid-Sept.: 9–9. Admission charged. (617) 487–1310.

24 *Bath Marine Museum, Bath, Maine.* Coastal I–95 becomes U.S. 1 at Bath; the museum, headquartered at 963 Washington St., is less than twelve years old and continues to grow. The Sewall Mansion houses varied displays, including a "please touch" room for children, also mementos from the Sewall family's link with the Hawaiian Islands which they helped get annexed to the United States. The Percy and Small Shipyard, opened in 1903, houses a collection of small craft, photos and tools; reactivation of its early electric-powered machinery is planned. The museum perpetuates the art of wooden shipbuilding in town through its apprentice shop; a view of ongoing work at the Bath Iron Works can be had from its ferry. May 25–Oct. 14, daily: 9–5. Admission charged. (207) 443–6311. The most colorful time to visit is during Bath Heritage Days: five days of band concerts, house tours, street dances and church suppers, timed to include July 4 each year. For details about local lodgings and other sites contact the Bath Area Chamber of Commerce (207) 443–9751.

25 *Searsport, Maine.* Rte. 1 on Penobscot Bay. The Penobscot Marine Museum here contains a number of treasures. The town's scant two mid-nineteenth-century business blocks give a deceptively sleepy impression of the town today. Its actual heart is Penobscot Bay itself, overlooking which grand old captains' homes are strung out for five miles. Nearby Brigadier's Island, connected by a natural causeway, is a picnic area. The museum is open Memorial Day through Oct., Mon.–Sat.: 9–5; Sun.: 1–5. Admission charged. (207) 548–6634.

26 *Camden, Maine.* Rte. 1, lower Penobscot Bay. This town sits dramatically on a curving shelf of coast between abrupt little Mount Battie and the Bay. A river cuts across town, shops have back porches overlooking the harbor; houses are all brightly painted and geraniums dangle from the lampposts. Camden's population more than triples in summer, and there are ample guestrooms in town, notably those at the Whitehall Inn which is the place poet Edna St. Vincent Millay gave her first public recital. Information about the excursion schooners which sail from this "Windjammer Capital of the World" is available from the Chamber of Commerce, town landing (207) 236–4404. Visitors wishing to economize can take advantage of Camden Hills State Park which also includes hiking and riding trails.

27 *Belfast, Maine.* Eight miles east of Searsport, U.S. 1. The city has its fair share of sea captains' homes, but remains a work-a-day coastal town rather than a resort. In the 1870s papermaking and other large industries upstaged shipbuilding and today it is most famous for its poultry, in honor of which it stages an annual mid-July "Broiler Festival."

28 *Thomaston, Maine.* U.S. 1. In 1840 two of the country's seven millionaires were Thomaston sea captains, and it retains both its large homes and elms. Visitors stop to see Montpelier (see details, Chapter 6) and the furniture outlet store at Maine State Prison (year round, daily: 9–5).

29 *East Boothbay, Maine.* U.S. 1 just east of Wiscasset, Rte. 27 to Rte. 96. Since the early nineteenth century this sheltered reach of the Damariscotta River has been a shipbuilding center, and some notable racing yachts continue to be produced here. Adjacent Boothbay is a lively summer resort, scene of Windjammer Days in mid-July and departure point for a number of excursion boats. Chamber of Commerce: (207) 633-2353.

30 *Friendship, Maine.* Tip of the peninsula accessible from U.S. 1 via Rte. 220 at Waldoboro and via Rte. 97 from Thomaston. A delightful small town, site of the annual July Friendship Sloop Days. The town's Historical Museum, full of marine exhibits, is housed in a former one-room schoolhouse, open weekends in summer.

31 *The Kennebunks.* I–95 and U.S. 1. Together these towns once formed the shipbuilding center for York, Maine's oldest and southernmost coastal county. Kennebunk is an unusually handsome but private town for which Kennebunkport forms the resort. Dock Square at its center is lined with Federal period buildings, many now boutiques and inns. The town library was built as a custom house in 1815 and the Arundel Yacht Club occupies a former rope walk. There are also a summer playhouse, golf club, historical society, the extensive Seashore Trolley museum (see Chapter 10) and the mid-eighteenth-century Perkins Grist Mill (see Chapter 7).

32 *Essex, Connecticut.* Exit 3 off Rte. 9 from I–95 at Saybrook. One of the most delightful main streets to be found anywhere. Local landmarks include the eighteenth-century Griswold Inn, one of the first three-story buildings in the country; it still offers food and lodging.

32a *Connecticut Valley Railroad, Essex, Connecticut.* The depot is just north of exit 3, so do not follow the sign into Essex. In summer months the last passenger car is an open gondola; others are mahogany inlaid, well restored. The narrated twenty-minute (one way) ride is along the Connecticut; passengers can transfer at the old Deep River Depot for either a one or two hour boat cruise aboard excursion boat *Silver Star*. Early May through Oct.; also Dec. 7–22, when Santa Claus rides all trains. Schedule available from the Valley Railroad, Railroad Ave., Essex, Connecticut 06426. (203) 767-0103.

33 *Essex, Massachusetts.* Rtes. 133 and 22, near Ipswich and Gloucester. The Story Shipyard on Main St., in business since 1813, marks the spot set aside in 1667 by the town of Ipswich for shipbuilding. It was Essex which actually built the lion's share of Gloucester fishermen. Today it is famous for its river clams, available at a long line of restaurants. Less well known is the 106-acre Agassiz Rock Reservation maintained by the Trustees of Reservations, off Southern Ave.

34 *Shiverick Shipyard, Dennis, Massachusetts.* Sesuit Neck Road off Rte. 6A. A bronze plaque depicts what this yard looked like in the 1860s and five of the yard owners' homes remain just across the road.

35 *Museum of the American China Trade, Milton, Massachusetts.* Exit 22 off Rte. 3 and follow Adams St. to 215. The museum's permanent collection includes exceptional Chinese import porcelain of the Federal era (featuring slant-eyed Revolutionary War heroes), Chinese imitations of English silverware, elaborately carved furniture, intricate ivory toys and puzzles and a library of more than 100,000 period papers related to the trade. There are also changing exhibits and a program of lectures and slide presentations. Year round except holidays; Tues.–Sat.: 2-5. Admission charged. (617) 696-1815.

36 *Salem, Massachusetts.* Rte. 1A north from Boston. Salem's Chamber of Commerce in the Hawthorn Hotel, Washington Square (617) 744-0004, dispenses leaflet guides and rents a taped tour of town. During 1976, visitor reception centers are set up in the city's churches. For Salem Bicentennial information: (617) 744-0798.

36a *Essex Institute, Salem, Massachusetts.* 132 Essex St. The museum building was built as a library in 1857 with a two-story-high gallery, ideally suited to display the cases full of exhibits depicting three centuries of local history. The library here contains outstanding source material on New England maritime history and the garden out back includes the city's first Quaker meetinghouse and the restored seventeenth-century John Ward House. The Institute maintains four other historic house museums in town. Year round, Tues.–Sat.: 9–4:30; Sun.: 2–5. (617) 744-3390.

36b *Peabody Museum,* 161 Essex St. See Chapter 6. Year round, weekdays: 9–5; Sun. and holidays: 1–5. Admission charged. (617) 745-1876.

37 *Bangor, Maine.* Maine Turnpike; fifty miles northwest of Maine's mid-coast area. If the city's famed "Devil's Half Acre" has disappeared, it still boasts some handsome streets, theoretically laid out by Charles Bulfinch. And it has more than its share of mansions, one of which

is now the Historical Society Museum, maintained by the D.A.R. (summer months, weekdays: 2–4 (207) 947-5766) and Symphony House across Union St., built by a lumberman with brick imported from England and slate from Wales, notable for its circular parlor paneled in Santo Domingo mahogany (recently restored and about to be opened to visitors at this writing). Bangor House, still the city's big hotel, was built in the 1830s on the pattern of Boston's now-vanished Tremont House. The city's largest collection of lumbering tools and memorabilia decorates its coffee shop. The Penobscot Heritage Museum of Living History occupies a gallery in City Hall; exhibits change periodically. Greater Bangor Chamber of Commerce, 55 Washington St. (207) 947-0307.

38 *Maine State Forest District.* A vast area encompassing the northwestern section of Maine, outlined on state maps. Hiking and camping are permitted within this area; maps which show campsites and private logging roads open to the public are available from the Paper Industries Information Office (133 State St., Augusta, Maine 04330) and the North Maine Woods Council (P.O. Box 113, Bangor, Maine 04401). The two conventional routes into the area are those to Baxter State Park (200,000 acres including the state's highest peak, Mt. Katahdin) and a two-week canoe trip up the ninety-two-mile Allagash Waterway. Details about both of these are available from Maine's State Park and Recreation Commission, Augusta, Maine 04330.

39 *Fort Kent, Maine.* Northern terminus of U.S. 1 at the Canadian border. The 1839 blockhouse here includes a small museum of lumbering and Indian artifacts. May–Labor Day, daily: 8–9 P.M.; rest of the year, weekends only.

40 *Fort Knox, Bucksport, Maine.* Rte. 174, marked from U.S. 1, just south of town. This extremely impressive granite complex includes barracks, storehouses and a labyrinth of passageways, even a granite spiral stairway. A delight for children and fort buffs, also a pleasant picnic spot. May through Oct., daily: 10–6. Admission charged per car.

41 *Lumberman's Museum, Patten, Maine.* Way up there, one hundred miles north of Bangor: I-95 to Sherman exit, then 10 more miles up Rte. 159. Named for the man who bought this land from Massachusetts back in the 1820s, this town is surprisingly handsome. The museum displays more than 1000 items in five buildings. Harvesting and processing plywood remain the town's industry; there is lodging in town and charter air service to fishing camps at Shin Pond. The museum is open May 20–Nov. 1, Tues.-Sat.: 9–4; Sun.: 1–6. (207) 528-2650.

42 *Greenville, Maine.* I-95 to Newport exit; Rte. 7 to Dover-Foxcroft, then Rte. 6 to 15 and on up. Located at the foot of Moosehead Lake which boasts four hundred miles of shoreline. Most of the lake's perimeter is owned today by Scott Paper Company, which offers a regularly scheduled six-hour tour of its nearby lumber camp and operations (contact Scott's Eastern District Woodlands Office, summer months, Rte. 15, just north of town: (207) 695-2514). Visit the camp and you discover instead of bearded men heaving axes, clean-shaven Canadians who man big machines and return home to their families every weekend. In Greenville, the big landmark is Sanders Store, in business since 1878 and still selling peavies along with hardware, flannels and sporting equipment. Greenville is also jump-off point for charter air service to otherwise inaccessible wilderness camps. The locally posh place to stay is Squaw Mountain (a ski area in winter), but the Greenville Chamber of Commerce furnishes details about hundreds of reasonably priced campgrounds and cabins. (207) 695-2702.

43 *Chesuncook Village, Maine.* Accessible by road from Millinocket; by boat via Moosehead Lake from Rockwood or Kokadjo. Typical of those early settlements predating the 1850s which were established deep in the wilderness with little outside communication through the winter months, Chesuncook is a genuine ghost town today; campsites are available nearby on Chesuncook Lake.

44 *Pownalborough Courthouse, Dresden, Maine.* Rte. 128 between Brunswick and Augusta. Built within Fort Shirley in the 1760s, a regional museum. July, Aug., daily: 10–5. Admission charged.

45 *Bristol, Maine.* From Rte. 1 at Damariscotta via Rtes. 129 and 130. Thompson Ice House dates from 1825; it is one of the earliest as well as one of the few surviving commercial ice houses in the state.

46 *Ice Harvest Festivals*

Brookfield, Vermont. I-89 Randolph exit, north on Rte. 12 to East Brookfield. The festival, annually the Sunday of Washington's Birthday weekend, brings horse-drawn sleighs, traditional and new-fangled harvesting tools to Sunset Lake. For details, contact Green Trails (see Chapter 7 details) (802) 276-2012.

Abbot Village, Maine. Twenty-five miles south of Moosehead Lake. Staged by Titcomb's

General Store, one of the last commercial ice harvesting operations and featuring use of a locally invented machine. The event is held at Piper Pond in February when the ice is right. Check with Titcomb's, which stores the ice in two-hundred-pound blocks and sells it to local dairymen and visitors throughout the summer (207) 876-4525.

47 *Boston and the Sea Film, New England Aquarium, Boston, Massachusetts.* Central Wharf. The film, produced by the Museum of the China Trade, is shown at twenty-minute intervals throughout Bicentennial years. It depicts the range of Boston's maritime interests and roles through the eighteenth and nineteenth centuries (617) 742-8870.

48 *Portland, Maine.* Maine Turnpike; from first Portland exits, follow ship signs to the dock area; Exchange, Fore and Commercial Sts. A few buildings predate the Great Portland Fire of 1866, but most were built immediately after. Outstanding landmarks include the Mariner's Church, Custom House, Commercial Row, Custom House Wharf and Thompson Block. Walking tour guides are available from the Greater Portland Chamber of Commerce (142 Free St.) and from Greater Portland Landmarks Inc. (485 Congress St.).

48a *Casco Bay Lines, Portland, Maine.* Custom House Wharf. In summer months the line offers a special, narrated cruise to Bailey Island and a Saturday night moonlight dance cruise; all six of its ferries are diesel-powered and cars can be taken as far as Peaks Island. (207) 774-7871.

49 *Donald G. Trayser Memorial Museum, Barnstable, Massachusetts.* Cobbs Hill, Rte. 6A, just east of the Hyannis Rd. traffic light. Built in 1856, it now houses marine paintings, ship models and other relics from the coastal traffic it was built to serve. July and Aug., Tues.-Sat.: 1-5. Admission charged.

50 *Stonington, Maine.* Tip of Deer Isle; from U.S. 1, northeast of Bucksport take Rte. 15. Stonington's wooden shops and houses, odd-shaped and varicolored, look like so many seagrowths on the smooth, pink granite rocks which slope to its harbor. Accommodations, notably Captain's Quarters, (207) 367-8766, are booked far ahead during summer months. Chamber of Commerce: (207) 348-2445. Oakland House (off Rte. 15 north of Stonington), a Victorian period hotel whose owners supplemented income with winter ice harvesting and summer quarrying. Defunct local quarries now make fine swimming holes. June 20-Sept. 10. (207) 359-8521.

51 *Vinalhaven, Maine.* Accessible by ferry from Rockland (see end of this chapter's details). Besides quarrying, this thirty-two-square-mile island's nineteenth-century industries included ice, the country's biggest horsenet factory, fishing, shipbuilding and farming. Its slabs of granite helped to build New York's Greenwich Village and Boston's North End. The library, the only granite building on the island, was a gift from Andrew Carnegie. At its post-Civil War peak, the island's population crested at four thousand. Today the town's Main Street is gap-toothed; you see through to Carver's Pond between the shabby Victorian buildings which survive. Its farmland has gone back to spruce and daisies. Spruce Island, just beyond town, is a nature preserve. Two clean but modest inns and a small motel offer lodging.

52 *Rockport, Massachusetts.* From Rte. 128 northern terminus, Rte. 127; just north of Gloucester on Cape Ann. The town's name and "Granite St." recall quarrying days. Just north of town the Granite Pier Wharf is an impressive outcrop on which you can drive and picnic, fish or watch summer regattas. Look sharp at the small stone bridge just opposite and you will see Swan Quarry, from which blocks were first hauled by oxen (it is now used for water storage). The Sewall-Scripture House (40 King St.), built from native granite in 1832, houses the Sandy Bay Historical Society and Museum with its collection of paintings, ship models and tools from the granite industry (July-Labor Day, daily: 2-5). The village itself is now best known for Bearskin Neck, a browsing mecca of boutiques and galleries, housed in former lobstering and fishing shacks.

53 *Gloucester, Massachusetts.* Terminus of Rte. 128 north from Boston. First settled by the Dorchester Company in 1623, Gloucester once encompassed all of Cape Ann. It is here that the schooner is said to have had its origin in 1713, deriving its name from a bystander at the launching who commented "see how she schoons" (glides smoothly). Gorton Company, ironically packagers of frozen fish, is the chief employer. The town's own vessels still specialize in fresh fish, supplying a major percentage of all that consumed by the American market. Sites include home of the artist Fitzhugh Lane and the collection of his work to be seen at the Cape Ann Historical Association Museum (Pleasant St., year round, Tues.-Sat.: 11-4). The Church of Our Lady of Good Voyage (124 Prospect St.) serves the Portuguese fishing community; built in 1893, it is patterned on the cathedral at San Miguel in the Azores and its twin steeples house the country's oldest carillon bells. Pricy restaurants line the waterfront, but eateries like the Cape Ann Diner also feature exceptional fresh fish. The best beach in town is Good Harbor and

the best time to visit is during the annual festival; for details, contact Gloucester Chamber of Commerce (617) 283-1601.

54 *Marblehead, Massachusetts.* Exit 25 off Rte. 128 or Rte. 1A and 129. This picturesque town's lure is still sailing vessels, but today it caters to yachtsmen. The narrow streets which cluster around Washington Square are crammed with little homes, built for eighteenth-century fishermen. Sites to see include Abbot Hall (the present town hall) built in 1876 and housing the famous "Spirit of '76" painting (June-Oct., Mon.-Sat.: 8-9 P.M.; Sun. and holidays: 1-5; Nov.-May, Mon.-Fri.: 8-9 P.M.: Sat.: 8-12); also eighteenth-century Fort Sewall, Old North Church built in 1824 with its gilded fish weathervane (year round, Mon.-Fri.: 9-5); the mansions noted in Chapter 6 and the drive past late-nineteenth-century summer "cottages" and yacht clubs on Marblehead Neck. The big annual event here is summer Race Week. For local guidance, contact the Marblehead Chamber of Commerce, Pleasant St. (617) 631-2868.

55 *Lighthouses.*

MAINE

A leaflet guide describing the state's seventy-three beacons and indicating which are accessible and open to the public is titled "Watchful Maine," available from the Maine Department of Commerce and Industry (see "Helpful Hints"). Among these, two are museums dedicated to local history and industries.

Monhegan Light, center of this delightful island (see Chapter 2). July-Labor Day, daily: 12:30-3:30.

Pemaquid Point Light (see Chapter 2 for Pemaquid). Memorial Day-last Sun. in Sept., daily: 10-5.

MASSACHUSETTS

Boston Light, Boston Harbor. Difficult navigation around this landmark precludes visits; the best view is available on harbor tours offered in summer months from the excursion boats based at Long Wharf. Contact Boston Harbor Cruises, (617) 227-4320, and the Bay State, Spray & Provincetown Steamship Co. (617) 723-7800.

Chatham Light, Chatham. Bridge St. A spectacular view from its base encompasses the grave of more shipwrecks than any to be found along the New England coast.

Highland Light, Truro. Highland Rd., off Rte. 6. Also known as Cape Cod Light. Another spectacular view, this one of the Peaked Hill Bars on which many a ship has come to grief. This is the first coastal light which Boston-bound vessels from Europe see. The first beacon here was erected in 1797, powered by twenty-four whale oil lamps; the present lighthouse dates from 1857.

Race Point Light, near Provincetown. Located within the Province Lands sector of the Cape Cod National Seashore and a favorite spot to photograph. The nearby Visitors Center dispenses information about nature trails, dune buggy safaris, biking, swimming and horseback riding in the area. Mid-May to mid-Oct., daily: 9-6; otherwise closed Mon., Tues.

CONNECTICUT

Old Lighthouse Museum, Stonington. Water St. The state's oldest lighthouse, a granite structure which is now a museum maintained by the town's historical society; exhibits range from Indian relics to Indian curios. July 1-Labor Day, daily: 12:30-4:40.

RHODE ISLAND

Beavertail Light, Jamestown. East Shore Rd. to southern tip of the island. Built in 1856 on a 1749 foundation; a good picnic site.

Point Judith Lighthouse, near Galilee. An octagonal building constructed in 1816. Visitors welcome on the grounds.

Watch Hill Light. North side of the eastern entrance to Fisher's Island Sound, now a U.S. Coast Guard Light; a white-washed granite beacon erected in 1858. Year round, daily: 1–5 except when the light and foghorn are working (401) 348-8923.

56 *Life-Saving Stations.*

Coast Guard Beach, Eastham, Massachusetts. Cape Cod National Seashore, accessible from Salt Pond Visitor Center. Last in the series of nine stations built here since 1872, now a museum exhibiting equipment used by members of the Lifesaving Service who had to row their boats out to wrecks or to haul in survivors by line, one by one, to shore. Summer months, daily: 1–5.

Life Saving Museum, Nantucket, Massachusetts. Polpis Rd. A reconstruction of the island's 1874 station, housing exhibits which include surf boats, quarterboards from ships wrecked off shore and mementos which tell the story of the Humane Society houses, life-saving stations and coast guard installations on the island. Year round, Tues.–Sun.: 10–5. Admission charged.

Block Island Life Saving Station, Mystic Seaport, Connecticut. A gingerbread-style building housing its original equipment, recently moved to the maritime museum from Block Island. (See detail 17.)

57 *Mount Washington Summit Road, Gorham, New Hampshire.* From Rte. 16 in Pinkham Notch, eastern base of Mount Washington between Jackson and Gorham. Opened in 1861, a gradual spiral upwards at an average grade of 12%. "Stages," a fleet of four-wheel-drive station wagons, ferry visitors to the top and back down at the same price charged for one car and driver (there is an additional charge for each passenger). (603) 466-4988. For Mount Washington see Chapter 10.

57a *Mount Washington Cog Railway, Mt. Washington, New Hampshire.* From Rte. 302 in Crawford Notch, two approach roads run to the Marshfield base station. The ride provides a dramatic view of changing flora and fauna between its starting altitude of 2569 feet and that of 6283 at the peak of New England's highest mountain. En route the trail halts twice, backtracking onto turnouts for down-coming traffic and taking on one thousand gallons of water. The base station includes a log restaurant and reasonably priced "rustic" cabins. Frequent departures June 29–Sept. 8 and less frequent June 15–28 and Sept. 9–Oct. 13; advisable to come in the morning when the wait is shorter. Steep admission charged but worth it. (603) 466-0004.

58 *Concord Coach,* displayed at the New Hampshire Historical Society, 30 Park St., Concord, New Hampshire. Year round, Mon.–Sat.: 9–4.

59 *Bellows Falls, Vermont.* Rte. 5 off I-91. The Connecticut River here plunges down through the narrowest channel in its entire length. The locks, begun by an Englishman in 1792 and America's first, have not been used since 1858, but are visible from the riverbank.

60 *Vermont's Northeast Kingdom* encompasses the northeasternmost counties of the state, largely untouched by both the recent tourist and ski booms. Ricker Mills within the town of Gorton here (Rte. 302 northwest from I-91) still produces softwood much the way it did a century ago; the adjacent Old Lake House was built in 1843 as a boardinghouse for lumberjacks.

61 *Indian Stream Republic.* Rte. 145 off Rtes. 26 and I-93. A disagreement about where the border actually lay left this territory between the United States and Canada up for grabs. Some three hundred residents declared themselves a republic in 1832 and the state did not get around to outlawing them until 1835. Today the area is known as New Hampshire's Connecticut Lakes region, much of it owned by the St. Regis Paper Co., which maintains private roads and permits day use only (camping prohibited). Reasonable lodging, geared to hunters and fishermen, can be found on Lake Francis, Back Lake and First Connecticut Lake. For a listing, write Colebrook and Pittsburg Chamber of Commerce, 12 Bridge St., Colebrook, New Hampshire 03576.

61 *Worcester, Massachusetts.* Rte. 9, central Massachusetts, accessible from Massachusetts Turnpike. The Blackstone Canal, which parallels the Blackstone River and Rte. 136 from Providence to Worcester, has been filled in at its northern terminus, but the Italian workmen who dug it built their homes and opened their shops on the spot, now the Italian section of Worcester. This city is New England's most racially varied. Besides its ubiquitous mills the city boasts an outstanding art museum (55 Salisbury St., year round, Tues.–Sat.: 10–5; Sun.: 12–6) and a Science Center (Harrington Way, year round, Mon.–Sat.: 10–5; Sun.: 1–5. Admission charged). Visitors' information booths are located in all the city's library branches. (Main Library, Salem Square.) Worcester Chamber of Commerce: (617) 753-2924.

63 *Farmington Canal.* This would-be alternate trade route to the Connecticut River runs through the towns of East Granby, Suffield, Simsbury, Avon, Plainville, Bristol, Southington, Cheshire, Hamden and Farmington. Its effect was felt in many of these towns, spurring Farmington itself into a variety of manufactures and even East Indies trade, giving it a cultural one-upmanship over its neighbors which is still evident in the elegance of its homes and museums. (See Chapter 3 for the Stanley-Whitman House; Chapter 10 for the Hill-Stead Museum.)

64 *Burlington, Vermont.* I-89 exits. Vermont's largest city, Burlington retains a late-nineteenth-century stamp in its Victorian houses, which line wide, tree-shaded streets above the brick commercial blocks which slope down to Lake Champlain. The waterfront itself has recently been obliterated by urban renewal, but plans to restore what tokens remain of its lumbering wharves are underway. Fleming Museum on the University of Vermont campus (Colchester Ave., open daily) is a mix of art, historic and scientific exhibits, and there is a Farmers' Market of crafts and fresh produce held regularly in town. For details about when and where (in flux at this writing) contact Burlington Chamber of Commerce (802) 832-2489.

64a *Lake Champlain Transportation Company, Burlington, Vermont.* King St. The company operates seven diesel-powered ferries which traverse the lake, east-west at three points: Grand Isle to Plattsburgh, Burlington to Port Kent, and Charlotte to Essex. Today it serves as a link between major highways (I-87 in New York; I-89 and Rte. 7 in Vermont). All three runs are for both passengers and cars; year round, daily except January to mid-March when the lake generally freezes. (802) 864-9804.

65 *Songo Lock, Naples, Maine.* Midway between Long Lake and Sebago Lake, built of stone masonry with wooden gates. It is adjacent to Sebago Lake State Park, which offers swimming and boating. Excursion through locks offered by *Songo River Queen.* See end of details.

66 *Granite Railroad, Quincy, Massachusetts.* This is generally cited as the country's first commercial railroad. In 1926 a full-scale replica of one of the original cars was built and eventually will be displayed in the Quincy Historical Society Museum, newly opened in the old Adams Academy Building (8 Adams St., April 19–Sept. 30, Tues.-Sun.: 10–5, [617] 773-1144) which also contains a number of mementos from the old line. More information about the three segments of the actual track which still survive is available from the Quincy Heritage Trail booklet; contact Quincy Heritage, Quincy Center MBTA Station (617) 773-1380.

67 *Wolfeboro Rail Road Co., Wolfeboro, New Hampshire.* Railroad Ave. The excursion takes you across an old millpond, through Falls Cut, across Crescent and Wentworth Lakes on stone dikes, over wooden trestles and through woods and meadows. Throughout the two-hour round-trip the line's owner-conductor gives forth with a steady stream of information about old railroading and steamboating days in the area. Year round; frequent departures in summer months, less frequent in off months. Admission charged and worth the slight extra price for a seat in the "Combine Car" with its plush upholstery, brass chandeliers and wood-burning stove. (603) 596-4884.

68 *Conway Scenic Railroad, North Conway, New Hampshire.* Rte. 16. Memorial Day–Oct.; frequent departures. Admission charged. For a schedule, write Conway Scenic R.R., P.O. Box 434, Conway, New Hampshire 03818. (603) 356-5251.

69 *Clark's Trading Post, Lincoln, New Hampshire.* Rte. 3. The trading post was opened in 1928 by Edward and Florence Clark who pioneered a very different sort of transport in the twentieth century – dogsleds! The complex includes trained bears, a haunted house and hodgepodge collection of nineteenth-century curios. The train ride is brief but takes you beneath an original Howe Truss covered bridge. July–Labor Day, daily; Sept., Oct., weekends. Admission charged. (603) 745-8913.

70 *South Royalton, Vermont.* Rte. 14, off I-89. Since the Vermont Central did not come to Royalton, a segment of the town moved to the side of the new tracks instead, forming the present cluster of homes and shops around a rectangular common with its brick depot and big wooden inn. All these buildings were built within one year. Today the inn (South Royalton House) and most of the buildings on the common are owned by Vermont Law School and Royalton College (related institutions); the inn does take guests and includes La Marmite French Restaurant (802) 763-8872.

71 *Barre, Vermont.* Rte. 14 from I-89. This self-styled "Granite Capital of the World" produces more than one third of the country's granite monuments. Visitors should not miss the city's cemetery, showplace for its product and famed for the statue of Robert Burns here. More intriguing is the figure of Elia Corti who sits atop his tomb; Corti carved the panels on the Burns monument but was killed by a stray bullet in a turn-of-the-century demonstration. Most visitors head for the Rock of Ages Quarry in Graniteville, south of the town center. What they come to see is the view: 350 feet down into the active quarry pit which covers twenty

acres. The nearby tourist center displays finished memorials and sells curios; here you buy tickets for the twenty-five-minute train ride: June–Sept., Mon.–Fri.: 9–4. (802) 476-3115.

72 *St. Albans, Vermont.* I-89 and Rte. 36. The principal town in Franklin County, Vermont's rolling, open northwestern corner. The city sits two miles in and above Lake Champlain. No longer New England's largest rail depot, St. Albans now claims to be "Maple Sugar Capital of the World." Leader Eva Partor, established 1818, is the biggest producer of syrup-making equipment and the Vermont Maple Festival is held at Taylor Park, the city's handsome common (first week in April). The Franklin County Museum (Church St., July–Aug., Tues.–Sat.: 2–5) offers mementos from the city's varied history. There is good food and board at the Governor Smith Inn, (802) 524-6566, and the summer resort around St. Albans Bay includes two state parks. St. Albans Chamber of Commerce: (802) 524-2444.

73 *St. Johnsbury, Vermont.* Rtes. 5 and 2. Largest town in Vermont's northeastern corner and known locally as "St. J." This is a major maple producer today; Carey Maple Sugar Co., Portland St., welcomes visitors year round, weekdays, and includes a little maple sugar museum. The Atheneum (30 Main St.) doubles as a handsome library and a little art museum displaying huge landscapes in the Hudson River School style. The Fairbanks Museum of Natural Science is unique (see Chapter 10) and St. Johnsbury House continues to offer food and lodging (802) 748-3181. St. Johnsbury Chamber of Commerce: (802) 748-3678.

74 *Danville, Vermont.* Rte. 2, west from St. Johnsbury. One cannot help but be grateful that the railroad did bypass Danville, leaving it high and unselfconsciously lovely atop its plateau. Grouped around the outsized common are the town hall (1805), the tiny square Caledonia Bank, a post office and general store. Abolitionist Thaddeus Stevens was born here, but the town is best known today as headquarters for the American Society of Dowsers which attracts thousands of people to try their luck discovering water with divining rods during the annual September convention. For details write the Society, Danville, Vermont 05828.

75 *Proctor, Vermont.* From Rutland, two miles west on Rte. 4, then eight miles north on Rte. 3. It is a disappointing fact but you cannot visit the marble quarries themselves since they are underground. Vermont Marble Company's exhibit is however spectacular in its own way, including a gallery of presidents and the Last Supper carved out of marble. A movie shows the quarrying process and a shop sells marble in various shapes. May 25–Oct. 21, daily: 9–6. Admission charged. (802) 459-3311.

76 *Pavilion Building, Montpelier, Vermont,* adjacent to the State House. The original hotel here was built in 1805 and subsequently entertained Lafayette and all the state legislatures until 1876 when the present building replaced it to serve the same purpose. The Tavern Motor Inn across the street continues in this role since the Pavilion was converted into state offices a few years ago, now also housing the Vermont Historical Society museum which includes delightful displays on most facets of Vermont history. Year round, Mon.–Fri.: 8–4:30.

77 *Steamtown Foundation, Riverton, Vermont.* Two miles north of Bellows Falls, Rte. 5. The collection includes thirty-one engines. The depot itself includes a major lineup of railroading stock and memorabilia. Excursions leave regularly June 22–Sept. 2 and Sept. 28–Oct. 20, daily; May 25–June 16 and Sept. 7–21, weekends only. You can also charter a steamtown train and board special long-run excursions offered periodically. Admission charged. (802) 463-3937.

78 *Vermont's Historic 1876 Transportation System.* Visitors would be encouraged to park their cars on entering the state, picking them up only when they are about to leave, be it after a two-day or two-month adventure. Reservations for the entire stay would be made by toll-free phone. They would be met at stations along the train route and taken to inns. Dining aboard would be 1876 style. For details, contact Steamtown (see 77).

79 *Edaville R.R., Carver, Massachusetts.* Rte. 58, between Rtes. 25 and 44. Cars are open in summer months, closed in winter. Excursions June 9–Labor Day; Labor Day–Oct. 9 a diesel engine replaces steam on weekdays and cranberries as well as passengers are hauled; weekends it reverts to steam and passengers only. Open again during December when the property is decorated with lights. April–June 9: an infrequent schedule. Check with the railroad, Box 7, South Carver, Massachusetts. (617) 866-4526.

80 *Mystic Valley Railway Society,* P.O. Box 32, Mattapan, Massachusetts 02126. This nonprofit group of Boston area rail buffs has staged a wild assortment of excursions in their five-year history. Destinations have included Cape Cod, Lake Winnipesaukee, Old Orchard Beach and Block Island. Besides simply offering a rail ride, these trips give passengers something to do at the other end; occasionally also include overnight lodgings. The excursions are offered on an average of one a month, reasonably priced. (617) 361-7114.

81 *Railroad Enthusiasts,* P.O. Box 136, Ward Hill, Massachusetts 01830. Trips are geared to the general public as well as to rail buffs; still worth getting on their mailing list.

82 *Boothbay Railway Museum, Boothbay, Maine.* Rte. 27 south of Rte. 1. The excursion is a 1.4 mile circuit on a narrow-gauge steamtrain of the "museum" grounds which also include an Olde New England village and railroading mementos, old cars and two genuine old rail stations. June 19–Labor Day, daily: 10–5; rest of year, Sat. only. Admission charged. (207) 633-4727.

83 *Portland, Maine to Island Pond, Vermont.* Annual autumn excursion. For details, contact the "420" Railroad Club, P.O. Box 641, Portland, Me. 04104.

84 *Narragansett Pier R.R., Peace Dale Depot, Narragansett, Rhode Island.* Rte. 1, May 30–Sept.; Mon., Wed., Fri., Sat. Admission charged. (401) 783-3391.

85 *Lake Morey, Fairlee, Vermont.* Rte. 5 off I-91. There are a clutch of outstanding resorts on and near the lake: Bonnie Oaks, Lake More Inn and Club and the Rutledge Inn and cottages; the first two are noted for their shared golf course, site of the annual Vermont Open Golf Tournament, mid-June. The Walker Museum in town houses a collection of Oriental and early American artifacts – July–mid-Sept., daily: 10–5.

86 *Ticonderoga at Shelburne Museum, Shelburne, Vermont.* Rte. 7 south from Burlington. In all the museum includes thirty-five buildings spread over forty-five acres (see Chapter 10). May 15–Oct. 15, daily: 9–5. Steep admission.

87 *The M/V Mount Washington, Weirs Beach, New Hampshire.* Today "the Mount" is powered by twin diesel engines and offers plenty of sunning space on her three decks, as well as an attractive saloon. During summer months she makes three daily circuits of the lake, connecting with the Wolfeboro Railroad and excursions up to the Castle in the Clouds (see Chapter 10). In high season she also offers Saturday night moonlight cruises. Her small sister vessels, the M/V *Sophie C.* (U.S. mail boat) provides a tour of the lake's islands and the M/V *Doris E.* offers short excursions. For details, contact Winnipesaukee Flagship Corp., P.O. Box 367, Weirs Beach, New Hampshire 03246. (603) 366-5531.

88 *Marine Museum at Fall River, Massachusetts.* 70 Water St., Battleship Cove. The museum is housed in an old mill, ideal space for its exhibit of 180 ship's models which vary in length from ½ inch to 14 feet. Nearby is the U.S.S. *Massachusetts*, famous World War II battleship (admission charged). The museum is open year round, weekdays: 9–5; Sun.: 12–5. Admission. (617) 674-3533.

89 *Woods Hole, Martha's Vineyard and Nantucket Steamship Authority, Woods Hole, Massachusetts.* Operates five diesel-powered ferries in summer, two in winter, all carrying cars. In Boston: (617) 426-1855; Woods Hole: (617) 548-5011.

90 *New England Steamboat, Inc., Haddam, Connecticut.* The diesel-powered *Yankee Clipper* carries passengers and bicycles on summer and fall cruises to Greenport and Sag Harbor, Long Island, allowing a three-hour stopover for sightseeing; also two-hour sunset cruises on the Connecticut. (203) 345-4507.

91 *More New England Ferries and Excursion Boats.*

CONNECTICUT

Bridgeport. Bridgeport & Port Jefferson Steamboat Co. This seasonal run takes one hour and twenty minutes and connects the two points signified by its name. (203) 367-8571 or 334-5993.

Groton. Whaling City Dredge & Dock Corporation. Across the river from New London the former Jamestown, Rhode Island, ferry now serves as a restaurant while a launch leaves regularly in season from its dock to tour construction sites of submarines at the mouth of the Thames River. (203) 445-7401.

New London. New London Ferry, 112 Pequot Ave. A seasonal service, four hours from New London to Orient Point, Long Island. (203) 443-5281 or 443-5053.

Block Island–New London. Foot of State St. June–Sept., cars carried. (203) 442-9553.

Fishers Island–New London. Foot of State St. Year round, cars carried. (203) 443-6851.

Essex. Excursion boat *Dolly Madison* offers Connecticut River cruises. (203) 767-8806/388-3280.

MAINE

Mt. Desert.

BAR HARBOR. Bluenose Ferry to Yarmouth, Nova Scotia. The M/V *Bluenose* makes one round trip daily, carrying six hundred passengers and up to 150 cars. Details from Canadian National Railways, toll-free: (800) 341-7981. In Boston (617) 742-5410 (weekdays, 9-5).

SOUTHWEST HARBOR. A choice of small ferries serves the Cranberry Isles in July, Aug.; a tour which includes a narrated visit to the Isleford Museum should be arranged through the Hull's Cover Visitors Center, Acadia National Park (207) 244-3575.

BASS HARBOR. Maine State Ferry Service maintains two runs in season; one to Frenchboro on Long Island where excursionists can enjoy beaching, and one to Swan's Island, a lobstering island with little to offer visitors who do not own their own "camps."

Naples. The *Songo River Queen* offers July and August excursions on the Songo River, through the Locks, on Long Lake and Brandy Pond. (207) 693-6861.

Stonington. A private line serves Isle au Haut, part of Acadia National Park, with hiking, swimming and camping facilities. Information is available both through park headquarters (see above) and from Capt. Stanley Dodge in Stonington (207) 367-2420.

Lincolnville. Maine State Ferry Service maintains service to Isleboro where visitors can enjoy swimming at a state park. (207) 789-2356.

Rockland. Maine State Ferry Service operates two runs, one to North Haven (a summer colony offering camping, picnicking and limited accommodations) and to Vinalhaven (see detail 51) and Matinicus (a genuine untouristed lobstering island) (207) 594-5543.

Port Clyde. The *Laura B.* serves Monhegan Island in season. (See Chapter 3.) Contact Capt. Earl S. Field (207) 372-6538.

New Harbor. *The Monhegan*, weekend service to Monhegan, mid-June to mid-Sept. (207) 799-1091.

Boothbay Harbor: *Linekin II* offers tours of the outer harbor in season and Captain Bob Fish operates a variety of excursions and fishing trips aboard a half dozen boats, also service (mid-June through Sept.) to Monhegan with the *Balmy Days* and to Squirrel Island (May to Oct.) with *Nellie G IV* and *Maranbo II*. (207) 633-5131.

Portland. Lion Ferry operates two little cruise ships, the M/S *Prince of Fundy* and M/S *Bolero*, both of which depart regularly in season for Yarmouth, Nova Scotia. Facilities aboard include comfortable cabins, a casino, dancing to a live combo and a restaurant. Weekend packages are available. May 1-Oct. 31. Toll-free: (800) 341-7595.

NEW HAMPSHIRE

Portsmouth. Star Island Corporation, Market St., exit off I-95. The new M/V *Viking Queen* carries passengers to Star Island, a religious conference center offering swimming and hiking (see Chapter 10). (603) 431-5500.

Lake Sunapee. The *Sunapee Belle*, a mini-copy of a Mississippi River sternwheeler, featuring buffet supper cruises during summer months; also luncheon cruises. (603) 763-5477.

MASSACHUSETTS

Boston. Bay State, Spray and Provincetown Steamship Co., 20 Long Wharf. The triple-decked *Provincetown* carries passengers from Boston to Provincetown June-Aug., daily, and May, Sept., Oct., weekends. The smaller *Bay State* specializes in lunch and cocktail cruises through the harbor islands. The *Spray*, a vintage 1897 windjammer, offers sailing tours in season. (617) 723-7800.

Boston Harbor Cruises. Daily tours of the harbor in season. (617) 227-4300.

Massachusetts Bay Line, Rowes Wharf. Harbor cruises and regular service to Nantasket; arrangements can also be made beforehand to be dropped off and picked up at George's Island. (617) 542-8000.

Hyannis. Nantucket Boat Inc., seasonal passenger service to Nantucket and Martha's Vineyard. (617) 775-7185.

Falmouth. Island Commuter Corporation offers day trips to Martha's Vineyard. (617) 548-4800.

New Bedford. Cuttyhunk Boat Line offers daily service in summer months to the island of Cuttyhunk (see Chapter 1). (617) 992-1432 or 992-4030.

Cape-Island Express. Daily passenger service to Martha's Vineyard. (617) 997-1688 or 997-3617 in Hyannis.

East Gloucester. Half-hour afternoon cruises aboard the *Dixie Belle*, from Lobster House Pier, Rocky Neck; June 15 to Sept. 15, daily. (617) 283-5893.

RHODE ISLAND.

Point Judith. Interstate Navigation Co. offers passenger service in season to Block Island. (401) 783-4613 or (203) 442-7891.

Newport. Viking Bus and Boat Tours offers regular excursions during summer months in Narragansett Bay. (401) 847-6921.

Providence. Interstate Navigation Co., Indian St. Pier, East Providence. Season passenger service to Block Island and Newport.

Warren. American Canadian Line. Luther Blount, who builds more than half the region's ferries and excursion boats, maintains the M/V *New Shoreham*, which carries 60 passengers on inland cruises up the Hudson, through the St. Lawrence passageway in summer, along the coast in spring and fall, and down the inland waterway to Florida at the onset of winter, returning that route in spring. (401) 245-1350.

MORE WINDJAMMER CRUISES.

In addition to the sailings offered out of Camden, Maine, (see detail 26) a choice of vessels and itineraries is available from scattered departure points. At this writing the five-day to week-long cruises average $250 per person; passengers must be aged 12 or older and reservations are usually necessary several months in advance of the summer season.

Massachusetts

MARTHA'S VINEYARD. Schooner *Shenandoah* carries up to 29 passengers on six-day cruises along the southern New England coast. Coastwise Packet Company, Vineyard Haven, Massachusetts 02568. (617) 693-1699.

Rhode Island

NEWPORT. The *Bill of Rights* makes weekly and some three-day weekend cruises along the southern New England coast; 30-person capacity. Box 477, Rhode Newport, Rhode Island 02840. (401) 724-7612.

Connecticut

MYSTIC. For details about the Mystic Whaler: (203) 536-4218.

Maine

ROCKLAND. Victory Chimes, billed as the largest windjammer under the U.S. flag, carries up to 45 passengers on weekly sailings; Maine Coastal Cruises, Box 368, Rockland, Maine 04841. (207) 596-6060. The *Richard Robbins Sr.* and the *Isaac H. Evans* also offer weekly cruises in Penobscot Bay; Box 482, Rockland, Maine 04841. (207) 594-8007.

ROCKPORT. The *Timberwind* offers six-day cruises in Penobscot Bay. Box 247, Rockport, Maine 04856. (207) 236-3639.

THOMASTON. The *Harvey Gamage* is a new schooner with a 34-person capacity. She cruises off the coast of Maine during summer months and in the Caribbean come winter. The Maine trips periodically feature historical narration by scholars. P.O. Box 375, Brewer, Maine 04412. (207) 989-6147.

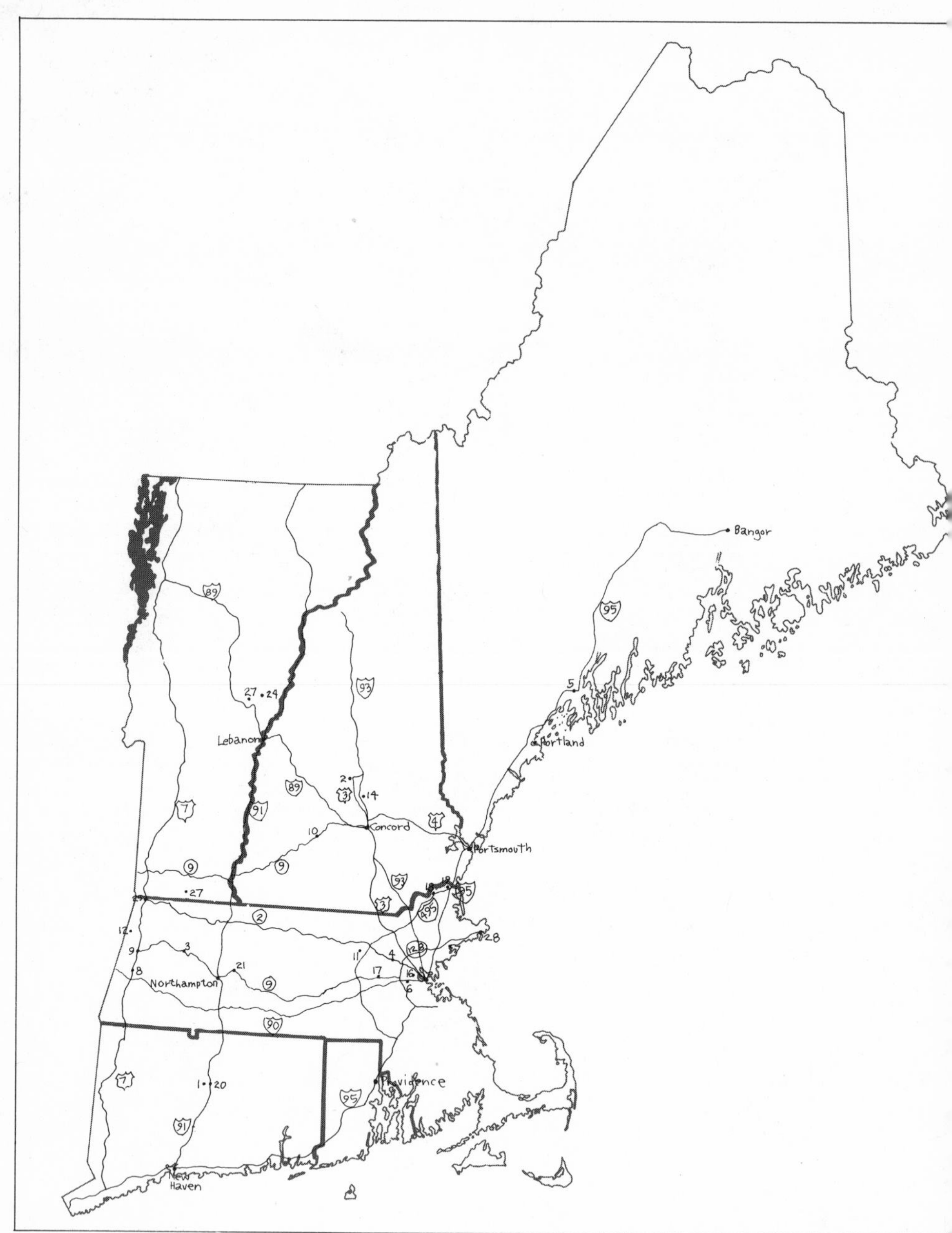

Bangor
95
5
Portland
Portsmouth
4
27
24
Lebanon
93
2
3
14
89
89
91
7
Concord
10
9
9
27
93
3
19
18
95
495
2
12
9
3
8
21
Northampton
9
11
4
128
28
17
16
6
90
Providence
1
20
7
95
91
New Haven

9

Intellect and Inspiration

The new nation's rush to establish economic self-sufficiency coincided with a restlessness to proclaim its own intellectual identity as well. Connecticut lexicog-
rapher *Noah Webster* had foreshadowed this spirit with 1
his 1780s publication of the *Blue-backed Speller*, declaring that "America must be as independent in literature as she is in politics, as famous for arts as for arms." In 1828 Webster's *American Dictionary of the English Language* proudly severed this country's speech from Old World roots.

In his classic, *The Flowering of New England*, Van Wyck Brooks describes the region's first intellectual rebels as a "buffer generation between the hard old Puritan ways and the minds of younger people." Around the turn of the nineteenth century, stark traditional Congregationalism had broken down into a prism of emotionally charged sects in rural areas. Religion remained the people's poetry. The bluff farmer-politician *Daniel Webster* 2
embodied the popular Yankee ideal.

In the 1820s America's oldest college became the first to break the provincial educational mold, geared to producing ministers and merchants. Harvard adopted new coldly rational Unitarianism, and a policy of teaching students to think and to write. Today it amazes us that so many literary greats of the ensuing decades – Emerson, Thoreau, the Alcotts, Melville, Hawthorne, Longfellow, Oliver Wendell Holmes and Whittier – all formed one Boston-based circle. Consider the temper of the times and it is less surprising. This was New England's first younger generation with the time and the education to philosophize and experiment with new life-styles. Young Bostonians who upbraided their elders for supporting slavery by importing cotton for their mills, or who simply devoted most of their time to high-minded discussion, were viewed much the way our present culture sees its counterculture.

Even friends found it difficult to comprehend Harvard student Henry Dana II's decision to sail as a common deckhand on a hide-collecting expedition to California. Occasionally, gentlemen sailed as "supercargoes" on fur-collecting voyages. But hides stank and the job of transporting them was even below the dignity of many a skipper. Dana eventually not only described his passage in *Two Years before the Mast* but dedicated his life as a lawyer to improving the lot of the common seamen, a lot which his social circle had created.

The status of literary endeavor, however, climbed quickly. In 1812 a doctor from western Massachusetts submitted a poem titled "Thanatopsis," penned by his
son *William Cullen Bryant*, to the new *North American* 3
Review. Van Wyck Brooks notes that "the American world had moved a step forward when village poets could produce verses and country doctors could be proud and happy, feeling that their sons were men of genius."

By the mid-century the impact of this first generation of thinkers, reformers and authors had proved dramatic. The founding of lyceums, libraries and new educational institutions on every level mirrored the general passion for learning. Boston's literary output commanded a world audience and bred a pride which can be felt in the city's streets today.

Historian Samuel Eliot Morison cites the 1836 publication of Ralph Waldo Emerson's "Essay on Nature" as "opening a period in American literary culture, corresponding to 1775 in American politics." Emerson's statement of transcendental philosophy declared the human soul innately capable of comprehending truth and beauty, keyed to an "over-soul": "That Unity . . . within which every man's particular being is contained and made one with all other; that common heart of which all sincere conversations is worship, to which all right action is submission."

Emerson came from a long line of Puritan divines. Four years before writing this proclamation he had resigned

his own post as minister to Boston's Second Church, itself once the bastion of Puritanism, but in 1832 a seat of Unitarianism. The new religion was a reaction to the old preoccupation with guilt and sin, but one which this young man found "vapid." Emerson missed the mysticism inherent in New England's bedrock religion. But he sought it in the one place which his ancestors had most feared and frowned on: solitude. In 1834 Emerson bought the house presently dedicated to his memory in
his ancestral hometown of *Concord*, setting an Aeolian 4
harp on the windowsill in his study to tap music from the wind and purchasing fourteen acres of pine and briar on nearby Walden Pond in which to commune with himself and nature.

Initially Emerson aroused shock, then intense interest from a few, and general curiosity throughout the region. The term "transcendentalism" has since been used to characterize the mood of literature, Utopian movements and many a reform of ensuing decades.

Among those who regularly met at *Emerson's house* 4a
and contributed to *The Dial*, mouthpiece for the new philosophy, was Henry David Thoreau, son of Concord's pencil manufacturer. With his brother Thoreau conducted classes at Concord Academy in the spirit advocated by Emerson: the children walked, rowed, and swam, questioned and discussed. In 1845 Henry accepted Emerson's
invitation to build a cabin at *Walden Pond* where he lived 4b
for two years, later explaining in *Walden, or Life in the Woods. A Manual of Self-reliance*: "I went to the woods because I wished to live deliberately, to front only the essential facts of life, and see if I could not learn what it had to teach, and not, when I came to die, to discover that I had not lived."

Thoreau's subsequent wanderings took him to live with the Penobscots in Maine, to camp on lonely New Hampshire mountaintops, and to trudge the length of Cape Cod. He continued to chronicle what he thought and saw with power and originality. In recent years his appeal as ecologist and mystic has eclipsed that of Emerson himself. In Concord you find his memory preserved through a *lyceum* dedicated to his spirit and 4c
writings.

In transcendentalism Nathaniel Hawthorne also found confidence to treat New England themes with his own keen sense of human tragedy. Hawthorne had been born in Salem at a time when the city's maritime glory had

just lapsed, leaving it a city of memories in which tales
of exotic exploits mixed with those of Puritan days and
witches. Hawthorne's own father, a skipper, had died in
Surinam, turning his mother into a recluse who rarely
left her room. During the year which he passed on a
Maine farm, this youth spent almost every winter night
skating on the pond by moonlight. Returning to Salem
from *Bowdoin College* he haunted Salem's streets, mu- 5
seums and waterfront taverns, traveled the length of the
White Mountains, Connecticut Valley and Erie Canal in
summer. He absorbed what he saw, filling notebooks
with details. In a covering letter which he sent with the
manuscript of *Twice-Told Tales* to a publisher in 1829,
Hawthorne attempted to explain: "You will see that one
of the stories is founded upon superstitions of this part
of the country. I do not know that such an attempt has
hitherto been made, but, as I have thrown away much
time in listening to such traditions, I could not help trying to put them into some shape. The tale is certainly
wild and grotesque, but the outlines of many not less so
might be picked up hereabouts."

There were two sides to Nathaniel Hawthorne: the melancholy, creative mystic and the practical, sociable young
man. He thrived alternately on solitude and companionship, and next joined *Brook Farm*, a Utopian community 6
which sought the "over-soul through community rather
than isolation." Founded in 1841 by George Ripley, like
Emerson a former Boston minister, the Brook Farm Institute of Agriculture and Education offered its one hun-
dred-odd young members a chance to explore nature
first-hand through manual chores, discussions and lively
interaction. Hawthorne invested $1,000 in the venture
which he later described in "Blithesdale Romance," but
after five months in the cowshed he shifted to an administrative post and thence out. Within a year he married
Sophia Peabody, the youngest of three socially and intellectually prominent sisters (the eldest founded the country's first kindergarten and the second married Horace
Mann). The young couple moved into the *Old Manse* in 4d
Concord built by Emerson's grandfather, but soon were
back in *Salem* again. After his short-lived job as *Customs* 7
Inspector, Hawthorne settled down to write the *Scarlet*
Letter. His *House of Seven Gables*, set in the romantically 7a
brooding house which is now one of New England's top
tourist attractions, he actually wrote in *Lenox*. Here he 8
lived in a small red cottage, presently reconstructed as a

musicians' practice studio on the grounds of Tanglewood, this region's summer music mecca which takes its very name from Hawthorne's *Tanglewood Tales.*

Here too Hawthorne and *Herman Melville* became 9
neighbors and friends. Melville, a native of New York City, was living at a farm near *Pittsfield* and transforming his experience aboard the Nantucket whaler *Acushnet* into a novel titled *Moby Dick*. Melville eventually returned to New York where, as Hawthorne had twice done, he found a sinecure in the city's custom house. Hawthorne himself returned to Concord, staying only briefly this time since his Bowdoin classmate – now
United States President *Franklin Pierce* – offered him 10
the post of consul at Liverpool.

Hawthorne is said to have lived in a total of seventeen
homes in New England. Just up the road from *Wayside* 4e
in Concord, his final home, stands *Orchard House*, me- 4f
morial to the Alcott family who had moved twenty-two times just within Massachusetts, living for a while in Wayside too.

Nathaniel Hawthorne Parlor, Concord, Mass.

Son of a poor Connecticut farmer, Bronson Alcott had spent his youth as a peddler, traveling through Virginia with a wagon full of Yankee notions, always on the lookout for a school in which he could exercise his novel theories of education. Since these coincided with those of the transcendentalists, he found a warm reception in Boston where he opened the Temple School in 1834 and with the help of Elizabeth Peabody, Sophia's eldest sister, set about shocking many good parents of the day. The school was closed in 1840 after public ire was aroused on two counts: Alcott had explained the facts of life to his pupils and also refused to expel a black pupil. He went off to England where he was gratified to find a school operating on his theories and a reformer named Charles Lane who agreed to return with him and finance a new Utopian experiment: a "Consociate family of New Eden."

In 1834 Lane bought a ninety-acre farm in the orchard town of Harvard, Massachusetts, and the Alcotts, including Bronson's long-suffering wife and his four daughters, moved in with Lane, his son and seven other adventurous spirits who included Isaac Hecker (subsequent founder of the Paulist Fathers). The "family" espoused a spartan regime of cold baths, manual labor and high-minded conversation. They dined on native grains, fruits, herbs and spring water, avoiding any food or clothing which "exploited" animals or human beings (thus cotton, picked by Southern slaves, was out). They grew only "aspiring plants," such as asparagus, which grow upwards.

The group proved far handier with their heads than hands: in autumn they neglected to harvest what they had clumsily sown, and in the blizzards of January the community, which Louisa May Alcott later described in *Transcendental Wild Oats*, foundered. The old farmhouse is now a museum dedicated to transcendentalism in general, centerpiece for an unusual complex of displays which make up *Fruitlands Museums.* 11

Charles Lane simply moved to another part of town to join a Shaker community which had successfully weathered some hard times itself: in 1782, four hundred Shakers had been driven and beaten the full ten miles from Harvard to Lancaster; those who wished to return got the same treatment on the way home. The sect had been brought from Manchester, England, by Ann Lee, a young millhand who saw herself as "mother of a new dispensation," no less a messiah than Jesus.

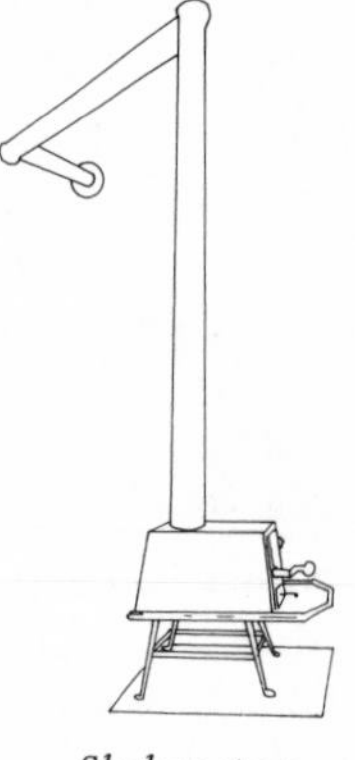

Shaker stove

That was in 1775 and the prophet who succeeded in prying followers away from their families (she strictly forbade physical contact between sexes) soon found herself the butt of persecution, ostensibly as an agent of the Crown. Ann Lee herself died, aged 48, in 1784. But with peace and the early nineteenth-century interest both in frenzied religious expression and spartan high living, the sect prospered. By the Civil War some 6,000 men and women were following Mother Ann's injunction to "put your hands to work and your hearts to God," in eighteen American communes, each a self-contained little world with its own farm, school and factories. At the time these extended from Kentucky to Maine and out to Ohio.

Today only six Shaker communities survive in shape enough to tell their story, four of them in New England.
One of these is a museum of a dozen restored *Shaker* 12
Buildings at Hancock, Massachusetts, and another the restored Shaker house at Fruitlands Museums and the traces of the actual community which Lane joined in Harvard. The remaining two are maintained by the
world's last surviving Shaker sisters at *Sabbath Day Lake,* 13
Maine, and at *Canterbury, New Hampshire*. Shaker fur- 14
niture, boxes and stoves, the likes of which you can also see in Boston's Museum of Fine Arts, are widely appreciated today for their spare beauty. It is also generally

known that Shakers invented the clothespin, circular saw, the flat broom, automatic spring, a threshing machine, pea-sheller, metal pen, and packaged seeds. But the four existing Shaker sites themselves must be visited to gain any understanding about these dancing monks and nuns who turned farming, craftsmanship and invention into visible prayers.

Throughout the past century "World's people" (non-Shakers) frequently visited these communes to buy produce and products, to bring orphans to be housed, or children to be reared, to seek alms (which they were never refused) or simply to witness the Sabbath ritual dance. Dickens described them as "grim." Hawthorne deplored their "utter and systematic lack of privacy." New Yorkers traveled up the Hudson by sidewheeler to see their shuffling dance. When the Hancock community
designed a *round barn*, the first, and although widely 15
copied, still the largest, Melville thought it amazing that each local hand was paid $500 and boarded for the duration of his work. Modern observers continue to be intrigued by glimpses into the lives of these unusual people.

Shaker round stone barn, Hancock, Mass.

The Alcott family today are remembered through *Little Women* as the model of a loving, close-knit family, the very antithesis of the communal alternative which Louisa May had had enough of. Bronson Alcott continued to experiment, finally finding acceptance for his educational theories. He became superintendent of Concord public schools and presided over a summertime "School of Philosophy" which he built in the backyard of Orchard House. On the proceeds of *Little Women*, written when she was 36, Louisa May filled the house with comforts; it remains a vivid record of the personalities of this family and the atmosphere in which they lived.

As such it resembles the sixteen-room mansion in which
Henry Wadsworth Longfellow first lodged as a young 16
Harvard professor, later received as a wedding gift from his father-in-law and filled with his own large family. Longfellow was professionally a linguist, America's first interpreter of German romance. Like Hawthorne, he looked to the region's past for inspiration but with far different results: melodious, up-beat poems such as "The
Courtship of Miles Standish," "Tales of a *Wayside Inn*," 17
and "Hiawatha" which quickly endeared him to the world at large.

Another local poet had begun writing lilting verse about New England even before Longfellow. Abolitionist Wil-

liam Lloyd Garrison read a few of these verses in a regional paper and drove out to Haverhill to find the author.
At the time *John Greenleaf Whittier* was searching for 18
eggs under the barn and Garrison pleaded with his father to give him an education. Later Whittier joined his patron on the Abolitionist journal *Liberator*, but he is best remembered for such poems as "Snow-bound" and "Barefoot Boy" which spoke to city folk of those past, simpler days – which many now began equating with the New England rural landscape.

Garrison himself was one of the most famous abolitionists of his day. In 1829, aged twenty-four, he had thundered his first public address from the pulpit in Boston's Park Street Church, crying: "I will be heard!" Shortly thereafter he landed in the city's Charles Street jail for his views, but a decade later public feeling had swung behind his cause. It was a novel, however, not a tract or newspaper salvo which is still debated as a cause of the Civil War. *Uncle Tom's Cabin* appeared in 1852 and was published simultaneously in three Paris newspapers.

Harriet Beecher Stowe was a mother of seven who had 19
just returned to New England from Cincinnati, Ohio, where her father had opened a seminary. While there she had observed life on the plantations just to the south, and when news of the Fugitive Slave Law reached her at Brunswick, Maine, she sat down and quickly penned her tale of a black family's attempt to escape oppression.

Harriet Beecher Stowe's bedroom, Hartford, Conn.

Visiting her subsequent home, you are struck by the domestic peace of it all. Harriet Beecher Stowe wrote a total of thirty books, in later years contenting herself with regional themes like *The Pearl of Orr's Island* (1862) and articles on creative housekeeping for magazines like *The American Woman's Home*. This earnest lady and the wit who invented Huck Finn may strike you as odd neighbors, but for nineteen years both Mrs. Stowe and Samuel Clemens, better known as Mark Twain, were part
of *Nook Farm*, a literary colony on the fringe of Hart- 20
ford.

"There was a constant running in and out of friendly houses where the lively hosts and guests called one another by their Christian names or nicknames," novelist William Dean Howells wrote about this enclave in the 1870s. Sam Clemens describes his own mansion here, in which he wrote both *The Adventures of Tom Sawyer*

Mark Twain House, Hartford, Conn.

and *Huckleberry Finn* as "the curious house that Mark built." A quote from Emerson above the library fireplace proclaims: "The ornament of a house is the friends who frequent it" and the home is at once a Victorian period piece and an expression of the hospitable man who seems to have lived in the spirit in which Mark Twain wrote. You are told that he frequently slept the wrong way around in bed, the better to see the elaborately carved headboard. His children were permitted to unscrew the cupids on the four posters, to wash and powder them.

In stark contrast to this celebrated extrovert stands the recluse who, in "polar privacy," wrote:

How dreary – to be – somebody!
How public – like a Frog –
To tell your name – the livelong June –
To an admiring Bog!

The dignified but spiritless brick mansion in Amherst, Massachusetts, where *Emily Dickinson* was born and lived 21
all but fifteen years of her life (never straying beyond the family compound, which includes her brother's adjacent home, for the last twenty-five), sheds little light on the life of this shadowy figure whose poetry continues to increase in stature while that of many other literary greats of her day shrinks. Anguished explanations for her solitary life can be found in her verse:

Before I got my eye put out
I liked as well to see
As other Creatures, that have Eyes
And know no other way.

With age her poetic sensitivity to the world immediately around her increased to a pitch which compelled both intense expression and fear of diluting it through the kind of stimulation which most of us require:

So safer – guess – with just my soul
Upon the Window pane
Where other Creatures put their eyes –
Incautious – of the Sun

On Emily's death her sister found nine hundred handwritten poems, tied in bundles in her dresser drawer. That dresser, with other Dickinson possessions, now sits in Harvard University's Houghton Library, but also fails to offer a clue to this poet's teasing, "gnomic verse."

Emily Dickinson is the exception. All the other authors described here found ready publication, most of them with the firm of Ticknor & Fields, which was housed in
the *Old Corner Bookstore* on Boston's Washington Street. 6a
Although the famed Harvard professor William Ellery Channing observed in 1842 that Hawthorne was the only American author who supported himself by writing, this situation had changed within the decade. Ticknor & Fields (parent of both the publishing firms Little, Brown and Houghton Mifflin) had pioneered the policy of paying authors royalties; it also acquired *The North American Review* (America's oldest magazine) and subsequently *The Atlantic Monthly*, most popular magazine of the day. The 1857 founding of *The Atlantic Monthly* is frequently pinpointed as the high point in Boston literary history. Its first edition contained contributions by Emerson, Longfellow, Whittier, also "Battle Hymn of the Republic" by Julia Ward Howe, *Man Without a Country* by Edward Everett Hale, and *Autocrat of the Breakfast Table* by *Oliver Wendell Holmes.* 22

Site of the original Old Corner Bookstore

Dr. Holmes might well be said to embody the final spirit of this era as Emerson does its launching. While still at Harvard Law School Holmes had written "Old Ironsides," a poem which, when widely reprinted in handbills and newspapers, saved the U.S.S. *Constitution* from demolition. Later he switched to medicine, hanging out

a shingle near Harvard Square which advertised: "The
smallest fevers thankfully received." While continuing an
active physician, Holmes produced classic poetry and
enthusiastically lectured around New England, to his
mind spreading around Boston's intellectual light.

Christian Scientist Church,
Boston

Emerson and Thoreau were also frequently to be found
on a lecturing circuit which at this time encompassed
New England. Private libraries such as the Redwood
Reading Room in Newport, the Boston, Portsmouth,
Salem and Nantucket *Atheneums* were also offering a 23
breadth of literature unavailable to the ordinary reader
until now. In 1837 Horace Mann closed his law office,
saying "let the next generation be my client." As secretary of the brand new Massachusetts Board of Education, he opened the country's first normal school and
reorganized public schooling in the state along lines
which other parts of the country soon began adopting.
In 1862 the Land Grant Act, sponsored by Senator Justin
Morrill of *Strafford, Vermont*, extended the principle 24
of free quality public education to the university level in
every state. In New England a clutch of private colleges
was founded in the first half of the century, among them
Amherst, Trinity, Holy Cross, Middlebury, Colby, Norwich and Mount Holyoke. With such earlier bastions of
learning as Harvard, Dartmouth, Yale, Brown and *Wil-* 25
liams, not to mention the late nineteenth-century *Mas-*
sachusetts Institute of Technology, their *campuses* 16a, 26
continue to attract students from throughout the world.

By its close the era can also be credited with spawning
three major religions. *Mormonism* was founded by one 27
Vermont farmboy (Joseph Smith) and firmly established
by another (Brigham Young). *Unitarianism*, an offshoot 28
of a Swiss sect, was first transplanted in America when
Boston's King's Chapel espoused it; in recent years it has
merged with Universalism, launched at the turn of
the nineteenth century in Gloucester, Massachusetts.
Christian Science was formally organized as the Church 29
of Christ, Scientist, in Lynn, Massachusetts, by Mary
Baker Eddy in 1879. In 1882 Mrs. Eddy moved the
church headquarters to Boston where it remains world
center for the religion and an integral part of the city
itself, while sites associated with its founder are scattered throughout the region.

DETAILS

1 *Noah Webster:* birthplace, West Hartford, Connecticut, 227 Main St. Typical, modestly furnished eighteenth-century farmhouse. Open year round, Thurs.: 10–4; Sun.: 2–4; otherwise by appointment. Small admission. (203) 521-1939.

2 *Daniel Webster:* birthplace, Franklin, New Hampshire, Rte. 127, west of Tilton exit off I-93. Small restored house with boyhood mementos. Memorial Day–Labor Day, daily: 10–4. (603) 934-2171.

3 *William Cullen Bryant:* homestead, Cummington, Massachusetts. (Directions marked from center of town.) Gracious white clapboard home set in 189 landscaped acres maintained as memorial to poet-journalist. Contains Victorian furniture, weights which he lifted a hundred times a day until past eighty. Stately sugar maples planted by brother still line driveway. June 15–Labor Day. (413) 634-2244.

4 *Concord, Massachusetts.* Rte. 2A. A town with a split personality; half the sites to see here have to do with the Revolution; the other half with nineteenth-century philosophers and writers. A pamphlet guide to the town is available from both the Minuteman Park headquarters (617) 369-6993 (see Chapter 5) and from the Concord Chamber of Commerce which mans an information booth off Walden St., Concord Center, May 30–Oct. 15, daily: 8:30–4:30, Sun.: 9–5.

4a *Emerson House.* Concord, Massachusetts, Cambridge Turnpike. Fine early nineteenth-century white clapboard home maintained by some eighty Emerson descendants. Center for transcendentalists' meetings. Burned in 1872, but friends raised money to restore it immediately and even to send Emerson abroad while repairs were made. House still feels lived in; filled with his books, notebooks, translations of his works into many languages including Japanese, round drum table with pockets for notes which he called his "savings bank." Mementos from friends include painting of young artist May Alcott (Amy of *Little Women*), chair designed by Thoreau with drawer for his gloves, picture of fanciful summer hut built on property by Thoreau and Bronson Alcott. April 19–Oct. 31, daily: 10–5. (617) Em 9-2236. Admission charged.

4b *Walden Pond,* Concord, Massachusetts. In 1922 Emerson's heirs gave his property on the pond to the County Commission. Beauty still essentially unspoiled. Plaque marks spot where Thoreau's cabin stood. Popular place for walking, swimming and cross-country skiing.

4c *Thoreau Lyceum,* Concord Massachusetts. 156 Balknap St. Not a museum, but a true "lyceum" (i.e., "gathering place of scholars") with quiet, friendly atmosphere, off the beaten track. Focus is on Thoreau and his interests: survey maps, letters, pictures and family possessions; library, natural history room, gift-bookshop. Lectures offered. Year round, weekdays: 10–5; Sun.: 2–5. (617) 369-5912. Small admission.

4d *Old Manse.* Concord, Monument St. (near Old North Bridge). Built 1770 by Rev. William Emerson, pastor of town's church (now First Parish Church). It is said that he urged the soldiers to battle from the upper windows of the house on April 19, 1775. When he died during the Revolution, his widow, Ralph Waldo Emerson's grandmother, married Rev. Ezra Ripley, the next pastor. It was Emerson who rented the house from Ripley's son for the newly wed Hawthornes. Hawthorne's *Mosses from an Old Manse* describes their happy life there, and Sophia scratched a note on one pane: "Una Hawthorne stood on this window sill January 22, 1845, while the trees were all glass chandeliers, a goodly view which she liked much, tho' only ten months old." Contains remarkable array of their mementos as well as those of Emerson family. April 19–May 31, weekends and holidays; June 1–Oct. 15, daily: 10–4:30; Sun.: 1–5; Oct. 16–Nov. 11, weekends and holidays. Admission charged. (617) 369-3909.

4e *Wayside.* Concord, Massachusetts, Lexington Rd. (next door to Orchard House). This was house immortalized by Louisa May in *Little Women.* When Hawthorne bought it he added a tower room, accessible only by trapdoor drawn up by him, as a study. He also added front gables and a marble fireplace brought back from Italy. Few mementos of Hawthornes or Alcotts present. House furnished as it was when Margaret Sidney (author of *Five Little Peppers and How They Grew*) lived there in 1880s. June–Aug., daily: 10–5:30. Also open April–May and Sept.–Oct. Admission charged. Inquire National Park Service (617) 369-6993.

4f *Orchard House.* Concord, Massachusetts, Lexington Rd. Pleasant lived-in atmosphere containing all vivid details of life described in *Little Women.* April 19–Nov. 15, daily: 10–5; Sun.: 1–5. Last tour one half hour before closing. Admission charged. (617) 369-4118.

5 *Bowdoin College.* Brunswick, Maine, Bath, College Sts. Founded in 1794, as private, nonsectarian college for men and named after Revolutionary War Governor of Massachusetts James Bowdoin.

Walker Art Building. A very fine art museum devoted to early American artists and nineteenth-century American artists of the Impressionist period such as Eakins and Homer. Perry MacMillan Arctic Museum in Hubbard Hall contains mementos of two famous Arctic explorers who were graduates of Bowdoin. Year round, daily: 10–4; Sun.: 2–5. July 4–Labor Day, daily: 10–5, 7–8:30; Sun.: 2–5.

6 *Brook Farm.* West Roxbury, Massachusetts, 670 Baker St. Entrance at cemetery to 168 acres of land devoted to wildlife refuge as well as eventual historical museum. Three of original buildings still stand: main building (which has been used as orphanage and has chapel added by Lutheran owners), Margaret Fuller cottage, and the shop which had a printing press and where shoes and pewterware were made. Although grounds open to public via nature trail leading from cemetery, buildings are *not.* Materials available for historic research on Brook Farm available for use on site at West Roxbury Public Library.

6a *The Old Corner Bookstore.* Boston, corner of Washington and School Sts. The building has been restored as an in-town office by the Boston *Globe.* Displays depict the building's history as nineteenth-century literary center of the city. Year round, Mon.–Fri.: 10–6.

7 *Customs House.* Salem, Massachusetts. See detail, Chapter 6. Visitors push button here and receive description of Hawthorne's stint as port surveyor.

7a *House of Seven Gables.* Salem, Massachusetts, 54 Turner St. Dates from 1668, and in 1800s owned by relatives of Hawthorne, the Ingersoll family. In 1910 it was restored and furnished, saving one wing for social workers. Six rooms are shown to public, including secret staircase. Furnishings date from seventeenth and eighteenth century and include a number of mementos of the Hawthornes, among them portraits of author and wife. Today receipts from admission tickets to this and two other homes on property (Hathaway House, 1668, and Nathaniel Hawthorne birthplace, 1750, moved from original site) still support settlement work. Consequently admission fees are high. July 1–Labor Day, daily: 9:30–7:30. (During summer and on Oct. weekends only, all three houses are open.) Rest of year, daily: 10–4:30. (617) 744-0991.

8 *Lenox, Massachusetts.* Rte. 7, Berkshires. Hawthorne's reconstructed cottage is part of a huge complex of 210 acres, with formal gardens and the Music Shed (summer home of the Boston Symphony Orchestra), a Chamber Music Hall, and a theater for a great variety of musical programs. The Berkshire Music Festival opens at Tanglewood in early July and runs through late August. (413) 637-1600.

9 *Herman Melville.* Melville's Pittsfield home, "Arrowhead," has recently been acquired as their headquarters by the Berkshire County Historical Society. (413) 442-1793. The new Pittsfield Library has a Melville Room with first editions of all his works (except *Billy Budd*), his desk, portrait, passport countersigned by Hawthorne (then the U.S. Consul at Liverpool), plus other mementos, and an outstanding collection of scrimshaw.

10 *Franklin Pierce Homestead.* Hillsboro, New Hampshire, Rte. 9 northwest of Manchester. Fourteenth President of the United States grew up in a Federal style wooden mansion. June–Oct., daily except Mon. (603) 478-3165.

11 *Fruitlands Museums.* Harvard, Massachusetts. From Boston, Rte. 2 to Harvard exit, then Rte. 120, ¼ mile south, right on Old Shirley Rd., and then bear left when it forks into Prospect Hill Rd. This is a complex of houses and artifacts including a restored Shaker home, a museum of American Indian artifacts and early American art and Fruitlands itself, the house lived in by the Alcotts during their ill-fated commune venture. There is a fine research library connected

with this museum complex. May 30–Sept. 30, daily except Mon.: 1–5. (617) 456-3924. Admission charged.

12 *Hancock Shaker Community, Inc.* Hancock, Massachusetts. Rte. 20, 5 miles west of Pittsfield; also exit 1, Massachusetts Pike, then Rte. 41, left on Rte. 20. More than a dozen buildings, including the handsome "Brick Dwelling" and the round barn, have been restored. Shaker crafts are demonstrated daily during summer season. During the first week in August "World's People Dinners" are also offered; meals are prepared from Shaker recipes and served up Shaker fashion. June 1–Oct. 15, daily: 9:30–5. Admission charged. (413) 443-0188.

13 *Sabbath Day Lake Shaker Museum.* Sabbath Day Lake, Maine. Community just east of Poland Springs, 23 miles north of Portland: Maine Pike I-95 to the Gray exit 11, north 8 miles to Rte. 26. The last active Shaker community (founded 1793) remaining in the world. There are 1,350 rolling acres of land plus ten buildings and a mill site. During summer season, student guides who have been trained by the sisters and who have spent time living in the community, offer regular tours of the meetinghouse, ministry shop (1839), boys' shop (1850) and Shaker store. May 30–Oct. 1, daily except Mon.: 10–4:30. Times may vary. Admission charged. (207) 926-4597.

14 *Canterbury Shaker Village, Inc.* East Canterbury, New Hampshire. 15 miles northeast of Concord; Rtes. 4 and 202 to Rte. 106, bear left about 7 miles, then left on road marked "Shaker Village" for about 3 miles. Founded in 1792, this village is still occupied by Shaker sisters as a museum rather than an active religious community. Includes eighteen buildings. There are tours through meetinghouse, sisters' shop, school and carriagehouse. May 28–Labor Day: 9–11 and 1–4. Also by appointment until Oct. 12. Admission charged. (617) 783-9822.

15 *Round Barns.* The Hancock Shaker barn is said to have been designed by one of the brethren who was a wheelwright, and it was widely copied by Vermonters in the late nineteenth century; surviving models can be found in the northern third of that state: in East Barnet, Passumpsic, Waterford, East Calais, Irasburg, Wells River, Grand Isle, Lowell, Coventry, North Troy and Enosburg Falls; ask around locally for precise locations. Also Haverhill, New Hampshire, and a reconstruction of the Hancock barn at Heritage Plantation, Sandwich, Massachusetts. (See Chapter 10.)

16 *Longfellow House.* Cambridge, Massachusetts, 105 Brattle St. Memorabilia such as a portrait of thirteen-year-old Edith, "the little girl with the little curl right in the middle of her forehead," drawings by the children, the round table at which Longfellow wrote "The Children's Hour," a chair supposedly made from the "spreading chestnut tree," all combine to make this a very hospitable warm house filled with the family presence. Year round, daily: 9–4:45. (617) 876-4491. Admission charged.

16a *Massachusetts Institute of Technology.* Cambridge, Massachusetts. 77 Massachusetts Ave. at Memorial Drive. Reputed to be the world's foremost science and engineering school. Sites to see include the Hart Nautical Museum (exhibits depict marine engineering development; year round, daily: 9–5) and Hayden Gallery (changing art exhibits; early June–Labor Day, daily: 1–5; rest of the year: Mon.–Thurs.: 10–5; Fri.: 10–9; Sat., Sun.: 1–5). Tours from the information center: year round; Mon.–Fri.: 10 and 2. (617) 253-4795.

17 *Longfellow's Wayside Inn.* South Sudbury, Massachusetts. On Rte. 20. From Marlboro take Rte. 20 off Rte. 295 east, and from Waltham, take Rte. 20 off Rte. 128 west. Longfellow is known to have been there only twice, but by using it as a setting for a group who gathered to tell stories (much as Chaucer did in *Canterbury Tales*) he forever linked his name to the place. The most famous of these *Tales of a Wayside Inn* is "Paul Revere's Ride," and the Inn has an annual ball at which Minutemen gather in uniform after April 19 festivities. The building was restored by Henry Ford, who made it the centerpiece for a mini-museum-village which includes a grist mill, the Redstone schoolhouse (which served as a setting for "Mary Had a Little Lamb"), and the Martha-Mary Chapel, a typical New England church, popular as a wedding site, convenient to receptions at the old ballroom of the Inn. Year round, daily. (617) 443-8846.

18 *John Greenleaf Whittier Homestead.* Haverhill, Massachusetts; 305 Whittier Road. Rte. 110, 4 miles outside Haverhill. This seventeenth-century house remains a working farm. Year round: 10–5; Sun.: 1–5; closed Mon. (617) 373-3979.

Whittier Home. Amesbury, Massachusetts. 86 Friend St. This too is a simple farmhouse lived in by the poet from 1836 to 1892, containing his manuscripts and possessions. Year round, daily except Sun. and Mon.: 10–5. (617) 388-1337.

19 *Harriet Beecher Stowe. Stowe House.* Brunswick, Maine, 63 Federal St. It was here that *Uncle Tom's Cabin* was penned.

Homestead: Hartford, Connecticut, see Detail 20. Middle-class Victorian home which reflects tastes of artistic occupant.

20 *Nook Farm.* Hartford, Connecticut, 351 Farmington Ave. Sisson St. exit off Rte. 44 west, right off ramp, Sisson to Farmington St., right until you see Mark Twain House. In 1927 grandniece of Harriet Beecher Stowe saved the Mark Twain House from demolition. Today it is restored to reflect the daily life of the author, who was thirty-nine in 1874 when he, his wife, three daughters and seven servants moved in. The nonprofit Stowe-Day Foundation maintains both the Stowe, (203) 525-9317, and Twain, (203) 247-0998, houses, a visitors' center and research library. June–mid-Aug., daily: 10–5; March–mid-June, Sept.–Dec., Tues.–Sat.: 10–5; Jan.–Feb., Wed.–Sat.: 10–5; Jan.–mid-June, Sept.–Dec., also Sun.: 2–5. Admission charged.

21 *Emily Dickinson House.* Amherst, Massachusetts, 280 Main St. The "Mansion," as it was known in Amherst at the time Emily's grandfather built it, modernized since; among the few mementos: her desk, the basket which she lowered with ginger cookies for neighborhood children. Guides describe the poet's life. Unfortunately "Evergreen," the yellow Victorian house next door which belonged to Emily's brother and which she frequently visited – while still retaining the interior she knew – remains private. The Mansion is open year round, Tues., through appointment with the secretary of Amherst College (413) 542-2000. Permission to visit the Dickinson Room at Harvard must be obtained from the office of the librarian at Houghton Library, Harvard University.

22 *Oliver Wendell Holmes.* In Cambridge, Massachusetts, a plaque commemorating Holmes's birthplace can be found to your left when facing Littauer Hall, off Massachusetts Ave. The property is now part of Harvard University. In Pittsfield, Massachusetts, the basement historical room in the Berkshire Museum exhibits the "One Hoss Shay" which inspired Holmes to write his famous poem. (39 South St.) Tues.–Sat.: 10–5; Sun.: 2–5. (413) 442-6373.

23 *Atheneums. Boston (Massachusetts) Athenaeum,* 10½ Beacon St. A private library opened in 1807, containing an outstanding collection of early manuscripts. The gracious reading rooms continue to be a favorite haunt for Boston literati. (617) 227-0270.

Wadsworth Athenaeum, Hartford, Connecticut, 600 Main St. Begun as a nineteenth-century private library, today one of the region's leading art museums, exhibiting Pilgrim furniture, sixteenth–twentieth century paintings. Feb.–Dec., Tues.–Sat.: 11–4; Sun.: 1–5. (203) 278-2670.

Other atheneums listed in previous details.

24 *Justin Morrill Homestead.* Strafford, Vermont, marked from Rte. 132, off I-91 at Thetford. A Gothic revival cottage built by Senator Morrill in the mid-nineteenth century. The community is an unspoiled hilltown clustered around its green and meetinghouse. Memorial Day–Labor Day, Tues.–Sun.

25 *Williams College.* Williamstown, Massachusetts. Founded in 1755. Notable buildings include Griffin Hall (1828), the Williams College Museum of Art (year round, Mon.–Sat.: 9–12, 2–4; Sun.: 2–5), and the Sterling and Francine Clark Art Institute (see Chapter 10). Campus tours: year round, weekdays: 10–12, 2–4 from Hopkins Hall. For *Harvard*, see Chapter 3; for *Dartmouth*, see Chapter 6; for *Yale*, see Chapter 3; for *Brown*, see Chapter 6.

26 *Campuses* of colleges dating from the first half of the nineteenth century. All offer campus tours, year round: Inquire admissions offices.

Amherst College, Amherst, Massachusetts. Founded in 1821. Mead Art Building stages changing exhibits (academic year: Mon.–Sat.: 9–5; Sun.: 11:30–5; summer months; Mon.–Fri.: 10–12, 1–4).

Trinity College, Hartford, Connecticut. Summit, Vernon and Broad streets. Founded in 1823. Austin Arts Center has changing exhibits (year round, daily).

Wesleyan College, Middletown, Connecticut.

College of the Holy Cross, Worcester, Massachusetts.

Middlebury College, Middlebury, Vermont.

Colby College, Waterville, Maine.

Mount Holyoke College, South Hadley, Massachusetts.

27 *Mormonism. Joseph Smith Memorial.* Sharon, Vermont, marked from Rte. 14, exit 2 off I–89. A thirty-eight-foot-high granite monolith commemorates his birth here.

Brigham Young Memorial. Whitingham, Vermont, off Rte. 100, near Massachusetts border. A plaque honors him.

28 *Universalism birthplace:* Sargent-Murray-Gilman-Hough House, Gloucester, Massachusetts, 49 Middle St. Open July–Sept. 15; weekdays: 11–5. Small admission. (617) 283–4505.

29 *Mary Baker Eddy Sites in New England.* An auto map and guide to dozens of sites connected with the foundress of the First Church of Christ Scientist is available from the visitors' center and the Mother Church complex, fifteen acres between Massachusetts Ave. and Huntington Ave. The original edifice here (1894) is now attached to a grandiose turn-of-the-century basilica, surrounded by later buildings which include the recent ultramodern administration headquarters and plaza. Tours are offered to the complex itself. (617) 262–2300.

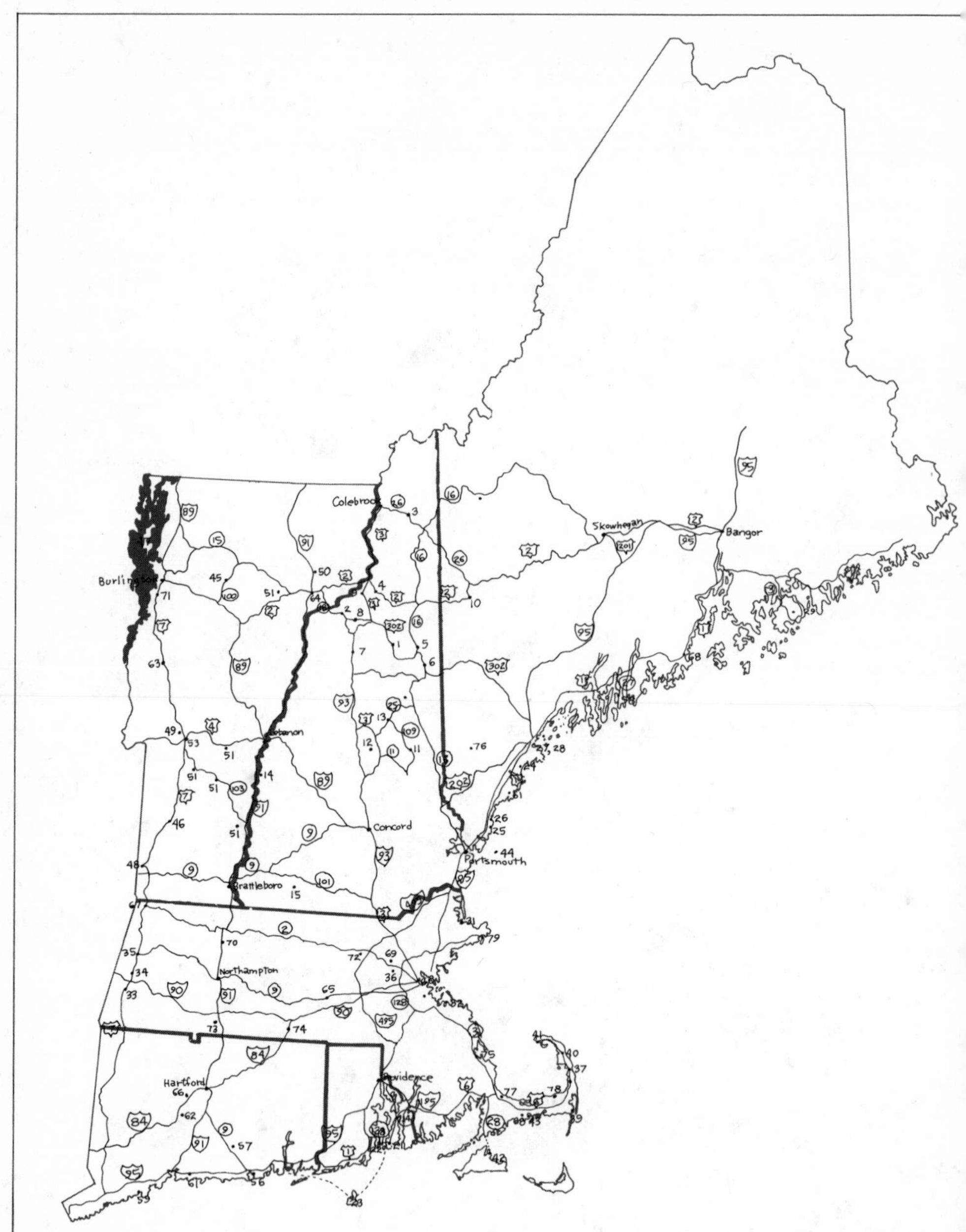

Skowhegan
Bangor
Concord
Portsmouth
Brattleboro
Northampton
Hartford

10

Victorian Vignettes

Just as seventeenth-century promoters like Captain John Smith and Samuel de Champlain had attracted settlers by raving about New England's natural beauty, now nineteenth-century artists and writers attracted city folk by celebrating the same. In their wake came steamboat- and trainloads of "rusticators" to spend the entire summer months in big hotels which suddenly mushroomed atop mountains and along the coast. The wealthiest built themselves sumptuous "cottages" in Newport, Bar Harbor and the Berkshires, while the middle class settled for tented camp meetings, boarding- and farmhouses. Wealthy Yankees themselves built their Victorian mansions, founded and filled museums with the art and curios collected on their own global jaunts.

The countryside reflected this region's fall from favor as a place to live. In 1810 it still accounted for one fifth of the nation's people; in 1870, for less than one tenth. In Massachusetts and Rhode Island alone more than 10,000 farms had been abandoned. Throughout the six states former pastureland acquired a shroud of second-growth forest.

To its new wave of tourists the countryside's ghostly aspect made it all the more picturesque. What lumbering still lingered on now sparked a reaction from influential "summer people" who formed the nation's first conservation groups. And a newfound pride in local history spawned pioneer preservation societies.

RUSTICATORS AND THEIR RESORTS

White Mountains

The artists of the Hudson Valley School first painted them in the 1820s. Thoreau, Emerson, Hawthorne and Whittier touted them through prose and poetry in the 1830s. Starr King's *The Great White Hills*, first serialized in the Boston *Transcript*, brought them local city dwellers by the drove. And after the Civil War, New Hampshire's White Mountains began offering through service via steam and train from every major city in the East.

Mount Washington, literally the high point of every 1
nineteenth-century visitor's expedition to New Hampshire, had actually been climbed by its first white hiker back in 1642. By 1819, that pioneer father-and-son team, Abel and Ethan Crawford, had cut a way to the top for tourists (now America's oldest, continually used hiking path). A decade before completion of the toll road up one side and the Cog Railway up the other, the first Summit House was built, 6,288 feet high on its bald, weathered pate.

"We used to average 100 diners a day. . . . One noon there were representatives of 13 different nations as guests at dinner," its proprietor wrote. In 1853 a rival "Tiptop House" opened. Cows were subsequently kept and a daily newspaper covering the region's resort scene was published on the summit.

Dozens of mammoth hotels dotted the region and although only a fraction survive, they typify the lot,
dating from 1843 *Thayers Hotel* in Littleton to the 1912 2
Balsams up in Dixville Notch. *Crawford House* at the 3, 1a
western base of Mount Washington was an 1859 prefab,

Mt. Washington Hotel, N.H.

cut in nearby towns and hauled overland, then assembled
in nine months on the spot, with neither pillars nor posts
in its grand dining hall. Just up the road stands the extravagant *Mount Washington Hotel*. "Look at me, gentle- 1b
men . . . for I am the poor fool who built all this," coal
baron Joseph Stickney is reported to have said at its
1902 dedication, and "laughed at his own folly." With
more than three hundred rooms, fifty outbuildings, its
own post office and telephone exchange, it is still New
England's biggest resort hotel.

North of Crawford Notch the rambling, wooden *Waum- 4
bec Hotel* still offers one of the area's most magnificent
views, and just southeast of Mount Washington the period
resort town of *Jackson* harbors some vintage inns, notably 5
Eagle Mountain House. *North Conway*, just below Jack- 5a, 6
son, remains the chief lodging and shopping center for
the Washington Valley. Some mountainous miles west of
Mount Washington is *Franconia Notch*, a tourist magnet 7
in its own right, ever since that day in 1805 when Franconia Village's tax collector happened to notice that a
local cliff resembled the profile of Thomas Jefferson,
the current president. A half dozen big hotels soon
sprouted around town, each offering outings, complete
with lavish picnics, to local sites like "*The Flume*." 7a

The Old Man of the Mountain continues to frown 7b
down on his admirers but most of these now tend to be
motorists in a hurry or skiers bound via the aerial tramway for the state ski area on his very mountain's slopes.
It is difficult to visualize life as it was passed for three
months at a time by nineteenth-century rusticators. Five-
course meals, supplied in many cases by the hotel's own
farm, were served up on the resort's own special china.
To work off these feasts, guests walked, played tennis or
golf, and explored the countryside in wagons and carriages. Come evening they listened to concerts by the
hotel's own orchestras or simply rocked to and fro in the
wicker rockers lining steamship deck-size verandas.

Many an entire town built on catering to this life has
all but disappeared. *Bethlehem, New Hampshire*, a hay 8
fever refuge which once boasted thirty-eight hotels, now
reaches to list six. But one self-contained resort on the
western fringe of the White Mountains vividly illustrates
the way a grand hotel evolved – and it is still grand. The
Mountain View near Whitefield dates from a stormy 9
1865 night when the Montreal stage capsized and its passengers found refuge in the nearest farmhouse. Most of

them so enjoyed the hospitality received from farmer
William Dodge and his wife that they were back next
summer. Photos within the present 190-room hostelry
(staffed by 250 long-time retainers) depict its gradual
expansion. The place, still operated by the Dodge family,
advertises itself as "a hotel run by ladies and gentlemen
for ladies and gentlemen" who appreciate its aura and
374 acres of manicured grounds. And on the extreme
eastern fringe of the White Mountains, the town of
Bethel, Maine, still conjures memories of those first 10
wealthy Bostonians whose visits were prescribed here by
prominent neurologist Dr. George Gehrind. The doctor
himself had discovered the sleepy lumbering town after a
nervous breakdown and so well did he recoup here that
he set up a handsome clinic – the core of the present
Bethel Inn. Guests are no longer encouraged to chop
down trees as part of their physical therapy treatment,
but the same atmosphere, genteel (fresh flowers on the
linen-decked tables), athletic (golf, swimming and hiking)
and restful (plenty of books and rockers), still prevails.

Lake Winnipesaukee and the Monadnock Region

Wolfeboro calls itself New Hampshire's oldest resort be- 11
cause Governor John Wentworth built his summer home
here in 1768. It remains a sleepy, picturesque town, and
Lake Winnipesaukee is still a popular but low-key resort
center. With few exceptions the big, late nineteenth-century hotels have vanished but *The Weirs*, begun as a meet- 12
ing spot for religious, temperance and military, is still a
wooden gingerbread cluster of little inns and shops along
the boardwalk which serves as home dock for the M/V 12a
Mount Washington, a reminder of the lake's glorious
"steamboatin'" days.

New Hampshire never did attract the flashy social set
and its few elaborate turn-of-the-century summer cottages which you can now visit are scattered. Above Lake
Winnipesaukee itself eccentric shoe manufacturer Thomas
Plant built his $7 million "*Castle in the Clouds*," import- 13
ing 400 Italian laborers just to lay its stonework; the
mansion enjoyed pioneer water, heating, refrigeration
and central vacuum cleaning systems! The estate spread
over seven mountains, crisscrossed by forty miles of
roads. And in an unfashionable Connecticut River Valley
corner of the state, sculptor *Augustus Saint-Gaudens* con- 14
verted a vintage 1800 tavern into another period mansion. The estate, which includes eighty-three rolling

acres, formal gardens and a templelike studio, is now the scene of evening picnic concerts throughout the summer.

Wealthy Bostonians tended to congregate in New Hampshire's southwestern corner, building Victorian
villas (all still private) in the shadow of *Mount Monad-* 15
nock. The mountain itself, however, was and continues to be an extremely popular and public place. It was a famous freak even before the Civil War.

Early settlers had trimmed its lower beard of hardwood and spruce, planting orchards and pasturing sheep between tidy stone walls, right up its rocky shoulders. After 1800 they took to firing the summit to kill off the wolves who proliferated there. The effect was to expose its rocky crest, thus creating an artificial timberline and alpine fauna usually found only on mountains twice as high.

By the 1840s Emerson, Kipling and Whittier had all eulogized the unique mountain, and Thoreau, who camped near the summit on three of his four trips here, noted the results: "One noon, when I was on the top, I counted forty men, women and children around me," he wrote. "Certainly more than one hundred ascended in a day . . . some playing cards – several busily engraving their names on the rocks with chisels." The indignant ecologist "heard tell of a party who hauled up their own dance floor and brought along a fiddler."

Neither "overuse" nor "ecology" were words anyone used in those days, but the more city folk explored the high country, the more outraged they became at the ugly gashes and clogged streams caused by lumbering. The new idea that forest cover influences a region's rainfall was also widely discussed. In 1810 New Hampshire had begun selling off its wild lands and by 1867 the last swath – 172 acres which included Mount Washington itself – had been auctioned for $25,000. Six major lumber companies, equipped with their own railways, were scientifically stripping and burning away.

The *Appalachian Mountain Club* (AMC), America's 16
first hiking group, began surveying trails and building mountaintop huts to accommodate foot traffic in 1876, thus further increasing awareness of the devastation. In 1910 a group of New Hampshire politicians and Boston
financiers founded the *Society for the Protection of* 17
New Hampshire Forests (SPNHF) which, in turn, lobbied to get the bill sponsored and passed which in 1911 created the *White Mountain National Forest*. The forest to- 18

day contains 725,000 acres, including 1,000 miles of
hiking trails. It is supplemented by smaller but crucial
state parks like Crawford Notch, Franconia, and Monad- 19
nock itself, all secured through efforts of SPNHF. As a
result the White Mountains continue to attract visitors to
dramatic waterfalls, wooded paths and dramatic vistas.
A couple of the old lumbering railbeds have even been
merged into a spectacular scenic drive, the *Kancamagus* 20
Highway, spotted with picnic, camping and hiking sites.
The AMC continues to serve hikers with bunks and board
at its eight "high huts" and its information centers in
Boston and Pinkham Notch, and with SPNHF to crusade
for conservation causes.

Rhode Island

The millionaires who built their stone palaces on *New-* 21
port's windy Ocean Drive would seem out to defy rather
than to explore or preserve nature. They filled these summer "cottages" with contrived magnificence and the season with a series of "social functions"; families spent
$100,000 on entertainment alone. Many of the mansions
remain private: the "400" very rich have their own telephone directory, subtitled "Numbers of Your Friends";
their Spouting Rock Beach Association (better known as
Bailey's Beach), their Reading Room and Country Club
(scene of America's first amateur golf tournament) are
still very private.

Marble House, Newport, R.I.

But now you can visit the *Tennis Hall of Fame* (the 21a
country's first tennis club) and six magnificent cottages,
maintained by the *Preservation Society of Newport* 21b
County, are open to the common visitor: The Elms (a
French chateau), Marble House (William K. Vanderbilt's
marble pile), the Breakers (a sixteenth-century Italian
palace built for Cornelius Vanderbilt), Chateau Sur Mer
(containing Newport's first ballroom), Rosecliff (with
the largest ballroom in town) and Kingscote (an 1820s
"stick Gothic" cottage, famed for its Tiffany glass).
Belcourt Castle, a Louis XIII palace full of antiques from 21c
various periods, is privately maintained, also the *San-* 21d
ford-Covell and *Edward King Houses*, early "cottages," 21e
are privately maintained. During the seventeen-day-long 21f
annual *Newport Music Festival*, you can cocktail and
enjoy candlelight performances of nineteenth-century
music and dance in these settings.

Nearby *Jamestown* also retains its nineteenth-century 22
flavor, but one other, less well known Rhode Island re-

sort remains pure Victoriana. No one thought of *Block* 23
Island as a resort until a Providence grocer organized a
steamboat load of excursionists to explore it in 1853.
Then suddenly it acquired a reputation for pure air,
spring water, and sandy beaches. Within a decade the Fall
River liners were making regular calls here, and Block
Island began calling itself "The Bermuda of the North-
east."

Its glory was shortlived. A low tolerance for "intemperance" soon put it out of style (a gilded statue of Rebecca at the Well, erected by the Women's Christian Temperance Union, still stands in the island's town, New Shoreham). But the mammoth frame hotels survive. Spring House and the Surf still require reservations well in advance, and a half dozen other arks cling to varying vestiges of dignity; a half dozen island restaurants also now offer spirituous liquor with their fish.

Maine

Maine's most famous resorts all date from the advent
of steamboat and rail service. By 1890 *Old Orchard* and 24
York Beaches had both built their famous boardwalks, 25
little altered to this day. Of the "westernmost" strip of
"Downeast" coastal resorts, *Ogunquit* bears its period 26
stamp better than any. Here the big hotels appeared
soon after a bridge linked the village with its three-mile,
dune-backed tongue of sand. Very few of these survive,
but the town's dozens of smaller inns and guesthouses
have been in business for generations. The boutiques,
now crowded into the old fishing shacks at Perkins Cove,
plus the early twentieth-century Ogunquit Playhouse,
two aging movie houses and two outstanding art galleries
represent the only new additions since Main Street shops
opened and the Marginal Way became a celebrated shore
path.

Captain John Smith named the *Calendar Islands*, claim- 27
ing that he saw one for every day in the year. But these
delightful hideaways off the city of Portland have long
since lost their hucksters. The fact is that they add up to
140, most as private as they can manage to be.

Back in 1895 the Casco Bay Lines offered its patrons
tickets priced from 5¢ to 25¢, depending on the quality
of the seat in the Gem Theater on *Peaks Island* which 27a
came with them. Peaks also offered the Greenwood Garden, a spectacular amusement park with a merry-go-
round, bandstand, and five-story observatory, plus

novelty stands, rare animals, frequent balloon ascents and a number of big hotels. On Peaks you can still find comfortable room and board, a bike, beaching and two unusual old cottages, now museums, which were built as summer spas for Portland's Civil War regiments. And
Chebeague, biggest of the group, does retain the vintage 27b
Hillcrest Hotel, now reduced to fourteen rentable rooms but proud of its huge, "rustic" lobby. But daytrippers wishing to explore the other four "Calendars" serviced by Casco Bay Lines had better bring their own picnic and bike. In Portland itself, no one with a taste for the plush
and gilt of this era should miss the "*Victoria Mansion*," 28
a period piece if ever there was one.

Popular artist Thomas Cole found his way from Ellsworth (seventy miles north of any other Maine coastal
resort of the day) across the new bridge to *Mount Desert* 29
in 1844. By 1859 the steamer *Rockland* was putting into
the little village of *Bar Harbor* regularly, and by the turn 29a
of the century this inconvenient haven rivaled Newport itself in social status. More than three hundred "cottages" were built, most of them "rustically" shingled but still with up to forty rooms, staffs of thirty servants, and one at least with a dining table which was lowered to the kitchen between courses. Humbler vacationers filled seventeen wooden hotels, the largest with five hundred rooms. Since Bar Harbor suffered a disastrous fire in 1947, sparing only the village Main Street, you must
scan photos in the museum room of *Jessup Memorial* 29b
Library to appreciate its lost look. But you can still enjoy popovers at the *Jordan Pond House*, which opened 29c
as a teashop in 1896 and hews strictly to its original menu and decor.

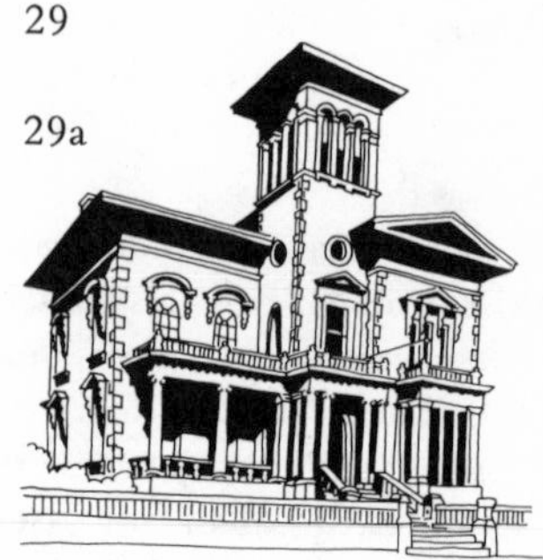

Victoria Mansion, Portland, Me.

Early Ecologists

You can also explore the countless waterfalls, more than two hundred miles of hiking and riding trails, and a dramatic forty-mile Ocean Drive on Mount Desert. It is all thanks to those wealthy cottagers who, in contrast to the Newport crowd, earnestly attempted to explore the island's natural beauty, in the process discovering unsightly gashes made by lumbering. In 1901, Dr. Charles Eliot (former president of Harvard University) rallied his friends to the idea of founding an organization to preserve the island; six thousand acres were soon donated to this purpose. John D. Rockefeller, Jr., built many miles of carriage paths and gave more than 11,000 acres.

In 1916, when the National Park Service was established,
Acadia National Park became the nation's first east of 29d
Mississippi.

Dr. Eliot's son and namesake left his own mark on
Massachusetts. In 1890 the young landscape architect
conceived the idea of preserving "bits of scenery which
possess uncommon beauty and more than the usual re-
freshing power" and "to hold small and well distributed
parcels of land, free from taxes, just as the public library
holds books and art museums, pictures, for the use and
enjoyment of the public." To accomplish this high-
minded end, the *Trustees of Reservations* was incorpo- 30
rated the very next year, quickly acquiring its first
acreage which, in turn, soon became part of the country's
first metropolitan park system (Boston's MDC), which
the Trustees helped to establish.

Today this low-profile, old Yankee group controls
more than 11,700 of the state's choicest acres, fifty-five
reservations in all. A few of these – the long, dune-backed
sweep of *Crane's Beach* in Ipswich and 250-acre *World's* 31, 32
End, a park landscaped by Frederick Law Olmsted in
Hingham – are popular summer escape hatches for Bostonians. The remainder, scattered from Cape Cod and
the islands to the Berkshires, remain unpublicized, quasi-
secrets.

The Trustees also maintain some of the state's most
genuinely interesting historic houses, among them *Naum-* 33
keag in Stockbridge, sole public representative of the
Berkshire's own gilded resort era. The mansion, built by
Stanford White for Joseph Choate (a New York lawyer
who twice served as ambassador to the Court of St.
James's), is shingled to blend with the seasonal display in
its forty-two-acre formal garden; its interior, as that of
Chesterwood, nearby mansion and studio of sculptor 33a
Daniel Chester French, hovers somewhere between the
flamboyance of Newport and the self-conscious rusticity
of Bar Harbor "cottages." The town's *Red Lion Inn*, un- 33b
mistakably 1890s, is pleasant and dignified. Stockbridge
residents themselves were obviously a proud and prosperous lot: their Laurel Hill Association, founded in
1853, served as a prototype for thousands of subsequent
town improvement societies throughout the country.

Berkshires, Cape Cod

Nearby *Lenox* dubbed itself the "inland Newport" and 34
formed, as it still does, social center of the *Berkshires*. In 35

the town library you can scan pictures of local cottages,
which numbered seventy-five by the turn of the century;
many survive as schools and convents; one is an *arts cen-* 35a
ter and two, *resorts*. The town remains a lively place 35b
during the eight-week *Tanglewood Music season*. 35c

Lenox also harbors *Pleasant Valley*, one of the fifty 35d
wildlife sanctuaries maintained by yet another of the period's pioneer conservation groups, the *Massachusetts* 36
Audubon Society. Founded by a few Boston women in
1896 – to discourage the use of wild birds' plumage as
hat decorations – this is the first of the country's Audubon Societies and one of the most active. Again, as with
the Trustees' reservations, only a fraction of the "sanctuaries" are widely known. *Wellfleet Bay*, lying as it does 37
smack in the center of the state's currently most popular
resort area – *Cape Cod* – attracts the lion's share of non- 38
New Englanders.

Cape Cod's fishing grounds had long been depleted, its
packet trade had been killed by the advent of the railroad, and its younger generation had been forsaking it
by the thousands in the first few decades after the Civil
War. Then the "summer people" began arriving. They
came "down Cape" on a spur railroad which is proudly
remembered in the town of *Chatham's Railroad Museum*. 39
They stayed in the old sea captains' homes and the (then)
new wooden hotels which still provide a delightful and
reasonable alternative to the Cape's modern crop of motels. *Highland House*, one of these first inns, now serves 40
as a museum for the town of Truro.

Luckily the natural beauty of this "bared and bended
arm of Massachusetts" which Thoreau explored on foot
twice in the mid-nineteenth-century has survived the
present era's tourist and realty boom. The *Cape Cod* 41
National Seashore, created in 1956, now encompasses
27,000 acres (roughly 40 percent of the "lower" or
"outer" Cape) including the vast, thirty-mile Outer
Beach, and offering a wealth of bicycle paths, nature
trails and programs for exploring and enjoying this unique
outcrop of sand, marsh, scrub meadow and forest.

Camp Meetings

Those grand old hotels seem reasonably enough priced by present standards: $20 to $30 a week bought a room and full board at most fashionable hostelries. But time as well as money were luxuries a working class family could not spare. Many chose to compress inspiration and relaxation into one brief summer respite: the camp meeting. Among the hundreds of tent colonies of the day, a few have survived, now encrusted with tradition, their tents transformed into little wooden cottages.

Oak Bluffs, the wooden, gingerbread community on Martha's Vineyard, remains the most famous. It began as the Methodists' Wesleyan Grove Camp Meeting in 1837 and by 1859, when it attracted more than 12,000 participants, a circus-style tent was erected for meetings; still worshipers continued to tent in a nearby grove of oaks. The present, glass-sided Tabernacle dates from 1870 as does the surrounding colony of seven hundred cottages (many of which retain flap-like ornaments on their facades). This actually is one of the country's first planned-resort communities. A couple of the period's neighboring hotels remain, along with the old-style shops along Circuit Avenue and the annual observance of "Illumination Night" when Japanese lanterns bedeck the entire village. 42

Craigville Conference Center, just outside Hyannis, is less well known but equally delightful. Established in 1872, it maintains a private beach house, its own piece of Cape Cod's most popular warm water beach, and offers rooms in its couple of little inns and village full of gingerbread cottages. Although maintained by the United Church of Christ, it welcomes "all people who enjoy pleasant and congenial surroundings." 43

One of the most attractive Conference Centers of this day was a fashionable resort of the latter. The *Isles of Shoals*, which we have noted as an early and rowdy fishing colony, had fallen on hard, fish-scarce times by the outbreak of the Revolution. The forty-four remaining residents were ordered to leave: Whigs and Tories alike feared that they might aid the opposition. Many took their houses with them (a few of which still stand in York, Maine) and few ever returned. The Isles were up for grabs in 1837 when a wealthy young Portsmouth politician bought them and moved his family to the new lighthouse keeper's cottage on White Island. Eventually he built sumptuous Appledore House on Hog Island (renaming it Appledore), which became a social mecca after his daughter Celia Thaxter's *Among the Isles of Shoals* became a best-seller. Encouraged by this success, a mustard millionaire bought Star Island across the way and built the equally lavish Oceanic Hotel in 1873. It quickly burned down and was quickly rebuilt, much as it 44

stands today. But by the 1890s the appeal of the Isles had
passed and the Unitarians, who now found it a reasonable
place to hold their summer meetings, bought it a decade
later (the Appledore had by then conveniently burned
down). Now the *Star Island Conference Center*, the old 44a
hotel and its adjacent cottages continue to attract three
hundred participants at a time during the ten-week-long
summer season. Day excursionists are also welcome,
even given a tour of the entire little island and permitted
to swim, or rock away on the vast veranda. Discussion
topics here, as at Craigville, are broadly based (including
literary and political themes) and the atmosphere is
family.

Vermont

The Green Mountain State drew its modest share of
the era's rusticators. The town of *Stowe* was as fashion- 45
able a summer resort as it is now a winter ski mecca. The
first Mt. Mansfield Hotel atop the state's highest mountain was built in 1858. There was also a scattering of
spas famed for their mineral water and hydraulic cures –
such as the handsome *Equinox Hotel* in Manchester which 46
still offers 250 rooms. And a few resort villages on the
Champlain Islands were spawned by steamboat traffic. 47
Vermonters themselves also built some "high Victorian"
mansions such as the *Park-McCullough* House in North 48
Bennington, *Wilson's Castle* near Rutland, and *Burklyn* 49, 50
way up above Lyndonville.

Park-McCullough Mansion, North Bennington, Vt.

But by 1890 four-fifths of Vermont towns were declining in population and less than two-thirds of those born in the state actually stayed on. Those who did mostly moved to the valleys where new inventions like the 1860s' hay bailer enabled them to tend the larger

spreads required for supplying big cities with milk, butter
and cheese. The state's famous *cheese factories* date 51
from this day as do the barns with their tall silos which
now spot Vermont's landscape. Enterprising city folk
now began finding their way to Vermont community
church suppers and agricultural fairs, finding ample and
reasonable board in farmhouses. (Both Vermont and
New Hampshire can still supply you with *lists of farms* 52
which accommodate guests.)

Hikers were initially far less attracted to the gentler
and more wooded Green Mountains. But in 1910 a couple
of dozen outdoorsmen formed the *Green Mountain Club* 53
with the idea of building a foot trail along the spine of
the range from the Massachusetts border to the Canadian
line; this 261-mile *Long Trail* is still maintained and pub- 54
licized by the Club, which also staffs a few of the high
huts to be found along the way. In the 1930s this now
famously ecology-minded state refused $18 million to
establish a national park down its middle; subsequently
it transferred some 35,000 acres to federal control and
its thirty-eight state *parks* and thirty-four state forests 55
encompass another 130,000 acres.

Connecticut

The old Connecticut coastal communities were discovered, along with "sea bathing," by New York's elite
in the 1870s. The present pattern of private "town" and
club-owned beaches with their adjacent waterside summer homes dates from this era. In *Old Lyme* you can visit 56
an early nineteenth-century Florence Griswold House in
which artists of the Barbazon School took to boarding,
decorating its walls with some forty seascapes. A short
ways up the Connecticut River stands the ornate Victorian *Goodspeed Opera House*, still in use with its vel- 57
vet seats, brass rails and a riverboat painted on its stage
curtain. With matching Gelston House next door, it
dates from the days when you could board Colonel
Goodspeed's steamers at the foot of State Street, Hartford, for dinner followed by an evening performance by
a New York opera company.

Goodspeed Opera House

Lacking movies and television, late nineteenth-century
Americans throughout the country enjoyed far more in
the way of live entertainment than our generation. Visit
the *Theater Museum in Boothbay*, Maine, and you will 58
see playbills advertising dramatic presentations in many
a Downeast town from which they have long since van-

ished. Visit the *P. T. Barnum Museum* in Bridgeport and you discover how this famous showman launched the world's biggest circus in his 70s after a full life spent politicking. 59

Boston

Boston – its downtown core rebuilt and its shape entirely changed in the late nineteenth century – retains more of the flavor of the period than any modern American city. 60 Step into the *Cyclorama Building*, now the 60a Boston Center for the Arts, and imagine what it must have been like back in 1884 to stand under its glass dome, completely surrounded by a life-size painting of the Battle of Gettysburg. You can still attend a performance of the Boston Pops and Boston Symphony (founded respectively in 1885 and 1881), now both housed in the turn-of-the-century *Symphony Hall.* 60b Across the street the matching *Massachusetts Horticultural Society Hall* 60c is still the scene for many a public exhibit (the Society dates from 1829).

The Public Garden's *Swan Boats* are exact replicas of 60d those first set in motion here in 1877, and the twenty-four-acre Garden itself, patterned on one at Versailles, was laid out on filled land in 1850. Two years later a parade of nineteenth-century townhouses began forming on land piled into *Back Bay*, eventually making their 60e way along the flanks of stately Commonwealth Avenue to the Fenway.

Copley Square, a centerpiece in this grand design, re- 60f tains its two period churches and the grandiose Boston Public Library building. It was also the original site of the *Boston Museum of Fine Arts.* 60g

THE COLLECTORS

In the decades immediately following the Civil War, most proper Bostonians made at least one visit to Europe, returning with a painful sense that their proud city had little to display of old world culture. So in 1870 a city museum was founded, initially to house collections of sculpture, engravings and paintings already amassed by Harvard, MIT and the Boston Athenaeum, which included important works by local artists, J. S. Copley, Gilbert Stuart, Jonathan Trumble and Benjamin West. But its first curators set about collecting copies and plaster casts of European masterpieces, believing "original works . . . beyond our reach." How they underestimated their Boston collectors and philanthropists!

These began by ferreting out and appropriating exotic treasures heretofore ignored by European collectors. One Harvard zoologist clippered off to Japan in 1876 and began amassing pottery, while a university colleague collected ancient scrolls. A Boston doctor, William Sturgis Bigelow, arrived in Japan a few years later, intending to stay seven months, returning seven years later with 50,000 prints, hundreds of paintings, swords and Noh costumes. Another local collector brought home 11,000 pieces of Latin American, Indian and Far Eastern art, and a Harvard classics scholar contributed an important collection of Greek sculpture. The museum itself joined Harvard in an expedition to Egypt which resulted in the finest Old Kingdom sculpture to be found this side of Cairo. Since Bostonian Lilla Cabot Perry happened to be studying painting under Monet in Paris, she naturally brought home dozens of works by her French impressionist friends.

Bostonians opened another art front in this country by staging the first national exhibit of crafts in 1897 at the museum; the group behind this novel show incorporated themselves as the *Society of Arts and Crafts* which today 60h
maintains a nonprofit gallery on Newbury Street (Back Bay), still Boston's most fashionable shopping area. One of the crafts group's first sponsors was *Mrs. "Jack"* 60i
Gardner, A Back Bay socialite whose own collections of Titians, Rembrandts, Whistlers and antiques eventually outgrew her two adjoining townhouses. The Venetian palace which she built to house them in is now an important little museum in its own right. It is a conveniently short walk from the present massive home of the Boston Museum of Fine Arts (which outgrew its first home within three decades) in Boston's Fenway, part of that "green necklace" designed by Frederick Law Olmsted.

Drop center barouche

The Yankee penchant for amassing treasures and deeding them to the public has spawned literally hundreds of intriguing museums dedicated to everything from *trolley* 61
cars to *buttons*, scattered through the region. Many we 62
have mentioned already and unfortunately space only permits noting the most outstanding members of this species.

In 1875 Henry Sheldon, a country storekeeper, church organist and town clerk, bought one of Middlebury, Vermont's finest Federal era homesteads and began moving

in vanloads of obsolete pianos, a dozen grandfather
clocks, odd old furnishings and hundreds of books, eventually hanging out a thirty-foot shingle: "Sheldon Art
Museum, Archeological and Historical Society," today
the delightful *"Sheldon museum"* which claims to be 63
the first incorporated village museum in the United States.

"I wish the museum to be the people's school . . . to
teach the village the meaning of nature and religion,"
explained Franklin Fairbanks at the 1890 dedication of
the *Fairbanks Museum* in St. Johnsbury, Vermont. This 64
neo-Romanesque building with its great, vaulted ceiling
is bursting with exhibits from Africa, Oceania, and South
America; there is a letter from Robert Louis Stevenson,
transferring his birthday to a young South Seas Island
neighbor (a St. Johnsbury girl), also a planetarium, live
animals and plants.

In *Worcester*, Massachusetts, where an outstanding *art* 65
museum also dates from this period, John *Higgins* found 65a
both his fortune and consuming hobby in steel. Here he
built a four-story, steel-framed building set with 10,000
panes of glass and topped by a steel knight, and filled it
with four hundred complete medieval suits of armor. His
hope was to inspire local industrial craftsmen the way
others did painters and sculptors. This remains the biggest
private collection of armor in the Western Hemisphere; a
total of 3,000 exhibits range from stone age weapons
through Roman gladiator trappings to early chain mail.

Although Downeast native Alfred Atmore Pope made
his millions in iron, his instinct for fine art is obvious:
Degas, Manet, Monet and Whistler masterpieces fill his
Farmington, Connecticut, mansion, now the *Hill-Stead* 66
Museum. A few decades later, a New York City couple,
the Clark family, heirs to the Singer sewing machine fortune, erected the marble Sterling & Francine *Clark Art* 67
Institute in north Berkshire's Williamstown, Massachusetts, to house their collections of fifteenth to twentieth
century European art, also an important collection of
French impressionist works. And although it did not
open until 1948, we must mention the *Farnsworth Mu-* 68
seum in Rockland, Maine, known for its Andrew Wyeth
paintings as well as outstanding nineteenth-century
marine paintings. It was donated by Lucy Farnsworth,
who died at the age of ninety-six, having passed most of
her life as a recluse in the Victorian mansion across the
street (now open for all to see its heavy layerings of satin,
velvet and gilt).

The very idea of preserving a historic building in the
way you would a work of art or piece of natural scenery
also dates from the 1880s. In 1876 Boston's *Old South* 60j
Meeting House was one of the country's first edifices to
be saved from demolition through public subscription. A
dozen venerable buildings were rescued by local societies
formed for the purpose in the following decade. In Concord, stationery store owner Davis Cummings, who had
been buying up old furnishings his neighbors thought
worthless for years, agreed to donate them to the town
if they would house the collection; thus the *Concord* 69
Antiquarian Museum was built in Emerson's former cow
pasture and now houses local memorabilia in period
rooms and one entire seventeenth-century one-room
plan house. Deerfield's local historian George Sheldon
met with similar success, founding the *Pocumptic Valley* 70
Historical Society with its extensive hodgepodge display
in Asher Benjamin's Deerfield Academy building, now
Memorial Hall.

"How can you, who have been brought up with Rembrandts and Manets, collect and live with such American
trash?" Electra Havermeyer's mother was overheard to
upbraid her eighteen-year-old daughter when the girl
bought her first cigar store Indian in 1906. Electra kept
on collecting, eventually founding the *Shelburne Mu-* 71
seum, today one of the country's most extensive as well
as first collections of Americana. American Indians,
communes and Shakers were far from themes of general
interest when Boston patrician Clara Endicott Sears
founded *Fruitlands Museums* in 1914. *Storrowtown* 72, 73
Village in West Springfield, not to mention *Old Stur-* 74
bridge Village and *Plimoth Plantation*, also helped pi- 75
oneer the idea of "outdoor museums." New complexes
dedicated to American history, notably *Willowbrook* 76
at Newfield in Maine, also *Heritage Plantation* and 77
the *Drummer Boy Museum* (both on Cape Cod) con- 78
tinue to open.

Perhaps the most unique, one-man, one-building collection of the early twentieth century is represented by
forty-room *Beauport* near Gloucester. Fashionable Bos- 79
ton interior decorator Henry Sleeper's idea was to "have
a house in which each room could recapture some of the
spirit of a specific mood or phase or period of our American life from the time of Plymouth down to the Revolution and early Republic." He went on to build just such
a house, incorporating pieces of seventeenth-, eighteenth-

and nineteenth-century buildings into one treasure-filled collage of a place.

Beauport is one among the thirty-five out of its sixty
properties which the *Society for the Preservation of* 80
New England Antiquities opens to visitors. The country's largest private holder of historic house museums, SPNEA was founded by Boston blueblood William Sumner Appleton in 1910 and continues to offer consulting service to hundreds of regional preservation projects annually; also to be an international pace-setter in its field.

Ironically, it's precisely because private, nonprofit groups pioneered the concept of preserving historic buildings, hiking paths and swatches of unusually beautiful land in New England that visitors find these difficult to locate and visit today. Elsewhere in the country such sites tend to be state or government owned, better publicized and open longer, more regular hours.

In recent years the *National Park Service* has in fact 81
been slowly acquiring a number of historic buildings in New England, moving its regional headquarters to Boston where it has begun the delicate job of managing the city's seven, still privately owned, Freedom Trail sites, incorporating them into a Boston National Historic Park, complete with a downtown National Park Service Visitor
Center. Each state does have its quota of *state parks*; 82
there are also a half dozen *National Wildlife Refuges* 83
within the region.

PROVINCIAL PASTIMES

This said, we can happily admit that current visitors find New England much the confusing and largely unspoiled place which their nineteenth-century counterparts did.

By the end of the century Americans had begun looking to New England as a region in which they could recapture a more traditional way of life than that found in newer parts of the country. They had begun searching out "unspoiled" villages, country fairs and church suppers, old-
time industries like *cranberrying* and *sugaring.* 84, 85

Tourism has since become so financially crucial to regional economy that state and local promotion groups now dispense free and valuable assistance (see "Helpful Hints") which includes annual listings of the thousands of small town happenings, which, if anything, seem to in-

crease each year. And recent years have seen a revival
both in nineteenth-century sports like *hiking*, *biking* and 86, 87
old-style skiing (reintroduced as "ski touring" or "cross- 88
country skiing") and in *traditional crafts*, all encouraged 89
by nonprofit, dedicated groups.

But there's an old Yankee maxim that nothing worthwhile comes easily, and it still applies to exploring this region. To stick to your car, to the most obvious "attractions" and to roadside motels, is to miss the authentic fabric of New England life, along with its wealth of natural and man-made beauty.

DETAILS

1 *Mount Washington, New Hampshire.* Between Rtes. 16, 302. The highest mountain in New England remains a hiking and a general tourist magnet. Half of those who reach the top come by foot over a choice of fifteen trails. See Chapter 8 for details on the Summit Road and Cog Railway. For information about hiking and accommodations in the two huts along the Crawford Path, check with the Appalachian Mountain Club at its Pinkham Notch Camp (603) 466-3994 (reservations) or (603) 466-2721 (information).

1a *Crawford House,* Crawford Notch, New Hampshire. Rte. 302. Today: three hundred guests, golf, swimming; worth a stop just to see old-style decor. Summer months. (603) 846-5511.

1b *Mount Washington Hotel,* Bretton Woods, Crawford Notch, Rte. 302. This old ark has been lucky. It was refurbished by the government for the 1944 United Nations conference at which the World Bank was established. Again in 1970 its 1890s decor was restored by the development company which has since created a ski area and plans to build a major condominium village on its 10,000 acres, an enclave which predates the surrounding national forest. The hotel closes winter months, otherwise: golf, horseback riding, tennis, swimming. In Boston: (617) 969-6407; in New Hampshire: (603) 278-1000.

2 *Thayer's Hotel,* Littleton, New Hampshire. Open year round: (603) 444-3923.

3 *Balsam Hotel,* Dixville Notch, Rte. 26, northeastern New Hampshire. Accommodates more than four hundred guests, offers golf, tennis; the region's first Victorian era hotel to winterize itself and offer skiing: Wilderness Ski Area has consistent snow cover. In Boston: (617) 227-8288. In New Hampshire: (603) 255-3400.

4 *Waumbec Hotel,* Jefferson, New Hampshire. Rte. 2. Maintained by the University of New Hampshire Whittemore School of Business as a hotel training school: golf, swimming and hiking; also site of special summer events. Open late June to mid-October. (603) 882-4763.

5 *Jackson, New Hampshire.* Rte. 16. Begun as a summer resort, now as famous in winter. Besides offering lodgings for downhill skiers at Wildcat Mountain (just across Pinkham Notch from Mount Washington: gondola which works year round) it has recently cut a 100-mile network of ski touring trails. For details contact Jackson Ski Touring Foundation (603) 383-9355.

5a *Eagle Mountain House,* Jackson. Reasonable: playroom, golf, tennis, swimming. (603) 383-4264.

6 *North Conway, New Hampshire.* Major accommodations center, year round. Sites include White Horse Ledge, Cathedral Ledge, Conway Scenic Railway (see Chapter 8) and Cranmore ski area. For details contact the Mount Washington Valley Chamber of Commerce: (603) 356-5524.

7 *Franconia Notch, New Hampshire.* Rte. 3. Its gilded era began with the advent of rail service; the station today is an outlet for the League of New Hampshire Craftsmen. The lone survivor of its grand hotels is now headquarters for Franconia College, which offers summer workshops in dance, music and photography. The country's oldest aerial tramway takes you to the top of Cannon Mountain, a ski area in winter; there's a state campground at the base of Lafayette Mountain; plenty of lodging in Franconia Village and adjacent Sugar Hill, notably the nineteenth-century Homestead: (603) 823-5564.

7a *The Flume.* Franconia Notch. An 800-foot-deep gorge within the present state park. Memorial Day–mid-Oct., daily: 9–5. Admission charged.

7b *Old Man of the Mountains.* One of New England's major landmarks, 1200 feet above Profile Lake.

8 *Bethlehem, New Hampshire.* Rte. 302. The seasonal Sinclair Hotel still offers swimming, golf. The grand old Upland Terrace is now a tennis camp.

9 *Mountain View House,* Whitefield, New Hampshire. Off Rte. 3 north of town. Features include an oval dining room, swimming, golf, tennis, sweeping views of the Presidential and Franconia ranges. May–Oct. 13 (603) 837-2511. The neighboring Spalding Inn Club is slightly newer, less formal, famed for its lawn bowling. Late May–late Oct.: (603) 837-2572.

10 *Bethel, Maine.* Junction Rtes. 2, 26, 5, 35. A town of big homes built by prosperous nineteenth-century farmers and lumbermen; the only Maine resort within the White Mountain National Forest. The Bethel Inn includes a half-dozen cottages; swimming, golf, hiking in nearby Grafton Notch. Summer season only (207) 824-2175, but local ski areas include Sunday River and Evergreen Valley.

11 *Wolfeboro, New Hampshire.* Rtes. 28, 109. A summer and fall resort; home of the Wolfeboro Railroad (see Chapter 8). Headquarters for Lakes Region Information. Box 300; (603) 569-1117.

12 *Weirs Beach, New Hampshire.* Rte. 3. An amusement center since its "grove meeting" days; honky-tonk but old-style; newer attractions include Animal Forest Park and Indian Village Funspot.

12a *M/V Mt. Washington.* For details see Chapter 8.

13 *Castle in the Clouds,* Moultonborough, New Hampshire. Rte. 171. Thomas Plant built this grandiose retreat on the proceeds from his shoe factory in Jamaica Plain (see details Chapter 7); worthwhile both for its mechanical contraptions and splendid view of the lake. Visitors drive part way up its steep entryway; take a four-wheel-drive vehicle the rest of the way. May 29–Oct. 13, daily: 9–4. Admission charged. (603) 476-2352.

14 *Saint-Gaudens National Historic Site,* Cornish, New Hampshire. Off Rte. 12A. A fine old brick tavern, transformed by the Irish sculptor in 1885 into a Victorian-style country retreat which he named "Aspet"; the formal gardens with their view of Mt. Ascutney are the site for Sunday picnic concerts. Late May–Oct. 15, daily: 8:30–5. Admission charged. (603) 675-2055.

15 *Mount Monadnock,* Jaffrey, New Hampshire. Rte. 124. The state maintains the park at its base and SPNHF, the top 40 acres with their 20 trails, and an Ecocenter near the parking lot.

16 *Appalachian Mountain Club,* Boston, Massachusetts. 5 Joy St. The AMC has published mapped guides to hiking trails in all New England states except Vermont. Its Pinkham Notch Base Camp sleeps 104 and offers family-style meals (by reservation); also showers, washing machines for hikers. Its "high huts" are scattered through the Presidential range, a day's hike apart. All offer food and bunks in summer months; some are open on a limited service basis in winter. Members receive publications, notice of hikes, and access to lodges. Boston: (617) 523-0636; Pinkham Notch: (603) 466-2721.

17 *Society for the Protection of New Hampshire Forests,* Concord, New Hampshire. 5 South St. SPNHF continues to crusade for ecology causes, also maintains nature conservation programs and Lost River, a spectacular gorge and series of caverns discovered in 1874 (jcts. I-93, Rte. 3, Kancamagus Highway at North Woodstock; mid-May mid-Oct., daily). (603) 224-0361.

18 *White Mountain National Forest,* outlined on highway maps of New Hampshire and Maine. Its 727,087 acres include 100 miles of roads, 128 miles of foot trails. The U.S. Forest Service administers 17 campgrounds on a first come, first served basis. Permits are required for all campfires, including portable stoves; camping permitted only in selected areas along trails. For details: White Mountain National Forest, Laconia, New Hampshire 03246; (603) 524-6450.

19 *New Hampshire State Parks.* Of the 32 parks, 14 include lake swimming. Among the most famous: Crawford Notch includes a wildlife exhibit, two campgrounds, an array of waterfalls and the Inn Unique, a little granite inn with a museum of local memorabilia (unpredictable hours: (603) 374-2323). Mt. Sunapee State Park includes a state ski area with a gondola operating year round, summer site for concerts, and the August Crafts Fair of the League of New Hampshire Craftsmen.

20 *Kancamagus Highway,* Lincoln to Conway. A spectacular, 34-mile slash through the National Forest; picnic areas, six camping areas, hiking trails. Late May–late Oct.; daytime traffic: Dec.–mid-April.

21 *Newport, Rhode Island.* This claims to be the country's first resort (see Chapter 4). For general guidance: Newport County Chamber of Commerce, 93 Thames St., Newport, Rhode Island 02840; (401) 847-1600.

21a *National Tennis Hall of Fame and Tennis Museum,* Newport Casino, 194 Bellevue Ave., Newport. Mid-May to late Oct., Mon.-Sat.: 9:30-5; Sun.: 11-5. Admission charged.

21b *Preservation Society of Newport County,* Washington Square, Newport. In addition to the mansions noted, the Society maintains Green Animals (outstanding topiary gardens, Corey's Lane, Portsmouth). All holdings: Memorial Day-mid-Nov., daily: 10-5; otherwise: weekends, same hours. Admission charged to all, combination ticket available. (401) 847-1000 or 847-7516.

21c *Belcourt Castle,* Bellevue Ave., Newport. Designed by Richard Morris Hunt, $3 million to build; features include a twenty-three-karat gold French coronation coach and elaborate antiques. April to mid-Nov., daily: 10-5; otherwise by appt.: (401) 846-0669.

21d *Sanford-Covell House,* 72 Washington St., Newport. "Pompeian," early Newport resort style featuring stenciled walls, original furnishings. June-Sept.; Tues., Thurs., Sat.: 1-5. Admission charged.

21e *Edward King House,* Aquidneck Park, Newport. Designed in 1845 by Richard Upjohn, Italianate villa. Year round, Mon.-Fri.: 9-4:30; summer weekends by appointment: (401) 846-7426.

21f *Newport Music Festival,* Newport. A program of nineteenth-century lesser-known music; three daily concerts held in various settings; early August. Details from 23 Bridge St. (401) 846-1140.

22 *Jamestown, Rhode Island,* Conanicut Island. From Newport, toll bridge ($2); from Saunderstown, Jamestown Bridge (free). Primarily nineteenth-century architecture; sites include an eighteenth-century windmill (see Chapter 7), Sidney L. Wright Collection of Indian Artifacts (see Chapter 2) and the old-style inns, the Bay Voyage, (401) 846-7426, and Jamestown Inn (401) 423-0400.

23 *Block Island, Rhode Island.* 12 miles off Point Judith. Seventeenth-century settlers chopped down all the trees and piled stones into endless low walls with a resulting Scotch heath look. Most of the eleven square miles invite exploration: dirt paths branch off the one paved road in all directions. Sites include Monhegan Bluffs, bird life, Crescent Beach and the town of New Shoreham. In addition to those mentioned we recommend the 1661 Inn. (401) 466-2421. Taxi service, rental bikes available. For details contact the chamber of commerce. (401) 466-2436. Accessible from New London, Galilee, Newport and Providence by ferry; see Chapter 8 details; also by New England Airlines from Westerly, Rhode Island (401) 596-2460.

24 *Old Orchard Beach, Maine.* U.S. 1, exit off I-95. Billed as the "cleanest, finest, safest beach in the world"; began as a Free Will Baptist camp meeting spot; still site of the annual Salvation Army meeting, August. Amusement center and the old pier have lost much of their gingerbread but not their honky-tonk; more than two hundred lodging facilities, every conceivable sport. Contact the chamber of commerce: (207) 934-2091.

25 *York Beach, Maine.* U.S. 1, off I-95. Centers around the old boardwalk featuring salt water taffy and fried clams; plenty of room on Long Beach and Short Sands; plenty of accommodations; contact the chamber of commerce: (207) 363-4422.

26 *Ogunquit, Maine.* U.S. 1, off I-95 at York. The town fills to overflowing summer weekends; plenty of lodging and room on the beach mid-week. Ogunquit Lobster Pound, one of best in the state. Chamber of commerce: (207) 646-5533.

27 *Calendar Islands, Casco Bay, Maine.* Just six, accessible by Casco Bay Line ferries (see Chapter 7); aside from those mentioned, none of the islands offers accommodations although summer rentals may be found. Long Island offers a state beach, general store and snack bar; details about clambakes on tiny House Island, dominated by massive Civil War Fort Scammel, are available from Bucaneer Lines, Box 592, Portland (207) 799-8188. On Eagle Island Admiral Robert Peary's home is open to visitors who can get there by private boat (June 20-Labor Day, daily).

27a *Peaks Island, Maine.* 15-minute ride from Portland. The lone surviving period hotel, now a convent. Accommodations limited to Fisher Lodge ("The Inn on Peaks," delightful rooms, meals by reservation) and to apartments available from Lionel Plant Assoc. Trefethen Evergreen Assoc. permits daytrippers to use its beach; Woodbury's Dairy Bar, good for sit-down as well as take-out meals.

27b *Chebeague Island,* Casco Bay. A half-hour ride from Portland. Taxis routinely meet the ferry but best to bring your bike; the Hillcrest By The Sea, open summer months, access to golf and tennis. (207) 846-9980.

28 *Victoria Mansion,* Portland, Maine. 109 Danforth St. Considered one of the outstanding examples of Victorian architecture in the country, built by a Maine native who made his fortune as a New Orleans hotelier. Cost $400,000 to build in 1863; elaborate detailing and furnishings.

Mid-June to mid-Oct., daily: 10-4; otherwise by appointment. Admission charged. (207) 772-4841.

29 *Mount Desert Island, Maine.* Rte. 3 off U.S. 1 at Ellsworth. In 1604 Champlain named this forty-two-square-mile island "Isle des Monts deserts," meaning: "Island of the bare mountains" for its distinctive; dome-shaped, rose-colored peaks which number eighteen; the highest, Cadillac Mt., 1,532 feet high. It also boasts five large lakes, dozens of ponds, streams and a cleft down its center, fjord-like Somes Sound. The entire history of the island from its early settlement as a mission is told in the Isleford Historical Museum on Little Cranberry Island (inquire: (207) 244-3575). Today Bar Harbor is the transient visitor center; Northeast Harbor is the fashionable yachting place and summer colony. Somesville remains a sleepy, clapboard village; Southwest Harbor and Bass Harbor are both fishing communities and ferry departure points (see Chapter 8).

29a *Bar Harbor, Maine.* Many of the now-vanished hotels were built quickly to make their owners' fortunes in a few years. Guests were routinely up at 6:30 and off by 7:00, playing golf (the Kebo Valley Golf Club, founded 1889, welcomes guests), walking, horseback riding (inquire from chamber about current stables) or maybe canoeing – with Indians doing the actual paddling. Between 1884 and 1893 there was also a narrow-gauge railway. For guidance to ample lodging places and restaurants contact the Chamber (Municipal Building, Bar Harbor, Maine 04609. (207) 288-5103).

29b *Jessup Memorial Library,* Mt. Desert St., Bar Harbor. The Historic room is well worth a stop. Year round, Mon.-Fri.: 10-4; also mornings, Wed., Fri.

29c *Jordon Pond House.* Opened in 1847, bought in the 1940s by John D. Rockefeller to preserve its atmosphere and quality; today administered by the Park Service, retaining its traditional menu: fresh fruit ice creams and popovers at high tea plus lobster and chicken, lunch and dinner. Usually a long wait but you can submit your name, then walk around Jordon Pond. (207) 276-3316.

29d *Acadia National Park.* At the Hulls Cove Visitors Center a film introduces the forty-square-mile park; famous sites include Anemone Cave, the Thunderhole and Cadillac Mountain. Ask here about horseback riding, hiking, guided and self-guiding nature walks, beaches and campsites; trails are kept open and fireplaces stocked with wood during winter months for ski tourers. For park details: (207) 288-3338 or in Boston: (617) 223-2793.

30 *Trustees of Reservations,* Milton, Massachusetts. These holdings differ essentially from state parks: all permit hiking and picnicking but the idea is to preserve the natural beauty, thus visitors are subject to a number of rules. A detailed listing is available from the Trustees' headquarters, 224 Adams St., Milton, Massachusetts 02186. (617) 698-2066.

31 *Crane's Beach,* Ipswich, Massachusetts. Argilla Rd., off Rte. 1A. Dune, salt marsh and steep upland as well as beach included in 1,326 acres plus the "Castle," an early twentieth-century mansion built by plumbing magnate Richard T. Crane with its formal garden, site of summer concerts. The beach is open mid-April–Labor Day, daily: 9-5. Steep admission charged but worth it except during Black Fly season. (617) 356-4354.

32 *World's End,* Hingham, Massachusetts. Unmarked road, ask directions from Rte. 3A. A 249-acre peninsula, landscaped by Frederick Law Olmsted in 1890 as a real estate development. Never developed, delightful walkways and plantings remain. Year round, daily: 10-5. Parking, horseback riding charges.

33 *Naumkeag,* Stockbridge, Massachusetts. Rte. 7. The mansion is furnished to period, outstanding formal gardens. June–Labor Day, Tues.-Sat.: 10-5; Sun.: 11-4. Admission charged. (413) 298-3239.

33a *Chesterwood,* Stockbridge. Rte. 102 west, 2 miles, left on Rte. 183. "I live here six months of the year – in heaven. The other six months I live – well – in New York," sculptor Daniel Chester French once said. A family friend of Emerson who helped him secure his first commission (the now-famous Minuteman in Concord) French is best known for his statue of Lincoln in the Washington memorial to that president. His elegant country home includes a studio at which visitors are invited to try their hand in clay. Maintained by the National Trust; June–Oct. 31, daily: 10-5. (413) 298-3579.

33b *Red Lion Inn,* Main St., Stockbridge. The original tavern on this site, in which Berkshire residents met to object violation of their rights in 1774, was replaced in 1897 by the present white, rambling inn. Its present owners saved it from demolition a few years ago: delightful lodging, meals or just to rock on its porch. (413) 298-5545.

34 *Lenox, Massachusetts.* Rte. 7. The Lenox Library (Main St.) built 1815 as a courthouse, contains a plush reading room, also photos of the period "cottages"; the Church on the Hill, just

north of town, is exceptionally handsome. The town's chamber of commerce, housed in the vintage 1803 Academy Building (Main St.) dispenses a leaflet guide to ample accommodations, restaurants and sports facilities (which include riding, golf, swimming). Write Box 646, Lenox, Massachusetts 01240.

34a *Lenox Art Center* at Wheatleigh, Lenox, Rte. 183. Hawthorne Rd. Restaurant, bar, theater presentations through summer months. P.O. Box 1787, Lenox, Massachusetts 01240. (413) 637-2227.

34b *Lenox Inns.* Two converted cottages which are now inns: Blantyre Castle (pool, tennis, dining), (413) 637-0475, and Eastover, complete resort (413) 637-0625.

34c *Tanglewood,* Lenox, West St. The Berkshire Music Festival summer season for the Boston Symphony Orchestra. Early July-late-Aug., Fri.-Sun., also weekday schedule of performances. Admission charged. (413) 637-1600.

34d *Pleasant Valley Wildlife Sanctuary,* Lenox. West Mt. Rd.; Rte. 20 off Rte. 7. One mile square with twelve miles of trails, featuring a beaver colony. (413) 637-0320.

35 *Berkshires, Massachusetts.* The state's westernmost region, with a history and atmosphere different from the rest, oriented toward New York City rather than Boston. For general information and a detailed, mapped guide to six circle tours contact Berkshire Hills Conference, Box 1170, Pittsfield, Massachusetts 01201. (413) 443-9186. A mapped "Westenhook Trail," geared to hikers, bicyclists and history buffs is available from Mrs. Angus McDonald, South Egremont, Massachusetts 01253.

36 *Massachusetts Audubon Society,* headquartered Lincoln, Massachusetts. The Society maintains more than forty sanctuaries within the state, thirteen staffed, offering camping, environmental programs. Membership receives publications, notice of excursions, lectures. This group inspired the formation of the National Audubon Society but today is unrelated. Within New England, details about activities are also available from the Audubon Society of New Hampshire (3 Silk Farm Rd., Concord, New Hampshire 02903; (603) 224-9909); the Audubon Society of Rhode Island (40 Bowen St., Providence, Rhode Island 02903; (401) 521-1670); the Maine Audubon Society (57 Baxter Boulevard, Portland, Maine 04101; (207) 774-8271) and the Connecticut Audubon Society (2325 Burr St., Fairfield, Connecticut 06430; (203) 259-6305). Headquarters of the Massachusetts Society is Drumlin Farm, a demonstration farm where children are permitted to pet the animals and encouraged to explore nature trails (South Great Rd., Lincoln, Massachusetts 01773; (617) 259-9500).

37 *Wellfleet Bay Wildlife Sanctuary,* South Wellfleet, Massachusetts. Rte. 6, just north of Eastham-Wellfleet town line. Some 650 acres of salt marsh, pond, meadow; self-guiding nature trails, guided walks, starting point for tours of the Outer Beach, Monomoy Island; during the mid-July-Aug. migrating season, 250 species of birds usually spotted. Year round, daily: 8 to sunset. Admission charged. (617) 349-2615.

38 *Cape Cod, Massachusetts.* Roughly seventy miles long, frequently described as shaped like a bent arm with its fist raised. Much of its 300-mile coastline is beach. Although the Cape's current tourist boom dates from the post-World War II days, Provincetown (the "fist" of this "arm") became a famous art colony just before the turn of the century. The Cape Cod Chamber of Commerce (just off Rte. 6, Hyannis, Massachusetts 02301; (617) 362-3225) is adept at handling its quarter million summer visitors and keeps lists of guesthouses, ideal accommodations for anyone without children, a substantial savings over motels.

39 *Chatham Railroad Museum,* Chatham, Massachusetts. Rte. 28, Depot St. Housed in the Victorian depot which operated 1887-1937; original dispatching and ticket office, timetables (three hours to Boston) and mementos. Late June-mid-Sept., weekdays: 2-4. (617) 945-0128.

40 *Highland House,* Truro, Massachusetts. Rte. 6. Lone survivor of many one-time small hotels in town. Collection includes fishing and whaling gear, ships models. Late June-early Sept., daily: 10-5. Admission charged.

41 *Cape Cod National Seashore,* Cape Cod, Massachusetts. Marked on highway maps. In all 26,666 acres which include six staffed beaches, also biking and self-guiding nature trails. Orientation film, map and program of daily seasonal lectures and guided hikes available from the Visitors Center at Salt Pond (Eastham, Rte. 6); mid-June-mid-Oct., daily: 8-6; otherwise, Fri-Tues.: 9-5) and Race Point (near Provincetown; summer months, daily: 9-7; rest of year, Wed.-Sun.: 9-5). For details write Superintendent, South Wellfleet, Massachusetts 02663. (617) 349-3785.

42 *Oak Bluffs, Martha's Vineyard,* Massachusetts. Cottages form concentric circles around the Tabernacle; many other cottages in town date from the era and reflect their ornate motifs. This is also one of the country's oldest black resort communities; the two surviving hotels are the Wesley and Seaview. Illumination night with its community sing, band concert, and Japanese

lanterns hung throughout is the third Wednesday evening, Aug. For details the island's chamber of commerce: Vineyard Haven, Massachusetts 02568; (617) 693-0085.

43 *Craigville Conference Center,* Craigville Village, Massachusetts. The "Village" centers on a formal green, includes both private, dorm-style accommodations at the Lodge, Manor, Seaside House and the Groves. Meals, family style; tennis courts, planned activities, famous beach; off-season lodgings extremely reasonable. Purpose defined as "re-creation of the whole person." For details: Craigville Village, Massachusetts 02636. (617) 775-1265.

44 *Isles of Shoals, New Hampshire and Maine.* Ten miles off Portsmouth, New Hampshire. See Chapter 3 for early history. Gosport had an unlucky time: pirates, notably Edward Teach (better known as Blackbeard), who is said to have escaped from here, leaving his bride behind to guard his treasures; islanders swear to see her periodically floating around. A less colorful pirate, name of Quelch, is said to have buried $100,000 here, too, and treasure hunters remain a summer fixture. The few people who did return here after the Revolution acquired a reputation as "harpies" for their habit of setting up false beacons to wreck ships for salvage. A mini-Washington monument on Star marks the grave of the minister sent out to work for that group. In all, the islands include Duck, Appledore, Malaga, Smuttynose, Cedar, Star, Lunging, Seavey and White; only Star is accessible to excursionists via M/V *Viking Queen* from Portsmouth. (603) 431-5500.

44a *Star Island, Isles of Shoals.* Daytrippers find a friendly reception but are told that the only way to appreciate the island is by staying overnight to see the evening candlelight procession to the chapel; the atmosphere attracts families generation after generation. Weekly programs, reasonably priced, sell out as soon as published in January (available from Star Island Corporation, 110 Arlington St., Boston, Massachusetts 02116; (617) 426-7988). Information about occasional vacancies during summer months by phoning the Dover-Mobile operator: (603) JE8-3544.

45 *Stowe, Vermont.* Rte. 100, off I-89 at Waterbury. Self-styled "Ski Capital of the East"; also a lively summer resort. From the summit of Mt. Mansfield, accessible via gondola and, during summer months, the old toll road (which once served the hotel on top) Lake Champlain stretches westward, a view which Emerson in 1868 described as "a perpetual illusion." The village is a cluster of shops, restaurants and inns, most famous among them, the Green Mountain Inn, (802) 253-7301, built in 1833 as a stage stop. Among forty-five other lodging places listed with the Stowe Area Assoc. (Box 1230, Stowe, Vermont 05672; (802) 253-7321) is Trapp Family Lodge, (802) 253-8511, owned by Maria Von Trapp of *The Sound of Music* fame. In winter the Mt. Mansfield Company maintains thirty miles of ski trails and year round offers a few pricy and choice resort motels, notably Toll House Motor Inn (802) 253-7311.

46 *Equinox House,* Manchester, Vermont. Junction Rtes. 30, 7. This mammoth white wooden landmark dominates gracious Manchester village; begun as a stage stop in 1801, it kept growing for a century. Mrs. Abraham Lincoln spent a month here after her husband's death, and her son bought an estate and died in town. The mineral spring is gone but its eighteen-hole golf course is one of five in town; also swimming, hiking, skiing, ski touring. Southern Vermont Art Center offers a full program of summer music, dance, art. (802) 362-3100.

47 *Champlain Islands.* Bridges from Rouses Point, New York, Swanton and Burlington, Vermont; ferry from Plattsburgh, New York. A string of flat islands, connected by bridges and causeways, mid-lake; hedged by the Adirondacks to the west, the Green Mountains to the east. St. Anne's Shrine, Isle La Motte on the site of Vermont's first settlement (see Chapter 2) was purchased by the Roman Catholic diocese of Burlington in 1853 and soon began attracting pilgrims who came by steamboat. The fourteen-acre point of land includes a beach, picnic sites and the gingerbread-style shrine maintained by the Edmundite fathers (May 15-Oct. 15; (802) 928-8284). The island is also famous for its black marble, exhibited along with local mementos in the Historical Society museum (July, Aug., Sat.: 2-5); many distinctive homes throughout the islands are made of this marble. The town of North Hero is a resort community on City Bay; here North Hero House (opened in 1891 to serve railroad and steamboat passengers) offers lakeside rooms and gourmet fare (802) 372-8237, summer months. North Hero State Park offers seventy-seven wooded campsites; for a pamphlet on the islands write: Lake Champlain Islands, Chamber of Commerce, North Hero, Vermont 05474. (802) 372-8722.

48 *Park-McCullough House,* North Bennington, Vermont. Rte. 67 off Rte. 7. The town is a mix of Greek revival and Victorian homes with an elaborate railroad station. The thirty-room mansion has been preserved as a setting for lectures, special exhibits, concerts, crafts programs and special celebrations. July-mid-Oct., daily except Sat., Tues.: 9-5; guided tours on the hour, 10-4. (802) 442-2747.

49 *Wilson's Castle,* Proctor, Vermont. Rte. 4, west from Rutland to Proctor Rd. A 32-room version of a European castle, noted for its stained glass windows, thirteen working fireplaces, antiques and an aviary stocked with Indian peacocks. Mid-May to mid-Oct., daily: 9–6. Admission charged. (802) 773-3284.

50 *Burklyn,* Burke, Vermont. Rte. 114 from Lyndonville. An elegant estate, originally 15,000 acres, now the site for periodic crafts shows, concerts and lectures. For details contact Darion Inn, part of the original working farm on the estate, now year round (skiing, ski touring, tennis, hiking) (802) 626-5641.

51 *Vermont Cheese Factories.* Cheddar cheese became a major industry in the late nineteenth century and remains one of the state's most distinctive products. The process remains essentially unchanged; free samples always offered.

Cabot Farmers' Co-Operative Creamery Co., Cabot. Posted from Rtes. 15, 2. New England's oldest, largest cheddar cheese plant. Year round, Mon.–Sat.: 8–4. (802) 563-2231.

Crowley Cheese Factory, Healville. Off Rte. 103, north of Ludlow. Housed in a picturesque wooden creamery; curds "cut" and "raked" by hand, using nineteenth-century tools. Best time to visit: 11–1. Year round, daily: 8–4. (802) 259-2340.

Grafton Village Cheese Co., Grafton. Townsend Road. A restoration, primarily for visitors to this resort village (see Chapter 7). Year round, Mon.–Fri.: 9–4:30.

Plymouth Cheese Corp., Plymouth Historic District, Rte. 100A near Bridgewater Corners. Part of the Calvin Coolidge restoration, actually opened by the late president's family in 1890. Year round, Mon.–Sat.: 8–5:30, Sun.: 9–5:30. (802) 672-3650.

Sewards Cheese Factory, East Wallingford. Rte. 140, south from Rutland. Factory tours limited to small groups, salesroom offers a range of Vermont-made eatables. Year round, daily: 8–4. (802) 259-2340.

52 *Farm Vacations.* Most of lodging is at working dairy farms, offering both horseback riding and swimming. A descriptive listing available from the Vermont Dept. of Agriculture, Montpelier, Vermont 05603. In New Hampshire a dozen "Farm Boarding Houses" listed on a sheet printed annually, available from the New Hampshire Dept. of Agriculture, Concord, New Hampshire 03301.

53 *Green Mountain Club,* Box 94, Rutland, Vermont 05701. The club was formed to break the Long Trail in 1910; members receive publications; proceeds from hut fees help maintain the trail. *The Long Trail Guidebook*, $3, available from the club. (802) 775-0495.

54 *The Long Trail.* A 278-mile hiking trail traversing the spine of the Green Mountains from the Canadian to the Massachusetts border. The forty shelters along the way range from three-sided lean-tos to sizable stone cabins, a few of which offer meals. Two free brochures, "Short Hikes on the Long Trail" and "Short Hikes on the Middlebury and Rochester Districts of the Green Mt. National Forest," are available at state information booths.

55 *Green Mountain National Forest and Vermont State Parks.* The National Forest encompasses 243,383 acres and includes most of the state's ski areas as well as summer camping sites on a first come, first serve basis. For details on these, also on fishing, hunting and campfire permits, contact: GMNF Supervisor, Box 519, Rutland, Vermont 05701. For details about the thirty-six campgrounds within the thirty-eight state parks, thirty-four state forests, contact the Dept. of Forests and Parks, Montpelier, Vermont 05602. All camping facilities are open Memorial–Labor days, daily: 10–9. Trails are maintained through these public preserves in winter for ski touring and snowmobiling.

56 *Old Lyme, Connecticut.* Exits off I-95. A genteel old shipbuilding town, also billed as the country's first art colony. The Florence Griswold House, Lyme St., built by a sea captain in 1817, became a boardinghouse and studio for famous artists at the turn of the century; about every inch of wallspace has been painted, there's a door by Childe Hassam. Also home for the local historical society. June 15–Sept. 10, Tues.–Sun.: 1–5. After Labor Day by appt. Admission charged. (203) 434-5542.

57 *Goodspeed Opera House,* East Haddam, Connecticut. Rtes. 82, 149. A centerpiece for a number of period resort hotels among which only the neighboring Gelston House (specializing in pre-theater dinners) survives. The two high-Victorian buildings together make a delightful

vignette and their interiors are far from disappointing. The Opera House is open for tours during its summer season when it also slates musicals and films (203) 873-8864.

58 *Theater Museum,* Boothbay, Maine. Rte. 27, Wiscasset Road. Billed as the country's only museum devoted to theater memorabilia; exhibits include a miniature nineteenth-century Boston theater interior. The museum is attached to Boothbay Playhouse, outstanding summer stock. July, Aug., daily: 10-10. (207) 633-3550.

59 *P. T. Barnum Museum,* Bridgeport, Connecticut. 804 Main St. Exit 37 off I-95. The elaborately carved 1890s building represents $100,000 left by the circus baron for this purpose on his death. It's filled with circus pictures, posters, exhibits like Tom Thumb's bed and clothes, a miniature five-ring circus and mechanized Swiss village which cost Barnum $30,000 a century ago and was exhibited at the Chicago World's Fair, 1871. The city celebrates Barnum's memory with a nine day Barnum Festival, timed to include July 4. The museum is open year round, daily: 2-5. (203) 576-7320.

60 *Boston, Massachusetts.* Much of the city dates from the late nineteenth century, largely because in 1872 fire destroyed the sixty acres on which its business and shopping core were quickly rebuilt. In addition to Back Bay (see detail 60e) its South End residential neighborhood dates from the 1850s when South Bay was filled in, still retaining its old townhouses and crescent-shaped squares. During 1976 a multimedia exhibit of late nineteenth-century life in Boston is on view in the drill hall of the castle-like First Corps of Cadets Armory, Arlington St. at Columbus Ave. Year round, daily: 9-5. For details contact Boston 200 (617) 338-1976.

60a *Cyclorama Building,* 543-547 Tremont St., Boston. A two-story brick and concrete landmark capped by a glass dome above a rotunda. The four-hundred-foot circular painting has since found its way to Gettysburg. Now the core of the Boston Center for the Arts, used for a variety of live performances and films. (617) 426-5000.

60b *Symphony Hall,* 251 Huntington Ave., Boston. Designed by McKim, Mead and White in 1900, famed for its acoustics. The interior, richly carved, gilded; classic statues peer from wall niches. Home of the Boston Symphony Orchestra with performances Sept.-April; then the Boston Pops (April 29 to mid-July) which play to an audience seated at round tables, refreshments served; also a special Christmas performance. The building is generally open to visitors year round, 9-5 when no performances scheduled. (617) 266-1492.

60c *Horticultural Hall,* 300 Massachusetts Ave. Renaissance style, brick and massive, the building is site for frequent exhibits and includes an outstanding library. (617) 536-9280.

60d *Swan Boats,* Boston Public Garden. Long wooden barges designed by Robert Paget in the 1870s and operated by the Paget family ever since; the graceful swan on the stern contributes to the Victorian flavor of the Garden which covers twenty-four acres, enclosed by a period railing.

60e *Back Bay.* Bounded by the Charles River, railroad, Public Garden and Fenway. Cited as America's first successful, large-scale city planning effort. This was tidal outwash, separating Boston from Brookline, until land reclamation began in 1856; forty years later it totaled 450 acres; eight blocks long. Its Commonwealth Ave. forms a part of Boston's green belt (running from the Public Garden to Franklin Park), articulated by landscape architect Franklin Law Olmsted in 1879. The most fashionable neighborhood of its day, partly because each townhouse was designed to individual tastes, today representing the evolution of American residential architecture from 1860 to 1910; Arlington to Clarendon Sts. are basically French Second Empire; Dartmouth to Fairfield, "Ruskin Gothic"; Fairfield and Gloucester, "Richardson Romanesque"; Gloucester and Hereford are a mix of revival styles. Initially Back Bay was also home for Harvard Medical School and MIT; present Bonwit Teller's was the Natural History Museum. Boylston and Newbury Sts. remain busy shopping strips, balancing residential Marlboro St. and Commonwealth Ave. Gibson House Museum, 137 Beacon St., Victorian furnishings. Year round, Tues.-Sun.: 2-5. Closed holidays. Admission charged.

60f *Copley Square,* Boston. Boylston St. Never a square, originally framed by an unbroken ring of noteworthy buildings among which the Renaissance-style Boston Public Library and Episcopal Trinity Church survive. The library was designed by McKim and White in 1892, noteworthy for its carved panels by Saint-Gaudens, bronze doors by Daniel Chester French and the center courtyard with its fountain and arched loggia. (Year round, Mon.-Fri.: 9-9; Sat.: 9-6; Sun.: 2-6.) Trinity Church was designed by Henry Hobson Richardson, built in the 1870s on 4,500 wooden piles; the rich interior contains carvings by John LaFarge and Saint-Gaudens, windows by LaFarge. (Year round, daily: 8-5.)

60g *Boston Museum of Fine Arts,* 465 Huntington Ave., Boston. Generally ranked second in the country after the Metropolitan Museum of Art, N.Y.C. Outstanding exhibits include Oriental, Egyptian, French impressionist and American (portraits by Gilbert Stuart, Copley and Sargent, Paul Revere silver, period rooms and American folk art). Inquire about introductory tours, monthly calendar of events, special exhibits. Year round, daily except Mon.: 10–6, Tues. until 9. Admission charged except Sunday morning (617) 267-9300.

60h *Society of Arts and Crafts,* 69 Newbury St., Boston. Founded by a local printer, a membership of seven hundred within the decade but now reduced and just resuming its place as an important catalyst in regional crafts since its gallery (first opened in 1900 but relinquished for many years) has only recently reopened. (617) 266-1810.

60i *Isabella Stewart Gardner Museum,* 180 Fenway, Boston. A Renaissance palace which has been left to the public on condition that nothing in it be changed. Paintings by Titian, Tintoretto, Rembrandt, Whistler, Corot and Matisse are crowded among antiques, lush flower displays; also site for concerts, Sept.–June, Tues. evening, Thurs., Sat. afternoons (for current program: (617) 734-1359). Museum open: Sept.–June, Tues. 1–9:30, Wed.–Sun.: 1–5:30; July, Aug., Tues.–Sat.: 1–5:30. Admission charged Sun. only. (617) 566-1401.

60j *Old South Meeting House,* Boston. See Chapter 4.

61 *Trolley Museums–Seashore Trolley Museum,* Kennebunkport, Maine. Log Cabin Road off U.S. 1. More than one hundred old streetcars; rides every 30 min. Mid-June–Labor Day, daily: 10–6; late May–June, Sept.–mid Oct., weekends only. Admission charged. (207) 967-2712.

Branford Trolley Museum, East Haven, Connecticut, 17 River St. Off U.S. 1 near the Green. More than 180 old streetcars, dating from 1878; also exhibits on electric railways, 3-mile rides. Late June–early Sept., Mon.–Fri.: 10–5; late May–early Sept., Sat.: 11–6; early April–mid Oct., Sun.: 11–6. Admission charged. (203) 469-9627.

Connecticut Electric Railway Association, Warehouse Point, Connecticut. Rte. 140. More than fifty streetcars dating from 1894; steam and electric locomotives; trolley rides. March–Nov. weekends: 12–5; July–Labor Day, also Tues.–Fri.: 11–4. Charge for rides, not museum. (203) 623-7417.

62 *Just Buttons,* Southington, Connecticut. Exit 32 off Rte. 84. An eighteenth century house containing the world's largest exhibit of American uniform buttons, thousands of buttons from the 1700s to twentieth century. Year round, daily, phone before coming. (203) 628-6337.

63 *Sheldon Museum,* Middlebury, Vermont. Park St. An 1829 brick mansion containing parlors, kitchen, children's rooms furnished to reflect nineteenth-century farm life; also a country store, research library. June–Oct. 15, daily except Sun.: 10–5; otherwise Tues.–Thurs.: 1–5. (802) 288-2117.

64 *Fairbanks Museum,* St. Johnsbury, Vermont. 83 Main St. A Romanesque-style red sandstone building, elaborately carved, the interior grand hall finished in solid, quartered oak. Exhibits include minerals, fossils, stuffed animals, birds, material from Africa, Oceania and the Orient plus local memorabilia; also a weather observation station and planetarium. Year round Mon.–Sat.: 9–4:30, Sun.: 1–5; planetarium lectures Sat. 2:30. (802) 748-3413.

65 *Worcester Art Museum,* Worcester, Massachusetts. See Chapter 8.

65a *John Woodman Higgins Armory Museum,* Worcester, 100 Barber Ave. Said to be the country's first steel and glass office building. The two-story Grand Hall contains four hundred suits of armor, dating from 1510; also a Gobelin tapestry, blacksmith shop. Year round, Tues.–Fri.: 9–4, Sat.: 10–3, Sun.: 1–5. (617) 853-6015.

66 *Hill-Stead Museum,* Farmington, Connecticut. Mountain Road, Farmington Ave. Elegantly furnished to period with an exceptional collection of French impressionist art. Year round, Wed.–Sun.: 2–5. (203) 677-9064.

67 *Sterling & Francine Clark Art Institute,* Williamstown, Massachusetts. South St. A 1950s museum but so in the tradition of late nineteenth-century philanthropy that it bears inclusion. Recently expanded, the museum contains one of the country's finest collections of nineteenth-century French and American art; also Italian, Flemish and Dutch works, fourteenth–seventeenth centuries and changing exhibits. Year round, Tues.–Sun.: 10–5. (413) 458-8109.

68 *William A. Farmsworth Library and Art Museum,* Rockland, Maine. Elm St. Permanent collection of nineteenth- and twentieth-century paintings includes works by Eastman Johnson, Fitz Hugh Lane, Winslow Homer and Thomas Eakins; special exhibits in summer. (Year round, Tues.–Sat.: 10–5, Sun.: 1–5.) Farnsworth House features ornate Victorian furnishings, detailing. June–Sept., Mon.–Sat.: 10–5, Sun.: 1–5. Admission charged.

69 *Concord Antiquarian Museum,* Concord, Massachusetts. Lexington Rd., Cambridge Turnpike. Exhibits include Emerson's study, a Thoreau room, Paul Revere's signal lantern and a diorama of the Concord battle; also period rooms. Year round, weekends: 2–4:30, mid-March–Oct., Mon.–Sat.: 10–4:30. (617) 369-9609.

70 *Pocumptic Valley Historical Society* and *Old Deerfield Village*. See Chapter 4.
71 *Shelburne Museum*. See Chapter 8.
72 *Fruitland Museums*. See Chapter 9.
73 *Storrowtown Village*. West Springfield, Massachusetts. 1511 Memorial Ave., Eastern States Exposition Grounds. An early nineteenth-century grouping of restored and reconstructed buildings including a school, general store, meetinghouse and tavern. Mid-June–Labor Day, Mon.–Sat.: 1–5. Admission charged. Old Storrowtown Tavern, a pleasant restaurant, year round, Mon.–Sat.: 11:30–10. *Village:* (413) 732-2361.
74 *Old Sturbridge Village*. See Chapter 7.
75 *Plimoth Plantation*. See Chapter 3.
76 *Willowbrook at Newfield*, Maine. Rte. 11, west of Portland. A dozen buildings include an 1850s farmhouse, general store, stable, creamery, schoolhouse and restaurant. May 15–Oct. 1, daily: 10–5. Admission charged. (207) 793-2784 or 793-2210.
77 *Heritage Plantation*, Sandwich, Massachusetts. Grove and Pine Sts. Basically one man's collections, ranging from early dolls to antique guns, spread in a variety of buildings over seventy-six acres. Early June to late Oct., daily: 9–5. (617) 888-0352.
78 *Drummer Boy Museum*, Brewster, Massachusetts. Rte. 6A, West Brewster. Twenty-one life-sized paintings depict events of the American Revolution, from the Boston Massacre to the Battle of Yorktown. Guides tell the story. Mid-May to Columbus Day, daily: 9:30–6. Admission. (617) 896-3823.
79 *Beauport*, Gloucester, Massachusetts. Eastern Point Boulevard (disregard "private" signs at entrance to Eastern Point). June–Sept., Mon.–Fri.: guided tours at 2:30, 3:30, 4:30. Admission charged. SPNEA, (617) 227-3956.
80 *Society for the Preservation of New England Antiquities*. Boston headquarters, 141 Cambridge St. Members enjoy free admission to SPNEA properties, receive the journal "Old-Time New England," and notice of lectures, special events. A booklet guide to properties is available. (617) 227-3956.
81 *National Park Service*, North Atlantic Regional Headquarters, Boston. 150 Causeway St. The office dispenses information on all Park Service holdings in New England, also reservation forms for camping in Acadia National Park. (617) 223-2915.
82 *State Parks*. **Massachusetts**: For details about the state's fifty state parks and forests, contact the Massachusetts Department of Natural Resources, Parks and Recreation, 100 Cambridge St., Boston. (617) 727-3180.

Connecticut: For a detailed listing of eighty-one state parks, twenty-nine state forests, contact Parks and Recreation Division, State Dept. of Environmental Protection, 165 Capitol Ave., Hartford, Connecticut 06115.

Rhode Island: More than eight thousand acres of state park and forest; for a map and detailed listing write the Division of Parks and Recreation, Dept. of Natural Resources, 83 Park St., Providence, Rhode Island 02903.

Maine: For details about some 190 campsites and picnic grounds, write: Division of Information and Education, Maine Forestry Dept., State Office Building, Augusta, Maine 04330. A pamphlet locating twenty-five state parks available from the Maine Publicity Bureau (see "Helpful Hints").

For New Hampshire see detail 19; for Vermont, detail 55.

83 *National Wildlife Refuges* within New England. For a detailed listing, contact the Fish and Wildlife Service, U.S. Post Office and Court House, Boston, Massachusetts 02109. (617) 223-5319.
84 *Cranberrying*. The Indians taught early settlers to harvest the wild cranberry but this didn't become a major industry on Cape Cod and southeastern Massachusetts until the mid-nineteenth century. Today modern machinery has replaced the old cranberry scoop but "wet harvesting," a process which entails flooding the bogs, causing thousands of bright berries to float to the surface, remains a sight to see. Guidance to the most colorful bogs is available in season (late September through mid-October) from the Cape Cod Chamber of Commerce and the Plymouth County Development Council. (See "Helpful Hints.")
85 *Sugaring*. Local Indians taught the settlers how to tap the maple tree and to turn its sap to sweet-tasting syrup. Over the years the process has changed, but remarkably little. Some three

hundred sugar houses invite visitors during the early spring sugaring season to watch both the "gathering" and "sugaring off" process and to sample the results. The big sugaring festival is in St. Albans, Vermont (see Chapter 8). The following sources furnish lists of "open sugar houses," noting the methods used; frequently horses and occasionally oxen still do the gathering. Vermont Agency of Development and Community Affairs, New Hampshire Dept. of Agriculture, Monadnock Region Association (New Hampshire), the Pioneer Valley Association (Massachusetts) and the Maine Department of Agriculture. (See "Helpful Hints.")

86 *The Appalachian Mountain Club* serves as a clearing house for hiking information and publications in all New England states. (See detail 16.)

87 *American Youth Hostels, Inc.,* 251 Harvard St., Brookline, Massachusetts, sponsors guided tours, also serves as a clearing house for touring information within New England (617) 731-5430. For details about ten selected bike routes within Massachusetts, write the Department of Natural Resources, 100 Cambridge St., Boston, Massachusetts 02202. For similar guides to bikeways in New Hampshire and Vermont, contact the New Hampshire Office of Vacation Travel and the Vermont Agency of Development and Community Affairs. (See "Helpful Hints.")

88 *Ski Touring.* Commercial touring centers continue to proliferate throughout the region, but the non-profit group responsible for the current popularity of this ancient sport in this country is the Ski Touring Council. It offers a series of nominally priced "workshops" geared to beginners, also guided tours for more advanced skiers. At least one of these is set for every winter weekend at sites scattered through New England. For details write the Council, c/o Rudolf Mattesich, Troy, Vermont 05868. (802) 744-2472.

89 *Crafts Groups.* **Connecticut**: The Society of Connecticut Craftsmen is headquartered in the Farmington Valley Arts Center, Avon, Connecticut. (203) 678-1771.

Massachusetts: Society of Arts and Crafts serves as a central information source for craftsmen in the state (detail 60h). There are two major crafts centers, Leverett Crafts, Leverett, Massachusetts, (413) 253-9062, and the Old Schwamb Mill (see Chapter 8). Polyarts, 868 Main St., Cambridge, (617) 492-2900, coordinates crafts fairs for the Boston region.

New Hampshire: The League of New Hampshire Craftsmen is one of the country's oldest, most active state crafts groups; its membership totals five thousand and work sold at its outlets and annual August fair is, subject to review, exceptional. Further information from the League headquarters, Concord, New Hampshire 03301. (603) 224-3375.

Maine. "Maine Handcraft Trails," listing major crafts outlets in the state, is free from the Maine Publicity Bureau (see "Helpful Hints"). United Maine Craftsmen sponsors an annual fair and offers information for and on its 850 members (28 Spring St., Yarmouth, Maine 04056).

Vermont: The Arts and Crafts Service supplies information about up-coming crafts events and individual craftsmen in the state. (State Department of Education, Montpelier, Vermont 05602. (802) 828-3291. An unavoidably outdated guide to crafts outlets is available from the Greater Vermont Association (see "Helpful Hints").

Helpful Hints

State and local groups listed here provide free maps, pamphlets, guides and information on specifics. Phone numbers, where given, indicate useful advice available.

CONNECTICUT

State of Connecticut Development Commission. 210 Washington Street, Hartford, Connecticut 06106. (203) 566-3948.

Connecticut Historical Commission. 59 South Prospect Street, Hartford, Connecticut 06106. (203) 236-5621.

MASSACHUSETTS

Massachusetts Department of Commerce & Development, Division of Tourism, 100 Cambridge Street, Boston, Massachusetts 02202. (617) 727-3201. Department of Agriculture, Fairs Division for current listings of town, county fairs, same address. (617) 727-3037.

Berkshire Hills Conference, 107 South Street, Pittsfield, Massachusetts 01201. (413) 443-9187.

For Boston: Boston Convention & Visitors Bureau. 900 Boylston Street, Boston, Massachusetts 02110. (617) 536-4100. Boston 200 (during 1976): (617) 338-1976.

Bristol County Development Council, 154 North Main Street, Fall River, Massachusetts 02722. (617) 676-1026.

Cape Cod Chamber of Commerce, Hyannis, Massachusetts 02601. (617) 362-3225.

Essex County Tourist Council, P.O. Box 21. Amesbury, Massachusetts 01913. (617) 388-1603.

Martha's Vineyard Chamber of Commerce, Vineyard Haven, Massachusetts 02568. (617) 693-0085.

Middlesex County Tourist and Development Council, 109 Concord Street, Framingham, Massachusetts 01701. (617) 879-5600.

Nantucket Island Chamber of Commerce, Pacific Club Building, Nantucket, Massachusetts 02554. (617) 228-0022. (Good for written information.)

Nantucket Information Bureau, 25 Federal Street, Nantucket. (617) 288-0925. (Good for phone inquiries about lodging, also for walk-in advice.)

Pioneer Valley Association, 333 Prospect Street, Northampton, Massachusetts 01060. (413) 586-0321.

Plymouth County Development Council, Box 1620, Pembroke, Massachusetts 02359. (617) 293-3551.

Worcester area: Central Massachusetts Tourist Council, Mechanics Tower - Suite 350, 100 Front Street, Worcester, Massachusetts 01608. (617) 753-2924. Bicentennial events hot-line during 1976: (800) 288-0925.

MAINE

State of Maine Publicity Bureau, 78 Gateway Circle, Portland, Maine 04102. Also an information center at Kittery on the Maine Turnpike. (207) 773-7266. It's advisable to check with toll-free information to find whether a free 800 number is in use.

NEW HAMPSHIRE

New Hampshire Office of Vacation Travel, Box 865, Concord, New Hampshire 03301. (603) 271-2343.

White Mountain National Forest, Box 638, Laconia, New Hampshire 03246. (603) 524-6450.

Dartmouth-Lake Sunapee Region, Box 346, Lebanon, New Hampshire 03766. Lakes Region, Box 300, Wolfeboro, New Hampshire 03894. (603) 569-1117.

Merrimack Valley Region Association, 48 Hanover Street, Manchester, New Hampshire 03103.

Monadnock Region Association, Box 269, Peterborough, New Hampshire 03458. (603) 924-3611.

Seacoast Regional Association, East Main Street, Box C, Newmarket, New Hampshire 03857.

White Mountains Attractions Association, Box 176, North Woodstock, New Hampshire 03262. (603) 745-8720.

White Mountains 93 Association, Lincoln, New Hampshire 03251. Mount Washington Valley Chamber of Commerce, North Conway, New Hampshire 03860. (603) 356-5524.

Sunapee Region Association, Mt. Sunapee, New Hampshire 03772. State turnpike information centers are located at Dover, Hooksett, Hampton, Merrimack and Rochester toll booths. Bicentennial events number: (603) 271-2730.

RHODE ISLAND

Department of Economic Development, Tourist Promotion Division, 1 Weybosset Hill, Providence, Rhode Island 02903. (401) 277-2611 for general information; (401) 277-2614 for answers to specific questions. Advisable to check with toll-free information to find whether a free 800 number is in use.

Newport Chamber of Commerce, 93 Thames Street, Newport, Rhode Island 02840. (401) 847-1600.

Providence Chamber of Commerce, 10 Dorrance Street, Providence, Rhode Island. (401) 521-5000.

VERMONT

Vermont Agency of Development and Community Affairs, Montpelier, Vermont 05602. (802) 828-3236.

A major walk-in information center is on I-91, northbound at Guilford.

The Greater Vermont Association, Box 37, Montpelier, Vermont 05602 publishes an attractions guide.

NEW ENGLAND COUNCIL

A non-profit, Boston-based group which publishes a small guidebook, *Historic Houses and Museums of New England*, listing open hours. Send 25¢ to the Council, 1032 Statler Office Building, Boston, Massachusetts 02116. (617) 542-2580.

NATIONAL PARK SERVICE

North Atlantic Regional Headquarters, 150 Causeway Street, Boston. The office gives information on all the historic sites and recreational areas which it maintains in New England. (617) 223-2915.

INDEX

GENERAL INDEX

PLACES INDEX

Praise for *Aztec Blood*

"Never less than spellbinding, this golden tale . . . follows the exploits of a mestizo boy (half Aztec, half Spanish) in seventeenth-century New Spain (Mexico), struggling for survival against Spanish nobles in league with the Inquisition.

[illegible] spins a dashing, glittering tale, sending th[illegible]
Indian mys[illegible]
ences to the picar[illegible] irrepressible Mateo [illegible]
[illegible]

Praise for [illegible]

"Ay de mi! Why is Cristo in a dank prison being tortured? What's all the mystery surrounding his birth? What's this business about treasure? The questions are all answered in *Aztec Blood*, Gary Jenning's latest historical novel set in Mexico . . . at the time of the Inquisition . . . This is a sprawling book, with lots of juicy historical tidbits . . . it's a wonderful mishmash of far-ranging esoterica, with were-jaguars the merest beginning."

—*The Washington Post Sunday Book Reviews*

"This lush, exotic page-turner fairly crackles with intrigue, romance and adventure. Following the pattern he established in *Aztec* and *Aztec Autumn*, Jennings continues to retrace the remarkable history of the Aztec Empire. Vanquished by the Spanish conquistadors, the once proud Aztec people are enslaved and condemned to toil on the grand haciendas owned by their conquerors.

The author has meticulously researched the torturous history of the colonization of New Spain, revivifying the all-forgotten era upon whose brutal foundation the modern nation of Mexico was forged."

—*Booklist*

"The sights, smells, and sounds of the era come alive in what is a true Tom Jones-style picaresque. Cristo is a lepero, a scorned mestizo beggar who lives by his wits, con-

niving and scheming merely to stay alive . . . Ultimately he fulfills his destiny by founding and leading a proud new people. Readers will lose themselves in this long, absorbing novel."
—*Library Journal*

"Highly entertaining . . . witty . . . charming . . . overflowing with interesting details about Spanish colonialism, heady [illegible] mysticism, and numerous puns and winking refer- [illegible]esque novels of the period."
—*Kirkus Reviews*

Aztec Autumn

"In this ambitious historical novel, a sequel to the bestselling *Aztec*, Gary Jennings picks up in the mid-sixteenth century, a generation after the conquest . . . Offered in the form of an as-told-to-first-person journal, Jenning's fascinating if often gory novel is guided by exhaustive research into practically every facet of life in sixteenth-century Mexico."
—*The New York Times*

"The long-awaited sequel to Jenning's bestselling *Aztec* is another assiduously researched, richly detailed, and robust recreation of a little-known era in ancient history. Jennings brings readers back in time to that world. Descriptions of landscape and culture, gruesome battle scenes and executions, have convincing immediacy. Showing us the transformation of the North America through the eyes of the Native People."
—*Publishers Weekly* (starred review)

"A plum pudding of historical information and detail set unobtrusively into brilliant and offbeat remarkable digressions."
—*The San Diego Union-Tribune*

"It has adventure, detail and a sense of historical authenticity, not to mention Jenning's smart, precise language. And it's a sequel that doesn't demand familiarity with the original to be enjoyable . . . This galloping book is savage and proud of it. And it's that very ferocity that contributes so much to its appeal." —*The Detroit Free Press*

And praise for *Aztec*

"A dazzling and hypnotic historical novel."
—*The New York Times*

"A first-class storyteller . . . Mr. Jennings has achieved true dimension." —*Atlantic Monthly*

"Anyone who reads, anyone who still lusts for adventure or that book you can't put down will glory in *Aztec*."
—*Los Angeles Times*

"*Aztec* is so vivid that this reviewer had the novel experience of dreaming of the Aztec world, in Technicolor, for several nights in a row." —*Chicago Sun-Times*

Forge Books by Gary Jennings

Aztec

Aztec Autumn

Aztec Blood

Spangle

Grand Promenade

Visit Gary Jennings at www.garyjennings.net.

GARY JENNINGS

AZTEC

BLOOD

A TOM DOHERTY ASSOCIATES BOOK
NEW YORK

AZTEC BLOOD

A Tor Book
Published by Tom Doherty Associates, LLC
175 Fifth Avenue
New York, NY 10010

www.tor.com

ISBN: 0-812-59098-8
Library of Congress Catalog Card Number: 2001040130

First edition: August 2001
First mass market edition: August 2002

Printed in the United States of America

0 9 8 7 6 5 4 3 2 1

For Joyce Servis

Also with gratitude to
Junius Podrug and Robert Gleason,
Gary Jennings's editor

A NOTE TO THE READER

Gary Jennings left behind a rich heritage of novel ideas and historical fiction when he passed away in 1999. Gary Jennings's estate and his editor worked with a carefully selected writer to organize and complete Gary Jennings's ideas to create this novel, inspired by his storytelling genius, in a manner faithful to Jennings's style.

The birth of a great people occurred after the conquest of Mexico and the mix of Spanish and indigenous blood:

All mixed bloods were called *castas* . . . These street people, who huddled, starved, and begged on every corner of the town . . . were known as *léperos*. Social lepers, they begged, did odd jobs, and robbed. By the seventeenth century, mobs of léperos thronged the capital and constituted a growing threat to public order. They could be wantonly destructive, even murderous . . . they were the first Mexican bandits . . .

The lépero lived as he could . . . ready to cut either a throat or a purse, begging for food or work, screaming under the whips of the town authorities . . .

Ironically, the léperos were to survive, grow, and finally inherit modern Mexico. They proved, not the degeneracy of man, but mankind's tenacity in the face of hideous adversity.

—T. R. Fehrenback, *Fire and Blood*

The birth of a great people occurred after the conquest of Mexico and the mix of Spanish and indigenous blood.

All mixed bloods were called castas. . . . These mixed people, who idled, starved, and begged on every corner of the towns . . . were known as léperos. [illegible] léperos, they begged, did odd jobs, and robbed. By the seventeenth century, mobs of léperos thronged the capital and constituted a growing threat to public order. They could be wantonly destructive, even murderous. . . . they were the first Mexican [illegible]. . . .

The léperos lived as [illegible] . . . partly in [illegible] or [illegible] begging for land or work [illegible] under the [illegible] of the town authorities. . . .

Eventually, the léperos were to number in [illegible], and [illegible] modern Mexico. They proved, not the [illegible] of man, but mankind's capacity for the [illegible] of [illegible].

—T. R. Fehrenbach, Fire and Blood

Does any man truly know who his father is?

—Homer, *The Odyssey*

PART ONE

Often not a whisper of trouble reached the accused until the blow actually fell . . . Kept in solitary imprisonment, cut off entirely from his friends outside, denied the sympathy of support he might derive from their visits or communications, he was left to brood despairingly, a prey to agonized doubts, in ignorance even of the charges brought against him.

—Maj. Arthur Griffiths, IN SPANISH PRISONS

ONE

To His Most Excellency Don Diego Veles de Maldonato y Pimentel, Conde de Priego, Marqués de la Marche, Knight of Santiago, Viceroy of New Spain by Appointment of His Most Catholic Majesty Emperor Felipe, our Lord King

As Capitán of the Guard for Your Most Excellency's prison, it has been my duty to examine one Cristóbal, known to all as Cristo the Bastardo, a notorious bandit, seducer of women and leader of rabble.

As Your Excellency knows, this Cristo is of tainted blood, specifically that category of mixed blood the law defines as a mestizo because his father was a Spaniard and his mother an Aztec india. As a mixed blood, he is without the protection of the law given to Spaniards and indios, and there are no legal prohibitions against either his torture or execution.

The examination of this thief and murderer of uncertain parentage and tainted blood has been neither pleasant nor profitable. Your instructions to me are to pry from his lips the location of the great hoard of booty that he seized by banditry, treasure acquired by insult to His Most Catholic Majesty in Madrid and to you and other citizens of New Spain, the rightful owners thereof.

You also commissioned me to obtain from his lips the whereabouts of the Aztec india who is said to be his mother. The woman has publicly denied birthing the bastardo but whether that is the truth or she has contrived such a story because of his tainted blood will not be answered until we find her and give her a taste of the truth-extractors we have in this dungeon prison.

I confess, Most Excellency, that the task you have given me is more difficult and odious than the Herculean labor of cleaning the cattle stables of King Augeas. It is most repugnant to have to question this half-caste son of a puta, a street whore, as if he were a legal person, rather than simply hanging him. However, the dead tell no tales and despite my ardent wish I am forced to simply seek the information by torture rather than dispatching him to *el diablo,* his master.

We began the interrogation with the cord-and-water method. As Your Excellency knows, we place the knotted cords around the prisoner's limbs and twist them with a rod. Five twists are generally sufficient to elicit the truth, but it did nothing to this madman except excite laughter. We then increased the twists and wet the cords to create shrinkage, but still no words of confession or repentance spilled from his mouth. We could not use the cords on his head for fear it would pop his eyes out and prevent him from being able to lead us to the treasure.

The water-and-cord treatment works well on shopkeepers and women, but it is not the equal of a determined rogue like this bastardo. Our small, colonial dungeon lacks the implements of a large prison. I have requested on a number of occasions instruments more suitable for the third degree of questioning than what we have available. My special interest is in one I observed when I was a young guard in Madrid's Saladero, that most famous of all prisons. I speak of the "Bull of Phalaris"; the mere threat of it often loosens the most silent tongues.

The bull is said to have been the invention of Phalaris, the tyrant of ancient Acragas in Sicily. To create this monster, Phalaris had a great bronze statue of a bull constructed, with the inside of the beast hollow. Those put to the question were shoved inside the bull through a trapdoor and roasted by a fire built underneath. Their shrieks thundered from the bull's mouth, as if he were roaring. It is said that Perilaus, the designer of this fiend's delight, was the first person to experience his own creation when Phalaris had him placed in it. And that Phalaris himself was ultimately roasted in it.

But I am certain you know all these facts, Excellency. Perhaps in the next dispatch to Madrid, we should request one of these bulls. Its bellowing would reverberate throughout our small prison and crack even our most recalcitrant felons.

Because I realized this Cristo the Bastardo was not an ordinary criminal but a demonio, with your permission I sought out a man who has experience dealing with those whose lips are sealed by the Dark Master. My search led to Fray Osorio, a Dominican monk in Veracruz who has gained great expertise at examining for the Holy Office of the Inquisition secret Jews, Moors, sorcerers, witches, warlocks, and other blasphemers.

Your Excellency may have heard of this priest. As a young man he was one of the examiners of none other than Don Luis Rodriquez de Carvajal, the notorious Judaizer who was burned along with his mother and sisters before a large crowd and all of the notables of our Most Loyal City of Mexico.

It is said that Fray Osorio heard the recantations of the Carvajales and personally strangled each one of them at the stake before the burning. As Your Excellency knows, once the condemned is tied to the stake, if they repent an iron collar is placed around their neck and twisted by a screw device from behind until the person dies. Garroting those who repent at the stake is not the province of a priest, but the fray acted with great piety and mercy in performing the task since strangulation kills quicker than the flames.

I was new in the viceroy's service at that time and can testify to the truth of this matter because I was assigned to the burning as a guard.

Fray Osorio answered our petición for assistance and graciously left his duties with the office of the Holy Office in Veracruz to interrogate this bastardo with the given name of Cristóbal. The good fray practices the dictates of the founder of his Dominican order, the sainted Dominic, the first inquisitor, who advised that when dealing with blasphemers and heretics, we must fight the devil with fire and told his followers that "when kind words fail, blows may avail."

The fray began by loosening the prisoner's tongue with blows from a gato desollar, a skinning cat. The hemp cords of this whip are soaked in a solution of salt and sulfur and imbedded with small, sharp pieces of iron. It can reduce the skin and flesh to pulp in a short time. *¡Qué diablo!* Most men would repent and beg for mercy at such a taste of this venomous tail, but lashing of this devil worshipper opened a flood of the most blasphemous and treasonous statements from his foul mouth.

He further insulted the entire royal realm of Spain by screaming that he is *proud of his mixed blood.* This state of mind by a mestizo is enough to have the man put to death immediately. As we of the City of Mexico know even better than the rest of New Spain, this infliction of tainted blood caused by the mixture of pure Spanish blood with the blood of indios creates a most foul and noxious deformity of character, often resulting in human lice who pollute our streets, social outcasts we call léperos, social lepers who are lazy and stupid, making their way in life by stealing and begging.

Mixed-bloods are *sin razón,* without reason, yet this bastardo claims that he has practiced the medical arts and has gained knowledge that mestizos and others of mixed bloods are stronger of body than those with *pureza de sangre,* the purity of blood that those of us capable of holding honorable positions in life possess.

He shouted under the lash that the mixture of Spanish and Aztec blood results in men and women who do not fall as sick to European diseases like the pox and the French disease that have killed nine out of ten indios, nor do they fall sick from the tropical fevers that have taken so many of our Spanish friends and family.

He has blasphemed that some day all of New Spain will be populated and governed by mestizos, who instead of being regarded as social lepers, will be the proudest in the land.

Dios mio! How did this lowly street leper conceive such ideas? I give no heed to this insane babbling of a madman and stand witness to these vile utterances and will testify to such before Your Excellency or an Inquisitor of the Holy Office.

Continuing his extraction, Fray Osorio obtained sulfur from the makers of gunpowder and placed it in the wounds and under the man's armpits. He burned the sulfur. Then the prisoner was hoisted upside down, hanging from his left leg with his hands tied behind him and his mouth gagged. While in this position, water was poured down his nose.

When these further methods failed to assist his powers of recollection or stem the flow of foul utterances and blasphemies, his fingers were put in thumbscrews. The thumbscrew is a favored device of persuasion because it exerts tremendous agony with little effort. The thumbs and fingers are put into a screw device between two crossbars with ribs, and the bars are slowly screwed down. This was done until the screws tightened and blood squirted from his thumbs and fingers.

The most agonizing persuasion, one that makes any man shiver in his skin, is often the most expedient. It is a particular favorite of mine, one that I have used since my days in the Saladero. It is deceptively simple but agonizing in the extreme: Each night my jailer sweeps up the vermin from the floor of the dungeon and spreads them on the prisoner's body. The prisoner is kept tied up so he cannot scratch or brush the creatures off.

I am pleased to report that never from the mouth of this devil had I heard more beautiful musica than his screams as they crawled over his naked body and squirmed into his open wounds.

All of this was performed the first day. But *¡ay de mí!*

Excellency, still no confession flowed from the prisoner's mouth.

After those methods failed to loosen his tongue for other than insults and profanos, Fray Osorio tried other and varied methods of persuasion he had learned from over three decades with the Inquisition. I regret to inform Your Most Excellency that after seven days of the most severe persuasion, this mestizo has not disclosed either the location of his hoard of stolen treasure nor the whereabouts of the Aztec bitch from whose útero this mal *hombre* dropped.

However, I am pleased to report that a physical examination has revealed even closer links between the mestizo and the devil. When the man was stripped naked to be bathed in hot oil, Fray Osorio made notice of the fact the man's male member not only was of extraordinary size, but was deformed—its foreskin had been cut back in a most unsightly manner.

Although neither of us had personally observed such an alteration of a man's body, we had heard of such blasphemy and realized that the unsightly deformity was a sign of the most foul evil and depravity.

At the good fray's suggestion, we requested an examination of the man's virile part by an *officio* of the Holy Office of the Inquisition with experience in such matters. In answer, Fray Fonséca, a most scholarly priest who had been successful at uncovering from their physical appearance Protestants, Jews, Moors, and other worshippers of the archfiend Mephistopheles, was sent to conduct further inquiry here in the dungeon.

We hoisted this Cristo the Bastardo up with his arms behind him and provided good light for Fray Fonséca to make a close examination of the man's male part. During the examination the recreant spieled an endless flow of the most foul words at the good priest, actually accusing him of fondling the *pene* for pleasure rather than purposes of holy inquiry.

The bastardo made outrageous boasts of the most loathsome kind, shouting that Spanish wives, mothers, and daughters have all tasted his oversized male member in every orifice of their bodies.

I swear by my father's grave, Excellency, when the bastardo shouted that my own wife had squealed with pleasure at the insertion of his pene into her, it took four men of the Guard to hold me from plunging my dagger into the man's heart.

In truth, Excellency, Fray Fonséca's investigation revealed that we were correct in our assessment that the deformity of the virile part is evidence of Satan's influence. It is exactly the type of mayhem that Jews and Moors do to their sons. The good fray suspects that rather than the pene having been intentionally deformed with a blade, as is customary among nonbelievers, that the bastardo's condition is a mark of Cain, revealing him as a devil worshipper.

Fray Fonséca found this case a most curious and important one and has requested that the prisoner be transferred to him and Fray Osorio at the conclusion of our interrogation so that he may make a closer examination of the suspicious male part.

Because this mestizo has neither recanted his evils nor revealed the hiding place of his treasure hoard, it is my recommendation that he be turned over to His Catholic Majesty's Holy Office of the Inquisition for further interrogation and repentance before he is executed.

While I await Your Excellency's instructions, I have given the prisoner pen and paper at his request. Can Your Excellency appreciate my astonishment when the devil made claim that he can read and write like a Spaniard? I confess my surprise was even greater after I had him compose a sentence and found that he indeed placed written words on paper like a priest. Teaching a mixed blood to read and write is, of course, offensive to Your Excellency's policy of providing a lifestyle for them commensurate to their station in life as servants and laborers.

However, because you believe that he may inadvertently provide a clue as to the location of the treasure he has hoarded, I have given him paper and quill to record his babbling.

As you have instructed, the writings of this madman, no matter how absurd, will be sent to Your Excellency for examination.

The Lord bears witness to the truth of this testament to Your Most Excellency, Viceroy of New Spain.

Para servir a Ud. May God our Lord watch over and preserve Your Most Excellency on this first day of February in the year of our Lord one thousand six hundred twenty and four.

Pedro de Vergara Garcia
Capitán of the Guard

TWO

NI THACA!" We are also human!

The Aztec words of a dying man who had been branded like a farm animal by his Spanish master cry in my mind as I prepare to record my thoughts on this fine paper the Viceroy's dungeon master has provided.

I am also human, are words I have spoken many times in my life.

As I sit in my cell, the light of a single flickering candle barely makes a hole in the darkness. The capitán has taken my clothes to give the vermin easier access to my flesh and wounds. Ay, what tortures the cunning of man can devise. It would be less agonizing to have my flesh frayed, cut away like a deer being skinned, than have these little creatures tickle me with their hairy legs and bite me with their snapping jaws.

Cold damp stone presses my naked flesh, and I shiver uncontrollably. The gnawing cold and the sounds of other prisoners keep me aware that I am still human. It is too dark to see their faces, but I hear the fear of other prisoners and feel their pain. If I was less deserving to be in this dungeon, perhaps I would feel more aggrieved at my captors' rough handling. But I confess, I have been many things in this life the good Lord has granted me and my shadow often climbed the gallows steps. No doubt I have earned every moment of pain given me.

But, *gracias a Dios,* today I am a king among prisoners for I have not just a candle, but quill, paper, and ink so I can record my thoughts. I do not think the viceroy is wasting fine paper as a gesture of mercy. He wants me to write my secrets, extorting the words by letting me dribble thoughts on paper when he could not extract them with hot pinchers. But perhaps my secrets will not be that easy for the viceroy to discover because I have *two* pots of ink: one pot as black as the spiders in this hell hole and the other pot of mother's milk.

You ask, Cristo, where do you get mother's milk in a dungeon?

From Carmelita, mi amigos. Lovely, sweet Carmelita. I have never gazed on her, but I am certain that she has the face of an angel. Yet we speak often, Carmelita and I, through the open crack in the wall between our cells. Poor sweet señorita, she was tried and sentenced to hang for opening the gut of a soldado, a king's soldier, who raped her without paying. *¡Oye!* Poor Carmelita. Imprisoned for defending her property against a thief, the right of any merchant.

Fortunately for Carmelita, the depravities of men are not just the vices of soldiers. The vile jailers of this dungeon, these carceleros, took turns with her when she was imprisoned and now she is with child. Ah! Clever girl—a woman with child cannot be executed! This puta knew exactly where the jailers kept their brains.

This angel of the dungeon is ever more clever than I. When I told her that I wished to leave a record of my presence on this earth but I did not want to reveal my secrets to the viceroy, she passed through the opening between our cells a cup of the milk from her breasts. She said the milky script would turn invisible even as I wrote—until an accomplice darkened it with heat and the words reappeared as if divined by a sorcerer. I had heard of this trick of invisible writing from an old fray many years ago but have never attempted it.

I shall write two versions of my life, one for the viceroy's eyes and the other as the scribbling on my tomb, those last words to be remembered by.

Sweet Carmelita will smuggle my pages out via a kindly guard to a man who claims her as his friend. In this way, from words written with mother's milk in a dungeon, the world may one day learn of my story.

Eh, amigos, will I not be as famous as Miguel Cervantes, he who wrote of that awkward knight errant who tilted with windmills?

What compels me to leave this history of my days before I face the fires of the infernal? Ay! My life is not just sorrow and regret. My travels from the harsh streets of Veracruz, to the palaces of the great City of Mexico and the towering wonders of Seville, the Queen of Cities, those memories are more golden than the treasures of El Dorado.

This is the true story of those times, of my days as a liar and thief, a street leper and a rich hidalgo, a bandit and a gentleman caballero. I have seen wonders and my feet have been scorched by the fires of hell.

As you will soon see, it is a wondrous tale.

THREE

MEN CALL ME Cristo the Bastardo. In truth I was not christened "Bastardo." I received on baptism the name Cristóbal in honor of God's only Son. Bastardo is an accusation that the bearer was conceived outside of holy matrimony, not a name.

Bastardo is merely one of my names. Even less flattering words have been used to describe my person. For some time I was known as Cristo the Lépero for my association in the dirt with those mixed-blood outcasts you of fairer society and purer blood call social lepers. The rape and union of Aztec women by Spanish men has created a great many half-castes—outcasts—who fall to begging or thievery because they are rejected by both the people of their mother and their father. I am one of these, but I admit to my arrogant pride in having the blood of two noble races in my veins.

Of my name, true and otherwise, and *other* treasures, I will say more later. Like the Persian princess who wove tales through the night to keep her head on her shoulders, I will not cast all of my pearls with a single toss. . . .

"Cristóbal, speak to us of jewels, silver and gold."

The words of the capitán of the guard come to mind like hot embers from the torturer's pyre for the not-yet-dead. Of those treasures I will speak, but first there is the matter of my birth. My youth. Dangers surmounted and a love that conquers all. These things must not be hurried but savored. Patience is a virtue I learned as a guest in the viceroy's dungeon.

One does not hurry a torturer.

You must excuse the awkwardness of the way in which I scratch words upon this fine paper. I am usually able to form letters on paper as well as any priest. Fray Osorio's ministrations, however, have impaired my script. After crushing my fingernails with thumbnails, I was forced to grip the quill between my palms.

Amigos, need I tell you what pleasure it would be to meet the good fray along the road on his way back to Veracruz? I would teach him some tricks that would no doubt be of use to the Holy Office of the Inquisition in its search for good and evil with pain. Those vermin devils that the dungeon master has swept off the floor and placed on my skin to create the almost unbearable ticklish agony, I would make good use of. I would slice open the fray's belly and slip a handful of the crawling vermin inside. . . .

Despite the corporeal damage, my soul is stalwart. It will still bethink truth, which is all that remains to me. All else has been taken from me—love, honor, clothes—so I sit naked before God and the rats that share my cell.

Truth still resides in my heart, in that sanctum sanctorum that no man can touch. The truth cannot be stolen from a man, even on the rack, because it is in the custody of God.

Like Don Quixote, an hidalgo whose dreams and ambitions were as strange as mine, I was destined from birth to play a role that made me different from other men. Secrets have always been shadows in my life. I was to find that even my birth was veiled by dark thoughts and foul deeds.

You say the great knight errant was nothing more than the ravings of Cervantes after he returned maimed from Moorish war and durance vile? Would you speak of my madness if I told you that in my adventures I fought for treasure beside the *real* Don Quixote?

Tell the fray to put away his hot pinchers and await this tale of treasure for I am not yet prepared to tell it. His embrace has left my thoughts in many pieces, and I need to mend them to remember this jewel of life and those worldly treasures the viceroy desires word of. I must go back, back to the days when I was suckled by a she-wolf and drank the wine of my youth.

I shall start at the beginning, my amigos, and shall share with you the gold of my life.

PART TWO

You have no mother.

—Fray Antonio

FOUR

CALL ME CRISTO.

I was born in the village of Aguetza in the vast Valley of Mexico. My Aztec ancestors built temples in the valley to please the sun, moon, and rain gods, but after the indio gods were vanquished by Cortes and his conquistadors, the land and the indios upon it were divided into large haciendas, feudal domains owned by Spanish grandees. Composed of a few hundred jacals—huts of sun-baked, mud-and-straw bricks—the village of Aguetza and all of its people belonged to the hacienda of Don Francisco Perez Montero de Ibarra.

The small stone church was near the riverbank on the village side. On the other side of the river were the shops, corrals, and the great house of the hacienda. The great house was built like a fortress with a high, thick wall, gun ports, and a huge door with iron braces. A coat of arms blazoned the wall beside the door.

In our time it is said that the sun never sets upon the Spanish Empire, for it dominates, not just Europe, but stretches around the world, encompassing most of the New World, then across to the Philippines and footholds in the land of the Hindu and Africa. New Spain, with its vast riches in silver and land, is one of the prizes of the empire.

The Spanish generally referred to all of the indios of New Spain as "Aztecs," even though there were many indio tribes—the Tarasco, Otomi, Totonac, Zapotec, Maya, and others, often with their own language.

I grew up speaking both Náhuatl, the Aztec tongue, and Spanish.

As I mentioned before, in my own veins was the blood

of Spain and the Aztecs. Because of that mixture, I was called a mestizo, a name that meant I was neither español nor indio. Fray Antonio, the village priest who had much to do with my upbringing and education, said that a mestizo was born into a border place between heaven and hell where dwell those whose souls are deprived of the joy of heaven. While the fray was rarely wrong, in this case he had misjudged the damnation of mestizos. Rather than limbo, it was a state of living hell.

The fray's church was built on the spot where there had once been a small temple devoted to Huitzilopochtli, the mighty Aztec tribal war god. After the conquest the temple had been torn down and its stones used to build a Christian temple on the same spot. From then on the indios gave praise to the Christian Savior rather than the Aztec gods.

The hacienda was a small kingdom in and of itself. The indios who worked the land grew maize, beans, squash, and other food stuffs, horses, cattle, sheep, and swine. Workshops created almost everything that was used on the hacienda, from the shoes for horses and plows for tilling the soil, to the rough carts with wooden wheels used to haul the harvest. Only the fine furnishings, china and linens of the great house used by the hacendado, Don Francisco, came from outside the hacienda.

I shared the hut of my mother, Miaha. Her Christian name was Maria, for the blessed Mother of Christ. Her Aztec name, Miahauxiuitl, meant Turquoise Maize Flower in our Náhuatl tongue. Except in the presence of the village priest, she was called by her Náhuatl name.

She was the *first* mother I knew. I called her Miaha, which was what she preferred.

It was common knowledge that Don Francisco lay with Miaha, and everyone believed that I was his son. The bastardos dropped by indias after intercourse with Spaniards were not favored by either race. To the Spaniard I was just an increase in his stock of dray animals. When Don Francisco looked at me, he saw not a child but a piece of property. The don proffered no more affection toward me than he did to the cattle grazing in his fields.

Accepted by neither Spanish nor indios, even children spurned me as a playmate, I learned early that my hands and feet existed solely to defend my mixed blood.

Nor was there sanctuary for me in the hacienda's main house. The don's son, José, was a year older than myself; his twin daughters, Maribel and Isabella, two years older. None of them were permitted to play with me, although they were allowed to beat me at will.

Doña Amelia was unrelentingly venomous. For her I was sin incarnate—living proof that her husband, the don, had stuck his garrancha between the legs of an india.

This was the world I grew up in, Spanish and indio by blood, but accepted by neither—and cursed by a secret that would one day shake the foundations of a great house of New Spain.

"What is this secret, Cristóbal? Tell it to us!"

Ayyo, the dungeon master's words appear on my paper like black ghosts.

Patience, Señor Capitán, patience. Soon you will know the secret of my birth and of other treasures. I will reveal the secrets in words the blind can see and the deaf can hear, but at present my mind is too weak from hunger and deprivation to do so. It will have to wait until I have regained my strength from decent food and sweet water. . . .

The day came when I saw with my own eyes how a person like me, who carried the blood taint, was treated when they rebelled. I was more than halfway through my eleventh year when I came out of the hut I shared with my mother carrying my fishing spear when I heard horses and shouting.

"*¡Andale! ¡Andale! ¡Apurate!*" Hurry! Hurry!

Two men on horseback were driving a man before them with whips. Running and staggering, the horses breathing down his neck, their powerful hoofs hammering at his heels, the man came toward me down the village path.

The horsemen were Don Francisco's soldados, Spaniards who protected the hacienda from bandits with their muskets and used their whips to keep the indios working the fields.

"Andale, mestizo!"

He was a half-breed like me. Dressed as a peasant, he was lighter of skin and taller than an indio, reflecting the infusion of español and indio blood. I was the only mestizo on the hacienda and the man was a stranger to me. I knew there were other mestizos in the valley. Occasionally one passed through the hacienda with the burro trains that bring supplies and haul away hides and the crops of maize and beans.

A horseman rode up beside the mestizo and quirted him savagely. The man staggered and fell, belly down. His shirt was torn and bloody, his back a mass of bleeding whip marks.

The other soldado charged with a lance and shoved the pole in the man's backside. The man struggled to his feet and staggered down the village lane toward us. He lost his footing again, and the horsemen wheeled, resuming their attack with whip and lance.

"Who is he?" I asked my mother as she came up beside me.

"A mine slave," she said. "A mestizo who has escaped from one of the northern silver mines. He came to some of the workers in the field asking for food, and they called the soldados. Mines pay a reward for runaways."

"Why are they beating him?"

It was a stupid question that required no answer from my mother. I might as well have asked why an oxen is whipped to pull a plow. Mestizos and indios were dray animals. Forbidden to leave the haciendas, they were the property of their Spanish masters. When they strayed, they were whipped like any other animal that disobeyed its master. The king's laws actually protected indios from being put to death, but there was no protection for half-bloods.

As the man got closer, I saw that his face was marred by more than blood.

"His face is branded," I said.

"Mine owners brand their slaves," Miaha said. "When they're traded or sold to other mines, more brands are burned on. This man was branded by many masters."

I had heard of this practice from the fray. He explained that when the Crown gave the conquistadors their original land grants, they also granted them tribute-paying indios. Many of these early settlers branded their indios. Some even burned their initials into the foreheads of the indios to ensure that they could not stray. The king finally forbade the branding of encomienda indios and it came to be used only for the forced laborers and criminals who work in the dreaded silver mines.

From the indios who had come out of their huts, I heard the word *casta* hissed as an insult. The insult was intended as much for me as the mine slave. When I looked toward the group, one of the men caught my eye and spat upon the ground.

"*¡Imbesil!*" my mother said angrily.

The man melted into the group to avoid my mother's ire. While the villagers may have viewed my tainted blood with repugnance, my mother was *india pura*. Of more importance, they did not want to antagonize her because it was known that Don Francisco slept with her from time to time. My own position as the supposed bastard of the grandee won me nothing—there was no blood-tie to Don Francisco that was recognized by him or anyone else.

The indios also believed in the myth of *sangre puro,* the purity of their own blood. But I represented more than tainted blood to them. A mestizo was a living reminder of the rape of their women and the ravaging of their land.

I was just a boy and it cracked my heart to grow up surrounded by contempt.

As the man was herded toward us, I got a closer look at the agony twisting his features. I had once watched men in the village beat a crippled deer to death with clubs. I saw in the man's eyes the same feral anguish.

I don't know why his tormented eyes locked on mine. Perhaps he could see his own corrupted blood in my lighter skin and features. Or perhaps I was the only one whose face was expressing shock and horror.

"*¡Ni Thaca!*" he shouted at me. We are also human!

He grabbed my fishing spear. I thought he was going to turn and fight the two soldados with it. Instead he shoved the spear against his stomach and fell on it. Air and blood bubbled from his mouth and the wound as he writhed in the dirt.

My mother pulled me aside as the soldados dismounted. One of them flogged the man, cursing him to hell for cheating them out of a reward.

The other drew his sword and stood over the man.

"His head, we can still get something for his head and branded face. The mine owner will post it on a stake as a warning to other runaways."

He chopped at the dying man's neck.

FIVE

THUS I GREW from baby crawling in the dirt to a young boy running in the dirt, neither brown nor white, neither español nor indio, welcomed nowhere save the hut of my mother and the little stone church of Fray Antonio.

My mother's hut also welcomed Don Francisco. He came each Saturday afternoon, while his wife and daughters visited the doña of a nearby hacienda.

At those times I was sent away from the hut. No village children played with me, so I explored the riverbanks, fishing and inventing playmates in my mind. Once I returned to the hut to retrieve my forgotten fishing spear and heard strange noises coming from the draped-off corner where my mother's pétat, her sleeping pallet, lay. I peeked through the reed curtain and saw my mother lying naked on her back. The don knelt over her, making wet, sucking noises with his mouth on one of her breasts. His hairy hind end glared at me, his garrancha and cojones swinging back and forth like those of a bull about to mount a cow.

Frightened, I fled the hut and ran to the river.

I spent most of my days with Fray Antonio. In truth, I found more love and affection from the fray than I did Miaha. While Miaha usually treated me with kindness, I never felt the warm, passionate bond between us that I saw with other children and mothers. Deep down I always felt that my mixed blood made her ashamed of me before her own people. I once expressed this feeling to the fray, and he told me it was not my blood.

"Miaha is proud to be thought of as having the don's child. It is the woman's vanity that keeps her from showing her love. She looked into the river once, and saw her own reflection and fell in love with it."

We both laughed over comparing her to the vain Narcissus. Some say he fell into the pool and drowned.

The fray taught me to read almost as soon as I was able to walk. Because most of the great classics were written in Latin and ancient Greek, he taught me my letters in both languages. The lessons always came with repeated warnings: I was never to let anyone, español or indio, know that I had such learning. The lessons were always conducted in the privacy of his room. Fray Antonio was a saint about everything but my education. He was determined to shape me into a scholar despite my mestizo blood—and when my mind did not grasp quick enough, he threatened to quicken my learning with a whipping stick but in truth, he never had the heart to strike me.

Such learning was not only forbidden to a mestizo; Spaniards were seldom lettered unless they were destined for the priesthood. The fray said that Doña Amelia could barely write her name.

Eh, the fray, at his personal peril, had educated me "beyond my means," as he put it. Through the fray and his books, I knew other worlds. While other boys followed their fathers to tend the fields as soon as they could walk, I sat in the fray's small chamber at the back of the little church and read Homer's *Odyssey* and Virgil's *Aeneid.*

But all must labor on a hacienda. Had I been indio, I would have joined the others in the field. But the fray chose me as his helper. My earliest memories were of sweeping the church with a bound-twig broom, a full head taller than I, and dusting the fray's small collection of leather-bound books and codices of Scripture, classics, ancient annals, and medicine.

Besides ministering to the souls of all on the haciendas in the valley, the fray was the chief source of medical advice. Spaniards from many miles and days of travel came seeking his medical attention, "as poor and ignorant as it is," he said, rather truthfully. Indios, of course, had their own shamans and witches to combat sickness. In our small village we had a witch-sorceress who could be called upon to put a curse on an enemy or drive off disease-inducing demons.

At an early age I began accompanying the fray as his servant on his medical missions to those who were too ill to come to the church. At first I only cleaned up after him, but soon I was able to stand by to hand him medicines or instruments as he worked on patients. I watched him mix his elixirs and later was able to make the same concoctions. I learned to set broken bones, dig out a musket ball, suture a wound, and restore the humors of the body through bloodletting, although always in the guise of a servant.

All these arts I mastered by the time I was spouting hair under my arms and between my legs. Don Francisco never took notice of my skills until I was almost twelve years old and made a mistake of revealing what I had learned.

That incident was to set off a chain of events that changed my life. Like so many times, changes came to me not with the tranquillity of a lazy river but with the volcanic bursts of those mountains the indios call fire mountains.

It occurred during the examination of a hacienda majordomo, who complained of abdominal pain. I had not seen this Spaniard before but knew from others that he was the new manager of the hacienda that was the largest in the valley. It was owned by Don Eduardo de la Cerda, a hacendado I had also never seen.

Don Eduardo de la Cerda was a *gachupín,* a wearer of spurs, so-called because he was born in Spain itself. Don Francisco, though of pure Spanish blood, had been born in New Spain. Under the rigid social code, Don Francisco, for all his purity of blood and ownership of a large hacienda, was legally a *criollo* because of his place of birth. Criollos were below gachupíns on the social scale because of *where* they were born.

Well, amigos, to the indios and mixed bloods, there was no difference between a gachupín and a criollo. The spurs of both drew blood equally.

One day, the fray had been called to the main house to administer to the majordomo, Enrique Gomez, who had been visiting with Don Francisco when he became ill after the noon meal. I came with the fray as his servant, carrying the leather bag in which he stored his medical tools and main jars of potions.

The majordomo was lying on a cot when we arrived. He stared intently up at me as the fray examined him. For some reason my features had attracted his curiosity. It was almost as if, despite his pain, he recognized me. This was an unusual experience for me. Spaniards never noticed servants, especially mestizos.

"Our guest," Don Francisco told Fray Antonio, "flinches when you press his stomach. He has strained a muscle in his abdomen, probably from lying on too many of Don Eduardo's india maidens."

"Never too many, Don Francisco," the majordomo said, "but perhaps too tough and too tight. Some of the women in our village are harder to mount than a jaguar."

From the smell of the man's breath as he had passed by me earlier, I realized that his stomach contents were boiling from chilies and spices he had consumed. The Spanish had adopted indio cooking, but their stomachs were not always in agreement. He needed a potion made from goat's milk and jalapa root to clean out his innards.

"It's an ache in his stomach from the noon meal," I blurted out, "not a muscle."

I realized my mistake immediately by the flush of anger on Don Francisco's face. I had not only refuted his diagnosis but had insulted the food of his household, literally accusing him of poisoning his guest.

Fray Antonio froze with his mouth agape.

Don Francisco slapped me hard. "Go outside and wait."

With my face stinging, I went outside and squatted in the dirt to await the inevitable beating.

In a few minutes Don Francisco, the majordomo, and Fray Antonio came outside. They looked at me and appeared to argue among themselves in whispers. I could not hear the words, but I could tell that the majordomo was making some contention about me. The assertion seemed to create puzzlement in Don Francisco and consternation in the fray.

I had never seen the fray in fear before. But today apprehension twisted his features.

Finally, the don motioned me over. I was tall for my age but thin.

"Look at me, boy," the majordomo said.

The man took my jaw in his hand and twisted my face from one side to another as if he were looking for some special mark. The skin on his hand was darker than the skin on my face because many pure blood Spaniards had olive-colored skin, but skin color meant less than the color of blood.

"You see what I mean?" he said to the don, "the same nose, ears—look at the side profile."

"No," said the fray, "I know the man well, and the resemblance between him and the boy is superficial. I know of this thing. You must trust my word."

Whatever contention the fray was making, it was apparent from the don's expression that he was not trusting it.

"Go over there," Don Francisco said to me, indicating a corral post.

I went to it and squatted in the dirt while the three men had another animated conversation and kept looking back at me.

Finally, all three went back inside the house. Don Francisco returned a moment later with a rawhide rope and a mule whip.

He lashed me to a post and gave me the worst beating of my life.

"Never again are you to speak out in the presence of a Spaniard unless you are told to. You forgot your place. You are a mestizo. You must never forget that you have tainted blood and that those of your type are lazy and stupid. Your place in life is to serve people of honor and quality."

He stared at me intently and then twisted my face from side to side as the majordomo had done. He uttered a particularly foul curse. "I see the resemblance," he said. "The bitch laid with him."

Flinging me aside, he grabbed his whip and rushed across the stepping stones to the village on the other side of the river.

My mother's wails could be heard throughout the village. Later, when I returned to our hut, I found my mother huddled in a corner. There was blood on her face from her mouth and nose, and one of her eyes was already swelling shut.

"*¡Mestizo!*" she yelled and struck me.

I recoiled in shock. To get a beating from others was bad enough, but to have my own mother blaspheme my mixed blood was unbearable. I ran from the hut to a rock hanging over the river. I sat and cried, stung more from my mother's words than the don's beating.

Later the fray sat down beside me.

"I'm sorry," he said. He handed me a piece of sugarcane to suck on. "You must never forget your place in life. Today you revealed medical knowledge. Had they known you read books . . . I can only shudder at the thought of what the don might have done to you."

"Why did the don and the other man look at me so strangely? What did he mean when he said my mother had lain with someone else?"

"Cristo, there are things you do not know about your birth, that you can never be told. To reveal them would place you in danger." He refused to say more to me, but he gave me a hug. "Your only sin is that you were born."

The fray's medicine was not the only kind practiced on the hacienda. The villagers and their sorceress had their own remedies. I knew the wide-leafed plants found in a few places along the riverbank had spiritual healing power over wounds. Feeling sorry because my mother had taken a beating for what I had done, I pulled a handful of these out, soaked them in water, and took them back to our hut. I spread them across my mother's cuts and welts.

She thanked me. "Cristo, I know it is hard on you. One day many things will be revealed to you, and you will understand why the secrecy was necessary."

That was all that she said.

Later, while the fray was still with the don and the majordomo, I sneaked into the fray's room and prepared a mixture of powder from his potions and applied them to my mother's face to reduce the pain. I knew the village sorceress used a potion of jungle herbs to cause sleep because she believed that good spirits enter the body during sleep and fight disease. I also believed in the healing power of sleep, so I went to her to obtain the herb to induce sleep for my mother.

SIX

THE HUT OF the sorceress was outside the village in a grove of zapote trees and bushes that had not been cleared for cornfields. A two-room mud hut with a maguey-thatched roof, it told the world it was the home of a witch-sorceress by the feathers and animal skeletons draped around the doorway. An eerie-looking creature that could only exist in a nightmare—the head of a coyote, the body of an eagle, the tail of a snake—hung above the doorway.

When I entered she was sitting crosslegged on the dirt floor. Before a small fire she heated green leaves on a flat rock. The seared, shriveling leaves gave off a pungent, smoky smell. Inside the hut was no less bizarre than the outer doorway. Animal skulls, some of which looked human and I hoped were monkeys, were scattered about and connected to a unearthly collection of misshapen forms.

Her name meant Snake Flower in the Aztec tongue.

Snake Flower was neither old nor young. Her india features were dark and sharp, her nose thin, her eyes black as obsidian but flecked with gold. Some villagers believed those orbs could steal souls and pull out eyes.

She was a *tititl,* a native healer skilled in herbal remedies and chants. She was also a practitioner of the darker arts—secret skills that Spanish law and logic would never comprehend. When the village cacique feuded with a mule train overseer, Snake Flower placed a curse on the overseer. After she shaped a clay doll in his image—but with the doll's guts hard as rock—the man's bowels impacted, and he was unable to eliminate waste. He would have died if the tititl in his own village had not made a duplicate doll with hard guts and smashed it to break the spell.

You say that this is foolishness and not magic? The play of childish savages? Is a tititl's magic anymore the work of savages than a priest's envisioning the devil in the shape of a man's garrancha? Or his dream of salvation from a dead man nailed to a cross?

Snake Flower did not look up when I entered her hut.

"I need a sleeping potion for my mother."

"You have no mother," she said, still not looking up.

"What? Even mestizos have mothers, witch-woman. It is sorcerers who are spawned from dirt and bat droppings. My mother needs a potion to help her sleep so the sleep spirits can fight the sickness."

She kept stirring the green leaves, sizzling and smoking on the rock slab. "A mestizo enters my hut and asks for favors and brings insults as his gifts. Have the Aztec gods grown so weak that a half-blood can insult one of pure blood?"

"My apologies, Snake Flower. My mother's injuries have made me forget my place." I had softened my tone. While I did not believe in the power of gods and spirits, there are many mysteries that sorceresses know and many secret paths they walk. I did not want to find a snake in my bed or poison in my bowl because I had offended her.

"My mother needs the sleep medicine that only an Aztec spirit woman can prepare. I offer not only gratitude but a gift of magic."

I tossed a small doeskin pouch on the dirt beside her.

She stirred the smoking leaves, not looking at the pouch or me.

"And what is this? The heart of a monkey? The ground bones of a jaguar? What magic does a mestizo boy know?"

"Spanish magic. A medical potion not as powerful as yours," I added hastily, "but *different*."

I could tell she was intrigued but too proud to admit it.

"Magic from pale-skinned weaklings who cannot withstand the sun god without burning and fainting?"

"I brought it so that you can show the others in the village how weak and foolish Spanish medicine is. The powder inside is used by Fray Antonio to burn off skin growths. It is mixed with water and spread over the growth. After it disappears, a lesser amount is applied to keep the growth from returning."

"*Bah!*" She flung the pouch across the room. "My medicine is stronger." She scraped green matter from the hot rock into a small clay cup. "Here, mestizo, take this to Miahauxiuitl. It is the sleeping potion you seek."

I stared at her. "How did you know I would come for sleeping medicine?"

She laughed shrilly. "I know many things."

I reached for the cup, but she withdrew it. She stared at me, taking my measure. "You shoot up like a corn stalk under a hot, wet sun. You are no longer a boy." She pointed a finger at me. "I give you this medicine to bring the sleeping spirits to Miahauxiuitl, but you will serve me in return."

"In what way?"

She laughed shrilly again. "You will see, mestizo, you will see."

I hurried back to my mother, leaving the doeskin pouch with the sorceress. She had a growth on the back of her hand, the same type of growth that I had seen Fray Antonio treat on Spaniards with the mixture of mercuriales I left her. I knew her concern. Because she was unable to get rid of the growth on her own hand, villagers had begun to question her skills. How could she drive away the demons that bring sickness, when she could not cure herself?

On the way back to our hut, I smelled her potion and was curious to learn its ingredients. My nose detected honey and lime and *octli,* a powerful drink similar to pulque made from the fermented sap of the maguey. There were other herbs in it, one of which I later realized was yoyotli, a concoction Aztec priests used to sedate sacrificial victims before their hearts were cut out.

SEVEN

THREE DAYS LATER the sorceress collected her debt. She came in the night and took me into the jungle to a place where children were once sacrificed to the gods by my Aztec ancestors.

She was covered from head to foot in a cape. I followed her with apprehension. I could not see her hands, but her toes were exposed and each toe had a claw attached. I wondered nervously what else was under the long cape.

It was with some relief that I was taken off on this unnamed adventure even though it raised the hair on the back of my neck. Fray Antonio and Miaha had argued on several occasions since the incident with the majordomo, each time sending me away so I could not hear what was being said. I did not have to hear the words to know that I was in some manner the source of their controversy.

For an hour I followed Snake Flower into the jungle—until we came to a pyramid that was almost covered by vines and other jungle growth. I had not been to an ancient Aztec shrine before but knew of this one from the village talk.

The fray forbade all from going to it, and to be discovered worshipping at it was blasphemy.

Under the glow of a half moon, Snake Flower bounded up the stepped slope of the temple like a jungle cat and waited for me near the large, flat, altar stone. She took off the reed cape, and I gawked at what she wore underneath. A snakeskin skirt covered her lower body. Above the dangling snakes, her breasts were bare, full and plump. Hanging between her naked breasts was a necklace of tiny hands and hearts. I stared intently in the darkness and could not readily see if the hands were those of monkeys or infants.

The temple was fifty feet high—a dwarf compared to many of the great Aztec temples I'd heard of—but it appeared gigantic to me in the moonlight. As we approached the top I trembled. On this summit children had been sacrificed by the thousands to angry Aztecs.

She was dressed as *Coatlicue,* Serpent Woman, the earth goddess who is the mother of the moon and the stars. Some say that the grisly necklace Coatlicue wears holds the hands and hearts of her own children, whom she had murdered when they disobeyed her.

We were at the right place for such dark deeds. Here was where young children were slaughtered, sacrificed to *Tlaloc,* the rain god. The tears of the children symbolized falling rain, and the more they cried, the better chances for rain to feed the life-giving maize.

"Why have you brought me to this place?" I put my hand on the bone knife I carried. "If you want my blood, witch, you will find it costly."

Her laughter shrilled.

"It is not blood I desire, young one. Pull down your pants."

I stepped back in fear, instinctively covering my virile part.

"Foolish boy, this will not hurt."

She took a small bundle from beneath the reed cape and removed the sacred deerskin she used in healing and a clay cup. To those items she added the rib bone of an animal and emptied a rawhide bag into the cup. She knelt on the sacrificial stone and began crushing the contents with the bone.

"What is that?" I asked, as I knelt beside her.

"A piece of dried jaguar heart."

She cut an eagle feather and deposited it into the cup. "The jaguar has power, the eagle soars. Both abilities are necessary if a man is to please his woman and produce many children." She sprinkled a fine, dark powder into the cup. "This is snake blood. A snake can unhinge its jaws, swell its belly, and devour something several times its size. A man needs a snake's expansive power to fill his woman's hole and satisfy her." She carefully stirred the mixture.

"I will not drink it."

Her laugh rang through the jungle night. "No, little fool, it is not for you to drink but to add to its power. The potion is for another man who can no longer swell his tepúli to please and impregnate his woman."

"He can't make babies?"

"No babies, no pleasure for him or his woman. The potion will make his tepúli grow long and hard."

Her gold-flecked eyes froze me to the bone; her dark power consumed me. I lay on my back on the sacrificial stone while she undid my rope belt. She pulled down my pants to expose my private parts. I felt no shame. While I had yet to lay with a girl, I had watched Don Francisco in the hut with my mother and knew that his garrancha grew as he suckled her breasts.

She gently stroked my pene. "Your young juice will make him strong like a bull when he lies with his woman."

Her hand was strong; her rhythm sure. A warm glow enveloped my extremities, and I smiled.

"You enjoy the touch of a woman on your man part. Now I must milk your juice like a calf sucking on its mother."

She put her mouth on my garrancha. Her mouth was hot and wet, her tongue ingeniously energetic. My garrancha became more and more eager for the sucking, and I shoved it deeper into her mouth. I jerked up and down as a firestorm roared in me, trying to push it deeper and deeper down her throat. Suddenly I was pumping with a rhythm of my own as my juices exploded into her mouth.

When the rhythm stopped, she leaned over and spit the juice into the clay cup that had the other ingredients. She then put her mouth back on my organ, licking up juice that had gone down the side and putting it into the cup.

"Ayyo, boy-man, you have enough juice to fill the tipíli of three women."

EIGHT

THE NEXT MORNING I was spit out of the mouth of a volcano.

"We are leaving the village," Fray Antonio said. He awoke me in the hut I shared with my mother. His features were pale and drawn, his eyes red from a lack of sleep. He was nervous and anxious.

"Have you been wrestling devils all the night?" I asked.

"Yes, and I lost. Throw your things in a sack; we are leaving now. A cart is being loaded with my possessions."

It took me a moment to comprehend that he did not just mean that we were going to a neighboring village.

"We are leaving the hacienda for good. Be ready in a few minutes."

"What of my mother?"

He paused at the doorway to the hut and stared at me as if he were puzzled at my question. "Your mother? You have no mother."

PART THREE

La Ciudad de los Muertos, the City of the Dead, is what the Spanish soon came to call Veracruz.

—Cristo the Bastardo

NINE

FOR A WHILE we were homeless, wandering from church to church as the fray sought food, roof, and sanctuary for us. Still short of twelve, I understood little of the misfortune that had been inflicted upon us other than the blisters on my feet from walking and the hollowness in my stomach when there was not enough food to fill it. From the conversations I overheard between the fray and his brethren in the church, an accusation had been made by Don Francisco that the fray had violated his faith and duties by impregnating an india maiden. Even at that age I was shocked to hear that the woman was Miaha, and I was said to be the child of that sin.

The fray was not my father, of that I was certain, although I loved him as a father. Once when the fray was besotted with wine, a not uncommon condition for him, he swore that my father was a *muy grande gachupin,* a very big wearer of spurs, but when the nectar of the gods has captured his mind, the fray was prone to say many things.

He told me that it was true that he had stuck his pene in Miaha, but that he had not fathered me. He further confounded the mystery of my birth in an enigma by saying that Miaha had not birthed me.

Sober, he refused to confirm or deny his drunken ravings.

The poor fray. Amigos, believe me when I say that this was a very good man. Eh, all right, he was not perfect. But do not cast stones. A few mortal sins, sí, but his sins hurt no one but himself.

On a day of great sadness for the fray, he was defrocked by a bishop of the Church. Those who take evil tales into their ears and spit them out their mouths had made many charges against him, few of which he bothered to defend, many for which he had no defense. I felt his sadness. His greatest sin was caring too much.

Although the Church rescinded his priestly authority to take confession and grant absolution, they couldn't stop him from ministering to the needs of the people. He finally found his calling in Veracruz.

Veracruz! City of the True Cross.

La Ciudad de los Muertos, the City of the Dead, is what the Spanish soon came to call Veracruz as the dreaded *vómito negro,* the black vomit, came like a poisonous wind from Mictlan, the underworld of the Aztec gods, and killed a fifth part of the population each year.

The vómito seeped out of the swamps during the hot, summer months, its foul miasma rising from the poisonous waters and floating over the city, along with hordes of mosquitoes that attacked like the frog plague of Egypt. The rotted air was the bane of travelers who came off the treasure ships and hurried to the mountains, clutching nosegays to their faces. Those whom this dark sickness struck suffered fever and terrible pains in the head and back. Soon their skin turned yellow, and they vomited black, coagulating blood. They found comfort only in the grave.

Believe me, amigos, when I tell you Veracruz is a hot ember that has been kicked out of hell, a place where the fiery tropical sun and fierce *el norte* winds turned earth to sand that flayed the flesh from bones. The festering fumes of the swamps, stagnating amid the dunes, combined with the stink of dead slaves—thrown into the river to avoid the cost of burial—to create a stench of death worse than the river Styx.

What would we do in this hell on earth? Have the fray marry some lonely widow, not a grass widow who changed her soft bed for one of straw after the death of her husband, but one who had a golden widowhood and would permit us to live as grandees in her fine home? No, never. My compadre the fray sucked in the troubles of others like the leeches barbers use to suck bad blood from people. It was not to a fine house that we went, but to a hovel with dirt floors.

To the fray it was Casa de los Pobres, the House of the Poor. To him it was as much a house of God as the finest cathedrals in Christendom. It was a long, narrow, wood shack. The planks that made up its walls and roof were thin and rotted from the brutal rains, winds, and heat. Sand and dust blew in, and the whole place shook during a norte. I slept on dirty straw next to whores and drunks and squatted near the fire twice a day to get a tortilla filled with frijoles. This simple meal was a fine feast for those who only knew the streets.

Turned out onto the streets of the meanest city in New Spain, over the next couple of years blows and curses would recast me from being a hacienda boy to a street leper, a lépero. Lying, thieving, conniving, and begging were only a few of the talents I acquired.

I confess that I was not a saintly boy. I sang not hymns but a cry of the streets—a cry for alms!

"Charity for a poor orphan of God!" was my song.

Often I covered myself with dirt, rolled back my eyes, and twisted my arms in obscene contortions, all but wrenching them out of their sockets, in order to extricate alms from fools. I was a mudlark with the voice of a mendicant, the soul of a thief, and the heart of a waterfront whore. Half español, half indio, I was proud to bear the noble titles of both mestizo and lépero. I spent my days barefoot and dirty, keening my alms cry, cadging filthy lucre from silken grandees, who, when they looked down at me at all, grimaced with contempt.

Do not cast stones at me like that bishop did to the poor fray when he took the holy cloth from him. The streets of Veracruz were a battlefield in which you could find riches . . . or death.

After a couple of years, the dark cloud that had come over us suddenly at the hacienda disappeared. I was past my fourteenth birthday when the shadow of death fell across our path again.

It was a day in which there was both death and riches on the streets.

I had writhed, contorted, and begged near the fountain in the center of the city's main plaza; and though my alms cup remained empty, I was not particularly chagrined. Early that morning I had struggled through Dante Alighieri's *La divina commedia.* Eh, do not think I read this tome for pleasure. The fray insisted I keep up my education. Because our library was so limited, I had to read the same books over and over. Dante's dark journey, guided by Virgil through the descending circles of hell, the inferno, to Lucifer at the bottom of the pit, were not unlike the baptism I received when I was first cast out onto the streets of Veracruz. Whether I would someday be purged of my sins and enter paradise were still unanswered questions.

The fray had been loaned the epic poem by Fray Juan, a young priest who had become his secret friend despite the fray's fall from grace with the Church. Fray Juan had been made party to my secret education. That morning, after I recited the poem in my bumbling Italian, Fray Antonio had beamed and boasted of my prowess with knowledge, and Fray Juan had agreed. "He drinks up knowledge like you do that fine Jerez wine I bring from the cathedral," Fray Juan had said.

Of course, my scholarship was a secret known only the between the friars and me. The punishment for lettering a lépero was prison and the rack. Had our secret leaked out, *we* could have been the entertainment of the day.

For entertainment it was. This day, half the city had gathered in their Sabbath finery—accompanied by small children, fine wines, and costly comestibles—to watch a flogging. Excited by the prospect of blood, they had a glow in their cheeks and malice in their eyes.

An overseer in a tan, buckskin jerkin, leather breeches, and black, knee-high boots was lining thirty bound and ragged prisoners up by sixes and loading them into caged, mule-drawn prison wagons. He had a dark beard, a dirty, low-slung felt hat, and mean eyes. He made promiscuous use of the cuarate-quirt, punctuating its cracks with bloodcurdling oaths:

"Get in there, you miserable sons of dray beasts and putas. In there or you'll curse the mothers you never knew for giving you birth—you murdering, thieving, pimping hijodeputa."

They lumbered painfully under his whip, with teeth gritted, into their portable prisons.

His charges were on their way to the silver mines of the north, but for the most part they weren't "murdering, thieving, pimping hideputas." Most were mere debtors, sold into peonage by their creditors. In the mines they were to work off their obligation. At least that was the illusion. In plain fact, when food, clothing, housing, and transport compounded their debt, the bill burgeoned irretrievably.

For most the mines were a death sentence.

Most of the prisoners were mixed bloods. The city alcalde—the viceroy's commander of the city—periodically swept the streets, throwing out of work léperos into jail. From there they were transported to the northern mines.

That could be me, I thought, with grim foreboding.

The alcalde peddled these unfortunates to the northern mines, lined his coffers, and, according to gachupins, reduced the city's infamous stink.

I stared at the mestizo prisoners, ill at ease. Indios had once comprised the entire mine force, until slavery and disease had killed them off in shocking numbers. The fray believed that ninety-five out of every hundred had beeen annihilated, and the king himself had at last forbade forcing them into bondage. Not that his decree had had much effect. Tens of thousands still died in tunnels, smelters, and pits, to say nothing of the cane fields and sugar mills. Others succumbed in the obrajes, small factories often occupied with the spinning or dying of wool and cotton, where they were chained to their workplaces.

The king could decree all he might, but in the jungles and mountains, where there were no laws, the hacendados held brutal sway.

The crowd cheered, and three guards dragged a runaway slave to the flogging post for his mandatory one hundred lashes. Once he was gagged and strung up, the sergeant-of-the-guard paced off the requisite distance, and the black-snake cracked. Blood bloomed, and his back was laid bare, his ribs and backbone shockingly white under the flayed flesh. Wine cups were raised, and the crowd thundered its approbation. Despite the gag, his screams soared above the crowd's roar.

The whip rose and fell, rose and fell, and I averted my eyes.

At last the hundredth lash was done.

"Lice," a man near me said. The voice belonged to a merchant, whose protruding belly and exquisite raiment bespoke great wealth, rich food, and rare wine. His delicate wife, garbed in silk and shaded by a parasol held by an africano slave, was at his side.

"These street léperos breed like bed bugs," she agreed, nodding her disdain. "If the alcalde didn't sweep them from the gutters, we would trip over them every third step."

The man was a gachupin, a wearer of spurs, born in Spain and representing the Crown's interests. The gachupin roweled us at every turn—whenever they wanted our women, our silver, our lives.

The king found criollos, the pure-blood Spaniard born in New Spain, too distant to trust, so he sent peninsulares to lord over them.

I heard a second commotion. A cocky, lépero street boy pelted a foraging vulture with a rock, shattering its right wing. A dozen lépero urchins, none older than nine or ten, now joined him, tethering the crippled bird to a tree. Once secured, they whipped it with a stick.

A big, ugly, bastard of a bird—over two feet tall and five across, even with its broken wing—it had been drawn by the smell of the mine prisoner's blood. As had its comrades, a dozen of whom spiraled above the plazula. As the crowd dispersed, they began a slow descent. Unfortunately, this one had been in too much of a hurry.

One of the boys had a twisted arm, mirroring the warped vulture wing. I'd heard on the streets that a beggar king, who bought the bastards off of whores, had disarticulated the elbow joint of this young beggar to increase his street value. Fray Antonio dismissed such allegations as "rumor and false report," describing the alleged Beggar King as "a luckless mendicant." He referred to lépero boys and girls, not as "lice" and "vermin," but as "Children of the Lord" since few of us knew who our fathers were. Conceived through rape or a whore's dissembled lust, we were despised by all save God.

The gachupin, however, loathed us, and in the end they held sway. The alcalde hanged that "luckless mendicant," the Beggar King, in the plazula, then dismembered him in fourths. His body parts were currently gibbeted above the city gate.

Whatever his disputed paternity, the crippled urchin was now impaling the zopilote's privates with a fishing spear.

I yanked it out of his hand. "Try that again," I said, shaking it in his young face, "and I'll bury this spear in your cojones."

The boys—younger and smaller than myself—instantly cowered. Such was life on the Veracruz streets. Might made right. We routinely awoke to find our closest compadres dead in the streets or in a transit jail en route to the mines.

I was, of course, better off than most. I had straw to sleep on and poor-house rations to eat. Furthermore, the fray, at personal peril, had educated me. Through the fray and his books, I knew other worlds.

I dreamed of Troy's fall and Achilles in his tent, not the torture of birds.

TEN

But even as I watched the muleteers haul the caged men to the northern mines, even as I watched the tethered vulture flop in circles on the ground, I knew *I was being watched.*

In a stately carriage of burnished oak and cedar, plush velvet and rich leather, gleaming fittings and magnificent dray horses, less than fifty paces away an old woman studied my every move. Haughtily aristocratic, she was accoutred in black silk, festooned with pearls, gold and gemstones; a coat of arms graced the carriage door.

She was thin as a reed—little more than parchment and bones—and all her money would never resurrect the blush of youth.

She was no doubt the doyen head of some great house, grown old and mean and murderous. She reminded me of some old raptor on the hunt, with talons arched, eyes ravenous, belly growling.

Fray Antonio was entering the square, and she turned to study him.

Bald, slope-shouldered, he was a man with troubled features. He not only worshipped the cross, he bore it. He absorbed the pain of others and carried it bleeding in his heart; New Spain had exacted from the fray a mortal toll.

To the léperos and other half castes, he was God's Mercy on Earth, his small, wooden shack in the casta barrio providing the only shelter and sustenance many of us would ever know.

Some said that Fray Antonio fell from grace through his ample sampling of the sacramental wine. Others said he had a weakness for easy women. But in the end, I believe, his insistence upon ministering to all equally, including indios and outcasts, was his sin.

The fray had seen the old woman staring at me and apparently did not like what he saw. He hurried to the carriage, his gray robe flapping, his leather sandals trailing dust.

A commotion to my right diverted my attention. The mestizo mine slave was cut free from the flogging post. He slid groaning to the ground. His ribs and backbone still glistened ivory white. The man who'd flogged him was cleaning his whip in a bucket of brine. Removing the whip, he shook it out, cracking it four or five times.

He then poured the bloody brine over the prisoners raw back. The mestizo howled like a pain-crazed dog, gone mad with feral suffering, after which the guards hauled him to his feet and dragged him off to a nearby prison wagon.

I turned back and the fray was standing next to the carriage. Both he and the matron stared at me. Fray Antonio shook his head, denying something. Perhaps she thought I'd stolen something from her. I quickly glanced at the caged mestizos. Did the alcalde send young boys to the northern mines? I suspected he did.

My fear quickly turned to anger. *I had stolen nothing from this gachupin!* It was true that I could not remember everything I had stolen on the streets. Life was hard, and you did what you could to survive. But this cheerless hag with her raptor eyes was no one I would rob.

Suddenly the fray was rushing for me in his alarmed shuffle, his eyes fearful. Slipping a pen knife from under his robes, he jabbed his thumb. *¡Santa Maria!* Mother of God! I wanted to howl like the man I'd just seen flogged. Had this rich matrona respectable stolen the friar's wits?

He gathered me against his musty robes. "Speak only Náhuatl," he whispered hoarsely. The wine on his breath was as rank as his rotting robes.

He jabbed his bleeding thumb against my face, each time leaving a small bloody mark.

"Mierda! What the—"

"Don't touch them!" His voice was as harried as his features.

He pulled my straw hat down to cover more of my face, and then grabbed me by the neck and rushed me to the old woman. I stumbled along with him, still clutching the fishing spear I had taken off the guttersnipe.

"As I told you, Doña, it's not him; this is just another street urchin. See, he's sick with the peste!" he said as he pushed my hat off of my forehead, exposing the red blotches on my face.

The old woman drew back in horror. *"Go!"* she barked to her driver.

She slammed the window shutter as the driver whipped the horses.

As the coach rumbled across the cobblestones, a wheeze of relief escaped from the fray. He mumbled *gracias a Dios* and crossed himself.

"What is it, Fray? Why did you make me look like a plague carrier?" I rubbed my face with both hands.

"It's a trick nuns have used to keep from being raped when their convent is attacked." Still in the grip of fright, he fingered his rosary, leaving bloody marks on the beads.

Gawking at the fray, I started to speak, but he waved away my questions. "Do not ask what I cannot answer. Just remember, bastardo chico, if a gachupin speaks to you, answer in Náhuatl and never admit you are a mestizo."

I wasn't sure I could pass for an indio. I was neither as dark as one nor as light as a Spaniard, but I was already as tall as most adult indios. I could more readily pass as a Spaniard.

My protests were silenced by a disturbance behind me.

The vulture I'd protected gave a sharp *squawk!* at a laughing street boy prodding it with a stick. The boy drove the stick into the bird's chest.

ELEVEN

ALL I KNEW in those days were the Veracruz streets and the fray's books. Not that I lacked cleverness or curiosity. As a beggar, my conniving was notorious. While many a lépero worked those same rough-and-tumble streets, none did so as ingeniously as I.

This day, a year later, I served my vigil in the doorway of a closed shop two streets up from the docks, and it should have been a lucrative perch. The treasure fleet was arriving, and spectators on their way to the harbor passed by the hundreds. Ships, laden with the goods of old Spain, were anchoring to unload and refill their holds with New Spain's treasure.

While the great City of Mexico, the place my Aztec ancestors called Tenochtitlán, was said to be the Venice of the New World, a city of canals and wide boulevards and palaces of the rich, Veracruz was the conduit through which all riches flowed, a temporary treasure trove, to be sure. The colony's wealth arrived in rough-stamped silver and gold, in rum kegs and molasses barrels, which were loaded aboard the treasure fleets, which carried it to Seville and to the king in Madrid. Of course, none of it enriched our City of the True Cross. For all its illusory wealth, Veracruz remained a pestilential sinkhole of sand, jungle heat, and el norte storms, whose incoming treasure had to be hidden from the marauding hordes of French and English pirates who lusted after her bounty as some men lust after a woman's flesh.

The city itself was continually in shambles. Its buildings—thrown together with wood, mud brick, and crude whitewash—were in constant disrepair. Frequently flattened by storms, routinely razed by fires, our city was forever rebearing itself like the phoenix.

Still the fleet arrived each year, escorted by flotillas of warships, and this year the fleet's arrival was even more dramatic. Aboard the admiral's flagship was the recently appointed archbishop of New Spain, the second most powerful man in all New Spain, nearly equal to the viceroy himself. If the viceroy died, became incapacitated, or was recalled, the archbishop often assumed the viceroy's mantle until the king chose a replacement.

Hundreds of priests, friars, and nuns from throughout New Spain were visiting the port to welcome the archbishop. The streets teemed with their sacred orders, sweating in their rough-spun robes of gray and black. They shared the streets with an army of merchants who had come to claim their goods from the ships and transport them to the great fair in Jalapa. High in the mountains en route to the City of Mexico, the Jalapa air was not poisoned by our pestilential swamps.

Nonetheless, pleading for alms was no easy matter—not even with the treasure fleet arriving. The streets were packed, the people distracted. A portly merchant with his equally prodigious wife threaded their way through the crowd. Expensively attired, they radiated riches. Léperos on all sides whined for handouts, but were ruthlessly spurned. Still I was nothing if not resourceful. An ancient East Indian—taken ill in our hospice—had taught me the art of contortionism, in which I soon excelled. By relaxing each joint, I could dislocate my elbows, knees, and shoulders, and contort my limbs into positions God never imagined. I quickly transmogrified myself into a monster.

As the merchant and his wife came abreast of my doorway, I crawled out of it and whimpered. They both gasped. As they hurried around me, I brushed up against the woman's dress and sobbed my alms cry: "Alms for the poor disfigured orphan!"

She almost jumped out of her skin.

"Give him money," the woman shouted at her husband.

The man threw a copper coin at me. It missed the woven basket, strung from my neck, and hit me in my right eye. I grabbed the coin with my one uncontorted hand—before one of the other street léperos sprang on it like a spitting diamondback.

I quickly realigned my limbs.

Should I have been ashamed of my life? Perhaps. But it was all I could do. Fray Antonio did his best for me, but his best was a bed of straw behind a dirty curtain on one side of the dirt-floored hovel and beyond that hovel no future at all. A lépero by definition lived by his wits—by begging, lying, stealing, conniving.

Ayya! A shove from behind suddenly sent me sprawling in the street.

A swaggering caballero with a stunningly beautiful mulatta on his arm, stepped over me without even looking down. To him I was less than a dog. He was a wearer of spurs, and I was something to rowel. Yet even at my tender age, I was more enthralled by his exotic, erotic woman than his sword and swagger. She was doubtless the offspring of an español father and africana mother, her father, most likely, a slave owner and her mother one of his chattels.

"Ah, we Spanish love the tawny ladies," the fray once told me while in his cups, and it seemed to be the case. The most ravishing became mistresses of the buena gente, the wealthiest of the gachupin. Those not so exquisite became household servants. Some women were passed hand-to-hand, loaned to friends, or hired out for breeding like blooded horses. When the flush of beauty faded, many were sold into houses of prostitution. Being a mulatta mistress was not a secure profession.

Still the woman on the Spaniard's arm played her role with knowing aplomb.

She, too, stepped over my sprawling remains, swinging her insolent hips like they were a silver mine, her flamboyant dress flouncing, her perfumed breasts bouncing, her thick, red-tinted hair flung casually over one shoulder.

Glancing over her shoulder, she allowed me a cruel, crooked grin.

I could not help but admire her apparel. Like mestizas and indias, mulattas were forbidden to wear European-style clothing, but while mestizas and indias wore simple peón garb—formless dresses, usually of white, coarse cotton—mulattas' clothes were as flamboyant as the brilliantly feathered mantles of the Aztec priests. This one wore her silk petticoat long and full, double ribbons trailing behind it like faithful retainers. Her waistcoat fitted her like a bodice, girdled with pearls and knots of gold, her skirts laced with vermilion and trimmed with gold thread. Her sleeves were broad and open at the end, draped with silvery silk. But her tawny breasts were what drew me. Covered only by long, twisted coils of red-streaked hair, into which gold and silver thread had been meticulously woven, their dark nipples darted artfully out of their hiding places, peeked briefly at the surrounding world, then discreetly receded from view.

In these areas mulattas were freer than our high-born ladies. Any Spanish woman daring to expose her flesh would have been horsewhipped, but mulattas were exempt property, not people.

Nor did the caballero's costume suffer from undue reticence. From his wide-brimmed, brilliantly plumed hat down to his high-topped, brightly burnished boots, jangling with silver spurs, his attire was almost as extravagant as the woman's.

"My brothers in the Church," the fray told me once, "bemoan the fact that so many men prefer mulattas over their wives. But many times I have seen these lovely women visit *them* through the church's back door."

Still I resented the way the caballero had pushed me aside. Léperos were treated worse than curs, but I resented it more than other half-castes because I was educated, which was more than most Spaniards and their silken ladies, even those living in palatial homes, could say. In fact, I not only read and wrote Spanish, I was fluent in Náhuatl, the language of my Aztec ancestors. I was proficient—no, I excelled—in Latin *and* Greek. I had read the classics in three languages, and on the waterfront had picked up smatterings of several more languages. My ear for foreign tongues was so acute, the goodly fray sometimes called me his "Little Parrot."

Of course, Fray Antonio had forbidden me to reveal these skills to anyone.

"Never divulge your learning," he warned me during my very first lesson—and during every lesson subsequently. "The Inquisition will not believe a lépero literate, without Lucifer's complicity, and they will reinstruct you according to their lights—and those who letter léperos as well. Believe me, theirs are lessons neither of us wish to learn. I know. So never flaunt your learning, unless you wish to while away your years in the Inquisition's dungeons. Unless you prefer to stretch your limbs on their strappados, whipping posts, and racks."

The fray's warning became as much a part of my lessons as *amo, amas, amat*.

The fray also taught me—through my mastery of the classics—the fallacy of *pureza de sangre,* the purity of blood so important to the spur wearers. Blood does not define our worth. With comparable instruction, a mestizo can equal, even surpass the purest blooded dons in Spain. I was living proof.

But like the indios, who hid their hatred behind stoic masks of indifference, I, too, repressed my rage. But all the while I knew the gachupin weren't my betters. Had I but silver and gold—and a fine carriage, a caballero's grand attire, a Toledo blade, and a mulatta mistress on my arm—I, too, would be *un hombre macho de le gachupin grande*, a great man of the big spurs.

A young Spanish girl in a green flowing gown laced with white silk came out of the goldsmith's shop nearby. I crossed the wharf to intercept her, preparing to do my crippled dog act for her. Until I saw her face. Her eyes stopped me dead in my tracks. I was no longer able to writhe on my hands and knees and play the fool than I could make the sun stand still.

She had dark, demure eyes, her face the soft pale of great ladies whose complexions never suffer from the sun. Her hair was long, brilliantly black, cascading over her shoulders in luxurious waves. She was but a girl, a year or two younger than my fifteen, but she carried herself with regal bearing. In a few years Spanish gente would die on swords for her favor.

Caballeros treated wellborn señoritas with gallantry, even in New Spain; and when a puddle of early morning rain blocked her path, I, too, felt called upon to play the chivalric fool. Undoing my manta, the indio blanket I wore slung over my right shoulder and under my left arm, I rushed to her.

"Señorita! Bernaldo de Carpio, Knight of Castile, salutes you."

Bernaldo, of course, was a Spanish hero second only to El Cid in the hearts of the people of Spain. He slew the French hero, Roland, at the Battle of Roncesvalles, saving the peninsula. As with so many epic tales of Spain, Bernaldo was wronged by the treachery of his own king and vanished into exile.

The girl's eyes widened as I rushed over to her. I flung my manta like a cape over the puddle. Bowing deeply, I gestured for her to step on the blanket.

She stood rooted like a tree, her cheeks flushing. At first I thought she was going to order me out of her sight. Then I realized she was fighting back a smile.

A Spanish youth came out of the goldsmith's behind her, a boy a year or two younger than me, but already as tall as me and more muscular. He was darker in complexion, his features pocked, and he seemed in a dark mood. He had apparently been out riding because he was wearing gray riding breeches, a red, sleeveless doublet over a matching linen shirt, knee-high, ebony riding boots with wickedly sharp rowels, and he carried a horsewhip.

When the crop struck my right cheek, I was caught flat-footed.

"Get out of here, you filthy lépero swine."

Rocked on my heels, anger overwhelmed me. If I hit him, I would be lashed to the whipping post, flogged senseless, then sent to die in the mines. There was no greater offense than to attack a gachupin. I did not care. When he raised the whip a second time, I clenched my fists and started toward him.

She stepped between us. "Stop it! Leave him alone."

She swung around to me. Taking a coin from her pocket, she handed it to me. "Take this. Go."

Grabbing my manta from the muddy water, I flung the coin in the puddle and walked away.

Pride goeth before a fall; and like a woman's smile, pride would return to haunt me.

TWELVE

CANNON FIRE FROM across the bay announced that the archbishop was coming ashore. The flowing crowd carried me to the docks to welcome in the big ships. The treasure fleet had left Spain six weeks earlier: forty-one ships sailing out of Seville. Sixteen were bound for Veracruz, while the others went to other Caribbean ports in places like Cuba, Puerto Rico, Hispaniola, and Jamaica.

For weeks mountains of goods had piled up at the waterfront, where they would be loaded aboard the ships. The treasure and other products of New Spain were unloaded in Seville once a year. The ships returned to Veracruz laden with skins of oil and wines, barrels of figs, raisins, olives, coarse wool called kersey, fine linen, and iron ingots. Endless kegs of quicksilver were also there for the mines—with which to leech the pure silver out of Zacatecas's earth and ore.

As I neared the harbor, I saw the products of New Spain ready to be loaded aboard the ships after the Spanish goods were unloaded. The colonies produced silver, sugar, molasses, rum, cochineal, indigo, chocolate, and hides.

Cochineal was a dye, developed by the Aztecs, its garish crimson prized by Spanish royalty. Its gaudy hue derived from a dark insect called the cochineal, which always resembled in my mind a dog tick. Our india women harvested the female cochineal from cactus pads with the flick of a feather. The insects were boiled to the bursting point, then dried and bundled into hemp bags.

Vertiginous stacks of sacked coca beans tottered above the waterfront, and in Spain they would be worth a fortune. There, the *chocolatl* would be pounded in a mortar together with small, very hot green chili, a vanilla pod, and some aniseed. Maize flour and water would be added, and the whole concoction brought to a boil.

The Spanish also added sugar to the drink, which made it as habit-forming there as it was here to our women—and here its hold over them is undeniably powerful. Our women drink so much of it in church, prepared by their servants, that the bishop had issued an edict prohibiting the practice. He became very sick afterward and rumors spread that some of the women had poisoned him.

The beverage, coco, was created by the Aztecs. Forbidden to the common people, *chocolatl* was imbibed solely by the nobility and considered sacred. The most famous of these Aztec connoisseurs was Montezuma, their emperor, who drank numerous cups a day, cold. Its beans, ubiquitously treasured, were used throughout New Spain as currency. Some even believed *chocolatl* to possess spirit power, that *chocolatl* mixed with menstrual blood was an irresistible love potion.

The exotic cargoes of the Manila galleons also poured into Veracruz. Ivory and sandalwood from East India; silk and tea from China; Chinese porcelain as well, packed in pepper grains and other spices to keep it from breaking—these were all hauled from the Acapulco port by mule train.

As I reached the waterfront, I saw the ships anchor and moor in the lee of San Juan de Ulúa, the island fort less than a musket shot from the city. Disembarking passengers in longboats were already coming ashore. Clambering out of their boats, they all dropped to their knees in prayer, many kissing the ground. Some priests broke down and sobbed, not because they'd survived the savage sea, but because they believed they'd landed on hallowed ground. By their lights Veracruz was indeed the City of the True Cross, welcoming them to a land where the Sacred Church claimed heathen souls by the millions.

In celebration of the archbishop's arrival, two thousand head of cattle had been driven through the city streets at dawn, their hooves all but shaking us out of bed. The streets still stank like a stable. The purpose for this cattle drive was ostensibly medicinal. The holy fathers held that cow respiration cleansed the air of pestilence, specifically the plague-infested swamp fumes befouling our city. Thus the heaving herd would deliver our sainted archbishop from the dreaded peste. When I asked the fray about the curative value of panting cattle, he grumbled, "The Lord acts in mysterious ways."

I wasn't so sure. Nor were some of my more skeptical indios friends. That the holy fathers deemed an out-of-breath bovine more health-giving than the Father, Son, and Holy Ghost I found a bizarre joke. Furthermore, the collective stench of swamp fumes, rotting river corpses, *and* cattle dung was an auto-da-fé worthy of Torquemada himself.

One group coming ashore was garbed not as clerics but servants. Two were full-grown men, one a dwarf, two women servants. They exuded a joie de vivre lacking in our own servants.

They must have very careless masters in Mother Spain, I thought. *Our gachupins would wipe those grins off their face in a hurry.*

Beatriz Zamba joined me. She had named herself Zamba

after her caste, not her parents. Since her father was a slave, she had no surname. Each day Beatriz strolled through Veracruz with bundled sugarcane packed on her back and cocuyo beetles hanging from her hat. Everywhere she went she sang out, "Sugar! Cocuyo! Sugar! Cocuyo!"

She peddled these vendibles in the streets.

The sugar was grown locally, and her lover—an africano sugarcane slave and father of her son—filched the cane she sold. In New Spain people lusted after it. Half the people around me sucked on cane or its various confections. And as Beatriz pointed out shortly after I arrived in Veracruz, "Soon they are sucking it up with no teeth."

Tooth loss among its enthusiasts was endemic. No doubt the worms that burrow holes in teeth had come from sugarcane.

Cocuyos, on the other hand, are harmless and, due to one strange trait, even decorative. A small black beetle with luminously green spots, when a cocuyo is captured, its back reflexively cracks, and a small loop protrudes beneath its shell. Through this rigid ring, hair, a necklace or a bracelet cord can be threaded. The owner of a beetle often treats the living beetle as a pet, as well as an ornament, feeding it bits of sugarcane or tortilla.

Beatriz fed the cocuyo strung around her neck sugarcane. "Sweets for the sweet," she said, smiling. Since Beatriz never indulged in sugarcane and still had all her teeth, her smile was resplendent.

Beatriz was a friend, and I called few people that—only she and the fray. Life on the streets was too hard for more than casual acquaintances. The friend you treasured today you found dead in a gutter tomorrow en route to the northern mines, which amounted to the same thing, or you found him picking your pocket and purloining your last tortilla.

But Beatriz was different. I once assisted Fray Antonio when he cured her baby of a soaring fever and a frightening assortment of peste blotches inflaming his face and body. When we brought the fever down and rid him of the dreaded bubos, she thought we had conjured miracles. She carried her child, Jacinto, on her hip this very day, and never forgot what we had done.

Her child's legal status was unclear. Nothing in the Spanish legal system was simple when it came to race. Spanish law acknowledged twenty-two racial categories, each governed by differing statutes, each category further subdivided into subcategories for predominately "white," "africano," and "indio" individuals.

A child with a Spanish father and an india mother was a mestizo.

A Spanish father and an africano mother yielded a mulatto.

Beatriz had an africano father and mulatta mother, and her category was zamba.

As people with mixed blood intermarried, it became increasingly difficult for the bureaucracy to categorize them. The strangest category was that of the child of a mulatto father and a zamba mother. The offspring of this union was called a *zambo miserable*. I do not know why the offspring should be called "miserable," but Jacinto's category was zambo miserable, because the law said he had "corrupted" blood.

Racial determinations could also be made when parentage or marriage records were in doubt. In that case a physical examination was conducted. Little attention was paid to skin color because many Spaniards were not light-skinned. More attention was given to hair shades and structure. Short, woolly hair indicated africano. Straight, coarse locks or an inability to grow bodily hair meant indio. Mestizos were a problem because they bore traits of both Spaniards and indios, and one trait occasionally stood out over the other.

The reason for this system, the fray explained, was that our traits and abilities were ostensibly passed along by blood. Pure Spanish blood inclined people to build ships, sail seas, and conquer empires. When the purity of the blood was diluted, these strengths were commensurably diluted; hence, Spain's strength was diluted.

"The obsession with pureza de sangre grew out of the centuries-long battle to force the Moors and Jews out of Spain, thereby unifying our kingdom," the fray once whispered to me while in his cups. "But what began as a holy crusade has ended in the rack, the gallows, and millions of graves. Our gachupin make the Ottomans look like cloistered nuns. It is all muy loco."

In the system of racial delineation, there were no categories for español women who wed indios, or africanas.

"Men who ruthlessly debauch our india, africana, and mixed-blood women," the fray said, "cannot conceive of Spanish women desiring men of differing blood. Hence, their offspring know no category. That child's life is purgatory on earth."

"So many people and so much happiness," Beatriz said, with a mocking smile.

"Maybe in the next world."

"You are such a fraud, Cristóbal," Beatriz said. She was one of the few street people who called me by my given name. "Where else could you make a living, playing the crippled clown?"

"Everyone needs someone to look down to."

"But those tricks—twisting the body God gave you into obscene contortions—are they not a mockery of His gift?" Her sly grin glittered derision.

"If I, a poor lépero, offend God's pride, we're all in more trouble than I thought."

Beatriz threw her head back and laughed. "That is one of the many things I admire about you, Cristóbal. You are utterly without virtue."

"I am practical."

I did not take offense, it was a game we played. She loved to tease and taunt me, then wait for my rejoinder. Everything I said she found funny.

But the old East Indian who had taught me the arcane arts of contortion did impugn my beliefs. Scrawny, gnarled, mango-bald, and with a scratchy voice of throat-sore gull, he'd been dubbed Gull by some long-forgotten wit, and the appellation stuck. Nor was Gull a partisan of the Christian faith. He believed in countless gods and goddesses, heavens untold, thousands of hells, often declaring that we suffered them all, returning to earth life after life, through afterworld after afterworld in infinite reincarnation—"like a dog unto its vomit," he once averred. He believed justice was nothing more than a Dark Diceman, casting lots for our souls, who spun our destiny on a Karmic Wheel, and that in the end all life was illusion—earth, death, life, karma, afterworld, even the Dark Diceman himself, even belief, *everything*, he'd said.

"The best way to survive so much chaos, falsehood, and pain is to conceal your True Self behind a mask," he used to say. "Oh, the mask might laugh and scream, rage and cry, but the face beneath the mask, your True Countenance, is impervious, impassive, heartless as void."

He also told me of Shiva, a god of creation and destruction. He had built and destroyed the world many times, would do it again, sooner than we thought, and yet paradoxically he was the most ardent of lovers—in the heavens, on earth, in all the hell worlds there ever were for all of time. Women everywhere worshipped his every move, look, and touch. When one of his wives mistook a pyre for his own burning ground, she flung herself onto the flames. Gull sang to me Kali's hymn to love and death:

Because you love the fire
I have made a burning-ground of my heart
Where you, oh Dark One,
Might dance.

In his India, Kali became the feminine avatar of lovers everywhere. Overnight widows, mistresses, and concubines all over India threw themselves on their lover's pyres. Like Kali, women chose the burning ground over bereavement.

"Death equals love?" I asked, incredulous.

"Its noblest exemplar."

I stared at him a long moment. Finally, shaking my head, I said, "In India, maybe, but don't voice those views too loudly around here. The Inquisition has a burning ground, too, and its glowing pinchers and blazing stakes have nothing to do with amour vincet omnia. Some of the women around here might not endorse your beliefs either."

"But you have Aztec blood in you as well. You carry in your heart the Aztec flame. They knew the truth of which I speak."

"They won't help you either when you're screaming on a rack or strung from a strapaddo."

Yet it was true about my indio ancestors. I had heard stories from Snake Flower and the woman I once called mother—stories of the many indio gods, of ancient worlds created and destroyed many times over, each new world "a Cycle of the Sun." Snake Flower told me our benighted world would one day die by fire.

And I knew, too, of Homer's Land of the Dead, his Elysian Fields, and gods on high.

I kept those views to myself as well.

But I listened with rapt fascination—and learned. Not only tales of his gods, but the secret arts of the mysterious East—stoicism, endurance, meditation, indifference to pain, and corporeal contortion. Contortion's skills alone took me hundreds of hours to perfect, but I practiced religiously. Eventually I was as supple as Gull. I could twist my joints as if they were the mellifluous sap that flows from the trees of our Rubber People.

Gull was a curious mentor. Tiny, with small delicate bones, he had for a time been a flyer of Papantla, that terrifying spectacle in which men swing from a rope around the towering tip of a vertiginous pole. Unfortunately for Gull, his line snapped one day, and like his namesake, he flew for real. Launched into space like a slung stone, he soared and soared and soared. For a while it seemed he might even take wing, until he dropped like a rock.

His doomed flight terminated against an abandoned pyramid, its stony slope breaking both his legs. Unconscious for a month—"wandering through the Aztec nether world," which was how Gull put it—when he came to, he told me he'd seen wondrous sights: Creation's dawn, the extinction of stars, the death of the gods, the end of time. But he never walked again. Not that he complained. He said those sights would inspire him all his days.

"I am content," he said simply. "The True Self behind the mask remains faithful to itself, remote, fearless, impervious as stone."

For a time he appropriated another's legs. A huge lépero nicknamed "Mountain"—because of his height and heft—conveyed him on his shoulders. Mountain, however, was an inept thief, who in the end was ambushed by his vindictive victims. This murderous mob stripped his hide with a flogging cat, hacked off both his hands, and cauterized the wrists in boiling oil. In the years to come his severed stumps grew even more scarified and unsightly, none of which affected his lust for life. He continually joked that his double amputations kept him out of the mines. Not even the alcalde wanted a handless slave. So Gull rode his mountainous shoulders, all the while contorting himself into monstrous convolutions, even as Mountain stuck his obscenely cauterized stubs under the nose of potential patrons and bellowed. "Alms! Alms for the handless, the legless, and the jointless!"

Gull was the brains, Mountain the feet, legs, and power. For a time they were the most successful beggars in Veracruz.

Until I came along and stole Gull's act.

The crowd parted for the vast procession of priests, friars, and nuns descending on the waterfront. Most of the priests wore a roughspun sackcloth of goat hair, wool, or burlap, their habits white, gray, brown, or black, depending on the order. Around their waists they wore rope belts. From their necks were strung wood-beaded rosaries. They held crosses before them. Cowls covered their heads. They favored hemp sandals, which kicked up dust as they marched. There seemed to be a contest as to whose robe could look the most threadbare. Several of the habits looked ready to dissolve off their bodies. Nor was much value placed on cleanliness. Sweat and dirt defaced habits and faces.

Fray Antonio had been one of them once—faithful to his vows of humility, good works, and poverty. Some of the priests and frays, however, clearly disdained that creed, clerics who rode in on horseback, wore shirts of fine linen and stockings of silk, whose monasteries were wealthy haciendas run by slave labor, and who lived like kings on the backs and sweat of the indio péons they had ostensibly come to save.

"The New World was conquered not only by the sword but by an army of priests," the good fray once told me. "Most gave everything they possessed, even their very lives, to bring Christ's cross to this benighted land. But these wicked ones arrive in silk and drive their flock like beasts of burden."

"For filthy lucre," I'd observed.

The fray nodded sadly. "And for a priest to pillage his flock, like a wolf on the fold, is a sin against God."

The great parade of priests and nuns swept by me. Holy men had arrived from all over New Spain, each order eager to outdo the other in hailing the new archbishop, and their music and dust billowed in the hot, warm air.

Their crosses extended before them, they sang "Te Deum" as they marched, a sacred paen to the Lord.

You are God:
We praise you.
You are the Lord:
We acclaim you.
You are the eternal Padre:
All creation worships you.

The religious orders commandeered the center of the street with great masses of lay people pressing on them from all sides—merchants, hacendados, doctors, abogados, planters, blacksmiths, tavern owners, soldiers, mulatta mistresses, africano slaves, street léperos such as myself, highwaymen, cutpurses, whores. People flocked here for the ships' mail, for money from relatives, to welcome long-lost friends. Mestiza and india wives of sailors who saw their husbands once a year while the ships were unloaded, repaired, caulked, refitted. Then there were the merely curious, such as I.

More ships were entering the harbor, dropping and securing their mooring cables to the heavy bronze mooring rings sunk into the fort wall, praying that in the fort's lee they might be safe from the violent el norte storms. Longboats from shore had ferried the king's custom inspectors and representatives of the Holy Office of the Inquisition. Already aboard, they examined all merchandise and baggage, except perhaps that of the archbishop and his entourage. The inquisitors quickly confiscated any works challenging or profaning church doctrine.

The crowd parted for another procession, and three pack horses trotted past us. Behind each rider were secured large clay jars in hemp baskets packed with straw. The jars were filled with la nieve, snow, from the great volcano Citlaltépetl, the highest mountain in all New Spain, and these riders were known as the *posta de nieve,* the snow post. This snow was packed into the jars along with tasty herbs and sugars and rushed from the mountain about thirty leagues away with continuous relays of fast horses to Veracruz, where it was served as a delicious concoction called sorbete. A special cold treat for the archbishop, it was a gift from the merchants of the town in hopes that it might help protect him from the dreaded vómito. It is only the second time I had seen the pack horses race through the streets with flavored snow. The last shipment had been to the deathbed of the previous alcalde. Dying of the vómito sickness, it was still said he died with his mouth full of cool sorbete and a smile on his face.

I could not imagine how sorbete tasted. I had never even held snow in my hand. Still my mouth salivated at the thought. Anyone who had such rare confections delivered to them from the high mountains was clearly blessed.

But then I felt blessed when Beatriz sold me stolen sugarcane for half the going rate.

The religious procession reached the docks. I wriggled my way to the edge of the procession, hoping to find enough space to do my crippled octopus act. I had my chance amid a bevy of sober-faced nuns, several of whom were strumming lutes, all of them singing the "Te Deum."

Their music and singing were serene, their smiles beatific, and their eyes fixed longingly at the heavens, but they were a tough audience for me to play to. They never stopped singing, never stopped smiling, but not one of them reached under her habit for a reale, a crumb of bread, a rosary bead, nada. Not one of them showed me anything resembling love or pity or tenderness. When one of them glanced my way at all, she looked through me as if I wasn't there. The only one who paid me any mind at all was a sinister-looking mother superior directly above me, who glared at me.

She was almost standing on top of me, and I was tempted to sink my lépero teeth into her ankle just to let her know . . . *I am also human.* But then a large black boot stomped on my ostensibly crippled hand.

"Aaak!" I roared.

As I scrambled to my feet, a man grabbed me by the hair and pulled me away from the nuns. I looked up into his dark eyes and even darker grin. There was much about the man that conveyed a caballero, those gentlemen knights whose swords were pledged to God and king. His attire was rakish. Upon his head sat a fawn-colored, broad-brimmed hat with a large, black, feather plume circling the brim and one of bloody crimson rising above it. His red velvet doublet he wore sleeveless, and his fancy shirt of black linen had sleeves that billowed all the way down to his wrists. His black velvet breeches were stuffed into black, thigh-high riding boots of brilliantly burnished snakeskin, bush racer to be exact, the deadly serpent whose caress kissed you to hell faster than a poxy strumpet. He wore no dress sword but a working weapon, a rapier of Toledo steel, its haft, like the backs of his wrists and hands, scored from hard use.

Yes, he radiated arrogance from horns to hocks. His red-gold mustache was exuberantly menacing, his beard short and pointed. His matching tresses cascaded over his shoulders in tight ringlets, one lock longer than the rest. This "love lock" he trussed with a ribbon, fashioned out of a lady's undergarment. He wanted the world to know he was a renowned rake and, as well, a seasoned swordsman.

But this was not a polished caballero, who slept on a fine bed with a treasure chest of gold at his feet. No younger son of a nobleman who spurned the priesthood to follow the god of war. This was a sword for hire—a sword *and* a garrancha that took what it wanted.

Any impression that he was a gentleman knight was illusory.

I knew what he was the moment I laid eyes on him—picaro. I had read the tale of that infamous picaro, Guzman de Alfarache. Everyone who could read had read it, and later I would also learn of other legendary picaros, including the poet-swordsman, Mateo Rosas de Oquendo. One day I would even learn the true identity of the man before me.

A picaro was an adventurous rogue who lived by his wits and his sword—often one step ahead of the law. Their reputation for knavery in Spain was as reprehensible as that of léperos in New Spain, and they were prohibited by law from entering New Spain. If detected aboard ship, they were detained and rerouted to the Filipinas, a hellhole certifying almost certain death by marauding clans or malaria. The islands, across the great Western Sea and nearly to China, the land of the chinos, were discovered by Ferdinand Magellan, who gave his life there. Named after good King Filipe II, the islands are said to be both lovely and deadly.

The reasons were pecuniary rather than moral. Silver was Mother Spain's life's blood, and the Crown did not want that silver lifeline jeopardized by armies of picaro swordsmen hijacking the silver trains along trails and highways.

Still, the lure of so much silver and gold combined with the chance to escape the Old World's warrants and jails was hard to resist. Despite the threat of deportation to the Filipinas, many ships contained rogues who had sneaked or bribed their way aboard and who arrived in Veracruz with plunder in their hearts.

Now the one before me might have fooled the Crown's agents, but I saw through him right away. He was a rogue in a caballero's clothes. His clothes might have been aristocratic—and I'm sure the nobleman he stole them from had paid dearly for them—but I recognized the worn heels, the fraying cuffs, the soiled sleeves. This was a man whose time and treasure went for fleshly pleasures, not fashionable dress.

Then there were his eyes. They had a reckless come-hither glint to them. They were the eyes of man who would buy you a drink one moment and cut your throat the next; who would accept your aid and comfort, then seduce your wife and daughters. These were the eyes of a killer, a highwayman, a rakehell, a debaucher of women, a man willing to sell his sword arm to the highest bidder. They were the eyes of a man who, unlike the rest of us, refused to cower in guilt and fear and who lived life on his own terms. Here was a man from whom I could learn much.

He treated me to a scintillating grin. It was quite overwhelming—wicked enough to break a bad woman's heart or turn a good woman bad. I was so taken by the singular dazzle of a flashing gold tooth, I almost missed him rubbing the two reales between his thumb and fingers. I naturally recognized his smile had the sincerity of a crocodile's tears.

"I have a mission for you, Chico Loco," he said.

"What mission?" I asked, my eyes fixed on the coins. Two reales was a day's wage for grown men and more than I'd ever possessed at one time in my whole life.

The rogue nodded toward a raised, covered pavilion. Under its canopy the alcalde of Veracruz and the city gentry gathered to greet the archbishop. Tables of food and drink had been set out for their pleasure.

Staring down at us from the top row was the alcalde's new young wife. His previous wife had recently died of fever. The woman saw us looking up at her, and she smiled coquettishly at my newfound employer, her eyes softly seductive. She was half-sitting, half-standing, in one of those great globelike dresses that puff out majestically and are not meant for walking, lying, or sitting but solely for gachupin admiration.

I thought the dress looked stupid but not the woman. I'd seen her once before in a passing carriage. She reeked of sensuality and looked to me as if she could snare the soul of a sinless saint. I said as much to the fray, who was with me at the time. He recognized her and described her as "the serpent who tempted Lucifer," which in this case, I suppose, was fitting. My newfound master needed no introduction to Satan.

The rogue handed me a small piece of folded paper. "Take this to the señora. Climb the shoring timbers *under* the grandstand to get to her. Do not be seen giving it to her. If you get caught, swallow it."

I hesitated.

"Yes?" he asked, smiling pleasantly.

"Your name if she asks?"

"Mateo."

"Mateo," I said softly.

He handed me the coins, then leaned down so that his garlic-and-wine breath reeked in my face. Smiling the entire time, he said, "If you tell anyone about this, I will cut off your cojones. *¿Comprende?*"

I had no doubt he had a whole collection of cojones.

"*Comprende.*"

The pavilion I was to enter featured three levels of wood tables and benches, each row higher than the previous one. The last row was ten feet off of the ground.

The alcalde table was in the middle of the top row. Each row had a wooden bench thirty or forty feet long and a table the same length. Atop the cloth-covered tables were a selection of food, fruits, and wine. Beneath the rows of benches and tables was a maze of boards and timbers shoring it up.

Two reales for storming this citadel? *¡Dios mio!* I could lose my head *and* my cojones. I deserved an entire treasure fleet. I looked back, and Mateo drew his dagger and pointed it menacingly toward his crotch.

I felt my own cojones tighten and looked back to the structure I had to scale. I realized why he had chosen me—only a contortionist would be able to twist and crawl and scurry through the maze of supporting timbers.

When I was out of his sight I eagerly read the note I was to deliver.

Your face is written in my soul
No rose is redder than your lips
Your eyes are burned into my heart
No goose is softer than your cheeks
Tonight, my love,
At the hour when your body is the warmest

"No goose is softer than your cheeks?" *¡Qué va!* Couldn't he have stolen better poetry than this?

I went beneath the pavilion and began twisting my way up through the boards, contorting my body every which way. Some of the boards weren't firmly fixed, and I had to continually test their stability, keeping my weight on the stout vertical bracing-timbers. Once a cross board came loose in my hand, and I had to meticulously work it back into place.

Any second I expected to be spotted by the gentry above or to have the entire jungle of shoring timbers come crashing down on top of me, killing everyone on the grandstand—myself in the process.

Finally, however, I reached the top level. I came up under the table so I wouldn't be seen. I was at one end, about fifteen feet from where the alcalde's señora sat, and I slowly crawled in her direction, avoiding the shoes of men and petticoats of women as I crawled.

I crawled until I recognized her dress. Puffing out like a big round ball an arm's length in each direction, this rose-colored raiment was supported underneath by cane spokes and wire loops. I have heard the dresses called both by their French name, farthingales, and their Spanish one, guardinfantes. Some of those I've seen flared out several feet on each side. The woman was not sitting naturally nor was she expected to, because the frame of the dress would not permit her. A wooden device had been constructed for her to lean back against in a half-sitting position.

I pulled on the hem of her dress to let her know I was there. I was reaching up to hand her the note, when her husband shouted, "Amigos! Don't doubt me when I tell you I am the greatest bullfighter in all New Spain. You've seen men fighting bulls with lances from the saddle of their horse. I stand with my feet on the ground and fight the bull with nothing but a cape."

I heard him stomping around to demonstrate his technique. "I need a cape. Clear this table," he told servants. "I will use the cover."

I needed the table cover! If I lost the cover, I lost my head!

Desperate and panicking, I hid in the only place available—even as the table cover was being pulled off by servants—under the woman's dress. I buried myself under her wire-framed tent and petticoats.

Ayyo, what saint did I fail to honor on their festival day to deserve this punishment? Dios mio, Holy Mother, Jesu Cristo! I am an innocent boy. A thief, yes. A conniver, true. A liar, often. But why must I have my head removed and impaled upon the city gates because of an affair of love that I was not involved in?

Furthermore, bullfights were done from horseback. Everyone knows that. Why must this fool of an alcalde have to pretend to fight bulls on foot? This was an offense not only to the bulls but to me, whom he had put in harm's way. Why couldn't he leave the pavilion and demonstrate his skill on a horse?

While he entertained the audience with his childish antics, I found myself under the tent of his wife's dress, squeezed in the warm, mysterious place between his wife's legs. Afraid that any part of my body might show, I squeezed in tighter against that sanctum sanctorum, and she spread her legs wide apart to allow entry. I quickly discovered that the woman wore nothing beneath the voluminous petticoats, and that I was flush against her most intimate of intimates.

I had seen naked little lépero girls urinating on the street, and I been told that women too had an opening between their legs. Yes, I knew now that was true. I could confirm that it was warm and moist, a wet lushness that was more tender and inviting than I would ever have imagined. I began to understand why men would want to place their garranchas in there.

Her hand grabbed my hair and pushed me deeper into the split between her legs.

Soon my nose was pushing up against the warm wetness, and she was pulling me harder and harder against her and wiggling more and more as she did. Something was between her legs that I did not know a woman had, a little button, a mushroom-sized pene of her own. From the woman's frantic movements I could tell that touching this was of great interest to her. This secret treasure seemed to have a hidden nerve. When I fondled it, her gyrations increased in proportion to the force of that touch. When I accidentally bumped my nose against it, her whole body trembled and shook. She squirmed, pushed it toward me, and the opening between her legs began to spread.

The alcalde's voice carried down to me as he stomped up and down the pavilion, fighting off a bull—played by a servant.

It was awkward, but somehow she managed to brace her backside against that board and hook a leg around the back of my head. The next thing I knew her treasure trove was in my mouth and between my lips. I fought to disengage, but her leg tightened its grip. My mouth and nose were now buried in that secret valley, and I couldn't get my breath. I opened my mouth wider, my tongue came out in a silent gasp, and—and—

That was what she wanted.

My tongue.

I was trapped. Her leg locked around the back of my neck. A mob of gachupins on all sides who would draw and quarter and castrate me if I was caught. I had Mateo below, who would likewise geld me if I failed to give her the note. My only recourse was to mollify her.

I began nervously, hesitantly, circling her nub with my tongue, almost afraid to touch it. But the more I circled and avoided it, the more her own hips began to tremble. Whenever I touched it, her body shook so hard I feared we'd be discovered.

Not that she seemed to care. She squirmed and gyrated, and her private parts became even hotter and wetter until my own garrancha grew, became *muy excitado,* throbbing uncontrollably.

Now the terrible fear was being replaced by something else: unbearable pressure. I had experienced these feelings before, and once a friendly puta, whom I'd slept beside one night at the house of the poor, had showed me how to touch it to relieve the pressure.

"Magnifico!" The crowd proclaimed as the alcalde "killed" the bull with his sword.

The more they screamed, the harder the señora locked onto the back of my head, the more my mouth and tongue worked at her source of joy.

"You have seen, amigos, the technique of fighting a bull with one's feet on the ground. I tell you that someday bullfights will no longer be from horseback. Our Portuguese friends say that will never happen, but mark my words—it will be hombre against el toro, facing the charging animal with nothing but his courage and cape to protect him."

He threw the cape-table cover back on the table, and

servants rushed to put it back in place. As the audience applauded, the woman's thighs and private parts were vibrating voraciously against my face.

I knew that my throbbing garrancha belonged in there. Although the fray expressly forbid any misconduct in the house of the poor and put up a blanket to partition off an area whenever a woman stayed, I had seen a lépero atop a puta pumping with his rump in the air, just as Don Fernando had mounted Miaha. My position now, on my knees with my head between her legs and her half-standing behind the table, made that impossible.

Unsure how to continue her pleasure, my coyote instincts took over, and I did what I felt was natural. I stuck my tongue into her hot, sultry opening.

It was a mistake.

She moaned and squirmed and a salacious shudder ran through her. God only knows what expression she had on her face. As I waited to be dragged out from under her dress and my throat slit, slowly, ever so slowly, her spasms began to subside. Panicking, I slipped out from under her dress as the alcalde addressed her.

"Mi amor, my love, your face is hot and flushed with excitement. It never occurred to me that you would get so excited by my performance!" The alcalde's voice was awed and gleeful at his wife's sexual excitement.

I lifted the tablecloth enough to make eye contact with the woman. Sweat lines from our antics were visible as trenches in the thick beauty powders on the sides of her face.

I held the note so she could take it. I smiled at her to show her that I was pleased to have given her pleasure. She allowed me a small, mischievous smile, half grin, half grimace, then lifting her knee, booted me in my face back through the wide opening in between the boards. On the way down I bounced and banged, careened and caromed off every cross beam, support joist, and shoring timber on my way down, hitting the ground with a resounding thump.

Slowly I rose and crawled out from under the pavilion.

I hurt in many places, but mostly in my soul. The rogue was nowhere to be seen. As I limped away, I considered my experience. I had made two important discoveries about women. They had a secret spot where they could be touched to give them pleasure. And once they had had their pleasure, a kick in the face was all you could expect.

I had gone only a short distance when the crowd parted for a coach. I saw a chance to ply my trade. But as I trotted toward the coach, an old woman in black stepped out of it and paused, looking down at me as she was being helped by attendants. Her raptor's eye caught mine, and an icy hand squeezed my heart.

The woman drew back in shock, but the surprise quickly left her face and alarm took over. I had once observed the same sort of reaction from a man bitten by an iguana—first the recoil in surprise, then revulsion, then anger as he beat the iguana to death.

I had no intimation as to why this aristocratic Spanish doña found me so loathsome, but my lépero instincts put wings on my feet. I raced into the cheering crowd as the archbishop reached tierra firma and bent to kiss the dirt.

I never looked back until I was clear of the crowds and well up an alley too narrow for a coach to follow. Even in the alley I felt naked and exposed, as if the sun itself were spying for this woman.

THIRTEEN

I WENT HOME to the House of the Poor, skulking along side streets, convinced the Angel of Death was everywhere. The hospice was empty. Fray Antonio and his charges, who would that night sleep on the floor's piled straw, were with the crowds honoring the archbishop. Soon the waterfront reception would move to the alcalde palace. The buena gente would attend the festivities inside, while in the plaza Veracruz's citizens, along with those in town for the treasure fleet, would celebrate through the night and into the next day. To miss the greatest celebration of my lifetime was deeply disappointing, but my fear outweighed my eagerness.

The Casa de los Pobres was little more than a large, rectangular room. One corner was blanketed off for the fray. Behind the hung blanket were his private quarters—a bed of straw in a wood frame, a small table with a reading candle, a chest with his personal effects, and several shelves for his modest library. The books weren't much—a few religious tomes, the rest classics from Greek and Roman antiquity. No doubt the local church and the alcalde had more books. Perhaps a few wealthy citizens as well, but it was a substantial collection of libros in a city where the vast majority of the people could not read their own names, let alone buy books.

My greatest pleasure was to sit in the fray's draped-off bolt-hole and read, but today I entered it to hide. I sat on his bed with my back to the corner and gathered my arms around my knees. Veracruz's streets had honed my survival instincts to a razor's edge, and I had felt stronger emotions emanating from the old woman than mere malice.

Fear.

Had I—or the parents I never knew—done anything to her? The fray never indicated any such thing, so her hatred, by itself, was inexplicable. But her fear? Why would an aristocratic, all-powerful matrona, the dowager of a great house, fear a lépero boy who cadged alms to earn his bread?

It was not the first time I had been mistaken for another. The day Don Francesco had beaten me within an inch of my life, his guest had claimed to recognize my true paternity. Perhaps the old woman saw the same similarities.

From time to time I'd questioned the fray about my father's identity, but he denied all knowledge. Once deep in wine he said my father had been a wearer of the spurs, but then grew angry, perhaps for having said too much.

But the old woman, like Don Fernando's guest before her, saw something in my face, knew what she saw, and it put me at risk. I now feared what she saw might cost me my life.

I tried to put the woman out of my mind, but I could not stop thinking about my parentage. That my mother might have been a thief and a whore made no special impression on me. We so-called "Children of the Lord" were notorious for base parentage. That my father might have been a wearer of spurs was also of no significance. The gachupins ceaselessly debauched our women, watching them drop their bastards without remorse, with contempt rather than love. To them, we were a slander against their stock and blood. They demonstrated their hatred in the laws they enacted *against* us, their own offspring. We bastardos had no rights in society. We could not inherit from our fathers; we were not even recognized as their children. Not just the streets of Veracruz—*¡Bueno Dios!*—one end of New Spain to the other, swarmed with the bastardos of Spanish hombres. If anyone had proven to a gachupin that I was his son, he would have stared right through me as if I'd never existed, because under the eyes of the law I did *not* exist. Our gachupin masters could use and abuse us at will.

Sometimes one heard the expression "son of a gun" applied to street children because their mothers were whores who did not know which men impregnated them. The term was first applied to the children born to prostitutes on ships. Large war galleons often carried putas to service the crew. When the women were about to give birth, they were laid next to one of the ever-burning braziers near the big guns, which had to be continually available to ignite the black gunpowder. Their propinquity to the cannons earned the appellation of "son of a gun."

Being the bastard son of a gachupin gave me no more rights than had I been the son of a gun.

And now I had met two people who apparently hated me for my parentage, as if I was responsible for parents I had never met, as if my very existence fomented blood feuds, as if *I* had committed the sins of my forebears.

Ayyo, perhaps the fray would tell me why this woman hated me. Perhaps he would find some way to take care of this problem. I knew he would if he could. Fray Antonio was a good man. He helped everyone. His only sin was that he was too good. After he was defrocked, he turned to the secular community for help. He talked a well-to-do merchant out of a rundown building in the heart of the mestizo barrio. In his spare time he solicited money, food, clothing, and medicine from the wealthy. He provided all that and lodging, too, to the poor.

In other words, like myself, he begged.

Once I accompanied the fray to these great houses and watched the contortions *he* performed wringing alms from parsimonious grandees. No, he did not twist his arms out of their sockets, but he twisted money out of their coffers, telling them all the time, with a serene smile and saintly eyes, that God hated doubt money but loved a cheerful giver and how the golden road to heaven was paved with loving largesse.

His doctoring skills were schooled in necessity, not academy, he often said. His surgical instruments consisted of carpentry tools and kitchen utensils. His medical knowledge he'd gleaned from a volume of Galen of Pergamum, a Greek physician a century after Christ. Translated from Greek into Arabic, then into Latin, Galen's works were frowned on by the Church for their Moorish taint, but they were the best guide the fray possessed. Occasionally, a real doctor—at the fray's behest—provided help and instruction. Beyond that all the fray had to go on was his experience in treating those whom other doctors spurned.

"I received my degree," the fray sometimes said, "from Galen and the School of Necessity."

The House of the Poor was no palace of the poor—just rough, unpainted boards nailed onto raw, unfinished timbers. I slept in the common area with those who were too starved or sick to find shelter elsewhere. Piles of straw and a few ragged blankets served as our beds. The fray had a few good blankets for when the nights turned cold, but he kept them hidden. The poor stole anything they could get their hands on.

But most nights the heat caused the very air to sweat, so much so it was hard to breathe in the hospice, though in truth it was hard to breathe anywhere on the tierra caliente except the cool, enclosed gardens of the rich. When it rained, which was often, water seeped throughout the main room. When it became too wet, I slept on the long table on which Veracruz's starvelings took their evening meals each night. When the weather was bad and people could not beg, we had more mouths to feed.

In one corner was a small fire pit. An indio woman came in each day and prepared tortillas and frijoles at the pit, which, along with occasional corn mush, were the only nourishment the fray could afford. Smoke from the open fire covered the ceiling, eventually working its way through the cracks between the roof and the walls.

Only the bookshelves were safe from the rain.

I turned and studied the titles on those shelves. A hacendado had given him most of them when he'd been the priest at a village church. There was the tome on medicine, a few religious works, notably San Augustine's *The City of God,* but most of the books were the classics of Greece and Rome. My favorites were Plutarch's *Bioi paralleloi (Parallel Lives)* in which he explored the character and noble deeds of Greece and Rome's greatest soldiers, legislators, orators, and statesmen; Homer's *Iliad* and *Odyssey;* Virgil's *Aeneid;* Dante's *Divine Comedy* and Aesop's *Fables.*

Other than what the fray and his books taught me, my possessions consisted of the dirty, ragged pants and shirt I begged in, and the only marginally cleaner garments and sandals I wore to church. The pants and shirt were made of coarse-spun indio cotton and maguey, the sandals were hemp. To save wear on the sandals, I only wore them *in* the church.

Then there was my silver cross. The fray confessed one

night, steeped in drink, that the crucifix did, in fact, belong to my mother, and that it had been given to her by my father. It was the only article of theirs I owned. The cross was pure silver, red stones adorning each corner. One would not expect "an india whore" to own so fine an ornament, but then my father was alleged to have been a wearer of spurs.

A lot of good it did me. If I wore the cross publically, I'd be killed for it or jailed as a thief. It wasn't even safe in the hospice. To disguise its worth, the fray finally covered it with pitch, and I strung it from my neck on a piece of hemp.

I fingered the blackened cross and thought of the fray. Had he been defrocked for fighting Church corruption? For opposing its exploitation of the indios and its oppression of the mixed bloods? Or had he fallen from churchly grace through his taste for wine and ladies of the night, as others have intimated?

To me the questions were fatuous. He did more good than anyone in all of Veracruz, and he had given me something, at great personal peril, even pure-blood Spaniards seldom enjoyed: the world of classical literature.

Nor had he neglected our more contemporary authors. The fray's priestly friend, Fray Juan, was a lover of such writers, most of whom were banned. He would loan the fray their illicit writings, which the fray concealed in a secret cache, and so through him I perused the books and plays of Miguel Cervantes sub rosa.

I knew Cervantes to be the creator of Don Quixote, the restive knight errant who tilted at windmills, and the fray had reluctantly permitted me to read the borrowed book. However, he forbade my reading the other banned authors—such as Lope de Vega and Mateo Altman—even though Fray Juan often brought their books to him. I, of course, perused them when he wasn't around.

I was asleep one morning when Fray Juan, greatly excited, visited and hid for the fray a copy of the book called

Guzman de Alferache. I asked Fray Antonio later why the book had to be hidden.

"Books like *Guzman de Alferache* are read only in Spain," he told me. "The Inquisition has banned the importation of them into New Spain because the Church believes that indios will be corrupted by such fare. Not even we pure-blood criollos are permitted to read them, for we, too, can be corrupted."

The fact that few indios read did not enter into the matter. And at fifteen years old, to be "corrupted" had a different meaning than that the fray put on the word.

A day later, when I was alone, I satisfied my curiosity.

The fray's "rabbit hole" was a secret storage hole under his bed with a trapdoor over it. Anything of value we kept in it—away from the thieving street people. Usually there was nothing in it except a few blankets. The blankets were donated to the fray for when the weather turned bitter. Sometimes when we did not have enough money to buy maize for the evening meal, he sold one of them.

I opened the trap and removed Fray Juan's book.

I sat with my feet dangling in the hole and began reading the book, which, to my surprise and pleasure, dealt with the adventures of a young rogue who found himself homeless and on the street of life. As I said, when I met the rogue, Mateo, my own *Guzman de Alfarache,* I learned much of Guzman's ways, of which I will apprise you later.

FOURTEEN

BY LATE AFTERNOON Fray Antonio had not returned to the house, which was not surprising. The fray loved festivals, and this one was unprecedented. The arrival of both the treasure fleet and the great man were a cause for jubilation, and a carnival atmosphere was everywhere. Furthermore, the church, which overlooked the main plaza, was packed with parishioners, and the archbishop himself had conducted the service. So the plaza teemed with congregational overflow as well as onlookers, all of them welcoming the archbishop. True, Veracruz had known many religious festivals, but this one, everyone agreed, was unique.

I knew I should have climbed down the rabbit hole and pulled the trapdoor shut. But I could not shake the memory of that menacing old woman. I needed the fray to explain my unsettling plight.

I donned a straw hat and an indio manta, a blanket tied over the right shoulder and under the left arm. Like the huipil blouse and skirt worn by the india and half-caste women, hundreds of male figures in the rough cotton shirt, pants, and woven maguey mantas would throng the plaza. That abundance offered more protection against discovery than any disguise I could conjure.

What a celebration! As I came onto the main square, the revelers roared. I heard their music, singing, and laughing voices a block away. Because the people of New Spain lived lives of hardship and uncertainty, when they had a fiesta at which to sing, dance, and drink, they did so with a passion. It did not matter whether the celebrations were religious or secular. Purveyors of pulque, sherry sack, and Jamaican rums lined the walkways around the square. Everyone partook. People too poor to feed their children parched corn imbibed as if they were heir to the Fleet's fortune.

A Caribbean rum, dubbed "kill-devil," was new to Veracruz. Decocted from sugarcane, this Luciferian liqueur stole the souls of all who did not sport the big spurs and hence could not afford the brandies of Spain. Well, not exactly all. I tasted it once and swore it would sear a hole in a crocodile's behind.

Cook fires blazed everywhere, boasting baked tortillas, boiling beans, red roasting chilis. Peddlers hawked bananas, papayas, sugarcane, and skewered mangos, skins peeled. Singers and guitarists worked the square, serenading lovers, cadging coppers.

Priests and nuns also packed the square, and as I squeezed through the crowds, I searched for Fray Antonio. He was nowhere to be found. He would not be at the archbishop's reception. Neither defrocked priests nor mendicant clerics were welcome, and the fray was both.

I stepped atop the low stonewall of a plaza fountain to get a better view and stared out over a floating sea of heads. Many were the shaved pates of friars, all of which looked alike.

A group of juglares, street actors who sang and danced, tumbled, and did magic tricks, were performing nearby. Their repertoire was rudely risqué, and I could not take my eyes off them.

My contortionist tricks paled beside theirs. One juglare unsheathed an arm-length sword, announcing he would swallow it. Tilting his head back, raising the inverted blade high overhead, he slid it inch by inch into his groaning gullet—until he'd swallowed three-fourths of his sword.

As I gaped in wide-eyed wonderment, I suddenly realized I was dangerously exposed. Hopping off of the fountain, I lost myself in the bustling crowd, head down but eyes up, searching for the fray.

I searched without luck. The only people I recognized were, incredibly enough, the dwarf and his four friends, two women and two men. He stood on a barrel while the others gathered around him. The rogue who'd slipped me two reales to messenger the love note was also there. A crowd gathered.

"Tomorrow, amigos," the dwarf roared with disconcerting power, "we of the acting group, La Nómadas, will perform for your personal delectation one of the noblest extravaganzas ever to grace the boards of Seville, Madrid, and Cadiz."

The group of actors gathered around the barrel cheered and stamped, clapped and brayed, as if their lives depended on it. The dwarf shyly raised his hands for silence.

"At that time the great autor, Mateo Rosas de Oquendo, legendary poet, swashbuckling swordsman, player par excellence, playwright extraordinaire, the toast of Church and Crown worldwide, will present one of the finest dramas ever to adorn the stages of Europe, England, and New Spain."

Ah, the man was a distinguished poet, swordsman, and actor! And he was my amigo and benefactor. I wondered how I could exact further emoluments from this rakish rogue.

Mateo took a deep bow, swirling his cape with garish flair. Applause detonated from assembled thespians, and the dwarf continued his pitch.

"Amigos, for your dauntless delight, at no cost but your pleasure and praise, the great autor will recite for you *el canto de mi Cid*."

A storm of applause and enthusiam swept through the crowd. And it was no wonder. El Cid was the preeminent hero of the Spanish people, and *The Song of My Cid* was his epic saga.

Even poor léperos knew fragments of it. The poem recalls the Cid's life and triumphs. A Castilian knight who lived over four hundred years ago, his deeds were deified throughout both Spain and New Spain, as if that very morning he'd beat back the Moorish hordes. In an age of chaos, when Spain was rent by feuding Christian kings and petty Moorish states, when war was continuous and peace a madman's dream, the Cid—also called El Campeador, the Champion—was the Perfect Knight Exemplar, who never lost a battle.

While Hernan Cortes was everywhere revered for sacking New Spain and slaying my ancestors by the millions with a ragtag band of barely five hundred men, even El Hernando paled before El Cid. The Champion was no mere man, but a mortal god.

The dwarf dropped from the barrel, and the rogue called

Mateo leaped atop it. Whirling his cape with almost preternatural aplomb, he addressed the crowd.

"There is none among you whose veins do not burn with the blood of Spain, whose hearts do not thunder like barbary steeds, when told how the Cid—betrayed by enemies at every turn—was banished forever from hearth and Crown."

A murmur of assent arose from the audience even though many were of mixed blood. I was less entranced than most. I too knew the poem—and his entire history—by heart. His name was actually Rodrigo Díaz de Vivar. *Mio Cid* was a Spanish-Arabic derivation of "My Lord," in honor of his noble birth and accomplishments. He was banished from court because of jealousy: He defeated a Moorish army without the king's authorization and then invaded Moorish Toledo. Neither his august family nor the king's niece, his wife, could save him.

"The poema de mio Cid begins with the champion's exile, exiting the shattered gates of his castle in compliance with the king's orders. Sixty men follow him."

Mateo performed the poem in the declamatory style, depicting betrayal and exile in starkly powerful cadences:

He turns to see the ruined hold, the tears fall thick and fast,
The empty chests, the broken gates, all open to the blast,
Without raiment are the wardrobes, reft of mantle and of vair,
The empty hollow of the hall of tapestry is bare.
No feather in the falconry, no hawk to come to hand,
A noble beggar must the Cid renounce his father's land.

Mateo paused as the dwarf and the actors around the barrel fanned out, their hats held out for contributions from the crowd. Mateo noisily cleared his throat. "It's parched and needs to be wetted if I am to persevere."

When enough money had flowed into the hats to buy whatever would wet the actor's voice, he continued, describing how the flight of a Raven was an ominous sign that they were exiles. His life was in a wreck from the lies and deceit of others, but someday he would have his revenge.

Mateo was handed a large goblet of wine. He took a long drink, tilting back his head as the sword swallower had done. He did not stop till he was sucking air, and when he upended the goblet it was empty.

"More wine for the 'Poema del Cid,' " the dwarf shouted, as he and the others of the troupe waded into the crowd with their hats.

Mateo drew his sword and gestured dramatically with it as he recited the poem.

The sixty lances of the Cid rode clattering through the town;
From casement and from turret top the townfolk look down.
Sad were their hearts and salt in their eyes as Rodrigo rode by;
"There goes a worthy vassal who has known bad mastery."
And many a roof that night had sheltered Rodrigo and his band
But for the dread in Burgos of the king's heavy hand.
The missive broad with kingly seals had run throughout the town;
"Who aid the Cid in banishment, his house shall be cast down."

I listened while the Cid and his small band slew Moors, sacked cities, and slaughtered Christian traitors. In a tumultuous battle with the count of Barcelona, who opposed him with Christian knights and a Moorish host, El Cid won the Kingdom of Valencia.

Mateo recounted how the Cid spurred his mighty war

horse, Babieca, against the dreaded Moorish horde of King Bucar:

The good blade shears the Moor in twain, down to the saddlebow;
So perish the Algerian lord—may every Moor die so!

The Cid had won the great sword Colada in battle with the Moors and then, in the battle against King Bucar, he added a second great sword, Tizon.

While listening to the poet master's impassioned tones, I chanced to study a balcony overlooking the plaza. A group of notables, doñas and caballeros, were on the balcony of the building next to where Mateo was giving his performance. An old woman in black was among them, staring down.

My blood ran cold.

I felt what King Bucar must have felt when the sharp blade of Colada sliced him down the middle.

I melted back into the crowd, risking only a shy, over-the-shoulder glance. Her eyes were locked on Mateo as he recounted the end of the poem.

So in Navarre and Aragon his daughters both did reign,
And princes of his blood today sit on the thrones of Spain.
Greater and greater grew his name in honor and in worth;
Until at last at Pentecost he passed away from earth.
Upon him be the grace of Christ, Whom all of us adore.
Such is the story, gentles, of the Cid Campeador.

Darkness was falling. I gave up my search for the fray. Fleeing the plaza, planning to return to the House of the Poor, I did not think the old woman had spotted me in the crowd. From the balcony I was just one more straw hat in a sea of such hats, but her mere presence in the plaza felt like a garrote strangling me.

What if I was being followed? Glancing over my shoulder, I veered from the hospice, sticking to the side streets. Hiding under cover of night, I was angry and frightened. What had I done to this doña? In my brief years on Veracruz's cruel streets I had suffered many adversities, but a gachupin dowager's blood vengeance was not one of them.

My only hope was Fray Antonio. Although criollo born, he was of pure Spanish blood. Compared to léperos such as myself, he was a king.

Life in the House of the Poor had moments of excitement. One never knew what to expect from street people. Three weeks before the archbishop's arrival, I arrived home after dark and heard laughter from inside. There I found Fray Antonio with a prostitute and her pimp lover. The woman lay on the table. Her left leg was black and swollen. They were plying her with pulque in hopes that she might pass out.

"She cut her foot weeks ago and the poison has spread," Fray Antonio said. "If I don't cut it off, she will die."

The woman did not have the money for the local surgeon barber who normally performed bleedings and medical amputations when he wasn't cutting hair. Fray Antonio, however, was not without medical skill. The street people preferred the skills and medicaments of our indio healers but did allow that Fray Antonio's powers surpassed those of most Spanish doctors. In any event Fray Antonio was now her last best hope.

The woman was drunk, snoring, flat on her back, and they were about to amputate her leg. The fray had a saw, an iron blade, and a pot of boiling oil heating on the coals. After they sawed off the leg, he would cauterize many of the veins with a hot blade. The raw stump he would char with boiling oil.

The fray tied her arms and legs, torso and neck to the table. He placed a thick wood stick between her teeth, and tied it tight behind her head. All the while her lover trembled convulsively, his face green as a jalapeño.

When the fray began to saw, the puta's screams rang through the night like screams of the damned. Blood detonated, and the man fled the hospice in terror.

"I can't blame him," the fray said.

Then he turned and looked at me. His hands were shaking, his face sweating. I was ready to give up, too, but he threw back a cup of pulque, then poured one for me.

"Cristóbal, you have to help or the woman will die."

He only called me by my proper name when he needed something urgent.

"The saw has to be steady, the cut even."

He gave me two small pieces of wood. "Hold these straight. I will pass the saw through them as I cut."

I had assisted in medical procedures before, but I had never seen a limb cut off. I held the two pieces of wood just above the knee, and the saw ripped through the woman's flesh. Her blood covered us both. When the fray hit her femur, it sounded as if he was tearing through a log. She passed out in shock, and at last her wailing ceased. When the leg was amputated, the fray removed the severed limb and dropped it on the floor at my feet. The fray quickly tightened the tourniquet and began to cauterize the severed veins with the red-hot knife.

After searing the stump with seething oil, he covered the convulsively unconscious woman with a blanket, saying to me, "Clean up."

He staggered out the door, no doubt to dull his mind with more pulque. I stared at the ashen-faced, comatose woman—and at the bloody piece of leg. What was I supposed to do with it?

FIFTEEN

At the House of the Poor I crept across the main room without lighting a candle. Rather than sleep in the big room, I went into the fray's enclosed corner and lay down on his bed. I lay there for over an hour, unable to sleep, when I heard men entering the house. No voices. They were trying to be quiet, but the straw gave them away.

Neither Fray Antonio nor our rope-sandaled street people had come in, men wearing *boots* had entered. I heard the jingle of spurs. A third man had entered, a wearer of spurs. That did not inevitably mean the man was a gachupin. Indio, mestizo, and africano vaqueros wore spurs as well, but they favored working rowels of honed iron. These were the silver spurs of a caballero.

The old woman had sent a gachupin and two helpers for me.

¡Así es! So be it.

The fray's rabbit hole was almost filled with blankets. I quickly removed enough to make room for me and slipped in, pulling the trapdoor and its rug over my head. The trapdoor would not completely close, but unless one was looking for it, it was unlikely they would spot it.

Through a crack in the opening, I saw someone enter with a lit torch. A Spaniard, about forty years old. From his clothes, it was obvious that he was a caballero, a gentleman and swordsman.

"No one here," he said. His voice was aristocratic, with that tone of cold command. Here was a man used to issuing orders.

"No sign of the boy or the priest in the main room, Don Ramon."

The second voice was that of an indio or mestizo vaquero, a horseman who drove cattle and sheep, perhaps even an overseer who commanded the hacienda's workers.

"They must all be at the festival, Don Ramon," he said.

"No way they can be found in that crowd," the don answered, "and anyway I have to get back to the reception. We will return in the morning."

A guest at the alcalde's reception itself. Truly a very big wearer of spurs.

I waited in the rabbit's hole until long after the crunch of boots had faded from the house. Climbing out of the hole, I crawled over to the blanket curtain and peeked into the darkness of the main room. Nothing moved. Still the fear that someone had stayed behind to watch kept me from going through the door. Instead I opened the wicker shutter that covered the window opening behind the fray's bed and climbed out into the alley. From the position of the moon, I estimated I had been in the rabbit hole for a good two hours and had been home from the festival for more than three.

I crept down the alley until I was two blocks from the House of the Poor, then positioned myself where I could watch the street leading to its front door. I was certain the fray would make his way home along this street.

I sat down with my back to a wall staring up the alley. Soon people came streaming back from the festival, many of them raucously inebriated.

Near dawn Fray Antonio and a rowdy group of neighbors staggered down the street. I rushed out and took the fray aside.

"Cristo, Cristo, what's the matter? Have you seen a ghost? You look like Montezuma upon learning that the Plumed Serpent, Quetzalcóatl, had claimed his throne."

"Fray, there is great trouble." I told him about the woman in black and the man named Don Ramon, who had searched the House of the Poor.

The fray crossed himself. "We are lost."

His panic fueled mine. "What are you talking about, Fray. Why do these people wish me harm?"

"Ramon is the devil himself." He grabbed my shoulders, and his voice shook. "You must flee the city."

"I—I can't leave. This is the only place I know."

"You must leave now, this moment."

Fray Antonio pulled me into the darkness of the narrow alley. "I knew they would come someday. I knew that the secret could not stay buried forever, but I did not think you would be found this quickly."

I was young and scared and ready to cry. "What have I done?"

"That does not matter. All that counts now is flight. You must leave the city by the Jalapa road. A steady stream of pack trains is hauling goods from the treasure fleet to the fair. There will be horsemen as well. You will not be noticed among the other travelers."

I was horrified. Go to Jalapa by myself? It was several days' journey. "What will I do in Jalapa?"

"Wait for me. I will come. Many people from the city go there for the fair. I will take Fray Juan with me. You stay near the fair until I arrive."

"But, Fray, I don't—"

"Listen to me!" He grabbed my shoulders again, his fingernails dug into them. "There is no other path. If they find you, they will kill you."

"Why—"

"I can't give you answers. If anything is to save you, it might be your very ignorance. From this moment on, do not speak Spanish. Speak only Náhuatl. They are looking for a mestizo. Never admit that you are one. You are indio. Give yourself an indio name, not a Spanish one."

"Fray—"

"Go—now! *Vayas con Dios.* And let God be your protector because no man will lift a hand to help a mestizo."

SIXTEEN

I LEFT THE city before dawn, walking quickly, sticking to the shadows. There were already a few travelers on the road, mule and donkey trains loaded with goods from the ships. I had not been far down the Jalapa road in years and what lay ahead for me was the unknown. While I was capable of taking care of myself on the streets of Veracruz, that was the only life I now knew. My confusion and dismay was aggravated by fear of the unknown and unfamiliar.

The Jalapa road trailed southwest out of the city, then cut across the sand dunes, swamps, and inlets before it slowly rose up the side of the great mountain range. Once the hot sands and swamps were passed, the trail ascended into the mountains. The heat of the tierra caliente slowly cooled.

Jalapa was a village high enough for travelers to escape the miasma that rose up from the swamps and annually killed one-fifth of Veracruz. Still the village's chief function was as a resting place on the road from Veracruz to the City of Mexico—except, of course, when the treasure fleet's fair was held.

I did not find carriages and wagons traveling all the way to Jalapa, though some would journey part of the way. The mountain roads would not accommodate them. People traveled by horse, mule, or Shank's mare. Or, in the case of the very wealthy, by litter-covered chairs suspended on two long poles. In the city a litter was commonly carried by servants, but over the mountains the poles were harnessed to mules.

At the time of the fair, long columns of the pack animals, piled high with goods, made the journey. Leaving Veracruz,

I took a position behind a mule train in the hopes of being thought of as one of the mule tenders. The arriero, the Spanish muleteer in charge of the pack train, rode a mule at the head of a train of twenty mules. Four indios were spread out along the line of the animals. The indio at the rear glared at me. Indios did not like mestizos. We were a living reminder of the Spaniards, who routinely defiled their women. Their hatred of these gachupin rapists they masked with feigned stupidity and heavy-lidded, empty-eyed stares.

I followed the pack train out of Veracruz, and all through the morning, the air heated up. By noon the dunes were a scorching inferno. In fact, a stone cliff, cutting through the sands, bore a hand-carved inscription, *EL DIABLO TE ESPERA*, the devil awaits you. I didn't know whether the message was meant for all travelers or if it was a special warning to me.

I left the House of the Poor without my straw hat, and now I walked with my head hanging down, the sun burning a hole in my brain, sick with dread. I had crossed the dunes before with Fray Antonio when we'd visited a village church on a nearby hacienda. As we crossed the burning dunes and walked through the foul stench of the swamps, having no finely scented nosegays, we tied rags across our faces to keep out the vómito fever. Fray Antonio told me tales of the "people of the rubber," who were even more ancient and more powerful than my Aztec ancestors.

"There is a legend," he said, "that the people of the rubber were giants who were created by the mating of a woman and a jaguar. You can tell from the statues they left behind, heads taller than a grown man, that they were a mighty race. They built a mysterious civilization called Tamoanchán, the Land of the Mist. Precious Feather Flower, Xochiquetzal, an Aztec goddess of love, resided there."

Fray Antonio did not believe in giants created by the union of a woman and a jungle cat, but he told the story with flair, waving his hands in dramatic emphasis.

"They are called 'people of the rubber,' because they constructed hard rubber balls from the sap of trees in that area. They organized teams and played each other in walled arenas the size of jousting fields. The object was for each team to knock the ball into the area behind the other team without using their hands. They could only propel it with hips, knees, and feet. The ball was so hard that it could kill if it struck a person on the head."

"Was anyone killed playing the game?" I asked.

"Every time. The losing team members were sacrificed to the gods at the end of the game."

He told me no one knew where the rubber people had gone. "My bishop said that they were vanquished by God because they were heathen sinners. But when I asked why God did not destroy all other heathen sinners worldwide, he became angry at me."

Yes, my trip to the hacienda with the fray had been a happy one. On this journey fear and melancholy were my staunchest companions.

SEVENTEEN

AT MIDDAY THE mule train stopped near a pulqueria to rest the animals and cook a noon meal. Other mules trains and travelers were already there.

I still had the two reales that the rogue poet had given me and some cocoa beans. The beans were a traditional form of money among the indios and were still used by them as currency. In fact, they had disdained the first Spanish coins, finding it difficult to place a value on something they couldn't eat or plant. Even though copper and silver coins were now in common use, the cocoa bean was still prized by the indios. Chocolate, a drink made from the beans, was the drink of kings.

Fermented pulque, the drink of the gods, was also highly

valued. Cheaper and more plentiful than chocolate, Fray Antonio believed it was the indio's salvation, because it dulled their senses and made their lives more bearable.

The pulqueria consisted of two thatched, mud-walled huts with two indio women cooking over an open fire. They served pulque from large, earthen jars. I had ten cocoa beans, enough to put a Veracruz whore on her back for as many minutes, and after much haggling I purchased a huge tortilla packed with pork stew and peppers for six beans. I told the woman she harvested the violento peppers in a volcano's molten heart.

I could have gotten a cup of pulque for the other four beans but also knew I could later have all I wanted for free.

I lay in the shade of a tree and ate the tortilla. I'd been up all night, but still I could not rest. Fray Antonio's frightened face haunted me. I was quickly on my feet and back on the Jalapa road.

In another hour the road wound around a sugar plantation. The endless expanses of sugarcane were not indigenous to New Spain but had been planted along the coasts by the Spanish. The cutting and refining of the cane was impossibly brutal, indisputably dangerous—all of it performed under temazcalli sweat hut conditions. Fantastic fortunes were born out of that cane, true, but no one worked those fields voluntarily. In the end the sugar trade came down to one irreducible determinant, slavery. The indios failed miserably as slaves, their death rate in the plantations and the mines so catastrophic that Crown and Church both feared their extinction. Only the africano bore up against such lethal servitude.

Two africanos accompanied the Cortes expedition of 1519—Juan Cortes and Juan Garrido—but turning jungles into sugar and mountains into silver required armies of slaves. Those glittering jewels, gilt carriages, fine silks, and splendid palaces that the gachupins so greedily lusted after, to say nothing of the Crown's foreign wars, were paid for in slave blood.

When the Spanish king inherited the Portugese throne in

1580, chained africanos, whipped and starved by Portugese slavers, arrived in New Spain by the thousands. They were brought to work the sugarcane haciendas after the Spanish discovered they could "grow" gold in the form of sweet sugar.

Yes, the sweet tooth of Europe made slavery inescapable.

As I walked past the cane, I saw men, women, and children, all africanos, working the fields. Up the road I neared *el real de negros,* the fenced-off slave quarters, a cluster of round huts with conical roofs made of straw.

I knew from Beatriz that slaves, even in their quarters, had almost no privacy. They lived communally, sharing the huts regardless of sex or marital status, surrounded by pigs and chickens. The owners wanted them to breed but discouraged family dwellings, fearing that privacy encouraged talk of rebellion, especially when slaves were sold to other hacendados. Consequently, few married even though the owners sought additional stock. Healthy slaves brought a price at auction.

On the sugar plantations slaves worked interminable hours with almost no free time. During busy periods the mills ran twenty-four hours a day and slaves worked until they dropped, often napping near their job so that the overseer could kick them to their feet and back to their jobs.

The plantation owners considered black slaves incomparable beasts of burden. Africanos were not only bigger and stronger than indios, but they survived the suffocating heat, back-breaking labor and deadly fevers that annihilated indios by the millions.

"But our blacks are likewise victims of that myth that each of them can do the work of four Indians," Fray Antonio told me when we had walked along the docks a few days ago and watched slaves piling sugar bags. Like the mestizo mine slave, each of the sugar plantation slaves had been branded like cattle with a hot iron with the initials of their owner. Most of the brands were on the shoulder. When I saw a brand on the face, I knew the slave had tried to escape once and was being marked as someone to watch.

"As a result overseers drive them four times as hard as indios," the fray continued. "They often drive these wretches mad. Many take their own lives. Others forswear children, abort those they do conceive, or resort to infanticide, sparing their children lives of living hell. Some rebel, which only leads to brutal reprisals by their owners.

"Many turn deeply melancholic, refusing water or sustenance, until they die. Others cut their throats. Those who endure keep the institution running."

Still Spaniards feared africano rebellion like the wrath of God.

I understood their fear. While indio docility had increased after the Mixton War, africano rebellion had never subsided.

Diego Columbus, the son of "the Great Discoverer," had endured the very first slave uprising when africanos on one of his Caribbean plantations rose up and slaughtered Spaniards. Each subsequent decade saw an africano uprising followed by savage reprisals from the wearers of spurs. And as the africano population grew disproportionate to that of the pure-blood españols, that fear spread.

Slaves were forbidden to assemble in numbers larger than three—public or private, day or night. The penalty was two hundred lashes each.

Fear kept me watching my back trail. The road was no longer able to handle a carriage but ay! who knows? Perhaps that predatory dowager would overtake me with eagle wings and raptor claws.

The ancient Greeks believed three goddesses determined our destiny. Not just the length of our days and years, but the breadth and depth of our misery. Those three shadowy women, whose hands and wheels spun the skein of fate, had allotted me more than an ordinary share of struggle, strife, and, yes, pleasure.

Again I posed as one of the drivers, attached myself to the rear of a mule train, and tried to avoid the dung. The sun slipped behind the mountains, casting shadows on the trail. Soon I would have to find a safe place to sleep. While the Spanish kept the towns and villages on a tight rein, on the roads and trails, banditry reigned. The worst of these bandits were my fellow mestizos.

Bad blood, you say? That was the general view, that mixed blood produced weak character, and it was easy to see why they thought that. We mestizos swarmed city streets like lice and robbed the gachupin blind on the rural roads.

The fray dismissed skin color as the key to character, believing that opportunity was the determining factor. However, he was a pure-blood Spaniard, while I was of mixed provenance and could not blithely dismiss a fact I'd heard since boyhood. The question of my corrupt blood had haunted me my whole life long.

Pack trains and travelers would soon be gathering by the roadside to cook their meals. Darkness was falling, and afterward wild animals—and wilder men—would have their way. The fact that I was a fellow mestizo would win me nothing from men who robbed, raped, and killed without scruple. Furthermore, mestizos were not the only highwaymen. Runaway africano slave bands, called maroons, terrorized travelers. The maroons were feared even more than mestizo road agents because they were not only bigger and stronger but had suffered more abuse than half-castes. They also had less to lose.

A dozen or so travelers had stopped near a maguey field to prepare their dinner fires and lay their bedding out. I stopped too. I had nothing to eat, nothing to unpack, and no tools for fire making. There was a good stream, however, so I would at least have water. After a long, thirsty drink, I lay down to rest under a dense conifer that might offer protection against a night rain, which seemed likely.

A pleasant river flowed lazily through a maguey field. It was no doubt part of some great hacienda, perhaps even one of the great holdings in which everything from sugar to cattle was raised.

As I walked along the river, I picked up a stick and swung it like a cane as boys do. I was about to turn back when I heard the giggle of girls. I froze and listened. It came again, laughing and splashing. Creeping half bent over, I made my way to the source of the sound. Through bushes at the edge of the river, I saw two young women splashing and swimming. They tossed a coconut between them as if it was a ball. One girl had the tawny color of a mulatta, the other the glistening ebony of a pure africana. They were in water about to their breast line and as they leaped, their entire upper bodies came out of the water, filling my young eyes.

They babbled back and forth in a language I did not understand but took to be one of the many africano tongues heard on the streets. After a moment the mulatta swam away, disappearing from my sight. I kept my eyes on the ebony girl. She had her back to me and seemed to be dealing with her hair, turning in the water so I would catch sight of her bare breasts and then turning back again.

A twig snapped behind me, and I turned as the mulatta rushed me and gave me a shove. Stumbling backward, I fell into the river. I sloshed in the water until I got my feet and came up spitting out river to the laughter of the two girls. The mulatta dove in and swam to where her friend was. They kept themselves up to their necks in the water.

I grinned at them. "Buenos dias."

"Buenos dias," the mulatta said.

"I am on my way to Jalapa. I am a merchant," I lied.

The mulatta returned my grin. "You look more like a boy than a merchant."

The girls were probably both about my own age, but they seemed older. The mulatta said words to the pure africana girl, and I took it that she was interpreting what we had said. If she was a field worker, she may know little or no Spanish.

"My father is a rich merchant. I work with his goods."

The mulatta laughed and shook her head. "You are dressed as a peón."

"I am in disguise so banditos do not try to rob me."

I found both women sensually appealing. The mulatta girl

was not the stuff of grande mistresses—she was not the Thoroughbred race horse demanded by rich caballeros, but was young and spirited. The darker-skinned girl was more attractive. She glistened like a precious black stone, statuesque and perfectly proportioned, her breasts young melons that were just becoming ripe.

Even though I had touched—and been touched—by Snake Flower and the alcalde's wife, I had never lain with a woman. Looking at the two girls, I wondered what it would be like to make love with them.

They must have read my thoughts. They looked at each other and broke out laughing.

My grin got wider and I felt my cheeks warm with embarrassment.

After more chatter in the strange tongue, the mulatta asked me, "Have you made love to many women?"

I shrugged and tried to look modest. "Many women seek my favors."

After more translation and laughter from the girls, the mulatta asked, "Have you made love to women whose roots go back to Africa?"

"No," I admitted, "but I would like to."

"Before you make love to an africana, you should know what gives us pleasure."

The ebony girl pulled herself onto a large rock and sat facing me. She kept an arm across her breasts and a hand covering the hair at the crevice between her legs.

"Love is upendo in our language," the mulatta said. "But fulfillment comes not just from the mind, but from mwili, the body." She waved her hand up and down at the other girl's nakedness. "The body is bustani, a garden; a garden of pleasure and delight. Each person, man and woman, have tools to work the garden." She pointed at the girl's lips. "They have mdomos, lips, and ulimi, the tongue. These permit one to taste the fruit of the garden."

The mulatta girl leaned over and brushed the lips of the other girl.

I had never seen two girls so physically intimate before. It stunned me.

"There are melons, tikiti, in the garden." She pushed aside the arm hiding the young melon breasts. "You can taste the whole melon," she kissed a breast, running her lips around its full curvature, "or you can taste just the namna ya tunda, the strawberries." She gently ran her tongue around the girl's nipples.

My virile part swelled and began throbbing. I stood perfectly still in the water, entranced by the performance the girl was putting on.

She caressed the girl's stomach with her hand, running her hand slowly down from the breast to where her legs split.

"This bush covers the marufuku bustani, the forbidden garden." She took the girl's dark hand away and placed her own hand on the pubis. "There is an ekundu eupe kipepeo in the garden." The ebony girl slowly spread her legs, exposing her vulva. "A pink butterfly."

The mulatta touched the pink area with her finger. "There is a secret mushroom, a kiyoga, that grows in the garden. When it is pressed, it helps to water the garden."

I could not see what her finger was doing, but the ebony girl reacted by writhing with pleasure. Surely it must be the same as the little pene I'd discovered on the alcalde's wife.

"There is a flower, ua, in the garden. It has an opening in the stem so that the honey, asali, can be obtained by the bee. The bee, nyuki, is the man. He is attracted to the nectar of the flower and desires to taste the honey."

She stopped and gave me a seductive smile. "Are you attracted to the flower?"

I felt a terrible urgency in my virile parts. My mouth was dry. I muttered yes as if I had a mouthful of cotton.

The mulatta girl looked sad for a moment. "But you see, a girl cannot let the bee taste the honey anytime he likes because the bee has a sting. Do you know what happens when the bee stings a woman?"

I shook my head numbly.

"She gets pregnant!"

The two girls splashed out of the water. I started for them but slipped on the muddy bottom and came up with another mouthful of water. By the time I got onto dry land, they had disappeared into the bushes.

Wet and chagrined, I made my way back to where the travelers camped. Women were a great mystery to me. While I could easily read men, I realized that I had not even begun the first chapter on the Book of Women.

EIGHTEEN

AS DUSK FELL I could not resist exploring. I disappeared into the maguey field out of sight of the travelers and any indio defending the field against thieves.

Maguey were enormous plants with leaves wider than my legs and taller than a grown man. To my boyish imagination, the plants were the gigantic crowns of Aztec gods. Some plants, like the maize that gave us life, had power stored within them. The maguey was a warrior of the plant world, not only because its tall, slender leaves rose like a bunch of spears, but because of the power of its nectar and the uses of its flesh.

Like a woman who could cook, sew, raise children, yet still pleasure a man, maguey provided the indio with cloth for rough clothes, blankets, sandals, and bags; needles from its spines; fuel and thatch from its dried leaves. But, ah, like that woman who provided the necessities of life, the maguey was also full of an intoxicating spirit.

At the fleshy heart of the plant, protected by the great spears, was agua miel, honey water. But this "honey" was craved not for its sweetness; to the contrary, the whitish, cloudy liquid was sour. In its natural state from the plant, unfermented, it tasted like swamp water to me. After fermentation, it acquired the taste of sour goat's milk. But *¡cho!* This milk captured your mind faster than Spanish vino, sending you reeling amid gods with a smile on your face.

The honey water we call pulque was well known to my Aztec ancestors. They called it *octli,* the drink of the gods.

The maguey grows slowly and flowers once after as long as ten years. When it flowers, a tall stem shoots up like a sword from the center. The indios who cultivate the plants know when the flower will appear. When the time is ripe, a man climbs into the plant among the thorny leaves to open the heart, creating a bowl to catch the raw juice.

Each plant can produce a dozen or more tall servings of pulque a day and can be nursed for several months. The *tlachiqueros* collect the raw juice several times a day, drawing it off with a long gourd, then putting it into pigskin bladders. Sometimes the juice is sucked into the mouth with a straw and then spit into the skins, which are emptied into hides or wood tubs to ferment several days.

Pure fermented pulque is called *pulque blanco.* My Aztec ancestors increased its bite with tree bark called *cuapatle. Pulque amarillo* is yellow pulque, created by adding brown sugar. Because this gave much power to the drink, our good King Filipe forbade putting cuapatle and sugar into pulque but the indios continue to do it.

My indio ancestors worshipped pulque because Quetzalcóatl, the Plumed Serpent, drank it. As with the tales of the Greeks and their tragedies, pulque was also born out of love lost. The Plumed Serpent fell in love with Mayahuel, a beautiful maid who was the granddaughter of one of the *Tzitzimime,* the star demons, and convinced her to run away with him. When they got to earth, Quetzalcóatl and Mayahuel entwined, transforming themselves into a single tree.

The Tzitzimime followed them. These demonicos were the most fearsome of all the beings who haunt the night, malevolent female spirits transformed into stars who kept baleful watch on the human world below them. Because they bore a grudge against the living, they brought down calamidads and miserías—sickness, droughts, and famines. They tried to steal the sun during solar eclipses, causing the Aztecs to sacrifice many fairskinned people to fortify the sun with fresh blood.

The Tzitzimime grandmother of Mayahuel recognized her as part of the tree. She ripped Mayahuel from the tree and fed her to the other demons. Quetzalcóatl, in sorrow, buried what was left of his beautiful Mayahuel and from her sprang the maguey plant that produces the intoxicating pulque. This gift brings joy to humans as Quetzalcóatl's and Mayahuel's love brought joy to each other.

If the Aztec gods drank pulque, in my mind it was the reason for their defeat by the Spanish God. The fray drank it when there was no vino to quench his thirst; he claims that unfermented it had the taste of rancid meat, but I still say it is as foul as the vomitó swamps.

The indios thrived upon it and even fed it to their children. The Aztecs were not tolerant of drunkenness but some indulgence was shown toward old people on the grounds that their blood was running cold. Besides the old, women in the days following childbirth and the sick were given the tonic to strengthen them. But adults found publicly drunk would have their hair cut off as punishment the first time, their houses demolished the second, and be put to death on the third. Dios mio! If the alcalde did this in Veracruz, there would be no indios or half-castes left in a week.

The fray found much sadness in the state of indio drunkenness. "They drink to forget their miseries," he often said. "And they drink differently from whites. My español hermanos think about the *amount* they consume. More the pity, indios drink for the *occasion* without considering the amount. They drink on Sundays, festival days, weddings, and other special occasions. And when they drink, they pour it down their throats until their minds have been captured by the heavenly waters and their bodies are pickled. It is said one indio could drink for a dozen Spaniards." He shook his finger at me. "This is no exaggeration, Bastardo. My brothers of the cloth say that drink is the wellspring of all indio vices. But why was this vice not widespread until we washed upon their shores?"

The fray threw his hands up in aggravation as he often did when religious doctrine conflicted with what he saw with his own eyes. "Sunday has become a day of public drunkenness for the indios. Why? Because it is their way of protesting the religion we have forced upon them. Did you know that a holy cross near the marketplace had to be removed because dogs and drunken indos urinated upon it?"

If drinking is so much a problem with the indios, one wonders why the Spanish masters did so much to profit upon it. The great maguey fields are owned by the hacendados. And it is said that Spanish wines cause the indios to lose their heads faster than pulque. These potent wines were brought to the villages by traveling Spanish traders, who find not only that the sale of the wine lines their pockets, but that indios can be persuaded to give up their land and gold when there is enough wine between their ears.

To the indio, pulque takes one to the threshold of the sacred; and along with corn, maguey is their staff of life. Perhaps there is something mystically akin to the Aztecs about the plant; it dies after flowering, which is what happened to the short-lived Aztec Empire.

My stomach growled irritably. It had been hours since I had eaten the tortilla with the volcanic peppers. The only nourishment available, without spending my treasure of two reales and a few cocoa beans, was pulque. My hunger would drive me to consume it raw . . . if I could not steal a fermented brew.

I knew from my trip with the fray to a village church on a maguey hacienda that indios who tended the fields often had a cache of the juice fermenting out of sight of the hacendado's overseers. I looked over the field and asked myself where I would have hid the contraband myself. Not in the large, bare, dirt areas between the plants, certainly. It would be hidden in the bushes, far enough in to be out of sight, but not so far that the bushes overgrew it.

Ay, with the eye of a well-practiced thief, I surveyed the lay of the land and began walking along what I considered to be the best candidates for a cache. It took me longer than I thought, a half an hour to find a clay pot of fermented pulque, but I attributed the excessive time not to any error in my plan of search but the ignorance of the indio who did not hide it as cleverly as I would have.

Soon after the pulque went down my throat, a warmth kindled in my belly that spread throughout my body. It was going to be cool tonight sleeping on the ground with only my manta for a blanket, so I drank a little more of the drink of the gods to help keep me warm.

Returning to camp, I went back to my spot under the conifer and sat with my back to the trunk. My head was spinning a bit, but my spirits were lifted. I thanked the Plumed Serpent for lightening my burdens.

A sugarcane hacendado had camped nearby with three of his vaqueros and an africano slave. A large fire shared with some other español travelers had been built. From the light of it I could see that the slave, a young, husky male, had been badly beaten. One side of his face was swollen, his right eye shut, and his ragged clothes were bloody and slashed by a whip. I had seen many africanos, indios, and half-castes beaten by their masters in a like manner. Violence and terror were how the few always subjugate the many.

I half-closed my eyes and listened as the slave owner, whose sugarcane hacienda lay east of Veracruz, talked to another spur wearer about the slave.

"An escapado," he said. "It took us three days to run him down. Now I'm going to take him back and flog him again in front of my other slaves. When I'm finished with him, no one will ever run away again."

"The countryside's full of runaways, maroons, who rob, rape, and murder every Spaniard they can get their hands on," the other man said.

As they talked, I realized I had seen the plantation owner before. He came to church occasionally in Veracruz. I knew him to be a brutal, stupid person, thick-chested, thick-necked, a hairy, hombre malo who liked to castrate male slaves, rape slave women, and flog everybody in sight. His reputation, even among his own people, was that of evil incarnate. I had had occasion to go to church—which I did whenever the fray berated me enough—when once this slave owner had appeared with a male slave, a boy about my own age, whom he had beaten savagely for some infraction. Qué diablo! He'd brought the boy to church naked, the boy's mouth gaping open, his pene bouncing, dragging him from a rope fastened to a dog collar.

When I told the fray, he said that the man would burn in hell. "Hate boils inside some people and comes to the surface by cruelty to others. This man hates people with black skin. He owns slaves to abuse them. He organized a Santa Hermandad, a militia of local swords to support the king's law, but in truth they are nothing more than men who hunt runaway slaves like others hunt deer."

I thought about the fray's words as I listened to the man loudly boast about all of the runaways he had tracked down and the africano women he'd sexually assaulted. What would it feel like to be a madman's slave, a man who could beat you at will and rape your wife on a whim? *Who could kill you when he got the urge?*

"This one claims to be a prince in his own country," the slave owner laughed. He picked up a rock and threw it, hitting the tied-up slave with it. "Eat that for dinner, Prince Yanga." He roared again with laughter.

"He's a tough one," the other Spaniard said.

"Not after I geld him."

No por Dios! *Castración!*

I glanced at the slave, and he stared blankly at me. He already knew his fate. But as I continued to look at him and his brown eyes met mine, I saw both intelligence and pain. Not just the pain of his bruises, but a much deeper hurt. His eyes told me that he was no animal but a man. *That he, too, was human!*

Not able to stand the sadness in his eyes, I looked away.

Slaves were castrated on the theory that it made them more malleable—just as bulls are gelded to soften their meat and make them more docile.

Another merchant, overhearing the conversation, recognized my look of revulsion.

"Slaves are property," the merchant said, glaring at me. "They are to be used in the fields or in bed, whatever suits the owners. They are like the indios, *gente sin razon.*" Without reason. Childlike. "But at least the africanos and indios have pure-blood. Mestizos, such as yourself, are the lowest."

I got up and found another tree to rest under, certain I would open my mouth and receive a beating if I stayed.

"His spurs are stuck up his own ass," Fray Antonio sometimes said privately of certain "wearers of the spurs." The fray's criollo resentment of those born on the Iberian Peninsula came out frequently. But as a mestizo, I knew that criollos were as harsh on slaves and half-castes as the other Spaniards. Because criollos were kept out of high office in the Church and government by the spur wearers, they tended, like the fray, to characterize anyone who wielded power ruthlessly or arbitrarily as spur wearers, forgetting about their own sharp spurs.

NINETEEN

I FELL INTO a deep sleep and awoke in the dark of the night. A ghostly moon navigated a sea of dark clouds, emerging for only a moment at a time. When she was obscured, the heavens were black as pitch. The night was filled with nocturnal birdcalls, the rustle of bushes as something bigger moved in the forest, and the noises made by the travelers—someone snoring, a mule snorting about something in its sleep.

A thought came to me, one born of madness. Perhaps it was the pulque, the drink that even intoxicated gods, warping my mind until I did things that any lépero would find insane.

When I was certain that no one was stirring in the area, I slipped my knife from its holder and arose from the ground. Crouching low, I went into the maguey field, away from the area where people were camped. If anyone saw me, they would think I was relieving myself or was stealing pulque.

Circling around, I came to the area where the slave Yanga was tied with his back to a tree. Down on my hands and knees, I crawled as quietly as a snake slithering up to the tree. Yanga twisted his head to watch my approach. I paused and put a hand to my mouth to signal silence.

Coughing erupted from the slave master, and I froze. I could not discern him in the darkness, but I believed he rolled over. A moment later he snored, and I moved forward.

The cough had put my heart in my throat. The pulque was wearing off, and I was starting to realize I was in danger. If caught, I would face the same flogging post and gelding knife.

My fear was overwhelming, and I longed to crawl back. But in my mind's eye I still saw Yanga's eyes, intelligent eyes, not those of a dumb animal but of a man who knew love and pain and knowledge and desire. Amigas, amigos, I wish I had had the courage of a lion, the strength of a tiger. But I was a boy of little consequence. It was time to return to my bed. Tomorrow, I would take to the road with the hounds of hell at my back. There was neither glory nor profit in helping a slave escape. Not even the fray would expect me to risk my own manhood to save the cojones of another.

Ah, the spur wearers are right. Mestizos are without reason, and without guidance, I succumbed to my baser instincts. I crawled to the tree and cut Yanga's ropes.

He didn't speak, but his eyes signaled his thanks.

Just as I reached my sleeping spot, I heard running and Yanga rushed by me into the bushes.

A moment later the slave master, stirred by the noise, shouted the alarm and ran into the same bushes. The man's sword was raised high and glinted when the moon peeked out of the clouds. Loud confusion erupted around me as other men shouted and drew their swords, not knowing what had caused the disturbance, assuming a bandit attack.

I did not know if I should run or remain at the tree where I had been sleeping. If I ran, the men in the camp surely would know that I had cut the slave's bonds. My panic demanded that I flee, but my survival instincts told me to remain still. When the slave master looked at the ropes, he would see that Yanga had not broken them, that someone had cut them for him.

From the bushes where the slave and his master had disappeared came the sounds of a struggle and cries of pain. No! What had I done? Cut Yanga free so the scoundrel could chop off his head? More cries, a whimpering sob, came from the bushes. It was too dark to see anything but the movement around me of dark figures until torches were lit. Brands blazing, the men went into the brush, following the sounds.

I followed close behind, determined to appear as part of the curious crowd rather than the culprit. As I got closer I could see men examining someone prone on the ground who was in severe pain.

Someone said, "Holy Jesu, he's been castrated!"

My heart sank. I had cut Yanga loose just to have his manhood cut off. I pushed my way into the crowd of men and stared down at the person on the ground.

It was the slave master, not Yanga. He was sobbing.

The crotch of his pants was bloody.

TWENTY

I HID IN the bushes and waited for the travelers to go on their way. When the last mule headed toward Jalapa, I walked over to a nearby indio hut and purchased a tortilla as my breakfast. The india woman—no doubt the wife of the maguey worker whose pulque I'd purloined—was young, little older than myself. Her harsh life, however—working the fields, preparing food, and dropping babies every year or two—had aged her prematurely. By age twenty-five she would be wizened beyond her years. That she had seen so little of youth weighed on me as she cooked the tortilla. She offered it to me with sad, dark eyes and lonely smile, refusing the cocoa bean I offered in trade.

The tortilla—without even beans or peppers or a little hint of carne—was my entire desayuno. From a nearby stream I washed it down, forgoing another trip to the pulque cache.

I then considered my plight. The fray would come for me; of that I was certain. I would wait at this spot, halfway to Jalapa, for the fray to catch up. It was a natural place for travelers to stop. I could also stay hidden and watch for the man named Ramon if he came looking for me. There was pulque to steal, and if I could no longer go without solid food, I could use one of my reales to buy enough tortillas and carne to last several days.

Although I was certain that the fray would *try* to come . . . I also feared that he might be in trouble because of me and that I might now be on my own. How would I eat? Where would I sleep? These thoughts dogged me as I lay in the bushes and watched the trail from Veracruz.

My own plight was not that different from *Vida del Pi-*

caro Guzman de Alfarache, the life and adventures of the picaro, Guzman de Alfarache. The book—also known as as *The Spanish Rogue*—was one of the titles the fray tried, and failed, to hide from me, a work whose popularity surpassed even that of Don Quixote whose misadventures delighted readers throughout Spain and New Spain alike.

If Cervantes sounded the death knell for the romantic knight, Guzman de Alfrache replaced that sentimentalized hero with a figure more in keeping with our cynical times: the picaro. As all know, the picaro is an amoral rascal who would rather live by his wits and his sword than the sweat of his brow.

Like the poet-swordsman-philandering rogue Mateo, Guzman's picaro was a casteless wanderer. An adventurer of neither peasant stock nor of aristocratic blood, he roamed the world at will, mingling with people of all classes and professions, barely escaping punishment for his lying, conniving, stealing, and womanizing.

Guzman's saga began in Seville, the crowning glory of Spain's greatest cities. All of the New World's treasure is shipped to Seville; and from that city, everything sent to the New World flows. A few years ago a sailor from the treasure fleet confided in me that the streets of Seville were paved in gold and only the most beautiful women in the world were allowed to enter its city walls.

At fourteen years of age our picaro's father, a profligate scoundel, squanders the family fortune and dies bankrupt. Our destitute hero must then set out to seek his own livelihood—following his father's ignoble example, it seems. Bad blood begets black blood, as the priests like to say.

Cheated by reprobate innkeepers, waylaid by highwaymen, he learns life's lessons while still a youth. But despite his inexperience, he is a born picaro, a rogue at heart. He is at home everywhere, at every level of society, whether begging a copper off of a hog farmer or supping with a count in a castle.

As he ambles from Spain to Italy, he loses his good clothes and money, joins a band of beggars, becomes a ne'er-do-well and gambler. He attempts honest labor as a kitchen scullion, but his baser instincts prevail even at that lowly station. When a silver goblet turns up missing—which our light-fingered friend has of course appropriated—the cook's wife is out of her head with fear, knowing that their master will beat her and her husband severely or even send them to jail. But the resourceful Guzman comes to her rescue. Cleaning and burnishing the goblet till it looks like new, he sells it back to her as a new one. Of course, these profits are not long for his purse. He quickly wastes his ill-gotten gain on bad women and worse cards.

On and on it goes. There is no end to this rogue's depravities. Gambling, begging, thieving his way to Italy. As adept at losing money as he is at stealing it, fortune *and* misfortune are his inevitable lot.

After many hair's-breadth escapes, he ends up in Rome, capital of the Catholic world. He joins a band of beggars who have turned begging into high art, even to the point of organizing a beggars' guild, complete with written laws and bylaws.

Would it not shock the alcalde of Veracruz if were I to present him with written rules for a lépero code of conduct? Of course he would declare me mad. Among other things, Veracruz street denizens would not be able to read the rules.

Guzman soon learns that while he has seen himself as a master of beggars, the Romans, who had once conquered the world, have much to teach him, including the different techniques for approaching men and women.

"Men," he is instructed by a mentor beggar, "are not in the least affected by the laments of most beggars. They will be much more likely to put their hands in their pockets when you implore their assistance boldly, for God's sake. As for women," he continued, "as some pay their devotions to Our Lady of the Rosary, it is by one of these exhortations that we wheedle them. It is frequently a good effect also to pray that they may be preserved from all mortal sin, from false witnesses, the power of traitors, and from slanderous tongues; such wishes as these, pronounced in energetic terms and in an impressive tone of voice, will almost always make their purses fly open to assist you."

He is taught to display ravenous hunger when eating before his patrons, which houses to approach for alms, and how to cadge convincingly. He is instructed never to wear anything new in public; to wrap a dishcloth over his head in winter instead of wearing a hat; to walk with crutches or one leg tied behind; to accept alms only in a cap, never in a purse or pocket; to hire and display small children in rags; a man is to carry one child in his arm and another by hand; a woman is to always have a child at her breast. He is taught to fake leprosy, even to the extent of erupting phony skin ulcers, causing his legs to appear swollen, to dislocate his arms, to render his face pale as death. He is taught these trade secrets and written rules only after swearing an oath of silence.

Guzman, however, tires of the mendicant life and once again joins the aristocracy. Through trickery, of course. Passing himself off as a young nobleman, he seduces their most desirable women, in the end fleeing with jealous lovers dogging his trail.

He applies to the priesthood when pious guilt overwhelms him. At the moment of his investiture, however, he runs off with a scarlet woman, who inevitably elopes with another, absconding with every peso of Guzman's ill-gotten savings.

Reconnecting with his mother, rather than dissuading him from his evil path, she joins forces with him. Captured and sentenced to the galleys, he escapes the oar locks when he informs on his fellow slaves, exposing their planned mutiny. He is rewarded with his freedom.

At the end of his memoir, he thus regales us: "Friendly reader, I have given you an account of the principal adventures of my life. What followed after the king was graciously pleased to grant me my liberty, you may expect to hear, should I live long enough to tell you."

Ah, Guzman, would I, too, live long enough to tell *all* of my adventures.

I am grateful for all he has taught me, permitting me to become the best beggar on the streets of Veracruz. And I can only hope that my problems in life will be solved by the way he overcame adversity with guile and guts.

Guzman was, in truth, a mentor, but in the end he taught me more than begging tricks; he showed me a way of life. As I lay in the shade—reflecting on Guzman, waiting for the fray, and wondering what I would do if he failed to show—I found the answer to my own life's journey in the picaresque saga. Like Guzman—expelled from a comfortable life—I would do what I had to do to survive. If it meant lying, stealing, conniving, womanizing . . . so be it.

Looking back on my lépero life, I was ashamed. I now believed my destiny demanded greater things that cadging alms. Among other things, I read Latin, Greek, and was conversant in waterfront tongues.

I realized at that moment that by exposing me to Guzman, God Himself had pointed out the path of my life.

TWENTY-ONE

NEAR MIDDAY I spotted the fray on the road. With him was Fray Juan, the two sharing a mule. I ran out from my place of hiding and shouted my joy but quickly restraining myself when Fray Antonio gave me a warning look. Obviously he had not revealed my troubles to his friend, and I can imagine why. Fray Antonio, while not a man of sword or fire, had the heart of a lion, a sometimes frightened lion, but one driven by his passion to confront injustice. Fray Juan was more ethereal, a sweet and gentle soul whose heart was faint and tender.

"Cristo, I told Fray Juan that you were so eager to accompany your friends to their village near the road to Jalapa that you asked to meet us along the way. Did your friends reach home all right?"

The fray was asking me if I had had any problems. "Yes, but we were unable to connect with the one named Ramon. He didn't show up."

The fray looked relieved.

I followed behind the mule of the two Spaniards, in accordance with my station.

Jalapa is north of Veracruz and inland. It was on the way to the City of Mexico, and several days' hard walk from Veracruz. I had covered less than half the distance when I met up with the two frays. It would take longer to cover the second part of the journey. After crossing the sands of the tierra caliente and starting up the mountain range, the path became steep and narrow. During the rainy season new streams sprang up along the trail, and the rivers jumped their banks.

There was little talk along the route. I had many questions for the fray, but they went unspoken. From the dark tightness of his features, I knew that all had not gone well in Veracruz. Even though Fray Juan had not been told of my troubles, he was quickly aware that something was wrong.

"Antonio says he has trouble with his stomach," Fray Juan said. "What do you think, Cristóbal, could it be that he is having a problem with a woman instead?"

He was only joking, but the fray's problem *was* a woman, though not in the way Fray Juan suggested.

Every hour up the foothills and mountains brought cooler air. The trip was almost pleasant until we reached a pulqueria. Like the one I had stopped at, it was conducted from an indio hut. A large clay pot of pulque and a stone oven cooking tortillas sat in the shade, flanked by logs, under shade trees. It might have been a pleasant respite if the frays, seated on a log, had not struck up a conversation with priest inquisitors.

There were three of them, Dominicans, two simple frays

dressed in black and a prior wearing the green cross of the Holy Office of the Inquisition. I was immediately taken for an indio or mestizo servant to the frays and as such was of no more interest to them than our mule. Their own six servants sat a distance.

The Dominicans greeted Fray Juan with friendly words but pointedly ignored Fray Antonio. I had seen this attitude toward him exhibited by other priests. Fray Antonio had fallen from grace with the Church. The fact that he shined in the eyes of God and the poor meant nothing to clerics who wore expensive hose, leather shoes, and silk shirts under their robes.

The inquisitors immediately began to torment Fray Antonio and Fray Juan, one for breaking the rules of the Church, the other for associating with the rule breaker.

"Fray Juan, tell us what news there is from Veracruz. We heard along the road that the archbishop has arrived."

"That is true," Juan said. "I'm sure the festival, celebrating his safe journey, still goes on."

"And what of sinners? Our good amigo of the Holy Office, Fray Osorio, is said to have his eye on a blasphemer in Veracruz who will test his faith in the fire of the stake."

Fray Juan noticeably flinched at the mention of the dreaded Veracruz Inquisitor. Fray Antonio kept his eyes averted from the Inquisitors, but his face reddened from anger at the mention of Osorio.

"What business brings you on the road?" Fray Juan asked, changing the subject. "Are you going to greet the archbishop and escort him to the City of Mexico?"

"No, God's call for us to hunt down blasphemers has prevented us from celebrating the archbishop's arrival," the prior said. His voice dropped down to a confidential level. "We are on our way to Tuxtla to investigate an accusation that some converted Portuguese Jews, marranos, are secretly practicing the black art of their devilish religion."

"Is the evidence forthcoming?" Fray Juan asked.

"The most serious since the Carvajales were sent howling into hell." The inquisitor's eyes narrowed when he spoke of unmasking Jews and dispatching them to el diablo. A marrano was a Jew who claimed to have converted to Christianity but continued to practice the forbidden religion in secret.

"New Spain seethes with Jews," the prior said, his voice strong with emotion. "They are the scourge of the land, false converts who pose as God-fearing Christians but who betray us. They conceal their foul deeds and hatred of us, but once the mask is torn off, their vile acts we invariably expose."

"They worship the devil and money," one fray muttered.

"They kidnap and commit fiendish acts on Christian children," the fellow fray remarked.

I felt an instant animosity toward the three brothers who took oaths of love and poverty but conducted themselves as murderous tyrants. I had heard of the Holy Office of the Inquisition and knew Fray Antonio's fear of the bestial inquisitor. Often I had heard the fray utter blasphemies about their overzealous work. Once, while in his cups, he told me that inquisitors were the hounds of the Church and that some of them were rabid.

I could see that both Fray Juan and Fray Antonio were intimidated by the inquisitors. At that time I didn't know how these Church dogs operated, whether they would attempt to strike down the fray or were merely bullies. I remained crouched nearby with my hand on the knife I carried under my shirt.

The prior gestured for Fray Juan to lean closer to hear a confidence but spoke loud enough for me to hear.

"Fray Osorio sent us a communication that while examining a woman under torture, he uncovered a sign of the devil that is of great interest to the Holy Office."

"What is it?" Fray Juan asked.

"A witch's teat!"

The young fray gasped, and Fray Antonio looked to see if I was listening. Seeing that I was, Fray Antonio promptly announced that we must continue our journey.

TWENTY-TWO

AS SOON AS we were out of sight of the pulqueria, I stepped up beside the mule carrying the two frays. I wanted to learn more of what I'd heard, so I boldly asked my question.

I knew what a woman's teat was. Many india and africana women worked naked to the waist in the fields or suckled their babies with their bare breasts on the street. But I had never seen a witch and didn't know what their teats looked like.

"What does a witch's teat look like?" I asked.

The young fray, Juan, made the sign of the cross and mumbled a prayer as Fray Antonio scowled at me. "Your curiosity will someday bring you trouble," he predicted.

"I fear it's already here," I mumbled, but quickly shut my mouth when the fray glared at me.

"There is much that you should know," Fray Antonio said, "to protect yourself from those who threaten you along life's path. There is evil in this world, and good men must fight it. Sadly, the institution the Church created to fight evil commits unspeakable atrocities in the name of our Lord."

"Antonio, you must not—" Fray Juan started.

"Quiet. I do not bow to ignorance as you do. The matter was mentioned before the boy, and he should know the workings of the Inquisition if he is going to survive in this world." His tone implied that my survival was not preordained.

He rode for a moment, gathering his thoughts. "You will discover, my young friend, that women's private parts are constructed differently from ours."

I almost laughed. Little india girls routinely ran naked on the streets. I would have to be blind not to have noticed that they lacked a pene. What would the fray say if I told him of my introduction to the alcalde's wife?

Once again the fray hesitated, weighing his words.

"When the Holy Office takes a person to their dungeons, they are stripped naked, and their bodies are minutely examined by inquisitors for signs of the devil."

"What are the signs of the devil?" I asked.

"The devil knows his own," Fray Juan says, "and places his mark on them. It may be in the form of a mold, a scar, the way wrinkles are formed on the skin—"

Fray Antonio scoffed and the younger fray gave him a pained look.

"You must not jeer at the Inquisition," Juan said. "Your blasphemous attitude is well known and someday they will remind you of that."

"I answer each day to God," Fray Antonio said. "Where Satan's signs reside, I know not. As for this beast, Orsorio," the fray's voice faltered with emotion as he spoke the name, "in examining naked women, he delights in peering between their legs and tormenting an appendage that is, in loving hands, their source of joy."

"Uno poco pene?" I timorously asked.

"No, not like that possessed of men. Something different. This inquisitor, in his ignorance, for he had never looked closely between a woman's legs before nor bedded with one, had heard of such a mushroom from other ignorant frays. These fools believed that what was found between the woman's legs was a teat, conceived, then suckled by Satan."

I gasped, remembering the little mushroom between the legs of the alcalde's wife that I had pressed with my tongue. "What—what if a man touches this teat? Will he die?"

"He becomes possessed by the devil!" Fray Juan exclaimed.

¡Ay de mí!

"Absurdo!" Fray Antonio cursed. "That is nonsense. All

women have the pleasure bump between their legs."

"No!" Juan said.

"Even our Virgin Mother had it."

Fray Juan quickly muttered a prayer and crossed himself.

"What I'm saying, Chico Bastardo, is that what Osorio found and reported as Satan's sign, a witch's teat, is God-given, something every woman possesses."

"It must have been terrible for the poor woman," I said.

"It was worse than terrible," Fray Antonio said. "When she did not confess, Osorio tortured her to death."

"Por Dios!" I said. "What was his punishment?"

"Punishment? There is none. God knows His own, they say. The woman is officially absolved, and she goes to heaven."

We walked in silence.

"Antonio," Fray Juan finally said, shaking his head, "your heretical opinions will one day bring the Inquisition down on the boy as well as yourself."

Fray Antonio shrugged. "All right, explain it to him in your own way."

Fray Juan said, "When our glorious monarchs, Ferdinand and Isabella, assumed the United Crown of Spain and captured the last Moorish strongholds on the peninsula, the land was heavily populated by Jews and Infidels. They threatened the foundation of our society. Our Most Catholic Monarchs created the Holy Office of the Inquisition to counter their demonic influence. Ultimately, it was decreed that Jews had to convert to the Christian faith or leave the country. At almost the same time that Cristóbal Colon—the great discoverer of the New World—was sailing from Spain to discover the New World, tens of thousands of Jews were forced out of the country and into the Islamic lands of North Africa."

"Torquemada, our Inquisitor General, introduced torture and confiscation of the victim's wealth as the means of conversion," Fray Antonio pointed out. "In other words, tens of thousands of Jews lost everything to Church and Crown, whether they converted or not."

Fray Juan shot Antonio a dark look and continued. "Muhammad's followers were also forced to convert or leave Spain."

"Violating the terms of their surrender," Fray Antonio said. "In any event, their property was likewise confiscated."

"From this time on," Juan persisted, "a new threat arose, the problem of false conversos—Jews who falsely subscribed to Christian beliefs, the ones we call *marranos,* and Moors who swear false allegiance to Christ, people we call *moriscos.*"

I recognized the word as meaning "little Moors."

"To stop these false conversos from spreading their evil ideas and Satanic rites, the the Church ordered the Holy Office to find the wrongdoers—"

"—through torture—"

"—and punish them."

"Burning them at the stake in front of the entire city," Fray Antonio said.

"Cristo, my son," Fray Juan said with weary patience, "auto-da-fé means 'act of faith,' and that is what it is. For those who repent and confess their guilt, the punishment is almost painless."

Fray Antonio snorted. "The victims are tied to the stake and wood piled around them. If they repent, they are garroted before they are burned."

I, too, had never understood the auto-da-fé. I had read the Gospels many times in the hospice and never saw suggestions that we burn people alive.

"The Inquisition, which is run entirely by men who have never slept with a woman, or who at least are forbidden to, is conducting a holy war against women," Fray Antonio said. He waved away the objections of Juan. "They accomplish this through what they call controlling devil worship among witches. Dominican monks have made passionate sermons in villages and towns, describing the demonic practices of witches, sowing a belief in the black arts. Because of these sermons, ignorant people see Satan's hand in everything. They report their neighbors, sometimes their own family members, to the Inquisition for the most trivial reasons.

"Once a woman is arrested, the inquisitors take as their Bible a book called *The Hammer of Witches,* which professes to teach one to recognize witches. They take the women to their dungeons, strip and search them for Satanic signs, even to the point of cutting off their hair.

"The inquisitors begin with simple questions from *The Hammer of Witches.* However, there are no correct answers, so the prisoners can never talk their way out of an accusation, even with the truth. A woman might be asked, "Do you believe in witches?" If she says yes, she has knowledge of witchcraft and is thus a witch herself. And if she says no, she is lying for the devil and is also tortured.

"A young girl's virginity they attack mercilessly. If she's chaste, they claim Satan protected his slut. If she isn't intact . . . she's been bedding Beelzebub.

"Young or old, they are tortured hard, even if they admit fornicating with Satan. Then they must describe how the fiend enters them, where he touches them, and where *they* touch their Dark Master, how it *feels.*"

When the Inquistion runs out of Jews, Moors, and witches, the fray told me, it censors books and tyrannizes people sexually—accusing people of polygamy, casting spells, blasphemy, sodomy.

"One woman, who smiled at the mere mention of the Holy Virgin, was denounced," Fray Antonio complained.

"They do God's work," Fray Juan said—but without much conviction.

"They are devils," Fray Antonio said to me. "Their obsession with Jews is unrelenting. Torquemada himself was from a family of conversos, and when King Felipe II made war on the pope, the pope reminded him that Spanish kings were also descendants of conversos."

Poor Fray Juan—he made the sign of the cross and prayed loudly to God for forgiveness.

The three of us traveled in silence, each closeted with

our own thoughts. I contemplated what it would be like being burned alive or for a woman to be sexually assaulted by demented monks. Both horrors were unimaginable.

Fray Antonio started another story of the Inquisition.

"There was a young priest who, despite the fact that he was criollo born, was headed for a brilliant career in the Church. Having an inquisitive mind, however, he asked too many controversial questions and read too many controversial authors—particularly the great Carranza, the Archbishop of Toledo, who believed that the common people should be given Spanish Bibles so that they might read and understand the word of God themselves rather than having a priest recite verses in Latin, a language they did not understand.

"The priest fought for Carranza's position even after the archbishop had been arrested by the Holy Office. Like Carranza, the young priest found the Inquisition at his door. Locked in a cell, he was left for days without food or water. Then the questioning and accusations began. Then the torture."

His face racked by emotion, he said, "The young priest was lucky. He came out of it with a few pains, some warnings, and banishment to a village church on a remote hacienda. But he never forgot. And he never *forgave*."

As I listened to the story, I realized that the young priest was Fray Antonio. At that time, still in the innocent blush of youth, I was surprised that the fray had felt the hand of the Inquisition. But as I sit in a dank dungeon, a man who has had his flesh shredded by the blazing pinchers and maggots thrust in the wounds, I know that any person of conviction and compassion is their likely prey.

TWENTY-THREE

WHEN WE ARRIVED at the Jalapa fair, the sun was at its zenith. Sprawled over a wide area, the merchandise of two worlds was vertiginously stacked under open sky or sail-cloth canopies. Magicians, acrobats, and charlatans vied for loose change alongside book stalls touting religious tomes and honor plays; tool sellers bragged about the strength of their hammers and saws; merchants peddling seed and farm tools debated prices with the majordomos of haciendas; clothiers purveying rare raiments of exquisite silk and fine lace, claimed that kings and queens throughout Europe accoutred themselves in identical finery. Religious vendors everywhere flogged crosses, paintings, statues, effigies, and icons of every description.

Stalls filled with honey and sugar treats competed with charms guaranteed to capture a person's love and "crucifixes blessed by Santa Lucy, on my word, a holy shield against infections of the eyes . . ." "Blessed by San Anthony of Padua, will vanquish diabolic possession and brain fevers . . ."

I felt like I had stumbled into the world of Scheherazade and the Arabian Nights.

Of course, the Inquisition was there in force. The *familiars,* its lay police, roamed the shops, perusing their list of libros proibidos and checking the authenticity of religious items. There were also the king's black-clad publicans, computing and collecting taxes for the Crown. Nor could I fail to note how much money changed hands beneath the table between booksellers and the familiars, the tax collectors and merchants; the inevitable una mordida that so ubiquitously underpinned New Spain's economy was universally condoned as an indispensable cost of doing business. With some truth. The tax collector purchased his office from the king. He was compensated not by merit, bonus, fee, or salary, but by legally sanctioned extortion. The same was true for most public offices. The jailer, who purchased his job, rented prisoners to the deadly sugar mills, the obrajas sweat shops, and the northern mines . . . dividing the dinero with the constable who arrested the prisoner and the judge who pronounced their guilt. Mordida, "the bite," a payment to a public official for him to do his duty—or ignore it—was the way of the world in New Spain.

"Face it," the fray told me while in his cups, "our public offices are sold at extortionate prices to raise money for our wars in Europe."

But for the moment I was entranced. I even forgot the old matron and the wicked Ramon. I roamed the fair, my eyes wide-open, my mouth agape. I'd seen Veracruz packed with people celebrating festivals and the arrival of the treasure fleet. I'd witnessed the fervid excitement of the archbishop's arrival, but the fair's affluence and ostentation was nonpareil. Even I, a veteran of everything Veracruz had to offer, who had seen so many bales and bundles trundled to and from the treasure fleet, was awed. It was different to see these uncrated items spread out individually—everything from gaudy silken garments to glittering swords, their jeweled handles and hafts sparkling in the sun—not hauled en masse out of a ship's bleak hold but invitingly displayed, waiting to be fondled, examined, closely inspected. Everything was so much more intimate here than on the waterfront docks: Spanish merchants haggling toe-to-toe and nose-to-nose with their customers; strolling pitchmen prating about their delicacies; acrobats doing back flips for tips; singers serenading passersby with impassioned ballads; indios scrutinizing the exotic goods and personages with the same wide-eyed wonder their ancestors had no doubt felt when they mistook Cortez and his horse-borne conquistors, riding into Tenochtitlan, for gargantuan gods.

Fray Antonio intercepted me to offer a word of caution. "I don't believe there is any threat here. Veracruz is consumed with the new archbishop's arrival, and Don Ramon and the widow should be busy for some time to come. Still we must be careful."

"I don't understand—"

"Good. Knowledge at this point can only get you killed. Ignorance is your sole ally." Then he left me stammering in confusion.

Heading for the book stalls, he began examining some newly arrived works of Plato and Virgil, while Father Juan was leafing through the romantic adventures of knights-errant and delectable damsels in search of God and Grail, some of these works banned, some not banned; but even those free of the censors, he dared not purchase and carry back.

Ordinarily, I, too, would have been at the booksellers' stalls, rifling through their tomes, but for the moment, at fifteen years of age, I was diverted by a strange gathering of magicians and sorcerers, proclaiming they could raise the dead, predict the future, and read the stars. Nearby a troupe of illusionists swallowed swords and devoured torches.

I was determined not to let fear ruin my fair. With the fray's coppers, I bought a flat, hard tortilla smeared with honey. Chewing on it, I strolled by the colorful booths and tables. Everything seemed to be for sale—from luscious putas to pulque fresh from the maguey's fleshy heart to rare wines that had survived both storm-tossed ocean voyage and jarring trek by pack train.

People flowed through the aisles like river currents. Merchants and mendicants, soldiers and sailors, whores and ladies, indios and mestizos, richly dressed españols, village headmen, caciques in colorful indio mantas, flamboyant africanas and mulattas.

Two española women stopped at a busy corner, shaking tambourines, flat musical instruments resembling drumheads but with jingling disks fitted around the rim. I recognized them as the picara dancers who had performed when that rogue, Mateo, had recited "El Cid." Their two male troupers dropped a barrel nearby and lifted the dwarf on top.

"Amigos, heed my call. Gather around and you will see and hear regal wonderments, oft performed for the crowned heads of Europe, the Infidel sultans of Arabia and Persia, and the heathen emperors of Asia.

"Remember a day in time when our proud land was overrun by the ravaging Moors. There were naught but a few small kingdoms where our lords held sway, and even these paid tribute to the Moors. That bitter tariff was not remitted in the gold dug from the earth but in the guise of gold-haired maidens, the fairest virgins in the land, whom each year the depraved Moorish king and his notables ruthlessly ravished."

With histrionic hands and wonder-wide eyes, the dwarf began his lurid tale.

"There was no Cid, no hero in our land, but, ah, there was a maiden who forswore the lewd lust of Moorish fiends. In alabaster garb, golden tresses trailing down her back, she burst into the council room where the Spanish king held court with his knights. Confronting them with their cowardly acts, she called them false men who sat on their swords while the flower of Spain's honor was desecrated and defiled."

The diminutive thespian eyed the intense men and outraged women now assembled.

"Do you know what this fair maid told them? She said to them that if they lacked the manhood to face the Moor, let women brandish Spanish steel and fight the Infidel in their stead."

Every man in the crowd—as well as youths such as I—raged at the shame of those knights. Spain's greatest treasure was the honor of her men—and the sanctity of her women. To give our women to our enemies as tribute? Ay! Better to rip out my tongue, gouge my eyes, cut off my cojones.

"Now, gather around all, as the dancers of La Nómadas sing for you 'The Maiden's Tribute.' "

While the crowd of men were primarily interested in the dancing women, and especially the flashes of thigh the women showed when they lifted their skirts, I saw that the dwarf kept a close eye out for the Inquisitors and other priests wandering around the fair, even as the two men circulated with a hat to collect money. Meanwhile the women dancers sang:

If the Moors must have tribute, make men your tribute money;
Send idle drones to tease them within their hives of honey;
For when 'tis paid with maidens, from every maid there springs
Some five or six strong soldiers to serve the Moorish king.
It is but little wisdom to keep our men at home;—

While the words of the song were innocent enough, the body language of the women, who occasionally paused in a whispered aside to describe what a Moor would do to a Spanish virgin, was enough to get them arrested.

They serve but to get señoritas, who when their time is come,
Must go, like all the others, the moor's bed to sleep in;—
In all the rest they're useless, and nowise worth the keeping.
'Tis we have manly courage within the breasts of women,
But you caballeros are all hare-hearted,
Thus spoke that fearless señorita—

The women dancing in front of me flung their skirts above their waists. They wore nothing beneath those swirling garments, and I gaped to glimpse that secret garden between their legs, which I'd so recently come to know. Of course, the men in the audience went wild and hurled their money into the hats.

What was it about Spanish women that drove Spanish men wild? Spanish men can see a naked india or africana woman and look through them as if they were never there or see them merely as receptacles for their lust. But one brief glance at a Spanish woman's ankle or a furtive glimpse of her delectable throatline, and these same men are beside themselves with rapture. And, of course, these two actresses displayed more than a little ankle.

"Pssss!" the dwarf hissed. "Cho!"

The dancers even drew the attention of the two priests. Pushing into the crowd, the women dropped their skirts and sang "The Song of the Galley," a tune about a woman waiting for her lover, a prisoner of the Moors, to return.

You mariners of Spain,
Bend strongly on your oars,
And bring my love again,
For he lies among the Moors!

You galleys fairly built
Like castles on the sea,
Oh, great will be your guilt,
If you bring him not to me.

The wind is blowing strong,
The breeze will aid your oars;
Oh, swiftly fly along—
For he lies among the Moors.

The sweet breeze of the sea
Cools every cheek but mine;
Hot is its breath to me,
As I graze upon the brine,

Lift up, lift up your sail,
And bend upon your oars;
Oh, lose not the fair gale,
For he lies among the Moors!

It is a narrow strait,
I see the blue hills over;
Your coming I'll await,
And thank you for my lover.

To San Maria I will pray,
While ye bend upon your oars;
'Twill be a sacred day,
If you bring him from the Moors.

No one reproached them for their lusty voices or whirling skirts, not even the two frays. Nor were these actors the same drab drudges in servant's livery disembarking from the treasure fleet. The traveling troupe had transformed itself. Gaudily attired, I realized now that their serving garb had been a disguise. The dockside inspectors diverted passengers of low character to Manila, almost certainly a death sentence, and actors were regarded as people of low, corrupting character. From time to time troupes had passed through Veracruz, and the fray had observed, "Not only does the king deny them entry here, in Spain when they die, the Church denies them entry into consecrated ground."

"They fear actors will corrupt the dead?" I asked, innocently.

"Actors, to the Church, are picaros by another name."

After my clandestine reading of *Guzman de Alfarache,* I knew what he meant. I also understood why I was drawn to these rogues. True, their lives were disreputable, but so was mine; but unlike me, they had fun, flair, and flamboyance. They never worked and weren't afraid. People applauded them enthusiastically and put money in their hats. I received for my bone-cracking contortions little more than kicks and derision. They looked forward to travel, adventure, and lascivious ladies. I would die in a gutter or a slave labor mine. They would die in featherbeds between the legs of a sensuous señorita with a jealous rival banging on the door. The most I could hope for when my end came was a belly full of pulque, a comfortable bridge to sleep under, and a clap-stinking puta to ease my pain.

But the picaros lived lives of high excitement, free as birds. Unlike the lépero, doomed to degradation by tainted blood, a picaro might pass as a duke—might become a duke! Picaros were not predetermined by blood. They were not simply *born* to their allotted fate; picaros were *made.* They did not gravitate to a structured life of perennial servitude. They did not die in the dark and the dust of silver mine cave-ins, lost, afraid, abandoned, alone. They relished their free will. They walked, talked, and addressed others, even their betters, with familiarity, a hopeful heart, irreverence, and most of all *no fear.* The picaro faced life with a free soul and a light step—even when he was stealing your purse or cutting your throat.

And picaras! Oh! I had never seen such women before! Their eyes were bold; their blood was hot. While there were women of every color and blood in New Spain, mestizas, indias, mulattas, africanas, and españolas who were as lovely to behold, none of these women showed any freedom in their actions, not even the flamboyant mulattas who were permitted to wrap themselves in garish garb of rainbow hues but would never think of changing their station and state, of challenging their class, their caste, the shackles of their sex.

All of these women may dress and adorn themselves up like scintillating flowers to please a man, but behind their manner and laugh, they know the man they flirt with is superior. But these picara women, who lifted their skirts, exposed their sex, and sang of women who mocked men and slaughtered Moors while their men cowered at home, these women were afraid of nothing. Not a man in that audience, unless his mind was reeling with vino, would have dared grab one of them. Nor would *they* have permitted it. They knew they were equal to these men—and more.

When women became more important to me than magicians and sword swallowers, the kind of woman who knew her own strength would be the one to draw me. Including the silken muchacha in Veracruz for whom I swirled my manta as a cape. Although she was still young, her eyes had bespoken the same fiery freedom as the dancers.

Often such women connoted danger, and—fool that I was—I knew even then I was drawn to them as to the edge of a smoking volcano, which could flare infernally at any time.

Ay! That was then and this is now. If the innocent fifteen year old knew then what this grown man with the quill in his hands knows today in prison, Dios mio, I could have lined my pockets with gold and my bed with women.

TWENTY-FOUR

When the women finished their respectful song and dance under the watchful eyes of the priests, the dwarf addressed the crowd again.

"For the special enjoyment of all, in the hour before darkness a special performance of a comedia will be performed."

A stir went through the crowd. A comedia was a play—a comedy, tragedy, or adventure story. I had never seen a play, and my heart jumped into my throat. I wondered if it was the same play they had announced in Veracruz.

"If you want to see a pirate punished, a good man's honor restored, come to the comedia." He waved his hand grandly in the direction of the man named Mateo, who had slipped through the crowd to stand beside the dwarf's barrel. "This comedia comes from the hand of that great master of the stage whose works have been performed in Madrid, Seville, and before royalty, Mateo Rosas de Oquendo."

Mateo took off his hat and made one of his grand sweeping bows.

"The admission to this masterpiece," the dwarf said, "a mere reale."

Ha! I had two reales in my pocket, obtained from the autor of the comedia itself. I could feast like a king and see the play. God was good. All is well in my life, I thought, momentarily forgetting that there was a snake in every paradise.

My wandering took me into the section where indio sorcerers and magicians were selling their magic, reveling in the excitement as I rubbed shoulders with priests and nuns, whores and dons, vaqueros and indios, spurred ones and lowly half-castes, rugged soldados and perfumed dandies.

I paused and watched a soothsayer predicting the future for people—an evil-looking, long-haired indio in a sinfully scarlet manta. Ugly slashes scarred both cheeks, and his face was streaked with jagged lightning flashes of flame yellow and blood crimson. He sat crosslegged on a blanket, shaking a dozen small bone fragments in a human skull, then throwing them across an indio blanket as if he were casting lots. From their pattern, he divined the course of a life or the answer to a prayer. I had seen tomorrow-tellers read their bones before on the streets of Veracruz. An indio now asked the magician to foretell his father's fate after a serious accident.

"On the way here, my father slipped off the mountain path and fell. He cannot walk and refuses to eat. He simply lies on his back in great pain."

The soothsayer betrayed no concern or care, questioning him dispassionately only about his father's Aztec birth name and sign.

The man handed him a coin. The fortune teller rattled the bones in the skull and threw them on a dirty blanket.

The pieces formed an obliquely oblong pattern.

"The shape of a grave," he told the indio. "Your father will soon pass beyond this life's travail."

I could not help but snort my skepticism. The old faker turned and gave me a menacing stare. Had I been an indio boy, I would have withered under his evil eye; but I was a lépero with a classical education—no, a picaro, which was how I now thought of myself. This new vision of myself as a gentleman-rogue gave my curiosity a freer rein. I should have walked away without tempting fate—and the grave's dark powers, which he clearly understood—but now I wanted to know more. So like Odysseus confronting the Cyclops, I taunted him.

"The course of a man's life is not determined by the throwing of old bones," I said haughtily. "That is magic for old women and fools."

Ay! The follies of youth. Fate's thread is woven for us all. That day so long ago at the fair, bones were cast for me and, unbeknownst to any but the gods, the paths of my life, my Aztec *tonal,* were laid out in the Tonalamatl, The Book of Fate. The friends and enemies I made that day I would meet throughout my life.

The old man's face twisted into a feral scowl, then erupted in the savage snarl of a jungle cat. He shook a handful of bones at my face and muttered some incantation in an indio dialect I did not know.

I quietly departed.

Why tempt fate?

"Mestizo. Your heart will be ripped out on the sacrificial block when the jaguars rise."

The words, barely whispered at my back, were spoken in Náhuatl. I swung around to see who made this threat. An indio was moving through the crowd, and I was certain he was the culprit.

I hurried away, not happy about my rash remarks and the omen they had provoked. It was not just the comment. It was the hateful tone in which it had been invoked. At the time I saw no connection between jaguars and sacrificial blocks, although I knew that the great jungle cats were sacred to the indios.

At any other time I would have laughed off the indio's comment as just another insult leveled at my mixed blood, but this was the second threat to my life in a short space. I was not frightened by the indio's threat but angered.

I wandered into the crowd, aggravated at both the insult and my hasty retreat in the face of what the fray would have derided as "superstitious foolishness." A picaro would have had a ready retort for a shaman's magical threats. Except the final threat had not come from the shaman but from a disembodied voice I still could not identify.

I headed for the bookstalls, searching for Fray Antonio and Fray Juan. Fray Antonio would be there, browsing the books but not buying any. Any dinero that came his way he used to purchase food for the poor. I could, of course, filch a fine libro for him, but he, of course, would not approve.

I spotted Fray Juan first, talking to a man near one of the bookstalls. As I approached, the man glanced around furtively, then led the fray to the area in back of the stalls.

I immediately broke into a run when I recognized the man—the picaro, Mateo. There was no telling what kind of trouble he had in mind for the fray. Look at the trouble he'd gotten me into already, my run-in with the alcalde's wife and her witch's teat. The dwarf who hawked comedias and ballads for him might boast that Mateo had written and performed before the crowned heads of Europe, but I was immune to such braggadocio. I knew silken devils when I met them. Naive Fray Juan, however, believed the best about everyone and would find himself Mateo's unlawful prey.

Behind the stalls Mateo was slipping him a book from beneath his cloak. When I approached them, Mateo reached for his dagger.

"The boy is a brother's servant," Fray Juan explained to Mateo.

Fray Antonio had described me the same way to the inquisitors to deflect their curiosity.

Mateo did not seem to recognize me, which was understandable. Léperos were objects, not people, and by definition unmemorable.

I hung back, subservient, but kept within earshot.

"This book," Mateo said, continuing his pitch, "is one of the classics of chivalric romance, a sweeping epic, towering above *Amadis of Gaul* and *Palmerin de Oliva.* See for yourself—the lavish cover of Moroccan leather, the elegant Gothic script, the exquisite vellum, all for a pittance: a minuscule . . . ten pesos."

Ten pesos! A pope's ransom. A month's wages for most men and for what? A chivalric romance? A stupid tale of knights and ladies, of dragons slain, kingdoms conquered, and damsals won. The very works that drove Quixote to joust with windmills.

Fray Juan examined it fondly. "It doesn't look like vellum—"

"You have my personal assurance as a lord of the realm that this paper was milled right on the Nile's venerable banks and shipped across the Mediterranean for the personal perusal of our saintly monarch in Madrid. Only by the most fortunate and auspicious of circumstances was this work of art diverted into my capable hands."

"The people of the Nile make papyrus not vellum," I said.

The picaro threw me a nasty look, but quickly returned to Fray Juan. The holy brother was now reading aloud the tome's flowery title.

> "Chronicle of the very remarkable Three Knights Tablante of Barcelona who defeated Ten Thousand Howling Moors and Five Frightful Monsters and set the rightful King upon the Throne of Constantinople and claimed a Treasure larger than that held by any King of Christendom."

I roared with derision. "The title is a jest and so is the book. Cervantes's *Don Quixote* exposed these chivalry romances for what they are. Who would read such gibberish? Only an imbecile. Who would write idiosy? Only a lunatic."

The fray, embarrassed, returned the book to Mateo and hurried away.

I had started after the fray when I heard Mateo quietly say, "Boy."

As I turned, his hand caught my throat with the speed of a striking snake. He jerked me toward him, his dagger already beneath my manta, probing my cojones.

"I should geld you like a steer, you dirty, half-caste beggar."

The point of the dagger cut into the soft flesh of my crotch, and a trickle of blood ran down my leg. He had the eyes of a pain-crazed animal insane with feral suffering. I was too scared to even beg.

He shoved me to the ground. "I will not rip your throat out because I don't want your whore's blood splattering my hands." His sword was out, and he stood over me, its blade flashing over my throat. I expected my head to drop and roll, but the sword tip froze stock-still against my Adam's apple.

"You spoke of that hijodeputa who wrote the saga of Quixote. If you mention his name one more time—the swine who plundered the stories, ideas, the truth, the very life of another, *my life*—I will not simply separate your head from your shoulders, I will strip your sorry hide an inch at a time and dress your carcass down with jalapeno and salt." The madman vanished, and I stared wall-eyed at the sky.

Ay! What had I done? True, I had spoiled his sale, but it was Cervantes's name that had driven Mateo muy loco ciego, almost costing me my cojones and my head. It suddenly occurred to me that perhaps the madman might be the author of the ridiculous novel.

Dios mio! Perhaps the fray can tell me about this church in India where one is punished for a past life's sins. I must have flung a thousand souls into hell's eternal furnace to have deserved this woe.

The fray, of course, claims I bring this hell of woe on myself by continually speaking out. He blames himself for my loose tongue, and there is some truth in that. He introduced me to the works of that indefatigable skeptic, Socrates. He challenged *everything* and passed this loathsome habit onto me like a disease.

Fortunately this lamp of truth seldom illuminates my own unrighteous life. One cannot tread the lépero path with truth as a guiding light; some truths no one can bear.

I dusted myself off and went back to the fair with less enthusiasm than I had had before.

TWENTY-FIVE

THEN I MET the Healer.

The first time I saw him he stood on the remains of an ancient Aztec monument, one of many scattered around the area. The stone slab elevated him several feet above the assembled onlookers, allowing him to perform his magic and work the crowds.

He was not old. He transcended such mundane concepts. He was ancient of days, a being of eons and millennia, not weeks or years.

I did not know what time or place or people spawned him, but to me he was *everything* Aztec or, more properly, Mexica, since the word Aztec was more Spanish than indio. One could not tell by his speech. Like a jungle parrot, he addressed questioners in their own tongue. I soon suspected he could speak the speech of birds and snakes, of rocks and trees, of mountains and stars.

The soothsayer I had encountered, the peruser of bones,

was, in contrast, a charlatan. The Healer abjured conjury. Written in the wrinkles of that old man's face and in the shadows of his veiled eyes were the secrets of the grave.

To me he was a god, not Greek or Roman replete with schemes and intrigues, but a darker deity, gentle in his wisdom but murderous in his scorn.

His cloak—reaching from his shoulders to his ankles—was fashioned of flamboyant feathers, all the colors of a glittering rainbow. His snakeskin belt was festooned with turquoise. The rope laces of his leather sandals coiled up his calves to his knees. He looked as I imagined Montezuma had, only more ageless and wise and weary and venerable.

He was "treating" a woman who was suffering from headaches. A mangy yellow dog, looking more coyote than hound, sprawled nearby on a frayed red blanket. The dog's head rested on crossed paws, his skeptical eyes taking in every movement, large or small, as if checking for enemies. I would soon learn much more about that strange animal and his even stranger companion.

The woman told the Healer that evil spirits had penetrated her brain and were screaming for her soul. In earlier times indio priests would have treated her with healing herbs, and even Fray Antonio acknowledged the power of some of these sacred remedies. The botanical garden of the Emperor Montezuma, he told me, had over two thousand different medicinal herbs. Much of this knowledge was lost to the world because the priests following the conquest incinerated its library of picture-writing scrolls collected by the Aztec doctors.

"They feared what they did not understand and burned what they feared," the fray once lamented.

Of course, failing herbal remedies, the ancient priests would have drilled into her skull and summoned the demon to leave.

The Healer was, of course, a *tititl,* a native doctor skilled in the use of herbs and chants; but unlike the Spanish herbalists called *curanderos,* a *tititl* used herbs, potions, *and* chants and magic ceremonies to heal. But that was the smallest part of the Healer's medical art. He had his own methods. At the moment he was whispering secret incantations into the woman's ears, designed to draw out her evil spirits.

While I know that the course of an illness, anymore than a life, is not determined by dice throws, we are from time to time engaged by demons. I have never confessed this to the fray, but I have seen people discourse with the devil; and it is an article of indio truth that fiends can spirit themselves into the brain through ears, nose, eyes, and mouth.

As I watched the old medicine man mouthing his sacred incantations, his lips brushed her ears. Suddenly, his eyes bulging, hand at his mouth, he jerked back. A writhing snake, which he'd sucked from her ear, thrashed in his teeth. The woman screamed, convulsing in his arms.

"Ahhhh!!!" rose from the crowd.

I dismissed it as legerdemain. The Healer had slipped a snake up his sleeve, then secreted it in his mouth. How could I think otherwise? I was by training and predilection a truth-teller. I'd studied Socrates; his disciple, Plato; and in my heart of hearts, I detested the mendacity surrounding me at every turn. I worshipped at Truth's Altar. Part of me wanted to roar with skepticism and expose him as a fraud. He was an indio puro, without power or protection. Yet I remained silent. Why, I do not know.

Then, as if reading my mind, his eyes picked me out amid all those faces in the crowd.

"Come here, boy."

Everyone stared at me—*even the yellow dog.*

The next thing I knew, I was standing on the rock slab beside him.

"You do not believe I drew the snake from her head?"

I could have said nothing. Given the plethora of enemies I was rapidly accumulating, I didn't need anymore. Dissimulation was undoubtedly the better part of valor. Somehow I couldn't lie.

"You hid the snake in your mouth or hand," I said evenly. "It was a trick."

The Healer's hold over the crowd snapped, and they began to hiss.

Still he was not chagrined. "I see indio blood in your veins," the old sage said, shaking his head sadly, "but you favor your Spanish ancestry."

"I favor knowledge over ignorance," I said.

"The question is," the old man said smiling, "how much knowledge can a boy bear?"

Chanting quietly in Náhuatl, his hands passed over my eyes. Swaying, my face flushed fevishly, and my eyes teared. Breath whooshed out of me, and all my skepticism died.

I was especially taken by his eyes. Black, bottomless wells filled with world weariness and tacit understanding, they gripped me like a vise. Helpless in their gaze, they wrung everything from me, knew everything about me, my people, my past, my blood—before the conquistadors, before the Aztecs, before the Mayans, time immemorial, time out of mind.

Reaching for my crotch—as if he was about to grab my garrancha—he drew a long, black snake out of my pants, writhing and hissing and spitting. The crowd erupted into laughter.

TWENTY-SIX

AFTER THE CROWD dispersed, I sat with him. Still dizzy from his magic spell, I now felt humbled. Handing me a piece of locust cake, a bit of maize, and a gourd of mango juice, he said gently, "Never forswear your indio blood," he told me. "The Spanish think they subjugate our flesh with whips and swords, with guns and priests, but there is another, separate world beneath our feet, above our heads, and dwelling in our souls. In this blessed realm, the sword slays not, and the spirit holds sway. Before the Spaniards, before the indio trod the earth, before the earth itself was blasted and forged out of the void, these sacred shades wrapped us round, nourished our souls, and gave us form. Forever they cry to us, 'Respect! Respect!' Forsake your blood, grovel before the Spaniard's inane gods, spurn the specters of our hallowed pale, you do so at your peril. Their memories are long."

He gave me a black stone—two fingers wide, one long and iron hard. One side glistened, a gleaming ebony mirror. Its interior glinted eerily, and I could feel myself falling into its lightless depths, as if its center were not mere rock but the pit itself—an infinite abyss, eternal as time, its heart the heart of an ancient star.

"Our indio ancestors traversed the stars," he said, "*were* the stars and carried in their hearts star-stones that foreordained our fate—*all* fate. Look into the smoking mirror, boy."

I was no longer of this earth but staring into a world before light and time. My hand trembled at its touch.

"It is yours," he said.

He had given me a piece of a star.

I dropped to my knees . . . overwhelmed.

"It is your *tonal,* your destiny, to have it."

"I am not worthy."

"Really? You have not asked what you must give in exchange."

"All I have are two reales."

His palm passed over mine without touching it, and the money vanished as if it had never been.

"The gift is immaterial. In the heart the blessing dwells, and your heart harbors the gods."

TWENTY-SEVEN

I FOUND FRAY Antonio under the tree where we had set up camp. I told him of my experience with the Healer, including the snake concealed in my loins. He was singularly unimpressed.

"Describe to me what happened—every detail."

I told him of the Healer's incantation, his hand sweeping by my face, my feeling of being both elated and dizzy—

"Ha! Your head went around in circles, you almost lost your balance, your eyes watered, your nose itched, you felt wonderful."

"Sí! From his incantation!"

"It was yoyotli, a powder that Aztec priests used to subdue sacrificial victims. Cortes first learned of it during the battle for Tenochtitlan, when he saw his indio allies, who had been captured by the Aztecs, singing and dancing on their way up temple steps where priests would rip out their hearts. Earlier the prisoners had been given a drink called obsidian knife water, a concoction made from cocoa, the blood of sacrifice victims, and a debilitating drug. Before they mounted the steps to the top, yoyotli dust was thrown in their face. Yoyotli makes one have visions. It is said that the warriors to be sacrificed not only went willingly but thought they were in the arms of the gods."

He explained that it was a trick known by enchanters. "Your 'Healer' had a little of it in his pocket. When he chants his incantations, he sweeps his hand in front of you so the dust flies in your face."

"No, I saw nothing."

"Of course. Only a tiny bit of dust is necessary. You were not going to be sacrificed. He just needed to stun you a little, weaken your mind, so you believed everything he told you."

"But he gave me the heart of a star!"

"Chico, Chico," the fray tapped his temple, "what have I taught you? Do you really think he steals stars from the sky? Or that he flew down to earth with Andromeda in his hand?"

I examined the black stone with the polished side.

"It is a shadow mirror," the fray said, "obsidian from a volcano, burnished until it blazes with a deep gloss. The indio magicians tell fools it foretells their tonal, their fate. If one breaks, they peddle the pieces to other idiots, saying they sell them the hearts of stars. You could buy mountains of them for a reale—or gather them by the wagonful on volcanic slopes. What did you offer the fraud for it?"

"Nothing," I lied.

The Healer was not at the stone slab, nor the spot where he robbed me of my dinero. I went looking where indios camped, ready to threaten him if he didn't return my money. I had never been so angry. Or embarrassed. Did this indio faker think he was a picaro? That was supposed to be my job.

Ay! I could not find the scoundrel. He was gone. With my two reales. My wounded pride would mend, but the money, the money was more sacred to me than the papal throne.

TWENTY-EIGHT

AN HOUR BEFORE sunset, I went to watch the play.

The play was put on in a tree-enclosed clearing with blankets hung to conceal the players from illicit onlookers. The sloped terrain allowed the players to occupy the high ground.

I didn't have a silver reale, the price of admission, but I found an affordable vantage point. Climbing a nearby tree, high above the blankets, I had my own private balcony, gratis. The dwarf taking admission at the entrance naturally shot me irate glances, but I was picaro-born and ignored him. After all several priests took up positions outside the blanket wall, folded the blanket drapes over their ropes and robbed the troupe of the admission fee as ruthlessly as I. And naturally no one challenged them.

Before the play began, the two attractive picaras hustled the mostly male audience, purveying sweetmeats. Flirtation went with the vending. Spanish men outnumbered Spanish females twenty to one in New Spain; and these Spanish women, though picaras, spellbound these hombres. I sometimes wondered if these Spaniards were as entranced with their women at home.

The dwarf ascended the grassy "stage."

"Poland, an ancient kingdom by the sea, lies northeast of our sunny Spain. The Alamanians, Danes, and Ruskies abut this arctic realm.

"Before our story begins, a prince is born to the king of Poland. His beloved queen dies in childbirth. Soothsayers at the court foretell of hellish wars enshrouding the king's enthronement; bloodtime, swordtime, destruction engulfing all until the king himself lies prostrate at the prince's feet.

"What was the king to do?" the dwarf asked the audience, his voice a stage whisper. "Should he have the babe killed? His blood-son of his beloved bride?"

The dwarf paused to quaff a goblet of wine. I already knew from Mateo's recital of "El Cid" that acting was a thirsty business.

"The king, knowing the prince would reduce his kingdom to ruin, erected a soaring, impregnable, windowless tower."

The dwarf's voice became darkly sinister. "In the bowels of this bleak and lightless bastion, the boy was raised in chains, swathed in animal skins. Only one mortal attended the boy, an aged sage who schooled him in arts and letters and in the ways of beasts and birds, but instructing him naught in the wiles and guiles of men."

"Some education," an audience wit groaned.

"Some play," another grumbled.

"Where's the marauding pirate?" another critic complained. "Where's the dauntless hero?"

"Mateo Rosas, whose name most of you know from the great theaters of Seville and Madrid, has personally selected Pedro Calderón de la Barca's masterwork for your delectation. As we all know, Calderón is second only to Lope de Vega as a master of the stage."

From the audience's grumbling I had the distinct impression that Mateo's august name meant nothing to them. Nor did I understand their antipathy to the drama. A prince imprisoned in a dark tower stirred my fertile, if fevered, imagination. I wanted to know how he would feel when he got out—and confronted both his father and life. I was on tenterhooks.

The dwarf continued, undismayed.

"As our story opens, the king of Poland is near the end. But who will succeed him? His legitimate heir has languished in chains his whole life long. If he dies, the next in line is the king's nephew, the duke of a land called Moscovy, a bitter, ruthless place at the edge of the world to the east of Poland.

"The king, the duke, and all the great men of the kingdom meet at the palace to debate the problem: Shall the prince be permitted to rule or be put to death because of the prophecy? The king decides to test the prince, who is now a grown man, to see if he is ruled by reason or by savage rage. To ensure he is kept under control—remember, not only have terrible things been prophesied, but he has been rigidly sequestered—the king sedates the prince and orders his tutors to tell him that his memories are but dreams.

"Also, Rosaura arrives, but she comes to avenge her honor's loss at the duke of Moscovy's hands. Disguised as a man, she plans to run the miscreant through herself.

"Now, amigos, we begin at the tower prison on a craggy mountain where Prince Segismundo languishes."

The dwarf waved his hand to where Mateo and the other actors were waiting "off stage." The actors, except Mateo, wore false beards, and the two actresses wore wigs.

"Mateo Rosas will play the prince and several other key roles. Now for your pleasure, La Nómada players present Pedro Calderón's comedia, *Life Is a Dream*."

With a sweep of his hat, Mateo addressed the audience as Segismundo, prince of Poland.

"I try, oh heavens, to understand what crime I committed . . . but since I was born, I understand my crime . . . for man's greatest crime is to have been born at all.

"I have less liberty than birds and beasts and fish. As I reach this pitch of anger, like a volcano, an Aetna, I could tear pieces of my heart from my own breast. What law, justice, or reason can deny to man so sweet a privilege, a freedom God has given a brook, a fish, a beast, and a bird?"

Other actors tell us that the king orders the prince released from the tower and brought to the palace to see if he is fit to rule or is a mad beast. If he fails the test, he will be put to death, and the duke of Moscovy will marry the beautiful Princess Estrella and assume the throne. But the king pleas with those around him to give the prince a chance. The king was being played by the dwarf with the powerful voice.

In the palace, for the first time unchained and interacting with people, the Prince considers vengeance on a servant who was cruel to him while he was held captive in chains. Another man tells him it's not the servant's fault, that he obeyed the king's orders.

But Segismundo thunders, "Insofar as the law was not just, he was not bound to obey the king."

A murmur went through the audience and I heard the word "treason" muttered. Even at my young age, disobedience to any king, even a bad one, was unthinkable.

But the evil servant challenges the prince, baiting him to fight him.

The prince struggles with the wrongdoer and throws him off of the balcony.

The prince is drugged and returned to the prison tower, where he is told by his tutor that all that occurred was nothing more than a dream, that he had never left the tower.

I could see the audience was constantly stirring and restless. "Where's the pirate?" a man yelled.

"Where are the gorgeous women?" another thundered.

I was enjoying the play and eager to find out about the woman who dresses like a man and whose sword thirsts for bloody revenge, but the audience of merchants and hacienda majordomos was little interested in a prince's struggle with the demons in us all.

Mateo ignored the grumbling. As Segismundo, he said, "To live is to dream . . . a king dreams he is king and in this deception spends his days, commanding, governing, disposing. But the renown he receives is only written on the wind. . . . The rich man dreams of his riches, which only brings him greater concern and worry. The poor man dreams that he suffers misery and want. All men dream the life they live. All life is a dream and dreams themselves are—"

"The hell with dreams! Where's the pirate?" someone shouted.

Mateo angrily drew his sword. "The next man who interrupts me will have this pirate spilling his blood."

This was no audience of city folk but rough colonists. A dozen men rose to the challenge, and Mateo was about to take them on when the dwarf and the other actors intervened, pleading with Mateo and forcing him off the stage.

Fray Antonio told me that when plays are presented in Spain, the common people stand closest to the stage and are called mosqueteros, musket bearers, because of the clamor they make and provoke. These vulgares, low vulgar people, pelt the actors with fruit and anything at hand if they do not like the play.

"Country boors!" Mateo yelled as he left.

There was something else he yelled back, a remark on their manhood and their mothers that I dare not repeat even in these secret words. The insult caused several men to draw their swords, which, however, they instantly sheathed when the two actresses placated them with honeyed words and seductive smiles, which implied everything but which would, I'm sure, deliver nothing.

In the meantime the troupe changed plays.

The dwarf explained that a simple Spanish soldier, rather than a Polish king, now trod their earthen stage.

"I am a simple soldier of the king," he said, "whose honor has been offended by the acts of an English pirate."

The actor-pirate bragged offstage, "I have enjoyed legions of Spanish women, by force at first but never with real resistance. They are all natural-born putas, endowed by their mothers in the harlot's art at birth."

The audience roared. Swords rattled, challenges were issued, and the audience was a howling mob. Shouts of ¡chinga su madre!—an aspersion proclaiming carnal knowledge of the man's mother—rocked the assemblage.

"This simple soldier," the dwarf said, waving his hands for silence, "returns from the Italian war to find his wife has been ravaged by an English brigand."

Gasps resounded. Several men shouted, "If he does not wreak vengeance on the Inglés son of a puta, he is no español."

"He is a mujer!" yelled a woman.

The Spanish soldier had no doubt raped and looted his way through Italy, just as the Spaniards to this very day raped and looted their way through New Spain, my very existence mortal proof of that sad fact; but given the temper of the audience, I kept that observation to myself.

The dwarf drew his sword. It was little more than a good-size dagger, but it looked like a broadsword in his diminutive hand. All the while his booming voice reverberated through us. "I have slit the throats of English, French, and Dutch swine, and my sword will drink their blood again."

Had there been a roof on the "theater," the audience's shouts would have blown it off. Men shook their swords and pleaded for the foul marauder to show his face. But discretion was the better part of showmanship. Either the actor was very good or he was very scared. He cowered offstage. I doubted that even the infamous mosqueteros of Seville were as menacing as our sword-swinging, dagger-slinging colonials.

The actresses, who'd sung, danced, seduced, and solicited hat money outright, now came on stage. This time they harmonized, not unmelodically, a ballad venerating the pristine honor and inviolable maidenhoods of Spanish women here, there, and everywhere. But even as they sang, they could not resist kicking up their heels, revealing a great deal of leg, including that now infamous garden of delights palpitating between their thighs. The two nearby priests pretended with elaborate insincerity to avert their voracious gazes.

The brutish English brigand revealed himself. Leaping to the stage, brandishing his sword, he accosted one of the dancers, roaring, "I've had you by force, and now I will have you again."

She was, of course, the wife of the simple soldier. Men in the audience implored her to take her own life rather than disgrace her husband's honor. It was not to be. As if confirming the corsair's earlier remarks, she yielded immediately, offering laughably little resistance. Murderous rage swept through the audience.

The Spanish soldier, played by the dwarf, continued his speech. Gesturing with much sweeping of his cape and doffing of his broad-brimmed caballero's hat, he spoke of the dauntless courage of Spanish men everywhere—of the righteousness of Spain's soldiers, merchants, and humble farmers. Like Mateo, the dwarf was more suited to play the peacock than the goose.

"Honor is not just the right and possession of the nobility," the dwarf orated, "it belongs to all of us who act as men should act. We Spanish are the greatest nation in the world. Our armies are the most powerful, our king the most generous, our culture the most glorious, our men the bravest, our women the fairest and the most virtuous."

Cheers erupted in the audience.

After each speech a singing guitarist serenaded us with ballads extolling the courage of Spanish men, particularly their love of women, honor, and war.

My ornaments are arms,
My pastime is in war,
My bed is cold upon the hill,
My lamp yon star;
My journeyings are long,
My slumbers short and broken;
From hill to hill I wander still,
Kissing thy token.
I ride from land to land,
I sail from sea to sea,—
Some day more kind my fate may find,
Some night kiss you!

Now the play moved quickly. The English freebooter returned again to ravish the soldier's clearly compliant wife, but this time found the soldier waiting for him.

After the dwarf took several bows and made another long speech, a sword fight flared between himself and the buccaneer. After dispatching the blackguard Britainer, he turned to the audience, saying it was now time to settle with his wife.

On this point the men in the audience were unrelenting. Male honor rose and fell on their women's fidelity. No matter how much he loved his wife or loathed her despoiler, her chastity's loss—or the rumor thereof—meant blood revenge. On this count his reputation brooked no slight or doubt or even hesitation.

The audience was blind hot. One man screamed for her head, complaining that she had not forced the brigand to kill her. Another shouted back at him that it wasn't her fault. The marauder's refusal to run her through revealed dishonor on his part, not hers. The two men started pummeling each other, which quickly led to drawn swords. Again the two actresses intervened. Separating the men, they lured each of them to the farthest corners of that blanketed alleyway with sugary words, sensuous smiles, and outrageously preposterous promises.

The actors had no more than got back into position when the dwarf suddenly stopped the action. "Amigos, my apologies. But I have been reminded that since we mount a second production, our troupe is due second recompense."

The picara women, who had extricated themselves from the swordsman with startling aplomb, again sashayed through the crowd, passing their hats. Despite jeering complaints, the money poured in torrents.

I stared at the women, dumbfounded. The performing of comedias seemed little more than rape, pillage, and highway robbery set in a theater—at least the way it was practiced in New Spain. As for the actresses, they only confirmed for me the incomprehensible power of women over men. Madre de Dios, the things these voluptuous vixens make us do worldwide, time out of mind. We are indeed helpless in their hands. At the drop of a garter, a quick come-hither smirk, or the flimsiest hint of chastity debauched, we are irretrievably lost.

True, most of the women I had known were Veracruz prostitutes, but I had seen great ladies from a distance. What little of them I had observed confirmed everything I glimpsed at the Jalapa fair. Women inevitably reduced the brave *and* the brilliant to drooling imbecility, all the while still believing that as machos hombres we were the ones in charge.

After the two actresses ransacked the crowd, our hero-soldier-dwarf returned to the stage. Not that he was any happier for it. The predacious pirate was now servicing the Spaniard's wife with such stupifying regularity that not even her oaf of a husband accepted her claims to "fanatical resistance" and "fighting the brute off."

"Ever hear of suicide?" the frustrated soldier-dwarf finally asked her, at his wit's end.

"I lacked the means, blessed husband," she responded, with an eager-to-please grin.

"You lying strumpet!" the actor-dwarf-soldier thundered. "All decent women hide poison in their bosoms for exactly these occasions, so when kidnapped by pirates, they can quickly dispatch themselves and not disgrace their cherished husbands, beloved brothers, and doting fathers."

Murmurs of approval rose from the men in the audience.

At last, under questioning, the truth came out. She was not his wife after all but a Moorish whore who, while he was away in Italy, had murdered his faithful bride and taken her place.

The good soldier promptly decapitated her, hurling her heretic soul howling into hell, her infernal descent daringly dramatized by a hideous hell-bent fiend, dragging her offstage, presumably to the bottomless pit. All this was enthusiastically enacted to the wild cheers of the audience.

I thought—and hoped and prayed—that the play was over, but then another character was summarily introduced, the daughter of the soldier. The daughter, a little girl, was portrayed by the shorter of the two dancing women.

The dwarf-soldier discovered that his little girl was dying from the plague. He went to her side and prayed for her. In answer to his prayers, an angel pulled her from her bed and up to heaven—with a rope hung over the branch of a tree.

"God recognizes His own," the hero told the audience, some of whom now had tears rolling down their cheeks.

The play was similar in theme to *Peribanez and the Comendador of Ocana,* one of Lope de Vega's masterpieces. Fray Juan had let me read the play because Vega was the great master of the Spanish theater, which of course was the greatest producer of comedias in the world. The point of Vega's play was that "honor" was not the exclusive possession of the noble class but could be found in a simple peasant. Peribanez, a peasant, was not noble by birth; but was noble in heart and soul. When his honor and human dignity were violated by the comendador who lusted for his wife, Peribanez avenged himself upon the powerful aristocrat.

The comendador made Peribanez a captain in order to send him away from Ocana and leave the coast clear for his seduction of Casilda, Peribanez's wife. But the crafty nobleman had not counted on the courageous loyalty of Casilda, who stood ready to fight and die for her honor. Peribanez uncovers the nobleman's wicked plot, witnesses his wife's willingness to sacrifice herself, and slays the comendador in mortal combat.

The play put on at the fair was a pale imitation of de Vega's tale, but it had the same result of theatrical fare everywhere: to separate the audience from their hard-earned lucre.

Apparently, this was the way it was done: Challenge a man's honor, then watch the feathers fly. Nothing inflamed the audience's emotions like chastity besmirched and vengeance exacted. I personally preferred the complex emotional struggle of a prince drugged, lied to, and raised as an animal. But emotional complexity failed to fire our hot macho blood. Clearly, a play had to dramatize manliness, courage, and *pureza de sangre,* purity of blood. Honor was derived from *who* one was and from *what* one was—all of which was contingent on bloodlines. Not even riches, titles, and family names could compare with purity of blood, particularly when it was backed up by the willingness to die for it, which was universally heralded as hombría, the quintessence of Spanish manhood.

While I had no honor myself, due to my impure blood, I understood the code of hombría. Wealth, learning, even great skill, such as that of a fine writer or an esteemed scientist, were dismissed by the gachupins as the paltry achievements of Jews and Moors. Fortitude was the true measure of a man, along with the lust to dominate—men by the warrior's sword, women by his passion.

I had started to descend from the tree when the dwarf announced an added attraction if further money could be raised.

"These beautiful señoritas will dance a zarabanda for you!" he enthused.

A zarabanda was a *deshonesto* dance—wicked, shameless, lecherous, and sly—in which women luridly flung their skirts and lasciviously pumped their hips. Of course, by now these women could show the men little they had not already seen. Still, everyone was game. The men cheered, stomped, and poured more money into the hats; and the deshonesto began.

The zarabanda blazed hotter and hotter, and the skirts flew higher and higher, driving the audience into an hysterical frenzy. Even the two priests could not look away. They feigned disapproval, rising as if to leave, but somehow never made it back beyond the blankets. Nor did they order the dance stopped, which was no doubt the better part of ecclesiastical zeal. The audience might well have ripped off their heads. In truth, they, too, were men and did not want the performance to stop.

Now the two male actors and the dwarf went into the audience with their collection hats. The more frequently the dinero flowed, the louder they shouted commands to the women, and the higher the skirts flew.

Only when the women were so exhausted that their legs no longer kicked and their skirts no longer soared and their secret gardens no longer filled the eyes did the priests rush up to the dirt stage and insist the show desist.

Even so, they met with opposition. A drunk knocked one of the priests out cold, while the other endured a withering barrage of obscene insults, culminating in his "manifest lack of hombria."

The altercation was ugly enough without physical *and* verbal assaults on the priests. It was time to part. Violence was common fare on the Veracruz streets and held no charm for me. The actors apparently concurred. On my way down the tree, I noticed them sneaking away.

In truth, I had enjoyed myself. I did wonder how the soldier could have mistaken the actress for his own wife. Maybe I had missed an important plot point. Or maybe she was simply more attractive. Who knows?

I burned with curiosity as to the prince of Poland. How *would* he turn out?

Nor were these idle questions. Though I did not know it at the time, from those two plays I had learned lessons that would prove invaluable.

TWENTY-NINE

NIGHT WAS FALLING as I left the comedia. Before returning to the encampment of the frays, I again sought the Healer, in search of my money. Hundreds of campfires surrounded the fair, but at last I recognized the Healer's donkey, dog, and the distinctive indio blanket that I'd seen the dog lying on, dyed imperial red from cochineal bugs. A full moon rode the brilliantly starry sky, affording me sufficient light to locate his campsite.

The Healer was nowhere around. I would have purloined his blanket and anything else I found to repay me for his fraud, but the little yellow dog gave me a vicious look. Yellow dogs were associated with very bad spirits. They accompanied the dead on the trip to the underworld, the Dark Place where one goes after death. This one stared as if he wanted to accompany *me* to the Dark Place.

I widened my search for the Healer and spotted him some distance behind his encampment. He stood with his back to me on the ruin of a forgotten Aztec monument, staring up at the gathering gloom of the dying day. I could only see the dark outline of his figure. As I walked toward him he raised his hands to the stars and uttered words in a language that was strange to my ear. It was not Náhuatl nor any indio dialect I had heard.

A wind gust, cold and unexpected, blew out of the north, a chill wind freezing my tierra caliente–brewed blood. As the wind buffeted me, I looked to the Healer. In the sky overhead a star streaked to earth, its fall a furious flash. I had seen shooting stars before, but never one that plummeted on mortal command.

My feet turned, and I hurried to the camp of the frays.

Fray Antonio would say it was, no doubt, a coincidence that the star fell just as the Healer appeared to command it. But what if the fray was wrong? The fray knew only an earthly realm, where Crown and Church held sway. What if there was another world, one that had been hidden in our jungles time immemorial, even before the Greek gods mocked us from Mount Olympus and a fruit-bearing snake ensnared Eve's fall.

I was not one to tempt fate. I already had enough enemies without angering the Aztec gods.

I had not gone far when I spotted the picaro, Mateo, sitting under a tree. He had a campfire before him and a dying torch hanging from a branch of the tree. The flickering light revealed fury on his face. Paper and a quill lay near him. I wondered if he had been writing a book, another romance of knights and adventure. "Romance" in books and ballads was not between a man and a woman, though such events were commonplace within their pages. The romance referred to was adventure, fighting evil, conquering a kingdom, and winning the hand of a beautiful princess.

I was intrigued by the idea that the man actually wrote a book. I knew, of course, that books were not hatched like eggs but crafted by men. Still the process was a mystery to me. Other than the frays, I had known few people, beside myself, who could write their name!

He lifted a wineskin and took a long drink.

Hesitating, pondering my move, I came close enough to him to risk a dagger's toss. He looked up at as I came into killing range; his expression darkened when he recognized me.

"I saw the play," I said quickly, "and *Life Is a Dream* was much better than that silly farce the dwarf put on. How could the soldier not recognize that another woman had taken the place of his wife? And his daughter—the autor did nothing to forewarn us that there was a daughter and that she was ill."

"What could a lépero cur like you know about a comedia?" He slurred his words drunkenly. Another sack of wine, this one flat and empty, lay beside him.

"I am not educated in comedias," I said haughtily, "but I have read the classics in Latin and Castile and even ancient Greek. And I've read two plays, one by Lope de Vega and the other by Mig—" My tongue tripped over the name because the only other play I had ever read was by Miguel Cervantes. The man had threatened my cojones once if I mentioned Cervantes's name again.

"What Spanish books have you read?"

"Guzman de Alfarache." The other book, *Don Quixote,* of course, I could not mention.

"What friend did Achilles permit to fight on his behalf in the *Iliad?*" Mateo asked.

"Patroclus. He was killed wearing Achilles's armor."

"Who killed him?"

"He told Hector that it was the gods and 'deadly Destiny.' "

"Who built the Trojan horse?"

"Epeius. He was a master carpenter and pugilist."

"Who was the Queen of Carthage in the *Aeneid?*"

"Dido. She killed herself after Jupiter ordered Aeneas to leave her."

"Ubi tete occultabas!"

He had switched to Latin and was asking me where I had been hiding. At first the question jarred me because I was, in fact, in hiding; but I realized that he was not referring to hiding my body. In his drunken state he was referring to the fact that I was dressed like a lépero but was educated like a priest.

"Veracruz," I answered. And then, with uncharacteristic honesty for me, I added, "It would not do for the gachupins to know that a mestizo speaks several languages and has read the classics."

He looked at me with new, if drunken, interest—then gave up the effort. The struggle was too much. Instead of further discourse, he raised the wineskin to his lips.

Who was this man? He was probably born in Spain, which presumably made him a gachupin, but I did not think of him as a wearer of spurs. He was first and foremost a rogue and actor. At the moment, a very drunk one.

"I respect you for your refusal to pander to that crowd of merchants and boors who did not understand how great the Calderón play truly was," I said. "Calderón is a true artist. But the other play," I asked, "what kind of person would write such twaddle?"

"I wrote it."

I froze in place, certain that my life had come to an end.

"But—but—"

"And I respect the fact you recognized it as preposterous."

"It was similar to *Peribanez and the Comendador of Ocana,* the play by Lope de Vega, but Vega's play was . . ."

"Better. I know. I took the skeleton of Vega's play and added different flesh to it. Why, you ask? Because audiences want simple plays about honor, and he has written so many, hundreds of them, that it is easier to put different clothes on them than to bother writing new ones." He belched. Impressively. "You see, my little street cur, this is what an audience wants, foolishness that fires their hearts but leaves their minds untouched. I give them what they want. If I didn't, the actors would go unpaid, and the theater would die. If a wealthy duke does not underwrite your art, you pander to the rabble or you starve."

"If you believed in your art, you would starve first!" I said.

"You are a fool, a liar, or both."

That was no doubt true. His comments, on the other hand, were made with pained sincerity. I now realized that he was drinking to deaden the pain of theatrical deceit.

"One thing bothers me though," I said. "You knew how the audience would react when you put on the dream play. Did you do it deliberately?"

He laughed. "Guzman taught you well. What is you name, muchacho?"

"They call me Cristo the Bastardo. My friend, the fray, a former fray, calls me Bastardo Chico."

"Then I shall call you Bastardo. It's an honorable name, at least among thieves and whores. I drink to you, Bastardo, and to your friend Guzman. And Odysseus. May you, like Odysseus, not die on the Siren's rocks."

He emptied the wineskin dry and threw it aside.

"I know audiences hate the dream play. I use it to heat up the blood. With all that anger blazing in their blood, they'll pay double to see the pirate get his just desserts."

"What happened to Prince Segismundo?" I said.

"Sit down, Chico, sit down and you shall be enlightened." He stared at me, glassy-eyed. "Do you have a name?"

"Uh, it's still Cristo the Bastardo."

"Ah, a good name. Christ's bastard is how I shall think of you." He fixed me with narrowed eyes. "Now for the prince of Poland, he killed a man, was drugged, and then told everything in his previous life had all been a dream."

He pulled out another wineskin. Acting was clearly a thirsty business.

"His father, the king, made a mistake. He thought that to put the prince in chains was to circumvent destiny, but none of us can cheat the Fatal Sisters who weave our woeful ends. Hearing that the king was to put the duke of Moscovy on the throne, Polish patriots rushed the prison tower and freed the prince. An army of outlaws and commoners stormed the prison tower, proclaiming to Segismunda, 'Liberty awaits you! Hearken to its voice!'

"Believing his life a dream, the prince says to himself, Why not do the right thing? Declaring that all power is borrowed and must return to its owner, the prince leads his ragtag army against the army of his father, the king. At his side is the beautiful woman, who seeks revenge against the duke. She has cast off her male clothes and goes into battle garbed as a woman but brandishing a man's sword.

"The king realizes that he is powerless against a populace aroused. 'Who can check a wild stallion's fury?' he asks. 'Who can hold back the current of a river, as it races proud and headlong to the sea? Who can stop a boulder as it falls, torn from a mountaintop?' All are easier to tame, he tells us, than the angry passion of a mob."

Mateo stopped, studying me, his eyes heavy with drink. "The king says, 'The royal throne has been reduced to horror, a bloody stage where the Fickle Sisters mock our every move.' "

He upended the wineskin and threw back his head. Squeezing its sides, he aimed the arcing geyser at his gaping mouth. Not all of it made its mark; wine dribbled down his beard. Tossing the sack aside, he lay back, his eyelids half open.

A chill was in the air, and I leaned closer to the fire to warm my hands as I waited for him to finish the tale. I was in suspense to find out what happened. Did the prince win? Did he kill his father? The woman warrior—did she avenge her honor with the duke?

I heard snoring and wondered what character performed

this unusual act in the play. After a moment I realized that Mateo was not acting. He had passed out.

With a groan of disappointment, I rose to leave the pícaro's encampment, no closer to finding out the fate of Prince Segismundo than when I had arrived.

As I turned I saw a man coming down the opening between campsites. He paused at every camp, peering at the occupants. I did not recognize the man, but the fact that he was searching for someone was enough to ignite fear in me. A tent was set up no more than a dozen feet from where Mateo had passed out, and I quickly surmised that it was his.

The entry flap was on the side where the man was approaching. Getting down on my hands and knees, I crawled to the rear of the tent, lifted up the bottom, and crawled into the darkness.

I realized immediately that someone was in the tent.

THIRTY

THE TENT HAD warmth inside, the subtle heat of a body. And fragrance. The smell of rose water. The scent of a woman.

I froze in utter terror. Bueno Dios! The whole camp will be aroused by the woman's screams.

Warm hands reached out and grabbed me.

"Hurry, my darling, before my husband returns."

She pulled me to her, throwing off her blanket, her naked flesh glowing in the dark. I recognized her voice! She was the taller of the two actresses.

Hot, wet lips found mine. Her lips were sweet, a hint of cherry. They swallowed my mouth, and her tongue pushed past my lips and tantalized my own. I pulled away, gasping for a breath. The tigress grabbed me and pulled me to her again, smothering my face in warm, soft, succulent breasts.

Reason flew from my head as my virile instincts erupted. I kissed the soft, warm mounds. As the mulatta girl had instructed at the river, my tongue found the strawberries at the tip of her breasts. To my delight they were firm and erect and delightful to kiss.

The woman pulled up my shirt and ran her hands up my chest. She leaned up and kissed my breasts, caressing one of my excited nipples with her tongue. I smothered a cry of pleasure and joy. Eh, no wonder the priests storm so much about carnal knowledge. The touch of a woman was heaven on earth! I thought a man was in command of love-making. Now I understood why men fight and die for a woman's smile.

Her hand slid into my pants and she grabbed my manhood. "Mateo, my darling, hurry, give me your garrancha before the beast comes."

Mateo's woman! *¡Ay de mí!* A voice of reason would have told me that my choices in life had been narrowed down to being killed by a jealous husband—or a jealous lover—whoever caught me first tasting forbidden fruit. But my mind had stopping commanding my actions—as my excitement and eagerness became acute, my garrancha started dictating my actions.

She pulled me atop her. Remembering the button on a woman that makes the fountain of lust flow, I reached down to the secret garden. Her little button was firm and erect, like the strawberries of her breasts. Touching it caused her body to convulse. A wave of heat swept through her that I felt against my own skin, and a moan of pleasure escaped her lips. She kissed me wildly, her mouth and tongue caressing, teasing, probing.

Her legs spread wide and she took hold of my garrancha, pulling me down between her legs. I was mindless with lust and desire. The head of my male organ touched her secret garden and—

Ay! A fire started in my virile parts and spread through

my body. My veins became liquid fire, my brains melted. My manhood pulsated on its own, squirting out virile juice.

I hovered over her, breathless, mindless, melting in her arms. I had been to Nirvana, to the Garden of Allah.

She groaned and pushed me off of her. "Estúpido! Why did you do that? You saved nothing for me!"

"I—I'm sorry!"

She gasped at the sound of my voice. "Who are you?"

The tent flap was jerked and both of us froze. Drunken curses accompanied more effort to open the flap.

I did not need to be told by a panicked gasp that her husband had arrived, the one she called a beast. The sound of his voice struck me as being that of the actor who played the English pirate. He wore a very big sword.

I edged away as the flap came open, pulling up my pants. Her husband flopped inside, falling to his knees. I could not make out his features in the darkness. Only her white flesh was visible in the tent. He unbuckled his sword and threw it aside.

"Been waiting for me, eh?"

If he only knew.

I froze in place, the demon called terror gripping me; holding my breath, I prayed that the ground would open up and swallow me before he discovered my presence.

He crawled onto her naked body, pulling down his pants. He climbed atop her without a word of affection, a caressing touch. The beast probably did not even know about the lust button.

A moment later he moaned and jerked as his virile juice exploded. Then he belched.

"Drunken animal!"

She hit him. I saw the flash of her white arm as she threw the punch. It caught him on the side of the head and he rolled off of her.

I slipped under the tent as she flew atop of him, screaming and clawing like a wildcat.

On shaky knees, I made my way back to the camp of the

frays. I did not see the man who I thought might be searching the camps.

As I lay in my blanket and stared up at the night sky, I realized I had learned another lesson about women. If a man takes pleasure from them, he had better be prepared to give back. They have the claws and temperment of a jungle cat.

THIRTY-ONE

THE NEXT MORNING, bundling their possessions, the frays prepared to leave the fair. Taking me aside, Fray Antonio said, "You cannot return to Veracruz, not until Ramon and the doña leave. On the way back to Veracruz, we'll take a detour, and I'll arrange for you to stay with an old friend who is the priest for several indio villages on a large hacienda. You will stay there until we decide what there is to be done with you."

"I can seek my fortune as a picaro," I said, with a wry smile.

But he saw no humor in my jibe. He shook his head sadly. "I have failed you. You should have been trained for household service or as a vaquero on a hacienda. I taught you Plato and Homer rather than how to shovel the manure from a stable."

"You haven't failed me. I do not want to shovel mierda."

"Still you must be careful. Someone at the fair may be searching for you. If they see me, they will look for you; so we must not be seen together. Juan has a list of religious items to buy for his church, so we cannot leave for a few more hours. Meet us at noon two leagues along the Veracruz road where it forks."

I drank water from the river and stole a mango for my breakfast. I ate the mango as I wandered into the fair. The fair was not over, but merchants who had sold out their stock were packing up to leave. They were quickly replaced by other merchants in from Veracruz.

I would not leave without confronting the Healer. While I was not completely skeptical about his powers, there was still the matter of my money. He had sold me that lump of common rock under false pretenses. Furthermore, it was now morning, and I was no longer frightened by the night. The light of day had steeled my courage. I set out for the area at the far end of the fair where the magicians and other fakers offered their services.

As I crossed the fairground, I saw the fray talking to a man on horseback. I only had caught a passing glimpse of Ramon when he searched our hospice, but I recognized him instantly. From his clothes—leather boots, pants, and shirt of rich but rugged cloth, a wide-brimmed hat without fancy trim—I inferred he was a majordomo, a hacienda boss. He was certainly no gachupin, the kind who sported fancy clothes and exotic mulatta mistresses. He had not grown soft living off the king's largesse and the fat of the land. I also knew he was looking for me.

Another horseman was with him, a Spaniard, who was dressed as an overseer, the kind who supervised the ranch hands who worked the livestock and crops.

There were so many people I could have easily blended into the crowd. Had I returned to the magician's area, I still might have accosted the Healer and reclaimed my lost reales. But the sight of Ramon froze me to my bones, and I headed back toward our camp. I intended to disappear into the surrounding river country.

Then I made a major mistake: *I looked back.* Glancing over my shoulder, I caught Ramon's eye. And made another mistake: I ran.

I was wearing a hat and was a couple of hundred steps away; so he could not have gotten a good look at my face. My actions, however, instantly caught his attention.

He spurred his horse in my direction. Fray Antonio grabbed the reins of Ramon's horse, but Ramon hammered him with the weighted buttstock of his riding quirt. His horse surged toward me, and the fray dropped to the ground like a rock, as if he'd been shot, not struck.

The hounds of hell were at my heels. I ran into the dense bushes, thick with thorny mesquite, and clambered up the steep hillside on hands and knees, badly torn. I heard the crash of bushes behind me and once more glanced frantically over my shoulder. Ramon's horse, lunging and bucking, had refused to enter the bushes, and Ramon was sawing at the reins. The other horseman, the overseer, passed him, charging up the rocky hill only to have his horse founder on shale.

Reaching the top of the hill, I discovered to my horror that I could not go any farther. A river gorge blocked my escape. Too steep to climb down, too high to jump into, I raced despairingly along the rimrock. Below, Ramon had reined in his mount. Pointing me out, vividly silhouetted against the ridgeline, he shouted something to his overseer. I could not see the overseer, but I heard him on foot in the bushes below me. Ahead of me the hill jutted a good fifty feet above the river. If I made it up the slope, I might have a shot at the river.

Running along the ledge I tripped and stumbled and flew headlong down the hill and back into the bushes. I hit the ground hard, but panic kept me from feeling pain. I crawled back up near the top edge of the brush, where I still had some concealment. I didn't return to the ridge top because I was too conspicuous up there.

The crash of the overseer through the bushes drove me on. I had a small knife, the size permitted a mestizo, but I had no illusion that I could fight the man. The Spanish overseer was not only bigger and stronger than a skinny, fifteen-year-old mestizo boy, but he would be armed with a sword.

Ramon's voice, commanding his overseer to find me, likewise inspired me. I ran with frenzied passion through the bushes, stumbling over rocks.

The slope became almost vertical, and I lost my footing.

Tumbling head over heels, I went over a ledge at the bottom and fell half-a-dozen feet. Landing on my back, I lay there inert, the wind knocked out of me. The sound of a man crashing through the brush got me dizzily to my feet, but I was too late.

The overseer, a tall, bony man with a ruddy face and short, red hair and beard, burst into the small clearing. His face and doublet were drenched in sweat, and his breath was labored. He had a wolfish grin, starkly white against his crimson beard, and a drawn sword. "I am going to cut out your heart, chico," he said.

As he stepped toward me, I backed up. I could hear Ramon, following him through the bushes. The overseer turned to greet him, but it wasn't Ramon. The picaro, Mateo, faced the overseer with sword in hand.

"What do you want?" The overseer crouched low, his sword at the ready.

Mateo's sword flashed. The movement was faster than my eyes could follow. The overseer didn't even lift his sword to parry. He just stood there, still as a statue. Then his head dropped from his body, hit the ground, and bounced once. His body collapsed in a heap beside it.

I gaped at the overseer's startled eyes, still blinking in stupified surprise.

Mateo gestured at a cutbank behind me, leading to the river. "The river! Vamos!"

Without a word I turned and ran through the cutbank. The river was a good fifty feet below, but I never hesitated. I hit the water like an Aztec altar stone—except this altar stone bobbed to the surface, the white, frothing current carrying me downstream. Above the river's roar, I still could hear Ramon shouting for his overseer.

THIRTY-TWO

WITH NO PLACE else to go, I followed the fray's instructions and waited for him by the fork in the road. At last he came along on mule back. Fray Juan was not with him, nor had my friend loaded his panniers. His face was frightened.

"You killed a man, cut off his head."

"I didn't kill him." I told the fray all that had happened.

"It doesn't matter. They blame you. Get on." He helped me climb on behind him and whipped the mule.

"Where are we going?" I asked, bouncing on the mule's back.

"Back to Veracruz."

"You said—"

"A Spaniard is dead, and you are blamed. I have no friend who will offer shelter to a mestizo wanted for such a killing. They will hunt you down and kill you when they find you. There will be no trial for a mestizo."

"What am I to do?"

"We have to go back to the city. Our only hope is for me to find the doña before she leaves the city and try to convince her that you will cause no harm. You must hide with your lépero friends while I try. If all else fails, I will put you on one of the boats that carries goods down the coast to the Yucatan, the land of the Mayas. It is the wildest part of New Spain. You could disappear into the jungles there, and an army would not find you. I will give you what money I can. My son, you will never be able to come back to Veracruz. There is no forgiveness for a casta who kills a Spaniard."

The fray was in hysterical panic. I didn't speak the language of the Mayas, and I knew nothing about jungles. I would end up being eaten by savages if I stepped foot into a Yucatan jungle. In a city I could at least steal food. In the jungle, *I would be food.* I told him so.

"Then go into the indio areas where you understand the Náhuatl tongue or similar dialects. There are hundreds of indio villages."

I wasn't indio; villages would reject me. Because of his fears, I was hesitant to express my own fright. Leaning forward against his back, as the mule went down a hill, I felt a shudder go through the fray's body.

"I should never have raised you. I should not have tried to help your mother. It has cost me my priesthood and now, perhaps, my life."

How had helping my mother cost him his priesthood? And why were Ramon and the doña after me?

I asked him, these questions but he only said, "Ignorance is your only hope. Mine, too. You must be able to honestly say you know nothing."

But I was not convinced that my ignorance would shield me. Had it not been for Mateo, I would have died where I stood in ignorance and blood.

He prayed a great deal on the long road back. He spoke hardly a word, even when we camped. Hiding in the bushes, we camped far, far from the trail.

An hour's walk from Veracruz, we stopped.

"Travel only at night," the fray said, "and enter Veracruz under cover of darkness. Stay off of the road and hide when it is light. Do not come to the House of the Poor until I send for you."

"How will you find me?"

"Stay in contact with Beatriz. I will pass a message through her when it is safe."

As I turned to leave him, the fray slipped off the tired mule and hugged me. "You have done nothing to deserve any of this—unless you can be blamed for being born. *¡Vaya con Dios!*"

Y el diablo, I thought grimly.

As I headed into chaparral, words trailed after me that were to haunt me for the rest of my life. *"Remember, Cristo, if they find you, nothing will save you!"*

THIRTY-THREE

I WAS TIRED from the hard ride. I was tired of hiding in bushes. I was sick to my soul from fleeing strangers and from being condemned for secrets I knew nothing about. I had gotten only a couple of hours sleep the night before, and I laid down and fell asleep almost as soon as my head hit the ground.

I awoke to darkness, the song of night birds, and the rustle of predators that kill by the light of the moon. Still thoughts nagged me. Ramon and the old matron clearly did not live in Veracruz. Had they, I would have recognized them. Apparently the archbishop's arrival had brought them. Therefore, I reasoned, Ramon and the old matron lived some distance away, perhaps as far as the City of Mexico.

Whatever events had spawned the terrible hate the old matron had for me had happened long ago, of that I was certain. The fray had intimated that the events went back to before my birth. In those days he was a priest on a great and powerful hacienda, one larger than Don Francisco's, the hacienda we left when I was about twelve. His priestly robes would protect him from all harm because the Church would have investigated and punished any who harmed a priest.

Yet events of the past had cost him his priesthood. He also said only ignorance of these events could protect me.

But the fray himself was not ignorant. And he no longer had the protection of the Church.

What would save *him?*

I set out on the road. I wanted one more conversation with the fray. He was clearly in danger. Perhaps he and I should leave Veracruz together. After seeing him, I would then go to Beatriz's. She was probably not back from the fair, but I could hide in her place. No one would look for me there. I had nothing to eat and no wish to stay alone in the wilderness.

The road was deserted—no travelers journeyed at night, and it was too close to the city for camps. The moon reflected off the dunes with brilliant luminosity, throwing off enough light for me to spot the snakes that slithered from the swamps.

By the time I reached the town, hunger gnawed at my stomach like a rabid wolf. Worse, I felt a blood-chilling drop in temperature. Then the wind sprang up, whipping my hair across my face, almost blowing my manta off. El norte was on the way.

A good el norte had the strength to knock down buildings, strip ships from their moorings, and blow them back to sea. Here in the dunes, wind-whipped sand would strip the skin from your hands and face. El norte was nothing anyone would wish to be caught in, and yet here I was, utterly exposed.

First I had to speak to the fray, before I went to Beatriz's room, a dingy little cubbyhole in a squalid building close enough to the water to suffer its fetid summer stink and the fury of hell when el norte blew. Her landlord was a former household slave who had been freed by a woman who manumitted all of her slaves upon her death. Having suffered the pain and misfortune of slavery had not made him a more understanding person when he bought his own house and rented pieces of it. But I was certain I could sneak in without him seeing me. Beatriz's hovel might hide and shelter me for the night, but there would be little or nothing to eat in it. She cooked her tortillas and beans every day on the ground outside, and I would find nothing there the rats had not sampled first.

I was on the edge of town, and the wind was now racketing through the Veracruz streets with cyclonic gusts, sweeping away the dirt and dregs that had accumulated since the last great blow.

By the time I reached the House of the Poor, clouds had blotted out the moon and turned the night black. The wind ripped at my clothes, and flying sand stung my face and hands.

I flew through the door yelling, "Fray Antonio!"

A single table candle lit the room, most of which was shrouded in shadows. I didn't see that Ramon and two other men were there until it was too late. The fray was seated on a stool with his arms and wrists trussed up behind his back with thick, hemp rope. A piece of the same heavily knotted hemp gagged his mouth tight. One of the men held the fray while Ramon beat him with the leaded buttstock of his wrist quirt. The fray's lividly distended face was covered with blood and contorted with pain. A third man apparently watched the door because the second I entered it slammed shut, and he grabbed me by the arms.

Ramon came toward me, unsheathing his fourteen-inch, double-edged, Toledo-steel dagger.

"I will finish what I started the day you were born," he said.

Fray Antonio broke free from the man's restraint. Charging the man holding me, he butted him in the side like an attacking bull. Both of them sprawled onto the floor. Ramon lunged at me, knife blade first, but I sidestepped, and he shot past me, stumbling over his partner, who was trying to regain his footing. Both went down together. Ramon, struggling to stand, furious at having missed me, suddenly spotted a second target in the bound and gagged fray, who was underneath him. Raising the knife high over his head with both hands, he drove the fourteen-inch blade into the fray's stomach all the way to the brass haft.

"Rot in hell, you son-of-a-whore!" Ramon screamed.

Gasping through his rope gag in agony, the fray rolled onto his back, his eyes walling, his mouth open, flooding with blood. His knees pulled up to his chest in mock genuflection. His chin fell slack, and his eyes rolled back till only the whites showed. All the while Ramon clung onto the knife handle and twisted the blade in and out, back and forth in a 180-degree semicircle. I raced for the door, running like the wind, my mind reeling in mute horror. I heard shouts behind me, but they meant nothing. Darkness, el norte's approaching wrath, and losing my pursuers were everything. Soon the shouts were lost, and I was left alone with the black of night and the howling wind.

THIRTY-FOUR

When I was certain that Ramon and his men were not on my trail, I went to Beatriz's room. There was barely enough space for a sleeping pallet and a wall crucifix. The wall was split with cracks and broken boards that let in wind, rain, and mosquitoes. The freed slave who owned the building and charged exorbitant rents, extorting one out of every three reales from the putas and sugarcane hucksters he boarded, clearly did not bother with repairs.

I clambered up the stairs along the side of the building that led to Beatriz's room. I paused in front of her door. None of us had anything of value, so no one locked their doors, at least none among the poor. In fact, if someone had found a lock, that would have been the only thing around here worth stealing.

The whole structure shuddered under the storm. Still the building had endured el nortes before and, I believed, would again. In any event its odds on survival were better than mine. Far better than the fray's—the only father I had known.

I entered the pitch-dark room, sat in a corner, and quietly cried. Over and over in my mind's eye, I saw the knife plunge and twist into the fray. The vision would not go away.

I held up my neck crucifix, my only valued possession, which Fray Antonio claimed to have been my mother's. I studied Christ on his cross and swore that one day vengeance would be mine, not the Lord's.

As I write these words with the mother's milk of a dungeon whore, I can again see the knife driving into the fray's gut, shock on his bloodied face, and Ramon's fist twisting the blade.

That scene was burned into my brain—forever.

Beatriz did not return from the fair until the morning of the next day. She was shocked to find me at her room. "Everyone knows," she said. "It's shouted on the streets. You killed Fray Antonio. And before that you killed a man at the fair."

"I killed no one."

"Do you have proof? Witnesses?"

"I'm a lépero. In both cases the killers were gachupins. It wouldn't matter if the Holy Mother backed me up."

What *was* the word of a mestizo? Even the sympathetic Beatriz doubted my story. I could see it in her eyes. She had been told from birth that Spaniards could do no wrong and that half-castes were innately treacherous. If a Spaniard said I was guilty, it must be true. And she cared for the fray.

"They say you murdered Fray Antonio after he caught you stealing charitable donations. You have a price on your head."

I tried to explain what had happened, but it sounded so crazy I found it hard to credit myself. I could see in Beatriz's eyes that she didn't believe me either. And if she didn't, no one would.

She took a bag of maize down to the street to fix tortillas. That I was accused of killing the finest man I knew wounded me deeply. I had no desire to leave her room or see anyone.

I paced back and forth in her room, then watched Beatriz through the window opening, rolling and cooking tortillas below. After a while, her landlord stopped to talk to her for a moment. I stepped back from the window for fear of being spotted, and it was a good thing. He looked up to where I was concealed, a quizzical expression on his face, and then hurried away down the street.

Her reaction to my story had, of course, troubled me. Not that I blamed her—what would I say if she told me she was wanted for two murders? But this was worse. That fat, lazy pig of a landlord never hurried anywhere, and now he was racing up the street like his pants were on fire.

She turned and stared at the window. I showed myself, and her features were a mix of guilt and confusion, fear and rage, confirming my worst fears. She had informed on me.

I leaned out the window. Up the street I could see him talking to three horsemen. It could not have been worse; their leader was Ramon.

THIRTY-FIVE

I ESCAPED OUT the back of the building, over rooftops, and down into an alley. Behind me men shouted and raced after me, sounding an alarm. I could hear fury in their voices and for good reason. The fray was universally beloved, while I was a lowly lépero, and *everyone* loathed léperos.

They would sell their mothers to a shipful of sailors for a few cocoa beans.

Veracruz was not a large city like Mexico, which the fray said was the largest city in the New World. The town swelled and shrank with the coming and going of the treasure fleet, its normal population only a few thousand. I was now exiting an alley into the heart of the city, not far from the main plaza, where our wealthiest citizens lived. I needed to get out of the city, but I was a long way from the outskirts and would be easily spotted here.

Up the street I saw a grand coach waiting in front of a great house. The coachmen were off to the side, pitching coins at a cup a dozen feet away, their backs to both me and the carriage.

I ran across the street and looked under the coach for a place to hide. Then I heard voices. In a panic I opened the door and slipped inside. Fur coverlets were draped over the two cushioned benches. The areas under the seats, used for storage, were empty. I pushed aside a coverlet, which reached all the way to the coach floor, and crawled under its bench seats. Turning onto my side, I let the fur drop back to the floor. I was hidden.

The voices outside faded. I felt something under me and discovered two books under my ribcage. I lifted the fur curtain just enough to get a little light and scanned the titles.

They were boring religious tomes. I recognized one as a book the fray owned from his days as a village priest, but something about the size of the book struck me as wrong. The fray's copy was much thicker. Opening the book, I discovered that after the title page and a couple of pages of religious doctrine, there was a second title page: *La Picara Justina*, Naughty Justina, The Tale of a Picara Who Deceives Her Lovers Just as a Picaro Does His Masters.

On the way to the fair, Juan had told Fray Antonio about this very book, that he had heard copies of it had arrived on the treasure fleet, smuggled past the inspectors of the Holy Office. It was a scandalous portrayal of a deshonesta woman who bedded and tricked men. He was eager to find a copy at the fair.

The second book, also disguised as a religious tome, was a play called *Burlador de Sevilla*, The Trickster of Seville, by Tirso de Molina. The frays had discussed it months before. Fray Antonio had dismissed it as "tripe." Its rogue was a despoiler of women named Don Juan, who tricked them into becoming his lovers then abandoned them. As with Naughty Justina, the play about Don Juan was on the Inquisition's banned book list.

A treasure fleet smuggler had obviously sold these two libros indecente as religious works. If the Inquisition got their hands on either seller or buyer, they would be in major trouble. Not only were the books themselves contraband, the false covers represented serious blasphemy.

Someone summoned the coachmen and servants, who had been tossing coins, to the house. They were to pick up the trunks and load them onto the coach. Their footfalls faded as they went to the house.

Should I get out of the coach and run? But run where? I asked myself. The answer was made for me. The coach door opened, and someone got in. I squeezed back as far as I could, barely breathing.

The carriage had barely shifted when the person stepped aboard, so I knew the person wasn't a grown man. Through a split in the fur cover I could tell from dress hem and shoes that a female had entered. A hand suddenly entered beneath the curtain—no doubt in search of Don Juan. The hand found my gaping face instead.

"Don't scream!" I pleaded.

A shocked gasp filled the carriage, but it wasn't enough to alert the attendants.

I drew the curtain and stuck my head out. "Please don't shout. I'm in trouble!"

The very girl who'd interceded between me and the pock-faced boy with the whip gaped at me.

"What are you doing there?" she asked in stunned surprise.

I stared once more at her dark eyes, sable tresses, and high, fine cheekbones. Despite the danger I was speechless at her beauty.

"I'm a prince," I finally said, "in disguise."

"You're a lépero. I'm calling the servants."

As she grabbed the door handle, I showed her the two books I had found.

"Are these what you were looking for under the seat? Two deshonesto books banned by the Holy Office."

Her eyes widened with guilt and fear.

"Ay, such a beautiful young girl. It would be a pity if the Inquisition stripped the flesh from your bones."

She struggled for control, terror and rage at war with each other.

"They burn people at the stake for having books like these."

Unfortunately, she would not bluff.

"Blackmail me? How do you know I won't say the books were yours, and that you were trying to sell them to me. If I say that, you'll be flogged as a thief and sent to the northern mines to die."

"Worse than that," I said. "there's a mob outside hunting me for something I didn't do. Being a lépero, I have no rights. If you call for help, they'll hang me."

My fifteen-year-old voice must have rung with sincerity because her anger instantly faded and her eyes narrowed.

"How did you know the books are banned? Léperos can't read."

"I read Virgil in Latin and Homer in the Greek. I can sing the song that Die Lorelei sang to lure sailors to their doom on the rocks of the Rhine, the Sirens' song Odysseus heard bound to his mast."

Her eyes widened once more but then flared incredulously. "You lie. All léperos are ignorant, unlettered."

"I'm a bastard prince, I am Amadis de Gaul. My mother was Elisena who, at my birth, set me adrift at sea on a wooden ark with my father Perion's sword by my side. I am Palmerin de Oliva. I, too, was raised by peasants, but my mother was a princess of Constantinople who likewise concealed my birth from her ruler."

"You are insane. You might have heard these stories, but you cannot claim to read like a scholar."

Aware that silken ladies succumb to pity as well as flattery, I quoted Pedro, the street lad from Cervantes's play, *Pedro, the Artful Dodger.*

A foundling too I was, or "son of the stone,"
And no father had I:
No greater misfortune a man may have.
I haven't a notion where I was reared,
I was one of those mangy orphans
At a charity school, I suppose:
On a slum diet and scourgings in plenty
I learnt to say my prayers,
And to read and write as well.

Foundlings were called "sons of the stone," because they were displayed on slabs in a cathedral. There people could view and acquire them if they wished.

She continued with the next lines:

But I learned on the side
To snaffle the alms,
Sell cat for hare and steal with two fingers.

To my misfortune she knew not only her poetry, but the lépero's larcenous heart as well.

"Why are you in this coach?"

"I'm hiding."

"What crime did you commit?"

"Murder."

She gasped again. Her hand went to the door.

"But I am innocent."

"No lépero is innocent."

"True, señorita, I am guilty of many thefts—food and

blankets—and my begging techniques may be questionable, but I've never killed anyone."

"Then why do they say you killed someone?"

"It is a Spaniard who killed them both, and it is his word against my own."

"You can tell the authorities—"

"Can I?"

Even at her innocent age she knew the answer to that one.

"They say I killed Fray Antonio—"

"Holy Maria! A priest!" She crossed herself.

"But he's the only father I've ever known. He raised me when I was abandoned and taught me to read, write, and think. I wouldn't hurt him; I loved him."

Voices and footsteps silenced my words.

"My life is in your hands."

I slipped my head back behind the curtain.

Trunks thumped on top of the coach, and it rocked as passengers climbed aboard. From the shoes and voices I was able to identify two women and a boy. From the boy's shoes, pants legs, and the sound of his voice I took him to be about twelve or thirteen and realized he was the boy who tried to hit me. Of the two women, one was quite a bit older.

The girl I had spoken to was addressed as Eléna. The voice of the older woman was commanding, an old matron.

The boy started to stow a bundle under the seat where I was hiding, and I heard the girl stop him. "No, Luis, I filled the space already. Put it under the other one."

Thank God the boy obeyed.

Luis sat next to Eléna and the two older women took the seat I was hidden under. Once the travelers were settled in, the coach started up the cobblestone streets. As the coach rumbled along, the older woman began questioning Eléna about remarks the girl had made earlier. The comments had angered the old woman.

I soon realized that Eléna was unrelated to the other passengers. The women were Luis's mother and his grandmother. I could not pick up the older woman's name.

As was the custom among genteel Spanish families, despite their age, a marriage between Eléna and Luis was already arranged. The union was deemed propitious, but it didn't seem that way to me. Among other things everything Eléna said irritated the old woman.

"You made a statement at dinner last night that disturbed Doña Juanita and me," the old matron said. "You actually said that when you were old enough, you would disguise yourself as a man, enter the university, and get a degree."

Cho! What a statement for a young girl to make—for *any* woman to make. Women were not allowed at universities. Even women of good families were frequently illiterate.

"Men are not the only ones with minds," Eléna said. "Women should also study the world around them."

"A woman's sole vocation is her husband, her children, and the management of her household," the old matron said sternly. "An education would put false ideas in her head and teach her nothing she can use. I, for one, am proud that we have never had our minds weakened and polluted with book learning."

"Is that all there is for us?" Eléna asked. "All we are good for—bearing babies and baking bread? Was not one of the greatest monarchs in the history of Spain, our beloved Isabella, a woman? Didn't the warrior called Joan of Arc lead the armies of France to victory? Elizabeth of England was on the throne of that cold island when our great and proud Armada was—"

A hard, sharp slap sounded and Eléna cried out in surprise.

"You impertinent girl. I shall advise Don Diego of your unladylike remarks. Like all of us, your place in life has been set by God. If your uncle has not instructed you of that, you will soon learn when you marry and your husband takes the strap to you."

"No man will take a strap to me," Eléna said defiantly.

Another slap, but this time Eléna did not cry out.

Ojalá! Had I been on the seat beside Eléna, I would have slapped that old woman's head off.

"Great Mother, she's only a girl with foolish ideas," the other woman said.

"Then it's time she learned her place as a woman. What kind of wife would she make for Luis with these crazy thoughts racing through her brain?"

"I shall marry whom I please."

Another slap. Dios mio, this girl had heart!

"You are not to speak again unless I speak directly to you. Do you understand? Not one word from you."

At which point Luis emitted a mean, malicious laugh, clearly amused at his bride-to-be's discomfort.

"Don Ramon has instructed me on the handling of a woman," Luis said, "and trust me, my hand will be firm."

I so recoiled at Ramon's name that I almost exposed myself.

"He told me they're like horses," Luis said. "When breaking them in your saddle, he said, do not forget to use your whip."

The older woman laughed, the mother's guffaws segued into a rasping, hacking cough. I had heard that grate before. On the streets they called it "a death rattle." One day she would expectorate blood. Soon after that she would be gone.

If the Dark Diceman cast lots for her soul, the lots would come up coffins.

Eléna's response to their ridicule was blood-chilling silence. What spirit the girl had! If Luis thought to break this one to saddle, he would be bitterly disappointed.

"I've heard from your married cousin that you've been writing poetry, Eléna," the old woman said. "She said it scandalizes the family. When we return you to Don Diego after your visit, I shall discuss this and other matters with him. These strange interests you evince are the devil's idle hands, not God's handiwork. If necessary, I shall whip that devil out of you—personally."

From my vantage point I could see Eléna's foot tapping,

tapping, tapping. She seethed under the lecture—but was not one bit cowed.

The side of Luis's boots bore his family's coat of arms, etched in silver: a shield featuring a rose and a knight's steel, mesh glove forming a fist. There was something vaguely familiar about the coat of arms, but many wealthy Spanish possessed them.

The city's cobblestone streets now yielded to the sandy Jalapa road, presently taking us through the dunes and swamps. Even though it was reinforced by timbers, the coach wouldn't follow it for long. The mountain foothills were impassable for anything larger than a donkey cart.

Where the passengers were ultimately headed, I had no idea. They could have been journeying to the City of Mexico for all I knew. Whatever their destination, they would not be continuing by coach. Soon they would choose between mule litter or horseback.

I was just starting to doze off, when the driver yelled down that we were being stopped by soldados.

A moment later one of them said to us, "We are checking all travelers departing the city. A notorious lépero thief has murdered a beloved priest in cold blood. Cut open his stomach and twisted the blade by the looks of it. Apparently, the priest caught him stealing."

Juanita gasped. I could see Eléna's legs stiffen. The heinous accusation put her conscience to the test. The fray's words echoed in my mind: *If they catch you, nothing will save you.*

"Are you sure he did it?" Eléna asked. She was clearly troubled, even forgetting to follow the old woman's injunction to remain silent.

"Naturalmente. Everyone knows he did it. He has murdered other men before."

Ay caramba! My crimes were growing!

"Will he get a fair trial if you find him?" she asked.

The man laughed. "A trial? He is a mestizo, a half-breed lépero. If the alcalde is merciful, he will not be tortured too severely before execution."

"What does he look like?" Eléna asked.

"The devil himself. Bigger than me, with an ugly face and murderous eyes. Looking into his eyes, you can see the devil grin. And his teeth are like a crocodile's. Oh, he is a mean one, that's for sure."

"But he's just a boy!" Eléna exclaimed.

"Hold on," the soldado told the driver, "a rider on horseback is signaling for you to wait."

I heard the man's horse move away from the coach, and the old matron directed questions at Eléna. "How did you know it was a boy?"

I froze with fear at the question and almost gasped.

"Why I—I heard men talking near the coach when I came out."

"Why do you ask so many questions?"

"I—I was just curious. A lépero boy begged from me while I was waiting for you. After my encounter with the street boy, who knows?"

"I hope you didn't give the lépero money," Juanita said. "Keeping them fed would be the same as feeding the rats who steal our grain."

Horse's hoofs pounded up to the coach.

"Bueno dias, your graces."

"Ramon!" Luis shouted.

"Bueno dias, Don Ramon," said the grandmother.

My blood raced. I almost shot out from under the seat, screaming. The murderer of Fray Antonio was here. Of all the thousands of Ramons on this earth, this one had to haunt me like a shadow wherever I went.

"How goes your hunt?" the old matron asked.

How did she know Ramon was hunting for me?

Ay, I did not have to stick my head out from under the seat to discover the color of the woman's dress. It would be solid ebony without even a hint of white lace at the cuffs. A crone who wore widows weeds as a badge of honor—and authority.

Now I remembered where I had seen the coat of arms on

Luis's boots—on the woman-in-black's coach door. I had escaped into the hands of my pursuers.

"He will not get out of the city," Ramon said. "I have offered a hundred pesos for his capture. We will have him dead by sunset."

"Dead? But what of a trial?" Eléna asked.

I heard a slap. Again, Eléna refused to cry out.

"I ordered you to be silent, girl. Do not speak unless spoken to. But if you must know, mestizos have no rights under the law. Ramon, send word to the hacienda the minute you know something. We will be there a few days before we leave for the capital. Come yourself when you have good news."

"Yes, Your Grace."

"Good news" would be news of my death.

The coach moved on. Behind me a killer was leading a city-wide search to find and kill me. Ahead of me was a hacienda where the killer would come when he couldn't find me in the city.

THIRTY-SIX

THE COACH RUMBLED on for two hours. From their talk I realized we were still on the Jalapa road. They had closed the wooden windows and put nosegays on to ward off the miasma swamp that causes the dread fever.

The grandmother gratefully slept.

Juanita tried to sleep but was continully awakened by her consumptive death rattle.

Eléna and Luis barely spoke. He was openly contemptuous of books, even the "religious" ones that he thought she read. From his sarcastic remarks, I inferred she had taken out a small book of poems and was reading. To him, horses, hunting, and dueling were all that mattered. Hombría was everything.

"Books teach us nothing that we need to know," he said condescendingly. "They are composed by quill pushers, by ink-stained wretches who would fold at the first sight of a spirited horse or an advancing swordsman."

"Your father writes beautifully," Eléna said.

"Which is why I have modeled my life on that of Don Ramon and your uncle."

"Do not belittle your father," his mother scolded gently.

"I will respect him when he trades that sharpened goose quill for a well-honed sword."

At midday the coach stopped at an inn. I understood from their comments that this was the coach's last stop. From here the women would mount mule litters, Luis a horse.

After they left the coach, I slipped out from under the seat. Peering out the window, I saw Eléna with the others standing in the shade of the inn porch, lined up to enter the inn. I exited the far door and raced for bushes a hundred steps away. I didn't look back until I reached them. When I did, I turned and saw Eléna. She had stayed outside on the patio while the others went in. I lifted my hand to wave to her as Luis stepped out and saw me.

Not looking back again, I ran deep into the bushes.

THIRTY-SEVEN

I HAD TO get off of the Jalapa road. With the treasure fleet and the excitement of the archbishop's arrival, it was no doubt the busiest road in New Spain. As was said about Rome, all roads ultimately led to the great City of Mexico in the heart of the valley of the same name. Despite the wondrous tales I had heard of the island city the Aztecs called Tenochtitlan, I would not dare venture there. Many times the size of Veracruz, the City of Mexico held not just the viceroy and his administrative offices, but most of the notables in the country owned a home—or more likely a palace—in the city. My chances of encountering the murderous doña and her henchmen there would be great.

If the black-hearted boy Luis suspected that I was the notorious killer lépero, or Eléna foolishly shared a moment of candor with him, searchers could already be on my trail. I hurried along, walking swiftly. I would not be able to leave the road until I came to one of the trails off of it that meandered through the scattered villages in the foothills and mountains. I was unfamiliar with the area and could not simply head off into the forest-jungle in search of a village. I was frightened, afraid of being captured, tortured, killed. But even at fifteen years old, I was also worried that I would die and leave wrongs unpunished.

I understood life is hard. That there is no justice for the poor, the indios, and the half-bloods. Injustices were a part of life, and wrongs created more wrongs like a rock dropped in a pond created ripples. But the memory of Ramon twisting the dagger in the fray infuriated me then and haunts me now. In my young mind, if I died with the fray's death unavenged, my grave would not be a resting place but a place where I thrashed in eternal discontent.

There was no one I could turn to. The alcalde would never believe a mestizo over a Spaniard. Even if someone listened to my woes, there would be no justice for me. Justice in New Spain was not administered by Themis, the Greek goddess of justice, who weighed the will of the gods on her scales. Mordida was the Mother of Justice in the colonies. Alcaldes, judges, constables, and jailers all purchased their offices from the king and were expected to collect the bribes called mordida, "the bite," to turn a profit on the public office. I could not even offer a nibble.

I heard the pound of horses and moved off the road quickly, hiding in the bushes. Four horsemen went by. I recognized none of them. They may have been vaqueros returning to a hacienda from the Veracruz festival—or hunters looking for a beggar boy with a hundred pesos on his head. Ay, that much money was a fortune. Vaqueros earned less for a year's work.

When silence returned to the road, I went back onto it and hurried along.

My only knowledge of New Spain was the Veracruz-Jalapa area. The village of my birth was in the northern part of the Valley of Mexico, and other than my memory of the group of huts themselves, I knew nothing of the region. Fray Antonio had told me that most of New Spain from Guadalajara to the end of the Yucatan region was either jungle, mountain, or deep valley. There were few cities of any note, and most communities were indio villages, many of which were on haciendas. He had once shown me a map of New Spain, pointing out that there were only a few cities dominated by the Spanish and that there were many villages, hundreds, that had little contact with the Spanish other than a priest somewhere in the area. The terrain in every direction, until one reached the dreaded northern deserts, lent itself much more toward donkey and mule trains over paths cut out by the tread of human and animal feet than for the use of carts with wheels.

Which was one reason, the fray said, the Aztecs never developed the wheeled cart, which is in such great use in Europe and other places in the world. They understood the function of a wheel and built wheeled toys for their children. But they had no use for carts because they had no beasts of burden to pull them—the horse, donkey, mule, and oxen are all brought to the New World by the Spanish. Without carts, there was no use for wide roads. The Aztec beast of burden was himself and slaves; and other than in cities, they needed only foot trails.

After an hour's walk I saw indios leaving the main road to take a small trail. A wooden sign at the head of the trail said HUATÚSCO. I had heard the name before, but did not know whether it was a village or town. Nor did I know how far it was, or what I would do when I got there. When I saw the sign on the way to the fair I had asked the fray whether Huatúsco was a place of importance. He was not familiar with the place, but told me that it was probably an indio village. "There are dozens of trails off the road between Veracruz and the Valley of Mexico," he had said, "and most lead from one indio village to another."

Plodding down the trail, no more than a foot-and-mule path, worries began to crowd out fear of pursuit. I had no money. How would I eat? One cannot beg for food from people who are so poor that a handful of maize and beans was a meal. How long could I steal before I got a spear in my back? Going into indio country was more frightening to me that hiding out in a city. As I had told the fray, in a jungle I would be food. But there were no cities for me to crawl into, and I had to get off the main road.

Ay, I was not too young for work, but I had no skills. I had two hands and two feet, which made me capable of only doing the simplest manual labor. In a land where an indio's only virtue, in Spanish eyes, was as a dray animal, a teenage boy was not going to be in demand. Not that I could work for a Spaniard. New Spain was a big place but the Spaniards in it were small in number compared to the indios. Word that a mestizo had killed Spaniards would spread like the pox. I would have to avoid all Spaniards.

I wondered how the picaro, Guzman, would have approached the problem. When he acted as a beggar one moment and an aristocrat the next, he changed the way he walked and talked.

My knowledge of the Aztec tongue was picked up from indios on the streets of Veracruz and had improved from mingling with so many indios at the fair. It was not perfect; but there were so many indio tongues and dialects, my speech itself would not be that suspect. However, my appearance would.

A mestizo was not an uncommon sight in towns and along the roads. But a half-blood would be noticeable in indio villages. I was taller for my age and lighter skinned that most indios, although I had spent years under the blazing sun of the tierra caliente and most of the year I was dark enough to be taken for an indio. The height was not as noticeable as the skin color because I would be taken for being older. My feet were already encrusted with enough dirt to hide their lineage.

My hair was not as black as most indios, so I pulled my hat down on my head. For those few times when my hair would be exposed, I would need something, perhaps the charcoal from a dead fire, to darken it, but for now my feet were driven by the necessity to keep moving. Most Spaniards would not notice the difference anyway.

Thinking about my appearance, as my dirty feet carried me along the trail, I decided that the way I walked and talked, the language of my body movements, were most likely to give me away. A lépero raised on the streets of a town would not have the quiet, stoic attitude that characterized the indio. Our voices were louder, our feet and hands moved faster. The indios were a defeated people, conquered by the sword, decimated by disease that killed nine out of ten of them, broken and slaughtered in mines and cane fields, shackled, branded, and ruled by the whip.

I needed to adopt that stoic indifference that ubiquitously characterized the indio—except when he was drunk. When I came into contact with people, I would have to appear quieter, less assertive.

I walked quickly and with no sense of direction except to keep one foot in front of the other and get away from whoever might be following. As I discovered during my earlier trip alone along the Jalapa road, I knew little of how to scrounge for food or find shelter in the wilds. An hour along the path I passed fields of corn. Indios who tended them gave me the same dark looks that I had experienced on the Jalapa road. Ay, these indios were stoic but not estúpido. Like a man watching another lusting after his woman, these peóns saw the hunger in my eyes when I gazed at their tall, slender, shapely stalks of corn.

In the city, many dark stories were told of Aztec tribes in the trackless jungles and mountains who still performed human sacrifices and ate the victims afterward. These tales were entertaining tales on a city street—not here in indio country.

It had rained earlier and the sky said it would rain again soon. I had nothing with which to light a fire, nor was there wood dry enough to burn. It came before I had trudged another hour, first in a mist and then as a downpour. I welcomed the rain because it would hinder and discourage a search for me. But I had to find shelter.

I came to a small village, no more than a dozen huts. I saw no one except a dark-eyed, naked child staring from a doorway, but I sensed other eyes on me. There was no place for me in this little village of indios and I kept going. If I had stopped to even beg a tortilla, I would be remembered. I wanted to be looked upon as just another person returning from the fair.

A fray on a mule followed by four indios servants on foot passed me. I was tempted to stop and tell him my story of woe but wisely kept going. As Fray Antonio told me, not even a priest would accept the word of a lépero accused of murdering Spaniards.

I walked through the mud of another village, rain still falling. Dogs barked at me and one chased me until I hit it with a rock. The indios raised dogs for food; and if I had had the makings of a fire, I would have butchered the mongrel and had a juicy leg of dog for dinner.

Soon my hat was wet atop my head, my manta soaked on my shoulders, and my pants and shirt equally as soaked. My sparse clothing was well enough to weather the heat of the coast, but I shivered in the cold rain that followed me like a bad omen.

More cornfields and thatched houses with corncribs overflowing tempted me as I went by. My stomach growled until it was too weak to complain. I came to a maguey field and looked around. Not seeing anyone, I went to one of the plants that was in the process of being harvested. I was too tired to search for a secret cache. There was probably no hidden supply anyway. A small field, it probably belonged to an indio who used it for his personal consumption and sold a little.

The heart of the plant had already been cut out. Hollowed pieces of reed were stacked nearby. I broke off a piece to suck out the juice of the plant. I tried repeatedly until I was finally able to extract juice. I hated the sour, rancid flesh taste and smell of the unfermented juice of the maguey, but it would ward off starvation.

The punishing rain from the gods came down harder and harder. I was forced to leave the trail to find cover under broad-leafed vegetation. I arranged the wide leaves over me and curled up in a ball. ¡Ay de mi! Again, it came to me how little I knew about the indio side of life, that part of my ancestry that had been connected to this land since time immemorial. I felt like an intruder in the land, someone the indio gods, who had retreated into the jungles and mountains, looked down on with contempt.

No matter what I did, how I shifted, the rains found me. I shivered wet and cold and miserable until I finally slipped into a troubled sleep.

I dreamt of dark things, things without shape but that left me with deep fear and foreboding when I awoke. It was still dark, the middle of the night. The rain had stopped. The air had turned warmer and the black night filled with fog. As I lay silently, trying to shake off the fright I still felt from the dream, I heard something moving in the bushes and my fears became ablaze.

I listened intently, not moving a muscle, barely breathing. The sound came again. Something was moving in the brush, not far from me. The dread raised by my dreams was still with me and my first thought went to evil. The most evil thing of the night was Night Ax, the ferocious Aztec forest spirit that waylaid travelers who were foolish enough to journey after dark. Night Ax—a headless entity with a wound in its chest that opened and closed with the sound of an ax striking wood—stalked the night, seeking the unwary. People heard someone chopping wood in the dark. When they went to investigate, Night Ax chopped off their head and stuck the head inside his chest opening.

Night Ax was a fiend mothers used to scare children into behaving. Even I had had the threat that unless I minded, Night Ax would come and chop off my head. The threat came not from Fray Antonio, of course, but from the street people who spent the night at the House of the Poor.

The noise I heard was not the sound of chopping wood but of something moving through the bushes, something big. As I listened I was certain that it was the sound of the New World tiger, the jaguar. A hungry jaguar was faster and as deadly as Night Ax.

I lay frozen in fear until the sound of movement was long gone. Even the silence that followed in the wake of the sounds was eerie. I had heard stories of other creatures, snakes that could crush every bone in your body and deadly spiders as big as a man's head. Neither made a sound before it was atop of you.

I told myself that the sounds were noises one would normally hear in the dark; the night birds, beetles, and crickets were silent because it was too wet for them to stick their heads out of their shelter, but the fear nagged me that they were silent because something bigger and more deadly was looking for a victim.

I slept fitfully and this time my dream took form—I dreamt I had amputated the fray's head instead of the prostitute's leg.

THIRTY-EIGHT

AT THE FIRST hint of dawn I left the bushes and got back on the trail. My clothes were wet, and I needed to hurry along to get my body warm. With the rising sun, the dampness of the vegetation turned to steam. For a while I could not see more than a couple dozen feet of trail ahead. As I walked the road climbed higher, and soon I broke out of the fog and into sunshine and blue sky.

I rubbed dirt on my face and hands to darken my skin and kept my head down when I passed people. Late in the afternoon, weak from hunger, I came to a clearing in which half a dozen different encampments were being set up for the night. They were all indio traders. Most carried their goods on their back and a few even had a donkey. There were no mules in sight. Few indios could afford a donkey, much less the larger animal that cost almost twice the price of a donkey.

I needed food but my fear was too great to even approach the indios. These men who traveled from village to town would be more sophisticated and in possession of much more information than simple farmers. I had determined that I was going to steal maize from the next unattended field I came to and eat it raw.

Shying away from the encampment, I started into the bushes to avoid contact with any of them when I saw a familiar figure. The Healer who used snakes to cure ills was unloading bedding and supplies from his donkey. The last time I had seen the man he had sold me a worthless piece of volcano excrement.

I hurried over to help him unload, greeting the old man in Náhuatl. He showed no surprise at my sudden appearance or my assistance.

"I'm happy to see you again," I said. "Do you remember me from the fair?"

"I remember, I remember. I have been expecting you."

"Expecting me? How did you know I would come?"

A flock of birds chattered overhead as they flew by. The old man pointed up at them. He made a throaty noise, akin to a raspy chuckle. He gestured at me to continue the unloading. As I unloaded the donkey, he knelt and began to make a dinner fire.

The sight of the fire brought a long, loud cry from my stomach. Any intention I had of coercing the Healer to return the money faded as I helped him prepare food. Guzman often traveled with an older person. The old indio sorcerer could no doubt use a young man to assist and serve him, both while traveling and in his act.

Soon I had my belly full from hot tortillas, beans, and chilies. My hunger cured, I squatted beside the dying fire while the Healer smoked a pipe. The pipe was elaborately carved in the shape of an Aztec god that was a common stone figure at many old ruins—Chac-Mool, laying on his back with his belly up. The hearts torn from the breasts of sacrificial victims were thrown into the bowl he held on his belly as food for the gods.

The bowl was now full of tobacco that the Healer lit.

I could see that the Healer was a sorcerer with many different types of magic in his sorcerer's bag. He was, of course, a Tetla-acuicilique, he-who-recovers-the-stone, a sorcerer who removed sickness-causing objects from the body. I had seen fakers retrieve small stones from the sick on the streets of Veracruz.

I had also heard of sorcerers who could understand the secret language of birds and could divine a person's fate from them. These sorcerers were considered preternaturally gifted and commanded high fees from indios. There was an Aztec word for those who divine by the flight and song of birds, but I did not know it.

"I ran away from my Spanish master," I told him. "He beat me much and worked me more than a pair of mules."

I elaborated upon the lie as only a lépero can. The old man listened silently, smoke curling from his pipe. It occurred to me that the smoke might tell him that I was lying, but the only sound that came from him was a low hum. Soon I felt the lies sticking in my throat.

Finally he got up and handed me a blanket from a pack removed from the donkey.

"We leave early tomorrow," he said. His face revealed nothing, but his voice was soothing. I felt both like crying and telling him the truth, but I was not sure how he would react to a tale of murder. I curled up under the blanket, relieved. More than just a full stomach, I had found a guide in the wilderness.

Again, I mourned Fray Antonio, my father in life if not in blood. It had not been a perfect life with the fray. Drinking and fornicating were numbered among his sins. But I never doubted the fray's love.

As I lay upon the ground, staring up at the night sky, I thought about the old matron and the killer Ramon. There was a living person who could provide the answers to their murderous rage toward me. The woman who raised me, Miahi. I assumed she was still alive. She would have the answers to what happened in the past that has erupted and spewn smoke and fire in my life. From years of listening to the fray when he had too much vino, I know she had left for the City of Mexico with some of his money and that there had been no word from her since. He called her a puta, but I did not know if that was his anger speaking or her occupation.

Before I dozed off I saw an indio merchant pull up his pant leg and prick his leg with a sharp piece of obsidian. He rubbed some of the blood on the tip of his walking staff and let more drops fall to the ground.

I looked over to the Healer with a question on my face. He made a low, chuckling sound like the song of certain birds. "You have much to learn about the Way of the Aztec. Tomorrow you will start learning how to walk the Path."

THIRTY-NINE

THE NEXT MORNING I heard hooves, and I went off into the bushes as if I needed to relieve myself. It was a mule train led by a Spaniard on horseback. After the last mule passed, I crept back out. I caught the eye of the Healer and turned away shamefaced.

The other travelers who had been camped around us moved on, but the Healer paused to smoke his pipe. I assumed he was going to tell me that I could not accompany him. When we were alone in the clearing and the donkey packed, the old man disappeared into the bushes for some time. When he came back he squatted next to a flat rock and worked berries and tree bark into a dark mush.

He motioned me over and applied the stain to my face, neck, hands, and feet. I took the rest of the paste and rubbed it on my chest. From a pack on the mule he gave me pants and a shirt that were made of a coarse maguey material to put on instead of my softer cotton clothes. An old hat of dirty straw went on my head to complete my conversion into a rural indio.

"Women use this to color their hair," he said about the dye. "It will not wash off, but it will wear off in time."

Still shamefaced at having tried to deceive him, or at least for having gotten caught at it, I mumbled my thanks.

He was not finished. Taking powder out of a pouch, he had me sniff it. I sneezed repeatedly, and my eyes teared. Still, he made me sniff it several times more. My nose burned and blood throbbed in it.

Before we set off down the road, he had me look into his mirror of polished obsidian. I swear he had a hint of a grin on his face when he gave me the mirror.

My nose was fat, puffed up. The fray would not have recognized me if we had passed on the street.

"It will stay swollen for a week," the Healer said.

"What do I do then?"

"Sniff more."

"I don't like that stuff. Is there something else we can do?"

His twittering hum grew a little louder.

"Cut off your nose."

We loaded the donkey. The last thing that went on the pack animal was a reed basket.

"What's in the basket?" I asked.

"Snakes."

I shuddered. Snakes. Eh, they could not be poisonous, otherwise the Healer couldn't do his act, handling them and even concealing them in his mouth. But who knew? Perhaps the old sorcerer had a special covenant with the Snake God that made him immune from the bite of a snake.

He handed me the donkey's lead rope and we went down the trail.

As we walked, the Healer told me that Spanish medicine does not work on indios.

"We are one with the land. The spirits of our gods are everywhere, in every stone, every bird, in the trees and the grass, the maize on the stalk, the water in the lake, and the fish in the stream. The Spanish have only one god."

"The Spanish conquered the indios." I spoke gently, out of respect for the old man's feelings.

"They have a powerful god, one who speaks through their muskets and cannons and horses that carry a man swiftly into battle. But the Spanish conquer only what the eye can see. Our gods are still here," he pointed to the jungle, "and there and all around us. Gods that carry sickness in the air, gods that warm the earth so the maize will feed us, gods that bring rain, and angry gods that throw fire down from the sky. These the Spanish never conquered."

It was the longest speech I had heard the old man make. I listened quietly, respectfully. Just as I had paid homage to Fray Antonio when he taught me how to wriggle lines on a piece of paper to form Spanish words, I paid honor to this old man whose feet had seen more of New Spain than an eagle's eye.

"Because we indio are one with the land, we must honor and pay tribute to the gods who bring illness and the ones who cure us. That tribute is blood. Last night you saw a merchant give blood to the gods, asking them to accept the small sacrifice in the hopes that he will get to his journey's end without sickness finding a way into his body or a jaguar dragging him off into the forest to devour him. Praying to the Spanish god would do him no good because the Spanish god does not protect the indios.

"*¡Ayya ouiya!* In my lifetime, nine of every ten indios have died from the diseases and punishments the Spanish have inflicted upon them. Spanish medicine poisons indio bodies. Indios are drained of their blood by the Spanish—it is spilled in their mines, their hacienda fields, their sugar mills, and workshops. More indio blood is spilled each day under the Spanish than had been spilt in a year of Aztec sacrifices, *but not a drop of it is in tribute to the Aztec gods.* This has angered the gods, and they believe the indios have abandoned them. They show their anger by letting the Spanish ravish them. Too many indios have forgotten the path that took them to greatness.

"Your blood has been salted by the Spanish. The indio spirits in you have been asleep, but you can awaken them and sweeten your blood with them. To awaken them you must walk the Way of your indio ancestors."

"Will you teach me the Aztec Ways?"

"One cannot be taught the Ways. One can be shown the direction, but only their heart will guide them to the truth. I will point you in the right direction, boy, but you must make the journey alone. The gods will test you," he twittered, "and sometimes the test is so severe that they rip the heart from your chest and throw your body to their favorites, the jungle cats. But if you survive you will know magic stronger than the fire the Spanish shoot from their muskets."

I had never given much thought to the indio side of my blood. In a world where the Spanish dominated, only their blood—or the lack of it—mattered. Now I found myself as fascinated about learning the Way of the Aztec as I was about Spanish literature and sword fighting. In truth, I had stepped from the world of New Spain to the world of the old Aztec. Just as I had had a guide in the fray, who led me through the culture of the Spanish, I was being offered help in learning the path of my indio side.

I was curious about the Healer. Where had he come from? Did he have a family?

"I came from the stars," he told me.

FORTY

AT MIDDAY WE arrived at a small village where the cacique, the indio headman, welcomed the Healer. We sat outside the cacique's thatched hut, along with several of the old men of the village. Most of the villagers were working in the fields.

The Healer gave the assembly a gift of tobacco. Pipes were lit and they spoke of the harvest and their fellow villagers. If we had come to the village for a purpose, it was not evident. Nor was it urgent. Life moved slowly for these old men; only death came at a gallop.

No one asked anything about me, and the Healer volunteered nothing. I squatted with my haunches on my heels and drew meaningless patterns in the dirt as I listened to the talk. I had difficulty understanding many of the words. My Veracruz Náhuatl was inadequate. Fortunately I am good with languages and was able to increase my ability to speak the tongue even as I listened to the chatter of the old men.

It was more than an hour before they got down to business, and the cacique told him of a woman who needed his services.

"She is suffering from the *espanto,*" the cacique said. His voice fell into a whisper as he spoke.

Eh, the espanto! This was something that even I knew something about. I have heard indios in Veracruz whisper of this terrible element. Like the cacique, they spoke the word only in a low voice—if they spoke it at all.

Espanto was *terror,* caused by witnessing something frightening. Not just an ordinary tragedy like the death of a loved one; usually it was something in the supernatural sphere, in the form of a ghost or other apparition. It was said that those who have seen Night Ax, the headless specter who stuffs heads in the hole in his chest, and Camazotz, the huge, blood-thirsty bat from the southern region who swoops down and rips people apart with enormous teeth and claws, suffer from espanto for the rest of their lives. People who had the infliction often are unable to eat and end up wasting away until they die.

There was more discussion between the Healer and the cacique on the way to the woman's hut, but I followed too far behind to hear. When we got to the hut, the woman came out and greeted the assembly. After the proper introductions, to which I deliberately kept out of the center, everyone sat on logs and tobacco was passed around.

A haze of smoke rose from the six people as they smoked their pipes. The woman puffed as much smoke from her pipe as any of the men.

She was a widow of about forty, a short, stocky india who had spent a lifetime working the fields, making tortillas, and nursing babes. She told the Healer that her husband had been dead for a year. This was her second husband, the one before having fathered her three children, two boys and a girl. One boy and the girl had died from the peste and the surviving boy was married, had a family, and lived in the village. The woman married the now-deceased second husband about five years ago. Their relationship had been a stormy one. "He was infected by Tlazoltéotl," she told the Healer.

I recognized the name of the goddess. Tlazoltéotl was the Aztec Venus, a goddess of love.

"He gave much blood to Tlazoltéotl," she said, "and the goddess rewarded him with the strength of many men in his lovemaking. He made constant demands on me for ahuilnéma." She dabbed tears in her eyes. "I did it so often that soon I could not sit down to roll tortillas. It was not decent. Even in the daylight, he would come home early from the fields and demand that he put his tepúli in my tipíli."

The Healer and the assembled old men murmured their sympathy for the woman's plight. I wondered what the problem was now that he was dead. But she soon enlightened us.

"He died last year and for a few months I had peace. But now he has come back."

I had been scratching meaningless designs into the dirt, but she suddenly had my attention.

"He comes to me in the middle of the night, takes my blanket off, and removes my nightclothes. While I lay naked, he takes off his clothes and gets on the bed with me. I try to keep him away from me, but he forces my legs apart."

She showed the old men how the ghost of her husband forced her legs apart, pushing at the inside of her thighs with her hands while her legs trembled and tried to resist the pressure. The old men as a group mouthed *aaayyyyo* as her legs finally split apart enough for her husband's pene to slip in. All eyes were on the area between her legs that she had exposed to get across her point.

"He comes to me not once a night but at least three or four times!"

A gasp of astonishment rose from the old men. Even I gasped. Three or four times a night! The continuous nocturnal struggles that the old woman went through showed on her face—dark circles under tired eyes.

"I cannot eat and my body is wasting away!" she wailed.

The old men confirmed excitedly that the woman was indeed wasting away.

"She was twice this size," the cacique said, "a woman of good proportion, who could work all day in the fields and still make tortillas."

The Healer asked her more questions about the apparition that raped her at night, going into minute detail about how he looked, the expression on his face, what he wore, and how his body felt to her.

"Like a fish," the woman said, "his tepúli feels cold and wet, slippery like a fish, when he slips it in my tipíli—"

She shuddered as if she could feel the cold fish inside of her, and we all shuddered with her.

After questioning her, the Healer got up and walked away from the hut, moving along the edge of a set of trees near a maize field. Birds flew in and out of the trees. His own gentle twittering was carried back to us on a breeze.

We all remained squatted by the woman as the Healer walked among the trees. Everyone had an ear cocked in the Healer's direction, quietly straining to hear what insight the Healer gained from birds. I, too, listened to the songs and chatters of the birds, but gained no wisdom about the woman's problem.

Finally the Healer came back to share what he had divined.

"It is not the dead husband who visits you at night," he told the woman, as we listened eagerly. "Tlazoltéotl has created a shadow image of the husband, and it is this shadow that comes at night." He held up his hand to shut off the woman's excited response that the ghost was solid. "The shadow is a reflection of your husband. He looks and feels like him, but he is a mirror image created with Tlazoltéotl's personal smoking mirror."

The Healer slipped out his own smoking mirror, and the woman and men drew back from it in fear and awe.

"We must burn her hut," the cacique said, "to rid her of this fiend. He must hide in a dark corner and come out at night to have his pleasure with her."

The Healer clicked his tongue. "No, it would do no good to burn the hut—not unless the woman was in it. *The shadow fiend is inside of her!*"

More gasps. The Healer was a true showman. He used his hands, eyes, and facial expressions to get across every point. I could imagine him on a comedia stage with the picaros at the fair, the audience alternately in awe and shock from his pronouncements, as he explained how life was but a dream. . . .

"Tlazoltéotl has hidden the shadow in you," he told the

woman. "We need to draw it out and destroy it so it cannot come back and violate you."

He instructed the cacique to get a fire going; then he led the woman into the hut. I followed inside, but he barred everyone else but the cacique.

"Lie down on the bed," he told the woman.

When she was on her back on the bed, he knelt down beside her and began to hum near her ear. His humming got louder and developed into a soft chant.

His mouth got closer and closer to her ear and finally his lips were brushing the woman's ear. She was wide-eyed and frozen in fear as if she expected him to mount her as her husband's ghost had done.

He slowly moved away from her ear, just inches, but enough so that the cacique and I could see that he was drawing a snake from her ear and into his mouth.

He suddenly stood up and spit the snake into his hand. Rushing by the cacique, he ran outside. I followed him outside with the cacique and the woman on my heels.

The Healer paused before the fire and held the wriggling snake in the air, hoarsely whispering an incantation of words that were completely unfamiliar to me. I knew it was not Náhuatl; no doubt they were magic words learned from secret sources and known only to those in the inner circle of magic.

He threw the snake into the fire. When the snake hit the flames, a whiff of green flame flashed. As he stood by the fire and made more proclamations in the strange tongue, I wondered if I had seen a little dust come out of his pocket and hit the flames just before the fire flashed green.

Sweating and trembling from ecstatic excitement, he turned to the woman. "The demon who has violated you each night, I have burned in this fire. It is gone and cannot return. Tlazoltéotl no longer has any control over your life. You will sleep well tonight and will never again be visited by the shadow creature."

After receiving his pay, a handful of cacao beans, the Healer led us back to the cacique's house, where pipes were once more lit and a jug of pulque passed around.

The old men were still discussing the oversexed ghost a little later when horsemen came into the village. I had heard the horses approaching and started up to flee but sat down at a look from the Healer. He was right. I could not outrun a horse.

Three men rode into the village: A Spaniard was on a horse. His clothes were similar to the man who had chased me at the fair, and I took him to be a hacienda overseer. The other two men were on mules, an indio and an africano. Both of these mule riders were dressed better than common indios and slaves. From their appearance I concluded that they were not simply vaqueros but a step above, men who held some authority over common workers.

I knew the moment I saw them that these men were hunters looking for me. Rather than simply passing through the village, they looked about with the wariness and intensity of men on a mission.

They paused their mounts by us. The cacique rose and greeted them, the mounted indio returning his greeting before he addressed all of us in Náhuatl.

"Have any of you seen a mestizo boy, about fourteen or fifteen years old? He would have passed through in the last couple of days."

I had to lift my head a little to look up to the indio on the mule. My hat was pulled down because of the sun, and I shaded my eyes with my hand in the hopes of concealing part of my face, hoping that the searchers would only see my big nose.

I waited gripped by fear as a general discussion ensued among the old men about who had passed through the village in the last two days. Finally the cacique said, "No mestizo has passed this way."

The elders murmured their assent.

"There is a reward," the hacienda indio said. "Ten pesos if you catch him."

Ayyo! The reward was a hundred pesos. These searchers were thieves who would cheat poor indios out of most of the reward.

FORTY-ONE

THAT EVENING AS we lay in our blankets, I said to the Healer, "The way you disguised my face fooled not only the Spaniard and the vaqueros, but even the cacique and the old men who were around me for hours."

"You did not fool the cacique or the elders; they know you are a mestizo."

I was shocked. "Why didn't they tell the Spaniard?"

"Their enemy is your enemy," the Healer said. "The cacique's son was forced to labor in a hole the Spanish have dug in the ground to steal silver. These holes are to the north, in the land of the Mictlán, the dark place where the dead go. The silver is put into the mountains by Coyolxauhqui, the Moon goddess. It is her excrement and she puts it in the mountains as a gift to her fellow god, Mictlantecuhtli, the god of the underworld. Digging the holes to steal the wealth of Mictlantecuhtli angers him, and he causes the tunnels to cave in. Many indios die there, some from the cave-ins and others from starvation and beatings. The cacique's son passed from sorrow to the Dark Place while working in one of the holes.

"The Spanish have recently come again to this small village and taken men. All are the sons, grandchildren, or nephews of the elders. The young men are being forced to dig a hole through a mountain to drain the lake surrounding Tenochtitlan, the city the Spanish called Mexico. Mictlantecuhtli is again angered by this violation, and many indios have died digging through this mountain."

"But there is a reward offered," I said. "Ten pesos is mucho dinero, probably more than the cacique or anyone else in the village see at any one time."

"The Spaniard's gold is stolen from Huitzilopochtli, the sun god, who excretes it for Mictlantecuhtli. The villagers do not want the gold. These are vengeful gods, who take many indio lives. The cacique and the other elders want their sons to live and the Spanish to stop forcing them to anger the gods."

Any Veracruz indio or mestizo, household servant, or street trash would have slit my throat and turned my dead body in for a reward of ten pesos. They would have revealed me to the Spaniard just in the *hopes* of a small reward. I learned something about the indios of New Spain: The domesticated indios, raised like work animals on haciendas and in cities, were different than the ones who were not corrupted by the conquerors. There were still indios who followed the old ways and to whom honor was more important than gold.

I asked the most important question. "How did the cacique know I'm not indio? The color of my skin? Hair? My facial features? Did I expose any pale skin? What was it?"

"Your smell."

I sat up. "My smell?" I was indignant. That morning I had washed with water from a creek. Late that afternoon both the Healer and I had used the cacique's temazcalli, his steam hut. While the Spanish did not bath as much as an indio, I bathed more than a Spaniard.

"How could he tell from my smell? Don't people all smell the same?"

The only response from the Healer was birdlike twittering.

"I must know," I insisted. "What do I have to do to make sure I smell like an indio? I don't have access to a temazcalli every day. Is there a special soap I can use?"

He tapped his heart. "Sweat and soap cannot take away what is in the heart. When you walk the Way of your indio ancestors, you will be an indio."

Before we left the village the Healer treated several others for ailments. Like Fray Antonio, who "doctored" the poor of Veracruz, the Healer was also a man of practical medicine, although the fray would not have recognized his methods.

A woman brought a small child to be examined for a stomach problem. The Healer held the child over a trough of water, studying the reflection. He twittered a bit and then prescribed pulverized avocado seed and crushed plantain in raw, unfermented maguey juice.

He examined a man suffering from a bad cough with his smoke mirror. The man, emaciated and in obvious discomfort, described pains in his chest, abdomen, and back. The Healer prescribed pulque and honey.

I was surprised that he had not drawn snakes from either person. "You told me that all illness is caused by the invasion of the body by evil spirits and they take the form of snakes that wiggle around the body. Why didn't you draw the evil snakes from the child and the man today?"

"Not all sickness can be sucked out. The woman whose dead husband has been forcing her to have sex at night believes his ghost is attacking her. When she sees the snake come out, she realizes that the ghost is gone. The man suffers from los aires, bad spirits in the air, which have entered his body. The snakes are too small and too many to suck out. They are everywhere in his body. He will die soon."

That shocked me. "The child will die, too?"

"No, no, the child's stomach is just upset. It would be a waste of a snake to use it with a child who would not understand that the evil had been withdrawn."

I knew that the snakes were not evil spirits in the body but were stored in a basket hauled around on the Healer's donkey. What he seemed to be telling me was that what he took from people's heads were bad thoughts. The thoughts themselves were maladies.

Although I had assisted the fray in cutting off a prostitute's leg and many lesser medical treatments, bad thoughts were a strange malady to me. Yet it seemed to work. Each person who had the snake removed smiled and was noticeably happier afterward.

The woman who suffered from the abuse of her husband brought us corn cakes and honey for breakfast and told the Healer that she had had the first good night's sleep in months. Had the woman gone to a Spanish doctor and complained of a ghost, he would have sent her to a priest for an exorcism. The priest would have used prayers and the cross to drive the evil from her—and perhaps solicited the help of the Inquisition to inquire whether the woman was a witch.

Whose method was the more humane? The more effective?

I was beginning to understand what the Healer meant when he said the Spanish had conquered the flesh of the indio but not the spirit.

FORTY-TWO

When I awoke in the morning, the Healer had already left his blanket. I went to the creek to wash and saw him in a small clearing between the trees. He was surrounded by birds, one of which was on his shoulder and eating from his hand.

Later, when we were traveling to the next village, he told me that he had been given knowledge about me.

"You have died once," he said, *"and you will die again before you know your name."*

I had no clue as to the meaning of this prophecy; he refused to say anything more.

The Healer began to guide me in learning the Aztec Ways as we journeyed between villages.

The Aztec way of life was to honor one's family, clan, tribe, and gods. Children were taught and strictly disciplined from birth about the way they must act and live and treat others.

The umbilical cord of a male child was given to a warrior who buried it on a battlefield, thus ensuring that the boy grew up to be a strong warrior. The umbilical cord of a girl child was buried under the floor of the house to keep her close to home.

"When an Aztec child is born," he said, "the father calls upon a soothsayer to read the child's path in life. The day sign the child is born under will affect him throughout life. There are good signs that bring happiness, health, and even wealth, and bad ones that bring failure and sickness."

"How are the paths determined?"

"The Tonalamatl, The Book of Fates, which sets forth the good and bad days, must be consulted. The day and week signs of your birth and other events surrounding it must be probed. A favorable birth sign brings rewards in life . . . but only if you lead your life according to the sign. An evil life will turn a fortunate birth sign bad."

He asked me questions about the day and time of my birth. That much I knew, along with the fact that the fray had hinted at ominous events surrounding my birth. I also knew from street talk something about good and bad days. The days of the Aztec calendar were numbered and named. One Crocodile, meaning the first time in the calendar day crocodile occurred, was considered a fortuitous day to be born on. Five Coatl, serpent, was a bad day. I was only familiar with the character of a few signs I heard street people talking about, but I knew there were days named for deer, rabbit, water, wind, and other things.

The Healer disappeared into the forest for two hours. Upon his return, we ate a meal I had prepared over our campfire. While he was gone, I had foretold the future for a pregnant india who had had two girls and was desperate to birth a boy. After examining the ashes in her cooking fire and muttering some Latin at a flock of birds, I advised her that she would indeed have a boy. The grateful woman gave me the duck I'd roasted for our meal.

I dared not tell the Healer that I was telling fortunes.

I listened to him as I attacked the duck with great enthusiasm.

He spoke solemnly. "Each of us has our destiny cast by the gods. For some there are clear signs of good fortune, while pain and misfortune will be the circumstance of others." He shook his head. "You fall within the Shadow Fates, the destines the gods have left uncompleted. Your day is Four and the sign is Ollin, motion. The gods do not cast the destiny of those born under this sign because motion is changeable. It runs here and there and changes direction many times. It is under the control of Xolotl, the Plumed Serpent's evil twin. You see Xolotl blazing in the night sky at certain times of the year, the dark side of the star, while the light side blazes in the morning."

From the description I assumed Xolotl was the evening star, the nighttime manifestation of Venus, as opposed to the morning star. Xolotl, a dog-headed monster, was another favorite character at mascaradas.

"It is said that those born under the motion sign change their path in life frequently and often become rogues and tale bearers."

Eh, that caught my attention.

"Because they are so fluid, they are able to change shapes. The darkest side of those born under the sign of motion are the shape changers who are able to take on different forms, even the shape of animals."

"Why is that considered the dark side?" I asked.

"Because there are evil persons who do much harm under the guise of animals or in the shape of another person."

The Healer also told me I needed an Aztec name.

I removed my mouth from the carcass of the duck I was gnawing and wiped duck fat from my chin. "What should my Aztec name be?"

"Nezahualcóyotl."

I recognized the name. Next to Montezuma, he was the most famous indio king. There were many tales about Nezahualcóyotl, the king of Texcoco. He was famous for his poetry and wisdom. But from the amused glint in the Healer's eye when he bestowed the name upon me, I realized I was not being honored for my wisdom or literary talents.

The name meant "Hungry Coyote."

Along the road the Healer showed me vegetation—plants and trees and bushes—that were useful in the healing arts, and the ways of the forest and jungle and the animals and people that inhabit them.

"Before the Spanish came, the revered speakers, what we called our Aztec emperors, had not only a great animal and serpent zoo, but vast gardens in which thousands of plants were grown that were used by healers. The potency and healing powers of the plant were determined by using them on criminals and prisoners who were to be sacrificed."

The great medical gardens and books suffered the same fate most Aztec knowledge did—the priests who followed the conquistadors destroyed them. What had the fray said about such ignorance? What they didn't understand, they feared and destroyed.

The Healer showed me plants that were used for wounds and ulcers, to heal the blisters of burns, reduce swelling, cure skin diseases and eye problems, cool fevers, soothe the stomach, calm the heart when it is too active and stimulate it when it is too quiet. Jalop was used to unlock the bowels, a plant called "urine of a tiger" to make water come when urination was difficult.

"Aztec doctors sewed up wounds with human hair. They set broken bones with pieces of wood and put a gum of ocozotl tree with resin and feather over the wood."

Not even the fish were free from the influence of Aztec herbs. Indios crushed a plant called barbasco and threw it into rivers and lakes. The herb stunned the fish and forced them to the surface, where the indios grabbed them.

Children were instructed to keep their teeth clean to avoid decay; salt and powered charcoal were used with a wooden instrument to clean teeth.

I saw an amazing example of Aztec tooth remedies in a village where another traveling healer had stopped at the same time we did. This healer's specialty was removing painful teeth—painlessly. He applied a substance to the teeth that instantly deadened the tooth. Within hours, the tooth had fallen out.

I asked the Healer what the man had applied that worked so well.

"The venom of a rattlesnake," he said.

The Healer told me not all the products of plants were used to heal. Veintiunilla, the "little twenty-one," caused death in exactly twenty-one days. Persons given the plant developed an insatiable thirst for potent drinks like pulque and cactus wine, and drank the intoxicating beverages until they died.

"Evil Aztec whores tricked men into drinking macacotal, the steeping from a snake. Ayyo, these men engage in ahuilnéma with six or seven women, one after another, and moments later are ready to have ahuilnéma with even more women. This goes on and on, with the man unable to control his urge, giving anything he owns to the whores, until the life is gone from him and his flesh hangs from his bones."

To have power to satisfy so many women. Muy hombre! What a way to die, eh, amigos?

Another indio aphrodisiac was the "witches rose." Medicine women used magic words to make roses open before their season. These were sold to men for a wicked purpose: the seduction of women. The rose was hidden under the woman's pillow. When she inhaled the scent, she became intoxicated with love for the person who put the rose there and called his name.

I asked him about the drugs that robbed one of their mind. His expression never changed, but when he was amused by something a glint came to his eye and he would emit a quiet, birdlike chuckle. He did so as he told me about yoyotli, the dust that made one so happy and pliable that you danced gaily to the sacrificial block where the priest was waiting with an obsidian knife to cut your heart out.

"Flower weavers are the sorcerers who bring our minds into contact with the gods," the Healer said. Peyotl, from the buds of cacti that grow only in the Place of the Dead, the northern deserts; and brown seeds from ololiuqui, a plant that climbs and clings to other plants, were used to "take people to the gods," which I understood to mean that the person entered a dreamlike state. From the babbling uttered and visions the person experienced, a healer could determine the person's malady.

Teunanacatl, a bitter black mushroom, was called the "flesh of the gods." Occasionally served with honey at feasts, it also took one to the gods, but the hallucinations were less than those created by peyotl. "Some people laugh hysterically, others image they are being chased by snakes or that their bellies are full of worms eating them alive. Others fly with the gods."

A plant that could be smoked was called coyote weed by the Healer. "It makes the smoker feel calm and soothes deep pains." A small smile on his face hinted that some of the tobacco he smoked was of the coyote weed variety.

The most powerful substance was teopatli, the divine ointment. The Healer spoke of it with a tone of awe. To the seeds of certain plants "are added the burnt ashes of spiders, scorpions, centipedes, and other noxious insects, petum to make the flesh painless, and ololiuqui to lift the spirits." When applied to the skin, it made the person invincible, as if an invisible shield was held in front of him. "The greatest warriors of the Aztec were the Jaguar Knights and Eagle Knights; it is said that the weapons of their enemies could not cut them when they had the teopatli ointment applied to their skin."

As the months passed by and we went from one small village to another, I never encountered another rider searching for me. Soon enough of the fear was gone for me to stop puffing up my nose. Because the sun darkened my skin so well, I needed little dye. But for safety's sake the Healer gave me a "sore" to wear on my cheek, a small, black piece of bark held on with sap.

We stayed away from the larger villages and towns while I learned how to think and act like an indio.

Even more than the Spanish, the indios were ruled by superstition and the whim of their gods. Nothing they did or experienced, from the sun overhead and ground beneath their feet, giving birth or to going to the marketplace to sell ears of maize, went without having some spiritual power involved. Sickness came mostly from evil spirits, bad aires, that one breathed in or was touched by. And the cure was to remove the spirits with the magic and herbs of a healer.

The Spanish priests battled the indio superstitions, trying to replace them with Christian rites. Most of the indio customs I found to be harmless or, in the case of herbal medical remedies, to be extremely beneficial. Occasionally I would be shocked.

In our travels to places little visited by outsiders, we came to a village where an old woman had been stoned to death just before our arrival. Her body, with bloodied stones lying about, was still on the ground when we walked in leading the donkey.

I asked the Healer what great crime the old woman had committed.

"She died not for her sins, but the sins of all the villagers. The oldest woman in the village is chosen each year to hear the confessions of all the people in the village. She is then stoned to death to win atonement for the entire village."

¡Ayya ouiya!

The gods were as involved in death as they were in life. Just as there was a Christian world of death, the Aztecs had their places where dead spirits resided, both an underworld and a heavenly paradise. Where you went, to the underworld or the celestial heaven, what happened to your soul, depended not upon conduct during life but on *how you died.*

The House of the Sun was a celestial paradise to the east of the Aztec world. Warriors killed in battle, people who were sacrificed, and women who had died in childbirth shared the honor of residing in this wondrous place after death. The house of the sun was filled with beautiful gardens, perfect weather, and the finest foods. It was the Garden of Eden, the Garden of Allah, paradise.

Warriors who dwelled there passed their time in bloodless battles. But each morning they assembled as a vast army on a great open plain that stretched almost endlessly to the horizon. They were waiting for the sun to rise in the East. When the first glow of light slipped above the horizon, the warriors greeted it by clashing their spears against their shields; then they escorted the sun on its journey across the sky.

After four years, the warriors, sacrifice victims, and women who'd died in childbirth returned to earth as hummingbirds.

Most people, those who succumbed to disease, accidents, and the maladies of old age, went to the Dark Place, the place of the dead, Mictlan.

This underworld, far to the north of the Aztec world, was a place of scorching deserts and winds that can freeze a person in place. The lord of Mictlan was Mictlantecuhtli, a god who wore a skull mask and a cloak of human bones. To reach Mictlan the soul had to journey through eight hells before arriving at the ninth hell, where Mictlantecuhtli and his goddess queen live.

Each of the journeys had the type of dangers Odysseus experienced and the ghoulish horrors of Dante's infiernal. The dead must first cross a wide and swift river. A red or yellow dog was needed for this task. After forging the river, they had to pass between two mountains which were clashing together. The tasks became more and more difficult—a mountain of razor-sharp obsidian to be climbed, a region of icy winds that could sear flesh from the bone; places where banners battered wayfarers, where arrows pierced the unwary, and savage beasts ripped open chests to eat human hearts. In the eighth realm, the dead had to climb narrow ledges of cliffs.

After four years of trial and torment, the dead achieve

the ninth hell, a place deep in the bowels of the earth. In this fiery bowel of the Lord Mictlantecuhtli and his queen, the essence of the dead—what the Christians called the soul—was burned to achieve eternal peace.

Eh, I would take the Christian heaven over Mictlan. Even thieving, murdering léperos make it there as long as they repent at the end.

The preparation for the journey after death also depends on the way one had died.

"Those who died in battle and childbirth were burned atop a pyre," the Healer told me. "This frees the spirit for its upward journey to the Eastern Heaven. Those who are to journey to the realm of the Lord of the Dead, Mictlantecuhtli, are buried beneath the ground. This gives them a start on their journey through the underworld."

Regardless of their destination, the dead were dressed in their finest ceremonial clothing and provided with food and drink for their journey. A piece of jade or other valuable placed in the mouth of the dead was money for buying whatever they needed in the hereafter. Even the poor were given food and water to help them on the long trip.

Those who could afford it made the journey to the House of the Sun or the underworld with a companion, a red or yellow dog.

When the Healer told me that, I glanced over at his yellow dog that never left his side, day or night.

Kings and great nobles made the journey surrounded by the wealth and splendor they'd enjoyed in life. Stone tombs were constructed and filled with food, chocolate, and sacrificed wives and slaves. Instead of a simple piece of jade, earthly treasure—objects of gold and silver and gems—were put in the tomb. The dead notable would be positioned seated in a chair with his weapons and golden breastplate or carried upon a litter.

The funeral customs of these people were not unlike those the fray had told me existed among the ancient Egyptians. "Because of the pyramids, funeral rites, and the fact that some Aztecs circumcised males in the manner of Semites, some scholars believed the Aztecs were originally from the Holy Lands, perhaps a lost tribe of Israel."

Aztec poets compared human life to the fate of a flower, rising from the earth, growing toward the sky, blooming, then swallowed up by the earth again.

"Our souls in your eyes are but as wisps of smoke or clouds rising out of the earth," they sang.

And they were fatalistic about death. It spared no one, rich or poor, good or bad. The Healer sang to me across the flames of a campfire:

Even jade will shatter,
Even gold will crush.
Even quetzal plumes will tear.
One does not live forever on this earth:
Only for an instant do we endure.

"Did they believe in life after death?" I asked the Healer. "Like the frays teach about the Christian religion?"

Where are we going, ay, *where are we going?*
Will we be dead there, or will we live still?
Will there be existence again there?
Will we feel again the joy of the Giver of Life?

"Your question," he said, "is answered by a third song."

By chance are we to live a second time?
Your heart knows it.
Only once have we come to live.

FORTY-THREE

ALONG WITH LEARNING the Ways of the Aztec, I slowly picked up the methods of the Healer, not just learning the art of treating wounds and sickness, but much more important in my eyes, the technique of pulling an "evil" snake from a person's head. I couldn't stomach putting one of the Healer's snakes in my mouth when doing the trick and instead I practiced with a twig.

I soon was able to put my "magic" into practice in a most delightful way.

The Healer had gone off to meditate with birds, and I was in the hut provided by the village cacique. Bored and with time on my hands, a dangerous combination for any youth, I had put on the Healer's colorful feather manta and elaborate headdress that covered most of my face. I was practicing the snake trick when the local cacique entered the hut.

"Great Sorcerer," he said, "I have waited for your arrival. I have problems with my new wife. She is very young, and is proving difficult for this old man to deal with."

The fray always claimed that I had a devil in me. At the old man's words, the devil in me awoke and took control. I could not resist finding out what problems this old man had with his young wife.

"I need you to come now to my hut and examine her. Some evil spirit has entered her tipíli and my tepúli is unable to penetrate into her."

Eh, I had seen the Healer deal many times with sex problems. It would be an easy task for me. Mumbling nonsense and gesturing with my hand, I sent him out of the hut. Once he was outside, I pocketed one of the Healer's pet snakes.

The notion of using the snake was repulsive to me, but he would expect it.

The cacique's house was the largest house in the village. While most of the village huts consisted of one or two rooms, his had four.

Ayya. The old man's wife was a surprise. A young, good-looking female, little older than me. Very ripe for ahuilnéma, even if it was an old pene being poked at her.

The cacique explained the problem. "She is too tight. I cannot get my tepúli into her. My tepúli is hard," he assured me, expanding his chest with air, "that is not the problem. And she is not too small. I can open her tipíli with my hand and put three fingers inside. But when I try to shove into her, the opening is not large enough."

"It is los aires," the young woman told me, using the Spanish phrase. "I was washing clothes by the riverbank when I breathed in an evil spirit. When my husband tries to put his tepúli in me, it will not go in even if I help it with my hand because the spirit closes my tipíli."

I muttered an incoherent response in a muffled voice.

She spoke impassively, but her eyes were very much alive. And those lively eyes were intently examining what little of my face was exposed by openings in the Healer's headpiece. No doubt she was picking up clues about my age that her husband's old eyes never caught.

I heard other men outside, the village elders gathering to see the magic. I ushered the cacique out to tell them they could not enter, mumbling the instruction so that I barely understood the words myself.

With him out of the room, I spoke to the girl. "Why are you not having ahuilnéma with your husband," I said, in a normal voice. "And don't tell me it's evil spirits."

"What kind of healer are you? They are always old men."

"A new type. I have knowledge not only of indio medicine but of Spanish as well. Tell me why you are not permitting your husband to have ahuilnéma with you."

She scoffed. "When I married, it was promised that I would have many presents. He is the richest man in the area, but he does not give me gifts. If he gives a chicken for me to pluck and cook for him, he thinks it is a present."

A woman after my own heart. The demon would go away if she got what she wanted. But *¡ay de mí!* I had presented myself as the Healer and the cacique was familiar with his technique. Neither he nor the village elders would be satisfied unless a snake was pulled from her. The slimy little green snake was wiggling in my pocket. From the feel, I was certain I now had snake mierda in the pocket, too. There was no possibility that I would put the horrible little creature in my mouth.

Obeying my instructions, the cacique entered alone. "The village elders wish to see you remove the evil spirit."

I put one of the Healer's talismans in front of my lips and spoke into it with the hoarse mutter I was affecting. "The elders cannot enter. The evil spirit must be removed from your wife."

"Yes, yes, they want to—"

"From her tipíli."

"Aaaak!" He gasped and gagged and began coughing. For a moment I thought he was going to drop dead on the spot. His health was important to me. If he died, I would probably never make it out of the village alive.

I was greatly relieved when he got his breathing going again.

"The demon is in her tipíli, and it is from there I must draw it. Being a doctor, it is of course proper and respectful that I perform the task. Of course, if you wish to never have ahuilnéma with your wife . . ."

"I don't know, don't know," he said, "perhaps I will try again—"

"Ayya! If you do, the demon will enter your tepúli!"

"No!"

"Yes. Until the demon is removed, she cannot even share her bed with you. Or cook for you. It might enter through your mouth with the food."

"*¡Ayya ouiya!* I must eat. Remove it from her."

"You may stay," I said, graciously, "but you must turn around and face the wall."

"Face the wall? Why must I—"

"Because the demon will seek another hole to enter after I remove it. It may go inside your mouth, up your nose, in your . . ." I patted my backside.

He groaned aloud.

"You must also keep repeating the chant I tell you. It is the only way to keep the demon from coming after you. Keep repeating these words over and over. Rosa rosa est est, rosa rosa est est."

I turned to examine his wife as he stood with his back to me, literally saying over and over that a rose is a rose is a rose . . .

I had the young wife lie down on a mat and remove her skirt. She had nothing on beneath it. Most of my experience with women had been in the dark, one might say, but the two girls at the river had instructed me well about the treasures to be found on a woman's body.

I put my hand on her mound of black hair and slowly allowed my hand to slip between her legs. As my hand moved down, her legs spread. I became instantly excited. My pene throbbed wildly. Her tipíli opened like a buttercup in the sun as my hand touched it. I let my fingers move in and around the lush, wet, warm opening. I found her witch's teat and began to gently caress it.

She began to flow with the movement of my hand, her hips moving up and down. Ayya! The only demon in this young woman's tipíli was the neglect she got from having to lay with an old man.

I heard the cacique tapering off from reciting roses. "You must keep the spirits away. Keep chanting."

He picked up immediately.

I turned back to the young woman. She was staring at me with eyes that told me she liked very much what I was doing. I started to lean down to take the witch's teat in my mouth, but she stopped me.

"I want your pene," she whispered, using the Spanish

word. Her eyes were as lush and lustful as her hot-wet tipíli. She may not have been opening for the old cacique, but I had the feeling more than one village boy had enjoyed her favors.

In truth, while I was a teller of tales, sí, a liar if you insist, I will admit honestly that I had little prior experience doing what the indios called ahuilnéma. The great opportunity at the fair had been lost when my garrancha got excited too quickly. Now, despite the danger of being caught—and not just skinned, but probably skinned and slow roasted—my pene was throbbing wildly, telling me that it wanted to explore new stimulation beyond what it had experienced by my own hand.

Her hand went to my pants and undid the cord holding them up. She pulled my pants down and took my pene in her hand, drawing it toward her tipíli.

The throbbing was so fierce that I thought my pene was going to explode.

I started to mount her and . . . and . . . mierda!

That juice that Snake Flower craved for her love potion exploded out of my pene. For a moment I convulsively jerked. The juice shot out and struck the young woman's stomach.

She looked down at her violated stomach and back into my eyes. She hissed something in Náhuatl. I did not recognize the word, but the meaning was clear.

Shamefaced, I slipped off of her and pulled up my pants.

"Rosas rosas rosas . . . can I stop now?" The cacique sounded exhausted.

I pulled the slimy little snake out of my pocket and told him to turn around.

"The demon is gone." I threw the demon into the fire, "but there is another problem. The demon got inside of your wife because she was weak from being unhappy. When she is happy, the demon cannot enter her. Each time you wish to do ahuilnéma with your wife, you must give her a silver reale. If you do that, the demon will not come back."

The cacique clutched his heart, and the girl grinned broadly as I left.

I hurried to the hut where we were staying to remove the headdress and cape before the Healer returned.

Fray Antonio had told me that a great king named Solomon had had the wisdom to order a baby chopped in two to determine which of the two women who claimed it was the baby's mother. I felt that my solution to the problem of the cacique and his wife had the same type of wisdom that this king of ancient Israel had possessed.

But *¡ay de mí!* my performance as a lover was a failure. I had lost honor. Sí, amigos, honor. I was learning the Aztec Ways, but I was still a Spaniard. At least half of one; and I had been shamed again by my pene.

Using Plato's logic, I determined that the problem lay with my inexperience. I knew from my days on the streets that young boys train their penes. I must perform more practice with my hand to ensure that my garrancha is ready the next time it is given the opportunity.

FORTY-FOUR

"YOU WILL NOT know the Ways of the Aztec until you speak to your ancestors," the Healer told me.

I had been with the Healer for over a year. My sixteenth birthday had come and gone, and I was nearing another birthday. We had traveled from village to village. I had learned the Náhuatl language as it should be spoken and could hold a conversation in other indio dialects. From all I had learned about the indio in our travels, I thought that I knew the Ways of my Aztec ancestors; but when I told this to the Healer, he would click his tongue and shake his head.

"How do I talk to the gods?" I asked him.

He twittered like a bird. "You must go to where they reside and open your mind. We are going to the Place of the Gods," he said.

We had entered the Valley of Mexico, the great cavity between high mountains that contained the most prized land in New Spain. The valley had been the heart and soul of the Aztec world, and now it was the same for the Spanish of the New World. In it were the five-great-lakes-that-were-really-one, including Lake Texcoco that the Aztecs had built Tenochtitlan upon—the great city the Spanish in turn razed to build the City of Mexico.

But it was not to that city-on-the-water that the Healer was taking me. As was our custom, we avoided all large towns. We were on our way to another city, one that once had more people than Tenochtitlan. Our destination was about two days' walk from the City of Mexico.

"Are there many people in this city that you're taking me to?"

"More than the sands along the Eastern Sea," he said, referring to the Veracruz coast, "but you cannot see them." He cackled.

I had never seen the old man so ecstatic. But it was no wonder because we were entering Teotihuacan, the place of the gods, the city that was holy to the Aztecs and which they called the Place That Men Become Gods.

"Teotihuacan is an not an Aztec city," the Healer told me. "It is much older than the Aztecs. It was built by a civilization older and mightier than all of the known indio empires. It was the greatest city in the One World."

"What happened to it? Why are there no people there now?"

"Ayya. The gods engaged in battles among themselves. People fled the city as the gods fought because death fell from the sky like the new rains. The city is still there, but only the gods walk its streets."

The Healer's knowledge of the city was based not upon learning found in books, but upon the knowledge found in legends and tales of old. A day would come when I would learn more about Teotihuacan. It would be no surprise to me that the Healer's knowledge of the city was correct.

Teotihuacan, lying about ten leagues northeast of the City of Mexico, was truly one of the wonders of the world. It was the great city of the classic era of the indio, a New World Rome and Athens. Sprawled over an immense area, the ceremonial center of the city alone was larger than many of the great Aztec and Mayan cities. It is said that the city rose about the time of the birth of Christ and fell about the same time the Dark Age was falling upon Europe.

The masters of the civilization that flourished in Teotihuacan were truly gods. The temples they built were the examples for all the great indio religious edifices that followed, but all that followed were dwarfed by the originals.

My breath left me and my heart jumped when Teotihuacan came into view. The two greatest pyramids of the One World, the monuments the Aztecs most feared and loved and worshipped, the Temple of the Sun and the Temple of the Moon, were the most stunning as we came upon the deserted city. These great pyramids were what the Aztecs copied for the ones they built.

The two main groups of temples were connected by a broad avenue, the Way of the Dead. Half a league long, it was wide enough for two dozen carriages to drive side-by-side. At the north end of the city was the Pyramid of the Moon, along with lesser pyramids. To the east, the greatest pyramid of all: the Pyramid of the Sun. Over seven hundred feet wide in each direction at its base, it rose over two hundred feet into the sky.

A great stairway at the Pyramid of the Sun, climbing up the five levels of the temple—stairs to the heavens—faced the Way of the Dead.

The Pyramid of the Moon was similar in appearance to that of the Sun, but not as large.

Near the center of the city, just east of the Way of the Dead, was the Ciudadela, the Citadel: a vast, sunken court surrounded on all four sides by temples. In the middle of this compound was the Temple of Quetzalcóatl. This temple—a stepped pyramid like those of the Sun and the Moon—had dramatic sculptured representations of Quetzalcóatl, the Plumed Serpent, and the Fire Serpent, the bearer of the Sun on its diurnal journey across the sky each day. The temple was frightening and majestic.

Each year the Aztec emperors came to Teotihuacan to pay homage to the gods. They walked down the Way of the Dead toward the Temple of the Sun amid other temples and the tombs of ancient kings who had become gods. Now the Healer and I walked in the footsteps of those Aztec rulers.

"The Sun and Moon, husband and wife, became gods when they sacrificed themselves to take the earth out of darkness, becoming the golden fire of day and silvery light of night," the Healer said.

We stood before the greatest pyramid on earth, the Temple of the Sun, covering ten acres of ground.

The old man cackled. "The gods are still here; you can feel them. They have your heart clutched in their fist, but they will not rip it out if you honor them."

He pulled up his sleeve and nicked the tender skin on the underside of his arm with an obsidian knife. He let the blood drip to the ground and handed me the knife.

I cut my arm and held it out so the blood would fall to the ground.

Three men and a woman came out of the shadows of a temple and slowly walked toward us. I recognized not their faces but their occupations: sorcerers and wizards, all of them. Each was as ancient and venerable as the Healer.

They exchanged the esoteric greetings of secret signs and veiled language known only to those who practiced the Dark Arts.

"These will be your guides to speak to your ancestors," the Healer said. "They will make your blood Aztec and take you to places where only those with true blood are permitted to enter."

Up to now I had not taken seriously the Healer's comments that I was to speak with the gods. Looking at the venerable faces and secretive eyes of the sorcerers who had come to guide me, I became anxious. How does one speak with the gods?

They led me to an opening in the great Sun pyramid, a hidden recess that I would not have found by myself even if I had been looking for it. The tunnel led to a huge cavern in the bowels of the pyramid, a cave as big as an indio ball court.

A fire in the center of the cave was waiting for us. I heard the trickle of water along the sides of the walls. The smell was of fire and water.

"We are in the womb of the earth," the woman said. "We came out of caves and into the light a thousand ancestors ago. This cave is the mother of all caves, the holiest of the holy. It was here before the Pyramid of the Sun was built." Her voice dropped to a whisper. "It was here during the darkness after each of Four Suns had gone dark and cold."

Blood from our arms was spilled into the fire. We sat before the fire, our legs crossed. A wind blew against me, a cold breeze that frightened the hair on the back of my neck and sent a cold serpent of fear shivering down my spine. Where the wind had entered the cavern, I could not tell, but never before had I felt a wind that seemed to be so *alive*.

"*He* is with us," the old woman chortled.

One of the sorcerers chanted an ode to the gods:

In heaven you live;
The mountains you uphold,
Anáhuac is in your hand,
Everywhere, always you are awaited,
You are invoked; your are entreated,
Your glory, your fame are sought.
In heaven you live:
Anáhuac is in your hand.

Anáhuac was the heartland of the Aztec Empire, the valley now called Mexico, with its five interlocking lakes, Zumpango, Xaltocan, Xochimilco, Chalco, and Texcoco. It was in the heart-of-the-heart of Anáhuac that they built Tenochtitlan.

Our Father the Sun,
In plumes of fire;
Our Mother the Moon,
In silver night.
Come to us,
Bring your light.

Wind as cold as the underworld caressed me again. I shivered down to my toes.

"The Feathered Serpent comes to us," the Healer said. "He is with us now. We called him with our blood."

The woman knelt behind me and put an Aztec warrior's cape of bright feathers, yellow and red and green and blue, over my shoulders. She put a warrior's helmet on my head and handed me a sword of hard wood with an obsidian edge so sharp it could split a piece of hair.

The Healer nodded approval after I was dressed. "Your ancestors will not honor you unless you come to them as a warrior. From the moment of birth, an Aztec was trained to be a warrior. That is why his birth cord was taken into battle and buried on the battlefield by a warrior."

He motioned for me to sit before the fire. The old woman knelt down beside me. She was holding a stone cup filled with a dark liquid.

"She is *xochimalca,* a flower weaver," the Healer said. "She knows the magic potions that let the mind bloom so that it can rise to the gods."

She spoke to me, but I did not understand what she said. I recognized the language as related to Aztec, but it was again the priestly language known only to the few. The Healer interpreted for her.

"She will give you a potion to drink, obsidian knife water. In it are many things, octli, the drink that intoxicated the gods, the cactus bud the white faces call *peyotl,* the holy dust called *ololiuhqui,* blood scraped from the sacrificial block at the temple of Huitzilopochtli in Tenochtitlan before the Spanish destroyed it. There are other things in it, substances that are known only to the flower weaver that came not from the ground we stand upon but the stars above us.

"Those whose hearts were ripped out at the sacrificial block were given this drink before they were sacrificed. As with warriors who die in battle and women who die in pregnancy, those sacrificed are paid the divine honor of living with the gods in the House of the Sun. Obsidian knife water takes one there, to the gods."

Seated before the blazing fire, surrounded by the chanting of sorcerers, I drank the potion.

¡Ayya ouiya! My mind became a river, a dark, flowing stream that soon turned into raging rapids and then into a black maelstrom, a whirlpool of midnight fire. My mind twisted and turned until it spun out of my body. When I looked back, I was soaring in the shadowy ceiling of the cavern. Below me was the fire with the wizards and my own familiar form gathered around it.

An owl flew by me. They were birds of evil omen, announcing death with their nocturnal hoots. I fled out of the cave to escape the death that the owl carried. Day had become night outside; a moonless, starless black shroud encased the earth.

The Healer's voice came to me, whispered in my ear as if I still sat beside him next to the fire in the cave.

"Your Aztec people were not born in this mother of caves in Teotihuacan but in the north, the land of winds and deserts where the Dark Place is found. They did not call themselves Aztecs. That was a name bestowed upon them by the Spanish conquerors. They called themselves Mexicas. They were driven from their northern land by bitter winds; storms of dust, because no rains fell. They were driven south by hunger and desperation, south to the land the gods favored and kept warm and wet. But there were already people in the south, people powerful enough to stop them and destroy the Mexicas. These people were blessed by the sun and rain god. They built a wondrous city called Tula. Not a place of the gods like Teotihuacan, but a city of beauty and pleasure, of great palaces and gardens that rival those of the Eastern Heaven."

It would be in Tula that our Aztec ancestors first understood their destiny, the Healer said.

Tula: the name was magic in my ears even as I listened to the haunted voice of the Healer. Sahagun, a Spanish priest who came to New Spain soon after the conquest, compared the legend of Tula to Troy, writing, "that great and famous city, very rich and refined, wise and powerful, suffered the fate of Troy."

"Quetzalcóatl had been at Teotihuacan, but he left it for Tula," the Healer said. "At Tula he angered and affronted Tezcatlipoca, Smoking Mirror, the god of wizards and sorcerers, and Tezcatlipoca took his revenge. He tricked Quetzalcóatl into getting drunk on pulque; and when lost in this drunken haze, Quetzalcóatl lay with his own sister. Shamed by his sin, he fled Tula and set sail on the Eastern Sea, swearing that he would return someday to reclaim his kingdom.

"Quetzalcóatl is one of your god-ancestors, but there are many others. The most important is Huitzilopochtli, the warrior god of the Aztecs. He took the form of a hummingbird and spoke to his tribe with the voice of a bird. Huitzilopochtli will be your guide."

Huitzilopochtli. Warrior. God. Hummingbird Wizard.

As I soared in the black shroud, I knew the truth.

I am Huitzilopochtli.

FORTY-FIVE

THE DOOR THE flower weaver's potion opened in my mind took me to a distant place and time. When I was leader of the Aztecs.

As I lay dying I saw the Way my people must follow.

I am Huitzilopochtli and the people called Mexicas are my tribe.

We came from the north, the Bitter Land, where the earth was hot and dry and the wind blew dirt in our mouths. Food was scarce in the Bitter Land, and we roamed south, hearing of green valleys that were lush with maize so fat a man's arms could not fit around a single ear. In the north we must fight the hard earth to raise corn so thin it doesn't nourish a cockroach. Many years ago the rain god refused to water our lands, and our people suffered hunger until they found the way of the hunter. Now we hunt with bow and arrow for game that cannot outrun our bolts.

We Mexicas are a small tribe, just two hundred cooking fires. Because we do not have land that can feed us, we wander in search of a home, to the green, lush south, coming into contact with the people who are already settled. All of the good land has been taken, and our tribe is not large enough to force others from their fields.

We move continuously in search of a refuge. We have no beasts of burden except ourselves. Everything we own is carried on our backs. Before the first light we are up and walk until the sun god has fallen. Each man must go out with bow and arrow and knife and kill food for the one meal we have. Our children die of hunger in their mothers' arms. Our warriors are so weak from hunger and fatigue that a single man cannot carry back a deer when they are favored by the gods and kill one.

We are hated everywhere we go. We must have a place of sun and water, but there are people in our path and they drive us away when we find a place where we can rest and grow maize.

The Settled People named us the Chichimecas, the Dog People, and poke fun at our crude ways, calling us barbarians who wear animal skins instead of cotton, who hunt instead of farm, eat raw meat instead of cooked over a fire. They do not understand that what we do is necessitated by our need to survive. *Blood gives us strength.*

The north is the place of the dead, the dark place feared by the people of the south, and they fear us starved barbarians who come from there. They claim we try to seize their land, and that we are wife stealers who grab their women when they are washing clothes along the riverbanks and take them as our own. Ayya, we are a lost tribe. So many have died from sickness, starvation, and war that we must replenish our people. The healthy women of the Settled People can give us children who could survive until we can find our home.

What we ask for is just a place with sun and water to grow food. We are not fools. We are not searching for the Eastern Heaven. We are told that in the south there are mountains that sometime roar and fill the sky and earth with smoke and fire, rivers of water that fall from the heavens and rush off of mountains to wash away everything in their path, gods who shake the ground underfoot and split the earth to swallow whole villages, and winds that howl with the ferocity of wolves. But it is also a land where food grows easily, where the fish and fowl and deer are plentiful, a place where we can survive and thrive.

To us, everything is alive—the rocks, the wind, the volcanoes, the earth itself. Everything is controlled by spirits and gods. We live in fear of angry gods and try to appease them. The gods have driven us from the north. Some say it is Mictlantecuhtli who drives us before his wrath, that he needs our northern lands because the Dark Place is filled with the dead. But I believe we have done something to offend the gods. We are a poor people and make few offerings to them.

I lay dying.

We were driven from a village of the Settled People who believed we lusted after their women and their food. One of their spears found my chest in the battle.

Fleeing their greater numbers and healthier warriors, we climbed to a hillside where it would be difficult for them to attack us. I am the tribe's high priest, wizard, king, and greatest warrior. Without me the tribe will not survive. Even as I lie dying, I can hear the victors below sacrificing Mexica prisoners that they captured. The sacrificed warriors and those who fell on the field of battle will go to the Eastern Heaven, a land filled with the honey of life, so my concern is for the survivors.

Although we are greatly outnumbered by our enemies, they were not able to completely destroy us because we have two things they lack: arrows and desperation. The bow and arrow was new to them. They fought only with spears and swords edged with obsidian. With plentiful food and more warriors, we would be invincible.

The Settled People celebrating their victory below were right. We sought their fields of ripe maize and their ripe women. We need the food to nourish us and the women to give us children. We have lost many warriors and need to replenish our stock.

As I, Huitzilopochtli, chief and priest of my tribe lay dying, surrounded by the lesser priests and headmen, I watched a hummingbird sucking the nectar from a flower. The hummingbird turned and spoke to me.

"Huitzilopochtli, your tribe suffers because it has offended the gods. You ask for food and shelter and victory over your enemies, but you offer nothing in return. The gods need food, too, and their food is the nectar of man. The Settled People are using the blood of the Mexicas to win the favor of the gods. If your people are to survive, you must offer us blood."

We of the north were ignorant of the needs of the gods. We did not know they demanded blood for their favors. We did not know the covenant between man and god:

Feed the Sun God blood and it shines on the land.
Feed the Rain God blood and it wets the crops.

I knew then the destiny of my people, and my own. My path would be to lead my people out of the wilderness to their destiny despite my mortal wounds. It had been prophesied by the high priest Tenoch, as he lay dying, that our destiny would be fulfilled at a place where an eagle fought a snake atop a cactus. Until we found that place, we would be wanderers.

I beckoned the priests and headmen to put their heads closer to me so I might instruct them.

"We must return and attack the Settled People. In the darkness before the dawn, when they are drunk and exhausted from their celebration, we will fall upon them and avenge ourselves."

"We don't have the strength," a headman said.

"We will surprise them. Our desperation will be our strength. We must attack and take prisoners. We have offended the gods because we have not offered them blood. To be strong, we must take many prisoners to sacrifice to them. Only then will the gods reward us."

I would not let them waver. If we fought, we had a chance.

"We must make an offering tonight in order to have victory on the morrow. We took two prisoners today. A woman and her baby. Sacrifice them. Rip out their hearts while the hearts are still beating. And let their blood soak the earth as tribute to the gods. Then cut up their bodies. Each of our strongest warriors is to get a taste."

I told them my body was dying, but I would still be with

them because my spirit would not die but would go through a transfiguration—to become a god.

"The gods have revealed to me the true meaning of my name. Huitzilopochtli is Hummingbird Wizard. In the future I will speak to you in the voice of a hummingbird."

The Mexicas were without a tribal god. I was to be their god, a vengeful god of war and sacrifice.

"The heart is where the spirit dwells," I told the priest, my son, who will wear the headdress of high priest when I die, "making its presence known by the rhythmic beating. Now, before Mictlantecuhtli grabs me and drags me down to the Dark Place, take your obsidian knife and open my chest. Rip out my heart and offer my blood and flesh to our warriors."

I instructed him as the hummingbird had me—my heart was to be put in a nest made of actual hummingbird feathers. My spirit would dwell in the feather nest, and no significant decision was to be made for the tribe without consulting me.

"I will speak to the high priest and, through him, to the rest of the tribe."

That night, with my heart carried high in a totem, my warriors made war upon the Settled People and captured many warriors to sacrifice and women to breed.

We retreated to the top of our hill and cut out the hearts of the warriors. We nourished the gods with their blood, and I gave my people another instruction, spoken to my son, the high priest.

"The blood belongs to the gods, but the flesh of the warriors belongs to the tribesman who captured him. Have a feast to celebrate the victory and the death of the warrior and feed his family and friends the flesh of the warrior."

Thus began the blood covenant between the Mexicas and the gods. In exchange for blood, the gods give victory and food to nourish our bodies.

There was only one way to supply the blood.

War.

FORTY-SIX

I WATCHED FROM the heart nest at the top of a totem as my people grew in strength and numbers. When several generations of my people had been born and died, we were no longer known as a small herd of mongrel people, but as a tribe with a name.

Mexicas were still a tribe without land, but now we had enough strength to demand women and food from lesser tribes. We were known as quarrelsome, cruel, unfaithful to our word; women stealers, and eaters of flesh.

Our reputation earned us more tribute than our arms because we were still a small tribe. Now four thousand campfires strong, with four different clans, we could gather a thousand warriors. Not a great number in a land where mighty kings could put a hundred times that many into battle, but we were growing.

I, Huitzilopochtli, was carried in a totem at the head of the tribe when it moved or its warriors went into battle. The Chosen One, a witch-priestess, carried the feather nest concealed inside a larger, colorful feather nest. Behind her came four priests carrying totems of each of the four clans. All other totems were inferior to mine.

Because of our reputation as fierce warriors, we were invited to join in war with others. Northern tribes, of which we were the smallest, had been hired by the Toltec king to make war on his enemies. To the Toltecs, we were crude barbarians, only worthy of fighting their battles—and dying for them.

In their days of conquest and expansion, the Toltecs were mighty warriors, but now lived off the hundreds of thousands of people who pay tribute to them or work as slaves in their fields. They had grown soft and fat. Rather than risking their own lives, they hired the barbarians from the north to do battle.

The war we came to fight was begun by Huemac, Big Hand, the Toltec king, because another tribe could not fulfill his demand that they send him a woman four hands wide in the buttocks. The tribe brought him a woman, but Huemac was not satisfied with the size and made war upon them. It was said the tribe had the finest carvers of jade in the One World, and that the woman's bottom was an excuse to enslave the carvers and steal their land.

The land of the enemy was in Anáhuac, the Heart of the One World. We were to get a share of the land after we killed the people who occupied it.

We Mexicas proudly marched behind the larger tribes commanded by the Toltec king to Tula, where we would join his army in the war upon the jade carvers.

Tula was not a city, but a paradise on earth. It was built after the gods had driven the people from Teotihuacan. With that great city abandoned by mortals, Tula became the queen of cities of the One World. Although its king ruled Anáhuac, the Heart of the One World, the fabled valley that we Mexicas had yet to set our eyes upon, Tula was not in the valley. It lay just outside the valley to the north, in the path of the tribes that for ten generations had been pushing south to escape the angry gods that were turning the northern region into a lifeless desert.

The Toltec kings of Tula were the richest and most powerful in the One World. They built Tula to resemble Teotihuacan, but they also populated the city with fabulous palaces as majestic as temples and lush gardens that flowed along the streets like rivers of flowers.

It was said that all the wealth of the One World came to Tula. From the tribute paid by those conquered or frightened by the bristling power of Tula's spears, came a portion of everything made or grown by the other Settled People.

Common peasants lived in the city in more luxury than the high priest of our tribe.

Tula was so beautiful that Quetzalcóatl, the Plumed Serpent, left Teotihuacan to reside there. And it was from Tula that Quetzalcóatl left, shamed by having known his sister, promising to return one day to reclaim the kingdom.

The Song of Quetzalcóatl, related by even our barbarian storytellers, speaks of the wonders of Tula, a paradise on earth where cotton grows in bright colors—red and yellow, green and azure—and the earth is a horn of plenty yielding food and fruit that could feed giants: Mangos and melons the size of a man's head, ears of maize so fat a grown man could not put his arms around one, cocoa beans for chocolate so plentiful that one just reached down and picked them off the ground.

Unlike we Mexicas who had no talents except for war, the Toltecs of Tula were the wonder of the One World—scribes, jewelers, stone cutters, carpenters, masons, potters, spinners, weavers, and miners.

This is the first great city my people and I have cast our eyes upon. We have heard that there are other cities, not as grand as Tula, but fabled in their own right. One was near the Eastern Sea where the People of the Rising Sun had lived. These people were stone giants from the stars. When they returned to the stars, they left behind statues of themselves that were as big as temples.

¡Ayya ouiya! We Mexicas had yet to find our place under the sun god. But I knew it was our destiny to someday have a city that put even Tula to shame. But for now, when we first saw Tula, we thought we were looking at the Eastern Heaven.

As our tribe marched by the great city, even I, their war god, was awed by the palaces and great temples honoring the Plumed Serpent and other gods. We have never seen anything like the grandeur of Tula, buildings with high, jeweled walls and people in rich clothing and jewelry.

Nor had they seen the Mexicas.

As we poor nomads from the north marched by, all of

our possessions on our backs, our small children in arms, the people of Tula laughed. They called us crude barbarians and poked fun at our animal skins.

I remembered that ridicule on another day.

After we passed the city, the army of the Toltec king marched behind us. It was a proud and colorful army. The common warriors wore quilted cotton armor, deerskin sandals, and wooden helmets painted bright colors. But, ayyo, the rich and nobles: their capes were of bright bird feathers, headgear trimmed with gold or silver; over their quilted cotton armor were plates of silver. The army marched with great discipline to the beat of drums and the blast of conch shells. Their weapons were not the crude clubs that we barbarians carried, but slender javelins and obsidian swords. But only the barbarians had bows and arrows; the civilized tribes considered the weapon too clumsy to use.

A proud and colorful army. But not a *fighting* army.

The Toltecs brought up the rear because they pushed us barbarians into the front of battle where many were killed or wounded. When the fighting reached their ranks, the Toltec nobles, who should have been leading their own men into battle, sent their common soldiers in first. The nobles entered the fighting only after most of the enemy were wounded or tired.

My totem was carried high into the battle. Our warriors in animal skins and crude weapons were the best fighters, but we were heavily outnumbered by the enemy and received no help from our Toltec masters. There was a great slaughter of barbarians as wave after wave of enemy fell upon us, another line of soldiers taking the place of each line we decimated. Finally, the enemy began to break. When it did, the Toltec army, fresh, fed, and rested, surged by us to complete the rout.

Ayyo. My Mexica stood in the battlefield, splattered with the blood of the enemy, and watched as the Toltecs cheated us out of our victory.

When it was over, we had few prisoners to sacrifice, and

no captured women to give birth to new warriors to replace our fallen comrades.

The gods would not be pleased by our meager sacrifice. Nor would they be satisfied by the Toltec offering. The greedy Toltecs sacrificed only a few prisoners, the wounded who would have died anyway. The common soldiers they kept as slaves, and the nobles they held for ransom.

The Toltec king "rewarded" us with inferior blankets, rancid maize, and bent spears. We were told before the battle that we could get a share of the land in the Anáhuac valley taken from the enemy, but the king and his nobles took all of the fertile land for themselves. We were given the side of a mountain, rough ground, too rocky to grow enough maize to fill our bellies.

The Heart of the One World was a great, green valley with five lakes. The dirt was soft and moist. Maize, beans, and squash grew as if the gods themselves had planted the seed. We Mexicas and other barbarians stared down at the fertile valley from our rattlesnake-infested rocks. And we looked back to Tula, just beyond the valley.

"Call a council of the Dog People," I told my high priest. "We must repay the treachery of the Toltecs, or they will treat us as whipped curs."

A dozen nomadic tribes had come from the north to fight for the Toltec king and claim their share of the spoils. We gathered together and swarmed upon Tula. There were no hired warriors to face us. The warriors of Tula had grown fat and lazy, and we slaughtered many—and took more as prisoners for the sacrificial block. Our vengeance was without mercy; we raped and burned the city.

When the barbaric horde left the city, it was no more. In a few generations, the winds and vines would cover the city, and Tula would forever be nothing more than a legend.

When it came to dividing up the spoils of land and prisoners, we Mexicas found that our barbarian allies were no more honorable than the Toltecs had been.

The other tribes claimed that we did not deserve a significant portion of the spoils because our tribe was small and had contributed little to the victory. My totem had been carried into the thick of the fighting, and I knew that lies were told about our warriors. But I had foreseen the treachery.

When the council of tribes made the accusation that we had done little to bring about the victory, our Revered Speaker, who spoke my words to Mexicas and others, called forth warriors who carried sacks.

The warriors came forward and dumped the contents of the sacks on the ground in front of the other council members.

"These are proof of our contribution to the victory."

Knowing that there would be treachery, I had instructed the Revered Speaker to have our warriors cut an ear from each enemy they killed and each prisoner they took.

Two thousand bloody ears were on the ground.

FORTY-SEVEN

WE HAD REPAID the treachery of the Toltecs and obtained land in the Anáhuac, but we had not fulfilled our destiny as masters of the One World.

Because we were the smallest of the northern tribes, our share of the valley, a portion next to Lake Texcoco, was the smallest. Maize and other food would grow on the fertile areas, but nearly half of that given to us was lake marsh upon which nothing grew but reeds and water flowers.

The Mexicas had been given the marsh to ensure that we did not grow and prosper as fast as other tribes. Although it was not long before that the other tribes were barbarians like us, who traded animal skins for cotton clothes; we were still hated by even our allies. They resented the way we sacrificed our prisoners to appease the gods rather than having them work our land and build our homes.

They claimed horror that we ate the bodies of sacrificed warriors to enhance the power of our own fighting men and that our greatest warriors cut off the skin at the tip of their pene and offer it to the gods as an extra sacrifice.

Blood-thirsty cannibals, they called us, and refused to marry their daughters to us.

But we prospered despite the poor quality of the land given us. Because we were next to the lake, we learned to fish and to trap ducks. Soon we were trading those items for food stuffs grown on higher ground. In a generation, our population doubled from plentiful food and raids that brought back women of other tribes.

To keep the gods appeased with blood, we carried on small wars constantly. Our neighbors in the valley were too powerful for us to attack. Instead, we sent our warriors outside the valley to attack other tribes.

As we were gaining our strength, a larger tribe gained domination over the valley. The Atzcapotazalco were a powerful tribe and we had to pay tribute to them.

Because we were now Settled People, I told the Revered Speaker it was time to build a temple to house my heart. No longer would it be carried on a totem.

It took over a year to build and when it was complete, my people had a special festival to honor me. The tribute collector for the Atzcapotazalco was the lord of Culhuacan. He was ambitious to be master of the valley himself and sought allies.

My people persuaded him to send one of his daughters to be honored at the festival by being wed to a god. Although we were still a small and unimportant tribe, our fighting prowess was known. To bind us to him, he sent his favorite daughter.

To receive the daughter of a great lord was an homage to us Mexicas. To pay our respects to her and her father, we prepared her in our usual custom.

When the lord of Culhuacan came to enjoy our festival,

we proudly showed him what we had done to his daughter.

She had been skinned like a deer to remove her outer coating, from her feet to her head. The carcass had been tossed aside and the skin was slipped into by a small-built male priest in tribute to the nature goddess.

¡Ayya ouiya! Rather than being pleased at the honor paid his daughter, the lord of Culhuacan went into a rage and called upon his warriors to attack us. We Mexicas were the finest warriors in the One World, but compared to the other tribes, we were still small in number. The Atzcapotazalco attacked us in great numbers. We were masters of the lake with our boats, and we used them to flee the onslaught. On the lake were two small islands, rocky islets, that no one cared about. Because they had no place else to go, my people landed on them.

When my totem was brought ashore on one of the islands, I saw an eagle atop a cactus, holding a snake in its beak.

It was a sign, a message from the gods that we had chosen the right place.

I called the island Tenochtitlan, Place of the High Priest Tenoch.

We could not return to the land that had belonged to us because the Atzcapotazalco had seized it as their own, and half of our people were taken prisoner and enslaved.

But I told my people that they had arrived at the place where their destinies would be fulfilled. I was shocked by the sacrilege of the Atzcapotazalcos. Like the other tribes in the valley, they did not honor their gods as they should; and they had insulted the Mexica god. We vowed revenge but knew that it would have to come when we were strong enough to overpower the enemy.

The islands were easy to defend and hard to attack. The lake gave us a bounty in fish, frogs, and fowl that could be traded for maize and beans.

By observing how tiny islets formed from trees in the shallow lake, we learned the chinampa method of farming atop the water. Large reed baskets, each longer and wider than the height of a tall man, were anchored to the bottom of the lake and filled with dirt. Crops grew in the rich dirt. Over time, the chinampas greatly increased the size of the islets themselves.

As Huitzilopochtli, the tribal god of war, it was my duty to instruct my Mexica people on how to fulfill their destiny now that they had arrived at the place Tenoch had prophesied. We would be a warrior society, with all efforts of our people directed toward creating the finest warriors in the One World.

Women were to be rewarded for becoming pregnant. Women who died in pregnancy were to be rewarded the same as warriors who died on the battlefield: They were to go to the paradise of the Eastern Heaven. From birth, male children would be inducted into warrior cults. They would be given swords and shields while still wet from their mother's blood and would grow up knowing no other life than that of a warrior.

FORTY-EIGHT

MOUNTED ATOP A high temple, I watched as generations were born and died and Tenochtitlan developed into a proud city. Through marriage and military assistance, my people had grown powerful but were still surrounded by larger empires. And we chaffed under the heel of the Atzcapotazalco Empire, of which we were still a vassal.

The basket farming had increased the size of Tenochtitlan until it was a large city. Through marriage and other inducements, we had also gained some land along the lake.

The warrior society I had ordained had created the finest fighting force in the One World. Despite its small size, the army of the Mexica was faster, had greater endurance, and were better fighters than any other tribe.

The gods had rewarded us, and we rewarded them. To gain the blood that was needed to appease the gods, our warriors needed constant warfare. Because that cannot be done with our neighbors, we hired our warriors out as mercenaries.

The Mexica name had become feared as it should. We did not retreat in battle. We would pursue an enemy until they dropped. When our warriors marched beyond the reach of our supplies, they marched prisoners with them and ate them to sustain their strength.

I, too, had learned lessons from the past. When an ambitious prince of Azapotzalco, Maxtla, rose to king by murdering his brother and other contenders, he aggravated other tribes by murdering their leaders and demanding more tribute. I instructed our Revered Speaker that we would need allies to go to war against the powerful empire.

With Texcoco and Tlacopan as our allies, we made war upon the Azapotzalco.

Maxtla believed he was a great warrior and maker of war, but he had never fought the Mexica way. After he discovered the power of our army, he sued for peace. My Revered Speaker held a feast to discuss the ending of the war. During the course of the meal, Maxtla asked what meat it was that he was eating.

"Ambassador stew," my Revered Speaker told him. "We are eating the man you sent with your overture of peace."

The peace negotiations were a failure.

The Azapotzalco were defeated. Maxtla fled the battle even while his warriors were fighting. At the sight of him running, they threw down their weapons and fled. My Mexica warriors found Maxtla hiding in a temazcalli, a mud hut used for steam baths.

They piled wood around the hut and baked him inside.

When the war was over, we Mexicas were the most powerful tribe in the One World. We were still in the spring of our bloom, but the rewards of empire were soon pouring into Tenochtitlan.

We had never been numerous people, and we lost many young men in war. We would never be able to control a great empire with a large army as all others before us had done. Instead, we spread out, conquered, and controlled with a reign of terror.

We defeated enemy armies, terrified their people, and then withdrew, leaving behind an administrator with a small force of warriors. The duty of the administrator was little more than collecting the annual tribute we assessed for the region. The local people were free to follow whatever lifestyle they wished—as long as the tribute was paid. When it was not, or our administrator was harmed or disobeyed, our army quickly subdued the rebellious people and punished them harshly.

Tenochtitlan became the greatest city in the One World. Not only did our armies march, but our merchants became travelers who brought back to the city the finest luxuries to be found in one corner of the One World to the other. If our merchants were harassed or murdered, the retribution was swift and harsh. When women of another city insulted our merchants by lifting their skirts and displaying their naked buttocks, we killed the inhabitants and razed the city.

Ayya, we had fulfilled our destiny. But our strategy was so successful, we found few enemies to fight. As the war god of my people, I knew that did not bode well for them. We needed a constant supply of war prisoners to sacrifice so we could continue to fulfill the covenant that had brought us food and prosperity.

I found a solution in the Flower Wars. These were friendly wars fought with our own allies. Their finest warriors would meet our finest in battle. Little effort was made to kill. Instead, the goal was to capture warriors so they could be sacrificed and then honored by having their captors cook and eat their remains.

But not even the Flower Wars were always able to satisfy our need for blood. We suffered a burning drought in which the rain god refused to water our crops, and the sun god blazed down until the crops shriveled and died. When the Revered Speaker came to meditate for guidance at my temple, I told him he must pour a river of blood to appease the gods. The gods had given us an empire, and they wanted their reward.

War had to be waged against even friends to obtain the necessary prisoners, but that year over twenty thousand sacrifices were made. An almost endless line of prisoners went all the way out to the causeways that led across the lake. The priests atop the temple who cut the still-beating hearts out and threw them into Chac-Mool's bowl were soaked in blood from head to foot. A river of blood ran down the temple steps.

The whole Mexica nation feasted on the flesh of the defeated warriors.

The gods were pleased. The rains came and the sun shined.

All was well with the Mexica people. It had taken us nearly twenty generations, but we had risen to hegemony over the One World.

But there was always one god who could never be satisfied. Quetzalcóatl, the Plumed Serpent, would not be satisfied with just blood. When he left Tula and sailed over the Eastern Sea, he had declared that he would be returning to claim his kingdom.

Although my people enjoyed the opulence of the masters of the One World, they always knew that someday Quetzalcóatl would return.

And the kingdom he would claim was the one they possessed.

FORTY-NINE

WE LEFT TEOTIHUACAN, left the dream, and I returned to being a servant boy to a traveling magician. The time I had been with the Healer turned into a year and then into another. After my experience with the potion of the flower weaver, I continued to learn the way of the indios, the dialects, the nuances of walk and talk and even thinking. The day came when the Healer paid me the compliment I had long waited for.

"You no longer smell like a white man," he said.

Besides knowledge of my indio ancestors' history, I gained respect for them. Aztec history was a bloody one, but besides war, the indios made astronomical discoveries, perfected a calendar, published innumerable books in the picture writing that resembled the hieroglyphics of the Egypt of the pharaohs, and made amazing discoveries in health and medicine. Tenochtitlan was said to be a clean, fresh-smelling city in which waste was hauled away in boats to be used as fertilizer. The floating gardens that took root and created man-made islands and temples larger than any on earth were marvels of engineering.

It was true that there were aspects of the Aztecs that were not to be admired. Their practice of the blood covenant was cruel and barbaric. But it was not any more brutal than the practices of the largest and most respected European empire in history: the Roman Empire. Not even the great Aztec sacrificial ceremony where twenty thousand people were killed overshadows the savageness and cruelty of the Roman arenas. The arenas were not just places where thousands of gladiators fought to the death, but many thousands of innocent Christians and other dissenters were murdered by professional warriors or torn apart by wild animals—all for the amusement of crowds.

The Aztecs were no more hated by the indio states they demanded tribute from than the Romans were hated by the peoples they had subjugated. The fray told me that the Romans crucified ten thousand Jews at one time after they rebelled against Roman tyranny and payment of tribute to Rome. Whole cities were decimated.

Even in my own enlightened time, how many thousands were *sacrificed* because of some unspoken blood covenant the Inquisition had with God? Is being *burned alive* at the stake less barbaric than having a knife plunged into your chest and your heart ripped out?

Ayya, I would not be the first to cast a stone at my Aztec ancestors.

There was more to the story of the Aztecs, the return of Quetzacóatl, and the attack by gods astride great animals, but that must wait for another time. But there was one custom of my indio ancestors that I found more repugnant than ripping out beating hearts. Aztec priests often slit their pene so that they could not have relations with women. And if they did have relations despite the cut, their virile juice spilled onto the ground. And many of their warriors cut off a piece of the skin at the front of their pene and offered the skin in sacrifice.

Eh, you think it was just a dream? This tale of Huitzilopochtli and blood, that I had walked with the gods? Perhaps so, but I carried away from that "dream" a mark placed upon me by the gods: The skin at the tip of my pene was severed. I had made the sacrifice of an Aztec warrior.

I learned more than indio ways and legends from the Healer. Besides practical facts about the plants and animals of New Spain, information that I could use if I ever had to survive from what I could find on the land, watching his wise and smooth manners gave me insights into dealing with people. Fray Antonio had dealt bluntly with people he had controversies with, often as a battering ram, driven by his passions. The Healer was a man of cleverness and cunning. Had he not deprived a master liar and thief of two reales? How he caught a thief with a snake trap gave me fresh perception about how greed can snarl a criminal. Later in life I would use the same trick. He called it "the snake trap."

In a village where we had stopped to heal local ailments, someone stole the Healer's prize pipe, the one that fed the belly of Chac-Mool. Only a fool would steal from a sorcerer, but fool he may have been. The Healer had had the pipe long before I was born. I could tell from the quiet intensity of his eyes that he was more upset about the loss than his impassive facial features revealed.

To catch the thief, he told me, he would use a snake trap.

"What's a snake trap?" I asked him.

"A snake trap is two eggs and a ring. The ring is attached upright to a piece of wood. Close to a snake hole, an egg is placed on each side of the ring. When the snake sees the egg, it swallows the first one. Snakes, like people, are greedy, and rather than stealing just one egg, as soon as the egg is worked down its body a little, it slips through the ring and swallows the second egg. It is now trapped because it can't go any farther forward or backward because the ring won't slip past either egg until they digest."

"You can't get a man to slip through a ring for an egg."

He twittered. "Not for an egg, but perhaps for tobacco to smoke in the pipe he stole."

The Healer placed a pouch of tobacco in our campsite at the spot where the pipe had been taken. He smeared red chili powder on the underside of some of the tobacco leaves.

"The thief already has his head through the ring, he did that when he slipped into our camp to steal my pipe. Now we shall see if instead of backing out of the ring, he takes the tobacco."

We left our camp for the cacique's hut, where those requiring the Healer's services had gathered. After an hour I went back to the camp under the pretense of getting something. The tobacco was gone. I ran and told the Healer.

Moments later the cacique ordered every person in the village out into the street and instructed them to hold up their hands.

One man had red powder on his hands. We found the pipe under the straw bedding in his hut.

We left the thief to his fellow villagers for punishment. I got another lesson in the Aztec Ways when the Healer explained how a punishment would be devised.

"Our people believe that a crime should be punished with the same instrument that the crime was committed with. If a man murders another with a knife, the killer will be stabbed with a knife, the same one if possible; that returns the evil the killer gave to the knife back to the killer himself."

Tobacco theft presented a less clear choice of punishment than murder. I wondered what punishment the cacique and village elders would devise.

They consulted in a circle while they drank pulque—and smoked the ever-present tobacco, of course.

Finally, they came to a conclusion.

The thief was tied to a tree and a cloth sack placed over his head. A small hole was cut in the sack and one by one the men of the village went up to the sack with their burning pipes and blew smoke into the hole.

At first I heard the tied man coughing. The coughing became a gasping hack. When it began to sound like a death rattle, I left and returned to our camp.

•

FIFTY

I WAS TO learn that there was a dark side to Aztec magic, a side as gruesome and bloody as anything imagined by Huitzilopochtli, evil so perverse, it was uncontrollable, even by the wielders. The fray used to accuse me of finding trouble like a bee finds pollen. Because of the tragic consequences that would follow, this was a time when I wished that I had not found trouble.

My introduction to the dark side of magic came when I encountered someone else I had also met at the treasure fleet fair.

We had come to a small town during the time of *día de los muertos,* the Day of the Dead festivities. This was a day the indios remembered their dead with food and drink and much gaiety in the cemetery where their dead are buried.

There are actually two days of the dead. The first day is called el día de los angelitos, the Day of the Little Angels, a day set aside for honoring children who have died. The next day honors adults.

After we unloaded the donkey and made camp, I wandered around the town, watching the festivities. The town square was crowded with people and music and fun. The town was much smaller than Veracruz, hardly more than a large village, but many people had come from the countryside to participate. Children ran around with candy "toys" in the shape of skulls, coffins, and other macabre items. Street vendors sold pan de muerto, the bread of the dead, small loafs with a decoration of cross and bones.

We celebrated the Day of the Dead in Veracruz and I knew its history from Fray Antonio. When the Spanish conquered the indios, they discovered that the Aztecs celebrated their dead children and adults in late summer. The celebration was similar to the All Souls Day and All Saints Day that the Church celebrated in November. The clever priests, wanting to ensure that it is a Christian holiday and not a pagan one that gets celebrated, moved the Aztec holiday to merge it with the Christian festivities.

The celebrations are partly done in the privacy of home, where altars are constructed for the dead, and partly at the graveyard, where friends and family hold candlelight vigils and el llorón, the weeping. Sometimes the vigils continue throughout the night; in other places church bells toll at midnight to call people home.

Many Spaniards are shocked by the macabre nature of this Aztec-Christian festival. They miss the point of the celebration. The indios believe that they can communicate their love to their departed loved ones by expressing the love at the deceased's grave site and in the home.

Like most festivals and fairs, the celebration enjoyed a carnival atmosphere. Late afternoon there would be a parade, with many people in costumes, like a máscara, but the costumes would emphasize skeletons, bishops, and devils.

In the center of the square, indios were putting on a play. Not the kind the picaro Mateo would recognize as a comedia, but one the indios understood well. The performers were men dressed as knights of the two great Aztec warrior orders, the Jaguar Knights and the Eagle Knights. Entrance into these noble orders was reserved for only those warriors who excelled on the field of battle, killing and taking prisoners.

Both sets of knights wore the traditional capes of bright feathers and heavy, quilted cotton armor, but each order had its own unique headdress. The Jaguar Knights wore headdresses of actual jaguar skins, a snarling face and teeth on top of the head with the rest of the dressed hide falling down the back. The Eagle Knights wore the head and feathers of eagles, the great, obsidian-sharp beaks of the birds of prey gaped open in a scream, their talons hanging down from around the neck of the warrior.

The jaguar and the eagle were appropriate symbols for the two greatest warrior castes of the Aztec Empire—the great cat ruled the ground, and the eagle was the king of the skies.

A tall religious monument, a tribute to some saint or another, was in the center of the square, and the mock battle took place around it. Lépero youths had climbed on the monument, and I dashed through the battling knights to climb up to get the best view. One of the léperos, believing I was an indio invading his territory, kicked at me. I grabbed his foot and dragged him off the monument. I took his place and glared at the others with Veracruz street toughness. No one else bothered me.

The knights fought with wooden swords and shields, swinging hard at each other, blocking, swinging again. The only purpose seemed to be battering each other since the swords could not inflict a serious injury.

Watching the mock battle, I spotted a person I had conflicted with at the treasure fleet fair: the caster of bones. The evil-looking creature was standing at the inner edge of the circle of people watching the fighting. His black hair hung down almost to his waist. Encrusted with dirt and grease, the hair was dirtier and no doubt smellier than a stable floor.

As the fighting went on, I noticed a curious phenomena: The combatants would continue until blood was drawn, usually a small cut on the hand, face, or legs that were bare from the knees down. The moment blood was seen, the victor and the bleeder would leave the battle. The curious thing was that each time it occurred, the victor looked to the magician. In return he got a nod of approval.

"Mestizo. Your heart will be ripped out on the sacrificial block when the jaguars rise."

That anonymous threat came to mind as I watched the magician giving silent blessing to the victors. Unlike the Healer, who had an aura of wisdom and knowledge of secret ways, the magician reeked of evil and malice.

I was staring at him, *glaring* at him, when he suddenly

looked up and caught me. I jerked back and looked away. I felt like I had just locked eyes with a snake. I sneaked another look at him, and he was still staring at me.

He had an evil eye that could burn through stone. I did not know if he recognized me from the fair or he had seen the contempt on my face when he caught me staring down a moment before. I was sure that he would not recognize me. Over two years had passed since the fair, and I had barely spoken to him at the time.

Whatever the reason, I had caught his attention; and that was unwelcome in my life. I got down from the statue base and slipped through the warriors to get away. As I was hurrying from the battling knights, a fray on a mule rode into the square. Behind him an indio rode another mule, dragging something behind on the ground with a rope. When they reached the area where the mock battle was taking place, they rode into it, scattering the warriors. It was then that I could see what the indio was dragging.

A body.

The priest stopped his mule and shouted to the crowd. "This man," he pointed down at the body, "died yesterday and was not buried with the rites of the Church. He was put into the ground with the *blasphemy of pagan rites*."

He paused to let his words sink in.

"I only learned of the disgrace because there are indios among you who are true to the Lord and tell me when such heresy occurs. His body has been dug up. It will be dragged through every street in this community for all to see what will happen to them when they offend God and the servants of the Church who serve Him.

"Afterward, the body will be chopped up and fed to dogs."

I had heard Fray Antonio speak of this crude practice by village priests. He said that most of the priests were less angry that the sinner had gotten buried without the proper rites than they were about not receiving payment for the last rites and Christian burial.

As the fray and the indio whose mule was dragging the

body rode by the dark magician, the reader-of-bones gave the two a look of such pure hate and malice that it frightened me.

I left the area, hoping I would not run into the dice man again.

As night was falling, I roamed the village to enjoy the celebration of the dead. When it was dark, people crowded into the cemetery to be near their departed loved ones. The graveyard blazed with hundreds of candles as people drank and danced, laughed and talked. They formed family groups at grave sites, passing around tamales, tortillas, pulque, and those hot peppers the Aztecs called chili.

I was not a part of a family group, but I enjoyed just strolling around, enjoying their joy. People were drunk and happy. At least most were happy. I watched a young woman arguing with her husband, who was very drunk. He was so drunk that he could hardly stand up. It brought to mind what the fray had told me was the difference between the way the Spanish drank and the indios drank: a Spaniard drinks to get a feeling of joy and well-being. An indio drinks until he passes out.

This young woman called her husband a stupid goat for getting so drunk and hit him. The blow sent him stumbling backward and he fell onto his backside. People nearby cheered and clapped the woman's action.

She stamped away, almost knocking me down. When she did, a handkerchief fell from her pocket. I grabbed the handkerchief and followed after her. She was out of the cemetery before I caught up with her and gave it back.

"Your husband is very drunk."

"I don't care if he drinks," she said. "He spent all the money I earned in a month of washing clothes. That is what I care about."

"It is a sin for him to get drunk and leave such a beautiful wife alone and unprotected. There are men who would take advantage of such stupidity."

She brushed hair from her forehead. "I have never seen you before."

I shrugged. "I am a wandering sorcerer. I am here today and shall be gone tomorrow."

"What kind of magic do you have?"

"Love magic. I keep it here." I touched the front of my pants. "Would you like to see it?"

Eh, where did I get the courage to say such things? I was seventeen years old and had never bedded a woman. But since my failure with the cacique's wife, I had practiced a great deal with my hand and was eager to see if my performance had improved.

She smiled and patted her own front. "I have a skull sewn onto my underwear today for my husband, but he is too drunk to see it. Or appreciate it."

We went to a grassy area to practice my magic—and see her skull.

She lay on her back on the warm grass. I knelt down beside her and leaned down to nuzzle her with my lips. *Ayya ouiya.* She jerked me down atop her and ravaged my mouth with her lips and tongue. When I was getting to like the lush wetness of her mouth, she rolled me over. Her mouth went back to my lips and her hand down my pants.

My garrancha was expanding to monstrous proportions—growing so hard, so fast, it hurt, which seemed to amuse the woman to no end. She giggled at the enormity of my erection—her fingers gripping it iron hard, tight as a vise.

She slipped a hand around my head, and as she kissed me open-mouthed, she began pulling down my pants.

Even at my tender age I was certain that rape was the man's job and not the woman's. I struggled to get up and mount her, so I could jab my pene in and pump it at least once before it exploded. "I want to—"

She swallowed my words with her mouth. Getting my pants down, her skirt went up and she straddled me. She rubbed her wet tipíli back and forth against my erection. As she slid back and forth on my virile part, she burst open her blouse. She bent down and guided a breast to my mouth. As she did, her legs spread farther apart and my pene suddenly slipped into her love opening.

All the lust of my pubescent youth was boiling up in me. My hips bucked up and down like a horse that had never felt a saddle.

She rode me, tightening her muscles around my member, gyrating on it erotically, with each twist and turn lengthening the stroke. Up and down, up and down, on my achingly long garrancha. She increased pressure, tempo, and heat with each rise and fall.

I began to lose control. And then my pene exploded inside her. It triggered something in her that at the time I did not understand, and her movements and moans became more frantic. She leaned forward, arching her back like a bent bow, but pumping with everything she had. Lights blazed in my eyes, thunder detonated in my ears, and the earth shook volcanically. My body erupted in turn, not an orgasm of the groin but of the entire corpus—of the entire planet. My entire being was breaking loose, coming apart, taking me on a Homeric odyssey I had never known I would make.

I might have other women subsequently—assuming I lived long enough—but this was my first. Come what may, she owned me body and soul. My soul had broken free, cut loose, its moorings forever slipped.

At which point she grabbed me by my backside and flipped me over on top of her. She pulled my hips forward, tilting them so that the top of my pelvis was rubbing what I would later learn to be what the poet Ovid called "the Venus Butterfly."

Her ministrations caused my garrancha to erupt into a long blade again. It went back inside of her, with me atop her. I pumped like el diablo was burning my buttocks, and she began exploding again.

Now she was delirious, her head rolling back and forth, her tongue lolling out of her head. Her hips were grinding desperately, her breath catching in her throat, and she was groaning. Raising her knees, clamping her legs over my shoulders, lifting her buttocks off of the ground, she pumped powerfully. Her nipples hard and swollen bit into my chest, and when I started to yelp, she grabbed me around the back of the neck and muted my groans with all-consuming kisses.

Only God knew what the next day would bring.

But in a sense I didn't care. I was just a boy and had had my first glimpse of bliss.

I had seen the elephant, soared with eagles, heard the owl—and touched the face of God.

If anyone had asked me, I was already dead.

¡Ay de mí! before the night was over, someone wanted me dead.

FIFTY-ONE

AFTER MIDNIGHT I joined the Healer at the campsite. I carefully gave no more hint of my activities with the woman on the grass than I would have to the pope. The Healer was otherworldly; matters of the temporal flesh were not in his realm.

Before hitting the ground with my blanket, I went into the bushes to relieve myself. We had camped on a knoll, and it gave me a view of the town below. The full moon gave good light to the night, casting the town in a ghostly glow. Candles moved around the graveyard like fireflies, and the sound of music floated up.

I sat for a while looking at the town, and it made me lonely. I had grown to love the Healer as a father, just as I had loved Fray Antonio, but neither was a real father. And I never had a real home. I wondered what it would be like to have a mother and father, brothers and sisters, to sleep each night on a bed and eat at a table with a plate in front of me and a fork and knife in hand.

Getting up to leave, I noticed the light of a fire on the knoll across the way and could see moon-shadowy figures moving. I knew that a small Aztec temple was on the hill, one of the hundreds of forgotten and abandoned religious relics left by the defeated empire.

I was curious about who would be at a pagan temple in the middle of the night. No doubt the village priest would like to know—and even pay a reward. Not that I would turn in someone for a reward . . . but maybe I could get the señorita who'd celebrated the Day of the Dead with me to get the reward and share it with me. That would satisfy my black heart and keep from having the Healer ask me too many questions.

I made my way down the knoll and moved up the other one, taking care not to make enough noise to wake the dead . . . or disturb whoever was at the temple.

As I neared the top I stopped and listened. I could hear a man speaking Aztec words, not words I understood but a magic incantation in a tone I have heard the Healer use many times. I crept closer and got a view of the temple, a small, stone pyramid with broad steps almost as wide as the pyramid itself.

Men had gathered at the top of the temple and back down the steps. I made out seven or eight men. A small fire had been lit atop the temple. I could see a bit of its flickering light, but my view was blocked by the men standing before it.

I quietly climbed up a tree to get a better view. A man still blocked much of my view, and I strained to see what blasphemy was going on. He moved out of my line of sight and I saw that rather than one large fire, there were several torches burning close together. The torches were kept low, no doubt to keep them from being seen from a distance. The flames illuminated a large, stone block. I heard hysterical laughter, the voice of a man drunk on pulque. He laughed again and I decided that whatever he had been given was not pulque, but a drug concocted by a flower weaver.

Four men suddenly grasped the laughing man, two taking his feet and two taking his arms. They held him outstretched over the block. As they lay him atop the block, I realized that the top of the block was slightly rounded so that the man's back was arched, and his torso extended up when he lay across it.

A dark figure stepped up to the block. He faced me but it was too far and too dark for me to see the person's features. But the figure was familiar. So was the long hair that came almost down to his waist. I was certain if it was daylight I could have seen just how dirty and greasy the hair was.

Fear and trepidation gripped me. I had already guessed what was about to happen at the strange, midnight ceremony. My mind told me that it was a mock ceremony, like the battle between the Aztec knights, but a tight, cold fist gripped my heart.

The magician lifted his hands over his head. The dark glint of an obsidian blade held by both hands reflected in the torch light. He plunged the long blade down at the prone man's chest. The man gasped. His body wriggled and thrashed like a snake whose head had been cut off.

His executioner cut open the chest and reached in. He jerked back and held up to the light a flapping heart. The men gathered on the temple let out a uniform sigh of awe.

My arms and legs turned to rubber, and I tumbled out of the tree. I crashed to the ground with a jolt and a cry of pain.

I ran, through the bushes, in the direction of our camp. I ran as I had when the overseer was chasing me with a sword. I ran as if all the hounds of hell were snapping at my heels.

As I ran I heard something behind me. Not something human, but something that was not stomping on two feet as I was.

It was coming up fast. I turned and swung my knife as

something swirled at me in a blur. I was knocked backward, breathless, and felt sharp claws on my chest. I put my arm across my throat to protect it.

Then the Healer was there, shouting something. The creature atop me was gone as quickly as it had come.

The Healer helped me off the ground and took me, sobbing, back to our camp. My explanation of what had happened spouted in a torrent along the way.

"I was attacked by a jaguar," I said, after telling him about the human sacrifice I had witnessed.

He had come looking for me when I failed to return.

We got together our possessions and the donkey and went down to the town, where many visitors were camped outside homes of friends. Had it been daylight, I would have kept going to the next town and beyond.

When we were settled near others camping in town, I quietly explained everything that had happened, this time going over it slowly and answering his questions.

"I'm sure it was that caster of bones I saw at the fair," I said. "I saw him again at the mock battle between the knights today."

He was strangely quiet. I would have expected him to expound upon the events, explaining them with his great storehouse of knowledge and wisdom. But he said nothing, and it increased my unease.

I slept little. I kept seeing the heart of a man being ripped out of his chest. And I kept seeing the face of the man who did it. It sickened me that I recognized the man whose heart was ripped from its chest while it was still warm and beating.

It was the Christian indio who'd dragged an Aztec worshipper behind his mule.

FIFTY-TWO

BEFORE WE SET out at the first break of light, making sure we attached ourselves to a mule train, the Healer put salves on the claw marks on my chest.

"It was bad luck that I ran into a jaguar as I was running away," I said, as he applied the ointment.

"It was no accident," the Healer said.

"It wasn't a man dressed up as a Jaguar Knight; it was a real animal."

"It was an animal, yes, but whether it was real . . ."

"Ayya, I saw it. So did you. It ran away on four legs. Look at my chest. No man did this."

"We saw an animal, but not all animals of the night are animal beneath the skin."

"What do you mean?"

"This man you call a magician, a caster of bones, is a *naualli.*"

"What is a naualli?"

"A sorcerer. Not a healer, but one who calls upon the dark side of the Tezcatlipoca magic that gives all sorcerers their power. They are about, but he is the most notorious. It is said that they terrify people and suck the blood of children at night. They can conjure clouds to make hail to destroy a man's crops, turn a stick into a serpent, a piece of stone into a scorpion. But of all these powers, the most terrifying is that of shape changing."

"Shape changing? You think the naualli turned into a jaguar to kill me?" My tone was that of a priest scolding an indio on a point of superstition.

The Healer twittered at my indignation. "Is it so certain that all we see is of the same flesh and blood that we ourselves are composed of? You took a journey to your ancestors. Was that a dream? Or did you really meet your ancestors?"

"It was a dream induced by the flower weaver's potion."

"The flower weaver's medicine created the bridge to your ancestors. But are you so certain that what you experienced was just a dream? That you didn't cross the bridge?"

"It was a dream."

He twittered again. "Then perhaps what you saw last night was just a dream."

"It had real claws."

"It is said that nauallis have a cloak made from the skin of jaguars, that when they put it on, it transforms them into the beast. They have a medicine more powerful than any flower weaver can prepare, an evil concoction prepared from every sort of poisonous vermin—spiders, scorpions, snakes, and centipedes. I told you about this, the divine ointment. But the nauallis know how to prepare the ointment for a different purpose than making them impervious to pain. They add the blood of a jaguar and pieces of a human heart. When it is drunk, it permits a wearer of the naualli's cloak to assume the body of the beast that the cloak is made from.

"I heard a story from the men at the village we were in four days ago. A rich Spaniard had kept an india girl as his lover for many years, having children by her and treating her in every way as his wife except marrying her. The Spaniard betrayed her by bringing a Spanish woman over from Spain to marry and returning the india woman in shame back to her village.

"The Spanish doña enjoyed riding a horse and would ride by herself on the vast property her husband owned. One day vaqueros heard her scream—she had been attacked by a jaguar. The vaqueros shot the jaguar before it killed her. As the beast lay on the ground dying, it turned into the india girl who had been betrayed."

"And the theory is that a naualli turned her into a jaguar." I laughed. "It sounds like an indio tale to me."

"Perhaps so, perhaps so. But last night you slashed the jaguar in the face. Today the naualli has a cut on his face. Perhaps you should ask him how he obtained his injury." He gestured to his left.

The evil old magician was coming down the street flanked by two husky indios I recognized as having worn Knights of the Jaguar costumes at yesterday's mock battle.

An ugly gash was on the magician's face.

He never said a word as he passed, nor did he or his henchmen look in our direction. But I felt his malignant animosity radiating at me. I was so frightened that I shook like a newborn foal testing its legs for the first time.

Down the road the Healer twittered and mumbled to himself for an hour. It was the first time that I had ever seen him so animated about anything. Despite his intense dislike for the naualli, he seemed to have professional respect for the man's magic.

Finally he said to me, "Tonight you must give extra blood to the gods." He shook his head sadly. "You should never laugh at the Aztec gods."

FIFTY-THREE

TWICE MORE IN our travels I heard stories about the search for the lépero who had killed the priest from Veracruz, but now the story had taken on the rudiments of myth. The lépero was not just a killer of many men, but a highwayman and a defiler of women. Now that a couple of years had passed and my fear of discovery was less, I found the stories of the terrible deeds of the infamous bandito, Cristo the Bastardo, to be almost amusing. But the larger the village or the closer to haciendas we got, the more careful I became about portraying my indio heritage.

Behind the tales was a true story of the murder of the only father I knew. As I had done since the foul deed occurred, each night I swore an unholy oath when I made my prayers that I would take revenge upon his killer. Like the indios who used the same instrument of revenge as the one the perpetrator used, I would plunge a knife in the man's gut and twist it.

FIFTY-FOUR

MY EIGHTEENTH YEAR occurred when I accompanied the Healer to a fair. The fair was once again held to sell merchandise that had arrived aboard ship but this time it was a smaller fair, and the merchandise came not from Europe but from Manila on the other side of the great Western Sea. Each year galleons, floating castles, sometimes several, other times just a single ship, made the crossing of the Western Sea, from Acapulco to Manila and back.

The Manila galleons took much longer to cross the ocean than the treasure fleet that coursed to Spain. Fray Antonio had showed me the two seas on a map of the world. The distance to Manila was several times farther than the route between Veracruz and Seville. Across the Western Sea, which the fray's map called the Southern Sea, were the islands called the Filipinas. From this outpost halfway around the world from Spain, trade was had with a land called China, where there are more chinos, people with yellow skin, than grains of sand—an island of short, brownish people who train warriors called samurai, who are the fiercest fighting men on earth—and the Spice Islands, where the beaches are composed not of sand, but of cinnamon and other spices, which can be shoved into buckets.

The incident at Veracruz was several years and many

leagues away. I felt safe going to the fair and was actually eager to be around more Spaniards again. For three years I had been enmeshed in the indio culture. While I learned much, there was still much I admired and desired to learn from my Spanish side.

I had grown inches and put on over twenty pounds in weight. I was tall and slender, as I had always been for my age, but had filled in some of the bones with the good food I enjoyed with the Healer. In the House of the Poor our meals consisted mostly of tortillas and beans, but on the road with the Healer we truly feasted. Often guests at village festivals, we dined on chicken, pig, and duck, and fine indio dishes like mole, the lusty sauce made with chocolate, chilies, tomatoes, spices and ground nuts. Eh, amigos, no king since Montezuma feasted better than the Healer and me.

While the Manila galleon fair was not as large as the one that took place in Jalapa for the treasure fleet because there were fewer ships on the Manila run, the cargo was much more exotic. The Manila galleons brought back silks, ivory, pearls and other luxuries that the rich of New Spain coveted. Best of all were the spices from the Spice Islands, pepper and cinnamon and nutmeg. The smell of the spices was exotic and tempted the thieving lépero in me. You ask if my years with the Healer had not separated me from the bad habits I learned on the streets of Veracruz? Let us just say that the Healer taught me new tricks . . . but I did not forget the old.

Because the products from the Far East were new and strange, there was much for me to wander about and gawk at. I bought a pinch of cinnamon and both the Healer and I tasted it on the tip of our tongues. Our eyes lit up in amazement at the strange taste. Dios mio, how many pesos would a shovelful be worth! I wondered if the sea that washed the Spice Islands tasted like spices.

But there was work to do and little time for daydreaming. The fair was held for only a few days and we had traveled far to get there. We had to make enough money in a short time to ensure the trip was worth it. The unusual sights and smells I could enjoy in stolen moments.

The Healer had come to practice his art, his healing and his magic, and I was his assistant. When business was slow, to draw a crowd I was sometimes a sick person who would loudly complain to him of pain and noise in my head. When enough people had gathered, the Healer muttered incantations and pulled a snake out of my ear. Once people saw my miracle cure, there was usually someone in the crowd who was willing to pay for a cure for themselves.

But the Healer did not take every person who stepped forward. He took patients only whom he believed he could help. And he did not require payment unless the patient could afford it. Neither practice filled our pockets. All of his patients were indios, anyway, and these people rarely had anything but copper coins jingling in their pockets. More often payment was in cocoa beans or a small sack of maize.

Like the Roman god Janus, there were two faces to the Healer. The snakes were a trick, but the healing was not.

I was still very loose and limber in my arms and legs, and privately I still practiced the art of twisting my joints, but I no longer performed in public, playing the cripple for alms. It was too dangerous because the man Ramon who killed Fray Antonio may have known of my skill. However, I inadvertently exposed my abilities.

Business was always better if the Healer could be elevated a bit above the onlookers. In this case there was a rocky mount about five feet off the ground. The area was heavily entrapped by large vines and other growth. I cleared away enough space atop to permit the Healer and his patients to stand.

During a performance in which a crowd had formed to watch the snake come out of a person's ear, the nervous patient accidentally kicked the Healer's pipe which was laying nearby, knocking it into the vines hanging down the side of the mound. I quickly scrambled to get it, slipping into the vines, twisting and turning to wiggle in and out like a serpent.

When I got back on top, I noticed a man, a Spaniard, staring at me. The man was not dressed in the cloth of a merchant nor in the rougher garb of a hacienda boss, but as a caballero—not the fancy clothes one usually sees them wearing on the streets, but the thicker fabric and leathers they wear when they are traveling or fighting. The Spaniard had hard and unforgiving features, his lips and eyes revealing a streak of cruelty. As he stared at me, another man came up beside him. I almost gasped aloud.

It was Mateo, the picaro who had put on the play at the Jalapa fair.

The mean-spirited Spaniard spoke to Mateo, and the two looked up at me with inquiring eyes. There was no explosion of recognition in the picaro's eyes. It had been three years since I had seen him, a long time ago for a skinny beggar boy who was fifteen at the time. I had no idea whether he recognized me. The last time I saw him, he had cut a man's head off for me. Perhaps this time he was going to cut my head off.

Fearful that I had exposed myself, I left the stage and pretended to walk along the rows of merchandise lined up for sale. Mateo and the other Spaniard followed slowly behind me. I ducked down behind bales of wool and crawled along until I reached the end and then ran low down another line of merchandise. I peeked up and saw Mateo looking around, trying to find me. I did not see the other man.

Running low along the merchandise, I saw a chance to make a dash to the heavy brush outside the perimeters of the fair. When I stood up to run, a rough hand grabbed me by the back of the neck and spun me around.

The Spaniard jerked me close to his face. He stank of sweat and garlic. His eyes bulged a little, like fish eyes. He put his knife under my throat and pressed until I was standing on my tiptoes and staring at him wide-eyed. He let go of my neck and smiled at me, keeping the pressure of the dagger under my chin. He held up a peso with his free hand.

"Do you want your throat cut or the peso?"

I couldn't open my mouth. I motioned at the peso with my eyes.

He released the knife from my throat and handed me the peso.

I stared at the peso—a veritable fortune. I had rarely had a silver reale in my hand, and a peso was worth eight reales. An indio would work a week for less. Men were sometimes killed for less.

"I am Sancho de Erauso," the Spaniard said, "your new friend."

Sancho was the friend of no one, of that I was certain. A large man but not tall, bulky, there was no piety in his eyes, no mercy in his face. The picaro Mateo was larcenous but had the manners and airs of a rogue and gentleman. Sancho had no pretense of being a gentlemen—or even human. He was a cutthroat, a man who could share with you a meal and a glass of wine and then kill you for dessert.

Mateo found us. No recognition showed on his face or in his eyes. Could he really not remember the boy he had killed a man for? Yet what would be his motive for not recognizing me? Perhaps he regretted his act and feared that I would expose him as the real killer. Perhaps he was going to kill me. And it was possible that like so many Spaniards, an indio or mestizo was as distinguishable to him as one tree from another in a forest of trees.

"What do you want of me?" My tone to Sancho was subservient, an indio speaking to a master who wielded a heavy hand.

Sancho put his arm around my shoulder, and we walked along together with Mateo on my other side. My nose was close to Sancho's armpit, and it smelled worse than a sewer hole. Did the man never bathe? Or wash his clothes?

"My friend, you are most fortunate. I need a small favor. You are a poor, miserable indio with no future except to break your back for the gachupin and die young. For this little favor, you will earn so much money you will never have to work again. No more stealing, no more whoring your mother and sister. You will have money, women, and not just pulque to drink, but the best Spanish wines and Caribbean rum."

The man was evil, el diablo and Mictlantecuhtli in one. His voice had the texture of Chinese silk, his face the charm of a rattlesnake smiling. His sincerity was as genuine as a puta's lust.

"We have a small task for you, something that only a slender youth who can twist his body like a corkscrew can do. We have to travel a few days to get to where you will perform your task. In less than a week you will be the richest indio in New Spain. How does that sound, amigo?"

It sounded like I was going to be roasted over a flame while wild dogs gnawed on my cojones. Still, I smiled at the bully. Elevating him to a man of respectability, I added the honorific "don" to his name. "Don Sancho, I am a poor indio. When you speak of great wealth, I thank all the saints that you will let me serve you."

"I don't like the looks of this one," Mateo said. "Something about him strikes me wrong—his eyes—he looks more conniving."

Sancho stopped and faced me, looking for the conniving in my eyes. "He's the best we've seen." He moved in closer and I forced myself not to be repelled by the smell. His grabbed me by the throat, and I felt his knife against my groin.

"The old man with the snakes, is that your father?"

"Sí, señor."

"You can run fast, Chico, but the old man can't. Each time you annoy me, I will cut off one of his fingers. If you run away, I will cut off his head."

"We have to travel south, to Monte Alban in the valley of Oaxaca," I told the Healer later. "Spaniards have hired me to do a task. They will pay me well."

I told him that Sancho wanted me to retrieve something he had lost. I couldn't tell him what the task was because I did not know, but as was his custom, he asked no questions. At these times I had the feeling that rather than a lack of curiosity, he knew exactly what was happening. No doubt a bird had been listening to the conversation and reported to him.

It was hours before the fair would close for the night, and I spent the time wandering around, looking at the many wonders, trying to figure a way out of the trap. There was no acting troupe in evidence, and I supposed that they had separated company with the poet-swordsman or by now had taken their turn on the gallows.

Mateo seemed grimmer than when I had first seen him. And his clothes were not as fancy and well kept. Perhaps the last several years had not been good to him. I had not forgotten that I owed him my life.

As I wandered about the fair, a commotion broke out and a crowd gathered. During an archery contest, a man, an indio, had been shot by an arrow that went astray. People surrounded him to stare, and I squeezed in close to watch. The man's friend knelt beside him and started to pull out the arrow. Another man stopped him.

"If you pull out the arrow that way, you will tear his insides and he will bleed to death."

The speaker, a Spaniard about forty years old and dressed like a wealthy merchant, knelt and examined the wound. I heard someone call him "Don Julio" when he instructed men to help him move the injured man.

"Move him over here. Stand back," he told those of us crowding around.

Always fascinated by medicine, I helped Don Julio and two others move the wounded man behind the line of merchant tents so he would be out of the sight and path of people.

Don Julio knelt and examined the arrow wound.

"What position were you in when you were shot?" Don Julio spoke Spanish with a slight accent, and I recognized that he was probably Portuguese. Many Portuguese had come to the New World after the Spanish king inherited the throne of that country.

"Standing up."

"Were you straight up? Standing tall? Or bent a little?"

He groaned. "Maybe bent a little."

"Straighten out his legs," he told us.

When we had the man's legs straight, he had us do the same for the upper body. Once he had the man in the position that most likely reflected what he was like when the arrow struck, Don Julio carefully examined and probed the area when the arrow met the flesh.

The man's friend impatiently snapped, "Pull it out before he dies." He spoke in the rough Spanish of rural indios.

I answered the man. "He has to remove it in the same line that it entered, or he will create a bigger wound."

By removing the arrow in the same path it entered, he would reduce tearing more flesh. The man already had a wound that would probably kill him no matter how carefully the arrow was removed. Increasing the size of the wound would reduce his chance of surviving.

Don Julio glanced up at me. I had inadvertently spoken in my polished Spanish rather than deliberately mispronouncing words as I had done with Sancho.

He tossed me a half-reale. "Run to a cloth seller. Get me a piece of clean white cotton."

I returned quickly with the piece of cloth. I did not offer the change.

After he removed the arrow, Don Julio dressed the open wound, cutting pieces of the cloth to create a cover for it.

"This man cannot walk or even ride a mule," he told the indio's friend. "He has to lie still until the bleeding stops." He took aside the man's friend. "He has only a small chance of survival, but he will not survive at all if you move him. He can't be moved for at least a week."

I saw the friend exchange looks with another man. Neither of the two men appeared to be indio farmers. They had the look of léperos, perhaps men hired from the streets by merchants to bring merchandise to or from the fair. The chances of them staying around until the man could travel were not good. As soon as the fair broke up, they would throw dice for his boots and clothes, smash his skull, and drag him into the woods for wild animals to dispose of.

As the crowd around the man moved away, I heard a man look in the direction of Don Julio and whisper contemptuously to another, *"Converso."*

I knew this word from discussions with Fray Antonio. A converso was a Jew who had converted to Christianity rather than leave Spain or Portugal. Sometimes the conversion had taken place generations before, but the blood taint was still there.

The fact that this wealthy doctor, which is what I took him to be, also had a blood taint naturally endeared him to me.

I left the fair and walked toward a mound that had once been a small temple for a military outpost or a merchant's rendezvous. I sat for a while deep in thought about the predicament I was in with Sancho and Mateo. I was less worried about myself than I was of any harm coming to the Healer. I had of course lied when I told Sancho that the Healer was my father, but in a way there was truth to it since I thought of both him and Fray Antonio like a father.

I had no illusions about what my reward would be once I had completed the task for Sancho. Both the Healer and I would be killed. Ay, it was not a happy situation. The Healer moved very slowly and would go nowhere without his dog and his donkey. My only recourse was to await the opportunity to stick a knife in Sancho's fat gut and hope that Mateo would not harm the Healer even if he cut off my head.

I spotted Aztec picture writing engraved in stone on the side of the wall of the ruins, and I moved aside brush to read it. I had learned to read Aztec picture writing from the Healer, who showed me pieces of paper with writing on it that was done before the conquest. He told me that the empire centered at Tenochtitlan required a vast amount of paper to run, for its army, merchants, government administration, and that hundreds of thousands of sheets of blank paper were received each year as tribute from vassal states.

The fray had also been interested in Aztec picture writing and paper. He had been excited once when another fray showed him a piece of it. Paper was made by soaking the bark of certain fig trees in water until the fiber separated from the pulp. The fiber was pounded on a flat surface, folded over with a sticky substance in between, flattened more, and then smoothed and dried. Good quality paper had a whitish substance spread over it.

A bundle of these papers bound together was called a codex by the Spanish, being a Latin word for a type of book. Only a few indio codices had survived the fanatical zeal of the Christian priests, Fray Antonio told me. Picture drawings were done in bright colors—red, green, blue, and yellow—and having seen a few pages possessed by the Healer, I can only envision that the codices saved from the ravages of the priests must be works of great beauty.

Aztec writing itself was nonalphabetical, picture writing much like the Egyptians used. A series of pictures had to be read together to reveal the message or story. Some objects were represented by a miniature of the object, but most situations required something more complex: a black sky and closed eye was night, a wrapped mummy figure was a symbol of death, seeing was expressed by an eye drawn away from the viewer.

The picture writing inscribed on the wall near the fair showed an Aztec warrior in full battle dress pulling the hair of a warrior from another city—thus war and battle were raging. An Aztec king or noble whom I could not identify, although I knew that each Revered Speaker had a personal symbol, was speaking. This was indicated by a little scroll coming from the mouth of the speaker. I had also seen it expressed as a wagging tongue. After he spoke, Aztec warriors marched, shown by footprints, toward a temple atop a mountain. The temple was burning, indicating that the tribe that owned the temple had been conquered.

As I read the tale aloud in Spanish, which was the language I thought in, I was startled when I caught another presence out of the corner of my eye. Don Julio was standing nearby watching me.

"You can read Aztec sign language?"

Pride loosened my tongue. "A little. The inscription is a boast—and a warning. Probably put here by the Aztecs to impress upon traveling merchants of other tribes what happens to towns that don't pay their tribute."

"Very good. I also can read the pictures, but it's almost a lost art." He shook his head. "My God, the history, the knowledge, that was lost when the frays burned them. The library at Texcoco was enriched with literary treasures gathered by the great king, Nezahualcoyotl. It was the New World equivalent of the great library of antiquity at Alexandria. And it was destroyed."

"My Aztec name is Nezahualcoyotl."

"An honorable name, even if it labels you a hungry coyote. Your namesake was not just a king, but a poet and writer of songs. But like so many kings, he also had human vices. Lusting for the wife of one of his nobles, he sent the man into battle with secret orders to his captains to see that the man was killed."

"Ah, the crime the Comendador Ocana tried to commit against Peribanez."

"You know Vega's comedia?"

"I—I heard it described once by a priest."

"A priest interested in any drama but a passion play? I must meet this man. What is your Spanish name?"

"Sancho," I said, without hesitation.

"Sancho, how do you, as an indio, feel about the fact that the Spanish have come and the indios' culture and monuments were destroyed or abandoned?"

He called me an indio. That made me comfortable talking to him again.

"The Spanish god was more powerful than the gods of the Aztecs."

"Are the Aztec gods all dead now?"

"No, there are many Aztec gods. Some were vanquished, but others merely went into hiding to wait until they regain their strength," I said, mimicking what the Healer had told me.

"And what will they do when they regain their strength? Drive the Spanish from New Spain?"

"There will be another great battle, like the wars in Revelations where fire and death and famine stalked the earth."

"Who told you that?"

"The priests in church. Everyone knows that there will be a great war between good and evil someday, and only the good will survive."

Don Julio chuckled and walked along the ruins. I followed along. I knew I was supposed to avoid being around gachupins, but the man had a depth of knowledge and wisdom not unlike that which I had sensed about the Healer and Fray Antonio.

It had been several years since I had been around people with the European-type knowledge that the fray had possessed. Like the fray, this man was a scholar. I bubbled over with enthusiasm to display my own knowledge.

"Besides the Bible," I said, "it is also said that the Jaguar Knights will drive the Spanish from this land."

"Where did you hear that?"

There was an inflection in his voice that suddenly made me cautious. But he only smiled when I looked at him with a question in my eyes.

"Where did you hear that?" He asked again.

I shrugged. "I don't remember. In the marketplace, I guess. There is always talk like that among the indios. But it is harmless."

Don Julio gestured at the ruins. "You should be very proud of your ancestors. Look at the monuments they left. There are many more like this, and many others that are the size of cities."

"The priests say we should not be proud; that our ancestors were savages who sacrificed thousands of people and even ate some. They say we must be thankful that the Church has stopped this blasphemy."

He murmured his accord to what the priests said, but I

had the impression that he was only giving the sort of respect everyone gives the Church, even if one disagrees.

We walked among the ruins for a moment before he spoke. "The Aztecs did practice savage rites, and for those there is no excuse. But perhaps they would look at us Europeans, at our wars with each other and the Infidels, at the cruelty and violence, and ask if we should cast the first stone. But regardless of how we judge their actions, there is no doubt that they built a mighty civilization and left behind monuments that, like those of the pharaohs, will survive the sands of time. They knew more about the movement of the stars and planets than we do today and had a more accurate calendar than us.

"Your ancestors were master builders. Along the eastern coast was a nation of people who harvested rubber from trees at a time when Christ was born. They were the ancestors of the Aztecs, Toltecs, and other indio peoples. They left behind great monuments. Like the Aztecs, they intricately carved the stone of monuments. But with what? They had no iron or even bronze tools. How did they etch the stone?

"Like the Aztecs, they were people without carts or beasts of burden. Yet they hauled great blocks of stones weighing as much as hundreds of men, stones so heavy no cart and team of horses in Christendom could carry them. They transported them great distances, up mountains and down the other side, across rivers and lakes, many leagues from the source of the stone. How? The secret was no doubt revealed in those thousands of books burned by the frays."

"Perhaps there was an Archimedes among them," I said. Fray Antonio had spoken of the accomplishments of the indios who built pyramids that violated the heavens and compared them to Archimedes. "Perhaps in those days there was such a man who, if he had had a long enough pole and a place to stand, could have lifted the world. Omnis homo naturaliter scire desiderat."

"Man naturally inclines to know more and more," Don Julio said, translating the Latin phrase. He stopped walking and locked eyes with me. There was a glint of humor in them. "You read Aztec picture writing, speak of an ancient Greek, quote Latin, and have knowledge of Spanish literature. You speak Spanish without an indio accent. A moment ago I lapsed into Náhuatl, and you spoke the language without even thinking about it. You are taller and lighter than most indios. These accomplishments are as mysterious as how these giant stones were moved over mountains."

Cursing my own stupid impulse to show off my knowledge, or Fray Antonio's knowledge to be more accurate, I had raised questions in the man's mind about me. *¡Ay de mí!* it had been three years since the murders and the hunt for me began, but this visit to a fair was bringing it back to me.

I fled the man called Don Julio, not looking back.

FIFTY-FIVE

WE LEFT THE next morning for the south, along a well-traveled, but frequently difficult to traverse road on which many of the fair merchants had already preceded us with their mule trains.

Besides Mateo, included in the band were two disreputable mestizos. These were stupid street scum who would be unwelcome in the meanest places in Veracruz—or quickly find their way to the gallows if they stayed around the town. Sancho and the mestizos were obviously a gang of banditos, the sort who laid-in-wait to ambush travelers, cutting throats for whatever was in the victim's pockets.

Again I wondered what had happened to the picaro poet to cause him to associate with these dregs.

Sancho and Mateo were mounted on horses and the two mestizos on mules. The Healer and I brought up the rear on foot, leading the mule and the yellow dog. The terrain was often such that the mounted men had to get down and lead their animals. Along the way, Mateo began to hang back with me and the Healer. I didn't know if it was for companionship or to watch us, but I suspected he could not stand too much of the company of Sancho.

"You speak good Spanish," Mateo said, as we walked along. "The priests taught you well."

The priests were the ones who taught indios, so it was a natural assumption to make. I did not take the statement to refer to Fray Antonio. It was just conversation on his part, not machination about my background, I hoped. He still had not given any hint that he knew my true identity. But as hard as I tried, my Spanish came across as better than most indios. I tried to speak the language in a loutish manner, but it was difficult when I was required to carry on a conversation rather than just make short responses. I had tried not to reveal to Mateo that my Spanish was as good as his own. I had made that mistake with Don Julio and was determined to keep up the mascarada.

I kept wondering if he knew who I was—and which of us he was protecting. The other question I knew the answer to: He would be the one to chop off my head after I performed the mysterious task for them. I had seen how quickly his sword can separate a man's head from his body.

I soon discovered that there were two things that Mateo loved most to do—besides making love and fighting duels—drinking and talking.

As we went along, he frequently imbibed from a goatskin and told many tales. Por Dios! This picaro caballero had had more adventures than Sinbad suffered setting out from Basra, and Odysseus sailing from Troy.

"He's like a songbird," the Healer said, when we were alone. "He likes to hear the music of his own words."

Mateo's tales were of his adventures as a sailor and soldier for the king.

"I've fought the French, English, Low Country rebels, and heathen Turks. Blasphemous Protestants, heretic Dutch, and Infidel Moors have all tasted my blade. I fought from the back of a horse, from the deck of a ship, and climbing a castle wall. I've killed a hundred men and loved a thousand women."

And told a million tales, I thought. I had great curiosity as to why the picaro *autor* of plays and books had ended up with Sancho, a common cutthroat, but it was not a subject I could broach.

They were a strange pair. I knew from personal experience that Mateo was lethal. And I could tell that Sancho was a killer. But the difference between them was that of a fine Toledo blade and an ax. Mateo was a picaro, a braggart, a swordsman, and an adventurer. But he was also a writer and actor, neither of which he appeared to excel at, but which gave him a rough quality as a scholar and gentleman.

Sancho had nothing of the scholar or gentleman about him. He was coarse and crude and pugnacious, filthy of word and body, arrogant and a bully.

And there was something else about him, something that didn't settle right in my mind, yet I could not figure out exactly what it was. His appearance bothered me. He appeared to be powerfully built . . . yet at times he seemed more fleshy than muscular, almost in a feminine sense. Years ago I heard Fray Antonio and Fray Juan talk about harem guards the Moors used called eunuchs, men whose cojones had been cut off. They said that the men grew soft and fleshy like a woman, even developing breasts. I supposed that the same thing happened to africano slaves who were castrated.

Despite his brutal manner and threats, Sancho had that feminine softness I imagined eunuchs had.

"As a boy younger than you, I sailed in the fleet of Medina Sidonia, who commanded the great Armada that fought the English in the northern waters. We were beaten by the weather, the wind howled like a mad dog, driving my ship ashore. I washed ashore and spent the next years in the guise of a French boy who had run away from his Scottish master. I joined a traveling group of actors on the road, first as a helper with their trunks and later as an actor and writer of plays.

"The English theater is not as brilliant as our Spanish one. They had a few modestly competent playwrights, one Will Shakespeare, another named Christopher Marlowe, but they lacked the genius of Spanish masters like Lope de Vega and Mateo Rosas de Oquendo. History will remember Mateo Rosas and sing his praise along with Homer long after the names of others have been blown away as dust."

I never knew if he was joking or boasting . . . or just plain drunk. His own peculiar "modesty" caused Mateo to often refer to himself as if he was talking about an entirely different person.

"I was captured by the Moors, by the Bey of Algiers himself, black heathen infidel devil that he be. I was tortured and starved until I made my escape."

I had heard this story before about an author whose name was sung more alongside that of Homer than Mateo's. Miguel Cervantes, the author of *Don Quixote,* had been captured by the Bey of Algiers and spent time in a Moorish prison. I had once spoken Cervantes's name in the presence of Mateo years prior and had nearly gotten my head lopped off. Only the devil knows why I do such stupid things, but I decided to demonstrate a little innocent knowledge to test a suspicion that Mateo borrowed other men's ideas just as casually as he did their purses and women.

"The priests at the church who taught me Spanish used to speak of another author of books and plays who had been captured—"

I suddenly found myself lying on the ground with a ringing in my head. Mateo had delivered a blow to my head.

"Never speak the name of this person in my presence," he said. "In a prison cell after enduring heinous tortures and deprivations, I revealed to this swine the story I would write about a knight-errant upon my return to Spain, the story of *my* life. He stole my life and published it before I got back—except, of course, he purloined my grandest accomplishments and held them up to ridicule, depicting my life before the entire world as the lunatic folly of a ridiculous buffoon. He stole my life, Chico. Eh, I admit I've done things the world deems dishonorable. Yes, I have helped myself to the coffers of the rich, drunk the wine of life to the bottom of the bottle, gambled my days, my years, my youth, my fears, my hopes, my dreams, my very soul far into mañana's dawn—and never looked back. I've killed men and seduced women. But some things I have never done. I have never stolen from a friend. I have never stolen a man's life. Now the world sings the praise of this thief, and none knows the name of poor Mateo Rosas de Oquendo." Mateo gave me a kick. "Now do you understand?"

Monte Alban crowned hills nearly fifteen hundred feet above the valley of Oaxaca and the city of that name. The hills were bare, almost bald of trees, and did not distract from the majesty of the ancient stone edifices.

Like other temple cities in New Spain, the example of Teotihuacan, the Place of the Gods, had been followed in building Monte Alban, a city dedicated to worship. The ancient stone structures were laid out in a rectangular plaza on the leveled mountaintop; about half a league long, the terraced plaza had pyramid temples, an observatory, ball court, and palaces.

Like so many of the holy places of my indio ancestors, Monte Alban was shrouded in mystery, a place of the gods, which more people visited than actually resided in. It was not Aztec, but Zapotec. South of the Valley of Mexico, the Zapotecs were not defeated by the Aztecs until about fifty years before Cortes's conquest. Beaten in battle, but not completely conquered, the Zapotecs and Aztecs were at each other's throats right up to the time of the conquest.

Today Monte Alban was devoid of life, the droppings of pack animals passing through and grass that had been crushed underfoot the only signs that anything but time had trespassed on the sacred grounds. At these ghostly stone cities of my ancestors, I got a sense of the forlorn, as if the people had left behind some of their sadness when they abandoned the city to snakes and tarantulas.

After the conquest, the people of the Oaxaca area traded masters as Cortes was granted tribute rights from indios. Granted the title of Marqués del Valle de Oaxaca and over twenty thousand tribute-paying indios, his actual feudal holdings came to be the size of some European kingdoms.

We made camp and later I walked among the ruins with the Healer. I felt a familiar chill breeze, the wind that I had felt in a cave below the Temple of the Sun in Teotihuacan.

"The gods are not pleased," the Healer said. "No good will come of this. These men have come here not to praise the gods but to offend them."

FIFTY-SIX

THE HEALER AND I camped away from the others. We were not alone on the hillside. A merchant from the fair had camped some distance from us with his peculiar merchandise: four prostitutes. He had rented them out at the fair and was returning to Oaxaca with his merchandise. I heard Sancho tell the man that he would use one of the putas.

While I knelt beside our fire preparing the midday meal for the two of us, I watched Mateo and Sancho walk to an enormous temple pyramid, the largest in the city. The pyramid glowed golden under the high sun. They carefully examined a side of the structure. I could not see a door where they stood. The sound of their voices, but not their words, carried to me. From their gestures and words, I had the impression that they were in disagreement upon how to enter the temple. And I made out the words "black powder."

I looked over at the Healer, who was quietly leaning back against a tree, smoking his pipe. His eyes were half-closed and his face as impassive as a pond on a windless day. I felt bad about misleading him, but there had been no other choice. Since arriving at Monte Alban, the "simple task" the españols had planned for me was becoming clear in my mind.

The two settled whatever differences they had with regard to the temple. Mateo gestured for me to join them. I trotted over.

Sancho indicated the spot they had been examining. Relief on the wall showed a god emerging from the jaws of a sacred jaguar. "Behind that wall is a sealed passageway. We opened it once at another spot, but a cave-in occurred when we resealed it. Now we're going to create another opening. The passageway leads down to the tomb of a Zapotec king who died about the time Pilate was crucifying Christ. In his tomb is his death mask with part of a breastplate attached. The object is solid gold and encrusted with gems and pearls."

Sancho paused to let the information sink in. I had already guessed that he was a tomb robber.

"Why didn't you get it out the last time you tried?" I asked.

"Ah, amigo, you are one smart man." Sancho put his arm around my shoulders and gave me a hug. I had a hard time keeping myself from gagging. "We should have had it in our hands, but there was treachery. We sent someone down, a man a little bigger than you, and he never came back."

I looked from Sancho to Mateo.

"What do you mean, he never came back? Is there another way out?"

Sancho shook his head no.

"Then he is still down there," I said.

"Sí, that is the treachery. He liked my prize so much, he decided to stay below and hug it. Some of the viceroy's soldados came along, . . ."

"You sealed him in and fled to avoid discovery."

Sancho grinned.

"How long ago?" I asked.

Sancho pretended to make a great effort at counting. "Thirty days."

It was my turn to nod and smile. "I see, I see."

Mother of God, I was in the hands of a madman.

"I met my good friend Mateo at the fair and enlisted his assistance because he can handle black powder. And he spotted you. We need someone slender enough to wiggle in the passageway and limber because there are sharp corners. The rest," Sancho raised both his hands in a gesture of finality, "you know."

The rest was that they were going to blow a hole into the passageway and send me in. If I managed to get out with the treasure, I would have my throat cut as my share of the reward. If Sancho was interrupted again by the viceroy's soldiers, I would be sealed inside to die. Worse, I feared for the Healer. Once Sancho got what he wanted, he would not leave the old man to be a witness. And the Healer was too old and slow to escape. Otherwise I would just have ran into the forest.

Sancho read my thoughts. "No, Chico, don't concern yourself with what has happened in the past. There will be enough gold for all of us. When you get your share, you will be able to buy your own hacienda."

Perhaps if I had had less of an education on the streets of Veracruz listening to people who lie every time their lips moved, I might have believed him. But I was raised shoulder to shoulder with léperos who would try to lie their way into heaven. And Sancho was the devil himself.

"I will crawl in your hole and bring out the treasure on one condition: my father leaves, now."

Sancho grabbed me by the throat and jerked me to him, putting his dagger to my gut. "There are no conditions. I will spill your guts in the dirt right now if you try to cross me."

"Cut me," I taunted, with more courage than I felt, "and you will never see your treasure."

"Let him alone, Sancho." Mateo spoke quietly. But he was never quiet unless he was deadly serious. I felt Sancho tense in anger, the point of his blade cutting into my side.

"We need him. We don't need his father. The old man's in the way."

"If I let him go, he'll inform the authorities."

"While we have his son? Not likely. Besides, the boy has courage; and he's not stupid. He doesn't believe you plan to reward him for his efforts."

Sancho released his hold. I stepped back as he looked up to the sky for heavenly confirmation of his honesty and sincerity. "Upon my sainted mother's grave, my martyr father's, too, I swear that I will reward you if you bring out the gold mask."

Eh, should I believe this hombre? It to easy to tell when he is lying. It happens every time he moves his lips.

"You'll get what you have coming," Mateo said. "Trust me."

I knelt beside the Healer. He continued looking straight ahead, smoking his pipe.

"You have to leave. Now." I wanted him gone before Sancho changed his mind. "Go to Oaxaca and wait for me. I'll be there in a couple of days."

"Why do we not go together?"

"Because I have to do something here, for the spur wearers."

He shook his head. "We travel together. You are my helper. My old eyes need you to show the way. I will wait here until you have finished your work."

Your old eyes are as sharp as an eagle's and your mind is sharper than a serpent's tooth, I thought.

"You cannot trust that Spaniard," he said, "the one with the fish eyes. If he is going to harm you, I will cast a spell on him. The dagger he points at you will come back to his own heart."

"Aztec magic doesn't work on the spur wearers," I said

quietly. "That's why they were able to destroy our temples and enslave our people."

Before he could speak more objections, I made a plea to him that I knew he would grant. "You have been my father and I love you as one. What I ask is that you honor that love by granting me this favor. Go to Oaxaca and wait for me. If you do not, you will be putting my life in danger."

He would not leave to protect himself, but he would to shield me.

I escorted the Healer with his donkey and dog to the trail to Oaxaca. I waited until he had disappeared down the trail before I returned to the campsite. I wanted to make sure that neither of the mestizos followed him. I considered escaping but knew too well Sancho would go after the Healer if I did. Only eighteen years on this earth, but I was ancient in terms of the treachery of men.

Sancho, Mateo, and the mestizos were huddled together when I came back.

"Wait for us over there," Sancho said.

I squatted and watched them, while I pretended to be preoccupied scratching an Aztec picture word in the dirt. As Sancho talked, Mateo's gaze occasionally went to the temple. I heard Sancho say that it didn't matter if it was day or night, but Mateo said it would take all night to prepare.

"Then I shall enjoy one of the putas camped down the hill," Sancho said.

The men scattered and Sancho called me to him. "We will need your services in the morning, Chico. Can I trust you not to run away tonight?"

"Señor, you can trust me as you trust your own sainted mother," I assured him, already planning my escape while the fool slept.

A rope looped over me and was jerked tight. One of the mestizos was on the other end of the rope.

Sancho shook his head with mock sadness. "Chico, my

mother was a witch full of devious tricks, and that is the best I could say about her."

Sancho tied my hands and feet. His mestizos carried me into his tent and dumped me on the ground. I lay on the ground for a couple of hours, trying to work my joints loose to slip out of the ropes, but Sancho had tied me securely.

He came into the tent at dusk.

"I have arranged for one of the putas to visit me, but I am tired tonight. I want to play with her, but not stick my pene into her. Comprende?"

I nodded. But I did not have the faintest idea what he was talking about. If he was too tired, why pay a whore for favors?

"If your pene will not turn into a garrancha, there is a potion I can get for you that will give it power."

He kicked me—hard. Several more times. Eh, telling a wearer of spurs that his pene is not as long and hard as a sword was an unusual—and ill-timed—moment of honesty on my part.

"I am going to explain what you are to do when I come back with the woman. I will explain only once. Then I will untie you and leave the tent. If you attempt to run away, not only will my mestizos cut off your head, but I will track down the old man and cut off his. Listen carefully for your duties with the woman. If you fail my instructions, I will cut off your pene."

Ojalá! God grant that someday this ugly ox feel my spurs!

Sancho had instructed me to be hiding under a blanket near the bed when he returned with the woman. They came with much laugher and singing, both very drunk. Sancho brought her into the tent, the two of them staggering. It was dark in the tent, a single candle glowed, barely breaking the darkness, but even in the dim I could see that she was not a young puta, but one old enough to be my mother. I took her to be mestizo rather than a full-blooded indio.

The moment he had her inside, he began undressing her.

Giggling, she tried to undress him, but he knocked away her hands. He stripped her naked and kissed and touched her in many places. He did not appear tired to me. I hoped that the excitement had put some power in his pene, and he would not need me.

Turning her around, he put her down on the bed on her chest with her feet on the ground and her buttocks arched up.

He waved to me. I silently groaned with reluctance. But aware I was dealing with a madman, I quietly slipped out from under the bed.

When he held her down and kissed her, I obeyed his instructions.

I inserted my pene into her tipíli.

Sancho breathed heavy and grunted, pretending he was doing ahuilnéma on the woman, as I pumped.

Dios mio!

FIFTY-SEVEN

SITTING ON THE ground with my back to a tree that I was tied to, I watched their preparations. Since first light they had been at the wall. The mestizos used an iron rod to poke a hole into the wall and then kept increasing the depth of the hole but not the width. The hole was barely big enough to stick my foot in, much less my whole body. Did these tomb robbers expect that I could shrink my body down to the width of my leg?

Mateo spent some time stuffing something into the hole. After he was finished, the mestizos piled wood and blankets against the hole. I watched all this in ignorance of what they were doing. Mateo poured a trail of something on the ground. It looked like the black powder I have seen solados stuff into the barrels of their muskets.

He knelt and lighted the end of the trail. Smoke rose from the powder as the fire moved to the wall. The smoke seemed to go out the moment it hit the stuffed hole. Than an explosion erupted, muffled by the wood and blankets. When the smoke cleared, a small hole in the wall became visible.

Mateo cursed. "These damn indios knew how to build so that bad hombres like us can't get in. I put enough black powder in to sink a galleon, and it barely damaged the stone."

After the two mestizos cleared the rubble, they dug again with their iron poles. Periodically Mateo used more black powder to lessen the resistance. By midday they had made a small tunnel several feet long through a block of solid rock. It was just wide enough for a slender contortionist to snake into. From the discussions between Sancho and Mateo, I learned that it had taken days and a large number of indios to work loose a great block enough for their previous helper to squeeze in. The activity had drawn the interest of authorities from Oaxaco. With Mateo's black powder, they had made an opening in a few hours.

I had heard many stories of tomb robbers from the fray and on the streets of Veracruz. Everybody knew someone else who had an acquaintance possessing a secret map to where Montezuma hid his treasures from Cortes. Or a similar tale about the tomb of a king of Texcoco, whose incredible riches were discovered by robbers who were turned to stone by the ghosts and spirits guarding the tomb.

It was well known that it was bad luck to break into the burial places of the notables of the past. It raised the wrath of gods. People who defiled the ancient holy places were cursed and came to a bad end, if the Spanish didn't punish them first. When I was seven years old, two men were hanged in the valley where I was born, thieves who'd broken into an ancient tomb in search of treasure.

¡Ay de mí! what had I become involved in? If we were

caught by the authorities, I would be hanged along with the rest of them, or worse, sent to the northern mines. If I found the treasure, my reward would be to have my throat cut. If I failed to find the treasure, I would pray for a quick death on the gibbet.

After the noon meal, Sancho and Mateo untied me and took me to the opening.

"After a few feet, this hole leads to a passage down to the tomb," Sancho said. "Your task is a simple one. You crawl down the passageway, get the breastplate, and crawl back. Comprende?"

"If it is so simple, why didn't your helper bring it to you?"

"I told you, we had to suddenly seal the opening."

"You couldn't have waited a moment for him to crawl out with the treasure?"

Sancho hit me. I stumbled backward and hit the ground hard. He threw his hands into the air. "Chico, Chico, see what you make me do? You ask too many questions. When I hear too many questions, my head hurts."

He led me to the opening. "When you are down there, fill your pockets with gems. I will let you keep all you find."

Eh, this hombre is generous, no? He would cut off his mother's nose if he could find a buyer.

He hung a sack with four candles and a small torch around my neck. He handed me a lighted candle. "Don't use the torch until you reach the tomb itself."

He tied part of a long coil of rope around my waist. The purpose of the rope was to guide me back if the passageway became a maze.

Before I stuck my head into the opening he grabbed me and gave me a powerful hug. "Amigo, if you don't find the treasure, don't come out," he whispered.

I crawled into the dark hole with grave misgivings. It was not midnight in the hole; it was as black as Mictlan, the underworld, as dark and silent as a grave. The air was as chill and unstirred as the breath of the dead. It *smelled* like the breath of the dead, a putrid, stagnant odor, like the bodies rotting in the Veracruz river where africanos and mestizos were thrown to save on burial effort.

The fray was right, I was raised badly. Trouble was waiting for me everywhere I went. While other mestizos are keeping warm and dry as household servants or at least mercifully dying at an early age, clutching a cup of pulque in the gutter, I am always tempting fate by taking a jaguar by the ear.

What would I find in this grave of ancient kings?

What would find me?

I had nothing with which to defend myself against the spirits of the temple but my ignorance.

The passageway was too small for me to continue crawling on my hands and knees. I lay flat on my stomach and pushed along, using my arms and elbows. My arms and legs were immediately cut and scraped as I crawled over the stone block that the hole had been blown through.

I prayed there was nothing in the tomb that became excited by the scent of fresh blood.

After a few feet of the rough hole that felt like I was crawling over obsidian spear heads, I was in another passageway. I could see only a few feet in front and was glad for the rope I was tethered to. No bigger than the blasted hole, it had been hewed an eon ago and was much smoother. I left one candle along the way and used it to light another. The candles barely broke the darkness.

Despite my youth and vigor, it was hard work dragging my body along on elbows and legs. Soon I was breathing hard not only from the exertion but an overwhelming sense of dread. The cold, rank, almost unbreatheable air and the dead blackness of the coffin-tight tunnel spooked me. Either the narrow passage was designed to discourage tomb robbers, or the early Zapotecs were as thin and lithe as snakes. The passageway twisted and turned nonsensically. If I encountered any danger and had to crawl backward, a feat ever more difficult than my excruciatingly painful forward progress, I would make the temple my tomb, just as my precessor—

Ay! I came to a pair of feet.

I hoped the dirty feet belonged to the decayed body of the man Sancho had sealed in the passage and not some ancient specter waiting for an intruder to happen along.

The dim candlelight exposed dirty feet that appeared more likely to belong to the recently departed than someone entombed an eon ago.

I was faced with a dilemma. I could crawl backward all the way out, and have Sancho cut my throat, or I could attempt to crawl over the body.

I would have crawled over the points of spears to avoid mounting this body. Cursing my own bad acts that brought me to this moment, and imploring all the gods that I would spend the rest of my life in devotion to them, I began to crawl over the body.

I pushed myself atop the body like I was a man making ahuilnéma to a man. The body was decayed and had lost its fluids. There was no room to maneuver. Gathering all of my strength, I pushed forward with a groan. My back hit the top of the passage and wedged in. I could go no farther. I tried to crawl back. I was stuck.

Santa Maria! Those past deeds in the past life Gull had warned me about were once more stepping on my heels. I was stuck atop the dried flesh and bones. *¡Ayya ouiya!* The indios believe that men who use each other as lovers will go to the underworld with one's pene stuck in the rear of the other one. What would some future tomb robber think if he found me mounted atop this other man?

I offered amends to the gods for whatever evil deeds I had done in past lives—and the present one. Then I pushed and pumped and groaned and moaned atop the dead man more than I did with the live woman I met in the cemetery on the Day of the Dead. My back scrapped the ceiling, my belly the body. When I felt the man's head against my stomach, I knew I was near victory. The head slipped down between my legs and I was free!

Ayyo, making ahuilnéma to a dead man was much work.

The passage slopped downward, and my progress improved. I came to the end of the tethered rope and had to untie it from my waist. The space around me widened and I could no longer see the walls with the candle. I got onto my feet and lit the pitch torch with the candle. As it flared, I knew I had reached the tomb.

White walls and ceiling reflected the torch light, revealing a long, narrow chamber. Along the walls a foot below the ceiling, picture writing described the heroic accomplishments of the ruler occupying the tomb. Food, weapons, and cocoa beans for the trip to the underworld were contained in open clay pots.

Along two walls stood statues of full-sized, battle-dressed warriors. As I peered closer, I realized they were not stone statues, but actual men who had been embalmed in a way that turned the person into a rigid monument.

At the end of the line of warriors were four seated women, ranging in age from a teenage girl to an old woman. Like the warriors, none of them looked particularly happy that they had been turned into statues. I took these to be the wives of the ruler. The ruler himself was seated in a chair on a flat space five steps up from the floor. He wore the golden mask-breastplate. The ornamental armor covered the face and extended about halfway down the chest.

A yellow dog was at the ruler's feet. So were a nest of the largest scorpions I had ever seen. They were the size of a man's foot. One sting and I would join the ruler in Mictlan. They made my flesh crawl as I stepped around them.

My torch was burning out. I quickly separated the golden treasure from the man and hurried back to the opening of the passage. I paused to take off my shirt and use it to capture a scorpion. It was more impulse than plan. Holding the mask-breastplate and shirt out in front of me, I crawled back, fighting my way back over the corpse.

As I neared the opening to where the robbers were waiting, I decided on my strategy. If I came to the opening with the treasure in my hand, Sancho would take it and cut my throat. If I did not have it, he would cut my throat. Ay, but if I did not have the treasure in my hands, I also might be able to make a run for it. It depended on where everyone was. I had been in the passageway for a couple of hours. If the gods decided to accept my offers of appeasement, they would not be waiting next to the opening.

As I neared the end I crawled slowly and quietly, pausing to listen for sounds of the robbers. A strange noise, something I could not identify, funneled down the passageway. Every couple of feet I paused to listen. The noise grew louder as I neared the entrance.

When I was still in the dark tunnel a dozen feet from the opening to the passageway, I saw Mateo and Sancho playing cards. They were under the shade of a tree about a hundred paces away. That left the two mestizos.

I inched closer to the end of the passageway. One of the mestizos came into sight. He was farther away than the two Spaniards, cooking. My heart started beating faster. With luck I would be able to get out and onto my feet to run before they spotted me.

I inched up to the opening. And saw a pair of legs.

The other mestizo was sitting near the opening. He had fallen asleep, sitting up, snoring, his head bobbling, his legs stretched out.

I had to slip out of the hole and get across the pile of rubble that the black powder explosions created. And run, before the mestizo could shout the alarm and grab me.

It couldn't be done, so I did the next best thing. I flung the shirt and scorpion onto his lap. Scrambling out of the hole, I grabbed a piece of the stone rubble bigger than my fist. The mestizo woke up immediately, nearly jumping out of his skin at the sight of the huge scorpion. He was still reacting in surprise when I hit him in the face with the stone.

I ran, with shouts from both Sancho and Mateo behind me. There was no heavy foliage for me to disappear into; I was forced onto the pyramid. I scrambled around the side, running for my life. The four in pursuit divided up to trap me. They slowly closed in, cutting off one way of escape, then another.

They squeezed my area of maneuvering until I was a dozen feet from Sancho.

"Where's my treasure?" he snarled. His temperament was murderous.

"I've hidden it. Let me go and I'll tell you."

"You'll tell me because I'm going to start slicing off pieces of your body, starting with your nose."

He charged me, his sword lashing at me, and sliced my chest.

"I'm going to slice one piece after another from you until you answer me."

I dodged around him and ran into Mateo.

He grabbed me. Sancho lashed out at me again, and Mateo blocked the blow with his own sword. "Stop! Killing him will get us nothing."

"It'll give me satisfaction." Sancho swung at me again and Mateo's sword flashed again. Mateo held onto me with one hand and crossed swords repeatedly with Sancho, driving Sancho back.

"Kill him!" Sancho shouted at the two mestizos.

The two mestizos charged Mateo. He slashed his sword at them, cutting the face of one of them. They both retreated.

Men came on horseback into the temple area.

"Soldados!" one of the mestizos yelled. The two mestizos ran. I saw Sancho disappearing down the other side of the temple. He must have seen the horsemen coming before the rest of us. Mateo kept his hold on me but made no attempt to run.

"We have to run!" I exclaimed. The penalty for tomb robbing was hanging.

He hung onto me but said nothing until the horsemen came up to us. Releasing his grip on me, he took off his hat and saluted the lead rider with a sweep of his hat and a bow. Other riders went in pursuit of the banditos.

"Don Julio, you are late. Our friend Sancho left a moment ago. From her speed, I suspect she is in the next town by now."

It was the man from the fair who'd pulled an arrow from a wounded indio, and to whom I had exposed my knowledge.

"Go after her," Don Julio told an officer in the uniform of a viceroy's soldado.

Her? Why did they call Sancho a *woman?* I wondered. I did not need the Healer to tell my fate from the songs of birds. I had fallen into the hands of the king's men. If they discovered I was wanted for murder, I would be tortured before they killed me.

"Our friend Sancho nearly killed me and this young devil," Mateo said. "The boy came out of the temple without the treasure piece."

Aha! Mateo had conspired to cheat the others with this don. The soldados must be in league, too. A very clever scheme.

"Where's the mask?" Don Julio asked me.

"I don't know, señor," I whined, in my best lépero voice. "I swear upon all the saints I could not find it." Eh, I could come back later and get the treasure myself.

"He's lying," Mateo said.

"Of course he is. He's even managed to forget how to speak good Spanish and speaks like a street person." Don Julio gave me a dark look. "You are a thief who has defiled an ancient tomb. The penalty is most severe. If you are lucky, you will be hanged *before* your head is removed to post as a warning to others."

"He made me do it!" I pointed at Mateo.

"Nonsense," Don Julio said. "Señor Rosas is an agent of the king, just as I am. He joined Sancho to trap her in the act of violating a tomb."

"Why do you keep calling Sancho a woman?" I asked.

"Answer my question, Chico. Where did you hide the treasure?"

"I found no treasure."

"Hang him!" Don Julio snapped.

"The passageway, it's in the passageway. I'll get it for you."

They shackled my ankle, securing it with a length of chain. I was sent into the tunnel like a fish that could be jerked back at any time. The two mestizos were chained at the same time I was. They were on their way to the jail in Oaxaca, as I entered the passageway.

With the mask-breastplate in hand, I crawled backward out of the passageway. My heart beat in my throat. I was crawling back into a hangman's noose. Don Julio, Mateo, and the soldados gathered around to view the treasure piece.

"Magnífica. It is a fine piece," Don Julio said. "It will be sent to the viceroy. He will send it to Madrid for the king the next time the treasure fleet sails."

On instructions from Don Julio, Mateo looped a rope around my neck with a wooden device where the knot should be. "If you try to run, the rope tightens it around your throat and strangles you. It's a trick I learned when I was a prisoner of the bey of Algiers."

"Why do you save my life just to get me hanged? You must tell the don the truth. I am innocent."

"Innocent? Perhaps not *completely* guilty this time, but innocent?"

There was still no word between us that Mateo had cut off a man's head for me. It was not something I could reveal to my advantage, or I would have done so.

"You betrayed Sancho," I said to him.

He shrugged. "One does not betray her. You merely take action to avoid her treachery. Were either of us to expect any reward from her but a dagger in the back? Eh, amigo. Don Julio has one of these ropes around my neck, too; you just can't see it. But he is a man of honor and of his word. If I am faithful to him, it will not strangle me."

"Who is he? I thought he was a doctor."

"He is many things. He knows of surgery and medicines, but that is just a small part of his knowledge. He knows how these monuments came to be built and why the sun comes up in the morning and goes down at night. But the main concern for you is that he is the king's agent who investigates plots to steal the king's treasures and other intrigues. And he can have a man hanged."

"What is he going to do with me?"

Mateo shrugged. "What do you deserve?"

Ay, that was the last thing I wanted the don to pass judgment on.

FIFTY-EIGHT

I SPENT THE night tied to the tree, a blanket thrown over me to ward off the cold. My anxiety and restrained posture made the night one of agony and worry. I knew how to deal with the Sanchos of this world. But this mysterious leader of the soldados was no one I wanted to tangle with. The next day before the noon meal, men from Oaxaca came to repair the temple.

Don Julio's angry curses drifted over me as I sat like a dog tied to a tree, the fiendish collar around my neck. His venom was directed at the absent Sancho for damaging the ancient monument. He ignored the fact that it was his own man Mateo who had blown the hole in the wall. He instructed the indios on making repairs with a mortar made from straw and dirt similar to the adobe used to build houses with. He did not like defacing a great stone monument with mock adobe, and cursed that the art of building stone temples was dead. The temporary sealing would have to suffice until indios skilled in working with stone could be brought from the City of Mexico.

Don Julio and Mateo sat down under the tree with me and took their midday meal.

"Take the rope off of him," Don Julio said. "If he runs, kill him."

I ate salted beef and tortillas in the shade of the tree and listened to Don Julio. I had come out second best when I tried to fool him at the fair because I said too much. This time I would select my lies carefully.

"What's your name, your real name?" he asked.

"Cristo."

"And your family name?"

"I have none."

"Where were you born?"

I made up a name for a village. "It's near Teotihuacan."

He went on to ask me about my parents and my education.

"*Ay de mí*, my father and mother both died from the peste when I was young. I was raised in the house of my uncle. He was a very learned man. He taught me how to read and write before he died. I am all alone in the world."

"What about that fake healer. You told Mateo and Sancho he was your father."

I almost groaned aloud. I needed to keep my lies consistent. "He's another uncle. I call him my father."

"When we spoke at the fair for the Manila galleons, you said that Jaguar Knights would drive the Spanish from New Spain. Who told you that?"

Before I could answer, he told Mateo, "Draw your sword. If he lies, chop off one of his hands."

Eh, another person who expects me to lie and wants to butcher me. What is it about these gachupins and chopping up people?

He asked the question again.

"I offended an indio magician, one who tells the course of an illness or other matters by casting bones. I poked fun at him when he was performing his magic. When I was leaving, someone I did not get a good look at told me that I would be killed when the Jaguar Knights rose."

"That is the only thing you know about the Jaguar Knights?"

I hesitated only long enough for Mateo to draw his

sword. I hastened with my tale, having seen what the man could do with a sword.

"I witnessed a terrible thing." I told them about the night I accidentally came upon a sacrifice ceremony.

"Interesting," Don Julio murmured. He seemed hardly able to contain his excitement. He said to Mateo, "I believe the boy stumbled onto the nest of the fanatics we seek."

"This magician must have frightened him greatly for the boy to believe he was actually attacked by a were-jaguar."

"What's a were-jaguar?" I asked.

"A man who changes into the shape of a jaguar. In Europe, there are many legends of werewolves, men who become wolves. Among the indios, there is a belief that certain people have the ability to change into jaguars. In the Veracruz area where the People of the Rubber flourished an eon ago, there are many representations in statues and etching of were-jaguars."

"Today it is the nauallis who shape-change," I said.

"Where did you hear that word?" Don Julio asked.

"From the Healer, my uncle. He, too, is a powerful magician, but he does not practice the dark magic. He says the change is made when a naualli drinks an elixir like the divine ointment."

"What does your uncle know about this naualli?"

"He doesn't like him. My uncle is a great healer, famous and welcomed in all of the indio villages. He told me that except for trips to fairs and festivals, the naualli stays in small villages in the area between Puebla and Cuicatlán. The town where the sacrifice took place is only a day from there. The naualli is known as a black magician. He can do killing curses. Put a curse on a dagger so that when you give it to an enemy, it stabs them. Of course I don't believe any of these things," I added hastily.

Don Julio asked many more questions, starting again with the first time I saw the naualli and going over everything I saw from when I watched the mock battle between the indio knights to the cut on the naualli's face.

When I was drained of information, Don Julio smiled at

me. "You have an amazing memory. No doubt that is the secret of your ability with languages and with scholarly matters when you never went to school. You're a mestizo, of course, not an indio."

I shot a glance at Mateo, but as usual, his eyes revealed nothing.

"A mestizo, but you can affect the manners and speech of an indio." Don Julio patted his beard. "And a Spaniard. If you had been dressed as a Spaniard when I talked to you among the ruins, I would have not doubted you were born in Seville or Cadiz. Mateo, you could have used this young man in your acting troupe before the viceroy sent them to the Filipinas."

Mateo visibly shuddered at the mention of the dreaded islands. Ah! I understood the hold Don Julio had on the picaro. Troublemaking Spaniards were not sent to the northern mines, but were vanquished to a place equally feared, a land Spaniards in New Spain without humor called the Infierno. The trip across the Western Sea that took a couple of months was so terrible that only half the prisoners on a galleon survived. After they landed, half of those who survived the voyaged died in the first few months from fevers, snakes, and pestilence as bad as that found in the jungles of the Veracruz coast and Yucatan.

Eh, the rope that jerks my amigo Mateo is banishment to this español hell on the other side of the great waters. He and his actors really must be muy mal hombres to deserve such a fate. And the women? Were they doing the deshonesto zarabanda dance for Filipinas crocodiles? What was the actress letting into her tent at night now?

"Only your generosity and kind spirit has kept me from joining my amigos, Don Julio. Because of your brilliance, insight, and wisdom, you recognized that I was as innocent as a newly ordained priest." Mateo spoke without a trace of sarcasm.

"Sí, as innocent as the two mestizo tomb robbers we will be hanging—and this one whose fate has not yet been decided."

I smiled humbly at Don Julio. "My kindly old uncle is half blind and nearly helpless. I must care for him, or he will perish."

"Your uncle, if that's what he is, is a fake and a fraud who has cheated people from Guadalajara to Mérida. You are also an incorrigible liar and thief. Even facing a rope around your neck, you dared to lie to me about the fact the treasure mask was in easy reach. Had I accepted your story, you would have returned to break into the tomb again to recover it. Do you deny this?"

"Don Julio," I whined, "you are a prince among—"

"Be quiet while I decide your punishment."

"I think the little scoundrel should get a hundred lashes," Mateo said. "It would teach him to have respect for the king's law."

"And how many lashes would teach you to respect the law?" Don Julio asked.

Mateo pretended to be examining a scuff on his boot.

The don cursed the workers at the wall and went to them, shouting that their ancestors were turning over in their graves at the sight of their sloppy work.

I glared at Mateo. "A hundred lashes, eh, amigo. Gracias."

"I'm not your amigo, you little street cur." He showed the point of the sword. "Call me that again, and I will cut off one of your ears."

Dios mio. Still the desire to slice me up.

"Your pardon, *Don* Mateo. Perhaps I will tell Don Julio that you told me to hide the treasure so *you* could come back for it later."

Mateo stared at me for a moment. I thought for certain that my ears were lost. His face convulsed and then he burst—into laughter. He slapped me on the shoulder so hard that I went over sideways.

"Bastardo, you are a man after my own black heart. Only a true rogue would have thought of such an outrageous lie. There is no doubt that someday you will come to a bad end.

Eh, but the stories you will be able to tell before they hang you."

"You will both end up making your last confession to a priest when you have a rope around your necks." Don Julio had returned from threatening the indios with everlasting damnation if they did not do better work. "But in the meantime, I have an assignment for both of you."

Mateo looked crestfallen. "You told me—"

"I told you that a very bad transgression against the king would be worked off if we caught that bandito Sancho. Do you see her in chains?"

"We saved a great treasure for the king."

"*I* saved a great treasure for the king. You were not told to use black powder."

"Sancho insisted that—"

"You should have refused. You did great damage to a temple that has resisted harm since Julius Caesar talked to the Sphinx. It has occurred to my suspicious mind that you used the black powder to quickly get into the temple before I arrived with soldados."

Don Julio was no one's fool. And I had not been wrong in my assessment of Mateo. Like Guzman, Mateo was unable to resist the temptation to acquire a treasure. All picaros shared the same fatal flaw: the soul of a knave.

Mateo looked hurt. "Don Julio, on my honor—"

"A dubious oath. Listen to me, amigos, like a priest I will grant you forgiveness for your sins; but unlike one, I can also keep you from the gallows—if you obey me and do the work I set out for you. These Knights of the Jaguar, as they style themselves, are well known to the viceroy. They are a small but violent group of indios who are determined to kill all Spanish and take control of the country."

"Give me a hundred men, and I'll bring you the heads of all of them," Mateo said.

"You couldn't do it with a thousand. You would never find them. The knights do not conduct themselves in the open. In the daytime they are simple indio farmers or hacienda workers. At night they are a murder cult that band together to kill Spaniards and indios who do not oppose Spanish rule."

"They have killed Spaniards?" Mateo asked.

"At least ten, perhaps more."

"I have never heard of such a thing!" Mateo said.

"The viceroy is withholding the information to keep people from panicking and spreading the fame of the cult. We are still dealing with scattered groups, but they must be stamped out. With the right leadership, an indio revolt could spread like wildfire. This naualli, despite his age, may be such a leader. We could have a widespread revolt on our hands, another Mixton War."

"Then let's roast the black magician's feet over a hot fire until he tells us the names of his knights," Mateo said.

"Amigo, you are so Spanish in your thinking," the don said. "That is exactly what the conquistadors did to Cuitláhuac, Montezuma's successor, after Tenochtitlan fell. They tortured him to find out where gold had been hidden. It didn't work after the conquest, and it would have even less effect today. These are no ordinary indio warriors, but fanatics. You," Don Julio indicated Mateo, "I am sure are familiar with the story of the Old Man and the Mountain. But," he smiled at me, "despite your wide range of knowledge, you may not be acquainted with this tale."

"I have not heard of an old man and a mountain," I said.

"Hundreds of years ago Christian armies went to the Holy Land to free it from the Infidels. During one of these crusades, a leader of a Muslim sect, Rashid ad-Din, sent his followers to murder his Arab enemies and Christian leaders. Because he had a mountain fortress, we called him the Old Man of the Mountain.

"Our people called his followers Assassins, a corruption of an Arabic reference to them being hashish smokers. Marco Polo, a traveler from Venice, learned that the Assassins used hallucinatory substances before committing their heinous crimes. While their minds were slaves to these drugs, the Assassins believed that they had traveled to Allah's Garden of Paradise. They then set out to murder their enemies, knowing they would be caught and killed themselves. But they believed that after they were killed, having completing their murder assignment, they would return to paradise.

"The Aztecs were even more adept at the use of drugs that control another's mind. One of the Jaguar Knights whom we managed to capture had taken drugs before his crime. Even under the most severe and enduring torture, he revealed little to the viceroy's men. The fact was that his mind was so altered by the drugs that he no longer knew the difference between his real existence and a place he called the House of the Sun."

"The House of the Sun is heaven beyond the eastern waters," I said. "When an Aztec warrior dies in battle, rather than going to the underworld, his spirit goes to this paradise."

Mateo tapped his sword on his boot. "This naualli may be the Old Man of the Mountain to these indios."

"Exactly," Don Julio said.

"And you want me to take this thieving little devil," Mateo waved the sword at me, "and find this practitioner of the black arts and get the truth from him."

"Almost. I want you to catch him in the act so we can hang him."

"I understand perfectly. But, of course, as a Spanish gentleman, I do not understand the language or the customs of these people. This fine young man should be sent to find this naualli. After he does, he can send for me. I will await his message at your house in the City of Mexico . . ."

Mateo stopped as Don Julio shook his head. "I think it would be better if you were nearby when the boy flushed out the Jaguars. That way you could protect him. Besides, as you pointed out, he is an untrustworthy cur who must be watched."

Mateo smiled at me; his eyes were not smiling. *¡Ay de mí!* Once again he blames me!

The man was a wolf in picaro's clothes. Someday I would tell him a secret, but this was not the time. But, amigos, I will let you in on the secret. Do you remember what he called me? Bastardo. But that is a name he had heard years ago at the treasure fleet fair. Sí, he knows I am the very one for whom he chopped off a man's head.

FIFTY-NINE

THE HEALER CLAIMED that all things were preordained in this world, that the gods had carved in stone books how our lives would unfold from the moment we were born. I believed that the gods had brought Don Julio into my life and sent me on this mission for a reason. Had I known the terrible consequences that were to occur because of my dealings with the dark magician, I would have tried to avoid the tragic fate by running into the forest and hiding from this strange Spanish don who was a doctor, scholar, and agent of the king.

That afternoon around the supper fire we received further instructions from Don Julio. Mateo plucked out little tunes on a guitar and drank wine from a goatskin as the don spoke.

"You are to direct yourselves to the indio town where you witnessed the sacrifice. There, find out where the naualli is. From what your uncle told you, he will be somewhere in the region. You will also come across other indio magicians, healers, and sorcerers. You can pick up gossip and information from them. We want to know about the Jaguar Knights, every bit of information you can learn.

"You are never to mention the Jaguar name. To do so in front of the wrong people would get your throat cut. Rather than questioning, which would do no good and raise suspicion, just listen. You are still a boy," he said to me, "and the indios will talk freely in front of you while they would not in front of a grown man. Keep your ears open, your mouth closed, and your feet ready to carry you quickly away.

"Mateo, you will need a cover identity, too." Don Julio thought for a moment. "Guitars. You will be a merchant of guitars. I will get you several mules. One of my indio vaqueros will be your assistant. I will send for him immediately. When you need me, he will ride to wherever I am."

Mateo hit an irritating series of chords on the guitar. "I am a swordsman and a poet, not a merchant."

"You are doing the king's work in exchange for not being sent to the Filipinas. If I want you to put on a dress and be a puta, you will do that, too."

Mateo drummed the guitar and sang an old Spanish ballad.

Yesterday I was King of Spain,
Today not one village;
Yesterday I had towns and castles,
Today I have not one;
Yesterday I had servants,
And people to wait upon me;
Today there is not a battlement
Which I can call my own.
Ill-fated was the hour
And the day luckless
When I was born and fell heir
To so great an heritage
Since I was to lose it
In one day, all together!
Why do you not come, Death,
And take this wretched body
Which would be grateful to you?

"Yes, like King Don Rodrigo," Don Julio said, "death will someday claim each of us. Sooner for some than others if the orders of the king's servant are not obeyed."

Don Julio started for his bedroll, and I stopped him with a question.

"What about my pay?"

"Your pay? Your pay is not to be hanged as a thief."

"I lost money because of Sancho. I will need money for expenses. To buy information in the marketplaces."

Don Julio shook his head. "If you have more money on you than usual, you will raise suspicion. Better that you remain poor. And heed my caution: To offer money in the marketplace for information about the Jaguar Knights would invite danger," Don Julio told me before he went back to shouting at the indios patching the wall, "but no more than robbing the burial places of kings. There may be some danger but also a reward if you are successful, however less than a king's ransom. Better than all of that, you won't be hanged for tomb robbing."

After he left, I lay on the ground and listened to Mateo's guitar and watched him drink wine. Knowing that his temper toward me was gentler when he had a bellyful of wine, I waited until the goatskin was empty before asking a question that had been burning in my mind.

"You and Don Julio referred to Sancho as a woman. How can that be? He's a man."

"Let me tell you, Bastardo, the story of a man that is a woman." Mateo drummed a tune on the guitar. "There was a woman named Catalina, and she became a man called Sancho. This is the story of a nun who became an army lieutenant . . ."

An amazing story. Some parts Mateo told me that night, the more profane parts I learned later myself. Sí, amigos, I would again meet up with the man called Sancho—the woman called Catalina. And like me, from a prison cell, she later wrote down the events that had shaped her life. Hers were to be published after careful censorship by the Holy Office. But I had heard her true story from her own lips, and now I embellish upon Mateo's account to share her actual words with you.

Share with me now the story of Catalina de Erauso, soldier, swordsman, womanizer, bandit, and scoundrel—the lieutenant nun.

SIXTY

DOÑA CATALINA DE Erauso was born in the town of San Sebastian in Guipúzoca province. Her parents were Capitán Don Miguel de Erauso and Doña Maria Pérez de Galarrage y Arce. When she was of the tender age of four years, they placed her in a convent of Dominican nuns. Her aunt, Sor Ursula Unzá y Sarasti, her mother's older sister, was the prioress of the convent.

Catalina lived in the convent until she was fifteen years old. No one asked her if she wanted to be a nun and spend the rest of her life cloistered behind the stone walls surrounding the convent. No one asked her if she had great curiosity about the world outside the gray walls. She had been given to the convent like a puppy, barely weaned.

In the year of her novitiate, when she was to make her final vows, she quarreled with one of the sisters, Sor Juanita, who had taken the veil after the death of her husband. There were those unkind who said that her husband willingly entered death to get away from her. She was a big, strong woman. When their quarrel became fisticuffs, it took all of Catalina's girlish strength to defend herself. When her strength failed her, God placed a heavy brass candleholder in her hand. Afterward, the nuns lay Doña Juanita on her bed to see if she would regain consciousness.

Doña Catalina's punishment depended upon Juanita's fate, and she pondered what was to become of herself. The answer, like another command from God, came on Saint Joseph's Eve when the entire convent rose at midnight to perform prayers through the night. Catalina went into the choir and found her aunt on her knees. She handed Catalina the keys to her cell and bid her to fetch her breviary. After she entered her aunt's cell, Catalina noticed that the key to the convent gate was hanging from a nail on the wall.

With the light from a lamp, she found a pair of scissors, needle, and thread, a quantity of pieces of eight that were lying about, and the keys to the convent doors and the gate beyond. Catalina left the cell and went through the prison-like doors, the voices of the choir following her from the chapel.

Through the last door, she shook off her veil and opened the gate. She stepped out of the gate and onto a street she had never seen before. Her heart was beating in her throat. For a moment Catalina was unable to move. Her most earnest desire was to turn and flee back into the convent. Gathering her courage and curiosity, she walked down the dark and deserted street, going in the direction her feet moved rather than with any organized plan.

Catalina passed farmhouses and barking dogs outside of town. An hour down the road, she came across a chestnut grove. There she remained in hiding for three days, eating chestnuts off the tree and drinking from a nearby river, but not venturing farther. Laying out her nun's garb, she planned and replanned before taking out the scissors and cutting out a suit of clothes. From the blue woolen habit, Catalina made a pair of knee-length breeches and a small cape; with a green petticoat, she created a doublet and hose.

Catalina often was asked why she chose to become a man. Perhaps it was because she had been in the exclusive company of women for her entire life and she wanted to experience something different. And it was easier to disguise herself as a man with a partition of nun's clothes than a woman.

Putting on the man's garb, perhaps she felt more comfortable with herself than she had ever been. After all, this was not a world for women; the world was for the enjoyment of men. To partake of her share of life's pleasures, perhaps she felt she needed to wear pants. On that day, at the age of fifteen, she resolved to never again wear the clothes of a woman. Catalina had found her true self.

Setting out again, still not knowing where her feet would take her, she tread this way and that way, down roads and past villages, until she came to the town of Vittoria, some twenty leagues from San Sebastian. She had no more idea of what she would do in Vittoria than any other place, but she still had a pocketful of pesos. Here Catalina indulged in food with substance. She remained in the town for several days and became acquainted with a certain professor of theology, Don Francisco de Cerralta.

Don Francisco, thinking she was a picaro lad, alone and wandering in the world, took her in as his personal servant. Discovering that she could read Latin, he kept Catalina in his quarters for long hours, working side-by-side with him. One night he awoke her and insisted she come to help him with an aged document he was translating. When she made to put on her pants, he grabbed her arm and told her to come along in her nightshirt, that he was in a hurry. He was dressed in his own nightshirt that, like hers, came down to the knees.

Seated next to him on a bench with the manuscript and candles on the table before them, she suddenly felt the man's hand on her thigh. On several occasions in the past, he had found a reason to pat her hindquarters, letting his hand linger as he did. He had made up for his indiscretion by buying her new clothes.

Now he leaned forward, straining to see a smudged bit of print, and as he did his hand slipped down to her knee and then back, pulling her nightshirt back, slipping his hand along her bare thigh.

"You're a handsome boy," he said, "soft as a girl."

At fifteen years of age, Catalina had had no experience being around a man, and the only thing she knew about men were stories of endless lust and disgust told by the nuns at the convent. She had heard stories of women sneaking into another woman's cell to be with her at night, and there was many a time when she lay in bed at night and wished that a particularly buxom nun would come to her bed, but she had never heard of a man wanting to fondle another man. In truth, she may have been more curious about what he had in mind than aroused by his behavior.

As he caressed her naked thigh with his hand, she saw that his other hand was also busy. He had pulled back his nightshirt and exposed his virile part. Occasionally at the convent the nuns had had to care for small children, so the shape of a pene did not come as a surprise to her. The surprise was how big, red, and angry his male member looked. He grasped it in his hand and pulled up and down on it, as one would pull on the teat of a cow to milk it.

He took Catalina's own hand and put it on his pene. Curious, she squeezed it and then pumped it for him. It seemed to give him great pleasure, but other than satisfying a little curiosity, she did not find the act stimulating.

As she pumped his pene, he pulled her nightskirt back all the way and explored between her legs to find her virile part. When he found the hole between her legs, he gasped in surprise.

"You're a girl!"

"And you are a sodomite."

Catalina punched him in the nose. Not because he was a pervert who thought she was a boy he could sodomize, but because he had insulted her by calling her a girl. Catalina had determined that she was no longer a girl.

A small built, skinny little man, he went backward off the bench. He got to his feet with blood running from his nose. "I'm calling the constable and having you arrested!"

"I will tell the constable what you do to boys and that you raped me."

He turned purple and his eyes bulged. Catalina thought he was going to fall dead before her eyes. "Get out of my house, get out!"

There was little of her own possessions to throw into a

small sack, so she added a silver candlestick holder from the fireplace mantle and some gold coins she found lying carelessly about.

More adventures and misadventures lay before her, though Catalina was soon to embark upon her greatest quest. Her wanderlust feet would take her to Valladolid where the king was holding court, and she worked as a page for a royal secretary, to Navarre where she spent two years as the secretary for a marqués, and even back to San Sebastian where she came face-to-face with her mother in Church but went unrecognized. What bitch cur would remember the puppy cast off when it was barely weaned?

Catalina had discovered her true romantic inclinations when the marqués' wife invited her into her bed when her husband was on a hunting trip. Although Catalina had filled out and was a strong youth, the marqués' wife was larger than her, at least in terms of her width. Knowing that she would expect Catalina to penetrate her, Catalina had appropriated a phallic-shaped ivory horn that the marqués used as a paperweight and used it to give her pleasure. Catalina soon devised a way to tie the horn to a leather strap around her belly and legs so that she did not have to hold onto it when it was inside a woman.

Ah, but the juices that flowed in her soul when her lips tasted the lips of another woman, when her tongue caressed her breasts. As for men, there were none who stirred her desires. And why should they? Was she not a man? Her one regret was that she could not grow a beard. Each morning she scraped her face with her knife to stimulate the growth of hair, but only a bit of dark fuzz appeared above her upper lip and a couple of strands on her chin.

Everywhere Catalina went people talked of the New World, of the fortunes to be made there, the adventures to be had. Finally she could no longer resist the call of the New World and set about to find passage.

She talked her way as a cabin boy aboard a ship setting out for Panama and Cartagena de Indias. But what a surprise awaited her aboard ship. It was a brutal, stinking existence. The food was rotten; the smell was foul. Half the seamen were criminals forced aboard, and the other half were too stupid and brutish to live ashore. There were no women aboard, and the young boys were looked upon by the grown sailors as keg holes to insert their lust.

As a cabin boy, she had the captain's ear, and she was left alone by the sailors. The only time one of them bothered her was when a swine in the galley put his hand on her buttocks when she was getting the captain's dinner. She sliced the offending hand with her dagger, and the captain had the man keelhauled after she told him that the villain had tried to enlist her in a mutiny. She watched as they keelhauled him, tying his feet to a rope and throwing him off the side of the ship, then pulling him under the keel with a rope that went under the ship to the other side. He came up bloodied with half his clothes torn off of him from scraping the barnacles and other crustaceans that make the wood bottom of the ship as rough and sharp as a bed of stones.

It came as no surprise to her that she would be able to draw a man's blood with a dagger. Catalina had become enthralled by manly sports of swords and dueling. Realizing that to a man, his steel blade was literally an extension of the garrancha between his legs, she acquired her own rapier and dagger. She spent all her spare time practicing with the sword and dagger. She had always been big-boned, and as she finished her growth, she was as tall as most men and carried nearly the muscle. What little she lacked in physical power she made up for with a violent temper that caused her to throw herself at a foe and strike the person down while they were still forming a plan of attack.

Of great importance to her was that her breasts did not expose her female origins, but she was fortunate to have no more breasts than those of a young girl. To ensure that they did not grow large enough to expose her, she applied a poultice sold to her by an Italian. It hurt a great deal, but her breasts never grew large enough to expose her.

* * *

When the ship entered the waters of the Indies, it broke off from the great flotilla that had sailed from Seville and set a course with others for Cartagena. Approaching the bay of Cartagena de Indias, they encountered a squadron of Dutch ships and drove them off. They arrived at Cartagena, where they were to stay for eight days to unload and take on cargo. From there they went north to Nombre de Dios on the Isthmus of Panama.

By the time the ship reached the Isthmus, Catalina had tired of the base life aboard a ship. She decided to abandon ship at Nombre de Dios. To ensure she would be able to present herself with some dignity, she went ashore, telling the guards that the captain was sending her ashore to fetch something for him. She had five hundred of the captain's pesos and his new silk doublet in her bag.

In Nombre de Dios she was cheated out of her money by unscrupulous card players, who took her for a fresh youth just off a ship. When it became apparent that the devil had dealt the cards, Catalina drew her sword and dagger and drew blood from two of the three scoundrels. She escaped with her life and the clothes on her back, and once more needed employment.

Her reputation as a fighter and ability to read and write held her in good stead with a merchant, who wanted her to protect his goods and act as his selling agent in another town. She set up shop doing the merchant's work, and things went along on an even keel for a while. She was actually beginning to enjoy being respectable when she was insulted at a comedia by a man named Reyes and sliced him bad enough to require ten stitches. Shortly thereafter Catalina drew Reyes's blood again and killed his friend. She was arrested for the offense. Her master attempted to extricate her from the mess, but in the end, money passed hands and he was forced to send her off to Lima to get her away from the blood feud and the constable.

Lima was a great city of the New World, capital of the opulent kingdom of Peru, which included over a hundred

Spanish towns and villages. The city was the home of the viceroy, an archbishop, a university, and many splendors.

Catalina went to work for a grand merchant of the city, who was very satisfied with her services. However, the merchant became concerned because there were two young ladies in the house, his wife's sisters, and she became accustomed to frolicking with them. One in particular had taken a fancy to her. One day the merchant caught her with her head up the girl's skirt and fired Catalina on the spot.

Abruptly she found herself homeless and with no friends or money. Six companies of soldados were being raised to fight in Chile and she joined on, receiving immediately an allotment of nearly three hundred pesos.

The soldiers shipped out to Concepción in Chile, a port that goes by the name "the noble and the loyal" and is large enough to have its own bishop. There, to her surprise, she met her brother, Miguel de Erauso. She had four brothers and four sisters, and she had never met Miguel. Naturally Catalina did not let him know that she was in any way related to him, much less his *sister*. When he found out that her name was also Erauso and the area she was from, he took her as a friend. She spent several idyllic years in Concepción. The good times came abruptly to an end when her brother caught her visiting his mistress and they fought. She ended up being banished to Paicabí, a miserable outpost where war was constant with the indios.

There was nothing to do in Paicabí except eat, drink, and fight. They even slept in their armor. Finally a force of five thousand was gathered to meet an indio army of much greater size. They engaged them on open ground near Valdivia, which the indios had sacked. They gained the upper hand and slaughtered many of the indios, but when the victory was nearly complete, indio reinforcements arrived and they were driven back. They killed many of her men, including her own lieutenant, and rode off with the company flag.

When she saw the flag being carried off, she rode after it, with two other horse soldados at her side. They chased the flag carrier through an almost solid wall of indios, trampling them under their horses' hooves and slashing them with their swords. They took wounds in return, and one of Catalina's companions took a spear in the throat. He went down but the remaining two of them hacked their way to the indio cacique who had stolen their company's standard. As she reached him, her companion was dragged from his horse by a dozen indios. She had taken a painful blow to her leg, but she surged on. She came up behind the cacique and slashed him in the back of the neck, grabbing the standard as he went down. She then turned to fight her way back.

Catalina spurred her horse on, trampling, killing, and slaughtering more indios than she could count. She took three arrows in the back and a gash from a spear in her left shoulder. When she broke out of the multitude of indios, she raced across to where her own men were assembled. They cheered as she brought back the company colors. Her horse had taken a mortal wound but drove on as if it had wings. It went down when she reached her own lines, and she went down with it.

Her wounds were well tended to, and she received the honor of being made a lieutenant. Catalina served five more years in that rank and fought many more battles. She fought and captured a Christian indio cacique named Francisco, who had done much damage to their forces and carried off much booty. He was said to be one of the richest indios in Chile. After she knocked him from his horse, he surrendered to her and she strung him up from the nearest tree.

The impetuous hanging of the rich indio outraged the governor, and she found herself sent back to Concepción. This was actually good fortune, but Chance had always made her life miserable, turning each piece of luck into a disaster.

Her fall from respectability began when she was frequenting a gambling house with one of her fellow officers. A small misunderstanding arose between her and her companion, who accused her of cheating and announced in a loud voice that every word out of her mouth was a lie. Catalina drew out her dagger and plunged it into his chest. Things became more complicated when the local judge attempted to arrest her on the spot. She drew her sword and slashed him, then as a dozen men in the room charged her, she backed to the door, holding them back with her sword. Outside she ran for the sanctuary of the cathedral.

The governor and his constables were forbidden to arrest her on church grounds. She stayed in the church for six months when one of her friends, a lieutenant by the name of Juan de Silva, came to her and asked her to be his second in a duel to be fought near midnight that very night. Assured that this was no trap to lure her from the church, she agreed to accompany him. Dueling had been forbidden by the governor, and they wore masks to hide their identity.

She stood by, as was the custom for seconds, while her friend dueled with the other man. When she saw that he was being bested and about to be killed, she drew her sword and joined the fight. The other man's second soon engaged her, and her point went through a double thickness of leather and into his left breast near the nipple. As he lay dying, she discovered to her horror that the man she had mortally wounded was Miguel de Erauso, her own brother.

Catalina left Concepción, with horse and weapons, and went onto Valdivia and Tucumán.

She set out along the coast, suffering greatly, first from thirst and second from a lack of food. She fell in with two other soldados, deserters both. As the leagues unfolded beneath them, they went over mountains and across deserts, driven by hunger and desperation, never seeing another human except an occasional indio who fled before them. They killed one of the horses for food, but found it to be nothing more than hide and bones. But they continued to press on, league after league, over three hundred in all, until they ate the other horses and her two companions fell and never got up. When her last amigo had dropped to the ground, sobbing that he could not get up, she left him, taking eight pesos from his pocket.

She was overcome by fatigue and hunger when two indio riders found her. Taking mercy upon her, they carried her to the cattle estancia of their mistress. The woman was a mestizo, the daughter of a Spaniard and an india woman. She restored Catalina to health and began to rely upon her in running her ranch. There were few Spaniards in the region, and she soon proposed that Catalina marry her daughter.

She had played a bit with the daughter, no more than touching her in private places and kissing her, but in truth, she was as ugly as the devil himself, quite the opposite to Catalina's own preference for pretty faces. She had to agree to the marriage, but she managed to delay it for two months. She was finally forced to flee in the night, taking the proposed dowry with her.

Catalina was again arrested for murder after other adventures, and this time her reputation as a swordsman, gambler, and rogue had spread to the point that she knew she would soon be dispatched to her Maker.

Seeking the protection of the Church a final time with a constable wanting to drag her to the gallows, Catalina confessed to him that she was, in fact, a woman and had spent her early life in a convent.

After much thought, he had Catalina examined by two old women, who confirmed not only her sex, but the fact that she was still a virgin.

Rather than the recriminations she had expected from her confession, the news that the notorious Sancho de Erauso was actually a woman soon made its way across the sea to Europe.

Catalina found herself on a ship again, this time taking her back to Spain—not to a prison, but for an audience with the king. And after that to Rome to see the pope.

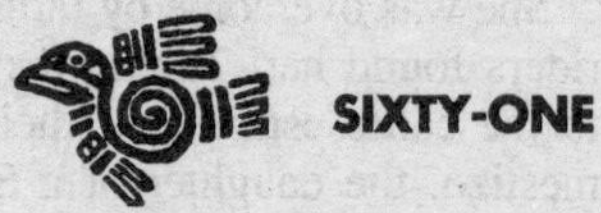

SIXTY-ONE

THE STORY OF Catalina de Erauso, of how she went to Madrid to meet the king and to Rome to be entertained by the pope, was told to me after I myself had made a trip across the great sea to Europe. I will finish the tale, but that meeting between us will come later. At this time we must rejoin the search for the naualli and the Knights of the Jaguar.

With Mateo, I rejoined the Healer at Oaxaca. We set out immediately toward Puebla because Don Julio said there was a festival soon to begin in Puebla that might attract the attention of the naualli. If we did not make contact with him there, we were to travel south toward Cuicatlán, keeping our eyes and ears open for signs of the naualli or his followers.

Jose, an indio vaquero, a trusted herder of cattle on the don's hacienda, joined us in the role of Mateo's servant. Jose would ride to carry any news we had of the naualli to Don Julio.

Mateo was mounted on a horse, Jose on a mule. There was talk of putting me on a mule, but I refused. The Healer would not travel in any other manner but to walk with his donkey's reins in his hand and his yellow dog beside him. I would not ride when he walked.

Mateo saw no detriment for us to travel together. "It will not create suspicion. It is common practice to travel together for safety."

In fact, we joined two mule trains that were heading for Puebla.

The Healer sought no explanation in why we were suddenly heading to Puebla. "I seek my mother," I told him. I weaved a tale that someone from Monte Alban had told me of seeing my mother in the Puebla area.

Little story was necessary for the Healer. He moved in whatever direction his feet were pointed; one road was the same as another to him.

"The roads are dangerous, and we will be joining others for protection." I gestured at Mateo and Jose.

Once again he said nothing. He had been traveling these dangerous roads for many times my lifetime, and he knew my reason was contrived. I suspected that the old man could read minds and knew my every lie.

We left the next day, walking behind Mateo, a mule piled high with guitars, a mule loaded with supplies, and Jose on another.

Along the way I casually questioned the Healer, asking him about his statement that someday the Aztec gods would rise up and drive out the Spanish. He told me it was something he had heard in his travels. He offered no more comments during the whole day, but that night after dinner, as he sat near the dying fire and smoked his pipe, he spoke of the naualli.

"In times long past," he said, "before the Great Deluge that covered the earth, the jaguar was the earth god. He dwelled in the stomach of the world. When he came out, he swallowed the sun and brought night upon the earth. After the Great Deluge, he was no longer in the bowels of the earth, but lived upon the land after the sun escaped. He stayed in caves and high in trees while his enemy the sun was in the sky, but the night belonged to him."

Mateo lay nearby with the sack of wine that seemed so often to be his bedmate, smoke curling up from tobacco he smoked without the use of a pipe. The tobacco had been twisted and rolled until it resembled a human turd. I had tasted one of the rolls, and it tasted much worse than I imagined mierda to taste. While he pretended to be half-asleep, gazing up at the night sky, I knew he was listening to the Healer.

"The power of the jaguar comes from the Heart of the World, a flawless green jade the size of a man's head. Inside the gem is a green flame, a fire so bright that to look at it would burn the eyes from a man. It is the power of this gem, this heart-of-hearts, that gives the jaguar magic."

I glanced over at Mateo. He continued to look up at the night sky, blowing rings of smoke. During the trip to Monte Alban he had told me a story about a priest into whose hands soon after the conquest came an incredibly bright jade that glowed green. The priest had been given the gem by indios. The superstitious priest, believing that the green fire was the power of Satan himself, smashed the stone despite an offer of thousands of ducats for the gem from another Spaniard. The point of the story to Mateo was that the priest's stupidity had destroyed a valuable gem.

"The Heart of the Land came from the stars," the Healer said. "The Heart was cast and brought to earth by the Tzitzimine, demons thrown out of heaven because of the evil they spoke and caused. The Tzitzimine lost the Heart to the Nine Lords of the Night; but because it had been made by the Tzitzimine, the Heart not only had magic powers, but was imbued with dark wizardry."

The Healer paused and looked at me in the waning light of the fire.

"It is from this source, the gem that is the Heart of the Land, glowing with the dark powers of the Tzitimine, that the naualli get their power. A naualli is a nanahualtin, one-who-knows how to use the power of the Heart."

"How does he know?" I asked.

"He has a book. It is like the Book of Fate, the Tonalamatl, but written in its pages are not the fates of men, but the incantations used by the Nine Lords of the Night to wield the power of the Heart of the Land."

I tried to imagine such a book. Aztec books, using picture writing, were often long scrolls, a single rolled page perhaps only two hands high, but very long; unrolled, they could be the length of several men lying head to foot.

"The naualli draws his power from the Book of the Nine

Lords of the Night. To gather his magic, he takes the book in darkness to a place where he will not be disturbed. The second, fifth, and seventh hours of night are considered the most auspicious for calling upon the Lords. When he has used the book to draw power from the Heart, he is able to perform his magic. One-who-knows can turn a stick into a snake, a flower into a scorpion, or even call ice stones from the sky to destroy crops. He can turn himself into a jaguar and rip the throat from any that oppose him."

"What was the difference between the Jaguar Knights and the Eagle Knights?" I asked.

"The Jaguar warriors and priests were identified with the night, with darkness. The jaguar ruled the night. The eagle hunted in the daytime. The Eagle Knights, like the Jaguar Knights, were fierce fighters, but the Eagle priests lacked the power of the elixir that made warriors feel no pain and the ability of the priests to shape-change."

I enjoyed listening to the Healer explain indio history. I compared it to what I had learned from Fray Antonio and others. To the Spaniards, history was a series of events. Kings and queens, wars, conquest and defeat, doctors writing down their cures, sailors drawing their charts and espousing their adventures, all recorded in books. To the Healer, history was magic and soul. Magic came from spirits and gods, and even a rock could harbor a spirit. Soul was how people were affected by the acts of the gods.

I knew that Spaniards had the force of reason on their side. But even when the Healer talked of magic books that turned men into jaguars and elixirs made a man invincible, I was inclined to see his tales as espousing another form of wisdom rather than being without reason.

Nor was I inclined to accept the Spanish version of the history of the indios over the Healer's knowledge. Fanatical priests had burned most of the Aztec books, so both the Spaniards and the Healer drew information from the stories passed down from generation to generation. The Spanish had an advantage in that they recorded the stories in books that were passed to generations of scholars, but the Healer had an even greater advantage: From one end of the old indio empires to the other were thousands of inscriptions on walls, temples, and other monuments. Some were disappearing every day, destroyed by ignorance or, even more common, broken up to use as building stone for new construction. But the Healer had spent a long lifetime walking from one end of the land to the other, reading the inscriptions. He had knowledge that was not known to the Spanish, and which never would be discovered because the inscriptions were crumbling to dust or smashed into pieces.

The Spanish had recorded vast amounts of facts into books. The Healer had lived history, not just that of his own days, but that of time immemorial. He slept, ate, spoke, and thought with little difference from what his ancestors had done for thousands of years. He was a walking, breathing temple of knowledge.

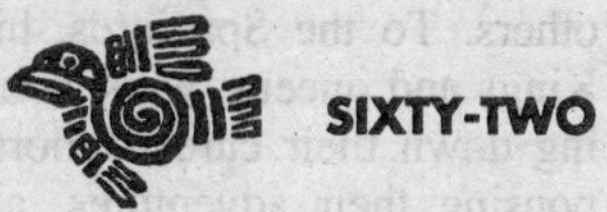

SIXTY-TWO

PUEBLA DE LOS Angeles, the Town of the Angels, was the largest city I had ever been in. To Mateo it was a small place compared to the City of Mexico.

"Mexico is a true city, not an overgrown provincial village like Puebla, Veracruz, and Oaxaca. It is a grand place. Someday, Bastardo, I will take you there. We will sup on the finest food and the most beautiful women. One whorehouse in that city has not only brown and white girls, but a yellow one."

I was awed that a whorehouse could actually have a chino. I had seen a woman with yellow skin at the fair for the Manila galleon, and I'd wondered what she was like without her clothes.

"Are they—the chino women—are they built like other women?"

He looked at me out of the corner of his eye. "No, of course not. Everything is reversed."

What does that mean? I wondered. Was everything that was usually on the front of a person, on the backside of a chino? I did not ask the question because I did not want to expose my ignorance further.

We camped outside Puebla in the same area where traders and indio magicians had converged. We did not see the naualli among them.

I accompanied the Healer and the others to the square at the city center where a harvest festival was to be held. Even though Mateo did not consider Puebla a grande city, it was enormous to me. As I had been told about the City of Mexico, Puebla was also high above the coastline, in a broad plain shouldered by distant mountains. Mateo said that the architecture was similar to that of the great city of Toledo in Spain.

"One of the finest voices of poetry died on the streets of Puebla," Mateo had told me earlier, when the city was in sight. "Gutierre de Cetina was a poet and a swordsman who fought in Italy and the German lands for the king. He came to Mexico after the conquest at the behest of his brother. Unfortunately, his poetry was better than his sword play. He was killed in a duel by a rival for the same woman. They say he was struck down after standing outside the woman's window praising her eyes with his poem, 'Ojos claros serenos.'

Eyes of clear serenity,
If your tender gaze endear,
Why for me is your gaze severe?
If the gazer be more to delight
When you gently stare,
Let your gaze be tender,
O torment wild!
Eyes of clear serenity,

Having gazed upon me thus,
at least now gaze at me.

I helped the Healer set up in the main square. He immediately attracted a crowd of indios, so there was no need for me to fake a miraculous recovery. I wandered about the square, unable to conceive that there could be a town enormously bigger than Puebla. What must the City of Mexico and the great cities of Spain be like?

Mateo hailed me. "Bastardo, the goddess Fortune smiles upon you. There is a comedia company in town. We are going to see their play. How many pesos do you have, compadre?"

After Mateo emptied my pockets, I followed eagerly beside him. He had never explained what happened that caused him and the troupe of players to find themselves on the wrong side of the king's justice. I picked up clues that they had been caught selling smuggled deshonesto and profano libros. From his attempt to sell Fray Juan a romantic adventure book that was on the prohibition list of the Holy Office, I knew that Mateo did these things. But for the others to be shipped off to Manila and him to be under the threat of the gallows, eh, it must have been more than a romance they were selling.

We went a few blocks off of the main street to the place of the comedia. I had expected to find a "wall" of blankets enclosing a small area, but it was much more elaborate. A vacant lot shouldered on three sides by two-story homes had been turned into a corral, a playhouse.

Against the wall of one house a wooden stage was elevated several feet above the ground. At ground level to the left and right were areas blanketed off. "Dressing rooms for the actors and actresses," Mateo said. Logs had been laid in many places for people to sit while others brought benches from home. The windows, balconies, and roofs of the adjoining houses served as theater boxes where people of quality watched the play. The stage was not protected from wind or rain. "If it rains too hard, they simply stop," Mateo said.

"So this is a theater for comedias," I said to Mateo, very impressed by the size. Several hundred people could view the performance.

"This is a temporary theater," he said, "but it is similar to corrales all over Spain. The difference is that there is often a canopy over the stage to protect from sun and rain and even canopies or roofs over some of the spectator areas. The stage would be a bit higher off the ground and wider, the dressing rooms more permanent. Empty space next to buildings are the best for creating a theater because the walls are already up on three sides. In some of the great cities, like Madrid and Seville, permanent buildings with wood walls and roofs have been constructed. Naturally, they cannot be completely enclosed as much as a house because some light is needed."

"Do you know these actors?" I asked Mateo.

"No, but I am sure they have heard of Mateo de Rosas Oquendo."

If they had not already, they would before long.

"The troupe pretends to be Spanish, but I can tell from their accents that they are not. I suspect they are Italians. Everyone wants to come to the Spanish stage. It is known everywhere that our plays and actors are the best in the world. This play is written by my amigo, Tirso de Molina. The *Trickster of Seville* is a comedia in three acts."

"Like what you put on—on," I stammered, "in Seville?" I almost said, 'at the fair.' I had already resolved in my mind that Mateo knew I was the boy from the Jalapa fair, but the matter remained a secret unspoken between us.

"Yes, like Seville, though a Puebla production will not be so grand."

The temporary theater was grand to my eyes. The only play I had ever seen other than ones put on by the churches during religious holidays was the one at the Jalapa fair, where a grassy knoll and some blankets served as a theater. The audience there had been rough muleteers and traveling merchants, but I could see from the balconies and rooftops that much more genteel people had come to see this play.

Mateo wanted seats on a balcony or roof, but none were left. We went to the far wall opposite the stage. Benches were available there for a few coppers more, and we stood on them to get a good look at the stage.

Close to the stage were what Mateo called the vulgos, the vulgar people.

"The mosqueteros are the lice of the theater," Mateo said. "When they step into a corral, suddenly a butcher and baker who sign their names with an X are experts on comedias. Men whose only acting has been to lie to their wives suddenly believe themselves as much a fault finder with an actor's performance as an Inquisitor with a blasphemer's denials."

The play began in a room in the palace of the king of Naples. We were told that we were in the Italian palace by an actor who indicated a hanging cloth that had an elaborate door painted on it. It was nighttime, the actor says, and Isabel, a duchess, was awaiting the arrival of her lover, Duke Octavio, in a dark room.

"Pretty wench," Mateo said, of the actress who played Isabel.

The main character in the play arrived. His name was Don Juan. He entered the room with his face concealed by his cloak and pretended to be Duke Octavio. When palace guards catch the two, Don Juan boasted that he had fooled Isabel into thinking he was Duke Octavio and made love to her.

The mosqueteros bunched near the stage yelled insults to the actors, attacking their accents. The mosqueteros had picked up on the same thing Mateo did—the actors had Italian accents. While the play was set in Italy, the area was under the control of the Spanish king; most of the characters were supposed to be Spanish. One particular vulgo was the loudest and the most aggressive. He was familiar with the play, having seen it in the Corral del Príncipe in Madrid, or so he claimed. He shouted corrections to the lines he believed the actors blundered.

Mateo grimaced at the noise made by the mosqueteros. "No autor or actor has failed to be a victim to this rabble."

But the play went on. Don Juan's jest ruined the duke and the Lady Isabel, and Don Juan fled Naples. He was shipwrecked and washed ashore near a fishing village, where he was taken to the hut of Tisbea, a fisher maid. When the young woman saw him, she fell in love with him. As he lay unconscious in her arms, she said, "Gallant and handsome youth of noble brow, return, I pray, to life."

With a change of dress and a different-colored wig, Tisbea is played by the same actress who played Isabel.

Don Juan tells her as he lies in her arms that he has fallen madly in love with her. "My country girl, I wish that God had drowned me in the waves that I might have been spared the madness of my love for you."

Convinced by him that although he is high born and she a peasant girl, his love is true, she yields to his demands that they share a bridal bed. As soon as he is through with the girl, he and his servant flee the village on horses they have stolen from her.

Tisbea, in anguish at the betrayal, cries, "Fire! Fire! I'm burning! Sound the alarm, amigos, while my eyes bring water. Another Troy is in flames. Fire, my compadres! May love have pity on a soul in flames. The caballero deceived me with his promise of marriage and soiled my honor."

The mosquetero who considered himself a master of the play ran to the stage. "You stupid woman! That is not her correct speech!" He threw a tomato at the woman.

Mateo moved with the speed of a jungle cat. One instant he was standing beside me, and the next he was at the stage with his sword in hand. He grabbed the mosquetero and swung him around. The brute stared at him, startled, and then grabbed for a dagger. Mateo hit him on the head with the hilt of the sword, and the man crumbled to the ground.

Mateo turned to the audience. He lashed the air with his sword. "I am Don Mateo Rosas de Oquendo, caballero for the king and autor of comedias. There is to be no more disturbance while this lovely lady with serene eyes," he turned and bowed to the woman, "speaks her lines." He nudged the unconscious man at his feet. "I would kill him, but a gentleman does not soil his sword with the blood of swine."

Clapping came from the balconies and rooftops. The vulgar people said nothing.

Mateo bowed once more to the actress, and she threw him a kiss.

Returning to Seville, Don Juan kept up his scandalous conduct. Betraying a friend, he deceived another young woman into believing that he was her lover. The woman shouted for help when she discovered the trick. Her father, Don Gonzalo, came to her rescue and was killed by Don Juan in a sword fight.

Despite the tragedy, Don Juan, driven by demons, unable to be the honorable gentleman that was his birthright, continued his intrigues, tricking women into surrendering their honor to him.

His downfall came, not at the hands of the living, but the dead. Don Juan came upon a statue of the fallen Don Gonzalo. Making fun of the stone statue, Don Juan pulled its beard and invited it to dine. Only to have the invitation accepted.

In a scene of ghoulish horror, Don Juan and the stone specter of the dead father have dinner. The dinner takes place in a dark church, and a tomb is the dinner table.

Eating a dish of spiders and vipers, and washing it down with bitter wine, Don Gonzalo said that all debts must one day be repaid:

Mark those well whom God has judged,
And punished for their crimes.
The day of reckoning arrives
When this world's debts are repaid.

The arrogant Don Juan at first challenges the ghost, showing no fear. But when the ghost clasps his hand, the fires of hell grip the seducer. With a clap of thunder, we were told the tomb is swallowed by the earth, taking Don Juan and the ghost with it. However, in this case the actors fell to the floor and they and the tomb were covered with blankets. The "thunder" was a drum.

When the play was over, I was eager to return to our campsite and discuss it with Mateo, but he had other plans. He twirled his mustache as he told me to go back alone, "I have some unfinished business." I followed his look to the stage where the actress was giving him the eye.

I trudged back to the camp alone and ate beans around a campfire, while Mateo, *caballero* and *autor,* lay in the arms of an actress and tasted a bit of heaven. Ay, there was another reason for my melancholy. This play about the scandalous Don Juan was the very play that the dark-eyed beauty Eléna had hidden under the seat of the carriage the day she saved my life.

SIXTY-THREE

WE DID NOT see the naualli magician at our encampment or in Puebla. Circulating among the other indio traders and magicians, I learned that he had been seen a week earlier on the road that leads south. One of the traders looked at me suspiciously when I asked about the naualli, and I told him that I was growing tired of assisting the old Healer and was looking for a new master.

Mateo was anxious to leave the area. He had not returned from his tryst with the actress until almost dawn. His doublet had a tear, and the side of his head was bruised.

"Did you bed with a den of wild cats?" I asked.

"In truth, there was one too many in the bed last night,

the woman's husband showed up at a most inopportune time."

Eh, amigos, was this a familiar tale with the picaro? I pretended to be shocked. "Dios mio. And how did he feel about you making love to his wife?"

"He found it very painful at the time. My problem is that I am not sure he feels anything anymore. He was bleeding profusely when I last saw him. We need to get on our way before his friends or the constable seek you out."

"Me? What have *I* done?"

He shook his head with feigned sadness. "You were born, Bastardo. I told the woman to tell them that a mestizo boy broke into the room and was raping her when her husband came to her rescue."

¡Ay de mí!

Along the road we stopped at villages and asked about the naualli. We traveled for three days before we obtained word that the naualli was in the area. Mateo and I had both questioned indios, mestizos and españols along the way and learned nothing. It was the Healer, speaking to a cacique, who obtained the information about the naualli.

I accompanied the Healer to his meeting with the cacique. We sat in the cacique's hut and were served a chocolate and chili drink by the cacique's nephew. At first I took the boy, who was about my own age, as a girl. He was dressed in woman's clothing and performed the duties of a woman. Later the Healer told me that when there are not enough women to perform household duties in a village because of losses to plagues, that at birth some male babies would be raised as girls and taught womanly chores. The Healer assured me that that did not include acting as a woman to perform ahuilnéma . . . but seeing the wrinkled old headman together with the boy-dressed-as-a-girl, I was reminded of the old cacique and young wife I had "healed" of the ahuilnéma problem they had with their marriage.

"My uncle has been told that the naualli is in the area," I told Mateo later. "He operates chiefly around here, serving a number of small towns and villages, leaving only to attend festivals and fairs."

"Did he learn anything about the Knights of the Jaguar?"

"The cacique said that the knights will rise and drive the Spanish from the lands of the indios. But other than such boasting, he had no real information."

Mateo decided we would camp at a larger village along a well-traveled road. From there we would hunt for the naualli within the areas he was said to traverse while we gathered information about him and the knights.

At the village cantina, Mateo spoke to three Spanish traders. The cantina was nothing more than a covered patio with two tables. I sat down in the dirt nearby as a priest joined them. I was always interested in listening to Spaniards talking. It fed my curiosity about that side of my blood. Because of the fray, I had seen maps of the world and knew that Spain was only one country among many. But, of course, Spain dominated most of Europe and was the greatest power in the world.

I soon discovered that the conversation was about strange events.

"Word of missing people is becoming more and more frequent," a trader said. "A hacienda owner rode out to inspect a fence and never returned. His horse came back without him, but searches could find no trace of his body. What is most suspicious is that after he disappeared, some of his indio vaqueros ran away. The overseer said that they believed the owner had been killed by an indio who could take the form of a jaguar."

"The number of suspicious deaths has risen steadily," another trader said. "I heard a similar story about a merchant who disappeared while traveling. His servants ran away with his goods. One was tracked down and tortured. To his dying breath, he claimed that his master had been attacked by a were-jaguar and dragged into the jungle. And it's not just we Spanish who are victims. My own servants are terrified unless we travel with mule trains and other merchants.

They tell me that indios and mestizos who work for Spaniards are being hunted down and devoured by jaguars that have been trained to kill Spaniards and those who support them."

Mateo made a listening response that showed his sympathy. "Have your servants told you who has trained these animals?"

There was general agreement that no names were ever mentioned. Mateo did not ask specifically about the Knights of the Jaguar. I supposed he was silent because he was seeking information, not providing it.

"The viceroy should be taking care of this problem," a trader said. "If he can't handle it, we should send our complaint to the Council of the Indies."

The third trader scoffed. "I have been traveling the roads and trails of New Spain for half my lifetime. There is nothing new about these stories. There is always talk among the indios that we will be driven from their land. And it is always by some magical means. A man who turns into a jaguar is nothing more than the fanciful imagination of these simple people."

"It is not fanciful. I believe it is true."

The pronouncement came from an unexpected source. The priest who had joined them took a deep gulp of wine and wiped his forehead with a handkerchief.

"I have worked among these savages," the priest said. "They hate us; hate us for taking their land, their women, their pride. They come to church on Sunday and lie about their adherence to our Savior. Then they go out and sacrifice babies. Did you know that? That they sacrifice babies with curly hair?"

"Babies with curly hair?" a merchant repeated.

"They sacrifice curly haired babies because the ripples in the hair are similar to the ripples in a lake. The curly hair pleases the lake god. When a baby cries when it's being sacrificed, the tears are symbolic of rain and it pleases the rain god."

"They do it because they believe the gods will give them

water for their crops," a merchant piped in. "It's been a dry year in this region. When it rains too little or too much, the crops don't grow and they starve."

"I can't stand dealing with these savages," the priest said, mopping his forehead again. "They practice the dark magic of Satan. I don't doubt they are in league with the devil and can turn themselves into were-jaguars, just as there are witches and warlocks in our own country who can take the shape of wolves. They are in the jungle when it gets dark. You never see their bodies but their eyes shine at you. It drove my companion priest mad. Three days ago he hanged himself from the bell rope. I ran into the chapel when I heard the bell tolling. There he was, dangling from the rope."

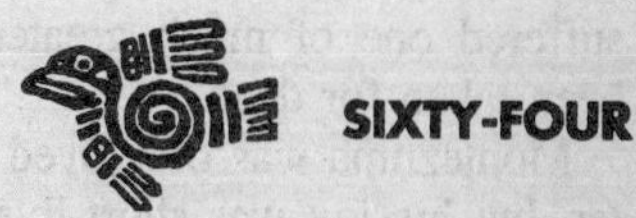

SIXTY-FOUR

THE NEXT DAY we had word that the naualli was seen at a nearby village.

We went there, the Healer and I to perform the snake magic, Mateo with Jose to sell guitars to Spanish living in the area.

The village turned out to be even bigger than the one where we had been staying, more of a small town than a simple village. I learned on the way to the magician's hut that the magician was a diviner of dreams. Along the way, the Healer told me the most famous dream in Aztec history. It concerned Montezuma's sister, who rose from the dead to prophesy the Spanish conquest.

Princess Papantzin was the sister of Montezuma. She was close to him as his friend and trusted advisor. When she died suddenly, Montezuma was in great shock. Because of his love and attachment for her, he had her entombed in an underground vault on the palace grounds. After the burial ceremony, the entrance to the tomb was covered by a slab of stone.

Early the next morning one of Montezuma's children saw the princess sitting by a fountain in a courtyard of the palace. She ran and told her governess, who, upon determining that it was indeed Princess Papantzin, roused the household.

Montezuma had the princess brought into his presence and she told him a strange tale. She said that she had become dizzy and passed out. When she awoke, she found herself in the black tomb. She made her way out and was able to push aside the stone slab enough to get out into the garden. She was resting when the child spotted her.

Before this event, the princess was known to have suffered a fainting malady in which she would fall to the floor and not awaken for several minutes. She had apparently suffered one of much greater duration this time and had been taken for dead.

Montezuma was overjoyed at the resurrection of his sister, but his joy was short-lived. She told him she had had a dream that she had walked with the dead in the underworld and they had taken her to the shore of the Eastern Sea. There she had seen boats bigger than a nobleman's house and strange men. The men had light eyes and pale skin and hair. They called themselves Sons of the Sun and said they had come from the House of the Sun beyond the Eastern Sea.

When they came ashore, their leader was no ordinary man, but a god dressed in a suit of gold. His shield shined with the fire of the sun.

"I am Quetzalcóatl, the Plumed Serpent," he said. "I have come to claim my kingdom."

Áyyo, poor Montezuma. Following his sister's dream, Hernando Cortes landed at Veracruz. No wonder he was frozen with fear when the news was brought to him that strange men with pale faces and shiny armor had arrived from the Eastern Sea. In dealing with Cortes, Montezuma's indecision was caused by his conviction that he was dealing with a god.

The Healer and the dream diviner talked and smoked, filling the magician's small hut so full of smoke I was forced to wait outside. Besides news that the naualli was in the area, I learned another interesting fact before I sought fresh air: a dwarf had disappeared from a neighboring village. The small person was the grown son of an old widow. He had been drinking pulque with a neighbor and had disappeared walking home.

"It is believed that Tlaloc has taken the dwarf," the dream reader said.

Eh, Tlaloc gets blamed for many things when the land is dry, I thought.

Tlaloc was that thirsty god who gives rain. His name means He Who Makes Life Grow. When he was happy, maize and beans grew tall and bellies were full. When he was angry, he let the crops die from thirst or flooded them with too much water. The traders had mentioned that little children were sacrificed to him because their tears looked like raindrops. Because statues of gods were often short, dwarfs were also especially favored by the gods as sacrifices.

The naualli had the weather working for him. The more people feared a drought and the famine that would ensue, the more they would pander to the old gods.

Meandering around a bit while I waited for the Healer, I spotted a buxom young girl about my own age. She gave me a smile that made my heart ping. I returned her smile and was sauntering toward her when two men came out of the hut she had exited. They saw that I had my eye on the girl and both of them gave me such unfriendly looks that I veered away.

They knew I was not an indio. My height and muscular frame was more that of a Spaniard or mestizo. And my beard made it obvious. Few indios had beards and the ones who grew a little facial hair tended to pluck it. The Aztecs considered body hair as a sign of low caste. Mothers rubbed hot lime water on babies faces to keep hair from growing.

"Go inside," the older man told the girl.

She shot me a sideways glance before she went back into the hut.

I wandered a little more aimlessly and suddenly realized coming around a house that I was behind the men I took to be the girl's father and brother. I slowed my pace to let them get ahead of me. We had not gone far when I saw a man ahead whom I believed to be the naualli. He was talking to four men. The five of them turned and went into the jungle. The two men in front of me followed.

I slowed my step down to a shuffle, trying to decide what I should do. I was certain that the naualli had disappeared into the jungle with the men to conduct a sacrifice. What other explanation could it be? They probably had the dwarf drugged and were going to rip out his heart on the sacrificial block.

Mateo and Jose had gone to a larger town to play cards, a pastime I had discovered was one of Mateo's many vices.

Cursing my bad luck and good intentions, my feet took me unwillingly to where I saw the men disappear into the forest. I had gotten no farther than a couple of dozen feet into the thickets when I came face-to-face with one of the indios. He pulled a big knife out of a sheath. I backed up. I heard the sounds of other men moving in the bushes. In a panic, I turned and ran. I ran back to where the Healer was with the dream diviner.

Mateo did not get back to camp until the next morning. He always came from these card games and drinking bouts looking like a wild animal who had taken on an entire pack. I suspected there was a great deal of truth to this impression.

I told him my suspicions about the dwarf while he took a swig from his goatskin of wine and crawled into his bedroll. "The dwarf was probably sacrificed last night."

"How do you know? Because the man is missing? That makes him a sacrifice victim?"

"I have not had the experiences of a world traveler and soldier, as yourself," I said to flatter him, "but even in my young life I have encountered many strange things. I witnessed a sacrifice once before, and I am certain that another one took place last night."

"Go find the body." He covered his head, ending any further discussion.

¡Ayya ouiya! I was no one's fool. I would lead Mateo and a troop of soldados into the jungle to find the body, but I was not about to do so alone. I walked down the dirt road, kicking rocks, when I saw the naualli ahead. He was camped with another man a few minutes walk from our own camp. I went into the bushes and found a spot from which I could sit and spy upon the camp.

After the two men left the campsite, heading for the village, I came out of hiding and slowly walked in the same direction. As I came by the camp, I saw a bundle lying on the ground, an indio blanket with ropes wrapped around it.

The bundle shook!

I kept walking, looking straight ahead. But my legs would not carry me any farther. I knew the dwarf was in that bundle. Mustering my courage, I turned on my heel and hurried back, drawing my knife. I broke into a run.

Kneeling beside the bundle, I began slashing at the ropes. "I'm cutting you loose!" I told the trapped dwarf, first in Spanish and then repeated it in Náhuatl. He began struggling to get free even as I was slashing the ropes.

When the last rope was cut, I jerked the blanket off. A pig looked up at me and squealed.

I gawked as it got to its feet to run. I threw myself at it, grabbing it with both arms and hands to keep it from escaping. The pig let out screeching squeals that would have disturbed the dead in Mictlán. Slipping out of my hands, it raced into the jungle. I got up to run after it, but it was hopeless. It was gone.

The noise had attracted some undesirable attention. The naualli was coming back, and he had been joined by several men.

I ran for our camp.

* * *

¡Ay de mí! To keep me from being arrested for pig stealing, Mateo had to give me his gambling winnings. This put my picaro amigo into a black mood, and I spent the day away from the camp to keep the wrath of his boot toe away from my backside.

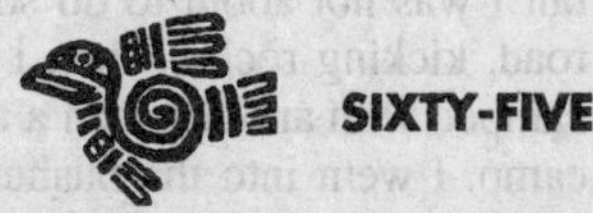

SIXTY-FIVE

INTENSELY INTERESTED IN my Spanish roots, I questioned Mateo frequently during our travels about the history of Spain and the conquest of the Aztec Empire. In order for me to understand Cortes and the conquest, I soon learned I had to know more about my indio roots. I had learned a great deal when the flower weaver sent me on a walk with the gods. In my discussions with Mateo, I learned not only about the conquest, but more about Aztecs.

My reverence for Doña Marina, an india girl who was Cortes's savior, was not only fed by my sympathy for the way she had been abandoned but because the fray would often tell me that like the doña, my mother was an Aztec princess.

I had learned much about Doña Marina and Cortes from Mateo. In truth, I had heard the names most often, especially that of the great conquistador, but like the Father, the Son, and the Holy Ghosts, the names were more legendary than real.

I knew that Tenochtitlan suffered the same fate as the other cities and villages of New Spain after the conquest—the indio character was destroyed and the name was changed to City of Mexico. The city was still the beating heart of the region, but the Aztec temples had been replaced by cathedrals.

While the Aztecs dominated the heart of preconquest

New Spain from Tenochtitlan, there were not only striking differences between the indio cultures but great hatred. No indio culture was as bloodthirsty as the Aztecs. They made war for booty, conquered and enslaved other cultures for tribute, but the main objective of the wars and tribute was not glory, territory, or gold—it was *human hearts.*

I had learned during the dream created by the flower weaver that my Aztec ancestors had a covenant with their gods—they gave the gods blood and the gods blessed them with rain for their crops. The more blood they gave the gods, the more hearts they ripped from sacrifice victims while the hearts were still hot and pounding, the more the gods favored the Aztecs over others.

The Aztecs had risen to dominance only about a hundred years before Cortes landed in 1519 on the coast of the Eastern Sea. The tale of how conquistadors conquered twenty-five million indios with about five hundred–odd soldiers, sixteen horses, and fourteen cannons has been told and retold many times to me—the priests speak of this miracle in almost as much awe as they do the birth of my namesake Jesus Christ. But often when I hear a Spaniard retell the story of the conquest, they leave out an important detail—the Aztecs were defeated not only by the men, horses, and cannons of Spain, but a coalition of indio nations who fielded thousands of warriors against them.

Today Spain is the greatest military power in the world, dominating not just the European continent, but ruling an empire that it is truly said the sun never sets upon. Christopher Columbus had laid the seeds of the empire by running into a whole new continent on his way to that vast land in Asia called India. But Columbus and the generation that followed were mostly concerned with Caribbean islands. Although they knew there was a great land mass to the west beyond the islands, little of it had been explored several decades after the 1492 discovery.

One of the men who followed in the wake of Columbus had been sent off to study law at a university but set aside his pen to take up the sword.

Hernando Cortes was born in Medellin, in the province of Estremadura, Spain, in 1485, seven years before Columbus sailed to the New World. He grew up in an almost fever-pitched atmosphere of tales of glory and adventure as more and more stories of riches and conquest came back from the early explorers. In truth, the Caribbean islands, which were the first conquests, were actually poor in everything but indios, whom the conquerors could use as slave labor.

Even though the New World had not yet fulfilled its promise of lands paved with gold, Cortes and his compatriots still dreamed of faraway places to be conquered. The fray said they had read too many "chivalric romances" in which a knight-errant found love, treasure, and glory. The most famous of these books I have mentioned before: *Amadis of Gaul.* Amadis was a prince cast out to sea on an ark at birth because his mother couldn't reveal who his father was. The prince grows up, falls in love with a princess, and has to go out into the world as a wandering knight and win her hand. He fights monsters, visits enchanted islands, and returns to his love.

To young men like Cortes, Amadis was not just a story, but a sign to seek to their God-given chance at "love, treasure, and glory" in the New World across the sea.

At the age of seventeen, Cortes left university and managed to get the promise of a berth aboard a ship bound for the New World, but fate—and his young man's lust—dealt him a bad hand. Scaling a stone wall to gain access to the apartment of a woman with whom he was engaged in an intrigue, the wall gave way and he fell, almost buried by the rubble.

Too injured to cross an ocean, two more years passed, and he was nineteen when he next got the opportunity. When he arrived at Hispaniola, the Caribbean island that was the main seat of Spanish rule, he went to see the governor and was told, because of family connections, that he would get a grant of land and a *repartimiento* of indios for slave labor. His reply to the governor's secretary was that he had not come to the New World to farm. "I came for glory and gold, not to till the soil like a peasant."

Mateo told me that this man of destiny, Hernando Cortes, was of medium height, slender, yet had a surprisingly deep chest and broad shoulders. His eyes, hair, and short beard were dark as any Spaniard's, yet his complexion was unexpectedly pale.

At first, he found no opportunity for conquering new worlds. While a number of Caribbean islands had been discovered, and the Crown was aware of a great, mysterious land mass beyond, no one realized that great empires already existed in what were to become New Spain and Peru.

Cortes impatiently worked his land and indios, but his hot-bloodied temperament kept him in trouble, mostly of a feminine nature. Amorous affairs turned into affairs of honor played out with swords, and he carried these scars to the grave.

During this time he obtained experience fighting against indios, putting down insurrections, and serving in the conquest of Cuba. Despite his good military record, he became embroiled in controversy with the new governor of Cuba, Velasquez, after a romantic entanglement with a daughter of the powerful Xuarez family. When Cortes refused to consummate the affair by marrying the girl, Governor Valasquez had him arrested and put into iron shackles. Cortes managed to work himself free of the fetters, pried apart iron bars, and leaped from his prison window. At a nearby church, he called upon the sanctuary of the Church—the civil authority could not arrest him while he was in God's house.

The governor placed guards near the church waiting for Cortes to make a move. When the young man got careless and wandered a few feet from the church grounds, one of the governor's men jumped him from behind and pinned his arms until other guards joined the fracas.

Put into irons again, he was put aboard a ship bound for Hispaniola, where he was to be tried for his defiance. He managed to get out of the shackles again, this time stealing a small boat being towed behind the ship, and made his way back to shore, abandoning the rowboat and swimming ashore when the small boat became unmanageable. He made his way back again to the sanctuary of the church.

Rather than maintaining a dispute he could not hope to win, he agreed to marry the wronged young woman, Catalina Xuarez, and reconciled with Governor Velasquez. Following his marriage, Cortes settled down to farm his land with several thousand repartimiento indios he had been granted. By this time he had a slash on his face from a duel over a woman.

He was thirty-three years old and a prosperous landowner when news came that an expedition had made contact with an indio culture along the Caribbean coast of what was to become New Spain. The news sent shock waves through the Spanish—another land to explore and plunder! An expedition was organized by Velasquez to explore the area and Cortes was granted his plea to lead it. Despite their past problems, Velasquez recognized in Cortes a bold, aspiring spirit who craved gold and glory.

Cortes immediately set out to put together the expedition, getting the men, supplies, and ships necessary, selling or borrowing off everything he owned to cover much of the cost. Velasquez, seeing the lengths of Cortes's efforts, realized that the man was likely not only to succeed but to claim all glory for himself. Jealous, he was about to revoke Cortes's authority when Cortes surprised him by setting sail without completing the preparations. Velasquez's orders to stop and arrest Cortes chased the adventurer as he went from port to port to gather men and supplies. Often he had to use his cannons to persuade the local authorities to ignore the governor's orders.

He finally set out for the area to be explored, landing on the west coast of New Spain with 553 soldiers, fourteen cannons, and sixteen horses. He told his men that they were setting out on a noble venture that would make them famous throughout the ages, that he was leading them to a land richer than any found before.

"Great things are achieved only by great exertion," he told them. "Glory was never the reward of the sloth!"

On April 21, 1519, Cortes landed at the place he called *La Villa Rica de la Veracruz,* the Rich Town of the True Cross. He came for glory, gold, and God.

Wrapped up in the religious zeal was the conception by the Spaniards that the indios were guilty of every kind of vice. But the most heinous crimes committed by the indios in the eyes of the Spanish were not on the battlefield or the sacrificial block but in bed. The Spaniards continuously charged them with the crime against nature, the crime that dare not speak its name: sodomy.

Despite the view of the Spanish, the practice of sodomy was not universal. The Aztecs punished sodomy harshly. The indio acting as a female had his virile parts cut off and a hole cut between his legs. Then his entrails were removed through the hole. I shuddered at the thought of someone taking a knife, spreading my legs, cutting out a hole, and sticking their hand up the hole to remove my guts.

After the insides were removed, the victim was tied down to a peg and covered with ash until he was buried. Wood was piled on top and burned.

The punishment for the indio acting as a man was simpler: He was tied down to a log and covered with ash, to remain there until he died.

Who had the worse punishment, you ask? The one who acted as a woman or the one who acted as a man? While the man-woman's punishment makes my flesh crawl, he would die quickly from the incision. The man tied down and left to die would wither slowly, his pain and suffering enduring much longer. But I would take a lingering death over someone cutting a hole between my legs and reaching up to rip out my entrails.

Not all indio groups prohibited sodomy, and a few openly practiced it. Some Mayan tribes trained their boys to engage in sodomy during their youth. Until a boy was old enough to marry, well-to-do parents provided him with a male companion, a slave boy, to meet his sexual urges. This way he did not pursue girls, permitting them to remain virgins until marriage.

Balboa, who discovered the Pacific Ocean after trekking through the jungles of Panama, found homosexuality practiced among the chiefs at Quarequa. When he discovered that the king's brother and the brother's friends wore women's clothing and entered each other through the backdoor, he threw forty of them to his savage dogs.

One Caribbean tribe first castrated their young male prisoners, then used them sexually until they grew to adulthood, at which point they were killed and eaten. Heinous behavior, but there are many tales told today of unscrupulous Christians in Spain conducting a trade in Christian penes and foreskins to the Moors.

I have heard the Christian priests damn sodomy. They tell the indios that if they practice the crime against nature and do not repent, when they die they will descend to hell joined with their lover.

The fray once recounted to me that Saint Thomas Aquinas sanctioned prostitution on the grounds that it saved men from sodomy.

Sodomy was not the only crime against nature the Spaniards found existed in the New World. Some indio nobles had special wives who were trained to use their mouth to suck on their husband's pene in the manner of vipers.

Of course, such matters of the flesh were not restricted to the indios. Fray Antonio told me that Pope Alexander VI of the Spanish Borgias had five children. He betrothed his daughter Lucrezia at twelve to one nobleman—then broke it off when the girl was thirteen in order for her to marry another. When that marriage did not bring the political and financial rewards the pope anticipated, he had the marriage annulled on the grounds of impotency—despite the fact that his daughter was pregnant. Not to be daunted by such trivialities, the good pope issued one bull stating that his son, Lucrezia's brother, was the father—and another naming *himself* as the father of his daughter's child. Poor Lucrezia—her next husband was the son of the king of Naples, but her jealous brother strangled the man with his own hands.

Good King Filipe III, who has sat on the throne of Spain and Portugal during most of my lifetime, is said to have had thirty-two children from consorts. That is more than most Aztec kings fathered.

SIXTY-SIX

IN ONE OF those marvelous acts of fate that seemed so often to clear the path for Cortes, he had the great fortune to take possession of a slave girl who had been born a princess. Doña Marina, as she came to be called, had been born in the province of Coatzacualco, on the southeastern border of the Aztec Empire. Her father, a rich and powerful cacique, died when she was very young. Her mother married again and had a son. She conceived the nefarious idea of securing for her son Marina's rightful inheritance.

She accordingly feigned that Marina was dead but secretly delivered her into the hands of some itinerant traders of Xicallanco. She availed herself, at the same time, of the death of a child of one of her slaves in order to substitute the corpse for that of her own daughter and celebrated the obsequies with mock solemnity. The merchants sold the india maiden to the cacique of Tabasco, who delivered her to the Spanish as tribute.

In a strange way, my own childhood speaks so much of the intrigues and tribulations of Doña Marina's that, while my indio ancestors considered her a traitor, she earned that special place in my heart that I have spoken about.

Cortes had landed on the coast and encountered the indio culture but soon discovered that he was on the fringes of a vast empire ruled by a mighty emperor. He was in desperate need of information from the indios he encountered and in need of allies because alone, with a few hundred men, he could not hope to overwhelm a large empire.

Doña Marina brought along with her charms—she was to become Cortes's mistress and mother of his son, Don Martin—a gift for languages. She not only spoke the language of the indios that she had been sold into slavery to, but her native Aztec tongue, Náhuatl, as well. She was able to quickly pick up enough Spanish to act as interpreter and negotiator with the indio leaders Cortes came into contact with.

And her experiences from noble woman to slave and finally lover of the Spanish leader, gave her insights that she used to lead Cortes from danger. It was she who realized that fifty indios sent ostensibly as peace delegates to him were spies and assassins. Cortes had the hands of the men chopped off and sent them back to their leaders as examples of how he would deal with treachery.

It was Marina, too, who would interpret for Cortes when he finally reached Tenochtitlan and stood before Montezuma II. The emperor, whose imperial title was Revered Speaker, was informed by his messengers of the Spanish landing. Cortes in turn learned that the ruler of the vast empire was in a golden city in a high valley far from the blazing sands of the Caribbean coastline.

Aztecs scribes painted picture writing so that the emperor would be able to see what the Spaniards looked like. It was the Spanish horses more than anything that struck fear in the hearts of the indios. There were no beasts of burden in Mexico, no horses, mules, donkeys, or even oxen. The horses, strange and terrifying to the indios, were as fearsome to them as the cannons. They saw the rider and horse moving in unison, as if parts of the same animal, and they assumed that gods were mounted upon these fearsome beasts.

But the seeds of Aztec destruction did not begin with the landing of Cortes, but hundreds of years before in a city, a time, and a place when Aztecs were nomadic barbarians who wore animal skins and ate meat raw. When Montezuma saw the picture writing he was deeply disturbed. He was fifty-two years old at the time Cortes arrived, and the news of the landing brought home to him a decade of growing fear and suspicion and to the indios at large the culmination of several hundred years of myth—the return of Quetzalcóatl, the Plumed Serpent.

Ay, poor Montezuma. He was a victim of his own fears—especially when his sister told him of her death dream in which she saw the return of a legend. The legend, of course, was that of the Plumed Serpent. Quetzalcóatl's story had as much love, murder, betrayal, and incest to have been written by Sophocles to entertain the ancient Greeks.

Quetzalcóatl was born in a One-Reed year. It was to become the most momentous date in indio history. He presided over Tula, the fabled Toltec city of gold and pleasure I visited in my dream. A great ruler, he erected wondrous temples and had artisans create sculptures, pottery, word-picture books, and other works of art that glorified the city. He was also a humane king who banned human sacrifice and permitted only the sacrifice of snakes and butterflies.

Those who favored human sacrifice feared that Quetzalcóatl was offending the gods by not giving them blood. They plotted his destruction, enlisting the help of three evil magicians. The evil magicians tricked Quetzalcóatl into becoming drunk on octli, the drink of the gods, now called pulque. In his drunken state he sent for his beautiful sister. He later awoke to find his sister naked beside him and realized he had bedded with her as he would a wife.

In pain and horror over his sin, Quetzalcóatl fled the golden city, setting sail upon the Eastern Sea with some of his followers on a raft made of intertwined snakes. Later he rose into the sky, becoming the Lord of the Dawn House, turning into the planet the Spaniards call Venus. He was a fiery eye in the sky, watching over the lands of the indios, waiting for the day when he would return to reclaim his kingdom. It was written that he would return in a One-Reed year.

For a decade before the arrival of the Spaniards, ominous signs had struck fear in the hearts of the indios as the One-Reed year approached—a fiery comet had appeared in the sky, earthquakes shook the land, and the mighty volcano Popocatépetl, the Smoking Mountain, had spit fire from the bowels of the underworld.

One of the most frightening events was a violent upheaval of the waters of Lake Texcoco, the lake that surrounds Tenochtitlan. Without warning or excessive rain, the waters of the lake suddenly swelled up as if lifted by a giant hand and overflowed into the island city, sweeping away many buildings.

Fire followed flood as one of the turrets of Tenochtitlan's great temple of Huitzilopochtli suddenly burst aflame without apparent cause and burned in defiance of all attempts to put it out.

Three comets were seen streaking across the night sky. Then, not long before the coming of the Spanish on the Eastern Sea, a strange golden light broke forth in the east. It glowed like a midnight sun, rising in the same pyramidal shape of an Aztec temple. The scribes recorded that fires burned so within it that it seemed "thickly powered with stars." Fray Antonio told me that it was the opinion of Church scholars that this event was a volcanic eruption, but some of the highest and most violent volcanoes in the world stood above the Valley of Mexico and one would think that the Aztecs would know the difference between volcanic eruption and heavenly fire.

At the same time of the golden pyramid of the night, low voices and doleful wailing was heard, as if to announce some strange, mysterious calamity.

Montezuma was terrified of the apparitions in the heavens and of his sister's death dream. When Cortes landed, a One-Reed year was coming around on the calendar wheel. Montezuma assumed that Quetzalcóatl had returned to claim his kingdom. Of course by now Quetzalcóatl's Tula was an abandoned city of ghostly stone temples, having been destroyed by invading barbarian armies, the Aztecs among them, hundreds of years before; but Montezuma thought he could pay tribute to Quetzalcóatl in goods and human hearts for the way the Aztecs had turned upon and devoured Tula.

Rather than driving the new arrivals into the sea with his overwhelming forces, gripped by fear and superstition, Montezuma sent an ambassador to salute Cortes and bring him gifts—while forbidding him to come to Tenochtitlan.

Among the gifts, Montezuma returned a Spanish helmet Cortes had sent to him. The helmet was overflowing with gold. There were also two great circular disks of gold and silver, as large as carriage wheels. The sight of golden gifts rather than force of arms did not pacify Cortes and his men; instead, it brought their greed to a boiling point.

But there was a great threat between them and the treasures of the Aztecs. The Spaniards realized that they were not dealing with a tribal chieftain but the monarch of a great nation, in size and population larger than most European countries. While the Spanish had superiority of weapons—the indio arrows and lances bounced off their armor—they were outnumbered a thousand to one. Any concerted attack by the Aztecs would succeed by sheer force of numbers.

The courage of his men wavered and Cortes, desperate that Velasquez would not get his prize, did the act of a man desperate for gold and glory—*he burned his ships.*

Now his men had only two choices—to fight or die. A handful of sailors and soldiers, around six hundred in all, found themselves stranded on the beach with their back to the water. To survive they had to defeat the army of an empire composed of millions of people.

One might fault Cortes on many levels. He was a womanizer, a slave master, a ruthless opponent, a man without respect for authority. But here was an act of daring and courage and brilliance that won a kingdom. To burn one's ships, to make him and his men cornered rats facing odds of a thousand to one, to have evaded the fate of an ordinary man, an ordinary leader who would have sent sail for reinforcements . . . this was the act of a *muy hombre,* very much man, worthy of Alexander the Great at Tyre, Julius Caesar at Munda, Hannibal crossing the Alps with elephants!

Another clever tactic was to work on the hatred the other indios had for the Aztecs to whom they paid tribute.

Using Doña Marina as his interpreter and mentor, Cortes convinced indio states that had been paying the Aztecs tribute in goods and sacrifice victims to ally themselves with him. The Aztec legions were dreaded much as the Roman legions and those of Genghis Khan, which had inspired fear into conquered people who were forced to pay tribute.

The strategy was successful. When Cortes marched upon Tenochtitlan, along with his men came indios numbering in the tens of thousands, the armies of Totonac, Tlaxcalans, and other nations anxious to use the Spanish to revenge countless aggressions by the domineering Aztecs.

Even with indio allies, the Aztecs were still the supreme fighting force in the New World. Without the quirk of fate that the indios believed that Cortes's arrival on the Eastern seashore fulfilled the Quetzalcóatl legend, Montezuma would have fielded an army that would have fallen upon the puny Spanish forces and its indio armies, sending the indios in terror from the dreaded Jaguar and Eagle Knights, who'd sworn to never retreat in battle. Montezuma's indecision cost him first his kingdom and then his life. He let the Spanish into his city without a fight.

One of the conquistadors, Bernal Diaz del Castillo, wrote a history of the conquest before my lifetime. A manuscript of it has circulated widely among the clerics of New Spain, and Fray Antonio had me read it so that I would learn the true story of how the Spanish had come to New Spain. Diaz's description of the city was the final fulfillment of the dream of Cortes and his men that he could find a fabled kingdom as had the hero of *Amadis of Gaul.* Diaz wrote that when the men saw Tenochtitlan for the first time, they realized that they had arrived at a golden city:

> When we saw so many cities and villages built in the waters of the lake and other large towns on dry land,

> and that straight, level causeway leading into Mexico City, we were amazed and we said that it was like the enchanted things related in the book of *Amadis* because of the huge towers, temples, and buildings rising from the water and all of masonry. And some of the soldiers even asked whether the things we saw were not a dream.

After permitting the Spanish to enter his city, Montezuma, held prisoner in his palace by his "guests," tried to address his people. While many fell to the ground in awe of his august presence, some began to taunt him as a man who had been turned into a woman by the white men—that he was only fit to suckle babies and knead maize! Rocks and arrows loosened from the crowd and Montezuma fell.

He was as mortally wounded in soul as in body for the way his people turned on him. He knew he had failed them. The Spanish tried to treat his wounds but he tore off the bandages. He refused to survive his disgrace. Dying, he rejected baptism into the Christian faith, telling a priest kneeling at his side, "I have but a few moments to live and will not at this hour desert the faith of my fathers."

Catastrophic disasters erupted in the wake of the Spanish conquest. First came the destruction of the fabric of indio society as almost everything they had ever known and worshipped was trampled by the conquerors. It wasn't just stone edifices that were torn asunder, but the very fabric of society—just as birth and marriage and death revolve around a Christian Church, so was almost every aspect of the indio's life caught up in the priests and temples of their faith. Those temples were torn down and ones of the new faith erected, administered by priests who spoke a strange language.

The second great catastrophe was the plagues that descended upon the indios in the footsteps of the Spaniards. Terrible epidemics of diseases that caused the indios' flesh to boil and insides to wither was the vengeful gift of the Spanish god. The Christian priests said that the diseases that struck down nine out of every ten indios in New Spain within a few generations of the conquest were fire and brimstone from God, punishing indios for their heathen ways.

The third disaster was greed. The Spanish king divided the most favorable parts of New Spain into feudal domains called encomiendas: grants of tribute from indios to each of the conquistadors.

Somewhere along the twisted road in which the entire structure of their society was destroyed, the indios lost their image of themselves as a great and mighty people.

Now I saw people who had once built dazzling cities and perfected science and medicine sitting with dull eyes in front of thatched huts, scratching the dirt with sticks.

SIXTY-SEVEN

MATEO BECAME CONVINCED that the naualli was not the leader of the Jaguar cult. "We have been watching him for weeks. If he was up to something, we would know it by now."

I did not agree. Mateo was prejudiced against investigating the naualli because he was tired and bored of being in the back country. I slowly learned more about what had happened to bring him within the grasp of the king's law. Jose confided that Mateo was not caught selling profano libros as the members of the acting troupe had been. Rather, Mateo's difficulties arose from gambling. In a heated moment he had accused a young man of cheating at cards. Swords were drawn and a moment later the young man's life poured out onto the cantina floor. While there was an official ban against dueling, it was commonly ignored; but in this case the dead man was the nephew of a member of the Royal Audiencia, the High Court that resided in the City of Mexico but had power over all of New Spain.

Jose told me that Mateo ran a risk of the gallows if he showed his face in the capital.

As for the naualli, I had taken a great dislike to him. He had nearly killed me once, and I had been humiliated by the pig incident. I also did not want to fail for another good reason: I did not know how I would be treated by Don Julio if I failed. Would he ship me off to the northern mines? The hell of the Filipinas? Or simply have me hanged and my head cut off afterward and impaled on a city gate as a warning to others?

Pondering the undesirable fates I was being swept toward, I nearly stumbled into the young girl I had previously seen with the two men who followed the naualli into the jungle. She had been kneeling picking berries and I nearly fell over her.

"Perdón," I said.

She did not reply but got up with her basket of berries and slowly walked into the dense forest. As she disappeared in the bushes, she looked back, with an inviting expression.

India women were washing clothes along the rocky riverbank and two men were smoking pipes and playing a dice game outside a hut. No one seemed to be paying any attention to me. Pretending to be just sauntering about, I moseyed into the bushes.

She followed the riverbank for ten minutes. When I caught up with her, she was sitting on a large boulder with her feet in the water.

I sat down on another boulder, kicked off my sandals, and cooled my own feet in the river.

"My name is Cristo."

"I am Maria."

I could have guessed that. Maria was the most common Christian name for females among the indias because it was a name they heard when they went to church. She was perhaps a couple of years younger than me, fifteen or sixteen. She struck me as a little unhappy.

"You don't look happy, muchacha." She was too old to

be called muchacha and I was too young to be calling her that, but being around a pretty young woman caused me to inflate into an hombre macho . . . at least in my own eyes.

"I'm getting married in a few days," she said.

"Eh, that's a time to celebrate. Don't you like the man you will marry?"

She shrugged. "He's neither good nor bad. He will provide for me. That is not what is making me unhappy. It is that my brother and uncle are such ugly men. I am not lucky like some of the other girls in the village who have handsome men in the family."

That brought up my eyebrows. "What do you care about your uncle and brother? You will not be marrying them."

"Of course not. But my father is dead and I will be making ahuilnéma with them."

I nearly fell off of the boulder. "What? You will be having ahuilnéma with your own uncle and brother?"

"Sí. They follow the old ways."

"I know of no Aztec ways that permit incest," I said hotly. Such an act would be considered sacrilegious among the Aztecs.

"We are not Mexica. Our tribe is older than the one you call Aztec. And here in this village, our elders make us practice the old customs."

"What old custom is this that you would bed your uncle and brother?"

"I will not bed both of them. Because I have no father, the act must be done by a male relative. The elders will decide whether it will be done by my uncle or brother before the wedding ceremony."

"Dios mio, you will bed your uncle or brother after the wedding? When will you lay with your husband?"

"Not until the next night. You do not have this custom among your people?"

"Of course not; it's blasphemous. If the priests found out about it, the men of your village would be severely punished. Have you ever heard of the Holy Office of the Inquisition?"

She shook her head. "We have no priest. To attend the Christian Church, we must walk for nearly two hours."

"This custom from the old ways, what is the purpose of it?"

"To ensure that our marriage does not offend the gods. The gods enjoy virgins, that is why maidens are sacrificed to them. If my husband bedded with a virgin, our marriage would be offensive to the gods and they might do bad things to us."

In the minds of people in a small, isolated village where it seemed that the spirits and gods of old were all around them, the idea of deflowering a young woman before she had ahuilnéma with her husband was not illogical.

"From your face I can see that you do not like our custom," she said.

I thought it was barbaric but did not want to offend the girl who had to live with the practice. "What do you think of bedding your uncle or brother?"

"They are both ugly. There are other men in the village I wouldn't mind making ahuilnéma with, but not those two." She splashed water with her feet. "I wouldn't mind making ahuilnéma with you."

Ayyo. Now this was a custom I understood.

We found a soft spot on the grass and took off our clothes. Our bodies were both young and supple. I was too eager and my virile juice flowed before I was ready, but she carefully caressed my tepúli and it grew again. And again.

After we had satisfied our desires for the time being, I asked her more questions about the "old ways" practiced in the village. I knew her male relatives were consorting with the naualli. Fearing I would frighten her, I let her talk about the old ways in general before leading her to the subject of sacrifices.

"There is a pyramid," she said, "put there by the gods long before there were any people in this valley. When the naualli comes, the men of the village go there and give blood in the old way."

"How do they give blood?" I asked, keeping my tone casual.

"They cut their arms and legs and sometimes their tepúli. Once a year they take blood from another. This year it was a dwarf."

Keeping the excitement out of my voice, I asked, "When did they sacrifice the dwarf?"

"Last night."

Dios madre! I had been right about the dwarf. With some gentle persuasion, I convinced her to show me this temple where the dwarf had been sacrificed.

She led me deep into the tropical forest. The farther we went, the more dense the vegetation became. Most of the ancient monuments of the indios were already swallowed by jungle throughout New Spain. One way the Spanish priests knew that a temple was still being used was if it had been cleared of the jungle growth.

We had walked a half an hour when she stopped and pointed. "Over there, another few hundred paces. I'm not going any farther."

She ran back the way we had come. I did not blame her. It was late afternoon, nearly twilight, with the sky dark from heavy black rain clouds. Rain would be falling soon and complete darkness on its heels. I had no more desire than she to be out in the jungle after the fall of night.

I crept slowly toward the pyramid, keeping my eyes and ears alert. Now that the girl was gone and the sky darkening, some of my courage and enthusiasm was slipping away. I had assumed that if there was a sacrifice here last night, there would be no need for anyone to be here now. But that was not necessarily true, I thought. Perhaps that was no more than wishful thinking.

When the pyramid temple came into view, I stopped and listened. I heard nothing but the freshening wind stirring the leaves. Knowing it was the wind did little to reduce my fears that every leaf that rustled was pressed upon by a were-jaguar.

The sides of the temple were overgrown with vines, but the growth had been cleared up the stone steps to the top. It was a little smaller than the temple at the town of the Day of the Dead festival, about twenty steps to the top platform where sacrifices would be held.

A light rain had begun to fall as I made my way to the temple. By the time I reached the bottom of the steps, it was coming down in a torrent. A thought about the rain nagged at me from a corner of my mind but stayed out of reach as I went up the steps.

By the time I was three-quarters of the way up the stone steps, a trickle of water was pouring down from the top. I stared in alarm and horror at the liquid. *It was bloody.*

I turned and flew down the steps, stumbling near the bottom. I lost my balance, falling to the ground. I ran like the night a were-jaguar had been chasing me. I ran as if all of the hounds of hell were yapping at the soft flesh at the back of my legs.

Dark night, as black as the naualli's eyes, had fallen by the time I got back, wet and muddy, to our campsite to find no one there. Mateo and Jose had no doubt decided to spend the rainy night playing cards at a cantina. The birds probably told the Healer he should stay at the hut of his dream-divining friend.

Without even a fire to warm me, I holed up under a tree, wrapped in wet blankets, shivering, my knife in my hand ready to strike anyone—or anything—that attacked me. The thought that had teased my mind back at the temple about the rain became clear. The drought was over. Tlaloc, the rain god, must be very pleased at the sacrifice given him.

Rain was still falling the next morning when I led Mateo and Jose back to the temple. I rode on the back of Mateo's horse. Refusing to go up the temple, I stood at the bottom and held the reins of the horse and Jose's mule while the two went up to the top.

"Is it terrible to see?" I shouted up to them. "Did they rip out his heart?"

Mateo nodded. "Yes, they ripped out his heart and left the body." He bent down and then stood up. "Here! See for yourself."

He tossed something down to me. It landed near my feet. It was the body of a monkey.

He came down the temple steps and I backed away from his anger. He shook his finger at me. "If you come to me with anymore dwarf sightings, I'm going to cut off your nose."

SIXTY-EIGHT

A*yya ouiya!* Unwise was I of the ways of the world despite my education on the streets of Veracruz. These simple country people were much more deceptive than any lépero. It occurred to me that it was time for me to be moving along. I would hate to leave the Healer—as with Fray Antonio, I loved him like a father. But I did not know what was going to happen to me when Don Julio was advised of our failure.

I was pondering my ill-begotten ways when the girl who was betrothed and who I had made ahuilnéma with came out of her hut. She gave me a knowing look and disappeared into the bushes. I followed her. My interest was not only in making ahuilnéma with her, but afterward I would take her to Mateo and force her to tell him about the sacrifices her uncle and brother have been involved in with the naualli.

I had gone no more than a hundred paces when I heard movement all around me. The girl's uncle leaped out from behind a tree and confronted me. He had an obsidian dagger in his hand. I turned to run and there were indios behind me. They grabbed me and wrestled me to the ground. While three of them held me down, another stood over me with a club. He raised the club over my head and swung down.

SIXTY-NINE

THEY CARRIED ME through the jungle, my hands and feet tied to a long pole that extended over their shoulders. I was as trussed as the naualli's pig had been. Even my mouth was gagged so I could not yell for help. At first I was only dimly aware that I was being carried but awareness came back quickly. The blow had been intended to daze me, not smash my head. They did not want me unconscious. What they had in mind would not give them pleasure if I was not awake to experience it.

They lowered me to the ground at the foot of the temple. The naualli stood over me. He wore a mask of human skin, the face of some prior victim who had been flayed, skinned so the priest can wear it. The face was of a stranger, but the cruel, diabolic eyes and the jeering lips were the naualli's.

The men around him were dressed as Jaguar Knights, the snarling jaws of the beasts atop their heads, their faces concealed by masks of jaguar skin.

I shouted at them that they were cowards, that they hid behind masks to do their foul deeds, but my words came out as a mumble through the gag.

The naualli knelt beside me. He opened a small pouch and took a pinch of something from it. One of the knights knelt behind me and trapped my head between his knees as the naualli put the substance from the pouch at one of my nostrils. I sneezed, and as I drew in my breath, he sprinkled more of it in front of my nostrils.

Fire went through me, brain fire, not unlike the sensation I felt when the flower weaver at Teotihuacan had sent me soaring to the gods. The fire subsided and a warm, comfortable feeling of well-being and love for all things filled me.

I was ungagged and the ropes were cut from my body. Helped to my feet, I got up, laughing. Everything around me, the indio costumes, the ancient temple, even the greenery glistened with sharp, brilliant colors. I put my arm around the naualli and gave him a hug. I felt good about everything.

The knights closed in on me, anonymous figures with their capes, headdresses, and masks. I struggled against their taking my arms. As I did, the sword of one of them was exposed, a steel blade like the Spanish carry. I gaily reached for it, but the knight knocked away my hand. They took my arms and directed me toward the stone steps. I went willingly, eagerly, happy to be with my friends.

My feet seemed to have a mind of their own, one that I did not control, and I stumbled and fell trying to mount the steps. My friends grabbed my arms and supported me up each step.

My will had been captured by the flower weaver's powder; but in my mind, despite my gaiety, I knew that something terrible awaited at the top of the temple. An unusual tale came to mind, one of the those preconquest stories I have heard waiting for Mateo outside cantinas. An india girl to be sacrificed was more clever than others who often not only went willingly but considered it a privilege. She told the priests preparing her that if she was sacrificed she would tell the rain god not to let it rain. The superstitious priests let her go. I giggled aloud at the idea of telling the naualli that if I was sacrificed, I would tell the rain god not to let it rain.

At the top I shook myself loose from their grip so I could look around at the grand scenery of the jungle. I laughed in delight at the striking colors. The different shades of green and brown glowed. A colorful songbird flew by, a flying rainbow of yellow, red, and green feathers.

My friends gathered around me again and tried to take my arms. I brushed aside their attempts and danced around, laughing at their efforts to restrain me. Four of them grabbed me, two taking my arms and tripping me backward. As I fell, they lifted me and carried me across to the sacrifice block.

They spread me over the arched block of stone, so my head and feet were lower than my chest.

A dark thought deep inside my mind stirred and told me that something was wrong, that what these men were doing was going to hurt me. I struggled against their holds, but it was to no avail; arched backward over the stone block, the position locked me in their grip with little effort.

The naualli hovered over me, chanting an ode to the gods, cutting the air with an obsidian knife. He brought the dagger down to my chest and cut my shirt, tearing it back until my naked chest was exposed. I struggled in earnest, but my arms and legs were trapped. The image of a man being sacrificed came to me, his chest ripped open by a razor-sharp blade, an Aztec priest reaching in and ripping out his heart and holding the blood-dripping vessel in the air while it was still beating.

The naualli's chant grew higher pitched until it sounded like the scream of a jungle cat. I sensed the heated anticipation, the bloodthirsty passions of those around me. Holding the sacrificial knife with both hands, he raised it high over his head.

One of the knights holding my arm suddenly let go. I saw the flash of a sword. The naualli staggered backwards as the knight with the sword swung at him. The blade missed the magician but struck a man holding one of my legs. The other hands released me as chaos erupted atop the pyramid. Wooden swords with razor-sharp obsidian edges were whipped out. The steel sword lashed out, slicing through the other blades.

Musket shots and shouts sounded from the bottom of the temple.

I rolled off of the sacrifice block and fell to the stone floor. As I got dizzily to my feet, the several Jaguar Knights still standing broke and ran from the one wielding the steel sword.

When the last knight had fled, the swordsman turned and faced me, saluting me with his sword. "Bastardo, you certainly know how to get yourself in trouble."

Removing the mask, Mateo grinned at me. I grinned back.

Don Julio came up the steps. "How is the boy?"

"The naualli got his mind drunk with something; but other than having a stupid grin, he appears all right."

"The naualli got away," Don Julio said. "My men are after him, but he moves faster than a jungle cat."

"He *is* a jungle cat," I said.

A lamb to slaughter. That is how they had treated me, I soon discovered.

Back at our campsite Mateo, Don Julio, Jose, and the don's other men drank wine and celebrated my rescue.

"We knew you had become an irritation to the naualli," Don Julio said. "You exposed your suspicions when you unleashed that pig, thinking it was the missing dwarf. The naualli no doubt did sacrifice the dwarf. Of that we will be certain after we question the followers we captured."

"Eh, chico, you are lucky I am a great actor. I knocked one of the guards over the head and took his costumes. We all looked the same with the costumes on, so I stepped in to help rip out your heart."

"No word of their evil master?" I asked.

"None." Don Julio smiled and shook his head. "That devil would have had to turn into a jaguar to avoid my men. He disappeared on foot with men on horses after him."

"So," I mused aloud, "you knew the naualli was going to take me."

"It was just a matter of time," Mateo said. "A mestizo

boy poking his nose in his secret doings. The indios hate mestizos almost as bad as us Spanish. It would have served his purpose doubly well to get rid of you on the sacrificial block."

I smiled at Don Julio and Mateo. I was burning with anger at them for nearly getting me killed, but could not show my temper because it would gain me nothing. But I could not keep from at least expressing a bit of displeasure. "Perhaps you moved too quickly to save my life. Had you waited until the naualli ripped out my heart, you might have been able to capture him."

"You're probably right," Don Julio said. "Keep that in mind, Mateo, next time you and the boy close in on the naualli. Waiting until the devil is actually extracting the boy's heart will give you time to chop off the naualli's head."

Don Julio spoke without his face exposing whether he was joking or not. But one thing was certain; we would not be finished with the naualli until he was captured or killed.

Mateo had caught the fact, too. "Don Julio, don't tell me that I must continue to remain in this backward area until that foul puta of a magician is found. I need to go to a city where there are people of my own kind, music, women—"

"Trouble," Don Julio said. "Isn't that what you usually find in cities? You are on this assignment because you have spent too much of your life in dark dens of iniquity, where cheating cards and loose women rise the heat in your blood. This assignment is good for you. Fresh air. Good country cooking . . ."

Mateo was no more pleased at being exiled to the netherlands than I was when I found out I had been literally staked out as a lamb for the naualli to devour.

SEVENTY

DON JULIO POSTED men at the main roads leading from the area and sent others into the brush looking for the naualli. Mateo occasionally joined the search on horseback but generally considered it a waste of his time.

"The devil knows the area and has followers everywhere. We will never find him."

Don Julio's estimation was that the naualli would not leave the area without his defeat avenged. "He would never be respected again." Avenging the setback, the don said, would be to kill a Spaniard, mestizo, or an indio who co-operated with the Spanish.

We were doomed to stay forever in this worthless land of backward indios. That was how Mateo described the situation. He found little comfort in wine and trips to the cantina in a nearby village, where he played cards with traveling merchants.

The Healer spent much of his time sitting in our campsite, smoking his pipe, staring up at the sky. Other times he would walk about where birds were nearby and twittered.

I had some concern for him. He took little interest in the solicitations for his services that came from the nearby villages. When I asked him what he was doing, he said he was "gathering his medicine."

Ayyo. That disturbed me. I suspected that he believed the naualli meant harm toward me and that he would use his magic to fight him. I did not want the Healer harmed trying to protect me.

I remained at the camp for a couple of days until I got a treasure in my hands.

A treasure, you ask? Perhaps a cup of emeralds or a golden mask? No, amigos, this was not a treasure of the purse but one of the mind. Mateo had won a copy of *Lazarillo de Tormes.* This book was the older brother to *Guzman de Alfarache,* the tale about the picaro lad in whom I found much to admire and hoped to emulate. The fact that this book, like *Guzman,* was on the Inquisition's prohibition list for New Spain made it all the more desirable to read.

Mateo told me that the author of *Lazarillo* was said to be Don Diego Hurtado de Mendoza, a man who had once studied for the priesthood but ended up as an administrator for the king and ambassador to the English. But that many people did not believe Mendoza was the true author.

"Mendoza became governor of the Italian state of Siena for King Carlos V. Mendoza was a brutal, arrogant ruler who was a tyrant to the people, so much so that they tried to kill him. I suspect that someone, perhaps one of his aides, had written the book, and Mendoza took it and had his own name put on it for vanity."

I took the book to a hillside that over looked the river. The sun was warm on the rocks and I seated myself among the boulders to read. As the adventures of Lazarillo unfolded, I found the tale often so dark a tyrant could have written the tale.

Lazaro, as he was called, had a background not unsimilar to Guzman. He was the son of a miller who plied his trade along the banks of the Rio Torme. Unfortunately for Lazaro, like Guzman, his father was a ne'er-do-well. After being caught cheating his customers, he was sent off as a mule driver to the Moorish wars and ended up getting killed.

Lazaro's mother ran an inn, but she was not a great businesswoman. She ended up getting involved with a Moor, who was a groom for a nobleman. She birthed a baby by the Moor, a dark-skinned child who brought scandal to Lazaro's mother and doom to the Moor when the nobleman found he was stealing to support his secret family. The

Moor was "soundly flogged, and his flesh tickled with drops of scalding fat."

Unable to support the family, Lazaro's mother apprenticed him to a blind beggar, who he is to lead about. The blind beggar immediately starts teaching Lazaro lessons in life. Before leaving town, he has Lazaro take him to the stone statue of a bull. Then he tells Larazo to put his ear close to the bull in order to hear a strange noise. As the naive boy does, the old man thumps his head against the stone. And then laughed at the trick he had played on the boy. "You scamp, you ought to know that a blind man's boy should have more cunning than the devil himself."

As I read, I came to believe that this mean-spirited blind man was the devil himself. But Lazaro came to admire the man's very churlishness and to understand what he was being taught.

"I have no silver or gold to give you, but what is far better, I can impart to you the result of my experience, which will always enable you to live; for though God has created me blind, He has endowed me with faculties that have served me well in the course of my life."

But Lazaro had also never met such an avaricious and wicked an old curmudgeon. "He allowed me to die almost daily of hunger, without troubling himself about my necessities; and, to say the truth, if I had not helped myself by means of a ready wit and nimble fingers, I should have closed my account from sheer starvation."

Life became a daily battle of wits between the stingy old man and the hungry boy eager to fill his belly. The old man kept his bread and meats in a linen sack he kept closed at the mouth by an iron ring and padlock. Lazaro created a small opening in a bottom seam and soon was feasting on choice foods. The boy learned to hide in his mouth alms tossed to the beggar and to steal wine by putting a hole in the bottom of the beggar's wine jar and plugging it with wax. Catching the boy drinking from the jug, the old man smashed the jug against the boy's face.

Over time, Lazaro suffered much abuse and developed

hatred for the blind man. He got some revenge by taking him along the roughest roads and through the deepest mud. Finally deciding to quit this tramp tyrant's service, and in disgust over all the beatings and starvation he had endured, Lazaro led the blind man to a place where it was necessary for the man to jump across a narrow stream. He positioned the old man so that when he leaped, the man would collide with a stone pillar. The blind man stepped back, then made a leap "as nimble as a goat" and collided with the pillar. It knocked him unconscious.

From this time on the luckless Lazaro went from the hands of one bad master to another. In one humorous account, Lazaro became the servant for a gentleman who was broke. By one devious scheme after another, the servant Lazaro found himself supplying the impoverished gentleman his daily bread!

For a time he served a pair of con artists who had a scam involving the pope's edicts called "bulls." One would go into a church and claim that he had holy bulls from the pope that could cure illnesses. A constable would charge into the church and call the other man a fraud. The constable would then collapse on the floor as if he had been struck dead. The man with the bulls would lay one of the papers on the constable's head and the man would recover. Seeing the "miracle," the people in the church would rush to buy the blessed edicts.

The good life would ultimately come to Lazaro when he married a servant of an archpriest. It was whispered in the community that the marriage had been arranged because the woman was the priest's lover, but Lazaro, to whom fortune was smiling by bequests of the priest, found the situation to his benefit. When his wife passed away, misfortune came back to Lazaro, but of these difficulties, he tells the reader that it "would be too cruel and severe a task for me to pretend to recount."

In truth, I found Lazaro was not as much fun to read as Guzman. The book was not as long, nor were the adventures as exciting, but the woes of Lazaro, including the blackness of the heart of so many he encountered, may have been a more realistic view of the world.

My eyes grew heavy after I finished the book, and I lay back and shut them. I awoke when I heard a rock bounce near me. I jerked awake, startled.

The girl who'd led me to the Jaguar Knights had flung the rock. She was on the hillside a little above me. She turned quickly when I looked up at her, and I got only a brief glimpse at her features.

"Señorita!" I yelled. "We must talk!"

I followed her. We had searched for her after the naualli disappeared but had not been able to find her. As I followed, I determined that I would not permit myself to be ambushed this time. If she disappeared into the bushes, I would run back to the campsite and get Mateo. If he was there.

I had gone no more than a hundred paces when she stopped. She kept her back to me as I approached. When she turned, I saw not a young girl, but a demon. The naualli had flayed her face, removing it in the manner of Aztec priests who skinned victims and wore the skin. The naualli had donned her face and clothes.

He screamed at me and charged, raising his obsidian knife high. The knife was still bloody from skinning the girl.

I pulled my own knife though I knew I would have little chance. My blade was much smaller, and he was a killer in a rage. I backed away from him, lashing out defensively with my knife. I was taller than him and my arms were longer, but his rage and insanity were vast. He swung his knife wildly, not caring if I slashed back. His blade sliced my forearm and I staggered backward. My heel caught on a rock and I stumbled, slipping down into a small crevice. I took a rough tumble, hitting jagged rocks that dug into my back, slamming my head against a rock.

The fall saved my life because it took me out of reach of the madman. He stood on the edge of the crevice. Letting out a bloodcurdling scream, he held the knife high as he prepared to leap down at me.

I saw a movement out of the corner of my eye. The naualli saw it too, and turned, swinging the knife.

The Healer came at the naualli, shaking a large feather, a bright green plume.

I gaped in shock and screamed for the Healer to stop. The old man had no chance waving a feather against the demon with a knife. I scrambled up the side of the crevice, yelling for the Healer to stop.

My movements were frantic, and I was slipping back a foot for every two I went up. The Healer shook the feather at the naualli, and the naualli swung his knife at the Healer. The knife hit the Healer in the stomach. It went in, up to the hilt.

For a moment the two old men stood perfectly still, like two stone statues embracing each other, the Healer with the feather in his hand, the naualli with his hand on the hilt of the knife. They slowly moved apart, and as they did, the Healer went down to his knees and the naualli moved away from him.

I made it up to the top and onto my feet. I charged the naualli but stopped and watched him in amazement. Instead of crouching in a knife fighter's stance to meet my attack, he pranced away, ripping off the girl face. He grinned gaily and danced and laughed.

Holding the knife again high in the air, he plunged it into his own heart.

I now realized why the Healer had been shaking a feather in the man's face. He had yoyotli or some other dream dust from a flower weaver on the feather.

The Healer lay on the ground on his back. His shirt was bloody. I knelt beside him with a heavy heart. "I will go for help," I said, but I knew it was useless.

"No, my son, stay with me. It is too late. This morning I heard the call of the uactli, the bird of death."

"No—"

"I will go now to the place where my ancestors have gone. I am old and tired and it is a long trip." He slowly faded, his breath leaving him as I held him in my arms and cried.

He had once told me that he had come from the stars. I believed that. There had been an otherworldliness to him. I had no doubt that he had journeyed to earth from the stars, and it would be to the stars that he returned.

Like the fray, he had been a father to me. As his son, it was my duty to prepare him for his journey.

I had to leave him to get help to move his body to a proper place for the burial I would give him. When I returned to the camp, both Don Julio and Mateo were there.

"I received a message from an indio," Don Julio said. "He had been sent by the Healer a couple of days ago. The message was that the naualli had died trying to attack you. I got here and found out Mateo knew nothing of it."

"That's because it just happened," I said. I told them about the fight with the naualli, and the feather that had "killed" the magician.

"How could the old man know about the fight before it ever happened?" Mateo asked.

I shrugged and smiled with sadness. "The birds told him."

The Healer would not go to Mictlán, the Dark Place of the underworld. He had died in battle as a warrior. He would go to the paradise of the Eastern Heaven.

With the help of the dream diviner, I prepared the Healer's body, dressing him in his finest clothes, his cape of rare feathers and his wondrous headpiece. I built a high pile of wood and laid the Healer's body atop the pile. Alongside the body, I placed a supply of maize, beans, and cocoa beans to sustain him on his journey to the Eastern Heaven.

His yellow dog had never left his side during all of the preparations. I killed the dog as gently as I could and laid him at the Healer's feet so the dog could guide him.

When the preparations were done, I lit the wood. I stood by as the pyre roared. The fire burned and the smoke raised into the night. I stayed until the last wisp of smoke, the last essence of the Healer, had risen to the stars.

Don Julio and Mateo came to the funeral place in the morning. Mateo led a horse that Don Julio indicated I was to ride.

"You are coming with us," the don said. "You have been a thief and a liar, a young rogue, old in the wrong ways of men. Now it is time for you to live another life, that of a gentleman. Get on your horse, *Don* Cristo. You are going to learn the ways of a caballero."

into the night. I stayed until the last wisp of smoke, the last essence of the Healer, had risen to the stars.

Don Julio and Mateo came to the funeral place in the morning. Mateo led a horse that Don Julio indicated I was to ride.

"You are coming with us," he announced. "Until now you have been a thief and a liar, a young rogue, old in the ways of men. Now it is time for you to live another life, that of a gentleman. Get on your horse, Don Cristo. You are going to learn the ways of a caballero."

PART FOUR

While I swam in a sea of knowledge, I lived in a world of ignorance and fear.

—Cristo the Bastardo

SEVENTY-ONE

SO BEGAN THE next phase of my life, the polishing of the scabrous soul of a lépero street urchin into a Spanish gentleman.

"You will learn how to ride a horse, fight with a sword, shoot a musket, eat with a fork, and dance with a lady. Perhaps along the way you will teach me a few things," Don Julio said. "Hopefully, none which will cause my head to be impaled upon a city gate."

And who was to be my teacher? Who else but a man who boasted he had killed a hundred men, loved a thousand women, stormed castle walls, bloodied the decks of ships, and wrote ballads and plays that made grown men weep?

Mateo did not suffer the new assignment with great pleasure. We were both banished to the don's hacienda and forbidden to enter the capital. No doubt the don reasoned that neither of us was ready to present ourselves in the City of Mexico.

Furthermore, neither of us were certain of the don's motives. It seemed evident Mateo was exiled to the hacienda because it was still not safe for him to show his face in the capital—the judge who wanted to hang him was still in power. I did not know why he sent me to the hacienda with a new identify—as his cousin.

"He likes you," Mateo said. "Don Julio has suffered much as a converso. He sees something in you beyond the lying, thieving lépero I know you to be."

Both of us had the suspicion that besides the desire to reward us for striking a lethal blow against the Jaguar Knights, the don had ulterior motives. We questioned whether he had an assignment so hazardous that those performing it would need new identities and be completely in his thrall, an assignment so dangerous no one else would accept.

Don Julio owned two great houses, one on a hacienda fifty leagues south of the City of Mexico and the other in the city itself. I was to learn that when he wasn't traveling, he spent most of his time at the hacienda while his wife remained in the City of Mexico.

Under the encomiendas, indios had to pay tribute granted to the conquistadors. They were often worked and branded as slaves. These grants slowly evolved into the hacienda system as conquistador blood lines died out, the vast grants were broken up, or tribute was replaced by land holdings. Many haciendas were as large as encomienda grants, having villages or even small towns within their borders. Other than the actual branding of indios and the direct payment of tribute, the old system had faded in name only. Indios paid tribute to the hacienda owner in the form of cheap labor. The indio was tied to the land. The land fed the family, clothed them, protected them. And the land belonged to a Spaniard. In essence, the feudal nature of the European baronial estates, in which nobles were served by peasants who worked the land, had been transferred to New Spain.

Few hacienda owners actually lived on their vast estates. Most, like Don Julio's wife, lived all or most of the year in the City of Mexico so they could enjoy the pleasures and conveniences of life in one of the grand capitals of the world. The unusual relationship between Don Julio and his wife, where they lived apart most of the time, was not discussed. I eventually discovered why the scholarly don would want to stay away from the tempestuous woman.

Don Julio's hacienda stretched a full day's ride in every direction. Popocatépetl, Smoking Mountain, and Iztaccíhuatl, White Lady—two great volcano mountains that pierce the very heavens with their snow-capped cones—were both in view from the window of my room at the great house. When I sat and watched them, I was always reminded of the enchanting tale of love and tragedy from Aztec lore that the Healer taught me.

Iztaccíhuatl was the legendary daughter of an Aztec king whose kingdom was under siege. Needing the enemy vanquished, he assembled all of his warriors at the foot of the great temple of Huitzilopochtli, the war god.

"Iztaccíhuatl is the most beautiful maiden in the land," he told the warriors. "He of you who is the bravest in the battle will claim her as his wife."

Popocatépetl was the bravest and strongest of all the warriors. And he had long loved Iztaccíhuat, but only from a distance, for he was of common stock, his father a simple farmer. He was so low in the social order that he had to avert his eyes when the princess was near him.

Iztaccíhuatl was aware of his love, and the two had met secretly in a garden near her quarters when Popocatépetl had been a palace guard.

In the battle that ensued, Popocatépetl was the mightiest warrior, turning the tide of the battle and driving the enemy from the walls of the city. Because of his bravery, he pursued the enemy beyond the walls and back to their own land.

While he was gone, jealous suitors got the ear of the king. Iztaccíhuatl was his only daughter and for her to marry a common soldier, the son of a farmer, was an insult to them. They convinced the king to send assassins to kill Popocatépetl. When the assassins left the palace, the king told Iztaccíhuatl that Popocatépetl had died in battle.

The grief-stricken princess died of love lost before Popocatépetl arrived back, having defeated the assassins. When Popocatépetl found his love dead because of treachery, he slew the king and all the nobles. Then he built a great temple in the middle of a field and laid the body of his beloved atop it. He set a torch over her body so that she would always have light and warmth. He built another temple for his own body and placed a torch above where he laid down to rest, joining his love in death.

An eon passed, the temples grew into tall mountains and

snow encrusted them for an eternity, but the fires within still burned.

I have never forgotten the girl in the coach who saved my life in Veracruz. When I look at White Lady, the mountain resembling the head, breasts, and feet of a sleeping woman, I wonder about what sort of woman the girl Eléna had become. . . .

The hacienda was not a fertile basin, although year round a river flowed through it. Wheat, maize, beans, peppers, and squash were raised near the river, maguey for pulque, and indio products grew in the more arid areas. Cattle roamed wherever they could find graze. Cattle were raised mostly for their hides because it was not economical to ship the meat great distances, even salted. Chickens and pigs were raised for the dinner pot, deer and rabbit hunted.

The great house was located at the top of a hill, a mound the shape of a monk's bald pate. At the bottom of the hill, a small indio village, about sixty jacals—mud-walled huts—sprawled along the riverbank. There were no slaves on the property.

"Slavery is an abomination," Don Julio told me, when I asked why he did not use slave labor. "I am ashamed to admit that my fellow Portuguese people dominate this trade, hunting poor africanos as if they were animals and supplying them to anyone with enough gold. I am also ashamed to admit that many slave owners are cruel and vicious people, who enjoy owning another human being, who get pleasure from the pain they inflict and would buy a slave just to abuse the poor soul. Many of these men breed with their female slaves, lying with them and even with the daughters they produced, without any thought that they are committing rape and incest."

Ayyo, well I knew the treatment of slaves, from seeing them on the streets of Veracruz, on visits to sugar plantations with the fray, and the incident in which I cut loose the slave called Yanga before he could be castrated.

* * *

A priest came once a month to service the village from a small chapel set at the foot of the hill. After meeting the priest, Mateo spit on the ground.

"Many brave frays have brought God and civilization to the indios. To this priest, there is only heaven and hell and nothing in between. Any transgression, no matter how small, is a mortal sin in this fool's head. He sees demons and devils in everything and everybody. He would turn his brother over to the Inquisition for missing confession."

I understood Mateo's concern. The priest had taken one look at Mateo and crossed himself and mouthed Hail Mary's as if he'd seen the devil. But I also agreed with Mateo about the priest. The priest had referred to me as a converso when I went to him for confession, believing of course that as Don Julio's cousin, my family stock had been Jewish. Naturally, I told him nothing of consequence in confession and instead made up small sins for him to redress with absolution. These little lies, of which I am certain God will forgive, were necessary because Don Julio insisted that both Mateo and I regularly attend church so that he could not be accused of running a Godless hacienda.

SEVENTY-TWO

EACH DAY THE men of the village left on horseback to tend cattle or on foot to work the fields. Some women stayed to nurture children and make tortillas, while others walked up the hill to cook and clean at the great house. Mateo became an overseer to the indio vaqueros, and I learned how to herd cattle. After a painful lesson, I also learned how to stay clear of a bull chasing a cow.

Those who lived in the City of Mexico or even Veracruz relied upon the viceroy and his army for protection, but the arm of the viceroy extends little beyond the large towns and main roads. Hacendados had to protect themselves, and their haciendas were as much fortresses as houses. The walls were made of the same mud-brick construction as the jacals of the indios, but many times thicker and higher. To protect against marauders—bands of mestizos, escaped slaves, and renegade Spaniards—the walls had to be thick enough so a musket shot could not breach them and high enough to make them difficult to climb. Timbers were used to support the walls and roofs of the inner building, but there was little wood in sight—visible was stone and the abode mud bricks.

Inside the walls, the L-shaped living quarters occupied two-thirds of the space; a small stable and large courtyard completed the walled area. The horses, except for the don's personal stock, and all of the oxen used to work the ranch were corralled near the village. Outside the village were also barns and shops where almost everything that was needed to run the hacienda—from shoes for horses to leather for tackle and plows for the fields—were made.

The courtyard trees were plentiful, while green vines and flowers climbed the walls and sprayed color everywhere but on the cobblestones themselves.

It was to this place, a fortress, a village, a small feudal kingdom, I came to be transformed from a mestizo caterpillar to a Spanish butterfly.

The don would teach me science, medicine, and engineering, but his would be the scholarly professor's approach—quiet discussions and books to read, as if I was at university. My other teacher was a madman.

Mateo was my mentor for all that would make a "gentlemen" outside the realm of the scholarly—riding horses, sword fighting, dagger stabbing, musket shooting, dancing, wooing, and even sitting down at a table with a knife, fork, and plate all of silver. I had to fight my instinct to fill my gut with as much food in the least time possible out of fear that my next meal might not come as soon as my stomach demanded.

While Mateo had all the surface breeding of a gentleman, he lacked Don Julio's calm temperament and patience. He paid me in bruises for every mistake I made . . .

It was two years before I met Isabelle, Don Julio's wife, and when I did it was not with the great pleasure I had in meeting the rest of Don Julio's family. To pay what respect I can, the woman was beautiful yet vain, perfumed sweetly but rude, and ultimately a Medusa who had a head of snakes and turned to stone those around her.

Don Julio had no children, but he did have a family. His sister, Inez, a couple of years older than him, and her daughter, Juana.

The sister reminded me of a nervous little bird, pecking here and there, always watching over its shoulder for a predator. A somber figure, she always wore widow's black. I assumed that it was due to her husband's death, but later learned she donned the color when her husband ran off with a serving maid only a few months before her daughter was born. The husband was never seen again.

Juana, the daughter, was four years older than me. She was livelier than her mother, who still mourned the loss of a scoundrel. Unfortunately, while Juana's mind was sharp and her smile large, our Maker had not provided her with a body of the same worth. She was rail thin and brittle-boned. Her limbs had fractured several times and had not healed properly, leaving her half-crippled. She walked with the support of two canes.

Despite her weakness in body, she maintained a joyous attitude toward life and possessed an intelligence that I found amazing. I had been raised to believe that a woman's boundaries were children and cooking. To learn that Juana could not only read and write but shared with Don Julio a knowledge of the classics, medicine, and matters of the world's physical phenomena and the sky above was of great import to me. It brought to mind that young girl who allowed me to hide in the carriage and talked boldly of disguising herself as a man to gain an education.

The breadth and depth of Don Julio's learning also changed the way I looked at the world. He made me realize that the world was more exciting and challenging than I had ever imagined. Fray Antonio told me that over a hundred years ago, before the conquest of the Aztecs, in Europe had flourished a great era in which knowledge and learning long forgotten was reborn. It had produced men like Cardinal Francisco Jiménez de Cisneros, who founded Alcalá University, and Leonardo de Vinci of Italy, who was not only a painter but a military engineer who designed fortifications and war machines while studying the human body more thoroughly than any man of medicine.

Don Julio, like Leonardo, was a man of all seasons. He painted, studied the plants and animals of New Spain, knew more about medicine than most medical doctors, drew maps, not only of the mountains and valleys, but of the stars and planets, and was an engineer.

His skill at engineering was so renowned that the viceroy had given him the task of designing a great tunnel to avert flood waters from Mexica. The city was built on an island in the middle of Lake Texcoco. When it rained heavily, it came under threat of flood, and in some years flood waters overwhelmed the city. The tunnel was built to direct the waters out of the lake to keep the city from flooding. It was the greatest engineering project in New Spain or anywhere else in the New World.

¡Ay de mí! it would ultimately drown us in tragedy.

My presence with the family had to be accounted for. I could not keep up the pretense of being indio with Don Julio and the people around him. A major problem, besides my skin color and features, was the fact that I was growing a heavy beard even in my late teens. Indios had little hair on their faces. Mateo tried to convince me to shave the beard, telling me that señoritas preferred a clean-shaven face that they could rub against. But I had already been stripped of my indio disguise to become a Spaniard. I kept the beard. Neatly trimmed beards, especially sharply pointed goatees with mustaches, were the fashion of gentlemen, but I kept my beard full and long to hide my face. I also believed it made me look older and wiser.

Juana, Don Julio's niece, joked with me about the beard, asking what crime—or what woman—I was hiding from.

Don Julio was silent on the subject of my beard. He was equally silent about the mestizo boy from Veracruz who was wanted for heinous crimes. Don Julio and Mateo continued to treat the subject as they had done so earlier—with complete silence.

My suspicion was always that Don Julio knew even more than he let on. Once when I hurried into his library in the great house of the hacienda to speak to him, he was standing by the fireplace looking at a piece of paper. As I approached, he threw the paper into the fire. As it burned, I saw that it was an old reward notice for a mestizo known as Cristo the Bastardo. Fortunately, Cristo was a nickname for Cristóbal, and the latter was a popular name among Spaniards and indios.

As I said, I believed part of the reason Don Julio took me in as family was because he also bore a blood taint. One day when I was defending my life against Mateo as he taught me how to fight with a sword, I asked him why someone would call Don Julio a Jew.

"Don Julio's family were originally Portuguese Jews. In order to stay in Portugal soon after the discovery of the New World, many Jews converted to Christianity. Both conversos, those who converted willingly and Jews who only converted for appearances, were tolerated for the blood money they paid until King Filipe of Spain inherited the throne in Lisbon. When pressures increased, many conversos and secret Jews, marranos, came to New Spain. Don Julio came here over twenty years ago and since has brought many family members with him. Conversos are frequently suspected of being secret Jews. And even if the conversion to Christianity was faithful, in most people's eyes they carry the blood taint no matter how long ago their family had converted."

I knew something of the fate of Jews and Moors in Spain from Fray Antonio. At almost the same time that Columbus was sailing from Spain to discover the New World, King Ferdinand and Queen Isabella ordered the Jews to leave Spain.

"Before the banishment," Mateo said, "Jews and Moors were not only the wealthiest merchants, but the most educated people on the Iberian Peninsula. They were most often the doctors and merchants found in every town of any size. But every Jew and Moor in Spain and Portugal was forced to either convert to Christianity or leave. When they left, they were not allowed to take their gold or jewels. My Christian blood runs deep, but I can sympathize with Jews and Moors who had to face death or exile over their religious beliefs."

As one whose own blood was deemed tainted, I, too, found sympathy in my heart for people who could not prove purity of blood, limpieza de sangre. With my knowledge of languages, literature, and medicine, had I been indio, Don Julio could have held me out as an example of what the indigenous peoples were capable of, sort of a tamed and erudite noble savage. But as a mestizo, a carrier of the blood taint, it would not amuse but infuriate the gachupins.

The don could have had me keep up my indio disguise or even revert to the mestizo that I was. But he knew that I would never be able to advance and display the talents and scholarship he recognized in me. So I became a Spaniard.

The don introduced me as the son of a distant cousin who came to stay with him when both my parents were carried away by peste. Because the don was a gachupin, a wearer of spurs, people would assume that I, too, was born on the Iberian Peninsula.

One day I was a social outcast and the next a wearer of big spurs.

SEVENTY-THREE

"PARRY LEFT!" MATEO shouted at me as he delivered a rain of blows.

Learning how to be a gentleman was harder than learning how to be a lépero, I soon discovered—and more painful.

"You are fortunate, Señor Bastardo," Mateo said, "that you dwell in the Empire of the Spanish."

Mateo used the tip of his sword to flick an imaginary object off the front of my shirt. I also had a sword, but other than using it as a club to bludgeon with, I had no idea what to do with it.

"The Spanish are the Masters of the Sword," Mateo said, "and all the world knows it. The English swine, may San Miguel burn their souls and cast them down to hell, use short, thick swords to deliver blows in the hope that they will beat their opponents to death. The French are dainty fighters, all lace and perfume. They wish to love their opponents to death. The Italians, ha, the Italians, those arrogant bastards full of hot wind and bravado, they *almost* succeed at being Masters of the Sword because of their speed and cunning, but they lack knowledge of the secret that makes Spaniards the greatest swordsmen on earth."

Mateo put the tip of his sword to my throat and lifted my chin an inch.

"I have been sworn to secrecy upon penalty of death by all the chivalric orders of Spain never to divulge this secret to anyone who does not have Spanish blood in his heart. You, my little bastardo-half-breed, are Spanish in a queer sort of way. But you must also swear an oath to God and all of his angels that you will never reveal this secret to anyone else because every man in the world wants to be a Spanish swordsman."

I was thrilled that Mateo had honored me with a secret of such magnitude.

He stepped back a couple of paces and drew an imaginary circle on the ground.

"The Circle of Death. You enter it with the Dance of the Blade."

I stared down at the ground where his sword had passed. Dancing? Deadly circles? Had Mateo been imbibing the don's wine again?

"The first thing you must understand is that there are two types of sword fighters, the quick and the dead." His sword flashed as a blur before my eyes. "What type of sword fighter are you, Bastardo?"

"The quick!" I slashed out with my sword like I was chopping down a tree. The sword flew out of my hand, and Mateo's sword was at my throat. The tip of his sword was under my chin; his dagger pushed against my gut. He put pressure on my chin with his sword and I stretched onto my tiptoes. Blood ran down my neck.

"You are dead, Chico. I ask God to grant you one more life so that I can teach you to fight with a sword, but when your training is over, there will be no more mercy. The next man you fight will either kill you—or be killed."

Mateo released the pressure on my throat.

"Pick up your sword."

I scrambled to get the blade, wiping blood from my neck.

"Stand before me with your feet together. Now take a step toward me. Extend your sword as far as you can and mark a spot in front of you and to each side."

After I scored the dirt with my sword, Mateo drew a circle around me, more to the front than to the back.

"That is the circle of death. It is not one circle, but a thousand, moving with you, moving with your opponent. It is liquid, like ripples in water, constantly moving, constantly changing, flowing toward you, flowing back."

Mateo faced me and stood at the edge of the circle. "The

circle begins at the point you can reach across and inflict a wound or death on your opponent. From here I can hit your face, your chest, your stomach." He moved slightly to the left. "From either side I can get the sides of your body. I move a little more and I can slice the hamstring behind your leg. Remember, Chico, the circle is fluid—it changes with every step.

"And it belongs to *both* of you. When you face another swordsman, one or both of you will close the space between you. When you get close enough to strike, the circle is created for both of you."

Along with the physical combat, Mateo gave me much verbal instruction about the uses of swords.

The dress rapier most men carried in town was lighter and fancier than the military swords and much less lethal.

"It will serve you well to fend off an attacker on a city street or in a duel of honor, and it is good for thrusting or cutting, but when you are in the thick of battle you need a weapon that will kill an opponent who may be wearing padding or even armor, one that can cut off an enemy's arm or head. A military sword will allow you to drive back a group of attackers or even cut your way through."

He demonstrated how the basket hilt protected the hand on a light sword. "The sword you duel with should have this type of hilt that protects your hand from a downward slice. But neither the dress sword you carry on the streets or the military sword you carry for protection outside a city should have an elaborate hilt. *Why not?*"

"Because, uh, becau——"

"Estupido!" He attacked with his rapier, the sword a blur as he struck me again and again, raising painful welts on my arms and legs.

"When you reach for a sword, whether it be from a sudden attack in battle or a sudden attack on a street from a robber, you may have only a split second to arm yourself. If there is a fancy hilt guard, you will grab it instead of getting a good grip on the hilt. When that happens, Bastardo, you will have a sword sticking in your throat before your own weapon is free of its scabbard. Most duels are arranged in advance. Thus you can use an elaborate hilt guard to protect your hand because you do not have to draw your sword to protect yourself from a sudden attack."

Not all swords are right for a particular man, he told me. The weight of the sword depends upon the strength of a man. "Much attention must be given to the length you need for your height and the length of your arms. If your sword is too long, you will not be able to uncross the blade from your opponent's without stepping back and putting yourself off balance. If it is too short, the circle of death will be smaller for your opponent because of his greater reach."

He showed me how to discover the length I needed. I held my dagger out arm length in one hand, the arm horizontal to the ground but the dagger held upward, and my other hand with my elbow crooked so the sword hilt was at my hip. "The sword should reach the grip of the dagger but not extend beyond," he said.

Everything else being equal, a tall man will prevail over a shorter man because he has a longer weapon and a longer reach.

"If your sword is too heavy, you will lack the speed to attack, parry, or counterattack. If it is too light, your opponent's blade will break it."

I had to build up strength, and I did this by practicing with a much heavier sword than either my dress sword or my military sword. "Your arm will think it is carrying the heavier sword, and you will be able to use your swords with greater speed and strength."

The dagger is a useless weapon for warding off blows. It has one good purpose: "When your blade is crossed with your opponent's, you stab him with your dagger before he can get his weapon uncrossed."

Ayyo, my Aztec ancestors would be proud to see that I was learning the fine art of killing from a true master. Mateo may have been a liar, a purloiner of poetry and women, but when it came to the art of killing, he was a master.

"You must always be the aggressor," he told me. "Not

that you should start all fights—but once they start, you must counterattack so aggressively your opponent is on the defensive. And when a fight is inevitable and your opponent chooses to talk about it, while he is still concentrating on insulting you with words, you must pay him the greatest insult of all—put your dagger in his gut."

The aggressor almost always wins a fight, he said. He who strikes first is most often the one who will live to fight again. "But what is aggression?" Mateo asked. "It is not the charge of a bull or mindless slashing. Successful aggression derives from a combination of great defensive maneuvers and brilliant offense. Even if you are hacking your way through a troop of the enemy, you must make every slash count because the one you miss may cost your life."

Mateo viewed fencing as another form of dancing.

"A swordsman must adopt the posture of a dancer, standing tall with body straight, but with knees flexible. Only then can we move quickly. Rapiers extended before us, our opponent at bay, our feet must move like a dancer's, never pausing, always in motion, but not capriciously. Dancers do not move their feet any which way but in harmony with the music, their partner, their mind, and the rest of the body. You must hear the music and dance to the rhythm."

"Where does the music come from?"

"The music plays in your mind, the tempo created by the movements of you and your opponent, and you dance to it. Thrust, parry, dance, standing straight up, your arm extended, keeping him from drawing a circle around you, dance, dance."

Mateo pranced like a young girl at her first ball, and I made the mistake of giggling—his sword whizzed by my cheek and cut a locket of my hair.

"Laugh again and they will call you One-Ear instead of Bastardo. *En garde!*"

When I stumbled with my footwork, Mateo cursed me. "It is my fault to ask a lowly lépero to wield anything more strenuous than a begging cup. If you cannot dance because your feet and your brain are not in the same body, then at least think of it as swimming. You must use all of your body at once when you swim. Swim toward me, Bastardo, step, step, thrust, parry, and step—*small steps, you oaf!* If you tread on your dance partner's toes, he will thrust his sword into your throat."

Each day I learned more about pain. And I noticed more and more scars on Mateo's face, arms, and chest when he took off his shirt to rinse the heat and sweat from his body. He had a name for every scar—Inez, Maria, Carmelita, Josie, and other women he had fought duels of honor for. There were even scars on his back, one particularly nasty one when an angry father's thrown dagger caught him in the back after he leaped from a girl's balcony.

I began to accumulate my own scars from Mateo's angry slashing.

"You must follow your body's instinctive reaction, not your eye. A flashing sword lies to the eye because it moves quicker than the eye can follow. You sword must be in position to ward the blow and counter, relying on the eye to follow the action. Your eye will lie to you and kill you.

"I have studied under Don Luis Pacheco de Narvaez, the greatest swordsman in all the world, he who was a student of Caranza himself. Caranza taught that the fluid, dexterous dance, what he called La Destreza, was the way of the swordsman."

After months of practice, Mateo made his judgment of me as a swordsman.

"You are *dead, dead, dead.* You might be able to hack your way through a side of beef with a two-handed sword or maybe an indio who has been tied up and thrown on the ground, but you are too slow and too clumsy to survive against a good swordsman."

That glint of cunning came into his eyes that I have seen when he is about to cut another man's purse or steal his woman.

"Since you will never be able to survive with the skills of a gentleman, you must learn how to be a tricky swine."

"I want to be a gentleman!"

"A *dead* gentleman?"

The lépero in me decided the issue. "Show me how to be a swine."

"You have as much strength and skill—or *lack* of skill—in your left hand as in your right. Swordsmen call the left hand the devil's paw for good reason—the Church frowns on the use of the left hand, and most men are taught to use the right hand for sword fighting only, even if their left hand is their superior one. You are not a gentlemen. You can fight with the left hand. But you must understand that simply using your left hand against a skilled swordsman will not give you a great advantage—unless you combine it with surprise.

"I will teach you a movement that you can use in desperation when you realize that the swordsman you are up against is going to slice pieces of meat off of you until you bleed to death standing up. You begin the fight with your sword in your right hand and your dagger in the left. When you are out of the circle, you suddenly let your dagger drop and switch the sword to your left hand as you step into the circle. It means dropping your guard for the briefest moment, and he would put his point in your heart if you did not ward off the thrust."

"How do I ward off the thrust?"

"With your shield."

"What shield?"

Mateo pulled up one of his sleeves. He had a thin piece of bronze metal strapped to his arm. "You will use your "armored" arm to knock away his blade."

Armor in a duel was dishonorable to the extreme. Switching to the left hand during a fight was ungentlemanly. But I would rather be a live swine than a dead gentleman.

SEVENTY-FOUR

THE FIRST TIME I saw the don's wife, Isabella, she was stepping down from a coach in front of the great house at the hacienda. A flutter of silks and petticoats, her Chinese satin bodice was encrusted with gem stones, and she had pearls strung around her neck and both wrists. Her red, shoulder-length hair was all curls from the ears down.

I have seen beautiful women before—colorful mulattas on the streets of Veracruz, beautiful, dark-eyed india women in out-of-the-way villages—but none of the Spanish women I had seen compared to Isabella.

I was beside Don Julio as he helped her step from the coach, and I gaped as she descended. Had a servant not laid out a carpet upon the dusty ground to protect her shoes, I would have flung myself on the ground for her to step on. My mind swirled and I nearly passed out as a whiff of her perfume found me.

Mateo and I stood with our hands on our swords, our backs ramrod, in our finest clothes, as if an honor guard for a queen.

Don Mateo took Isabella by the arm and paused before us as he escorted her into the hacienda.

"May I present my young cousin, Cristobál, and my aide, Mateo Rosas de Oquendo."

Isabella looked at us, her green eyes inspecting Mateo and me thoroughly, before turning back to Don Julio.

"Another poor relative to feed, and a blackguard to hide the silver from."

That was my introduction to Doña Isabella.

* * *

The great house had been an oasis of tranquillity since I had first been brought there to be molded into a gentleman. Other than the scholarly challenges of Don Julio, and an occasional kick or insult from Mateo when he became frustrated by my clumsiness, I was well-fed, slept in an actual bed, and begged the good Lord each night not to send me back to the streets of Veracruz—or the gallows.

With the arrival of Isabella, the house stopped being an oasis and became an el norte tempest. She was the center of everything—demanding and irritable to the servants, sweet and manipulative with Don Julio, rude to the don's sister, niece, and "cousin"; downright hateful to Mateo, who she treated as if he was going to abscond with her jewels at any moment. She referred to him not by name but as "that picaro."

We soon discovered that she had not come to be sociable. From overhearing a conversation between Don Julio and Isabella in the library, I learned she had grossly overspent her household budget for their home in the City of Mexico and had come demanding more money. The don was angry because it was no small amount of money Isabella needed. She had gone through a year's household expenses in a few months, a sizable amount since the house had a full staff of servants and Isabella surrounded herself with considerable luxury.

She told the don that the money had been stolen but admitted, when he questioned her, that she had not reported the loss to the viceroy or anyone else. The don was clearly incredulous, but when it came to dealing with Isabella, he was as helpless as everyone else.

After Isabella had been in residence for three days, I inadvertently was able to look upon her hidden beauty. I entered the antechamber next to the don's bedroom looking for a book the don had left there and found myself staring at Isabella naked from the waist up. She soaked in a small bathtub. The steamy brew smelled of roses.

I was struck dumb, but Isabella, without bothering to cover her bare breasts, simply looked at me. "You're a handsome boy, aren't you," she said, "but you need to shave that vulgar beard."

I ran from the room in terror.

"She's the don's wife," Mateo told me. "We must respect her. And we must never lust for her. One does not have passion for the wife of a friend."

Mateo spoke with such heated emotion that I feared he suspected me of such thoughts. I found this odd. Mateo had loved the wives of a dozen men. I found it interesting that he had such strong feelings about the wife of a friend. Such distinctions were part of the code of honor that I was learning, the code of *hombria* in which honor and amorous conquest both play large roles. A true *man* has loved many times—but only honorably. One does not scale the wall to the bedroom of a friend's wife . . . but any other woman is fair game.

A code for women existed, too. A woman was to remain a virgin until marriage—and never be tempted afterward. Eh, amigas, did I say life was fair?

At times Mateo felt that he was a prisoner at the hacienda. He was a man of action and bossing vaqueros was not his brand of excitement. He would disappear for weeks at a time, and when he came back his clothes and body looked like the fur of a cat that had tangled with a pack of voracious dogs. Once he let me come with him, and we rode hard for days following a treasure map in search of Montezuma's legendary gold mine.

He had won the treasure map in a card game. The fact that the map could be a fake was not in the cards. We went near no large towns, but it was an exciting experience to jump on the horse and seek a lost treasure. We never found the mine. My suspicion was that Mateo had been duped into letting a fake map be used as a bet. Naturally, I was careful not to suggest the idea.

"Only the emperor knew the location of the mine," Mateo said, "The miners were indio slaves who were permanently locked in. They worked the mine, never leaving, never seeing the light of day or another human being. Once a year they passed the gold to Montezuma alone without ever seeing another human face."

Questions like how the miners ate if they were locked in and how Montezuma carried away gold all by himself only resulted in my getting cuffed by Mateo. Tolerance of facts that conflicted with his own notions was not a gift the Lord gave him.

SEVENTY-FIVE

ISABELLA HAD BEEN at the hacienda a week when she announced that she was attending a social gathering at another hacienda. Don Julio said that he had to attend a sick patient, the name and exact illness of whom I was never able to ascertain. Since it would not be proper for Mateo, a notorious picaro, to escort the don's wife for a social visit, the duty fell to me as the don's cousin.

"You've had two years of education as a gentleman," the don said, after informing me that I would be accompanying Isabella. "But the only practice you have had is on the hacienda. There is a time when you will not have this cocoon to protect you, and you must know if you can carry yourself as a person of quality among others. This will be a test for you. Isabella is a difficult woman to please; she demands the respect given a queen."

Later that afternoon I walked into the library and gave the don a start as he bent over examining a strange instrument. It was a tube of brass with glass at each end and set on metal legs. He put a cloth over it immediately.

At first he appeared hesitant to show me the instrument, but after he gave me instructions about Isabella, he removed the cloth. He had the excitement of a child thrilled with a new toy.

"It's a starscope," Don Julio said. "It was developed in Italy where a cosmographer named Galileo used it to look at planets in the heavens. He has written a book, *Sidereus Nuncius,* The Starry Messenger, telling of his discoveries."

"What do you see when you look into this . . . this starscope?"

"Heaven."

My jaw dropped and Don Julio laughed.

"You see the planets, even the moons of Jupiter. And you learn something so shocking to our Church that men burn at the stake for possessing one of these instruments."

Don Julio lowered his voice into a conspiratorial tone. "The Earth is not the center of the heavens, Cristo. The Earth is just a planet revolving around the Sun as other planets do. A Polish mathematician named Copernicus discovered this many years ago but feared to reveal his works until after his death. *De revollutionibus orbium coelestium,* On the Revolutions of the Celestial Spheres, published in 1543 on Copernicus's deathbed, refutes the Ptolemaic presumption that the Earth is the center of the heavens.

"The starscope proves Copernicus's theory. The Church is so frightened of the starscope that a cardinal has refused Galileo's request that he look in the starscope because the cardinal fears he will look into the face of God!"

"What about the face of God?"

A musket shot in the room could not have been more startling. Isabella stood at the door to the library.

The don recovered first. "Nothing, my dear, we are talking about philosophy and religion."

"What is that thing?" She pointed at the starscope. "It looks like a tiny cannon."

"Just a device for measuring. It assists me in making maps." He put a cloth over the starscope. "As you know I cannot attend the gathering at the Velez hacienda. I am sending Cristo with you. He will escort you in my place."

She did not give me the look of derision I expected. She

pointed her fan at me. "You dress like a peasant. If I am to be forced to have your company on this trip, you are to dress as if you were going to a party in Spain instead of a social gathering in this wilderness."

After she left the room Don Julio shook his head. "She is a woman who knows how to command. But she is right. You dress like a vaquero. I will have my manservant ensure that you are a properly clothed gentleman."

The road to the Velez hacienda was little more than a rural path that rarely felt the wheels of a carriage. Doña Isabella and I rocked back and forth inside the carriage, as the wheels found every rut on the road. It was hot and dusty inside the carriage, and the doña held a nosegay to her face.

There was little conversation for the first couple of hours. An early departure was necessary to reach the other hacienda before nightfall and Isabella slept.

Don Julio's valet had indeed made a gentleman of me, at least the turtle's shell of one. He cropped my hair, removing it from my shoulders so it fell to about chin length, and curled the ends. A white, linen shirt with billowing sleeves, wine red doublet that had slashes for the white shirt to show through, matching short cape, black Venetian breeches that were pear-shaped, wide, almost bombasted at the hips and narrow at the knee, black silk stockings, and round-toed shoes with bow ties . . . it was a reasonably modest outfit, but the street lépero in me felt that I was dressed as a dandy. The valet had refused to let me carry my heavy sword and instead saddled me with a slender rapier that would hardly cut the head off of a frog.

Isabella made no comment about my clothing. It was several hours before she gave any indication that she was sharing the coach with anything but a mote of dust. When she finally awoke and had to acknowledge my presence, she looked me over from the ostrich feathers in my hat to the silken bows on my shoes.

"Did you enjoy sneaking in to watch me in my bath?"

My face turned redder than my doublet.

"Bu—bu—but I didn't—"

She waved away my innocence.

"Tell me about your parents. How did they die?"

I related the carefully concocted story that I was an only child, orphaned at the age of three, when my parents were swept away by a plague.

"What was your parents' house like? Was it large? Are you heir to nothing?"

Doña Isabella was not questioning me out of suspicion but boredom, but while lies often leaped to my lépero tongue, I did not want to risk so much for idle chatter.

"My family is not as illustrious as yours, Doña. Nor as exciting as your life in the City of Mexico. Tell me about the city. Is it true that eight coaches could drive side-by-side at the same time down the grand avenues?"

A flood of words about her life in the city—the clothes, the parties, her grand home—erupted. Diverting her from inquiries about my past was not difficult. Isabella enjoyed talking about herself much more than hearing about others. Despite her queenly mannerisms and pretensions to being a great lady, I knew from household gossip that her father had been a petty merchant and her only claim to gentility was the fact that she had married well.

But she was always full of surprises. Startling inquiries or comments occasionally dribbled from her mouth without warning. "Tell me about the little cannon you can see heaven with," she said.

"It's not a cannon. It's a starscope, an instrument for gazing at the sky."

"Why does Julio keep it hidden?"

"Because it's banned by the Church. One could have much trouble with the Inquisition for possessing such an instrument."

I went on to tell her about Galileo seeing the moons of Jupiter, and the cardinal who was afraid to look into the scope for fear he would see the face of God.

Doña Isabella asked no further questions about the starscope and soon she had dozed off again. Some doubts had crept into my mind about telling her about the instrument. Don Julio had had the opportunity to do so and did not. A few days before he showed me the telescope, he had caught me opening a cabinet in the library. The cabinet was usually kept locked, but he had been in it earlier and left it unlocked.

The cabinet contained books that were on the prohibition list of the Inquisition. They were not scandalous *libros deshonesto,* but works of science, medicine, and history that the Inquisition found offensive but most men of learning did not.

He was showing me a science tome banned because it was written by a English Protestant when we discovered that Isabella was listening. On that occasion he had also the opportunity to draw her into the discussion or explain the contents of the cabinet and had not.

I put away my doubts and fears about Isabella. What could come of it? She was the don's faithful wife, was she not?

SEVENTY-SIX

THE VELEZ HACIENDA and its main house were larger than Don Julio's. To my lépero eyes, the house was a palace. En route Isabella told me that the hacendado, Don Diego Velez de Maldonato, was a very important gachupin in New Spain.

"It is said that he will someday be viceroy," she said.

Don Diego was not at the hacienda, but Isabella assured me that she socialized with him frequently in Mexico. Socializing with prominent people seemed to be important to her.

"There will be families from two other neighboring haciendas," Isabella said. "The gathering is hosted by the majordomo of the don's estates. You would learn much by sitting at his feet and listening to him. He is not just a majordomo for Don Diego, and brilliant in all forms of commerce, but is considered the best swordsman in New Spain."

We arrived at the great house late in the afternoon. As soon as the coach pulled up, we were greeted by several women, all of whom, like Isabella, were absentee owners of haciendas and their daughters. Their husbands followed in their wake.

I was bored, dusty, and stiff from the long ride and was introduced to Don *this* and Doña *that,* but none of the names stuck. Isabella had been in a state of hibernation during most of the carriage trip and came alive the moment the coach pulled up in front of the house.

She introduced me as Don Julio's young cousin without much enthusiasm. Without expressly stating it, her tone deplored having another of the don's poor relatives in the house. The moment she implied my penurious circumstances, the warm attention I was getting from the mothers suddenly turned to frowns and their daughters' smiles became cold as a frog's flesh. Once more she had made me feel like dirt.

Ah, Doña Isabella, what a woman! It was no wonder the don was captured by her wiles—nor that he stays as far away from her as possible. Mateo claims that some women are like the poisonous black widow spiders—they, too, have beautiful bellies, but they devour their mates. And Isabella was a master spinner of webs.

But I was not as dismayed as some poor relative would have been; inside I was laughing at the fact that the great lady had been escorted by a lépero. Until I heard a voice from the past.

"It's so good to see you, Isabella."

* * *

Life is a crooked road for some of us, twisting over dangerous cliffs and vertiginous crags, with sharp rocks waiting below.

The Church tells us we have choices in life, but I sometimes wonder if the ancient Greeks were not right, that there are playful—and sometimes spiteful—gods who weave our fate and wreak havoc in our lives.

How else could one explain that I had fled my enemy five years ago, ran from his dagger and his killers, only to find myself in the same house with him?

"Don Julio's cousin."

She introduced me with so much disdain that Ramon de Alva, the man who cut the life from Fray Antonio, barely glanced in my direction. She would never know the debt of gratitude I owed her.

We were given time to freshen our clothes and bodies before dinner. News of my pecuniary status must have preceded me because the room I was given was a servant's bedroom that was smaller than most gentlemen's clothes closet. The room was dark, cramped, insufferably hot, and well-seasoned with the smell of the stable underneath.

I sat on the bed with my head on my lap and pondered my fate. Would Ramon de Alva recognize me if I looked him squarely in the eye? My instinct was that he would not. I was five years older, a very important group of years that took me from adolescence to young manhood. I had a full beard. And I had been introduced and was dressed as a Spanish gentleman and not a lépero street urchin.

The chances of him recognizing me were small indeed. But *any* chance at all set my heart trembling in my chest. My best ploy would be to stay completely out of harm's way.

I had already ascertained that all of the guests were friends of Isabella's from the city and were making their annual visit to their haciendas. We were only staying one night and would leave very early to make it back while the sun was still in the sky. I only had to stay out of sight for the few hours it took to dine and engage in the drinking and mindless social chatter that ensues.

To stay away from dinner would be to stay away from Ramon de Alva and the chance he would carve me with his sword in front of his guests. An ingenious plan unfolded in my mind: *I would be too sick to attend dinner.*

I sent a servant with my regrets to Doña Isabella that my stomach was upset from traveling and that I wished permission to stay in my room. Of course, if she insisted, I told the servant, I would attend her at dinner.

He returned a few moments later with Isabella's reply: She would manage without me.

I was ravenous and I told the servant to bring a plate of food. He looked at me in surprise and I told him it was a stomach ailment that food would cure, but my doctor had told me I had to lie down when partaking.

Collapsing on the bed, I thanked San Jerome for having extended his mercy.

I had sworn to achieve revenge on the man, but this was neither the time nor the place. Any action I took against him would reflect back on Don Julio and Mateo. While my passions urged me to strike down the man, even if I had to give my life in the fracas, my good sense dictated that I would not repay the kindness of my friends by bringing misery into their lives. New Spain was a big place, but the Spanish population was not large compared to the land. Ramon de Alva was going to come back into my life again. I would have to bide my time until the opportunity for cutting him down without destroying those who had shown kindness to me presented itself.

I fell asleep with the smell of manure in my nose and the sound of music from the party in my ears. Awakening hours later, I sat up in the dark room. The party noise was gone. Looking at the moon, I adjudged that I had slept past midnight.

I was thirsty and left the room in search of water, walking quietly for fear I would rouse the house and call attention to myself.

Earlier I had seen a well located in a small patio off the main courtyard of the compound. Our carriage was parked next to the courtyard. No doubt the well was used for the stables, but in my life I have drank worse than stable water.

I paused at the bottom of the steps from my room and savored the cool night air for a moment. Keeping my step soft, I located the well in the moonlight and drew water from it, pouring a bucket over my head after I had drank my fill.

Going back and sweating in the room was not inviting—it was as hot and humid as an indio's sweat hut. An alternative was our coach. The coach offered better air, and a seat that was no harder than the straw bed in the room. I climbed aboard. I had to scrunch down on the seat, but at least I could breathe.

Sleep was darkening my mind when I heard whispered voices and a giggle. Fearful that I would expose my presence in the carriage if I moved too quickly, I carefully unwound my body and sat up to peer outside.

Two people had entered the little courtyard. My eyes were adjusted to the dark, and I was able to quickly identify them from their clothes: Isabella and Ramon de Alva.

The blackguard took her into his arms and kissed her. His lips slipped down to her breast area, and he pulled apart her bodice to expose the white breasts that I had once seen.

The man treated a woman like a dog in heat. He threw her on the ground and tore at her clothes. Had I not observed that she had come voluntarily with him and that she enjoyed his hard touch, I would have grabbed my dagger and flung myself on him to stop him from raping her.

Her undergarments flew as he flung them away. When he had exposed the dark area between the glistening whiteness of her thighs, he dropped his own pants and fell upon her. He inserted his pene between her legs, and both of them began to pump and pant.

I slowly lay back, cringing as the springs of the coach squeaked. I shut my eyes and put my hands over my ears to shut out the sounds of their dog noises.

My heart bled for Don Julio. And for myself.

What terrible thing had I done to cause this evil man in black to come into my life again.

The next morning I got a handful of tortillas from the kitchen rather than joining the guests at breakfast. Coming down the great hall of the house, I saw a portrait on the wall that caused me to stop and stare.

The person in the painting was a handsome young girl, about twelve years old, not yet in the flush of womanhood, but in that late stage of balancing on the line between child, girl, and young woman.

I was certain that the young woman in the picture was Eléna, who had smuggled me out of Veracruz. As I stared at the picture I realized that in the coach the older women had referred to her uncle as "Don Diego."

¡Santa Maria! No wonder I had encountered the beastly Ramon de Alva. It had been said in the coach that de Alva was employed by her uncle.

The resemblance of the girl in the picture to my savior in the coach was too great for there to be any mistake. A servant came by and I asked, "This girl, is she Don Diego's niece?"

"Yes, señor. Very nice girl. She died of the pox."

I left the house and made my way to the coach with tears in my eyes. Had de Alva crossed my path, I would have thrown myself on him and ripped out his throat with my dagger. While no sense could be made of such logic, I blamed de Alva even for the death of Eléna. In my eyes he had taken two people I love from me and was dishonoring a third. I again swore an oath to someday take vengeance on him in a way that would not harm Don Julio or Mateo.

My heart now knew why this land called New Spain was a land of tragedy and tears as well as gaiety and song.

SEVENTY-SEVEN

AFTER ISABELLA RETURNED to the city, Don Julio took Mateo on an undercover assignment with him, and I languished at home with boredom and jealousy.

"You are in charge of the hacienda while I am gone," Don Julio told me, "a heady assignment for one so young—and tempestuous."

I begged to go, but the don's ears were deaf to my pleas.

As I was helping Mateo load his gear on a pack horse, he talked about the task.

"Don Julio is not interested in the ordinary crime that plagues the country, petty highwaymen who rob a bishop's purse or a merchant's goods. The don reports directly to the Council of the Indies in Spain. He is given assignment when there are threats to public order or the king's treasure."

I already knew this about the don, having learned it during the time we pursued the Jaguar cult. And I had slowly put together the fact that his converso status was one of the reasons the Crown used him. He was easier to control since he always had the accusation of Judaism hanging over him.

"There is talk that pirates are planning to launch an attack on the silver stockpiled for the treasure fleet. My job will be to hunt out information in inns where men drink too much and boast to barmaids and whores. For a few well-placed coins, and a few well-placed kisses, the women repeat what they heard."

"Where will you be going?"

"Veracruz."

I realized that I was being left behind because the don worried that I would be recognized by someone in Veracruz. Once again my past had become an unspoken issue between us. Until Mateo or Don Julio raised the subject, I would not embarrass or belabor them with my problems. Harboring one wanted for murder could get both to the gallows—with me as their companion.

The pirate attack turned out to be just another rumor that plagued the treasure fleet. Mateo came home with another scar. This one was called Magdalena.

I never told Mateo about Isabella's tryst with de Alva. I was too embarrassed for the don to share the information even with Mateo. I also knew that if I told Mateo, he would have killed de Alva. Not only was the man's death to be my sport, but I feared setting Mateo upon the man who was called the best swordsman in the land. Mateo would have insisted upon fighting him fairly because he would be doing it for the don. I had no intention of fighting honorably.

The hacienda ran itself, I soon learned, and my efforts at making it run more efficient almost always caused the indios to slow down or stop work. Rather than make more of a fool of myself, I retired to the don's library to increase my knowledge and ease my boredom for the month that Mateo and the don were gone.

The don said I soaked up knowledge like a sponge.

"You are developing into a Renaissance man," he once told me, "a man who has knowledge of not just one discipline, but of many."

My face lit up that day like the noon sun. Don Julio himself was a true Renaissance man, a possessor of knowledge of art, literature, science, and medicine. He could set a broken arm, expound upon the Peloponnesian wars, quote Dante's *La divina commedia,* chart a course on land or sea with stars and planets. I was intensely proud of the don, whose genius as an engineer had made him the designer of the great tunnel project that was one of the wonders of the New World.

With the don's encouragement, I devoured books like a great whale swallowing a school of fish in one gulp. Fray

Antonio had, of course, already given me many lessons in the classics, history, and religion. But the fray's library had been small, less than three dozen volumes. Don Julio's library was one of the largest private libraries in New Spain and contained over fifteen hundred books. It was a cornucopia, a horn of plenty, for a person with an insatiable appetite for knowledge.

I read and reread not only the great works that had been contained in the fray's library, almost all of which the don had also, but practical books like Father Agustin Farfan's treatise on medicine, the works of the great pharmaceuticist Mesue, the ninth-century Arabic doctor at the court of Harun-Al-Raschid at Bagdad, the secrets of surgery revealed by the Spaniard Benavides, Sahagun's history of the indios, and Bernal Díaz del Castillo's history of the conquest.

The don's library was stuffed with the works of Galen, Aristotelian science, and Arabic doctors; writing of the Greek philosophers, Roman lawgivers, and the Renaissance poets and artists; tomes on engineering and the cosmos. Of the most fascinating works were those of the technique of surgery to put a nose on a person after it was cut off, the story of the sinful French disease, also called syphilis, and Ambroise Paré's battlefield surgery techniques.

A surgeon in Italy had developed a procedure to replace the noses of those who had had them cut off. Don Julio said that the surgeon was motivated by the plight of a young woman from Genoa whose nose had been cut off by some soldiers who were enraged at the resistance she offered to the rape they were conducting.

Gaspare Tagliacozzi, the Italian surgeon, died about the time I was being born. He had studied a Hindu method of surgery in which a flap of the skin of the forehead was draped down and shaped to form a nose. The upper part of the flap, still attached to the forehead, was left attached until the nose part grew on the flesh. The Hindus had developed this art from necessity—many Hindu woman lost their noses for real or imagined infidelities.

The Hindu method left a large, pyramid-shaped scar on the patient's forehead. Tagliacozzi developed a method of using the same amount of skin but obtaining it from under the forearm. Because the forearm was mobile, a frame was built around the person's head to hold the forearm against the nose area until the forearm flap of skin attached itself to form a new nose.

He also performed similar operations for repair on the ears, lips, and tongue.

As for the young woman from Genoa whose defense of her virtues caused the loss of her nose, it is said that the operation was a complete success, except that in cold weather her nose developed a rather purplish hue.

Tagliacozzi relates his techniques in *De Chirurgia Curtorum Per Insitionem*, published a couple of years before his death, a copy of which in Spanish found its way to the don's library.

One of the worst contagions on the face of the earth is commonly called syphilis, or the French disease. It is said that the disease got its name from the shepherd Syphlius, who insulted Apollo; the angry god inflicted upon Syphlius a loathsome disease that spread like wildfire.

Syphilis has struck the hearts of every man and woman in the New World and the old. Acquired through copulation, many men have carried it home to their wives. The priests chide us that syphilis is a disease of sin, put on earth by God to punish the promiscuous, but what sin does an innocent woman commit who gets this dreaded affliction because the husband she has no control over carries it home from a whore or an amorous adventure?

For those who do not shake it in its early stages, there is no cure for the disease except death. For some the death comes slowly, eating away the life of the person; others are carried away mercifully—but painfully—quickly. One out of every two persons who get the contagion dies from it.

The treatment is as horrible as the frightful, raw, painful rash and ulcers that cover an infected person's body. When the sores are present on the body, the infected person is placed in a barrel or tub with mercury in it. A tub ordinarily used for the salting of meat so that it would last longer was often utilized. Tub or barrel, the container was large enough to contain the body of a man and so it was used for sweating out the malady and fumigating syphilitics. The contents of the container, man and mercury in powder or liquid form, were heated.

It is said the cure kills as many as the disease. Many of those who survive the cure have tremors of the hands, feet, and head along with frightening grimaces, death's head skull grins.

Don Julio told me that alchemists, who supplied the mercury compound to barbers and others who gave the treatments, finally realized their dreams of turning mercury into gold by the treatment of syphilis.

Some claim Columbus's men brought the dreaded disease back from America. On their return to Spain, many of them chose to become mercenaries and had hurried to join King Ferdinand of Naples, who was defending his kingdom against King Charles of France. After Naples fell, the Spaniards entered the service of the French king and carried the disease along with them to France. Because of its early prevalence in the French army, it earned the common name of the "French disease."

The indios deny that the disease is a New World one and claim that the Spaniards brought it with them and that it killed as many indios as the peste and vomitó.

Who knows? Perhaps both are right—the Lord acts in mysterious ways.

Another wonderful story of medicine fascinated me, that of the French battlefield surgeon, Ambriose Paré. This was another man who died not too long before my birth.

When Paré was a young army surgeon, the common way to stop bleeding of a gunshot wound was to cauterize it with boiling oil. The black powder used in cannons and smaller weapons was considered poisonous; boiling oil was applied to eliminate the poison, stop the bleeding, and cure the wound. Applying hot oil to a wound was extremely painful to the soldiers who were already suffering great pain.

During a period of heavy casualties, Paré ran out of oil and improvised, applying a salve made from egg yolks, rose essence, and turpentine. To stop the bleeding, he took the radical step of *sewing* closed the damaged arteries. To his surprise, and the surprise of the surgeons working around him, his patients almost all survived, while the death rate on those who had boiling oil applied was exceptionally high.

Like many heroes of medicine and science, Paré was not immediately proclaimed a hero. Careful to give the Inquisition its due, he always denied he had cured the men. To avoid a charge that he was in league with the devil, after every treatment, he said, "I dressed his wound; God healed him."

It is from Paré that Don Julio learned the technique of removing a musket ball or arrow with the person in the same position as when the object entered.

Alas, the price of fame and success: Paré's fame grew, jealous surgeons tried to poison him.

After reading of Paré's skills and knowledge and seeing Don Julio's educated application of medicine, I was struck by how miraculous it was that Fray Antonio was able to perform surgery with little knowledge of anatomy and kitchen utensils for instruments. Eh, no doubt the Lord was guiding his hands.

Thinking about the miracles the fray performed, the tale of another medical miracle came to mind. Suffering from a gangrenous left leg, a farmer named Roberto fell into a coma at the door of a church. In his unconscious state, he dreamt that saints had come and removed him to a hospital. The saints performed an operation to amputate the leg below the knee and performed the same operation, postmortem, on a patient who had died in an adjoining bed. They sewed the leg from the dead man onto the farmer. When Roberto awoke the next day, he discovered he had two sound legs.

When he returned home from the hospital, Roberto told his family and friends about the incident. Each time he told them that he had been the recipient of a miracle, that saints themselves had sewed the leg of a dead man to replace his amputated one, people scoffed. When they did, he lifted up his pants to prove his story.

One of his legs was white, the other black.

The man on the bed beside him had been africano.

SEVENTY-EIGHT

WHILE I SWAM in a sea of knowledge, I lived in a world of ignorance and fear. It was dangerous to display any sort of knowledge outside of the tight circle formed by Don Julio, Mateo, and myself. I learned this painful lesson from Don Julio, whom I am sad to say claims that I am the only friend he has ever had who incites him to violence.

The incident occurred when a woman Don Julio had treated died in a town a day's ride from the hacienda. I accompanied Don Julio to the woman's home, where she was being prepared for burial. The woman was not of a great age, about forty years old, which is about what I calculated Don Julio's own age to be. And she had appeared to be in good health immediately prior to her expiration.

To further complicate matters, she was a wealthy widow who had recently married a younger man, who had a reputation as a profligate and womanizer.

Upon arrival at the house, Don Julio sent all but the alcalde and her priest out of the death room and examined the body. He suspected arsenic poisoning because of the smell of bitter almonds from her mouth.

The priest announced that the woman had expired from sinfulness because she had married so soon after the death of her husband and to a man whom the Church frowned upon.

I laughed at the priest's prognosis. "People don't die from sin."

The next thing I knew I was nearly knocked across the room by a blow from Don Julio. "Young fool! What do you know about the mysterious workings of God?"

I realized my folly. This was the second time in my life that I had gotten into trouble for exposing medical knowledge.

"You are correct, padre, the woman died of her sins," Don Julio said, "in the sense that she brought into her own house the scoundrel who poisoned her. Like almost all poisons, it will be extremely hard to prove that he administered it. However, with the permission of the alcalde, and the blessing of the Church, I would like to lay a trap for the killer."

"What trap do you wish to lay, Don Julio?" the alcalde asked.

"The bloodguilt?"

Both men murmured with approval. I remained quiet, in ignorance and humility.

"If I could get the padre and your excellency to prepare the husband by sowing the seeds of his fear . . ."

When the two left the room to converse with the husband, Don Julio said, "We have to hurry."

He began to examine the body. "The palm of her hand has a cut, probably when she broke this cup in her pain." The cut was a jagged one, but there was little blood in it.

Pieces of the cup were on the table next to the bed and on the floor beside the bed. He examined the cup part, sniffing them.

"I suspect that the poison came in this cup."

"How will you prove it? What is bloodguilt?"

"Bloodguilt is an old wives' tale, but one that many people believe." He took a copper tube and a small, round copper ball out of his medical case. I had seen him put liquid in the ball and attach the tube in it for insertion in the back side of a person's body when he was applying medicine to that place. "When a person dies, for some strange and unknown reason, blood sinks to the lowest part of the body. As she is lying on her back, the blood will gather all along her back, behind her legs, and so forth."

"Why?"

He shrugged. "No one knows. Many doctors believe that it is part of a process in which the body is drawn toward the earth for its burial. As you know from the books in the library that you read with my permission—and those you read by stealth—there are more mysteries than answers in life."

"The sinking of the blood—that is bloodguilt?"

"No. Help me turn her a little." He took his dagger from his belt. "I'm going to draw blood."

He filled the ball with blood and inserted the tube, keeping the device upward so the liquid would not run out. Pulling back the woman's sleeve, he sat the device on her bare arm, keeping his finger over the end so the blood would not run out.

"Here, put your finger where mine is."

I traded places with him, keeping the end of the tube sealed while he pulled the sleeve down until the ball and tube were covered.

"When you remove your finger, blood from the hidden container will slowly flow into her palm. To someone just entering the room, it will appear that the wound to her hand is bleeding."

"Why would the wound bleed?"

"Many people believe wounds to a body will bleed if the person's killer comes close. When that happens, the killer is unveiled. That is the bloodguilt, the blood of the victim pointing to the killer."

"Is this true? Does the blood really flow?"

"It does when you arrange for it to flow, as we just did. I sent the fray and the alcalde out to arouse the husband's fears about the bloodguilt. It is time to call them back with the husband in tow. When the husband steps into the room, remove your finger and step back, and I will point out that the palm is bleeding."

A moment later the husband ran from the room in terror. The last I saw of him, he was babbling incoherently as the alcalde's men tied his hands behind him. I did not attend his hanging; I had seen enough death in my life.

On the way back to the hacienda, Don Julio instructed me on the proper way to deal with medicine with a priest.

"The medical lore of a priest is found in the Scriptures."

"Scriptures have medical information?"

"No. That is exactly my point. To most priests, a doctor does not heal—God does. And God is stingy about how many He saves. If a doctor saves too many, the suspicion may arise that he is in league with the devil. When you challenged the priest, you were right in your knowledge, but wrong in your wisdom. It is dangerous for any doctor to demonstrate too much medical knowledge or effect too many cures. When the doctor is a converso, as I am, and as others believe you are, familiars from the Inquisition may pull you from your bed in the middle of the night if you expose too much medical skill."

I apologized profusely to the don.

"The same approach must be taken in regard to your knowledge of indio healing herbs. The herbs are often more effective than any European medicine, but care must be taken not to arouse the ire of priests or jealous doctors."

Don Julio told me something that I found shocking: He sometimes proscribed remedies that he knew were nonsense—but appeased patients and priests.

"There is a concoction called *mithradatium* that has several dozen ingredients and is believed to be a cure-all for everything, including poison. One of the main ingredients is the flesh of a viper on the theory that a snake is immune to its own poison. I find the medicine not only a fraud, but often harmful. When I administer it, I do so in such a weak dose that it can do no harm.

"Our doctors have more knowledge of poisons that kill

people than of drugs to cure illness. The fools will often ignore an indio remedy that has been known to cure and apply something that has no medicinal value. The viceroy himself and half the grand men in Spain have bezoar stones to put into their drinks because they believe that the stones are an antidote that absorbs poisons."

"Bezoar stones? I have not heard of this antidote," I said.

"They're stones found in the organs of dead animals. Men who plot the course of nations, kings who rule empires, often will not drink anything unless their bezoar stone has been placed in their cups."

"They keep one from being poisoned?"

"Bah! They're useless. Some even have horns they believe are from unicorns. They drink from the horns or stir their drinks with the horns in the belief that the horns can neutralize poisons."

I shook my head in wonderment. It was for this very type of men that the Healer's snake trick was suited.

The don went on, not hiding his disgust.

"When the archbishop was dying a few years ago, men who were called the best doctors in New Spain were at his bedside. One of the medicines given to him to help him sleep and reduce his pain was mouse dung, the droppings of mice." He shook his head as if the fact still did not fit well into his brain. "I am certain this foul substance helped speed the poor man to his reward in heaven."

After listening to the don, I realized that he and the Healer were not as far apart in their medical practices as one might suppose.

Or in their cunning. Bloodguilt was no doubt the Spanish equivalent to an indio snake trap.

One era in my life closed and another opened when I was twenty-one years old. I had dreamt a thousand times of seeing the New Spain city that was called a wonder of the world, a city of canals and palaces, of beautiful women and grand caballeros, of champion horses and golden carriages.

The day finally came when I was to see the Venice of the New World.

SEVENTY-NINE

"WE'RE ALL GOING to the city," Don Julio informed us one day.

Mateo and I exchanged looks of surprise.

"Pack all of your personal possessions. I will instruct the servants what to take of the household. Cristo, you are to supervise packing of the library and some other items I will point out. Mateo and I will leave tomorrow for the city. You will follow with my sister and niece after you get everything packed and loaded. You will have to hire extra mules to carry the loads. Inez and Juana will go as far as possible by carriage and then by litter when the coach can go no farther."

"How long will we be in the city?" Mateo asked.

"I don't know. Perhaps forever. Perhaps we will be buried there."

I had never seen the don so grave and introspective. Beneath his sober demur, I sensed anxiety and urgency.

"What is the urgency, Don Julio?" I asked. "Is Doña Isabella ill?"

"My wife is still healthy enough to spend two pesos for every one I earn. No, it's not the doña. The viceroy commands my presence. The heavy rains of the past few weeks has resulted in flooding parts of the city."

"What of the drain tunnel?" Mateo asked.

"I don't know what's happened. Too much water for the tunnel, cave-ins; I won't know until I inspect it. I designed the tunnel to handle heavy rainfalls."

While I was concerned about the don's tunnel problem, I was elated that we were going to the great city. The years spent on the hacienda had turned me into a seasoned gentleman—in my own eyes—but the hacienda was a place of cattle and corn. Mexico! The name itself glittered with excitement for me.

I could see from a look Don Julio gave me that he had considered leaving me on the hacienda. I, too, feared the dark shadows in my past, but so many years had passed that I no longer kept an eye on my back. Besides, I was no longer a mestizo boy but a fine Spanish gentleman!

Mateo, too, was eager to get back to city life. And it was safer for him. The don said that the audiencia member who would have caused problems for Mateo had returned to Spain. But the excitement we felt was tempered by our concern for Don Julio. Mateo expressed some of my own fears that night after dinner.

"The don is worried, more than he allows us to see. The command from the viceroy must be serious. The tunnel was the most expensive project in New Spain's history. We know the don is a great man, the best engineer in New Spain—the tunnel must be a marvel."

Mateo tapped my chest with the tip of his dagger.

"But, Bastardo, let us hope that the tunnel the don *designed* is the tunnel that got *built.*"

"You believe the workmanship was faulty?"

"I believe nothing—yet. But we live in a land where public offices are sold to the highest bidder and mordida buys any favor from a government official. If the tunnel fails and the city is severely damaged, the viceroy and his underlings will not accept the blame. Who better to blame than a converso?"

A fortnight after the don and Mateo departed, I set out on horseback for the city with a train of mules behind me. In my eagerness, I had the servants pack quickly; but while I moved with the speed of a jaguar, Inez dragged her feet like a prisoner setting off for an execution. The prospect of living with Isabella rankled. She did not want to leave the hacienda; but even with a loyal staff of indios, the don feared for the safety of two Spanish women alone.

"I would rather be murdered by bandits than sleep in the same house with that woman," Inez declared.

Personally, I would have slept under the devil's roof for the chance to see Mexico.

I rushed Inez and Juana through their packing, with Inez making excuse after excuse for her slow progress. When the two were packed, we set out, two women, myself, and a train of mules and tenders. I had been at the hacienda for three years. I came as a mestizo outcast and left as a Spanish gentleman. I could ride, shoot, use a sword and even a fork! I could not only herd cattle but had learned the miracle of how sun and water nourished the land.

Another stage of my life was about to begin. What would the gods hold for me this time?

EIGHTY

I FIRST SAW the grand city from atop a hill in the distance. It shimmered on a lake like a fine jewel on a woman's bosom.

Mexico! I asked myself, as the conquistadors had before me, *Was it real?*

Juana spoke to me from her litter carried by two mules.

"Bernal Díaz del Castillo, the conquistador who wrote a history of the conquest, described what the conquistadors thought when they first saw Tenochtitlan. He spoke of enchanted things . . . 'great towers, temples, and buildings rising from the water.' Cristo, we, too, must ask ourselves if these things we see now, the City of Mexico towering from the ruins of Tenochtitlan, are not a dream."

The towers and temples below were not Aztec, but were marvels of the world anyway, at least the small part of the world my eyes had set upon. Mateo claimed that he had loved and fought in half the great cities of Europe, and the city we call Mexico was as tall and proud as any of them. Churches and palaces, homes so large the great house at the hacienda would have fit in their courtyard, wide boulevards, canals, green fields, and lakes. Causeways ran from the shore to the city, one meeting a great street. But no! Not a street like those in Veracruz or Jalapa, but a grand avenue long enough and wide enough to set both of those miserable towns upon it. Six carriages could travel it abreast. Even the narrower streets could easily have allowed three carriages side-by-side.

In the heart of the city I made out a large square that I knew was called the Zocalo, the main plaza. It was the largest and most important square in the city, distinguished by fine buildings like the viceroy's palace and the cathedral that was still being improved upon.

And the canals! As if an artist had drawn them with his hand directed by God. The lake and canals swarmed with canoes and barges, supplying the city like a fleet of water bugs, while the broad causeways streamed with coaches, litters, horsemen, and pedestrians.

Joaquin, Don Julio's indio valet, who served him both at the hacienda and the town house, accompanied us. He pointed at the main plaza. "The largest marketplace is in the square. There are many shops besides the places of the Church and viceroy. The great houses of the nobles and rich merchants are on adjoining streets."

He indicated a large, green area not a great distance from the plaza.

"The Alameda. In the afternoon the ladies wear their best silks in their carriages and the men dress as gallants upon their finest horses and parade up and down the Alameda. It is a place where many times men draw their swords and," he leaned closer to whisper to me, "women lift their dresses!"

If Mateo was not at the don's house when we arrived, I knew where I would find him.

* * *

We joined people on a main road leading to one of the causeways that stretched across the lake to the city. Foot, horse, mule, carriage, and litter traffic increased as we drew closer to the causeway. The largest number of people on the road were indios carrying fruits, vegetables, and handmade household items. As the indios approached the causeway, dozens of africanos and mulattos diverted them to an area off the side of the road where cargo was being piled and examined on the ground. An indio carrying a large sack of corn on his back tried to proceed around the men and was roughly shoved to the roadside with the others.

I asked Jose what was going on.

"Recontonería."

The word meant nothing to me.

"Africanos buy the fruits and vegetables from the indios and resell the goods in the city for two or three times as much."

"Why don't the indios take the stuff into the city themselves?"

"One who defies the Recontonería is found floating in a canal. Everyone, the bakers and innkeepers, all buy from them. Some indios try to bring the products into the city with their canoes, but few can slip by the Recontonería's boats."

These bandits and pirates robbed the indios through brute force. I was outraged. "Why doesn't the viceroy put a stop to this crime! It not only cheats the indios, but raises the cost of food for everyone. I shall complain to the viceroy personally."

"Everyone knows but nobody will stop it, not even the viceroy."

"Why not? A few soldados with muskets—"

Joaquin studied me with amused forbearance. I suddenly realized how stupid I must have sounded.

"Obviously, the scheme is not stopped because it is profitable to people *besides* the africanos, people high enough that even the viceroy tolerates the practice."

The Spanish blood in my veins told me that people who

shared that blood would not permit africanos and the like—slaves, ex-slaves, and mulattos—to profit. No doubt many of the africanos involved were not freed men but slaves, who left their masters' homes in the morning to walk to the end of the causeway empty handed and return that night with a pocketful of money after buying vegetables cheap and selling them dear. Of course, it would be the masters who profited.

Indios hated and feared the africanos because of the way the Spanish used the blacks to intimidate them.

"It's sad," I told Joaquin, "that the indios and africanos, both of whom are maltreated by the Spanish, cannot find some common ground that would lessen their mutual suffering."

Joaquin shrugged. "It doesn't matter to us who takes our land, our women, and our money, anymore than which fox steals the chicken. They are gone anyway, are they not, señor?"

EIGHTY-ONE

WE CROSSED THE causeway and my heart beat faster. I had entered the greatest city in the New World. The avenue before me pulsated with people, sounds, and color.

"Do you know about the *Arabian Nights?*" I asked Joaquin.

"No, señor."

"A tale of brave men and beautiful women, gold and jewels, exotic places, fascinating people, and strange beasts. I will be satisfied if I die tomorrow, Jose, for I have seen the Arabian Nights today."

What sights! What color! What sounds!

Exquisite women in woven gold-and-silk dresses traveled

in silver carriages that would not have shamed a duchess in Madrid; caballeros and caballos rode past, gallant men on magnificent prancing horses—reddish-brown sorrels, dark-stripped grays, black-and-white piebalds—with jingling silver spurs, silver bridles, and Joaquin told me, often even *silver horseshoes.* Uniformed bearers, africanos in livery, trotted not just beside carriages but could be seen behind men on horseback, stepping in the horse's droppings as they carried whatever items the men needed for business or social gatherings that day.

Four things in Cuidad Mexico are fair to behold—the women, the apparel, the horses, and the carriages. I had heard this saying many times in my life, but now I understood that it was not an old wives' tale. Not that all the pomp and display was necessary or a sign of good breeding.

Mateo, who himself is not adverse to pomp, says that every cobbler with a helper and every muleteer with six mules will swear that he is a descendant from a great house in Spain, that the blood of the conquistadors runs in his veins, and now, though fortune has frowned upon him and his cloak is threadbare, he should be addressed with the honorific "Don" and his pompous airs recognized as good breeding. If that were so, Mateo said, New Spain boasts enough "great lords" to fill the ranks of every noble house on the peninsula.

Frays sweated in grays and black and brown habits, while lordly gentlemen strutted with swaggering arrogance under large, plumed hats and brandished silver-and-pearl hilt swords as a mark of their station in life. Ladies in hooped skirts and white petticoats, their faces layered with French powder and bright red lip coloring, carefully made their way over the cobbled stones in heeled slippers, followed by pages holding silk parasols to shade their mistresses' delicate faces from the sun.

Ponderously heavy, squeaking carts, world-weary oxen, baying donkeys, cursing muleteers—is there any other profession that knows more bad words? Wrinkled old women selling tortillas dripping with salsa, mulattas selling peeled papayas on a stick, whining, avaricious léperos beseeching alms—*damn their larcenous souls!* Why don't they work as honest people do like me?

Deeper into the city the evil smells attacked me, and I realized that the canals were open sewers, often so filled with refuse and *God-knows-what*—things that I didn't even want to guess the true nature of—that boatmen were having a difficult time making way with their canoes. But I didn't care if boiling lava flowed in the canals. I had so long smelled only hay and manure that the stench of a great city was a nosegay to me.

Like heroes of those sultry exotic nights in Arabia, I had found a green oasis, Allah's paradise on earth. I started to tell Joaquin my thoughts about Allah and his garden but quickly reined in my words. I had already blasphemed in mentioning the Arabian Nights. If any more profanation dribbled off my tongue, the next smell I suffered would be the Inquisition dungeon.

We crossed the main plaza. Two sides were lined with covered passageways to shelter merchants, government officials, and shoppers from the sun and rain. Grandees filled with smug importance carried papers to meetings with the viceroy, while household servants haggled with women squatting by mats covered with fruits and vegetables, and great ladies entered the shops of merchants who sold everything from Chinese silk to Toledo blades.

Across the square was the viceroy's palace and prison, the complex looking much like a stout fortress with its stone walls and great gateways.

To the left of the palace, was the house of God, a great cathedral that had been started long before I was born and was still rising in the rubble and dust accompanying its construction.

Despite the grandeur of the city, its buildings do not challenge the heavens like Babel's Tower. I commented to Joaquin that I saw few buildings more than two stories high.

He waved his hands up and down. "The ground shakes."

Of course, earthquakes. New Spain has as much passion

in its earth—earthquakes that shake the world beneath our feet and volcanoes that spit fire—as in its people who blaze with the fires of love and hate.

The shops of merchants and government buildings slowly faded as we made our way toward the Alameda, the great greenway in the heart of the city where the caballeros and ladies showed off their clothes, horses, and smiles.

Our train of mules and the litter chairs of my two charges passed by houses so magnificent to call them palaces is not to boast. In front of the great gates stood africano servants in finer clothes than any I possessed.

When we got to the Alameda, the parade of gallants and ladies had commenced. I was embarrassed to be leading a mule train. I was now a young Spanish gentlemen, in name if nothing else, and we did not soil our hands with work.

I pulled my hat down over my eyes in the hopes that later, when I returned as a caballero, I would not be remembered as a mule driver.

The greenway was pleasant, a place of grass and trees and a fine pond, but I barely noticed the natural surroundings—my eyes were on the men and women, on the sly and shy glances, the unspoken but communicated invitations, the flirtatious giggles, and masculine snorting of gallants and horses. Ah, what spirit, mettlesome steeds, mettlesome men, horse and man, high-spirited, fiery, sexually vigorous, stomping, pawing, rearing, a sword on the hip, love sonnets on the lips!

Eh, this was the man I wanted to be—brave and arrogant, a fiery demon in a woman's bed, a deadly swordsman on the dueling field. To be outgoing and charming, a swan with a blade, contending for a lady's favor, drawing my sword and dagger to best a rival—or two—or three. I would fight a dozen of these perfumed dandies for a minute in the arms of a beautiful woman!

No actor of comedias could have put on more mystery or romance than these gallants and ladies. Each gentlemen had his train of africano slaves following the prance of their proud horse, some as many as a dozen waiting on them.

Each lady had a like number by her coach, in brave and bright apparel, almost as garnish as her own clothes and coach.

"Before the night is over, someone will draw a sword in anger and jealousy," Joaquin said, "and blood will follow."

"Do the authorities punish such acts?"

"The viceroy's men make much ado, rushing toward the assailant with their swords drawn, telling him that he is under arrest, but there is never an arrest. The friends of the gentlemen surround him with drawn blades and escort him to a nearby church where he seeks sanctuary. Once inside the church, the viceroy's men cannot follow. After a few days all is forgotten. The blade is back on the Alameda, this time drawing his sword to defend a friend or fight off the viceroy's men."

I was marveling to myself at the wonder and justice of such a fine system of honor when a horseman suddenly came up beside me and slapped me on the back so hard I nearly fell off my horse.

"Mateo!"

"It is about time you got here, Cristobál." In private he referred to me only as Bastardo, but Joaquin was in listening range. "I have many fine adventures to tell you. I spent the last three nights in a church. Does that tell you that I am ready to be a priest?"

"That tells me that you were one step ahead of the viceroy's men. What is that? A new woman?" I indicated a small but ugly gash on the side of his neck.

"Ahhh," he touched the raw wound. "This is Julia. For a moment in her arms, I braved a dagger thrown on the Alameda. The cowardly blackguard who threw it thought he could increase his life span by at least a few moments by wounding me."

"And Don Julio? Doña Isabella? They are well?"

"There is much to talk about, my young friend. The don has been anxiously awaiting your arrival. We have work to do!" He slapped me on the back again, hard enough to knock my breath away.

I noticed he was riding a horse that was different than the one he'd left the hacienda on. It was a fine sorrel, more red than brown. I was instantly envious that he had such a beautiful animal. I would need such a horse to prance about the Alameda.

"Is that fine animal part of the don's city stable?"

"No, I purchased it from my winnings at cards. I paid twice what any sorrel in the city would go for, but it was worth it. Its pedigree goes back to a famous sorrel of a conquistador. Ahh, my young friend, is it not true that even a woman cannot satisfy a man's pride and ego like a horse?"

He threw back his head and sang Balbuena's ode to the horses of New Spain:

Their glory here is such
that we're moved to declare
they must come from the stud farm of Mars . . .

Half the horses in New Spain are claimed by its owner to have a bloodline traceable back to one of the fourteen horses of the conquistadors who terrorized the indios during the conquest. And most of the nags had as much claim to such a grand bloodline as muleteers who struck it rich hauling supplies to the silver mines and started calling themselves "dons."

I clicked my tongue. "Amigo, you have been defrauded. Did you forget that there were no sorrels in the company of Cortes?"

He looked at me and his face turned so black that I felt fear down to my spurs.

"That knave who sold it to me shall be dead by sunset!"

He spurred his horse. In panic I shouted after him. *"Stop! I was only joking!"*

EIGHTY-TWO

DON JULIO'S CITY house, while not as magnificent as a palace, was more stately than the house at the hacienda. Like most fine homes in the city, it had a garden courtyard with bright flowers and fountains, vine-covered arched passageways whose shadows provided coolness even when the sun was high in the sky, a large stable for the carriages and horses, and, of course, in the main house, a grand, sweeping stairway.

A servant showed me to my room—over the stable, with heat and manure smell. Mateo grinned.

"My room is next to yours. Doña Isabella wants us to know our place."

Don Julio was waiting for us in his library, already instructing servants on the unpacking and shelving of his books. We followed him into a sitting room. He stood as he spoke to us.

"The city suffered flood damage during the heavy rains because cave-ins occurred, fouling the tunnel. A tunnel, like a piece of pipe, will only conduct as much water as its narrowest portion."

More for my benefit than Mateo's, who already had some knowledge of the tunnel project, he went on to tell us about it.

The city is set upon a lake, or what many people thought of as a series of five interlocking lakes. The lake is on a flat plain, deep in a vast valley, over seven thousand feet high, shouldered by mountains, many of which are a league high. Tenochtitlan was originally built on a soggy island and was slowly expanded by the floating gardens that took root in the shallow lake. Because the city was so low to the waterline, the Aztecs built an elaborate system of canals and dikes to protect the city from floods.

Almost from the time of the conquest, the city began to suffer periodic flooding. The indios thought of the flooding as having a spiritual source. In revenge for the Spanish defilement of Aztec gods, Tlaloc, the blood-thirsty god of rain, brought torrential precipitation that threatened the city. To build a large city on the footprint of Tenochtitlan, the Spanish deforested the tree-covered slopes. It was said that Cortes's palace alone absorbed nearly ten thousand trees.

With the slopes stripped of vegetation; water cascaded off the mountains, carrying soil to fill the lakes, raising the waterline. The first floods led to reconstruction of the Aztec dikes. But as the lake beds filled with more and more dirt from the mountainsides, the dikes could not keep back the rising water.

"Every decade since the conquest has seen torrential rains and flooding of the city," the don said. "Most of the valley went underwater during one unusually wet season a few years ago, and the city was nearly abandoned—only the cost of rebuilding an entire city kept us from moving Mexico to higher ground."

It had long been envisioned that a canal and tunnel be built through the mountains to drain off the rainwaters before the city floods. Don Julio, noted for his engineering skills, was commissioned to design the project.

"As you both know, I drew up the plans for the project, a canal that ran six miles from Lake Zumpango to Nochistongo, with four miles of it cut through the mountains."

"Were those plans followed?" Mateo asked.

"The size and position of the canal and tunnel were to my specifications. But instead of shoring up the tunnel with iron-supported timbers and lining it with masonry-hardened brick, the walls of the tunnel were composed of mud-and-straw bricks similar to those used to construct a house." Don Julio's face twisted with grief. "We did not know the constitution of the mountain, which turned out to be subject to cave-ins. I did not get involved in the actual construction, but I am told many indios died digging the tunnel. Their smothered screams will haunt me when I am burning in hell for my part in this disaster."

Unfortunately for the indios, the mountain was not composed of rock but of loose and crumbling earth. I had heard that fifty thousand indios had died digging the tunnel, but rather than increase Don Julio's grief and guilt, I merely looked away.

"As you know, the rains were high this year, not as bad as they have been in the past, but above the normal rainfall. There was minor flooding."

I felt instant relief. "Minor flooding! Then the situation is not as drastic as we thought."

"It is worse. Because of the cave-ins, the tunnel was unable to carry waters that were only slightly above normal. A severe storm may result in the whole city flooding."

"What can be done?" Mateo asked.

"That is what I am working on. There is already an army of indios clearing the debris from the cave-ins and patching the violated areas with masonry bricks and using wood beams to shore up. But by the time we attack one weak point, there is a cave-in a few feet away."

"What can we do to assist?" Mateo asked.

"At the present, nothing. I need to know more about how the tunnel was constructed, and I do not need your help in doing the tests. It will be months before I know anything, and even then I may never be able to determine exactly what went wrong. But if what I suspect is true, I will have need of your skills. In the meantime, I have received a commission from the Council of the Indies to investigate possible insurrection against His Majesty's authority.

"The viceroy contacted the council and requested assistance in regard to rumors of a plot by africanos, slaves, mulattos, and the like to revolt and kill all of the Spanish and make one of their own choosing king of New Spain."

Mateo scoffed. "There has been such talk since the day

I arrived in New Spain. We Spanish fear the africanos because they outnumber us."

Don Julio shook his head. "Do not so easily discount rebellion. Several times in the past the africanos have risen up against their masters, burned plantations, murdered the owners. When one group in a plantation rebelled, others nearby joined. Fortunately, the insurrections have always been put down—brutally—at an early stage, before enough africanos could unite to resist the soldados sent to correct the situation. One reason is that they have never had a leader capable of uniting them into an organized military unit. But such a man may exist, and word of his accomplishments has spread like wildfire among the blacks until he has the status almost of a god."

"Yanga," Mateo said.

"Yanga!" I almost jumped out of my chair.

"What's the matter, Cristo? Why does the name surprise you?"

"Well, I—I heard of a slave named Yanga, a runaway. But that was many years ago."

"This Yanga is a runaway, I believe from the Veracruz area; but Yanga may be a common name among africanos. You have been tucked away at the hacienda for so long, you didn't hear the growing stories about the man. This particular Yanga escaped from a plantation. He made his way into the mountains and over a period of years he gathered other runaways, what we call *cimarrones,* enough to form a small band of highwaymen, *maroons,* who preyed on the roads between Veracruz, Jalapa, and Puebla.

"Yanga claims to have been a prince in Africa. Regardless of his heritage, he has a knack for organization and fighting. His band is now said to number over a hundred. They maintain a village in the mountains. When the viceroy's troops finally reach the village, after suffering many casualties, Yanga's men set fire to the village and disappeared into the jungle. A few weeks later they had another village high in the mountains from which they terrorized the roads below.

"They have a fearsome reputation, not only among us Spanish, but the indios. They steal indio women and conduct what has become to be called 'mountain marriages,' in which the women are forced—sometimes with eagerness on their part—to marry them. Recently a merchant, his son, and his indios were attacked near Jalapa by maroons. The runaway slaves took a strongbox containing over a hundred pesos. The merchant's young son was killed in the attack, his head cut off, along with some of the male indios. Several of the indio women were carried off. It's said that one of the maroons grabbed a baby from a woman's arms, smashed its skull on a rock, and carried off the woman on a stolen pack animal.

"This attack was supposed to have been done by Yanga's men, but Yanga gets blamed for so many attacks that he would have to be in three places at the same time. And the stories grow and grow of the savageness of the maroons until one has to wonder whether those parts of the tales grew in the telling, too. About the time this attack was occurring near Jalapa, a hacienda near Orizaba was attacked, and the Spanish majordomo was killed, along with indios. Survivors said that after the majordomo fell to the ground, a slave split open his head with a machete, then scooped down and cupped out blood with his hands and drank it. That attack, too, of course, was attributed to Yanga."

We were all silent for a moment. I hoped, of course, that the Yanga of the maroons was a different man than the Yanga I had helped free, but I remember the plantation owner chortling over the slave's claim that he had been a prince. But even if it were the same man, I would feel no guilt over his actions. The greedy hacendados created maroons, not me.

Don Julio stared at a corner of the ceiling and pursed his lips. When he spoke, it was as if he had read my mind.

"It seems as if the Lord gives us back twofold the evils that we sow. Spanish men outnumber Spanish women twenty-to-one in New Spain, thus the natural outlet for a man's sexual needs is native women. Male slaves also have sexual needs, and the africano men also outnumber the slave women twenty-to-one. The only women to fill this shortage are india. We revile the offsprings of these matings, by Spaniards and slaves, as less than human, not because they do not walk and talk and think like us, but because in the deepest part of our soul, our greed for New World treasure has inflicted these inequities.

"The second generation of settlers in the New World was already experiencing slave revolts. Africanos owned by Diego Columbus, son of the Discoverer, revolted and killed Spaniards on the island of Hispaniola. Yet thousands, tens of thousands more slaves were imported since then. Was there no lesson to be learned from this inauspicious beginning with slavery?

"But enough of philosophy. I have need of men who can go out on the streets and investigate, not philosophers. Cristo, it's been many years since you were a thief and a beggar. Do you still have the talent?"

"I could swindle a widow out of her last peso it you have such a need, Don Julio."

"Your assignment may be more difficult, and dangerous, than swindling widows. I want you to go back on the streets as a lépero. You will keep your eyes and ears open as you mingle with the africanos. Listen to their talk; watch their actions. I need to know if this talk of revolt is bravado from pulque-loosened tongues or if an actual revolt is being planned."

"I've had experience with africanos in Veracruz. That experience tells me that those in this city are unlikely to express their desires to a lépero."

"I don't expect them to confide in you. Just keep your eyes and ears open. Most of these africanos and mulattos speak a corrupt tongue among themselves because there is no one language a large number of them share. They speak a little of various africano tongues, some Spanish, and words picked up from indios. You can better understand what they say than Mateo or me."

"But wouldn't it be better if you hired a slave or a mulatto to mingle with them and report their words?" I asked.

"I've done that. Mateo will be dealing with several we've paid to report. But the viceroy will not take the word of an africano. Nor would he take the word of a lépero who, in his eyes, is more untrustworthy than even a slave. He would only listen to a Spaniard, and I have two—my young cousin and an overseer from my hacienda."

"Besides supervising the africanos you've hired, how else can I serve you in this investigation?" Mateo asked Don Julio.

"Keep Cristo alive. He is new to the city, and I fear that his lépero survival instincts may be as eroded as the walls of the tunnel. Also, think about going into the pulque business."

"Pulque?"

"What do you think africanos drink? Fine Spanish wines?"

"But it would be illegal for a slave to drink pulque." The foolish remark came from me, and I got an amused and incredulous stare from each of them.

"Murder, banditry, and insurrection are also illegal," Don Julio murmured.

"So is being an unsavory lépero," Mateo said, "yet the streets—and this house—harbor such trash. But, Don Julio, what do you have in mind about this pulque business?"

"Two things are certain to close a man's eyes and loosen his tongue—a woman and drink. You find both in a pulqueria. I have it on good authority that there are a thousand pulquerias in the city, if one counts all the old women who sell from a jug outside their front door. There are no doubt a number of them operating clandestinely who serve africanos exclusively. You will rent one of these establishments, or buy it if necessary. You will uncover others and send our hired africanos into them to drink and listen."

"How do I locate such a place?"

"Cristo will soon learn of them from street talk, but there is an easier way. They would not be owned by africanos, only run by them. Most illicit profits in this city pass through the hands of us Spanish. I will give you the name of a man, a Spaniard, very respectable on the surface. He no doubt will be able to arrange for your needs in regard to a *pulqueria*."

"Is he associated with the Recontonería?" I asked.

Don Julio shook his head in wonderment. "An hour in the city and already you know the name of the organization that controls most of the corruption. I am no longer worried that you have lost your skills as a miscreant."

As Mateo and I were leaving the room, the don asked, "How do you find your rooms? Isabella chose them especially for the two of you."

I exchanged looks with the picaro. "Very fine, Don Julio; they are excellent."

He struggled to keep his lips from cracking with a smile. "Feel privileged that you are only *above* the stable."

EIGHTY-THREE

MATEO RUBBED HIS hand together with zeal as we made our way back to our grand suites over the stable. "Adventure, intrigue, who knows what this assignment will hold for us, amigo. I smell romance and danger in the air, a woman's lace, a dagger at my throat."

"We've investigating a revolt of slaves, Mateo, not a duke's love affair."

"My young friend, life is what you make of it. Mateo Rosas de Oquendo can make a golden ring out of pig's tail. I will show you. Tonight I will take you to a place where you can get the hacienda dust off your garrancha. You have been lying with india village girls so long that you have forgotten what it is like to rub your nose between the breasts of a woman who doesn't smell of tortillas and beans."

"What is this place, Mateo? A convent of nuns? The viceroy's wife's bedroom?"

"A casa de las putas, naturally. The best in the city. Do you have any pesos, amigo? They have a game of cards there called primera that I am a master at. Bring all your money, and you will enjoy every woman in the house and still go home with your pockets full."

I glowed in the brilliance of Mateo's camaraderie. What a friend! He was not only going to take me out to enjoy the riches of a woman's body but would ensure that my pockets were full when I returned home.

There are times, however, when I should slap myself when I get caught up in Mateo's enthusiasm for life and love. Times when I should remember that enough money has passed through Mateo's hands in his lifetime to fill one of the king's treasure ships—without any of it sticking to his fingers.

The first hint that this night might not be as enriching as he promised was when he asked me for my money pouch on the way to the house of gambling and prostitution.

"For safekeeping," he told me, "and profit. I know this card game like I know my mother's face."

New Spain, like Old Spain, is a very Christian country. We thrive upon righteousness and piety. Our conquistadors carried the sword and the Cross. Our priests braved torture and cannibalism to bring the Word to heathens. But we are also a very lustful people with romance in our hearts and a certain practicality when it comes to matters of the flesh. Thus we find nothing inconsistent about having as many whorehouses as churches in the city.

The House of Seven Angels was the best, Mateo assured me. "They have mulattas who are the color of milk and chocolate, whose breasts are fountains that gods would yearn to be suckled upon, whose pink place is as sweet and juicy as a ripe papaya. These women have been bred for bloodlines like the finest horses—for the shape of their haunches, the curve of their breasts, the length of their legs. Cristo, Cristo, such females you have never encountered outside of the spells you were in when the Healer worked his magic potions."

"Are there Spanish women, too?"

"Spanish women? What Spanish woman would be in a whorehouse? Must I cut your throat to teach you respect for the women of my country? Of course there are no Spanish women, although some of the houses are owned by Spanish women, who run them with the permission of their husbands. A Spanish whore would get a hundred offers of marriage her first day in New Spain. There are a few india for those whose luck at the gambling tables was bad. But they do not compare to the mulattas."

An africano almost as big as the front gate of the House of Seven Angels let us in after Mateo flipped him a reale of my money. I memorized the arrogant way Mateo sneered at the man and the contemptuous manner in which he flipped the coin, as if money grew from the lint in his pockets.

The reception area of the house had four card tables set up with men crowded around each.

"Wander around, select the puta who tickles your pene the most. I will run your pesos up so we can each have the best women."

The women of the house were in a room off to the left. They sat on benches padded with red silk cushions. Another slave, almost as large as the one outside, guarded the entry. One could look, but no touching until the financial arrangements had been agreed upon.

Mateo had not lied about the quality of these women. Mulattas like I had never seen, women whose legs could wrap around a man's waist and nearly reach the ceiling after he mounted her. Off to the side were several india girls, of a more delicate nature than the girls I knew, who developed powerful arms and legs from working in the fields and rolling tortillas, but to me they were as pulque is to a fine

Spanish wine. I had had pulque, now it was time to taste another intoxicant.

Several of the women had half masks covering their face. I did not know whether the masks were meant to ape the fashion of well-to-do ladies—or if the women believed their faces were less attractive than their bodies.

One of the masked women, an india, smiled at me. I suspected she wore the mask because she was much older than the other girls, probably in her late thirties, old to be in whorehouse, although she was still firm and reasonábly attractive. Her body was pleasant, but lacked the eroticism of the other women.

I asked the guard about her.

"She's a bondservant, sold to the madam by the magistrate after she was arrested for theft."

Criminals were sold for harsh punishment, men even to the mines, but I was shocked that a woman cóuld be sold into prostitution.

"It was her choice," the guard said. "She could have sewed clothes in an obraje labor shop, but she asked for prostitution because she is allowed to keep extra money given to her by the customers and the work is easier. At her age she would have been better off in a house with only india putas. The owner of this establishment keeps her for only one reason—men who lose at the tables."

I pointed at a particularly lusty wench, a mulatta who I intended to mount and ride as if she were one of Cortes's fourteen famous horses. "That is the one I will sample as soon as my friend is finished playing."

"Good selection, señor. The finest puta in the house, but she is also the most expensive—and there is usually a small token paid to me because she is my wife."

"Naturally," I sniffed, trying not to sound provincial by being shocked that he was renting out his wife.

Pleased that I had made my choice and looking forward to a tryst with a creamy goddess of love, I sought out Mateo at the tables. As I approached he rose from a table with a black look on his face.

"What's the matter?"

"Santo Francisco did not guide the cards to me tonight."

"How did you do?"

"I lost."

"Lost? How much?"

"Everything."

"Everything? *All of my money?*"

"Cristo, not so loud. Do you want to embarrass me?"

"I want to kill you!"

"All is not lost, my young friend." He fingered the cross I wore, the one that Fray Antonio told me was my only memoir of my mother. I had removed the false coloring to expose its beauty. "This fine, holy necklace would bring enough pesos to get me back into the game."

I slapped away his hand. "You are a knave and a blackguard."

"True, but we still need to raise money."

"Sell your horse, the one Cortes rode."

"I can't. The beast is lame. As will be the scoundrel who sold him to me when I catch him. But I wonder if the madam would give me a few pesos for him? She can sell him to the indios for meat."

Walking away from him, I was so angry, if I had had the courage—and the insanity—I would have drawn my sword and asked him to step outside.

The guard was still at the doorway to the harem. I showed him a silver ring with a small red stone that I had gotten in my travels with the Healer.

"This is a powerful ring; it brings luck to those who wear it."

"Give it to your friend who plays cards."

"No, uh, he doesn't know how to use the magic. It is worth ten pesos. I will give it to you for time with the tawny beauty." My tongue refused to refer to her as his wife.

"The ring is worth one peso. You can have fifteen minutes with a one-peso girl."

"One peso! That is thievery. It is worth at least five."

"One peso. *Ten* minutes."

I was desperate. I needed the smell of a woman's perfume in my nostrils as a nosegay to get me through the night of smelling manure in my room at the don's house. Besides, I had stolen the ring after refusing to pay a peso for it.

"All right. Which girl."

He pointed to the oldest india, the masked woman who had selected prostitution over sewing in a labor shop. "Her name is Maria."

"You are a handsome boy. Do you have more money?" she panted.

I lay flat on my back on a hard bed with her bouncing atop me like she was riding a horse after it stepped on hot coals.

"Oh, you are a beast—*pant! pant!*—you have the pene of a horse, the thrust of a bull—*pant! pant!* How much money will you pay if I make your juice come twice?"

We only had ten minutes and while I was capable of exploding juice from my virile part in seconds, I needed to last the full ten minutes to get my peso's worth. She talked continuously from the moment I hurriedly took off my breeches, mostly about how much more money she should get from me. While I had modestly flattered myself as one of the great lovers of New Spain, she was leaving me with the impression that she was more interested in the size of my pocketbook than the precious jewels I carried in my pants.

"You are a fine, handsome boy. It's too bad you don't have more money."

She stopped panting. The ten minutes were almost up.

"More! I need more! I've been holding it, now I need to spend it."

"You have one more peso?" she asked.

"I have nothing!"

She started rocking again and reached down and took hold of the cross I wore. "A beautiful necklace. I'm sure the madam would let you have me all night for this."

"No!" I slapped her hands away from it. I could feel the stirring in my pene, the power building up, ready to gush. "It belonged to my mother," I moaned, thrusting.

"Perhaps God wants me to have it. My own son had one like it."

"Ask him for his."

"I haven't seen him in years. He lives in Veracruz," she panted.

"I lived in Veracruz. What's his name?"

"Cristóbal."

"My name is Cristo—"

She stopped cold and stared down at me. I stopped thrusting and stared up at her. Two dark eyes in the mask stared down at me. The volcano between my legs was shaking my whole body, ready to erupt and pour lava into her.

"*Cristóbal!*" she screamed.

She leapt off the bed and ran from the room. I lay numb, my volcano slowly shrinking. Maria. My mother's Christian name was Maria.

I struggled into my clothes and staggered out of the room to find Mateo. My mind and body were in the grip of a growing sense of horror.

EIGHTY-FOUR

I LEFT THE House of the Seven Angels feeling cold and depressed. Mateo was waiting for me in the courtyard. He sat on the edge of the fountain, flipping his dagger. His face told the story of his luck.

"I lost the horse. When the madam finds out he's lame, she'll send her underlings to rip off my privates, stick them in my mouth, and sew my lips shut."

He noticed my dejected state. What had occurred was too

horrible to reveal, too heinous to share even with a good friend, too infamous to acknowledge even to myself.

He slapped me on the back. "Don't feel so bad. Tell me the truth. You could not get your garrancha up, eh? Don't worry, compadre. Tonight you could not get your sword up, but tomorrow, I swear, when a woman passes within ten feet of you, your sword will reach out of your pants and slip into her."

Morning came and I stayed in my hard bed in my stinking room, refusing to leave, hoping that miasma from the stables would kill me. I had found my mother and then—no! It was too awful to think about. She had not seen me since I was a young boy. Today, I was just a bearded young stranger to her, but a good son would have recognized his own mother. Like Oedipus, I was damned and doomed, tricked by the gods, and deserved only to stick needles into my eyes and spend my days as a blind beggar, tormented by my sins.

Midday I sent a servant to the House of Seven Angeles to ascertain the price of Miaha's freedom. The servant returned with news that the woman had fled during the night, leaving the madam unpaid for her bond debt.

There would be no use searching for her on the streets of the city; she would not be foolish enough to run from her legal bond master and stay around the city. Besides the horror of the act we had committed, my appearance in her life would have ignited anew the troubles that had driven us from the hacienda when I was a boy. As an india, she could disappear forever into the land.

Among his many babblings, Fray Antonio claimed I had no mother. From that I took it to mean that Maria was not my mother. But last night she had claimed me as her son. *¡Ay de mí!* I felt so miserable.

Late in the next afternoon Mateo took me to go to the Alameda. "The don's horses are well enough for pulling a carriage or working cattle, but we can't ride such animals on the Alameda. We would be laughed off of the green."

"Then what will we do?"

"We walk, as if our servants were tending our horses while we stretched our legs."

"Perhaps the señoritas will not notice our poverty."

"What! A Spanish woman not knowing the amount of gold in a man's pouch? Would God not notice the man who murdered the pope? I said that we would walk, not that we would fool anyone."

We strolled along the cool greenery, watching the champion horses and champion women. How envious I was of everything! To be born and raised basking in the reflection of silver and gold—rather than rags and straw. I had chosen the best clothes that the don had handed down to me and a dress sword he had given me. What I had thought on the hacienda was a fine blade with a fancy basket hilt was little more than a kitchen knife on the Alameda. My confidence began to fade as I suspected that people saw the lépero under my clothes.

No matter how I thought of myself as the peacock, there was always something to give away my lack of breeding. Even my hands betrayed me. The hands of the proud men on the Alameda were as soft and delicate as a woman's. They probably had never even lifted on a pair of breeches. My hands were hard and callused from working cattle. I kept them closed, hoping no one would notice that I had used my hands for honest labor.

Women saw my ordinary clothes and lack of a horse, and their eyes slid past me as if I was invisible. But Mateo grabbed their attention no matter how worn the heels of his boots or how frayed the cuffs of his doublet. He had an arrogance about him, not the haughtiness of a dandy, but an aura of danger and excitement that told a woman he was a scoundrel who would steal her heart and jewels but leave her smiling.

I noticed that some of the women and men wore masks,

full-face ones and the type that only covered the upper half of the face.

"Fashion," Mateo said, "it is all the rage. New Spain is always years behind Europe. Masks were the fashion ten years ago when I fought in Italy. Many women even wear them smeared with oil to bed, believing it eases the wrinkles on their faces."

As we walked Mateo told me that he had already been working on the investigation for Don Julio.

"I contacted the man that the don says acts for the Recontonería. He is a strange little man, not at all the cutthroat or with the appearance of blackguard, but more the type who counts sheep and writes down the pounds of wool for a merchant. The don says he is merely a go-between for several notables in the city to whom the pesos taken from illegal pulquerias, whorehouses, and control of the marketplace ultimately passes."

Mateo was describing his negotiations with the man for a pulqueria when I saw a familiar figure. Ramon de Alva rode high in the saddle, a big man on a big horse. I cringed first at the sight of him and then straightened my spine. I was not a young picaro on the streets of Veracruz, but a Spanish gentleman with a sword strapped to my side.

Nothing got past Mateo, and he followed my gaze.

"De Alva, the right hand man of Don Diego de Velez, one of the richest men in New Spain. Alva's said to be rich as Croesus himself, also the best swordsman in the colony—except for myself, of course. Why do you stare at this man as if you wished to put your dagger in his gullet?"

At that moment Alva stopped beside a carriage. The woman in the carriage was wearing a half mask, but I recognized the carriage. Isabella, laughing gaily at something Alva said, carrying on her flirtation and the don's disgrace in plain sight for all the notables of the city to see.

Someone snickered off to my left. A group of young hidalgos were watching the exchange between Alva and Isabella. The one who snickered wore a gold doublet and breeches with red and green slashes that made him look like a bright jungle bird.

"Look at Alva with the converso's wife," the canary said. "We should all let her do our penes in the viper way. What else is a converso's wife good for?"

I flew at the yellow bird and punched him in the face. He staggered backward.

"You are a woman," I told him, uttering the worse insult one could give an hombre, "and I'm going to use you as one."

He snarled and went for his sword. I grabbed for mine—*and my hand fumbled with the basket on the hilt!* My sword was only half drawn when the yellow bird lunged with his for my throat.

A sword flashed between us and, the bird's sword was countered. Mateo followed with lightning thrusts that cut the hidalgo's arm. The man's sword fell to the ground, and his friends drew their swords. Mateo was quickly on them, and soon all three were in full retreat.

From across the Alameda, the horn of the viceroy's soldados blew.

"Run!" Mateo shouted.

I ran behind him into a residential area. When there were no sounds of pursuit, we walked in the direction of the don's house.

Mateo was angrier than I had ever seen him and I kept silent, shamed at my failure. He had warned me not to play the fop and wear a fancy sword, but I had done so and would now be bleeding to death on the Alameda if it were not for his quick blade.

When we were near the don's house and his face was no longer the color of the Smoking Mountain when it spit out fire. I mumbled my amends.

"You warned me about the basket guard. I was too concerned with playing the dandy than being the swordsman that you taught me to be."

"*Tried* to teach you," he corrected. "I told you that as a swordsman, you are a dead man. I am not angry about your foolish attempt at swordplay. I am enraged about the position you put the don in."

"The don? I was defending his honor!"

"You were defending his honor? *You?* A half-blood who is just a few steps from the sewers? You defend the honor of a Spanish gentleman?"

"They didn't know I'm a mestizo. They think I'm Spanish."

He grabbed me by the throat. "I don't give a damn if you are the Marqués de la Valle himself. The code of hombria demands that a man fight his own battle for a woman." He shoved me away.

"I don't understand what I did wrong."

"You put the don in danger."

I was still in a fog. "How did I affect the don by defending his honor?"

"By putting his honor at issue, you foul and disgusting lépero. The don is not a fool—he knows his wife is spreading her legs for Alva, and other men before him. They have no marriage; he stays away from the city to keep from being disgraced."

"Why doesn't he do something about it?"

"What is he to do? Ramon de Alva is a master swordsman. He was weaned with a dagger in his teeth. The don is a man of letters; his weapon is the quill. If he confronts Alva, he is a dead man. And it is not just Alva. If it were not the majordomo, it would be a dozen other men. Or some fool who smirks and calls him a converso as if it were a form of leprosy.

"The don is an honorable man. He is a brave man. But he is intelligent, and he chooses his fights because he is not a fool. When you attack a man in his name, you create not just a blood feud but bring the intrigue between Isabella and Alva into the open, forcing the don to take action."

To say I was shocked and devastated by my stupidity would not describe my agony.

Mateo sighed. "It is not as bad as I have portrayed. You did not say why you attacked the man, and you are new and unknown in the city. I recognized one of his friends as the brother of a lady I have become acquainted with. Tomorrow I will tell her that you attacked the man because you thought he was the culprit who was singing love songs to your betrothed. Without identifying you, I will pass the message that you were mistaken and regret the incident. That will not keep you from getting killed if the man I wounded finds you, but it will protect the don."

We reached the house and paused in the coolness of the courtyard, while Mateo lit one of those tobacco leaves that the indios rolled into a turd.

"More was in your face when you looked at Alva than his affaire d'amour with Isabella. I saw hate, the kind one gives to a man who has violated his mother."

I flinched at the reference to mothers. "I knew about the intrigue between Isabella and Alva," I told him in a low tone after making sure no servants were in the area. When I described the romping in the courtyard at the Velez hacienda, Mateo muttered a curse that if it came true, Isabella would burn eternally in the fires of hell.

"Then that is it? The affair with Isabella?"

"Yes."

"You are a lying dog of a lépero. Tell me the truth before I cut off your testicules and feed them to the fish in the fountain."

Defeated, I sat down on the edge of the fountain and told Mateo the whole story—almost. I left out Maria and the whorehouse. It had been bottled up in me for so long, it came out in a gush of words and hand wringing—the strange vendetta of the old woman in black, being told my father was a gachupin, the questioning by Ramon de Alva, the murder of Fray Antonio, the search for me.

After I was finished, Mateo called for a servant and instructed him to bring us wine. Then he lit another foul-smelling tobacco leaf.

"Let us assume for a moment that your fray was correct, that your father was a gachupin." He shrugged. "There are thousands of half-blood bastards in New Spain, mestizos, mulattos, even ones with chino blood from women brought on the Manila galley. A bastard of even pure blood cannot inherit from his father unless he is recognized and made an heir. If that were the case, you would not have been raised by a defrocked priest in the gutters of Veracruz."

"I have had these same thoughts. I have no rights under the law and am hardly considered human. The reason why Alva wants to kill me remains as big a mystery to me as why someone would want to breathe in foul smoke from a plant leaf."

"The tobacco comforts me when there is no woman around to caress me." He stood up and stretched and yawned. "Tomorrow you must go back out onto the streets and become a lépero again. And I must buy a pulqueria."

Mateo was usually so full of advice—often bad—that his failure to offer a solution to the matter of Ramon de Alva left me . . . empty.

"What do you think, Mateo? Why would Alva kill the fray and want to kill me?"

"I don't know, Bastardo, but we shall find out."

"How?"

He stared at me as if I had asked him the color of his sister's petticoats.

"Why, we will *ask* him!"

EIGHTY-FIVE

THE NEXT MORNING I was happy to be out of my Spanish clothes and into the rags of a lépero. From an indio currando I procured a pinch of the powder that the Healer had used to inflate my nose. I had stopped bathing after the don gave me the assignment, and even stopped washing my hands. Still, I would have had to roll in a pigsty for a week to have gotten back the true feel of the gutter.

I was anxious to test my old begging skills and was quickly disappointed as one person after another walked by me without dropping a single coin into my dirty palm. Contorting my limbs was out of the question. Not only might I be recognized, but lack of practice had stiffened my joints.

Weeping, wailing, pleading, whining—nothing brought a coin to me. Mexico was a city like Veracruz, but it was twenty times bigger and I assumed that gave me twenty times the opportunity to swindle. I soon learned that it merely increased the number of times I would be quirted or kicked.

Perhaps it is me, I thought. Being a lépero was like being a gentleman—it was not just the clothes one wore, not even just the way one walked or talked, but the way one *thought.* I no longer thought like a lépero and it showed to those I approached.

Giving it another try, I spotted a fine corner for begging at an inn near the marketplace. Inns catered to visitors, and visitors were more likely to open their purses. I was turned down immediately by a fat merchant—and then spotted an angry bull of a lépero ready to slit my belly for invading his territory.

I hurried away, deciding to take Don Julio's advice. I would wander among the people on the streets, especially the africanos and mulattos, keeping my ears and eyes open.

Veracruz had as many africanos and mulattos on the street as indios and español combined. Ciudad Mexico did not have that high a percentage of blacks, but their presence was significant. Black-skinned household servants were considered more prestigious than brown-skinned ones, and those with white skin were extremely rare. No lady of quality could call herself such unless she had at least one personal maid of African heritage.

And the Spanish bureaucracy, which categorized everyone according to blood and place of birth, created three different classes of africano. Bozales were blacks born in Africa; ladines were "acculturated" blacks who had lived in other Spanish domains, such as the Caribbean islands, before coming to New Spain; negros criollos were born in New Spain.

Even the Church had forsaken the poor africano. Unlike the feverish effort to save the soul of the indio, little effort was made to instruct the africano in Christianity. Africanos and mulattos were barred from the priesthood.

Fray Antonio believed that africanos were deliberately not taught Christ's message that all of us were equal in God's eyes.

Even more than the indio, the africanos thus continued their own, often strange, religious practices, some of which they had learned on the Dark Continent and others that they had acquired here—witchcraft, worship of strange objects, deviltry. They followed their own set of healers, sorcerers and pagan rites not dissimilar to those of the indio.

I encountered an africano woman selling love potions from where she sat on a blanket next to a building wall. She stirred the potion with the forefinger of a hanged man . . . *shades of Snake Flower!* I hurried along, determined not to donate a piece of my virile organ to her pot.

It is said that the Bozales, born in Africa and brought here aboard Portuguese slave ships, are much more submissive than either the ladines brought from the Caribbean or the criollos born here. Friendless, homeless, without family, pursued and captured like animals by slave hunters, starved and brutalized in the holes of slave ships, and then beaten into submission by vicious slave masters in the New World, africanos had been dehumanized into a work animal.

No large groups of africanos assembled on the streets, and I had to move among the smaller groups of two or three. The viceroy had forbidden africanos from assembling on the street or in private in groups of more than three. The penalty for a first offense was two hundred lashes while the slave's left hand was nailed to the whipping post. For a second offense, castration.

Even at a slave's funeral, no more than four male slaves

and four female were allowed to come together to mourn the dead.

Almost all of the servants I observed were negros criollo. Not one had the fire expected from a slave fresh off a ship and still not broken to the yoke of slavery. What I heard was everything from amused contempt for their white masters to smothering hatred.

Don Julio had arranged for me to work a day in an *obrajes.* A small factory, usually no larger than a hacienda stable, the obrajes produced inexpensive products—cheap, coarse wool clothing and the like, goods that were not barred by finer imports from Spain.

The obrajes owners contracted with the authorities for prisoners. One arrested for a minor offense was sold to the shop owner by the authorities for a specific time. A sentence of three or four years for stealing something of little value or failing to pay a debt was common.

The system had great merit in the public mind. The officer who sold the prisoner had himself bought his position from the Crown. The sale helped him recoup his investment, and the prisoner earned his keep. It permitted the shop owners to produce goods cheaply while still turning huge profits. Most of the bond workers were chained to their work station for all their waking hours, being released only to take in food and eliminate waste.

Some workers were slaves who were not chained to their workplace but spent their days unloading raw materials and loading finished goods or running errands to pick up food or supplies. Investigating a shop for rumors, after a few hours I realized it was useless. The shop owner and his overseers kept the workers going at full speed at all times. I left and went back onto the streets.

I saw Ramon de Alva walking along the arcade on the main plaza. A young man about my own age was with him and at first I supposed him to be Alva's son, but realized that the similarity was in style, not physical appearance. They walked like predators, sizing up the next kill, and studied the world with hardened eyes. I followed them, puzzling over Mateo's remark that one day Ramon would tell me why he wanted me dead.

The younger man stirred a memory in me, but the recollection stayed out of reach, slipping away like a fish each time I reached to grab it. Noting the coach's coat of arms inscribed on its doors, I knew who the young man was. Luis. The last time I saw him he was the proposed betrothed of Eléna in Veracruz. His facial scars, the result of pox or some type of burning, remained with him. He was handsome despite them, but they coarsened his appearance.

On impulse, I followed the coach. It moved no faster in the heavy traffic than quick-footed pedestrians. I wanted to know where he lived. He was not only involved with Ramon, but was related to the old woman.

The palatial house that the coach stopped at bore the same coat of arms on the stone wall near the main gate. The house was near the Alameda on a street that held some of the finest palaces in the city. Clearly, Luis belonged to one of the most prominent families in New Spain.

I noted the house well, determined to investigate it further, and turned to leave after the carriage had entered the premises and the street guard went inside to assist the occupants. Another carriage pulled up as I started to walk away, and I stopped and pretended to examine something on the ground in the hope that it held the elderly matron and that I would get a fresh look at her.

Rather than entering the compound, the carriage stopped beside the main gate and a young woman stepped down from it unassisted. I shuffled toward her, toying with the idea of practicing my beggar skills on her, when she turned and looked at me.

Holy Mother of Christ! I stared into the face of a ghost.

The years since last I saw her had not left her food for worms in the grave but had turned her into a woman. What a woman! *¡Bella!* Beautiful! The beauty Michelangelo created when God directed his hand to paint angels.

Gaping, I staggered to her, my knees weak. *"I thought you were dead!"*

A small scream escaped her lips as she saw me rush toward her in my lépero guise.

"No! No! It's me—from Veracruz. They told me you were dead."

The gate guard came at me with a whip. "Filthy beggar!"

I caught the blow on my forearm. Before going out on a street mission to expose violent insurrectos, I'd put on the metal forearm guard Mateo recommended. I blocked the whip with my right forearm, stepped in, and hit the guard across the face with the metal of my left one.

Eléna's carriage driver leaped off the coach, and I heard the pounding of footsteps from the courtyard. Scrambling around the carriage, I dashed across the street and ran between houses.

I returned home to shave my beard and change my filthy ragged hat and shirt for different filthy rags before I returned to the street to continue the slave investigation. In a few days my nose would be back to normal size, but I would not be recognized—they would be looking for a full-bearded lépero. It would be assumed that I had intended to attack Eléna. A lépero who attacked a gachupin would be sent to the silver mines for a life sentence at the hardest imaginable labor—if he was not hanged instead.

I wished I had struck Luis's face rather than the guard's. But I was more excited about Eléna than my increased peril.

"*She's alive!*" I thought, my heart pounding.

Why did the servant say she was dead? Was the servant merely mistaken—or was the picture not of Eléna? I rolled my memory over and over and decided that there was a good resemblance between Eléna and the girl in the picture, but no more than one might expect between sisters. Regardless of the solution to the mystery, the truth was that Eléna lived.

How was a half blood, a breed lower than a cur, filthier than a pig, with the habits of sloths and the rats that eat their own babies, to claim a Spanish beauty betrothed to nobleman? *¡Ay de mí!* It suddenly struck me. She may already be married to Luis. If she was, I will kill him and marry his widow.

But she had seen me back on the streets as a lépero. Would I never shed my scabrous outer shell? Dirty feet, dirty hands, dirty face, dirty hair, unkempt, unbathed, how would I ever find a dark-eyed Spanish beauty like Eléna to love me if I am forever the Marqués de Beggars?

The only way I would ever be able to stand in the same room with her was if I possessed wealth and power.

My mind began to toy with ideas on how to become wealthy. Mateo had also condemned our lack of money and had spoken of the days when he made much dinero selling libros deshonestos.

Eh, amigos, I would have to sell many dirty books to make my fortune. But as with Hercules shoveling mierda from stables, there would be a reward after the dirty work was finished.

After spending a day on the streets, listening to the strange mélange of slave languages, I came to the conclusion that the africanos in the city were indeed agitated. A young servant girl had been beaten to death by an older Spanish woman, who believed that her husband was having sex with the girl. The Spanish woman did nothing to her husband because he forced sex on a servant girl, and of course, the authorities did not prosecute the woman for killing the girl.

I heard the words, "red frog," a number of times, as if it were a meeting place and I soon concluded that it might be a pulqueria.

Rushing back to the don's house, I found Mateo sleeping on a hammock in the shade of fruit trees. From the pile on the ground near the hammock, he looked like he had had a hard day drinking wine and smoking dog droppings.

"I know where the slaves meet secretly. A pulqueria called 'the Red Frog.' "

Mateo yawned and stretched his arms. "And you wake me from a wondrous dream for this? I had just slayed two dragons, won a kingdom, and was making love to a goddess when you interrupted me with your jabber."

"Excuse me, *Don* Mateo, Knight of the Golden Cross of Amadís of Gaul, but as one who would like to pay Don Julio back for the gracious food he provides, not to mention his hospitality above the stable, I learned a vital piece of information almost at the cost of my life. Tonight we must investigate fire-breathing africano rebels who meet at a den called the Red Frog."

Mateo yawned, took a long draw from a wine bottle, smacked his lips, and lay back. "I rented the establishment for the next several nights from the owner with the assistance of the Recontonería. We are offering free pulque to the slaves. If that doesn't get them talking, nothing will. The owner was most accommodating. Not even swine who run illegal pulquerias for slaves want a rebellion—bad for business."

Mateo went back to fighting dragons and rescuing beautiful princesses. I encountered Isabella going to my room. Feigning an interest in coats of arms, I described Luis's to her and asked her if she knew the family. She told me it was the family of Don Eduardo de la Cerda and his son, Luis. Isabella was a storehouse of gossip and rumor, and I quickly ascertained that Luis and Eléna were about to be betrothed.

That meant, that if I hurried, I could kill Luis without making her a widow.

EIGHTY-SIX

THAT NIGHT I was a server of pulque to slaves. The lowest possible grade of pulque, barely fermented and watered down, was the usual swill served to the slaves. But thanks to the generosity of Mateo Rosas, pulqueria proprietor extraordinare, they had pure pulque in which both cuapatle and brown sugar had been added to give it gusto.

Mateo took a taste of it before we opened the doors and spit it out.

"This stuff would burn the hair off a mule."

I soon discovered that the fifty africanos in the room, forty men and ten women, had a better constitution for strong drink than the indios. It took barrel after barrel before I could detect its affect in their eyes and voices. Soon, though, they were laughing and dancing and singing.

"We're going to run out of this swill pretty soon," Mateo whispered to me. "Get the agitators working."

Two africanos who had been recruited to obtain information were in the room. At my signal, one of them climbed atop a table and shouted for silence.

"Poor Isabella was killed by her master, beaten to death because the woman's husband raped her, and no one does anything about it. What are we going to do about it?"

Angry roars came every corner of the room.

Isabella? Too bad it was the wrong Isabella.

Soon the room was in an uproar as one person and another shouted solutions, most of which involved killing all the Spanish in the country. No one seemed to take notice that the generous bartender was Spanish.

More pulque made the rounds, and someone yelled that they needed a king to lead them. One candidate after another was shouted down, when one stood up and said his name was Yanga. It wasn't the Yanga I had known, and one of our agitators whispered to me, "His name's Allonzo and he's owned by a goldsmith."

But the name worked magic, and he was quickly elected "King of New Africa." His woman, Belonia, was elected queen on the first shout.

After that, everyone got drunker.

There were no plans made to obtain weapons, to recruit soldiers, establish a timetable, kill anyone.

We broke open the last barrel of pulque and walked out, letting the slaves enjoy themselves at no expense. We did this routine three more nights without any suggestion of insurrection. What we did confirm was that the slaves were victims of hopelessness.

"Tavern talk," Mateo said, disgusted. "That's all it is, just as the don thought. They are angry over the death of the girl and the injustices to themselves, but it's not enough of a spark to ignite them. These slaves are well-fed, little worked, and sleep on more comfortable beds than Isabella provides us. They are not like their brothers and sisters on the plantations, who are starved and worked to death. Bah! A friend's husband was not returning until late night from Guadalajara. Such a woman! And I missed a night of bliss to serve swill to slaves."

Don Julio returned from inspecting the tunnel the next day and Mateo and I reported to him.

"Talk, that is all I thought it was. I will report immediately to the viceroy. I'm sure he will be relieved."

The don had no assignment for us. I had suggested to Mateo that it was time for us to earn some money so we could live as gentlemen instead of stable boys, and he said he would think the matter over. I soon learned that he did more than think about it.

"The Recontonería representative is willing to finance the importation and sale of libros deshonesto, the more indecent the better. I have Seville contacts from the days when I was one of the great autors of comedias in that city. It would be little work for them to arrange for the purchase and shipment from Spain and for me to arrange to clear customs in Veracruz. The Recontonería operates there, too, and will provide me with names of each person who must be given a bite."

"What does the Recontonería get out of this?"

"Our heads if we cheat them. They have their own version of the royal fifth—they get one peso for every five that we earn."

"Is there any competition for this business?"

"There was, but we no longer have to worry about him."

"Why did he leave the business?"

"The Inquisition burned him in Puebla a week ago."

Life seemed bright as I went to bed that night. Don Julio was pleased with our work on the slave revolt rumors. Mateo had a scheme to make us rich enough to afford the horses and clothes we needed to prance on the Alameda. I intended to become the richest man in New Spain by smuggling books banned by the Inquisition. And to marry the best woman in the colony.

¡Ay de mí! We mortals make many plans for our puny lives, but the Dark Sisters weave the Fates's shroud, not ourselves.

EIGHTY-SEVEN

LATE THAT NIGHT I was awakened by noise on the streets and in the house. I instantly assumed that the house had been attacked. Don Julio had gone back to the tunnel, taking Mateo with him, leaving me as master of the house, at least in name, since Isabella barely permitted me into the main part of the house.

I grabbed my sword and found Isabella, Inez, Juana, and the servants huddled in terror.

"The slaves have revolted!" Isabella cried. "Everyone is fleeing to the viceroy's palace for protection."

"How do you know?"

Inez, the nervous little bird, flapped her wings and announced that we would all be murdered, with the women raped first.

Juana said, "People heard an army of slaves running through the streets, and the alarm has spread."

Clutching a strongbox, Isabella told the servants to follow her to the viceroy's and protect her.

"I need the servants for a litter for Juana!" I told her.

She ignored me and left, taking the frightened servants with her, even the africano servants trembling in fear at the slave revolt.

Carrying Juana on my back with her frail sticks of legs around my waist, I left the house with her and Inez. People were hurrying by, women with their jewel boxes and men with swords and strongboxes. All around me I heard word of one neighborhood after another entirely wiped out, murdered by the rampaging slaves, who were cutting up the victims and performing frightful rites over the remains.

Where had Mateo and I gone wrong? How could we have so misjudged the intent of the slaves? Even if the city survived, Don Julio and his two trusty spies would end up with our heads rolling off the chopping block.

Times like this caused my lépero instincts to surface, and my first thought was to get a fast horse out of the city—not out of fear of the slaves, but racing to the tunnel to warn Don Julio and Mateo that we had guessed wrong and must flee. I would have willingly left Isabella and Inez to the unkind hands of the slaves, but I could not abandon poor Juana.

The whole city appeared to have poured into the main plaza. Men, women, and crying children, most, like us, in bedclothes, screaming at the viceroy to put down the rebellion.

From a balcony of the palace, the viceroy called for silence. Criers at high places around the square one after the other repeated the viceroy's words.

"An hour ago a herd of pigs being brought into the city for market got loose and ran through the streets. People heard the pounding hooves and thought it was an army of slaves."

He was silent for a moment.

"Go home. There is no rebellion."

Among more primitive people, great moments in history are remembered and retold or sung time and time again around the night fire. Civilized peoples write the events down and pass their history onto their descendants in the form of marks on paper.

The night the people of the City of Mexico were panicked into believing a slave revolt was occurring because a herd of pigs had run through the city has been immortalized in a thousand diaries and recorded by historians at the university. Else who would believe that the people of one of the great cities of the world could behave so foolishly?

Would the tale have ended there, our children's children and thereafter could have laughed a little at the image of the great dons and ladies of the city running through the streets in their bedclothes, clutching their coin and jewels to their bosom. But the Spaniard is a proud beast, a conqueror of empires, a ravager of continents, and he does not take humiliation without drawing his sword and spilling blood.

Demands went to the viceroy to take care of the slave "problem." Don Julio's report that a king and queen had been elected and the tavern talk of rebellion were deemed proof that a rebellion was still imminent. Something had to be done by the viceroy to calm the fears and redress the shame.

The Audiencia, the high court of New Spain over which the viceroy presided, ordered the arrest of thirty-six africanos whose names had been recorded at the pulqueria the night Mateo and I got them drunk. Of those arrested, five men and two women were quickly found guilty of insurrection and hanged in a public square. Afterward, their heads were chopped off and displayed on pikes at the entrance to the causeways and the main plaza. The others were severely punished, the men whipped and castrated, the women beaten until blood flowed freely and bone on their backs glistened.

I did not attend the hangings and floggings, although most of the gentry of the city had been there, but I had the misfortune to come face-to-face with King Yanga and Queen Isabella. Their eyes followed me as I walked across the main plaza. Fortunately their impaled heads could not swivel on the pikes, and I was able to hurry away from their accusing gaze.

Mateo left for Veracruz to send off a letter to an old friend in Seville who would arrange for the purchase of books prohibited by the Inquisition. He would send the letter on one of the lobo ships that raced to avoid pirates between Veracruz and Seville in between voyages of the great treasure fleet.

To obtain a proper list that we thought would be appealing to buyers, we consulted the Inquisition's list of banned books, the *Index Librorum Prohibitorum.*

Mateo's eye went to the chivalric romances. Instead, I advised that we order some books for women who are married to bores and suffered unrequited passions, books in which a man is virile but whose hands are gentle yet forceful, and in whose arms the woman finds all the passion she will ever desire.

For persons whose tastes ran more to Roman orgies, I selected two books that would have made Caligula blush.

Added to that was a book on casting horoscopes, the casting of spells, and two of the scientific tomes I knew Don Julio harbored secretly in his library.

Though not all of the books were banned in Spain, they were all on the prohibited list in New Spain under the theory that they would pollute the mind of the indios. How many indios could afford to buy a book, and how many could read more than their name, had clearly not been taken into account. In truth, few indios could even read the *list* of banned books!

Eh, you ask, what is the motive for prohibiting the importation of books to keep indios who could not read from reading them? The real motive was to control the reading and the thoughts, not of the indios, but of the colonists. Permitting the criollos free rein in their thinking might stimulate contrary thoughts, such as those that festered in the

Low Countries where the Dutch and others battled the Crown over religious and other differences.

Even using lobo boats, we waited over six months for the first shipment of books. Don Julio spent most of his days supervising the work on the tunnel, with an occasional visit to the city to argue with the viceroy's staff for the workers and supplies needed to do the work.

He left Mateo and me to our own vices, and we went quickly went to work when the books arrived. The man who had sold the banned libros had run a print shop just off the main plaza, near the building of the Inquisition. His shop had been abandoned, and his widow soon found there were no buyers for the business. Printing was not a popular profession anywhere in New Spain. Books could not be printed in the colony because the king had granted the exclusive right to sell books to a publisher in Seville. New World printers could only print items required by merchants and religious materials needed by the frays. The fact that this print shop was located almost adjoining the headquarters of the Inquisition and that its last owner had been burned meant no one was eager to acquire the business.

Before the books arrived, Mateo had arranged with the widow of the printer to rent the business in exchange for a percentage of our profits.

"It is a perfect cover for us," Mateo said.

"But it's nearly on the doorstep of the Inquisition!"

"Exactly. The Holy Office knows no one would be foolish enough to operate a prohibited business under their nose."

"Isn't that what the last printer was doing?"

"He was a drunk and a fool. He was supposed to send a case of religious printing to a convent in Puebla and a case of banned books to his partner in crime. Unfortunately, he had drunk enough wine that night to make him cross-eyed when he marked the boxes. So you can imagine what the nuns received . . ."

I wondered what he thought when the familiars of the

Inquisition showed him the box that was supposed to contain pious tomes and instead had libros written by the devil himself. Had the printer been a lépero, he would have shown shock at the discovery and been aghast that Lucifer could turn prayers into lust.

"I still don't understand why we need the printer's business," I said.

"How did you plan to sell the books? Spread a blanket under the arcade in the plaza and lay the books out? The widow has a list of customers that the printer supplied. And customers know how to contact the printer's establishment."

While Mateo occupied himself in making contact with the printer's former customers, I found myself fascinated with the mechanism called a printer's press. I was intrigued both with the history of printing and how a press was used to put words on paper.

Without letting Don Julio know about my motives, I steered him into a conversation about the history of printing. He told me that words—and picture words like the Egyptians and Aztecs used—were originally etched in stone or marked on leather with dye. While the Aztecs and the Egyptians used bark and papyrus to make paper, better methods were known to the Chinese and learned by the Arabs from Chinese prisoners taken at the Battle of Talas in 751. The Arabs spread the knowledge of paper making across their Islamic world, and Moors carried it to Spain where the art was highly perfected. The Chinese were also the ones who perfected the art of printing by the use of moveable type.

The peoples of China have given the world many wonders, the don told me. The society was so amazing that when Marco Polo came back from their land and told his fellow Europeans of the things he had seen, they called him a liar.

"But the Chinese," Don Julio said, "like the Aztecs, were prisoners of their own writing techniques. Aztec picture writing and the thousands of marks used by the people of China does not lend itself easily to printing. It was a

German named Gutenberg who used the Chinese techniques of moveable type and paper to print large numbers of books. He was doing this forty or fifty years before Columbus discovered the New World."

While the Chinese had originally used hardened-baked clay for type, the type in use for printing today was a mixture of lead, tin, and antimony, an alchemists combination of metals soft enough to be easily turned molten and molded into letters but hard enough to give thousands of imprints on paper before wearing out. The pieces of type are formed by pouring the molten lead into molds made from a special mixture of hard iron.

"Another great step in printing was the use of a codex rather than a roll," he said. Rolls of paper were difficult to handle and print on. When clever printers cut the rolls into sheets to be attached on one side like books are now done, the sheets could be run through a printing press.

"Book selling and making are not considered honorable trades," Don Julio said. He surprised me by informing me that he had once owned a print shop. "I used it to publish my scientific findings on the geography of New Spain and the mining industry. You will find the works in my library. I sold the press after it was discovered that my pressman was coming in at night to print libros deshonestos, showing people having sex with animals. He was arrested by the Inquisition and fortunately he had done the printing at a time when I had returned to Spain and hence could not involve me. I sold the press immediately for a pittance, happy that I had not been burned at the stake, with the scandalous sheets used to get the fire going."

He told me the viceroy called printing and book selling, which were customarily done out of the same shop, a vulgar profession.

And the Inquisition took special interest in those who printed books and other documents. Bishops often referred to it as a "black art" and the reference was not just to the color of ink. The Church frowned on reading other than that necessary for religious training and good moral character, which of course, is why the libros de caballerias like Amadís of Gaul were banned in New Spain.

The Inquisition paid particular attention to the printing business in New Spain and decreed that no book be printed or sold without permission of the Church. Since the king had sold away New World printing rights to Seville publishers, the range of books one could have published was few indeed even before the Inquisition became involved. One could even get in trouble for printing religious works, for Christian doctrine to appear in any language but Latin was considered heresy. Even a translation of the Bible into Náhuatl was seized. The Church wanted to ensure that it controlled what the indio read, just as it insisted upon not having the Bible translated into Spanish.

Permission to publish had to be obtained from the Inquisition, and the name of the bishop giving permission was to be noted on the front page of the book along with other information that had come to be included in the colophon—the title itself, the name of the author, the name of the publisher, and sometimes a sentence or two praising God.

Don Julio had told me that this title page originated from the days when medieval scribes placed their names, the date they finished their labors, and quite often a notation about the book or a short prayer at the end. He had several medieval works in his library, and he showed me the inscriptions at the end of the codices.

His library also contained the first book that was printed in the New World. Referred to as a Short Doctrine on Christianity, the *Breve y más compendiosa doctrina christiana en lengua mexicana y castellana* was published in 1539 by Juan Pablos, a printer from Italy, for Juan de Zumárraga, the first bishop of the City of Mexico. "The first book we *know* of," the don said, "but there are always rogues who would print their mother's sexual confessions and sell them for a few pesos."

The don's comments about book rogues only earning a "few pesos" proved to be prophetic. Mateo and I soon learned that after we paid off the book publisher and go-between in Seville, customs and Inquisition officials on two continents, the ravenous Recontonería in the colony, and the grieving widow who sold us the right to be criminals in her husband's shoes, we had almost nothing left for ourselves.

This put Mateo into a black mood and sent him off to drink and lust and fight. The failure of my first large criminal scheme, and with it my dream of being a hidalgo who could at least stand in the same room with Eléna without being horsewhipped, had left me pensive. My own dark mood was aggravated every time I thought about what had happened with the woman Maria. I refused to even think of her as my mother. As the fray said, I have no mother. I carried that mood with me to the print shop, where it had become my habit to tinker.

For some time I examined and experimented with the printing press in the shop we had acquired. Books had made me something more than a social outcast, at least in the minds of Fray Antonio, Mateo, and the don. Because books carried so much power, so many thoughts and ideas and knowledge, I had always considered that there was something divine about their construction, that perhaps they came into being in a blaze of heavenly light and fire, as I imagined the Ten Commandments must have come to Moses.

It was a shock to sit down at the printing press, take the six letters that formed the word "**C-r-i-s-t-o**," place them in a type holder and attach the holder to one of the two metal plates of the press, brush a few drops of ink over the letters, slip in a piece of paper, and bring the other plate of the press so the letters and the paper pressed together . . .

Santa Maria! When I saw my name in print, saw that like what God had done for Moses, I had created a work that could be passed down the ages, something of me that could be read by future generations besides the name on my headstone, I was so impassioned tears came to my eyes.

After that I played with the press, experimenting with

type setting, until I had become rather proficient at it. All this knowledge came to fruit when I awoke Mateo to tell him what scheme had captured my thoughts.

He came out of sleep and bed with a dagger in hand, but lay back after threatening to quarter me with a dull blade.

"I have found our fortune."

He moaned and rubbed his forehead. "I am no longer interested in *earning* a fortune. A true hombre wins treasure with his sword."

"Mateo, it has occurred to me that if the works we spend so much money to import from the peninsula were printed here, we could make great profit on them."

"And if the king offered you his daughter and Castile, you could wear fancy clothes and eat the best food."

"It's not that difficult. We have imported copies of some of the best indecent books available in Spain. If we printed them, we would avoid the great expense of getting them here."

"Have you been kicked in the head by one of the don's horses? It takes a printing press to print books."

"We have a printing press."

"It takes knowledge."

"I have learned how to use the press."

"Workers."

"I can buy a bond servant that is heading for the obrajes."

"Someone to burn at the stake if the Inquisition finds out."

"I will obtain a very stupid bond servant."

We selected a very thin volume of lewd nonsense as our first project. Appropriately enough, our bond servant's name was Juan, the same as the printer of the first book in New Spain. He was not as stupid as I would have liked him to be, but he made up for it with greed. He had been sentenced to four years in the silver mines and to have been diverted to a print shop had saved his life—the average life span in the mines was less than a year for those sentenced to penal servitude.

Like myself, he was a mestizo and lépero, but unlike me, who had claims to being a gentleman, he epitomized the common concept that léperos are the product of abuse of pulque.

The fact that I had saved his life from the dreaded northern mines had not endeared me to him because he was a street animal. However, knowing how the mind of a lépero works, not just the avarice but the tainted logic, rather than paying him in the hopes he would not run away but remain faithful to the sentence imposed, I provided the opportunity for him to occasionally steal from me.

One of his most important benefits, besides the fact that his criminality and fear of going to the mines gave him a small amount of obedience, if not loyalty, to me, was the fact that he could not read or write.

"That means he won't know what's he's printing. I told him we are printing nothing but copies of the lives of saints and I have an engraving of the stigmata of San Francis that we will use over all our books."

"If he can't read or write, how can he set type?" Mateo asked.

"He doesn't read the books he's setting the type for, he's merely duplicating the letters in the book with letters from the type tray. Besides, I will set much of the type myself."

The first book we published in New Spain, which while not having the solemn tone of Bishop Zumárraga's work on Christian doctrine, and would have been considered scandalous by respectable people, was a great success.

Mateo was deeply impressed by the pile of ducats that was left over after paying our expenses. "We have cheated the author of his due, the publisher of his profit, the king of his fifth, the custom officials of their bite. . . . Cristo, you are a gifted scoundrel. Because of your talent as a publisher, I am permitting you to publish my own novel, *Chronicle of the very remarkable Three Knights Tablante of Seville who defeated Ten Thousand Howling Moors and Five Frightful Monsters and set the rightful King upon the throne of Con-*

stantinople and claimed a Treasure larger than that held by any King of Christendom."

My dismay was revealed on my face.

"You do not want to publish a literary masterpiece that was proclaimed the work of angels in Spain and sold better than anything those dolts Vega and Cervantes ever wrote—or stole—from me?"

"It's not that I don't *want* to publish it, it's just that I don't think our little printing venture could do justice to—"

Mateo's dagger blade appeared under my chin.

"Print it."

We had been in the business for some months when we received our first visit from the Inquisition.

"We did not know you were in the business of printing," a fish-faced man wearing the uniform of a familiar of the Inquisition told me. His name was Jorge Gomez. "You have not submitted your materials to the Holy Office and obtained from it permission to print."

I had carefully prepared a cover story and had prominently displayed, the "book" on saints that we were printing. I apologized profusely and explained that the owner of the shop was in Madrid to obtain exclusive rights to print and sell in New Spain matters concerning saints.

"He left Juan and me here to prepare for full printing of the tomes when he returns with the royal license and presents it to the viceroy and the Holy Office."

I again expressed my regret and offered the man a gratis copy of the book when printing was completed.

"What else do you print while your master is gone?" the Inquisition official asked.

"Nothing. We cannot even print the complete book on saints until our master returns with enough paper and ink to finish the job."

Familiars were not priests but technically just "friends" of the Holy Office, volunteers who assisted the inquisitors. In truth, they wore the green cross of the Inquisition and acted as a secret constabulary who performed services ranging from acting as bodyguards to inquisitors, to breaking into homes in the middle of the night to arrest those accused and haul them to the dungeon of the Holy Office.

Familiars were feared by all. Their reputation was so dreadful that the king occasionally used the terror they strike to keep those around him from swaying in their loyalty.

"You understand that you are forbidden to print any books or other works without first obtaining the proper permission. If it should be found out that you were in fact involved in any illegitimate printing . . ."

"Of course, *Don* Jorge," I said, rewarding the honorific to a peasant whose closest encounter with being genteel was stepping in the manure of a gentleman's horse. "Frankly, we have so little to do until our master returns, if there are any simple printing jobs that we are capable of and can do as an accommodation for the Holy Office, we would be happy to do so."

Something stirred deep in the familiar's eyes. The eye motion, which I could not have defined at the time but that I have come to realize is a slight widening of the inner circle of the eye, is a reaction that few people except successful merchants and successful léperos would recognize.

The common name for the phenomena is *greed.*

I had been trying to think of a way to offer the official mordida but had hesitated. Some of these familiars had the reputation of being such zealots that they would refuse their own mother the mercy of the garret and let them burn slowly from the toes up. None the less, I had given "Don Jorge" an opening.

"The Holy Office does need assistance with certain printing jobs. We once used the printer who occupied these very premises, but he proved to be a tool of the devil."

I crossed myself.

"Perhaps I can assist until my master returns . . ."

He took me aside so that Juan could not hear.

"Is that mestizo a good Christian?"

"If his blood were untainted, he would be a priest," I

assured him. He had assumed I was Spanish, and of course that made me a defender of the Faith unless I acted contrary.

"I shall return later with two documents that I will need copies of for priests and nuns throughout New Spain. The contents change occasionally and will need to be updated." He stared at me narrow-eyed. "To uncover blasphemers and Jews, the workings of the Holy Office must remain a secret. Any failure to maintain the secrecy would be akin to doing the devil's work."

"Of course."

"You must take an oath of secrecy never to reveal what you have been given to print."

"Of course, Don Jorge."

"I will bring you two documents today. These documents require a large number of copies, and you will be paid a modest recompense to cover the cost of ink. The Holy Office will supply the paper."

"Thank you for your generosity, Don Jorge."

So that was it. He would be collecting the full amount of printing costs from the Holy Office but only passing on to me enough to pay for supplies to keep me in business. And assuredly the excess would not find its way to a poor box.

Oh, the wiles and intrigues of men! While this sort of intrigue is expected from any official in the realm, one would think that those who served the Church would hold themselves in better stead with God.

"What are these documents?"

"The list of people suspected of being blasphemers and Jews," he said, "and the list of books prohibited by the Holy Office."

EIGHTY-EIGHT

"Converso. Suspected marrano. Accused by Miguel de Soto."

Mateo finished reading the entry about Don Julio on the Inquisition's black list. I had naturally kept a copy of the list of suspect people after printing it.

"Who is Soto and why has he made an accusation that Don Julio is a secret Jew?" Mateo pondered.

"I spoke to an auditor in the viceroy's countinghouse, whose tastes in reading would make Lucifer blush and repent. He says Soto buys and sells workers. He deals in bond servants, landless indios, luckless mestizos, anyone or group that is helpless and can be roped into a project. He contracted with the tunnel project to provide indios—thousands of them. Even considering that he had to bribe half the city's officials to get the contract, he still made an enormous amount of money. Why he would make an accusation against the don, I don't know, but I can guess."

"The don has accused him of providing poor materials and workmanship on the tunnel, causing it to fail?" Mateo said.

"No, he only provided workers for others. My guess is he's doing Ramon de Alva a favor."

"What does Alva have to do with Soto?"

"Miguel is his brother-in-law. So is Martín de Soto, who hauled timber and materials for bricks."

"What service did Alva provide on the tunnel project?"

"None—on the surface, at least. He appears to be only involved in running the business affairs of Don Diego Velez, Marqués de la Marche." Eléna's uncle, but my connection to Eléna was a better kept secret the Inquisition's list of accused. "Alva appears to have made himself a very rich man along with the Marqués. The auditor says that whatever the Soto's are involved in, you will find Alva."

"Your nemesis."

"My tormentor. And now the don's. Don Julio believes that failure to follow his instructions and poor workmanship and materials caused the tunnel to collapse. But he has difficulty proving it."

"He is accusing the ones who did the work of the misdeeds. Miguel Soto probably charged for ten workers for every one he provided. And his brother-in-law no doubt delivered half the bricks and timber he was paid for. If a scapegoat is ever needed, a converso will fall faster than anyone else. Soto and the others are blackening the don's name with their accusations about Judiasm. There is no better way to destroy a man's life than to be dragged out of bed by familiars in the middle of the night."

"We must do something to help the don," I said.

"Unfortunately, this is not a matter that I can handle with a sword. The accusation has already been made, and to kill Soto would not remove it—to the contrary, it might raise more suspicion against Don Julio. We have to let the don know about the accusation so he is forewarned."

"How are we to do that? Shall I tell him that you and I are now the printing masters for the Holy Office?"

Mateo found no humor in my joke. "I suggest you dig deep into those tales you told on the street for your daily bread most of your life. Lying to a friend should not be difficult for a lépero."

"I will tell him I was walking by the Holy Office and saw the list on the street where someone had dropped it."

"Excellent. That is no more stupid a lie than any of the others you have used." Mateo yawned and stretched. "I think it is time to have that conversation with your friend Alva that I mentioned earlier."

"How do you plan to get him to talk to us?"

"Kidnap him. Torture him."

* * *

Don Julio looked up from the accusation list.

"You found this document on the street? You swear to me on the grave of your sainted mother?"

"Most assuredly, Don."

He threw the list into the fireplace and carefully stirred the ashes as it burned.

"Do not bother yourself about this. I have been accused twice before and nothing has come of it. The Holy Office will conduct an investigation and that can take years."

"Is there nothing we can do?"

"Pray. Not for me, but for the tunnel. If the tunnel fails again, it will be a contest as to who will be first—the viceroy who would have me hanged or the Holy Office who would burn me."

Busy with the printing of books banned by the Holy Office and the lists prepared by it, I left it to Mateo to devise a plan for the kidnapping of Ramon de Alva. Alva is not only a famous swordsman but rarely leaves his house unless surrounded by retainers, thus the plan must have the daring of El Cid and the genius of Machiavelli.

Working late at the print shop, I heard something drop at the back door. The door had a wooden slot in it that the previous owner, may he rest in peace, had used to receive orders from merchants when the shop was closed.

Though I had no intention of filling any orders, I went to check and found a package on the floor. I unwrapped it to find it contained a collection of handwritten poems and a note.

Señor Printer
Your predecessor would occasionally publish and sell my works with the money going to feed the poor on festival days. They are yours if you wish to continue the relationship.

A Lonely Poet

The note was written in a fine hand, as were the poems. The poems stirred my heart—and my virile place. I read each of them over and over. I would not call the poems deshonesto, perverted; some of the books I publish have men and women coupling with animals—that is most foul. But while the poems that came through the back door were not of this scandalous nature, they could not be published in the ordinary course because they were of a very provocative tone. To me they had grace and beauty and truly defined the power and passion between a man and a woman. And they told of a woman's honest desires, not the emotion of the Alameda where women play at love while counting the pesos in your family tree, but the passion of real people who know nothing of each other but their touch.

Several people had asked about the poems of this "lonely poet," who was known by no other name. Having never heard of him, I made promises I never intended to keep to obtain the poems. Now I would have a market for a few of them, but unlike scandalous books, these poems would appeal to a small group that had more interest in passion than perversion. I doubted I would make enough money to feed one hungry lépero at festival time, but in publishing these poems I felt rather like the publisher of fine books.

The secret would have to remain with me. If I let Mateo know, he would insist we print his silly love poems. Or he would steal them.

I began the typesetting immediately. This was not a task I could leave to Juan the lépero—he would not be able to translate the handwriting into type print. Besides, I did not want his dirty hands on such beautiful words.

"I have a plan," Mateo said. He spoke quietly over a goblet of wine in a tavern.

"Alva owns a house that he keeps vacant for his trysts. The house is unoccupied except for a housekeeper who is half-blind and almost deaf. When he arrives, his retainers stay in the coach. If we were waiting for him instead of a woman, we could have a private conversation."

"How did you find out where he meets women?"

"I followed Isabella."

I was sorry I asked, sorry for the don.

Mateo had more of an *idea* than a plan. How to get us into the house without being detected was a major problem. Half blind, almost deaf, did not mean that she was dead—or stupid. We also had to know when a tryst was scheduled.

"Isabella is subject to Alva's schedule. Other than having her hair endlessly dressed or social functions, she has no time commitments. His personal attendant carries a message here to the house and will deliver it only to her maid. Her maid attends all of the assignations."

That was natural. No lady of quality would leave her house for shopping or to meet her lover unless she was accompanied by a servant woman. The maid was a large africano woman who had a strong-enough back to keep from being crippled when Isabella flew into rages for trivial mistakes and whipped the woman.

I gave the matter thought for two goblets of wine. Life on the streets in which I had to lie, cheat, steal, and connive had prepared me for these later roles in life. While Mateo was an autor of comedias for playhouses, I, Cristo the Bastardo, was an autor of *life*.

"Here is the plan," I said.

EIGHTY-NINE

THREE DAYS LATER I received instructions at the print shop to hurry home. I knew what the message meant: The lookout that Mateo had posted told him that Isabella had received a note to meet Ramon de Alva.

Mateo was waiting with the items we needed to implement the plan. He was a man who was never nervous, but for once his anxiety revealed itself. He would not have flinched to face the greatest swordsmen in Europe . . . but poisoning a woman terrified him.

"Did you put the herb in her soup?" he asked.

A little soup was all that Isabella ate before she left the house for her intercourse with Alva. They would have a full meal after they had satisfied their lust.

"Yes. Are you sure it will work?"

"Absolutely. In a few minutes Isabella's stomach will hurt so bad she will have to send for a doctor. She will also send her maid to Alva to let him know that she will not be at the love house."

"If this doesn't work, I will flay you like that naualli sorcerer flayed people and use your skin for a pair of boots."

I went to check on Isabella. The maid was leaving Isabella's bedroom as I approached. Before she closed the door behind her, I saw Isabella doubled up on her bed. Her groans made my heart leap with joy. She would only be sick for a few hours, and I had been tempted to make the poison strong enough to kill her.

"Is your mistress sick?"

"Yes, señor. I have to go for the doctor." She hurried away.

"The maid has gone for the doctor. I suspect from there she will walk directly to Alva's and pass the message to his man."

Mateo and I left the house and walked down the street to a coach awaiting us. It was not a fancy coach, but the carriage of a petty merchant who was happy to get three banned books for a night's use of it.

Inside the coach, we put on cloaks and full face masks, the type commonly used at the Alameda and parties. Mateo waited inside the coach; I, on the street, as the maid approached. As she came by me, I pretended to cough and then shook out a large handkerchief, shaking it so that dust from the cloth hit her in the face.

She kept walking, trying to brush away the dust with her hand.

I got into the coach and looked back as we rolled down the cobblestone street.

The maid was staggering.

The same indio herbal seller who sold me the herb that had gotten Isabella sick had supplied yoyotli, the hallucinatory dust that stole the mind of sacrifice victims and that the Healer had once used on me.

A few minutes later the coach rolled away from the love house, leaving Mateo and me in front.

We entered the unguarded gate and went directly to the main door. I pulled a cord that rang a bell inside. The bell was almost loud enough for a church tower. A few minutes later the housekeeper opened the door.

"Buenas tardes, señora," the housekeeper said.

Without saying a word, as none was needed in reply to a servant, Alva's love partner for the night, me, and my maid, Mateo, entered the house.

We were dressed as women and wearing masks.

We would not have fooled Alva for a moment.

We would not have fooled a one-eyed pirate a musket shot away.

We fooled an old woman who was half blind and almost deaf.

The old woman left us at the foot of the stairs to the bedrooms and wandered off, thoughts dribbling out of her head, something about the size of the don's new woman.

The bedroom selected for trysts was easy to determine—it was lit with candles, the bed linen had been freshly turned, and wine and sweetmeats were laid out.

We performed our preparations and sat down to wait.

"Remember, Alva is a famed swordsman," Mateo said. "If he is able to draw his blade, I will kill him. But he will kill you before I am able."

Ah, Mateo, always a comfort to a friend. And truthful.

Had he not always said that as a swordsman I was a dead man?

Bedroom windows overlooked the courtyard below. We watched Alva arrive in his carriage, walk across the courtyard, and disappear under the covered way that led to the main door. Two of his men remained in the courtyard.

I sat with my back to the door at a small table that held wine and sweetmeats. We had discarded our female clothes except for a woman's hooded cape that I kept on to present a feminine back when Alva came in the door. My sword was in hand and so was my heart. I feared Alva less than I feared whatever revelations from the past he may possess.

The door opened behind me and I heard his heavy step as he entered.

"Isabella, I—"

The man had the instincts of a jungle cat. Whatever he could see from a rear view of me instantly put him on guard and he went for his sword.

I leaped from the chair, flashing my own sword, but before we could engage Mateo hit him on the back of the head with an ax handle. Alva fell to his knees and Mateo hit him again, not enough to knock him out but to stun him. We were immediately on him with rope, tying his hands behind him. Mateo looped another rope through the large round candleholder, as big as a carriage wheel, hanging from the ceiling. With a knife at Alva's throat, we maneuvered him under the chandelier. The end of the rope dangling from the ceiling was tied into a noose and we slipped it over Alva's head.

Together we hoisted him up by the neck until his feet were dangling. I slipped a chair under his feet and he was able to stand on the chair and keep from strangling.

When we were finished, Alva stood on the chair with his hands tied behind him and his neck in the noose. Mateo kicked the chair out from under him. He swung, wrenching for air; the candleholder creaked, and stucco fell from the ceiling.

I put the chair under his feet and let him struggle onto it.

Because I did not intend to kill the man unless it was necessary, besides wearing a mask I had pebbles in my mouth to disguise my voice.

"You killed a good man in Veracruz nearly seven years ago, a fray named Antonio, and you tried to kill a boy whom Antonio raised. Why did you do this? Who put you up to these black deeds?"

His voice was a gutter of anger that spewed filth.

I kicked the chair out from under his feet and he bounced and swung, his face red. When his features were convulsed with pain and nearly black from being strangled, I replaced the chair.

"Let's cut off his testicules," Mateo said. He poked the man in the groin with his sword to get across the point.

"Ramon, Ramon, why must you make us turn you into a woman?" I asked. "I know you killed the fray for someone else. Tell me who you performed the deed for, and you can go on using this place as your private whorehouse."

More filth spewed from his mouth.

"I know one of you is that bastard boy," he gasped. "I fucked your mother before I killed her."

I went forward to kick the chair out from under him. As I stepped up to the chair, Alva kicked me in the stomach. His boot caught me just below my sternum and took my wind and, for a moment, my life from me. I staggered backward and fell onto my rear on the floor.

The momentum caused by kicking me sent Alva swinging wildly off the chair. The carriage wheel candleholder broke loose as an entire section of the ceiling collapsed to the floor. A storm of debris and dust blinded me.

Mateo yelled and I saw Alva's dark form run by me and then the crash of wood as he flung himself headfirst through the closed window shutters. I heard his body hit the tiles on the roofed part of the courtyard. He yelled for help.

Mateo grabbed me. "Hurry!"

I followed him into the adjoining sitting room and onto

a balcony. He had the rope we had been hanging Alva with in hand. He looped the noose around a post and swung over the side, sliding down the rope with his hands and feet. I followed before he hit the ground, grateful that this was not the first time Mateo had had to leave a bedroom with a threat behind him.

After discarding our clothes and masks and reassuming our roles as workers of Don Julio, we sat in a tavern and played primero, a card game Mateo was brilliant at losing money playing.

"Bastardo, we learned one interesting piece of information tonight—other than the fact that Alva is a tough hombre."

"Which is?"

"He killed your mother."

I never knew my mother and I had no real image of her, but the fact that this man claimed to have raped and murdered her were more nails in his coffin. The statement, even if I assigned it as a taunt, increased the mystery surrounding the past. What did Alva have to do with my mother? Why would it be necessary for a gachupin to kill an india girl? And the most mysterious of all—I knew for a fact that he had not killed her. As far as I knew, she was still alive.

"It will be a long time before we could ever hope to trick Alva into falling into our hands again," he said. "If ever."

"Do you think he will connect us back to Isabella?"

Mateo shrugged. "I think not. The conclusion will be that Isabella and the maid both were victims of bad food. But to ensure that there is no connection, I will be leaving tonight for Acapulco."

The Manila galleon was due in from the Far East. What his joining the excitement of the arrival of the galleon with its treasures from China, the Spice Islands, and India had to do with Alva discovering the identity of his attackers was another mystery to me. I had the unkind, but true, thought that he was leaving for Acapulco just to enjoy himself.

NINETY

WITH MATEO IN Acapulco, the don at the tunnel project, and Isabella in a foul mood, I stayed away from the house as much as possible. When I was not in the print shop, I would take a walk along the arcade, stopping in a shop now and again.

I was working late in the shop when I heard the flap on the back door and the sound of a package dropping. Realizing it was probably the author of the romantic poems that I found so provocative and compelling, I raced to open the door and run into the alley. I saw the person fleeing, a slender built, short man with his hooded cape flapping as he ran. He disappeared around a corner. When I reached the corner, a carriage was already moving down the street. It was too dark to see any identifying marks on the carriage.

Walking back I was struck by the presence of the scent of a French water that I knew was popular with young women in the city. At first I thought it odd that a man would wear a scent, but there were many fops who wore not just French water, but such silks and lace that on inspection of their genitals one would expect to find a witch's teat instead of a pene. That a writer of romantic poetry might be the type who found other men attractive, entering by the back door as it is said, would not surprise me. Eh, the poems came through the back door, did they not?

The poems were once again visions of love that touched my romantic soul—the one well-hidden behind my lépero's scabrous one. I put aside a deshonesto play that I had been checking Juan's typesetting on and began typesetting the poems. No profit was made from the poet's books, but what a pleasure to lose one's self in the images of lovers in a heat of passion. Printing his works of honest passions, I felt that I was making amends for the works of lesser quality—and lesser morality—that I printed only to make money. It was much work for me to set the type for all of the poet's works, but I had found it very rewarding.

As I set the type, I thought about the play we were surreptitiously publishing. We printed more plays than books. While comedias were rarely performed in New Spain, they were more popular to read than books.

It occurred to me that money could be had quicker and easier simply by putting on plays, rather than selling printed copies. Plays had not reached the level of popularity or profitability in New Spain that they had in the mother country because those the Holy Office approved for the colonies were insipid comedies of manners or religious works. To have even submitted a play like the ones we print to the Holy Office for a permit to perform would have resulted in our immediate arrest.

I wondered if there was a play we could present that would prove popular yet yield the needed approval. A group of actors had come to town to present a play in a vacant area between the mint building and residences, but the play had only lasted a few performances. I watched the play while Mateo was in Acapulco and found it to be a very uninteresting rendition of Lope de Vega's *Fuente Ovejuna.* I had been forewarned that the censor's knife had cut the heart from Vega's brilliant work and that a familiar would be in the audience with a copy to ensure that the deleted dialogue did not find its way back into the presentation. Added to this, the actors did not have their lines well rehearsed. I heard the actors had disagreed over which play was to be presented and who was to perform the lead roles. It was sad to watch such a wonderful, stirring play mouthed by people who were unable to instill within themselves the spirit of the character they were playing.

No nation had ever produced a writer as prolific as Vega. Cervantes called him a monster of nature because he was able to write plays in hours and had composed perhaps a couple of thousand. *Fuente Ovejuna* was a stirring tale, much in line with Vega's other great works that demonstrated how Spanish men and women of all classes can be honorable. I had read a true copy of the play, smuggled into the colony under the dress of an actress.

The name of the play, Fuente Ovejuna, was the name of the village where the action took place. Here again a nobleman was trying to dishonor a peasant girl, who was betrothed to a village youth. Laurencia is the peasant girl, but she is a smart, resourceful one. She knows what the nobleeman, the commander, is really after when he sends his emissaries to her with gifts. He plans to dishonor her and cast her aside after he has had his pleasure. As she says about men in general, "All they want, after giving us much trouble, is their pleasure at night and our sorrow in the morning."

She can be a sharp-tongued wench. As one character puts it, "I bet the priest poured salt on her as he christened her."

When the commander returns triumphant from war, the village greets him with gifts. But the gift he wants are Laurencia and another peasant girl. Struggling against his adjutant who is trying to pull her into a room where the commander can take advantage of her, Laurencia says, "Isn't your master satisfied with all the meat he was given today?"

"He seems to prefer yours," the servant says.

"Then he can starve!"

The commander catches Laurencia in the forest and tries to take her by force, when a peasant boy who loves her, Frondoso, grabs a bow and arrow the commander had laid down, and holds off the knight until the girl escapes.

The commander is disgusted by the way the peasant girl resists him. "What boors these peasants are. Ah, give me the cities, where nobody hinders the pleasures of lofty men, and husbands are glad when we make love to their wives."

He discusses women with his aide, speaking of the women who will surrender themselves to him without a struggle. "Easy girls I love dearly and repay poorly. Ah, Flores, if they only knew their worth."

The cruel nobleman takes village girls by force as he pleases, but Laurencia manages to avoid him. He shows up at her wedding and has her bridegroom, Frondoso, arrested. The commander carries off Laurencia and beats her when she resists his rape.

She returns to her father and the men in the village, calling them "sheep" for permitting the commander to violate village girls. She tells the men of the village that after the commander hangs Frondoso, he'll come and hang the spineless men of the village. "And I'll be glad—you race of half men—that this honorable town will be rid of effeminate men and the age of Amazons will return."

Picking up a sword Laurencia rallies the women of the village around her, and declares they must take the castle and free Frondoso before the commander kills him. She tells another woman, "When my courage is up, we don't need a Cid."

Women knock down the castle door and storm in, facing the commander, just as he's starting to have Frondoso hanged. The village men enter with their weapons to help. But a woman says, "Only women know how to take revenge. We shall drink the enemy's blood."

Jacinta, a girl raped by the commander, says, "Let us pierce his corpse with our lances."

Frondoso says, "I won't consider myself avenged until I've pulled out his soul."

The women attack the commander and his men. Laurencia says, "Com' on women, dye your swords with their vile blood!"

Vega had the literary courage to put swords in the hands of women. I suspect that was why the audience, which was composed mostly of men, did not appreciate the play as much as I did.

Another great moral point of the play was the way the villagers stood together when they are tried for the commander's death before the king and queen, Ferdinand and

Isabella. When the villagers are questioned and tortured to reveal who slayed the evil nobleman, each of them in turn names the culprit: Fuente Ovejuna. The village itself had taken justice in its hands.

Faced with an impossible situation, the king and queen leave the death of the commander unpunished.

From what few seats were sold for the play, I had no doubt that the rest of the city were not stirred by the actors.

The thought of putting on a comedia had been on my mind from the time I had been clandestinely printing offensive ones. But no matter how I struggled with the thought, I was always blocked by how I knew Mateo would react. He would insist that we do some foolish tale of hombria—if I had to sit through another hour of an honorable Spaniard killing an English pirate who had raped his wife . . .

I would have presented a play by Beelzebub if it made money, but besides their lack of artistic merit, Mateo's plays had the added disadvantage of being financial disasters.

I went home that night struggling with the idea of putting on a play that would provide great profit yet not run us afoul of the Inquisition. Restless, I grabbed a copy of Montebanca's *Historia of the Roma Empire* and read it by candlelight as I breathed the sweet fumes of the stable below. As the empire became more and more decadent, decomposing as its social and moral fabric rotted under one bad leader after another, the emperors had gotten more and more extreme in the entertainment they provided the people in the arena; no longer did it entertain people to see gladiators killing each other, soon small armies fought and men were pitted against wild beasts. I found among the more interesting gladiatorial contests the sea battles in which the arena was flooded and warships with gladiators aboard fought.

Dozing off, I wondered how one would flood a comedia de corral, which was often little more than the space between houses, to put on a battle of gladiators.

I awoke in the middle of the night with the realization that I already had the flooded arena.

* * *

Mateo returned from Acapulco after two weeks. He was in bad temper and had no scar to which he had ascribed a woman's name.

"Pirates sank the Manila galleon; I made the trip for nothing."

"Mateo, Mateo, my friend, my companion in arms, I have had a revelation."

"Did you walk on water, amigo?"

"Exactly! You have guessed it. We are going to put on a comedia—on water."

Mateo rolled his eyes and pounded the side of his head. "Bastardo, you've been inhaling some of that yoyotli that steals the mind."

"No, I've been reading history. The Romans sometimes flooded the arena and put on gladiatorial sea battles with warships."

"Did you plan to put this comedia on in Rome? Has the pope given you San Pedro's to flood?"

"You are such a doubter of genius. Have you looked around and seen that Ciudad Mexico is surrounded by water?—not to mention a dozen lagoons in and around the city."

"Explain this madness to me."

"We take great risk for small profit printing deshonesto plays and books and selling them. It occurred to me that we could put on our own comedia and make our fortune."

Mateo's eye lit up. "I will write the play! An English pirate rapes—"

"No! No! No! Everyone from Madrid to Acapulco has seen that story. I have an idea for a play—"

His hand brushed his dagger. "You don't want *me* to write the play?"

"Yes, of course, but based on a different story." That fortunately needed very little dialogue, I added silently to myself. "What is the greatest moment in the history of New Spain?"

"The conquest, of course."

"Besides those famous horses whose blood you invest in, Cortes had a fleet of warships. Because Mexico, Tenochtitlan, was an island with a causeway that could be easily defended by the Aztecs, Cortes had to attack the city over water. He had timber felled and beams cut and built a fleet of thirteen boats; installed them with masts, rigging, and sail. While the boats were being prepared, he employed eight thousand indios to dig a canal by which the boats could be launched on the lake."

Mateo, of course, knew the story better than me. Cortes put twelve rowers aboard each vessel, along with twelve crossbowmen and musketeers, a total of about half of the conquistadors in his army. None of the conquistadors wanted to be rowers, and he'd had to coerce men with sea experience to man the oars.

He equipped each boat with cannon taken from the ships that had carried him to New Spain and put the boats under the command of captains. He invested himself as admiral of the fleet and led an attack on the city as the rest of his force and indio allies attacked the causeway.

The fleet of little warships was countered by an Aztec armada, over five hundred war canoes, hosting thousands of warriors. As the two fleets closed the distance between them, Cortes knew all would be lost if the good Lord did not give them a fresh breeze to propel their ships into battle with such speed that they would not be overwhelmed by the enormous number of Aztec war canoes.

The Hand of God did enter the battle. A breeze came up that sent Cortes's ships crashing through the Aztec armada with a ferocity only matched by the fierceness of the conquistadors themselves.

"How did you plan to pay for the thirteen ships and five hundred canoes, not to mention several hundred conquistadors and five thousand Aztec warriors?"

"We need but one warship and two or three canoes. A lake barge can be turned into a warship by adding some false lines of timber and wooden cannon. Indios with canoes can be had for a few pesos each night."

Mateo had the nervous intensity of a jaguar on the prowl. He paced, seeing himself as the man who won an empire.

"Cortes would be the main player," he said, "fighting with the strength of ten demons, killing a dozen—*no!*—a hundred of the enemy, exhorting his men not to waiver, in his most desperate moment, on his knees, calling upon God to deliver wind."

"Naturally only a fine actor like yourself could pay the conqueror."

"There is a company of players in the city, stranded, their bellies getting thinner each day," he said. "They could be had for a place to sleep and a little wine and food until our boat is prepared."

"I leave matters requiring artistic judgment to one who has performed before royalty in Madrid. I will occupy myself with mundane matters of getting the warship built, printing announcements, and the selling of tickets."

And, praise God, collecting enough money to become the gentleman I had always wanted to be.

Preparations for the play proved to be easier than I had imagined. The viceroy's office and the Holy Office were more than willing to license a play that extolled God and the glory of Spanish conquerors. All of the negotiations were done in my persona of a print shop assistant commissioned by the fictitious autor of the play. Because of our connection to the don, we decided not to use our real names.

Late at night, while I was printing up handbills advertising the play, I heard the telltale drop of a package through the back door slot and I again rushed to the alley.

The poet was nearly to end of the alley when a dark figure jumped out in front of him. The poet screamed and ran back toward me.

A woman's scream.

Terrified, looking back where an attack was expected, the poet ran nearly into my arms. I grabbed the mask from the person's face.

"Eléna!"

She stared at me wide-eyed. *"You!"*

She spun around and ran back down the alley, flying around Juan the lépero whom I had posted in the alley.

No wonder the words of the poet had so inflamed my heart—they flowed from the heart and hand of the woman I loved! That Eléna was the author of the poetry was a shock. That she was capable of writing poetry in no way surprised me. As a young girl she had talked of disguising herself as a man to write poetry.

The drudgery of typesetting the poems had been rewarded by a moment in which we stood only inches apart.

What did she mean when she had exclaimed, *You!* Shock that she had seen the lépero again who had accosted her on the street? Or did she recognize me as the youth from Veracruz? I toyed with the word, "you," listening in my mind to her speaking it, sometimes in a tone of familiarity, other times a tone of derision creeping in.

Finally, sighing, realizing my thoughts of someday courting Eléna were more fanciful than Mateo's battles with dragons, I sat down with the papers she had delivered.

The material she left were not in fact poems but a play. Called *Beatriz de Navarre,* it was the tale of a woman with a jealous husband. He suspects her of infidelity after finding what appears to be a love note.

Determined to catch the two lovers red-handed, he spies on his wife's every move. He had truly loved his wife and their love had been passionate before his suspicions arose. But with suspicion eating at him, he treats her coldly, keeping his doubts to himself so he can catch her in the act. His wife reaches out for him but is rejected.

While lurking outside his wife's bedroom, he hears her telling someone how much she loves him, using very erotic language. Enraged, he breaks down the door. He finds no one but his wife in the room and assumes her lover has fled. Still in a rage, certain that the woman has been unfaithful to him, he draws his sword and thrusts it through her heart.

As she lies on the floor, her life slowly draining from the

wound in her chest, she whispers to her husband that she has always been faithful to him, that she loved him, and had been immortalizing her love for him in a poem. She had been afraid to show it to him because he had forbidden her to even read poetry, much less write it.

After her last breath escapes from her, he picks up papers on the table where she had been writing. Reading the poem aloud, he realizes that the words he overheard outside her door were not to a man in her room, but a lover in her heart—she had been reading aloud the poem.

He had doubted her because he never realized that a woman was capable of placing her heart on paper in a poem. Women had neither the inclination nor the need to experience literature.

Heartbroken by having spilled the blood of his beloved, he kneels beside her and begs forgiveness, then plunges a dagger into his own heart. . . .

Was I touched by the play because it was penned by a certain young woman in a carriage who saved my life and yearned to get an education? Perhaps, but the language, the words of the love poem Beatriz wrote to her husband, was also quite appealing to me. Eléna the poet had a talent for bringing words between lovers that were poignant, provocative, and, yes, with an eroticism that titillates the ear and private places.

Another one of the ideas that seize my mind and soul and bring the hounds of hell yapping at my heels came to me, an idea even more outrageous than Mateo's tales. I would put on a play that would tickle the fancy of Homer and Sophocles. From the money earned from Cortes's spectacular sea battle, I would produce Eléna's play. Not in her name, of course, but one I would make up to protect her. And I would have to devise a way to let her know that the poor lépero boy she had helped had repaid her by giving her everlasting glory—in anonymity.

Of course, I would have to trick the Holy Office and the viceroy to get the play performed and not let Mateo know I had stolen money to put on someone else's play. He would carry through his threat to flay me and rub my raw flesh with salt if he knew.

Eh, amigos, I had nothing to risk. I would simply replace the money I diverted from our play with the admissions sold for Eléna's play.

The thought of the sacrifices I would be making for love choked me up as I reread the play.

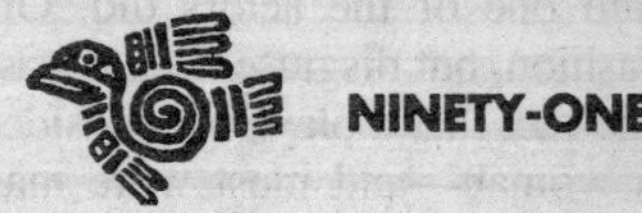

NINETY-ONE

WE CHOSE A lagoon near the Alameda for the reenactment of the lake battle between Cortes's fleet and the Aztecs. Handbills advertising the play had been distributed throughout the city, and criers proclaimed the magnificence of the play in every plaza.

I personally collected the admission price. Vendors of blankets for sitting on the grass, since there were only a few benches available, and the sale of candy and sweetmeats, owed me a percentage of all dinero collected.

The preparations went well and there was no room to sit or stand by the time I collected the last admission. But my fears were not relieved. Despite the simplicity of the story, Mateo was anything but a simple actor, managing to embellish even the most ungarnished role. I feared that the Mexico audience would boo him off the stage—or worse, Mateo might draw his sword at the audience instead of the other actors.

The play began with the conquistadors floating in on a warship that looked much like a barge that had been temporarily converted into a warship. Mateo-Cortes stood valiantly at the bow, sword in one hand, Holy Cross in another. Beside him was "Doña Marina," the india interpreter who had been so vital in forming alliances with indio nations, giving Cortes's little band the armies he needed to defeat the dreaded Aztec legions.

The "doña" had originally been cast from a woman in the troupe of traveling actors, but her husband and Mateo had fallen out, for reasons I never bothered to inquire about. Her replacement was a pretty young india girl. I had the misfortune of asking Mateo where he'd found her—a casa de las putas, of course.

I wore a mask, as a number of people in the audience and one of the actors did. Of course, mine was not for fashion, but disguise. Eléna was a lover of plays and despite the fact that a play was considered vulgar entertainment for a woman—and most wore masks to them—I was certain she would not pass up the opportunity to see so heralded a play.

My fears—and rapture—at seeing her again came true as she arrived in a coach with Luis and an older woman chaperone. I did not recognize the older woman, it was not the elderly matron who had been in the coach many years before. A servant followed them, with cushions and blankets for them to sit on.

I sold Luis tickets, careful not to meet eyes with him or Eléna, even with my face covered by a mask.

After the last admission had been collected, I posted myself so that I could abscond with the admission money if the audience became so inflamed over Mateo's bad acting that blood was drawn rather than just vegetables thrown. I could not see Eléna from my position. It hurt to know she was with Luis, and I was the better for not seeing them together.

As the barge-warship came into sight, the ominous beat of drums set the mood for the dark battle that was to come.

When the barge-warship was close enough, Mateo-Cortes told the audience that before he was old enough to kill an Infidel with a sword, the Moors had been defeated and driven from Spain. But while Spain was no longer threatened by the bloody Islamic horde, the nation had not found its place under the sun as a great empire. The opportunity came when Columbus discovered a whole new world to conquer.

"Because I sought fortune, adventure, and to bring the Cross to pagans, I, too, crossed the great ocean to the New World."

As with any Mateo speech, he talked so long that my eyes were beginning to get heavy and difficult to keep open. I had insisted upon inserting action between his long discourses, and to my relief, three indio war canoes, all I could afford, came into the lagoon. And the battle began—the wooden cannons on Cortes's ship coughed black powder smoke; more powder was lit on board the barge to create noise and a haze. A man hiding behind a blanket banged on a large metal drum to create the sound of cannon and musket fire, arrows without sharp heads flew, indios shouted curses and banged the Spanish with wooden spears, while the four conquistadors fought back. As an added touch, we had set several pieces of pitch-covered wood afire floating around the boats.

The indios mounted a surprisingly aggressive attack on "Cortes" and his men, who fought back just as aggressively. I watched, horrified, as the battle between indios and conquistadors intensified into actual combat. A conquistador was dragged off the ship and into the water and barely got away with his life as the triumphant indios tried to spear him like a fish.

Then another conquistador went into the water. A roar of delight came from the indios on the canoes as they threw themselves at men on the mock warship.

¡Ay de mí! This disaster was not planned. With the smoke, the fire, the shouting, the clash of swords and spears, the impression of a real battle was supposed to be created. But only the impression!

I clutched the money pouch, ready to flee, but stood rooted by fascination as I watched all my work in putting together the play being destroyed by the sudden inflamed passions of indios and españols, who forgot they were acting.

¡Santa Maria! A conquistador was stunned by a spear blow to the head and dragged off the warship. Indios swarmed up the sides of the ship. Only Mateo was left on his feet. The invaders grappled with Doña Marina, and her dress was torn off of her in the struggle.

I had a horrible thought. *The indios are going to win!*

If that happened, Mateo would not be booed from the "stage," his ticket collector would not be robbed, the crowd would tear us limb from limb.

My eyes sought out the familiar who sat with a copy of the play to make sure that the dialogue did not deviate from what had been approved. If he leaped to his feet and stopped the play, there would be a riot over the admission money.

Suddenly, Mateo-Cortes was here—there—everywhere, his sword flashing. One by one the indios abandoned the barge, mostly over the side and into the water. When there were no more indios aboard to fight, he leaped aboard a canoe and battered the indios left on it. Commanding the indios left in his canoe to bring him and the almost disrobed Doña Marina to land, he stepped ashore with his sword in one hand and a cross in the other. The cross was bloodied from breaking an indio's head.

The audience was on its feet roaring its approval.

We had constructed a six-foot-high model of Tenochtitlan's great temple to their war god and thrown red paint on it to create the impression of sacrificial blood. Mateo-Cortes climbed the steps and stood atop, holding sword and cross high. He gave a stirring speech about the glory of God and Spain, and how the riches of the New World and the bravery of its colonists had made Spain the most powerful country on earth.

The audience went wild with cheers and clapping.

Mateo had found his gift on the stage: *action*. He was not suited for standing on a stage talking to other actors or to the audience. Put a sword in his hand and an enemy before him, and he became . . . *himself* . . . a man with the courage of a lion, the daring of an eagle.

I leaned back against a tree, folded my arms, and looked up to the early evening sky, feeling the weight of the coins in the pouch around my neck.

Apologizing to my Aztec ancestors, I thanked God for not letting the indios win.

NINETY-TWO

With a hit play in the lagoon, even after paying expenses—including the burning of two canoes and half the barge a few days later—I was able to steal enough money from the pile I was saving for Mateo and me to put on Eléna's play.

I hired the actor and actress who had created the rift on the Cortes play and rented the same space and stage near the mint where they had put on their failed comedia.

The play had to be timed perfectly. I had submitted a written copy to both the Holy Office and the viceroy's staff to obtain the requisite permission and license. Naturally, I had to alter Eléna's story and dialogue because there was no possibility that either authority would grant permission as it was written. I changed the plot so that the woman read her husband's poetry rather than her own, because it would have been an unacceptable portrayal of women to have them intellectually superior to their husbands. I also toned down some of the passion in the woman's lines and gave the tale a happy ending—with their child, who only appeared at the end of the play, being hauled up to heaven after dying of the plague.

Of course, the version of the play I gave to the actors was Eléna's. My plan was to stage the play the following week when both the viceroy, archbishop, and bishop inquisitor were all in Puebla for the investiture of a bishop there. I would run the play for several nights, and then close it before they returned. As for the familiar whose duty it was to follow the script . . . I would post a lépero who would sprinkle him with a small amount of flower weavers' dust to disorient him as he approached.

Eléna would have her triumph, but the play would be closed by the time the most powerful men in New Spain got back to the city. Even if frays saw the play and found it profane, it would take several days to get a messenger to Puebla and back with permission to close it.

It would not do to get Eléna in trouble with the Inquisition for authoring what would be considered an indecent portrayal of a woman, yet I wanted her to know that her play had not been stolen but was being attributed to her. I also needed a scapegoat to take the blame when the inquisitors took action. I solved the problem by creating an autor named Anele Zurc, who had written and financed the play. The name was neither male nor female, and appeared to be vaguely foreign, perhaps Dutch, some of whom were citizens of the king. I would get a message to her, through her maid, that would subtly let her know that the name is hers, Eléna de la Cruz, written backward. The note would be signed, *Son of the Stone,* in reference to the lines from the Miguel Cervantes's play I had quoted to her in the carriage an eon ago.

Other than a couple of minor servant roles, Eléna's play only required two actors, the husband and wife, and I left to them artistic preparation of the play. I was busy collecting admissions to the Cortes play, and rounding up conquistadors and Aztecs for the roles as more and more became injured in the battles.

When the night came for the opening of the play, I was more excited than a man at the birth of his first son. I had hoped and prayed that Eléna had understood my message and would attend. After signing Son of the Stone, I could not risk letting her see me even under a mask—uncertain as to who I was and what my intentions were, she may have come with representatives of the viceroy and the Inquisition.

Needing someone to collect the admission money from the patrons, I choose an indio who worked for a shopkeeper near the print shop. After worrying about using a priest or other Spaniard to trust with the money, I chose the indio. I hid myself in the curtains beside the stage.

Eh, amigos, did you really think that I would risk my sweetheart's play being ruined by vulgar mosqueteros shouting down the hack actors and pelting them with tomatoes? And run the risk that the play would close almost as quickly as it opened? I sent Juan the lépero into the streets with free admissions slips for anyone who would come to the play. Giving a group of street people instructions on how to cheer the play as it went along, I passed coins among them with promises of more for those who showed the most enthusiasm.

When I saw Eléna come into the theater, I had to restrain myself from breaking from my hiding place and running to her. As usual, my fervor was dampened by the presence of Luis, who escorted her everywhere. I now knew it was common knowledge that they would marry, a circumstance that was a blade twisting in my heart.

When I saw the familiar sent to monitor the play walk by with his eyes watering and a great grin on his face, I knew it was safe to proceed. As usual, frays showed up, walking past the admission taker as if they were invisible.

During the play, my eyes were on Eléna rather than the actors. I could see that she was as thrilled about it as Luis was bored. She sat on the edge of her seat and stared at the action on the stage, her lips often moving, silently voicing the lines as the actors spoke them. She was radiant and beautiful and I felt privileged to have had the opportunity to repay the great debt—and pleasure—she gave me.

Halfway through the play the frays rushed out, no doubt offended by the words spoken by the actress. It was a long way to Puebla, I gloated to myself.

As the final scene unfolded, with the heroine lying on the floor, dying, revealing that she was the author of the poem, a group of frays and familiars suddenly entered. From my hiding place, I gawked as the bishop of the Holy Office of the Inquisition came in behind his priests and familiars.

"This comedia is canceled," the bishop announced. "The autor is to present himself to me."

The bishop had not gone to Puebla after all.

I fled with great haste.

Mateo was waiting for me in my room. "The Inquisition closed our play," he told me.

"Our play?" What was he talking about? He knew about the play I put on for Eléna! "How did you know? When did you find out?"

He threw up his hands in a plea for God to recognize the injustice. "The greatest performances of my life, and the bishop himself closed us. He took the admission money, too."

"He closed *our* play? Why did he close the play?" I was devastated. How could the bishop close a play that glorified Spain?

"Because of the love scene with Doña Marina."

"Love scene? There's no love scene with Doña Marina."

"A small rewrite," Mateo said.

"You added a love scene in the battle for Tenochtitlan? Are you insane?"

He tried to look remorseful. "At the conclusion of battle, a man needs a women in his arms to lick his wounds."

"At the conclusion? Your love scene took place on top of the temple? What happened to the sword and cross you were supposed to be holding?"

"I kept them in hand. Doña Marina, uh, assisted by getting down on her knees as I—"

"Dios mio. And I thought I had been foolish with my play."

"Your play?"

Once while traveling with the Healer I had stepped on a snake, and I looked down and saw that my foot was holding it down just behind the head. I had nothing in my hand to strike it and was terrified and perplexed—if I moved my foot it would bite me, yet I could not keep the pressure on it forever.

I had just stepped on another snake.

Pretending I hadn't heard Mateo, I started for the door. He grabbed me by the back of my doublet and pulled me back.

"You have been acting very strange, Bastardo. Please sit down and tell me what you have been doing while I was making us rich conquering the Aztecs." His voice was soft, almost mellow, like the purring of a tiger—just before it eats you. He never said "please" unless he was ready to rip out my throat.

Weary of intrigues, I sat down and told him everything—starting with Eléna in the carriage so many years ago, to discovering she was the erotic poet and putting on her play as a tribute to her.

"How much is left of our money?" he asked.

"I spent all that I had. The Inquisition took the rest. How much do you—"

He shrugged. It was a foolish question. What I did not steal and lose, he no doubt lost to cards and women.

I expected, no, I deserved, to be beaten for my treachery. But he seemed to take it all with the air of a philosopher as opposed to the mal hombre loco that I knew him to be.

He lit a stinking, rolled tobacco leaf. "If you had stolen it from me to buy a horse, I would kill you. But to buy a jewel for a woman, which is what you did, that is different. I cannot kill a man for loving a woman so much he would steal or kill for her." He blew foul smoke in my face. "I do it frequently."

The next morning I found that the Inquisition had seized the print shop and arrested Juan the lépero. He was ignorant of my identity and would be unable to put the inquisitorial hounds on my trail and too ignorant himself to be burned for blasphemy.

Overnight Mateo and I found ourselves out of the comedia business, out of the book business, out of money, and no longer the printers for the Inquisition.

The gloom worsened as rains fell heavily and Lake Texcoco began to rise. Our concern turned to Don Julio at a time when he suddenly needed our help.

NINETY-THREE

DON JULIO, BUSY with the tunnel project, knew little of our activity except that Mateo had obtained a role in a play. Isabella refused to see the play, saying that it would be belittling for her to attend a play in which one of her "servants" appeared.

The don's lack of interest in our activities was out of character. He was usually concerned with our staying out of trouble. His preoccupation with the tunnel worried us because it meant things were not going well. We heard stories on the street that the tunnel continued to suffer problems.

The don called the swordsman and me into his library at the city house.

"You are to be a lépero again," Don Julio told me, "and once again be my eyes and ears and those of the king's."

This time it was silver train robberies. The silver area was centered about a hundred leagues north in Zacatecas. I knew something about the mining business despite having never seen one. Mateo claimed that I was like Don Julio in that I lusted for knowledge more than women, and there was much truth in his accusation. The don's library contained several books on mining techniques and included short histories of mining in New Spain; I read all that there was to know about silver mining, even though I was after a silver thief not a prospector, and I cajoled the don into sitting down with me and telling me more.

In 1546, Juan de Tolosa found a fantastic mountain of silver, La Bufa, at Zacatecas in the Chichimeca indio region. The discovery, and the many dozens that followed, turned New Spain into the richest silver-bearing place on earth.

Tolosa, the commander of a detachment of soldiers, established camp at the foot of a mountain called La Bufa by the indios. Tolosa gave gifts to the indios, trinkets and blankets, and in turn they took him to a place where they said the rocks were "living." The glowing spirit in the rocks was silver, and Tolosa went on to become one of the richest men in New Spain.

Soon a new type of conquistador arose in New Spain, prospectors who ventured north into dangerous indio country, where the savage Chichimeca were unconquered. The men braved bloodthirsty indios, who ate their captives, and fellow prospectors, who would have put a knife in their back for a silver lode. Often they worked in pairs, and when a find was made they constructed a small tower over the claim where one man stood with a musket while the other rushed to register the claim.

Zacatecas was considered by some to be the second city of New Spain, outshined only by the greater glory of Ciudad Mexico. But Don Julio said the boom city was like a barrel of fish—when the last bit of silver is pulled from it, there would be no more city. But until then it was a place where one day a man might be in mud up to his knees cursing mules as he carried supplies to the mines and the next find that he is a fine "gentleman" of New Spain, referred to as "Don," and perhaps purchase a noble title in the process.

Don Julio said, "We first had a landed nobility in New Spain when each conquistador was given a domain from which to collect tribute, then a merchant class when cities began to rise atop Aztec ruins. Now we have a silver nobility, men who discovered that the dirt in their fingernails was silver ore. These men buy titles and wives from noble families and build palaces. One day they heard the bay of mules and had manure stuck to the bottom of their boots, and the next their dirty ears were titillated by murmurs of "Señor Marqués," as they went by with a new coat of arms on the side of their carriage."

The don told me the story of a muleteer he knew who became a count. "With his earnings from his mule trains, he bought a mine abandoned because it had become flooded and no one knew how to drain the water. He consulted me, but I was too busy designing a way to keep Mexico City from being deluged to help him. However, he and a friend devised a way of tunneling the water out. He became wealthy enough that when his daughter married, he paved the way from his house to the church in silver."

The silver nobles sent to Spain, the king's fifth, aboard the treasure fleet that bought the luxuries of Spain—the finest furniture, swords, jewelry. From the Far East the Manila galleons brought them silk and ivory and spices.

"In a country of chinos named China, a great wall, hundreds of miles long, is being built to hold back barbarians from the north. It is said that the chino emperor is financing the building of this wall with New Spain silver obtained from the sale of silk."

I knew something of the place called China, or Cathay, because the don's library contained a copy of the travels of Marco Polo. Christopher Columbus, of course, thought his voyage would take him to China and had a copy of Marco Polo's book on the voyage with him.

Silver was not just for buying noble titles, but the king's fifth financed the perpetual wars that the Mother Country fought in Europe. To get that money, the silver was mined and refined in the north country and hauled to the capital on the back of mules. There, some of the bars were minted into coins and others were shipped whole to Spain on the treasure fleet.

The transfer of the plate to Veracruz once a year was done with a troop of soldados, and no bandit dared attack. But the metal came to the mint from the mining country in so many mule trains during the course of a year that it was impossible to protect all of them. A system had been set up in which bags of dirt were transferred in mule trains as decoys. When the banditos attacked, they were met with strong resistance by soldados pretending to be indio mule herders.

"The robbers have begun avoiding the false mule trains and attacking those only carrying silver. The viceroy wants to know why. The schedule for the false trains is made in the mint and sent by messengers to the mines. My suspicion is that someone in the mint is selling the information to the banditos."

"How about the messenger? Or at the mines?"

"Unlikely as to either. There are different instructions to the various mines, all in sealed pouches. From the way the bandits avoid the traps, they know the entire schedule, not that of just one mine. The only source of the complete schedule in one place is the mint."

"Am I to go into the mint and investigate?" My eyes were lit up envisioning stacks of gold and silver, some of it finding its way into my pockets.

"That would be putting a fox in to watch the chickens. No, your work will be on the outside, on the street as is the custom. Besides the mint director, who is above suspicion, there is only one man who has access to the list. You are to watch him for any suspicious contacts he makes. A new list is prepared weekly, and the suspect has access to it. He's the one who prepares the individual lists for the mines and gives them to the north country messenger. After that, he must pass it almost immediately to a conspirator who carries it north to the bandit gang. He may do it on his way home from the mint, sometime during the night, or even on his way to work in the morning. After that, it will be too late to have it in the hands of the bandits. I expect you to watch the man at the mint to see who he passes the information to."

He turned to Mateo. "You are to relieve Cristo during his watches. And have horses ready for both of you when it is time to follow the person carrying the stolen information north."

We told him we would start watching the mint official immediately. I said, "You look tired, Don Julio. More than tired. You must get away from the tunnel and rest."

"I will rest in the grave soon. The rains are falling heavily. Each day the water level for the city rises."

"The tunnel?"

"My plans were not followed. I have tried to patch it in a dozen places, but after I patch it in one place, the old water-logged adobe bricks permit it to cave in elsewhere. The earthquake a few days ago undid a year's work of clearing the tunnel. Have you heard that we have a prophet who says the tunnel will fail because a Jew built it? He doesn't even call me a converso."

I knew of the man, a Franciscan fray who had ran afoul of his holy order and no doubt had lost his mind. He became a wanderer in the streets, living off the charity of those who fear madmen. Earthquakes always frighten people because they are so severe in the valley. After the big earthquake, the monk preached in the plaza mayor, telling people that the city was Sodom and God was going to destroy it. Numerous small quakes followed the big one, and people panicked, crowding into churches.

Our surveillance of the mint employee did not reveal who he passed the silver trains list to. Yet the list had been passed, because robberies erupted again by a bandit gang that knew exactly what mule trains were carrying silver.

The more we observed the employee, the more we doubted that he was the culprit—yet he was the only one with the information. The messenger who delivered the lists to the mines was given sealed pouches by the employee.

Had the messenger opened the pouches, the recipients would have known it.

The employee lived alone in a modest house with just one servant. Between the two of us, Mateo and I kept a close eye on him and his servant. There was never any opportunity for him to pass the information on.

Mateo let his beard grow, and I stopped trimming mine. Neither of us were anxious to be identified as the autors of the closed plays that were the talk of the town.

A visit to a goldsmith's shop finally revealed to me who the mint employee was passing the information on to. Don Julio had sent me to the goldsmith to pick up a gold chain and medallion he had purchased for Isabella's birthday. While I waited inside the shop, a man came in and ordered a gold ring for his wife, a very expensive ring. The purchaser was the messenger who carried the lists to the northern mines.

The only way the messenger could get his hands on the complete list was if the mint employee gave it to him. It struck me as to how the deed was done. The mint employee we watched was conspiring with the northern rider, giving him not just the individual lists to deliver to the mine owners, but a separate copy of the complete list for delivery to the bandits. We never saw the lists passed because the illicit transaction took place inside the mint when the rider was given the sealed pouches he was to legally carry.

When a new list was issued, Mateo and I followed the rider to the north. We had a copy of the man's schedule—all except for the rendezvous with the robbers.

We rode north toward Zacatecas, following the mint rider. It was a well-traveled road and we blended in with the merchants, mule trains, and officials on their way to the northern mines. Leaving the Valley of Mexico, the area the Aztecs called Anáhuac, Land by the Water, we rode into a more arid land. Not the great northern deserts that stretched endlessly, the vast sands of Francisco Vázquez de Coronado and the fabled Seven Golden Cities of Cíbola, but a land that was neither as wet as the valley nor as dry as the deserts.

Indios still ran wild in the territory surrounding Zacatecas, but they were naked and afoot, and it was rare that they would attack two well-armed men on horseback.

The indios of the region were called Chichimeca, a name the Spanish applied to many barbaric, nomadic tribes who still ate raw meat—some of it human. When thousands of miners invaded their territory, a fierce war had been fought with the indios. The battles had gone on for decades. Even after the viceroy's troops put down the last large-scale resistance, the fighting never stopped. The indios continued to live and war in small packs, claiming scalps, weapons, and women as their trophies.

"They are as naked as sin," Mateo told me. "The frays can't get them to put on clothes, much less live in houses and plant maize. But they are great fighters, masters with bows, fearless in an attack. No indios in New Spain are as fierce."

All of the attacks by bandits on the mule trains carrying silver had been in the Zacatecas area, and we were confident that the list would not leave the rider's hands until we reached the city called the Silver Capital of the World.

Zacatecas had the reputation of being the wildest place in New Spain, where fortunes were won and lost with the turn of a card, and men died just as quickly. A paradise for Mateo, but I was surprised that he was not excited about visiting the town.

"It lays claim to being a great city, but it has no spirit. Barcelona, Seville, Roma, Mexico, these are *cities* that survive the ages. As the don says, Zacatecas is a barrel of silver fish. When the fish are all caught, no more Zacatecas. Besides, there are a hundred men to every woman. What place can call itself a city in which men must find love in the palm of their own hand? There is no love or honor in the city."

I should have known that women would be behind his feelings for the city. To live for love and honor, or to die defending it, was the way of the chivalric knights.

Zacatecas was built in a basin of hills, at an altitude even higher than the Mexico valley. The hills were places of scrub brush and stunted trees. The entire mining region was an arid wilderness with few rivers and little cultivation of maize and other crops. The town was laid out with a plaza in the center where a church stood along with the alcalde palace. The better houses, and some were palaces, spread out from the central plaza. Beyond the heart of the city were an indio barrio and a barrio of freedmen and mulattos.

We had not kept close to the rider during the journey but now that we had arrived at a place where we believed the list would be passed, we closed the distance to keep him in sight. He went to an inn near the central plaza and we followed. We were taking our packs from the back of the horses to release the beasts to the care of the stable when we heard a loud, shrill laugh that had an abrasive, but familiar, ring to it.

Two men coming down the street were talking, and the larger of the two, an exceptionally ugly, corpulent man wearing a bright yellow, silk doublet and breeches, entered the inn.

They had not seen us and Mateo had ducked down, pretending to check something on the side of his horse. When he stood up, we looked at each other.

"Now we know who is getting the mint list," he said.

Sancho de Erauso, whose real name was Catalina de Erauso, the man-woman for whom I once violated an ancient tomb, was now in the business of robbing the king's silver.

"We can't go into the inn; she'll recognize us," I said.

Mateo shrugged. "It's been years since she saw us. We both now have beards, which is the fashion of this cold, dismay place. We look like a thousand other miners and muleteers."

I was not anxious to tempt fate with a woman who pretended to be a man and who was as strong as a bull and had the temperament of a spitting viper. "I don't think we should go in. Let's get the alcalde to arrest her."

"On what evidence? That she robbed a tomb years ago? We have no proof yet that she's involved with the silver robberies except that she frequents the same inn as the mint rider. We need to know where her gang is hiding so we can put them out of business."

Forced to enter the inn or play the coward, I followed Mateo inside. We took a table in a dark corner in the tavern area. Catalina and her companion were at a table across the room with the mint rider. We paid no attention to them, but I was certain Catalina's eyes put musket shots in us as we walked to our table.

Mateo ordered bread, meat, a slab of cheese, and a jug of wine.

As we ate, Mateo watched the people out of the corner of his eye. "He passed the list to Catalina and she gave him a pouch, probably gold."

"What do we do?"

"Nothing yet. When Catalina leaves, we'll follow her to see if she reports to anyone else and where her gang is hiding."

She left a few minutes later with her companion, and we followed slowly. They went to a stable at another inn, and we returned for our own horses. They left town on the road to Panuco, a mining town three leagues to the north. The richest mines in New Spain were in the area. But it was not to a mine, but another inn, a much smaller one, that their horses carried them. A carriage was stationed next to the stable. The carriage was not as rich and luxurious as the one bearing the same coat of arms that I had ridden in in Veracruz and seen in Mexico, but the heraldic bearings were unmistakably: the coat of arms of the de la Cerda family, the noble clan of Luis. Son of a marques, he was the grandson of a woman who had an unfathomable murderous vendetta against me, and if rumor proved true, was soon to be the husband of the woman I loved.

Mateo noticed the intensity of my feelings, and I told him who owned the coach.

"Luis may not be connected to the robberies," Mateo said.

"He is. And so is Ramon de Alva."

"Have you learned from a witch the power of mind reading?"

"No, the power of silver. What was the name of the mint official who provides the list to robbers?"

"Soto, the same as Alva's brothers-in-law, but it's a very common name."

"I'm certain we'll find there's a relationship. Luis's family is also known to be involved in business dealings with Alva."

"All the dons of New Spain deal with each other."

I knew in my heart that Luis was involved. I could not explain to Mateo, but there was a certain darkness of heart to Luis that matched the same trait in Alva. Both men struck me as cold and ruthless. Eh, robbing silver trains was less reprehensible then killing thousands of indios with poor and inadequate materials in the tunnel, an activity I was certain Alva was involved in. And now I was certain he and Luis were involved in the silver robberies.

I got off my horse and handed the reins to him. "I'm going to find out for sure."

Sneaking around to the side of the inn, I gained access to a window. Not more than a few feet away, Catalina and Luis drank and talked like old friends—and conspirators. The man-woman suddenly turned and looked me in the eye. I gave myself away by panicking and running back to the horses.

"Luis and Catalina, they spotted me. What should we do?" I asked Mateo.

"Ride like the wind back to Mexico and report to Don Julio."

A fortnight later, after three changes of horses and cursed rain that dogged us the moment we crossed the mountains into the Valley of Mexico, we rode across a causeway into the city. Rain had pounded us as if the rain god had decided to wreak vengeance on us for the work we did in denying him blood sacrifices. Often we had to seek high ground to avoid meadows that had turned into small lakes. We sloshed through a foot of water crossing the causeway into the city. On some streets the water was up to our horses bellies.

Neither of us spoke. We were too tired, and too aware of the consequences that might follow to the don. The fact that we had solved the silver robberies would help the don's problem with the viceroy, I assured myself. But that a lépero, wanted for two murders, and a picaro, who should be banished to Manila, both employed by a converso, were to accuse rich, powerful men . . . ay, who was I fooling with my thoughts of truth and justice?

Worry ached my chest and stomach as we approached the don's house. It was only nine o'clock in the evening when we reached it. We were surprised that no light shone from the house. Isabella insisted upon maintaining the house with blazing candles inside and outside to let the world know how *she* shines, but none of the lights were lit. My lépero instincts would normally have been aroused by the difference in lighting, but we had rode as if the devil was on our tail. We were hungry and exhausted.

We dismounted at the main gate and opened it, two wet, muddy men walking their wet, muddy horses to the stable. The first indication of danger I had was movement in the darkness. Then Mateo's sword was drawn. I clutched clumsily at my own sword, but stopped as Mateo lowered his own.

A dozen men surrounded us, armed with swords and muskets. They wore the green cross of the Inquisition.

NINETY-FOUR

THE INQUISITORS TOOK our swords and daggers and tied our hands behind our backs as I plied them with questions.

"Why are you doing this? We've done nothing."

The only answer was a sudden rain burst, lashing us like a cat-o'-nine-tails from the sky. I knew very well who they were, but silence is considered guilt in the face of an accusation, so I was loud about my innocence, demanding that they present their credentials to Don Julio.

When my hands were tied, they pulled a black hood over my head. Rough hands steered me to a carriage. Before the hood went down, I saw Mateo hooded and being put into another carriage. When the hood went down, my ears became my eyes. The only sounds were the violent rain and the shuffling of feet. The sole words I heard when they separated us was a familiar calling me "the marrano," a secret Jew. That told me we were not being arrested for deshonesto books and plays but as part of Don Julio's tunnel problems. The Inquisition burned Jews. Of course, I could avoid being burned at the stake. I could tell them I was not really a converso Spaniard at all, that I have only been pretending to be a gachupin. That I was actually a mestizo wanted for the murder of two Spaniards. That way I would only be tortured, hanged, and my head mounted at the city gate.

Tlaloc, the rain god, wanted to drown the city. Don Julio, with his grand ideas to save the city with a tunnel, had gotten in the way of the god's vengeance.

My mind and body were strangely calm. True, I felt panic pull in my heart, but my thoughts were for Don Julio and his family, sweet, delicate little Juana and the nervous bird,

Inez. Poor Inez. She had waited all her life for a terrible disaster to happen and now it came to her door in the middle of the night.

No concern stirred in me for Isabella. I was certain she would find a way to avoid the Inquisition, perhaps even collect a reward for turning in Don Julio. With her connection to Alva, no doubt she had already given a statement to the Inquisition. One did not need an Aztec diviner to fathom that, if it would help her, the don's wife would have told the Inquisitors we were devil worshippers who ate the flesh of Christians.

The coach rumbled on cobblestone streets, rain beating on the roof. I rocked back and forth in my seat and kept up questions in the hopes of learning something about the don's fate. The silence was not ignorance, but intimidation. Each unanswered question generated more anxious questions, more fear, and that was the intent. Fray Antonio had told me about his own experiences with the Inquisition, about the silence. But to have heard about it happening to someone else was different than experiencing it yourself.

I wanted to tell the men beside me that I knew what foul creatures they were. The secret army of the green cross. The hounds of the Holy Office of the Inquisition. Men in black who came in the dark of night to drag you from your bed and take you to a place where you might never see the sun again. I wondered if "Don" Jorge was among them. If he identified me as the printer of profane books, they would burn me at the stake twice.

The heavy downpour stopped, and my world of sound became the heavy breathing of a man beside me and the hiss of water beneath the carriage wheels. I knew we had entered the main plaza when the sound of the carriage wheels changed. The dungeon of the Holy Office was not far.

The carriage stopped and the door opened. The man on my right got out and pulled me out after him. As I tried to cautiously step down, he gave me a jerk, causing me to miss the step. I twisted sideways as I fell, smacking the street stones with my left shoulder.

Silent hands lifted me up and directed me through a doorway. The floor suddenly was not there and I started falling, crashing against a wall. Hands grabbed me again and stabilized me. I was on a stairwell. Starting down it, my feet went out from under me and I began to stumble. I fell against someone in front of me, breaking my fall. I hit the steps, banging my head, and slamming down on the same shoulder that I had injured on the cobblestones.

Jerked to my feet, I was half dragged down a stairway. When we reached a floor, I was guided against a wooden frame. My hands were untied and retied, my doublet and shirt removed, so I was naked from the waist up. The hood came off. I was in a room, shadowy, almost dark, with large candles burning in the upper corner of two walls. The wood frame I was tied to was the notorious instrument called a rack. The room was a torture chamber.

The walls of stone glistened wetly. Water ran in streams on the floor. It made the dungeon atmosphere more gruesome. Even in normal weather conditions, the city's water table was so high that graves filled with water before the dirt was thrown in. The dungeon defied the tendency of any hole to fill with water more than a few feet deep. No doubt the Inquisition had the funds to construct a room that did not flood. Or, as the bishop of the Holy Office probably claimed, God kept the room from flooding so the inquisitors could do their work.

When I was securely tied, my mouth was gagged. The sound of struggling and Mateo cursing came from an adjoining room. The sounds stopped and I assumed he was gagged also. I wondered how many of these little chambers of horror were in this hellhole.

The familiars conferred across the room with two frays. The frays wore dark robes with hoods. I could not hear exactly what was being said, but again I made out the word "marrano."

The familiars left and the two frays slowly approached

me. There was nothing hurried about their movements. I felt like a lamb staked out with jungle beasts about to rip out its guts.

They stood in front of me. The hoods went over their heads but did not completely cover their faces. Behind the edges of the cowls, their faces were as vague as fish in dark water. One pulled down the gag enough so that I could speak.

"Are you a Jew?" he asked. The question was asked in a very gentle tone, a fatherly tone, a father asking a child if it had been bad.

The kindly tone caught me by surprise and I stammered out a response, "I am a good Christian."

"We shall see," he murmured, "we shall see."

They began removing my boots and breeches.

"What are you doing? Why are you taking my clothes?"

Silence greeted my questions. The gag was pulled back over my mouth.

When I was naked, my legs were tied to the frame. The two frays began a minute examination of my body. One stood on a bench and parted my hair to view my scalp. They slowly moved down my body, looking at each mark, not just only scars, but moles and blotches, the shape of my eyes, even the few wrinkles on my face. Each carefully traced the lines on my palms. As they silently worked, one would gesture to the other to double-check a blemish or wrinkle.

They were looking for a sign of the devil on my skin.

The silliness of their actions struck me. I started to laugh and choked on the gag. The indignity of what these two priests were doing, touching my body, examining my skin, hair, even my virile part. Is this what they became priests for? To find the devil in a mole? To see demons in a wrinkle of skin?

As they examined my virile part, I realized that I was fortunate that the Aztec gods had stolen a piece of foreskin. The frays believed I was a Jew—with their twisted logic, had I *not* appeared circumcised, they would have concluded that as a Jew, I had been earlier circumcised and Lucifer had restored my foreskin so I could disguise myself as a Christian.

When they finished in front, the rack was swiveled so they could examine my backside. Ay! Did they think the devil was hiding up my back door?

They handled me like two butchers deciding how to carve a side of beef. No conclusions as to whether I bore the mark of the devil were stated to me.

Working my jaw, I slipped the gag far enough down my chin to mumble. I asked again, why I was being held, what the charges against me were.

The two frays were deaf to all but their own utterances and whatever messages they believed God whispered to them.

"The girl, Juana, has she been seized? She has special needs; her body is fragile. God would punish anyone who harmed a poor sick child like her," I threatened.

The mention of God's punishment got the attention of one fray. He looked up from checking for the devil between my toes. I could not discern his hooded features, but for a brief moment his eyes met mine. His eyes were black, blazing fire pits, dark flames in a fathomless well, a brooding wrath that invited me . . . nay, tried to suck me in. His eyes shared the same macabre madness of Aztec priests who tore out throbbing hearts and fed on blood like vampires.

After they had finished their examination, they unfastened my arms and legs and gave me my shirt and breeches to put back on. I was taken down a few steps to a stone corridor of cells behind iron doors with Judas windows. It was wetter at this level and my feet splashed in water above my ankles. Moans escaped through one of the judas windows as I walked by. An agonized voice came from another.

"Who's there? Please tell me, what is the date? The month? Have you heard of the family of Vicento Sanchez? Are they well? Do my children know their father still lives? Help me! For the love of God, *help me!*"

They opened a rusted iron door and gestured for me to enter. A shapeless black void lay before me. I hesitated to enter, fearful that it was a trick, that I was being dropped into a deep pit to die. One of the frays pushed me, and I stumbled into the cell, splashing in water up to my knees before my outstretched hands found a wall for support.

The door banged shut behind me, and I was immersed in complete darkness. Mictlan, the Land of the Dead, could not have been blacker. Hell could not frighten me anymore than I was by the complete absence of light.

Using my hands to feel, I slowly oriented myself to the room. Nay, not so much a room as a cesspool for vermin. With my arms stretched out on each side, I could touch the walls. A stone bench was my only refuge from the water.

The bench was not long enough to lay down on. I sat with my back against a wall and my legs outstretched on the bench. The wall beside me continually bled water. *Drip-dripdripdrip!* from the ceiling was unceasing and never failed to find my head no matter how I positioned myself.

No blanket, no place to pass body waste except the cesspool itself. I already guessed that I would taste no water except what I excreted in.

The place was wet and cold, but the rats did not mind. Moreover, I sensed another presence in the room. Something cold and slimy slithered across my legs, and I cried out in terror. My first impression was a snake, but even a snake would turn its nose up at this hellish place. If it was not a snake, I wondered . . . what else felt cold and clammy and slithered?

¡Ay de mí!

Fear crawled up my skin. I breathed slowly in and out, keeping my panic from overwhelming me. I knew what they were doing, those fiends in the robes of mendicant brothers, creating fear and panic to demoralize me. I laughed to myself. They were certainly succeeding. The only thing that kept me from a complete breakdown was that Fray Antonio had told me of these horrors.

Cold and shivering, I made a small prayer that God take

my life but spare the others. I had not prayed much in my life, but I owed it to the don and his family who had treated me as one of their own. How was the don taking this abuse? Inez and poor Juana? What about my friend, Mateo? He was a strong man, stronger than me, certainly much stronger than the don and the women. He would do as well as anyone who suddenly awakens to find that sometime during the night he had been dragged to Dante's *Infierno,* only this cold Hell was administered by the Church, who had blessed his birth and would bless his death.

The world is a cruel place.

NINETY-FIVE

DAYS AND NIGHTS passed. I saw no one and heard no sounds except my own fears and the soup ladle at my judas window. I counted the days by the meals, one in the morning, one at night, each time a cold gruel—sewer water with a few kernels of maize. Supper included a tortilla.

The fray bringing the food tapped on the window, and I put my bowl through the opening for him to fill. Straining to see through the small opening, all I saw was his dark cowl. I realized the anonymity served two purposes: The lack of human contact heightened the fear of those trapped in this nightmare, and it protected the monks from the revenge of prisoners who won their freedom but remembered the torture they'd suffered.

The food server never spoke. I heard others in cells calling out to him, sometimes wailing that they were dying or pleading for mercy, but there was no sign that a human being resided beneath the dark robe.

On the fourth day of my confinement, a bang on my door came even though I had already finished my morning gruel.

I waded across as the food door flapped opened. Candlelight flooded through the slot. The light was dull, but my light-starved eyes felt stabbed with maguey needles as I stared at it.

"Come into the light so I can see your face," the man holding the candle said.

I did as instructed. After a moment the candle was removed. I heard the scrap of wood as he moved a stool into position so he could sit and speak to me through the window. *Human contact!* I was close to tears at the notion that someone wanted to speak to me. Now I would find out what had happened to the don and his family and what the charges were against me.

"I have come to hear your confession for the transgressions you have committed against God and His Church," the man said. His voice was a monotone, the tone of a priest reciting a prayer that he had recited a thousand times before.

"I have committed no crimes. What am I charged with?"

"I am not permitted to tell you the charges."

"Then how can I confess? If I don't know the charges, what should I confess to? I can confess to impure thoughts when I saw a woman. Frequenting a tavern when I should have been in mass."

"Those are for the confessional booth. The Holy Office demands that you confess to crimes. You know the true nature of those crimes."

"I have not committed any crimes." Standing in the cold water, my body shivered and the words came out with a stutter. Of course, I was lying. I had committed many crimes. But none against God.

"Your denial will not do. If you were not guilty, you would not have been arrested and brought here. This is a House of the Guilty. The Holy Office investigates each charge thoroughly before taking a person into custody. It does not hunt down the sacrilegious, they are drawn to it by God's hand."

"I was brought here by devils, not angels."

"That is blasphemous! Speak not that way—you will not

gain the Lord's mercy vilifying His servants. Understand this: If you do not confess your crimes against God and His Church, you will be put to the question."

"You mean tortured?" Anger was rising in me because I realized the helplessness of my situation. If I confessed to religious crimes, I would find myself at an auto-da-fé stake with a fire roaring around me. And if I refused to confess to things I never did, I would be tortured until I confessed to them.

"Like all men who have lived and loved and fought," I said, "I may have transgressed at some time. But these are not insults to God, nor do they jeopardize my mortal soul. I confessed my sins to the Church and have been granted absolution. If there are other matters, you must tell me of what I am accused so I may tell you whether there is any truth to the tales."

"That is not how the Holy Office does its sacred work. I am not authorized to tell you the charges. You will learn those when you appear before the tribunal. But it will go easier on you if you confess now so you can put yourself at their mercy. If you do not confess, the truth will be wrenched out of you."

"What is the value of words drawn with pain? How can the Church treat its children like this?"

"The Church does not inflict pain. God guides the instruments; thus, the pain derives from the instrument, not the Church's holy hand. When blood is spilled or pain inflicted, it is the fault of the person, not the Church. Torture is not inflicted as punishment but to secure testimony."

"How does the Holy Office justify this?"

"San Dominic tells us that when words fail, blows may prevail."

I almost laughed and asked him to point to anywhere in the Bible where Jesus advocated violence, but held my tongue.

"Who is authorized to tell me the charges?"

"The tribunal."

"When will I see the tribunal?"

"After you confess."

"That is insane!"

"You have a bad attitude," he scolded. "You are trying to use reasoning that merchants use when they are buying bales of wool. This is not a negotiation over a side of beef or a game of primero. We do not worry about what cards are being held across the table or who is bluffing. *God knows your sins.* Your duty is to confess your transgressions. When you fail in that duty, the truth will be drawn from you."

"Your tortures draw confessions from the innocent, and I am innocent. I have nothing to confess. What happens then? Do you torture me to death?"

"God recognizes His own. If perchance you die without sin under torture, you will find everlasting peace. It is a just system, one approved by the Lord Himself. We are merely His servants. You are given an opportunity to confess before the truth is drawn from you. No one is punished until they have an opportunity to repent. Later, you will be brought before a tribunal and told the charges. The prosecutor will call witnesses who have made accusations against you. Your advocate will be able to call witnesses in your favor. Until that is done, you will not be punished."

"When will I be called before the tribunal?"

"After you confess."

"And if I don't confess?"

The man made a nasal sound that expressed his impatience with my stupidity.

"If you fail to confess, you are deemed guilty. The tribunal will determine the degree of your guilt and your punishment."

"All right," I said, "what if I confess right now? When will I be brought before the tribunal?"

"When it is ordered. For some, the call comes quickly. For others . . ."

"What have people said about me that makes you think I am a bad person?"

"You will be told at the time of the trial."

"But how can I prepare a defense to what people say if I don't even know who they are until the time of my trial?"

"We speak in circles, and I am tired of the game." He leaned closer to the opening and spoke in a whisper. "Because of the severity, I will tell you one of the charges so you can confess and hope for mercy. It concerns the Christian child."

"Christian child?"

"A missing child has been found dead in a cave, a little girl. The child was nailed to a cross in the same manner as our Savior. Unspeakable things had been done to her naked body. Within a foot of the terrible crime, Jewish wine and cups with the sign of the Jews was found. One cup was filled with wine and the blood of the child."

"What have I to do with this horror?"

"Witnesses saw you leaving the cave."

My shout of denial must have been heard all the way to the viceroy's palace. I threw up my hands, beseeching God in the darkness.

"*No!* I have nothing to do with this evil. Yes, I have transgressed. Holy Father in Heaven, I sold a few deshonesto books, I put on a play that offended some, but that is the extent of my crimes. I never touched a—"

My mouth snapped shut. A look of smug satisfaction had spread on his face. The story of the child had been a ruse, designed to shock me into confessing to true crimes. He had succeeded.

"New Spain seethes with Jews," he hissed. "They pretend to be good Christians, but they are plotting the death of all Christians. It is the duty of good Christians to denounce all false Christians, even in their own family."

"Why are you here?" I demanded.

"I have come to hear your confession so that I may advise the tribunal you have repented."

"You have heard it. I am a good Christian. I sold some profano books. I regret my transgressions. Send a priest in and I will confess to those matters I have stated. I have no others to reveal."

"I heard nothing about the Jewish activities of Don Julio and the rest of his family."

"You will hear no more from me because the tale you want to hear is a lie. When will I meet my advocate?"

"You already have. I am an abogado de los presos. Your advocate."

Later I was taken from my cell and brought to a room where racks and other torture implements were applied. Waiting for me was Don Jorge, the familiar who paid me to print the banned lists, and an old friend—Juan the lépero.

"That's him," Juan said. "He said the master of the print shop had gone to Madrid. I never saw anyone but him run it."

"To your knowledge, this man practices witchcraft and has shift with the devil?"

"Yes, yes," the lying lépero said. "I have seen him talking to the devil. Once I saw him swirling in the air with the devil sodomizing him."

I laughed. "This lépero trash would sell you his mother's love hole for a copper."

Juan pointed an accusatory finger at me.

"He cast spells on me. Forced me to do the devil's work."

"You are a work of the devil, you swine. Do you think anyone would believe such a crazy story from a social scab?"

I looked at the familiars standing by us for confirmation that no one would believe a lying street trash with such a ridiculous story. Their faces told me that the lépero would indeed be believed.

After being returned to my cell, day and night became one again, and I no longer knew how long I had been imprisoned as I lost track of the monotonous food servings. Body fat accumulated from years of feasting at the don's table slipped off my bones. Anxiety never left me. When would I be taken out from my cell and tortured? Would I be able to back up my brave words and endure it or cry like a baby and confess to whatever they asked? Worse than my anxieties, I wondered how the don and the poor ladies fared. If confessing to sex with the devil would have gotten them released, I would have willingly done so. But I knew that anything I confessed to would be used against them as members of the household. I considered implicating that puta bitch Isabella as having had sex with the devil, but again, when I made myself even an innocent witness to blasphemy, I was sealing my doom.

Being in the cold, wet cell twenty-four hours a day was torture in and of itself. Isabella, in her wildest imagination, could not have found me a more miserable place to bed down. Ay, I would have given several toes for a night stretched out in my warm, dry bed above the stable. I would have given them just to have slept with the horses.

When they came to get me, I knew not the day or the hour. My cell door suddenly opened, and I was painfully blinded by torchlight.

"Come forward," a voice instructed me. "Stretch out your hands."

I closed my eyes and crawled out of the cell. My hands were chained together. I had to be lifted to my feet because my legs would not support me. I no longer had feeling or strength in my limbs. The two frays, wearing what I had come to think of as demon robes, assisted me to the torture room.

My abogado was waiting.

"You have an opportunity to confess before you are put to the question," he said. "I am here to witness it."

"I confess that I have seen you suck men's pene in the manner of vipers," I said. "I confess that I have seen these two devil priests sodomize sheep. I confess—"

"You may proceed," he said to the frays. Nothing in his voice betrayed that he was in anyway offended by my insults. "He should not be wearing this." He removed my mother's cross.

As I was being strapped to a rack, he stood beside me and spoke in a conversational tone. "You are lucky you are in New Spain. This dungeon is no worse than a stroll on the Alameda compared to prisons on the peninsula. I once served in a prison in Spain whose dungeon is so deep it is called el infierno, hell itself. Nowhere could a face be made out without striking a light."

"Is that where your mother conceived you?" I asked, in a most polite tone.

"Cristo, Cristo, you should not speak badly of one whose only mission in life is to help people like you."

My laughter was interrupted as the chain on my wrists was attached to a hook. Frays raised me until my feet were off the ground. Weights were attached to my feet. I was lifted into the air as the hook was raised and then allowed to fall toward the floor, but stopped with a jerk just before my feet touched solid ground. I screamed as my arms and legs were almost pulled from their joints by the weights.

My attorney sighed. "You wish to tell me about Don Julio and the Jewish rites he practices?"

I do not remember what my reply was, but it angered him and delighted my torturers. No torturer likes an easy victim because it keeps them from demonstrating their skills. I do not even remember all that was done to me—at some point I was lying flat as if in a bed, my mouth was propped open with a piece of wood, and a linen cloth was put down my throat. Water was slowly poured onto the cloth and it drained into my stomach. I could breathe only with difficulty, and I was certain my stomach was going to burst. When vómito erupted, it gushed out my mouth and nose and choked me. To my regret, my advocate sidestepped the flow I directed at him.

No more words flowed from me, either in confession or condemnation, and they worked on me until they tired. When they finished, I was too weak and dizzy to walk to my cell, and they chained me to a rack until I could regain my feet.

I could have told them that they were wasting their time torturing me. They had drained me of all human feeling by the time they began pounding me with questions. I merely drooled and laughed insanely at their questions because I was too weak and in agony to formulate answers or insults.

The walls separating my torture chamber from the adjoining one were full of wide cracks. I heard the whimper of a female voice, and I strained to maneuver into a position where I could see into the chamber. When I did, I gasped from what I saw.

Juana was strapped naked to a rack. The poor soul's skinny, little body showed all of its bones. Two frays were examining her, and I could see that they had spread her legs and were using an instrument to see if she was a virgin. I remembered what Fray Antonio told me: If an unmarried girl's hymen was broken, they would accuse her of having had intercourse with the devil. And if it was intact, she still was accused of having the intercourse—they claimed the devil had repaired it with his black magic.

Fire from somewhere deep in my soul exploded, and life erupted in me again. I screamed obscenities at the frays and resisted the gag they tried to put on my mouth. I did not shut up until I was beaten into unconsciousness.

But, of course, as my advocate had so thoughtfully apprised me in our first interview, it was not the frays inflicting the pain by swinging the clubs, it was the clubs themselves.

NINETY-SIX

MORE DARKNESS. DRIPDRIPDRIPDRIP from the ceiling.

More torture. Questions that went unanswered. I was so weak they now had to drag me out of my cell and down the passageway to where the rack awaited.

My body now anticipated the tortures so well that I screamed before they inflicted pain. I don't know exactly all that flew off of my tongue; but since the torture continued, they must not have liked my answers. I had picked up an extensive vocabulary of gutter expressions on the streets of Veracruz, comments about one's wife, daughters, sons, mother, and father. I applied these liberally to my lawyer and the priests.

I confessed many things. Each day I confessed more and more, screaming my sins to them, demanding that they burn me at the stake so I would not be cold anymore. But my confessions did not please them because I never implicated the don or his family.

Then it stopped—no more dragging me from my cell, no more screaming. I no longer had any sense at all of the passage of time or if it even passed. But life goes on even in the most dire of situations, and soon I had enough sense back to realize how many places I hurt. I had sores on my body from unhealed wounds and the constant dampness.

But then one day I saw him again, the man who claimed to be my advocate. He came after a food serving that I knew was breakfast only because there was no tortilla.

"You appear before the tribunal today for trial. They will bring you up in a few minutes. Do you have any witnesses in your favor?"

It was a long time before I answered him. Not because my mouth worked slowly, but because I wanted to form the words correctly. When I spoke, it was calmly and quietly.

"How can I know what witnesses to call if I am not told the charges? How can I call witnesses if I cannot leave my cell to speak to them? How can I call witnesses if you tell me the trial is about to start? How can I put on a defense if my advocate is a whore in the pay of the devil?"

I don't know how long I spoke to the closed food door. I believe my advocate left after my first sentence, but I continued to talk logically and reasonably to the door. It did not answer me back.

* * *

Inquisitors must develop the eyes of bats. The room where the tribunal met was as ill lit as the rest of the dungeon. Half a dozen men in secretive cowls were in the room. Their faces were lost in shadows, and their function hardly had meaning to me. My impression was that there were two inquisitors, a prosecutor, and a number of other people whose precise function escaped me, but they may have been judges. Scribes were also present, taking down the words spoken.

I was chained to the chair I was sat upon. My advocate sat away from me, as if I would give him some foul disease if he crept too close. Perhaps it was my smell. He did not look pleased with me. I suppose he is usually able to inform the tribunal that he had been successful at obtaining a confession from an accused, and my denial was demeaning to his skills as my abogado.

I heard the prosecutor read the charges, but they made no sense to me—vague allegations about heresy, being a secret Jew, blasphemy, and devil worship. That I was a corrupt person who sold banned books and put on two offensive plays were the only charges they had right.

My advocate rose and informed the tribunal that he had dutifully asked me to confess the truth of the charges three times, and I had refused. "Persuasion on the rack failed to loosen his tongue. He is now in the hands of God."

"I don't see God in this room," I said. "I see men who believe they serve God but do the Lord an injustice."

My statements were not greeted with the applause of a well-received comedia but a frown from one of the judges.

"If the prisoner speaks without permission again, give him the mordaza," he told the constable. A mordaza was a gag. I shut my mouth.

The chain of evidence against me began with testimony from inquisitors who had questioned me verbally about the Church, God, Christ, Jews, Satan, witches, and only heaven knows what else. The questions sounded like those that Fray Antonio had described as the Witches Hammer, in which there were no real answers and every response could be twisted.

"He was asked how many horns Satan has," the fray testified at the Inquisition hearing. "He replied that he didn't know. As we all know, Satan has two horns."

"Had I said two horns, he would have accused me of having personally seen Satan!" I shouted.

"The mordaza," the constable was told.

"I meant no offense, Monseñor. Please, I promise to keep my lips sealed."

Once more I avoided being gagged.

The first witness was called. She was masked, but I could tell from her voice it was a servant from Don Julio's house. She was a crazy old woman who was always seeing devils and demons everywhere she looked. We all knew she was harmless, but she had the queer sort of insanity that Inquisitors fed upon.

"I saw them dancing," she told the tribunal, "that one," meaning me, "the don, his sister, and his niece. They each took turns dancing with the devil."

The judges asked her questions about Jewish customs in the house, whether we observed the Sabbath on Saturdays, ate meat on Fridays; the old woman confirmed that we ate meat on Fridays, a lie, but in response to other questions she kept telling them about different acts with the devil. She was obviously crazy, babbling on about demonic things when asked about Jewish rites.

I don't think even these judges were impressed with her tales, other than specifically noting the violation of the proscription on eating meat on Fridays.

Poor Juana could not have danced with her weak legs if the devil had propped her up, but I kept my mouth shut.

The next witness was another masked woman, this one well dressed. I knew her identity immediately.

Isabella had come to help nail down my coffin lid. From her well-kept appearance, she had not tasted the Inquisition's dungeon, but I had expected no less.

I cringed as I listened to her testimony because there was some truth to it.

"You call this metal tube a 'starscope'?" a judge asked.

"That is what Don Julio called it. I knew nothing of such things, of course. My belief is that this blackguard," she indicated me, "had brought the foul instrument from Spain, smuggling it by the officials of the Holy Office who inspect for such blasphemies."

"And you say that the purpose of the instrument was to spy on heaven?"

"Yes, that and many other evil things that I have no knowledge of."

No knowledge but she could testify to them? Like the birth of our Savior, was this Immaculate knowledge? I could tell from the testimony that the inquisitors had not found the instrument. I suspected that Don Julio, fearful that he could encounter problems in the city over the tunnel, had hidden his banned books and the starscope on the hacienda.

She was asked questions about Jewish practices, and she denied them for good reason—such practices would incriminate her, too. But she got a blow in against Don Julio in another way.

"He forced me to lay with him during times when I was with my monthly blood."

Engaging in coitus during a woman's monthly disablement was a sacrilege because conception could not be had at that time. It was generally believed that Jews and Moors conducted themselves in this manner to keep from fathering children that would necessarily be raised as Christians.

"You have no children, señora?" a judge asked.

"That is true. But it is not my fault. My husband was a brutal man with a terrible temper. I lived in constant fear of him."

I had to fight myself to keep from leaping out of my chair and going for her throat. If there ever was a man who walked with angels in his relationship with his family and friends, it was the don.

A book was shown to her.

"This book is one that you turned over to the familiars, is that correct?"

"Yes. I never saw the book before; but after my husband was taken into custody, I noticed it in the library. He had kept it in a secret place."

"The book sets forth the rites of the practice of Judaism," the judge said.

"I know nothing of that. I am a good Christian. The book belonged to my husband. I am certain it must be the book he used when he and his family, including this one"—I could feel her glare through the mask—"practiced their dark rites."

This time I leaped from my chair.

"That's a lie. The book does not belong to the don, and I can prove it." I pointed at it. "The don brands his books with his initials along the edge, as is the custom among book owners. There is no brand. *The book is false evidence!*"

They gagged me.

Isabella was deliberately incriminating Don Julio and me with false evidence. The woman was motivated in life only by money and vanity. The Holy Office seized the property of those found guilty. It took no imagination to conclude that an arrangement had been made by which Isabella received property back in exchange for her testimony. Or Ramon de Alva could be behind her, getting rid of his lover's husband and the threat of exposure on the tunnel project at the same time.

The third witness was a man who I could not identify. He stated he worked for Don Julio on the tunnel project and that he had observed Don Julio and me scoff when he said that we should dedicate the tunnel to San Pablo. That he had later seen us carry an object into the tunnel, a six-pointed star. The object had no significance to him at the time; but now that a fray had enlightened him, he realized that what we carried was a mystic Jewish symbol, the Shield of David, that Jews attributed magical properties to.

I had never been to the tunnel, had never seen this six-pointed star-shield, but I would not have taken exception even if my mouth wasn't sealed. The matter of my guilt, and that of Don Julio, was predetermined. Nothing I could do or say, no appeal to reason, would suffice.

My advocate never asked a question of any witness.

My gag was removed and a judge asked if I wished to speak about the charges.

"The charges are nonsense," I said. "This trial has the same validity as the trial of another Jew a long time ago."

"Then you admit you are a Jew," the judge said.

"The Jew I referred to is our Savior, Jesus Christ, whose name was chosen for me to bear. I now see why I bear his name. I am to be martyred by false witnesses as He once was."

The tribunal was not pleased with my response. I was returned to the blackness of my cell. I was only in the cell for the night. My door opened and I was escorted out to be burned at a stake, I was certain. But instead I was taken to a large, ground-level cell that held five prisoners, including one I knew well.

Ignoring his embarrassment, I gave my amigo a great hug. Mateo took me into a corner and spoke to me in whispers.

"You have escaped the stake, but not severe punishment. You will get a hundred lashes and sentenced to the northern mines."

"How do you know?"

"My cousin in Oaxaca, who made his fortune buying land from indios after getting them drunk, has paid the Holy Office for my sins. He has proof our family line has purity of blood. I will be taken to Acapulco and placed aboard the Manila galleon. The ocean crossing is rivaled only by Charon's trip across the river Styx. Many of those who survive the brutal trip are eaten by the natives.

"I asked an accommodation for you, and he was told you were a suspected marrano, so exile to Manila was not possible. But he discovered that someone had paid for your life. A sentence to the mines is hardly less painful than being burned at the stake, but at least you live another day and . . . who knows?" He shrugged.

"And what of the don? Juana and Inez?"

His face darkened and he wouldn't look at me.

"The stake. They will be burned at the stake? Santa Maria," I whispered. "Is there no way to ransom them?"

"Inez and Juana are marranos."

"I don't believe it."

"They had a book of Jewish rites Isabella found."

"It was lying evidence. The don's initials were not on the book."

"The book was theirs, not the don's. I saw it at the hacienda. I also know they commonly practiced the rites. I have seen them. That's why the don banished them to the hacienda. And he forbade them from bringing any of their Jewish instruments or books with them. They brought it to the city, and Isabella found it and used it against them. I was shown the book by the frays and denied I had ever seen it."

"I don't care if they're Jews. They're my friends."

"Not friends, Bastardo, they're our family. And while we don't care, there are many who do."

"Nothing can be done?"

"If they repent, they will be strangled at the stake before the fire is lit. Because they are women, they might elude the stake altogether by repenting, but they refuse. It's Inez. The nervous little bird is determined to die a martyr for her beliefs, and little Juana, I think, is just tired of living. The don will not permit his sister and niece to die alone, so he also refuses to repent."

"Madness! These are ravings from a play written by a madman."

"No, Cristo, this is no play. Life is sadder than any comedia. And the blood is real. This is a living nightmare."

NINETY-SEVEN

AN AUTO-DA-FE WAS not just a burning, but a grand show in which different levels of punishment were issued. And while all in the cell were to be punished at the auto-da-fé, none were to die at the stake.

Mateo warned me that no one in the cell could be trusted. Those who were not already spies for the Inquisition would become spies to reduce their punishment.

After a few days my advocate came to see me. He informed me of the sentence that Mateo had already advised me of. I pretended surprise at hearing that I would be spared the stake. Hoping that I did not sound contrite, I asked why I had been spared.

"The Lord acts in mysterious ways," he said.

Auto-da-fé, act of faith.

A *quemadera,* a burning place, was established in a corner of the Alameda, with a wooden pavilion similar to that I seen erected for the notables to watch the landing of the new archbishop. Only this time they will hear a sermon by a fray of the Holy Office and the charges read; then they will watch human beings burned as if they were pigs roasted for a party.

Mateo, who had an eye and an ear at the Alameda even when the rest of him was encased with me in a cell, said that preparation for the auto-da-fé had been going on for over a week, and the whole country was excited about it. People would be traveling from all over New Spain to witness the punishments, the burning as the climax of the celebration. I say "celebration" because the event came replete with the fervor of a holy festival.

On the fateful day, the frays had us dress in *sambenitos,* a shirt and pants of rough cotton dyed yellow and decorated with red flames, devils, and crosses. We were led outside and placed on donkeys with our shirts lowered so that we were first naked from the waist up. Even the upper bodies of two convicted women were naked.

Drum beats, horns, and criers preceded us, then high officials of the Holy Office in their finest robes and silk stockings, carried in sedan chairs. Then came the familiars on horseback, in chivalry, finery, and armor, as if they were the highest knights of the land.

The balconies of the houses on our path were draped with brilliant tapestries and banners bearing the coat of arms of the owners. Wealth was displayed, too, as candelabras and vessels of the purest silver and gold were set upon the railings. The purpose of this ostentation escaped me, but my only wealth for most of my life had been a cross placed around my neck by my mother when I was a baby. Now even that was gone. My advocate had taken it.

Then came those of us wearing the sambenito. I soon found out why our torsos were left bare. People lining the streets threw rocks and rotten vegetables at us. With our shirts down, it hurt more. Lépero street riffraff who were used to the kicks and blows of their betters flung the sharpest stones.

Each of us carried a green candle, another sign that the Holy Office had conquered the devils within that had made us sin. Behind us came a cart carrying Don Julio, Inez, and Juana. I cried when I saw them and a familiar taunted me as a coward, thinking I wept for myself.

"Do not cry," Mateo told me, "the don wants to be honored by a man for his courage, not cried over by a woman. When he looks at you, show him with your eyes and face that you respect and pay homage to him."

The words did no good. I cried for the don, for the frightened bird of a sister who had finally found her courage, and for the niece woman-child whose bones broke easier than straw.

In the quemadera area, those of us to receive lashes were tied to posts. As I was tied, I looked up and saw the coat of arms of Don Diego Velez hanging from a balcony that a group of people stood upon. Ramon and Luis, the assassins of my life, were there. There was a movement beside Luis, and suddenly I was looking into the eyes of Eléna. She stared down at me for a moment, her eyes not going anywhere else in the quemadera. Before the first blow struck my back, she slipped away and disappeared from my sight.

I knew now who my savior was. I had suspected that she had ransomed me, but now I was certain. She had come not to see the suffering, but to see that her deed had not been betrayed and my punishment had not included the stake. And perhaps to let me know that she was repaying the Son of the Stone for the comedia.

Not to faint from the lashing was the sign of much man, but I prayed God to cause me to pass out so that I would not bear witness to the horror to be done to my family. My eyes I could avert, but my hands were tied and my ears wide open. My lashing post was closest to the pyres, and I would hear all.

At times my mind was lost as the whip struck my back. Men and women have died under the lash, but there were shouts from the crowd that my back was being spared because so much of the skin was still intact despite the hundred lashes. Eléna's mercy had also reached the hand that held the whip, but in this case I wished that I had died rather than remain awake.

Don Julio got off the cart and walked to the stake. A great roar went up in the crowd, a bloodthirsty howl as if each one of those thousands gathered had been personally harmed by the don. He ignored the crowd and walked as a king on his way to a coronation.

I suddenly realized what the bloodthirsty event reminded me of. In the reading of the classics under Fray Antonio's tutelage, I had read stories about the bloody sacrifices in the arena the emperors provided to entertain and appease the public. The Aztec sacrifices had also been done to entertain the public. Eh, man has not changed in thousands of years, he is still a beast.

Inez had to be helped along, and I knew not whether that was because of physical weakness or if her zeal was faltering. When I saw her face, brave and unafraid, I knew that the weakness was of body and not of spirit. She glowed with courage, and I shouted my admiration to her and again the whip tore at my back.

Juana I could not bear to even look upon. She was so tiny a single guard was able to gather her in his arms and carry her to her place of honor. A murmur swept through the crowd, and people turned their heads to avoid looking at her.

I averted my eyes and only know what I was told. Each stake had a garret strap wire around it connected to a turn handle on the backside of the post. If one repented, the executioner put the strap around the throat and twisted the handle, tightening the strap until the victim died of strangulation.

This act of mercy was performed only on those who repented and only by the viceroy's men rather than frays because clerics could not kill. Or so they claimed.

Don Julio and Inez refused to repent and were not given the act. I have been told by one close enough to hear that Juana also refused to repent, but that the executioner, whose black heart broke at her plight, pretended she had repented and strangled her, saving her from the slow excruciation of the flames. Another story was that a wealthy benefactor in the crowd had sent gold ducats to the executioner to ensure that Juana's suffering was short.

I heard the fires ignite, first the tinder, then the kindling, then the soaring flames. I heard the gasps, the screams; the sizzle of flesh, the terrible pop of exploding blisters and detonating fat. I tried to keep out the sounds of suffering by filling my mind with one word that I repeated over and over.

Revenge, revenge, revenge . . .

PART FIVE

... engendered in some prison, where wretchedness keeps its residence, and every dismal sound its habitation ...

—Miguel Cervantes, *Don Quixote*

NINETY-EIGHT

I DID NOT journey to the northern mines on a pure-blood horse but on the floorboards of a mule-drawn prison-train, coffle chained to the wagon bed. I shared my corner of the wagon bed with a sambenito from the auto-da-fé who had gotten a hundred lashes and two years at the mines for sodomy. My sentence was for life; but since few survived more than a year in the mines, a life sentence was no great matter.

I waved good-bye to Mateo as I was taken to the prison-train. He would soon leave the Inquisition prison himself for his ocean voyage to Manila in the Filipinas, the place of banishment for New Spain's undesirables. Between the tropical fevers and the warring natives, the Filipinas was likewise regarded as a death sentence.

A dozen other men were chained with me, but other than the sodomite and myself, they were all petty criminals sold to the mines by the civil authority. The term of service for each was no more than a year, and most expected relatives to suborn their early release. One of them, a mestizo sentenced for stealing a sack of maize to feed his family, was making his second trip to the mines. The first had been a six-month's stretch for an overdue debt. Rather than extending the due date or adding on additional interest, the creditor had had him arrested, jailed, then sold to a mine for the amount of the debt.

At times the terrain was too steep and rugged for the wagon to carry us, and we had to get out and walk, our legs coffle chained one prisoner to the other. For the most part, though, we bounced in the rocking wagon, our backs an agony of whip welts, our spines jolted out of place by the hard shocks of the springless wagon.

The mestizo reminded me of the mine slave who'd been murdered before my eyes when I was a boy. I told him about the incident, and he told me stories of the mines. They were not pretty tales, but I needed to know all I could about my new prison. I had sworn to avenge my family and was determined not to die in a mine.

"We will be beaten on arrival so that we learn submission," he told us, "but not beaten so severely that we cannot work."

My back was still raw from the auto-da-fé's flogging—the one the crowd felt was not ruthless enough. The crowd's opinion notwithstanding, I knew even then I would carry those scars for the rest of my life—however long that was.

"For those with a life sentence, or who are slaves, they brand their faces just in case they try to escape," the mestizo said.

I can still see the brands that scarred the face of the mine slave when he was killed before me at the hacienda. One of the brands was a small "S" that probably was the initial of a Sanchez or Santos or a dozen other potential "S" names who owned the mine.

"Africano slaves and those given life sentences work the most dangerous job—breaking ore out of the mine face."

The mestizo looked at me as he spoke because everyone in the wagon knew of my life sentence. His coloring was almost the same as mine; but I was known as a Spaniard, a converso, and carried myself as one, and he gave no indication whether he knew we were both of mixed blood.

"The ore is broken out with iron picks then loaded into burden baskets with shovels," he said. "Cave-ins occur constantly, and many slaves die the first time their pick strikes."

Don Julio had told me that the mine owners do minimal timber-shoring because of the expense. Vast quantities of timber were required in the smelting process, and the wood had to be hauled over great distances. It was cheaper to replace workers than pay for timber.

We reached the hacienda de mina in slightly under two weeks. It overlooked a high, sheer cliff top, and a river ran through its land, bringing reliable water to this otherwise barren waste. However, it was quickly apparent that this hacienda was not a typical land estate, supported by crops and livestock. The gate swung open, and we entered a vast, smoking, self-sufficient compound, dedicated to wresting silver from an uncooperative mountain, then forcing the unwilling metal from the reluctant rock, which only grudgingly gave it up. The excavation of tunnels, the mining ore, and hauling it out—thousands upon thousands of loads—and then the refinement of that ore, separating the silver from the unprofitable dross, was what the hacienda de mina was about.

We entered the compound's soaring walls in chains and shackles. All the while I scrupulously studied everything—the black, gaping mouth of the mine shaft; the thunder of the stamping mill; the fuming roar of the refinery; the clanging, filthy, smoke-shrouded blacksmith shop; the long, malodorous, soot-fouled prisoners' barracks. Towering above us, the mine owner's huge, high, massively walled house, gessoed a stark white against so much squalor and darkness.

I contemplated the compound's surrounding whitewashed walls of thick adobe brick with special care. One day I would scale those soaring white walls and leave this obscene hellhole forever.

Indios came out of the hole in the ground like enslaved ants, one after another, sacks and burden baskets slung over their backs and tumplined across their foreheads, which, according to the mestizo, averaged a hundred pounds apiece—four-fifths the weight of the wiry men who carried them.

The ants dumped their loads in a pile near the stamping mill. I could see only a little of it as I was marched toward a barrack, but I was familiar with the process from reading the book Don Julio had written on the mining industry.

The rock and dirt carried out of the mines was crushed in the stamping mill then spread into large heaps across a stone-paved courtyard called a patio. Water was added to the minerals until they became muddy. Then an azoguero, a refiner, mixed mercury and salt into the mud. The mud was spread into thin cakes that were stirred and left to "cook." Later the silver was washed and heated until the mercury separated out. This amalgamation process took weeks to months, depending on the skill of the mixer and the grade of the silver.

Mercury, or quicksilver, was vital to the mining process, and the king held a royal monopoly on it. Most of it came from the Almaden mine in Spain.

In the outdoors area, where meals were taken, we were assigned to work crews. Each crew was overseen by an africano slave.

The man I was assigned to was several inches taller than I. He was powerfully built, had survived a decade of overseeing mine slaves, and currently commanded a dozen or so. His body was scarred from innumerable mining accidents. He invariably reminded me of Rome's arena gladiators. His name was Gonzalo.

"Take off your shirt," he told me, whip in hand.

I removed my shirt. The scars on my back were red but no longer bled and were healing.

The whip lashed the back of my legs. I cried out, startled from the pain. Two men grabbed my arms and held me as he beat me five more times across the calves and the backs of my thighs.

"You are here to work, not to be flogged. I whip you so that you will work harder. I did not whip your back because it has not healed. I don't want you hurt so much that you can't work. Do you understand?"

"Yes."

"As long as you work, you will be not be whipped—too often—and will be given decent food so you can work hard. If you try to escape, you will be killed. This is not a jail. You earn more time in jail for attempting to escape. Here you will be killed. Do you understand?"

"Yes."

"If you are lazy and do not work, I will flog you worse than the familiars at the auto-da-fé. The second time I will cut off your ear. When you go below, you will see a nailing post where we impale the ears. Do you know what will happen the third time?"

"You will cut off my head."

Gonzolo grinned and struck me across the face with the buttstock of his whip. Blood squirted down my cheek. "You are right, but it is not good to be right too much. You are a work animal, not a man. When you talk to me, you must keep your eyes looking down so I know you respect me."

Indio dog handlers brought their mastiffs closer, snarling hell-hounds with snapping jaws.

"Some plot to escape from the sleeping house in the middle of the night. We had one man try that. He dug a hole through the house wall and ran for the hacienda wall. The dogs ate well that night."

He hit me again on the back of the legs.

"Do not attempt to hide any silver; you have nothing to spend it on. The first time you are caught hiding silver, you will lose an ear. The second time your head."

The whip lacerated my legs below the knees.

"Take him to be branded."

The two men held me as a blacksmith shoved a glowing hot iron with the initial "C" about the size of the first joint of my little finger. I flinched away from the iron and instead of a perfect "C," it smeared the letter across my cheek on the same spot where I was bleeding from the whip handle.

And so I began my life as a mine slave. Branded and flogged, I was allowed to eat and sleep only because dray animals need food and rest to work. The sleeping house was a windowless mud-brick building with only one door. Its purpose was imprisonment, and it succeeded admirably. No beds or rooms, it was just a long, narrow room with straw and scattered blankets on the floor.

There were two twelve-hour shifts down below plus more work topside, moving ore from the stamping-mill piles to where it was amalgamated on the patio. When one crew came in from its twelve-hour shift, the men ate, then went into the barracks, where they slept until it was time for their shift.

The crew I was assigned to shared the same sleeping space and blankets. When one crew left, another found a blanket in the straw and slept. We had no personal possessions except the clothes we wore. When our clothes rotted off, a ragged shirt or pants was provided from a pile gathered from men who had already died.

Each day we filed into the shaft head and descended by ladder from one tier to another, down to the main tunnel. In the mine, it was dark, damp, cold, dusty, and dangerous—and then, as we descended, it became so infernally hot that the sweat flooded from us in cataracts, and men dropped dead from lack of water. Our only light came from candles and small torches, and once beyond their glow we vanished into darkness.

Because of the darkness, escape would be easy; but there was no place to run to. The only way out was topside, where guards and dogs awaited.

Being a lifer, I spent part of my time working on blasting crews. We chipped and hammered and dug holes several feet deep into the mine face, then packed in the black powder—the same explosive used in cannons and muskets. We poured a line of black powder, lit it, and ran like hell.

A recent innovation, we were not adept at it, and given the lack of shoring timber, blasting carried with it serious problems. Whereas it did loosen a lot of rock—a single blast broke up more rock than a dozen men could loosen in a day with picks—it also loosened tunnel walls *throughout* the mine. Suffocating clouds of dust and debris blew through the tunnels with hurricane force, and cave-ins were commonplace. Men were routinely buried alive.

I was trapped by cave-ins every few days and only through the luck of the draw was able to dig my way out. Many were not so lucky. The mestizo who'd tried to educate me in the ways of the mines was buried alive the first week.

After blasting, we returned to the mine face with picks, shovels, and double-headed hammers to break up the rock and dirt.

The work was so excruciatingly arduous, we were fed not only beans and tortillas, but on alternate nights, meat. Consequently, after initial bouts of pain, dizziness, and the bite of the lash, my stamina improved. Any caballero who saw the muscles harden on my hands, arms, and back would instantly know I was no gentleman.

The mine owners used the de rato, or shortest route, method of mining. An ore vein was found and a tunnel began that followed the vein—twisting, turning, up the mountain, suddenly down it. Wherever the silver went, we went.

When I entered the mine, it was predawn and dark. And the sun was down when I came out. I no longer knew from personal experience whether the sun still warmed the earth or eternal night had fallen.

My world became one of darkness and drudgery. I was often too tired to even think and that helped heal the horror in my brain, forged by the fiery holocaust that had consumed Don Julio and his family.

Once I learned to deal with the arduous cycle of work, eating, sleep, and intermittent floggings, I began to think about breaking out. I knew escape could mean my death, but that was of no consequence. My greatest fear was dying anonymously in a cave-in, buried eternally under a mountain of rock—and never avenging Don Julio.

Escape would not be easy. The harsh physical conditions were more than matched by the brutal vigilance of the guards. Nonetheless, I gradually saw a way. Once, while waiting in an abandoned tunnel for the blasting to finish, I noticed a slender thread of light slanting through a crack about the thickness of a fingernail.

How did light penetrate a tunnel that was hundreds of feet beneath the earth's surface?

Gonzolo saw me staring at the light and laughed. "Do you think it's magic, marrano?"

"I don't know what it is," I confessed.

"It's coming through the mountainside. Crawl through that crack for ten or twelve feet, and you'll be standing above a river. Tell you what. Make it through that crack, and I'll let you leave this mine."

He laughed long and hard at his witless jest.

Someday I will not only walk out, I will strangle you with your whip, I promised myself.

But that certain slant of light stayed with me. Maybe it was Don Julio's training. He had taught me to question physical phenomena, and every question I asked myself about that stream of light produced the same answer: Beyond that wall of rock stood freedom.

All I had to do was work my way through the crack.

Obviously, hammering through a dozen feet of stone was not an option. But I did have something that would widen that crack in a heartbeat, and as a lifer I knew how to use it: black powder.

The crack already existed. I'd have to widen it by cramming enough powder in. After blowing that mountainside to kingdom come, I'd have to work my way out through all that rock . . . assuming the mountain did not fall upon my head . . .

Stealing the black powder would be difficult. The powder was stored in a windowless adobe hut with a locked iron door. As for the powder we used, it was brought in in small quantities and heavily guarded.

But when I packed the charges into the mine face, I was alone with it. If before each blasting, I could steal a pinch of the powder, secret it on my body, and hide it later, the small thefts would add up.

If I was caught, there would be hell to pay.

If I didn't try, I would die in the mine.

NINETY-NINE

OVER A PERIOD of months I collected and hid the powder a thimbleful at a time near the crack in the abandoned tunnel. With a little of my wet urine, I created cakes out of it. After the cakes dried I broke them up and crushed them into what Don Julio called "maize" powder because each chunk was about the size of a kernel of maize.

With each surreptitious trip to the abandoned tunnel, I packed some black powder into the crack.

Stealing the powder, sneaking brief moments in the tunnel, packing the crack, the beatings, the cave-ins, sheer physical exhaustion were all taking a toll on me. By the time I was ready to make my move, I was more than just frantic, I was now deranged by the sheer horror and impossibility of what I was doing.

Furthermore, Gonzolo was after me. In order to pull all this off, I was increasingly late for work, and though once at the mine face I was among the hardest of workers, lateness was something Gonzolo would not tolerate.

That last afternoon when I arrived late at the mine face he struck me across the head with the buttstock of his quirt so hard my ears rung, then said, "Tonight, when I finish with you at the flogging post, marrano, you'll never be late to the mine face again. And you'll remember the Inquisition as angels of mercy. Assuming, that is, you survive what I give you."

So that was that; it was today or never.

For the rest of the shift, he would not let me out of his sight. When I carried back my burden baskets of ore, when I went to get black powder, tools, anything, everything, he was on me like a shadow. And when it was time for the shifts to change, he walked me back personally, his right hand locked on my elbow.

We were just passing the abandoned tunnel, when I turned to him and stopped. "I just want to ask you one favor," I said, in my most contrite voice, my eyes downcast.

I needed to make sure we were alone. Gonzolo was always the last man to leave the tunnels, and he automatically looked around for stragglers. The last men rounded the bend in the tunnel ahead, and we were alone.

"You have the right to ask nothing, marrano!" he hissed, and swung the whipstock at me again.

Mateo's fencing lessons at last bore fruit. I parried the blow with my double-headed mine hammer, then smashed him in the nose with its iron top. Grabbing him by the throat, I dragged him into the abandoned tunnel and slammed him into the wall.

"Die, you son of a whore, die!" I hissed in his face.

I backhanded the hammer into his left temple, killing him instantly—a death far more merciful than any he had dispensed.

Now I had two choices: blow this mountain to kingdom come or be tortured to death by an army of mine guards.

I hurriedly packed the rest of the hidden black powder into the crack and inserted the fuse. Down tunnel was the fire stove where we lit the brands we used to light the powder. I hurried down tunnel. I had to get to it before the next shift reached the shaft.

At the stove I took a brand—a small shank of wood soaked in pitch at the tip—from the brand box and lit it.

A guard shouted, "You, prisoner, what are you doing here? Where's Gonzolo?"

Another guard's voice said. "Why aren't you with the rest of your shift?"

I raced back to the abandoned shaft as fast as I knew how.

I beat them to the shaft and lit a fuse. I had no idea how effective it would be. It was little more than twine soaked in urine and black powder. I had no idea how fast it burned.

It might burn in five seconds. It might not burn at all. I hadn't had time to test it.

Cupping the blazing brand, I lit the fuse as the two guards charged into the tunnel.

Both were armed with short swords, and again Mateo's instructions saved my life. When the first guard—a short, skinny africano with close-cropped hair and no front teeth—thrust at my throat, I slipped into my fencing-dancing posture and ducked. His momentum carried him into me, throwing him off balance and, at the same time, blocking any assault the other guard might be planning.

I drove my fist into his Adam's apple—while my heavy hammer pulverized his pelvis. He screamed and went limp in my arms.

Using his body as a shield I dodged his partner's sword blows while I groped for the short sword his partner had dropped on the tunnel floor. At last I had it in my hand. Letting the guard fall groaning, I faced the other guard, sword in one hand, hammer in the other.

Mateo had taught me that when fighting with rapier and dagger, the only practical use for the dagger was as a stabbing weapon. In other words, I was to occupy my opponent with my rapier, then kill him with my knife.

Well, this short sword wasn't a rapier and my hammer wasn't a dagger, but the strategy still seemed sound. Especially when combined with Mateo's other piece of irrefutable wisdom: Always stay on the attack.

I sprung at the man like a crazed tiger, the hammer raised and pulled back in my left hand, the sword blade flashing and feinting, cutting and thrusting in my right.

Seeing himself closely confined with an armed maniac, he turned and fled; and I raced after, thirsting for blood, crazed with rage.

Which was the only thing that saved my life. For the fuse worked all too well. It's two-foot length exploded in less than half a minute, sympathetically detonating a full two pounds of black powder I had hidden in the tunnel wall but had not had enough time to relocate down the tunnel and well out of the blast radius.

The explosion buried the guard and myself in a small mountain of collapsing rock. I came to slowly, groggily. By now I could hear voices coming from up the shaft. The next shift, plus guards, would be coming straight here to clear the rubble and learn what had happened.

I had killed a supervisor, two guards, and blown up half the shaft. I had to make good my escape. I scrambled back down the shaft to the abandoned tunnel. It had caved in too and was filled with rock and rubble almost to the ceiling. But through rock and rubble something else had broken through: light.

I scrambled over the deadfall like a cat. With hands and hammer I began clearing a jagged, foot-high crawl space. I could make it to the outside, I thought, except for one rocky scarp jutting up near the exit. I hoped and prayed I could break it off with my hammer.

The shouts up shaft were growing louder, and the crevice was groaning and shaking. I didn't have much time. Soon the guards would be here—and the mountain would come back down, resealing my escape hatch.

I shouldered my way into the crevice.

It was a tight, jagged, bloody crawl to the light, and what lay beyond God only knew. By the time I reached the bloody scarp, I was a mass of cuts and blood. Furthermore, I could hear men entering the abandoned shaft, meaning they would hear my hammer blows.

To hell with it.

I laid into the rocky scarp with both hands as hard as I knew how. The din of my hammer blows was loud enough to wake the damned, and the screams behind me grew louder. On the fourth blow, the scarp broke off and went flying off through the crevice. At the same moment, some man behind me grabbed my sandaled foot, crawled up the tunnel, and grabbed my thigh. I turned and was about to hammer his skull to pieces, when he shouted, "I'm coming with you!"

"Then come along," I shouted, "wherever the hell we're headed!"

Grabbing the outside edge of the crevice, I poked my head out. I had had several minutes to gradually adjust to the light, but still it was blinding. I shielded my eyes and kept moving. I had to get out before the guards came and grabbed us both.

I was halfway out of the crevice when my eyes adjusted enough that I could see the escape route. To my right, perhaps a hundred feet away, was a slanting fissure in the cliff face, transversing a good four or five hundred feet. I couldn't see how far down it went, but it was my only shot. I had to scramble across that vertical cliff and then work my way down the fissure.

Now the prisoner behind me was in hysterics. A guard had worked his way into the crevice and had his ankle.

"No, no!" he screamed. "I can't go back."

I shared his sentiments completely. The crevice—with a million tons of rock pressing down on it—was groaning and screaming like a dying animal. I groped a couple of handholds and swung out over the abyss. My sandals went flying off my feet, falling what looked to be forever into the roiling, white-water rapids below. It was just as well. My bare feet would be better in feeling out footholds.

I found one and started out across the cliff face toward the fissure.

One hundred feet, a foot at a time, as I worked my way across that wall of rock, it seemed more than a hundred miles. My feet and fingers trembled in agony, bled profusely, and, as if in sympathy, the mountain itself groaned, moaned, vibrated, as if agonizing over all the horrible pain I'd caused it.

Still I almost reached it. I was within five feet of the slanting fissure, down which I could climb, perhaps to safety. At least I wouldn't have to crawl across this cliff face like a frightened bug.

But the mountain would have none of it. I had hurt her too badly; and being a mountain, her vengeance was vast.

My black power blasts had collapsed tunnels all over the mountain. Long-forgotten cracks and holes and fissures along that cliff face were exuding smoke and dust. To my right black smoke was still pouring out of the crevice I'd crawled through.

In fact a guard's head was poking out of the opening. He was black with mine dust, as was I, and he was screaming obscenities I could not hear because the mountain was also screaming. It was shaking and trembling, thundering and roaring—and a million tons of rock came down on the crevice, sealing it forever. From my perch I could hear and feel more and more tunnels collapsing all up and down the mountain. More puffs of smoke and dust billowed out of the cliff face.

A wolfish grin split my face, and I could not resist laughing. I had not only rid the mine of Gonzolo, I'd rid the mountain of the mine.

I reached out with my left hand for the slanting fissure, but instead of grabbing its edge, I was hit by the reverberation of a shaft cave-in on the other side of my piece of cliff. My left hand reached only air. The mountain shook me like a jaguar shaking a jungle rat. The outcrop my right hand clung to broke off, and I was holding onto nothing. The mountain was now vibrating furiously and shook me loose. It rid itself of its despoiler, and I was falling, falling, falling.

I felt so free, soaring through space, I did wonder for a brief second if this was how angels felt—except then I reminded myself, angels don't fall, they fly. And I was definitely falling. In fact, looking down I could see the foaming river rushing up at me with dizzying speed.

My last coherent thought was whether I would meet Don Julio and his family in hell.

ONE HUNDRED

AT THE LAST second I had the presence of mind to lower my legs and straighten my back, so I did not belly flop or cannon ball. I hit the cataract upright, feet first, arms at my sides. Even so, the earth shook as the plummeting plunge into the white-water rapids knocked me senseless.

Eventually the icy, white water brought me to my senses. The cataract was in violent turmoil from the spring snow-melt from the mountains. Madre de Dios, it was cold. The pain was bracing as well. The plunge had wrenched both ankles, twisted a knee, and almost dislocated my left shoulder.

Still, when I came to, the first thing I heard above the river's din were the muffled explosions above me, which sounded like Mount Olympus in her death throes and the roar of gods gone mad. My detonation had apparently hit some sort of nerve in that mountain, perhaps an entire spinal cord. Every shaft, tunnel, cavern, crack, crevice, nook, and cranny was collapsing. The riverbanks, even the water trembled with the blasts, and the only semicoherent thought banging in my brain was: *The mountain has reclaimed her mines.*

But then I was rocketing downstream. Everything was moving so fast I wasn't able to focus on anything except trying to stay above water and stay alive. My whole world was suddenly that river. It was as if I had always been in the river and had never had a life except the river. I couldn't even remember hitting the water—just the pain and the cold and the cataract's power. I couldn't even think about the mountain and the mine. I was out of sight, touch, and ear-shot of that hellhole. I was in the midst of white-water, and it was growing whiter and wilder by the minute. That was all that mattered.

Rocks and outcrops were growing in size and number, and I was now bouncing off of them with painful regularity. The river turned, angling right, hard right, and the white-water now was ferocious. Swimming was not an option. It was all I could do to keep my head above the surface.

More rocks, more outcrops, then a protracted din. I butted my head against a barn-sized boulder and was again knocked semiconscious. I came to to a roar that made me think of the mine explosions, but the din was protracted as well as ear-shattering.

The river curved and there it was: falls. I was now angling down toward it and could actually see over the rim.

I was going over.

Again, I was falling. This time I had no illusions about flying angels. I was dropping like a rock, except that this rock was now pain-wracked and hard-used. And falling.

I hit the river below like a black-powder explosion bringing down a mountain of rock.

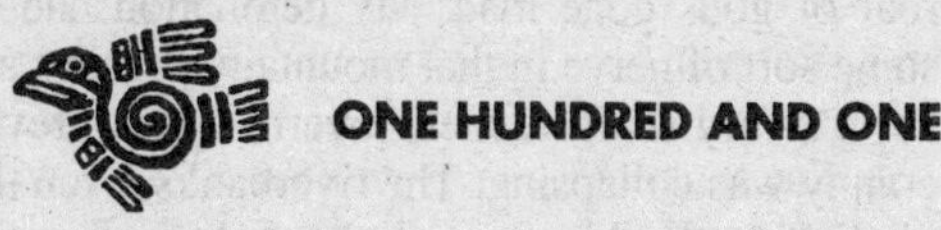

ONE HUNDRED AND ONE

How long I lay snarled in that deadfall dam of rocks and logs there beside the riverbank, I do not know. For a long time I thought I heard the mine detonating, but I finally realized those explosions were only in my head.

I was aware almost as soon as I regained consciousness that I had to get up and walk. Lying there in the freezing water was not an alternative. To rest was to get caught. To get caught was to be flogged, castrated, dismembered, killed. To rest was to suffer and die. I crawled out of the deadfall and clambered up onto the shore. *Follow the river,*

I thought, *away from the mine.* Aimlessly, mindlessly, almost senselessly, I began walking downstream.

When I came to the tributary, I followed it away from the river. I had to get away from civilization, away from Spaniards, and become just another indio. Alone, dressed in dirty, torn, water-logged rags, bruised, battered, I didn't have much. But I was still alive. If I could find food, clothes, shelter, I might make it awhile longer.

I followed the tributary downstream, downhill. To survive in the wilds, always go downhill, the Healer had told me; and I found no reason to doubt him now. But even going downhill, the land was still relatively high, and now it was approaching dusk and growing chill. Furthermore, the surrounding terrain provided almost no cover—no jungle, dense brush, or forest, but only a few scraggly, stunted trees and scattered clumps of low brush.

For a time this bothered me. I was a wanted man, and naturally I feared pursuit; but then it finally dawned on me, was I wanted? Was I being pursued? Surely no one in the mine had survived that cataclysm. No one would know I had. *I was a dead man.* No one would pursue me because I was dead.

Not only was I cold and in rags, the temperature falling, my stomach was rumbling and I was growing faint with hunger and exhaustion. No, I was long past exhaustion. I was the snake operating without a head, wriggling around on raw nerves.

That night I found a stand of trees. The ground beneath their limbs was covered with leaves and deadfall. I used an old trick the Healer once taught me. I gouged out a body-sized depression with a rock, filled it with leaves and twigs, then covered myself with leaves and branches. It wasn't the cleanest bed I had ever slept in, but it kept me warm.

I went in the only direction that I had strength enough to drag myself: Just like the Healer. It was comical, but all I could think of was his advice. It ran over and over in my brain, like a prayer, and would not let me go:

"When lost, go downhill, always go downhill. You will

eventually come to a valley, and in the valley you will find water, and where there is water you will find provender and people, and where you find people you will find companionship. You will not be alone."

Down the mountain foothills I stumbled, fell, crawled, and rolled. True to the Healer's word, I reached another river, this one not a mountain cataract but a peaceful, meandering stream. Since I was traveling downhill, the weather warmed. Of course, now that I no longer feared pursuit, I did find something else to worry about: the Chichimecas. Dreaded untamed savages, they hunted in small bands and often their prey was two-legged, and the northern mines were in their territory. It would be a great pity to have escaped a death sentence in the mines only to end up in the bellies of the Dog People. The Healer would have likewise found a wry irony in that one; if a man, who carried Aztec blood in his veins, ended up nourishing his own Aztec cousins in one of their infamous rituals.

I followed the river farther downstream. The Healer could not have been more correct about where such declivities led. The river sprouted streams and creeks, spreading out into a narrow valley, which included a lush field of maize. A haze of smoke curling upward told me the location of the mud hut of a farmer. I hid and watched the hut. The farmer was a big, stupid-looking, half blood, with a belly bloated from too much pulque and too many tortillas. When I saw him he was chopping wood outside the hut. His wife came out of the hut while I watched. She was a full-blooded indio, small build, youngish, pretty. I did not see any children. When the woman came out of the hut, the mestizo told her that she had not brought enough wood down from the hills. His voice toward his wife was as spiteful and stupid as his face. She took the criticism with the silent passivity that was the lot of indias. Life was hard and speaking out against a husband who might beat you solely because you were smaller and physically weaker did not make your life any easier.

The maize was barely ripe, but I took an armful and

found shelter in a cave formed by river-eroded boulders. I peeled the cobs and ate the raw kernels, attacking them as if I was one of the Dog People. My Aztec bloodline traced their own roots back to these barbaric northern tribes, so perhaps it was natural that I would act like one of them.

Eating the raw corn and washing it down with river water bloated my belly, but did little else to assuage my hunger. It rained later, and I spent the night in the cave. Cold, clammy, I curled up in a fetal position and tried to keep my teeth from chattering. Exhaustion is, however, the best soporific; and though awakened periodically, I did sleep.

I stayed in the cave until the sun was well up, then lay atop a flat rock to soak up its rays. Like reptile limbs, my arms and legs began to operate better as the sun warmed my blood. When my body was warm, I took off the rags and went into the river water to bathe.

The river was cold, but I'd been so filthy for so long that even my trip down the rapids hadn't scrubbed me clean. Eh, for a few moments in a steam hut, I would have bartered my soul to Beelzebub.

Along the riverbank I found a dry tree limb that made a serviceable spear, and I sharpened the tip with a sharp rock. I stood on the edge of a small, clear pool and tried repeatedly to spear a fish. After what must have been a hundred tries, I impaled a foot-long bottom-feeder with whiskers and insane eyes. I ate it raw, whiskers, bones, scales, all—after which I passed out from exhaustion.

I was still naked from my bath and now tried to wash my rags. I tore them even more beating them on the rocks and wringing out the water. I at last gave up. Laying them on the rocks to dry, I likewise lay myself out naked and dozed in the sun.

I awoke with a sense of unease, with the strange feeling I was being watched. I did not see or hear anything. It may have been simply the chronic on-edge fear that had been my lot for so long. Still I was apprehensive. A moment before some birds had taken sudden flight, and I could not help but wonder what had started them. I did not want to startle my watcher either by sudden moves, so I sat up slowly.

I did not see her at first. She was in the bushes on the far riverbank. How long she had watched me, I did not know. I was still undressed, but did not bother to cover myself. My nakedness had not bothered her so far.

My eyes found hers. I expected her to bolt like a startled deer. Instead she remained crouched in the bushes, returning my stare as impassively, studying me as if I were a bug on the rock.

"Hello," I said, first in Náhuatl, then in Spanish. She said nothing. She could not have lived this long in mining country without knowing what an escaped mine slave looked like. But something told me that she would not turn me in for a reward. Unlike other women, an india would not think in terms of earning money unless she was forced into prostitution. Had this one been driven by greed or fear, she would have fled long ago.

I rubbed my stomach and said in Náhuatl, "I'm hungry."

Again, she stared at me, silent, her eyes expressionless. Finally she got up and left.

I debated whether I should grab my rags and flee. Or grab a rock, run her down, and crush her skull before she spread the alarm. Neither alternative was workable. In my weakened state I could not run far; and in a fair fight, she would have probably taken me.

As far as fleeing went, the headless snake was no longer running on raw nerves. I had no strength left, nerve, muscles, brain, heart, anything. I needed rest. Lying down on a broad, flat rock, I went back to sleep, soaking up the sun's warmth. Awaking at midday, I was still tired. I feared I would always be tired. Worse, I hurt—everywhere. My entire body was a single aching wound.

I slipped off the rock. Unable to rise, I slid down to the riverbank for a drink. At the water's edge, I spotted a small reed basket on the rock across the river where the woman had hid. I could see tortillas sticking out.

I had been so wary for so long, I first wondered whether

it was a trap. Maybe her vicious husband was waiting with a machete and dreams of a rich reward. But I didn't see that I had much choice. I had to eat. Somehow I managed to stand. Sloshing across the hip-deep river, I grabbed the basket. I was eating a tortilla before I got back to the other side.

Like a primal beast, I took the food to my cave. There were plain tortillas, a tortilla wrapped around a piece of beef, a tortilla filled with beans and peppers, and even a tortilla smeared with honey. Gracias Dios, a feast for a king. I ate until my belly almost burst. Then I crawled back onto the rock in the sun. Like a crocodile with its belly full, I basked in the sun, my spirits soaring, giving my muscles new strength.

I fell asleep again and slept for another couple of hours. When I awoke, she was sitting on a rock across the riverbank. Nearby was a pile of clothing.

I waded across to her and sat down beside her, not bothering to cover my nakedness.

"Gracias," I said, "muchas gracias."

She said nothing but looked at me with sad, dark eyes.

I knew what her life was like. Just as the españols treated indios and mestizos as their work animals, a farm woman was a work animal to her husband. They lived a life of hard work and silent desperation, aged fast, died young.

We talked just a little, only a few sentences. I repeated my "muchas gracias." She gave me her obligatory "Por nada." I asked her how many children she had. She answered, "None." When I expressed surprise that a young woman so beautiful did not have scores of muchachos, she answered:

"My husband's pene is muy malo, mucho por nada, no bueno. And so he beats me, as you were beaten."

She pivoted her hips, and her back bore the broad white stripes of her abuse.

The human body is a strange animal. I had previously been too worn out to even stand, but apparently the male garrancha is immune to such weakness. As I sat beside the river talking to this young woman, my garrancha rose.

We lay together by the riverbank that afternoon—and every afternoon for the next five days. When I finally left her, I wore pants and a shirt of coarsely woven cotton, and a straw hat. I carried the traditional indio manta over my right shoulder and under my left arm and a blanket rolled up around a woven maguey rope over my left shoulder. The blanket would ward off the cold at night, and the tortillas, rolled up in the blanket, would last me for days.

Working in the mines had burned every bit of fat from my bones, but the work had left my muscles hard. A few days of nourishment did not fill out my frame, but combined with rest I was now able to walk.

If I could avoid the local cannibals, I would survive awhile longer.

Before leaving my riverbank cave, I foraged a bit and found a thick tree limb, a little longer than my leg. I could use it as a walking staff and a club. A long, straight sapling, sharpened at the end, served as a spear. I lashed a split-wood handle to a long, slender piece of obsidian, given to me by the girl, and sharpened it into a blade.

I wore my straggly hair shoulder-length, and my beard was creeping down past my Adam's apple. I know I looked like a mountain beast that had escaped from the Place of the Dead.

With instructions from the girl, I crossed the nearby hills, where I intersected a trail leading to the Zacatecas' main road. I kept a weather eye out for the Chichimeca during the entire trip. They were nowhere to be found. If the Dog People saw me, they were no doubt frightened off by my lunatic appearance.

In the far distance smoke curled up to the sky. The girl had warned me this way led to mines. I knew the smoke meant silver smelters. I touched the scar on my cheek, the brand that mine slaves wore. I was fortunate that the brand was neither large nor deep and that my beard was exceptionally heavy, but while the scar would not be noticeable to a casual observer, I would not fool anyone who knew the mines.

I sat hidden by bushes on a hillside and studied the road until dark. Mule trains constituted the heaviest traffic, which was to be expected on any major road in New Spain. The trains came up the road loaded with supplies for the mines. None came back down empty. Not every mule was loaded with silver. Some packed tools or parts to be repaired. Others carried sulfur, lead, and copper ores, which would be transferred to the appropriate refineries.

Except for the occasional indio, packing maize, beans, and maguey to market on mule back, the only four-footed traffic was the infrequent Spaniard on horseback. The two-footed traffic consisted of mine workers, indios, mestizos, and africanos, going to or from the mines. These men traveled in groups, usually about ten or twelve at a time. Even the horsemen rode with companions for protection.

It was to be expected. The mine roads attracted not only the usual run of banditos, but renegade indios and escaped mine slaves added to the hordes of highwaymen.

I fell asleep that night studying the road. The next morning I continued my vigil. I debated joining a cadre of mine workers, returning to other parts of New Spain after their stint in the mines was over. However, since they were hired for pay and were neither convicts nor slaves, none of these workers would wear a brand; and if they noticed mine, they might turn me in for the reward.

As I watched the road, a lone, elderly woman appeared, leading a donkey bearing reed baskets. It suddenly occurred to me that if I had her donkey and baskets, I, too, could be a native trader.

Dios mio! It was the perfect disguise. I would naturally have to find some way to repay the old woman when I had dinero. God would bless her, of course, and if nothing else, I was probably saving her from those bands of banditos, who would rob her blind and slit her throat.

I veered off cross-country and, reaching the road, hid in the bushes. She was good-sized for an india, but I was sure

I could frighten her out of her wares and not hurt her. I could not see her face; but from her clothing and her grandmotherish scarf, she appeared ancient. She walked slowly, her head bent down, leading the donkey in no particular hurry.

Not wanting to scare her too badly, I threw aside my spear and club. When she reached my hiding place, I drew my obsidian knife and leaped out of the bushes.

"I'm taking your donkey!" I shouted at her.

"That's what you think!" a male voice shouted back.

I stared into the dark features of an africano.

He drew a sword. "Drop your knife!"

I heard hooves in the distance; I had walked into a trap.

The man closed in on me with his sword extended.

"Drop your knife, mestizo, or I'll cut off your head."

I turned and ran, heading back up the hill. In less than a minute men on mule back roped me like a steer and bound my arms and legs. When the dust settled, I was tied up and on the ground and surrounded by six africanos. I assumed they were maroons, a highwaymen gang of escaped slaves, and I was half right.

Their leader, a husky africano, who had lassoed me from the back of a mule, bent down and grabbed my face with his hand, twisting it so he could examine my mine slave brand.

He grinned with pleasure. "Just as I thought, an escaped mine slave. But the brand is not readable. What mine did you escape from?"

I did not answer. He let me go and stood up. He gave me a kick. "It doesn't matter. He's strong and healthy. Any of the mines will pay us a hundred pesos for him."

I knew he was right. They would pay a hundred pesos and consider it cheap. A black slave would cost them four times that much.

¡Ay de mí! I had forgotten an important lesson in life, one the fray always preached. When things are too good to be true . . . they are not true. Only a fool would have been duped by the little india with the donkey. I should have

seen from the length of her stride and the swing of her arms that the old crone was a man.

I had blown up a mine, shattered a mountain, survived a river at full flood, escaped certain death only by the personal intervention of God, bedded down a beautiful india saint . . . only to stumble—no!—race into the hands of slave hunters.

The donkey "woman" caught up with us.

"I get credit for the capture!" he shouted to the others. "I get the bonus dinero." He ran up to the man who had examined my face and whom I took to be the leader of the band. "Yanga, I get the bonus dinero for making the capture. Isn't that true!"

The name jolted me.

"I caught him with my rope," the man called Yanga said. "You let him get away."

"But I was the bait that lured him out of hiding!"

I paid attention to the man as the donkey man argued with him. Could it be the same Yanga whom I had aided years ago? What about the maroon bandit leader named Yanga?

After the two men resolved their differences, Yanga announced that it was too late to head for a mine; that they would make camp on the spot. Supplies were unpacked and a fire started for dinner. I eyed Yanga until my staring caught his attention.

He gave me a kick. "Why do you stare at me? You try to poison my soul with the evil eye, and I will cut you into little pieces."

"I know you."

He grinned. "Many people know me. My name is sung all over New Spain."

"Your name was ridiculed when I last saw you, the night I saved your life." I had actually saved the man's testicles, but for most men it was the same thing. He was older and his beard was streaked with white, but I was convinced it was the same man.

He stared down at me narrowly. "Explain yourself."

"You were tied to a tree along the Jalapa road. A plantation owner was going to relieve you of your testicles. I cut you loose, and you removed his instead."

He muttered something in his native tongue that I did not understand. He knelt beside me again and stared at me. I could see that he was trying to subtract the years and the beard from the face.

"Ridiculing you as a prince," I went on, "he boasted of castrating you in front of his other slaves, so they would understand the consequences of disobedience, what would happen to them if they disobeyed. You were beaten, then tied to the tree. The man threw a rock at you and told you to eat that for dinner."

His face revealed that my guess was right; he was the Yanga of the Jalapa road. "Life is a circle," the fray used to say. "If one has enough patience, everything that goes by him once will return. The chinos in China on the other side of the world believe that if you wait by a river long enough, the body of your enemy will float by. Like the body of your enemy, the good deed you do today, the evil you sow, everything comes full circle."

I started to say something else, and he hushed me. "Quiet. Don't let the others hear such talk."

He left and did not return for another hour. When he came back, he had food for each of us. He loosened my left hand so I could eat.

The others were gathered around the campfire, exchanging boasts and dreams about what they would do with the prize money they would collect for capturing me. From their talk I understood that they had bagged a few indios and an africano mine slave in the past, but none had been as big and healthy as I was. Ay, I wish they had seen me before the india farm woman had fattened up my body and soul.

"How did escaped slaves come to be slave hunters?" I asked.

"I have fought the gachupins for seven years," he said. "Over those years my band grew to more than a hundred.

We could not live by thievery alone but needed food and families. That meant that we could not flee as fast from danger. We made our village high in the mountains, and when the soldados came, we drove them back into the jungle. But we always paid a price. And each time we fled, our village was burned, and we had to find another home.

"Finally the viceroy offered us peace. We would be forgiven our past crimes and would be declared freedmen. In return we had to return all escaped slaves that came our way. The plantation owners pay little for this service, but the mines continually run out of workers and pay well."

Eh, it's a brutal world, is it not, amigo? Avaricious slave owners flog and rape their human "property." The españols mistake a pig stampede for an africano rebellion and hang innocent blacks out of ignorance and fear. Ex-slaves, who once fought to be freed, now hunt other slaves for a bounty. A short time ago I was going to rob an old india of her donkey and goods.

"Returning me to the mines is a death sentence," I said, testing the waters.

"What did you do to get sent to the mines?"

"I was born."

Yanga shrugged. "Death cures all ills. Perhaps dying quickly in the mines is more merciful than dying on the outside."

"And perhaps I should not have risked my life for your manhood. I did not save a man anyway but a woman."

He hit me across the head so hard I blacked out for a moment. He retied my hands. Before he left, he gave me another kick.

"You get to eat only because we want to kept you fat until we are paid for you. But don't speak your bad words to me again. The mine owners will not miss your tongue when we sell you back to them."

The men around the campfire laughed at my punishment.

I lay very still, bringing the world back into focus. The man had fists the size of cannonballs. And maybe harder.

However, when I rolled to my side, I felt a knife tucked

between my ribs and my right arm. The rope Yanga had retied around my left hand had enough slack in it for me to grasp the knife.

The maroons drank and sang and argued late into the night. Eventually they passed out. If they had selected a sentry, he was passed out too—and snoring. They were all snoring. I cut myself free, picked up my manta and retied it around over my shoulder. I crept over to the mules, who knew me by now and did not spook.

There were four mules, still saddled and bridled in case the maroons needed to mount up in a hurry. I cut the reins and cinches on three of them. As soon as I was in the saddle of the fourth, I let out a yell that would have awakened people in the Place of the Dead, and booted the mule's ribs with my heels. I left the shouts of men behind me. Hopefully, by the time they rounded up their mules, I would be long gone.

ONE HUNDRED AND TWO

THUS BEGAN AN era of my life in which my name became famous once again in New Spain. Famous for charity? you ask. For works of scholarship? Amigos, you joke with me, of course, when you ask such questions. You know that the first time I became famous in the land it was for two murders I did not commit. Do you expect anything less from me? This time it was as a bandit leader that lips spoke my name and tongues wagged my fame.

Not long after I escaped Yanga's slave hunters, I began my new life. And why not? I was a man of property, possessing a mule and a steel knife. But I could not eat the mule I needed to carry me, and a knife is not a sword. Furthermore, I lacked money.

Finding an ax along the road gave me an idea. I would become a woodcutter, and on the Zacatecas road I had my first chance.

I spotted a very fat priest traveling by mule litter. He must have been an important fray, perhaps the prior of a church or convent in the mining capital. His litter was transported by two mules, front and back, with an indio walking beside each animal with rein in hand. Ten more indios, armed with knives and spears, marched with the litter.

Not too far in front of the priest's procession was a large mule train. The priest no doubt camped with the muleteers at night for added protection and traveled near them by day. But at the moment his litter and indios had dropped behind the mounted mule train, because they were climbing a steep hill, and his indios on foot could not keep up.

I was one man armed with a knife against a dozen indios. If I attacked them, they would impale me like thorns in a maguey branch. But I possessed a secret weapon: my axe.

The sun had set below the rimrock, casting the road below in shadowy twilit gloom, when the comedia began. As the priest's procession approached the top of the hill, his indios were forced to stop. At which point they heard the chopping sounds. No houses were evident, so the chopping was a little strange. To the fray, of course, the chopping sounds were nonetheless insignificant, but to an indio steeped in superstition, Night Ax, the headless apparition, evoked nothing less than hell on earth. During childhood their parents told them continually that if they weren't good children, Night Ax would come for them. They, in turn, passed the same threat on to their children: Night Ax stalking the evening forests, pounding his chest with his ax as he looked for victims.

As the chopping continued, I studied the indios from my hiding place uphill. The indios looked at one another, clearly distraught. Each of them had chopped wood on almost a daily basis. They understood that the ax wasn't splitting wood but . . . spilling blood.

The procession came to a halt. The priest, oblivious to

the drama, continued to sleep, his head slumped forward. I mounted my mule and came out of hiding at a swinging gallop, the ax in hand, my blanket covering my head—with holes punched out for my eyes—making me appear in the deepening dusk as a headless, ax-swinging fiend.

The indio bodyguards ran. The ones guiding the mules dropped their reins and quickly followed suit. The startled mules even took off running. I intercepted the lead animal, reaching down to get its reins. With the priest in the litter shouting and waving frantically, I led the mules off of the road and into the forest.

When I had gone far enough to elude would-be rescuers, I halted the mules. When I dismounted, the fat priest climbed out of the litter. He was the kind of priest that Fray Antonio hated, the ones with silk and lace and heavy gold chains.

"God will punish you for this!" he screamed.

I confronted him with my knife, putting it against his big belly. "God punishes me, fray, with the likes of you—priests who grow rich and fat and wear silk while poor people starve. How many indio babies starved for this silk shirt?"

I now poked his throat with the steel blade.

"Don't kill me!"

"Hey, amigo, do I look like a killer to you?"

From the look on his face, I'm afraid I did.

But while I left his life intact, yes, I must confess I robbed a priest—very thoroughly. I took not only his jewelry and money, I made him strip naked and appropriated all his silks and linens, along with a pair of exquisite calfskin shoes. I honestly believe that Fray Antonio, Fray Juan, and most of the priests of New Spain, men who conquered an empire of the soul with faith and guts, would have secretly cheered the man's downfall.

"Fray, when they ask you who did this foul deed, tell them it was Cristo the Bastardo who robbed you. Tell them I am a prince of mestizos and that no Spaniard is safe with his gold or his women while I am alive."

"You can't leave me alone in this wilderness! I have no shoes!"

"Eh, padre, if you have led a good life, the Lord will provide. Consider the lilies of the field, who neither toil nor do they spin."

When I left, he was standing barefoot and naked by his litter damning me to hell in a language that was most unpriestly.

So began the new career of Cristo the Bandito. I was so successful at my newfound trade that soon I had a half-dozen highwaymen assisting me. I am sad to say that not all of my new friends were as scrupulous and efficient as I. Those who could not avoid a sword or musket ball with my fabled alacrity or who showed their bad judgment and lack of character by trying to steal from me, I quickly dismissed or killed. In fact, the first mestizo trash who tried to cut my throat for a larger cut of the till, I killed. I then lopped off his right ear and wore it on my sword scabbard as a warning to future miscreants. Not that it did much good. Within weeks I had three more ears hanging—a vivid rebuttal of the ancient maxim espousing honor among thieves.

We moved quickly, hitting the same piece of road several times in succession, then riding like the wind to an entirely different part of the country. To keep from arousing suspicion, I became a guitar merchant, using the trick that Don Julio had us use when we were tracking the naualli magician. A few guitars make a tall load on a mule yet they are very light, so the mule can, if required, depart in a hurry.

Do you think it was exciting to be a bandito? It was wait in ambush, hit and run, keep on the move, stay one step ahead of the viceroy's soldados, drink too much, love too little, guard your back against comrades who would knife it in a heartbeat if there was one maravedí or the arms of a half ugly woman in it for them. Ay, for me it was worse. While I admit to having the larcenous soul of a lépero;

unlike the riffraff I rode with, I have been a gentleman, a scholar, a wearer of spurs.

Never far from my mind were my memories. Painful memories. Fray Antonio—tortured and slaughtered for protecting me. The Healer, who taught me how to be proud of my indio heritage. I thought of Don Julio, who saved my life, made me a gentleman—and then I thought of the holocaust that took him and his family before my eyes. Of my compadre, Mateo, who saved me from killers, taught me the theater, made me a man, and who either perished crossing the great ocean or died of fever in the Filipinas' jungles. And of a woman with radiant eyes and a smile like the rainbow's end, who wrote with poetry of soul, saved my life twice, whom I loved with all my heart but would never know, let alone, possess . . . and who, wed to a monster, would never know peace.

Throughout everything, all I wanted to do was turn my horse toward the City of Mexico, plunge a dagger into Ramon de Alva, and pray for one last glimpse of the woman I loved. But it was not to be. Not that I had given up on my revenge. The time was not ripe, that was all. Alva had grown even richer and more powerful since the don's death. He was now heralded as one of the most powerful men in New Spain. None of which meant he could not die, but when I did exact my vengeance, it would not be by way of an anonymous blade. That would be too kind. I wanted his fortune, his women, his pride, then his life. Death was not enough—not for what he had done.

I tried not to think of Eléna. Marriages among the rich and noble were arranged by family heads, whose words were law. By now she would be sharing Luis's life and bed. The thought of her in his arms was a knife in my heart, like the one Ramon thrust into the fray and twisted.

Still I had pride—even as a bandit. Eh, what the devil! I assumed I would die soon. Why not spread my name across the length and breadth of New Spain?

Among other things, I brought originality to the ancient profession of banditry. The way I invoked the Night Ax in my robberies was a singular example. My favorite techniques, however, were typically more grandiose, often conjuring explosive effects for which I owed an inestimable debt to Don Julio, Mateo, and I suppose my abysmal stint in the mine. From all three I had learned the art of black powder detonation.

No one had seen anything like it before. Explosions placed in mountain passes, bringing down half a mountain on a mule train's protectors. Bridges blown with guards still crossing, leaving carriages and pack trains behind them still on the trail. Black powder bombs, hurled by hand, stampeding horses, indios, and Spaniards alike, convincing them all that troops and artillery were on the offensive.

But my favorite raid had been on the wife of Veracruz's alcalde—the same woman whose witch's teat I had so meticulously titillated so many years ago. The alcalde was long dead—gored to death while challenging a bull on foot. His widow, however, had lost none of her cold beauty, had left Veracruz, and resided in the City of Mexico, to which she was returning after a visit to a hacienda.

We attacked just as the carriage was stopping for the noon meal. The lady was still inside the carriage when one of my men climbed aboard and took the reins. I jumped up to take her jewels and encountered my old friend. As the carriage rocked and swayed from the ruts in the road, the woman assaulted me verbally.

"You filthy animal! Get away from me!"

"Filthy?" I smelled my clothes under my arm. "I am not unclean. I bathe more than your Alameda friends do."

"What do you want? Take this!" She took off her least valuable ring and handed it to me. "That ring means more to me than life itself. It was given to me by my sainted husband before he died."

"It is not the cold jewels you wear on the outside, but the hot gem of your love I seek."

"My love? No, por Dios!" She crossed herself. "You are going to rape me."

"Rape? Never. Do I appear to be less than a gentleman

than the dons who curry your favor on the Alameda? You have mistaken me for an ordinary bandit, possibly that villain and murderer Cristo the Bastardo. But I am a gentleman. I am Don Juan Tenorio of Seville, son of the king's chamberlain." Eh, I am sure Tirso de Molina would forgive me for borrowing the name of the rogue he gave birth to with his quill and ink.

"You are a liar and a blackguard."

"Ah, yes, my beautiful one, I am those things, too." I kissed her hand. "But we have met before."

"I've never met a bandit before."

"Oh yes, you did, my love. During one of your husband's early bull-fighting performances."

"Nonsense. My husband was an important man. You would not be permitted in our presence."

"It was not your husband who permitted me. It was you who invited me under your dress."

She stared deeply into my eyes, mesmerized by the hint of familiarity she saw there.

"The last time you stared so intently into my eyes, you gave me a kick that made me fall and nearly break my neck."

She gaped. "No! It can't be!"

"Yes. I remember that day very well." I put my hand on her knee and slowly worked it up her thigh. "I remember that you wore no . . . oh, you still do not."

Her witches teat was still there, as diamond-hard as an aroused garrancha. After my hand found it, I slipped off of the seat and knelt between her legs. I pushed up her dress to expose her naked parts. Her legs spread, and my head descended into her innermost recesses. I playfully tongued that oh-so-titillating teat. It was as delicious as it had been years before.

My tongue was intently exploring a deeper, even more depraved domain when a shot was fired. My bandit comrade let out a yelp of pain and fell dead from the driver's seat. The horses bolted and we had a wild ride until soldados had caught up with the carriage.

A moment later one of them jerked open the door to the carriage.

"Are you all right, señora?"

"Yes."

"Did they harm you?"

"No, I am untouched."

"There was one who jumped into the carriage. Where did he go?"

Ah, that was the question. Where I had gone was under her dress. She was not wearing one of those dresses big enough to hide an elephant under. But with a blanket over her lap and my legs and feet under the seat, I was reasonably hidden. Until she turned me in, and the soldados dragged me out of the coach and chopped off my head.

"Where did he go?" she repeated. I could hear the question in her voice. Not as to my whereabouts—I was still between her legs. But whether I should lose my head.

"He's gone," she said, "leaped from the carriage."

The soldados escorted the carriage to an inn. The alcalde's widow refused to get out of the carriage. She told an officer she wanted to stay aboard and "rest" in privacy. Eh, amigos, it was no rest for me. She kept me busy until I escaped into the dark night.

To this day I do not know whether she protected me because she did not want to be exposed herself . . . or because she loved my tongue.

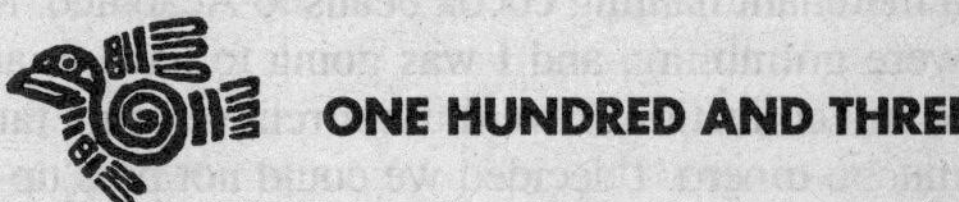

ONE HUNDRED AND THREE

IN TRUTH, THE big robberies were very few and very far between. For the most part my life was a dangerous, ill-trod mountain path, trailing sheer cliffs and split by forks. In my second year as a bandit, I came to one of those forks.

New Spain was a big land, but like Rome, all roads eventually lead to Ciudad Mexico. If one stayed around the main roads, or in my case, committed acts of banditry along them, one would eventually encounter one's past, just as I had met the alcalde's wife. It occurred on one of those roads, which was little more than a trail through a mountain pass.

When the treasure fleet arrived from Seville and the galleon with the riches of the Orient from Manila, my amigos and I made sure we got some small piece of the riches. Ay, it was not an easy task, and by that second year of banditry those pieces were getting smaller. More soldados were patrolling the roads now due to my fame, and especially patrolling the roads when the treasure fleets were in. Everyone on the roads proceeded with extreme caution. The silver trains were heavily guarded. Travelers joined in massive caravans, like those of the Arabian deserts. With each month the pickings had grown increasingly slim.

In those hard times we often had to content ourselves with easy targets—well-to-do travelers foolish enough to travel alone. Most often these solitary wayfarers were well-mounted and relied on their animals to outrun any bandits. But this one time the traveler journeyed by litter and was such a sitting duck I wondered if it was a trap, such as the one Yanga had sprung on me.

We saw the litter from where we had been camped the night before. It had been more than two weeks since we had stolen anything significant and even that had been only a merchant hauling cocoa beans to Acapulco. My three men were grumbling, and I was going to have to add more ears to my collection if we did not relieve some fat merchant of mucho dinero. I decided we could not pass up such an easy target.

We studied him from above and determined his sex by a protruding arm. *A very foolish man,* was my basic impression. The litter was carried by two mules and two indios guided them, but that was all. He was unprotected.

Eh, amigos, perhaps our luck was changing.

We came down like the Four Horsemen of the Apocalypse, waving our swords, our war screams terrifying. The two indios naturally fled, but rather than some plump priest or merchant climbing out of the litter, a caballero flew out of it with his sword flashing. My best bandito, who got to the litter ahead of me, lost his horse and his life. As I charged, the caballero leaped on my dead amigo's horse and wheeled to face me. When I saw his face, I was so shocked I nearly lost my life. I steered my horse just in time to avoid Mateo's sword.

"Mateo! It's Bastardo! *Your Bastardo!*"

"Santa Maria," he whispered. Then he roared with laughter. "Cristo! Didn't I teach you how to be a better thief?"

His hair was streaked with gray as was his beard. He was almost as gaunt as I had been after I escaped from the mines. When he told me his story that night around the campfire, I saw why.

"The trip west across the great Southern Sea, the one you called the Western Sea, is hell afloat. Acapulco to Manila is three times farther than Veracruz to Seville. It takes several months to make the trip. Many died aboard. The return trip along the famous monk-navigator Urdaneta's route is even farther and takes over four months. Many more died. When we were told that the viceroy sent the lice of New Spain to the Filipinas to die, we were lied to. They were sent to die at sea."

"And Manila? What of it?" I asked.

"A pretty place but not a great city, a place to lie in the shade and wait to grow old and die while a native girl fans you with a palm leaf. For a man like me who loves the excitement of comedias and the romance of the Alameda, Manila was barren."

We camped high in the mountains to ensure that we would not be surprised by soldados. The two of us sat up most of the night around a fire in a cave talking about our lives and adventures.

Already weakened from months in the hands of the Inquisition, Mateo had barely survived the voyage across the great sea. In the Filipinas, he was sent to a country farm to act as an overseer; but as soon as his strength returned, he was in much demand by the viceroy in Manila as a swordsman.

"My days as a prisoner ended. I fought Malay pirates, yellow devils, tougher than the most bloodthirsty pirates terrorizing the Spanish Main. I killed a hundred of them and saved a chino princess. Her father gave her to me in marriage and my own kingdom. But the princess had a jealous suitor with a big army, and I ended up escaping with just the crown jewels to keep me warm. I went to China, the land of the chinos, and stood upon a great wall that is long enough to enclose all of Spain. I visited an island where the people call themselves Japonés and their warrior class, called samurai, are the toughest fighters on earth. I came back to New Spain with enough wealth to buy the entire City of Mexico and turn it into my personal hacienda."

My compadre had not changed, had he? Still the liar and braggart. Samurai warriors and winning a kingdom! But there were always a few beans of truth in his pot of frijoles. His last adventure was the most truthful.

"I arrived in Acapulco with my pocket full of priceless gems. There was a card—"

"—game and a woman and some wine. How much do you have left?"

"I used my last peso to hire that litter. I didn't have the dinero to buy a horse. And you, amigo? How much treasure have you accumulated from leading a gang of notorious banditos?"

I cleared my throat. "I, uh, have some cocoa beans."

He groaned out loud and long. "Bastardo, you learned nothing from all of my teachings."

"No, that's not true. I did learn much from you. *All of the wrong things.*"

The next day we set out on the trail toward the Valley of Mexico. The Manila galleon road had not been profitable, and we headed for the other side of the valley. On the Jalapa-Veracruz road we looked for our fortunes to change with the arrival of the treasure fleet.

"If I had significant funds, I could return to the City of Mexico by paying a 'fine' to one or two of the viceroy's underlings," Mateo said.

"I have a handful of cocoa beans," I said.

"It would take a handful of gold. I heard of the black legend of Don Julio even in Manila."

We had not talked much about the don. The subject was too painful. It was unspoken between us that we would kill Ramon de Alva.

"But you," Mateo said, "you could not show your face in the city even if you had a mountain of gold. The first thing I heard when arriving at Acapulco was to beware of Cristo the Bandito. There are many Cristos, but still I hoped against hope that this Cristo would turn out to be my old friend the Bastardo."

Mateo's plan for us was to continue robbing until we had enough dinero to leave New Spain for Seville. To him, Seville was the queen of cities.

"We need to get out of New Spain for a couple of years. We dare not confront Alva until we can walk down the Alameda and the main plaza without fear of being arrested."

We did not discuss these plans in the hearing of my three men.

While I joined Mateo's enthusiasm for a trip to Seville, his concept was that we would take our New World fortune back to Spain and live like kings. So far we had accumulated only a handful of cocoa beans. The more I had robbed, the more my fame spread, the more precautions the rich merchants took.

"One advantage to robbing arrivals from the treasure fleet," I told Mateo, "is that for most of them it is their first time in New Spain, and they do not always follow the advice of more experienced travelers. We should be able to pick up a fat purse or two in a week's time."

"Bah! What would we do with a couple of purses? A few

hands of cards? A couple of putas for a night? For this we risk the gallows everyday?"

"No," I expounded, "for this you keep a little food in your belly, and you sleep with one arm out of your blanket and your sword in your hand. The life on the road is not for a gachupin, I know that. Whatever we get, you can have my share, too. Maybe it will be enough to buy your way back to the capital."

Mateo slapped me so hard on the back, I was nearly knocked off my horse. "Eh, compadre, I have hurt your feelings. It is for both of us that I want to acquire wealth. Instead of many small attacks, we must make one big theft that gives us enough dinero to fulfill our needs. Being a gentleman and caballero is expensive."

"The only way we could get enough money in one robbery would be to attack a silver train. But they are heavily guarded," I said. "In the past when troops were needed for war with the Chichimecas, the viceroy did not have enough soldados to protect all of the silver trains, and he used trickery to deceive robbers. Now the silver trains are so well-armed that even with black powder bombs, it would be suicide for a small group like ours to attack one. We would have a better chance of walking into the mint in Mexico City and carrying out an armful of silver bars."

"You would have a better chance of stealing gold from heaven than the mint's silver," Mateo observed. "The place has no windows on the ground floor, the upper windows are barred, and the place is encased with thick walls. It's said to be guarded more dearly than a sultan's harem."

The pickings on the Jalapa road continued to dwindle, which did nothing to improve anyone's temperament. Mateo, who was the most averse to our hit-and-run robberies and to the life of the bandito in general, was unrelentingly sarcastic about a change in strategy.

"I will find a rich widow who will provide me with the lifestyle of a gentleman in return for my services in bed. I would get you employed in the household, of course. You can be my servant, empty my bedpan, and shine my boots."

What an amigo!

The first attack Mateo and I made together was clearly a bad joke from the gods. Our victims turned out to be a troupe of actors from Madrid. Mateo refused to rob them, telling me it would be sacrilegious for us to plunder fellow thespians. Our three fellow brigands balked at Mateo's refusal to rob the actors and would not concur until Mateo turned his sword on them.

The acting troupe incident only increased Mateo's dissatisfaction with the highwayman's life. In truth, it stirred in both of us the urge to return to the stage. Mateo agreed to only one more robbery, after which he would seek other ways of filling his purse.

Our luck changed when we spotted stragglers making the journey from the treasure fleet along the Jalapa road. We roared down on them, a Spaniard in a mule litter, his Spanish servant on a donkey, and a host of indios to serve as guards and servants on foot.

We discovered that rather than a rich merchant, the man was an official from the Council of the Indies in Spain.

"A mint inspector!" Mateo exclaimed with disgust. "Instead of mint money, we capture an inspector who oversees that the mint is operating correctly."

We kept the mint inspector and his español servant tied up while we pondered whether we might be able to obtain ransom for the man. The inspector was to present his papers at the mint in the capital, do a complete inspection of all aspects from its security to the quality of its coin-stamping, and then proceed to Lima, Peru, for an inspection there, after sending a report back to the council.

"The possibilities of getting ransom are slim," Mateo said. "From the papers outlining his authority, he is making a surprise inspection of the mint. No one, not even the mint director or the viceroy, knows he is coming. Worse, if we ask the viceroy to ransom him, he'd probably refuse and hope we kill the inspector. With communications only through the treasure fleet, it would be a year or two before the council found out its inspector was dead and another year or two before another one arrived. The viceroy would benefit because no inspector would come all the way to New Spain to make an inspection and not make sure he found deficiencies that needed to be corrected."

"We need to sleep on the matter," I told him.

Wrapped in our mantas, we lay down with our alternatives in mind. Cut the throats of the two captives and leave the bodies where they would advertise the futility of resisting us. Attempt to obtain a ransom. Or let them go.

I awoke in the middle of the night with a way to use the mint inspector in an entirely different way. I awoke Mateo.

"When we questioned the inspector, he claimed that he has no relatives or friends in New Spain who could ransom him."

"Eh, you woke me up to tell me what I already knew?"

"The man who appears at the mint with the Council of the Indies authority in his hand will be accepted as the inspector."

He grabbed me by the throat. "I am going to rip out your throat if you do not get to the point."

I knocked his hand away. "Listen, you dolt, the mint is filled with enough silver to buy a small kingdom. It can't be stormed, but you could walk into it with the inspector's papers!"

He shook his head. "I have not had enough wine or pleasure with a woman to keep my head clear. My mind and ears are playing tricks on me. I thought perhaps you said I could walk into the mint with the inspector's papers."

"Mateo, no one knows the inspector. His only identification is the council's letter of authority. If you present the paper, you are the inspector."

"Bravo Bastardo! A brilliant plan. I present the papers of this inspector; I have you along as my servant. We walk into the mint. We fill our pockets—no! We lead in a mule and load it with silver bars and walk it out. Is that the loco plan you have devised?" He fondled his dagger.

"Ah, Mateo, Mateo, you jump to conclusions too quickly. I have not finished my plan."

"Then tell me, whisper into my ear exactly how we are to take the treasure from the mint once we are inside."

I yawned, suddenly very tired. Turning my back on him, I crawled back into my bedroll. When I was comfortable, I said, "I have only figured out a way to get into the mint. We do not even know what it looks like inside. Once we are in there, we can figure out how to take the treasure with us."

Mateo said nothing. He lit a tobacco twist and smoked it. That was a good sign. Much better than him fingering his dagger and looking at my throat.

The next morning he gave me his verdict.

"Your idea of using the mint inspector's papers is foolish and stupid. It is exactly the sort of loco idea that has gotten me close to the gallows so often."

"Then we will do it?"

"Of course."

ONE HUNDRED AND FOUR

WE STUDIED THE mint inspector and his servant at great length, making them walk and talk.

"This is how an actor prepares his part," Mateo said, tapping his head. "Makeup and costume do not make an actor. It is the mental attitude." He gestured at the mint inspector. "Notice that when this worthless dog of a bureaucrat talks to you, how he lifts his nose as if disdaining your lowly odor? How he walks stiffly like he has a stick up his ass? Now watch this." Mateo paced back and forth for a moment. "What do you see, Bastardo?"

"I see a man with wary eyes, watching for a surprise attack, one hand on his sword, his step bold."

"Exactly! But the creature I am to impersonate has spent

his life in the safe haven of the king's treasure. He is a man of numbers, not action. He has permanently stained his fingers with ink and has a callus between his fingers from holding a quill. His eyes are bad from reading documents in candlelight, and he has to bend down close to read anything. But of the greatest importance, because he carries the king's authority in a matter more dear to the king's heart than the treasure to be found in his mistresses' bed, the little swine of an inspector is caught up with his own importance. Hiding behind the king's authority, having stained his hands with ink rather than blood, he has the audacity to be rude to even caballeros who could slice him into pieces."

Now that Mateo pointed out the man's characteristics, I could see the truth of his statements. And his own acting ability. I remembered, too, how impressed I had been when I saw Mateo on the stage as the mad prince of Poland.

"Now, Bastardo, watch the servant, see his hesitant step, the way he looks down when the eyes of authority are on him, the way he flinches when spoken to harshly, his whine when he has been caught at wrongdoing."

Eh, I, too, was an experienced actor. Did I not play the role of lépero trash in Veracruz? An indio faker with the Healer? A gentleman-cousin of the don's? It would be easy for me to assume the guise of a mere servant. I demonstrated my ability for Mateo.

"No, you stupid bobo! You are supposed to be a servant, not a whimpering lépero. Servants are humble, not sly."

We left the mint inspector and his servant in the hands of our three fellow banditos and left for the City of Mexico with their clothes and papers. We didn't know if we would need the inspector again, and warned our men that if any harm came to him, we would skin all three banditos and pack their carcasses in salt.

Mateo insisted that we travel to the city with him in a mule litter and me on a donkey, maintaining our disguises in terms of our speech and actions even when we were alone. I was taller than the servant, and I looked ridiculous with my long legs almost touching the ground. I felt like Don Quixote's "servant," Sancho. But I carefully avoided comparing Mateo to the knight-errant.

To match the inspector's hair, I reddened Mateo's hair with a bark juice indias used to color mantas. The inspector had a small monocle, a piece of ground lens he could put up to one eye to inspect papers with. Mateo would keep the glass up to his eye during much of the visit. He had told me that he wanted to make sure he wasn't recognized when we returned to the city someday as a gentlemen.

I used the disguise taught to me by the Healer: a pinch of flower dust that would make my nose swell up and distort my face. No one noticed a servant, but I wanted to ensure that at the least they would search for one with a big nose.

Mateo composed a story he would use at the mint limiting our interaction with the employees. "The mint director will want to entertain the inspector, soften him up with fine wine and maybe even female companionship. We will tell him, however, that our trip from Veracruz was delayed because I got an attack of the black vomit. I am now not only in a hurry to get out of this accursed colony and return to Spain, but I must inspect the mint without delay so I can be in Acapulco in time for a sailing to Lima."

Finally we crossed onto the causeway and entered the city. Hard as I tried to focus on the mint, images from the past intruded into my thoughts. Had I seen faces from the past, Eléna, Luis, de Alva, or even Isabella, I do not know that I would have been able to keep my composure—or my dagger in its sheath.

Mateo walked stiffly into the mint like a man with a sword handle up his rear.

I came behind him, shuffling my feet a bit as if I was too lazy and too stupid to pick them up and put them back down. I carried his kidskin bag that contained his letter of authority and instructions.

We soon discovered that the mint director was not in. He was in Zacatecas, reviewing the procedures used to prepare and ship the silver bars that made their way to the mint and ultimately to the treasure fleet.

The assistant director greeted us with great apprehension. "Five years ago we endured a surprise inspection," he complained, "and nothing but lies were sent back to the Council of the Indies about our management. We run the finest mint in the Empire of Spain at the least expense."

Mateo was irritably haughty. "We shall see how efficient your operation is. Our sources report that your stamping operation is mismanaged, rife with peculation, and that silver is systematically shaved from all bullion passing through your mint."

The poor man nearly had a coronary. "Lies! Lies! Our coins are works of art. Our bars are true weight!"

I did not know anything about the bars, but the gold and silver coins looked like fine art to my avarice lépero eyes.

Prior to leaving the real mint inspector, we had obtained some information from him about the operation of the mint, roasting his feet over a fire for a time until the information flowed from his mouth.

The mint had several functions. Bars of silver mainly, but also some gold and copper were shipped from the mines to the mint. At the mint, the assayers were in charge of weighing and determining the purity of the precious metals, the treasurers collected the king's fifth from the value, and the engravers turned some of the bars into thousands of coins.

The mint was supposed to only coin silver reales and copper maravedies of several denominations, but it was well known that it occasionally did stamp gold. The maravedíes had little value, a handful could barely buy a few tortillas. The silver reales ranged in size from a quarter reale to eight reales, popularly known as pieces of eight.

Like the other government positions, the director of the Casa de Moneta, the House of the Mint, was a position purchased from the king. While mint fees for assaying and stamping supplied income for the director, the income was supplemented by cheating.

The mint inspector had revealed what he was looking for after we toasted his feet over a campfire: gold residue to indicate the mint was illegally coining gold in defiance of the exclusive royal license granted to mints in Spain; evidence that coins were being tossed in a cloth pouch to grind off minute amounts of silver. The process was called "whirling" because indio workers would whirl the coins in the pouches for hours. The loss of silver from the process was too small to affect scales, yet when a tiny bit of silver was ground off of tens of thousands of coins by this method, the silver dust became significant.

More significant was the use of altered scales for weighing, and under the table deals in which the weights were understated. Less weight meant less of the king's 20-percent tax collected. Of course, the mint director and the owner of the silver split the thefts.

Mateo and I, as seasoned criminals, were better equipped to uncover nefarious acts than the bureaucratic mint inspector. Given the time, we would have uncovered each and every way the mint people were cheating, but our duty was not to find their criminal activities—we were there to plan our own.

Our interest was in security measures and the location of the treasure within.

The building was more secure than a castle. The walls were two feet thick. There were no windows on the ground level. The second-floor windows had iron bars. Both the lower and upper floor were wood. Only one exit door existed, and it was more than a foot thick and located in front of the building. No buildings bordered the mint on any side. Two guards slept in the building at night. Everyone who entered was searched upon exiting.

The silver and gold was stacked in bars on iron shelves and heavy iron tables. It sat there in the open, ready to be carried off, by anyone who could walk through walls.

There were only two ways to breach the security at night:

batter down the door or blow a hole in the wall. Either method would bring a hundred of the viceroy's soldados running.

Mateo discovered a hidden bolthole where the cloth bags—used to hold batches of new-minted silver coins—were kept. In some of them he found traces of silver shavings and bullion dust. It was a minor matter, but Mateo acted as if he had uncovered many other violations. He gave the assistant director a severe tongue lashing, frequently referring to dungeons and hanging. The man was sickly green and sweating profusely by the time he and Mateo disappeared into his office. Mateo came out a moment later, and we "left for Lima."

"How much did you squeeze him for?" I asked, after we had crossed back over the causeway. We were heading southeast for Acapulco but would soon buy horses and reverse our direction.

He save me a sideways glance. "How do you know I got anything?"

"How do I know the sun will rise? You are a picaro. You had the poor man almost on his knees praying for forgiveness and the chance to see his family once again. Of course you intended to share it with your partner."

"A thousand pesos."

I gasped. "*¡Santa Maria!*" In our state of poverty, it was a literal fortune. I did some quick calculations. That much money could last the two of us a year if we lived modestly and were careful. It would last no more than a week if Mateo was permitted to indulge in gambling and women.

"If we are prudent—"

"We will double it on the way back to our camp, compadre. There used to be a place in Texcoco. I'm sure it's still there. Three gambling tables and five of the most beautiful women in New Spain. There is a mulatta from Hispaniola that . . ."

I groaned and put my hands over my ears.

* * *

I underestimated Mateo's ability to lose money. We left the Texcoco gambling cantina three days later with our pockets empty and fresh blood on Mateo's sword. He had caught the owner's son cheating him at cards. The son would never shuffle another deck of cards again because it takes *two* hands. We fought our way out of the town with the owner, the constable, and two dozen of their friends trying to stop us.

Leaving town as quickly as our horses could carry us, I spotted the acting troupe that we had detained briefly along the Jalapa road before releasing them. They had set up the traditional playhouse called a corral in an empty lot—an elevated stage a couple of feet off of the ground with its back to one of the buildings. The roofs, windows, and patios of the other buildings formed the area where the audience stood or sat on logs or benches.

This, of course, was exactly how we had put on comedias. And it gave me a flash of insight as to how we could relieve the mint of its treasure.

"Act II!" I yelled to Mateo as we road out of town.

"What?"

"Act II. I know Act II for the mint."

He twirled his hand near his head to advise me that I was loco.

ONE HUNDRED AND FIVE

I WAS HAPPY to be back in the business of being the autor of comedias, even if they were bandit extravaganzas.

To implement our plan to rob the mint, we would need our three bandito amigos. They were stupid, greedy mestizos, but their strong backs would be necessary. That meant we had to do something about the two prisoners. The obvious solution would be to kill them, but Mateo had more sympathy for the españols than the rest of us. At his insistence, we chained them together in a small cave and hired nearby indios to feed them twice a day. The indios were told to wait ten days, and then release the two men. Recalling that indios sometimes had trouble with numbers—their coins often had slash marks on them to indicate denomination so the indios would understand their value—I gave them ten pebbles to ensure that they understood that the prisoners were not to be released for ten days.

While we were arranging confinement for the prisoners, we put indias to work sewing scenery for the play. The easiest play to get permission to put on would be one with a familiar religious theme. We chose a play similar to an auto sacramentale, a play with a sacred theme, the type usually performed as part of the Corpus Christi Feast Day celebration. Only our version involved Mateo having the only speaking part, that of a narrator who describes the action as God wreaks vengeance on sinners by casting down a great deal of heavenly thunder and lightning.

The chance that anyone would pay for an admission for the play after the first performance was negligible, but we only needed one performance. And with a religious theme, there would be no problem getting the comedia licensed by the viceroy and the Holy Office.

We needed disguises again. It was Mateo, the consummate actor, who came up with simple disguises.

"Lay monks."

"Lay monks?"

"There is a Basque order of secular monks called the Brothers of Good Hope. They are something of vagabonds, not picaros, who travel around doing good deeds. They wear mouse-brown robes with the cowls covering their heads and full beards. The Church tolerates them because they are considered harmless. It would not be unusual for them to put on a bastardized version of a sacred play."

"*¡Viva!* Mateo, you are a genius. Even these stupid léperos we ride with would be able to hide in monks robes with a hood over their heads."

Mateo grinned and took a long swig from his ever-present goatskin. "Eh, Bastardo, did I not tell you that if you stuck with me, you would get all that you deserve in life? Look at you now. In a couple of weeks you have gone from a bandito to a servant, from a servant to a monk. Soon you will be a gentleman in our madre Spain. When our pockets are loaded with the gold and silver of the king, we will go to Seville, the Queen of Cities. Did I tell you that the streets of Seville are paved in gold? That the women are . . . ?"

We needed money for the mordida to be paid to the viceroy's licensing representative for permission to use the vacant lot next to the mint, for the wood to build a stage, and even to have indias turn coarse brown blankets into monk's robes. I came up with the plan.

"You have lost enough money to last several lifetimes at the cheating card tables of the cantinas. Would it not be right to retrieve some of those losses? Besides, we need more practice with black powder."

We chose a mining town no more than three days' journey from the capital. It was not a large, rich town like Zacatecas, but there would be many times more silver on the cantina tables than in an ordinary town that thrived on trade or agriculture.

Mateo went into the cantina, while I went to the back. One of the mestizos held our horses in back. After giving Mateo enough time to have one drink and look over the tables to see where the big bets were, I placed a black powder hand bomb at the back door of the cantina. I hoped Mateo remembered to stay on the other side of the cantina. When the explosion went off, it blew down the door and part of the wall. I immediately threw another bomb inside and ran for my horse.

The plan was that the men in the cantina would run outside in panic, leaving money on the tables.

A moment later we picked up Mateo on the side of the

building and rode out of town, leaving behind us a great deal of confusion. Mateo had a pocketful of silver and a lot of bad temper.

"*¡Ay de mí!* Look how I have fallen. A gentleman and caballero of Spain, grabbing money from a gambling table like a common thief. This is what I get for associating with those with tainted blood."

"Eh, hombre, look at it this way. For once you left a cantina with money in your pockets."

I left "Brother Mateo" to negotiate the mordida. As we predicted, the play's subject matter guaranteed prompt approval. I meanwhile erected the stage and scenery. I placed the stage ten feet back from the outside wall of the mint, as instructed by the assistant mint director. With my nose swollen from the same substance used by the Healer to disguise me, my beard cut differently, and dressed as a monk, I managed to fool the assistant mint director.

We did not want the stage set against the building anyway. Instead, we closed that space off with blankets and scenery, creating a dressing room.

Eh, amigos, you believe we are going to blow our way into the mint? But you wonder, how will we blow a hole in the wall and sneak out the treasure without disturbing the guards inside? How can we do this when we will have an audience of a couple hundred people watching? Even if we succeed in getting our hands on the treasure, how would we get it across one of the causeways when the viceroy's soldados guarding the causeways have orders to search all baggage leaving the city at night? Would we be trapped on the island-city, hunted down like rats?

Loco, you say. The fact that I have spent so much of my life at the tender mercy of torturers in dungeons may shade your opinion of my abilities as a criminal. Ayya ouiya, as the Healer would say. Even my own opinion of my criminal abilities was low. The treasure that we sought was for more than silk doublets and gilt-adorned coaches, it was for revenge. And this lowly lépero still had some tricks.

* * *

Feeling secure in my monk's garb, my face half hidden by the cowl, I took a walk in the great city. I feared confronting Eléna and Luis, so I avoided the Alameda. I strolled the main plaza under the arches and across the wide, stone-paved square. Memories strolled beside me, especially those of a dark-eyed girl for whom I had once spread a manta on a puddle and whom I had once chased down an alley out of love of her poems.

My feet brought me back to the side street, where I had run the print shop and sold profano and deshonesto banned books. It was still a print and bookshop, and I went inside. The proprietor asked me if I needed help.

"Gracias, but I would like to look at the books you offer."

His stock of books took up five wall shelves. While I examined them, a customer entered. He loudly asked for a certain religious tome, a book of the lives of saints, and the printer answered in a loud voice he would get him a copy. Nothing changes, does it, amigos? If I was not wanted from one end of New Spain to the other, I would have had some fun telling the two men that I was from the Inquisition and insisted upon inspecting the "book of saints."

My eye caught the title of a book that was familiar to me. It was Gaspare Tagliacozzi's *De Chirurgia Curtorum Per Insitionem*, published in Italy in 1597. Tagliacozzi was the surgeon who learned the secret of the Hindu doctors who were able to reconstruct noses and cover scars by taking skin from one part of the body and putting it on the affected area. I pulled the book off the shelf and examined the front edge.

Don Julio's initials were burned into it.

My hands shook so bad I nearly dropped the book. Tears burned my eyes.

"Have you found something you like, fray?"

Getting my emotions under control, I bargained for the book and left the store.

That night I showed the book to Mateo at the inn where we were staying. He pushed it away and went to the inn's cantina to get drunk.

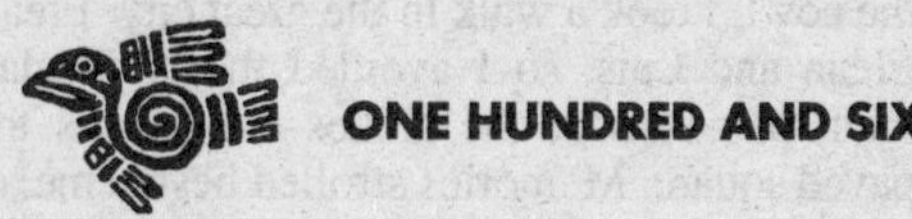

ONE HUNDRED AND SIX

WE WERE ALL nervous the night of the play. The play itself was not expected to curry audience favor. Because of the religious theme, the mosqueteros would grumble but would fear to shout down Mateo too loudly as he stood on the stage and spoke of God's revenge.

Mateo was to narrate the tale. Two of our banditos would help Mateo present the play. Our bandit-thespians would repeatedly drop dead on the stage and set off explosions of mock thunder and manufacture lightning by passing a torch in front of a large mirror.

Another would be working the tunnel with me.

Eh, did I catch you by surprise? Tunnel, you ask? Sí, just as you thought, the explosions were our admission into the mint. But did you think we were going to blow our way into the building? We were not *that* loco. The guards would certainly be on the second floor or on the roof watching the play, but an explosion against a wall would shake the whole building. The explosions would be used to attract the attention of the guards inside the building and make noise to cover our clandestine activities.

True, the walls were thick, the windows upstairs barred, but amigos, did I not tell you that the lower floor was wood? Do you not remember that the dirt of the city is so soft and moist you can dig it with a spoon? The dirt was hauled away in the same wagons that brought our wood for the stage.

The entire tunnel was only seven or eight feet long and less than three feet wide. Hardly a challenge to a human mole like myself who had tunneled through a hard-rock mountain and had squirmed down the narrow passageway of an ancient tomb to rob it. The tunnel led from a covered hole behind the stage, under the wall, and into a room—the room noted during our inspection, where the gold and silver were stored until they were taken to be assayed or processed.

Our biggest fear was that it would fill with water.

In these situations I sometimes feared that the Aztec gods would repay me for desecrating their temple at Monte Alban.

When the play commenced, I looked out from the curtain for Eléna. Most plays were performed during the day, but this time we needed the darkness. The stage was ablaze with candles and torches, so the audience could see Mateo and the other actors struck by thunderbolts.

I knew that the subject matter would not interest her, but since so few plays were presented, I hoped she would appear out of simple curiosity. As a lady of quality, she would have sat in a window or balcony of a building, fronting the lot. In the darkness I could not distinguish any of those people. I could not see much of the audience. They sat shrouded in darkness while the stage was ablaze with light. But my eye caught two familiar figures in the front roll—*the mint inspector and the mint director's assistant.*

I realized that the indios had drastically miscounted the days.

Ay! It only got worse. Mateo, damn his thespian soul, was of course not one to put on a simple performance, but was determined to win accolades. As he strutted back and forth on the stage, his cowl had slipped down and his face was exposed.

¡Madre de Dios! The mint inspector had spent days with us when we wore no disguise. He could see Mateo's face now. My heart thumped in my throat as panic gripped me. I could not run without warning my friend, but each time I hissed his name the explosions drowned me out. I would have had to light the black powder under his feet to get his attention anyway—he was so overtaken by his role as the

voice of God that he would pay no attention to me.

My eye darted to the mint inspector to see if he was on his feet denouncing Mateo. To my astonishment, the man was calmly sitting and staring up at the stage as if nothing was wrong. Eh, perhaps there was nothing wrong. *In his eyes.* The man was blind as a bat, was he not? I watched him intently. Nothing in his expression revealed that he found anything amiss. He stared blankly up at the stage, his head moving to follow Mateo's dynamic strutting.

But what if the servant was in the crowd? *He* had good eyes.

And how many others could identify the picaro who was supposed to be sweating or buried in Manila?

I ran for the hole behind me. Enrique, my bandito helper, was waiting. We used a bucket tied to a rope to reduce the water in the hole so I would not drown if my progress was slow.

Taking hold of an iron bar and a hooked pole, I crawled into the hole. The tunnel was already filled with water, but I wiggled through it quickly and into the darkness on the other side. I could see nothing, but quickly felt where the joints were. I timed my prying to the explosions at the comedia, quickly tearing out enough of the floor so I could squeeze into the room. From inside the room, the explosions were amazingly muted.

Using a flint and steel and a small vial of oil, I lit a fire and used it to light candles in the room. I knew from the inspection that the walls of the room were about a foot thick, double the thickness of the other interior walls of the mint. The door was closed and bolted by the mint director when he left at night, deterring the night guards from gaining access. I could light the room and move around without fear of disturbing the guards, who were undoubtedly watching the play from the upper windows.

I fished into the water with my hook and brought out a heavy leather sack filled with empty bags that Enrique extended to me with a hooked pole from his end. I filled the empty bags with gold, most of it from chests filled with coins, because it was many times more valuable than silver. Filling a sack, I pushed it down into the water of the hole and splashed the water to signal Enrique to pull it out. When I had sent five sacks of gold out, I turned to the silver and filled six more with silver coins and bars.

A black metal box with its key inserted caught my eye. I opened the box, and it took my breath away. It was filled with gems, diamonds, rubies and pearls. A paper inside the box listed the inventory of the valuables and the name of the owner: Holy Office of the Inquisition. There was also a list containing the names of the previous owners—people who had been tried and convicted by the Holy Office and who had had their property confiscated.

I locked the box, put the key in my pocket and placed the box in my last sack. After the sack was pulled through, I got down on my stomach to wiggle back through the tunnel. It was now more than half filled with water. As I started down I realized something was terribly wrong. Dirt and rocks were being thrown in from the other side.

Our plan included a pile of dirt and rocks to fill the tunnel with once we finished so it would not be noticeable to someone entering the rear area of the stage. But Enrique was not supposed to fill it until *after* I emerged.

Léperos were not intelligent beasts, but unlike the indios who released the mint inspector prematurely, they could do simple arithmetic. Dividing the treasure four ways gave them a greater share than dividing it five ways. I did not know if trapping me in the mint was Enrique's idea or he had schemed with the other two. The move was too clever for Enrique to have planned. I suspected that the three banditos had decided to kill Mateo and myself after the robbery, and the opportunity to eliminate me suddenly arose.

The dirt and rocks thrown into the other side rose the water level on my side until it came up to the floor. I could not even get into the tunnel and try to dig through because I would drown.

The door to the rest of the mint was locked. Only the mint director had the key. When it was unlocked, he would find me in their treasure room with a rather large hole in the floor and a good portion of the treasure missing.

Even the Inquisition would be outraged because their box of gems was gone. The only controversy would be whether the viceroy had me drawn and quartered or the Inquisition burned me at the stake.

I was completely trapped.

ONE HUNDRED AND SEVEN

THE EXPLOSIONS OUTSIDE had stopped. That meant I would be abandoned momentarily. The plan was for us to move out as soon as the play was finished. We had a donkey cart standing by. Under the pretense of putting our costumes in it to take back to the inn, we would load the treasure aboard and start back toward the inn.

But halfway back we would detour.

It would not be possible to get the cart off the island across the causeways because it would be searched. So we had bought an indio boat to load the gold and silver aboard. We would take it across the lake ourselves where we had horses waiting.

Mateo would not willingly abandon me, but what was he to do when the lépero swine told him the tunnel had both filled with water and caved in? I knew how Mateo's mind worked. Once I was captured, he would do something to help me. Perhaps try to ransom me with the treasure. Or bribe the jailers.

But he would never get that chance. The moment the gold and silver were loaded on the boat, they would knife him in his back.

I sat down on the floor and gave the matter some thought. I could make another hole in the floor and tunnel out. I had no shovel and, in truth, while the ground was soft enough to be dug with a spoon, it would take a shovel to get me out by morning. I could use the iron bar and my hands, but the digging would go so slow, the water would probably fill the hole as quickly as I cleared it, and I had no bucket to empty it.

Ay, curse the classical education the fray gave me. An unpleasant comparison with my own perilous situation came to me from those books I'd devoured with my eyes and mind so long ago. King Midas had a love for gold. He was known to the Greeks for his greed and foolishness. He had an opportunity to exercise both of his vices when he captured Silenus, a satyr who was the companion of Dionysus, the god of wine and ecstasy. To gain Silenus's release, Dionysus had granted Midas a wish. The king's wish was that everything he touched turn to gold. But Midas of the golden touch soon regretted his wish. He had to touch food in order to eat it, and it turned to gold.

Eh, the gold was all gone, but I had plenty of silver to eat.

If I could not dig my way out, the only other exit was through the door. The door was thick, locked, and iron plated. But wait—it was iron plated on the outside. There had been no reason to plate the *inside.*

I examined the door with candlelight.

A slender crack existed between the door and the frame. Wiggling back and forth with the iron bar, I would be able to widen it. If I could break away enough of the wood, I would be able to push back the metal locking device with the bar. But I would not have the noise from the explosions to cover my prying. And the guards would no longer have their attention drawn to the play.

During the inspection, we had failed to ask where the guards slept. I tried to remember if I had seen beds anywhere, but nothing came to mind. It made sense that one would sleep on the ground floor and the other on the upper floor. But when it came to the Spanish bureaucracy, common sense and common practice were not always the same.

There was also the front door to consider, but it would be an easier task than the vault door. It was held by two iron bars rather than a lock, because a lock would not be strong enough. If the front door of the mint was to be attacked, it would be by battering ram from the outside. But inside, the bars were easy to slip aside.

I had no choice but to attack the storage vault door immediately, praying that the two guards would drink a little wine or beer and discuss the play before going to bed.

Using the bar, I broke away wood, making as little noise as I could. When the bar scraped the iron lock, my excitement increased, but it would only scrape. I could not get the lock to slide back. Anxiety took the place of excitement, and panic threatened to overwhelm me. Aaaak! I jabbed the iron bar in deep enough to kill the door and jerked the bar to the side. The lock broke, and I swung the door open. But I had made enough noise not only to wake the guards, but the twenty thousand sacrificial victims of the last great Aztec human feast.

I ran down the mint hallway for the front door, the cool air on my sweaty face. Pushing aside the door bars, I heard a shout behind me. A club smacked the door as I flung it open and rushed out. I ran by the corral. It was deserted.

Shouts followed me, but I paid no heed to them as I ran down the street and around a corner. I had to make it to where the boat would be loaded before Mateo got a knife in his back and I was captured by soldados.

Three men were beside the boat when I came running up to it. They were shadowy figures to me in the darkness. I could not tell if Mateo was among them.

"Mateo!" I shouted.

"Bastardo! You made it."

Bravo! Mateo was still alive.

"Did you think that—" I heard footfalls behind me and spun out of the path. Enrique was behind me. His dagger caught air as I twisted away.

My own dagger was in my hand, and I charged against

him, shoving it into his gut. He grunted and stared at me. I could see the whites of his eyes and smell sour salsa on his breath as he gasped.

I jerked the knife out and stepped back. Another of the banditos was on the ground in a gathering pool of blood. Mateo's sword flashed in the moonlight, and the other one caught the blade on the side of his neck. The wounded man staggered backward and fell into the lake.

"Are you all right?" I asked Mateo.

"A scratch to my back. I suspected Enrique's story was false. When I started to question him with my blade, he ran into the darkness."

Horses hooves and shouts filled the night air.

"Andale!" Mateo said. "We have a lake to cross."

After we reached the other side of the lake where our horses were pastured, Mateo was philosophical about the loss of our three comrades in arms.

"We would have had to kill them even if they did not try to stab our backs. After we divided the treasure, they would have soon been captured with their share because they would have exposed their wealth to others. It would have been a waste of thievery to give treasure back to the viceroy after we so cleverly stole it."

We packed most of the Holy Office's confiscated gems and enough gold ducats to fulfill our needs to be gentlemen of quality for a lifetime. The rest of the booty, a great quantity of gold and silver and the remainder of the jewelry, we placed in a cave, carefully concealing the existence of the cave with rocks and brush.

We rode for Veracruz, hoping our booty would not be found by an indio who thought he'd stumbled onto Montezuma's lost mine.

We had booked passage with a lobo boat that crisscrossed the ocean in between the annual voyages of the treasure fleet.

Our destination was Seville, the queen of Cities.

ONE HUNDRED AND EIGHT

I WOULD RIDE a dragon across the Fire Mountains before crossing an ocean in a boat. For three weeks we were tossed like a cork on waves the size of mountains, blown by winds sent by the gods to punish me for my innumerable transgressions. The sea's vomit-sickness ravaged me. What little I could eat, I vomited. By the time we reached the peninsula that housed Spain and Portugal, I had lost weight and any interest I ever had in being a sailor.

Mateo had served on both land and sea for the king. He was singularly unaffected. "I was just a boy when I had to leave the city of my birth and find sanctuary from a blood feud and the king's constables," he told me during the voyage. "A fleet was leaving to fight the Turkish sultan, and I had a berth on one of the ships."

He declined to reveal what had caused his youthful flight from justice, but my experiences with Mateo told me that a woman was somewhere in the comedia of his early life.

"The captain disliked me instantly, no doubt for some youthful indiscretion, and assigned me to the fireboats during the battle with the Infidel fleet. The boats were equipped with wooden cannons painted black, but we were the vanguard of a great naval victory over the Turks."

Wooden cannons? Fireboats? I had never heard of these machines of war and found Mateo's tale fascinating.

"In our age of ships that are the size of small castles, it is hard to sink a ship in battle. A lucky shot to the powder room will send a ship to the bottom, in pieces. But ships are made of wood and wood *burns,* compadre. Fire is a greater threat to a ship than being outgunned. You can sail out of cannon range, but you can't flee fire onboard. And there is no place to go if the fire gets out of hand. I have seen men onboard ships engulfed in flames throw themselves into the sea to drown rather than have the flames tickle their feet."

A "fireboat," he explained, was a ship refitted so it burned quickly and easily. "Ships are equipped to minimize the flammable material on board. But a fireboat is equipped to maximize burning."

The refitted ships were typically merchant vessels of little value in a battle. "We gutted the ship below deck and built wood chimneys from the hole to above the main deck. We constructed wood troughs in the hole that led to the portholes and the chimneys; then we packed the hole with anything that would burn easily.

"But we had to keep a ship looking like a man-of-war. We painted logs black and mounted them at gunports to make it appear that we were heavily gunned when, in fact, we were unarmed."

"What was the purpose of the troughs under the deck?"

"We poured oil in the troughs and lit it. The oil fires ran down the troughs, spreading the fire throughout the hole, even pouring out of the portholes to put the sides of the ship ablaze. The chimneys were stuffed with flammables and a little black powder."

When the sea battle began, the fireship would set a course for its victim. It would take many hits as it came at the opposing ship, but by the time the enemy realized the danger, that it was not engaging an ordinary warship, the fireboat was beside it. When it came alongside, topside grappling hooks would snag the other ship's rigging, locking them in a lethal embrace.

"We had to set the fires before our lines tangled with those of the other ship, and the timing had to be perfect," he said. "We had to abandon ship in a rowboat and were at the mercy of the enemy guns if we left too soon. We would be consumed by fire and explosions if we were too late."

Once the hooks had tangled the other ship's masts, a

powder charge in the chimneys was ignited. "That blasted fire out of the chimneys' mouths into our own sails and the other ship's rigging. The flaming sails meant the end of both ships. Only half a dozen of us manned the vessel; and as soon as the chimneys blew, we jumped into a longboat we had been towing."

Fireboat crews got double pay and bonuses. "But our casualty rates were 50 percent. Most often the crews consisted of men like me who were being punished."

Mateo stared out at the sea, remembering the past. "We Spaniards were the masters of the fireboats, using them against the Infidels in many battles, but we became victims of our own cunning when we fought the English."

A great armada of ships and troops had been assembled by the Spanish king to invade England and restore the Catholic religion to that blasphemous country, Mateo said. "We were the greatest power in the world then and now. We ruled the land and sea, and our empire embraced the world. The great fleet our king amassed for the invasion was the Armada Invencible, the largest and most powerful ever assembled. And it was defeated. But it was not English guns that caused our fleet to break formation and paved the way for a storm to overpower our ships. It was five miserable fireboats. When our fleet was anchored off Calais, the English sent five blazing ships into their midst. Our captains were so terrified of the fiery ships that many of them pulled anchor and fled without firing a shot."

We were a week at sea when Mateo shocked me with an attack.

I awoke to find him bending over me with his dagger in his hand. Before I could move, he slashed my face. I came out of bed with my arms flailing, blood flying from my face.

I grabbed my own dagger and crouched in a corner. "This is what it has come to, eh, compadre? All the treasure is better than half?"

Mateo sat on his own bed and wiped blood from his

dagger. "You will thank me when we arrive in Seville, and you no longer have a mine brand."

My hand went to the bleeding cut on my cheek.

"Sailors know that fresh salt air and seawater heals wounds with less infection than foul miasma of cities." He stretched out on his berth. "If you do not bleed to death by morning, you should be thinking of a story to tell the women in Seville about how your face got scarred."

My first surprise as we came upon Seville was that the great port was not on the sea but was about twenty leagues up the Rio Guadalquivir, pass the marshy plains of Las Marismas.

"Seville is the biggest city in Spain. Perhaps only Rome and Constantinople are equal in size to it in all Europe," Mateo said. "It is a city of riches. Through its gates poured the gold of the Incas and the silver of the Aztecs. Stored in the Archivo de Indias are the documents of every nature concerning the discovery and conquest of the New World, from the shipping manifesto of its discoverer, Cristóbal Colon, to letters from Cortes to the king and the few Aztec codices that had survived the wrath of the priests. Everything that is sent to the New World and sent back must pass through Seville. The Casa de Contratación, the House of Trade, controls all aspects of shipping, from what ships may sail, to what they may carry and how much they must pay. Even a Portuguese slave ship must get a license from them to ship slaves from the west coast of Africa to the New World."

Amigos, Seville was more than I could ever have imagined. The City of Mexico was an elegant gem set on a blue lake. Seville was the bulwark of empire. It was larger, grander, greater, not just in size but in stature. Its massive fortifications were built to withstand armies and the ravages of time—thick, high, defiant. When we disembarked and walked the crowded streets, I played the role of colonial simpleton, my mouth agape, my ears open to every sound. If Mateo had not been beside me, the rapacious street people would no doubt have stripped me of my money, clothes, and honor in a few blocks.

"That's the Torre del Oro," Mateo said, pointing to a ten-sided stone tower near the river, the Tower of Gold. It appeared strong enough to have flaunted the armies of even the Great Khan, a safe haven of the riches that poured in from the New World and Far East.

"You could ransom a king with its floor sweepings," Mateo said.

In the heart of the city was the Alcázar Palace, the fortress-castle of kings. It had stood for hundreds of years, built even before Tula was sacked by barbarians. I had thought the viceroy's palace in Mexico was an edifice for kings, but it was a peón's hovel compared to the Seville palace. The Alcázar did not even house the king.

"His palace in Madrid is of a much grander scale," Mateo said.

After sainted King Ferdinand III conquered Seville, he made the city his capital. But the Moorish influence in architecture gave the city a taste of the alien to me, a cast I found provocative. Until I saw that city's Moorish heritage, the Infidels had been little more than a name to me. I saw now that they were a race imbued with grace and beauty, its architects designing buildings with the grace used by poets and artists.

Near the palace was the Cathedral of Santa Maria, exotic and venerable, with Gothic and Moorish influences. Said to be the second church of Christendom, only San Pedro's in Rome was more colossal. San Sophia in Constantinople was not comparable, of course, now that it was in the hands of the Infidels and turned into a mosque. Like the cathedral in the City of Mexico, which rose from the site of an Aztec temple, Santa Maria was built on heathen ground, the space previously occupied by a mosque. The city itself was once the capital of the Moors. It was only fitting that someday a Christian church would stand atop the vanquished Moorish mosques. Gazing on Santa Maria, I could almost believe what so many Spaniards professed: that God favored Spain and therefore had made her the most powerful nation on earth.

The people were as different from the colonists of New Spain as the buildings were. The city vibrated with raw power, with *arrogance.* The arrogance was visible everywhere. In the carriages that charged through the city carrying men who decided the fate of nations. In the merchants who held a monopoly on half the world's trade. And even in the street trash. Dios mio! Such haughty swine! No whining, no pleading, instead *demands* for alms, as if begging was a royal grant. I shouldered them aside, as did Mateo. The lazy lice should work for their food!

The differences between Spain and New Spain were stark. New Spain colonists were ambitious, earnest, hardworking, God-fearing. They were people who treated their religion and government with homage and fear, their family life with respect and dedication. In Seville, I saw the opposite: a surprising amount of irreverence and freedom of spirit. Men sold libros deshonestos openly on the street—in full view of the Inquisition. And the profanity! *¡Ay de mí!* If I had spoken such words as a youth, the fray would not have washed out my mouth, he would have cut out my tongue!

"In small towns and villages," Mateo explained, "people are more under the sway and fear of the Church and the king, but in the large cities, like Seville, Cadiz, and even Madrid, they are more worldly. Half the men on the streets have fought in foreign wars. The finest ladies have to rub shoulders on the streets with sailors and soldiers who travel around the world. Inquisitors are ever more careful about whom they accuse on the peninsula. Unless they are certain the person is a Jew or a Moor, they tread carefully because they may get their own throats cut."

Cutting the throat of an inquisitor? I crossed myself at the spoken sacrilege without thinking. Eh, had I been educated on the streets of Seville!

"To milk a cow," Mateo said, "you must keep it penned up so no one else gets the milk. The king keeps tight control on the colonies because they are the cows that are milked. Not only iron control of the ships so that everything that goes in or out is ruthlessly regulated, but the viceroy's soldados, the Holy Office, the Santa Hermandad's constables, all are expressions of the king's power. All of those controls are also in Mother Spain; but after centuries of fighting the Moors, the people have little tolerance for petty tyrannies."

In the City of Mexico, thousands of indios scuffled along, dignified and polite, their heads bowed, their shoulders weighed down from the collapse of their culture and way of life. No such humility was evident in the City of Riches. Nor was the quiet charm of the colonial capital evident in the loud, brash, smelly streets and alleys of Seville.

Seville, I decided, was a strutting bull—rich and fat, but also crude, rude, and disgustingly indecent.

"Eh, Bastardo, if you think that the comedia audiences in Mexico City were boisterous and troublesome, wait until you experience them in Seville. Actors have been killed over the way a line is uttered."

"You promised we would not get involved in comedias," I said. "A visitor from New Spain may spot us."

"You are too cautious, compadre. And I did not promise. To stop your incessant whining, I *pretended* to agree with you."

"You told me that you had to stay clear of the comedias because you owed money and had slashed a creditor who insulted you."

Mateo patted the gold in his pocket. "I knew an alchemist who believed that gold could cure disease. He was right—but it is social diseases like debts and public offenses money cures. Bastardo, wait until you see the great playhouse of Seville. Those little corrals we toyed with—eh, you could put half of the City of Mexico under the roof of the Corral de El Coliseo. My favorite is the Doña Elvira, built by the count of Gelves. It is older than the Coliseo, and without as much roof, but an actor can be heard in it much better. But it is the play that will determine where we attend. Depending on what is playing, we will patronize de las Atarazanas, the Don Juan . . ."

I sighed. Arguing with him was futile. Plays were in the autor's blood. And my own inhibitions were weakening. I had spent years in hell, and now I shared his excitement. My blood was on fire just hearing about plays.

"Our attire must first fit our station as rich caballeros. Nothing but the finest silks and linens, the softest wool, for our doublets, pants, and capes. Boot leather smoother than a baby's bottom, hats with the rarest of plumage. And swords! Fine Toledo blades that draw blood with the ease of a clumsy barber. And jeweled daggers. One cannot kill another gentlemen with a woodsman's ax!"

¡Ay de mí! We possessed a king's ransom, but to a man whose views of money came from the grandiose fantasy of *Amadis de Gaul,* even the riches of Croesus were a pittance.

Our plan to live modestly and avoid attention was already in tatters. I would feel fortunate if Mateo did not storm Seville in a chariot like Caesar returning to Rome with his legions.

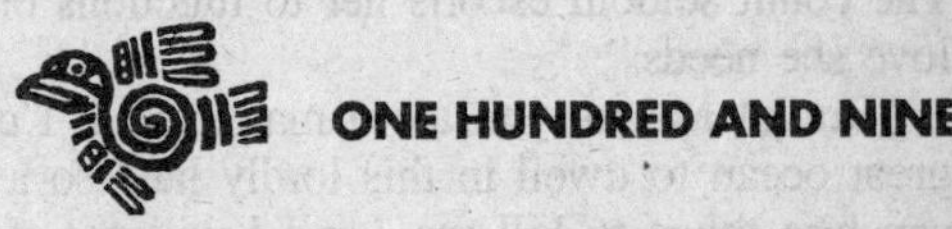

ONE HUNDRED AND NINE

DON CRISTO, MAY I present Doña Ana Franca de Henares."

"My lady." I greeted her with a low, sweeping bow.

Eh, amigos, did you think it would be long before Mateo and I enjoyed the charms and arms of feminine companionship?

Mateo had warned me about Doña Ana. Her ennobled title of doña was as genuine as my own beknighted donhood. The daughter of a butcher, an elderly nobleman had retained her as a serving wench at age fourteen. Most of her services were performed in his bedroom. He was so decrepit he used her primarily as a foot warmer, mostly employing the private place between her legs for his cold feet.

She ran away at the age of seventeen with an itinerant acting troupe, instantly assuming the role of the autor's mistress. She had talent though and soon commanded leading roles in Madrid, Seville, and Barcelona. With fame, power proliferated, and her liaisons turned legion.

I admit to Mateo's warning not to get romantically involved with her. Not because she was a fortune hunter; that was to be expected. Not because she was immoral; that was to be desired. Nor because she had had many lovers; that made her knowledgeable. But because of the danger.

"The Count of Lemos is her current lover," Mateo told me before he introduced me. "He is a bad lover and an even worse swordsman. He makes up for his lack of ability in bed by being generous with his money to his mistresses. He makes up for his dueling deficiencies by engaging thugs to kill or cripple all would-be challengers."

"Why are you telling me these things?"

"Because she is an old friend who needs a new friend. The count seldom escorts her to functions or provides the love she needs."

"Bravo! Mateo, you are a mastermind. I come across a great ocean to dwell in this lordly land so a jealous lover can hire thugs to kill me—and I will not even desire the death by having pillaged the man's woman. Is that what you have in mind?"

"No, Bastardo, actually, what I had in mind is that for once in your life you associate with a *real* woman, a woman who can teach you things about being a gentleman that are impossible for me to convey. When she finishes with you, the colony clod will be gone and a polished gentleman standing in his place. This is a woman who was made for love. Sadly, she is also intelligent, scheming, and greedy like a man, but in bed she would singe Ero's wings."

"Then why don't you keep her for yourself?"

"Because I consider my compadre's comfort and delight before my own."

I gave him my best horselaugh.

"Besides," he said, "I have another woman, one with a jealous streak as wide as the Rio Guadalquivir, who requites faithless lovers with a knife in their testiculos. The count knows Ana needs an escort for social functions but wants assurance that her charms will not be poached. She has described you to perfection, but I do not fit her august description." He grinned slyly. "She told the count that her escort prefers other *men*."

Ay, and I was chosen to play the sodomite. While I had no intention of playing this woman's fool, Mateo at last browbeat me into meeting her.

After one look in her eyes, I was ready to don motley and play a lunatic idiot.

Unlike so many famous actresses, there was none of the coquette in her. Those women flirted and teased their way into wallets and coffers. Ana Franca, on the other hand, was quiet and reserved, very much the lady. But of course she was that—with elegant silks, dazzling jewels, and demure eyes, fluttering behind an ivory-handled Chinese fan. Her lure was not beauty, though her looks were exquisite—skin softly white, lush chestnut hair piled high and cinched by pearls, an aquiline nose, while high, slanting cheekbones framed her extraordinary emerald eyes. Still it was not her beauty that drew me to her but the radiance of her being. She was muy grande mujer, a very great woman.

Not that I don't appreciate beauty, but a wise man soon learns that cold beauty means a cold bed. I have been eternally drawn to the inner essence, the warmth of the fire within, not the ephemeral look of skin arrestingly stretched on bone.

Ana's central allure was her eyes. Like the Sirens, the *Odyssey's* winged bird-women who lured sailors to their death by the sweetness of their song, Ana Franca's eyes doomed men to perdition. But while Odysseus was warned to deafen his ears against the Sirens' song, Mateo had left my ears and eyes wide-open.

I cannot say I fell in love with Ana Franca. My heart was forever pledged to another. But at the very least I fell hopelessly in lust with her. I could well understand why she would be a count's mistress. Despite her humble beginnings, she had nothing of the working class about her. At our first meeting, she set down the terms of our relationship.

"Mateo describes you as a colonial bumpkin, and your sole experience is with the crudity of New Spain. We see these unrefined oafs all the time. They come off a ship with their pockets full of gold and the belief that newfound wealth is a substitute for breeding. They are met with sardonic amusement and outright contempt."

"And how does one acquire the countenance of culture?"

"One is a gentleman when one *thinks* like a gentleman."

Shades of the Healer. Could she tell I was not a gentleman by my smell?

"You have the clothes of a gentleman. You are not particularly handsome, but the scar from your pirate battles bequeaths boldness to your features. But remove the clothes, and one knows you are not a gentleman."

The story I had concocted had been a romantic one—a duel for a lady's charms. But Mateo disliked the duel story because other men might view it as a challenge, in his eyes, a self-pronounced death sentence for one of my sword skills. A fight with French pirates had the right measure of dash, without threatening the manliness of others.

The face that bore the pirate's scar was a stranger to me. From the time I first started growing hair on my face, I had had a beard. But a beard was no longer a disguise. Most of my sins had been committed with facial hair. Nor did I need to conceal the mine slave brand because Mateo had cleverly—and painfully—disguised it. Now a colorfully scarred, clean-shaven stranger stared back at me in a mirror.

The fashion of the New World had been long hair, but men in Spain for the past several years had been wearing their hair short. The short hair made me even more of a stranger to myself. I felt confident I could stroll through the dungeon of the Holy Office in the City of Mexico without being recognized.

"Doña Ana, what cure is there for this coarseness of soul?" I asked her.

"For you, there is no cure. Look at your hands. They are rough and hardened, not at all the fine, soft hands of a true gentleman. I suspect your feet are harder than your hands, and your arms and chest. Common laborers, not gentlemen, have such unsightly muscles. Your soldierly past might explain some of that, but not an *army* of defects."

"What else am I doing wrong?"

"Everything! You lack the cold-blooded arrogance of one who has never struggled. You show no contempt toward the lower classes, whom God has denied the privileges of exalted birth. God prescribes a place for all of us. Quality people are born to rule. Common people are born to serve. Your most obvious defect is that you only *act* like a gentleman. One cannot *play* the role. You must *think* like a gentleman. If you have to act, then your roots will constantly intrude and people will see through the pretense."

"Tell this colonial bumpkin one mistake I've made," I demanded hotly. "Tell me what I've done to give you license to call me coarse and unrefined."

She sighed. "Cristo, where should I begin? A moment ago my maid brought you a cup of coffee."

I shrugged. "All right. Did I spill it down my chin? Stir it with my finger?"

"You thanked her."

"Never! I never spoke a word to her!"

"You thanked her with your eyes and a smile."

"What nonsense is this?"

"A person of quality would never show appreciation to a servant. No true gentleman would even acknowledge she *existed,* unless of course they were interested in exploiting her sexually. Then they would leer at her and perhaps comment on her feminine endowments."

Ayyo. When I thought about it, I knew she was correct.

"And other than my courtesy toward servants?"

"Your lack of hubris. Have you seen Mateo enter a room? He enters a fine salon as if it were a pigsty, and he was dirtying his boots in it. When you entered my salon, you looked on it admiringly."

"Ah, but Mateo is older and wiser than me and has had much more practice playing the gentleman."

"Mateo does not have to play the gentleman; he was born one."

"Mateo? The picaro? A gentleman?"

She put her Chinese fan to her face. Her eyes told me that she had said something that she had not intended. Doña Ana was not a woman you could coerce information from, so I let it pass though I suddenly realized I knew nothing about Mateo's background and family—not even where he was born.

But I now understood that she and Mateo went back a long ways.

"As a young girl, you ran off with the autor of an acting troupe. Do I call this man my friend?"

She smiled her answer.

"Doña, while you are giving me lessons in gentlemanship, what I can do for you?"

Her fan fluttered in front of her face again.

"The count's mouth boasts of his abilities as a lover better than his virile parts deliver."

She left her chair and sat on the small couch beside me. Her hand went between my legs. I wore fashionable tight silk hose rather than woolen pants. My virile part swelled as she caressed it.

"He will have you killed if he finds out you are my lover. Danger makes lovemaking so much more exciting, don't you think?"

Mateo had warned me of her charm—and the count's jealousy. But I admit that I am weak in rebuffing the wiles of a woman.

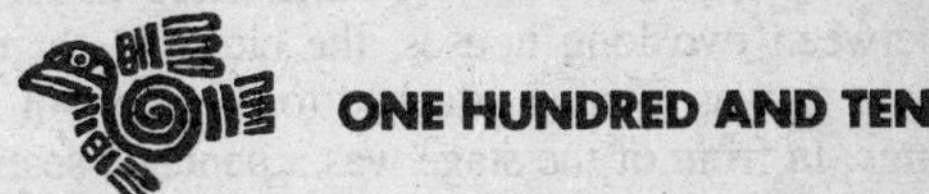

ONE HUNDRED AND TEN

SO IT CAME to be that a colonial oaf was made into a gentleman of Seville.

The main resentment I had about Ana's tutelage was playing the necessary role of the lover of men to appease her count. For that particular costume, after some argument we settled upon a dandified yellow silk shirt and a doublet of what Ana termed "provocative pink."

"The count's younger brother is a back-door man," Ana told me. "This is how he dresses. If you dress this way, it will convince the count."

¡Ayya ouiya! What strange paths life takes.

In return for my commitment to play the dandy, I was invited into Ana's *front door* many times—and to join the profane life of Seville's theater community. At a party following one play's opening, I understood why the Church denied actors burial in consecrated ground. Furthermore, such parties underscored the differences between Spain and New Spain. Aftertheater festivities, such as the one I was attending, would have been unimaginable in the City of Mexico. At that particular party in Seville, people dressed like characters from Don Quixote and Amadis de Gaul, and behaved like Roman satyrs at an orgy.

I wanted to participate in the life of the theater, and Ana was happy to let me escort her in the milieu. Even though she no longer trod the boards, she socialized with actors and had strong opinions about their performances. She was often as caustic as the mosqueteros.

The first play she took me to was an eye-opener. Mateo had taught me that the best position for a corral de comedias was in a vacant area enclosed by two or three houses, which approximated the corral's layout. In Seville, theaters had the same posture, but were much more elaborate. Positioned between two long houses, the elevated stage was covered by a canvas awning attached to the roofs of the two buildings. In front of the stage was a benched seating area called the banco. Behind the banco was the patio, more commonly called the pit. In this area the common men, such as the butchers and bakers, stood. In the pit, of course, were the dreaded mosqueteros, whose whistles, hoots, thrown garbage, and drawn swords could bring any play to an abrupt end.

Below the vulgar pit were raised seats called the grada. Covered by a wood roof supported by pillars, people of higher quality sat in the terraced seating. Above the amphitheater-type seating of the gradas were aposentos, box seating, where the very rich sat.

"The aposentos were originally windowed rooms in the adjoining house, but the theater owner built these to ensure he collected admissions," Ana told me. To the side of the terraced seating was the infamous cazuela. "The stewing pan," Ana said. "This is where the lower-class women watch the play. Mateo says you have attended some plays and have experienced the vulgar antics of the mosqueteros. But you have not experienced true vulgarity until you hear the women of the stewing pan express their disappointment in a play or an actor."

We went to the play in Ana's carriage. We took along her friend, Felicia, a woman a few years younger than Ana and almost as sensual. To my surprise, the two women went to the play wearing masks—and dressed as men. Not as caballeros, but commoners.

"Unless it's a religious play, decent women wear masks to performances," Ana said.

"To keep people from recognizing them?"

"No, they want to be recognized by their friends. It's for modesty sake. A lady of quality cannot be seen at a play. Except by other ladies of quality."

"Oh." I did not understand, but it was just another mystery about women of which I was ignorant. "And the men's clothing. Do the women of Seville always dress as men when they attend plays?"

"Of course not. The purpose of the disguise is to permit us to publicly comment on the play," Felicity said.

Again, I did not understand how men's disguises gave Ana and Felicity the right to critique a play, but when they stepped from the carriage, carrying bags of tomatoes, I began to suspect there was more to these guises than met the eye. Particularly, when they told me to buy tickets for the patio.

"We are to stand in the pit?" I asked. "With the mosqueteros."

Ay, the gleam in their eyes told me that I was in the hands of Mateo-style maniacs. Except I was soon to discover that his dementia had nothing on these two women-in-men's clothing.

The play was regarded as second only to the tale of Don Quixote as a great masterpiece of Spanish literature. But it was also controversial.

"The Holy Office vacillates about La Celestina, and it is on and off the Inquisition's banned list," Ana said. "And when they do ban it, their edicts are ignored, troubling them to no end. The familiars would not dare take the autor or his cast into custody. The people would not permit it. *Don Quixote* incited us to laughter by mocking the hidalgos and the insane chivalry that dominated their writing, but La Celestina touched our souls. The people of Spain are made of blood and fire. They are greedy and generous, foolish and brilliant. They have God in their hearts and the devil in their thoughts. The devious slut, Celestina, and the two lovers represent the best and the worst of us."

Referred to generally as La Celestina, the *Comedia de Calisto y Melibea* was not a new play. It was first presented eons ago, in 1499, seven years after the discovery of the New World and over twenty years before the fall of the

Aztec Empire. The tragedy of the two lovers was set forth in an astounding twenty-one acts.

Celestina was a bawd who served as a go-between for two young lovers, Calisto and Melibea. Calisto was from the minor nobility; Melibea was of higher status and wealth, making them unsuitable marriage partners. But they came together as lovers and defied convention, not just by speaking words of love, but by physically consummating their passions.

The true star of the comedia was Celestina, who was both evil and cunning. Her coarse humor and ironic commentary fascinated audiences everywhere. But her cunning and greed ultimately betrayed her. Paid for her role as go-between, she refused to share her gold with her conspirators. After killing her, they were themselves murdered by an angry mob.

But nothing would free the lovers of their own fate. Their uncontrolled passions were the instrument of their doom. Calisto was killed in a fall from a ladder to Melibea's window. Melibea—her lover dead, her honor ruined by her virginity's loss—throws herself from a tower window.

"Their attempt to defy destiny was doomed," Ana explained in the carriage ride to the theater. "Fate and custom foreordained their end—foreordains all our ends, demonstrating the futility of opposing the gods."

"Who was the author?" I asked.

"A converso Jew, a lawyer. He first published anonymously because of fear of the Inquisition."

As I watched it, I could well understand the author's fear. The language of the play was often coarse. Celestina made bawdy comments about a young man's "scorpion tail" pene, whose sting produces nine months of swelling. A character accuses Celestina and a girl who lives with her of having "calluses" on their stomach from all of the men who visit. There are suggestions of female bestiality, though not in regard to the lovely and innocent Melibea.

Those pompous inquisitors from New Spain would throw fits were they to watch twenty-one acts of La Celestina, in which lust, vice, superstition, and evil were main characters. As a sort of heavenly justice, I imagined myself tying them up, pinning their eyes open, and forcing them to watch the play repeatedly.

The tomatoes? You wonder what they did with the tomatoes? When we entered the pit it was filled with men who chattered endlessly. All of them appeared not only to have seen the play performed before, but some appeared to have come to this particular presentation on more than one occasion. These street merchants and common laborers discussed the actors, the way they delivered their lines, their mistakes and triumphs, as if they themselves were the play's autor. The play was conducted in the middle of the afternoon in order to utilize sunlight. Why were these louts going to a play in the middle of the day instead of working?

But I, too, soon got used to expecting good performances.

"It's what we paid our money for," Ana said. "When I first acted, my pay was the coins tossed on the stage during my performance. I went hungry until I learned how to play a character. *¡Bolo!"* she screamed at the actress playing Areusa and threw a tomato when she did not deliver a line to her liking.

Ana and Felicity were not the only ones who knew the exact lines from the play. Some of the favorite lines, usually those which were deshonesto, were spoken by the mosqueteros at the same time the actor uttered them.

I was quickly enthralled. Soon I was throwing tomatoes myself. . . .

After the performance we rode back to Ana's large home. On the way I noticed Felicity looking at me more and more with a small smile and seductively bold eyes.

When we arrived back at her house, Ana instructed us, "Come, we will use my pool to refresh ourselves."

Her "pool" was an ancient Roman bath. The city had many Roman ruins, and Ana's was not the only house built upon a bath or other edifice.

I had taken many baths in the warm pool with Ana. I

was startled when she suggested that the three of us enjoy a bath together.

"Felicity's lover has been in Madrid for a month," Ana said.

He was none other than the younger brother of the count who was Ana's own benefactor and lover, the brother who Ana said preferred men.

"But he has to keep up an appearance of propriety," she said. "Hence Felicity, who is a fine actor."

I did not understand what Ana meant by Felicity being a fine actor.

Ana was already in the water when I slipped into the pool, putting my towel aside as the warm water engulfed me. Felicity sat on the edge with her towel wrapped around her as Ana and I came together.

Ana leaned out of my arms and pulled aside Felicity's towel. Before she slipped into the water, I saw and understood what Ana meant when she called Felicity a good actor.

Eh, if Catalina the Bandito could fool kings and popes, why couldn't Felicity—or whatever *his* name was—dupe the dons of Seville?

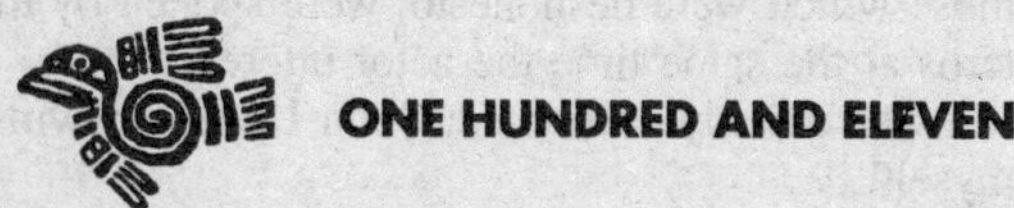

ONE HUNDRED AND ELEVEN

ANA'S ENTHUSIASM FOR plays, parties, and lovemaking was inexhaustible, and she kept me busy with all three. My sole regret was that I saw so little of Mateo. At first his name was on everyone's tongue. Stories of a caballero who had returned from the New World with his pockets full of gold made him an instant legend. The stories they told about him! I heard that Mateo had found the lost Island of California, where an Amazon queen sits upon a throne of gold with her feet on the skulls of men who had the misfortune to shipwreck on her shores. But the most notorious tale was that he had found the Seven Golden Cities of Cíbola while exploring the deserts north of the Rio Bravo.

Ana expressed curiosity about the fabled cities, and I told her the story.

After the conquistadors had looted the Aztecs and the Incas, they looked further for more golden conquests. In 1528, a party of Spaniards landed on the peninsula that earlier Juan Ponce de León had named Florida, which meant "flowery," when he searched for the Fountain of Youth. Alvar Núñez Cabeza de Vaca was one of them. This man with a strange name—Cabeza de Vaca, "Head of Cow"—and an africano slave named Estéban, were among sixty men shipwrecked on the coast of Florida. Núñez, Estéban, and two others traveled eight years across the continent, over a thousand leagues, to an area far north of the settled areas of New Spain. There, in a desert land beyond the Rio Bravo, near where the present settlement called Santa Fe is located, they claimed to have seen in the distance seven golden cities. Expeditions to find the cities, including one led by Francisco Vázquez de Coronado, failed to find anything but poor indio pueblos.

Eh, but Mateo found the seven cities, had he not?

I would have expected Mateo to become deeply involved in the Seville theater scene, but although I did encounter him occasionally in the world of plays, he had become engrossed in another one of his other favorite enterprises.

"Mateo is involved with a duchess," Ana said, "a cousin to the king."

"Is she married?"

"Of course. Her husband is the duke, who is in the Low Countries inspecting the army. The duchess is very lonely and demanding of Mateo's time, and energy. Mateo believes that for the first time in his life he is truly in love."

"Is there anyone in Spain who is married and does not have a lover?"

Ana thought for a moment. "Only the poor."

On several occasions, Ana had made cryptic references to Mateo's dark past. During a discussion about a Miguel Cervantes play, Ana cast a little light on Mateo. Ultimately, I was able to draw secrets from her that stunned me and changed my whole perspective about Mateo.

I knew, of course, a small part of his past, that he was bitter toward Cervantes. However, his hatred for Cervantes related to something deeper. Ana explained Mateo's anger while we rode in her carriage to the play.

"When Mateo knew Cervantes, he of course was very young and Cervantes quite old. You are familiar with the background of the author of *Don Quixote?*"

Ana, who seemed to know everything about the literature of Spain since Roman times, enlightened me. Cervantes had been born into reasonably humble circumstances. The fourth of seven children, his father was a barber-surgeon who set bones, performed bloodlettings, and attended lesser medical needs. The young Cervantes did not attend university but acquired an education through priests.

After hearing of Cervantes's military service, I was surprised that Mateo would not have more respect for the man. Both had served in Italy and had fought the Turks. Cervantes had been a soldier in a Spanish infantry regiment stationed in Naples, a possession of the Spanish crown, and served in the fleet under Don Juan of Austria, when it routed the Turkish fleet at the Battle of Lepanto near Corinth. Though stricken with fever, Cervantes refused to stay below. On deck, he received two gunshot wounds in the chest and a third rendered his left hand useless for the rest of his life. He later fought at Tunis and La Goleta. Sent back to Spain, recommended for a captaincy, Barbary corsairs captured the ship carrying Cervantes and his brother, Rodrigo. They were sold into slavery in Algiers, the Muslim center for Christian slave trafficking. Unfortunately for Cervantes, Letters of Recommendation magnified his importance in the eyes of his captors. But while the letters raised his ransom price, they also protected him from punishment by death, mutilation, or torture when his four daring bids to escape were frustrated.

Five years of captivity under the Bey of Algiers, four heroic escape attempts, his resounding success in battle, all brought him nothing. He arrived home to find that Prince Don Juan de Austria was both dead and out of favor with the king. The prince's recommendations for promotion were worth nothing.

Cervantes found humdrum employment. An affair with a married woman produced a daughter out of wedlock, whom he raised himself. He married a farmer's daughter nearly two decades younger than him. The girl had a small piece of property in La Mancha. While visiting La Mancha, he conceived his first published work of fiction, *La Galatea,* in the fashionable genre of pastoral romance. It would be another twenty years, at the age of fifty-eight years, before his masterpiece, *El ingenioso hidalgo Don Quixote de la Mancha,* was published. In those twenty years he wrote poetry, plays, and worked as a tax collector—and was once imprisoned for discrepancies in his tax-collection account ledgers.

"One of the plays he wrote was La Numantia," Ana said, and took me to see a performance. "Numantia was a Spanish town that withstood a terrible seize by the Romans. For ten long, bloody years, three thousand Spaniards defended the town with desperate courage against a Roman force of over one hundred thousand. Cervantes chose to set his play in the final days of the siege, at a time when the dead and starving lay in heaps in the city. Infants sucked blood from their mothers' breasts rather than milk. Two Numantian youths fight their way into the Roman camp to steal bread. One is killed, but the other, fatally wounded, comes back with blood-stained bread before dying.

"Think of the image," she said, "blood-stained bread and babies drinking the blood of their mothers."

For this play Ana dressed as a woman of quality, wearing a mask of course, and we sat in a box. The mosqueteros were even quiet during the play. "It is a story of great patriotism, of the courage of the Spanish people," she said. "One does not throw refuse at our people. When I first saw this play, I was just a girl. A drunk yelled an insult at the way one of the boys who had given their lives for bread had acted his death scene. The men in the pit almost tore him to pieces."

Watching the play, I barely breathed during that scene for fear of antagonizing those around me.

No single hero dominated the four-act tragedy. The people, the city, and Spain herself were the heroes. Characters included Spanish ladies, Roman soldiers, even the Rio Douro.

I was impressed by Cervantes's mastery in blending dark pagan superstitions with the Spanish people's heroism in resisting the Roman invaders. In one scene the earth opened and a demon appeared and scurried away with a sacrificial lamb. Marquinio the Sorcerer, a black lance in one hand, a book of magic in another, summoned a dead youth from the Place of the Dead. The lad speaks to the people of their duty and their fate. They must destroy their city, denying Rome both victory and spoils. Neither gold nor gems nor women must fall to the invaders.

Ana pointed out an interesting little man in the audience. "Juan Ruiz de Alarcón, one of your fellow colonists. He came here from New Spain to study law and theology and ended up writing plays. One of his plays, *The Truth Suspected,* will open next week."

Ruiz was a bowlegged hunchback with a flame-red beard. He had the blazing stare of a religious fanatic, the body of a dwarf, and the curled upper lip of a starving wolf.

I said as much to Ana.

"His hunger is for fame and glory, but his body precludes both the battlefield and the dueling field. So he puts all of his energy into his quill and garrancha."

"His what?"

"He believes he's a great lady's man."

"Santa Maria." I crossed myself. "Poor devil."

"Poor women! They say he is hung like a bull."

After the play, Ana and I relaxed in her Roman bath. I rubbed her feet while she smoked hashish. She had offered me the Moorish dream smoke early in our relationship, but it gave me a headache. Perhaps my Aztec blood was requited only by the dream-making of flower weavers.

"Tell me about Cervantes and Mateo," I pleaded.

"Mateo was a young autor, the manager of a travel troupe, and—"

I interrupted. "The troupe of actors you ran away and joined?"

"Exactly. As you already guessed, he was my first lover. Not the first man to enjoy my body, but the first I wanted to make love to me."

I smiled at the thought of the two hellions in a theater and in bed. Dios mio, it would have been a volcano colliding with a tidal wave.

"So why does he hate Cervantes?"

"Cervantes was a writer of plays, but he had not gained the fame that was to come after the publication of Don Quixote. Mateo was the manager of a troupe of actors and desired to have his own plays performed. He showed some of his plays to Cervantes."

"The tale of a knight-errant," I asked, "an old hidalgo who jostled with windmills?"

"I never knew exactly what Mateo's comedia plots were about. He said Cervantes spoke well of them, and for a while they were friends."

"Close enough that Mateo might have poured out his heart to Cervantes? Told him of all the adventures and misadventures he had known in the pursuit of wine, women, and glory?"

"Yes, Mateo's told me that too, that the old man 'borrowed' our friend's adventures; and I have no reason to doubt him. Mateo's life would fill many books. But it is also true that while Mateo's plays about knights and dragons and beautiful princesses were popular with audiences, they were everything that Cervantes loathed. In *Don Quixote* he parodied Mateo and his writing mercilessly."

"So Cervantes 'borrowed' his life and ideas and presented them with mockery."

"Mateo hasn't forgiven him."

"For certain," I said, "Mateo goes muy loco whenever the name of Miguel Cervantes is mentioned."

"If he knew that you and I went to see La Numantia . . ."

"Sí, he would remove an ear from each of us. And, Ana, you said to me once that Mateo was not a picaro, but a gentleman. Of course, he told me his whole life story during our wanders and battles with pirates, but I wonder if he told you the same tale—"

"He told me nothing. I learned it from one who knew Mateo when he was a marqués."

A marqués! A nobleman above a count and below a duke. A great personage. Even those who bore an empty title because their estates had been lost or confiscated could sell themselves in marriage to a very rich widow or merchant's daughter.

"You know the tale from Mateo's own lips," she said. "He was an orphan at five, his father dying in battle and his mother taken by the plague. His father, the marqués, was a general for the king, one with a fine reputation. After the death of his parents, Mateo was raised in the house of his cousin, a count. At a very early age, he was pledged in marriage to the count's daughter, who was a year or two older than him. When Mateo was seventeen, a servant awoke him and informed him that a man had been seen sneaking into the house. Grabbing his sword, he made a search for the intruder. The intruder turned out to be his closest friend. He found the man in the arms of his betrothed.

"Por Dios, can you imagine the scene, Cristo? The hot-blooded, idealistic young nobleman, raised in the tradition of hombria, that a man must be honorable and his honor is inexorably linked to the honorable behavior of the women in his life. He finds his wife-to-be making love with his good friend? Can you guess what happened next?"

I knew Mateo too well to have to guess. "He killed the man, of course."

"Cristo, had he simply killed the man, he would be a marqués today instead of a picaro. He killed not just the friend but his betrothed. She got in the way of the fighting men and was slain. Ay, men and women throughout the land praised his act of honor, but it was the old count's only child. To save his own family's honor, he saw to it that Mateo became a hunted man."

I was quiet for a long time after listening to Ana. Closing my eyes, I imagined what it must have been like for Mateo—and the two lovers. The shock of discovery. Fear as the wronged man bloodies his sword. The hapless woman on the floor.

The thoughts depressed me, and I was relieved when Ana asked me to move my massaging farther up her body.

ONE HUNDRED AND TWELVE

SEVILLE WAS ENLIGHTENING for me. I even learned how to see through a servant without seeing the person. But my heart tugged more and more toward New Spain. I had given up the notion that Eléna would ever be mine. Like Calisto and Melibea, we could not resist fate and custom. She would be married to Luis, bear his babies, but would never achieve her dream of being fully realized as a poet and writer of plays. Grasped in Luis's tight fist, she would slowly wither into a dried-up old woman whose dreams had turned to dust.

Hopefully, I would be able to make her a widow.

Some days I would go down to the docks and watch the ships come and go. Their destinations were to different places in the Spanish Empire, scattered about the four corners of the world, but in my own mind each was sailing for Veracruz.

The matter hung so heavily on me that Ana complained I was no fun, telling me not to come around until I learned how to laugh again. I suspected that the Italian count, who was courting her, had more to do with her comments than my love-struck moodiness.

My desire to return home came to a head when a familiar name became the talk of Seville: Catalina de Erauso, the woman-man who'd escaped from a convent and become a soldier for the king.

Listening to the tales of her in cantinas and the theaters, I separated in my own mind some of the fact from fiction. While the stories told of her incredible adventures as an army lieutenant and her many duels and escapades, they left out the fact that she had led a bandit gang that robbed the king's silver, and that she wore men's clothes to seduce women.

She passed through Seville to appear before the king in Madrid. He awarded her a pension and paraded her before the court as a heroine of the Spanish Empire. She was returning here to set sail for Italy, where she would be received by the pope. I sent a note to her at her inn, asking if she had spent all the silver she'd stolen in Zacatecas.

She would not know who sent the note until she faced me. Even if she recognized me, I was not worried she would report me to the king's officers as an escaped mine slave. While she would stick a knife in my back if she had the opportunity, she would not want me questioned about my activities in New Spain for fear of exposure of her own criminal acts.

My message was returned with word that she would meet me at her inn. I was to accommodate her by having a carriage at our disposal, at my expense, of course. Had this woman-man forgotten that she had once tried to murder me?

* * *

Catalina came out of the inn dressed in a nun's habit, but I was having none of it. For one thing I'd never known a nun with crisscrossing knife scars creasing her face, one with a nose reddened from decades of drink, broken and rebroken so many times it looked like a badly busted knuckle. The nuns I'd known typically had their front teeth. A nun's eyes, fixed on Eternity, were serenely beatific. This nun had the stare of a sheep-killing dog.

If you're a Bride of Christ, I muttered to myself, *I'm the pope.*

She did not recognize me when I presented myself to her in front of the inn. It was too many years, too many *lives* ago for her to identify me as the mestizo boy who'd robbed a temple for her. And she had gotten only a brief glance at me when I saw her through the window. In my mind there was no risk in confronting her about Luis and much to gain.

"I need some information about Luis de la Cerda. My brother spied on you when you met with him last in New Spain. You spotted my brother watching you through a window at an inn in the silver country."

I saw the bulge of a long dagger under her habit. She looked at me with a blank face, but her eyes perceptibly narrowed. No doubt her mind buzzed with thoughts of cutting my throat.

"The man who saw me through that window was arrested by the Inquisition."

"Arrested and sent to the mines, where he died. He told me about you and Luis before he died."

"But his brother seems to have prospered."

"God protects His own," I said, modestly, "and rewards them." I pulled out a pouch bulging with gold ducats. "I want you to tell me about the silver robberies. I want to know how you came to get involved with Luis and the name of everyone else you were involved with."

"Why should I tell you anything? For a little gold? I would get it as a reward if I turned you into the Holy Office."

"You would get more than that for a reward. I wonder

how the pope would receive you if he knew you lusted for the flesh of women?"

Her narrowing eyes now widened in surprise. She still had not identified me as the mestizo boy who robbed temples. I did not want her to make that connection, but I needed to frighten her.

"And the king? Would he give me a pension or a hangman's noose if he was told you robbed not only his silver but ancient tombs?"

Her face would not maintain the stoic countenance. Her lips twisted into a feral sneer. "A man whose tongue has been cut out tells no tales."

I chuckled. "Sister, such impure thoughts must not come from your holy lips." I turned around and gestured at two men in a cart following our carriage. "I see that you hired two felons to murder me. Do you see the four men in the king's uniform on horseback behind them?"

I waved my hand back at the horsemen. They rode forward and stopped the cart. They were dragging the two men off of the cart when I turned back to her. Her right hand was hidden in the folds of her habit.

I threw her the pouch of gold. "Put away your dagger. The brother to that pouch will be yours if you give me the information I request."

Her mind worked like a slow-witted dog with sharp teeth. Her first instinct was to rip with the teeth. Only after that passed, did her mind evaluate the situation.

"Why do you want this information?"

"Revenge on those who wronged my brother."

A blood feud was a simple, honorable circumstance that any Spaniard would understand.

She smiled at me. During the voyage from the New World the seamen had landed a denizen of the sea whose smile was a sharp-toothed grin. Catalina, even when pretending to be friendly, had that same razor-fanged smirk.

"Perhaps the good Lord will help me remember those days when I helped convey the king's silver, but for now I am in great need of something."

She instructed the driver to take us to one of the twisting alleys left over from the days when Seville was a Moorish city.

"Why are we going there?" I asked.

"An acquaintance has fallen in love with a very lonely widow. But the widow needs some encouragement to consummate the relationship."

I did not need the ashes of an owl to divine that Catalina herself was the person lusting after the lonely widow.

"What kind of encouragement do you seek?"

"A love potion."

Shades of Snake Flower.

The narrow streets, where the love witch's shop was located, could not accommodate our carriage, so we continued our travel on foot. The driver did a double take when he saw Catalina. A nun had entered the carriage; a short, husky caballero left it. I told the driver to wait for us. We left her nun's habit on the seat.

The love witch was a dark, elderly woman, seething with shadowy mysteries and esoteric secrets. In her little shop, reeking of incense and awash in alchemist's jars full of unnamed things, she might have seemed intimidating, at least by Seville's standards, but compared to Aztec love witches, who gleefully cut off pieces of penes, she was a babe in arms.

From theater talk, I knew that love magic was the rage in Spain and practiced openly without interference from the Inquisition.

Catalina, who identified herself as Don Pepito, explained the problem with the lonely widow. Gold quickly exchanged hands, one of the coins from the pouch I had given "Don Pepito," and the love witch immediately recommended ways to spellbind the widow.

"You may have to try several different spells," she said, "because people are affected differently. The most successful for widows is the enchanted lamp oil wick."

She explained that the man would "gather" some of his

semen. I assumed after stimulating himself. I hid a grin behind my hand. Catalina would not like this remedy.

A lamp wick was soaked in the semen and burned in the widow's presence. "She is driven to instant uncontrollable desire when she breathes in your male essence, while you are invoking the sacred—"

"I don't like that one. Give me another incantation."

The love witch held out her hand for another gold coin.

"When you are in the widow's presence, without her seeing what you are doing, you stick your hand in your pants and pull on your pubic hair. You recite, 'Come to me, hot as an oven, wet as a . . .' "

We left the love witch several gold coins short but Catalina armed with incantations.

Catalina told me of her involvement in the silver robberies.

"I was arrested for a minor offense and sentenced to hang," she said.

I did not ask what sort of "minor" offense would result in a death sentence.

"Instead of dancing on the gallows, I was sold by the constable to a man who, rather than putting me to honest labor, offered me criminal employment."

"Who was the man?"

She did not know.

"Describe him."

She did and I was certain that it was not Ramon de Alva. I didn't mention his name. If she betrayed me, I did not want everyone I sought vengeance upon to be aware of my mission.

"The crime they forced me to commit was robbery of the silver trains. A messenger from the mint would bring me the schedule for shipments, and I would lie in wait with my comrades."

"Who else did you come into contact with?"

"The man your brother saw me with at the cantina. His name is Luis. That is all I know about him."

"You have not earned your second pouch of gold. I need more information."

"Do you wish me to lie?"

"My desire is that you dig into your memory and tell me more about the man named Luis. I want to know if you ever saw him in the company of the man who paid the constable for your release."

She thought for a moment. "No, I never saw them together." She stopped and faced me. "My memory is coming back. If you give me that second pouch of gold, I will tell you the name of the person who bought my freedom."

I gave her the pouch.

"Miguel de Soto."

Eh, the man who bought and sold workers for the tunnel project, Ramon de Alva's brother-in-law.

Catalina hurried away from me, perhaps to pull her pubic hair for the widow, but I did not bother calling after her. I had made a connection between Luis, Alva, the silver robberies, and the tunnel project. It was not evidence I could go to the authorities with. With my sins, real and imagined, I could not have gone to them if God had been my witness.

My mind flashed to little Juana naked on a rack being examined by devils in priest's robes, and the courageous don being marched toward his fiery death.

It was time to return to New Spain.

Mateo was out of the city. I knew that he was elated about being back in Spain, among his own. I would not disturb him, but leave word with Ana. I would miss my compadre, but in the great circle of life, perhaps we would meet again.

I had heard that one of the lobo ships that ply the Caribbean was sailing soon for Cuba. From there I could get passage to Veracruz.

"You have not earned your second pouch of gold. I need more information."

"Do you wish me to lie?"

"My desire is that you dig into your memory and tell me more about the man named Luis. I want to know if you ever saw him in the company of the man who paid the constable for your release."

She thought for a moment. "No, I never saw them together." She stopped and faced me. "My memory is coming back. If you give me that second pouch of gold, I will tell you the name of the person who bought my freedom."

I gave her the pouch.

"Miguel de Soto."

Eh, the man who bought and sold workers for the tunnel project. Ramon de Alva's brother-in-law.

Catalina turned away from me, perhaps to pull her [illegible] hair for the widow, but I did not bother calling after her. I had made a connection between Luis, Alva, the silver robbery, and the tunnel project. It was not evidence I could go to the authorities with. With my sins, real and imagined, I could not have gone to them if God had been my witness.

My mind flashed to little Juana, naked on a rack, being [illegible] by devils in priest's robes, and the courageous old man marched toward his fiery death.

It was time to return to New Spain.

Mateo was out of the city. I knew that he was elated about being back in Spain, among his own. I would not [illegible] that I leave word with Ana [illegible] this [illegible] in the great circle of life perhaps we would meet again.

I had heard that one of the [illegible] ships that [illegible] was sailing soon for Cuba. From there I could get passage to Veracruz.

PART SIX

. . . he wanted nothing but a lady, on whom he might bestow the empire of his heart . . .

—*Miguel Cervantes,* **Don Quixote**

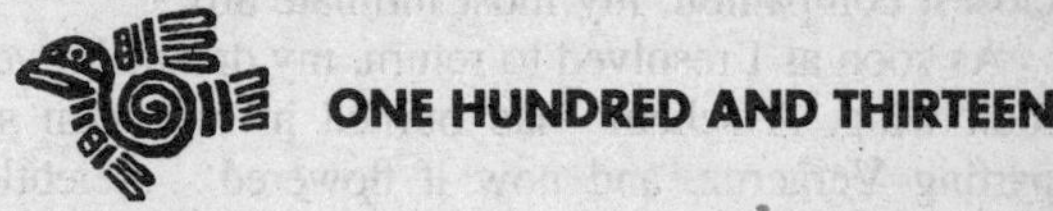

ONE HUNDRED AND THIRTEEN

THE VOYAGE FROM Seville to Veracruz took three weeks aboard a dispatch boat. Sent ahead of the treasure fleet, the boat was to notify New Spain that the fleet had set sail.

Two years had passed since I watched Veracruz fade from view and drop beneath the horizon line. Now the snow-capped volcanic cone of Citlaltépetl, the highest mountain in New Spain, appeared apparitionlike above that same horizon's rim, a white solitary finger, beckoning me to God only knew what.

New Spain had been a hard master, killing almost everything I'd cared about. The only woman I would love—a creature of radiant grace and poetic sensibility—was sentenced to a marital servitude as thoroughly abominable, for someone of her sensitivity, as my own years in the colony's dungeons and mines.

Still, New Spain was my home. Staring at that white, beckoning finger of volcano, my heart begrudgingly softened. Seville was a proud and grand city, one of the cornerstones of a great European empire, but my heart and soul were bound to the New World with hoops of steel. That hard, benighted land had brought my Aztec ancestors sustenance, had made me who I was and what I might become. And despite its whips and racks and dungeons and mines, it had taught me courage, loyalty, friendship, honor, even learning. Against all odds, I had prospered. I was returning home a rich and cultured gentleman.

Yes, I was returning home.

The pleasure of my return, however, was tempered by my debt of retribution. I did not want eye for an eye but a *head* for an eye—and the revenge I sought for the killers of Fray Antonio, Don Julio, and his family never left my side, not once, not for a heartbeat. Bloody revenge was my closest companion, my most intimate ally.

As soon as I resolved to return, my dreams of vengeance took wing. A scheme had burned in my brain since departing Veracruz, and now it flowered . . . relentlessly . . . incessantly . . . like the fatal nightshade. Like the Healer's snake trap and Don Julio's blood rite, I saw a way to bring these murderers to terms—and destroy them root and branch.

As the dispatch vessel dropped anchor in the channel between the island fortress of San Juan de Ulúa and the city, my twenty-fifth birthday came around. I spent the morning of that birthday interviewed by a customs officer and an inquisitor from the Holy Office. I had been careful to bring nothing with me that would offend anyone. The only book in my baggage was a history of the life of San Francis, a genuine history, not the type I once printed with a saintly title and a salacious text.

Before leaving Seville I had chosen a name and background for myself but abandoned both at sea. A better opportunity arose in the guise of a young man close to my own age. The third son of an impoverished Spanish nobleman, he had fled Spain to avoid the priesthood. He jumped ship when, after being blown off course, we briefly dropped anchor off an idyllic isle. His plan for life was to spend his days on the island, basking in the sun in the arms of native girls. Don Carlos, a name I found suitable, was an easygoing rascal who had been talkative about his family and history during our weeks together. I soon knew the name of his father and mother, brothers and sister, family history, and status in the community. On the pretense of planning to purchase a New World house that would evoke a fine Spanish style, I had him draw me a floor plan of his family home and coat of arms.

Well-dressed, respectable, well-mannered, with no contraband but with the unmistakable arrogance of an hidalgo,

I quickly passed muster. I granted each official the modest gratuity that only the truly honest render.

A ship's tender carried me to the jetty. I saw that the merchants were already piling their goods on the dock. The silver treasure was already in the city, stored in a locked room in the alcalde's palace—or would be here soon. The treasure fleet was not due for a week, but ships had been spotted from the island fortress in the bay with a spyglass. God had blessed it with favorable winds. Soon the fleet would arrive, unload, and then commence reloading.

For my stay in Veracruz, I chose the inn at the main plaza, the very one that I had once fought for the right to beg in front of. None of the harbor léperos who pleaded with me for alms were familiar to me. That was not a surprise—the life span of a lépero is often brief. I had left Veracruz as a boy of fifteen, and now I was a man almost twice that age. Léperos are frequently swept away by life in the gutter, enslavement in the mines and cane fields, as well as the waves of vómito fever and the other pestes that plague the city.

I tossed the beggars a few coppers. It would have amused me to reward them with some silver, but such benevolence would have drawn both suspicion and thieves. Not that I feared recognition. I had left Veracruz as a boy. During my subsequent years in Mexico, I favored a heavy beard and long hair. Clean-shaven, facially scarred, my hair not only short but streaked prematurely gray, I was not the same person as Cristo the Bastardo. I *was* Don Carlos, a hidalgo, the son-of-somebody, seeking his fortune in the New World, perhaps by marriage to the daughter of a rich merchant who was willing to give a fat dowry to add the son-of-somebody to the family tree.

But beyond mere clothes, money, and hair, I would not be recognized. Two years in Seville had taught me not to act like a Spaniard but to *be* one. As the Healer would say, I now "smelled" like a gachupin. The color of my skin was darker than many Spaniards, but the Iberian Peninsula had hosted so many peoples—from Romans and Visigoths, to

Moors and Gypsies—for so many centuries that its people's skin color ranged from white-as-milk to café con leche. The disparity in skin color was only one reason why bloodlines, not appearance, determined people's worth.

As with all travelers in this region, I was anxious to get out of the hot, humid, sickly city and into the cool mountains beyond the dunes. But first I would need a horse, pack animals, servants, and supplies.

I arranged with the innkeeper for a room overlooking the plaza and to take my dinner in my room. He offered me the services of a mulatta of fine proportions, but my mind was too full of memories to seek carnal pleasures. Not far from here I had watched de Alva cut the life out of Fray Antonio and a young girl, with a poet's soul, who dreamed of reading and writing like a man and who had risked her life to hide a beggar boy, solely because he recited poetry.

After I established myself in Ciudad Mexico with a house suitable for a gentleman of not immodest means and a staff of servants, I would replace my Veracruz horse with one of the bloodline of the conquistadors' Fourteen. And I would present myself on the Alameda, not as a silk dandy, a criollo full of masculine pride because their only glory had been parading up and down the greenway, but as a wearer of spurs who had lived life and sported action.

The greater portion of the money we took from the mint was still buried. I would take only my share and leave the rest for Mateo. After I was settled in my new identity, I would write and ask if he wished me to send his share on the next voyage of the treasure fleet. By that time he would be very broke, despite the large amount we had brought to Seville.

As the sun fell behind the western peaks, I stood by the window of my room overlooking the plaza, drinking a goblet of good Spanish wine. It felt strange to be drinking good wine in a well-appointed room in Veracruz.

Of course, I still had a plan for revenge—that thought was never far from my mind—one that would appeal to the greed and venality of men like Ramon and Luis. This time

I would not kidnap and torture nor would I kill them surreptitiously. That would only end their earthly travail. They had stripped Don Julio not only of his life, but his honor, money, and even family. They would suffer in a like manner. To lose honor and position was more painful to a proud Spaniard than to lose his head.

My revenge would also be a personal quest to unravel the mystery of my birth.

Sleep came to me in troubled fragments. My dreams were cruel monsters from my troubled past.

While the sun was still struggling to rise, trapped by Aztec gods below the Eastern Sea, with gray half light wavering on its horizon line, I heard the rumble of massed footfalls on the plaza cobblestones. For a moment I thought I was reliving, in a dream, the night the City of Mexico mistook stampeding swine for rampaging slaves and slaughtered guiltless blacks like they were devils loosed from hell.

Musket shots exploded, echoing off the plaza walls, and I jumped from my bed. Grabbing my sword and dagger, I ran to the window.

Black powder blazed from muskets, and glittering swords flashed in the dim predawn. Dark figures, scores of them, attacked the alcalde palace fort across the plaza.

Was it war? I wondered. But then realized that it was less likely war than attacking pirates, here to rape and loot as they had done in a dozen cities in the Caribbean and along our coast. The ships that had been spotted were not the treasure fleet but an invading force.

While the marauders attacked the palace fort, others dashed into buildings and homes. I barred the door and wedged a chair under the handle. It would not keep out determined men but would delay entry. Hanging my money pouch from a cord around my neck, I dressed quickly and put a dagger in a belt scabbard and another in a secret sheath in my boot. I grabbed my sword and slipped out the window onto a ledge a couple of feet wide. My room was on the top floor, and from the ledge I made my way to the roof.

On the roof I had a good view of the city. Daylight was spreading, and I could see Veracruz was under attack by as many as two or three hundred men. Men—whose only uniforms were pirate motley—invaded homes in small units, while a larger force attacked the alcalde's palace. His guards offered only token resistance, firing their muskets perhaps once or twice before running.

The fort was barely a musket shot from shore. I could see men lined up on the walls, but no boats filled with soldados disembarked. The corsairs had confiscated their longboats with their own dinghies.

Shouting, screams, musket fire, and explosions rang in the early dawn. As I hid on the roof, people ran into the presumed safe haven of the church without realizing that blackguards respected no sanctuary. Others tried to flee in carriages and on horseback. Most were stopped by the freebooters, shot from their mounts or dragged screaming from their coaches.

I saw a carriage rushing from one of the wealthier districts into the plaza in a mad dash for the alcalde's palace. Careening around the corner, it nearly overturned. The indio handling the reins was thrown from the driver's seat. Panicking from the gunfire, the horses galloped into the middle of the square, the carriage wheels rumbling across the cobblestones.

A pale, frightened face appeared in the carriage window.

"Eléna!" The name tore from my lungs in a hoarse scream.

A pirate stood in the path of the oncoming horses and fired a shot. The startled horses reared, then bolted as other buccaneers grabbed their harnesses.

I was already leaping from the roof to the top of the arcade overhanging the sidewalk and from there to the ground.

Four freebooters dragged Eléna from the coach and were

ripping off her clothes. She was screaming, clawing, biting, swinging furiously at them.

At a dead run I hurled my dagger into the back of one of the buccaneers, and as the man next to him turned, drove my sword into his throat. I jerked it out and parried the sword of the third man. Stepping out of the circle of death, I switched hands, taking my sword into my left hand and dagger in the right, leaped at the man. Feinting toward his face, I hamstrung him.

A blade slashed my left arm. I cried out in pain and dropped my blade. The last man standing had sliced my upper arm to the bone. As I swung around, off balance and open to the next blow, Eléna pulled something from the folds of her dress.

His sword came up to whack off my head when Eléna struck him in the back with something. He gaped at me in wide-eyed surprise. When he turned to face her, he had a jeweled dagger protruding from his back. I relieved him of his sword as he fell to his knees. Other blackguards were now running toward us.

"Into the carriage!" I yelled to her.

Climbing aboard, I grabbed the reins with my good hand, throwing my sword on the boards at my feet. Holding the reins with my knees, I jerked the driver's whip from its holder and lashed out at the horses. A pirate cannon had been rolled into the plaza, and now it boomed, smashing the main gate of the government palace. More from the cannon than my whip, the horses bolted. I hung onto the reins with my one good hand as the terrified horses thundered across the plaza, scattering privateers in their path.

A marauder leaped aboard by grabbing onto the carriage door. Eléna screamed, and I leaned down with the sword and swung at him. I missed but he released his hold and fell.

"Eléna! Are you all right?"

"Yes!" she shouted up.

We raced out of the plaza and down a residential street. After a few blocks we hit the road to Jalapa. My pain was intense, and I was dizzy from loss of blood, but knowledge of who my passenger was redoubled my strength.

When we were safely down the road, I brought the horses under control and slowed them to a walk. They were soaked from sweat and ready to fall. I was soaked in blood *and* sweat, weak from the loss of blood, and I was slowly fading as the horses came to a stop.

"Are you injured?" a voice called up.

This voice of an angel was the last thing I heard when a black cloud swept over me, and I was tumbling, tumbling, tumbling into a bottomless pit.

ONE HUNDRED AND FOURTEEN

"SEÑOR, SEÑOR, CAN you hear me?"

Was it the voice of an angel—or a siren? One of those half-woman creatures who seduced sailors to their doom with the sweetness of their song. The question ran through my mind as I hovered between light and dark. As light returned to my mind, I realized I was still sitting on the driver's bench. Eléna had climbed up beside me.

"I'm trying to stop the bleeding," she said. A piece of white linen, blood-soaked, was tied around my arm, and she was tearing another piece off of her petticoat.

My mind was still foggy, but my medical training came to play. "Put it above the wound," I instructed her. "Take something . . . the handle to one of your combs. Twist the cloth with it so it tightens against my arm."

As she tightened the cloth, her eyes came up and met mine, the eyes of my personal angel. Darkness was falling again for me. In a daze I was sure I heard the clop of horse's hooves and the swaying of the carriage.

As light came to my eyes and things took shape, I found

Eléna still at my side. She was holding the reins, and the horses slowly led the carriage. Funny, I thought, I'd never seen a woman handle reins, and for a moment I wondered if I was dreaming again. But, of course! This was a woman who could not just read and write, but who wrote poetry and plays! "And who stabbed a pirate with a dagger?"

"What did you say?" she asked.

I did not realize I had spoken aloud. "I said—I wondered where you got the dagger that saved my life."

"A friend told me that prostitutes carry a dagger to defend themselves. I don't see why a prostitute should be more effectively protected than a lady."

She pulled back on the reins and spoke gently to the horses, telling them to stop.

"Where are we?" I asked.

"A league, perhaps two, from the city. You have been slipping in and out of consciousness for the past hour. There is a sugarcane hacienda owned by an acquaintance perhaps another hour ahead. The road is firm enough for carriage wheels. We will go there for shelter and the treatment of your wound."

I was still weak, and my arm was in agony. I loosened the linen tourniquet she had twisted above the wound and tightened the one that pressed on it.

"The wound needs to be cauterized with hot oil," she said.

"No, oil harms the flesh even more. The French doctor, Paré, proved that. If it does not stop bleeding, the veins that leak will need to be stitched."

"You're a doctor?"

"No, although I have some medical knowledge. My fa— uncle, was a doctor and on occasion I assisted him."

She gave me a long look, a searching stare that took me in my entirety. "Have we met? Perhaps in Mexico City? A reception?"

"No, I just arrived in New Spain for the first time on the dispatch boat. But I thank God that he permitted me to meet you now."

"Strange . . ."

"You think you know me? Perhaps someone who looks like me?"

"You seem a little familiar, in a way I feel but cannot express. Also you called me by my name earlier."

Fortunately she had turned to pull back on the reins as she spoke, or she would have seen the shock on my face. I pulled my features back into control and smiled at her when she turned back to me.

"Your name was shouted by someone near the inn when you were being pulled out of the coach."

"Someone must have recognized me."

"Do you live in Veracruz?"

"No, in Mexico. I've been visiting friends."

"Your husband is back in Veracruz . . ."

"I am not married." She was silent for a moment. "From your look I can see that you wonder why I am not married when I am past the age that most women marry. My uncle expects me to marry, but I have been undecided whether I will marry a man or God."

"You mean you are considering becoming a nun?"

"Yes, I am in discussions with the prioress of the Sisters of Mercy."

"No!"

"Señor?"

"I mean, well, you shouldn't become a nun. There is so much to life—"

"The spirituality of the convent I would never find in marriage."

I almost blurted out that she could write plays and poetry outside of a cloister, but then held my tongue. I could not reveal that I knew too much about her. Disclosing my true identity would win me nothing. Nor was the absence of a husband any reason to buoy my spirits. She was still the daughter of a great house of Spain and could only marry an equal. There would be few social equals in all New Spain. Luis was of that rank. My intuition told me that she would rather enter a convent than marry him.

Again, she probed my soul with her eyes.

"Señor, I do not know why you risked your life for me, but for reasons only you and God know, I am not ravished or dead. You will find my uncle, the viceroy, very grateful."

Don Diego Velez had been appointed viceroy a year ago when I was in Seville. Ramon de Alva was closely associated not only with Luis but with Don Diego. Considering the way governmental services and positions were bought and sold, Don Diego was probably involved in the tunnel debacle. If so, bringing down Alva and Luis would destroy Eléna.

"Is the pain worse, señor? Your features darken."

"No, señorita, but for a moment I remembered a friend and was sad."

She smiled knowingly. "I see. You left behind on the peninsula a piece of your heart. I hope, señor, that like so many of the men who come to the colonies, you did not leave her heartbroken."

"I can assure you, señorita, mine is the heart that was torn."

"Perhaps now we are friends, we could be less formal and use out names. Mine, as you know, is Eléna . . ."

¡Ay de mí! I could have given all the gold in Christendom to have said to her that my name was Cristo the Bastardo; that I had loved her the first moment I saw her nearly a dozen years ago on a Veracruz street. But it was "Don Carlos," a young hidalgo, whom she took to the sugarcane hacienda.

I passed out again on the road, and it was several days before I was able to travel. During most of that time, Eléna, with help from the majordomo's wife, treated my wound.

After my first excitement at seeing her, I had become silent and morose. She took this to be a natural reaction to my wounds. But my wounds ran deeper. I had returned to New Spain seeking retribution. Until I saw Eléna, I had not considered how my revenge might affect her or how seeing her could divert me from my path.

During those days that she nursed me, Eléna and I became close. To the scandal of the majordomo's wife, she insisted upon laying cool, wet compresses on my head and bare chest when the fever raged. When I was weak, but conscious, she sat by my bed and read poetry to me. No well-born, unmarried woman would have done either.

I could see that the majordomo's wife had noted the growing closeness between us. If word got to the viceroy that I was romantically pursing her, the viceroy would not be pleased. Instead of hailing me as a hero, he would examine my background with a jeweler's eye, and unfortunately, my past would not stand scrutiny. Ay, and Luis. His jealousy would jeopardize my new life, too.

I finally realized that my love for Eléna could only end in tragedy for us both. I resolved to terminate my friendship with Eléna in a way that would brook no further contact. My lying lépero tongue served me well.

"Eléna," I said, when she brought me dinner, not permitting a servant to bring it, "something lies heavily on my conscience."

"What is it, Carlos? Are you going to tell me that you hate the way I read poetry to you every night?"

"An angel could not read more eloquently than you." I did not mention that I had recognized some of the poems as her own. "No, this concerns another matter. Having come close to death recently—the ocean-crossing, pirate raid, the fevers—it all seems like terrible premonitions. I have decisions I can no longer put off."

"Is there something I can help you with?"

"Yes. I need your advice. Should I bring over my wife and child now, or at a later time."

I deliberately looked away as I spoke the lie. I did not want her to see my face nor did I wish to see hers.

I managed to blunder out the rest of the lies. I had left behind my family to seek a fortune in the New World, but I was already lonely for them. I soon faked dozing off to sleep so I would not reveal my distress with my voice.

* * *

The next day she returned in the carriage to Veracruz. Word had come that the pirates had left after looting the city and the alcalde's soldados were now in control. We also learned why the pirates had found the city such easy prey: The money allotted to the alcalde for defense of the city had been misappropriated. When the attack came, most of his soldados lacked sufficient black powder and musket balls to resist. The failure of the fort commander to recognize the ships earlier, and the easy manner in which the pirates had marooned the fort's troops by stealing their longboats, had also exacerbated the disaster.

"The alcalde and fort commander are both under arrest," the hacienda majordomo informed me before he left for Veracurz with Eléna.

I had deliberately pretended to need more healing time to avoid accompanying her. Eléna felt I should be transported to the capital by mule litter when she returned there in the company of a troop of soldados. I needed to get to the City of Mexico alone.

"The alcalde and fort commander will be lucky if they ever reach the capital for a trial," the majordomo said. "The shame of it. People are angry. Money for the city's protection went into their pockets. We have the finest army in the world. Spain dominates the world. How could this happen?"

It happened, I thought wearily, because the alcalde and fort commander bought their offices from the king. They paid for the right to embezzle city funds, including tax money for musket balls. The king used their bribes to fight wars in Europe. It was all arranged, all agreed on. Nobody was naive.

But I said nothing.

Eléna now planned for me to ride triumphantly into the capital city, where she would organize the hero's welcome worthy of Achilles *and* Odysseus, all of which would draw more attention to my counterfeit background as well as generating rivalries I could not afford.

As soon as the majordomo returned from delivering her to Veracruz, I convinced him to sell me a horse. "It will help me regain my strength, so I can make the journey to Mexico City as a caballero instead of an old woman in a litter."

With a horse under me, I set out for the City of Mexico, planning to arrive there a week ahead of Eléna.

ONE HUNDRED AND FIFTEEN

YEARS HAD PASSED since I had last crossed a causeway into the City on the Five Lakes. Little had changed. The city still inspired awe at a distance, as magical as Tenochtitlan when the conquistadors first viewed it. The Recontonería still plundered the indio farmers at the causeway's entrance. Blood and money still ruled.

After obtaining lodging at an inn, I went to work. I needed several things immediately: Locate an attractive residence, a couple of servants, a good horse, and a stylish carriage. I needed to present myself to the city as well-born and modestly well-to-do.

I visited several respected merchants, telling them what I needed. To my surprise, word of my actions in Veracruz had preceded me. Everyone was eager to help. Unfortunately, I was also overwhelmed with invitations to dinners and parties.

I made arrangement for a modest house. As a single man, I was not expected to live in a palace. After running a large hacienda, I knew how to deal with furnishings and kitchen supplies. It would take several weeks to prepare the house to be occupied, and in the meantime I would stay at the inn.

I begged off from all invitations, using my still-bandaged arm as an excuse.

After the house arrangements were completed, I hired

servants and gave them a list of everything necessary to make a house livable. Arranging for credit with the local merchants, I left the city. My destination was our concealed treasure cave. I deliberately traveled by horseback rather than boat. It took me a week longer, but I wanted to be sure I was not followed. The cave was now completely overgrown and more hidden than ever. After assuring myself that everything was intact, I filled my saddlebags and money belt with gold.

On my return to the city, I went to the still unfurnished house I had rented and removed bricks in the fireplace hearth and dug a hole under them—just enough room to hide the trove when resealed. I was now ready for my plan.

It was in the blood of Luis and Alva to steal. Now that the opportunity for silver robberies was gone, and the tunnel misappropriations were history, they would be eager. I needed to find something else to excite their greed.

Those first days in the city, I kept my ears open. Over and over, I heard one consistent complaint. Maize, the staff of life for the poor and common people, had risen astronomically in price, and while price increases were expected in times of flood and drought, the weather for the growing season had been normal.

Amigos, you want to know why the price would rise when the supply and demand remained constant, eh. So did I.

Maize, I discovered upon inquiry, was controlled in price by the viceroy, who administered the system through an official empowered to set the price. The maize was purchased from growers by middlemen who in turn sold it to warehousers licensed by the viceroy's administrator. These warehousers released it in quantity as it was needed for consumption and at a price set by the viceroy's administrator. The higher the demand, the more the middlemen, warehouses, and people paid to the producers.

A reasonable system, so it appeared.

So why in a year in which the supply was normal and the demand had not increased, did the price rise? I soon learned from my first inquiry that the man most responsible for getting the maize to the marketplace was Miguel de Soto—the viceroy's administrator.

Is there no end to human greed? These devils not only stole silver, but plundered the tunnel-drainage project, almost flooding the entire capital by their skullduggery. Now they were plundering the city's food supply. But what bothered me most was, not that they were acquiring a stranglehold on the food supply and would soon charge outrageous prices that would provoke massive famine, but who would they blame afterward. Who, like Don Julio and his daughters, would burn at the stake?

Perhaps they would look for another converso?

I gave the matter much thought, and hired a twelve-year-old lépero, Jaime. Léperos of all ages were untrustworthy, but the younger they were, the less cynical they were likely to be. I hired this one to hang around outside of Soto's place of business on the main plaza.

Then I sent a note to Soto, saying that a friend of his in Spain had referred him to me. I also used Eléna's name, mentioning that I had intended to look him up earlier, but I had been delayed in Veracruz "assisting" the viceroy's niece. He set up an appointment for that very afternoon.

Soto was a stocky-built man, about forty years old, whose waistline was bursting at the seams from inactivity and fine food.

"It is a pleasure to meet you, Don Carlos," he said. "Your rescue of Eléna at Veracruz is on everyone's lips. They call you 'the hero of Veracruz,' and speak of you in the same breath as Cortes—as if killing pirates was the same as conquering the Aztecs and carving out an empire."

I murmured a modest reply.

We sat at a table in his counting room. While his clerks busied themselves with paperwork, he offered me wine.

"You say that a friend in Spain referred you to me?"

"Yes, I met her in Seville."

"Ah, a woman. Not one my wife would object to, I hope." He laughed.

"I doubt she would make your wife jealous. It is of, course, your amiga, Catalina de Erauso."

I had deliberately looked away when I mentioned the name, but caught his reaction in the corner of my eye. His expression was that of a man who had startled a snake. I turned back to him in all innocence.

"The name is vaguely familiar, Don Carlos. Who did you say this woman was?"

"My apologies, señor, my apologies. She was the talk of Madrid and Seville, and I assumed you knew her true name. She is the nun who fled a convent to become a soldier and adventurer. You must have heard the tale . . ."

"Ah, sí, sí, the infamous lieutenant nun. Yes, everyone in the New World and the old has heard of her." He squinted at me, a contrived, puzzled expression on his face. "But I have had no dealings with this woman . . . man . . ." He shrugged. "Whatever she is."

"Again, my apologies, I did not mean to suggest this curious woman was your friend. I met Catalina in Seville recently when we were guests at the same inn. As you might have heard, she has become both famous and honored for having so cleverly disguised herself—and served Spain."

"Yes, very clever."

"When I told her that I was departing for the great Ciudad Mexico, she advised contacting you. She said you were a man both discreet and clever . . ."

He tried to smile, but his facial muscles were too tense.

". . . at making money," I finished.

"Ah, I see, I see. Did she tell you how I, uh, made money?"

"No, merely that you were a skilled businessman. She did mention that you were both in the silver business together." I leaned closer and spoke in a confidential tone. "Frankly, Don Miguel, I had the impression that you and she had not parted on the best of terms, and that she wanted to send her regrets and hope to make peace with you. Considering her dubious reputation, I assume she cheated you at some transaction."

De Soto's tense features softened. He shook his head and waved his hands. "Don Carlos, you would not believe how much difficulty I had with this woman. I have heard that the king has rewarded her because her antics amuse him, but if he knew her true character, he would have rewarded her with the gallows."

"You have my regret, señor, that I have intruded upon you under false pretenses. Apparently the disreputable wench was amusing herself with her story. I hoped to increase my wealth by establishing a relationship with one knowledgeable of the business practices in the colony, but instead I have intruded upon you."

I got up to leave and Soto insisted I sit down. "It is not your fault, amigo. That woman is the devil herself. Tell me more about what you have in mind?"

"My family is an old and honorable one. I was fortunate to marry the daughter of a swine grower who gave a handsome dowry. The marriage is a happy one as she is the love of my life, my Aphrodite."

He would, of course, interpret my statements as meaning that I had married far beneath my station for a rich dowry, and that my new wife was uglier than the swine her father raised. He would assume that once I had the dowry in hand, I had fled the father, the daughter, and the swine.

But he would be impressed that I had money, which was becoming an increasingly scarce commodity. Spain's foreign empire had made a few people incredibly rich, but the cost of such adventures was prohibitive. Foreign wars had all but bankrupted the treasury. Taxes and exorbitant prices had impoverished the people, including the lower nobility and merchant classes.

He made sympathetic noises with his tongue. "I see, I see. You have brought the dowry to New Spain to increase your fortune. That was wise of you. Money decays in Spain, but in the colony, it can sprout wings and fly."

"Exactly, Don Miguel. But I have to tell you that I am

inexperienced in the art of commerce. Naturally, my family avoided such entanglements."

"Have you thought about a position with the government? Your actions in Veracruz would no doubt get you a captaincy in a regiment."

This was the opening I was waiting for. I deliberately avoided his eye, trying to appear evasive.

"A commission would not suit me nor any other position with the government until I clear up a small matter."

Soto nodded knowingly. "I see." He leaned toward me, duplicating my confidential tone. "You may speak frankly with me, Don Carlos. As that evil woman no doubt told you, I am a man of great discretion."

I hesitated and then, with obvious reluctance, confessed my predicament. "I would not be able to hold an honorable position with the viceroy at this time. My blood is pure back to mio Cid, but you know how these things can be mixed up and confused. One of my urgent needs is to make my funds not only significant to maintain a gentleman's lifestyle, but to clear this small matter of blood."

Soto's mind was traveling so fast I could see the hooves flying. I had literally confessed to having Jewish ancestry. The taint would be especially awkward for me if family members were accused of practicing Judaism.

"I understand perfectly," Soto said. "Such accusations, no matter how lacking in substance, are costly to clear up. And, until it is . . ." He spread his hands.

I started to leave. "Again, Don Miguel, I regret disturbing your day with my troubles."

"Sit down, amigo, sit down. How much did you intend to invest in a business venture?"

Again, I avoided his eyes. "My finances are very modest. Four or five thousand pesos, perhaps a little more." No true Spaniard revealed the truth about his fortune. Soto would multiply the amount I stated many times.

He shook his head. "Not a significant sum for a business venture of the sort I had in mind. You would need at least twenty-five thousand pesos."

"A sum that large is, of course, out of my reach"—I contrived a cunning look—"but I would like to know a little more about the venture. It may be that I could squeeze a little more from my limited funds."

He smiled broadly, no doubt already planning how he would spend the twenty-five thousand pesos he would cheat me out of. "I need to talk to other investors before I permit myself to disclose confidential information."

"That would be expected. But can you at least give me some idea of the subject matter? I need to make a decision as to whether I will even stay in the city or go north to seek my fortune in the mining country. I am interested only in a venture that will bring large returns quickly."

"I can only tell you that it concerns speculation in maize, and that it will be extremely profitable. *Extremely* profitable. Naturally, only one whom we consider a brother would be invited to participate."

After giving him my address so he could contact me, I left Don Miguel de Soto's smiling. Coming out of the building, I gave Jaime, the lépero boy, a knowing look as I walked away.

He would follow Soto when the man left his office. It would not matter if Soto left by foot, horse, or carriage. With the crowded streets, the boy would be able to keep up.

I had no illusions that the cabal involved in maize speculation would permit me in because of brotherly love. And I did not know if they needed the additional pesos I offered, although for certain Soto's innate greed would compel him to reach for it.

The true bait I had offered them was that of a converso scapegoat. If things went bad, they would need a lamb to sacrifice. I had just offered myself.

ONE HUNDRED AND SIXTEEN

I DID NOT hear from Soto for two days, but the third morning he asked to meet me. A second message asked me to appear at the viceroy's palace that afternoon.

Jaime had followed Soto to the house of Ramon de Alva soon after I had left Soto. Later, Luis had shown up at the house. All of my suspicions were confirmed. I only had to wait to see if the bait had been taken.

Soto greeted me again in his office, drawing me to the side so that his clerks could not hear us. "I regret to inform you that my compadres have declined your offer to join our enterprise."

My disappointment was genuine.

Soto spread his greedy hands in a gesture of his own frustration.

"I assured them that, through mutual friends, I could vouch for your honesty and honor, but this business venture we are involved in is a very delicate one, requiring some knowledge of each investor's background."

In other words, they were afraid they could not trust me—trust me to take the blame quietly, that is.

"Well, amigo, perhaps another venture sometime . . . ," I said.

Soto padded my sleeve. "Perhaps you and I could do some business together."

I could barely suppress a grin.

"The men who are my partners in this venture are, shall we say, more solvent than I. Last year I purchased a large hacienda in the Taxco area. Ay, amigo, it has drained me of dinero."

"What do you propose, Don Miguel?"

Those expressive hands of his spread again. "That we be partners, private partners. I sell you a piece of my share of the venture."

"Tell me more about this venture I would become involved in."

"My good friend, I have barely met you, but I love you like a brother. You will be informed fully as to all details of the enterprise. However, I must move cautiously; I have only known you for a couple of days."

"But, Don Miguel, as you say, we are brothers."

"Eh, but Abel also had a brother. We shall sup and drink together a few times and get to be fine friends. Doña María Luisa, my wife, wishes you to honor our table tomorrow night. Someone you know will be there."

No surprise was a pleasant prospect, even if the mystery guest was Eléna, but I could not avoid the invitation. Soto would not cut me in until he knew me better.

"I would be honored. But please, tell me which friend of mine will be there. Not my father-in-law, the swine farmer?"

He laughed. "If he shows up in New Spain, we will sew him up in one of his own pig bladders and ship him home. No, it's your father's old friend, Don Silvestre Hurtado."

I felt a grave opening at my feet. My face signaled my dismay.

Soto slapped me on the back. "You forgot that Don Silvestre lived here, eh? Of course, you were just a boy when he left Spain. Were you seventeen or eighteen?"

"Sí, about that."

"Do not fret, amigo. I have spoken to the don and those matters your father wrote him about are our secret. It was very clever of you to account for your money as the dowry from a swine maid." He made a gesture of sewing his lips shut. "My lips are sealed, amigo. The matters are most serious, but enough about money . . ." He shrugged. "After we do business, you will be able to avoid arrest by repaying the money. You can restore the girl's stolen honor, or at least permit her and the child to live in greater comfort."

I left Soto's after promising to present myself at his house on Saturday. Today was Thursday, so I still had one day in which to live before an angry mob tore me to pieces for being a fraud. I had no idea what Soto was talking about. Secrets? Dowry? A girl's stolen honor? *¡Ay de mí!*

Jaime the lépero was crouched nearby as I came onto the street, and I gestured him to me.

"I will be needing your help later. Come to the inn when it is dark."

"Sí, señor. Now I will need an extra payment, my mother is very sick."

"You have no mother. You were spawned by el diablo." I tossed the little liar a reale. "Direct me to an indio sorcerer who sells potions."

He grinned up at me. "Do you need a love potion?"

I groaned. "I need something to calm stormy waters."

¡Ay de mí! An old family friend, eh. Soto told me the old man lived with his daughter. He was half blind and used a single ground glass, a monocle, to assist his vision. My first instinct was to hire thugs to smash his eyepiece, but even half blind he would know me for a fraud. I even thought of having the old man killed or at least beaten unconscious. Unfortunately, I had neither the time nor the stomach for it. The old man was just the beginning of my troubles. What evils had my namesake Don Carlos perpetrated? Avoid arrest? Repay the money and restore the girl's honor? Comfort for her and the child?

I had already discovered in my two conversations with Miguel de Soto that secrets pour from his mouth like water over a dam. By now the whole city would know that my swine maiden tale was a cover for dastardly deeds.

Por Dios! Why had I not kept the identity I had originally planned? I had assumed the skin of a scoundrel. Apparently a thief and spoiler of women. I had worked hard all of my life to shed my thief's persona and become a gentleman. I had now come full circle. I was a gentleman *and* a thief!

Ay, what had Fray Antonio said about those strange people who live in the land of elephants and tigers, the Hindu?

That bad acts in a past life determine present fortune—or misery? That our many lives formed a circle and that bad acts would eventually return us to the same point—or one worse.

I made my way back to the inn to rest before my meeting with the viceroy. Eléna would be back in town by now. Had she already heard the swine maiden's tale? I had already told her of my concern for my "wife and child." Now she would know that, not only had I lied to her about my background, but was a rogue who treated women heartlessly.

I wanted to avoid being a hero, to enter the city quietly. Now I would be the talk of the city, as the dons and doñas argued over whether I should be praised or hanged. Something also told me that the miseries that were being heaped upon me were not over.

When I arrived back at the inn, the innkeeper gave me more startling news.

"Your brother has arrived. He is waiting in your room."

I graciously thanked him. As I walked toward the stairway, my feet moved in a straight line, but my mind screamed for me to run. First, an old friend of the family. Now, Don Carlos's brother. Had his whole family, his whole province, moved to New Spain?

In the hallway above, I drew my sword. I did not want to spill strange blood, but there was no longer any alternative. If I did not kill the brother, the alarm would sound and I would not make it past the causeways before the viceroy's soldados threw me in irons.

I steadied my nerves and drew a deep breath. Then I burst through the door of my room, my blade at the ready.

A one-eyed man looked up at me from the bed where he was enjoying a sack of wine and the mulatta I had refused.

"Eh, Bastardo, put down that sword. Did I not always tell you that as a bladesman, you were a dead man?"

ONE HUNDRED AND SEVENTEEN

MATEO SENT THE *puta* out, and I sat in a chair with my feet on the end of the bed as he relaxed back against the pillows. His left eye was covered by a black patch.

I shook my head at the sight of the patch. "And what is the name of that wound, compadre? Margarita? Juanita? Sofia?"

"This one is the duchess."

"Ah, so the duke came back from the wars and caught you in bed with his wife. A cousin to the queen, no less."

"A cousin to the devil, for sure. She sent the duke an 'anonymous' message soon after I began bedding her, thinking, no doubt, that jealousy would win him back."

"How bad is the eye?"

"Bad? There is nothing wrong with it." He lifted the patch to expose a blood red, empty socket. I winced.

"The eye is fine. I just don't have it anymore."

"A sword fight?"

"Nothing so honorable. The duke's men held me while he gouged it. He was about to do the other eye when I broke lose."

"Did you cut his throat or gouge his eyes out?"

"Neither. His throat is fine and so are both his eyes. However, he now pees through a straw."

"Well done. And how did you manage to maim a duke and live?"

He grinned. "By moving very quickly. The last ship of the treasure fleet had sailed from Seville when I reached the docks. I hired a fast coastal runner to chase it down. I caught up to a boat that was having difficulty with its rigging. It had a destination of Hispaniola, not Veracruz. From there a boat put me into Veracruz. When I heard about a clean-shaven man with a scar on his cheek who had saved a lady from pirates, eh, who could it be but my old compadre? Who else would be so foolish as to fight pirates rather than join them?"

"Mateo, I'm in trouble."

"So I have heard, *Don Carlos.* Even the puta mulatta knows you stole your wife-to-be's dowry from her father's house and fled, leaving her pregnant."

"I did that? What a thief!"

"Worse than a thief. It was cowardly and not honorable. Had you killed the father in a duel, men would hide you from the king's agents in their homes. But to steal a dowry from the father? And severely wound him by hitting him over the head with a candlestick? A candlestick! How can he hold his head up to his friends after he had been felled by a candlestick? It was a silver candlestick and you stole that, too. Oh, Don Carlos, you are a bad one. You would be in chains right now if Eléna's uncle had not become viceroy."

I advised Mateo of my activities since I left Seville, right up to Soto's dinner invitation. "Those chains and noose you mentioned are still waiting for me. I am going to dinner Saturday at the house of Miguel de Soto's. Another guest will be an old friend of my family."

"Which family?"

"The one in Spain."

"Someone knows Don Carlos here in Mexico City?"

"One person for certain. An old man who knows all of my sins. I'm told he's half blind, but he could tell I'm a fake in the dark. The way Fortune is laughing at me, there may be another intimate or victim of Don Carlos on every street corner, waiting to expose me."

"Ah, Bastardo, this is what comes of thinking for yourself. Had you told me you were returning to reap revenge, I would not have let you come alone. I would still have my eye, and you would not be in this mess. What is your plan? To murder the old man? Gouge *his* eyes out before dinner?"

"I considered both. But I have neither the heart nor the nerve for either."

"Silencing the old man before he can tell the world of your sins would throw suspicion on you."

"I've thought of that, too. I'm also considering using yoyotli dust. If I can find it." I reminded him how we used the dream dust to disorient Isabella's maid.

"It's risky. And it fails to do one thing: validate you as Don Carlos."

"You think this old man will do that? He has not seen Don Carlos for seven or eight years, but I have seen Carlos, and I look nothing like him. His skin, hair, and eyes are all lighter than mine. This old man could smell me and know I'm not the son of his old friend."

"Soto is trying to find a way to justify dealing with you, even if it's behind the back of his compadres. So far he has heard stories about you that intrigue him. You are a thief and a scoundrel. That fits in nicely with his own plans. But he needs to know more about you. If he doesn't get enough information from the old man, he may keep inquiring. You could do worse than an old man who depends upon a monocle to see."

"A single eyeglass will let him see enough of me to know I'm a fraud."

"Perhaps. But what if it were broken? Ground eyeglasses are rare and expensive. No one here in New Spain can make such a thing. It would take at least a year to replace if something happened to his only glass."

"I don't know. Perhaps the best course for me is to forget Luis and Alva. I could kidnap Eléna and take her to some deserted paradise."

"And as which scoundrel would you present yourself to her? The mestizo bandit who terrorized the roads of New Spain? Or the worthless son of a hidalgo who beat an old man with a candlestick to steal his daughter's dowry?"

Mateo stayed at the inn when I left for the viceroy's palace. He told me to have the innkeeper send the puta back up. Lust helped him think, he said.

A soldado at the main gate escorted me into the reception area of the palace, turning me over to the viceroy's aide. The viceroy's household, both premises and staff, had a regal presence. Rugs and tapestries were lavish, artistically embroidered, gold thread predominating. A fieldstone fireplace had a massive maw from which hung a variety of fire tools. Great silver candlesticks on the fireplace mantel in the reception room were almost as tall as me. Against a wall stood stiff, straightback chairs of mahogany and darkly polished leather.

Most people would be impressed with how many pesos such luxury was worth. I wondered how many lives such affluence cost.

It was only to be expected that the viceroy lived like a king. In truth, he was one. He ruled with near-absolute power a land five times the size of Spain. While the high court called the Audiencia and the archbishop both had a say, the viceroy could overrule either. Complaints about his conduct had to be presented to the king in Madrid through the Council of the Indies. The process could take a year for matters of some urgency and forever for lesser matters.

I waited nervously for the summons to appear before him. Would Eléna be there? Would her eyes be full of contempt? Probably no more than I already felt myself. My entire life was now one huge house of lies, each stacked atop another. Not even I knew the truth.

I felt eyes on me and turned around to find Eléna had entered the room. She paused just inside the door and had stopped to look at me with concern. With a smile, she came to me, her hand held out in greeting. I kissed it.

"Doña Eléna, we meet again."

"Don Carlos, I am happy to see you are well. You gave us a fright when you left the hacienda. At first we thought you had taken a wrong turn and became lost."

"My apologies, my lady, I was sneaking away to stop being a trouble for so many people."

"You caused no fuss, only concern for a man who had risked his life for me. I realize that you wish to maintain your privacy. However, my uncle learned that you were to be the guest of Don Miguel de Soto. He has asked Don Miguel to invite you another time so you may attend a reception here at the palace."

I murmured my assent, maintaining my smile, while I cringed at the prospect of being displayed before all the notables in the city.

As we looked into each other's eyes, my heart melted. She started to say something and looked away as she hesitated. A cross hung from a silver chain around her neck. I was jolted when I saw it; it was my mother's cross, the one the Inquisition lawyer had taken from me. Seeing the cross shook me, and I had difficulty keeping my composure.

Her eyes were moist when they met mine again. A blush had pinked her cheeks. She spoke in a low, confidential tone. "That problem you left in Spain. I've spoken to my uncle; he will help."

"Eléna," I took her hand, my heart was tearing at what she must think of me, "I'm so sorry."

"Eléna!"

We both snapped to attention.

Luis had entered the reception area.

For a moment I was flustered. I instinctively reached for my sword and cleared the scabbard by several inches before I caught myself.

Luis's lips formed a smile, but his eyes were as I remembered. Hard. Snake eyes staring up from a luckless throw of the dice.

"I didn't mean to startle you. The viceroy is waiting."

"Don Carlos, may I present my fiancé, Don Luis de la Cerda."

I exchanged bows with him, barely able to keep my face neutral. The word "fiancé" had caught me off guard.

"You have the appreciation of all New Spain for your efforts on behalf of Doña Eléna. And you especially have the thanks of her future husband."

He bowed again. The words were spoken with sincerity. But each one grated on me and set my teeth on edge. I did not doubt that he was attracted to Eléna, but I knew the man was incapable of truly loving a woman. I remembered his comments from so long ago when I was hidden under the seat of a carriage.

"We had better join the viceroy," Eléna said.

Eléna led the way, with Luis behind me. The hair on the back of my neck bristled. I had seen something in Luis's eyes when he spoke his thanks to me—jealousy. When Eléna and I had looked into each other's eyes, Luis had spotted something beyond my saving her life.

Unlike myself, Luis's appearance had not changed. His beard covered many of the pox scars, but his eyes betrayed the harshness of his dark soul.

I was consumed by anger at the tragic murders of the people I loved. But even at that I felt no animosity for the world at large. What twists of fate, what disappointments had caused this scion of wealth and power to stain his birthright with common thievery. I knew the stories of his need to involve himself in business. True, his father had squandered the family fortune. If Luis had not accumulated one of his own, he would have traded his title for a rich man's daughter and dowry rather than marrying into the viceroy's family.

What had caused Eléna to change her mind about entering a convent? My suspicion was that the change in plans had to do with Eléna's pleas to her uncle on my behalf. In a convent she would be safe from the monster, and I could dream of stealing her away. Ay, my new disguise as a gentleman of Spain had driven her farther from me and into the arms of a villain.

Don Diego Veles de Maldonato was short, no taller than Eléna, but he made up for his diminutive stature with aristocratic arrogance and a steely gaze of cold command. He wore his mustache and beard short, his hair as close cropped as a monk's. He ruled as a king a wild land as large as half a dozen European countries combined. Although he was known to have mistresses, the viceroy was a widower without children. He had raised Eléna as his own daughter.

After proper introductions had been made, the viceroy came around from his gilt desk to personally inquire as to the status of my wound.

"Don Carlos, your boldness and courage were most noble. Had there been a dozen more like you in Veracruz, the entire pirate army would have been summarily routed."

"I am sure there were greater acts of bravery that morning, Your Excellency. In fact, if your niece had not stabbed the man who was about to chop off my head, I would be buried in Veracruz rather than standing before you today."

"In truth, naked greed not lost courage stripped our soldados of their weapons. And as for my niece, I have lectured her many times about carrying daggers and other unladylike conduct. Fortunately for you both, my niece ignores my advice."

"Uncle, that is not true. I listen to all your commands."

"But *obeying* them is something else."

Eléna murmured her dissent . . . quietly.

"But as we know, this time her disobedience proved expedient. In any event custody of her iron will soon fall to another's hand; I am certain Don Luis will invite you to the place of honor at his wedding table."

Luis bowed. "We would be most honored if Don Carlos graced our banquet table."

"I live for the day," I said evenly.

"I will see Don Carlos alone for a moment," the viceroy said.

When Luis and Eléna had left the room, he dropped his veneer of grace and reverted to an administrator dealing with a problem.

"Your rescue of Eléna was fortuitous on several counts. You saved my niece from unspeakable horrors and perhaps even death. The debacle of our soldados being without powder and ball to resist the attack will resound all the way to Madrid and back. The alcalde and fort commander will be punished, though not to the extent that the people are crying for. Your daring rescue of my niece has in a small way overshadowed the shame of defeat. The rescue has figured prominently in the dispatch that has been sent to the king. As soon as he receives it, the news will quickly make its way to your home province."

And when it did, word would fly to Madrid that I was a wanted man.

"I related the story of your daring in the most compelling language, giving it all the praise it deserved. I also hinted at a matter of youthful indiscretion that must be cleared up. Until we hear from Madrid, I will not know what honor to bestow upon you."

Or whether to remove my head, I thought.

"You, of course, will remain in the city until word comes."

Eh, I was not to leave town. It would take six months to a year for Madrid to sort it all out.

The viceroy clasped my good hand. "Understand this, young man. In my mind, what you did for my niece makes up a thousand-fold for whatever acts you committed in Spain. But we must move slowly and carefully to ensure that this grand gesture wipes away the sins of the past. If nothing further comes of this, I praise God that the situation has enabled me to convince Eléna to marry one of the finest young men of New Spain."

Luis was waiting for me when I came out of the viceroy's chamber.

"I will escort Don Carlos from the building," he told the viceroy's secretary.

As we walked, Luis asked if the viceroy had given me adequate assurances concerning my "difficulties."

"He has been most generous," I said.

"Eléna has suggested that you may wish to meet some of our city's more eligible women. Few places on earth boast women and horses that are as well-bred and beautifully proportioned as in this city. As your own father may have told you, there is a great deal of similarity between how one handles a fine woman and a fine horse."

I could not suppress a grin. If Eléna could have heard this again!

"I'm afraid my father never compared my mother to a horse; but perhaps he was not the master of either, which I'm sure your own father was."

"My father is the master of nothing, not even the cards and drink he squanders his life on."

Luis's voice had turned hard and angry. His short temper inspired me to provoke him further.

"Your gracious offer to introduce me to the ladies of your city is most generous. And as soon as my wound has healed, I shall accept your kindness." I stopped and faced him. "You know, señor, I fell in love with the lovely Eléna and had hoped she would return my affection. I was saddened to learn she was betrothed."

Luis's veneer of civility vanished. For a tense moment I believed he would draw his sword in the viceroy's palace, all of which pleased me greatly.

"Good day, señor," I said, with a curt nod and bow. I turned my back to him and left, bearing an uneasy feeling between my shoulder blades that a dagger might find its way there.

ONE HUNDRED AND EIGHTEEN

YOU DID WHAT?" I directed my exasperation at Mateo in the courtyard of my newly rented quarters. He was not a man who spent his life walking toward the gallows—he *ran* for the noose.

Mateo fondled his ever-present wine goblet, an expression of smug self-righteousness on his face. He smiled thinly at me through a haze of smoke. "Do you wish to discuss this matter calmly and quietly or would you rather we trumpeted it to your servants and neighbors."

I sat down. "Tell me what madness drove you to visit Don Silvestre. Start at the beginning so I will know whether to leave town . . . or garrote you."

He shook his head and tried to look innocent, which hardly rang true: His face was a battlefield of those scars that each bore a woman's name.

"Bastardo, my compadre—"

"Ex-compadre."

"I went to the house of your old family friend, Don Silvestre, a fine old caballero. There is snow on his head, his legs are weak at the knees, not to mention bowed from a lifetime on the saddle, but fire still burns in his heart. He is as you imagined him—mostly blind. I made the pretense of asking to examine his eyepiece. Without it, he could not count my fingers a foot from his nose."

"I hope you broke the glass."

"Of course not. Would a caballero like myself do that to an old knight?"

"Not unless it would assist you at a cantina's card table or into a woman's bed."

He sighed and emptied the goblet with a long drink. He refilled it before he went on with his story.

"We shall save breaking the old man's eyepiece to another day," he said.

"Soto's party has been changed to the viceroy's palace. The old man will probably attend."

"I already know that. He will not just attend, he is riding with us in our carriage."

"Santa Maria, Holy Mother of God." I got down on my knees and prayed before a stone angel pouring water into the patio fountain. "Save me from this madman, Holy Madre, and have God send lightning to strike him down."

"Bastardo, you panic too easily. You must face life's setbacks with equanimity, not hysteria. Now get up off your knees. I am not your priest."

I got to my feet. "Tell me how I am to ride in a carriage

to the viceroy's ball with a man who will expose me as a fake the moment he sees me."

"The old man already believes you are Don Carlos because I have told him you are Don Carlos. You do not have to convince him. What you have to do is avoid *un*convincing him. It will be dark when we pick him up. The street boy who spies for you will suddenly rush out of the darkness, grab his eyeglass, and run away. Even if, God forbid, the attack fails, Don Silvestre still will not recognize you. He has to get very close even to see with his eyeglass. Like any old caballero, he is vain about his age and physical condition. He is not only half blind but half deaf. If you speak quietly when you are forced to speak, he will not notice. Also, I will be there to carry the conversation. Don Silvestre does not like you because you have violated the caballero's code of honor. He will not speak to you unless he has to. However, after explaining to him the true circumstance of the crimes in Spain . . ."

"Sí, the *true* circumstance of my crimes. Why don't you let me know those circumstances."

He nicked ashes off the end of his tobacco roll. "What you did, of course, was protect the family honor."

"I beat my fiancé's father with a candlestick and stole her dowry."

"Ah, Bastardo, you believe everything you hear, and so does Don Silvestre. A friend writes him from Spain and says young Don Carlos is a thief and a blackguard. He believes it. But now another friend, me, has come and told him the truth."

"What is the truth? Will you tell me before I put my sword in *my* throat."

"The truth is that you took the blame for your older brother."

It stunned me. I repeated the words carefully. Than a second time, savoring them. "I took the blame for my older brother—to protect the family name."

I paced back and forth, feeling the words, getting into the mood of the comedia that Mateo was constructing. "Eh, my brother, the heir to the title and the family fortune, the possessor of our family's good name and honor, is a scoundrel. He violates my bride-to-be and steals my dowry. What is the honorable thing to do? If I kill him, as he so well deserves, the truth will come out, and our proud family name will be ruined. No, there is only one thing for me to do. I am the younger brother, heir to nothing, possessor of nothing. I assume the blame for my brother's foul deeds, save the family honor, and incur the punishment."

I bowed and saluted my friend with my hat. "Mateo Rosas, you are a true genius. When you told me you had constructed a comedia for the don, I saw only disaster. If we presented this play in Mexico City and Seville, we would be hailed as heroes of the quill and paper. This play would gain us the fortune we never acquired—at least legally."

Mateo tried to appear modest. "Don Silvestre accepted the story as readily as Moses accepted the word of God. It is now chiseled in stone in the old man's mind. He was embellishing upon it as I explained it to Eléna."

Did I hear him right? Did he just say that he had explained it to Eléna? Did he also whisper it in the viceroy's ear? Amigos, was I correct in my assumption that Mateo would someday get me hanged if I was not duly punished for my own crimes?

"Bastardo, you better have some of this wine. Your face was the color of death, and now it is turning to fire."

"When did you see Eléna?"

"This afternoon, when she came to Don Silvestre's after your meeting with the viceroy."

"Why did she go to Don Silvestre's?"

"To talk to the old man about you. She wanted the details of your crimes, to see if she could assist you in gaining pardon."

"And you told her this tale about taking the blame for my brother after you had convinced the don?"

"Actually, the inspiration for the tale came when I saw the lovely Eléna. Bastardo, you have supreme taste in women. She is a little delicate and intelligent for me, with a little more above the neckline and a little less below it than I prefer, but her eyes would conquer the soul of Eros himself."

"Explain exactly what occurred. Do not leave out any details. When I murder you, I want to have no feelings of guilt."

"This beautiful woman came in. She pled her case before me and the don, telling us in every detail how you had fought off a dozen pirates—"

"A dozen?"

"Some number like that. As I listened to her, I realized she loved you."

"Don't say that; I can't stand the hurt."

"We must face the truth. We have come back for revenge, but hate is only on one side of life's coin. The other side is love. When I heard the love in her voice, I knew I had to ensure that her love did not go unfulfilled. Did you know that my comedias always had happy endings? Eh, it's the truth. In matters of love, tragedy is so ubiquitous that I wrote only endings in which love triumphed."

"What did she say when she learned I had taken the blame for my brother?"

"She cried, Bastardo, she cried from joy and relief. She said that she knew that you were a good and honorable man from the very moment she looked into your eyes."

"*¡Ay de mí!*" I sat down and buried my face in my hands. The angel was so blinded by my saving her that she saw a half blood lépero as a man of honor. If she knew the truth about me, she would run in horror.

"And Don Silvestre? He did not deny the story?"

"He embellished upon it himself. It caught the old knight's fancy. And come to find out, the older brother was a scoundrel, too. But his black deeds were always washed away to save the family honor. It was right and proper to the don that a younger brother would make such a sacrifice. He got so caught up in the tale, he began to imagine that every black deed Don Carlos stood accused of was done in the name of honor. Your innocence, however, must never be disclosed, not if you are to protect the family name. I did, of course, agree that the viceroy should know. Eléna rushed to tell him the news."

I groaned. "And Luis. She will tell Luis. And she will tell her maid, who will tell the maid next door . . ."

Mateo shrugged. "And in a few weeks we will be gone."

"But Eléna will be left with the scandal. Today I deliberately insulted Luis by implying I was romantically interested in Eléna. While I angered him, I was no serious threat as the disgraced Don Carlos. Now I am doubly a hero. I sacrificed myself for my brother and almost threw down my life for Eléna. When she tells Luis that I am twice the hero, he will see me as a threat."

Mateo shook his head. "The viceroy would never let you marry Eléna even if you had repelled that entire pirate attack singlehandedly. You are still the third son of a minor family. Luis will be a marqués when his father dies. Socially, his claim to nobility is as strong as the viceroy's. That's why he is forcing her to marry him. It is Luis's pride that will make him kill you, not the threat to his marriage. Of course, if he finds out you are meeting Eléna, he will kill you sooner rather than later."

Another knife went into my gut. "Tell me that you have not done something as foolish as setting up an assignation with her."

He said nothing. I waited until he'd drained another goblet full of wine.

"What did you do?"

"Luis is a swine."

"What did you do?"

"The girl wishes to talk to you, to beg for forgiveness in ever doubting you. If you handle the matter right, you will partake of her favors before Luis gets the chance."

"Are you loco? Do you think I would use Eléna to avenge myself on my enemies?"

"You ask if I am loco? You have come back to New Spain to kill her husband-to-be and perhaps destroy her uncle, who raised her as a daughter. And you think you can do these deeds without damage to her?"

He got up from sitting on the edge of the fountain. "Bastardo, I will have to work very hard, very hard indeed, to write a happy ending to the tragic-comedia that you have begun."

ONE HUNDRED AND NINETEEN

THE MEETING MATEO had set up between Eléna and myself was arranged at the house of Don Silvestre's widowed daughter. Mateo said the widow, who was only a few years older than me, rarely used the house; she spent most of her time at the household of her father. The widow had many charms, Mateo told me, alluding to the fact that he would ensure she did not wither from lack of love.

I was nervous as I waited in the courtyard. An elderly india and her husband appeared to be the only servants at the house. On a small table, they had set out sweetmeats and wine. Darkness had fallen and they illuminated the area around me with candles. Protected by high walls, the location was private. A perfect place for a rendezvous with another man's woman.

I felt as if I had stepped onto a stage featuring the doomed lovers, Calisto and Melibea, if not an even more tragic comedia called *Romeo and Juliet,* a play Mateo said was written by an Englishman named Shakespeare. The quandary Mateo spoke of, that I could not destroy the others without harming Eléna, weighed heavy on my heart. The Fates were casting lots for my soul.

I heard the carriage outside and tensed with anticipation.

When she came through the gate, I got up slowly from where I had been sitting at the edge of the fountain. She had changed into a black dress and wore a long, silk shawl over her head and draped down her shoulders. I had half expected her to wear a mask as was so common among the ladies of the city when traveling to an assignation, but no one would have recognized her with the shawl anyway.

"Doña Eléna." I bowed.

"Don Carlos."

To give my hands something to do, I gestured at the table of sweetmeats. "Our hostess is not at home, but she kindly provided a table of delicacies."

"I have met Doña Teodora. She is a good woman who cares well for her elderly father."

"I understand you were with the father today."

She came to me, holding out her hand. "Oh, Carlos, I am so happy you are not the scoundrel others claim you to be. Your sacrifice to protect your family name was that of a martyred saint."

I took her hand and kissed it.

"Eléna, I have to tell you the truth"—at least part of it—"I am not the person you think I am."

"I know that."

"You do?"

"Of course. The man I met at Don Silvestre explained about your brother."

"No, no, it's not just that, it's . . ."

"Yes?"

It was impossible. If I told her the truth, she would run screaming from the house. But I hated living a lie. My entire life had been a lie, and with her I wished to lay my soul naked.

"There are things about me that I cannot reveal, things that you would never understand, some that would make you hate me. But there is one truth that you may depend upon. From the moment I first saw you, I loved you."

"And I, you."

She said it so simply, I was caught by surprise.

"Did you want me to hide my feelings?" she asked.

"It's impossible for us, you're betrothed to another."

I was holding onto her hand. I drew her closer and she pulled away. She walked around the courtyard for a moment.

"Don't you find it strange," she said, "how we of the higher class of society have less freedom? Our possessions, even our names, entrap us. A man and a woman of common blood can love and marry whom they like." She turned and faced me. "My uncle can make me marry Luis, but he can never make me love him. I do not hate Luis, and I believe he truly loves me. He has refused offers of marriage from families whose daughters have larger dowries and certainly fairer looks. But for me, marriage to him would be a prison. That's why I was willing to go to another type of prison, a convent, where at least I would have had the freedom to read books and write what I have the vanity to call poetry."

"Your poems are the songs of angels."

"Fine words, Don Carlos, but I hardly think you have heard of my poems all the way in Spain. My poems have been rarely published even in the colony."

"You do yourself an injustice. I was given this book to read when I was sailing from Seville."

I showed her a book of poems I had printed for her.

She shook her head, her eyes glowing. "I wrote that years ago. There must be a book or two still in existence. And it made it all the way to Seville?"

"To the whole world. I'm certain there is a copy right now in the queen's boudoir in Madrid."

"More likely on the Inquisition's evidence table. Who gave you the book?"

"I don't know the man's name. He was reading a book in a cantina and offered it to me when he learned I was to take a sea voyage." Eh, amigos, do lies flow like honey off my tongue?

I heard a noise at the wall bordering the street. A head popped into view for just the briefest moment before the man dropped back down. I ran out the gate, but the man was on a horse galloping away before I was able to seize him.

Eléna came out behind me. "I recognize him. One of Luis's servants set to spy on me."

She left without further word. Concerned for her reputation, I did not try to stop her. Under ordinary circumstances, I would soon be receiving Luis's seconds to deliver the challenge for a duel, and I would welcome the opportunity to kill him. I suspected, though, that the challenge would not come. Not because Luis feared me, but because of the scandal it would create so soon after I had saved Eléna.

I stood for a moment in the courtyard and closed my eyes, listening again to her saying that she loved me. But who did she love? The martyr-hero Don Carlos? Or the poor lépero boy grown into a notorious bandit?

ONE HUNDRED AND TWENTY

We used the hired coach to pick up the old caballero and take him to the party. I was very nervous, more than I had been in any other social situation in my life. Mateo had thoroughly investigated the arrangements for the party and had a plan for every contingency. He was still caught up in the idea that we were all actors in a play that he had written. He even had written in a part for the lépero boy, Jaime, to play that night.

"If the old man recognizes that I am not Don Carlos, what will we do?" I asked, as the carriage wheels brought us closer and closer to Don Silvestre's door. I already knew his answers. I had bemoaned the questions over and over, and finally he was just responding with curtness.

"Murder him."

"And Isabella? If we encounter the Bitch of Babylon?"

"Murder her."

Fine advice, none of which he and I were mentally capable of carrying out, although I would be sorely tempted in regard to Isabella. Mateo had learned that the Church had agreed to annul her marriage to Don Julio, and the woman had married a Zacatecas silver king within a year of the don's death. Naturally, she had a house, not only in the City of Silver, but in the capital. As best as Mateo could discover, she had the Ciudad Mexico house torn down and was in the process of building a palace built to rival the viceroy's. He assumed that she would stay in Zacatecas during the renovations, but he was not certain. As for myself, I was certain that she would be in the party's reception line, ready to clutch her chest and scream the moment she saw us.

Mateo doubted she would recognize either of us. He had removed his beard and left only a rather large mustache. Like me, his hair was closely cropped. The putas at the tavern where we had been staying had dyed his hair and mustache red. With a red eye patch, red hat, red doublet, and red pants, he was as inconspicuous as a peacock in a flock of pigeons.

"Flamboyance defines my disguise," he said earlier, as I gawked at the clothes he intended to wear to the viceroy's ball. "I learned the art of disguise when I had to play several roles in the same play. If Isabella sees me, she will not recognize me for the don's friend."

"You will hide in plain sight?"

"Exactly so."

Eh, we had seen Mateo on stage, had we not, amigos? He is a fine actor—sometimes. Other times he commits the actor's sin of overdramatizing his role. Like everything else about Mateo, there was no middle ground. When he was good on stage, he was the best. And when he was bad, Dios mio, he incited riots.

If the Book of Fates determined that Isabella would be at the party, I hoped Isabella would, as usual, be too caught up in herself to recognize us.

"I will kill myself if I am exposed before Eléna."

Mateo twirled one of the ends of his mustache. "Compadre, your problem is that you do not accept women for what we really need them for. You want her to be puta and angel. I'm happy with just the woman of sin."

When we pulled up in front of the gate to Don Silvestre's house, I waited inside the coach while Mateo went to fetch the don. I tapped my knee nervously with the tip of my dagger, more inclined to cut my own throat than the old man's if he exposed me.

The only light at the gate was a large candle in a bronze and glass holder. It threw no light more than a couple of feet, but I skulked inside the dark coach anyway.

Despite my apprehensions, there had been one encouraging event. Miguel de Soto had shown up unexpectedly at my door. Profusely begging my pardon, he said his unnamed associates were cutting me in as a partner. But the ante had risen: I needed fifty thousand pesos to buy in.

Provoking Luis had tipped the scale. Realizing the viceroy would never permit him to kill me in a duel, he wanted to break me financially then put a dagger in my back. It was an enormous amount of money, and I agreed to only thirty thousand. I gave him three thousand pesos in gold ducats to show good faith and told him I would have the rest in a few days. Handing over the gold, I asked for more details concerning my investment.

"The price of maize is soaring," he said.

It was. Maize had all but vanished in the markets—when the warehouses were full. My new servants grumbled about it. No doubt it cut into the profits they made cheating me on food purchases.

"My partners own the maize in the warehouses. I control its distribution."

They were keeping it out of the marketplace—literally starving people—in order to drive the price up. When the price reached its peak, they would flood their brokers with grain and reap a prodigious profit. I had suspected this, but to hear it put bluntly increased my quandary about harming

Eléna. Evil manipulation of the staple could not be done without the knowledge and assent of the viceroy.

When I heard Mateo and the don, I peered out the coach window, tense. Mateo let the old man go through the gate first and hung back to fasten it.

Don Silvestre came alone toward the coach, and I opened the door.

"Carlos—" he began.

Someone shot out of the darkness and pawed at the old man's face. The don tried to grab him and the assailant shoved him back, sending him staggering back on weak knees. Mateo caught the don as he fell backward.

"Thief!" Don Silvestre yelled. "He took my eyepiece!"

I shot out of the carriage and joined Mateo and the carriage driver in a pursuit of the thief. It was hopeless, the thief had disappeared. To my relief Jaime the Lépero had played his role well.

I exchanged looks with Mateo as we hurried back to where the don was waiting by the carriage. This was the test. Taking a deep breath, I walked straight up to the old man and gave him an abrazo, a great hug.

"Don Silvestre," Mateo said, "how regretful it is that you two meet after all these years in the midst of this dreadful theft."

"My eyeglass, he took my eyeglass—and it was my only one. Only God knows when I can get a replacement."

"I heard that an eyeglass grinder had come aboard the last treasure fleet and took samples of glasses to the mining country," Mateo said. "We shall look into it, eh, Carlos."

"Carlos." The old man patted my face with his palm.

"We shall not let this tragic theft ruin the reunion of you and Carlos," Mateo said. "Off to the viceroy's palace," he told the driver, "the entire city is awaiting the guest of honor."

Mateo kept up a continuous flow of chatter all the way to the palace. What little I said was in such soft tones, the half deaf don missed most of it. Along the way, Mateo lit a tobacco twist with a candle kept lit in a glass enclosure on the side of the carriage. He deliberately held the candle up to illuminate my face in the dark coach. The ball would be brilliantly lit, and we were better off testing the don's eyesight here than in front of a hundred people.

"What do you think, Don Silvestre?" Mateo asked. "Has Carlos changed much since you saw him as a teenager?"

The don leaned forward and squinted at me. "The spit and image of his father," the don said. "I would have picked him out of an army of a thousand as his father's son."

I had to resist the impulse to cross myself and thank God aloud for making the old caballero so vain he would not admit to the infirmities of old age.

One test had been passed. But I knew the Dark Sisters who weaved our fates were not to be so easily appeased. A strange feeling gripped me as we passed through the palace gates. I had always wondered who I really was. Telemachus, the son of Odysseus, asks in the *Odyssey:* "Does any man truly know who his father is?" I had asked such questions my whole life long, about my father, my mother, and a loco old matrone who dressed in black and sought to drink my blood.

Well, the fray often said God's greatest gift was unanswered prayers, and at last I understood the wisdom in that dictum.

Now I feared God would answer those questions.

ONE HUNDRED AND TWENTY-ONE

I HAD ATTENDED the ribald parties of Seville's theater people, but this was the first grand society ball I had attended. We were greeted by an officer of the guard who stepped smartly in his magnificent uniform as he escorted us to the palace entrance. There, aides to the viceroy were waiting to accompany us to the ballroom. Both aides looked askance at Mateo's crimson garb and eye patch. Mateo's hard-edged swordsman comportment shined through the silk clothes. Had he not been with me, the guest of honor, no doubt they would have been more inclined to call the capitán of the guard before permitting him into the ballroom.

The hall mirrors leading to the ballroom glittered from the candlelight and torches as well as reflecting the brightly trimmed uniforms of the honor guards lining the way.

At the end of the hall, we passed through open doors into a three-story ballroom that could have housed several residences comparable to my rented one, grounds included. Like the mirrored hallway, it blazed with candlelight and torches. The ceiling, fittings, and moldings glistened with silver and gilt, and for a moment I was stunned by the ballroom's magnificence. I found it hard to feign the arrogant indifference of a hidalgo.

Several hundred people drank and talked and strolled around the floor. Still, every eye turned to me as I paused at the top of the sweeping marble staircase leading down to the ballroom floor. I had never in my life felt so out of place, and I was sweating from every pore.

The viceroy came up beside me. With a grand gesture, he proclaimed, "Señoras, señoritas, and caballeros, I present Don Carlos Vasquez de Monterey, the hero of Veracruz."

The audience lined up on two sides of the room, leaving only a narrow walkway between. The orchestra struck up music. The viceroy took my arm and guided me down the steps. I was to be paraded through the party so that everyone could get a close look at me.

Ay, how many in the room could identify me? Was one of the fat merchants I had robbed along the Jalapa road waiting to greet me? A bishop whose clothes I had stolen, along with his purse and mule? A lady from whose neck I had ripped a pearl necklace?

Life is a circle and as I listened to the applause from the audience, I had the terrible feeling that the victim of every evil deed I had ever committed had assembled in the ballroom to expose me before the woman I loved.

I moved stiffly down the steps, a frozen smile on my face, my mind a shambles. I kept a tight hold on Don Silvestre's arm to slow our step. My eye had caught a familiar figure on the other side of the room and I almost stumbled.

Isabella.

I saw a flash of red out of the corner of my eye. I assumed the red caballero, my compadre, had just fled the room.

Fighting the impulse to run, walking down the aisle, nodding at the smiling people on both sides, I knew it would soon turn ugly. I feared it in my bones. Isabella was on the far end of the receiving line. When I reached her, all hell would break loose. I did not care what Mateo said about her not recognizing me without a beard. She was nothing if not cunning. My eyes would give her pause. She would put her Chinese fan up to her face and her eyes would narrow as she searched my face. There would be a moment of puzzlement, then astonishment, and horror that brought forth a scream.

Even my friend, Mateo, who had faced a thousand heathen swords, or so he said, had fled the witch.

Eléna stood next to Luis. She smiled her love. Luis' face held no expression, but I did not need a sorcerer to divine his thoughts. When Isabella began screaming and the party goers turned rabid against me, Luis would be the first to unsheathe his dagger.

My worse nightmare was that I was to be exposed in front of Eléna. What would she think when her hero was dragged to the dungeon by palace guards? The next time she saw my head it would be impaled atop the city gate.

My instinct to run was overwhelming but my knees were buckling. All the while I drew closer to Isabella. Thoughts raced through my mind. Was this how it would end? Instead of bringing down Luis and Ramon, I would end up being exposed and arrested? Where was Ramon? No doubt he was in the audience somewhere. Would he recognize the mestizo boy he had tried to kill half a lifetime ago. Would he join Isabella in exposing my frauds?

A woman screamed.

Isabella dashed into the open aisle I was coming down with Don Silvestre and the viceroy.

I nearly jumped out of my skin.

Her dress was on fire.

As men beat at the flames, I saw a figure in red disappearing into the back of the crowd. I grinned like a monkey, most impolite considering the lady's distress, but I could not suppress it.

Eh, amigos, did you really think that my old compadre would abandon me?

Sadly, the fire did not consume Isabella, merely the back of her dress and some petticoats. However, it did require that she retire from the party. She left in a state of hysterics. The assumption was that she had gotten too close to a candle.

"Music," the viceroy instructed an aide. "tell the orchestra to play gay music. I want people to dance, to forget this unfortunate incident."

He apologized profusely and spoke darkly of Isabella. "That woman will not be invited again to the palace." He leaned closer and whispered. "Her former husband was a marrano."

As the dancing began, with Luis and Eléna leading the procession, I left Don Silvestre with friends of his and faded back against a wall. The silly grin had faded from my face. My nerves were raw, and I struggled to get my breath back. I looked around to see if there was anyone else I recognized. Ramon was not present as far as I could tell.

I grabbed a goblet of wine to calm my nerves and then another. And another. Soon my head felt lighter. But my heart was still heavy from watching Luis and Eléna dance time and again. She glanced at me once and I smiled. I knew he was deliberately monopolizing her dancing.

Stepping aside to avoid servants with a food cart, I brushed against a man.

"Perdón!" I said.

"It is I who should beg for pardon," the man said. "Like Agesilan of Colchos who mounted a hippogriff to save the beauteous Diana, you deserve all of the praise Constantinople can reap upon you."

The man looked vaguely familiar to me. Not as if I knew him, but as if *I should have known him.* There was something about his features, his eyes, that stirred a memory in me.

"Thank you, señor, but I'm afraid that I'm not as lucky as Agesilan or any of the other caballeros of old. You see, in the tales of old, the hero always wed the beautiful woman that he had saved. In my case . . ."

"You're right. Instead of the hero, the princess will wed a villain."

The wine and the man's sympathetic remark loosened my tongue.

"Truer words were never spoken. Eléna must marry a man who believes a woman should be broken like a horse."

"I see you know Don Luis well despite your short time in the city. And I'm afraid your assessment of him is correct. Poor Eléna. She was willing to hide away in a convent to avoid marriage him because he will never permit her the freedom to read and write. And she's a fine poet. The words that are smothered inside her will be a loss to the world. But you must not put the entire blame on Luis. He was raised poorly for the heir of a great name and title. People believe it is his father's fault. The father is a notoriously bad gambler. A bad poet. Even a drunk. If it wasn't for Luis, the family coat of arms would be for sale to swine merchants."

"Eh, I've heard the father was a bad one, a man who squandered his wealth on gambling and women. Only his title has kept him from the poorhouse. But that is no excuse for the son. There are those of us who were born with so much less and who have had to deal with so much more adversity than a father who was a ne'er-do-well."

"Of course, and you are one of them. Eléna has told me

how you sacrificed yourself for your older brother."

"I—you know Eléna?"

"I am also a writer of poetry. Though unlike Eléna, I am a writer of bad poetry. But our mutual interest over the years has given us the opportunity to speak many times. To the point where I count her as a friend."

"Then as a friend, how do we keep her from marrying that blackguard Luis?"

"Ah, amigo, you are new to the city. Be here awhile and you will find out that what Luis wants, he gets. He performed many services for the viceroy to gain Eléna's hand after she refused him repeatedly. No, I am afraid nothing can be done. Hopefully Eléna will have the courage and determination to insist upon writing her poetry after marriage."

"If there is a marriage," I said, darkly.

The man patted me on the shoulder. "You should not speak in such terms. If it gets back to Luis, he will have to challenge you. You showed great courage in Veracruz, but dueling is another sport. Besides being a fine swordsman, Luis is a scoundrel who doesn't always play fair. If he could not beat you honorably, he would have you murdered by assailants. I speak now as a friend and admirer of Eléna's and a man grateful for your services."

"You must know Luis well," I said.

"Very well. I'm his father."

I sipped my wine slowly, watching the dancers. I knew of him, of course. Don Eduardo Montez de la Cerda. After a moment I turned back to him.

"Don't take offense," he said, "I truly am Eléna's friend. I love her like the daughter I never had." He looked away from me. "I love her like the son I wish I had, instead of the one I deserved."

What I heard in his voice was not pity for himself but regret—and recrimination toward himself.

"I speak to you as a friend, Don Carlos, because I know Eléna is your friend." He locked eyes with me. "Perhaps in a way that must remain unspoken, she is more than a friend.

And because of your own sad family situation"—he saluted me with his goblet—"my lips are also no doubt steered by the wine I've imbibed this day. I feel I can reveal a little of the troubles in my heart. I truly do wish that something would happen to prevent the marriage, but it is impossible. And I do not blame Luis for all that he became. Luis never had the father he deserved. Nor mother. His mother died while he was relatively young. His grandmother, my mother, dominated the household. My own father had been weak and produced a weak son. My mother made up for my weaknesses by instilling her ruthless ambitions on Luis when she failed to drive them into me. While this was happening, I hid my head deeper in the wine keg and the card tables. Each year as Luis became stronger, I became weaker." He saluted me again with his goblet. "And that, Don Carlos, is the sad story of my life."

I became aware of something as he spoke. "Eléna asked you to speak to me. She told you of my love for her."

"Yes. She loves and respects you enough to want to ensure that you live a long and happy life. That will not occur if you antagonize Luis with attention toward her. She will not dance with you tonight, nor see you again except in public. This is to protect you."

I started to tell him that I did not need her protection when he grabbed my arm.

"Ah, my mother has spotted us talking. Come along and meet her." He guided me toward an old woman seated in a chair across the room. "You will learn more about Luis in a few minutes with her than pondering for a year."

I followed along, but my attention was drawn to Eléna. She was dancing with another partner, and I smiled at her as she swirled by. She gave me a small smile and quickly turned her head. It took a moment to clear my head and remember that his mother was the old matrona who wanted me dead.

"My mother probably wants to meet you because Luis has mentioned you unfavorably. Don't be offended if she seems like she is sizing you up for the scaffold. She has worked as hard for this marriage with Eléna as Luis has."

Could I have avoided the confrontation? Yes. But after spending half of my life fleeing from the old woman's unnamed wrath, I permitted my feet to move forward.

A humorless rasp of a chuckle escaped my lips. "Your mother and Luis are vipers."

He shot me a look. Regardless of his candor about his own life, it was not gentlemanly of me to speak disrespectfully of his mother. In other circumstances he would have called me to the dueling field for such a remark.

"Do not blame my mother. Any mother who birthed a son like me would wonder why God had damned her."

The old woman's eyes met mine as we approached, and despite having steeled my nerves, I was jolted. The old matrona sent my anger racing. This woman had sent Ramon to kill Fray Antonio. Overcome by rage, I jerked my arm from Don Eduardo's at the same time the old woman gaped and started up from her seat.

"Wha—what's the matter?" Don Eduardo asked.

An audible gasp of pain emitted from the old woman. She took a step, her face ashen, her eyes wide, her lips trying to form words. She fell forward, collapsing on the floor.

Don Eduardo rushed to her, crying her name. In a second Luis was beside him. I pushed through the crowd that had immediately gathered around her. Lying on the floor, she refused offers of aid and gestured her son and grandson closer to her trembling lips. The old woman whispered her last words. As she spoke, both Don Eduardo and Luis looked at me with as much shock as the old woman had when she recognized me.

I glared back at them, defiantly. I do not know what words were spoken, but I know they were to throw my life into more turmoil. She had whispered a secret to her son and grandson, a terrible secret that had plagued my life from the day I was born. While I had not heard the words, I had felt them. They twisted my heart and raised the hair on the back of my neck.

My eyes went from the two kneeling beside the old woman to a mirror behind them. I saw my own reflection.

And knew the truth.

ONE HUNDRED AND TWENTY-TWO

THE OLD WOMAN'S eyes haunted me in a troubled sleep that came after hours of even more troubled consciousness.

Mateo was not at the rented house when I returned from the viceroy's ball. I had left while the room was still buzzing about the death of the matrona. Eléna had tried to ask me a question as I pushed through the crowd, and I had ignored her.

At my house a message awaited me that Mateo had gone to "comfort" Don Silvestre's daughter. Mateo's idea of comforting the woman was to give her pleasure in bed. And take a bit himself.

A gallery of the dead—Fray Antonio, the Healer, Don Julio, Inez, and Juana—shared my night, invading my dreams and waking moments. Only the Healer seemed at peace. The others were restless because they were unavenged.

But mostly I saw the old woman. The Fates had brought me full circle. Back to the woman who had started it all in Veracruz. I never understood the old woman's hatred for me. I always assumed that it was a blood feud. But I no longer believed that. Looking at the three of them, the dying old woman with her son and grandson, I had gained an insight into the mystery that had dominated my life. And felt the earth heating up under my feet.

Early in the morning a servant brought me a message.

Don Eduardo was waiting in his carriage. He asked that I take a ride with him so that we might speak. The summons was neither expected nor a surprise. It was just another hand the Dark Sisters had dealt me. I joined him in the carriage.

"Do you mind if we ride along the Alameda?" he asked. "I enjoy it in the cool of the morning. Quiet and peaceful. So unlike the parade of male egos and female vanities that dominate it in the afternoon."

I sat quietly, listening to the carriage wheels, not really looking at him nor avoiding his eyes. A strange calmness had grasped me despite my troubled night. I actually felt more at peace than I had felt since I began a fugitive life in Veracruz half a lifetime ago.

"You have not expressed condolences at the death of my mother, but I suppose that is to be expected."

I met his eye. "Your mother was evil. She will rot in hell."

"I am afraid, Cristóbal, that we, and Luis, shall join her. But you are right about her. I actually hated her myself. One is supposed to love and honor one's mother, but I never truly loved her, nor her, me. She hated me because I was too much like my father, too much inclined to words than actions. He brought her to the New World because he had nearly beggared them in the old. She sent him to an early grave with her hate. When I turned out to be worse than my father, she set me aside in her mind and kept the reins of the family tightly in her fist.

"Have you seen Pedro Calderón's dramatic comedia, *La hija del aire?*" he asked.

I shook my head. "I was told of the play in Seville."

The Daughter of the Air was said to be Calderón's masterpiece. It was the story of the Babylonian warrior queen, Semiramis. Her greed for power led her to conceal and imprison her own son when it came time to ascend the throne. She then assumed the throne herself, dressed as a man, impersonating her son.

"If my mother had been able to get rid of me and wear my face, she would have done so."

"Murder you? As she has tried to murder me?" The words were wrapped in bitterness that suddenly welled up in me.

"I have always been weak." He spoke not to me but to the open window of the carriage.

"Why was it so important to murder me? Why was it so important that Fray Antonio had to be murdered to find me?"

"Fray Antonio,"—he shook his head—"a good man. I didn't know my mother was involved. When I heard he was murdered by the boy he raised, I assumed the truth of the accusation."

"Assumed the truth? Or hid behind it?"

"I told you I was not a good father. To Luis. Or to you."

I knew he was my father when I saw my reflection in the mirror while he and Luis were kneeling at the side of the old woman. Looking from their faces to mine had brought home the truth of the disturbance that had plagued me each time I looked at their faces.

"It doesn't make any sense. I am your son, but I'm also just another mestizo bastard in a land full of such bastardos. To have lain with my mother, Maria, and made her with child . . . that's no more than what thousands of other españols have done. Why would this bastardo create enough hate to spawn murder?"

"Your mother's name was Verónica, not Maria." He spoke the name quietly.

"Verónica." I rolled the name off of my tongue. "Was my mother Spanish?"

"No, she was india. Very proud india. My family—your Spanish family—is related to royalty. My grandfather was a cousin to King Carlos. Your mother was of royalty, too, indio royalty. Her blood traced back to one of Montezuma's sisters."

"Eh, that's wonderful. But that does not make me a prince of two races, but merely another bastardo without land or title."

"I was deeply in love with your mother, a lovely flower.

I have never seen another woman who had her natural beauty and grace. Had she been born in Spain, she would have ended up as the concubine of a prince or duke." He had stopped talking to me and had gone back to talking to the window.

"Tell me about my mother."

"She was the only woman I ever loved. She was the daughter of a cacique of a village on our hacienda. Like most other hacendados, we were rarely at the ranch. But after my father died, when I was twenty years old, my mother exiled me to the hacienda for a time. She wanted to get me out of the city and what she considered corrupt influences, to get me away from books and poetry and make me what she considered to be a real man, un hombre. There was a man at the hacienda, the majordomo, whom my mother considered to be just the person to turn her boy into a wearer of big spurs."

"Ramon de Alva."

"Yes, Ramon. Then, just a hacienda manager. Eventually one of the richest men in New Spain, a man not just with the viceroy's ear, but who knows the dirty secrets of half the noble families in the colony. And from what I've heard, one who has filled Don Diego's pockets many times."

"Little of it honestly gained."

Don Eduardo shrugged. "Honesty is a gem with many facets. It sparkles differently for each of us."

"Try telling that to the thousands of indios who died in the mines and the tunnel project." There was still poison in my words, but my own heart was slowly softening toward the man who was my first father. He did not seem to harbor malice. Instead, his greatest sin was that he looked away—and walked away—from evil.

He grinned with resignation. "As you can see from the human toad who sits beside you, not even the renowned Ramon de Alva could create a miracle and make a decent man of me. My mother wanted me to love the smell of gold, while I instead sniffed roses. It was not saddle leather I wanted between my legs but the soft touch of a woman.

Obeying my mother's command, I went to the hacienda and came under the tutelage of Ramon. To my mother's eternal horror, instead of getting me away from trouble in the city, I carried it with me like an old trunk. I opened that trunk the first time I saw your mother.

"Verónica was coming to church the first time I saw her. As the hacendado, it was my duty to greet the flock as they came for Sunday service. I was standing next to the village priest when she came forward with her mother."

"The village priest was Fray Antonio."

"Yes, Fray Antonio. The fray and I became close, like brothers, during my time on the hacienda. He had an interest in the classics as I did. I had brought almost my entire library with me, and I gave him a number of books as a gift."

"They were branded with your initial. The same books that the fray used to teach me Latin and the classics."

"Bueno. I am glad they saw good use. As I was saying, I was standing by the church door when Verónica came forward. When I looked into her eyes that first time, my heart was torn out of my chest faster than any Aztec priest ever ripped the heart from a sacrifice victim. We live in a world in which who we choose to marry is decided upon rationally, but there is no rational judgment involved in who we love. I was completely helpless. I saw her. I loved her. The fact that she was an india and I was a Spaniard with a centuries-old title mattered not. No alchemist, no sorcerer, could have concocted a potion that put me deeper into a state of love enchantment than I went into the moment I saw her. I even told Ramon about my affection for the girl."

My father shook his head. "Ramon encouraged my feelings for her. Not in an honorable way, of course, but in the way Spaniards look at india girls, with the eye in their crotch. He never really understood me, or my affection for Verónica. I truly loved her, worshipped her. I would have been content living on the hacienda for the rest of my life at the feet of your mother. Ramon never understood because he is not capable of love. Nor was my mother. Had their ages been closer, he would have made a fine consort for her. They would never have married because of their different social positions, but they could have lain in bed at night and excited each other with their passions of greed and corruption."

Don Eduardo turned back to the window. "Fray Antonio, poor devil. He should never have been a priest. He had the sort of loving heart toward all people that makes a saint, but he also had desires that were human. He was a friend and companion to Verónica and me as we trod the road of young love, discreetly leaving us alone in green meadows when we lay down to consummate our feelings for each other. If the fray had been more Spanish and less a humanist, tragedy would have been avoided."

"It should be some comfort to him in his martyr's grave that he was too good a man," I said, not hiding the sarcasm in my voice.

He turned back to me, his sad and lonely eyes moist. "You want me to take responsibility for the fray's death. Yes, Cristóbal, it is just another one of many mortal sins I shall answer for. Did you ever wonder how you came to be named Cristóbal?"

I shook my head.

"One of your late great-great-great-ancestors was a Cristóbal. Of all the marqués' in our bloodline, he was the one I admired the most. After his death, no other marques in our family was given his name because he had left a stain on the family honor. He married a Moorish princess, a blood taint that took two centuries to purge."

"I'm honored," I said, without feeling. "How appropriate that another with a blood taint should bear the name."

"I understand your feelings." He peered closely at me. "You have led a rare life, perhaps the most unusual in the history of the colony. You have walked the streets as an outcast and ridden in a carriage as a caballero. You must know things about the peoples and places of New Spain that the viceroy and his advisors cannot even imagine."

"I know so little about life that I actually believe in the

ultimate goodness of people. Fortunately for mankind, the world is not entirely composed of people like you and your mother."

My words seemed to strike a chord with him. Hurt was expressed in his eyes and lips. "I am the harshest critic of myself. Not even Luis or my mother were able to point out my deficiencies better than I have been able to myself. But coming from you, my son who is a stranger, it cuts me deeper than from the others. I sense that you have seen so much of life that you have knowledge and wisdom beyond your years, and that you see my faults more clearly than they do because you are so innocent yourself."

"Innocent?" I laughed. "You know my name is Cristóbal. But I am also known as Cristo the Bastardo. Liar and thief are my better qualities."

"Yes, Cristóbal, but which of your many wrongful deeds were not done under coercion? You have the excuse of ignorance and necessity to justify your actions. What excuse do those of us who were born to luxury have for our excesses? Our greed?"

"Eh, thank you, Don Eduardo." I shrugged. "I am relieved that I am a more *honorable* scoundrel than the rest of you."

He turned back to the window. It provided less animosity than me.

"I was young and foolish. Not that much has changed. Today I am just more older and foolish, but in a different way. In those days my head was full of love, and I thought that nothing else mattered. But, of course, it did. As nature would have it, the consummation of our love resulted in a child. Such a fool I was. Such a fool. My mother was visiting at the hacienda when you were born. You were only hours old when I told her and Ramon the news.

"I still remember the horror spreading across her features as I told her. For the first time in my life, I had felt power in dealing with my mother. When she understood what I had done, she turned purple. I actually feared that she would fall dead on the floor. In one of the those strange twists of fate that have plagued our lives since that day, she dropped dead at the sight of you, the child she thought she had killed."

"How did Maria come to be called my mother?"

"My boyish glee at shocking my own mother had worse consequences than I could ever have imagined, consequences that would have taxed the mind of the devil to conjure. My mother immediately sent Ramon out to kill Verónica and the baby."

"Holy Mother of God."

"No, unholy mother, my unholy mother. Ramon went out to kill her and the baby. One of the servants overheard my mother's plans and ran and told Fray Antonio. The good fray was resourceful, if nothing else. Another woman had given birth within hours of Verónica birthing you."

"Maria."

"Yes, Maria. She gave birth to a stillborn child. It was said to be the fray's child. I don't know; I suppose it was. Like you, it was a boy."

"Verónica switched babies."

"Yes, she switched babies. She gave you to Maria and took the dead baby. She ran into the jungle with the dead baby and Ramon pursuing her. She came to a cliff overlooking a river. With Ramon almost to her, she threw herself and the baby over the cliff."

With tears flooding my eyes, I reached over and slapped Don Eduardo. He stared at me with the same sort of shock I had seen on his mother's face when she saw me standing next to him and recognized me.

"And what did you do while my mother was sacrificing her life for your sins? Playing cards? Drinking wine? Wondering what india girl you could use to shock your mother with again?"

He stared at me in agony, a whipped dog. I could imagine the rest of the story. A hurried marriage to a suitable woman of Spanish blood. The birth of an heir.

"You've left one thing out of your story, haven't you? You have not told me all of the truth. You have not told me why my birth was different than the army of bastardos left behind by you Spanish who dug your spurs into india girls."

The coach came to a halt. I didn't notice it, but we had pulled through the entrance of a home. There was something familiar about the house. I realized it almost at the same moment the coach door opened.

It was the house where Isabella had her trysts with Ramon de Alva. The house that Mateo and I had entered disguised as women to beat the truth out of Ramon.

The other coach door opened.

Ramon was on one side. Luis on the other.

I looked to my father. Tears flowed down his cheeks.

"I'm sorry, Cristóbal. I told you. I am not a strong man."

ONE HUNDRED AND TWENTY-THREE

CRISTO THE BASTARDO, I salute you."

My admirer was Ramon de Alva. Sitting in the carriage, I had no opportunity to draw my sword. Not that it would have served me well. Besides Ramon and Luis, there were two tough-looking hombres I took to be Ramon's henchmen and the carriage driver to deal with.

They took me into the house and strung me up to the carriage wheel–sized candleholder that hung from a chain to the ceiling. They put a noose around my neck and a chair under my feet. The irony of being subjected to the same torture Mateo and I had put Ramon through was not lost on me.

Once I was tied, only Ramon and Luis stayed in the room. My father never got out of the carriage.

"I salute you," Ramon said, "because you have risen above all adversity. Except for now, of course. Who would have imagined that a lépero boy would become the colony's most notorious bandit? And the bandit would become it's most celebrated hero, a man of such courage that the viceroy gives a grand ball so the entire city can honor him for fighting off pirates."

"Chingo tu madre!" It was the most provocative insult I could think of as I stood on my tiptoes with a nose around my neck and my time on earth in short supply.

"As I told you, amigo, it was your mother who got fucked."

He kicked the chair out from under me. My body dropped for a split second, falling just a few inches. When it jerked to a stop, it felt as if my head was being wrenched from my shoulders. The jerking tightened the noose around my neck like an iron garrote. I could not breathe. I could not think. The rest of my body was electrified. My legs shook uncontrollably. Through the fog I heard my father yelling. The chair was put back under my feet. I swayed dizzily as I gasped for air and tried to maintain my balance on the chair.

"You said he would not be hurt!" Don Eduardo shouted.

"Get him out of here," Ramon told Luis.

Ramon walked around my chair, a jungle cat pacing around a staked-out lamb, calculating which part of the body it would rip apart first.

Luis joined him a moment later. "When we are through with this one, I'm going to send my father to his grave. My grandmother is not here to deal with him, and I have nothing but contempt for him."

Ramon took a gold coin from his pocket. He held it up to show it to me.

"Do you recognize this coin?" he asked me.

I sputtered an insult, something from my street days, but it came out as gibberish because the noose was still too tight. Why was he showing me the coin? Why didn't he just kill me?

"An interesting coin." Ramon examined the coin, turning

it over. "A very special coin. Do you know why it's a special coin, Cristo?"

"Why are we delaying?" Luis asked. "Let's torture the truth out of him and then kill him."

Eh, this was my brother talking. I gibbered an incoherent insult to him.

"Patience, compadre," Ramon said to Luis, "remember that patience is a virtue. This is a tough hombre we are dealing with. Eh, Cristo, you are a tough hombre, no? You have survived everything thrown at you and come out stronger. Until now."

He kicked the chair out from under me. I strangled and kicked. Again, it felt as if my head was going to separate from my shoulders. After a moment the chair came back under my feet.

"You know what the worse part is of this dilemma you are in? Each time I kick the chair from your feet, your neck stretches a little more. After three or four times it will snap. But no, not with the big break your neck gets when you drop on a gallows. This fall will not kill you, not right away. Amigo, it will leave you crippled. You will not be able to move your arms and legs. You will be totally helpless. Not even able to feed yourself. You will die slowly, begging those around you to kill you because you can't do it yourself."

Ramon spoke slowly, enunciating each word carefully so I would not fail to understand completely what he was saying. Despite the noose around my neck, I was horrified at what he was saying. I had the courage to die, but I did not have the courage to be totally paralyzed and die slowly, like a piece of meat rotting.

Ramon showed me the coin again.

"I want to talk to you about this coin. As I told you, it is a very unusual coin."

I was completely mystified as to why he was so interested in the coin.

"Do you know where I got the coin? From my brother-in-law, Miguel. Do you know where he got it?"

He looked up at me. I stared back passively. His foot went to the chair, and I nodded frantically.

"Me," I gasped.

"Ah, you see, Luis, he has decided to cooperate with us." Ramon grinned sadly up at me with contrived regret. "Luis is so impatient, always in a hurry. He wanted to kill you immediately. You have me to thank for the moments your life has been extended."

He flipped the coin in the air and caught it. He examined it again, turning it over in his hand. "Sí, a very unusual coin. Do know why it is unusual?"

I shook my head.

"You don't know? Eh, I believe you, I didn't think you knew. One reason it is unusual is that it is presently the only thing in the world keeping you alive." He tossed the coin and caught it again. "If it were not for this coin, I would have let Luis run his sword through you the moment the coach door opened."

He bounced the coin in his hand. "To you, it is just a gold coin. It appears to be exactly like so many other gold coins of the same size and weight. But, amigo, if you look at it carefully, examine it closely, you will see that there is a difference. Whose face is on the gold coins minted where the Spanish flag flies anywhere in the world?" His foot went back to the chair. "Tell me, amigo, whose face?"

"The king," I gagged.

"Sí, our Most Catholic Majesty." He held up the coin to me. "But you see, if you look at the coin, the king's face is not on it. It is another face. Do you know whose face? No, I know you don't. It is the not very handsome features of one Roberto Baltazar, Count de Nuevo Leon. Not a caballero of one of the old houses of Spain, but what we call our silver nobility, a mule team driver who staked a prospector who found a vein of pure silver. Enough for a man with mule mierda on his boots to buy a grand title.

"Count Roberto, besides having the vanity of a purchased title, turned some of the silver he hoarded into gold coinage for his own private use, with his features on them. He delivered the silver bars to the mint and had the mint stamp out gold coins in exchange for the silver."

I was still completely in the dark as to why I was being told a story about a rich man who wanted his face on coins.

"Do you know what happened to Count Roberto's coins?"

It hit me. Now I knew why my past had crashed down so quickly after the old woman identified me at the ball.

"Ah, I can see that you have grasped the situation. A man has arrived in the city and is spending privately minted gold coins. Eh, the merchants don't care, gold is gold. But these coins were stolen. They were stolen with enough other gold, silver, and gems to ransom a king of Christendom from the Moors. Now, amigo, you see the way the cards are falling? You gave a large number of these stolen coins to Miguel. That means you are the thief who emptied the mint."

When I went into our horde to get the money to finance my revenge, I had grabbed a sack of gold coins. It had been no accident that I had inadvertently grabbed the bag containing the Count Roberto's ugly face. The Fates and Lady Fortune were guiding my hand, laughing as they did.

"Now you understand why I do not succumb to my young compadre's impatience to have you dead? He worries that a street beggar will claim his inheritance and his woman. Being of tainted blood, you would not comprehend the abhorrence of those with pure blood to be connected in any manner to those of your kind."

Ramon shook his finger at me. "It is fortunate that we were able to grab you before the viceroy's soldados did. The merchants who you gave the coins to have been questioned and identified you as the one who passed them. Now you are a very smart hombre, Cristo. You have to know that no matter what promises we make, we are ultimately going to kill you once we have our hands on the treasure. Your choices are clear. You can tell us where the treasure is, lead us to it if necessary, and live a short time in the hopes that we will relent from killing you, or you will miraculously escape, or—" he put his foot back on the chair—"you will die slowly, not able to move your arms or legs."

He was right. My choice was clear. I had to die to keep them from profiting from the treasure and hoped that Mateo punished them. I kicked the chair out from under my feet.

"He'll choke to death!" Ramon shouted.

He shoved the chair back under my feet. I lifted my feet so it would not touch the chair.

"He's trying to kill himself!"

Ramon grabbed my legs and lifted me so that the pressure was off of my neck.

"Cut him down!" He screamed.

Luis hacked at the rope with his sword. After the rope was cut, they lowered me to the floor, my hands still tied behind me.

"Tougher than I even imagined." Ramon looked at Luis. "Or maybe he just hates us so much that he is willing to die to cheat us out of the treasure."

Luis kicked me. "I'll get the information from him. When I get through with him, he will beg me to kill him."

An explosion sounded that rocked the room.

"What is it?" Ramon exclaimed.

The two ran to the bedroom door, unbarred it, and went out. I heard one of their men below yell, "A black powder bomb hit the house. Street people are trying to break down the gate!"

Someone came through the window and flew across the room. As I twisted to get a look at the person, he slammed the bedroom door and threw the bar across. Pounding immediately began on the door. But Ramon had had the door constructed sturdily to ensure that he would not be surprised during his trysts with other men's wives.

"Eh, Bastardo, once more you have fun without me."

"Cut my bonds!"

He cut the ropes holding my arms and helped me to my feet. He guided me through the window, and we dropped down into the alley below. Two horses were waiting. Holding them were Jaime the lépero. Mateo tossed him a pouch heavy with coins as we mounted.

"Jaime followed the carriage when it left the house this morning. He also gathered the street people who are harassing your friends."

I grinned my thanks and waved as we rode off. I quickly took a mortal oath to ensure that Jaime was properly rewarded when I was able.

"To the causeway!" Mateo shouted. "Soldados were already at the house searching for you."

The horses could not carry us in a full gallop on the stone pavement. We checked their speed so that they did not slip on the stones. We would not run far on foot in the city.

As we approached the entrance to the causeway, I saw three men wearing the uniform of the viceroy's guards talking to the two causeway guards. A man I recognized as one of the viceroy's aides was with them.

Mateo and I spurred our horses on. The causeway guards lifted their muskets as we charged. Mateo knocked one down with his horse. A musket shot sounded from the other man, and I felt my horse falling out from under me. I kicked out of the stirrups and threw myself to the side to keep from being crushed as the horse went down.

Dios mio! My breath was knocked from me and pain exploded on my entire right side as I hit the road. I rolled and struggled to get my feet beneath me. Looking up, I saw a musket being swung at my head. I ducked, but it hit me a glancing blow that sent me back down.

My hands were quickly tied by soldados.

The viceroy's aide glared down at me. "Take this bandito to the dungeon. He has many questions to answer."

ONE HUNDRED AND TWENTY-FOUR

DID I NOT tell you life is a circle? I began this secret tale after I was given quill and paper by the capitán of the guard. After using my mind to journey out of the cell as I recall my memories, and revealing my innermost secrets, I am still in the cell. Unlike what Mateo can do when he creates his plays, I cannot write a role that permits me to walk through the iron bars.

I have been stalling the capitán, even telling him some of my tales, to keep from being returned to the untender mercies of the Inquisitor priest who seeks God's favor by inflicting pain on others. I saw Fray Osirio often while I was writing this history of a life of lies. Like a vulture waiting for a wounded animal to die, he often waddled back and forth and flapped his wings outside my cell, waiting for the command that he could attach hot pincers back on my flesh.

Ay, all tales must have an end. And it would not be honorable of me to have you come this far, sharing these little inconveniences and tribulations that seem to dog my heels, without being with me when the cards dealt me by the Fates are finally turned face up. Eh, amigos, there is money on *all* the hands on the table, is there not? Sí, I can understand if some of you are betting against me. For good reasons, there are those among you who would like to see this thief and liar end his days hanging from a gallows with his heels kicking. But no matter what hand you are backing, you will want to be there to see if you win your bet as to my fate.

With that in mind, I have stuck a good quantity of the viceroy's fine thick paper inside my shirt to hide it. My intention is to put down the words in stolen moments at the hidden places where life would take me.

ONE HUNDRED AND TWENTY-FIVE

DO YOU REMEMBER my amiga, Carmelita? The puta in the next cell who supplies me with mother's milk for my secret writing? I received my last cup from her today. She is to have her baby at any moment, and they have taken her to a convent to drop it. The guards say that after she is through nursing the baby, she will return to prison and her punishment. What do you want to bet that she will be pregnant again when she returns. Eh, I know she's going to a *convent* . . . but stranger things have happened, no?

This was the second dungeon I had been in, and despite the painful reminders from the viceroy's torturers of my many trespasses, it is far superior to the black pool that the Holy Office maintained. A dark, ugly place, in the hands of the viceroy I was at least at ground level, so my cell was dry. And because there were bars rather than iron doors, my cell was not as dark as that black Hades maintained by the inquisitors.

Had they not insisted upon dragging me from my cell and applying tortures that only el diablo himself could have devised, I might have found my time waiting for the ultimate punishment bearable.

As it was, whenever I was not occupied writing the secret story of my days, or thinking—and worrying—about Eléna, I fantasized about how I would deal with Fray Osorio from Veracruz, who had tortured me with his devilish instruments. Of special interest to me was a device that I had heard the capitán of the dungeon guard boast about, one that he said existed in Madrid's Saladero, that infamous of all prisons, and that he has asked the viceroy to obtain. The capitán called this demonic contrivance the "Bull of Phalaris," and claims that it tickled the fiendish fancy of every torturer who used it.

The bull is said to be a great hollow, bronze statue. Torture victims were shoved into it through a trapdoor and roasted by a fire built underneath. Their shrieks were heard from the bull's mouth, making it seem that the bull was bellowing. The capitán claimed that Perilaus, the designer of this fiend's delight, was the first person to experience his own creation and that Phalaris, it's commissioner, was ultimately roasted in it.

Many a night as vermin ate at my wounds and sores, in the privacy of my mind I put Fray Osorio into the bronze bull and built a fire beneath. I would not build a large fire, but a small one, just enough to roast the fray slowly as I listened to the sweet music of his screams.

Are these not grand thoughts for a dungeon rat, who does not know what day it is? I had been unconscious so often that I had lost all track of time. By my estimate it was more than a month after my incarceration that I received my first visitor, other than torturers. No doubt the visitor had paid a bribe for the privilege of visiting the colony's most notorious criminal, coming caped and hooded to hide his identity.

When I first saw the dark figure approaching my cell, my immediate reaction was that it was Mateo. I had been writing when the person approached. I leaped from my stone bench to meet him at the bars, my quill still in hand. But it was not my compadre come to rescue me.

"Are you enjoying your stay with your brother rats and cucaraches?" Luis asked.

"Very much. Unlike my two-legged brother, they are not consumed with hate and greed."

"Don't call me your brother. My blood is pure."

"Perhaps someday I shall see the color of it, I suspect it is yellow."

"I don't think you will live long enough to spill my blood."

"Did you come here for a reason, *brother?*"

His face was a map of hate. His eyes were meaner than a cornered rat's, his lips pulled back with contempt.

"The marriage bans are being published. While you rot in this dungeon, or trade it for a grave, I will be married to Eléna."

"You can force her into marriage but never to love you. No one could love you, no one except that evil old woman who bloodied her hands with the lives of anyone who stood between her and her greed."

"Eléna will love me. You don't think she could really love a mestizo, do you, a lady of pure blood loving a thing with tainted blood, a creature like you who is hardly human?"

"Eh, my brother, it cuts deep, doesn't it? You know she loves me and that you can only possess her through her uncle's coercion. Is that what you want, brother? To possess a woman by fraud and force? Is rape your idea of love?"

He visibly trembled from the rage toward me that boiled in him.

"How does it feel to know you have to buy her from her uncle because she cannot stand you. What is the viceroy's share of your maize scheme? How many children will die of starvation because of your greed?"

"I came here to tell you how much I hate you. You have been a black shadow in my life since I was a boy. My grandmother told me of my father's folly, that he had put a stain on one of the proudest families of Spain by marrying an india girl."

A bolt of shock hit me. *¡Santa Maria! Don Eduardo had married my mother!* I understood now, I was not a bastard. The marriage legitimized me. No wonder Luis and his grandmother had always feared me. Eduardo, dreamer and poet that he was, had not taken advantage of my mother but had married her, creating a mestizo who was legally heir to a noble house with ties to royalty.

"You fear me because I'm the eldest son," I said. "By law I'm heir to the title when Eduardo dies." I threw back my head and howled with laugher. "I possess everything you ever wanted, the grand titles, the houses, and haciendas, everything that you take pride in—even the woman you desire!"

"You possess nothing but the mierda you lie in and the vermin that eats your flesh."

He said nothing for a moment and then took a piece of paper out of his pocket.

"As a peace offering to my bride-to-be, I agreed to come here and deliver a message to you. She is still grateful for the services you performed in Veracruz."

I stepped close to the bars, sticking my hand through, eager to take the note. He dropped the paper and grabbed my arm, pulling me against the bars. At the same time his other hand came through the bars and shoved a dagger in my gut.

For a long moment we stared at each other, barely a breath apart. He twisted the dagger into my gut. I screamed with rage and swung my other hand through the bars, the hand holding my writing quill. He let go of me and jerked back but the obsidian-sharp goose quill caught him in the face, slicing his cheek.

We stood staring at each other for a moment. Ink and blood ran down his cheek. I touched the scar on my own cheek.

"A scar is on my face because I bear the mark of a mine slave. Now you carry my mark."

He continued to stare at me, his eyes on my abdomen. I pulled open my shirt. The packet of paper I had hidden inside my shirt bore the cut left by his blade.

ONE HUNDRED AND TWENTY-SIX

FOR A LONG time after Luis left, I gave thought to what he had inadvertently revealed. It unraveled the twisted mysteries of my past. I had been forced in life to live many lies. What I never realized was that the biggest lie of all had been foisted upon me at my birth.

Don Eduardo never mentioned to me that he had married my mother. That was how I thought of him, as Don Eduardo, not as my father.

Perhaps he assumed that I knew or that Fray Antonio had told me the truth. But Fray Antonio's great hope was that ignorance would protect me. He had been wrong of course. There was too much at stake to rely upon the truth remaining buried.

I tried to imagine how the tragic play of family honor and family heritage came about. The old matrona had sent the young Don Eduardo to the hacienda managed by Ramon to be taught the traits of a knight.

Eh, amigos, what marks a caballero as a man? His woman, his sword, and his horse, and not always in that order. Ramon must have been elated when his young protégé selected a pretty india to lie with. Perhaps he even reported it to the old woman, telling her that her son was acting like a true Spanish gentleman.

Ramon, of course, while not of noble blood himself, had spent his entire life in the service of nobility, and he knew them well. What he did not realize is that not all nobles are like Count Roberto's coins, all bearing the same face. Eduardo, like Eléna, had been molded differently than others of their class. God had put thoughts in their hearts that they were impelled to write down and share with the world. And those thoughts did not always agree with what others demanded.

Eduardo's mother—it is not in me to think of her as my grandmother—arrived for a visit at the hacienda, perhaps to see firsthand what progress Ramon had made in molding Eduardo. No doubt Fates played a hand here, timing the visit with my birth.

I tried to imagine what went on in Eduardo's mind as to my mother. My first instinct was that he had married my mother to defy his own mother, but my heart told me that was not true. His voice in the carriage carried true feeling for my mother. I believed that he had truly loved her. Perhaps, like so many poets and those who have led their lives guided by their words, he thought that love would conquer all. In that he has misjudged the old matrona. She was a product of her place in society. On the death of her husband, perhaps even much sooner, since her husband had some of the traits she found so noxious in her son, she took the reins of the noble house of the Marqués de la Cerda and struggled to keep it from fading.

How had Eduardo presented himself when he told his mother that he had not only married an india maiden but she had borne him a son and heir? The hate I saw in Luis' face outside the bars no doubt paled in comparison to the old woman's volcanic rage when she learned that the next marqués of the ancient line would be a mestizo.

What had Eduardo thought when Ramon was sent to murder his wife and child? Did he believe these killings were retribution for his sins? Did he even try to protect them? Did he even know that they would be murdered?

These were not questions I had answers to, but ones for which I conjured truths, at least to my own satisfaction.

I refused to believe that Don Eduardo knew my mother was going to be murdered. For the sake of his soul, I prayed that he had not known and failed to stop the act.

And I believed that after the foul deed was done, he blamed himself.

We all act differently, all take different roads in life.

When everything went to hell in my father's life, he simply gave up. He married the Spanish belle his mother decreed, produced a son whose blood was not tainted, and retreated into his poetry, the words of his heart.

Eh, amigos, do you see what I just wrote? I called him my father instead of Don Eduardo. In my own heart I had found enough understanding of him to speak of him as my father. Understanding, but not forgiveness.

Days passed slowly in the dungeon. Unlike the Inquisition's chamber of horrors, most of the prisoners in the viceroy's jail were minor criminals and debt peonasjers, with an occasional wife murderer or bandito thrown in. Many of them were grouped together in the larger cells. Other than myself, only one other prisoner was celled privately. I never knew his real name, but the guards called him "Montezuma" because he believed he was an Aztec warrior. His delusions had brought him to the viceroy's dungeon and soon to the gallows because he killed and ate a priest's heart when he took him to be an enemy warrior. The man's only language appeared to be animal growls and howls, which the guards often elicited by provoking and beating him. As a joke, the guards would throw a new prisoner into the man's cell, then pull him out at the last second as Montezuma was about to cannibalize him.

As I rotted in the dungeon, awaiting my death, I felt a little jealous of the madman. What a relief it would be to escape into a world created by one's own mind.

Several days after Luis's murder attempt, I received more visitors. At first I thought the two priests at my bars were Father Osirio and the other vulture fray who were waiting to rip off my flesh. They came up to my cell bars, cloaked in their priestly robes, and stood without speaking.

I ignored them, remaining on my stone bench, pondering what ignominious insults I could hurl at them.

"Cristo."

The whispered words were spoken by an angel. I leaped

from the bench and grabbed the bars with both hands.

"Eléna."

She drew close to the bars and her hands took mine. "I'm sorry," she said. "I have brought so much trouble into your life."

"I made my own trouble. My only regret is that I tainted you with it."

"Cristo."

I stepped away from the bars, certain a dagger was about to be thrust.

"Did you come here to murder me when your son failed?" I asked my father.

"I came with Eléna to assist in *this* son's escape. I know what Luis tried. He taunted me that he had failed, but he would arrange for it to be done. Money can buy murder in places like this. He will find a guard who will do the deed for enough gold. We are here today because a palm was crossed with a piece of gold."

"It would be easier to pay for my murder than my escape. The murderer would probably go unpunished because I am condemned to death anyway. But an escape would result in all the guards being punished. And escape without cooperation of the guards would not be possible. These bars are iron and the walls are two feet thick."

"We have a plan," Don Eduardo said.

"You will need a miracle more than a plan," I said.

Eléna took my hands again. "I prayed for that, too."

"To me it is miracle enough that I see and touch you once again. But tell me why you think I can escape."

We huddled together while they whispered their plan to me.

"Our partner in this matter is your friend Mateo," Don Eduardo said. "He assures us that he has engineered many escapes, even from the Bey of Algiers. He sought Eléna's help and she came to me, knowing that I am desperate to redeem my sins."

I almost groaned aloud. Mateo's escapes were composed on paper and performed on stage.

"Mateo has gained access to the palace roof through a trapdoor in my bedroom," Eléna said, "created to allow escape in case of fire or attack. From the palace roof he can cross other roofs, eventually reaching the prison roof."

"What will he do on the roof?"

"The chimneys from the dungeon and every other part of the compound are there. He's made black powder bombs that he'll drop down chimneys, including the one at the guard's station. They'll not explode like cannonballs, but cause great smoke."

"Other than make me choke to death, what will these smoke bombs do?"

"Conceal your escape," Don Eduardo said. "My carriage is outside. When the smoke is created, we will rush outside, board the carriage, and leave."

I stared at them. "And these bars? Will the smoke widen them, so I can slip through?"

"I have a key," Eléna said. "My maid's lover is a guard. I obtained a key from him that fits the cells and doors."

I thought for a moment. "The guards will recognize me and grab me."

"We have a priest's robe," Eléna said. "You will be able to slip through in the initial confusion."

"But if they check my cell—"

"They will find me," she said.

"What!"

"Shhh," she whispered. "Your father wanted to be the one to take your place in the cell, but they would hang him after they found him. They won't harm me."

"You'll be tried for the escape."

"No. I'll tell them I came here to thank you for saving my life and bid you farewell, and that you had somehow gotten a key to the cell and forced me in when the smoke erupted."

"They'll never believe you."

"They have to believe me. My uncle would not permit any other interpretation of my actions. If his niece and ward was involved in the escape of a criminal under his authority, he would be recalled to Spain in disgrace. He will not only believe me, he will herald the story."

"Your friend Mateo will be outside the palace grounds with an extra horse," Don Eduardo said. "After dropping the black powder, he will use a rope to slip down to the street on the other side of the palace walls."

"We'll never make it over the causeway."

"He has a plan."

"He has many plans." Eh, amigos, don't we know that some of Mateo's plans are pure disasters?

Eléna squeezed my hands and smiled. "Cristo, do you have a better plan?"

I grinned. "My plan is your plan. What have I got to lose but a life that's already been condemned? So, my friends, tell me, when will this grand scheme hatch?"

Don Eduardo took a small hourglass from his waist coat and set it on a horizontal bar of the cell. "Mateo has a duplicate hourglass. When the top glass is empty, he will start dropping bombs."

I gaped at the glass. "It is almost empty!"

"Exactly. So prepare your mind," he said. "In a moment you will leave here in the fray's robe Eléna is wearing. Keep your head down. There's a handkerchief in the pocket of the robe. Keep the handkerchief close to your face at all times. Rub your face with it. Eléna put black cosmetic powder on it so it will appear your face is smoke blackened."

Eléna slipped the cell key into the door and slowly turned it. When I was unlatched, she handed it to me through the bars.

"Vaya con Dios," she whispered.

The grains of sand in the hourglass were quickly diminishing. We waited with intense anticipation for the last grain to fall. And nothing happened.

"Mateo has—" I started.

An explosion hit that shook the dungeon. And then another. Stone and mortar fell from the ceiling, and a black cloud blew through the corridors.

Eléna jerked open the cell door and handed me her robe.

I gave her a kiss. Don Eduardo pulled me away from her.

"Hurry. We must use the surprise."

Dense smoke had already taken what little light the candles gave off in that gruesome stone passageway. I could barely see Don Eduardo as I followed behind him. All around me prisoners were coughing and screaming to be let out, fearful that a fire had somehow ignited the stone walls. To my right I heard the mad howl of Montezuma the Cannibal. He seemed to delight in the fact that the dungeon had turned midnight.

Muffled explosions came from other parts of the palace. Mateo was making sure the viceroy's guards were kept busy everywhere.

I crashed into someone, and my first instinct was that it was a guard.

"Help me! I can't see!" The man yelled, grabbing me with both his hands.

I recognized the voice. *Fray Osorio.* Sí, the man who had peeled my skin and ripped my flesh with hot pincers.

The Fates had finally dealt me a good hand.

"This way, Padre," I whispered.

I steered him to the cell of Montezuma and opened it with the passkey.

"Fray Antonio and Cristo the Bandit have arranged a special treat for you."

I shoved Osorio into the cell.

"Fresh meat!" I yelled to Montezuma.

I ran to find my father. Behind me was the sweet music of Montezuma's feral howls, and the fray's screams of horror and pain.

I stumbled out of the dungeon behind Don Eduardo. Others were already there, coughing and choking. Guards lay on the ground. The prisoner section had been inundated with smoke, but Mateo's bombs had blown wood, charcoal, and stone from the fireplace in the guard's room, wounding several of them.

I followed Don Eduardo's hurried steps to a waiting carriage. The driver was not in sight. He jerked open the carriage door and stopped.

Luis grinned at him from inside the carriage.

"I saw the carriage parked near the dungeon and figured you were paying this swine a visit. But I'm surprised you had the courage to help him escape. *Guards!*"

Don Eduardo grabbed him and pulled him from the carriage. As Luis came out, his dagger appeared in his hand. He drove it into Don Eduardo's stomach.

The older man let go of Luis and staggered back. Luis was still off balance from being pulled from the carriage. I hit him with my fist. He fell back against the carriage, and I slammed my elbow into his face. Luis fell to the ground.

My father was kneeling, clutching his stomach. Blood ran through his fingers.

"Run!" he gasped.

Guards had already started for us, and I could delay no longer. I climbed onto the driver's seat and grabbed the reins. *"Andale! Andale!"* I whipped the horses.

The carriage shot across the cobblestone courtyard with the two startled horses in the lead. They headed in a straight line for the main gate, which lay two hundred feet ahead. Behind me guards were shouting the alarm and muskets fired.

Ahead of me guards rushed to close the main gate. As it slammed shut, I turned the horses. More muskets sounded as I whipped the horses along the high wall separating the palace grounds from the street. A musket round found one of the horses and he went down, tipping the carriage and causing it to crash against the wall. The driver's box was as high as the wall, and I leaped from the driver's seat up atop the wall, then dropped into bushes on the streetside below.

"Compadre!"

From up the street, Mateo galloped two horses toward me.

one hundred and twenty-seven

WE'LL NEVER MAKE it over a causeway!" I shouted, as we charged through the streets.

Mateo shook his head, as if fleeing this island city was an inconsequential detail. Night was rapidly falling, but that would not get us past the causeway guards. The whole city—having heard the explosions and musket fire at the viceroy's palace—would be on the alert.

Mateo did not lead me to a causeway. Instead, I followed him to a familiar location: The lakeside dock where we had once fled the city aboard a boat filled with mint treasure.

A boat was waiting. As we neared, two mestizos in the boat pushed off and began paddling away from shore. I cursed their black hearts. We were stranded!

I followed Mateo's lead and climbed off my horse. He spooked the horses, sending them back toward the heart of the city.

The thunder of other horse hooves was coming toward us.

"The boat's leaving! We're trapped!"

"That was us on the boat," Mateo said calmly.

He steered me toward a donkey cart where Jaime the lépero was standing with a big grin. The cart was empty except for indio blankets.

"Under the blankets, quickly. The boy will lead us out of here."

"We will never get past the guards at the causeway. They're not that stupid."

"We're not going over the causeway." Mateo glared at Jaime.

The boy had his hand out.

"What do you want?"

"More dinero."

With the sound of the hooves of the soldado's horses in our ears, Mateo cursed the boy and threw him a coin. "Bandito!"

We climbed into the cart and covered ourselves as the boy guided the donkey away.

We went to the house of Don Silvestre's widowed daughter.

"She stays all the time now with her father, only coming here to bring me food and comfort," Mateo said. "I came back into the city and holed up until I made contact with Eléna and, through her, Don Eduardo."

For the next two days, Jaime came each afternoon for a few minutes with news of the day—and for an additional payment. I had the distinct feeling that he would have sold us to the highest bidder if in this case the highest bidder hadn't been us. As a street boy, I would have admired his thieving spirit. As a victim of his avarice, *¡ay de mí!* We paid.

"I should cut your thieving little throat," Mateo growled at the boy.

The first news we had was that Cristo the Bandit and his accomplice had escaped from the city on an indio boat. Since there were hundreds of such boats plying the city each day, it was impossible to determine which boat we had left in and where we took to land.

With that news also came bad tidings. Don Eduardo had died of his wound; the death was attributed to me. It made me both sad and angry. Once again I had lost a father to a dagger. And again I was blamed for spilling the blood.

Reports about the hunt for Cristo became a daily fare. He was spotted fleeing in the direction of the four winds. He was already back up to his old tricks, robbing silver trains and ravishing women. Eh, if I had just committed half the deeds and loved half the women the rumors spoke about.

The other news was about Eléna. The tale being told in

the marketplace was that the viceroy's niece had taken food to a sick guard and had been at the guard station when the bomb exploded. I had to give the Spanish bureaucracy some credit. They had taught Don Diego well. After all my years on the streets, lying about everything, including my very existence, I could not have come up with a more clever lie.

The other news about her was less heartening. Her betrothal to Luis was announced, and the marriage was being rushed so that they could journey to Spain on the next treasure fleet. Luis, whose own mother had returned to Spain to give him birth, thus ensuring that he was a Spain-born gachupin rather than a colony-born criollo, was to present himself at the Royal Court in Madrid for an appointment of some substance.

While I sulked in the house, not daring to leave it, Mateo journeyed out and came back with other news.

"The mood on the streets is mean. The price of maize is rising each day."

"They've started the squeeze," I said.

"Exactly. Hired rumormongers go into the marketplace and tell stories of droughts and floods that have destroyed the maize crops, but no one believes them. Travelers, who have come from the areas, shake their heads and repudiate the rumors out of hand. And in the meantime, Miguel de Soto refuses to release maize from the government's warehouses, claiming that they are almost empty and what little is in them is needed for emergencies."

"How are they keeping maize from individual farmers out of the city?"

"The Recontonería. They are buying it and hauling it away instead of into the city. They burn it."

"Burn it?"

"To keep it from increasing the supply and lowering the price for the maize they keep in the warehouse. The people hurt most are the poor, mestizos and indios who work as laborers. They cannot afford to buy enough maize to feed their families. Your lépero brothers and the poorest of the poor are also starving. They all blame the viceroy."

"Why the viceroy? Do you think he is really involved?"

Mateo shrugged. "Do I think he is directly involved, no. But he paid a great price to the king for his office. Men who pay the great amount required for the position usually go into debt to buy the office until they have collected back enough to pay off the loans. And who would he borrow from?"

"His old majordomo and business partner, Ramon de Alva."

"And Luis, the Soto's. The huge profits these bandits reap have to be connected to the viceroy's loans."

"So is Luis' marriage to Eléna," I said with bitterness. Though I had to admit that Luis, with *my* marques title, was a plausible candidate.

"Is there anything being done?"

"Hunger makes even calm people angry and mean. When the grumbling gets too loud and people take to the streets, the cabal suddenly—miraculously—finds more maize in the warehouse and distributes a little at a fair price. As soon as that is eaten, they cut the supply and raise the price again. The warehouse is well-guarded, but Jaime has spoken to a warehouse worker who claims it is almost bursting from the maize packed into it."

"I can understand the greed of my beggar brothers," I told Mateo. "When a bone was thrown into the gutter, we all ran for it because it may have been the only food we would see that day. But how can the greed of Ramon and the others be explained?"

"They are pigs, who will eat at the trough even when their bellies swell and threaten to burst. They are never full. There is always a need for *more*."

"Amigo, I have been cooped up in this casa for an eternity. If I do not get out of it soon, I will die from boredom."

"Eh, I understand. Your señorita is marrying a pig in a few days. You want to hang him by his feet and cut his throat so you can watch him bleed, no?"

"Something like that. I also want to hang Ramon beside him."

"So let's do it."

"Tell me your idea," I said.

"What idea?"

"The one you always have. The tragic-comedia of revenge that you have concocted and that is no doubt beyond our ability to perform."

"Have you not cheated death because of my dramatic skill?"

"Cheated, yes. But I am still in the city, surrounded by hundreds of soldados, and will be back in captivity as soon as Jaime the lépero finds someone who will pay for our heads more than you are paying."

"Bastardo—"

"Eh, I'm not a bastard anymore."

"You will always be a bastard to me. But excuse me, Señor Marqués." Mateo stood and bowed. "I forgot I am speaking to the head of one of the great houses of Spain."

"You are forgiven. This time. Now tell me your plan."

"Listen closely, compadre, and you will discover why on the peninsula princes and dukes speak of my comedias with the same reverence they reserve for the Holy Bible. Because of your rashness in saving la bella Eléna from pirates, you have been exposed as the liar and thief that you are. Now that we are hunted criminals, we no longer have the freedom to swindle the cabal into financial ruin."

"Is your plan to talk me to death?"

"Sorry, Señor Marqués, I must keep aware of the fact that you wearers of spurs are very impatient."

As I listened to Mateo's jest about the noble title I "inherited" when my father died, I remembered Ana's comment that Mateo was an outlaw nobleman. I had never mentioned it to him. There are some things too private to probe. Had Mateo wanted me to know, he would have told me. He was a man who boasted of many things. His disgraced nobility was not something he bragged about.

Mateo tapped his head. "Think, Bastardo, other than cutting off their heads with a fine sword stroke, what would most hurt these pigs the worst?"

"Emptying their money chests."

"And who is protecting them?"

"The viceroy."

"Eh, Bastardo, I taught you well. So to make these devils vulnerable, we must rid them of their gold and the viceroy's protection." He took a deep swig of what I had learned long ago was his brain food. "Now tell me, where is all their dinero?"

"Uh, buying up maize to control the market."

"Sí, their pesos have all turned into maize. They control maize."

I began to see his plan. "We will take control of the maize. Buy everything that comes into the city. Pay the Recontonería more for it. Distribute it to the people. We break the stranglehold on their monopoly of maize, drive down the price, their maize, their pesos, rot in the warehouse."

Mateo shook his head in mock disappointment. "Bastardo, Bastardo, I thought I taught you better than this. That is a wonderful scheme, but there is one big flaw to it."

"What?"

"It would take too long. It would take weeks for us to gather enough maize from what is brought to the Recondonería by small farmers. By that time they will have doubled and tripled their money and your amor will be on her way to Spain with her new husband. No, we must strike boldly and quickly. We will do that by burning the maize warehouse and making the supply of maize scarce."

I gaped at him in astonishment. "You have lost your mind. That would play right into their hands. The less maize, the more it will raise the price. They will bring in maize from other areas and make a fortune."

Mateo shook his head. "I told you, they are squeezing the supply in the city. They hold it back to drive up the price. When it appears, the poor are going to riot, as they have done in the past, they release enough to take off the pressure. But if we destroy their supply, they will not only have none to sell, but none to take the pressure off. It would take a week or more to get maize here from the nearest warehouses, the ones in Texcoco. By that time people will be very hungry."

"I don't know . . ."

"Listen, it is a masterful play. We beat them at their own game. To drive up the price, they use the maize in their warehouse like a bucket of water to put out a fire. They make those on fire pay dearly for the water and only splash a little extra when it looks like the fire will spread. We will take away their bucket. When that happens, they will have nothing to keep the fire from spreading. Starving people are not passive. The evils of men or gods will not make the people of this city rebel—but empty bellies will."

"They have rioted before," I said.

"And will do it again. We destroy the supply of maize. Our hired rumormongers go into the streets, saying the viceroy himself has burned the maize. Eh, soldados of the palace guard will be seen firing the building."

I broke out laughing. "Mateo, you are the greatest autor of plays in the civilized world."

"You underestimate my talents," he said in a tone of false modesty.

ONE HUNDRED AND TWENTY-EIGHT

WE WILL USE the mascarada as cover for our plan," Mateo told me.

Eh, amigos, did I not tell you that there was always an excuse for a celebration in the colony? We took to the streets to celebrate the dead, the arrival of the treasure fleet, good news of victories in the wars in Europe, the birth dates of saints, investitures of bishops and viceroys . . . and any other momentous events we could use as an excuse.

Of all the celebrations, the colorful atmosphere of the mascarada carnival was my favorite. The excuse for this mascarada, Mateo said, was the queen's delivery of a healthy baby prince. Don Silvestre's widowed daughter told him about the celebration during one of her visits.

"She says the reason for the mascarada is to take the people's minds off their empty stomachs. The viceroy knows the temper of the street. Every time he levies a special tax for the king's wars, he throws a carnival. So he called the city notables together last week and told them they were going to put on a mascarada to celebrate the royal birth. It will permit us to go out onto the streets dressed in costume. She is purchasing costumes for us."

When her servants brought our costumes, Mateo looked at them in shock and then flew into a rage.

"I refuse to wear such rubbish!"

"Of course," I agreed, barely able to keep from laughing.

He kicked the bundle of costumes. "The Fates are laughing at me."

Don Silvestre's daughter had actually chosen the most popular mascarada costumes for our disguises: Don Quixote and his companion-servant, the rotund Sancho. Eh, how was she to know about Mateo's anger toward the doleful knight's creator.

The genius of the selection was not apparent to Mateo but came instantly to me: There would be a great number of Quixotes and Sanchos at the mascarada. We would blend in.

With no other alternative, he grudgingly agreed. Naturally he selected the main role, that of the knight, and left me with the fat, little peasant Sancho. "But do not mention the name of that blackguard who stole my soul," Mateo warned me.

We left the house dressed in our costumes.

"We will go to the main square. It will be packed, so when the parade moves, no one will notice when we veer off toward the warehouse."

The square was mobbed with people, some in costumes,

most just there to watch the show others put on with their costumes and antics. At the head of the parade were trumpeters. Behind them came a long procession of carts that had been turned into scenes from the pages of history, literature, and the Bible, along with hundreds of costumed figures.

The scenery carts were elaborately designed, the gaudiest drawing the most attention from the on-lookers. Those on the street tended to be the small merchants, laborers, and the poor, while the people of quality watched from decorated balconies or rooftops.

The first exhibition parading past was indio. Men and women in the costumes of the various indio nations marched by, the warriors in battle garb, the women in traditionally festive attire. One group, wearing only enough clothes to avoid arrest, had smeared brightly hued clay paints on their bodies and marched down the street swinging clubs. From the crowd's comments, I took them to be votaries of the vicious Dog People.

Following the indios was Cortes astride his horse and surrounded by indio kings, some of whom he had killed or vanquished: Netzahualcóyotl, the poet-king of Texcoco who died before the conquest, Montezuma, who died at the hands of his own angry people, the ill-fated Chimalpopoca, who died from torture at the hands of the conquistadors, and the war god Huitzilopochtli, who took a heavy toll in lives before his temple finally fell to the Spanish.

After the scenes and characters from history, came vivid recreations of great scenes from literature. Following tradition, the first was a cart that showed mio Cid coming to the rescue of the fighting Bishop Jerónimo, who had charged the Moors singlehandedly. The scenery cart showed the bishop striking down an Infidel with a cross, rather than the lance mentioned in the poem, while Cid came charging up on horseback.

Then came Amadis de Gaul, the seminal chivalry character. The scene showed Amadis in the magic archway on Firm Island that no knight except the most valorous on earth could enter. Amadis was fighting invisible warriors, their ghostly nature shown by sheer, spider weblike cloth covering their uniforms.

"Do you hear the poor people around you," Mateo said. "They know the meaning of each scene and can even repeat words from the books—yet they have never read a book. They have heard of these characters and scenes from others. The mascarada brings them alive, making them real for people who cannot even read their own name."

Eh, it was bringing them alive for me, too, and I had read most of them.

Bernaldo de Carpio came along, slaying the Frankish champion Roland at the Battle of Roncesvalles, and a bittersweet scene came to my own mind: When I first saw Eléna at the plaza in Veracruz, I had pretended I was Bernaldo.

Along came Explandian, the hero of the Fifth Book of Amadis. This was one of the books Don Quixote read. The chivalric nonsense led the knight-errant's mind astray and was among the romances his friend, the curator, burned. The scenery cart showed an enchantress conveying the sleeping Esplandian to a mysterious vessel called the Ship of the Great Serpent. The ship was a dragon.

"Palmerin de Oliva," someone said as the next cart came by. The heroic Palmerin de Oliva had gone on an adventure to find a magic fountain guarded by a giant serpent. The waters of the fountain would cure the king of Macedonia from a deadly illness. Along the way he met beautiful fairy princesses who cast a spell to protect him from the enchantments of monsters and magicians.

The Palmerin cart was the most cleverly done and awes and shouts of approval followed it. It showed Palmerin standing by the fountain and surrounded by the scantily clad fairies. Wrapped around the entire cart was a giant, coiled serpent, the monster that protected the fountain. The monster's head had risen behind Palmerin as if it were about to attack the young knight.

And, of course, there was our friend from La Mancha bringing up the rear, following in the footsteps of the literary characters that had twisted his mind. The adventures of the knight-errant was the newest of the characters on parade but had already gained legendary stature. And everyone there, few of whom had ever read a book, knew the story.

Don Quixote was Alonso Quixano, a middle-aged hidalgo, a man who spent his life idle and not at all wealthy, living in the dry, almost infertile region of La Mancha. He became consumed with a passion for reading books of chivalry. These books of knights and princesses in distress and dragons to slay were so farfetched and irrational the poor gentlemen lost control of his mind reading them. Soon he was burnishing his grandfather's ancient armor and preparing his trusty knight's "steed," Rosinante, a poor, skinny old stable horse, to carry him into battle. Needing a princess to rescue and love, a necessity for any knight-errant, even ones who confuse windmills for giant monsters, he dubs a simple country lass, Aldonza Lorenza, a duchess. For a page and servant, he induced a peasant, the gullible Sancho, to accompany him.

On his first outing, the don came to a country inn, which, in his fanciful world, he imagined to be a great castle with a moat and lofty towers. There he is waited on by two prostitutes, whom he fantasizes are great ladies from noble families. That night the two "ladies" help him undress.

The float shows the good don in night clothes but wearing his knight's helmet. Two women are next to him. The women, the inn's prostitutes, had helped him get off his rusty armor but were unable to get off his helmet, which he must sleep in.

The women are costumed so that the side of their clothing facing Don Quixote is that of great ladies and their backside, the side he does not see, are the cheap, gaudy clothes of prostitutes.

I barely got a glance at the scenery cart.

"Let's go," Mateo commanded.

Ay, faithful, stupid, pudgy Sancho trudged away, following Don Quixote on another mission to joust with windmills.

ONE HUNDRED AND TWENTY-NINE

WE MET WITH Jaime and a prostitute a block from the warehouse.

"You have given the puta her instructions?" Mateo asked.

"Sí, señor. But she requires more money to do the task." Jaime held out that ever-demanding hand.

"Do you remember what I told you about your ears?" Mateo asked. "You and she are to do what I tell you, or you will both lose your ears and noses. Here," Mateo said, giving him a single coin, "this is the last. Finito!"

The hand dropped. But I did not like the look in the boy's eyes. I said so when Mateo and I left them to get into position.

"You should have given the boy more money," I said.

"No. The little thief's rich already. He's gotten enough."

"You don't understand the mind of a lépero. There is always famine after feast, so there is never enough."

Four guards were at the front of the warehouse. Only one was on duty. The other three were around a fire, two of them asleep and one dozing on and off, waiting for his shift to begin. One guard was at the back. Only one was needed because a yell from him would bring the others.

Jaime and the puta went to work, walking near the back of the warehouse, attracting the guard's attention. Jaime went over to speak to the guard, offering him the woman's service for a nominal amount. It was to be expected that the guard would refuse, not wanting to risk severe punishment by leaving his post. And that is exactly what happened: The boy gave us a subtle hand signal that the guard would not leave his post.

As the boy kept the guard talking, we approached in our costumes.

The guard grinned at us as we came near. Jaime jerked on his sleeve. "Eh, I offer you a good deal."

"Get out of here, lépero—"

That was all the guard got out before Mateo put him out with a blow from the hilt of his sword.

"Quick now," Mateo told Jaime.

The boy and the prostitute left to attract the attention of the men in front of the warehouse, while Mateo and I broke the lock on the back door. With the lock off, I dumped on the ground the contents of a sack I had been carrying. It contained a dozen torches dipped in pitch. Mateo lit straw and used it to light a torch. From it we lit the others.

The earth floor was blanketed with chaff and husks, and corn dust was thick in the air.

"Ah, Chico loco," Mateo said, grinning, "this place is a tinder box ready to blow!"

Even as we lit the torches, these remnants and leavings began to ignite, and by the time we threw the blazing brands into the corns sacks, the floor was aflame. I counted us lucky that all that air-borne corn dust hadn't exploded like gunpowder, blowing us all to Mictlan. By the time we left the warehouse, everything was burning. The floor chaff and corn-sack conflagrations were converging into lakes of fire.

We fled that inferno for our lives, tongues of flame licking the sky.

Returning to the house where we were holed up, darkness was falling. Behind us the sky was filled with explosions of shooting flame and high, twisting coils of billowing smoke as the huge warehouse turned into a single hell-fired holocaust.

By now Jaime would be telling people that the viceroy's guards had been seen starting the fire. So would other street people paid to spread the story.

"What if the city burns down?" I asked Mateo.

"Mexico is not a city of wood hovels like Veracruz. It

will not burn down. And if it did"—He shrugged—"it would be God's will."

He was in a jolly mood by the time we were back at the house. I had to argue to keep him from going to a cantina to find trouble and a card game. Still something about the night's work had left me uneasy.

I awoke in the middle of the night, my paranoia as much afire as the warehouse had been. I went into Mateo's room and shook him awake.

"Get up. We're leaving."

"Are you loco? It's still dark."

"Exactly. The viceroy's soldados will be here soon."

"What? How do you know?"

"How do I know the sun will rise in the East? It's in my mind and my blood. I used to be a lépero. This well may be running dry for Jaimie, but not if he sells us to the viceroy. We're worth a fortune to the little beggar."

He looked at me for a long moment and then flew out of bed. "Andando!"

We left dressed as poor street people.

We were walking away from the house, when a group of soldados on foot and on horse converged on the house.

Under ordinary circumstances, we would have been challenged on the street because we were out past the ten o'clock curfew the viceroy mandated. On this night people were still on the streets because of the celebration following the parade and an extra attraction: The warehouse still glowed and smoldered from the fire.

We had to get off the street and had no place to go. I led Mateo to a place where the door was always open: A House of the Poor.

This one was larger than the dirt-floored hovel in Veracruz. Each of us secured a bed with a straw mattress rather than just straw flung on the ground.

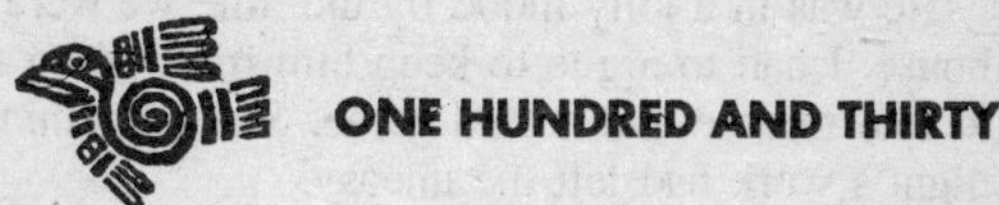

ONE HUNDRED AND THIRTY

THE NEXT MORNING we stayed in the House of the Poor until the streets were alive with people. The day had special significance to me. It was the day of Eléna's wedding to Luis. Rather than the formal wedding involving all of the great families of the colony, the wedding was to be a simple affair in the viceroy's chambers. The archbishop would preside.

"Your face looks like Montezuma's after he discovered Cortes was not an Aztec god."

"It's Eléna's wedding day. She may be getting married at this very moment."

"It is also the day of reckoning for us. The viceroy's men will be on the streets looking for us. We will not last long if our plan to start a riot does not work."

Jaime the lépero knew some of our sins, but nothing of our plans. As for Ramon, Luis, and the viceroy, they might conclude that I'd fired the warehouse, but they would not know about my larger plans.

We went onto the streets dressed as léperos, our swords hidden under ragged cloaks. We headed for the marketplace where maize would be sold. What we found there was turmoil. A large crowd had gathered before the stalls of the maize sellers. The dealers were literally auctioning off the maize to the highest bidders. And the bidders were the servants from the wealthiest families in town.

"Nothing will be left for us," I heard people mutter.

"It's not fair!" Mateo shouted. "My babies will starve! Food and justice!"

"My family's hungry!" I roared. "What can I feed them? The soles of my shoes?"

"The viceroy's men fired the warehouse to raise prices!" That from someone, I imagined, who had been paid by us.

A group of ten guards from the viceroy's palace stood by at the edge of the crowd, uneasy. They were outnumbered by fifty to one. An officer on horseback watched me and Mateo.

"We will all starve!" Mateo shouted. "It's the viceroy's fault. He eats fatted calves while our children cry and die in our arms!"

"I need food for my babies!" an old hag yelled. The woman looked many years from having birthed any babies, but I took up her cry and soon other women were shouting for food.

Arguments broke out between the food sellers, and people demanding they be sold maize at an affordable price. Pushing and shoving ensued and tempers flared. The crowd was already enraged, and with each new indignity, the fury grew, people gathering strength from others around them. People who would normally scurry away like whipped dogs from a spur wearer's whip were shouting for food and justice.

The officer ordered his men to follow him as he cut through the crowd in a straight line for Mateo and me. We pried stones from the pavement and let them fly. The crowd parted as the officer quickened his horse. My stone went wide, but Mateo's hit the man's helmet. As he came up to us, Mateo pulled the officer from the horse.

A musket went off and the old hag crying about her imaginary babies fell to the pavement.

"Murder!" Mateo shouted. "Murder!"

The cry was picked up by a hundred voices. Violence spread like the fire in the warehouse. As the other soldados came forward, pushing their way through the crowd to try and reach their officer, people grabbed them. The last I saw of the viceroy's men was a mob of street people beating them.

The anger and frustrations, not just of a food shortage, but a lifetime of being treated as little more than curs, erupted like a volcano. People attacked the stalls of the maize merchants.

Mateo climbed onto the officer's horse and raised his sword. "To the viceroy's palace," he shouted, "for food and justice!"

He helped me up behind him on the horse. The mob followed us out of the marketplace, growing bigger with every step it took. Soon it was a thousand strong, then two thousand as it poured into the main plaza, looting merchant shops.

A wild frenzy seized the crowd as it neared the palace.

"Gold!" Mateo shouted and pointed at the palace. "Gold *and* food!"

The cry was picked up by the mob and shouted by thousands of voices.

The palace was not a fortress. The city had no walls, and the palace walls were designed more for privacy than protection. The city was in the center of New Spain, a week's journey at least for any invading force. No one had ever challenged the city, so there had been no need for a fortress.

The viceroy's gates offered little resistance to the mob. A cart filled with paving stones being used by laborers to repair ruts was grabbed and slammed through the gate; nor did the vastly outnumbered palace guards, who melted away at the sight of two thousand angry people marching at them, offer resistance. Not even the futile shots that would have been fired at foreign invaders were expended at the crowd.

"That bench!" Mateo shouted at those who followed us to the front door of the palace, "we'll use it to knock down the door!"

A dozen hands lifted the heavy wooden bench and sent it crashing against the tall double doors. Two more times it was rammed before the doors flew open. Mateo and I rode the horse into the palace, followed by an army of looters.

While the mob surged down the great hall, we dismounted and went up the stairway. Coming out of the viceroy's chambers at the top, I saw a group of people: The viceroy, archbishop, and aides were hurrying down the upstairs hallway. Behind them came Ramon, Luis, and Eléna.

"Eléna!" I shouted.

The three of them turned to us. Mateo and I saluted the two men with our swords.

"Go!" Mateo yelled. "Run like women from their husbands' penes. Return with a rolling pin to fight us."

Ramon stared down at us calmly. "You two have caused me a great deal of trouble, but killing you will be worth something."

He came down the hallway with Luis beside him as we went up the stairs. I stole one frantic glance at Eléna in her wedding dress before we met the two swordsmen.

Mateo was a step ahead of me and immediately engaged Ramon as I squared off against Luis. The sound of our striking blades played above the sounds of the mob below. We heard musket shots. Apparently the viceroy's guards had decided to take a stand.

Luis's features were contorted with hate yet also a strange sort of glee.

"I'm going to show my new bride how a gentleman handles lepéro scum," he said.

His swordsmanship was dazzling. He was far better than I would ever be. I could not believe my own rage had sucked me into this. I would be cut to pieces in front of Elena. Only raw hate kept me going, giving me speed and strength and cunning I never dreamed I had. Still it was not enough. He slashed my forearm, cut my right shoulder, and reopened the wound I had gotten from the Veracruz pirate.

"I am going to carve you into pieces, not kill you quickly," Luis said. "I want her to see every drop of your tainted blood spill."

His blade sliced my knee. I was bleeding in four places, and he was backing me up with sword work I could never hope to match. He touched his newly shaved cheek with his sword—the cheek I had impaled with my writing quill.

"Sí, you cut my face so I would look like you, and I hate you even more for that," he said. He backed me against a wall, and his blade cut my other knee. My leg collapsed, and I went down on one knee.

"Now your eyes and then your throat," he said.

He suddenly expelled air from his mouth as if he had been struck in the back and lost his breath. He stared at me with wide eyes and then slowly turned around.

Eléna was standing behind him.

As he turned, I saw the dagger in his back. It had not gone in far and, he shook it off.

"Bitch!" he screamed.

I leaped forward and hit him with my shoulder. He flew backward and hit the railing. I kept my momentum going and hit him again. He burst through the railing and fell to the floor below. I staggered to the edge and looked down. He was on his back, still alive, moaning and moving his arms and legs, but nearly unconscious. The pox marks on his face were not visible from the top of the stairs. With his shaven face and cheek scar, it was as if I was looking down at myself.

Luis had made the same mistake that the pirate had: He had underestimated a woman.

"Eléna." I held out my hand to her. She grabbed me around the waist and I leaned on her for a few seconds before pulling away. "I must help Mateo."

The picaro was faring no better with Ramon than I had with Luis. Mateo was a better swordsman than I, an extraordinary bladesman for certain, but Ramon was said to be the best sword fighter in all New Spain.

As I limped toward the action, Mateo suddenly moved into the circle of death, lunging at Ramon. Ramon's blade swung around to Mateo's neck, and Mateo's left arm went up and caught the blade against his forearm. At the same time Mateo stuck his dagger in the man's abdomen.

The two stood face-to-face, almost nose to nose, Ramon staring at Mateo in wide-eyed disbelief, unable to accept that he'd been bested, let alone killed. Mateo's thrust had set the man onto his tiptoes.

Mateo twisted the dagger.

"This is for Don Julio."

He twisted the dagger again.

"For Fray Antonio."

He stepped back and faced Ramon, who rocked back and forth on his heels, the dagger still stuck in him. He grinned at Ramon and held up his forearm, pulling back his sleeve to expose the metal guard on the arm. "I regret that I am no gentleman."

Ramon collapsed.

Musket sounds became epidemic, and the mob was pouring out of the palace in retreat from the palace guards.

"Take him out of here," Mateo told Eléna. "Get him to the stables and into a carriage. Get him away from here."

"Where are you going?" I asked.

"I have an idea." He whispered to Eléna, not letting me hear.

Before we went out the door I turned back and saw Mateo bending over Luis. He stood up and shouted to guards coming down the hallway.

"Here! Take this man! *It's Cristo the Bandito!*"

ONE HUNDRED AND THIRTY-ONE

ELENA COMMANDEERED A coach and frightened coachman, instructing him to take us out of the city. We went to a hacienda owned by Luis. It was the closest place where we could find shelter and help with my wounds.

"Luis rarely visited the hacienda. He had only recently acquired this one and seldom visited any of them."

"The people there, they'll know I'm not Luis."

"The servants and vaqueros would not know you from Luis. If we say you are Luis, they will not question it. The majordomo was recently fired. Luis frequently fired majordomos."

She wrapped a piece of petticoat around my face after staining it with blood from my other wounds. "There. I could tell them you were the viceroy, and they would not know the difference."

She refused to tell me what Mateo had whispered to her.

She doctored my wounds again, just as she had after I was wounded in Veracruz. I lay in bed all day, healing.

To me it was a temporary sojourn from reality. I expected at any time that the viceroy's men would be coming to get me. Mateo had erred in not killing Luis. The idea that he would turn the man over to the guards and they would accept the fact that Luis was Cristo the Bastardo was nonsense. There was a physical resemblance but the moment Luis recovered his senses he would tell them who he was.

I cursed Mateo for his stupidity.

Several days later Eléna came to the room. She looked a little distraught.

"He is dead."

"Who?"

"Cristo the Bastardo. My uncle had him almost immediately put to death as a lesson to the rioters."

"You mean Luis? But . . . how? How could they not believe him when he told them who he really was?"

"I don't know."

She cried, and I held her in my arms.

"I know he was the devil," she said, "but I blame that evil grandmother of his as much as I do him. I never loved him. In truth, he was not really even likable. He had no true friends, which was one reason I tried to be his friend. But he has been with me almost all of my life. And no matter how he talked, I know that his love for me was real."

There was more news. Mateo had been rewarded by the viceroy. He was a hero of the city, having almost singlehandedly driven the mob from the palace and capturing Cristo the Bastardo after the bandit killed Ramon de Alva.

I gaped when I heard the story. Dios mio! Why would it

surprise me? No doubt Mateo had written the act as part of his original plan for the riot.

That night, when I was tucked in bed, Eléna had a servant bring a pot of boiling hot oil. After the servant left, Eléna barred the door. She sat down beside me on the bed.

"You asked me what Mateo whispered. He gave me instructions, ones that will hurt you."

I looked over at the hot oil. "You're not intending to cauterize my wounds with that—"

"No, you've told me that is not the proper way. I'm going to drip the oil on your face."

¡Santa Maria!

"Have you gone as loco as Mateo? You intend to conceal my identity by wiping away my face."

She leaned down and kissed me with soft, cool lips. Then she caressed my cheeks with her fingers. "Remember when I told you that you reminded me of someone?"

"Yes, first I assumed it was that lépero swine, Cristo the Bastardo, whom you helped to escape. Now I know my resemblance to Don Eduardo inspired you."

"No, Don Cristo-Carlos-Luis, whatever your name is, it was none of those. It took a long time for me to realize that you reminded me of Luis. Neither of you were as handsome as Don Eduardo."

"Thank you."

"But you both shared some of his features."

I looked back at the hot oil. She was going to scar my face with pox marks.

"No, I won't let you do it."

"You must. It is the only way. It will not hurt for long."

"It will be with me the rest of my life. Each time I see those pox marks, I will think of Luis and hate my own face."

"It is the only way."

"It'll fool no one."

"Cri—uh, Luis, think about this. He had no close friends except Ramon, and that mal hombre is in hell. He has no more family except relatives in Spain, none of whom have seen him for years. My uncle was the only one who even knew him reasonably well. Luis was a man who did not seek the company of others, not even women. His grandmother, and myself to a lesser extent, were the only ones with whom he was close."

"You said it yourself, your uncle would recognize him. He's seen both of us together."

"And what is my uncle to report to the king? That he mistook a marques for a beggar-bandit and imprudently hanged him? My uncle will not blink an eye when my husband, Luis, returns to the city after his wounds heal. I will let him know subtly before you walk into his presence, so he will not faint dead when he sees you."

I shook my head. "This is insanity. I cannot just take the place of another man. The last time I tried this it got me into more trouble than it was worth."

"That is what is wonderful about this plan of Mateo's. Who is the Marqués de la Cerda?"

"The marqués? Why I . . . I . . ."

"Say it."

"I am the rightful Marqués de la Cerda—by birth."

"Can't you see? My love, you will be impersonating *yourself!*"

I thought for a moment.

"I am also your lawful wedded husband. It is time I claimed my conjugal rights." I pulled her to me and began removing her clothes.

"Wait," she said. She pushed me away. "As your wife, will I be allowed to read what I like and write what I wish?"

"As long as I get what I want, you may read and write."

"To make sure I get what *I* want," she said, "I shall keep a dagger hidden in my petticoats."

¡Ay de mí! I had married a jungle cat.

ONE HUNDRED AND THIRTY-TWO

FIVE MONTHS LATER, recovered from my wounds—and the hot oil to my face—we left the City of Mexico to board the treasure fleet at Veracruz.

Don Diego had welcomed me into the family without meeting my eye. Mateo had contrived a heroic feat for me in the riots, one only slightly less awesome than his own singlehanded defense of the palace. With my ancient bloodline, which was in a small way tied to the throne of Spain, and my recent act of heroism—along with a substantial contribution to the king's war purse—I was ordered to the Royal Court in Madrid to assume a position on the Council of the Indies for three years. With the travel time between Europe and the colony, and visits to my peninsular relatives, it would be a good five years before we returned. By that time, all but the legend of Cristo the Bastardo will have faded.

Mateo sailed on the same ship. Extricating our secret hoard from the cave, he boasted that he would build a great arena and fill it with water in Madrid. Then he would perform before the king the great sea battle for Tenochtitlan. Would I worry what mischief this would result in? Sí.

You say this is all a fairy tale? That the poor street child cannot become a nobleman with a beautiful wife? Eh, amigos, was not Amadis of Gaul cast out as a child? And did he not win a princess and a kingdom?

Do you expect any less from Cristo the Bastardo?

Have you forgotten that a great autor of plays was manipulating all the events to ensure that there was a happy ending? I told you it was a wondrous tale, as colorful and exciting as any of the chivalric romances that drove poor Don Quixote loco.

And in truth, I have not told it all. I could not, of course. You see, like Jaime the lépero, I am such a product of my youth on the streets that I could not help lying. Amigos, forgive me, but I confess that sometimes in my secret narrative, I have even lied to you.

I leave now—

Eh, wait, you say. I have left out part of the story. You want to know why the guards did not believe Luis when he told them that he was not Cristo the Bastardo.

Well, you see, he never told them he was really Luis. He tried, but the words would never come out. Mateo told me the reason before Eléna and I boarded the galleon for Seville. When he bent over Luis on the floor of the viceroy's palace, he cut out Luis's tongue.

It is now time to put down my pen. As a high nobleman of Spain and New Spain, I am now a man of the sword and not the quill.

¡Vaya con Dios, amigos!

AFTERWORD

The major historic events related in the novel occurred during the seventeenth century in Mexico, then known as New Spain. Incidents such as the manipulation of the price of maize resulting in the food riot in which the viceroy's palace was attacked, the pirate raid on Veracruz, the Jaguar Knight murder cult, and the adventures of the nun-bandit Catalina de Erauso were of this period.

Eléna, of course, was inspired by Sor Juana Inés de la Cruz. Beautiful, brilliant, a bastarda ("daughter of the Church" was how her birth certificate put it), the great poetess threatened to disguise herself as a man and sneak into a university because women were not permitted an education.

The author has been liberal in presenting the chronology of the events.